Hugh Finlay

After deciding there must be more to life than a career in civil engineering, Hugh took off around Australia in the mid-70s, working at everything from spray painting to diamond prospecting, before hitting the overland trail. He joined Lonely Planet in 1985 and has written *Jordan & Syria*, coauthored *Morocco, Algeria & Tunisia* and *Kenya*, and contributed to several other LP guides. Hugh coordinated this edition of *Australia* and wrote the features on Aboriginal Art and Fauna & Flora, as well as updating the introductory chapters and the Northern Territory chapter. He has recently written LP's *Northern Territory* guide, and updated the *Nepal* guide. When not travelling, Hugh lives in central Victoria with partner, Linda, and daughters Ella and Vera.

Mark Armstrong

Mark was born in Melbourne and completed his tertiary studies at Melbourne University. Among other things, he has worked in computer sales and marketing, as a restorer of old houses, as a fencing contractor and in the hospitality industry. He lived for a while in Barcelona and has travelled in South-East Asia, Europe and North America. In 1992 he wrote and published *Where to Wine, Dine and Recline in Central Victoria* before beginning work on Lonely Planet's *Victoria* and *Melbourne* guides. Most recently he wrote Lonely Planet's *Queensland* guide and he updated the Victoria and Queensland chapters for this edition of the *Australia* guide.

John & Monica Chapman

As an escape from full-time employment, John and Monica have combined their skills and spare time to become authors. Their writings and photographs appear regularly in newspapers and magazines. John has written and published bushwalking guides to Tasmania. He and Monica are authors of Lonely Planet's *Tasmania* guide and *Bushwalking in Australia* and they updated the Tasmania chapter of this book.

David Collins

David was born in England and left as soon as he could. He settled in Sydney and muddled his way through several years writing scintillating news stories about fibre optic cables. After an unproductive stint freelancing, when his desire to go bodysurfing always outweighed his capacity to meet deadlines, he was rescued from a life of idle luxury and wrenched to Melbourne by Lonely Planet, where he currently works as a member of LP's web site team. David updated the Sydney section of this book.

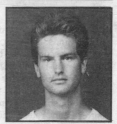

Denis O'Byrne

Denis was born in the Adelaide Hills, South Australia, and raised at Robe in the state's south-east. He left SA when he was 17 but returns home often to visit family in Adelaide or to go fishing on the Eyre Peninsula. He describes his career as a zigzag path leading nowhere, having worked as a surveyor, plant operator, national park ranger, builder's labourer, building consultant and freelance writer among other things. Denis worked on Lonely Planet's *Outback Australia* and *Vanuatu* guides, before heading south from Alice Springs to update the South Australia chapter of this book.

62·95

Dani Valent

When Lonely Planet needed an invoicer, Dani escaped the topsy-turvy world of Port Melbourne pie-making to join the sales department team. When in Melbourne, Dani now works on LP's web site. She researched and wrote the Bulgaria chapter of Lonely Planet's *Eastern Europe* guide, and updated the ACT chapter and the Snowy Mountains section of the New South Wales chapter of this book.

David Willett

David is a freelance journalist based near Bellingen on the mid-north coast of New South Wales. He grew up in Hampshire, England, and wound up in Australia in 1980 after working on newspapers in Iran and Bahrain. After two years as a sub-editor at the Melbourne *Sun* newspaper he decided to trade a steady job for a warmer climate. Between jobs, David has travelled extensively in Europe, the Middle East and Asia. He has coordinated and co-updated Lonely Planet's *Greece* guide, as well as updating Tunisia for the *North Africa* guide and Sumatra for the *Indonesia* guide. He has also contributed to the *Mediterranean Europe* and *Africa* shoestring guides. David assisted in updating the New South Wales chapter in this edition.

Jeff Williams

Jeff is a Kiwi, originally from Greymouth on New Zealand's wild west coast. He lives in Queensland and tries to keep abreast of the enthusiasm of his toddler son, Callum. When not travelling for Lonely Planet, he amuses himself walking, mountaineering, skiing and birdwatching on whichever continent will have him. Jeff wrote Lonely Planet's *Western Australia* guide and coauthored the *South Africa, Lesotho & Swaziland, Outback Australia, New Zealand* and *Tramping in New Zealand* guides. He updated the Western Australia chapter of this edition.

From the Authors

Hugh Finlay Hugh would like to thank partner, Linda, and their daughters Ella and Vera, who accompanied him in the Northern Territory and helped in many ways; thanks also to Alan Withers, for his help and hospitality in Borroloola and the Gurig National Park; to Denis O'Byrne for tips on the Centre; Peter Yates, who put him in touch with a number of interesting people he would otherwise have missed; and to the staff at the Darwin office of the Northern Territory Tourism Commission. Thanks also to Nick Bryce for his help on the Tanami.

Mark Armstrong Mark would like to thank all the travellers he met who helped with information and advice. The staff of the tourist offices in Queensland and Victoria were extremely helpful, as were many national park rangers in both states. Thanks also to Paul, Hope, Laura and Annalise Hayes, and Phil Barr and Janet in Cairns, John 'Sardines-on-the-Jardine' Meckiff for companionship on the trip to Cape York, Michael and Andy Todd for hospitality in Sydney, and Jodie Dunphy and Peter Marsh for support on the home front.

John & Monica Chapman John and Monica would like to thank the Tasmanian travel and information centres, in particular staff at the travel centres in Melbourne, Exeter and Wynyard. Thanks to Kevin Pierce at Wilderness Air for his hospitality and to all those who provided good service in their travels around the state.

Denis O'Byrne Denis would like to thank Phil Brennan of the Department of Environment & Natural Resources; Adam Best of Recreation SA; Peter Caust at the Underground Bookshop, Coober Pedy; Peter Erxleben at the Pine Grove Motel, Ceduna; Friends of the Heysen Trail; Jenny Genrich at the Ceduna Travel Centre; Rosemary Gower at the Barmera Travel Centre; Evelyn Gray at Bicycle SA; Sheree Hannam at Eyre Travel, Port Lincoln; Brett Knuckey; Barry and Jane Matthew of the Bunkhaus, Nuriootpa; Harvey Neal; Noel Saxby of the SA Police; Doug Sprigg; Anne Weddle of the Clare Tourist Centre; and Rugby Wilson of the Blue Gum Cafe, Kingscote. Denis would also like to thank his family, especially Peter, Kristy and Jenny, and her friend Dick; and his business partner, Allan O'Keefe.

Jeff Williams Jeff would like to thank Stef and Angela Frodsham in East Fremantle for great hospitality; Porky and Scott for the wildflower tour; Jon 'Yeager' Frodsham in Kalgoorlie for the Harleys and the 'nightlife' tour; Pete Flavelle in Mosman Park for good company at the Cottesloe; Steve Mackie in Kalbarri; Pete Turner in Exmouth; tourist bureau staff at Perth (especially Murray and Janis), Kunanurra, Broome, Albany, Mt Barker, Kalgoorlie, Geraldton, Carnarvon, Bunbury and Busselton; and Alison and Callum.

Dani Valent Dani would like to thank Leone, Ed, Nina and mates in Wollongong, Michael for a timely phone call in Canberra, and Catherine for insider info in Broken Hill.

This Book

Australia was first written by Tony Wheeler in 1977 and has been through successive transformations. Among the major contributors to past editions were Simon Hayman and Alan Samalgaski (3rd edition), Mark Lightbody and Lindy Cameron (4th edition), Susan Forsyth, John Noble, Richard Nebesky and Peter Turner (5th edition), Alan Tiller and Charlotte Hindle (6th edition) and Hugh Finlay, Mark Armstrong, Michelle Coxall, Jon Murray and Jeff Williams (7th edition).

From the Publisher

This edition was edited by Anne Mulvaney, Chris Wyness, Karin Riederer, Brigitte Barta, Suzi Petkovksi, Lindsay Brown and Miriam Cannell. Mapping and design were coordinated by Rachel Black, with the assistance of Jenny Jones and Tony Fankhauser. The Aboriginal Art section was coordinated by Matt King and designed by Vicki Beale, and the Fauna & Flora section was edited by Lindsay Brown and laid out by Rachel Black, with assistance from Ann Jeffree. The Australian Ecosystems section was illustrated by Ann Jeffree and written by Lindsay Brown; thanks to David Curl for assistance and advice. The cover was designed by David Kemp and Adam McCrow. Thanks to Mary Neighbour, Michelle Stamp, Jane Hart, Bethune Carmichael and Rob van Driesum. Thanks also to the readers whose letters helped with this update. Their names are listed at back of the book.

Warning & Request

Things change – prices go up, schedules change, good places go bad and bad places go bankrupt – nothing stays the same. So if you find things better or worse, recently opened or long since closed, please write and tell us and help make the next edition better. Your letters will be used to help update future editions and, where possible, important changes will also be included in an Update section in reprints.

We greatly appreciate all information that is sent to us by travellers. The Lonely Planet readers letters team – Shelley Preston and Julie Young in Australia, Greg Mills in the USA and Sarah Long in the UK – sorts through the many letters we receive. The best letters will be rewarded with a free copy of the next edition, or another Lonely Planet guide if you prefer. We give away a lot of books but, unfortunately, not every letter/postcard receives one.

Contents

Map Legend

BOUNDARIES

.... International Boundary
.... Regional Boundary

ROUTES

.... Freeway
.... Highway
.... Major Road
.... Unsealed Road or Track
.... City Road
.... City Street
.... Railway
.... Underground Railway
.... Tram
.... Walking Track
.... Bicycle Track
.... Ferry Route
.... Cable Car or Chairlift

AREA FEATURES

.... Parks
.... Built-Up Area
.... Pedestrian Mall
.... Market
.... Cemetery
.... Reef
.... Beach or Desert
.... Rocks

HYDROGRAPHIC FEATURES

.... Coastline
.... River, Creek
.... Intermittent River or Creek
.... Rapids, Waterfalls
.... Lake, Intermittent Lake
....Canal
.... Swamp, Salt Lake

SYMBOLS

✪ **CAPITAL**		.... National Capital
◉ **Capital**		.... Regional Capital
▬ **CITY**		.... Major City
● **City**		.... City
● Town		.... Town
● Village		.... Village
■ ▼		.... Place to Stay, Place to Eat
☕ 🍴		.... Cafe, Pub or Bar
✉ ☎		.... Post Office, Telephone
❶ ⑤		.... Tourist Information, Bank
◯ 🅿		.... Transport, Parking
🏛 ⌂		.... Museum, Youth Hostel
⚏ ⚑		Caravan Park, Camping Ground
✝ ✚		.... Church, Cathedral
☪ ✡		.... Mosque, Synagogue
⛩ 卍		Buddhist Temple, Hindu Temple
✛ ★		.... Hospital, Police Station

◔	⌷	.... Embassy, Petrol Station
✈	✛	.... Airport, Airfield
▤	✿	.... Swimming Pool, Gardens
❖	☜	.... Shopping Centre, Zoo
❦	↑	Winery or Vineyard, Golf Course
←	A25	One Way Street, Route Number
🏛	▲	..........Stately Home, Monument
♜	✕	.... Castle, Mine
⌒	⌂	.... Cave, Hut or Chalet
▲	☀	...... Mountain or Hill, Lookout
🗼	⌘	.... Lighthouse, Shipwreck
)(	◉	.... Pass, Spring
🐾	⚑	.... Beach, Surf Beach
	∴	...... Archaeological Site or Ruins
		.... Ancient or City Wall
		... Cliff or Escarpment, Tunnel
		.... Railway Station

Introduction

It may be cliched to say Australia is a big country, but there are few places on earth with as much variety as Australia has to offer. And not just variety in things to see – in things to do, places to eat, entertainment, activities and just general good times.

What to see and do while tripping around this island continent is an open-ended question. There are cities big and small, some of them amazingly beautiful. If you fly in over its magnificent harbour, for example, Sydney can simply take your breath away.

To really get to grips with the country, however, you must get away from the cities. Australian society may be largely urban but, myth or not, it's in the outback where you really find Australia – the endless skies and red dirt, and the laconic Aussie characters. And when you've seen the outback, that still leaves you mountains and coast, bushwalks and big surf, the Great Barrier Reef and the Northern Territory's Top End.

Best of all, Australia can be far from the rough and ready country its image might indicate. In the big cities you'll find some of the prettiest Victorian architecture going; Australian restaurants serve an astounding variety of cuisines with the freshest ingredients you could ask for (it's all grown here) and it's no problem at all to fall in love with Australian wines. Australia is exciting and invigorating. There's some fantastic travelling waiting for you: go for it.

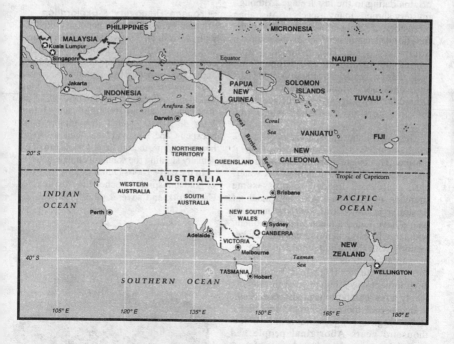

Facts about the Country

HISTORY

Australia was the last great landmass to be discovered by the Europeans. Long before the British claimed it as their own, European explorers and traders had been dreaming of the riches to be found in the unknown – some said mythical – southern land *(terra australis)* that was supposed to form a counterbalance to the landmass north of the equator. The continent they eventually found had already been inhabited for tens of thousands of years.

Aboriginal Settlement

Australian Aboriginal (which literally means 'indigenous') society has the longest continuous cultural history in the world, with origins dating to the last Ice age. Although mystery shrouds many aspects of Australian prehistory, it seems almost certain that the first humans came here across the sea from South-East Asia. Heavy-boned people whom archaeologists call 'Robust' are believed to have arrived around 70,000 years ago, and more slender 'Gracile' people around 50,000 years ago. Gracile people are the ancestors of Australian Aboriginal people.

They arrived during a period when the sea level was more than 50 metres lower than it is today. This meant more land between Asia and Australia than there is now, but watercraft were still needed to cross some stretches of open sea. Although much of Australia is today arid, the first migrants would have found a much wetter continent, with large forests and numerous inland lakes teeming with fish. The fauna included giant marsupials such as three-metre-tall kangaroos, and huge, flightless birds. The environment was relatively non-threatening – only a few carnivorous predators existed.

Because of these favourable conditions, archaeologists suggest that within a few thousand years Aboriginal people had moved through and populated much of Australia, although the most central parts of the continent were not occupied until about 24,000 years ago.

The last Ice age came to an end 15,000 to 10,000 years ago. The sea level rose dramatically with the rise in temperature, and an area of Greater Australia the size of Western Australia was flooded during a process that would have seen strips of land 100 km wide inundated in just a few decades. Many of the inland lakes dried up, and vast deserts formed. Thus, although the Aboriginal population was spread fairly evenly throughout the continent 20,000 years ago, the coastal areas became more densely occupied after the end of the last Ice age and the stabilisation of the sea level 5000 years ago.

European 'Discovery' & Exploration

Captain James Cook is popularly credited with Australia's discovery, but a Portuguese was probably the first European to sight the country, while credit for its earliest coastal exploration must go to a Dutchman.

Portuguese navigators had probably come within sight of the coast in the first half of the 16th century; and in 1606 the Spaniard, Luis Vaez de Torres, sailed through the strait between Cape York and New Guinea that still bears his name, though there's no record of his actually sighting the southern continent.

In the early 1600s Dutch sailors, in search of gold and spices, reached the west coast of Cape York and several other places on the

Archaeological Treasures

The early Aboriginal people left no stone buildings or statues to tickle our fancy, but archaeologists have unearthed many other treasures. The best-known site by far is **Lake Mungo**, in the dry Willandra Lakes system in the south-west of New South Wales.

Mungo (the name is Scottish) is a living, evolving excavation. The true archaeologists here are time and weather. This area was once a vast system of inland lakes, dry now for some 20,000 years. The embankment of sand and mud on the eastern fringe of the ancient lake system, named the 'Walls of China' by homesick Chinese workers, has been eroded by wind in recent years, revealing human and animal skeletal remains, ancient campfires and evidence of inter-tribal trading.

The remains prove that ritual burial was practised here, 15,000 years before the construction of the Egyptian pyramids. The fireplaces reveal that sophisticated, tertiary-chipped stone implements were fashioned by the dwellers at the edge of this now dry lake. The food they ate can be discovered in the fireplaces, and the long-extinct animals they preyed on are found in skeletal form on the dunes. This area is so important that the Willandra Lakes are now a UN World Heritage area.

Another fascinating area of study has been **Kow Swamp** in northern Victoria. This site has a rich collection of human remains which date from the late Pleistocene epoch. One body, buried 12,000 years ago, had a headband of kangaroo incisor teeth. In the lunette of **Lake Nitchie**, in western New South Wales, a man was buried 7000 to 6500 years ago with a necklace of 178 pierced Tasmanian-devil teeth.

The west and north of Australia have many significant sites. Groove-edged axes dating back 23,000 years have been found in the **Malangangerr** rock-shelter in Arnhem Land. Other rich sources of artefacts are **Miriwun** rock-shelter on the Ord River in the Kimberley; the **Mt Newman** rock-shelter in the Pilbara; and the **Devil's Lair** near Cape Leeuwin in the far south-west of the continent. Fragments and stone tools dating back 38,000 years were found in the nearby **Swan Valley**.

Ice-age rock engravings (petroglyphs) are found throughout the continent. Those in **Koonalda Cave**, on the Nullarbor in South Australia, are perhaps the oldest. Flint miners often visited the cave 24,000 to 14,000 years ago, and unexplained patterns were left on the wall – perhaps it's art, perhaps not. Other places where petroglyphs are easily seen are on the **Burrup Peninsula** near Dampier, Western Australia; **Mootwingee National Park**, between Tibooburra and Broken Hill in far western New South Wales; the **Lightning Brothers** site, Delamere, Northern Territory; and at the **Early Man shelter** near Laura in Queensland.

Josephine Flood's *Archaeology of the Dreamtime* (Collins, Sydney, 1983) provides a fascinating account of archaeological research into Australia's first inhabitants.

Warning: It might be OK in other parts of the world, but in Australia it is illegal to remove archaeological objects or to disturb human remains. Look but don't touch. ■

west coast. They found a dry, harsh, unpleasant country, and rapidly scuttled back to the kinder climes of Batavia in the Dutch East Indies (now Jakarta in Indonesia).

In 1642 the Dutch East India Company, in pursuit of fertile lands and riches of any sort, mounted an expedition to explore the land to the south. Abel Tasman made two voyages from Batavia in the 1640s, during which he discovered the region he called Van Diemen's Land (renamed Tasmania some 200 years later), though he was unaware that it was an island, and the west coast of New Zealand. Although Tasman charted the coast of New Holland from Cape York to the Great Australian Bight, as well as the southern reaches of Van Diemen's Land, he did not sight the continent's east coast.

The prize for being Australia's original Pom goes to the enterprising pirate William Dampier, who made the first investigations ashore, about 40 years after Tasman and nearly 100 years before Cook.

Dampier's records of New Holland, from visits made to Shark Bay on the west coast in 1688 and 1698, influenced the European idea of a primitive and godless land, and that perspective remained unchanged until Cook's more informed and better documented voyages spawned romantic and exotic notions of the South Seas and the idealised view of the 'noble savage'.

The dismal continent was forgotten until 1768, when the British Admiralty instructed Captain James Cook to lead a scientific expedition to Tahiti, to observe the transit of the planet Venus, and then begin a search for the Great South Land. On board his ship *Endeavour* were also several scientists, including an astronomer and a group of naturalists and artists led by Joseph Banks.

After circumnavigating both islands of New Zealand, Cook set sail in search of the Great South Land, planning to head west until he found the unexplored east coast of New Holland.

On 19 April 1770 the extreme southeastern tip of the continent was sighted and named Point Hicks, and when the *Endeavour* was a navigable distance from shore Cook turned north to follow the coast and search for a suitable landfall. It was nine days before an opening in the cliffs was sighted and the ship and crew found sheltered anchorage in a harbour they named Botany Bay.

During their forays ashore the scientists recorded descriptions of plants, animals and birds, the likes of which they had never seen, and attempted to communicate with the few native inhabitants, who all but ignored these, the first White people to set foot on the east coast. Cook wrote of the Blacks: 'All they seemed to want was for us to be gone'.

After leaving Botany Bay, Cook continued north, charting the coastline and noting that the fertile east coast was a different story from the inhospitable land earlier explorers had seen to the south and west. When the *Endeavour* was badly damaged on a reef off north Queensland, Cook was forced to make a temporary settlement. It took six weeks to repair the ship, during which time Cook and the scientists investigated their surroundings further, this time making contact with the local Aboriginal people.

After repairing the *Endeavour*, navigating the Great Barrier Reef and rounding Cape York, Cook again put ashore to raise the Union Jack, rename the continent New South Wales and claim it for the British in the name of King George III.

James Cook was resourceful, intelligent, and popularly regarded as one of the greatest and most humane explorers of all time. His incisive reports of his voyages make fascinating reading even today. By the time he was killed, in the Sandwich Islands (now Hawaii) in 1779, he had led two further expeditions to the South Pacific.

Convicts & Settlement

Following the American Revolution, Britain was no longer able to transport convicts to North America. With jails and prison hulks already overcrowded, it was essential that an alternative be found quickly. In 1779 Joseph Banks suggested New South Wales as a fine site for a colony of thieves and in 1786 Lord Sydney announced that the king had decided upon Botany Bay as a place for convicts under sentence of transportation. That the continent was already inhabited was not considered significant.

Less than two years later, in January 1788, the First Fleet sailed into Botany Bay under the command of Captain Arthur Phillip, who was to be the colony's first governor. Phillip was immediately disappointed with the landscape and sent a small boat north to find a more suitable landfall. The crew soon returned with the news that in Port Jackson they had found the finest harbour in the world and a good sheltered cove.

The fleet comprised 11 ships carrying about 750 male and female convicts, 400 sailors, four companies of marines and enough livestock and supplies for two years.

Australia

a Lonely Planet travel survival kit

Hugh Finlay
Mark Armstrong
John & Monica Chapman
David Collins

Denis O'Byrne
Dani Valent
David Willett
Jeff Williams

Australia

8th edition

Published by
    Lonely Planet Publications
    Head Office: PO Box 617, Hawthorn, Vic 3122, Australia
    Branches: 155 Filbert St, Suite 251, Oakland, CA 94607, USA
                 10 Barley Mow Passage, Chiswick, London W4 4PH, UK
                 71 bis rue du Cardinal Lemoine, 75005 Paris, France

Printed by
    Pac-Rim Kwartanusa Printing
    Printed in Indonesia

Photographs by

Greg Alford	Hugh Finlay	Jon Murray	Richard Stewart
Mark Armstrong	Healesville Wildlife	Richard Nebesky	Tourism NSW
Glenn Beanland	Sanctuary	NT Tourism	John Turbill
Lindsay Brown	Richard I'Anson	Commission	WA Tourism
John Chapman	Matt King	Denis O'Byrne	Commission
David Collins	Chris Klep	Ray Stamp	Tony Wheeler
David Curl	James Lyon	Paul Steel	Jeff Williams

Front cover: Wind-sculpted sand in the Simpson Desert, SA (Denis O'Byrne)
Title page: The Sydney Opera House from the harbour, NSW (Richard Nebesky)

First Published
    February 1977

This Edition
    August 1996
    Reprinted with March 1997 Update Supplement

**Although the authors and publisher have tried to make the information as
accurate as possible, they accept no responsibility for any loss, injury or
inconvenience sustained by any person using this book.**

National Library of Australia Cataloguing in Publication Data

    Australia

    8th ed.
    Includes index.
    ISBN 0 86442 362 4.

    1. Australia – Guidebooks.
    I. Finlay, Hugh.
    (Series: Lonely Planet travel survival kit).

919.40463

text & maps © Lonely Planet 1996
photos © photographers as indicated 1996

JAMES LYON

JAMES LYON

TONY WHEELER

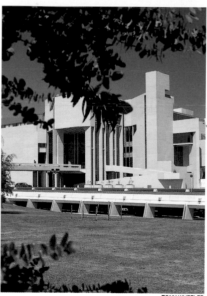
TONY WHEELER

<table>
<tr><td>A</td><td>B</td></tr>
<tr><td>C</td><td>D</td></tr>
</table>

Australian Capital Territory
A: Black Mountain tower, Canberra
B: Waterfall near Canberra
C: Statue, Canberra
D: National Gallery of Australia, Canberra

AUSTRALIA

0   250   500 km

PAUL STEEL

TONY WHEELER

TONY WHEELER

<table>
<tr><td>A</td></tr>
<tr><td>B</td></tr>
<tr><td>C</td></tr>
</table>

Australian Capital Territory
A: New Parliament House, Canberra
B: High Court building, Canberra
C: Old Parliament House, Canberra

It weighed anchor again and headed for Sydney Cove to begin settlement.

For the new arrivals New South Wales was a harsh and horrible place. The crimes punished by transportation were often minor and the sentences, of no less than seven years with hard labour, were tantamount to life sentences as there was little hope of returning home.

Although the colony of soldiers, sailors, pickpockets, prostitutes, sheep stealers and petty thieves managed to survive the first difficult years, the cruel power of the military guards made the settlement a prison hell.

At first, until farming could be developed, the settlers were dependent upon supplies from Europe and a late or, even worse, a wrecked supply ship would have been disastrous. The threat of starvation hung over the colony for at least 16 years.

The Second Fleet arrived in 1790 with more convicts and some supplies, and a year later, following the landing of the Third Fleet, the population increased to around 4000.

As crops began to yield, New South Wales became less dependent on Britain for food. There were still, however, huge social gulfs in the fledgling colony: officers and their families were in control and clinging desperately to a modicum of civilised British living; soldiers, free settlers and even emancipated convicts were beginning to eke out a living; yet the majority of the population was still in chains, regarded as the dregs of humanity and living in squalid conditions.

Little of the country was explored during those first years; few people ventured farther than Sydney Cove, and though Governor Phillip had instructed that every attempt should be made to befriend the Blacks, this was not to be. See Devastation of the Aborigines later in this section.

Phillip believed New South Wales would not progress if the colony continued to rely solely on the labour of convicts, who were already busy constructing government roads and buildings. He believed prosperity depended on attracting free settlers, to whom convicts could be assigned as labourers, and

in the granting of land to officers, soldiers and worthy emancipists (convicts who had served their time).

This had begun by the time Phillip returned to England and his second in command, Grose, took over. In a classic case of 'jobs for the boys', Grose tipped the balance of power further in favour of the military by granting land to officers of the New South Wales Corps.

With money, land and cheap labour suddenly at their disposal the officers became exploitative, making huge profits at the expense of the small farmers. To encourage convicts to work, the officers paid them in rum. The officers quickly prospered and were soon able to buy whole shiploads of goods and resell them for many times their original value. New South Wales was becoming an important port on trade routes, and whaling and sealing were increasing.

Meeting little resistance, the officers did virtually as they pleased. In particular, one John Macarthur managed to upset, defy, outmanoeuvre and outlast three governors, including William Bligh of the *Bounty* mutiny fame.

As governor, Bligh actually faced a second mutiny in 1808 when the officers rebelled and ordered his arrest. The Rum Rebellions, as it became known, was the final straw for the British government, which dispatched Lieutenant-Colonel Lachlan Macquarie with his own regiment and orders for the return to London of the New South Wales Corps.

John Macarthur, incidentally, was to have far-reaching effects on the colony's first staple industry, wool. His understanding of the country's grazing potential fostered his own profitable sheep breeding concerns and prompted his introduction of the merino, in the belief that careful breeding could produce wool of exceptional quality. Though it was his vision, his wife, Elizabeth, did most of the work – Macarthur remained in England for nearly a decade for his part in the Rum Rebellion.

Governor Macquarie, having broken the stranglehold of the Corps, set about laying the groundwork for social reforms. He felt that the convicts who had served their time should be allowed rights as citizens, and began appointing emancipists to public positions.

While this meant the long-term future for convicts didn't appear quite so grim, by the end of Macquarie's term in 1821 New South Wales was still basically a convict society and there were often clashes between those who had never been imprisoned and those who had been freed.

During the 1830s and 1840s the number of free settlers to the colonies of New South Wales, Western Australia, Van Diemen's Land (present-day Tasmania) and Port Phillip (Victoria) was increasing, although it was the discovery of gold in the 1850s that was truly to change the face of the young country.

By the time transportation was abolished (to the eastern colonies in 1852 and to the west in 1868) more than 168,000 convicts had been shipped to Australia.

Colonial Exploration & Expansion

Australia never experienced the systematic push westward that characterised the European settlement of America. Exploration and expansion basically took place for one of three reasons: to find suitable places of secondary punishment, like the barbaric penal settlements at Port Arthur in Van Diemen's Land; to occupy land before anyone else arrived; or in later years because of the quest for gold.

By 1800 there were only two small settlements in Australia – at Sydney Cove and Norfolk Island. While unknown areas on world maps were becoming few and far between, most of Australia was still one big blank. It was even suspected that it might be two large, separate islands and it was hoped there might be a vast sea in the centre.

The ensuing 40 years was a great period of discovery, as the vast inland was explored and settlements were established at Hobart, Brisbane, Perth, Adelaide and Melbourne. Some of the early explorers, particularly

those who braved the hostile centre, suffered great hardship.

George Bass had charted the coast south of Sydney almost down to the present location of Melbourne during 1797 and 1798. Also in 1798, he sailed around Van Diemen's Land with Matthew Flinders, establishing that it was an island. Flinders went on in 1802 to sail right round Australia.

The first settlement in Van Diemen's Land, in 1803, was close to the present site of Hobart; by the 1820s Hobart Town rivalled Sydney in importance. The island was not named Tasmania, after its original European discoverer, until 1856 when, after the end of transportation, the inhabitants requested the name be changed to remove the stigma of what had been a vicious penal colony.

On the mainland, the Blue Mountains at first proved an impenetrable barrier, fencing in Sydney to the sea, but in 1813 a track was finally forced through and the western plains were reached by the explorers Blaxland, Wentworth and Lawson.

Port Phillip Bay in Victoria was originally considered as the site for a second settlement in Australia but was rejected in favour of Hobart, so it was not looked at again until 1835 when settlers from Tasmania, in search of more land, selected the present site of Melbourne. Perth was first settled in 1829, but as it was isolated from the rest of the country, growth there was very slow.

The first settlement in the Brisbane area was made by a party of convicts sent north from Sydney because the (by then) good citizens of that fair city were getting fed up with having all those crims about the place. By the time the Brisbane penal colony was abandoned in 1839, free settlers had arrived in force.

Adelaide, established in 1837, was initially an experiment in free-enterprise colonisation. It failed due to bad management and the British government had to take over from the bankrupt organisers and bail the settlement out of trouble.

In 1824 the explorers Hume and Hovell, starting from near present-day Canberra, made the first overland journey southwards, reaching the western shores of Port Phillip Bay. On the way they discovered a large river and named it after Hume, although it was later renamed the Murray by another great explorer, Charles Sturt. In 1829, Sturt established how the Murrumbidgee and Darling river systems tied in with the Murray, and where the Murray met the sea. Until that time there had been much speculation that many of the inland rivers might in fact drain the anticipated inland sea.

Twelve years later the colony's surveyor-general, Major Mitchell, wrote glowing reports of the beautiful and fertile country he had crossed in his expedition across the Murray River and as far south as Portland Bay. He dubbed the region (now Victoria) Australia Felix, or 'Australia Fair'.

In 1840 Edward Eyre left Adelaide to try to reach the centre of Australia. He gave up at Mt Hopeless and then attempted a crossing to Albany in Western Australia. This formidable task nearly proved too much as both food and water were virtually unobtainable and Eyre's companion, Baxter, was killed by two Aboriginal guides. Eyre struggled on, encountering a French whaling ship in Rossiter Bay, and reprovisioned he managed to reach Albany. The road across the Nullarbor Plain from South Australia to Western Australia is named the Eyre Highway.

From 1844 to 1845 a German scientist by the name of Ludwig Leichhardt travelled through northern Queensland, skirting the Gulf of Carpentaria, to Port Essington, near modern-day Darwin. He failed in 1846 and 1847 to cross Australia from east to west, and disappeared on his second attempt; he was never seen again.

In 1848 Edmund Kennedy set out to travel by land up Cape York Peninsula while a ship, HMS *Rattlesnake*, explored the coast and islands. Starting from Rockingham Bay, south of Cairns, the expedition almost immediately struck trouble when their heavy supply carts could not be dragged through the swampy ground around Tully. The rugged land, harsh climate, lack of supplies, hostile Aboriginal people and missed supply drops, all took their toll and nine of the party of 13 died. Kennedy himself was speared to death by Aboriginal people when he was only 30 km from the end of the fearsome trek. His Aboriginal servant, Jacky Jacky, was the only expedition member to finally reach the supply ship.

Beginning in Melbourne in 1860, the legendary attempt by Robert Burke and William

Robert O'Hara Burke (left) and William John Wills led an ill-fated expedition south to north across Australia in 1860

Wills to cross the continent from south to north was destined to be one of the most tragic. Unlike earlier explorers, they tried to manage without Aboriginal guides. After reaching a depot at Cooper Creek in Queensland they intended to make a dash north to the Gulf of Carpentaria with a party of four. Their camels proved far slower than anticipated in the swampy land close to the gulf and on their way back one of the party died of exhaustion.

Burke, Wills and the third member, John King, eventually struggled back to Cooper Creek, at the end of their strength and nearly two months behind schedule, only to find the depot group had given up hope and left for Melbourne just hours earlier. They remained at Cooper Creek, but missed a returning search party and never found the supplies that had been left for them. Burke and Wills finally starved to death, literally in the midst of plenty; King was able to survive on food provided by local Aboriginal people until a rescue party arrived.

Departing from Adelaide in 1860, and chasing a £2000 reward for the first south-north crossing, John McDouall Stuart reached the geographical centre of Australia, Central Mt Stuart, but shortly after was forced to turn back. In 1861 he got much closer to the Top End before he again had to return. Finally in 1862 Stuart reached the north coast near Darwin. The overland telegraph line, completed in 1872, and the modern Stuart Highway follow a similar route.

Devastation of the Aborigines

When Sydney Cove was first settled by the British, it is believed there were about 300,000 Aboriginal people in Australia and around 250 different languages, many as distinct from each other as English is from Chinese. Tasmania alone had eight languages, and tribes living on opposite sides of present-day Sydney Harbour spoke mutually unintelligible languages.

In such a society, based on family groups with an egalitarian political structure, a coordinated response to the European colonisers was not possible. Despite the presence of the Aboriginal people, the newly arrived Europeans considered the new continent to be *terra nullius* – a land belonging to no-one. Conveniently, they saw no recognisable system of government, no commerce or permanent settlements and no evidence of landownership. (Had there been such systems, and if the Aboriginal people had offered coordinated resistance, the English might have been forced to legitimise their colonisation by entering into a treaty with the Aboriginal landowners, as happened in New Zealand with the Treaty of Waitangi.)

Many Aboriginal people were driven from their land by force, and many more succumbed to exotic diseases such as smallpox, measles, venereal disease, influenza, whooping cough, pneumonia and tuberculosis. Others voluntarily left their lands to travel to the fringes of settled areas to obtain new commodities such as steel and cloth, and experience hitherto unknown drugs such as tea, tobacco and alcohol.

The delicate balance between Aboriginal people and nature was broken, as the European invaders cut down forests and introduced numerous feral and domestic animals – by 1860 there were 20 million sheep in Australia. Sheep and cattle destroyed water holes and ruined the habitats which had for tens of thousands of years sustained mammals, reptiles and vegetable foods. Many species of plants and animals disappeared altogether.

There was still considerable conflict between Aboriginal people and White settlers. Starving Aboriginal people speared sheep and cattle and then suffered fierce reprisal raids which often left many dead. For the first 100 years of 'settlement' very few Europeans were prosecuted for killing Aboriginal people, although the practice was widespread.

In many parts of Australia, Aboriginal people defended their lands with desperate guerrilla tactics. Warriors including Pemulwy, Yagan, Dundalli, Jandamarra (known to the Whites as 'Pigeon') and Nemarluk were feared by the colonists for a time, and some settlements had to be abandoned. Until the 1850s, when Europeans had to rely on inaccurate and unreliable flintlock rifles, Aboriginal people sometimes had the benefit of superior numbers, weapons and tactics. However, with the introduction of breach-loading repeater rifles in the 1870s, armed resistance was quickly crushed (although on isolated occasions into the 1920s, Whites were still speared in central and northern Australia). Full-blood Aboriginal people in Tasmania were wiped out almost to the last individual, and Aboriginal society in southern Australia suffered terribly. Within 100 years of European settlement all that was left of traditional Aboriginal society consisted of relatively small groups in central and northern Australia.

Gold, Stability & Growth

The discovery of gold in the 1850s brought about the most significant changes in the social and economic structure of Australia, particularly in Victoria, where most of the gold was found.

Earlier gold discoveries had been all but ignored, partly because they were only small finds and mining skills were still undeveloped, but mostly because the law stated that all gold discovered belonged to the government.

The discovery of large quantities near Bathurst in 1851, however, caused a rush of hopeful miners from Sydney and forced the government to abandon the law of ownership. Instead, it introduced a compulsory diggers' licence fee of 30 shillings a month, whether the miners found gold or not, to ensure the country earned some revenue from the incredible wealth that was being unearthed. Victorian businesspeople at the time, fearing their towns would soon be devoid of able-bodied men, offered a reward for the discovery of gold in their colony.

In 1851 one of the largest gold discoveries in history was made at Ballarat, followed by others at Bendigo and Mt Alexander (near Castlemaine), starting a rush of unprecedented magnitude.

While the first diggers at the goldfields

that soon sprang up all over Victoria came from the other Australian colonies, it wasn't long before they were joined by thousands of migrants. The Irish and English, as well as Europeans and Americans, began arriving in droves, and within 12 months there were about 1800 hopeful diggers disembarking at Melbourne every week.

Similar discoveries in other colonies, in particular Western Australian in the 1890s, further boosted populations and levels of economic activity.

The gold rushes also brought floods of diligent Chinese miners and market gardeners onto the Australian diggings, where violent White opposition led to race riots and a morbid fear of Asian immigration which persists, to some extent, to this day. Although few people actually made their fortunes on the goldfields, many stayed to settle, as farmers, workers and shopkeepers. At the same time the Industrial Revolution in England started to produce a strong demand for raw materials. With its vast agricultural and mineral resources, Australia's economic base became secure.

Besides the population and economic growth that followed the discovery of gold, the rush contributed greatly to the development of a distinctive Australian folklore. The music brought by the English and Irish, for instance, was tuned in to life on the diggings, while poets, singers and writers told stories of the people, the roaring gold towns and the boisterous hotels, the squatters and their sheep and cattle stations, the swagmen, and the derring-do of the notorious bushrangers, many of whom became folk heroes.

Federation & WW I

During the 1890s calls for the separate colonies to federate became increasingly strident. Supporters argued that it would improve the economy and the position of workers by enabling the abolition of intercolonial tariffs and protection against competition from foreign labour.

Each colony was determined, however, that its interests should not be overshadowed by those of the other colonies. For this

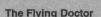

The Flying Doctor

Before the late 1920s the outback's far-flung residents had little or no access to medical facilities. The nearest doctor was often weeks away over rough tracks, so if you fell seriously ill or met with a bad accident, your chances of recovery were slim. Difficult pregnancies and illnesses such as rheumatic fever and acute appendicitis were almost a death sentence. If you were lucky, you fell ill near a telegraph line, where your mates could either treat you or operate under instructions received in morse code. This pointed to another harsh truth of life in the outback: reliable and speedy communications over long distances were available to very few.

In 1912 the **Reverend John Flynn** of the Presbyterian Church helped establish the outback's first hospital at Oodnadatta. Flynn was appalled by the tragedies resulting from the lack of medical facilities and was quick to realise the answer lay in radios and aircraft. However, these technologies – particularly radio – were still very much in their infancy and needed further development.

Flynn knew nothing of either radios or aviation but his sense of mission inspired others who did, such as radio engineer **Alf Traeger**. In 1928, after years of trial and error, Traeger developed a small, pedal-powered radio transceiver that was simple to use, inexpensive and could send and receive messages over 500 km. The outback's great silence was broken at last.

Aircraft suitable for medical evacuations had become available in 1920 but it was the lack of a radio communication network that delayed their general use for this purpose. Traeger's invention was the key to the establishment of Australia's first Flying Doctor base in Cloncurry, Queensland, in 1928. Cloncurry was then the base for the **Queensland and Northern Territory Aerial Services** (Qantas), which provided the pilot and an aircraft under lease.

The new service proved an outstanding success and areas beyond the reach of Cloncurry soon began to clamour for their own Flying Doctor. However, the Presbyterian Church had insufficient resources to allow a rapid expansion. In 1933 it handed the aerial medical service over to 'an organisation of national character' and so the **Royal Flying Doctor Service** (RFDS) was born. Flynn's vision of a 'mantle of safety' over the outback had become a reality.

Today, 12 RFDS base stations provide a sophisticated network of radio communications and medical services to an area as large as western Europe and about two-thirds the size of the USA. Emergency evacuations of sick or injured people are still an important function, but these days the RFDS provides a comprehensive range of medical services, including routine clinics at communities that are unable to attract full-time medical staff. It also supervises numerous small hospitals that normally operate without a doctor; such hospitals are staffed by registered nurses who communicate by telephone or radio with their RFDS doctor.

The administration of RFDS bases is divided between seven largely independent sections, each of which is a nonprofit organisation funded by government grants and private donations. ■

reason, the constitution that was finally adopted gave only very specific powers to the Commonwealth, leaving all residual powers with the states. It also gave each state equal representation in the upper house of parliament (the Senate) regardless of size or population. Today Tasmania, with a population of less than half a million, has as many senators in Federal parliament as New South Wales, with a population of around six million. As the Senate is able to reject legislation passed by the lower house, this legacy of Australia's colonial past has had a profound effect on its politics, entrenching state divisions and ensuring that the smaller states have remained powerful forces in the government of the nation.

With federation, which came on 1 January 1901, Australia became a nation, but its loyalty and many of its legal and cultural ties to Britain remained. The mother country still expected military support from its Commonwealth allies in any conflict, and Australia fought beside Britain in battles as far from Australia's shores as the Boer War in South Africa. This willingness to follow Western powers to war would be demonstrated time and again during the 20th century. Seemingly unquestioning loyalty to Britain and later the USA was only part of the reason. Xenophobia – born of isolation, an Asian location and a vulnerable economy – was also to blame.

The extent to which Australia regarded itself as a European outpost became evident with the passage of the Immigration Restriction Bill of 1901. The bill, known as the White Australia policy, was designed to prevent the immigration of Asians and Pacific Islanders. Prospective immigrants were required to pass a dictation test in a European language. This language could be as obscure a tongue as the authorities wished. The dictation test was not abolished until 1958.

The desire to protect the jobs and conditions of White Australian workers that had helped bring about the White Australia policy did, however, have some positive results. The labour movement had been a strong political force for many years, and by 1908 the principle of a basic wage sufficient to enable a male worker to support himself, a wife and three children had been established. By that time also, old age and invalid pensions were being paid.

When war broke out in Europe in 1914, Australian troops were again sent to fight thousands of km from home. From Australia's perspective, the most infamous of the WW I battles in which Diggers took part was that intended to force a passage through the Dardanelles to Constantinople. Australian and New Zealand troops landed at Gallipoli only to be slaughtered by well-equipped and strategically positioned Turkish soldiers. The sacrifices made by Australian soldiers are commemorated annually on Anzac Day, 25 April, the anniversary of the Gallipoli landing.

Interestingly, while Australians rallied to the aid of Britain during WW I, the majority of voters were prepared to condone voluntary military service only. Efforts to introduce conscription during the war led to bitter debate, both in Parliament and in the streets, and in referenda compulsory national service was rejected by a small margin.

Australia was hard hit by the Depression; prices for wool and wheat – two mainstays of the economy – plunged. In 1931 almost a third of breadwinners were unemployed and poverty was widespread. Swagmen became a familiar sight, as they had been in the 1890s depression, as thousands of men took to the 'wallaby track' in search of work in the countryside. By 1933, however, Australia's economy was starting to recover, a result of rises in wool prices and a rapid revival of manufacturing.

Also on the rise was the career of Joseph Lyons, who had become prime minister after defeating the Labor government, headed by James Scullin, at elections in 1932. Lyons, a former Labor minister, had defected and formed the conservative United Australia Party, which stayed in power through the 1930s. The death of Lyons in 1939 saw the emergence of a figure who was set to dominate the Australian political scene for the next 25 years – Robert Gordon Menzies. He was prime minister from 1939 until forced by his own party to resign in 1941, after which time he formed a new conservative party, the Liberal Party, before regaining office in 1949, a post which he held for a record 16 years.

'Protection' of Aboriginal People

By the early 1900s, legislation designed to segregate and 'protect' Aboriginal people was passed in all states. The legislation imposed restrictions on the Aboriginal people's rights to own property and seek employment, and the Aboriginals Ordinance of 1918 even allowed the state to remove children from Aboriginal mothers if it was suspected that the father was not an Aboriginal. In these cases the parents were considered to have no rights over the children, who were placed in foster homes or childcare institutions. Many Aboriginal people are still bitter about having been separated from their families and forced to grow up apart from their people. An upside of the ordinance was that it gave a degree of protection for 'full-blood' Aboriginal people living on reserves, as non-Aboriginal people could enter only with a permit, and mineral exploration was forbidden.

WW II and Postwar Australia

In the years before WW II Australia became increasingly fearful of Japan. When war did break out, Australian troops fought beside the British in Europe but after the Japanese bombed Pearl Harbor, Australia's own national security finally began to take priority.

Singapore fell, the northern Australian towns of Darwin and Broome and the New Guinean town of Port Moresby were bombed, the Japanese advanced southward, and still Britain called for more Australian troops. This time the Australian prime minister, John Curtin, refused. Australian soldiers were needed to fight the Japanese advancing over the mountainous Kokoda Trail towards Port Moresby. In appalling conditions Australian soldiers confronted and defeated the Japanese at Milne Bay, east of Port Moresby, and began the long struggle to push them from the Pacific.

Ultimately it was the USA, not Britain, that helped protect Australia from the Japanese, defeating them in the Battle of the Coral Sea. This event was to mark the beginning of a profound shift in Australia's allegiance away from Britain and towards the USA. Although Australia continued to support Britain in the war in Europe, its appreciation of its own vulnerability had been sharpened immeasurably by the Japanese advance.

One result of this was the postwar immigration programme, which offered assisted passage not only to the British but also to refugees from eastern Europe in the hope that the increase in population would strengthen Australia's economy and its ability to defend itself. 'Populate or Perish' became the catch phrase. Between 1947 and 1968 more than 800,000 non-British European migrants came to live in Australia. They have since made an enormous contribution to the country, enlivening its culture and broadening its vision.

The standard of living improved rapidly after the war (due largely to rapid increase in the demand for Australian raw materials), and the Labor government of Ben Chifley put in place a reconstruction programme, which saw, among other things, the establishment of the massive Snowy Mountains Hydroelectric Scheme.

Postwar Australia came to accept the American view that it was not so much Asia but *communism* in Asia that threatened the increasingly Americanised Australian way of life. Accordingly Australia, again under Menzies by this stage, followed the USA into the Korean War and joined it as a signatory to the treaties of ANZUS and the anti-communist Southeast Asia Treaty Organization (SEATO). During the 1950s Australia also provided aid to South-East Asian nations under the Colombo Plan of 1950, a scheme initiated by Australia but subscribed to by many other countries (including the USA, Britain, Canada and Japan) as a means to prevent the spread of communism throughout the region.

In the light of Australia's willingness to join SEATO, it is not surprising that the Menzies government applauded the USA's entry into the Vietnam War and, in 1965, committed troops to the struggle. Support for involvement was far from absolute, however. Arthur Calwell, the leader of the Australian Labor Party, for example, believed the Vietnam conflict to be a civil war in which Australia had no part. Still more troubling for many young Australian men was the fact that conscription had been introduced in 1964 and those undertaking national service could now be sent overseas. By 1967 as many as 40% of Australians serving in Vietnam were conscripts.

'Assimilation' of Aboriginal People

The process of social change for Aboriginal people was accelerated by WW II. After the war 'assimilation' of Aboriginal people became the stated aim of the government. To this end, the rights of Aboriginal people were subjugated even further – the government had control over everything, from where they could live to whom they could marry. Many people were forcibly moved from their

20th-Century Exploration

Around the turn of the century, Baldwin Spencer, a biologist, and Francis Gillen, an anthropologist, teamed up to study the Aboriginal people of central Australia and Arnhem Land. Other expeditions to northern Australia and Arnhem Land were led by the British polar explorer G H Wilkins (in 1923) and Donald Mackay (in 1928). Donald Thomson led his first expedition to Arnhem Land in 1935 and his work in northern Australia still receives accolades from anthropologists and naturalists.

In the 1930s, aerial mapping of the Centre began in earnest, financed by Mackay. Surveys were carried out over the Simpson Desert, the only large stretch of the country still to be explored on foot. In 1939, C T Madigan led an expedition that crossed this forbidding landscape from Old Andado to Birdsville.

In 1948 the largest scientific expedition ever undertaken in Australia was led by Charles Mountford into Arnhem Land. Financed by the National Geographic Society and the Australian government, it collected over 13,000 fish, 13,500 plant specimens, 850 birds and over 450 animal skins, along with thousands of Aboriginal implements and weapons.

During the 1950s the Woomera Rocket Range and the atomic-bomb test sites of Emu Junction and Maralinga were set up. This vast region was opened up by the surveyor Len Beadell, who is widely regarded as the last Australian explorer. ■

homes to townships, the idea being that they would adapt to European culture, which would in turn aid their economic development. This policy was a dismal failure.

In the 1960s the assimilation policy came under a great deal of scrutiny, and White Australians became increasingly aware of the inequity of their treatment of Aboriginal people. In 1967 non-Aboriginal Australians voted to give Aboriginal people and Torres Strait Islanders the status of citizens, and gave the Federal government power to legislate for them in all states. The states had to provide them with the same services as were available to other citizens, and the Federal government set up the Department of Aboriginal Affairs to identify and legislate for the special needs of Aboriginal people.

The assimilation policy was finally dumped in 1972, to be replaced by the government's policy of self-determination, which for the first time enabled Aboriginal people to participate in decision-making processes by granting them rights to their land. See the Government section later in this chapter for more on Aboriginal land rights.

Although the outcome of the Mabo case (see Aboriginal Land Rights under Government later in this chapter) gives rise to cautious optimism, many Aboriginal people still live in appalling conditions, and alcohol and drug abuse remain widespread problems, particularly among young and middle-aged men. Aboriginal communities have taken up the challenge to try and eradicate these problems – many communities are now 'dry', and there are a number of rehabilitation programmes for alcoholics, petrol-sniffers and others with drug problems. Thanks for much of this work goes to Aboriginal women, many of whom have found themselves on the receiving end of domestic violence.

All in all it's been a tough 200 years for Australia's Aboriginal people. One can only be thankful for their resilience, which has enabled them to withstand the pressures placed on their culture, traditions and dignity, and that after so many years of domination they've been able to keep so much of that culture intact.

The 1970s and Beyond

The civil unrest aroused by conscription was one factor that contributed to the rise to power, in 1972, of the Australian Labor Party, under the leadership of Gough Whitlam, for the first time in more than 25 years. The Whitlam government withdrew Australian troops from Vietnam, abolished national service and higher-education fees, instituted a system of free and universally available health care, and supported land rights for Aboriginal people.

The government, however, was hampered by a hostile Senate and talk of mismanagement. On 11 November 1975, the governor-general (the British monarch's representative in Australia) dismissed the Parliament and installed a caretaker government led by the leader of the opposition Liberal Party, Malcolm Fraser. Labor supporters were appalled. Such action was unprecedented in the history of the Commonwealth of Australia and the powers that the governor-general had been able to invoke had long been regarded by many as an anachronistic vestige of Australia's now remote British past.

Nevertheless, it was a conservative coalition of the Liberal and National Country parties that won the ensuing election. A Labor government was not returned until 1983, when a former trade union leader, Bob Hawke, led the party to victory. In 1990 Hawke won a third consecutive term in office (a record for a Labor prime minister), thanks in no small part to the lack of better alternatives offered by the Liberals. He was replaced as prime minister by Paul Keating, his long-time Treasurer, in late 1991.

By 1991 Australia was in recession, mainly as a result of domestic economic policy but also because Australia is particularly hard hit when demand (and prices) for primary produce and minerals falls on the world markets. Unemployment was the highest it had been since the early 1930s, hundreds of farmers were forced off the land because they couldn't keep afloat financially, there was a four-million-bale wool stockpile that no-one seemed to know how to shift, and the building and manufacturing areas faced a huge slump amid a general air of doom and gloom. The federal election in 1993 was won by Paul Keating, against all expectations. The economy took a slight turn for the better, but not enough for the electorate to maintain its faith in the Labor government. With unemployment remaining high at around 9%, in early 1996 Keating was defeated in a landslide victory to the Coalition, led by John Howard.

Despite the economic problems, however, most non-Aboriginal Australians have a standard of living which is extremely high; it's a disgrace that the same can't be said for most of their Aboriginal counterparts. Many Aboriginal people still live in deplorable conditions, with outbreaks of preventable diseases and infant mortality running at a rate higher even than in many Third World countries. While definite progress has been made with the Federal government's Native Title legislation (see the Government section in this chapter for details), there's still a long way to go before Aboriginal people can enjoy an improved standard of living.

Socially and economically, Australia is still coming to terms with its strategic location in Asia. While it has accepted large numbers of Vietnamese and other Asian immigrants during the past two decades, it has never really considered itself a part of Asia, nor has it exploited the area's economic potential. With the boom in the economies of South-East Asia, regionalism is fast becoming the focus for the Australian economy.

Another issue dominating Australian thinking in the 1990s is that of republicanism, as increasing numbers of people feel that constitutional ties with Britain are no longer relevant. This is especially true with Sydney having been awarded the Olympic Games in the year 2000. Many feel it would be fitting that the games be opened by the constitutional head of a new Republic of Australia. But the election in 1996 of a conservative government with strong traditional ties to the monarchy means it may be a long time yet before the governor-general is done away with.

GEOGRAPHY

Australia is an island continent whose landscape – much of it uncompromisingly bleak and inhospitable – is the result of gradual changes wrought over millions of years. Although there is still seismic activity in the eastern and western highland areas, Australia is one of the most stable land masses, and for about 100 million years has been free of the forces that have given rise to huge mountain ranges elsewhere.

From the east coast a narrow, fertile strip merges into the greatly eroded Great Dividing Range, that is almost continent-long. The mountains are mere reminders of the mighty range that once stood here. Only in the section straddling the New South Wales border with Victoria, and in Tasmania, are they high enough to have winter snow.

West of the range the country becomes increasingly flat and dry. The endless flatness is broken only by salt lakes, occasional mysterious protuberances like Uluru (Ayers Rock) and Kata Tjuta (the Olgas), and some starkly beautiful mountains like the Mac-Donnell Ranges near Alice Springs. In places, the scant vegetation is sufficient to allow some grazing. However, much of the Australian outback is a barren land of harsh, stone deserts and dry lakes with evocative names like Lake Disappointment.

The extreme north of Australia, the Top End, is a tropical area within the monsoon belt. Although its annual rainfall looks adequate on paper, it comes in more or less one short, sharp burst. This has prevented the Top End from becoming seriously productive agriculturally.

The west of Australia consists mainly of a broad plateau. In the far west a mountain range and fertile coastal strip heralds the Indian Ocean, but this is only to the south. In the north-central part of Western Australia, the dry country runs right to the sea. The rugged Kimberley region in the state's far north is spectacular.

Australia is the world's sixth-largest country. Its area is 7,682,300 sq km, about the same size as the 48 mainland states of the USA and half as large again as Europe, excluding the former USSR. It constitutes approximately 5% of the world's land surface. Lying between the Indian and Pacific oceans, Australia is about 4000 km from east to west and 3200 km from north to south, with a coastline 36,735 km long.

CLIMATE

Australian seasons are the antithesis of those in Europe and North America. It's hot in December and many Australians spend Christmas at the beach, while in July and August it's midwinter. Summer starts in December, autumn in March, winter in June and spring in September.

The climatic extremes aren't too severe in most parts of Australia. Even in Melbourne, the southernmost capital city on the mainland, it's a rare occasion when the mercury hits freezing point, although it's a different story in Canberra, the national capital. The poor Tasmanians, farther to the south, have a good idea of what cold is.

As you head north the seasonal variations become fewer until, in the far north around Darwin, you are in the monsoon belt where there are just two seasons – hot and wet, and hot and dry. In the Snowy Mountains of southern New South Wales and the Alps of north-east Victoria there's a snow season with good skiing. The centre of the continent is arid – hot and dry during the day, but often bitterly cold at night.

A synopsis of average maximum and minimum temperatures and rainfall follows. Note that these are *average* maximums – even Melbourne gets a fair number of summer days hotter than 40°C.

Adelaide Maximum temperatures are from 26°C to 30°C from November to March; minimums can be below 10°C between June and September. Rainfall is heaviest, 50 to 80 mm per month, from May to September.

Alice Springs There are maximums of 30°C and above from October to March; minimums are 10°C and below from May to September. Rainfall is low all year round; from December to February there's an average of 40 mm of rain per month.

Brisbane Maximums average 20°C or more year round, peaking around 30°C from December to February; minimums are around 10°C from June to September. Rainfall is fairly heavy year round, with more than 130 mm per month from December to March.

Cairns Maximums are about 25°C to 33°C year round, with minimums rarely below 20°C; rainfall is

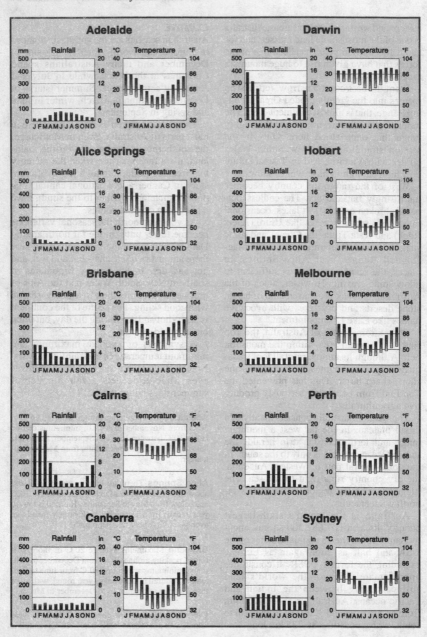

below 100 mm a month from May to October (lowest in July and August), but peaks from January to March at 400 to 450 mm.

Canberra Maximums are in the mid to high 20s in the summer and minimums are often near freezing between May and October; rainfall is usually 40 to 60 mm a month, year round.

Darwin Temperatures are even, year round, with maximums from 30°C to 34°C and minimums from 19°C to 26°C; rainfall is minimal from May to September, but from December to March there's 250 to 380 mm a month.

Hobart Maximums top 20°C only from December to March, and from April to November minimums are usually below 10°C; rainfall is about 40 to 60 mm a month, year round.

Melbourne Maximums are 20°C and above from October to April, minimums 10°C and below from May to October; rainfall is even year round, at 50 to 60 mm almost every month.

Perth Maximums are around 30°C from December to March, but minimums are rarely below 10°C; rainfall is lightest from November to March (20 mm and below) and heaviest from May to August (130 to 180 mm).

Sydney Usually only in the middle of winter are minimums below 10°C; summer maximums are around 25°C from December to March; rainfall is in the 75 to 130 mm range year round.

NATIONAL PARKS & RESERVES

Australia has more than 500 national parks – nonurban protected wilderness areas of environmental or natural importance. Each state defines and runs its own national parks, but the principle is the same throughout Australia. National parks include rainforests, vast tracts of empty outback, strips of coastal dune land and long, rugged mountain ranges.

Public access is encouraged if safety and conservation regulations are observed. In all parks you're asked to do nothing to damage or alter the natural environment. Approach roads, camping grounds (often with toilets and showers), walking tracks and information centres are often provided for visitors. In most national parks there are restrictions on bringing in pets.

The gum nut adorns the famed Australian eucalypt, or gum tree

Some national parks are so isolated, rugged or uninviting that you wouldn't want to do much except look unless you were an experienced, well-prepared bushwalker or climber. Other parks, however, are among Australia's major attractions and some of the most beautiful have been included on the World Heritage List (a United Nations list of natural or cultural places of world significance that would be an irreplaceable loss to the planet if they were altered).

Internationally, the World Heritage List includes 440 sites such as the Taj Mahal and the Grand Canyon, and 12 Australian areas: the Great Barrier Reef; Kakadu and Uluru-Kata Tjuta national parks in the Northern Territory; the Willandra Lakes region of far western New South Wales; the Lord Howe Island group off New South Wales; the Tasmanian Wilderness (Franklin-Gordon Wild Rivers and Cradle Mountain-Lake St Clair national parks); the Central Eastern Rainforest Reserves (15 national parks and reserves, covering 1000 sq km in the eastern highlands of New South Wales); the Wet Tropics of far north Queensland, in the Daintree-Cape Tribulation area; Shark Bay on the Western Australian coast; Fraser Island off the Queensland coast; and the Fossil Mammal sites at Riversleigh (western Queensland) and Naracoorte (coastal South Australia).

The Great Barrier Reef, the Tasmanian Wilderness, the Wet Tropics of Queensland and

Shark Bay meet all four World Heritage criteria for natural heritage, with Kakadu National Park, Uluru-Kata Tjuta National Park, Willandra Lakes and the Tasmanian Wilderness being listed for both natural and cultural criteria. These sites are among the very few on the World Heritage List selected for both natural and cultural heritage reasons, or for meeting all four natural criteria.

Before a site or area is accepted for the World Heritage List it has first to be proposed by its country and then must pass a series of tests at the UN, culminating, if it is successful, in acceptance by the UN World Heritage Committee which meets at the end of each year. Any country proposing one of its sites or areas for the list must agree to protect the selected area, keeping it for the enjoyment of future generations even if to do so requires help from other countries.

While state governments have authority over their own national parks, the Federal government is responsible for ensuring that Australia meets its international treaty obligations, and in any dispute arising from a related conflict between a state and the Federal government, the latter can override the former.

In this way the Federal government can force a state to protect an area with World Heritage listing, as it did in the early 1980s when the Tasmanian government wanted to dam the Gordon River in the south-west of the state and thereby flood much of the wild Franklin River.

For national park authority addresses see Useful Organisations in the Facts for the Visitor chapter.

State Forests

Another form of nature reserve is the state forest. These are owned by state governments and have fewer regulations than national parks. In theory, state forests can be logged, but often they are primarily recreational areas with camping grounds, walking trails and signposted forest drives. Some permit horses and dogs.

The logging of state forests for woodchips has long been a contentious issue in Australia, and in recent times has once again come to the fore. The Federal government issues the woodchip licences. and decides which forests will go and which will stay. Its most recent forest policy in late 1995 set aside a number of areas for woodchipping, while protecting others. The loggers say more should be logged, the conservationists naturally enough say it should be less, and the confrontation often gets quite ugly. One of the more high-profile campaigns by the pro-logging lobby in recent years saw hundreds of logging trucks descend on Canberra, blockading Parliament House and forcing the politicians to walk the last bit to work.

GOVERNMENT

Australia is a federation of six states and two territories. Under the written Constitution, which came into force on 1 January 1901 when the colonies joined to form the Commonwealth of Australia, the Federal government is mainly responsible for the national economy and Reserve Bank, customs and excise, immigration, defence,

The grey kangaroo can be seen at dusk in many national parks and state forests

foreign policy and the postal system. The state governments are chiefly responsible for health, education, housing, transport and justice. There are both federal and state police forces.

Australia has a parliamentary system of government based on that of the UK, and the state and federal structures are broadly similar. In Federal parliament, the lower house is the House of Representatives, the upper house the Senate. The House of Representatives has 147 members, divided among the states on a population basis (NSW 50, Victoria 38, Queensland 25, South Australia 12, Western Australia 14, Tasmania five, ACT two and Northern Territory one). Elections for the House of Representatives are held at least every three years. The Senate has 12 senators from each state, and two each from the ACT and the Northern Territory. State senators serve six-year terms, with elections for half of them every three years; territory senators serve only three years, their terms coinciding with elections for the House of Representatives. Queensland's upper house was abolished in 1922. The Federal government is run by a prime minister, while the state governments are led by a premier and the Northern Territory by a chief minister. The party holding the greatest number of lower house seats forms the government.

Australia is a monarchy, but although Britain's king or queen is also Australia's, Australia is fully autonomous. The British sovereign is represented by the governor-general and state governors, whose nominations for their posts by the respective governments are ratified by the monarch of the day.

Federal parliament is based in Canberra, the capital of the nation. Like Washington DC in the USA, Canberra is in its own separate area of land, the Australian Capital Territory (ACT), and is not under the rule of one of the states. Geographically, however, the ACT is completely surrounded by New South Wales. The state parliaments are in each state capital.

The Federal government is elected for a maximum of three years but elections can be (and often are) called earlier. Voting is by secret ballot and is compulsory for persons 18 years of age and over. Voting can be somewhat complicated as a preferential system is used whereby each candidate has to be listed in order of preference. This can result, for example, in Senate elections with 50 or more candidates to be ranked.

The Constitution can only be changed by referendum, and only if a majority of voters in at least four states favour it. Since federation in 1901, of the 42 proposals that have been put to referendum, only eight have been approved.

In Federal parliament, the two main political groups are the Australian Labor Party (ALP) and the coalition between the Liberal Party and the National Party. These parties also dominate state politics but sometimes the Liberal and National parties are not in coalition. The latter was once known as the National Country Party since it mainly represents country seats.

The only other political party of any real substance is the Australian Democrats, which has largely carried the flag for the ever-growing 'green' movement. The Democrats have been successful in recent times. Although the 1996 election gave a massive majority to the Coalition in the House of Representatives, the balance of power is held in the Senate by the Democrats. But independent politicians with no affiliation to a particular party who had made it into the traditional political structure in 1993 lost their seats in 1996.

The Cabinet, presided over by the prime minister, is the government's major policy-making body, and it comprises about half of the full ministry. It's a somewhat secretive body which meets in private (usually in Canberra) and its decisions are ratified by the Executive Council, a formal body presided over by the governor-general.

Aboriginal Land Rights

Britain founded the colony of New South Wales on the legal principle of *terra nullius*, a land belonging to no-one, which meant that Australia was legally unoccupied. The settlers could take land from Aboriginal people without signing treaties or providing compensation. The European concept of landownership was completely foreign to Aboriginal people and their view of the world in which land did not belong to individuals: people belonged to the land, were formed by it and were a part of it like everything else.

After WW II, Australian Aboriginal people became more organised and better educated, and a political movement for land rights developed. In 1962 a bark petition was presented to the Federal government by the Yolngu people of Yirrkala, in north-east Arnhem Land, demanding that the government recognise Aboriginal peoples' occupation and ownership of Australia since time immemorial. The petition was ignored, and the Yolngu people took the matter to court – and lost. In the famous Yirrkala Land Case 1971, Australian courts accepted the government's claim that Aboriginal people had no meaningful economic, legal or political relationship to land. The case upheld the principle of *terra nullius*, and the common-law position that Australia was unoccupied in 1788.

Because the Yirrkala Land Case was based on an inaccurate (if not outright racist) assessment of Aboriginal society, the Federal government came under increasing pressure to legislate for Aboriginal land rights. In 1976 it eventually passed the Aboriginal Land Rights (Northern Territory) Act – often referred to as the Land Rights Act.

Land Rights Acts The Aboriginal Land Rights (NT) Act of 1976, which operates in the Northern Territory, remains Australia's most powerful and comprehensive land rights legislation. Promises were made to legislate for national land rights, but these were abandoned after opposition from mining companies and state governments. The act established three Aboriginal Land Councils, which are empowered to claim land on behalf of traditional Aboriginal owners.

However, under the act the only land claimable is unalienated Northern Territory land outside town boundaries – land that no-one else owns or leases, usually semi-desert or desert. Thus, when the traditional Anangu owners of Uluru (Ayers Rock) claimed traditional ownership of Uluru and Kata Tjuta (the Olgas), their claim was disallowed because the land was within a national park and thus alienated. It was only by amending two acts of parliament that Uluru – Kata Tjuta National Park was handed back to traditional Anangu owners on the condition that it be immediately leased back to the Australian Nature Conservation Agency (formerly the Australian National Parks & Wildlife Service).

At present almost half of the Northern Territory has either been claimed, or is being claimed, by its traditional Aboriginal owners. The claim process is extremely tedious and can take many years to complete, largely because almost all claims have been opposed by the NT government. A great many elderly claimants die before the matter is resolved. Claimants must prove that under Aboriginal law they are responsible for the sacred sites on the land being claimed.

Once a claim is successful, Aboriginal people have the right to negotiate with mining companies and ultimately to accept or reject exploration and mining proposals. This right is strongly opposed by the mining lobby, despite the fact that traditional Aboriginal owners in the Northern Territory only reject about a third of these proposals outright.

The Pitjantjatjara Land Rights Act 1981 (South Australia) is Australia's second-most powerful and comprehensive land rights law. This gives Anangu Pitjantjatjara and Yankunytjatjara people freehold title to 10% of South Australia. The land, known as the Anangu Pitjantjatjara Lands, is in the far north of the state.

Just south of the Anangu Pitjantjatjara Lands lie the Maralinga Lands, which comprise 8% of South Australia. The area, largely contaminated by British nuclear tests in the 1950s, was returned to its Anangu traditional owners by virtue of the Maralinga Tjarutja Land Rights Act 1984 (South Australia).

Under these two South Australian acts, Anangu can control access to land and liquor consumption. However, if Anangu traditional owners cannot reach agreement with mining companies seeking to explore or mine on their land, they cannot veto mining activity; an arbitrator decides if mining will go ahead. If mining is given the green light, the arbitrator will bind the mining company with terms and conditions and ensure that reasonable monetary payments are made to Anangu.

In South Australia, other small Aboriginal reserves exist by virtue of the Aboriginal Land Trust Act 1966 (South Australia). This act gives Aboriginal people little control over their land.

Outside the Northern Territory and South Australia, Aboriginal land rights are extremely limited. In Queensland, less than 2% of the state is Aboriginal land, and the only land that can be claimed under the Aboriginal Land Act 1991 (Queensland) is land which has been gazetted by the government as land available for claim. Under existing Queensland legislation, 95% of the state's Aboriginal people can't claim their traditional country.

Since the passing of the Nature Conservation Act 1992 (Queensland), Aboriginal people in the state also have very limited claim to national parks. If Aboriginal people successfully claim a Queensland park, they must permanently lease it back to the government without a guarantee of a review of the lease arrangement or a majority on the board of management. This is quite different to the arrangements at Uluru – Kata Tjuta National Park, where the traditional owners have a majority on the board, with a 99-year lease-back that is renegotiated every five years.

In Western Australia, Aboriginal reserves comprise about 13% of the state. Of this land about one-third is granted to Aboriginal people under 99-year leases; the other two-thirds is controlled by the government's Aboriginal Affairs Planning Authority. Control of mining and payments to communities are a matter of ministerial discretion.

In New South Wales, the Aboriginal Land Rights Act 1983 (New South Wales) transferred freehold title of existing Aboriginal reserves to Aboriginal people and gave them the right to claim a minuscule amount of other land. Aboriginal people also have limited rights to the state's national parks, but these rights fall short of genuine control and don't permit Aboriginal people to live inside parks. In Victoria and Tasmania, land rights are extremely limited.

Mabo & the Native Title Act It was only very recently that the non-Aboriginal community, including the Federal government, came to grips with the fact that a meaningful conciliation between White Australia and its indigenous population was vital to the psychological well-being of all Australians.

In May 1982, five Torres Strait Islanders led by Eddie Mabo began an action for a declaration of native title over the Queensland Murray Islands. They argued that the legal principle of *terra nullius* had wrongfully usurped their title to land, as for thousands of years Murray Islanders had enjoyed a relationship with the land that included a notion of ownership. In June 1992 the High Court of Australia rejected *terra nullius* and the myth that Australia had been unoccupied. In doing this, it recognised that a principle of native title existed before the arrival of the British.

The High Court's judgment became known as the Mabo decision, one of the most controversial decisions ever handed down by an Australian court. It was ambiguous, as it didn't outline the extent to which native title existed in mainland Australia. It received a hostile reaction from mining and other industry groups, but was hailed by Aboriginal people and the prime minister of the time, Paul Keating, as an opportunity to create a basis of reconciliation between Aboriginal and non-Aboriginal Australians.

To define the principle of native title, the Federal parliament passed the Native Title Act in December 1993. Despite protest from the mining industry, the act gives Australian Aboriginal people very few new rights. It limits the application of native title to land which no-one else owns or leases, and also to land with which Aboriginal people have continued to have a physical association. The act states that existing ownership or leases extinguish native title, although native title may be revived after mining leases have expired. If land is successfully claimed by Aboriginal people under the act, they will have no veto over developments, including mining. It will no doubt take a number of years and court cases before the implications of the Native Title Act are fully understood.

ECONOMY

Australia is a relatively affluent, industrialised nation but much of its wealth still comes from agriculture and mining. It has a small domestic market and its manufacturing sector is comparatively weak. Nevertheless, a substantial proportion of the population is employed in manufacturing, and for much of Australia's history it has been argued that these industries need tariff protection from imports to ensure their survival.

Today, however, efforts are being made to increase Australia's international competitiveness. This has become more important as prices of traditional primary exports have become more volatile. During the 1980s and early '90s, Labor sought to restrain the growth of real wages with the assistance of the Australian Council of Trade Unions (ACTU), to make Australian products more competitive overseas, but this Accord, as it was known, ended with the 1996 election of the conservative Howard government.

An important source of income is the tourism industry, with the numbers of visitors rising each year and projections for even greater numbers in the future. The other bright spot is the booming economies of South-East Asia, with Australia perfectly positioned to enter these markets – 55% of Australia's exports go to the Asian region.

Agriculture, formerly the cornerstone of the Australian economy, today accounts for about 4% of production, while mining contributes about 8% and manufacturing about 16%. Major commodity exports include wool (Australia is the world's largest supplier), wheat, barley, sugar, coal and iron ore.

Japan is Australia's biggest trading partner, but the economies of China, Korea and Vietnam are becoming increasingly important. Regionally, Australia recently initiated the establishment of the Asia-Pacific Economic Cooperation (APEC) group, a body aimed at furthering the economic interests of the Pacific nations.

The Australian economy is growing at the rate of around 4% per year and inflation is low, at around 4%.

POPULATION & PEOPLE

Australia's population is about 18 million. The most populous states are New South Wales and Victoria, each with a capital city (Sydney and Melbourne) with a population of around three million. The population is concentrated along the east coast from Adelaide to Cairns and in a similar, but smaller, coastal region in Western Australia. The centre of the country is very sparsely populated.

There are about 230,000 Aboriginal people and Torres Strait Islanders, most heavily concentrated in central Australia and the far north. Aboriginal affairs are handled mainly by the Federal government body ATSIC (Aboriginal & Torres Strait Islander Commission).

Until WW II Australians were predominantly of British and Irish descent but that has changed dramatically. Since the war, heavy migration from Europe has created major Greek and Italian populations, also adding Yugoslavs, Lebanese, Turks and other groups.

More recently Australia has had large influxes of Asians, particularly Vietnamese after the Vietnam War. In comparison to its population Australia probably has taken more Vietnamese refugees than any other Western nation. On the whole these 'new Australians' have been remarkably well accepted and 'multiculturalism' is a popular concept in Australia.

If you come to Australia in search of a real Australian you will find one quite easily. He or she may be a Lebanese cafe owner, an English used-car salesperson, an Aboriginal artist, a Malaysian architect or a Greek greengrocer. And you will find them in pubs, on beaches, at barbecues, in mustering yards and at art galleries. And yes, you may meet a Mick (Crocodile) Dundee or two but he is strictly a rural model – the real Paul Hogan was a Sydney Harbour Bridge painter, a job where after you finish at one end you just start again at the other.

ARTS & CULTURE
Aboriginal Society
Australia's Aboriginal people were tribal, living in extended family groups or clans, with clan members descending from a common ancestral being. Tradition, rituals and laws linked the people of each clan to the land they occupied and each clan had various sites of spiritual significance, places to which their spirits would return when they died. Clan members came together to perform rituals to honour their ancestral spirits and the creators of the Dreaming. These beliefs were the basis of the Aboriginal peoples' ties to the land they lived on.

It is the responsibility of the clan, or particular members of it, to correctly maintain and protect the sites so that the ancestral beings are not offended and continue to protect the clan. Traditional punishments for those who neglect these responsibilities can still be severe, as their actions can easily affect the well-being of the whole clan – food and water shortages, natural disasters or mysterious illnesses can all be attributed to disgruntled or offended ancestral beings.

Many Aboriginal communities were semi-nomadic, others sedentary, one of the deciding factors being the availability of food. Where food and water were readily available, the people tended to remain in a limited area. When they did wander, however, it was to visit sacred places to carry out rituals, or to take advantage of seasonal foods available elsewhere. They did not, as is still often believed, roam aimlessly and desperately in the search for food and water.

The traditional role of the men was that of hunter, tool-maker and custodian of male law; the women reared the children, and gathered and prepared food. There was also female law and ritual for which the women were responsible. Ultimately, the shared efforts of men and women ensured the continuation of their social system.

Wisdom and skills obtained over millennia enabled Aboriginal people to use their environment to the maximum. An intimate knowledge of the behaviour of animals and the correct time to harvest the many plants they utilised ensured that food shortages were rare. Like other hunter-gatherer peoples, Aboriginal people were true ecologists.

Although Aboriginal people in northern Australia had been in regular contact with the fishing and farming peoples of Indonesia for at least 1000 years, the cultivation of crops and the domestication of livestock held no appeal. The only major modification of the landscape practised by Aboriginal people was the selective burning of undergrowth in forests and dead grass on the plains. This encouraged new growth, which in turn attracted game animals to the area. It also

Bark painting of a long-necked turtle from western Arnhem Land

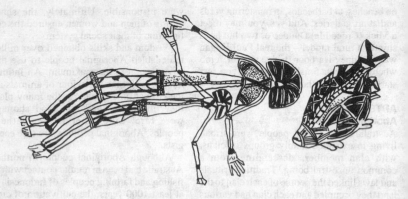

Blue Paintings at Little Nourlangie, Kakadu

prevented the build-up of combustible material in the forests, making hunting easier and reducing the possibility of major bushfires. Dingoes were domesticated to assist in the hunt and to guard the camp from intruders.

Similar technology – for example the boomerang and spear – was used throughout the continent, but techniques were adapted to the environment and the species being hunted. In the wetlands of northern Australia, fish traps hundreds of metres long made of bamboo and cord were built to catch fish at the end of the wet season. In the area now known as Victoria, permanent stone weirs many km long were used to trap migrating eels, while in the tablelands of Queensland finely woven nets were used to snare herds of wallabies and kangaroos.

Contrary to the common image, some tribes did build permanent dwellings, varying widely depending on climate, the materials available and likely length of use. In western Victoria the local Aboriginal people built permanent stone dwellings; in the deserts semicircular shelters were made with arched branches covered with native grasses or leaves; and in Tasmania large conical thatch shelters which could house up to 30 people were constructed. Such dwellings were used mainly for sleeping.

The early Australian Aboriginal people were also traders. Trade routes crisscrossed the country, dispersing goods and a variety of produced items. Many items traded, such as certain types of stone or shell, were rare and had great ritual significance. Boomerangs and ochre were other important items. Along the networks which developed, large numbers of people would meet for 'exchange ceremonies', where not only goods but also songs and dances were passed on.

Aboriginal Beliefs & Ceremonies

Early European settlers and explorers usually dismissed the entire Aboriginal population as 'savages' and 'barbarians', and it was some time before the Aboriginal peoples' deep, spiritual bond with the land, and their relationship to it, was understood by White Australians.

The perceived simplicity of the Aboriginal peoples' technology contrasts with the sophistication of their cultural life. Religion, history, law and art are integrated in complex ceremonies which depict the activities of their ancestral beings, and prescribe codes of behaviour and responsibilities for looking after the land and all living things. The link between the people and the ancestral beings are totems, each person having their own totem, or Dreaming. These totems take many forms, such as caterpillars, snakes, fish and magpies. Songs explain how the landscape contains these powerful creator ancestors, who can exert either a benign or a malevolent influence. They tell of the best places and the best times to hunt, and where to find water in drought years. They can also specify kinship relations and correct marriage partners.

Ceremonies are still performed in many parts of Australia; many of the sacred sites are believed to be dangerous and entry is prohibited under traditional Aboriginal law. These restrictions may seem merely the result of superstition, but in many cases they have a pragmatic origin. One site in northern Australia was believed to cause sores to break out all over the body of anyone visiting the area. Subsequently, the area was found to have a dangerously high level of radiation from naturally occurring radon gas. In another instance, fishing from a certain reef was traditionally prohibited. This restriction was scoffed at by local Europeans until it was discovered that fish from this area had a high incidence of ciguatera, which renders fish poisonous if eaten by humans.

While many Aboriginal people still live in rural areas, those living an urban life remain distinctively Aboriginal – they still speak their indigenous language (or a creolised mix) on a daily basis, and mix largely with other Aboriginal people. Much of their knowledge of the environment, bush medicine and food ('bush tucker') has been retained, and many traditional rites and ceremonies are being revived.

See the Religion section later in this chapter for more on Aboriginal beliefs, ceremonies and sacred sites. See also the Aboriginal Art section following this chapter.

European Art

In the 1880s a group of young artists developed the first distinctively Australian style of watercolour painting. Working from a permanent bush camp in Melbourne's (then) outer suburb of Box Hill, the painters captured the unique qualities of Australian life and the bush. The work of this group is generally referred to as the Heidelberg School, although the majority of the work was done at Box Hill. In Sydney a contemporary movement worked at Sirius Cove on Sydney Harbour. Both groups were influenced by the French plein-air painters, whose practice of working outdoors to capture the effects of natural light led directly to Impressionism. The main artists were Tom Roberts, Arthur Streeton, Frederick McCubbin, Louis Abrahams, Charles Conder, Julian Ashton and, later, Walter Withers. Their works can be found in most of the major galleries and are well worth seeking out.

In the 1940s, under the patronage of John and Sunday Reed at their home in suburban Melbourne, a new generation of artists redefined the direction of Australian art. This group included some of Australia's most famous contemporary artists, such as Sir Sidney Nolan and Arthur Boyd.

More recently the work of painters such as Fred Williams, John Olsen and Brett Whiteley has made an impression on the international art world. Whiteley, probably Australia's most well-known modern artist, died in 1992.

Literature

Aboriginal Song & Narrative Aboriginal oral traditions are loosely and misleadingly described as 'myths and legends'. Their single uniting factor is the Dreamtime, when the totemic ancestors formed the landscape, fashioned the laws and created the people who would inherit the land. Translated and printed in English, these renderings of the Dreamtime often lose much of their intended impact. Gone are the sounds of sticks, dijeridu and the rhythm of the dancers which accompanies each poetic line; alone, the words fail to fuse past and present, and the spirits and forces to which the lines refer lose much of their animation.

At the turn of the century, Catherine Langloh Parker was collecting Aboriginal legends and using her outback experience to interpret them sincerely but synthetically. She compiled *Australian Legendary Tales: Folklore of the Noongah-burrahs* (1902).

Professor Ted Strehlow was one of the first methodical translators, and his *Aranda Traditions* (1947) and *Songs of Central Australia* (1971) are important works. Equally important is the combined effort of Catherine & Ronald Berndt. There are 188 songs in the Berndt collection *Djanggawul* (1952), and 129 sacred and 47 secular songs in the collection *Kunapipi* (1951). *The Land of the Rainbow Snake* (1979) focuses on children's stories from western Arnhem Land.

More recently, many Dreamtime stories have appeared in translation, illustrated and published by Aboriginal artists. Some representative collections are *Joe Nangan's Dreaming: Aboriginal Legends of the North-West* (Joe Nangan & Hugh Edwards, 1976); *Milbi: Aboriginal Tales from Queensland's Endeavour River* (Tulo Gordon & J B Haviland, 1980); *Visions of Mowanjum: Aboriginal Writings from the Kimberley* (Kormilda Community College, Darwin; 1980); and *Gularabulu* (Paddy Roe & Stephen Muecke, 1983).

Modern Aboriginal Literature Modern Aboriginal writers have fused the English language with aspects of their traditional culture. The result is often carefully fashioned to expose the injustices they have been subjected to, especially as urban dwellers. The first Aboriginal writer to be published was David Unaipon in 1929 *(Native Legends)*.

Aboriginal literature now includes drama, fiction and poetry. The poet Oodgeroo Noonuccal (Kath Walker), one of the most well-known of modern Aboriginal writers, was the first Aboriginal woman to have work published *(We Are Going*, 1964). *Paperbark: A collection of Black Australian writings* (1990) presents a great cross-section of modern Aboriginal writers, including dramatist Jack Davis and novelist Mudrooroo Narogin (Colin Johnson). The book has an excellent bibliography of Black Australian writing.

There are a number of modern accounts of Aboriginal life in remote parts of Australia. *Raparapa Kularr Martuwarra: Stories from the Fitzroy River Drovers* (1988) is a Magabala Books production. This company, based in Broome, energetically promotes Aboriginal literature.

Autobiography and biography have become an important branch of Aboriginal literature – look for *Moon and Rainbow* (Dick Roughsey, 1971) and *My Country of the Pelican Dreaming* (Grant Ngabidj, 1981).

The Aboriginal in White Literature Aboriginal people have often been used as characters in White outback literature. Usually the treatment was patronising and somewhat short-sighted. There were exceptions, especially in the subject of interracial sexuality between White men and Aboriginal women.

Rosa Praed, in her short piece *My Australian Girlhood* (1902), drew heavily on her outback experience and her affectionate childhood relationship with Aboriginal people. Jeannie Gunn's *Little Black Princess* was published in 1904, but it was *We of the Never Never* (1908) which brought her renown. Her story of the life and trials on Elsey Station includes an unflattering, patronising depiction of the Aboriginal people on and around the station.

Catherine Martin, in 1923, wrote *The Incredible Journey*. It follows the trail of two Black women, Iliapo and Polde, in search of a little boy who had been kidnapped by a White man. The book describes in careful detail the harsh desert environment they traverse.

Katharine Susannah Prichard contributed a great deal to outback literature in the 1920s. A journey to Turee Station in the cattle country of the Ashburton and Fortescue rivers, in 1926, inspired her lyric tribute to the Aborigine, *Coonardoo* (1929), which delved into the then almost taboo love between an Aboriginal woman and a White station boss. Later, Mary Durack's *Keep Him My Country* (1955) explored the theme of a White station manager's love for an Aboriginal girl, Dalgerie.

More recent works incorporating Aboriginal themes include Rodney Hall's *The Second Bridegroom* (1991), Thomas

Keneally's *Flying Hero Class* (1991) and David Malouf's *Remembering Babylon* (1993).

Bush Ballads & Yarns The 'bush' was a great source of inspiration for many popular ballads and stories. These were particularly in vogue at the turn of the century but they have an enduring quality.

Adam Lindsay Gordon was the forerunner of this type of literature, having published *Bush Ballads and Galloping Rhymes* in 1870. This collection includes his popular *The Sick Stockrider*.

The two most famous exponents of the ballad style were A B 'Banjo' Paterson and Henry Lawson. Paterson grew up in the bush in the second half of the last century and became one of Australia's most important bush poets. His pseudonym 'The Banjo' was the name of a horse on his family's station. His horse ballads were regarded as some of his best, but he was familiar with all aspects of station life and wrote with great optimism. *Clancy of the Overflow* and *The Man From Snowy River* are both well-known, but The

Banjo is probably best remembered as the author of Australia's alternative national anthem, *Waltzing Matilda*, in which he celebrates an unnamed swagman, one of the anonymous wanderers of the bush.

Henry Lawson was a contemporary of Paterson, but was much more of a social commentator and political thinker and less of a humorist. Although he wrote a good many poems about the bush – pieces such as *Andy's Gone with Cattle* and *The Roaring Days* are among his best – his greatest legacy is his short stories of life in the bush, which seem remarkably simple yet manage to capture the atmosphere perfectly. Good examples are *A Day on a Selection* (a selection was a tract of crown land for which annual fees were paid) and *The Drover's Wife;* the latter epitomises one of Lawson's 'battlers' who dreams of better things as an escape from the ennui of her isolated circumstances.

There were many other balladeers. George Essex Evans penned a tribute to Queensland's women pioneers, *The Women of the West*; Will Ogilvie wrote of the great

Waltzing Matilda

Written in 1895 by the 'bard of the bush', Banjo Patterson, *Waltzing Matilda* is Australia's unofficial national anthem. Most people know it as a catchy but meaningless ditty about a jolly swagman who stole a jumbuck (a sheep) and later drowned himself in a billabong rather than be arrested, but historians have suggested that Patterson actually wrote the tune as a political anthem. The Waltzing Matilda Centenary Festival, held in Winton in 1995, fuelled the controversy over the origins of the song.

The 1890s was a period of social and political upheaval in Queensland. Along with nationalistic calls for the states to amalgamate and form a federation, the decade was dominated by an economic crisis, mass unemployment and a series of shearers' strikes in outback Queensland which led to the formation of the Australian Labor Party to represent workers' interests.

Patterson visited Winton in 1895, and during a picnic beside the Combo Waterhole he heard stories about the violent 1894 shearers' strike on Dagworth Station. During the strike, rebel shearers had burned down seven woolsheds, leading the police to declare martial law and place a reward of £1000 on the head of their leader, Samuel Hofmeister. Rather than face arrest, Hofmeister drowned himself in a billabong.

While there is no direct proof that Patterson was writing allegorically about the strikes, the song's undeniable anti-authoritarianism and the fact that it was adopted as an anthem by the rebel shearers weigh in heavily in support of the theory. ■

cattle drives; and Barcroft Boake's *Where the Dead Men Lie* celebrates the people who opened up never-never country where 'heat-waves dance forever'.

Standing apart from the romanticism of these writers is Barbara Baynton. She is uncompromising in her depiction of the outback as a cruel, brutal environment, and the romantic imagery of the bush is absent in the ferocious depiction of the lot of *Squeaker's Mate* in *Bush Studies* (1902).

Outback Novelists The author's name if not the content would have encouraged many overseas visitors to read D H Lawrence's *Kangaroo* (1923), which, in places, presents his frightened images of the bush. Later, Nevil Shute's *A Town Like Alice* (1950) would have been the first outback-based novel that many people read. Other Shute titles with outback themes are *In the Wet* (1953) and *Beyond the Black Stump* (1956).

Perhaps the best local depicter of the outback was the aforementioned Katharine Susannah Prichard. She produced a string of novels with outback themes into which she wove her political thoughts. *Black Opal* (1921) was the study of the fictional opal mining community of Fallen Star Ridge; *Working Bullocks* (1926) examined the political nature of work in the karri forests of Western Australia; and *Moon of Desire* (1941) follows its characters in search of a fabulous pearl from Broome to Singapore. Her trilogy of the Western Australian gold-fields was published separately as *The Roaring Nineties* (1946), *Golden Miles* (1948) and *Winged Seeds* (1950).

Xavier Herbert's *Capricornia* (1938) stands as one of the great epics of outback Australia, with its sweeping descriptions of the northern country. His second epic, *Poor Fellow My Country* (1975), is a documentary of the fortunes of a northern station owner. Through the characters, Herbert voices his bitter regret at the failure of reconciliation between the White despoilers of the land and its indigenous people.

One of the great nonfiction pieces is Mary Durack's family chronicle, *Kings in Grass Castles* (1959), which relates the White settlement of the Kimberley ranges. Her sequel was *Sons in the Saddle* (1983).

Australia's Nobel prize-winner, Patrick White, used the outback as the backdrop for a number of his monumental works. The most prominent character in *Voss* (1957) is an explorer, perhaps loosely based on Ludwig Leichhardt; *The Tree of Man* (1955) has all the outback happenings of flood, fire and drought; and the journey of *The Aunt's Story* (1948) begins on an Australian sheep station.

Kenneth Cook's nightmarish novel set in outback New South Wales, *Wake in Fright* (1961), has been made into a film.

20th-Century Novelists Miles Franklin was one of Australia's early feminists and decided early in life to become a writer rather than the traditional wife and mother. Her best-known book, *My Brilliant Career*, was also her first. It was written at the turn of the century when the author was only 20, and brought her both widespread fame and criticism. On her death she endowed an annual award for an Australian novel; today the Miles Franklin Award is the most prestigious in the country.

A contemporary writer of note is Peter Carey, who won the Booker Prize for *Oscar and Lucinda* in 1988.

Thomas Keneally is well-known for his novels which deal with the suffering of oppressed peoples, for example *The Chant of Jimmy Blacksmith* and the Booker Prize-winning *Schindler's Ark*, upon which the Spielberg film *Schindler's List* was based.

Thea Astley is far from a household name, yet she is one of the finest writers in the country. Her books include *Vanishing Points*, *The Slow Natives*, *An Item from the Late News* and *It's Raining in Mango*, the last of which is probably her finest work and expresses her outrage at the treatment of Aboriginal people.

Elizabeth Jolley is well known as a short-story writer and novelist with a keen eye for the eccentric. Her works include *Mr Scobie's Riddle* (1983), *My Father's Moon* (1989),

Cabin Fever (1990) and *The Georges' Wife* (1993).

Tim Winton, from Western Australia, is one of the most exciting writers in Australia today. His works include *Cloudstreet* (1992) and *The Riders* (1994), which was shortlisted for the Booker Prize.

Cinema

The Australian film industry began as early as 1896, a year after the Lumiere brothers opened the world's first cinema in Paris. Maurice Sestier, one of the Lumieres' photographers, came to Australia and made the first films in the streets of Sydney and at Flemington Racecourse during the Melbourne Cup.

Cinema historians regard an Australian film, *Soldiers of the Cross*, as the world's first 'real' movie. It was originally screened at the Melbourne Town Hall in 1901, cost £600 to make and was shown throughout the USA in 1902.

The next significant Australian film, *The Story of the Kelly Gang*, was screened in 1907, and by 1911 the industry was flourishing. Low-budget films were being made in such quantities that they could be hired out or sold cheaply. Over 250 silent feature films were made before the 1930s when the talkies and Hollywood took over.

In the 1930s, film companies like Cinesound sprang up. Cinesound made 17 feature films between 1931 and 1940, many based on Australian history or literature. *Forty Thousand Horsemen*, directed by Cinesound's great film maker Charles Chauvel, was a highlight of this era of locally made and financed films which ended in 1959, the year of Chauvel's death. Early Australian actors who became famous both at home and overseas include Errol Flynn and Chips Rafferty (born John Goffage).

Before the introduction of government subsidies during 1969 and 1970, the Australian film industry found it difficult to compete with US and British interests. The New Wave era of the 1970s, a renaissance of Australian cinema, produced films like *Picnic at Hanging Rock*, *Sunday Too Far Away*, *Caddie* and *The Devil's Playground*, which appealed to large local and international audiences.

Since the '70s, Australian actors and directors such as Mel Gibson, Nicole Kidman, Judy Davis, Greta Scacchi, Paul Hogan, Bruce Beresford, Peter Weir, Gillian Armstrong and Fred Schepisi have gained international recognition. Films like *Gallipoli*, *The Year of Living Dangerously*, *Mad Max*, *Malcolm*, *Crocodile Dundee I* and *II*, *Proof*, *Holidays on the River Yarra*, *The Year My Voice Broke*, *Strictly Ballroom* and most recently *Priscilla – Queen of the Desert*, *Muriel's Wedding* and *Babe* have entertained and impressed audiences worldwide.

Music

Popular Music Australia's participation in the flurry of popular music since the 1950s has been a frustrating mix of good, indifferent, lousy, parochial and excellent. However, even the offerings of the most popular acts have done nothing to remove the cultural cringe: the highest praise remains 'it's good enough to have come from the UK/USA'. And it's true that little of the popular music created here has been noticeably different from that overseas.

Which is why the recent success of Aboriginal music, and its merging with rock, is so refreshing. This music really is different. The most obvious name that springs to mind is Yothu Yindi. Their song about the dishonoured White-man's agreement, *Treaty*, perhaps did more than anything else to popularise Aboriginal land rights claims. The band's lead singer, Mandawuy Yunupingu, was named Australian of the Year in 1993.

Other Aboriginal names include Coloured Stone, Kevin Carmody, Archie Roach, Ruby Hunter, Scrap Metal, the Sunrise Band, Christine Anu (from the Torres Strait Islands), and the bands that started it all but no longer exist, No Fixed Address and Warumpi Band.

White country music owes much to Irish heritage and American country influences, often with a liberal sprinkling of dry outback humour. Names to watch out for include Slim Dusty, Ted Egan, John Williamson, Chad Morgan, Lee Kernaghan, Neil Murray, Dirty Hanks, Trailblazers, Gondwanaland and Smokey Dawson.

Having written off White popular music, the live-music circuits of Australia really are something to crow about. The bands playing around the traps can be just as exciting as those found in London or LA, pardon the comparisons! Popular bands to look out for include: Midnight Oil, Cruel Sea, Hunters & Collectors, You Am I, The Black Sorrows, Spider Bait, silverchair, Magic Dirt, and Custard.

Folk Music Australian folk music is derived from English, Irish and Scottish roots. Bush bands, playing fast-paced and high-spirited folk music for dancing, can be anything from performers trotting out standards such as *Click Go The Shears* to serious musicians who happen to like a rollicking time.

Fiddles, banjos and tin whistles feature prominently, plus there's the indigenous 'lagerphone', a percussion instrument made from a great many beer bottle caps nailed to a stick, which is then shaken or banged on the ground. If you have a chance to go to a bush dance or folk festival, don't pass it up.

Architecture

Australia's first European settlers arrived in the country with memories of Georgian grandeur, but the lack of materials and tools meant that most of the early houses were almost caricatures of the real thing. One of the first concessions to the climate, and one which was to become a feature of Australian houses, was the addition of a wide verandah which kept the inner rooms of the house dark and cool.

The prosperity of the gold rush era in the second half of the last century saw a spate of grand buildings in the Victorian style in most major towns. Many of these buildings survive, and are a fine reminder of a period of great wealth, confidence and progress. The houses of the time became much more elaborate, with ornamentation of all sorts gracing the facades.

Increasing population in the major towns saw the rise of the terrace house, simple single and later double-storey houses which, although cramped at the time, today provide comfortable dwellings for thousands of inner-city residents.

By the turn of the century, at a time when the separate colonies were combining to form a new nation, a simpler, more 'Australian' architectural style evolved, and this came to be known as Federation style. Built between about 1890 and 1920, Federation houses typically feature red-brick walls, and an orange-tiled roof decorated with terracotta ridging and chimney pots. Also a feature was the rising-sun motif on the gable ends, symbolic of the dawn of a new age for Australia.

The Californian bungalow, a solid house style which developed in colonial British India, became the rage in the 1920s and '30s, and its simple and honest style fitted well with the emerging Australian tendency towards a casual lifestyle.

Differing climates led to some interesting regional variations. In the tropical north the style known as the Queenslander evolved – elevated houses with plenty of ventilation to make the most of cooling breezes. In the 1930s the first buildings in Darwin appeared with the same features, and have developed into the modern 'Troppo' (tropical) style of architecture.

The immigration boom which followed WW II led to urban sprawl – cities and towns expanded rapidly, and the 'brick veneer' became the dominant housing medium, and remains so today. On the fringe of any Australian city you'll find acres of new, low-cost, brick-veneer suburbs – as far as the eye can see it's a bleak expanse of terracotta roofs and bricks in various shades.

Modern Australian architecture struggles to maintain a distinctive style, with overseas trends dominating large projects. Often the most interesting 'modern' buildings are in fact recycled Victorian or other era buildings. There are some exceptions, notable ones being the Convention Centre at Sydney's Darling Harbour, which was designed by Phillip Cox, and the new Cultural Centre at Uluru-Kata Tjuta National Park in central Australia, which was designed in consultation with the traditional owners of the national park.

RELIGION

A shrinking majority of people in Australia (around 70%) are at least nominally Christian. Most Protestant churches have merged to become the Uniting Church, although the Church of England has remained separate. The Catholic Church is popular (about a third of Christians are Catholics), with the original Irish adherents now joined by large numbers of Mediterranean immigrants.

Non-Christian minorities abound, the main ones being Buddhist, Jewish or Muslim.

Aboriginal Religion

Traditional Aboriginal cultures either have very little religious component or are nothing but religion, depending on how you look at it. Is a belief system which views every event, no matter how trifling, in a nonmaterial context a religion? The early Christian missionaries certainly didn't think so. For them a belief in a deity was an essential part of a religion, and anything else was mere superstition.

Sacred Sites Aboriginal sacred sites are a perennial topic of discussion. Their presence can lead to headline-grabbing controversy when they stand in the way of developments such as roads, mines and dams. This is because most other Australians still have great difficulty understanding the Aboriginal peoples' deep spiritual bond with the land.

Aboriginal religious beliefs centre on the continuing existence of spirit beings that lived on Earth during the Dreamtime, which occurred before the arrival of humans. These beings created all the features of the natural world and were the ancestors of all living things. They took different forms but behaved as people do, and as they travelled

about they left signs to show where they had passed.

Despite being supernatural, the ancestors were subject to ageing and eventually they returned to the sleep from which they'd awoken at the dawn of time. Here their spirits remain as eternal forces that breathe life into the newborn and influence natural events. Each ancestor's spiritual energy flows along the path it travelled during the Dreamtime and is strongest at the points where it left physical evidence of its activities, such as a tree, hill or claypan. These features are sacred sites.

Every person, animal and plant is believed to have two souls – one mortal and one immortal. The latter is part of a particular ancestral spirit and returns to the sacred sites of that ancestor after death, while the mortal soul simply fades into oblivion. Each person is spiritually bound to the sacred sites that mark the land associated with his or her ancestor. It is the individual's obligation to help care for these sites by performing the necessary rituals and singing the songs that tell of the ancestor's deeds. By doing this, the order created by that ancestor is maintained.

Unfortunately, Aboriginal sacred sites are not like Christian churches, which can be desanctified before the bulldozers move in. Neither can they be bought, sold or transferred. Other Australians find this difficult to accept because they regard land as belonging to the individual, whereas in Aboriginal society land is regarded as belonging to the community. In a nutshell, Aboriginal people believe that to destroy or damage a sacred site threatens not only the living but also the spirit inhabitants of the land. It is a distressing and dangerous act, and one that no responsible person would condone. See Aboriginal Beliefs & Ceremonies earlier in this chapter for more on sacred sites.

Throughout much of Australia, when pastoralists were breaking the Aboriginal peoples' subsistence link to the land, and sometimes shooting them, many Aboriginal people sought refuge on missions and became Christian. However, becoming Christian has not, for most Aboriginal people, meant renouncing their traditional religion. Many senior Aboriginal law men are also devout Christians, and in many cases ministers.

LANGUAGE
Australian English

Any visitor from abroad who thinks Australian (that's 'Strine') is simply a weird variant of English/American will soon have a few surprises. For a start many Australians don't even speak Australian – they speak Italian, Lebanese, Vietnamese, Turkish or Greek.

Those who do speak the native tongue are liable to lose you in a strange collection of Australian words. Some have completely different meanings in Australia than they have in English-speaking countries north of the equator; some commonly used words have been shortened almost beyond recognition. Others are derived from Aboriginal languages, or from the slang used by early convict settlers.

There is a slight regional variation in the Australian accent, while the difference between city and country speech is mainly a matter of speed. Some of the most famed Aussie words are hardly heard at all – 'mates' are more common than 'cobbers'. If you want to pass for a native try speaking slightly nasally, shortening any word of more than two syllables and then adding a vowel to the end of it, making anything you can into a diminutive (even the Hell's Angels can become mere 'bikies') and peppering your speech with as many expletives as possible. Lonely Planet publishes an *Australian phrasebook*, which is an introduction to both Australian English and Aboriginal languages, and the list that follows may also help:

arvo – afternoon
avagoyermug – traditional rallying call, especially at cricket matches
award wage – minimum pay rate

back o' Bourke – back of beyond, middle of nowhere
bail out – leave
bail up – hold up, rob, earbash
banana bender – resident of Queensland

barbie – barbecue (bbq)
barrack – cheer on team at sporting event, support (as in 'who do you barrack for?')
bastard – general form of address which can mean many things, from high praise or respect ('He's the bravest bastard I know') to dire insult ('You rotten bastard!'). Avoid if unsure!
bathers – swimming costume (Victoria)
battler – hard trier, struggler
beaut, beauty, bewdie – great, fantastic
big mobs – a large amount, heaps
bikies – motorcyclists
billabong – water hole in dried up riverbed, more correctly an ox-bow bend cut off in the dry season by receding waters
billy – tin container used to boil tea in the bush
bitumen – surfaced road
black stump – where the 'back o' Bourke' begins
bloke – man
blowies – blow flies
bludger – lazy person, one who won't work
blue (ie 'have a blue') – to have an argument or fight
bluey – swag, or nickname for a red-haired person
bonzer – great, ripper
boomer – very big, a particularly large male kangaroo
boomerang – a curved flat wooden instrument used by Aboriginal people for hunting
booze bus – police van used for random breath testing for alcohol
bottle shop – liquor shop
Buckley's – no chance at all
bug (Moreton Bay bug) – a small crab
bull dust – fine and sometimes deep dust on outback roads, also bullshit
bunyip – mythical bush spirit
burl – have a try (as in 'give it a burl')
bush – country, anywhere away from the city
bushbash – to force your way through pathless bush
bushranger – Australia's equivalent of the outlaws of the American Wild West (some goodies, some baddies)
bush tucker – native foods, usually in the outback

camp oven – large, cast-iron pot with lid, used for cooking on an open fire

cask – wine box (a great Australian invention)

Chiko roll – vile Australian junk food

chocka – completely full, from 'chock-a-block'

chook – chicken

chuck a U-ey – do a U-turn

clobber – to hit

cobber – mate (archaic)

cocky – small-scale farmer

come good – turn out all right

compo – compensation such as workers' compensation

counter meal, countery – pub meal

cow cocky – small-scale cattle farmer

cozzie – swimming costume (New South Wales)

crook – ill, badly made, substandard

crow eater – resident of South Australia

cut lunch – sandwiches

dag, daggy – dirty lump of wool at back end of a sheep; also an affectionate or mildly abusive term for a socially inept person

daks – trousers

damper – bush loaf made from flour and water and cooked in a camp oven

dead horse – tomato sauce

deli – milk bar in South Australia & Western Australia, but a delicatessen elsewhere.

dijeridu – cylindrical wooden musical instrument traditionally played by Aboriginal men

dill – idiot

dinkum, fair dinkum – honest, genuine

dinky-di – the real thing

divvy van – police divisional van

dob in – to tell on someone

donk – car or boat engine

don't come the raw prawn – don't try and fool me

down south – the rest of Australia, according to anyone north of Brisbane

drongo – worthless or stupid person

Dry, the – dry season in northern Australia (April to October)

duco – car paint

dunny – outdoor lavatory

dunny budgies – blowies

earbash – talk nonstop

eastern states – the rest of Australia viewed from Western Australia

esky – large insulated box for keeping beer etc cold

fair crack of the whip! – fair go!

fair go! – give us a break

flake – shark meat, used in fish & chips

floater – meat pie floating in pea soup – yuk

flog – sell, steal

fossick – hunt for gems or semiprecious stones

from arsehole to breakfast – all over the place

furphy – a rumour or false story

galah – noisy parrot, thus noisy idiot

game – brave (as in 'game as Ned Kelly')

gander – look (as in 'have a gander')

garbo – person who collects your garbage

g'day – good day, traditional Australian greeting

gibber – Aboriginal word for a stone or rock, hence gibber plain or desert

give it away – give up

good on ya – well done

grazier – large-scale sheep or cattle farmer

grog – general term for alcoholic drinks

grouse – very good

homestead – residence of a station owner or manager

hoon – idiot, hooligan, yahoo

how are ya? – standard greeting, expected answer 'good, thanks, how are *you*?'

icy-pole – frozen lolly water on a stick

jackaroo – young male trainee on a station (farm)

jillaroo – young female trainee on a station

jocks – men's underpants

journo – journalist

jumped-up – full of self-importance, arrogant

kiwi – New Zealander

knock – criticise, deride
knocker – one who knocks
Koori – Aboriginal person (mostly south of the Murray River)

lair – layabout, ruffian
lairising – acting like a lair
lamington – square of sponge cake covered in chocolate icing and coconut
larrikin – a bit like a lair
lay-by – put a deposit on an article so the shop will hold it for you
lollies – sweets, candy
lurk – a scheme

manchester – household linen
mate – general term of familiarity, whether you know the person or not
middy – 285 ml beer glass (New South Wales)
milk bar – general store
milko – milkman
mozzies – mosquitoes

never-never – remote country in the outback
no hoper – hopeless case
no worries – she'll be right, that's OK
north island – mainland Australia, viewed from Tasmania
northern summer – summer in the northern hemisphere

ocker – an uncultivated or boorish Australian
off-sider – assistant or partner
OS – overseas, as in 'he's gone OS'
outback – remote part of the bush, back o' Bourke
OYO – own your own (flat or apartment)

paddock – a fenced area of land, usually intended for livestock
pastoralist – large-scale grazier
pavlova – traditional Australian meringue and cream dessert, named after the Russian ballerina Anna Pavlova
perve – to gaze with lust
pinch – steal
piss – beer
piss turn – boozy party, also piss up
pissed – drunk

pissed off – annoyed
piss weak – no good, gutless
plonk – cheap wine
pokies – poker machines
Pom – English person
postie – mailman
pot – 285 ml glass of beer (Victoria, Queensland)
push – group or gang of people, such as shearers

ratbag – friendly term of abuse
ratshit (RS) – lousy
rapt – delighted, enraptured
reckon! – you bet!, absolutely!
rego – registration, as in 'car rego'
ridgy-didge – original, genuine
ripper – good (also 'little ripper')
road train – semitrailer-trailer-trailer
root – have sexual intercourse
rooted – tired
ropable – very bad-tempered or angry
rubbish (ie *to rubbish*) – deride, tease

Salvo – member of the Salvation Army
sandgroper – resident of Western Australia
scallops – fried potato cakes (Queensland, New South Wales), shellfish (elsewhere)
schooner – large beer glass (New South Wales, South Australia)
scrub – bush
sea wasp – deadly box jellyfish
sealed road – surfaced road
session – lengthy period of heavy drinking
sheila – woman
shellacking – comprehensive defeat
she'll be right – no worries
shonky – unreliable
shoot through – leave in a hurry
shout – buy a round of drinks (as in 'it's your shout')
sickie – day off work ill (or malingering)
slab – plastic shrink-wrapped package of beer containing 24 cans
smoko – tea break
snag – sausage
squatter – pioneer farmer who occupied land as a tenant of the government
squattocracy – Australian 'old money' folk,

who made it by being first on the scene and grabbing the land

station – large farm

sticky beak – nosy person

stinger – (deadly) box jellyfish

strides – daks

stubby – 375 ml bottle of beer

Stubbies – popular brand of mens' work shorts

sunbake – sunbathe (well, the sun's hot in Australia)

surfies – surfing fanatics

swag – canvas-covered bed roll used in the outback; also a large amount

tall poppies – achievers (knockers like to cut them down)

tea – evening meal

thingo – thing, whatchamacallit, hooza meebob, doo velacki, thingamajig

thongs – flip-flops, an ocker's idea of formal footwear

tinny – 375 ml can of beer; also a small, aluminium fishing dinghy (Northern Territory)

togs – swimming costume (Queensland, Victoria)

too right! – absolutely!

Top End – northern part of the Northern Territory

trucky – truck driver

true blue – dinkum

tucker – food

two-pot screamer – person unable to hold their drink

two-up – traditional heads/tails gambling game

uni – university

up north – New South Wales and Queensland when viewed from Victoria

ute – utility, pick-up truck

wag (ie *to wag*) – to skip school or work

wagon – station wagon, estate car

walkabout – lengthy walk away from it all

wallaby track (on the) – to wander from place to place seeking work (archaic)

weatherboard – wooden house

Wet (ie *the Wet*) – rainy season in the north

wharfie – dockworker

whinge – complain, moan

wobbly – disturbing, unpredictable behaviour (as in 'throw a wobbly')

woomera – stick used by Aboriginal people for throwing spears

yabbie – small freshwater crayfish

yahoo – noisy and unruly person

yakka – work (from an Aboriginal language)

yobbo – uncouth, aggressive person

yonks – ages; a long time

youse – plural of you, pronounced 'yooze', only used by the grammatically challenged

Aboriginal Language

At the time of European contact there were around 250 separate Australian languages, comprising about 700 dialects. Often three or four adjacent tribes would speak what amounted to dialects of the same language, but another adjacent tribe might speak a completely different language.

It is believed that all the languages evolved from a single language family as the Aboriginal people gradually moved out over the entire continent and split into new groups. There are a number of words that occur right across the continent, such as *jina* (foot) and *mala* (hand), and similarities also exist in the often complex grammatical structures.

Following European contact the number of Aboriginal languages was drastically reduced. At least eight separate languages were spoken in Tasmania alone, but none of these was recorded before the native speakers either died or were killed. Of the original 250 or so languages, only around 30 are today spoken on a regular basis and are taught to children.

Aboriginal Kriol is a new language which has developed since European arrival in Australia. It is spoken across northern Australia and has become the 'native' language of many young Aboriginal people. It contains many English words, but the pronunciation and grammatical usage are along Aboriginal lines, the meaning is often different, and the spelling is phonetic. For example, the

English sentence 'He was amazed' becomes 'I bin luk kwesjinmak' in Kriol.

There are a number of generic terms which Aboriginal people use to describe themselves, and these vary according to the region. The most common of these is Koori, used for the people of south-east Australia.

Nunga is used to refer to the people of coastal South Australia, Murri for those from the north-east, and Nyoongah is used in the country's south-west.

Lonely Planet's *Australian phrasebook* gives a detailed account of Aboriginal languages.

Aboriginal Art

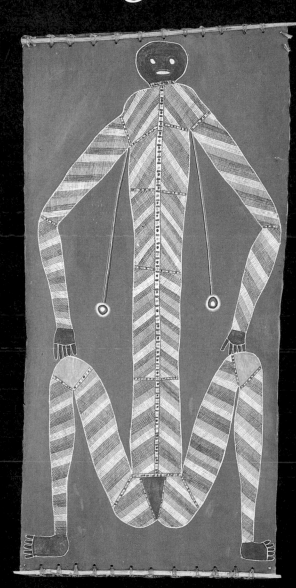

Namarrkon, Lightning Spirit by Curly Bardagubu, c. 1931-1987, Born clan; Kunwinjku language, Namokardabu, western Arnhem Land; earth pigments on bark; 156 x 75cm; 1987; purchased through the Art Foundation of Victoria with assistance from Alcoa of Australia Limited, Governor 1990; National Gallery of Victoria.

ABORIGINAL ART

Aboriginal art has undergone a major revival in the last decade or so, with artists throughout the country finding both a means to express and preserve ancient Dreaming values, and a way to share this rich cultural heritage with the wider community.

While the so-called dot paintings of the central deserts are the most readily identifiable and probably most popular form of contemporary Aboriginal art, there's a huge range of material being produced – bark paintings from Arnhem Land, wood carving and silk-screen printing from the Tiwi Islands north of Darwin, batik printing and wood carving from central Australia, and more.

The initial forms of artistic expression were rock carvings, body painting and ground designs, and the earliest engraved designs known to exist date back at least 30,000 years. Art has always been an integral part of Aboriginal life, a connection between past and present, between the supernatural and the earthly, between people and the land.

All early art was a reflection of the various peoples' ancestral Dreaming – the 'Creation', when the earth's physical features were formed by the struggles between powerful supernatural ancestors such as the Rainbow Serpent, the Lightning Men and the Wandjina. Not only was the physical layout mapped but codes of behaviour were also laid down, and although these laws have been diluted and adapted in the last 200 years, they still provide the basis for today's Aborigines. Ceremonies, rituals and sacred paintings are all based on the Dreaming.

A Dreaming may take a number of different forms – it can be a

Pampardu Jukurrpa
by Clarise Poulson;
acrylic on linen;
150 x 90cm; 1993;
Warlukurlangu Artists
Association, Yuen-
dumu, NT; courtesy of
DESART.

Left: Lightning Brothers rock art site at Katherine River; courtesy of the NT Tourist Commission.

Below: Ewaninga rock engravings, south of Alice Springs; courtesy of the NT Tourist Commission.

person, an animal or a physical feature, while others are more general, relating to a region, a group of people, or natural forces such as floods and wind. Thus Australia is covered by a wide network of Dreamings, and any one person may have connections with several.

CENTRAL AUSTRALIAN ART
Western Desert Paintings

The current renaissance in Aboriginal painting began in the early 1970s at Papunya (honey ant place), at the time a small, depressed community 240 km north-west of Alice Springs, which had grown out of the government's 'assimilation' policy. Here the local children were given the task of painting a traditional-style mural on the school wall. The local elders took interest in the project, and although the public display of traditional images gave rise to much debate amongst the elders, they eventually participated and in fact completed the *Honey Ant Dreaming* mural. This was the first time that images which were originally confined to rock and body art came to be reproduced in a different environment.

Other murals followed this first one, and before long the desire to paint spread through the community. In the early stages paintings were produced on small boards on the ground or balanced on the artist's knee, but this soon gave way to painting on canvas with acrylic paints. Canvas was an ideal medium as it could be easily rolled and transported, yet large paintings were possible. With the growing importance of art, both as an economic and a cultural activity, an association was formed to help the artists sell their work. The Papunya Tula company in Alice Springs is still one

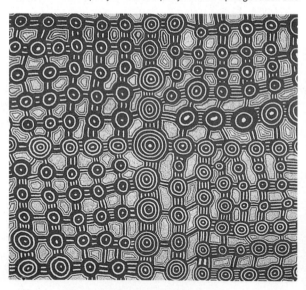

Untitled by Dini Campbell Tjampitjinpa; acrylic on linen; 182 x 152cm; 1993; Papunya Tula Artists Pty Ltd, Alice Springs, NT; courtesy of DESART.

of the few galleries in central Australia to be owned and run by Aborigines.

Painting in central Australia has flourished to such a degree that these days it is an important educational source for young kids, as they can learn aspects of religious and ceremonial knowledge. This is especially true now that women are so much a part of the painting movement.

The trademark dot-painting style is partly an evolution from 'ground paintings', which formed the centrepiece of traditional dances and songs. These were made from pulped plant material, and the designs were made on the ground using dots of this mush. Dots were also used to outline objects in rock paintings, and to highlight geographical features or vegetation. Over time the use of dots has developed, sometimes covering the entire canvas.

While the paintings may look random and abstract, they have great significance to the artist and usually depict a Dreaming journey, and so can be seen almost as aerial landscape maps. One feature which appears regularly is the tracks of birds, animals and humans, often identifying the ancestor. Various subjects, including people, are often depicted by the imprint they leave in the sand – a simple arc depicts a person (as that is the print left by someone sitting), a coolamon (wooden carrying dish) is shown as an oval shape, a digging stick by a single line, a camp fire by a circle. Males or females are identified by the objects associated with them – digging sticks and coolamons are always used by women, spears and boomerangs by men. Concentric circles are usually used to depict Dreaming sites, or places where ancestors paused in their journeys.

Liru Tjara by Mary Ungkaipai Forbes; watercolour on paper; 102 x 82cm; Kaltjiti Crafts, Fregon, SA; courtesy of DESART.

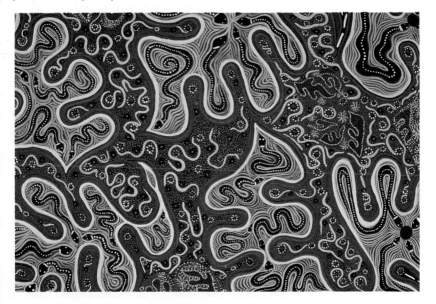

Kadaitja Man by
Ronnie Tjampitjinpa;
acrylic on linen;
122 x 61cm; 1993;
Papunya Tula Artists
Pty Ltd, Alice Springs,
NT; courtesy of
DESART.

While these symbols are widely used and are readily identifiable, their context within each individual painting is known only by the artist and the people closely associated with him or her – either by group or by the Dreaming – and different groups apply different interpretations to each painting. In this way sacred stories can be publicly portrayed, as the deeper meaning is not evident to any but those with a close association with the image.

The colours used in dot paintings from central Australia may seem overly vivid, and inappropriate to the land or story depicted. However, they are not meant to be true representations of the landscape, but variations in that landscape. The reds, blues and purples which often dominate the outback scenery, and which were so much a part of Albert Namatjira's painting (see below), feature prominently.

Albert Namatjira (1902-59) Australia's most well-known Aboriginal artist was probably Albert Namatjira. He lived at the Hermannsburg Lutheran Mission, about 130 km west of Alice Springs, and was introduced to European-style watercolour painting by a non-Aboriginal artist, Rex Batterbee, in the 1930s.

Namatjira successfully captured the essence of the Centre using a heavily European-influenced style. At the time his paintings were seen purely as picturesque landscapes. These days, however, it is thought he chose his subjects carefully, as they were Dreaming landscapes to which he had a great bond.

Namatjira supported many of his people on the income from his work, as was his obligation under tribal law. Because of his fame he was allowed to buy alcohol at a time when this was otherwise

Ngapa Manu Warna Jukurrpa (Water & Snake Dreaming) by Rosie Nangala Flomming; acrylic on linen; 180 x 120cm; 1993; Warlukurlangu Artists Association, Yuendumu, NT; courtesy of DESART.

illegal for Aborigines. In 1957 he was the first Aborigine to be granted Australian citizenship, but in 1958 he was jailed for six months for supplying alcohol to Aborigines. He died the following year aged only 57.

Although Namatjira died very disenchanted with White society, he did much to change the extremely negative views of Aborigines which prevailed at the time. At the same time he paved the way for the Papunya painting movement which emerged just over a decade after his death.

The Utopia Batik Artists

The women of Utopia, 225 km north-east of Alice Springs, have become famous in recent years for their production of batik material. In the mid 1970s the Anmatyerre and Alyawarre people started to reoccupy their traditional lands around Utopia cattle station, and this was given a formal basis in 1979 when they were granted title to the station. A number of scattered outstations, rather than a central settlement, were set up, and around this time the women were introduced to batik as part of a self-help program. The art form flourished and Utopia Women's Batik Group was formed in 1978.

Silk soon became the preferred medium for printing, and the batiks were based on the traditional women's designs which were painted on their bodies.

In the late 1980s techniques using acrylic paints on canvas were introduced to the artists at Utopia, and they have also become popular.

Other Central Australian Art

The making of wooden sculptures for sale dates back to at least early this century. In 1903 a group of Diyari people living on the Killalpaninna Lutheran Mission near Lake Eyre in South Australia

Handcrafted decorative central Australian carvings made from river red gum root; Maruku Arts & Crafts, Uluru (Ayers Rock), NT; courtesy of DESART.

were encouraged by the pastor to produce sculptures in order to raise funds for the mission.

The momentum for producing crafts for sale was accelerated by the opening up and settlement of the country by Europeans. Demand was slow to increase but the steady growth of the tourist trade since WW II, and the tourist boom of the 1980s, has seen demand and production increase dramatically.

The most widespread crafts seen for sale these days are the wooden carvings which have designs scorched into them with hot fencing wire. These range from small figures, such as possums, up to quite large snakes and lizards, although none of them have any Dreaming significance. One of the main outlets for these is the Maruku Arts & Crafts centre at the Uluru National Park rangers' station, where it's possible to see the crafts being made. Although much of the artwork is usually done by women, men are also involved at the Maruku centre. The Mt Ebenezer Roadhouse, on the Lasseter Highway (the main route to Uluru), is another Aboriginal-owned enterprise – and one of the cheapest places for buying sculpted figures.

Terracotta pots by the Hermannsburg Potters; 1992; represented by Alcaston House Gallery, Melbourne.

The Ernabella Presbyterian Mission in northern South Australia was another place where craftwork was encouraged. A 1950 mission report stated that: 'A mission station must have an industry to provide work for and help finance the cost of caring for the natives'. As the mission had been founded on a sheep station, wool crafts were the obvious way to go, and to that end the techniques of wool spinning, dyeing and weaving were introduced. The Pitjantjatjara (pigeon-jara) women made woollen articles such as rugs, belts, traditional dilly bags (carry bags) and scarves, using designs incorporating aspects of women's law (*yawilyu*). With the introduction of batik fabric dyeing in the 1970s, weaving at Ernabella virtually ceased.

The Arrernte people from Hermannsburg have recently begun to work with pottery, a craft which is not traditionally Aboriginal. They have incorporated moulded figures and surface treatments adapted from Dreaming stories.

Old Man – Young Man – Very Big Story by Djambu Barra Barra, born about 1946; language group Wagilak related to Ritangu; domicile Ngukurr, NT; synthetic polymer paint on lanaquarelle paper; 63 x 67cm; 1992; represented by Alcaston House Gallery, Melbourne.

ARNHEM LAND ART

Arnhem Land, in Australia's tropical 'Top End', is possibly the area with the richest artistic heritage. It is thought that rock paintings were being made as much as 40,000 years ago, and some of the rock art galleries in the huge sandstone Arnhem Land plateau are at least 18,000 years old.

Although Arnhem Land is famous for its rock art, the tradition of bark painting is equally strong in the region. In fact in recent years, this portable art form has become very popular, probably because the boom in tourism has led to a high demand for souvenirs. As is the case in many communities throughout the country, producing art works for sale is an important form of employment in a place where there are generally few opportunities.

The art of Arnhem Land is vastly different from that of the central deserts. Here, Dreaming stories are depicted far more literally, with easily recognisable (though often stylised) images of ancestors, animals, and even Macassans – early Indonesian mariners who regularly visited the north coast long before the Europeans arrived on the scene.

Rock Art

The paintings contained in the Arnhem Land rock art sites range from hand prints to paintings of animals, people, mythological beings and European ships, constituting one of the world's most important and fascinating rock art collections. They provide a record of changing environments and Aboriginal lifestyles over the millennia.

In some places they are concentrated in large galleries, with paintings from more recent eras sometimes superimposed over older paintings. Some sites are kept secret – not only to protect them from damage, but also because they are private or sacred

Rock paintings, Nourlangie Rock, Kakadu National Park; courtesy of the NT Tourist Commission.

to the Aborigines. Some are even believed to be inhabited by dangerous beings, who must not be approached by the ignorant. However, two of the finest sites have been opened up to visitors, with access roads, walkways and explanatory signs. These are Ubirr and Nourlangie Rock. Park rangers conduct free art-site tours once or twice a day from May to October. (For more information see the Ubirr and Nourlangie Rock sections in the Northern Territory chapter.)

The rock paintings show how the main styles succeeded each other over time. The earliest hand or grass prints were followed by a 'naturalistic' style, with large outlines of people or animals filled in with colour. Some of the animals depicted, such as the thylacine (or Tasmanian tiger), have long been extinct in mainland Australia. Other paintings are thought to show large beasts which roamed the world and which were wiped out millennia ago.

After the naturalistic style came the 'dynamic', in which motion was often cleverly depicted (a dotted line, for example, to show a spear's path through the air). In this era the first mythological beings appeared – with human bodies and animal heads.

The next style mainly showed simple human silhouettes, and was followed by the curious 'yam figures', in which people and animals were drawn in the shape of yams (or yams in the shape of people/animals!). Yams must have been an important food source at this time, about 8000 years ago, when the climate was growing increasingly damp. As the waters rose, much of what is now Kakadu National Park became covered with salt marshes. Many fish were depicted in the art of this period, and the so-called 'x-ray' style, which showed the creatures' bones and internal organs, made its appearance.

By about 1000 years ago many of the salt marshes had turned into freshwater swamps and billabongs. The birds and plants which provided new food sources in this landscape appeared in the art of this time.

From around 400 years ago, Aboriginal artists also depicted the human newcomers to the region – Macassan fisherpeople and, more recently, the Europeans – and the things they brought, or their transport such as ships or horses.

Bark Paintings

While the bark painting tradition is a more recent art form than rock art, it is still an important part of the cultural heritage of Arnhem Land Aborigines. It's difficult to establish when bark was first used, partly because it is perishable and old pieces simply don't exist. European visitors in the early 19th century noted the practice of painting the inside walls of bark shelters. The bark used is from the stringybark tree (*Eucalyptus tetradonta*), and it is taken off in the wet season when it is moist and supple. The rough outer layers are removed and the bark is then dried by placing it over a fire and then under weights on the ground to keep it flat. Drying is complete within about a fortnight, and the bark is then ready for use. Most bark paintings made today have a pair of sticks across the top and bottom of the sheet to keep it flat.

The pigments used in bark paintings are mainly red and yellow (ochres), white (kaolin) and black (charcoal). Because these were

Kumoken (Freshwater Crocodile) with Mimi Spirits by Djawida, b.c. 1935, Yulkman clan; Kunwinjku language, Kurrudjmuh, western Arnhem Land; earth pigments on bark; 151 x 71cm; 1990; purchased 1990; National Gallery of Victoria.

the only colours available their source was an important place. The colour could only be gathered by the traditional owners, and it was then traded. Even today it is these natural pigments which are used, giving the paintings their superb soft and earthy finish. Binding agents such as birds' egg yolks, wax and plant resins were added to the pigments. Recently these have been replaced by synthetic agents such as wood glue. Similarly, the brushes used in the past were obtained from the bush materials at hand – twigs, leaf fibres, feathers, human hair and the like – but these too have largely been done away with in favour of modern brushes.

One of the main features of Arnhem Land bark paintings is the use of cross-hatching designs. These designs identify the particular clans, and are based on body paintings of the past. The paintings can also be broadly categorised by their regional styles. In the west the tendency is towards naturalistic images and plain backgrounds, while to the east the use of geometric designs is more common.

The art reflects Dreaming themes, and once again these vary by region. In eastern Arnhem Land the prominent ancestor beings are the Djangkawu, who travelled the land with elaborate dilly bags and digging sticks (which they used to create waterholes each time

Some Animals Have Secret Songs by Amy Johnson Jirwulurr, born about 1953; language group Wagilak; domicile Ngukurr, NT; synthetic polymer paint on cotton duck; 90 x 106cm; 1988; represented by Alcaston House Gallery, Melbourne.

Gabal Ritual *by Willie Gudabi, born about 1916;*
language group Alawa; domicile Ngukurr, NT;
synthetic polymer paint on lanaquarelle paper;
75 x 55cm; 1993;
represented by Alcaston House Gallery, Melbourne.

they stopped), and the Wagilag Sisters, who are associated with snakes and water holes. In western Arnhem Land the Rainbow Serpent, Yingarna, is the significant being (according to some clans), but one of her offspring, Ngalyod, and Nawura are also important. The *mimi* spirits are another feature of western Arnhem Land art, both on bark and rock. These mischievous spirits are attributed with having taught the Aborigines of the region many things, including hunting, food gathering and painting skills.

Fibre Art

Articles made from fibres are a major art form among the women. While the string and pandanus-fibre dilly bags, skirts, mats and nets all have utilitarian purposes, many also have ritual uses.

Hollow-Log Coffins

Hollowed-out logs were often used for reburial ceremonies in Arnhem Land, and were also a major form of artistic expression. They were highly decorated, often with many of the Dreaming themes, and were known as *dupun* in eastern Arnhem Land and *lorrkon* in western Arnhem Land.

In 1988 a group of Arnhem Land artists made a memorial as their contribution to the movement highlighting injustices against Aborigines – this was, of course, the year when non-Aboriginal Australians were celebrating 200 years of European settlement. The artists painted 200 log coffins – one for each year of settlement – with traditional clan and Dreaming designs, and these now form a permanent display in the National Gallery in Canberra.

Ngukurr Contemporary Painting

Since the late 1980s the artists of Ngukurr (nook-or), near Roper Bar in south-eastern Arnhem Land, have been producing works using acrylic paints on canvas. Although ancestral beings still feature prominently, the works are generally much more 'modern' in nature, with free-flowing forms and often little in common with traditional formal structure.

TIWI ISLAND ART

Due to their isolation, the Aborigines of the Tiwi Islands (Bathurst and Melville islands off the coast of Darwin) have developed art forms – mainly sculpture – not found anywhere else, although there are some similarities with the art of Arnhem Land.

The *pukumani* burial rites are one of the main rituals of Tiwi religious life, and it is for these ceremonies that many of the art

Tiwi art is derived from ceremonial body painting and the ornate decoration applied to funerary poles, *yimawilini* bark baskets and associated ritual objects made for the *pukamani* ceremony, which is held at the grave site approximately six months after burial. The ceremony marks the conclusion of formal mourning and the lifting of complex taboos associated with death.

Traditionally, the participants decorate themselves with a variety of ochre designs so as to conceal their true identity from the malevolent *mapurtiti*, the spirits of the dead. Tiwi art generally avoids specific reference to totems, dreamings or stories connected with the *palaneri* (Creation period).

Pukamani funerary poles and bark baskets installation; Milikapiti, Melville Island, NT; represented by Alcaston House Gallery, Melbourne.

works are created – *jimwalini* (bark baskets), spears and *tutini* (burial poles). These carved and painted ironwood poles, up to 2.5 metres long, are placed around the grave, and represent features of that person's life.

In the last 50 or so years the Tiwi islanders have been producing sculptured animals and birds, many of these being Creation ancestors. (The Darwin Museum of Arts & Sciences has an excellent display.) More recently, bark painting and silk-screen printing have become popular, and there are workshops on both islands where these items are produced. (For more information see the section on the Bathurst and Melville islands in the Northern Territory chapter.)

KIMBERLEY ART

The art of the Kimberley is most famous for its Wandjina images – a group of ancestor beings who came from the sky – but other styles also exist.

The Wandjina generally appear in human form, with large black eyes, a nose but no mouth, a halo around the head (representative of both hair and clouds), and a black oval shape on the chest. These beings were responsible for the formation of the country's natural features, and were also thought to control the elements. The images of the Wandjina are found on rock as well as on more

Rock painting, Carisbrooke (Qld). The apparently non-figurative motifs on this piece of rock art distinguish this type of painting from the more figurative rock galleries in the north of the state; courtesy of the Queensland Tourist & Travel Corporation Resource Centre.

recent portable art media, with some of the rock images being more than six metres long.

Another art form from the western Kimberley is the engraved pearl-shell pendants which come from the Broome area. It is believed that the Aborigines of the area were using pearl shell for decoration before the arrival of Europeans, but with the establishment of the pearling industry in Broome late last century the use of pearl shell increased markedly. Traditionally the shells were highly prized, and so were engraved and then used for a number of purposes – ceremonial, personal decoration and trade – examples of this art have been found as far away as Queensland and South Australia.

The designs engraved into the shells were usually fairly simple geometric patterns which had little symbolic importance. The practice of pearl-shell engraving has largely died out, although the decorated shells are still highly valued.

Art in the eastern Kimberley also features elements of the works of the desert peoples of central Australia, a legacy of the forced movement of people during the 1970s. The community of Warmun at Turkey Creek on the Great Northern Highway has been particularly active in ensuring that Aboriginal culture through painting and dance remains strong.

NORTH QUEENSLAND ART

In North Queensland it is once again the rock art which predominates. The superb 'Quinkan' galleries at Laura on the Cape York Peninsula, north of Cairns, are among the best known in the country. Among the many creatures depicted on the walls, the main ones are the Quinkan spirits, which are shown in two forms – the long and stick-like Timara, and the crocodile-like Imjim with their knobbed, club-like tails.

A number of ceremonial items were also traditionally produced in this area, with perhaps the best known being the men's decorated shields. These were mainly used for ritual purposes, but they were also put to practical use when fighting between clans occurred. Other items included clubs, boomerangs and woven baskets, many of which also carried painted designs.

URBAN ART

While the works of rural artists based on traditional themes is the high-profile side of Aboriginal art, another important aspect is the works produced by city-based Aborigines. As much of this work has strong European influences, it was often not regarded as an authentic form of Aboriginal art – this view has since changed.

A major impetus in the development of urban art was the Aboriginal land rights movement, which started to gain momentum in the 1970s. Images depicting the dispossession of the Aborigines and the racist treatment they had received became powerful symbols in their struggle for equality.

Although much of the work being produced still carries strong political and social comment, these days the range has become broader.

David Mpetyane paints and writes within the context of his joint ancestral background and his awareness of present and past. He lives and works in Alice Springs, and is influenced by the contemporary life of the community around him, while also using first-contact stories and his strong identification with the land. His imagination is fired by the anger and beauty of the natural environment, as he relives the Creation period journeys of his ancestors and weaves their stories into his present life. David's painting *Perfect Place for Philosophy and Waste* was inspired by the following poem.

Fertility

Alice lost her virginity
Witness by
The old man gum tree
While the dog sat confused
Patiently licking its wounds
She gave birth
To one stone room
Next a shed then a house

She then stepped one step south
Before the caterpillars knew
Alice grew
With the scenery so strong
The old man gum tree
Witness Alice lose her virginity
Long before me

David Mpetyane, 1992

Perfect Place for Philosophy and Waste by David Mpetyane, born 1963; language group Central/Western Aranda; domicile Alice Springs, NT; synthetic polymer paint on linen; 110 x 183cm; 1992; represented by Alcaston House Gallery, Melbourne.

Facts for the Visitor

VISAS & EMBASSIES

All visitors to Australia need a visa. Only New Zealand nationals are exempt, and even they receive a 'special category' visa on arrival.

Visa application forms are available from either Australian diplomatic missions overseas or travel agents, and you can apply by mail or in person. There are several different types of visas, depending on the reason for your visit.

Australian Embassies

Australian consular offices overseas include:

Canada
Suite 710, 50 O'Connor St, Ottawa (☎ (613) 236 0841; fax 236 4376)
also in Toronto and Vancouver

China
21 Dongzhimenwai Dajie, Sanlitun, Beijing 100600 (☎ (10) 532 2331; fax 532 6959)
also in Guangzhou and Shanghai

Denmark
Kristianagade 21, DK 2100 Copenhagen (☎ 3526 2244; fax 3543 2218)

France
4 Rue Jean Rey, 75724 Paris Cedex 15 Paris (☎ (01) 4059 3300; fax 4059 3310)

Germany
Godesberger Allee 107, 53175 Bonn (☎ (0228) 81 030; fax 810 3130)
also in Frankfurt and Berlin

Greece
37 Dimitriou Soutsou, Ambelokipi, Athens 11521 (☎ (01) 644 7303; fax 646 6595)

Hong Kong
23/F Harbour Centre, 25 Harbour Rd, Wanchai, Hong Kong Island (☎ 2827 8881; fax 2827 6583)

India
Australian Compound, No 1/50-G Shantipath, Chanakyapuri, New Delhi 110021 (☎ (11) 688 8223; fax 688 5199)
also in Bombay

Indonesia
Jalan H R Rasuna Said Kav C 15-16, Jakarta Selatan 12940 (☎ (021) 522 7111; fax 522 7101)
Jalan Prof Moh Yamin 51, Renon, Denpasar, Bali (☎ (0361) 23 5092; fax 23 1990)

Ireland
Fitzwilton House, Wilton Terrace, Dublin 2 (☎ (01) 676 1517; fax 678 5185)

Italy
Via Alessandria 215, Rome 00198 (☎ (06) 852 721; fax 8527 2300)
also in Milan

Japan
2-1-14 Mita, Minato-ku, Tokyo 108 (☎ (03) 5232 4111; fax 5232 4149)
Twin 21 MID Tower, 29th floor, 2-1-61 Shiromi, Chuo-ku, Osaka 540 (☎ (06) 941 9271; fax 920 4543)
7th floor, Tsuruta Keyaki Bldg, 1-1-5 Akasaka Chuo-ku, Fukuoka City 810, Kyushu (☎ (092) 734 5055; fax 724 2304)
8th floor, Ikko Fushimi Bldg, 1-20-10 Nishiki, Naka-ku, Nagoya 460 (☎ (052) 211 0630; fax 211 0632)
also in Sapporo and Sendai

Malaysia
6 Jalan Yap Kwan Seng, Kuala Lumpur 50450 (☎ (03) 242 3122; fax 241 5773)
also in Kuching and Penang

Mauritius
Rogers House, 5 Pres John Kennedy St, Port Louis (☎ 230 1700; fax 208 8878)

Nepal
Banshari, Kathmandu (☎ (01) 41 3076; fax 41 7533)

Netherlands
Carnegielaan 4, 2517 KH The Hague (☎ (070) 310 8200; fax 310 7863)

New Zealand
72-78 Hobson St, Thorndon, Wellington (☎ (04) 473 6411; fax 498 7118)
Union House, 32-38 Quay St, Auckland 1 (☎ (09) 303 2429; fax 377 0798)

Papua New Guinea
Independence Drive, Waigani NCD, Port Moresby (☎ 325 9333; fax 325 6647)

Philippines
Dona Salustiana Ty Tower, 104 Paseo de Roxas, Makati, Metro Manila (☎ (02) 817 7911; fax 817 3603)

Singapore
25 Napier Rd, Singapore 1025 (☎ 737 9311; fax 733 7134)

South Africa
292 Orient St, Arcadia, Pretoria 0083 (☎ (012) 342 3740; fax 342 4222)
also in Cape Town

Sri Lanka
3 Cambridge Place, Colombo 7 (☎ (01) 69 8767; fax 68 6453)

Sweden
> Sergels Torg 12, Stockholm (☎ (08) 613 2900; fax 24 7414)

Switzerland
> 29 Alpenstrasse, CH-3006 Berne (☎ (031) 351 0143; fax 352 1234)
> also in Geneva

Thailand
> 37 South Sathorn Rd, Bangkok 10120 (☎ (02) 287 2680; fax 287 2029)

UK
> Australia House, The Strand, London WC2B 4LA (☎ (0171) 379 4334; fax 465 8210)
> also in Edinburgh and Manchester

USA
> 1601 Massachusetts Ave NW, Washington DC 20036 (☎ (202) 797 3000; fax 797 3168)
> also in Atlanta, Boston, Chicago, Denver, Honolulu, Houston, Los Angeles, New York and San Francisco

Vietnam
> 66 Ly Thuong Kiet, Hanoi (☎ (04) 25 2763; fax 25 9268)
> also in Ho Chi Minh City

Zimbabwe
> 4th floor, Karigamombe Centre, 53 Samora Machel Ave, Harare (☎ (04) 75 7774; fax 75 7770)

Foreign Embassies & Consulates

The principal diplomatic representations to Australia are in Canberra and you'll find a list of the addresses of relevant offices in the Canberra section of the ACT chapter. There are also representatives in various other major cities, particularly from countries with major connections with Australia like the USA, UK or New Zealand; or in cities with important connections, like Darwin which has an Indonesian consulate. Big cities like Sydney and Melbourne have nearly as many consular offices as Canberra, although visa applications are generally handled in Canberra. Look up addresses in the Yellow Pages telephone book under 'Consulates & Legations'.

Tourist Visas

Tourist visas are issued by Australian consular offices abroad; they are the most common visa and are generally valid for a stay of either three or six months. The three-month visas are free; for the six-month visa there is a $35 fee.

The visa is valid for use within 12 months of the date of issue and can be used to enter and leave Australia several times within that 12 months.

When you apply for a visa, you need to present your passport and a passport photo, as well as signing an undertaking that you have an onward or return ticket and 'sufficient funds' – the latter is obviously open to interpretation.

You can also apply for a long-stay visa, which is a multiple-entry, four-year visa which allows for stays of up to six months on each visit. These also cost $35.

Working Visas

Young, single visitors from the UK, Canada, Korea, Holland and Japan may be eligible for a 'working holiday' visa. 'Young' is fairly loosely interpreted as around 18 to 25, although exceptions are made and people up to 30, and young married couples without children, may be given a working holiday visa.

A working holiday visa allows for a stay of up to 12 months, but the emphasis is supposed to be on casual employment rather than a full-time job, so you are only supposed to work for three months. This visa can only be applied for from outside Australia (preferably but not necessarily in your country of citizenship), and you can't change from a visitor visa to a working holiday visa.

Conditions attached to a working holiday visa include having sufficient funds for a ticket out, and taking out private medical insurance; a fee of about $140 is payable when you apply for the visa.

See the section on Working later in this chapter for details of what sort of work is available and where.

Visa Extensions

The maximum stay allowed to visitors is one year, including extensions.

Visa extensions are made through Department of Immigration & Ethnic Affairs offices in Australia and, as the process takes some time, it's best to apply about a month before your visa expires. There is an application fee of $135 – and even if they turn down your application they can still keep your money. To qualify for an extension you are required to take out private medical insurance to cover the period of the extension, and have a ticket out of the country. Some offices are more strict than others in enforcing these conditions.

If you're trying to stay for longer in Australia the books *Temporary to Permanent Resident in Australia* and *Practical Guide to Obtaining Permanent Residence in Australia*, both published by Longman Cheshire, might be useful.

CUSTOMS

When entering Australia you can bring most articles in free of duty provided that Customs is satisfied they are for personal use and that you'll be taking them with you when you leave. There's also a duty-free per person quota of one litre of alcohol, 250 cigarettes and dutiable goods up to the value of A$400.

With regard to prohibited goods, there are two areas that need particular attention. Number one is, of course, dope – Australian Customs have a positive mania about the stuff and can be extremely efficient when it comes to finding it. Unless you want to make first-hand investigations of conditions in Australian jails, don't bring any illegal drugs with you. This particularly applies if you are arriving from South-East Asia or the Indian Subcontinent.

Problem two is animal and plant quarantine. You will be asked to declare all goods of animal or vegetable origin – wooden spoons, straw hats, the lot – and show them to an official. The authorities are naturally keen to prevent weeds, pests or diseases getting into the country – Australia has so far managed to escape many of the agricultural pests and diseases prevalent in other parts of the world. Fresh food is also unpopular, particularly meat, sausage, fruit, vegetables and flowers. There are also restrictions on taking fruit and vegetables between states (see the aside on Interstate Quarantine in the Getting Around chapter).

Weapons and firearms are either prohibited or require a permit and safety testing. Other restricted goods include products (such as ivory) made from protected wildlife species, non-approved telecommunications devices and live animals.

There are duty-free stores at the international airports and their associated cities. Treat them with healthy suspicion. 'Duty-free' is one of the world's most overworked catch phrases, and it is often just an excuse to sell things at prices you can easily beat by a little shopping around.

MONEY
Currency
Australia's currency is the Australian dollar, which comprises 100 cents. The dollar was introduced in 1966 to replace the old system of pounds, shillings and pence. There are coins for 5c, 10c, 20c, 50c, $1 and $2, and notes for $5, $10, $20, $50 and $100.

Although the smallest coin in circulation is 5c, prices are still marked in single cents, and then rounded to the nearest 5c when you come to pay.

There are no notable restrictions on importing or exporting currency or travellers' cheques, except that you may not take more than $5000 cash out of the country without prior approval.

Exchange Rates
The Australian dollar fluctuates quite markedly against the US dollar, but it seems to stay pretty much in the 70c to 80c range – a disaster for Australians travelling overseas but a real bonus for inbound visitors.

Canada	C$1	=	$0.96
Germany	DM 1	=	$0.88
Hong Kong	HK$10	=	$1.69
New Zealand	NZ$1	=	$0.89
United Kingdom	UK1	=	$2.03
USA	US$1	=	$1.31
Japan	Y100	=	$1.24

Changing Money
Changing foreign currency or travellers' cheques is no problem at almost any bank or

licensed moneychanger such as Thomas Cook or American Express.

Travellers' Cheques

There is a variety of ways to carry your money. If your stay is limited, then travellers' cheques are the most straightforward and generally enjoy a better exchange rate than foreign cash in Australia.

American Express, Thomas Cook and other well-known international brands of travellers' cheques are all widely used. A passport will usually be adequate for identification; it would be sensible to carry a driver's licence, credit cards or other form of identification in case of problems.

Fees for changing foreign currency travellers' cheques seem to vary from bank to bank and year to year. Currently of the 'big four' (ANZ, Commonwealth, National and Westpac), ANZ and Westpac do not charge any fee, while at the National it's $5 and at the Commonwealth $6 per transaction, regardless of amount or number of cheques.

Buying Australian dollar travellers' cheques is an option worth looking at. These can be exchanged immediately at the bank cashier's window without being converted from a foreign currency and incurring commissions, fees and exchange rate fluctuations.

Credit Cards

Credit cards are widely accepted in Australia and are an alternative to carrying large numbers of travellers' cheques. Visa, MasterCard, Diners Club and American Express are all widely accepted.

Cash advances from credit cards are available over the counter and from many automatic teller machines (ATMs), depending on the card.

If you're planning to rent cars, a credit card makes life much simpler; they're looked upon with much greater favour by rent-a-car agencies than nasty old cash, and many agencies simply won't rent you a vehicle if you don't have a card.

Local Bank Accounts

If you're planning to stay longer than just month or so, it's worth considering othe ways of handling money that give you mor flexibility and are more economical. Thi applies equally to Australians setting off t travel around the country.

Most travellers these days opt for a account which includes a cash card, which you can use to access your cash from ATM all over Australia. Westpac, ANZ, Nationa and Commonwealth bank branches are found nationwide, and in all but the mos remote town there'll be at least one place where you can withdraw money from a hole in the wall.

ATMs can be used day or night, and it is possible to use the machines of some othe banks: Westpac ATMs accept Common wealth Bank cards and vice versa; Nationa Bank ATMs accept ANZ cards and vice versa. There is a limit on how much you can withdraw. This varies from bank to bank bu is usually $400 to $500 per day.

Many businesses, such as service stations supermarkets and convenience stores, are linked into the EFTPOS system (Electronic Funds Transfer at Point Of Sale), and where you can use your bank cash card to pay for services or purchases direct, and sometimes withdraw cash as well. Bank cash cards and credit cards can also be used to make local, STD and international phone calls in special public telephones, found in most towns throughout the country.

Opening an account at an Australian bank is not all that easy, especially for overseas visitors. A points system operates and you need to score a minimum of 100 points before you can have the privilege of letting the bank take your money. Passports, driver's licences, birth certificates and other 'major' IDs earn you 40 points; minor ones such as credit cards get you 20 points. Just like a game show really! However, if visitors apply to open an account during the first six weeks of their visit, then just showing their passport will suffice.

If you don't have an Australian Tax File Number (see Work later in this chapter), interest earned from your funds will be taxed at the rate of 48% and this money goes straight to our old mate, the Deputy Commissioner of Taxation.

Costs

Compared to the USA, Canada and European countries, Australia is cheaper in some ways and more expensive in others. Manufactured goods tend to be more expensive: if they are imported they have the additional costs of transport and duties, and if they're locally manufactured they suffer from the extra costs entailed in making things in comparatively small quantities. Thus you pay more for clothes, cars and other manufactured items. On the other hand, food is both high in quality and low in cost.

Accommodation is also very reasonably priced. In virtually every town where backpackers are likely to stay there'll be a backpacker hostel with dorm beds for $10 or less, or a caravan park with on-site vans for around $25 for two people.

The biggest cost in any trip to Australia will be transport, simply because it's such a vast country. If there's a group of you, buying a second-hand car is probably the most economical way to go.

On average you can expect to spend about $30 per day if you budget fiercely and *always* take the cheapest option; $50 gives you much greater flexibility. Obviously if you stay for longer periods in each place and can take advantage of discounts given on long-term accommodation, or even move into a share-house with other people, this helps keep your costs to a minimum.

Tipping

In Australia tipping isn't entrenched. It's only customary to tip in more expensive restaurants and only then if you feel it's necessary. If the service has been especially good and you decide to leave a tip, 10% of the bill is the usual amount. Taxi drivers don't expect tips (of course, they don't hurl it back at you if you decide to leave the change).

WHEN TO GO

Any time is a good time to be in Australia, but as you'd expect in a country this large, different parts are at their best at different times.

The southern states are most popular during summer (December through February), as it's warm enough for swimming and it's great to be outdoors. In the centre of the country it's just too damn hot to do anything much, while in the far north the summer is the Wet season and, even though it is usually not as hot as down south, the heat and humidity can make life pretty uncomfortable. To make matters worse, swimming in the sea in the north is not possible due to the 'stingers' (box jellyfish) which frequent the waters at this time. On the other hand, if you want to see the Top End green and free of dust, be treated to some spectacular electrical storms and have the best of the barramundi fishing while all the other tourists are down south, this is the time to do it.

In winter (June through August) the focus swings to the north, when the humidity has faded and the temperature is perfect. This is the time for visits to far north Queensland and the Top End. Central and outback Australia are also popular at this time, as the extreme heat of summer has been replaced by warm sunny days and surprisingly cool – even cold – nights. The cooler weather also deters the bushflies, which in the warmer months can be an absolute nightmare. The southern states, however, are not without their own attractions in winter. Snow skiers can head for the Victorian Alps or the Snowy Mountains in New South Wales for good cross-country or downhill skiing – although snow cover ranges from excellent one year to virtually nonexistent the next.

Spring and autumn give the greatest flexibility for a short visit as you can combine highlights of the whole country while avoiding the extremes of the weather. Spring is the time for wildflowers in the outback (particularly central and Western Australia) and these can be absolutely stunning after rains and are worth going a long way to see.

The other major consideration when travelling in Australia is school holidays.

Australian families take to the road (and air) en masse at these times and many places are booked out, prices rise and things generally get a bit crazy. (See the Holidays section for details.)

TOURIST OFFICES
There are a number of information sources for visitors to Australia and, like many other tourist-conscious Western countries, you can easily drown yourself in brochures and booklets, maps and leaflets.

Local Tourist Offices
Within Australia, tourist information is handled by various state and local offices. Each state and the ACT and Northern Territory has a tourist office of some form and you will find information about these centres in the state chapters. Apart from a main office in the capital cities, they often have regional offices in main tourist centres and also in other states. Tourist information in Victoria is handled by the Royal Automobile Club of Victoria (RACV) in Melbourne.

As well as supplying brochures, price lists, maps and other information, the state offices will often book transport, tours and accommodation for you. Unfortunately, very few of the state tourist offices maintain information desks at the airports and, furthermore, the opening hours of the city offices are very much of the 9-to-5 weekdays and Saturday-morning-only variety. Addresses of the main state tourist offices are:

Australian Capital Territory
    Canberra Tourist Bureau, Jolimont Centre, Northbourne Ave, Canberra City, ACT 2601 (☎ toll-free 1800 026 166)
New South Wales
    NSW Government Travel Centre, 19 Castlereagh St, Sydney, NSW 2000 (☎ 13 2077)
Northern Territory
    Darwin Region Tourism Association, 33 Smith St, Darwin, NT 0800 (☎ (08) 8981-4300)
Queensland
    Queensland Government Travel Centre, Cnr Adelaide and Brisbane Sts, Brisbane, Qld 4000 (☎ (07) 3221 6111)

South Australia
    South Australian Travel Centre, 1 King William St, Adelaide, SA 5000 (☎ (08) 8212 1505)
Tasmania
    Tasmanian Travel & Information Centre, Cnr Davey and Elizabeth Sts, Hobart, Tas 7000 (☎ (002) 30 8233)
Victoria
    RACV Travel Centre, 230 Collins St, Melbourne, Vic 3000 (☎ (03) 9650 1522)
Western Australia
    Western Australian Tourist Centre, Forrest Place, Perth, WA 6000 (☎ (09) 483 1111)

A step down from the state tourist offices are the local or regional offices. Almost every major town in Australia seems to maintain a tourist office or centre of some type or other and in many cases these are really excellent, with much local information not readily available from the state offices. This particularly applies where there is a strong local tourist trade.

Overseas Reps
The Australian Tourist Commission (ATC) is the government body intended to inform potential visitors about the country. There's a very definite split between promotion outside and inside Australia. The ATC is strictly an external operator; it does minimal promotion within the country and has little contact with visitors to Australia. Within the country, tourist promotion is handled by state or local tourist offices.

ATC offices overseas have a useful free magazine-style periodical booklet called *On the Loose* which details things of interest for backpackers around Australia.

The ATC also publishes *Australia Unplugged*, which is a good introduction to Australia for young people, giving some information about the country in general and snapshots of the major cities.

As well, it publishes a number of Fact Sheets on various topics, such as camping, fishing, skiing, disabled travel and national parks – and these can be a useful introduction to the subject. They have a handy map of the country, which is available for a small fee. This literature is intended for distribution overseas only; if you want copies, get them before you come to Australia.

The ATC maintains a number of Helplines, which independent travellers can ring or fax to get specific information about Australia.

Addresses of the ATC offices for literature requests are:

Hong Kong
Suite 1501, Central Plaza, 18 Harbour Rd, Wanchai (☎ 2802 7700)
Helpline: ☎ 2802 7817; fax 2802 8211

Japan
Australian Business Centre, New Otani Garden Court Bldg 28F, 4-1 Kioi-cho, Chiyoda-ku, Tokyo 102 (☎ (03) 5214 0720)
Helpline: ☎ (03) 5214 0730; fax 5214 0719
Twin 21 MID Tower 30F, 2-1-61 Shiromi, Chuo-ku, Osaka 540 (☎ (06) 946 2503)
Helpline: ☎ (06) 946 2500; fax 946 2473

New Zealand
Level 13, 44-48 Emily Place, Auckland 1 (☎ (09) 379 9594; tax 307 3117)
Helpline: ☎ (09) 527 1629; fax 377 9562

Singapore
Suite 1703, United Square, 101 Thomson Rd, Singapore 1103 (☎ 255 4555)
Helpline: ☎ 250 6277; fax 253 8431

UK
Gemini House, 10-18 Putney Hill, London SW15 6AA (☎ (0181) 780 2227; fax 780 1496)

USA
Suite 1200, 2121 Ave of the Stars, Los Angeles, CA 90067 (☎ (310) 552 1988; fax 552 1215)
25th floor, 100 Park Ave, New York, NY 10017 (☎ (212) 687 6300; fax 661 3340)
Helpline: ☎ (708) 296 4900; fax 635 3718

USEFUL ORGANISATIONS
Automobile Associations

The national Australian Automobile Association is mainly an umbrella organisation for the various state associations and to maintain international links. The day-to-day operations are all handled by the state organisations which provide an emergency breakdown service, literature, excellent maps and detailed guides to accommodation and camp sites.

The state organisations have reciprocal arrangements with other states in Australia and with similar organisations overseas. So, if you're a member of the National Roads &

Motorists Association (NRMA) in New South Wales, you can use RACV facilities in Victoria. Similarly, if you're a member of the AAA in the USA, or the RAC or AA in the UK, you can use any of the state organisations' facilities. Bring proof of membership with you. More details about the state automobile organisations can be found in the relevant state chapters. Some of the material they produce is of a very high standard. In particular there is a superb set of regional maps to Queensland produced by the Royal Automobile Club of Queensland (RACQ). The most useful state offices are:

New South Wales
NRMA, 151 Clarence St, Sydney, NSW 2000 (☎ 13 2132)
Northern Territory
Automobile Association of the Northern Territory, 79-81 Smith St, Darwin, NT 0800 (☎ (08) 8981 3837; fax 8941 2965)
Queensland
RACQ, 300 St Pauls Terrace, Fortitude Valley, Qld 4006 (☎ (07) 3361 2444)
South Australia
Royal Automobile Association of South Australia (RAA), 41 Hindmarsh Square, Adelaide, SA 5000 (☎ (08) 8202 4500; fax 8202 4521)
Tasmania
Royal Automobile Club of Tasmania (RACT), Cnr Patrick and Murray Sts, Hobart, Tas 7000 (☎ (002) 38 2200)
Victoria
Royal Automobile Club of Victoria (RACV), 422 Little Collins St, Melbourne, Vic 3000 (☎ (03) 9607 2137)
Western Australia
Royal Automobile Club of Western Australia (RACWA), 228 Adelaide Terrace, Perth, WA 6000 (☎ (09) 421 4444)

National Parks Organisations

Australia has an extensive collection of national parks. In fact, the Royal National Park just outside Sydney is the second-oldest national park in the world; only Yellowstone Park in the USA predates it.

The Australian Nature Conservation Agency (ANCA), formerly the Australian National Parks & Wildlife Service, is a Commonwealth body responsible for Kakadu and Uluru national parks in the Northern Territory, offshore areas such as the Cocos

(Keeling) Islands and Norfolk Island, and also international conservation issues such as whaling and migratory bird conventions. To some extent it also coordinates projects which involve more than one state body.

The individual national parks agencies are operated by the states. The offices tend to be a little hidden away in their capital city locations, although if you search them out they often have excellent literature and maps on the parks. They are much more upfront in the actual parks where, in many cases, they have very good guides and leaflets to bushwalking, nature trails and other activities. The state offices are:

Australian Capital Territory
    Australian Nature Conservation Agency, GPO Box 636, Canberra, ACT 2601 (☎ (06) 250 0200; fax 250 0242)
New South Wales
    National Parks & Wildlife Service, 43 Bridge St, Hurstville, NSW 2220 (PO Box 1967, Hurstville, NSW 2220 (☎ (02) 585 6444)
Northern Territory
    Parks & Wildlife, PO Box 496, Palmerston, NT 0831 (☎ (08) 8999 5511; fax 8999 4558)
    Australian Nature Conservation Agency, Smith St, Darwin, NT 0800 (GPO Box 1260, Darwin, NT 0801 (☎ (08) 8981 5299; fax 8981 3497)
Queensland
    Department of Environment & Heritage, 160 Ann St, Brisbane, Qld 4000 (☎ (07) 3227 8186)
South Australia
    Department of Environment & Natural Resources Information Centre, 77 Grenfell St, Adelaide, SA 5001 (☎ (08) 8204 1910)
Tasmania
    Department of Parks, Wildlife & Heritage, 134 Macquarie St, Hobart, Tas 7000 (PO Box 44A, Hobart, Tas 7001 (☎ (002) 33 6191)
Victoria
    Department of Conservation & Natural Resources, 240 Victoria Parade, East Melbourne, Vic 3002 (PO Box 41, East Melbourne, Vic 3002 (☎ (03) 9412 4011)
Western Australia
    Department of Conservation & Land Management (CALM), 50 Hayman Rd, Como, Perth, WA 6152 (☎ (09) 334 0333)

Australian Conservation Foundation

The Australian Conservation Foundation (ACF) is the largest nongovernment organisation involved in conservation. Only 9% to 10% of its income is from government; the rest comes from memberships and subscriptions, and from donations, which are mainly from individuals.

The ACF covers a wide range of issues including the greenhouse effect and depletion of the ozone layer, the negative effects of logging, the preservation of rainforests, the problems of land degradation, and the protection of the Antarctic. It frequently works in conjunction with the Wilderness Society and other conservation groups.

With the growing focus on conservation issues and the increasing concern of the Australian public in regard to their environment the conservation vote is increasingly important to all political parties.

Wilderness Society

The Tasmanian Wilderness Society was formed by conservationists who had been unsuccessful in preventing the damming of Lake Pedder in south-west Tasmania but who were determined to prevent the destruction of the Franklin River. The Franklin River campaign was one of Australia's first major conservation confrontations and it caught the attention of the international media. In 1983, after the Australian High Court ruled against damming the Franklin the group changed its name to the Wilderness Society because of its Australia-wide focus.

The Wilderness Society is involved in issues such as forest management and logging. Like the ACF, government funding is only a small percentage of its income, the rest coming from memberships, donations and merchandising. There are Wilderness Society shops in all states (not in the Northern Territory) where you can buy books, T-shirts, posters, badges etc.

The Wilderness Society can be contacted at 130 Davey St, Hobart, Tas 7000 (☎ (002) 34 9366)

Australian Trust for Conservation Volunteers

This nonpolitical, nonprofit group organises practical conservation projects (such as tree planting, track construction and flora and fauna surveys) for volunteers. Travellers are welcome and it's an excellent way to get involved with the conservation movement and, at the same time, visit some of the more interesting areas of the country. Past volunteers have found themselves working in places such as Tasmania, Kakadu and Fraser Island.

Most projects are either for a weekend or a week and all food, transport and accommodation is supplied in return for a small contribution to help cover costs. Most travellers who take part in ATCV join a Banksia Package, which lasts six weeks and includes six different projects. The cost is $650, and further weeks can be added for $105.

Contact the head office (☎ (053) 33 1483) at PO Box 423, Ballarat, Vic 3350, or the state offices listed below:

New South Wales
    23-33 Bridge St, Sydney, NSW 2000 (☎ (02) 9228 6461)
Northern Territory
    4 Burnett Place, Darwin, NT 0800 (☎ (08) 8981 3206)
Queensland
    Old Government House, QUT Grounds, George St, Brisbane, Qld 4000 (☎ (07) 3210 0330)
South Australia
    PO Box 419, Campbelltown, Adelaide, SA 5074 (☎ (08) 8207 8747)
Victoria
    13 Duke St, South Caulfield, Vic 3162 (☎ (03) 9532 8446)

National Trust

The National Trust is dedicated to preserving historic buildings in all parts of Australia. It owns a number of buildings throughout the country which are open to the public. Many other buildings are 'classified' by the National Trust to ensure their preservation.

The National Trust produces some excellent literature, including a fine series of walking-tour guides to many cities, large and small. These guides are often available from local tourist offices or from National Trust offices and are usually free whether you're a member of the National Trust or not. Membership is well worth considering, however, because it entitles you to free entry to any

National Trust property for your year of membership. If you're a dedicated visitor of old buildings this could soon pay for itself. Annual membership costs $44 for individuals ($31 concession) and $62 for families ($44 concession), and includes the monthly or quarterly magazine put out by the state organisation that you join. Addresses of the National Trust state offices are:

Australian Capital Territory
    GPO Box 3173, Manuka, ACT 2603 (☎ (06) 239 5222; fax 239 5333)
New South Wales
    Observatory Hill, Sydney, NSW 2000 (☎ (02) 258 0123)
Northern Territory
    4 Burnett Place, Myilly Point, Darwin, NT 0820 (☎ (08) 8981 2848)
Queensland
    Old Government House, QUT Grounds, George St, Brisbane, Qld 4000 (☎ (07) 3229 1788)
South Australia
    Ayers House, 288 North Terrace, Adelaide, SA 5000 (☎ (08) 8223 1655)
Tasmania
    Franklin House, 413 Hobart Rd, Launceston, Tas 7249 (☎ (003) 44 6233)
Victoria
    Tasma Terrace, 6 Parliament Place, Melbourne, Vic 3002 (☎ (03) 9654 4711)
Western Australia
    Old Observatory, 4 Havelock St, West Perth, WA 6005 (☎ (09) 321 6088)

WWOOF

WWOOF (Willing Workers on Organic Farms) is a relatively new organisation in Australia, although it is well established in other countries. The idea is that you do a few hours work each day on a farm in return for bed and board. Some places have a minimum stay of a couple of days but many will take you for just a night. Some will let you stay for months if they like the look of you, and you can get involved in some interesting large-scale projects.

Becoming a WWOOFer is a great way to meet people and to travel cheaply. There are about 200 WWOOF associates in Australia, mostly in Victoria, New South Wales and Queensland.

As the name says, the farms are supposed

to be organic but that isn't always so. Some places aren't even farms – you might help out at a pottery or do the books at a seed wholesaler. There are even a few commercial farms which exploit WWOOFers as cheap harvest labour, although these are rare. Whether they have a farm or just a vegie patch, most participants in the scheme are concerned to some extent with alternative lifestyles.

To join WWOOF send $15 (A$20 from overseas) to WWOOF, W Tree, Gelantipy Rd, Buchan, Vic 3885 (☎ (051) 55 0218), and they'll send you a membership number and a booklet which lists WWOOF places all over Australia.

ANZSES

The Australian & New Zealand Scientific Exploration Society is a nonprofit organisation which undertakes scientific expeditions into wilderness areas of Australia. Each year over 100 volunteers are sent into the field, always under the guidance of an experienced leader.

The organisation offers volunteers the opportunity to participate in the collection of scientific data and the experience of living and working in remote areas of Australia generally not accessible to the average traveller.

Recent studies have included flora and fauna gathering west of Coober Pedy and in Witjira National Park (outback South Australia), Eungella National Park, Cedar Bay National Park, Fraser Island, Sturt National Park (NSW), south-west Tasmania and far-east Gippsland (Vic).

The ANZSES postal address is PO Box 174, Albert Park, Vic 3206 (☎ (03) 9690 5455).

BUSINESS HOURS

Most shops close at 5 or 5.30 pm weekdays, and either noon or 5 pm on Saturday. In some places Sunday trading is catching on, but it's currently limited to the major cities. In most towns there are usually one or two late shopping nights each week, when the doors stay open until 9 or 9.30 pm. Usually it's Thursday and/or Friday night.

Banks are open from 9.30 am to 4 pm Monday to Thursday, and until 5 pm on Friday. Some large city branches are open 8 am to 6 pm Monday to Friday. Some are also open to 9 pm on Friday. Of course there are some exceptions to Australia's unremarkable opening hours and all sorts of places stay open late and all weekend – particularly milk bars, convenience stores, supermarkets, delis and city bookshops. The big chain supermarkets in large city shopping centres are also often open 24 hours.

HOLIDAYS

The Christmas holiday season, from mid-December to late January, is part of the long summer school vacation and the time you are most likely to find accommodation booked out and long queues. There are three other shorter school holiday periods during the year but they vary by a week or two from state to state, falling from early to mid-April, late June to mid-July, and late September to early October.

Public holidays also vary quite a bit from state to state. The following is a list of the main national and state public holidays:

National
New Year's Day
   1 January
Australia Day
   26 January
Easter
   Good Friday, and Easter Saturday, Sunday and
   Monday (March/April)
Anzac Day
   25 April
Queen's Birthday (except WA)
   2nd Monday in June
Queen's Birthday (WA)
   1st Monday in October
Christmas Day
   25 December
Boxing Day
   26 December

ACT
Canberra Day
   March

Bank Holiday
    1st Monday in August
Labour Day
    1st Monday in October

New South Wales
Bank Holiday
    1st Monday in August
Labour Day
    1st Monday in October

Northern Territory
May Day
    1 May
Alice Springs Show Day
    1st Friday in July *
Tennant Creek Show Day
    2nd Friday in July *
Katherine Show Day
    3rd Friday in July *
Darwin Show Day
    4th Friday in July *
Picnic Day
    1st Monday in August

Queensland
Labour Day
    1 May
RNA Show Day (Brisbane)
    August *

South Australia
Adelaide Cup Day
    May *
Labour Day
    1st Monday in October
Proclamation Day
    Last Tuesday in December

Tasmania
Regatta Day
    14 February
Eight Hours Day
    1st Monday in March
Bank Holiday
    April
Launceston Show Day
    October *
Hobart Show Day
    October *
Recreation Day (northern Tasmania only)
    1st Monday in November *

Victoria
Labour Day
    2nd Monday in March
Bank Holiday
    April

Melbourne Cup Day
    1st Tuesday in November *

Western Australia
Labour Day
    1st Monday in March
Foundation Day
    1st Monday in June

(* indicates holidays are only observed locally)

CULTURAL EVENTS
Some of the most enjoyable Australian festivals are, naturally, the ones which are most typically Australian – like the surf-lifesaving competitions on beaches all around the country during summer; or the outback race meetings, which draw together isolated townsfolk, the tiny communities from the huge stations and more than a few eccentric bush characters.

There are happenings and holidays in Australia year round – the following is just a brief overview. Check the relevant state tourist authorities for dates and more details.

January
    Sydney to Hobart Yacht Race – Tas. The arrival (29 December to 2 January) in Hobart of the yachts competing in this annual New Year race is celebrated with a mardi gras. The competitors in the *Melbourne to Hobart Yacht Race* arrive soon after.
    Huon Valley Folk Festival – Tas. Popular music festival in a great setting by the Huon River.
    Australia Day – This national holiday, commemorating the arrival of the First Fleet, in 1788, is observed on 26 January.
    Survival Festival – NSW. This is the Aboriginal version of Australia Day. It also is held on 26 January, and is marked by Koori music, dance and arts and crafts displays in Sydney.
    Sydney Festival & Carnivale – NSW. A three-week arts, music, food and dance festival.
    Australasian Country Music Festival – NSW. Tamworth *is* country music in Australia, and this festival held on the Australia Day long weekend is the showcase for the country's top C & W artists.
    Montsalvat Jazz Festival – Vic. Australia's biggest jazz festival is held at the beautiful Montsalvat artists' colony at Eltham.
    Alpine Wildflower Festival – NSW. Held at the skiing village of Thredbo, this festival focuses on arts and the environment.

February

Royal Hobart Regatta – Tas. This is the largest aquatic carnival in the southern hemisphere, with boat races and other activities.

Sydney Gay & Lesbian Mardi Gras – NSW. It's fun – there's a huge procession with extravagant costumes, and an incredible party along Oxford St.

Festival of Perth – WA. This huge cultural festival features three weeks of performances by local and international artists.

Melbourne Music Festival – Vic. The main contemporary music festival in the country.

Hunter Valley Vintage Festival – NSW. Wine enthusiasts flock to the Hunter Valley (north of Sydney) for wine tasting, and grape-picking and treading contests. Runs throughout February and March.

March

Adelaide Arts Festival – SA. Held on even-dated years, this is three weeks of music, theatre, opera, ballet, art exhibitions, light relief and plenty of parties. The *Adelaide Fringe Festival* accompanies the main festival.

Moomba – Vic. This week-long festival in Melbourne culminates in a huge street procession, usually on the Victorian Labour Day holiday.

Port Fairy Folk Festival–Vic. Every Labour Day weekend the small coastal town of Port Fairy comes to life with music, dancing, workshops, storytelling, spontaneous entertainment and stalls. Australia's biggest folk music festival attracts all sorts of people and for three days the population swells from 2500 to over 10,000.

Australian Formula One Grand Prix -Vic. This premier motor race takes place on a circuit around Albert Park Lake in inner suburban Melbourne. There are also festive events, concerts and street parties.

Australian Motorcycle Grand Prix – NSW. This round of the 500 cc world championships is held at Eastern Creek.

March to April

Royal Easter Show – NSW. Livestock contests and exhibits, ring events, sideshows and rodeos are features of the Sydney show, which is held at Easter.

Bell's Beach Surf Classic – Vic. The longest-running professional surfing event in the world is held over the Easter weekend at Bell's Beach, south-west of Melbourne.

National Folk Festival – ACT. Large music festival held at Easter in Canberra.

April

Anzac Day – This national public holiday on 25 April commemorates the landing of Anzac troops at Gallipoli in 1915. Memorial marches by the returned soldiers of both world wars and the veterans of Korea and Vietnam are held all over the country.

Melbourne Comedy Festival – Vic. The comedy capital of Australia puts on a terrific three-week festival with local, out-of-town and international comedians, plays and other funny events.

May

Torres Strait Cultural Festival – Qld. Month-long Aboriginal festival featuring music, dance and exhibitions.

Outback Muster – Qld. Held at the famed Stockman's Hall of Fame in Longreach, this unusual three-day festival features a variety of events related to droving. It also incorporates an outback performing arts show.

June

Melbourne International Film Festival – Vic. This is Australia's longest-running international film event, presenting the best in contemporary world cinema.

Barunga Wugularr Sports & Cultural Festival – NT. For the four days over the Queen's Birthday long weekend in June, Barunga, 80 km south-east of Katherine, becomes a gathering place for Aboriginal people from all over the Territory. There's traditional arts and crafts, as well as dancing and athletics competitions.

Merrepen Arts Festival – NT. In June or July, Nauiyu Nambiyu on the banks of the Daly River is the venue for this festival where several Aboriginal communities from around the district, such as Wadeye, Nauiyu and Peppimenarti, display their arts and crafts.

July

NT Royal Shows – Agricultural shows in Darwin, Katherine, Tennant Creek and Alice Springs.

August

Darwin Rodeo – NT. This includes international team events between Australia, the USA, Canada and New Zealand.

Darwin Beer Can Regatta – NT. Races for boats constructed entirely out of beer cans, of which there are plenty in this heavy-drinking city.

Yuendumu Festival – NT. Aboriginal people from the central and western desert region meet in Yuendumu, north-west of Alice Springs, over a long weekend in early August. There's a mix of traditional and modern sporting and cultural events.

Sydney City to Surf – NSW. Australia's biggest foot race takes place with up to 25,000 competitors running the 14 km from Hyde Park to Bondi Beach.

Shinju Matsuri (Festival of the Pearl) – WA. Held in the old pearling port of Broome, this week-long festival is a great event and highlights the town's Asian cultural heritage.

Oenpelli Open Day – NT. Oenpelli is in Arnhem Land, not far from Jabiru in Kakadu National Park. On the first Saturday in August an open day is held where there's a chance to purchase local artefacts and watch the sports and dancing events.

September

AFL Grand Final – Vic. Sporting attention turns to Melbourne with the Grand Final of Aussie rules football, when a crowd close to 100,000 assembles at the MCG. It's the biggest sporting event in Australia.

Royal Melbourne Show – Vic. This attracts agricultural folk for the judging of livestock and produce, and lots of families for the sideshows.

Royal Perth Show – WA. Has agricultural displays and demonstrations, with sideshows, novelty rides etc.

Royal Adelaide Show – SA. One of the oldest royal shows in the country, with major agricultural and horticultural exhibits and entertainment.

Birdsville Races – Qld. Famous outback race meeting where visitors flock in from around the country for a weekend of horse races and heavy drinking. Proceeds go to the Royal Flying Doctor Service.

October

Australian Bush Music Festival – NSW. Performances by Aboriginal and non-Aboriginal singers, dancers and musicians at Glen Innes.

Melbourne Writers Festival – Vic. Readings and discussions of works by Australian and international authors.

Melbourne Festival – Vic. An annual festival offering some of the best of opera, theatre, dance and the visual arts from around Australia and the world.

Melbourne Fringe Festival – Vic. Three weeks of theatre, dance, comedy, cabaret, writers' readings, exhibitions and other events help Melbourne celebrate the 'alternative' arts.

Henley-on-Todd Regatta – NT. A series of races for leg-powered bottomless boats on the (usually) dry Todd River.

Tooheys 1000 Touring Car Race – NSW. Motor racing enthusiasts flock to Bathurst for the annual 1000-km, touring car race on the superb Mt Panorama circuit.

Royal Shows – Tas. The royal agricultural and horticultural shows of Hobart and Launceston are held this month.

November

Melbourne Cup – Vic. On the first Tuesday in November Australia's premier horse race is run at Flemington Racecourse. It's a public holiday in Melbourne but the whole country comes to a virtual standstill for the three minutes or so when the race is on.

Indigenous Arts Festival – SA. Week-long Aboriginal festival in Adelaide.

Festival of the Bogong Moth – Vic. Held at Mt Beauty in Victoria, this three-day Aboriginal festival features the art, music, dance and language of seven regional Aboriginal groups.

Wangaratta Jazz Festival – Vic. A popular jazz and blues festival.

December to January

These are the busiest summer months with Christmas, school holidays, lots of beach activities, rock and jazz festivals, international sporting events including tennis and cricket, a whole host of outdoor activities and lots of parties.

Sydney to Hobart Yacht Race – NSW. Sydney Harbour is a sight to behold on Boxing Day (26 December) when boats of all shapes and sizes crowd its waters to farewell the yachts competing in this gruelling race. It's a fantastic sight as the yachts stream out of the harbour and head south. In Hobart there's a mardi gras to celebrate the finish of the race.

POST & TELECOMMUNICATIONS
Sending Mail

Post offices are open from 9 am to 5 pm Monday to Friday, but you can often get stamps from local post offices operated from newsagencies or from Australia Post shops, found in large cities, on Saturday mornings as well.

Letters Australia's postal services are relatively efficient but not too cheap. It costs 45c to send a standard letter or postcard within Australia.

Air-mail letters/postcards cost 75/70c to New Zealand, 85/80c to Singapore and Malaysia, 95/90c to Hong Kong and India, $1.05/95c to the USA and Canada, and $1.20/1 to Europe and the UK.

Parcels The rates for posting parcels are not too extortionate. By sea mail a 1/2/5 kg parcel costs $14.50/18/28.50 to New Zealand and India, and $15/19/31 to the USA, Europe or the UK. Each kg over five kg costs $3.50 for New Zealand and India, and $4 for the USA, Europe or the UK, with a maximum of 20 kg for all destinations. Air-mail rates are considerably more expensive.

Receiving Mail

All post offices will hold mail for visitors, and some city GPOs (main post offices) have very busy poste restante sections. You can also have mail sent to you at American Express offices in big cities if you have an Amex card or carry Amex travellers' cheques.

Telephone

Local Calls Local calls from public phones cost 40c for an unlimited amount of time. You can make local calls from gold or blue phones – often found in shops, hotels, bars etc – and from payphone booths. Local calls from private phones cost 30c.

STD Calls It's also possible to make long-distance (STD – Subscriber Trunk Dialling) calls from virtually any public phone. Many public phones accept Telstra (formerly Telecom) phonecards, which come in $5, $10, $20 and $50 denominations, and are available from retail outlets such as newsagents and pharmacies which display the phonecard logo. Otherwise, use coins and be prepared to feed them through at a fair old rate. STD calls are cheaper in off-peak hours

– see the front of a local telephone book for the different rates.

Some public phones are set up to take only bank cash cards or credit cards, and these too are convenient, although you need to keep an eye on how much the call is costing as it can quickly mount up. The minimum charge for a call on one of these phones is $1.20.

STD calls are cheaper at night. In ascending order of cost:

Economy – from 6 pm Saturday to 8 am Monday;
   10 pm to 8 am every night
Night – from 6 to 10 pm Monday to Friday
Day – from 8 am to 6 pm Monday to Saturday

International Calls From most STD phones you can also make ISD (International Subscriber Dialling) calls. Dialling ISD you can get through to overseas numbers almost as quickly as you can access local numbers and if your call is brief it needn't cost very much

Dial 0011 for overseas, the country code (44 for Britain, 1 for North America, 64 for New Zealand), the city code (171 or 181 for London, 212 for New York etc) and then the

---

Telephone Number Changes

Since 1995 a new telephone numbering system has been gradually introduced throughout Australia, to meet the demand for new numbers. Every phone and fax number in Australia is gaining an extra one or two digits, so that all numbers will have a total of eight digits. In metropolitan areas an extra digit is being added to the front of the existing seven-digit number. In regional areas, generally the last two digits of the current area code are being added to the front of the local number to form a new eight-digit number. The original 54 area codes will be merged into just four: (02) for New South Wales and the ACT, (03) for Victoria and Tasmania, (07) for Queensland, and (08) for Western Australia, the Northern Territory and South Australia.

Most of the new numbers are now in use, and all should be in use by November 1997. In this book, new numbers are listed for most areas, except Western Australia, the ACT and some regions of Queensland and New South Wales. See the Phone Changes box at the start of each state or territory chapter for more detailed information.

There is a six-month period when both the old and new numbers are accessible, and then for three months a recorded message will refer the caller to the White Pages information section.

When dialling a long-distance number, remember to use the area code, even if it's the same as the code for the area you are calling from. For example, you need to dial the 02 code when dialling a NSW number from outside NSW, *and* when dialling long-distance within NSW (eg from Sydney to Newcastle).

The change does not affect the cost of calls: a long-distance call is still charged at long-distance rates. If in doubt, you can call AUSTEL's information hotline on ☎ toll-free 1800 888 888. ■

telephone number. And have a phonecard, credit card or plenty of coins to hand.

It's possible to make ISD calls with either of Australia's two telecommunications companies, Optus and Telstra (formerly Telecom). The fee structure varies slightly between the two, and if you are phoning one country constantly it may be worth comparing the two. This option is only available from private phones in certain areas. Phone Optus (☎ toll-free 1800 500 005) for details on how to access their services.

International calls from Australia are among the cheapest you'll find anywhere. A Telstra call to the USA or Britain costs $1.35 a minute ($1.03 off-peak); New Zealand is $1.09 a minute ($0.72 off peak). Off-peak times, if available, vary depending on the destination – see the back of any White Pages telephone book, or call ☎ 0102 for more details. Sunday is often the cheapest day to ring.

Country Direct is a service which gives travellers in Australia direct access to operators in nearly 50 countries, to make collect or credit card calls. For a full list of the countries hooked into this system, check any local White Pages telephone book. They include: Canada (☎ 1800 881 150), Germany (☎ 1800 881 490), Japan (☎ 1800 881 810), New Zealand (☎ 1800 881 640), the UK (☎ 1800 881 440) and the USA (☎ 1800 881 011).

Toll-Free Calls Many businesses and some government departments operate a toll-free service, so no matter where you are ringing from around the country, it's a free call. These numbers have the prefix 1800 and we've listed them wherever possible throughout this book. Many companies, such as the airlines, have six-digit numbers beginning with 13, and these are charged at the rate of a local call. Often these numbers are Australia-wide, or may be applicable to a specific STD district only. Unfortunately there's no way of telling without actually ringing the number.

Mobile Phones Phone numbers with the prefixes 014, 015, 016, 018 or 041 are mobile or car phones. The three mobile operators are the government's Telstra, and the two private companies Optus and Vodaphone. Calls from mobile numbers are charged at special STD rates and can be expensive.

Information Calls Other odd numbers you may come across are those starting with 0055 and 190. The 0055 numbers, usually recorded information services and the like, are provided by private companies, and your call is charged in multiples of 25c (40c from public phones) at a rate selected by the provider. These rates are: Premium 70c per minute, Value 55c per minute, and Budget 35c per minute.

Numbers beginning with 190 are also information services, but they are charged on a fixed fee basis, which can vary from as little as 35c to as much as $30!

Internet If you want to surf the Net, even if it's only to access your e-mail, there are service providers in all the capital cities, and in many regional areas too. On-line costs vary, but a typical price structure is a $25 joining fee then $5 per hour on-line, with no minimum charge. A few of the current major players include:

Australia On Line
　　☎ toll-free 1800 621 258; www.ozonline.com.au
On Australia (Microsoft Network)
　　☎ (02) 9934 9000
Oz Email
　　☎ (02) 9391 0480; www.ozemail.com.au
Pegasus Networks
　　☎ toll-free 1800 812 812; www.peg.apc.org

CompuServe users who want to access the service locally should phone CompuServe (☎ toll-free 1800 025 240) to get the local log-in numbers.

TIME
Australia is divided into three time zones: Western Standard Time is plus eight hours from GMT/UTC (Western Australia), Central Standard Time is plus 9½ hours (Northern Territory, South Australia) and Eastern Standard Time is plus 10 (Tasmania,

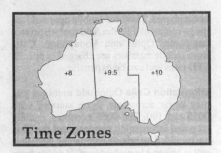

Time Zones

Victoria, New South Wales, Queensland). When it's noon in Western Australia it's 1.30 pm in the Northern Territory and South Australia and 2 pm in the rest of the country.

During the summer things get slightly screwed up as daylight saving time (when clocks are put forward an hour) does not operate in Western Australia, the Northern Territory or Queensland, and in Tasmania it starts a month earlier and finishes up to a month later than in the other states.

ELECTRICITY

Voltage is 220-240 V and the plugs are three-pin, but not the same as British three-pin plugs. Users of electric shavers or hairdryers should note that, apart from in fancy hotels, it's difficult to find converters to take either US flat two-pin plugs or the European round two-pin plugs. Adaptors for British plugs can be found in good hardware shops, chemists and travel agents. You can easily bend the US plugs to a slight angle to make them fit.

WEIGHTS & MEASURES

Australia uses the metric system. Petrol and milk are sold by the litre, apples and potatoes by the kg, distance is measured by the metre or km, and speed limits are in km per hour (km/h). Colloquially, distance is often measured in the time it takes to get there, rather than in km, eg Geelong is two hours drive away.

For those who need help with metric there's a conversion table at the back of this book.

BOOKS

In almost any bookshop in the country you'll find a section devoted to Australiana with books on every Australian subject you care to mention. Australia has a lot of bookshops and some of the better-known ones are mentioned in the various city sections.

At the Wilderness Society shops in each capital city and the Government Printing offices in Sydney and Melbourne you'll find a good range of wildlife posters, calendars and books.

History

For a good introduction to Australian history, read *A Short History of Australia*, a most accessible and informative general history by the late Manning Clark, the respected Aussie historian, or *The Fatal Shore*, Robert Hughes' bestselling account of the convict era.

Geoffrey Blainey's *The Tyranny of Distance* is an engrossing study of the problems of transport in this harsh continent and how they shaped the pattern of White settlement: transporting produce 100 miles by bullock cart from an inland farm to a port, cost more than shipping it from there around the globe to Europe – a handicap that only wool, and later gold, was profitable enough to overcome.

Finding Australia, by Russel Ward, traces the period from the first Aboriginal arrivals up to 1821. It's strong on Aborigines, women and the full story of foreign exploration, not just Cook's role. There's lots of fascinating detail, including information about the appalling crooks who ran the early colony, and it's intended to be the first of a series.

The Exploration of Australia, by Michael Cannon, is a coffee-table book in size, presentation and price, but it's a fascinating reference book about the gradual European uncovering of the continent.

The Fatal Impact, by Alan Moorehead, begins with the voyages of Cook, regarded as one of the greatest and most humane explorers, and tells the tragic story of the European impact on Australia, Tahiti and Antarctica in the years that followed. It details how good intentions and the economic imperatives of the time led to disaster, corruption and annihilation.

Cooper's Creek, also by Moorehead, is a classic account of the ill-fated Burke and Wills expedition which dramatises the horrors and hardships faced by the early explorers.

John Pilger's *A Secret Country* is a vividly written book which deals with Australia's historical roots, its shabby treatment of Aboriginal people and the current political complexion. It also posits an interesting theory on the dismissal of the Whitlam government in 1975.

To get an idea of life on a Kimberley cattle station last century, *Kings in Grass Castles* (1959) and *Sons in the Saddle* (1983), both by Dame Mary Durack, are well worth getting hold of. Other books which give an insight into the pioneering days in the outback include *Packhorse & Waterhole* by Gordon Buchanan, son of legendary drover Nat Buchanan who opened up large areas of the Northern Territory; *The Big Run*, by Jock Makin, a history of the huge Victoria River Downs cattle station in the Northern Territory; and *The Cattle King* by Ion Idriess, which details the life of the remarkable Sir Sidney Kidman, who set up a chain of stations in the outback early this century.

Aboriginal People

The Australian Aborigines by Kenneth Maddock is a good cultural summary. The award-winning *Triumph of the Nomads*, by Geoffrey Blainey, chronicles the life of Australia's original inhabitants, and convincingly demolishes the myth that Aboriginal people were 'primitive' people trapped on a hostile continent. They were in fact extremely successful in adapting to and overcoming the difficulties presented by the climate and seeming lack of resources – it's an excellent read.

For a sympathetic historical account of what's happened to the original Australians since Europeans arrived read *Aboriginal Australians* by Richard Broome. *A Change of Ownership*, by Mildred Kirk, covers

similar ground to Broome's book, but does so more concisely, focusing on the land rights movement and its historical background.

The Other Side of the Frontier, by Henry Reynolds, uses historical records to give a vivid account of an Aboriginal view of the arrival and takeover of Australia by Europeans. His *With the White People* identifies the essential Aboriginal contributions to the survival of the early White settlers. *My Place*, Sally Morgan's prize-winning autobiography, traces her discovery of her Aboriginal heritage. *The Fringe Dwellers*, by Nene Gare, describes just what it's like to be an Aborigine growing up in a White-dominated society.

Don't Take Your Love to Town by Ruby Langford and *My People* by Oodgeroo Noonuccal (Kath Walker) are also recommended reading for people interested in the experiences of Aboriginal people.

Songman, by Allan Baillie, is a fictional account of the life of an adolescent Aboriginal boy growing up in Arnhem Land in the days before White settlement.

Fiction

You don't need to worry about bringing novels from home for your trip to Australia; there's plenty of excellent recent Australian literature including the novels and short stories of writers such as Rodney Hall, Dorothy Hewett, Janette Turner Hospital, Elizabeth Jolley, Gillian Mears, Drusilla Modjeska and Frank Moorhouse. Popular genres include crime (Peter Corris, Garry Disher, Marele Day, Susan Geason and Kerry Greenwood), dirty realism (Andrew McGahan and Justine Ettler) and anthologies (from collections of works by up and coming authors such as *Picador New Writing* to Dale Spender's *The Penguin Anthology of Australian Women's Writing* and Robert Dessaix's *Australian Gay and Lesbian Writing*).

Peter Carey is one of Australia's most successful contemporary writers and all his books are worth looking for. His rambling novel *Illywhacker* (1985) is set mostly in

Melbourne, while *The Tax Inspector* is set in an outer suburb of Sydney.

Tim Winton is widely regarded as one of the best writers in Australia today. Winton's evocation of coastal WA is superb, particularly in works such as *Shallows* and *An Open Swimmer*. Other writers with a strong sense of place include Helen Garner (*Monkey Grip* – Melbourne), Peter Corris (the Cliff Hardy stories – Sydney), David Ireland (*The Glass Canoe* – Sydney) and David Malouf (*Johnno* – Brisbane).

There are many Australian classics (those listed here have also been made into films), including *The Getting of Wisdom* by Henry Handel Richardson, *Picnic at Hanging Rock* by Joan Lindsay and *My Brilliant Career* by Miles Franklin. *For the Term of his Natural Life*, written in 1870 by Marcus Clarke, was one of the first books to be made into a film, in 1926. See the Literature section in the Facts about the Country chapter for more on Australia's best-known fiction writers.

Travel Accounts

Sean & David's Long Drive, a hilarious, offbeat road book by young Australian author Sean Condon, is one of the titles in Lonely Planet's new 'Journeys' travel literature series.

Other accounts of travels in Australia include the marvellous *Tracks*, by Robyn Davidson. It's the amazing story of a young woman who set out alone to walk from Alice Springs to the Western Australia coast with her camels – proof that you can do anything if you try hard enough. It almost single handedly inspired the current Australian interest in camel safaris!

Quite another sort of travel is Tony Horwitz's *One for the Road*, an entertaining account of a high-speed hitchhiking trip around Australia (Oz through a windscreen). In contrast, *The Ribbon and the Ragged Square*, by Linda Christmas, is an intelligent, sober account of a nine-month investigatory trip round Oz by a *Guardian* journalist from England. There's lots of background and history as well as first-hand reporting and interviews.

Howard Jacobson's *In the Land of Oz* recounts his circuit of the country. It's amusing at times, but through most of the book you're left wondering when the long-suffering Ros is finally going to thump the twerp!

The late Bruce Chatwin's *The Songlines* tells of his experiences among central Australian Aboriginal people and makes more sense of the Dreamtime, sacred sites, sacred songs and the traditional Aboriginal way of life than 10 learned tomes put together. Along the way it also delves into the origins of humankind and throws in some pithy anecdotes about modern Australia.

The journals of the early European explorers can be fairly hard going but make fascinating reading. The hardships that many of these men (and they were virtually all men) endured is nothing short of amazing. These accounts are usually available in main city libraries. Men such as Sturt, Eyre, Leichhardt, Davidson, King (on the Burke and Wills expedition), Stuart and many others all kept detailed journals.

Travel Guides

Burnum Burnum's Aboriginal Australia is subtitled 'a traveller's guide'. If you want to explore Australia from the Aboriginal point of view, this large and lavish hardback is the book for you.

For trips into the outback in your own vehicle Lonely Planet's *Outback Australia* is the book to get. Brian Sheedy's *Outback on a Budget* includes lots of practical advice. There are a number of other books about vehicle preparation and driving in the outback, including *Explore Australia by Four-Wheel Drive* by Peter & Kim Wherrett (Viking O'Neil).

Surfing Australia's East Coast by Aussie surf star Nat Young is a slim, cheap, comprehensive guide to the best breaks from Victoria to Fraser Island. He's also written the *Surfing & Sailboard Guide to Australia*, which covers the whole country. Surfing enthusiasts can also look for the expensive coffee-table book *Atlas of Australian Surfing*, by Mark Warren.

If you want to really understand the Barrier Reef's natural history, look for *Australia's Great Barrier Reef*. It's colourful, expensive and nearly as big as the Barrier Reef itself. There's also a cheaper abbreviated paperback version. Lonely Planet's *Islands of Australia's Great Barrier Reef* book gives you all the practical info you'll need for making the most of the reef. *Australia's Wonderful Wildlife* (Australian Women's Weekly) is the shoestringer's equivalent of a coffee-table book – a cheap paperback with lots of great photos of the animals you didn't see, or those that didn't stay still when you pointed your camera at them.

Lonely Planet's *Bushwalking in Australia* describes 35 walks of different lengths and difficulty in various parts of the country. Lonely Planet also has *Victoria*, *Western Australia*, *New South Wales*, *Queensland*, *Northern Territory*, *South Australia* and *Tasmania* state guides and *Melbourne* and *Sydney* city guides.

There are state-by-state Reader's Digest guides to coasts and national parks, such as the *Coast of New South Wales*, and Gregory's guides to national parks, such as *National Parks of New South Wales* (a handy reference listing access, facilities, activities and so on for all parks).

Souvenir Books

If you want a souvenir of Australia, such as a photographic record, try one of the numerous coffee-table books like *A Day in the Life of Australia*. *Local Color – Travels in the Other Australia* (1994) by Bill Bachman is a photographic essay which includes fine descriptive prose by Tim Winton. There are many other Australian books which make good gifts: children's books with very Australian illustrations like Julie Vivar and Mem Fox's *Possum Magic*, Norman Lindsay's *The Magic Pudding*, and *Snugglepot & Cuddlepie* by May Gibbs (one of the first bestselling Australian children's books), or cartoon books by excellent Australian cartoonists such as Michael Leunig and Kaz Cooke.

MAPS

There's no shortage of maps available, although many of them are of pretty average quality. For road maps the best are probably those published by the various oil companies – Shell, BP, Mobil etc, and these are available from service stations. The state motoring organisations are another good source of maps, and their's are often a lot cheaper than the oil company maps. See Useful Organisations earlier in this chapter for addresses. Commercially available city street guides, such as those produced by Melways, Gregorys and UBD are also useful.

For bushwalking, ski-touring and other activities which require large-scale maps, the topographic sheets put out by the Australian Surveying & Land Information Group (AUSLIG) are the ones to get. Many of the more popular sheets are available over the counter at shops which sell specialist bushwalking gear and outdoor equipment. AUSLIG also has special-interest maps showing various types of land use such as population densities or Aboriginal land. For more information, or a catalogue, contact AUSLIG, Department of Administrative Services, Scrivener Bldg, Fern Hill Park, Bruce, ACT 2617 (☎ (06) 201 4201).

MEDIA

Australia has a wide range of media although a few big companies (Rupert Murdoch's News Corporation and Kerry Packer's Consolidated Press being the best-known) own an awful lot of what there is to read and watch.

The ownership of media enterprises is closely monitored by the Federal government, and foreign ownership is limited to 15%. The laws regarding cross-media ownership are also tight, and both laws have led to recent clashes between the government and interested parties, particularly Canadian Conrad Black and Australian Kerry Packer over their level of ownership of the Fairfax group.

Newspapers & Magazines

Each major city tends to have at least one important daily, often backed up by a tabloid and also by evening papers. The Fairfax group's *Sydney Morning Herald* and Melbourne *Age* are two of the most important dailies. There's also the *Australian*, a Murdoch-owned paper and the country's only national daily. The *Australian Financial Review* is the country's business daily.

Weekly newspapers and magazines include an Australian edition of *Time* and a combined edition of the Australian news magazine the *Bulletin* and *Newsweek*. The *Guardian Weekly* is widely available and good for international news.

The Independent is a monthly magazine which explores current social and lifestyle issues in depth, while the *Business Review Weekly* does the same with business matters on a weekly basis.

Good outdoor and adventure magazines include *Wild* and *Outdoor Australia*, published quarterly, and *Rock*, published monthly.

Magazines from the UK and USA are also available, but usually with a delay of a month or so.

Radio & TV

The national advertising-free (so far) TV and radio network is the Australian Broadcasting Corporation (ABC). In most places there are a couple of ABC radio stations and a host of commercial stations, both AM and FM, featuring the whole gamut of radio possibilities, from rock to talkback to 'beautiful music'. Triple J is the ABC's youth FM radio station which broadcasts nationally and is an excellent place to hear music (Australian and overseas) which is outside the pop mainstream and plug in to Australia's youth culture.

In Sydney and Melbourne there are the ABC, three commercial TV stations (the Nine, Ten and Seven networks) and SBS, a government-sponsored multi-cultural TV station which is beamed to the capital cities and some regional centres. Around the country the number of TV stations varies from place to place; there are regional TV stations but in some remote areas the ABC may be all you can receive.

Imparja is an Aboriginal owned and run commercial TV station which operates out of Alice Springs and has a 'footprint' which covers one-third of the country (mainly the Northern Territory, South Australia and western NSW). It broadcasts a variety of programmes, ranging from soaps to pieces made by and for Aboriginal people.

On the pay TV front Australia is really dragging its feet. Only in 1995 did the first pay TV operation start, and even now it's only available to a fraction of the population, and at relatively high cost. The major players in the industry are still jockeying for position, and until the dust settles pay TV is a bit of a non-starter.

Internet

The World Wide Web is rapidly expanding to become one of the major sources of information on anything you care to name. Although things on the Net change rapidly, some sites which currently provide a range of information on Australia include:

Guide to Australia
  This site, maintained by the Charles Sturt University in NSW, is a mine of information, with links to Australian government departments, weather information, books, maps, etc.
  URL: www.csu.edu.au/education/australia.html
The Aussie Index
  A fairly comprehensive list of Australian companies, educational institutions and government departments which maintain Web sites.
  URL: www.aussie.com.au/aussie.htm
Australian Government
  The Federal government has a site, which is predicably unexciting, but it is wide-ranging and a good source for things like visa information.
  URL: gov.info.au
Lonely Planet
  Our own site is not specific to Australia but is still definitely worth a look. Well, we would say that, wouldn't we?
  URL: www.lonelyplanet.com.au

FILM & PHOTOGRAPHY

Australian film prices are not too far out of line with those of the rest of the Western world. Including developing, 36-exposure Kodachrome 64 or Fujichrome 100 slide film costs around $25, but with a little shopping around you can find it for around $20 – even less if you buy it in quantity.

There are plenty of camera shops in all the big cities and standards of camera service are high. Processing standards are also high, with many places offering one-hour developing of print film. Melbourne is the main centre for developing Kodachrome slide film in the South-East Asian region.

Photography is no problem, but in the outback you have to allow for the exceptional intensity of the light. Best results in the outback are obtained early in the morning and late in the afternoon. As the sun gets higher, colours appear washed out. You must also allow for the intensity of reflected light when taking shots on the Barrier Reef or at other coastal locations. Especially in the summer, allow for temperature extremes and do your best to keep film as cool as possible, particularly after exposure. Other film and camera hazards are dust in the outback and humidity in the far north tropical regions.

As in any country, politeness goes a long way when taking photographs; ask before taking pictures of people. Note that many Aboriginal people do not like to have their photographs taken, even from a distance.

HEALTH

Australia is a remarkably healthy country to travel in, considering that such a large portion of it lies in the tropics. Tropical diseases such as malaria and yellow fever are unknown, diseases of insanitation such as cholera and typhoid are unheard of, and even some animal diseases such as rabies and foot-and-mouth disease have yet to be recorded.

So long as you have not visited an infected country in the past 14 days (aircraft refuelling stops do not count) no vaccinations are required for entry. There are, however, a few routine vaccinations that are recommended worldwide whether you are travelling or not, and it's always worth checking whether your tetanus booster is up to date.

Medical care in Australia is first-class and only moderately expensive. A typical visit to the doctor costs around $35. If you have an immediate health problem, phone or visit the casualty section at the nearest public hospital.

Visitors from the UK, New Zealand, Malta, Italy, Sweden and the Netherlands have reciprocal health rights in Australia and can register at any Medicare office. This entitles them to free or heavily subsidised medical treatment at public hospitals and from clinics which 'bulk bill' (ie the bill for the treatment is sent direct to Medicare).

Travel Insurance

Ambulance services in Australia are self-funding (ie they're not free) and can be frightfully expensive, so you'd be wise to take out travel insurance for that reason alone. Make sure the policy specifically includes ambulance, helicopter rescue and a flight home for you and anyone you're travelling with, should your condition warrant it. Also check the fine print: some policies exclude 'dangerous activities' such as scuba diving, motorcycling and even trekking. If such activities are on your agenda, you don't want that policy.

Medical Kit

While facilities in cities and towns are generally of a very high standard, doctors and hospitals are few and far between in the remote areas. If you're heading off the beaten track, at least one person in your party should have a sound knowledge of first-aid treatment, and in any case you'll need a first-aid handbook and a basic medical kit. Some of the items that should be included are:

- Aspirin or Panadol – for pain or fever.
- Antihistamine (such as Benadryl) – useful as a decongestant for colds and allergies, to ease the itch from insect bites or stings, and to help prevent motion sickness. Antihistamines may cause sedation and may interact with alcohol so care should be taken when using them.
- Kaolin preparation (Pepto-Bismol), Imodium or Lomotil – for stomach upsets.

- Antiseptic such as Betadine, which comes as impregnated swabs or ointment, and an antibiotic powder or similar 'dry' spray – for cuts and grazes.
- Calamine lotion – to ease irritation from bites or stings.
- Eye drops.
- Sterile gauze bandages.
- Triangular bandages to support limbs and hold dressings in place.
- Other assorted bandages and Band-aids – for minor injuries.
- Adhesive tape and cotton wool.
- Scissors, tweezers and a thermometer (note that mercury thermometers are prohibited by airlines).
- Insect repellent, sunscreen, suntan lotion, chap stick and water purification tablets.

Optional items include:

- Cold and flu tablets
- Antacid indigestion tablets.
- Ear drops.
- Vinegar for jellyfish stings
- Burn cream

Health Precautions

The contraceptive pill is available on prescription only, so a visit to a doctor is necessary. Doctors are listed in the Yellow Pages phone book or you can visit the outpatients section of a public hospital. Condoms are available from chemists, many convenience stores such as 7-Eleven, and vending machines in the public toilets of many hotels and universities.

Heat Travellers from the northern hemisphere need to be aware of the intensity of the sun in Australia. Those ultraviolet rays can have you burnt to a crisp even on an overcast day, so if in doubt wear protective cream, a wide-brimmed hat and a long-sleeved shirt with a collar.

In northern and outback areas you can expect the weather to be hot between October and April, and travellers from cool climates may feel uncomfortable, even in winter. 'Hot' is a relative term, depending on what you are used to. The sensible thing to do on a hot day is to avoid the sun between mid-morning and mid-afternoon. Infants and elderly people are most at risk from heat exhaustion and heatstroke. Australia has a high incidence of skin cancer, a fact directly connected to exposure to the sun. Be careful.

Water People who first arrive in a hot climate may not feel thirsty when they should; the body and 'thirst mechanism' often need a few days to adjust. The rule of thumb is that an active adult should drink at least four litres of water per day in warm weather, and more when physically very active, such as when cycling or walking. Use the colour of your urine as a guide: if it's clear you're probably drinking enough, but if it's dark you need to drink more. Remember that body moisture will evaporate in the dry air with no indication that you're sweating.

Tap water is safe to drink in towns and cities throughout the country. In outback areas, bore water may not be fit for human consumption, so seek local advice before drinking it.

Always beware of water from rivers, creeks and lakes, as it may have been infected by stock or wildlife. The surest way to disinfect water is to thoroughly boil it for 10 minutes.

Health Problems

Sunburn In the tropics, the desert or at high altitudes you can get sunburnt surprisingly quickly, even through cloud. Use a sunscreen and take extra care to cover areas which don't normally see sun, such as your feet. A hat provides added protection, and you should also use zinc cream or some other barrier cream for your nose and lips. Calamine lotion is good for mild sunburn.

Prickly Heat Prickly heat is an itchy rash caused by excessive perspiration trapped under the skin. It usually strikes people who have just arrived in a hot climate and whose pores have not yet opened sufficiently to cope with greater sweating. Keeping cool but bathing often, using a mild talcum powder or even resorting to air-conditioning may help until you acclimatise.

Heat Exhaustion Dehydration or salt deficiency can cause heat exhaustion. Take time to acclimatise to high temperatures and make sure you get sufficient liquids. Wear loose clothing and a broad-brimmed hat. Do not do anything too physically demanding.

Salt deficiency is characterised by fatigue, lethargy, headaches, giddiness and muscle cramps, and in this case salt tablets may help. Vomiting or diarrhoea can deplete your liquid and salt levels. Anhydrotic heat exhaustion, caused by an inability to sweat, is quite rare. Unlike the other forms of heat exhaustion it is likely to strike people who have been in a hot climate for some time, rather than newcomers.

Heatstroke This serious, sometimes fatal, condition can occur if the heat-regulating mechanism of the body breaks down and the body temperature rises to dangerous levels Long, continuous periods of exposure to high temperatures can leave you vulnerable to heat stroke. You should avoid excessive alcohol consumption or strenuous activity when you first arrive in a hot climate.

The symptoms are feeling unwell, not sweating very much or at all and a high body temperature (39°C to 41°C). Where sweating has ceased the skin becomes flushed and red. Severe, throbbing headaches and lack of coordination will also occur, and the sufferer may be confused or aggressive. Eventually the victim will become delirious or convulse. Hospitalisation is essential, but meanwhile get victims out of the sun, remove their clothing, cover them with a wet sheet or towel and fan them continually.

Fungal Infections Fungal infections, which occur with greater frequency in hot weather, are most likely to occur on the scalp, between the toes or fingers (athlete's foot), in the groin (jock itch or crotch rot) and on the body (ringworm). You get ringworm (which is a fungal infection, not a worm) from infected animals or by walking on damp areas, like shower floors.

To prevent fungal infections wear loose, comfortable clothes, avoid artificial fibres, wash frequently and dry carefully. If you do get an infection, wash the infected area daily with a disinfectant or medicated soap and water, and rinse and dry well. Apply an antifungal powder like the widely available Tinaderm. Try to expose the infected area to air or sunlight as much as possible and wash all towels and underwear in hot water as well as changing them often.

Cold Too much cold is just as dangerous as too much heat, particularly if it leads to hypothermia. If you are trekking in cold areas, such as the alpine areas of Tasmania, Victoria and NSW, be prepared.

Hypothermia occurs when the body loses heat faster than it can produce it and the core temperature of the body falls. It is surprisingly easy to progress from very cold to dangerously cold due to a combination of wind, wet clothing, fatigue and hunger, even if the air temperature is above freezing. It is best to dress in layers; silk, wool and some of the new artificial fibres are all good insulating materials. A hat is important, as a lot of heat is lost through the head. A strong, waterproof outer layer is essential, as keeping dry is vital. Carry basic supplies, including food containing simple sugars to generate heat quickly and lots of fluid to drink. A space blanket is something all travellers in cold environments should carry.

Symptoms of hypothermia are exhaustion, numb skin (particularly toes and fingers), shivering, slurred speech, irrational or violent behaviour, lethargy, stumbling, dizzy spells, muscle cramps and violent bursts of energy. Irrationality may take the form of sufferers claiming they are warm and trying to take off their clothes.

To treat mild hypothermia, first get the person out of the wind and/or rain, remove their clothing if it's wet and replace it with dry, warm clothing. Give them hot liquids – not alcohol – and some high-kilojoule, easily digestible food. Do not rub victims; instead allow them to slowly warm themselves. This should be enough to treat the early stages of hypothermia. The early recognition and treatment of mild hypothermia is the only way to prevent severe hypothermia, which is a critical condition.

Motion Sickness Eating lightly before and during a trip will reduce the chances of motion sickness. If you are prone to motion sickness try to find a place that minimises disturbance – near the wing on aircraft, close to midships on boats, near the centre on buses. Fresh air usually helps; reading and cigarette smoke do not. Commercial motion-sickness preparations, which can cause drowsiness, have to be taken before the trip commences; when you're feeling sick it's too late. Ginger is a natural preventative and is available in capsule form.

Jet Lag Jet lag is experienced when a person travels by air across more than three time zones (each time zone usually represents a one-hour time difference). Jet lag occurs because many of the functions of the human body (such as temperature, pulse rate and emptying of the bladder and bowels) are regulated by internal 24-hour cycles called circadian rhythms. When we travel long distances rapidly, our bodies take time to adjust to the 'new time' of our destination, and we may experience fatigue, disorientation, insomnia, anxiety, impaired concentration and loss of appetite. These effects will usually be gone within three days of arrival, but there are ways of minimising the impact of jet lag:

- Rest for a couple of days prior to departure; try to avoid late nights and last-minute dashes for travellers' cheques, passport etc.
- Try to select flight schedules that minimise sleep deprivation; arriving late in the day means you can go to sleep soon after you arrive. For very long flights, try to organise a stopover.
- Avoid excessive eating (which bloats the stomach) and alcohol (which causes dehydration) during the flight. Instead, drink plenty of noncarbonated, non-alcoholic drinks such as fruit juice or water.
- Avoid smoking, as this reduces the amount of oxygen in the aeroplane cabin even further and causes greater fatigue.

- Make yourself comfortable by wearing loose-fitting clothes and perhaps bringing an eye mask and ear plugs to help you sleep.

Diarrhoea A change of water, food or climate can all cause the runs; diarrhoea caused by contaminated food or water is more serious. Despite all your precautions you may still have a mild bout of diarrhoea but a few rushed toilet trips with no other symptoms is not indicative of a serious problem. Moderate diarrhoea, involving half-a-dozen loose movements in a day, is more of a nuisance.

Dehydration is the main danger with any diarrhoea, particularly for children where dehydration can occur quite quickly. Fluid replacement remains the mainstay of management. Weak black tea with a little sugar, soda water, or soft drinks allowed to go flat and diluted 50% with water are all good. With severe diarrhoea a rehydrating solution is necessary to replace minerals and salts. Commercially available ORS (oral rehydration salts) are very useful. In an emergency you can make up a solution of eight teaspoons of sugar to a litre of boiled water and provide salted cracker biscuits at the same time. You should stick to a bland diet as you recover.

Lomotil or Imodium can be used to bring relief from the symptoms, although they do not actually cure the problem. Only use these drugs if absolutely necessary – eg if you *must* travel. For children Imodium is preferable, but under all circumstances fluid replacement is the most important thing to remember. Do not use these drugs if the person has a high fever or is severely dehydrated.

Worms These parasites are most common in rural, tropical areas and a stool test when you return home is not a bad idea. They can be present on unwashed vegetables or in meat which has been prepared on a farm and not been inspected by the proper authorities.

Infestations may not show up for some time, and although they are generally not serious, if left untreated they can cause severe health problems. A stool test is necessary to pinpoint the problem and medication is often available over the counter.

Tetanus This potentially fatal disease is found in undeveloped tropical areas. It is difficult to treat but is preventable with immunisation. Tetanus occurs when a wound becomes infected by a germ which lives in the faeces of animals or people, so clean all cuts, punctures or animal bites. Tetanus is also known as lockjaw, and the first symptom may be discomfort in swallowing, or stiffening of the jaw and neck; this is followed by painful convulsions of the jaw and whole body.

Sexually Transmitted Diseases Sexual contact with an infected sexual partner spreads these diseases. While abstinence is the only 100% preventative, using condoms is also effective. Gonorrhoea and syphilis are the most common of these diseases; sores, blisters or rashes around the genitals, discharges or pain when urinating are common symptoms. Symptoms may be less marked or not observed at all in women. Syphilis symptoms eventually disappear completely but the disease continues and can cause severe problems in later years. The treatment of gonorrhoea and syphilis is by antibiotics.

There are numerous other sexually transmitted diseases, for most of which effective treatment is available. However, there is no cure for herpes and there is also currently no cure for AIDS.

HIV/AIDS HIV, the Human Immunodeficiency Virus, may develop into AIDS, Acquired Immune Deficiency Syndrome. Any exposure to blood, blood products or bodily fluids may put a person at risk. Transmission in Australia is mostly through contact between homosexual or bisexual males, or via contaminated needles shared by IV drug users. Apart from abstinence, the most effective preventative is always to practise safe sex by using condoms. It is impossible to detect the HIV-positive status of an otherwise healthy-looking person without a blood test.

HIV/AIDS can also be spread through infected blood transfusions, although in Australia all blood is screened for HIV. It can also be spread by dirty needles – vaccinations, acupuncture, tattooing and ear or nose piercing can potentially be as dangerous as intravenous drug use if the equipment is not clean.

Fear of HIV infection should never preclude treatment for serious medical conditions. Although there may be a risk of infection, it is very small indeed.

Cuts & Scratches Skin punctures can easily become infected in hot, humid weather and may be difficult to heal. Treat any cut with an antiseptic such as Betadine. Where possible avoid bandages and Band-aids, which can keep wounds wet. Coral cuts are notoriously slow to heal, as the coral injects a weak venom into the wound. Avoid coral cuts by wearing shoes when walking on reefs, and clean any cut thoroughly with sodium peroxide if available.

Bites & Stings Bee and wasp stings are usually painful rather than dangerous. Calamine lotion will give relief and ice packs will reduce the pain and swelling. There are some spiders with dangerous bites but antivenenes are usually available. Scorpion stings are notoriously painful; scorpions often shelter in shoes or clothing.

Certain cone shells found in Australia can sting dangerously or even fatally. There are various fish and other sea creatures which can sting or bite dangerously or which are dangerous to eat. Again, local advice is the best suggestion. (See the Dangers & Annoyances section later in this chapter for information on snakes, jellyfish and insects.)

Women's Health
Poor diet, lowered resistance due to the use of antibiotics for stomach upsets and even contraceptive pills can lead to vaginal infections when travelling in hot climates. Keeping the genital area clean, and wearing

Australia for the Disabled Traveller

The general level of disability awareness in Australia is encouraging, however, information about accessible accommodation and tourist attractions is fragmented and available on a regional basis only. The practical level of awareness is generally high and new accommodation must meet standards set down by law.

Information

The Australian Tourist Commission (see the Tourist Offices section earlier in this chapter for contact details) publishes an information fact sheet *Travel in Australia for People with Disabilities* containing addresses of organisations (such as the Paraplegic and Quadriplegic Associations, Multiple Sclerosis Society, Arthritis Society, Blind, Deaf and Spastic Societies) in each state or territory, which provide assistance to the disabled.

NICAN (National Information Communications Awareness Network), PO Box 407, Curtin, ACT 2605 (☎ (06) 285 3713; fax 285 3714) is an Australia-wide directory providing information on accessible accommodation, sporting and recreational activities. ACROD (Australian Council for the Rehabilitation of the Disabled), PO Box 60, Curtin, ACT 2605 (☎ (06) 282 4333; fax 281 3488), can provide information about state-based help organisations, accommodation and tour operators providing specialised tours.

Publications to look for include:

Access in Brisbane and *Darwin Without Steps,* both available from the local council
Accessing Sydney, available from ACROD NSW
Easy Access Australia – A Travel Guide to Australia ($24.80), a book researched and written by wheelchair users (order from PO Box 218, Kew, Victoria 3101)
Smooth Ride Guides – Australia & New Zealand, published in the UK but available in Australia
A Wheelie's Handbook of Australia, another book written by a wheelchair user (order from Colin James, PO Box 89, Coleraine, Victoria 3315).

Places to Stay

Accommodation in Australia is generally good, the difficulty is finding out about it. Always ask at information centres for lists of accessible accommodation and tourist attractions.

The capital cities are well represented by international hotel chains such as Hyatt, Hilton, Sheraton etc, which provide accessible rooms. Motel chains such as Flag and Best Western are also well represented.

There are other accommodation providers which have accessible rooms and most proprietors will do what they can to assist you. The publication guides published by the state motoring organisations are very comprehensive and give wheelchair-access information. However, it is best to confirm that the facilities suit your needs.

Some YHA youth hostels have accessible accommodation. Contact YHA Travel Membership (☎ (03) 9670 7991), 205 King St, Melbourne, Victoria 3000.

The Wheel Resort (☎ (066) 85 6139; fax 85 8754), at 39-51 Broken Head Rd, Byron Bay in NSW, was designed and is operated by wheelchair users for disabled travellers.

Getting Around

Air Travel by air is easy; Qantas and Ansett welcome disabled passengers. Qantas staff undergo disability training and Ansett has instituted ANSACARE, a system of recording your details once only, eliminating repetition at booking and obviating the need for further medical certificates. Neither airline requires a medical certificate for long-term, stable disabilities. All Australia's major airports have facilities for the disabled traveller; parking spaces, wheelchair access to terminals, accessible toilets and skychairs convey passengers onto planes. Some Qantas jets carry the skychair and some even have an accessible toilet on board.

Bus Interstate travel on buses is not yet a viable option for the wheelchair user.

Train The Indian Pacific train runs twice-weekly between Sydney, Adelaide and Perth, a journey of 65 hours and including three nights. One 'cabin' in a carriage provides wheelchair access. Train doorways are narrow so a skychair-type chair is used for boarding, and for movement between carriages. An en suite bathroom with grab rails over the toilet and shower is available but will not suit everyone. Contact the Passenger Service Managers at: Sydney (02) 9255 7833, Adelaide (08) 8217 4240 and Perth (09) 227 9064.

NSW Countrylink (☎ (02) 9379 4850) operates the XPT to Melbourne, Brisbane via Murwillumbah, Coffs Harbour, Dubbo and Wagga Wagga, while the Xplore travels to Tamworth and Canberra. Each train has at least one carriage with a seat removed for a wheelchair and an accessible toilet. Countrylink's *Guide for People with Special Requirements* details this and other services.

In Victoria the Public Transport Corporation's *Disability Services For Customers with Specific Needs* is available from Disability Services, Spencer St Railway Station, Melbourne 3000 (☎ (03) 9619 2354, toll-free 1800 131 716). V/Line's country trains and stations are equipped with ramps and some rural services employ hoist-equipped accessible coaches. Twenty-four hours advance booking is required; V/Line Reservations & Enquires, at Spencer St Station (☎ 132 232, ask for wheelchair reservations). The Travellers Aid Society at Spencer St Station (☎ (03) 9670 2873) and at Level 2, 169 Swanston Walk (☎ (03) 9654 2600) provides advice, assistance and toilets for the disabled traveller.

Car Rental Avis and Hertz offer hire cars with hand controls at no extra charge for pick-up at the major airports, but advance notice is required.

Parking The International Wheelchair Symbol for parking in allocated bays is widely recognised. Mobility Maps of central business districts showing accessible routes, toilets etc are also available from major city councils.

Taxi Most taxi companies in the major cities and towns have modified vehicles which take wheelchairs. In Melbourne, Norden Transport Equipment (☎ (03) 9793 1066) has a self-drive van equipped with a lift and lock-down attachments for up to three wheelchairs, and this is available for long or short-term rentals.

Ferry TT Line's *Spirit of Tasmania* which operates between Melbourne and Devonport in Tasmania, has four accessible cabins and wheelchair access to the public areas on the ship.

Bruce Cameron

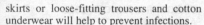

skirts or loose-fitting trousers and cotton underwear will help to prevent infections.

Yeast infections, characterised by a rash, itch and discharge, can be treated with a vinegar or lemon-juice douche, or with yoghurt. Nystatin suppositories are the usual medical prescription. Trichomoniasis is a more serious infection; symptoms are a discharge and a burning sensation when urinating. Male sexual partners must also be treated, and if a vinegar-water douche is not effective medical attention should be sought. Metronidazole (Flagyl) is the prescribed drug.

WOMEN TRAVELLERS

Australia is generally a safe place for women travellers, although it's probably best to avoid walking alone late at night in any of the major cities. Sexual harassment is unfortunately still second nature to many Aussie males, and it's generally true to say that the farther you get from 'civilisation' (ie the big cities), the less enlightened your average Aussie male is going to be about women's issues; you're far more likely to meet an ocker than a Snag!

Female hitchers should exercise care at all

times (see the section on hitching in the Getting Around chapter).

GAY & LESBIAN TRAVELLERS

Australia is rapidly becoming a popular destination for gay and lesbian travellers. Certainly the profile of gay and lesbian travel has risen significantly in the last few years, partly as a result of the publicity surrounding the Gay & Lesbian Mardi Gras in Sydney. Throughout the country, but especially on the east coast, there is a number of tour operators, travel agents, airlines, resorts and accommodation places which are exclusively gay and lesbian, or gay friendly.

Certain areas are the focus of the gay and lesbian communities: Cairns and Noosa in Queensland, the Blue Mountains and the south coast in New South Wales, and Melbourne, Daylesford and Hepburn Springs in Victoria, are all currently popular areas.

As is the case with the attitude to women, the farther into the country you get, the more likely you are to run into fairly rampant homophobia. Homosexual acts are legal in all states, except Tasmania.

Gay Publications

There's a wide range of publications produced by the gay community. All major cities have free gay newspapers, available through subscription, from major gay and lesbian venues and some newsagents in gay and lesbian residential areas.

The *g'day accommodation guide* gives state by state listings of a whole range of items which may be of interest to the gay traveller, such as transport, bars, pubs, entertainment, tours and accommodation. It can be purchased from newsagencies in Australia and New Zealand and gay book shops in Europe and the USA.

National gay lifestyle magazines include *OutRage*, *Campaign*, *Lesbians on the Loose* and art magazine, *Blue*.

Tour Operators

A number of tour operators cater exclusively or partly for gay and lesbian travellers. They include:

BreakOut Tours
GPO Box 3801, Sydney, NSW 2001 (☎ (02) 9558 8229; fax 9558 7140)
Destination DownUnder
40 Miller Street, (PO Box 429) North Sydney, NSW 2060 (☎ (02) 9957 3811; 9957 1385)
also offices in Europe, the UK and the USA.
Friends of Dorothy Travel
2nd floor, 77 Oxford Street, Darlinghurst, NSW 2010 (☎ (02) 9369 3616; fax 9332 3326)
Graylink
PO Box 3826, Darwin, NT 0801 (☎ (08) 8948 0089; fax 8948 1777)
Beyond the Blue
Suite 205/275 Alfred St, North Sydney, NSW 2060 (☎ (02) 9955 6755; fax 9922 6036)

Gay Organisations

The Australian Gay & Lesbian Tourism Association (AGLTA, PO Box 208, Darlinghurst, NSW 2010; ☎ (02) 9955 6755; fax 9922 6036) promotes gay and lesbian travel within Australia and is well worth contacting.

EMERGENCY

In the case of a life-threatening situation dial 000. This call is free from any phone and the operator will connect you with either the police, ambulance or fire brigade. To dial any of these services direct, check the inside front cover of any local telephone book.

For other telephone crisis and personal counselling services (such as sexual assault, poisons information or alcohol and drug problems), check the Community pages of the local telephone book.

DANGERS & ANNOYANCES
Animal Hazards

There are a few unique and sometimes dangerous creatures, although it's unlikely that you'll come across any of them, particularly if you stick to the cities. Here's a rundown just in case.

Snakes The best-known danger in the Australian outback, and the one that captures visitors' imaginations, is snakes. Although there are many venomous snakes there are few that are aggressive, and unless you have the bad fortune to stand on one it's unlikely that you'll be bitten. Taipans and tiger snakes, however, will attack if alarmed. Sea snakes can also be dangerous.

To minimise your chances of being bitten always wear boots, socks and long trousers when walking through undergrowth where snakes may be present. Don't put your hands into holes and crevices, and be careful when collecting firewood.

Snake bites do not cause instantaneous death and antivenenes are usually available. Keep the victim calm and still, wrap the bitten limb tightly, as you would for a sprained ankle, and then attach a splint to immobilise it. Then seek medical help, if possible with the dead snake for identification. Don't attempt to catch the snake if there is even a remote possibility of being bitten again. Tourniquets and sucking out the poison are now comprehensively discredited.

Spiders There are a couple of nasty spiders too, including the funnel-web, the redback and the white-tail, so it's best not to play with any spider. Funnel-web spiders are found in New South Wales and their bite is treated in the same way as snake bite. For redback bites, apply ice and seek medical attention.

Insects Among a splendid variety of biting insects the mosquito and march fly are the most common. The common bush tick

(found in the forest and scrub country along the east coast of Australia) can be dangerous if left lodged in the skin, as the toxin the tick excretes can cause paralysis and sometimes death – check your body for lumps every night if you're walking in tick-infested areas. The tick should be removed by dousing it with methylated spirits or kerosene and levering it out intact.

Leeches are common, and while they will suck your blood they are not dangerous and are easily removed by the application of salt or heat.

Crocodiles Up north saltwater crocodiles can be a real danger and have killed a number of people (travellers and locals). They are found in river estuaries and large rivers, sometimes a long way inland, so before diving into that inviting, cool water find out from the locals whether it's croc-free.

Box Jellyfish In the sea, the box jellyfish, also known as the sea wasp or 'stinger', occurs north of Great Keppel Island (see the Queensland chapter) during summer and can be fatal. The stinging tentacles spread several metres away from the sea wasp's body; by the time you see it you're likely to have been stung. If someone is stung, they are likely to run out of the sea screaming and collapse on the beach, with weals on their body as though they've been whipped. They may stop breathing. Douse the stings with

Redback spider

Funnel-web spider

vinegar (available on many beaches or try a nearby house), do not try to remove the tentacles from the skin, and treat as for snake bite (see Snakes entry earlier in this section). If there's a first-aider present, they may have to apply artificial respiration until the ambulance gets there. Above all, stay out of the sea when the sea wasps are around – the locals are ignoring that lovely water for an excellent reason.

Stings from most other jellyfish are simply rather painful and dousing in vinegar will deactivate any stingers which have not 'fired'. Calamine lotion, antihistamines and analgesics may reduce the reaction and relieve the pain.

Other Sea Creatures The blue-ringed octopus and Barrier Reef cone shells can also be fatal so don't pick them up. If someone is stung, apply a pressure bandage, monitor breathing carefully and conduct mouth-to-mouth resuscitation if breathing stops.

When reef walking you must always wear shoes to protect your feet against coral. In tropical waters there are stonefish – venomous fish that look like a flat piece of rock on the sea bed. Also watch out for the scorpion fish, which has venomous spines.

Flies & Mosquitoes For four to six months of the year you'll have to cope with those two banes of the Australian outdoors – the fly and the mosquito.

In the cities the flies are not too bad; it's in the country that it starts getting out of hand, and the farther 'out' you get the worse the flies seem to be. In central Australia the flies start to come out with the warmer spring weather (late August), particularly if there has been any amount of spring rain, and last until winter. They are such a nuisance that virtually every shop sells the Genuine Aussie Fly Net (made in Korea), which fits on a hat and is rather like a string onion bag but is very effective. It's either that or the 'Great Australian Wave' to keep them away. Repellents such as Aerogard and Rid go some way to deterring the little bastards.

Mossies too can be a problem, especially in the warmer tropical areas. Fortunately none of them are malaria carriers.

On the Road
Kangaroos and wandering stock can be a real hazard to the driver. A collision with one will badly damage your car and probably kill the animal. Unfortunately, other drivers are even more dangerous, particularly those who drink. Australia has its share of fatal road accidents, particularly in the countryside, so don't drink and drive and please take care. The dangers posed by stray animals and drunks are particularly enhanced at night, so it's best to avoid travelling after dark. See the Getting Around chapter for more on driving hazards.

Bushfires & Blizzards
Bushfires happen every year in Australia. Don't be the mug who starts one. In hot, dry, windy weather, be extremely careful with any naked flame – no cigarette butts out of car windows, please. On a Total Fire Ban Day (listen to the radio or watch the billboards on country roads), it is forbidden even to use a camping stove in the open. The locals will not be amused if they catch you breaking this particular law; they'll happily dob you in, and the penalties are severe.

If you're unfortunate enough to find yourself driving through a bushfire, stay inside your car and try to park off the road in an open space, away from trees, until the danger is past. Lie on the floor under the dashboard, covering yourself with a wool blanket if possible. The front of the fire should pass quickly, and you will be much safer than if you were out in the open. It is very important to cover up with a wool blanket or wear protective clothing, as it has been proved that heat radiation is the big killer in bushfire situations.

Bushwalkers should take local advice before setting out. On a day of total fire ban, don't go – delay your trip until the weather has changed. Chances are that it will be so unpleasantly hot and windy, you'll be better off anyway in an air-conditioned pub sipping a cool beer.

If you're out in the bush and you see smoke, even at a great distance, you should take it seriously. Go to the nearest open space, downhill if possible. A forested ridge is the most dangerous place to be. Bushfires move very quickly and change direction with the wind.

Having said all that, more bushwalkers die of cold than in bushfires! Even in summer, temperatures can drop below freezing at night in the mountains (see the Health section earlier in this chapter). The Tasmanian mountains can have blizzards at almost any time of year.

WORK

If you come to Australia on a 12-month 'working holiday' visa you can officially only work for three out of those 12 months, but working on a regular tourist visa is strictly *verboten*. Many travellers on tourist visas do find casual work, but with a national unemployment rate of around 9%, and youth unemployment as high as 40% in places, it can be difficult to find a job – legal or otherwise – in many areas.

With the current boom in tourism, casual work is often easy to find in the peak season at the major tourist centres. Places like Alice Springs, Cairns and various other places along the Queensland coast, and the ski fields of Victoria and NSW, are all good prospects, but opportunities are usually limited to the peak holiday seasons.

Other good prospects for casual work include factory work, bar work, waiting on tables, washing dishes (kitchenhand), other domestic chores at outback roadhouses, nanny work, fruit picking and collecting for charities.

Although many travellers do find work, if you are coming to Australia with the intention of working, make sure you have enough funds to cover yourself for your stay, or have a contingency plan if work is not forthcoming.

The Commonwealth Employment Service (CES) has over 300 offices around the country, and the staff usually have a good idea of what's available where. Try the classified section of the daily papers under Situations Vacant, especially on Saturday and Wednesday.

The various backpacker magazines, newspapers and hostels are good information sources – some local employers even advertise on their notice boards.

Tax File Number

It's important to apply for a Tax File Number (TFN) if you plan to work (or open a bank account – see the Money section earlier in this chapter for details) in Australia, not because it's a condition of employment, but without a TFN tax will be deducted from any wages you receive at the maximum rate, which is currently set at 48.5%! To get a TFN, contact the local branch of the Australian Taxation Office for a form. It's a straightforward procedure, and you will have to supply adequate identification, such as a passport and driving licence. The issue of a TFN takes about four weeks.

Paying Tax Yes, it's one of the certainties in life! If you have supplied your employer with a Tax File Number, tax will be deducted from your wages at the rate of 29% if your annual income is below $20,700. As your income increases, so does the tax rate, with the maximum being 48.5% for incomes over $50,000. For nonresident visitors, tax is payable from the first dollar you earn, unlike residents who have something like a $6000 tax-free threshold. For this reason, if you have had tax deducted at the correct rate as you earn, it is unlikely you'll be entitled to a tax refund when you leave.

If you have had tax deducted at 48.5% because you have not submitted a Tax File Number, chances are you will be entitled to a partial refund if your income was less than $50,000. Once you lodge a tax return (which must include a copy of the Group Certificate all employers issue to salaried workers at the end of the financial year or within seven days of leaving a job), you will be refunded the extra tax you have paid. Before you can lodge a tax return, however, you must have a Tax File Number.

Fruit & Vegetable Picking Seasons

The table below lists the main harvest times of the crops where casual employment is a possibility. Enquire at the local CES office.

New South Wales

Crop	Time	Region/s
Grapes	Feb-Mar	Griffith, Hunter Valley
Peaches	Feb-Mar	Griffith
Apples	Feb-Apr	Orange
Cherries	Nov-Jan	Orange
Oranges	Dec-Mar	Griffith
Bananas	year round	North Coast

Queensland

Crop	Time	Region/s
Bananas	year round	Innisfail
Grapes	Jan-Feb	Warwick
Pears	Feb-Mar	Warwick
Apples	Feb-Mar	Warwick
Various fruit & veg	May-Nov	Bowen
Asparagus	Aug-Dec	Warwick
Tomatoes	May-Nov	Bundaberg
Stone fruits	Dec	Warwick

South Australia

Crop	Time	Region/s
Dried fruits/ peaches	Feb-Mar	Riverland
Wine grapes	Feb-Apr	Riverland, Barossa, Clare
Apples/pears	Feb-Apr	Adelaide Hills
Strawberries	Oct-Feb	Adelaide Hills
Apricots	Dec-Feb	Riverland

Tasmania

Crop	Time	Region/s
Apples/pears	Feb-May	Huon Valley, Tasman Peninsula
Soft fruit	Dec-Jan	Huon Valley, Kingston, Derwent Valley

Victoria

Crop	Time	Region/s
Peaches	Jan-Mar	Shepparton
Grapes	Jan-Apr	Mildura
Tomatoes	Feb-Apr	Shepparton, Echuca
Strawberries	Oct-Apr	Echuca, Dandenongs
Cherries	Nov-Feb	Dandenongs

Western Australia

Crop	Time	Region/s
Grapes	Feb-Apr	Albany, Midland
Apples/pears	Mar-May	Manjimup
Melons, Vegies	May-Oct	Kununurra

ACTIVITIES

There are plenty of activities that you can take part in while travelling round the country. Here we've just given an idea of what's available; for specifics, check the Activities section at the start of each chapter.

Skiing

Australia has a flourishing skiing industry – a fact that takes a number of travellers by surprise – with snowfields straddling the New South Wales-Victoria border. There's information in the Victorian Alps section of the Victoria chapter, and in the Snowy Mountains section of the New South Wales chapter. Tasmania's snowfields aren't as developed as those of Victoria and New South Wales, but if you do want to ski while in Tassie you can read all about it in the Activities section of the Tasmania chapter.

Bushwalking

One of the best ways of really getting away from it all in Australia is to go bushwalking. There are many fantastic walks in the various national parks around the country and information on how to get there is in Lonely Planet's *Bushwalking in Australia*, as well as in the Activities section of each chapter.

Surfing

If you're interested in surfing you'll find great beaches and surf in most states.

Scuba Diving

There's great scuba diving at a number of places around the coast but particularly along the Queensland Great Barrier Reef where there are also many dive schools. Many travellers come to Australia with the goal of getting a scuba certificate during their stay.

Horse Riding

In Victoria you can go horse riding in the High Country and follow the route of the Snowy Mountains cattle people, whose lives were the subject of the film *The Man from Snowy River*, which in turn was based on the poem by Banjo Paterson.

In northern Queensland you can ride horses through rainforests and along sand dunes and swim with them in the sea. You can find horses to hire at any number of places around the country.

Cycling

You can cycle all around Australia; for the athletic there are long, challenging routes and for the not so masochistic there are plenty of great day trips. In most states there are excellent roads and helpful bicycle societies, which have lots of maps and useful tips and advice. See the Getting Around and state chapters for more details.

Camel Riding

Camel riding has taken off around the country but especially in and around Alice Springs in the Northern Territory. If you've done it in India or Egypt or you just fancy yourself as the explorer/outdoors type, then here's your chance. You can take anything from a five-minute stroll to a 14-day expedition.

Birdwatching

You can contact the Royal Australasian Ornithologists Union, which runs bird observatories in New South Wales, Victoria and Western Australia. Its headquarters is at 415 Riversdale Rd, Hawthorn East, Victoria (☎ (03) 9882 2622).

Other Activities

Windsurfing, paragliding, rafting, hot-air ballooning, bungy jumping and hanggliding are among the many other outdoor activities enjoyed by Australians and available to travellers. For information on any of these or other activities see the relevant chapters or contact any of the state tourist bureaus.

HIGHLIGHTS

In a country as broad and geographically diverse as Australia the list of highlights is virtually endless, although one person's highlight can easily be another's disappointment. There are, however, a number of features in each state which shouldn't be missed.

In Queensland there's the Great Barrier Reef and its many water-based activities. The state's varied terrain offers visitors the choice of secluded beach and island resorts, the rainforested Daintree, inland desert and 'one-horse towns', cattle country and the remote Cape York Peninsula.

Sydney, the capital of New South Wales and host for the year 2000 Olympic Games, has simply one of the most stunning locations you're likely to come across. The coastal beaches, the northern rainforests, southern Alps and wide expanse of the interior also have plenty to offer.

No visit to Victoria would be complete without a visit to the enchanting Grampians (Gariwerd) mountain range, famous for its natural beauty and great bushwalks. Other highlights include the fairy penguins at Phillip Island, the period gold-mining township of Sovereign Hill at Ballarat, and the Great Ocean Road, one of the world's most spectacular coastal routes. Melbourne, too, is often overlooked, yet it has a charm not found in other Australian cities.

Heading south to Tasmania there's the rich heritage of the convict era at places such as Port Arthur, as well as some of the most beautiful wilderness areas in the country. The Cradle Mountain-Lake St Clair World Heritage area is popular with bushwalkers, as is the rugged south-west corner of the state.

South Australia's big drawcards are the Barossa Valley, with its excellent wineries, and the Flinders Ranges, which offer superb bushwalking and stunning scenery. In the northern areas of South Australia you can get a real taste of the outback along famous tracks such as the Strzelecki, Oodnadatta and Birdsville, while the opal-mining town of Coober Pedy, where many people not only work underground but also live in subterranean houses, is totally unique.

The Northern Territory has the obvious attraction of Uluru (Ayers Rock), probably Australia's most readily identifiable symbol after Sydney's Opera House. There's also the World Heritage-listed Kakadu National Park with its abundant flora and fauna and superb wetlands. The Territory is also where Australia's Aboriginal cultural heritage is at its most accessible – the rock-art sites of Kakadu, and Aboriginal-owned and run tours of Arnhem Land, Manyallaluk (near Katherine) and Kings Canyon are just a few of the possibilities.

Lastly there's Western Australia with its vast distances and wide open spaces. In the south of the state is Fremantle, an eclectic little port city not far from the state capital, Perth. The eucalypt forests of the south coast are simply spectacular, while the Kimberley region in the far north is ruggedly picturesque – the Bungle Bungle (Purnululu) National Park here is unforgettable.

ACCOMMODATION

Australia is very well equipped with youth hostels, backpacker hostels and caravan parks with camp sites – the cheapest shelter you can find. Furthermore, there are plenty of motels around the country, and in holiday regions like the Queensland coast intense competition tends to keep the prices down.

A typical town of a few thousand people will have a basic motel at around $50 for a double, an old town centre pub with rooms (shared bathrooms) at say $30, and a caravan park – probably with camp sites for around $10 and on-site vans or cabins for $35 for two. If the town is on anything like a main road or is bigger, it will probably have several of each. You'll rarely have much trouble finding *somewhere* to lay your head in Oz, even when there are no hostels, although some surprisingly small and seemingly insignificant towns have backpacker hostels. If there's a group of you, the rates for three or four people in a room are always worth checking. Often there are larger 'family' rooms or units with two bedrooms.

There are a couple of free backpacker newspapers and booklets available at hostels around the country, and these have fairly up-to-date listings of hostels, although they give neither prices nor details of each hostel.

For more comprehensive accommodation listings, the state automobile clubs produce directories listing caravan parks, hotels, motels, holiday flats and a number of backpacker hostels in almost every city and town in the country. They're updated every year so the prices are generally fairly current. They're available from the clubs for a nominal charge if you're a member or a member of an affiliated club enjoying reciprocal rights. Alternatively, some state tourist offices (notably Tasmania and Western Australia) also put out frequently updated guides to local accommodation.

In 1995 the Federal government funded a survey by the state motoring organisations of all backpacker hostels in Australia (including YHA hostels) and gave them a 'backpack' rating – ranging from one to five backpacks, depending on the facilities offered. The results have been published in a small pocket-sized booklet which should be available at hostels and tourist offices. While it could be handy to know what grading a hostel has been given, the survey gives no idea about what each hostel is really like, nor does it take into account important intangibles such as atmosphere and popularity. The other drawback of the grading system is that there is no plan to keep the listing current, so any change in the state of things as at 1995 will not be reflected in the listing.

There's a wide variation in seasonal prices for accommodation. At peak times – school holiday in particular – prices are at their peak, whereas at other times useful discounts can be found. This particularly applies to the Top End, where the Wet season (summer) is the off season and prices can drop by as much as 30%. In this book high-season prices are used unless indicated otherwise.

Camping & Caravanning

The camping story in Australia is partly excellent and partly rather annoying! The excellent side is that there is a great number of caravan parks and you'll almost always find space available. If you want to get around Australia on the cheap then camping is the cheapest way of all, with nightly costs for two of around $8 to $15.

On the downside, camp sites are often intended more for caravanners (house trailers for any North Americans out there) than for campers and the tent campers get little thought in these places. The fact that most of the sites are called 'caravan parks' indicates who gets most attention. In many Australian caravan parks gravel is laid down to make the ground more suitable for cars and caravans, so pitching a tent becomes very hard work.

Equally bad is that in most big cities sites are well away from the centre. This is not inconvenient in small towns, but in general if you're planning to camp around Australia you really need your own transport. Brisbane is the worst city in Australia in this respect because council regulations actually forbid tents within a 22-km radius of the centre. Although there are some sites in Brisbane within that radius, they're strictly for caravans – no campers allowed.

Still, it's not all gloom; in general, Australian caravan parks are well kept, conveniently located and excellent value. Many sites also have on-site vans which you can rent for the night. These give you the comfort of a caravan without the inconvenience of actually towing one of the damned things. On-site cabins are also widely available, and these are more like a small self-contained unit. They usually have one bedroom, or at least an area which can be screened off from the rest of the unit – just the thing if you have small kids. Cabins also have their own bathroom and toilet, although this is sometimes an optional extra. They are also much less cramped than a caravan, and the price difference is not always that great – say $25 to $30 for an on-site van, $30 to $50 for a cabin. In winter, if you're going to be using this sort of accommodation on a regular basis, it's worth investing in a small heater of some sort as many vans and cabins are unheated.

Camping in the bush, either in national parks and reserves or in the open, is for many people one of the highlights of a visit to Oz. In the outback you won't even need a tent – swags are the way to go, and nights spent around a campfire under the stars are unforgettable.

Youth Hostels

Australia has a very active Youth Hostel Association (YHA) and you'll find hostels all over the country, with more official hostels and backpacker hostels popping up all the time.

YHA hostels provide basic accommodation, usually in small dormitories or bunk rooms although more and more are providing twin rooms for couples. The nightly charges are very reasonable – usually between $12 and $18 a night.

Very few YHA hostels still have the old fetishes for curfews and doing chores, but many retain segregated dorms. Most also take non-YHA members, although there may be a small 'temporary membership' charge. To become a full YHA member in Australia costs $26 a year (there's also a $16 joining fee, although if you're an overseas resident joining in Australia you don't have to pay this). You can join at a state office or at any youth hostel.

The YHA also has the Aussie Starter Pack, whereby Australian residents joining the YHA receive two vouchers worth $8 each to use at a hostel in their state. International visitors joining the YHA at a hostel receive

their first night at that hostel for free. Under the scheme, the additional nightly fee charged to non-YHA members is $2 per night. When staying at a hostel nonmembers receive an Aussie Starter Card, to be stamped each night by the YHA. Once the card has been stamped 12 times, you are given a year's free membership.

Youth hostels are part of an international organisation, the International Youth Hostel Federation (IYHF, also known as HI, Hostelling International), so if you're already a member of the YHA in your own country, your membership entitles you to use Australian hostels. Hostels are great places for meeting people and great travellers' centres, and in many busier hostels the foreign visitors will outnumber the Australians. The annual *YHA Accommodation Guide* booklet, which is available from any YHA office in Australia and from some YHA offices overseas, lists all YHA hostels in Australia, with useful little maps showing how to find them.

You must have a regulation sheet sleeping bag or bed linen – for hygiene reasons a regular sleeping bag will not do. If you haven't got sheets they can be rented at many hostels (usually for $3), but it's cheaper, after a few nights stay, to have your own. YHA offices and some larger hostels sell the official YHA sheet bag.

All hostels have cooking facilities and 24-hour access, and there's usually some communal area where you can sit and talk. There are usually laundry facilities and often excellent notice boards. Many hostels have a maximum-stay period – because some hostels are permanently full it would hardly be fair for people to stay too long when others are being turned away.

The YHA classes its hostels as simple, standard or superior, and also uses the back-pack grading symbol ranging from one to five backpacks. Rural hostels also get a gum-leaf rating, from one to three gum leaves depending on how much of a wilderness experience the visitor can expect. The hostels range from tiny places to big modern buildings, from historic convict buildings to

a disused railway station. Most hostels have a manager who checks you in when you arrive and keeps the peace. Because you have so much more contact with a hostel manager than the person in charge of other styles of accommodation they can really make or break the place. Good managers are often great characters and well worth getting to know.

YHA members are also entitled to a number of handy discounts around the country – on things such as car hire, activities, accommodation etc – and these are detailed in the *Discounts* booklet, published each year.

Accommodation can usually be booked directly with the manager or through a Membership & Travel Centre. The YHA handbook tells all.

The Australian head office is in Sydney, at the Australian Youth Hostels Association, 10 Mallett St, Camperdown, NSW 2050 (☎ (02) 9565 1699). If you can't get a YHA hostel booklet in your own country write to them but otherwise deal with the Membership & Travel centres:

New South Wales
    422 Kent St, Sydney, NSW 2001 (☎ (02) 9261 1111; fax 9261 1969)
Northern Territory
    Darwin City Hostel, 69A Mitchell St, Darwin, NT 0821 (☎ (08) 8981 6344; fax 8981 6674)
Queensland
    5 Northpoint, 231 North Quay, Brisbane, Qld 4000 (☎ (07) 3236 1680; fax 3236 1702)
South Australia
    38 Sturt St, Adelaide, SA 5000 (☎ (08) 8231 5583; 8231 4219;
    e-mail yhasa@ozemail.com.au)
Tasmania
    1st floor, 28 Criterion St, Hobart, Tas 7000 (☎ (03) 6234 9617; 6234 7422)
Victoria
    205 King St, Melbourne, Vic 3000 (☎ (03) 9670 7991; fax 9670 9840)
Western Australia
    65 Francis St, Northbridge, Perth, WA 6003 (☎ (09) 227 5122; fax 227 5123)

Not all of the 140-plus hostels listed in the handbook are actually owned by the YHA. Some are 'associate hostels' which generally abide by hostel regulations but are owned by other organisations or individuals. You don't need to be a YHA member to stay at an associated hostel. Others are 'alternative accommodation' and do not totally fit the hostel blueprint. They might be motels which keep some hostel-style accommodation available for YHA members, caravan parks with an on-site van or two kept aside, or even places just like hostels but where the operators don't want to abide by all the hostel regulations.

Backpacker Hostels

Australia has a large number of backpacker hostels, and the standard of these hostels varies enormously. Some are run-down inner-city hotels where the owners have tried to fill empty rooms; unless renovations have been done, these places are generally pretty gloomy and depressing. Others are former motels, so each unit, typically with four to six beds, will have fridge, TV and bathroom. When the climate allows, there's usually a pool too, and they're often air-conditioned, at least at night. The drawback with these places is that the communal areas and cooking facilities are often lacking, as motels were never originally designed for communal use. You may also find yourself sharing a room with someone who wants to watch TV all night – it happens!

Still other hostels are purpose-built as backpacker hostels; these are usually the best places in terms of facilities, although sometimes they are simply too big and therefore lack any personalised service. As often as not the owners have backpackers running the places, and usually it's not too long before standards start to slip. Some of these places, particularly along the Queensland coast, actively promote themselves as 'party' hostels, so if you want a quiet time, they're not the place to be. The best places are often the smaller, more intimate hostels where the owner is also the manager. These are usually the older hostels which were around long before the 'backpacker boom'.

With the proliferation of hostels has also come intense competition. Hop off a bus in any town on the Queensland coast and chances are there'll be at least three or four touts from the various hostels, all trying to lure you in. To this end many have introduced inducements, such as the first night free, and virtually all have courtesy buses. Even the YHA hostels have had to resort to this to stay in the race in some places.

Prices at backpacker hostels are generally in line with YHA hostels – typically $12 to $18, although discounts can reduce this.

There's at least one organisation (VIP) which you can join where, for a modest fee (typically $15), you'll receive a discount card (valid for 12 months) and a list of participating hostels. This is hardly a great inducement to join but you do also receive useful discounts on other services, such as bus passes, so they may be worth considering.

Nomads Backpackers (☎ (08) 8224 0919; fax (08) 8232 2911) is another organisation which runs a number of revamped pubs around the country. It has an Internet site at 'gateway.eastend.com.au/nomads'.

As with YHA hostels, the success of a hostel largely depends on the friendliness and willingness of the managers. Some places will only admit overseas backpackers. This happens mostly in cities and when it does it's because the hostel in question has had problems with locals treating the place more as a dosshouse – drinking too much, making too much noise, getting into fights and the like. Hostels which discourage or ban Aussies say it's only a rowdy minority that makes trouble, but they can't take the risk. If you're an Aussie and encounter this kind of reception, the best you can do is persuade the desk people that you're genuinely travelling the country, and aren't just looking for a cheap place to crash for a while.

The Ys

In a number of places in Australia accommodation is provided by the YMCA or YWCA. There are variations from place to place – some are mainly intended for permanent accommodation, others are run like normal commercial guesthouses. They're generally excellent value and usually conveniently located. You don't have to be a YMCA or YWCA member to stay at them, although sometimes you get a discount if you are. Accommodation in the Ys is generally in fairly straightforward rooms, usually with shared bathroom facilities. Some Ys also have dormitory-style accommodation. Note, however, that not all YMCA or YWCA organisations around the country offer accommodation; it's mainly in the big cities.

Another organisation that sometimes offers accommodation is the CWA (Country Women's Association), which operates mainly in the country and is usually for women only.

Guesthouses & B&Bs

This is the fastest growing segment of the accommodation market. New places are opening all the time, and the network of alternatives throughout the country includes everything from restored miners' cottages, converted barns and stables, renovated and rambling old guesthouses, up-market country homes and romantic escapes to a simple bedroom in a family home. Many of these places are listed throughout the book. Tariffs cover a wide range, but are typically in the $40 to $100 (per double) bracket.

Hotels & Pubs

For the budget traveller, hotels in Australia are generally older places – new accommodation is usually motels. To understand why Australia's hotels are the way they are requires delving into the history books a little. When the powers that be decided Australia's drinking should only be at the most inconvenient hours, they also decided that drinking places should also be hotels. So every place which in Britain would be a 'pub' in Australia was a 'hotel', but often in name only.

The original idea of forcing pubs to provide accommodation for weary travellers has long faded into history and this ludicrous law has been rolled back. Every place called a hotel does not necessarily have rooms to rent, although many still do. A 'private hotel', as opposed to a 'licensed hotel', really is a hotel and does not serve alcohol. A 'guesthouse' is much the same as a 'private hotel'.

New hotels being built today are mainly of the Hilton variety; smaller establishments will usually be motels. So, if you're staying in a hotel, it will normally mean an older place, often with rooms without private facilities. Unfortunately many older places are on the drab, grey and dreary side. You get a strong feeling that because they've got the rooms they try to turn a dollar on them, but without much enthusiasm. Others, fortunately, are colourful places with some real character. Although the word 'hotel' doesn't always mean they'll have rooms, the places that do have rooms usually make it pretty plain that they are available. If a hotel is listed in an accommodation directory you can be pretty sure it really will offer you a bed. If there's nothing that looks like a reception desk or counter, just ask at the bar.

You'll find hotels all around the town centres in smaller towns, while in larger towns the hotels that offer accommodation are often to be found close to the railway stations. In some older towns, or in historic centres like the gold-mining towns, the old hotels can be really magnificent. The rooms themselves may be pretty old-fashioned and unexciting, but the hotel facade and entrance area will often be quite extravagant. In the outback the old hotels are often places of real character. They are often the real 'town centre' and you'll meet all the local characters there.

A bright word about hotels (guesthouses and private hotels, too) is that the breakfasts are usually excellent – big and 100% filling. A substantial breakfast is what this country was built on and if your hotel is still into serving a real breakfast you'll probably feel it could last you until breakfast comes around next morning. Generally, hotels will have rooms for around $25 to $35. When comparing prices, remember to check if it includes breakfast.

In airports and bus and railway stations, there are often information boards with direct-dial phones to book accommodation. These are generally for the more expensive hotels, but these will sometimes offer discounts if you use the direct phone to book. The staff at bus stations are helpful when it comes to finding cheap and convenient places to stay.

Motels, Serviced Apartments & Holiday Flats

If you've got transport and want a more modern place with your own bathroom and other facilities, then you're moving into the motel bracket. Motels cover the earth in Australia, just like in the USA, but they're usually located away from the city centres. Prices vary and with the motels, unlike hotels, singles are often not much cheaper than doubles. The reason is quite simple – in the old hotels many of the rooms really are singles, relics of the days when single men travelled the country looking for work. In motels, the rooms are almost always doubles. You'll sometimes find motel rooms for less than $40, but in most places they'll be at least $50.

Holiday flats and serviced apartments are much the same thing and bear some relationship to motels. Basically holiday flats are found in holiday areas, and serviced apartments in cities. A holiday flat is much like a motel room but usually has a kitchen or cooking facilities. Usually holiday flats are not serviced like motels – you don't get your bed made up every morning and the cups washed out. In some holiday flats you actually have to provide your own sheets and bedding but others are operated just like motel rooms with a kitchen. Most motels in Australia provide at least tea and coffee-making facilities and a small fridge, but a holiday flat will also have cooking utensils, cutlery, crockery and so on.

Holiday flats are often rented on a weekly basis but even in these cases it's worth asking if daily rates are available. Paying for a week, even if you stay only for a few days, can still be cheaper than having those days at a higher daily rate. If there are more than just two of you, another advantage of holiday flats is

that you can often find them with two or more bedrooms. A two-bedroom holiday flat is typically priced at about 1½ times the cost of a comparable single-bedroom unit.

In holiday areas like the Queensland coast, motels and holiday flats will often be virtually interchangeable terms – there's nothing really to distinguish one from the other. In big cities, on the other hand, the serviced apartments are often a little more obscure, although they may be advertised in the newspaper's classified ads.

Colleges

Although it is students who get first chance at these, nonstudents can also stay at many university colleges during the uni vacations. These places can be relatively cheap and comfortable and provide an opportunity for you to meet people. Costs are typically from about $20 for B&B for students, twice that if you're not a student.

This type of accommodation is usually available only during the summer vacations (from November to February). Additionally, it must almost always be booked ahead; you can't just turn up. Many of Australia's new universities are way out in the suburbs and are inconvenient to get to unless you have transport.

Other Possibilities

There are lots of less conventional accommodation possibilities. You don't have to camp in caravan parks, for example. There are plenty of parks where you can camp for free, or (in Queensland at least) roadside rest areas where short-term camping is permitted. Australia has lots of bush where nobody is going to complain about you putting up a tent or rolling out a swag – or even notice you.

Australia is a land of farms (known as 'stations' in the outback) and one of the best ways to come to grips with Australian life is to spend a few days on one. Many farms offer accommodation where you can just sit back and watch how it's done, while others like to get you more actively involved in day-to-day activities. With commodity prices falling daily, mountainous wool stockpiles and a general rural crisis, tourism offers the hope of at least some income for farmers, at a time when many are being forced off the land. The state tourist offices can advise you on what's available; prices are pretty reasonable.

Finally, how about life on a houseboat? See the Murray River sections in the Victoria and South Australia chapters.

Long-Term Accommodation

In the cities, if you want to stay longer, the first place to look for a shared flat or a room is the classified ad section of the daily newspaper. Wednesday and Saturday are the best days for these ads. Notice boards in universities, hostels, certain popular bookshops and cafes, and other contact centres are good places to look for flats/houses to share or rooms to rent.

FOOD

The culinary delights can be one of the real highlights of Australia. Time was – like 25 years ago – when Australia's food (mighty steaks apart) had a reputation for being like England's, only worse. But miracles happen and Australia's miracle was immigration. The Greeks, Yugoslavs, Italians, Lebanese and many others who flooded into Australia in the '50s and '60s brought their food with them. More recent arrivals include the Vietnamese, whose communities are thriving in several cities.

In Australia today you can have excellent Greek moussaka (and a bottle of retsina to wash it down), delicious Italian saltimbocca and pasta, or good, heavy German dumplings; you can perfume the air with garlic after stumbling out of a French bistro, or try all sorts of Middle Eastern treats. The Chinese have been sweet & souring since the gold-rush days, while more recently Indian, Thai and Malaysian restaurants have been all the rage. And for cheap eats, you can't beat some of the Vietnamese places.

Australian

Although there is no real Australian cuisine there is certainly some excellent Australian food to try. In recent years there's been a great rise in popularity of exotic local and 'bush' foods, and for the adventurous these dishes offer something completely different. So in a swish Melbourne restaurant or Sydney bistro you might find braised kangaroo tail samosas, emu pâté, gum-leaf smoked venison, salt-bush lamb, native aniseed frittata, Warrigal-greens salad or wattle-seed ice cream.

All major cities also have a selection of cafes and restaurants serving food which can be termed 'modern Australian'. These are dishes which borrow heavily from a wide range of foreign cuisines, but have a definite local flavour. At these places seemingly anything goes, so you might find Asian-inspired curry-type dishes sharing a menu with European or Mediterranean-inspired dishes. It all adds up to exciting dining.

Australia also has a superb range of seafood: fish like John Dory and the esteemed barramundi, or superb lobsters and other crustaceans like the engagingly named Moreton Bay bugs! Yabbies are freshwater crayfish and very good.

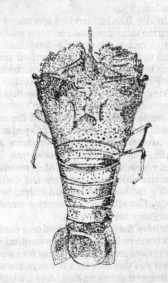

The Moreton Bay bug is a delicious Australian seafood

Another positive aspect of Australian food is the fine ingredients. Nearly everything is grown locally so you're not eating food that has been shipped halfway around the world.

At the bottom end of the food scale is the Australian meat pie – every bit as sacred an institution as the hot dog is to a New Yorker. The standard pie is an awful concoction of anonymous meat and dark gravy in a soggy pastry case. You'll have to try one though; the number consumed in Australia each year is phenomenal, and they're a real part of Australian culture. A pie 'n sauce at the 'footy' on a Saturday afternoon in winter is something plenty of Aussies can relate to.

Even more a part of Australian food culture is Vegemite. This strange, dark yeast extract looks and spreads like thick tar and smells like, well, Vegemite. Australians spread Vegemite on bread and become positively addicted to the stuff.

Vegetarian

Vegetarians are generally well catered for in most areas. While there are few dedicated vegetarian restaurants, most modern cafes and restaurants have a few vegetarian dishes on the menu.

Where to Eat

Takeaway Food Around the country you'll find all the well-known international fast-food chains – *McDonalds, KFC, Pizza Hut* etc – typically conspicuous.

On a more local level, you'll find a milk bar on (almost) every corner, and most of them sell pies, pasties, sandwiches and milkshakes. There are speciality sandwich bars, delicatessens and health-food shops worth seeking out if you want something a little more exotic than a pie.

Most shopping centres have a fish & chip shop and a pizza joint, and most of the latter seem to do home deliveries.

Absolute rock-bottom is the kept-luke-warm-for-hours food found at roadside cafes and roadhouses across the country. Give it a miss unless you have absolutely no choice.

Restaurants & Cafes The best Australian eateries serve food as exciting and as innovative as any you'll find anywhere, and it doesn't need to cost a fortune. Best value are the modern and casual cafes, where for less than $20 you can get an excellent feed.

Restaurants – and there's no shortage of them – range from the ordinary to the utterly extraordinary, and it's just a matter of finding one which suits your tastes and budget.

While eating-out is a pleasure in the big cities, in many smaller country towns it can be something of an ordeal. The food will be predictable and unexciting, and is usually of the 'meat and three veg' variety.

All over Australia, but particularly in Melbourne, you'll find restaurants advertising that they're BYO. This stands for 'Bring Your Own' and means they're not licensed to serve alcohol but you are permitted to bring your own. This is a real boon to wine-loving but budget-minded travellers because you can buy a bottle from the local bottle shop or from that winery you visited last week and not pay any mark-up. Most restaurants make only a small 'corkage' charge (typically $1 to $1.50 per person) if you bring your own.

Pubs Most pubs serve two types of meals: bistro meals, which are usually in the $10 to $15 range and are served in the dining room or lounge bar, where there's usually a self-serve salad bar; and bar (or counter) meals which are filling, simple, no-frills meals eaten in the public bar; these usually cost less than $10, and sometimes as little as $4.

The quality of pub food varies enormously, and while it's usually fairly basic and unimaginative, it's generally pretty good value. The usual meal times are from noon to 2 pm and 6 to 8 pm.

Markets Where the climate allows there are often outdoor food stalls and markets, and these can be an excellent place to sample a variety of cuisines, with Asian being the most popular. Darwin's Thursday evening Mindil Beach market is probably the largest of its type in the country, and the range of cuisines is very impressive.

DRINKS
Nonalcoholic

Australians knock back Coke and flavoured milk like there's no tomorrow and also have some excellent mineral water brands. Coffee enthusiasts will be relieved to find good Italian cafes serving cappuccino and other coffees, often into the wee small hours and beyond.

Beer

Australian beer will be fairly familiar to North Americans; it's similar to what's known as lager in the UK. It may taste like lemonade to the European real ale addict, but it packs quite a punch. It is invariably chilled before drinking.

Fosters is the best-known international brand with a worldwide reputation, but there's a bewildering array of Australian beers. Among the most well-known are XXXX (pronounced 'four-ex'), Tooheys Red, Fosters, Carlton Draught and VB (Victoria Bitter). Recent additions to the stable of old favourites include lower alcohol beers such as Carlton Cold, Diamond Draught and Lite Ice, and styles other than your average Aussie lager, such as Blue Bock and Old Black Ale, both made by Tooheys.

The smaller breweries generally seem to produce better beer – Cascade (Tasmania) and Coopers (South Australia) being two examples. Coopers also produces a stout, popular among connoisseurs, and their Black Crow is a delicious malty, dark beer.

Small 'boutique' beers have become very popular recently so you'll find one-off brands scattered around the country. Beers such as Redback, Dogbolter and Eumundi, while being more expensive than the big commercial brands, are definitely worth a try. For the homesick European, there are a few pubs in the major cities that brew their own bitter. Guinness is occasionally found on draught.

Standard beer generally contains around 4.9% alcohol, although the trend in recent years has been towards low-alcohol beers, with an alcohol content of between 2% and 3.5%. Tooheys Blue is a particularly popular light beer. And a warning: people who drive under the influence of alcohol and get caught lose their licences (unfortunately, drink-driving is a real problem in Australia). The maximum permissible blood-alcohol con-

A Beer, By Any Other Name...

All around Australia, beer, the containers it comes in, and the receptacles you drink it from are called by different names. The standard bottle is 750 ml, and costs around $2. Cans (or tinnies) hold 375 ml and come in shrink-wrapped packets of 24, known as a slab, and these cost around $20, although you can of course buy them singly. Half-size bottles with twist-top caps are known as stubbies (echoes in South Australia), except in the Northern Territory where a stubby is a 1.25 litre bottle, although these are not in everyday use and are really only a novelty souvenir. Low-alcohol beer is marginally cheaper than full-strength beer. Boutique beers generally only come in stubbies, and are significantly more expensive than your average common or garden variety.

Ordering at the bar can be an intimidating business for the newly arrived traveller. Beer by the glass basically come in three sizes – 200, 285 and 425 ml – but knowing what to ask for is not quite so simple. A 200-ml (seven ounce) beer is a glass (Vic and Qld), a butcher (SA) or a beer (WA or NSW). Tasmanians like to be different, and so there they have a six-ounce glass. A 285-ml (10 ounce) beer is a pot (Vic and Qld), a schooner (SA), a handle (NT), a middie (NSW and WA) or a 10 ounce (Tasmania – they're very original down there!). Lastly, there's the 425-ml (15-ounce) glass, which is a schooner (NSW and NT) or a pint (SA). ■

centration level for drivers in most parts of Australia is 0.05%.

While Australians are generally considered to be heavy beer drinkers, per capita beer consumption has fallen quite considerably in recent years. In the past decade per capita consumption has decreased by 20%.

Wine

If you don't fancy Australian beer, then turn to wines. Australia has a great climate for wine producing and Australian wine is rapidly gaining international recognition – it's also one of our fastest-growing exports.

The best-known wine-growing regions are the Hunter Valley of New South Wales and the Barossa Valley of South Australia, but there are plenty of other areas too. In Victoria the main region is the Rutherglen/Milawa area of the north-east, but there's also the Yarra Valley (where the French company, Moët et Chandon, makes top-quality sparkling wines), the Mornington Peninsula and the Geelong area, all within easy reach of Melbourne. South Australia also has the beautifully picturesque Clare Valley, and the Coonawarra area south of Adelaide. In Western Australia increasingly sophisticated wines are being produced in the Margaret River area, and there's even a winery in Alice Springs in the Northern Territory.

Australia's wines are cheap and readily available. For $8 you can get a perfectly acceptable bottle of wine which you could happily take to someone's place without having to hide the label; $20 gets you something very good indeed.

It takes a little while to become familiar with Australian wineries and their styles but it's an effort worth making. The best – and most enjoyable – way to do this is to get out to the wineries and sample the wine at the cellar door. Most wineries have tastings: you just zip straight in and say what you'd like to try. However, free wine tastings do not mean open slather drinking – the glasses are generally thimble-sized and it's expected that you will buy something if, for example, you taste every Chardonnay that vineyard has

ever produced. Many wineries, particularly in the main areas, have decided that enough is enough and now have a small 'tasting fee' of a couple of dollars, refundable if you buy.

Each wine-growing area is generally renowned for a particular style of wine, although there's much more experimentation and blending of grapes these days. The Hunter Valley is famous for its whites, especially Chardonnay, the Clare Valley and Coonawarra regions produces excellent reds and fortified wines, and the Rutherglen region of Victoria is great for port and Muscat.

Designer Drinks

So-called 'designer drinks' are all the rage in the hip cafes and bars. Two Dogs Lemonade, an alcoholic lemonade, was the first on the scene in what was thought to be a novelty part of the market. This was followed by the phenomenally popular Sub Zero, a basically tasteless alcoholic soda which, when mixed with the obligatory dash of raspberry cordial, is *de rigueur*.

Other alcoholic oddities include Strongbow White, a cider with a real kick; a shandy (half beer, half lemonade) called Razorback Draught; XLR8, an alcoholic cola; and there's even an alcoholic spring water! (Strange, a few years ago the fashionable reason for drinking spring water was that it was supposedly good for you!)

ENTERTAINMENT
Cinema

Although the cinema took a huge knock from the meteoric rise of the home-video market, it has bounced back as people rediscover the joys of the big screen.

In main cities there are commercial cinema chains, such as Village, Hoyts and Greater Union, usually in two to 10-screen complexes. Smaller towns have just the one cinema, and many of these are almost museum pieces in themselves. Seeing a new-release mainstream film costs around $11 ($7.50 for children under 15) in the big cities, less in country areas and less on certain nights at the bigger cinema chains.

Also in the cities you'll find art-house and independent cinemas, and these places generally screen either films that aren't made for mass consumption or specialise purely in re-runs of classics and cult movies. Cinemas such as the Kino and Astor in Melbourne, the Valhalla and Paddington Academy Twin in Sydney, the Chelsea in Adelaide and the Astor in Perth all fall into this category.

Discos & Nightclubs
Yep, no shortage of these either, but they are confined to the larger cities and towns. Clubs range from the exclusive 'members only' variety to barn-sized discos where anyone who wants to spend the money is welcomed with open arms. Admission charges range from around $6 to $12.

Some places have certain dress standards, but it is generally left to the discretion of the people at the door – if they don't like the look of you, bad luck. The more 'up-market' nightclubs attract an older, more sophisticated and affluent crowd, and generally have stricter dress codes, smarter décor – and higher prices.

Live Music
Many suburban pubs have live music, and these are often great places for catching bands, either nationally well-known names or up-and-coming performers trying to make a name for themselves – most of Australia's popular bands started out on the pub circuit.

The best way to find out about the local scene is to get to know some locals, or travellers who have spent some time in the place. Otherwise, there are often comprehensive listings in newspapers, particularly on Friday.

Spectator Sports
If you're an armchair – or wooden bench – sports fan, Australia has plenty to offer. Australians play at least four types of football, each type being called 'football' by its aficionados. The seasons run from about March to September.

Aussie Rules Aussie Rules is unique – only Gaelic football is anything like it. It's played by teams of 18 on an oval field with an oval ball that can be kicked, caught, hit with the hand or carried and bounced. You get six points for kicking the ball between two central posts (a goal) and one point for kicking it through side posts (a 'behind'). A game lasts for four quarters of 20 minutes each. To take a 'mark' a player must catch a ball on the volley from a kick – in which case the player gets a free kick. A typical final score for one team is between 70 and 110.

Players cannot be sent off in the course of a game; disciplinary tribunals are usually held the following week. Consequently there can be spectacular brawls on field – while the crowds, in contrast, are noisy but remarkably peaceful (a pleasant surprise for visiting soccer fans).

Melbourne is the national (and world) centre for Australian Rules, and the Australian Football League (AFL) is the national competition. Ten of its 16 teams are from Melbourne; the others are from Geelong, Perth, Fremantle, Sydney, Brisbane, and Adelaide, which is also a stronghold of Aussie Rules. But it's nowhere near as big-time there as it is in Melbourne, where crowds regularly exceed 30,000 at top regular games and 80,000 at finals.

Australian Rules is a great game to get to know. Fast, tactical, skilful, rough and athletic, it can produce gripping finishes when even after 80 minutes of play the outcome hangs on the very last kick. It also inspires fierce spectator loyalties and has made otherwise obscure Melbourne suburbs (Hawthorn, Essendon, Collingwood etc) national names.

Soccer Soccer is a bit of a poor cousin: it's widely played on an amateur basis but the national league is only semiprofessional and attracts a pathetically small following. It's slowly gaining popularity thanks in part to the success of the national team. At the local level, there are ethnically based teams representing a wide range of origins.

Rugby Rugby is the main game in New South Wales and Queensland, and it's rugby league, the 13-a-side professional version, that attracts the crowds. The Winfield Cup competition produces the world's best rugby league – fast, fit and clever. Most of its teams are in Sydney but there are others in Canberra, Wollongong, Newcastle, Brisbane and on the Gold Coast. Rugby union, the 15-a-side game originally for amateurs, also has a steady following.

Cricket During the other (non-football) half of the year there's cricket. The Melbourne Cricket Ground (MCG) is the world's biggest, and international Test and one-day matches are played every summer there and in Sydney, Adelaide, Perth, Brisbane and Hobart. There is also an interstate competition (the poorly attended Sheffield Shield) and state-wide district cricket.

Basketball Basketball too is growing in popularity and there is a national league, the NBL. Australia's women's netball team won the world cup in 1995, and Australia also has world-class hockey teams (both men and women).

Horse Racing Australians love a gamble, and hardly any town of even minor import is without a horse-racing track or a Totalisator Agency Board (TAB) betting office. Melbourne and Adelaide must be amongst the only cities in the world to give a public holiday for horse races. The prestigious Melbourne Cup is held on the first Tuesday in November.

Other Sports The Australian Formula One Grand Prix is held in Melbourne each March, the Australian round of the World 500 cc Motorcycle Grand Prix is held at Eastern Creek in NSW annually in March, and the Australian Tennis Open is played in Melbourne in January.

Surfing competitions, such as that held each year at Bell's Beach, Victoria, are world-class.

THINGS TO BUY
There are lots of things definitely not to buy – like plastic boomerangs, fake Aboriginal ashtrays and T-shirts, and all the other terrible souvenirs which fill the tacky souvenir shops in the big cities. Most of them come from Taiwan or Korea anyway. Before buying an Australian souvenir, turn it over to check that it was actually made here.

Aboriginal Art
Aboriginal art has been 'discovered' by the international community, and prices are correspondingly high.

For most people the only thing remotely affordable are small carvings and some very beautiful screen-printed T-shirts produced by Aboriginal craft cooperatives. Dijeridus and boomerangs are also popular purchases, but just be aware that unless you pay top dollar, what you are getting is something made purely for the tourist trade – these are certainly not the real thing.

Australiana
The term 'Australiana' is a euphemism for all those things you buy as gifts for all the friends, aunts and uncles, nieces and nephews, and other sundry bods back home. They are supposedly representative of Australia and its culture, although many are extremely dubious as such.

The seeds of many native plants are on sale all over the place. Try growing kangaroo paws back home (if your own country will allow them in).

For those last-minute gifts, drop into a deli. Australian wines are well known overseas, but why not try honey (leatherwood honey is one of a number of powerful local varieties), macadamia nuts (native to Queensland) or Bundaberg rum with its unusual sweet flavour.

Also gaining popularity are 'bush tucker' items such as tinned witchetty grubs, or honey ants.

Opals
The opal is Australia's national gemstone, and opals and jewellery made with it are popular souvenirs. It's a beautiful stone, but buy wisely and shop around – quality and prices can vary widely from place to place.

Getting There & Away

Basically, getting to Australia means flying, although it is sometimes possible to hitch a ride on a yacht to or from Australia.

Australia is a long way from anywhere. Coming from Asia, Europe or North America there are lots of competing airlines and a wide variety of air fares, but there's no way you can avoid those great distances. Australia's current international popularity adds another problem – flights are often heavily booked. If you want to fly to Australia at a particularly popular time of year (the middle of summer, ie Christmas time, is notoriously difficult) or on a particularly popular route (like Hong Kong or Singapore to Sydney or Melbourne) then you need to plan well ahead.

Australia has a large number of international gateways. Sydney and Melbourne are the two busiest international airports with flights from everywhere. Perth also gets many flights from Asia and Europe and has direct flights to New Zealand and Africa. Other international airports include Hobart in Tasmania (New Zealand only), Adelaide, Port Hedland (Bali only), Darwin, Cairns and Brisbane. One place you can't arrive at directly from overseas is Canberra, the national capital.

Although Sydney is the busiest gateway it makes a lot of sense to avoid arriving or departing there. Sydney's airport is stretched way beyond its capacity and flights are frequently delayed on arrival and departure. Even if you can organise your flights to avoid Sydney, unfortunately many intercity flights (Melbourne in particular) still go via Sydney. If you're planning to explore Australia seriously then starting at a quieter entry port like Cairns in far north Queensland, or Darwin in the Northern Territory is worth considering.

TICKETS
Discount Tickets
Buying airline tickets these days is like shopping for a car, a stereo or a camera – five different travel agents will quote you five different prices. Rule number one if you're looking for a cheap ticket is to go to an agent, not directly to the airline. The airline can usually only quote you the absolutely by-the-rule-book regular fare. An agent, on the other hand, can offer all sorts of special deals, particularly on competitive routes.

Ideally an airline would like to fly all its flights with every seat in use and every passenger paying the highest fare possible. Fortunately life usually isn't like that and airlines would rather have a half-price passenger than an empty seat. When faced with the problem of too many seats, they will either let agents sell them at cut prices, or occasionally make one-off special offers on particular routes – watch the travel ads in the press.

Of course what's available and what it costs depends on what time of year it is, what route you're flying and who you're flying with. If you're flying on a popular route (like Hong Kong) or one where the choice of flights is very limited (like South America or, to a lesser extent, Africa) then the fare is likely to be higher or there may be nothing available but the official fare.

Similarly the dirt cheap fares are likely to be less conveniently scheduled, go by a less convenient route or be with a less popular airline. Flying London-Sydney, for example, is most convenient with airlines like Qantas, British Airways, Thai International or Singapore Airlines. They have flights every day, they operate the same flight straight through to Australia and they're good, reliable, comfortable, safe airlines. At the other extreme you could fly from London to an Eastern European or Middle Eastern city on one flight, switch to another flight from there to Asia, and change to another airline from there to Australia. It takes longer, there are delays and changes of aircraft along the way, the airlines may not be so good and furthermore the connection only works once a week and that means leaving London at 1.30 on a

Wednesday morning. The flip side is it's cheaper.

Round-the-World Tickets

Round-the-World tickets are very popular these days and many of these will take you through Australia. The airline RTW tickets are often real bargains and since Australia is pretty much at the other side of the world from Europe or North America it can work out no more expensive, or even cheaper, to keep going in the same direction right round the world rather than U-turn to return.

The official airline RTW tickets are usually put together by a combination of two airlines, and permit you to fly anywhere you want on their route systems so long as you do not backtrack. Other restrictions are that you (usually) must book the first sector in advance and cancellation penalties then apply. There may be restrictions on how many stops you are permitted and usually the tickets are valid from 90 days up to a year. A typical price for a South Pacific RTW ticket is around £760.

An alternative type of RTW ticket is one put together by a travel agent using a combination of discounted tickets from a number of airlines. A UK agent like Trailfinders can put together interesting London-to-London RTW combinations including Australia for between £690 and £800.

Circle Pacific Tickets

Circle Pacific fares are a similar idea to RTW tickets, using a combination of airlines to circle the Pacific – combining Australia, New Zealand, North America and Asia. Examples would be Qantas-Northwest Orient, Canadian Airlines International-Cathay Pacific and so on. As with RTW tickets there are advance purchase restrictions and limits to how many stopovers you can make. Typically fares range between US$1760 and US$2240. Possible Circle Pacific routes are Los Angeles-Bangkok-Sydney-Auckland-Honolulu-Los Angeles or Los Angeles-Tokyo-Kuala Lumpur-Sydney-Auckland-Honolulu-Los Angeles.

TO/FROM THE UK

The cheapest tickets in London are from the numerous 'bucket shops' (discount ticket agencies) which advertise in magazines and papers like *Time Out*, *Southern Cross* and *TNT*. Pick up one or two of these publications and ring round a few bucket shops to find the best deal. The magazine *Business Traveller* also has a great deal of good advice on air-fare bargains. Most bucket shops are trustworthy and reliable but the occasional sharp operator appears – *Time Out* and *Business Traveller* give some useful advice on precautions to take.

Trailfinders (☎ (0171) 938 3366) at 46 Earls Court Rd, London W8, and STA Travel (☎ (0171) 581 4132) at 74 Old Brompton Rd, London SW7, and 117 Euston Rd, London NW1 (☎ (0171) 465 0484), are good, reliable agents for cheap tickets.

The cheapest London to Sydney or Melbourne bucket-shop (not direct) tickets are about £385 one way or £638 return. Cheap fares to Perth are around £330 one way and £550 return. Such prices are usually only available if you leave London in the low season (March to June). In September and mid-December fares go up by about 30%, while the rest of the year they're somewhere in between. Average direct high-season fares to Sydney, Melbourne or Perth are £468 one way and £875 return.

Many cheap tickets allow stopovers on the way to or from Australia. Rules regarding how many stopovers you can make, how long you can stay away, how far in advance you have to decide your return date and so on, vary from time to time and ticket to ticket, but recently most return tickets have allowed you to stay away for any period between 14 days and one year, with stopovers permitted anywhere along your route. As usual with heavily discounted tickets, the less you pay the less you get. Nice direct flights, leaving at convenient times and flying with popular airlines, are going to be more expensive than flying from London to Singapore or Bangkok with some Eastern European or Middle Eastern airline and then changing to another airline for the last leg.

Air Travel Glossary

Apex Tickets Apex stands for Advance Purchase Excursion fare. These tickets are usually 30% to 40% cheaper than the full economy fare, but there are restrictions. You must purchase the ticket at least 21 days in advance and must be away for a minimum period (normally 14 days) and return within a maximum period (90 or 180 days). Stopovers are not allowed, and if you have to change your destination or dates of travel, there will be extra charges. As well, if you have to cancel your trip, the refund is often considerably less than what you paid for the ticket. Take out travel insurance to cover yourself in case you have to cancel your trip unexpectedly.

Baggage Allowance This will be written on your ticket; you are usually allowed one 20-kg item to go in the hold, plus one item of hand luggage. Some airlines which fly transpacific and transatlantic routes allow for two pieces of luggage (there are limits on dimension and weight).

Bucket Shops At certain times of the year and/or on certain routes, many airlines fly with empty seats. As it's more cost-effective for them to fly full, even if that means having to sell a certain number of drastically discounted tickets, the airlines off-load tickets onto bucket shops (UK) or consolidators (USA), travel agents who specialise in discounted fares. The agents, in turn, sell the tickets at reduced prices. These tickets are often the cheapest you'll find, but you can't purchase them directly from the airlines. Availability varies widely, so you'll have to be flexible in your travel plans.

Bucket-shop agents advertise in newspapers and magazines and there's a lot of competition – especially in places like Amsterdam and London – so it's a good idea to telephone first to ascertain availability before rushing from shop to shop. You have to be quick off the mark, as by the time you get there the tickets may be sold out.

Bumped Just because you have a confirmed seat doesn't mean you're going to get on the plane – see Overbooking.

Cancellation Penalties If you have to cancel or change an Apex or other discount ticket, there may be heavy penalties; insurance can sometimes be taken out against these penalties. Some airlines impose penalties on regular tickets as well, particularly against 'no show' passengers.

Check In Airlines ask you to check in a certain time before the flight departure (usually two hours on international flights). If you fail to check in on time and the flight is overbooked, the airline can cancel your booking and give your seat to somebody else.

Confirmation Having a ticket written out with the flight and date on it doesn't mean you have a seat until the agent has confirmed with the airline that your status is 'OK'. Prior to this confirmation, your status is 'on request'.

Courier Fares Businesses often need to send urgent documents or freight securely and quickly. They do this through courier companies which hire people to accompany the package through customs and, in return, offer a discount ticket – sometimes a phenomenal bargain. In effect, what the companies do is ship their freight as your luggage on a regular commercial flight. This is perfectly legal, but there are two shortcomings: the short turnaround time of the ticket is usually not longer than a month; and you may be required to surrender all your baggage allowance for the use of the courier company, and be only allowed to take carry-on luggage.

Discounted Tickets There are two types of discounted fares – officially discounted (such as Apex; see Promotional Fares) and unofficially discounted (see Bucket Shops). The latter can save you more than money – you may be able to pay Apex prices without the associated Apex advance booking and other requirements. The lowest prices often impose drawbacks, such as flying with unpopular airlines, inconvenient schedules, or unpleasant routes and connections.

Economy-Class Tickets These tickets are usually not the cheapest way to go, though they do give you maximum flexibility and are valid for 12 months. Most unused tickets are fully refundable, as are unused sectors of a multiple ticket.

Full Fares Airlines traditionally offer 1st-class (coded F), business-class (coded J) and economy-class (coded Y) tickets. These days there are so many promotional and discounted fares available that few passengers pay full fare.

Lost Tickets If you lose your ticket, an airline will usually treat it like a travellers' cheque and, after enquiries, issue a replacement. Legally, however, an airline is entitled to treat it like cash, so if you lose a ticket, it could be forever. Take good care of your tickets.

MCO An MCO (Miscellaneous Charges Order) is a voucher for a value of a given amount, which resembles an airline ticket and can be used to pay for a specific flight with any IATA (International Air Transport Association) airline. MCOs, which are more flexible than a regular ticket, may satisfy the onward ticket requirement, but some countries are now reluctant to accept them. MCOs are fully refundable if unused.

No Shows No shows are passengers who fail to show up for their flight for whatever reason. Full-fare no shows are sometimes entitled to travel on a later flight. The rest of us are penalised (see Cancellation Penalties).

Open Jaw Tickets These are return tickets which allow you to fly to one place but return from another, and travel between the two 'jaws' by any means of transport at your own expense. If available, this can save you backtracking to your arrival point.

Overbooking Airlines hate to fly with empty seats, and since every flight has some passengers who fail to show up (see No Shows), they often book more passengers than they have seats available. Usually the excess passengers balance those who fail to show up, but occasionally somebody gets bumped. If this happens, guess who it is most likely to be? The passengers who check in late.

Promotional Fares These are officially discounted fares, such as Apex, which are available from travel agents or direct from the airline.

Reconfirmation You must contact the airline at least 72 hours before departure to 'reconfirm' that you intend to be on the flight. If you don't do this, the airline can delete your name from the passenger list and you could lose your seat.

Restrictions Discounted tickets often have various restrictions on them, such as necessity of advance purchase, limitations on the minimum and maximum period you must be away, restrictions on breaking the journey or changing the booking or route etc.

Round-the-World Tickets These tickets have become very popular in the last few years; basically, there are two types – airline tickets and agent tickets. An airline RTW ticket is issued by two or more airlines that have joined together to market a ticket which takes you around the world on their combined routes. It permits you to fly pretty well anywhere you choose using their combined routes as long as you don't backtrack, ie keep moving in approximately the same direction east or west. Other restrictions are that you (usually) must book the first sector in advance and cancellation penalties then apply. There may be restrictions on how many stopovers you are permitted. The RTW tickets are usually valid for 90 days to up to a year.

The agent ticket is a combination of cheap fares strung together by a travel agent. These may be cheaper than airline RTW tickets, but the choice of routes will be limited.

Standby This is a discounted ticket where you only fly if there is a seat free at the last moment. Standby fares are usually only available directly at the airport, but sometimes may also be handled by an airline's city office. To give yourself the best possible chance of getting on the flight you want, get there early and have your name placed on the waiting list. It's first come, first served.

Student Discounts Some airlines offer student-card holders 15% to 25% discounts on their tickets. The same often applies to anyone under the age of 26. These discounts are generally only available on ordinary economy-class fares. You wouldn't get one, for instance, on an Apex or an RTW ticket, as these are already discounted.

Tickets Out An entry requirement for many countries is that you have an onward or return ticket, in other words, a ticket out of the country. If you're not sure what you intend to do next, the easiest solution is to buy the cheapest onward ticket to a neighbouring country or a ticket from a reliable airline which can later be refunded if you do not use it.

Transferred Tickets Airline tickets cannot be transferred from one person to another. Travellers sometimes try to sell the return half of their ticket, but officials can ask you to prove that you are the person named on the ticket. This may not be checked on domestic flights, but on international flights, tickets are usually compared with passports.

Travel Periods Some officially discounted fares, Apex fares in particular, vary with the time of year. There is often a low (off-peak) season and a high (peak) season. Sometimes there's an intermediate or shoulder season as well. At peak times both officially and unofficially discounted fares will be higher, or there may simply be no discounted tickets available. Usually the fare depends on your outward flight – if you depart in the high season and return in the low season, you pay the high-season fare. ■

From Australia you can expect to pay around A$1200 one way, and A$1800 return to London and other European capitals, with stops in Asia on the way. Again, all fares increase by up to 30% in the European summer and at Christmas.

TO/FROM NORTH AMERICA

There is a variety of connections across the Pacific from Los Angeles, San Francisco and Vancouver to Australia, including direct flights, flights via New Zealand, island-hopping routes and more circuitous Pacific rim routes via nations in Asia. Qantas, Air New Zealand and United fly USA-Australia; Qantas, Air New Zealand and Canadian Airlines International fly Canada-Australia. An interesting option from the east coast is Northwest's flight via Japan.

One advantage of flying Qantas or Air New Zealand is that on the US airlines, if your flight goes via Hawaii, the west coast to Hawaii sector is treated as a domestic flight. This means you have to pay for drinks and headsets in this sector on the US airlines – goodies that are free on international sectors.

To find good fares to Australia check the travel ads in the Sunday travel sections of papers like the *Los Angeles Times*, *San Francisco Chronicle-Examiner*, *New York Times* or *Toronto Globe & Mail*. You can typically get a one-way/return ticket from the west coast for US$830/1000, or from the east coast for US$1000/1400. At peak seasons – particularly the Australia summer/Christmas period – seats will be harder to get and the price will probably be higher. In the USA good agents for discounted tickets are the two student travel operators, Council Travel and STA Travel, both with lots of offices around the country. Canadian west-coast fares out of Vancouver will be similar to those from the US west coast. From Toronto fares go from around C$2230 return, from Vancouver C$1700.

If Pacific island-hopping is your aim, check out the airlines of Pacific Island nations, some of which have good deals on indirect routings. Qantas can give you Fiji or Tahiti along the way, while Air New Zealand can offer both and the Cook Islands as well. See the Circle Pacific section for more details.

One-way/return fares available from Australia include: San Francisco A$1000/1360, New York A$1150/1660 and Vancouver A$1000/1360.

TO/FROM NEW ZEALAND

Air New Zealand and Qantas operate a network of trans-Tasman flights linking Auckland, Wellington and Christchurch in New Zealand with most major Australian gateway cities. You can fly directly between a lot of places in New Zealand and a lot of places in Australia.

Fares vary depending on which cities you fly between and when you do it but from New Zealand to Sydney you're looking at around NZ$450 one way and NZ$565 return, and to Melbourne NZ$529 one way and NZ$730 return. There is a lot of competition on this route, with United, British Airways, Qantas and Air New Zealand all flying it, so there is bound to be some good discounting going on.

Cheap fares to New Zealand from Europe will usually be for flights via the USA. A straightforward London-Auckland return bucket-shop ticket costs around £950. Coming via Australia you can continue right around on a Round-the-World (RTW) ticket which will cost from around £1050 for a ticket with a comprehensive choice of stopovers.

TO/FROM ASIA

Ticket discounting is widespread in Asia, particularly in Singapore, Hong Kong, Bangkok and Penang. There are a lot of fly-by-nights in the Asian ticketing scene so a little care is required. Also the Asian routes have been particularly caught up in the capacity shortages on flights to Australia. Flights between Hong Kong and Australia are notoriously heavily booked while flights to or from Bangkok and Singapore are often part of the longer Europe-Australia route so they are also sometimes very full. Plan ahead. For more information on South-East Asian travel, and travel on to Australia, see

Lonely Planet's *South-East Asia on a shoe-string*.

Typical one-way fares to Australia from Singapore are S$585 to Darwin or Perth, S$785 to Sydney or Melbourne.

You can also pick up some interesting tickets in Asia to include Australia on the way across the Pacific. Qantas and Air New Zealand offer discounted transpacific tickets.

From Australia return fares from the east coast to Singapore, Kuala Lumpur and Bangkok range from $700 to $900, and to Hong Kong from $900 to $1300.

The cheapest way out of Australia is to take one of the flights operating between Darwin and Kupang (Timor, Indonesia). Current one-way/return fares are $198/330. See the Darwin Getting There & Away section for full details.

TO/FROM AFRICA

The flight possibilities between Africa and Australia have increased markedly in the last few years, and there is a number of direct flights each week between Africa and Australia, but only between Perth and Harare (Zimbabwe) or Johannesburg (South Africa). Qantas, South African Airways and Air Zimbabwe all fly this route.

Other airlines which connect southern Africa and Australia include Malaysia Airlines (via Kuala Lumpur) and Air Mauritius (via Mauritius), both of which have special deals from time to time.

From East Africa the options are to fly via Mauritius, or via the Indian subcontinent and on to South-East Asia, then connect from there to Australia.

TO/FROM SOUTH AMERICA

Two routes operate between South America and Australia. The Chile connection involves Lan Chile's Santiago-Easter Island-Tahiti twice-weekly flight, from where you fly Qantas or another airline to Australia. Alternatively there is the route which skirts the Antarctic circle, flying from Buenos Aires to Auckland and Sydney, operated twice-weekly by Aerolineas Argentinas.

ARRIVING IN AUSTRALIA

Australia's dramatic increase in visitor arrivals has caused some severe bottlenecks at the entry points, particularly at Sydney where the airport is often operating at more than full capacity and delays are frequent. One answer to this problem is to try not to arrive in Australia at Sydney. You can save yourself a lot of time and trouble by making Brisbane, Cairns, Melbourne or another gateway city your arrival point. A $3.40 'noise pollution' tax is included in the price of international and domestic flights arriving in Sydney

For information about how to get to the city from the airport when you first arrive in Australia, see the To/From the Airport section under the relevant city. There is generally an airport bus service at the international airports and there are always taxis available.

LEAVING AUSTRALIA

There is a $27 departure tax when leaving Australia, but this is incorporated into the price of your air ticket and so is not paid as a separate tax.

WARNING

The information in this chapter is particularly vulnerable to change – prices for international travel are volatile, routes are introduced and cancelled, schedules change, rules are amended, special deals come and go, borders open and close. Airlines and governments seem to take a perverse pleasure in making price structures and regulations as complicated as possible and you should check directly with the airline or travel agent to make sure you understand how a fare (and any ticket you may buy) works.

In addition, the travel industry is highly competitive and there are many lurks and perks. The upshot of this is that you should get quotes and advice from as many airlines and travel agents as possible before you part with your hard-earned cash. The details given in this chapter should be regarded only as pointers and cannot be any substitute for your own careful, up-to-date research.

Getting Around

For schedules of all land and sea transport services throughout Australia, there's the publication *Travel Times*, which is published twice yearly and is available from newsagents ($7.95).

AIR

Australia is so vast (and at times so empty) that unless your time is unlimited you will probably have to take to the air sometime. It has been calculated that something like 80% of long-distance trips by public transport are made by air.

There are only two main domestic carriers within Australia – Qantas and Ansett – despite the fact that the airline industry is deregulated. For 40-odd years Australia had a 'two-airline policy'; the former Australian Airlines and Ansett had a duopoly on domestic flights. With this cosy cohabitation the airlines could charge virtually what they liked, and operate virtually identical schedules. All this meant that for the traveller, domestic airline travel was expensive and the choice of flights limited, particularly on the low-volume routes.

With deregulation came another player, Compass, and a fierce price war. The net result was that Compass folded (twice!) and we're back to a two-airline industry and relatively high prices, although discounting is now a regular feature of the domestic flights scene.

Note that all domestic flights in Australia are nonsmoking. Because Qantas flies both international and domestic routes, flights leave from both the international and domestic terminals at Australian airports. Flights with flight numbers from QF001 to QF399 operate from international terminals; flight numbers QF400 and above operate from domestic terminals.

Cheap Fares

Random Discounting A major feature of the deregulated air travel industry is random discounting. As the airlines try harder to fill planes, they often offer substantial discounts on selected routes. Although this seems to apply mainly to the heavy-volume routes, that's not always the case.

To make the most of the discounted fares, you need to keep in touch with what's on offer, mainly because there are usually conditions attached to cheap fares – such as booking 14 or so days in advance, only flying on weekends or between certain dates and so on. Also the number of seats available is usually fairly limited. The further ahead you can plan the better.

The places to which this sort of discounting generally applies are the main centres – Melbourne, Sydney, Brisbane, Cairns, Adelaide and Perth – but deals come and go all the time.

It is fair to say that on virtually any route in the country covered by Qantas or Ansett the full economy fare will not be the cheapest way to go. Because the situation is so fluid, the special fares will more than likely have changed by the time you read this. For that reason we list full one-way economy fares throughout the book, although you can safely assume that there will be a cheaper fare available.

Discounts are generally greater for return rather than one-way travel.

Some Possibilities If you're planning a return trip and you can save 14 days up your sleeve then you can save 45% to 50% by travelling Apex. You have to book and pay for your tickets 14 days in advance and you must stay away at least one Saturday night. Flight details can be changed at any time, but the tickets are nonrefundable. If you book seven days in advance the saving is 35% to 40% off the full fare.

For one-way travel, if you can book three days in advance a saving of around 10% is offered; for seven-day advance booking the discount is around 20%.

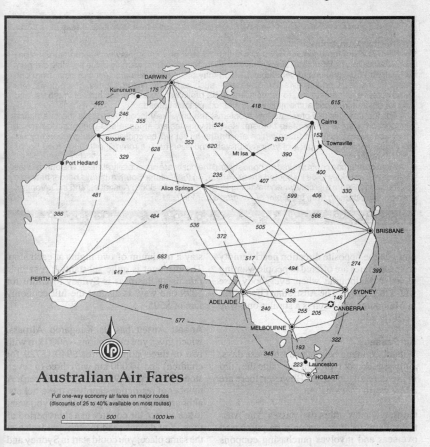

Australian Air Fares

Full one-way economy air fares on major routes
(discounts of 25 to 40% available on most routes)

0   500   1000 km

University or other higher education students under the age of 26 can get a 25% discount off the regular economy fare. An airline tertiary concession card (available from the airlines) is required for Australian students. Overseas students can use their International Student Identity Card.

All nonresident international travellers can get up to a 40% discount on internal Qantas flights and 25% on Ansett flights simply by presenting their international ticket when booking. It seems there is no limit to the number of domestic flights you can take, it doesn't matter which airline you

fly into Australia with, and it doesn't have to be on a return ticket. Note that the discount applies only to the full economy fare, and so in many cases it will be cheaper to take advantage of other discounts offered. The best advice is to ring around and explore the options before you buy.

Another thing to keep your eyes open for is special deals at certain times of the year. When the Melbourne Cup horse race is on in early November and when the football AFL Grand Final is held (also in Melbourne) at the end of September lots of extra flights are put on. These flights would normally be

---

Interstate Quarantine

When travelling throughout Australia, whether by land or air, you may well come across signs (mainly in airports, interstate railway stations and at state borders) warning of the possible dangers of carrying fruit, plants and vegetables, which may be infected with a disease or pest, from one area to another. Certain pests and diseases – such as fruit fly, cucurbit thrips, grape phylloxera and potato cyst nematodes, to name a few – are prevalent in some areas but not in others, and so for obvious reasons authorities would like to limit their spread.

For the traveller this presents few problems; the only likely inconvenience is the quarantine inspection posts on some state borders. Here all vehicles are stopped and you must declare all fruit and vegetables, and those which are on the hit list will be confiscated. Inspection officers may ask to look in the back of your car or van, and even have a rummage through food boxes and containers.

Most quarantine control relies on honesty and the posts are not actually staffed. The only places where you are likely to be inspected are at Yamba, on the Victoria-South Australia border between Mildura and Renmark (only when travelling from Victoria into South Australia), and in Devonport when disembarking from the *Spirit of Tasmania* car ferry. ■

---

going in the opposite direction nearly empty so special fares are offered to people wanting to leave Melbourne when everybody else wants to go there. The Australian Grand Prix in Melbourne in March is a similar one-way traffic event.

Air Passes

With discounting being the norm these days, air passes do not represent the value they did in pre-deregulation days. However, there are a few worth checking out.

Qantas Qantas offers two passes. The Australia Explorer Pass can only be purchased overseas and involves purchasing coupons for either short-haul flights (eg Hobart to Melbourne) at $170 one way, or for long-haul sectors (such as just about anywhere to Uluru) for $220. You must purchase a minimum of four coupons before you arrive in Australia, and once here you can buy up to four more.

There is also the Qantas Backpackers Pass, which can only be bought in Australia with identification such as a YHA membership or a VIP Backpackers or Independent Backpackers Card, or a Bus Australia card. You must purchase a minimum of three connecting sectors (such as Melbourne-Sydney, Sydney-Brisbane and Brisbane-Cairns), and

stay a minimum of two nights at each stop. The discount is quite substantial; a sample fare using this pass is Sydney to Uluru for $279 one way, as against the full economy fare of $505.

Ansett Ansett has its Kangaroo Airpass, which gives you two options – 6000 km with two or three stopovers for $949 ($729 for children) and 10,000 km with three to seven stopovers for $1499 ($1149 for children). A number of restrictions apply to these tickets, although they can be a good deal if you want to see a lot of the country in a short period of time. You do not need to start and finish at the same place; you could start in Sydney and end in Darwin, for example.

Restrictions include a minimum travel time (10 nights) and a maximum (45 nights). One of the stops must be at a non-capital-city destination and be for at least four nights, and you can only stay at each destination once. All sectors must be booked when you purchase the ticket, although these can be changed without penalty unless the ticket needs rewriting, in which case there's a $50 charge. Refunds are available in full before travel commences but not at all once you start using the ticket.

On a 6000-km air pass you could, for example, fly Sydney-Alice Springs-Cairns-Brisbane-Sydney. That gives you three stops and two of them are in non-capital cities. The regular fare for that circuit would be $1569, but with current discounts (seven day advance purchase) it's $1217, so you save $368. A one-way route might be Adelaide-Melbourne-Sydney-Alice Springs-Perth. There are three stops, of which one is a non-capital city. Regular cost for that route would be $1484, but with discounts it's $1187, so the saving is $238.

Other Airline Options

There are a number of secondary airlines. In Western Australia there's Ansett WA with an extensive network of flights to the mining towns of the north-west and to Darwin in the Northern Territory. Kendell Airlines services country areas of Victoria, South Australia and Tasmania, as well as Broken Hill (NSW) and Uluru (NT).

There are numerous other smaller operators. Sunstate operates services in Queensland including some to a number of islands. They also have a couple of routes in the south to Mildura and Broken Hill. Skywest has a number of services to remote parts of Western Australia. Eastern Australia Airlines operates up and down the New South Wales coast and also inland from Sydney as far as Bourke and Cobar. Airnorth connects Darwin and Alice Springs with many small towns in the Northern Territory.

Airport Transport

There are private or public bus services at almost every major town in Australia. In one or two places you may have to depend on taxis but in general you can get between airport and city reasonably economically and conveniently by bus. Quite often a taxi shared between three or more people can be cheaper than the bus.

BUS

Bus travel is generally the cheapest way from A to B, other than hitching of course, but the main problem is to find the best deal.

There is only one truly *national* bus network – Greyhound Pioneer Australia (☎ 13 20 30).

McCafferty's (☎ (07) 3236 3033; 13 1499), operating out of Brisbane, is certainly the next biggest, with services virtually right around Australia except for the long haul across the Nullarbor between Perth and Port Augusta (South Australia), but here you can take the Indian Pacific train using a McCafferty's bus pass.

There are also many smaller bus companies operating locally or specialising in one or two main intercity routes. These often offer the best deals – Firefly costs $45 for Sydney to Melbourne, for example. In South Australia, Stateliner operates around the state including to the Flinders Ranges. Westrail in Western Australia and V/Line in Victoria operate bus services to places trains no longer go.

A great many travellers see Australia by bus because it's one of the best ways to come to grips with the country's size and variety of terrain, and because the bus companies have such comprehensive route networks – far more comprehensive than the railway system. The buses all look pretty similar and are equipped with air-conditioning, toilets and videos.

In most places there is just one bus terminal. Big city terminals are usually well equipped with toilets, showers and other facilities.

Greyhound Pioneer and McCafferty's have a variety of passes available, so it's a matter of deciding which suits your needs.

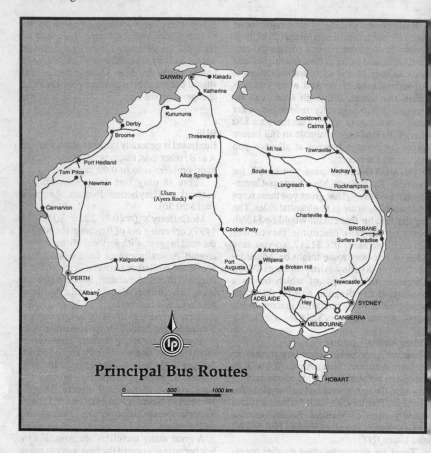

Principal Bus Routes

0   500   1000 km

Greyhound Pioneer Passes

Unlimited Travel Pass This gives you a set number of days travel within a specified period, the shortest being seven days travel in 30 days ($450), and the longest 90 days travel in six months ($2225). The advantages of these passes are that you can travel one route as many times as you like, and have unlimited km. The disadvantages are that you may feel obliged to travel farther than you might otherwise like to, simply because you have the days free to do so.

Set-Route Passes These are more popular, giving you six or 12 months to cover a set route. You haven't got the go-anywhere flexibility of the Unlimited Travel Pass but if you can find a set route which suits you – and there are 33 to choose from – it generally works out cheaper than the Unlimited Travel Pass. When a pass follows a circular route, you can start anywhere along the loop, and finish at the same spot.

The main limitation is that you can't backtrack, except on 'dead-end' short sectors such as Darwin to Kakadu, Townsville to Cairns and from the Stuart Highway to Uluru.

The Aussie Highlights pass allows you to loop around the eastern half of Australia from Sydney taking in Melbourne, Adelaide, Coober Pedy, Uluru, Alice Springs, Darwin (and Kakadu), Cairns, Townsville, the Whitsundays, Brisbane and Surfers Paradise for A$690. Or there are one-way passes, such as the Go West pass from Sydney to Cairns via Melbourne, Adelaide, Uluru, Alice Springs, Katherine, Darwin (and Kakadu), and Townsville for $550; or Across the Top, which goes from Cairns to Perth via the Top End and Kimberley, for $490. There's even an All Australia Pass which takes you right around the country, including up or down through the Centre, for $1200.

McCafferty's Passes

McCafferty's has 15 set-route passes to choose from. On the routes which cross the Nullarbor, the pass includes travel on the Indian Pacific train service between Perth and Adelaide.

The Travel Australia Pass is the equivalent of Greyhound Pioneer's All Australia Pass and costs $1160. The Point to Point Pass takes in a loop from Cairns via Sydney, Melbourne, Adelaide, Uluru, Alice Springs and Tennant Creek for $600, while the Best of the East & Centre is the same but with the addition of travel to Darwin and Kakadu, for $700. Top End Safari gives you six months to travel from Cairns to Darwin and Kakadu for $200 ($180 without Kakadu), while the Tassie Discovery gives you a circuit of the island for seven, 15 or 30 days, and includes the ferry fare from Melbourne. The West Coast Adventurer does the trip from Darwin to Perth for $275, and you can include Monkey Mia, Coral Bay, Kalbarri and Kakadu for an additional $205.

Other Bus Options

There are a few companies which offer flexible transport options in various parts of the country, and are a good alternative to the big bus companies. Their trips are generally aimed at budget travellers and so are good fun – a combination of straightforward bus travel and an organised tour. The buses are generally smaller and so not necessarily as comfortable as those of the big companies, but it's a much more interesting way to travel.

The three main companies are:

Oz Experience (☎ (02) 9977 2688). Basically a backpackers' bus line offering frequent service up and down the east coast of Australia to all the major destinations, with off-the-beaten-track detours to cattle stations and national parks. You buy one of their 18 passes, which range from $110 to $833 depending on the distance, and are valid for six to 12 months. Their buses travel set routes, but your pass entitles you to unlimited stops, which means you can get on and off whenever and wherever you like. The drivers act as guides, providing commentary and advice, and they can also pre-book your hostels, stop at supermarkets so you can do your shopping, and arrange discounts on most tours and activities along the way.

The Wayward Bus (☎ toll-free 1800 882 823). Offers transport between Adelaide and Melbourne via the Great Ocean Road (three days, $150), Alice Springs (eight days, $560) and Perth (12 days, $770). Unlike the Oz Experience runs, these trips include sight-seeing, meals and accommodation.

Straycat (☎ (03) 9348 9244). Has three-day Melbourne to Sydney trips via the Victorian Alps and the Snowy Mountains for $149, or two-day trips via the coast road for $79. The prices include meals but not accommodation, which is booked for you and costs around $13 per night.

TRAIN

Australia's railway system has never really recovered from the colonial bungling which accompanied its early days over a century ago. Before Australia became an independent country it was governed as six separate colonies, all administered from London. When the colony of Victoria, for example, wanted to build a railway line it checked, not with the adjoining colony of New South Wales, but with the colonial office in London. When the colonies were federated in 1901, by a sheer masterpiece of misplanning not one state had railway lines of the same gauge as a neighbouring state.

This misfortune has dogged the railways

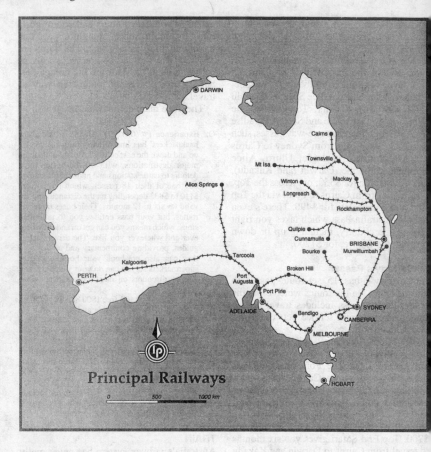

Principal Railways

0   500   1000 km

ever since. When New South Wales started to lay a line from Sydney to Parramatta in 1850, it began with a wide gauge – five feet three inches. Victoria also started building to this gauge, in order to tie in with the New South Wales system. But when New South Wales changed railway engineers and subsequently switched to standard gauge – four feet eight inches – Victoria decided its railway construction had gone too far to change. When the two lines met in Albury in 1883 the Victorian tracks were seven inches wider than the New South Wales ones. For

the next 79 years a rail journey between Melbourne and Sydney involved getting up in the middle of the night at the border to change trains!

In 1962 a standard gauge line was opened between Albury and Melbourne and standard gauge lines have also been built between the New South Wales-Queensland border and Brisbane. In 1970 a standard gauge rail link was completed between Sydney and Perth and the famous, and very popular, Indian Pacific run began.

There are also, however, narrow gauge

railways, built because they were believed to be cheaper. The old Ghan line between Adelaide and Alice Springs was only replaced by a new standard gauge line in 1980.

Apart from different gauges there's also the problem of different operators. The individual states run their own services, or a combination of them for interstate services. Australian National Railways is an association of the government-owned systems in Queensland, New South Wales, Victoria and Western Australia, and this body goes some way to coordinating the major services.

Rail travel in Australia today is basically something you do because you really want to – not because it's cheaper, and certainly not because it's fast. It's generally the slowest way to get around. On the other hand the trains are comfortable and you certainly see Australia at ground level in a way no other means of travel permits.

Australia is also one of the few places in the world where new lines are still being laid or are under consideration; the task of finally completing the north-south, transcontinental rail link between Alice Springs and Darwin is still being considered.

Rail Passes

There are a number of passes which allow unlimited rail travel either across the country or just in one state. With the Austrail Pass you can travel anywhere on the rail network for a set number of days, in either 1st class or economy. The cost is $530/320 in 1st/economy class for eight days of travel over a 60-day period, and $750/475 for 15 days of travel over a 90-day period.

The Austrail Flexipass allows a set number of travelling days within a six-month period. The cost is $620/360 in 1st/economy class for eight days of travel, $870/520 for 15 days, $1210/735 for 22 days and $1540/945 for 29 days. The eight-day pass cannot be used for travel between Adelaide and Perth or between Adelaide and Alice Springs.

For travel within a limited area, the passes which just cover travel in one state may be more suitable. These are available for Victoria and Queensland; see the relevant Getting Around sections for details.

As the railway booking system is computerised, any station (other than those on metropolitan lines) can make a booking for any journey throughout the country. For reservations telephone ☎ 13 2232 during office hours; this will connect you to the nearest mainline station.

CAR

Australia is a big, sprawling country with large cities where public transport is not always very comprehensive or convenient – the car is the accepted means of getting from A to B. More and more travellers are also finding it the best way to see the country – with three or four of you the costs are reasonable and the benefits many, provided of course you don't have a major mechanical problem.

Road Rules

Driving in Australia holds few real surprises. Australians drive on the left-hand side of the road just like in the UK, Japan and most countries in South-East Asia and the Pacific. A main road rule is 'give way to the right' – if an intersection is unmarked (unusual), you must give way to vehicles entering the intersection from your right.

Trams are a special hazard in Melbourne. You can only overtake trams on their left and must stop behind them when they stop to pick up or drop off passengers. In central Melbourne there are also a number of intersections where a special turn, known locally as the 'hook turn' and mastered only by native Melburnians, must be employed when making right-hand turns. You must wait until the light of the road you're turning into turns green, and then turn from the left-hand side of the road; this is so you don't hold up trams. Somewhat inconspicuous signs suspended above the intersection indicate if the hook turn must be used.

The general speed limit in built-up areas in Australia is 60 km/h and on the open highway it's usually 100 or 110 km/h, although in the Northern Territory there is no speed limit outside built-up areas. The police have speed radar guns and cameras and are very fond of using them in carefully hidden locations in order to raise easy revenue. However, far from the cities where traffic is light, you'll see a lot of vehicles moving a lot faster than the speed limit. Oncoming drivers who flash their lights at you may be giving you a friendly warning of a speed camera ahead.

All new cars in Australia have seat belts back and front and if your seat has a belt you're required to wear it. You're liable to be fined if you don't. Small children must be belted into an approved safety seat.

Although overseas licences are acceptable in Australia, for genuine overseas visitors an International Driving Permit is preferred.

On the Road

Road Conditions Australia is not criss-crossed by multilane highways. There simply is not enough traffic and the distances are too great to justify them. You'll certainly find stretches of divided road, particularly on busy roads like the Sydney to Melbourne Hume Highway or close to the state capital cities – eg the last stretch into Adelaide from Melbourne, the Pacific Highway from Sydney to Newcastle, the Surfers Paradise-Brisbane road. Elsewhere Australian roads are well-surfaced and two lanes (though a long way from the billiard-table surfaces the Poms are used to driving on) on all the main routes.

You don't have to get very far off the beaten track, however, to find yourself on dirt roads, and anybody who sets out to see the country in reasonable detail will have to expect some dirt-road travelling. If you seriously want to explore, you'd better plan on having four-wheel drive (4WD) and a winch. A few useful spare parts are worth carrying if you're travelling on highways in the Northern Territory or the north of Western Australia. A broken fan belt can be a damn nuisance if the next service station is 200 km away.

Drink-Driving Drink-driving is a real problem, especially in country areas. Serious attempts have been made in recent years to reduce the road toll – random breath tests are not uncommon in built-up areas. If you're caught with a blood-alcohol level of more than 0.05 (0.08 in the Northern Territory) then be prepared for a hefty fine and the loss of your licence.

Distances by Road (km)

	Adelaide	Brisbane	Canberra	Darwin	Melbourne	Perth	Sydney
Adelaide		2130	1210	3215	745	2750	1430
Alice Springs	1690	3060	2755	1525	2435	3770	2930
Brisbane	2130		1295	3495	1735	4390	1030
Broome	4035	4320	5100	1965	4780	2415	4885
Cairns	2865	1840	3140	2795	3235	6015	2870
Canberra	1210	1295		4230	655	3815	305
Darwin	3215	3495	4230		3960	4345	4060
Melbourne	755	1735	655	3960		3495	895
Perth	2750	4390	3815	4345	3495		3990
Sydney	1430	1030	305	4060	895	3990	

These are the shortest distances by road; other routes may be considerably longer. For distances by coach, check the companies' leaflets.

Fuel Fuel (super, diesel and unleaded) is available from stations sporting the well-known international brand names. Prices vary from place to place and from price war to price war but generally they're in the 65c to 75c a litre range (say around $2.70 to $3.20 an imperial gallon). In the outback the price can soar and some outback service stations are not above exploiting their monopoly position. Distances between fill-ups can be long in the outback.

Signposting Between cities signposting on the main roads is generally quite OK, but around cities it's often abysmal. You can spend a lot of time trying to find street-name signs, and as for indicating which way to go to leave the city – until recently you were halfway to Sydney from Melbourne before you saw the first sign indicating you were travelling in the right direction.

Hazards Cows and kangaroos are two common hazards on country roads, and a collision is likely to kill the animal and seriously damage your vehicle. Kangaroos are most active around dawn and dusk, and they travel in groups. If you see one hopping across the road in front of you, slow right down – its friends are probably just behind it. Many Australians try to avoid travelling altogether between 5 pm and 8 am, because of the hazards posed by animals. Finally, if one hops out right in front of you, hit the brakes and only swerve to avoid the animal if it is safe to do so. The number of people who have been killed in accidents caused by swerving to miss an animal is high – better to damage your car and probably kill the animal than kill yourself and others with you.

Outback Travel

You can drive all the way round Australia on Highway 1 or through the Centre from Adelaide to Darwin without ever leaving sealed road. However, if you really want to see outback Australia, there are lots of roads where the official recommendation is that you report to the police before you leave one end, and again when you arrive at the other,

so if you fail to turn up they can send out search parties.

Nevertheless many of these tracks are now much better kept than in years past and you don't need 4WD or fancy expedition equipment to tackle them. You do need to be carefully prepared and to carry important spare parts. Backtracking 500 km to pick up some minor malfunctioning component or, much worse, to arrange a tow, is unlikely to be easy or cheap. When travelling to really remote areas it is advisable to travel with a high frequency outpost radio transmitter which is equipped to pick up the Royal Flying Doctor Service bases in the area.

You will of course need to carry a fair amount of water in case of disaster – around 20 litres a person is sensible – stored in more than one container. Food is less important – if space is tight it might be better allocated to an extra spare tyre.

The state automobile associations can advise on preparation, and supply maps and track notes. Most tracks have an ideal time of year – in the Centre it's not wise to attempt the tough tracks during the heat of summer (November-March) when the dust can be severe, chances of mechanical trouble are much greater and water will be scarce and hence a breakdown more dangerous. Similarly in the north, travelling in the wet season may be hindered by flooding and mud.

If you do run into trouble in the back of beyond, stay with your car. It's easier to spot a car than a human being from the air, and you wouldn't be able to carry your 20 litres of water very far anyway.

For the full story on safe outback travel, get hold of Lonely Planet's *Outback Australia*. Some of the favourite tracks are:

Birdsville Track Running 499 km from Marree in South Australia to Birdsville just across the border in Queensland, this is one of the best-known routes in Australia and these days is quite feasible in any well-prepared conventional vehicle.

Strzelecki Track This track covers much the same territory, starting south of Marree at Lyndhurst and going to Innamincka, 473 km north-east and close to the Queensland border. From there you can loop down

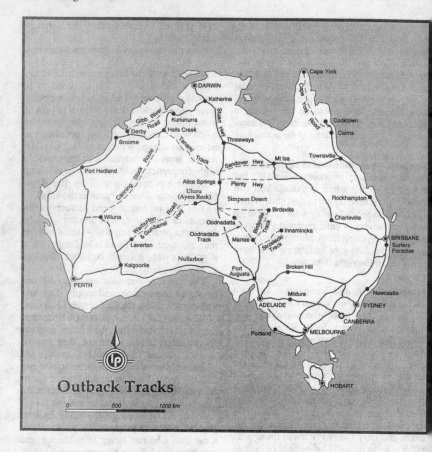

Outback Tracks

0   500   1000 km

to Tibooburra in New South Wales. The route has been much improved due to work on the Moomba gas fields. It was at Innamincka that the hapless early explorers Burke and Wills died.

Oodnadatta Track Parallel to the old Ghan railway line to Alice Springs, this track is comprehensively bypassed by the sealed Stuart Highway to the west and south. It's 465 km from Marree to Oodnadatta and another 202 km from there to the Stuart Highway at Marla. Any well-prepared vehicle should be able to manage this route.

Simpson Desert Crossing the Simpson Desert from Birdsville to the Stuart Highway is becoming

increasingly popular but this route is still a real test. Four-wheel drive is definitely required and you should be in a party of at least three or four vehicles equipped with long-range two-way radios.

Warburton Road/Gunbarrel Highway This route runs west from Uluru by the Aboriginal settlements of Docker River and Warburton to Laverton in Western Australia. From there you can drive down to Kalgoorlie and on to Perth. The route passes through Aboriginal reserves and permission to enter them must be obtained in advance if you want to leave the road. A well-prepared conventional vehicle can complete this route although ground clearance can be a problem and it is very remote. From the Yulara resort at Uluru to Warburton is 567 km, and it's another 568 km from there to Laverton. It's then

361 km on sealed road to Kalgoorlie. For 300 km near the Giles Meteorological Station the Warburton Road and the Gunbarrel Highway run on the same route. Taking the old Gunbarrel (to the north of the Warburton) all the way to Wiluna in Western Australia is a much rougher trip requiring 4WD. The Warburton Road is now commonly referred to as the Gunbarrel – just to make life simple.

Tanami Track Turning off the Stuart Highway just north of Alice Springs this track goes north-west across the Tanami Desert to Halls Creek in Western Australia. It's a popular short-cut for people travelling between the Centre and the Kimberley. The road has been extensively improved in recent years and conventional vehicles are quite OK although there are occasional sandy stretches on the WA section. Be warned that the Rabbit Flat roadhouse in the middle of the desert is only open from Friday to Monday.

Canning Stock Route This old stock trail runs south-west from Halls Creek to Wiluna in Western Australia. It crosses the Great Sandy Desert and Gibson Desert, and since the track has not been maintained for over 30 years it's a route to be taken seriously. Like the Simpson Desert crossing you should only travel in a well-equipped party and careful navigation is required.

Plenty & Sandover Highways These two routes run east from the Stuart Highway, to the north of Alice Springs, to Mt Isa in Queensland. They're suitable for conventional vehicles.

Cape York The Peninsula Developmental Road (Cape York Road) up to the top of Cape York, the farthest northerly point in Australia, is a popular route with a number of rivers to cross. It can only be attempted in the dry season when the water levels are lower. The original Cape York Road along the old telegraph line definitely requires 4WD. Conventional vehicles can take the new 'Heathlands' road to the east beyond the Wenlock River, which bypasses the most difficult sections, but the Wenlock River itself can be a formidable obstacle.

Gibb River Road This is the 'short cut' between Derby and Kununurra, and runs through the heart of the spectacular Kimberley in northern Western Australia. Although fairly badly corrugated in places, it can be easily negotiated by conventional vehicles in the dry season and is 720 km, compared with about 920 km via the bitumen Northern Highway.

Car Rental

If you've got the cash there are plenty of car-rental companies ready and willing to put you behind the wheel. Competition is pretty fierce so rates tend to be variable and lots of special deals pop up and disappear again. Whatever your mode of travel on the long stretches, it can be very useful to have a car for some local travel. Between a group it can even be reasonably economical. There are some places – like around Alice Springs – where if you haven't got your own transport you really have to choose between a tour and a rented vehicle since there is no public transport and the distances are too great for walking or even bicycles.

The three major companies are Budget, Hertz and Avis, with offices in almost every town that has more than one pub and a general store. A second-string company which is also represented almost everywhere in the country is Thrifty. Then there are a vast number of local firms, or firms with outlets in a limited number of locations. The big operators will generally have higher rates than the local firms but it ain't necessarily so, so don't jump to conclusions.

The big firms have a number of big advantages, however. First of all they're the ones at the airports – Avis, Budget, Hertz and, quite often, Thrifty, are represented at most. If you want to pick up a car or leave a car at the airport then they're the best ones to deal with. In some but not all airports other companies will also arrange to pick up or leave their cars there. It tends to depend on how convenient the airport is.

The second advantage is if you want to do a one-way rental – pick up a car in Adelaide and leave it in Sydney, for example. There are, however, a variety of restrictions on these. Usually it's a minimum-hire period rather than repositioning charges. Only certain cars may be eligible for one-ways. Check the small print on one-way charges before deciding on one company rather than another. One-way rentals are generally not available into or out of the Northern Territory or Western Australia.

The major companies offer a choice of deals, either unlimited km or a flat charge plus so many cents per km. On straightforward off-the-card city rentals they're all pretty much the same price. It's on special deals, odd rentals or longer periods that you find the differences. Weekend specials – usually three days for the price of two – are usually good value. If you just need a car for three days around Sydney make it the weekend rather than midweek. Budget offers 'stand-by' rates and you may see other special deals available.

Daily rates are typically about $50 a day for a small car (Holden Barina, Ford Festiva, Daihatsu Charade, Suzuki Swift), about $75 a day for a medium car (Mitsubishi Magna, Toyota Camry, Nissan Pulsar) or about $100 a day for a big car (Holden Commodore, Ford Falcon), all including insurance. You usually must be at least 21 years old to hire from most firms.

There is a whole collection of other factors to bear in mind about this rent-a-car business. For a start, if you're going to want it for a week, a month or longer then they all have lower rates. If you're in Tasmania there are often lower rates, especially in the low season. If you're in the really remote outback (places like Darwin and Alice Springs are only vaguely remote) then the choice of cars is likely to be limited to the larger, more expensive ones.

OK, that's the big hire companies, what about all the rest of them? Well, some of them are still pretty big in terms of numbers of shiny new cars. In Tasmania, for example, the car-hire business is huge since many people don't bring their cars with them. There's a plethora of hire companies and lots of competition. In many cases local companies are markedly cheaper than the big boys, but in others what looks like a cheaper rate can end up quite the opposite if you're not careful. In the Northern Territory, Territory Rent-a-Car is at least as big as the others, and its rates are very competitive.

And don't forget the 'rent-a-wreck' companies. They specialise in renting older cars and have a variety of rates, typically around $35 a day. If you just want to travel around the city, or not too far out, they can be worth considering.

Be aware when renting a car in Australia that if you are travelling on dirt roads you are generally not covered by insurance. So if you have an accident, you'll be liable for all the costs involved. This applies to all companies, although they don't always point this out. This does not apply to 4WDs.

4WD Rental Having 4WD enables you to get right off the beaten track and out to some of the great wilderness and outback places, to see some of the Australian natural wonders that most travellers don't see.

Renting a 4WD is within a reasonable budget range if a few people get together. Something small like a Suzuki or similar costs around $100 per day; for a Toyota Landcruiser you're looking at around $150, which should include insurance and some free km (typically 100 km per day). Check the insurance conditions, especially the excess, as they can be onerous – in the Northern Territory $4000 is typical, although this can often be reduced to around $1000 on payment of an additional daily charge (around $20). Even in a 4WD the insurance of most companies does not cover damage caused when travelling 'off-road', which basically means anything that is not a maintained bitumen or dirt road.

Hertz and Avis have 4WD rentals, with one-way rentals possible between the eastern states and the Northern Territory. Budget also rents 4WDs from Darwin and Alice Springs. Brits: Australia (☎ 1800 331 454) is a company which hires fully equipped 4WDs fitted out as campervans. These have proved extremely popular in recent years, although they are not cheap at $120 per day for unlimited km, plus Collision Damage Waiver ($15 per day). Brits: Australia has offices in all the mainland capitals, as well as in Cairns and Alice Springs, so one-way rentals are also possible.

Renting Other Vehicles There are lots of vehicles you can rent apart from cars and motorbikes. In many places you can rent campervans – they're particularly popular in Tasmania. Motorscooters are also available in a number of locations – they are popular on Magnetic Island and in Cairns for example – and you only need a car licence to ride one. Best of all, in many places you can rent bicycles.

Buying a Car

Australian cars are not cheap – a result of the small population. Locally manufactured cars are made in small, uneconomic numbers and imported cars are heavily taxed so they won't undercut the local products. If you're buying a second-hand vehicle reliability is all important. Mechanical breakdowns way out in the outback can be very inconvenient (not to mention dangerous) – the nearest mechanic can be a hell of a long way down the road.

Shopping around for a used car involves much the same rules as anywhere in the Western world but with a few local variations. First of all, used-car dealers in Australia are just like used-car dealers from Los Angeles to London – they'd sell their mother into slavery if it turned a dollar. You'll probably get any car cheaper by buying privately through newspaper small ads rather than through a car dealer. Buying through a dealer does have the advantage of some sort of guarantee, but a guarantee is not much use if you're buying a car in Sydney and intend setting off for Perth next week. Used-car guarantee requirements vary from state to state – check with the local automobile organisation.

There's a great deal of discussion amongst travellers about where the best place is to buy used cars. It's quite possible that prices do vary but don't count on turning it to your advantage. See the section on buying cars in Sydney for the situation at that popular starting/finishing point.

What is rather more certain is that the farther you get from civilisation, the better it is to be in a Holden or a Ford. New cars can be a whole different ball game of course, but if you're in an older vehicle that's likely to have the odd hiccup from time to time, life is much simpler if it's a car for which you can get spare parts anywhere from Bourke to

Bulamakanka. When your fancy Japanese car goes kaput somewhere back of Bourke it's likely to be a two-week wait while the new bit arrives fresh from Fukuoka. On the other hand, when your rusty old Holden goes bang there's probably another old Holden sitting in a ditch with a perfectly good widget waiting to be removed.

In Australia third-party personal injury insurance is always included in the vehicle registration cost. This ensures that every vehicle (as long as it's currently registered) carries at least minimum insurance. You'd be wise to extend that minimum to at least third-party property insurance as well – minor collisions with Rolls-Royces can be amazingly expensive.

When you come to buy or sell a car there are usually some local regulations. In Victoria, for example, a car has to have a compulsory safety check (Road Worthiness Certificate – RWC) before it can be registered in the new owner's name – usually the seller will indicate if the car already has an RWC. In New South Wales and the Northern Territory, on the other hand, safety checks are compulsory every year when you come to renew the registration. Stamp duty has to be paid when you buy a car and, as this is based on the purchase price, it's not unknown for buyer and seller to agree privately to understate the price! It's much easier to sell a car in the same state that it's registered in, otherwise you must re-register in the new state. It may be possible to sell a car without re-registering it, but you're likely to get a lower price.

One way of getting around the hassles of buying and selling a vehicle privately is to enter into a buy-back arrangement with a car or motorcycle dealer. However, dealers will often find ways of knocking down the price when you return the vehicle, even if a price has been agreed in writing – often by pointing out expensive repairs that allegedly will be required to gain the dreaded RWC needed to transfer the registration. The cars on offer have often been driven around Australia a number of times, often with haphazard or minimal servicing, and are generally pretty tired. The main advantage of these schemes is that you don't have to worry about being able to sell the vehicle quickly at the end of your trip, and can usually arrange insurance, which short-term visitors may find hard to get. See the Sydney Getting There & Away section in the New South Wales chapter for more details.

A company that specialises in buy-back arrangements on cars and motorcycles, with fixed rates and no hidden extras, is Car Connection Australia (☎ (03) 5473 4469; fax (03) 5473 4520). Here a second-hand Ford Falcon or Holden Kingswood station wagon or Yamaha XT600 trail bike will set you back a fixed sum of $1950 for any period up to six months; a Toyota Landcruiser, suitable for serious outback exploration, is $3500, also for up to six months. Information and bookings are handled by its European agent: Travel Action GmbH (☎ (0276) 47824; fax 7938), Einsiedeleiweg 16, 57399 Kirchhundem, Germany.

Finally, make use of automobile organisations. They can advise you on local regulations you should be aware of, give general guidelines about buying a car and, most importantly, for a fee (around $70) will check over a used car and report on its condition before you agree to purchase it. They also offer car insurance to their members. See the Facts for the Visitor chapter for more details.

MOTORBIKE

Motorbikes are a very popular way of getting around. The climate is just about ideal for biking much of the year, and the many small trails from the road into the bush often lead to perfect spots to spend the night.

The long, open roads are really made for large-capacity machines above 750 cc, which Australians prefer once they outgrow their 250 cc learner restrictions. But that doesn't stop enterprising individuals from tackling the length and breadth of the continent on 250 cc trail bikes. Doing it on a small bike is not impossible, just tedious at times.

If you want to bring your own motorcycle into Australia you'll need a *carnet de passages*, and when you try to sell it you'll get less than the market price because of restrictive registration requirements (not so severe in Western Australia, South Australia and the Northern Territory). Shipping from just about anywhere is expensive.

However, with a little bit of time up your sleeve, getting mobile on two wheels in Australia is quite feasible, thanks largely to the chronically depressed motorcycle market. The beginning of the southern winter is a good time to strike. Australian newspapers and the lively local bike press have extensive classified advertisement sections where $2500 gets you something that will easily take you around the country if you know a bit about bikes. The main drawback is that you'll have to try and sell it again afterwards.

An easier option is a buy-back arrangement with a large motorcycle dealer in a major city (Elizabeth St in Melbourne is a good hunting ground). They're keen to do business, and basic negotiating skills allied with a wad of cash (say, $4000) should secure an excellent second-hand bike with a written guarantee that they'll buy it back in good condition minus $1500 or $2000 after your four-month, round-Australia trip. Popular brands are BMWs, large-capacity, shaft-driven Japanese bikes and possibly Harley-Davidsons (very popular in Australia). The percentage drop on a trail bike will be much greater (though the actual amount you lose should be similar), but very few dealers are interested in buy-back schemes on trail bikes.

You'll need a rider's licence and a helmet. Some motorcyclists in New South Wales have special permission to ride without a helmet, ostensibly for medical reasons. A fuel range of 350 km will cover fuel stops up the Centre and on Highway 1 around the continent. Beware of dehydration in the dry, hot air – force yourself to drink plenty of water, even if you don't feel thirsty. If riding in Tasmania (a top cycling and motorcycling destination) you should be prepared for rotten weather in winter, and rain any time of year.

The 'roo bars' (outsize bumpers) seen on

interstate trucks and many outback cars tell you one thing: never ride on the open road from early evening until after dawn. Marsupials are nocturnal, sleeping in the shade during the day and feeding at night, and road ditches often provide lush grass. Cows and sheep also stray onto the roads at night. It's wise to stop riding by around 5 pm.

Many roadhouses offer showers free of charge or for a nominal fee. They're meant for truck drivers, but other people often use them too.

It's worth carrying some spares and tools even if you don't know how to use them, because someone else often does. If you do know, you'll probably have a fair idea of what to take. The basics include: a spare tyre tube (front wheel size, which will fit on the rear but usually not vice versa); puncture repair kit with levers and a pump (or tubeless tyre repair kit with at least three carbon dioxide cartridges); a spare tyre valve, and a valve cap that can unscrew same; the bike's standard tool kit for what it's worth (aftermarket items are better); spare throttle, clutch and brake cables; tie wire, cloth tape ('gaffer' tape) and nylon 'zip-ties'; a handful of bolts and nuts in the usual emergency sizes (M6 and M8), along with a few self-tapping screws; one or two fuses in your bike's ratings; a bar of soap for fixing tank leaks (knead to a putty with water and squeeze into the leak); and, most important of all, a workshop manual for your bike (even if you can't make sense of it, the local motorcycle mechanic can). You'll never have enough elastic (octopus) straps to tie down your gear.

Make sure you carry water – at least two litres on major roads in central Australia, more off the beaten track. And finally, if something does go hopelessly wrong in the back of beyond, park your bike where it's clearly visible and observe the cardinal rule: *don't leave your vehicle*.

BICYCLE

Whether you're hiring a bike to ride around a city or wearing out your Bio-Ace chainwheels on a Melbourne-Darwin marathon, you'll find that Australia is a great place for cycling. There are bike tracks in most cities, and in the country you'll find thousands of km of good roads which carry so little traffic that the biggest hassle is waving back to the drivers. Especially appealing is that in many areas you'll ride a very long way without encountering a hill.

Bicycle helmets are compulsory wear in all states and territories.

It's possible to plan rides of any duration and through almost any terrain. A day or two cycling around South Australia's wineries is popular, or you could meander along beside the Murrumbidgee River for weeks. Tasmania is very popular for touring, and mountain bikers would love Australia's deserts – or its mountains, for that matter.

Cycling has always been popular here, and not only as a sport: some shearers would ride for huge distances between jobs, rather than use less reliable horses. It's rare to find a reasonably sized town that doesn't have a shop stocking at least basic bike parts.

If you're coming specifically to cycle, it makes sense to bring your own bike. Check your airline for costs and the degree of dismantling/packing required. Within Australia you can load your bike onto a bus or train to skip the boring bits. Note that bus companies require you to dismantle your bike, and some don't guarantee that it will travel on the same bus as you. Trains are easier, but supervise the loading and if possible tie your bike upright, otherwise you may find that the guard has stacked crates of Holden spares on your fragile alloy wheels.

You can buy a good steel-framed touring bike in Australia for about $400 (plus panniers). It may be possible to rent touring bikes and equipment from a few of the commercial touring organisations.

Much of eastern Australia seems to have been settled on the principle of not having more than a day's horse ride between pubs, so it's possible to plan even ultralong routes and still get a shower at the end of the day. Most people do carry camping equipment, but, on the east coast at least, it's feasible to travel from town to town staying in hostels, hotels or on-site vans.

You can get by with standard road maps, but as you'll probably want to avoid both the highways and the low-grade unsealed roads, the Government series is best. The 1:250,000 scale is the most suitable but you'll need a lot of maps if you're covering much territory. The next scale up, 1:1,000,000, is adequate. They are available in capital cities and elsewhere.

Until you get fit you should be careful to eat enough to keep you going – remember that exercise is an appetite suppressant. It's surprisingly easy to be so depleted of energy that you end up camping under a gum tree just 10 km short of a shower and a steak.

No matter how fit you are, water is vital. Dehydration is no joke and can be life threatening. One Lonely Planet author rode his first 200-km-in-a-day on a bowl of cornflakes and a round of sandwiches, but the Queensland sun forced him to drink nearly five litres. Having been involved in a drinking contest with stockmen the night before may have had something to do with it, though.

It can get very hot in summer, and you should take things slowly until you're used to the heat. Cycling in 35°C-plus temperatures isn't too bad if you wear a hat and plenty of sunscreen, and drink *lots* of water. In the eastern states, be aware of the blistering hot 'northerlies', the prevailing winds that make a north-bound cyclist's life uncomfortable in summer. In April, when the south-east's clear autumn weather begins, the Southerly Trades prevail, and you can have (theoretically at least) tailwinds all the way to Darwin.

Of course, you don't have to follow the larger roads and visit towns. It's possible to fill your mountain bike's panniers with muesli, head out into the mulga, and not see anyone for weeks. Or ever again – outback travel is very risky if not properly planned. Water is the main problem in the 'dead heart', and you can't rely on it where there aren't settlements. That tank marked on your map may be dry or the water from it unfit for humans, and those station buildings probably blew away years ago. That little creek

marked with a dotted blue line? Forget it – the only time it has water is when the country's flooded for hundreds of km.

Always check with locals if you're heading into remote areas, and notify the police if you're about to do something particularly adventurous. That said, you can't rely too much on local knowledge of road conditions – most people have no idea of what a heavily loaded touring bike needs. What they think of as a great road may be pedal-deep in sand or bull dust, and cyclists have happily ridden along roads that were officially flooded out.

Useful Organisations

In each state there are touring organisations which can help with information and put you in touch with touring clubs:

Australian Capital Territory
    Pedal Power ACT, PO Box 581, Canberra, ACT 2601 (☎ (06) 248 7995)
New South Wales
    Bicycle Institute of New South Wales, 209 Castlereagh St, Sydney, NSW 2000 (☎ (02) 9283 5200)
Queensland
    Bicycle Institute of Queensland, 491 Stanley St, South Brisbane, Qld 4102 (☎ (07) 3844 1144)
South Australia
    Bicycle Institute of South Australia, GPO Box 792, Adelaide 5000 (☎ (08) 8346 7534)
Tasmania
    Pedal Power Tasmania, c/o Environment Centre, 102 Bathurst St, Hobart, Tas 7000 (☎ (03) 6234 5566)
Victoria
    Bicycle Victoria, 19 O'Connell St, North Melbourne, Vic 3051 (☎ (03) 9328 3000)
Western Australia
    Cycle Touring Association, PO Box 174, Wembley, WA 6014 (☎ (09) 382 1961)

There are many organised tours available of varying lengths, and if you get tired of talking to sheep as you ride along, it might be a good idea to include one or more tours in your itinerary. Most provide a support vehicle and take care of accommodation and cooking, so they can be a nice break from solo chores.

HITCHING

Hitching is never entirely safe in any country in the world. It is in fact illegal in most states of Australia (which doesn't stop people doing it) and we don't recommend it. Travellers who decide to hitch should understand that they are taking a small but potentially serious risk. Australia is not exempt from danger (Queensland in particular is notorious for attacks on women travellers), and even people hitching in pairs are not entirely safe. Before deciding to hitch, talk to local people about the dangers, and it is a good idea to let someone know where you are planning to hitch to before you set off. If you do choose to hitch, the advice that follows should help to make your journey as fast and safe as possible.

Factor one for safety and speed is numbers. More than two people hitching together will make things very difficult, and solo hitching is unwise for men as well as women. Two women hitching together may be vulnerable, and two men hitching together can expect long waits. The best option is for a woman and a man to hitch together.

Factor two is position – look for a place where vehicles will be going slowly and where they can stop easily. A junction or freeway slip road is a good place if there is stopping room. Position goes beyond just where you stand. The ideal location is on the outskirts of a town – hitching from way out in the country is as hopeless as from the centre of a city. Take a bus out to the edge of town.

Factor three is appearance. The ideal appearance for hitching is a sort of genteel poverty – threadbare but clean. Don't carry too much gear – if it looks like it's going to take half an hour to pack your bags aboard you'll be left on the roadside.

Factor four is knowing when to say no. Saying no to a car-load of drunks is pretty obvious, but you should also be prepared to abandon a ride if you begin to feel uneasy for any reason. Don't sit there hoping for the best; make an excuse and get out at the first opportunity.

It can be time-saving to say no to a short ride that might take you from a good hitching point to a lousy one. Wait for the right, long ride to come along. On a long haul, it's pointless to start walking as it's not likely to increase the likelihood of your getting a lift and it's often an awfully long way to the next town.

Trucks are often the best lifts but they will only stop if they are going slowly and can get started easily again. Thus the ideal place is at the top of a hill where they have a downhill run. Truckies often say they are going to the next town and if they don't like you, will drop you anywhere. As they often pick up hitchers for company, the quickest way to create a bad impression is to jump in and fall asleep. It's also worth remembering that while you're in someone else's vehicle, you are their guest and should act accordingly – many drivers no longer pick up people because they have suffered from thoughtless hitchers in the past. It's the hitcher's duty to provide entertainment!

Of course people do get stuck in outlandish places but that is the name of the game. If you're visiting from abroad a nice prominent flag on your pack will help, and a sign announcing your destination can also be useful. Uni and hostel notice boards are good places to look for hitching partners. The main law against hitching is 'thou shalt not stand in the road' – so when you see the law coming, step back.

Just as hitchers should be wary when accepting lifts, drivers who pick up fellow travellers to share the costs should also be aware of the risks involved.

BOAT

Not really. Once upon a time there was quite a busy coastal shipping service but now it only applies to freight, and apart from specialised bulk carriers, even that is declining rapidly. The only regular shipping service is between Victoria and Tasmania and unless you are taking a vehicle with you the very cheapest ticket on that often-choppy route is not all that much cheaper than the air fare. You can occasionally travel between

Australian ports on a liner bound for somewhere but very few people do that.

On the other hand it *is* quite possible to make your way round the coast or even to other countries like New Zealand, Papua New Guinea or Indonesia by hitching rides or crewing on yachts. Ask around at harbours, marinas or yacht or sailing clubs. Good places on the east coast include Coffs Harbour, Great Keppel Island, Airlie Beach/Whitsundays, Cairns – anywhere where boats call. Usually you have to chip in something for food.

A lot of boats move north to escape the winter, so April is a good time to look for a berth in the Sydney area.

TOURS

There are all sorts of tours around Australia including some interesting camping tours. Adventure tours include 4WD safaris in the Northern Territory and up into far north Queensland. Some of these go to places you simply couldn't get to on your own without large amounts of expensive equipment. You can also walk, ski, boat, raft, canoe, ride a horse or camel or even fly.

YHA tours are good value – find out about them at YHA Travel offices in capital cities (see Accommodation in the Facts for the Visitor chapter for addresses). In major centres like Sydney, Darwin and Cairns there are many tours aimed at backpackers – good prices, good destinations, good fun.

There are several good operators offering organised motorcycling tours in Australia. One of these is Bike Tours Australia, which also operates under the name Car Connection Australia (see Buying a Car in this chapter for contact details). Another company which offers tours as well as a motorcycle sell-and-buy-back scheme is Australian Motorcycle Adventures (☎ (07) 3865 3176; fax 3865 3154) at Unit 2, 58 Pritchard Rd, Virginia, Brisbane, Qld 4014.

STUDENT TRAVEL

STA Travel is the main agent for student travellers in Australia. They have a network of travel offices around the country and apart from selling normal tickets also have special student discounts and tours. STA Travel doesn't only cater to students, they also act as normal travel agents to the public in general. The STA Travel head office is in Melbourne, but there are a number of other offices around the various cities and at the universities. The national telephone sales number is ☎ 1800 637 444, and the main offices are:

Australian Capital Territory
    Shop 208, Level 3, Westfield Shopping Mall, Belconnen, ACT 2616 (☎ (06) 251 4688
New South Wales
    1st floor, 732 Harris St, Ultimo, Sydney 2077 (☎ (02) 9212 1255)
Northern Territory
    Shop T17, Smith St Mall, Darwin 0800 (☎ (08) 8941 2955)
Queensland
    Shop 25-26, Brisbane Arcade, 111 Adelaide St, Brisbane 4000 (☎ (07) 3221 3722)
South Australia
    235 Rundle St, Adelaide 5000 (☎ (08) 8223 2426)
Victoria
    224 Faraday St, Carlton, Melbourne 3053 (☎ (03) 9349 2411)
Western Australia
    100 James St, Northbridge, Perth 6003 (☎ (09) 227 7569)

Australian Capital Territory

HIGHLIGHTS

- Taking a tour of the grass-topped Parliament House
- Following the Aboriginal plant trail through the National Botanic Gardens
- Listening to a Carillon recital from the sculpture garden of the National Gallery
- Cooling your inline-skating heels at Captain Cook Water Jet
- Going koala-spotting in the Tidbinbilla Nature Reserve
- Cycling around Lake Burley Griffin
- Camping in the dense forest of Namadgi National Park

Population 300,000
Area 2366 sq km

When the separate colonies of Australia were federated in 1901 and became states, the decision to build a national capital was part of the Constitution. The site was selected in 1908, diplomatically situated between arch rivals Sydney and Melbourne, and an international competition to design the capital was won by the American architect Walter Burley Griffin. In 1911 the Commonwealth government bought land for the Australian Capital Territory (ACT) and in 1913 decided to call the capital Canberra, believed to be an Aboriginal term for 'meeting place'.

Development of the site was slow and it was not until 1927 that parliament was first convened in the capital. From 1901 until then, Melbourne was the seat of the national government. The Depression virtually halted development and things really only got under way after WW II. In 1960 the population topped 50,000, reaching 100,000 by 1967. Today the ACT has just on 300,000 people and it is the fastest growing state or territory in Australia.

Canberra

Population 295,000

Canberra is well worth visiting. Some of the best architecture and exhibitions in Australia are here and the whole city is fascinating because it is totally planned and orderly. It also has a beautiful setting, surrounded by hills, and is close to good bushwalking and skiing country. It is a place of government with few local industries and it has that unique, stimulating atmosphere that's only to be found in national capitals.

Canberra has all the furnishings of a true centre of national life – like the exciting National Gallery, the splendid Parliament House and the excellent National Botanic Gardens. What's more, Canberra has quite a young population, including a lot of students, and it is livelier than we're usually led to expect. Finally, this is the only city in Australia where it really is possible to bump into kangaroos – they've been spotted swimming across Lake Burley Griffin and grazing in the grounds of Parliament House.

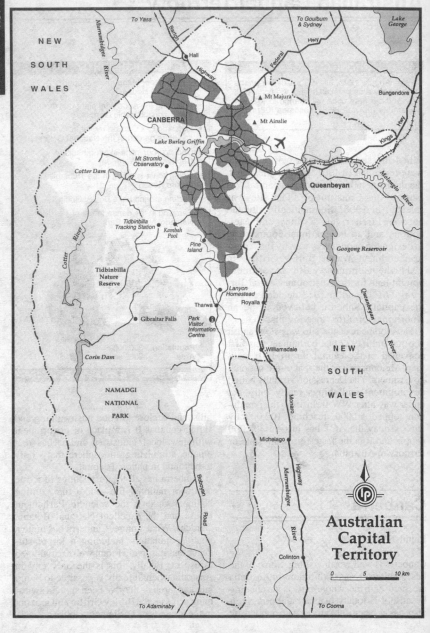

Australian Capital Territory

Orientation

Civic, the city centre, is on the northern side of Lake Burley Griffin (an artificial waterway). Civic's centre is Vernon Circle and the nearby post office, banks and bus terminals. The pedestrian malls east of the circle are Canberra's main shopping areas. The mirror-image Sydney and Melbourne buildings flank the beginning of Northbourne Ave, the main artery north of the lake.

From Vernon Circle, Commonwealth Ave runs south over the Commonwealth Ave Bridge to Capital Circle, which surrounds the new Parliament House on Capital Hill. Capital Circle is the apex of Burley Griffin's parliamentary triangle, formed by Commonwealth Ave, Kings Ave (crossing the lake on the northeastern side) and the lake. Many important buildings are concentrated within this triangle, including the National Library, the High Court, the National Gallery and Old Parliament House. South-east of Capital Hill is Manuka Circle, a pleasant shopping and dining district.

As well as the many neighbourhoods (Canberra's basic unit of urban structure) north and south of the lake, the city includes the large 'towns' of Belconnen, Woden and Tuggeranong.

Information

Tourist Office The information centre (☎ 1800 026 166) is on Northbourne Ave, Dickson, about two km north of Vernon Circle. It's open daily from 9 am to 5 pm (from 8.30 am on weekends). There are free phones to call various places to book accommodation. There's also a small information booth in the Canberra Centre shopping mall.

There's a Women's Information and Referral Centre (☎ 205 1075) on the corner of London Circuit and Petrie Plaza.

Tune to 98.9 FM for tourist information.

Post & Telecommunications Have mail addressed to poste restante at the Canberra City Post Office on Alinga St, Civic. There are plenty of payphones here. Canberra's STD area code is 06 (until August 1997).

Foreign Embassies There are about 60 embassies and high commissions in Canberra.

A few are worth looking at, although many operate from rather nondescript suburban houses. Most are in Yarralumla, west and north of Parliament House. On the Sundays of long weekends in January (Australia Day), June (Queen's Birthday) and October (Labour Day) there are embassy open days, when you can visit a few of them for about $5.

The US Embassy is a facsimile of a southern mansion, in the style of those in Williamsburg, Virginia. Just opposite is the Mughal-inspired High Commission of India. The Thai Embassy, with its pointed, orange-tiled roof, is in a style similar to that of temples in Bangkok. Papua New Guinea's high commission looks like a 'haus tambaran' spirit-house from PNG's Sepik region. A display room with photos and artefacts is open weekdays from 9 am to 1 pm and 2 to 5 pm.

Embassy and high commission addresses include:

Canada
    Commonwealth Ave, Yarralumla (☎ 273 3844)
China
    15 Coronation Drive, Yarralumla (☎ 273 4878)
Germany
    119 Empire Circuit, Yarralumla (☎ 270 1911)
India
    3 Moonah Place, Yarralumla (☎ 273 3999)
Indonesia
    8 Darwin Ave, Yarralumla (☎ 250 8600)
Israel
    6 Turrana St, Yarralumla (☎ 273 1309)
Japan
    112 Empire Circuit, Yarralumla (☎ 273 3244)
Malaysia
    7 Perth Ave, Yarralumla (☎ 273 1543)
Netherlands
    120 Empire Circuit, Yarralumla (☎ 273 3111)
New Zealand
    Commonwealth Ave, Yarralumla (☎ 270 4211)
Norway
    17 Hunter St, Yarralumla (☎ 273 3444)
Papua New Guinea
    39 Forster Crescent, Yarralumla (☎ 273 3322)
South Africa
    Corner State Circle and Rhodes Place, Yarralumla (☎ 273 2424)
Thailand
    111 Empire Circuit, Yarralumla (☎ 273 1149)
UK
    Commonwealth Ave, Yarralumla (☎ 270 6666)
USA
    21 Moonah Place, Yarralumla (☎ 270 5000)

ACT

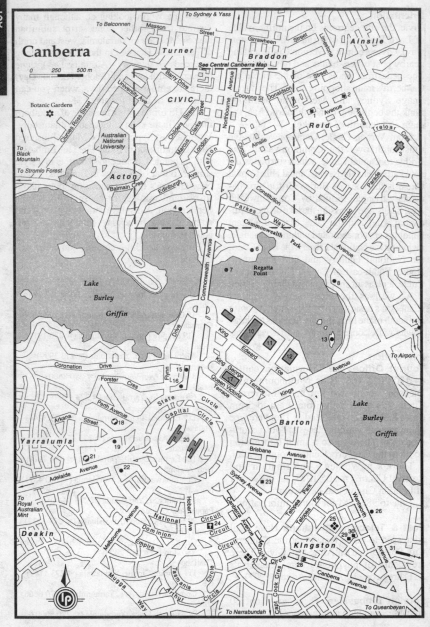

Canberra

0   250   500 m

Botanic Gardens

To Black Mountain

To Stromlo Forest

To Belconnen

To Sydney & Yass

Masson   Street

Girrawheen   Street

Turner   Braddon

Ainslie

See Central Canberra Map

Barry Drive

University Ave

CIVIC

Childers Street

Clarke Street

Marcus

London

Ave

Vernon

Circle

Northbourne   Avenue

Cooyong St

Donaldson

Ainslie

Street

Limestone

Street

Avenue

Reid

Treloar Cres

Clunies Ross Street

Australian National University

Acton

Balmain Cres

Edinburgh   Ave

Parade

Anzac

Constitution

Parkes   Way

Commonwealth   Park

Avenue

Commonwealth   Avenue

Lake Burley Griffin

Drive

King   Edward

Regatta Point

King   George   Terrace

Queen Victoria   Terrace

Tce

Kings   Avenue

To Airport

Lake Burley Griffin

Coronation   Drive

Forster   Cres

Flynn

State   Circle

Capital   Circle

Perth Avenue

Arkana

Street

Yarralumla

Barton

Brisbane   Avenue

Adelaide   Avenue

To Royal Australian Mint

Deakin

Melbourne   Avenue

National

Dominion   Circuit

Empire   Circuit

Mugga   Way

Arthur   Circle

Tasmania   Circle

Hobart   Ave

Canberra   Avenue

Sydney Avenue

Manuka   Circle

Capt. Cook Cres

Kingston

Telopea   Park

Wentworth   Avenue

To Narrabundah

To Queanbeyan

To Sydney & Yass

PLACES TO STAY

1	Acacia Motor Lodge
2	Olim's Canberra Hotel
23	Macquarie Private Hotel
28	Kingston Hotel
29	Motel Monaro
30	Victor Lodge

OTHER

3	War Memorial
4	Acton Park Ferry Terminal, Bike & Boat Hire
5	Church of St John the Baptist
6	National Capital Exhibition
7	Captain Cook Memorial Water Jet
8	Blundell's Farmhouse
9	National Library
10	National Science and Technology Centre
11	High Court
12	National Gallery
13	Carillon
14	Australian–American Memorial
15	UK High Commission
16	PNG High Commission
17	Old Parliament House
18	US Embassy
19	India High Commission
20	Parliament House (on Capital Hill)
21	Thai Embassy
22	The Lodge
24	Serbian Orthodox Church
25	Kingston Shopping Centre
26	Old Bus Depot Market
27	Manuka Shopping Centre
31	Train Station

Bookshops There are many good bookshops. Dalton's, on the corner of Rudd and Marcus Clarke Sts, and Paperchain, on Furneaux St in Manuka, are two of the best. The Ocean Bookshop in Garema Place is small, select and superb and there's an excellent second-hand bookshop in Lyneham shopping centre.

The Commonwealth Government Bookshop, on the northern side of the Melbourne Building, has handy publications plus some glossy books that make good souvenirs. Canberra is well stocked with overseas information centres and libraries – good places to keep up with foreign news.

Maps The NRMA (☎ 243 8800) at 92 Northbourne Ave has excellent maps of Canberra. For topographic maps of the ACT try the information centre, or the ACT Government City Shopfront near the Civic bus interchange. Travellers Maps & Guides is in the Jolimont Centre on Northbourne Ave.

Medical Services There's a Traveller's Medical & Vaccination Centre (☎ 257 7156) upstairs in the City Walk Arcade, near the Civic bus interchange. It's open weekdays from 9 am to 5 pm. There are several other clinics nearby.

Emergency Emergency phone numbers are ☎ 000 for ambulance, fire and police; ☎ 257 1111 for Lifeline (emergency counselling); and ☎ 247 2525 for the Rape Crisis Centre.

Lookouts

There are fine views of Canberra from the surrounding hills. West of Civic, **Black Mountain** rises to 812 metres and is topped by the 195-metre Telstra Telecommunications Tower, complete with a revolving restaurant. There's also a display on telecommunications history. The tower is open daily from 9 am to 10 pm ($3). There are also splendid vistas from the approach road. Bus No 904 runs to the tower or you can walk there along a two-km trail through bush, starting on Frith Rd. Other bushwalks, accessible from Belconnen Way and Caswell Drive, wander round the back of the mountain. The information centre has a brochure with a map.

Other lookouts, all with road access, are **Mt Ainslie** (843 metres), **Red Hill** (720 metres) and **Mt Pleasant** (663 metres). Mt Ainslie is close to the city on the north-eastern side and has particularly fine views, day or night. There are foot trails up Mt Ainslie from behind the War Memorial, and out behind Mt Ainslie to **Mt Majura** (888 metres) four km away. You may see a kangaroo or two on the hike up.

Lake Burley Griffin

The lake was named after Canberra's designer but was not created until the Molonglo River was dammed in 1963. Swimming in the lake is not recommended

Liz & Phil and the Republican Debate

The republican debate is well up there with the major issues keeping Australian politicians in Canberra busy. It's certainly an issue that arouses high passions in many people, as demonstrated when a Melbourne artist displayed a sculpture of the Queen and Prince Phillip on a park bench *(Down by the Lake with Liz & Phil)*. This in itself was nothing to get worked up about; what some people took issue with was that, between the two of them, the Queen's crown jewels were all that the royal pair had on! Within a very short time the ire of monarchists was raised and, to add injury to insult, an anarchistic vandal beheaded the Queen.

Further lunacy followed when an off-duty Sydney police sergeant – in what he described as 'an act of loyalty' – drove the four hours to Canberra and attempted to clothe the figures in T-shirts and a quilt! ■

but you can go boating (beware of sudden strong winds) or cycle around it. You can hire boats, bikes and inline skating at the Acton Park Ferry Terminal, on the northern side of the lake.

There are a number of places of interest around the 35-km shore. The most visible is the **Captain Cook Memorial Water Jet** which flings a six-tonne column of water 140 metres into the air, and will give you a free shower if the wind is blowing from the right direction (despite an automatic switch-off which is supposed to operate if the wind speed gets too high). The jet, built in 1970 to commemorate the bicentenary of Captain Cook's visit to Australia, operates daily from 10 am to noon and 2 to 4 pm and, during daylight saving time, from 7 to 9 pm. At **Regatta Point**, nearby on the north shore, is a skeleton globe with Cook's three great voyages traced on it.

The **National Capital Exhibition**, also at Regatta Point, is open daily from 9 am to 5 pm (to 6 pm in summer) and has displays on the growth of the capital. It's free and interesting. Farther around the lake, to the east, is **Blundell's Farmhouse** (c1860). The simple stone and slab cottage is a reminder of the area's early farming history and is open daily except Monday ($2).

A little farther around the lake at the far end of Commonwealth Park, which stretches east from the Commonwealth Ave Bridge, is the **Carillon**, on Aspen Island. The 53-bell tower was a gift from Britain in 1963, Canberra's 50th anniversary. The bells weigh from seven kg to six tonnes. There are recitals on Wednesday from 12.45 to 1.30 pm and on weekends and public holidays from 2.45 to 3.30 pm.

The southern shore of the lake, along which the impressive National Gallery and High Court are situated, forms the base of the parliamentary triangle.

Parliament House

South of the lake, the four-legged flag mast on top of Capital Hill marks Parliament House. This, the most recent aspect of Burley Griffin's vision to become a reality, sits at the apex of the parliamentary triangle, at the end of Commonwealth Ave. Opened in 1988, it cost $1.1 billion, took eight years to build and replaced the 'temporary' parliament house lower down the hill on King George Terrace, which served for 11 years longer than its intended 50-year life. The new Parliament was designed by the US-based Italian Romaldo Giurgola, who won a competition entered by more than 300 architects.

It's built into the top of the hill and the roof has been grassed over to preserve the shape of the original hilltop. The interior design and decoration is splendid. A different combination of Australian timbers is used in each of the principal sections. Seventy Australian art and craft works were commissioned and a further 3000 were bought.

The building's main axis runs north-east to south-west, in a direct line from the old parliament, the War Memorial across the lake, and Mt Ainslie. On either side of this axis two high, granite-faced walls curve out from the centre to the corners of the site. The House of Representatives is to the east of these walls, the Senate to the west. They're linked to the centre by covered walkways.

Extensive areas of Parliament House are open to the public daily from 9 am to 5 pm. You enter through the white marble Great Verandah at the north-eastern end of the main axis, where Michael Tjakamarra Nelson's *Meeting Place* mosaic, within the pool, represents a gathering of Aboriginal tribes. Inside, the grey-green marble columns of the foyer symbolise a forest, while marquetry panels on the walls depict Australian flora. From the 1st floor you look down on the Great Hall, with its 20-metre-long Arthur Boyd tapestry. A public gallery above the Great Hall has a 16-metre-long embroidery, created by over 500 people.

Beyond the Great Hall you reach the gallery above the Members' Hall, the central 'crossroads' of the building, with the flag mast above it and passages to the debating chambers on each side. One of only four known originals of the Magna Carta is on display here. South of the Members' Hall are the committee rooms and ministers' offices. The public can view the committee rooms and attend some of the proceedings.

Other visitor facilities include a cafeteria, a terrace with views over the city, and a small theatre telling the story of Australian democracy. You can also wander over the grassy top of the building. If you want to make sure of a place in the House of Representatives gallery, book by phone (☎ 277 4890) or write to the Principal Attendant, House of Representatives, Parliament House, Canberra. Some seats are left unbooked but on sitting days you'd have to queue early to get one. Seats in the Senate gallery are almost always available.

There are free guided tours every half-hour, somewhat curtailed on sitting days.

Bus Nos 901, 234 and 352 run from the city to Parliament House.

Old Parliament House

On King George Terrace, halfway between the new Parliament House and the lake, this building was the seat of government from 1927 to 1988. Its parliamentary days ended in style: as the corridors of power echoed to the defence minister's favourite Rolling Stones records, the prime minister and leader of the Opposition sang together arm in arm, and bodies were seen dragging themselves away well after dawn the next morning – and that's just what got into print! There are tours of the building and regular exhibitions in the old parliamentary library.

Old Parliament House is now home to the **National Portrait Gallery** (☎ 273 5130). The gallery is open daily from 9 am to 4 pm. Temporary exhibitions from the National Museum's archives are also staged here. The admission charge ($2) covers all the exhibits.

National Gallery of Australia

At the bottom of the parliamentary triangle, on Parkes Place, beside the High Court and Lake Burley Griffin, is the excellent art gallery, which opened in 1982. The Australian collection ranges from traditional Aboriginal art through to 20th-century works by Arthur Boyd, Sidney Nolan and Albert Tucker. Aboriginal works include bark paintings from Arnhem Land, *pukumani* burial poles from the Tiwi people of Melville and Bathurst islands off Darwin, printed fabrics by the women of Utopia and Ernabella in central Australia, and paintings from Yuendumu, also in central Australia. There are often temporary exhibitions from the Kimberley and other areas where Aboriginal art is flourishing.

In addition to works from the early decades of European settlement and the 19th-century romantics, there are examples of the early nationalistic statements of Charles Conder, Arthur Streeton and Tom Roberts. The collection is not confined to paintings: sculptures, prints, drawings, photographs, furniture, ceramics, fashion, textiles and silverware are all on display. The Sculpture Garden, which is always open, has

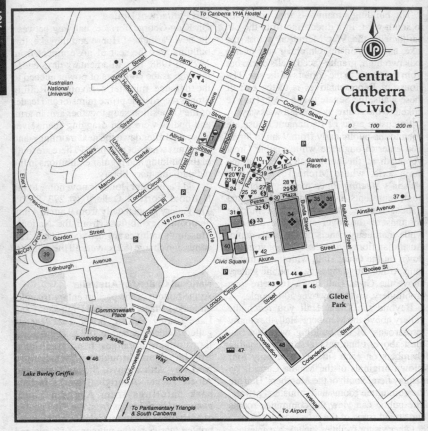

a variety of striking sculptures. The garden is a great place to listen to Carillon recitals.

The gallery is open daily from 10 am to 5 pm. Admission is $3 (free for children and full-time students). There are tours at 11 am and 2 pm. Every Thursday and Sunday at 11 am there is a free tour focusing on Aboriginal art. Free lectures are given on Wednesday and Thursday at 12.45 pm and most weekends at 2 pm. Most Friday afternoons there is a free film screening. Phone the gallery for details (☎ 240 6411) or check Saturday's *Canberra Times*. There are two restaurants at the gallery.

High Court

The High Court building, by the lake next to the National Gallery, is open daily from 9.45 am to 4.30 pm. Opened in 1980, its grandiose magnificence caused it to be dubbed 'Gar's Mahal', a reference to Sir Garfield Barwick, Chief Justice during the building's construction. In truth, there is a touch of Indian Mughal palace about the ornamental watercourse burbling along-side the entrance path to this grand building.

PLACES TO STAY		7	Jolimont Centre (Countrylink, Airlines, Bus Station)
10	City Walk Hotel	8	Commonwealth Government Bookshop
45	Parkroyal Hotel	9	Pandora's
		11	Traveller's Medical and Vaccination Centre
PLACES TO EAT		15	Ocean Bookshop
3	Barocca Cafe	17	Private Bin
4	Psychodeli	18	Civic Bus Interchange
12	Mama's Trattoria, Happy's, Dorettes Bistro & Caffé della iPiazza	19	Police Station
13	Sammy's Kitchen & Gus's	22	ACT Government City Shopfront
14	Asian Noodle House & Ali Baba	23	Asylum, Phoenix & Terminus
16	Noshes & Heaven	24	Moosehead's
20	Imperial Court Chinese Restaurant	27	ANZ Bank
21	Thai Lotus	29	Commonwealth Bank
25	Bailey's Corner & Tosolini's	30	Merry-Go-Round
26	Antigo	31	Women's Information and Referral Centre
28	Chairman and Yip, Red Sea Restaurant & Club Asmara	32	Westpac Bank
35	Sizzle City	33	National Australia Bank
41	Cafe Chaos	34	Canberra Centre
42	Anarkali Pakistani Restaurant	36	City Market & Supermarket
		37	Gorman House Community Arts Centre
OTHER		38	National Film and Sound Archive
		39	Academy of Science
1	Drill Hall Gallery	40	Canberra Theatre Centre
2	Environment Centre	43	Electric Shadows Cinema
5	Dalton's Bookshop	44	Canberra Blade Centre
6	Post Office	46	Acton Park Ferry Terminal
		47	Swimming Pool
		48	Casino

Questacon – National Science & Technology Centre

This is a 'hands on' science museum in the snappy white building between the High Court and the National Library. It's open daily from 10 am to 5 pm and entry is $8 ($5 students). There are 200 'devices' in the centre's five galleries and outdoor areas where you can use 'props' to get a feeling for a scientific concept, and then see its application to an everyday situation. It might be educational but it's also great fun.

National Library

Also on Parkes Place, beside the lake, is the National Library, one of the most elegant buildings in Canberra. It has more than five million books, and displays include rare books, paintings, early manuscripts and maps, Captain Cook's *Endeavour* journal, a fine model of the ship itself and special exhibitions. The library is open Monday to Thursday from 9 am to 10 pm and Friday to Sunday from 9 am to 5 pm. Guided tours run from Tuesday to Thursday at 2 pm. On Tuesday at lunchtime and on Thursday night there are free films – phone for programmes (☎ 262 1156). There's also a restaurant, and a cafe with free Internet access.

Royal Australian Mint

The Mint, on Denison St, Deakin, south of the lake, produces all of Australia's coins. Through plate-glass windows (to keep you at arm's length from the cash) you can see the whole process, from raw materials to finished coins. There's a collection of rare coins in the foyer. The Mint is open on weekdays from 9 am to 4 pm and on weekends from 10 am to 3 pm (free). Bus Nos 230 and 231 run past on weekdays; on weekends take No 267.

Australian War Memorial

The massive war memorial, north of the lake and at the foot of Mt Ainslie, looks directly

ACT

along Anzac Parade to Old Parliament House across the lake. It was conceived in 1925 and finally opened in 1941. It houses an amazing collection of pictures, dioramas, relics and exhibitions. For the less military-minded, the memorial has an excellent art collection. The Hall of Memory is the focus of the memorial and in 1993 the body of the Unknown Australian Soldier was brought from a WW I battlefield and entombed here.

The memorial is open daily from 10 am to 5 pm (when the *Last Post* is played) and admission is free. Several free tours are held each day, some focusing on the artworks. Phone ☎ 243 4268 for times. Bus Nos 901 and 302 run from the city; No 303 runs nearby.

There are memorials to several conflicts and campaigns along Anzac Parade.

Australian National University
The ANU's attractive grounds take up most of the area between Civic and Black Mountain and are very pleasant to wander through. The information centre (☎ 249 2229) on Balmain Crescent is open on weekdays. The University Union on University Ave offers a variety of cheap eats and entertainment. Near the junction of Kingsley and Hutton Sts is the **Drill Hall Gallery**, an offshoot of the National Gallery with changing exhibitions of contemporary art. It's open Wednesday to Sunday from noon to 5 pm. Admission is free.

National Film & Sound Archive
The archive is housed in an Art-Deco building on McCoy Circuit at the eastern edge of the university area. Interesting exhibitions (some interactive) from the archive's collections are shown. There's also a trendy cafe. The archive is open daily from 9 am to 5 pm. Admission is free. Over the road is the Australian Academy of Science (not open to the public), known locally as the Martian Embassy – it looks like a misplaced flying saucer.

National Botanic Gardens
On the lower slopes of Black Mountain, behind the ANU, the beautiful 50-hectare botanic gardens are devoted to Australian flora. There are educational walks, including one amongst plants used by Aboriginal people. The eucalypt lawn has 600 species of this ubiquitous Australian tree. Another highlight is the rainforest area, achieved in this dry climate by a 'misting' system.

The gardens are reached from Clunies Ross St (take bus No 904) and are open daily from 9 am to 5 pm. Guided tours are held on Wednesday, Friday and Sunday at 11 am, and on Saturday and Sunday at 2 pm. The information centre (☎ 250 9540) has an introductory video about the gardens and there's a cafe.

Australian Institute of Sport
Founded in 1981 as part of an effort to improve Australia's performance at events like the Olympics, the AIS is on Leverrier Crescent, in the northern suburb of Bruce. It provides training facilities for some of the country's top athletes, who lead hour-long tours of the institute daily at 11 am and 2 pm ($2.50). The public can use the tennis courts and swimming pools; phone ☎ 252 1281 for times. Bus No 431 runs to the AIS from the city centre.

National Aquarium & Wildlife Sanctuary
On Lady Denman Drive near Scrivener Dam, the western end of the lake, the impressive aquarium (☎ 287 1211) also includes a wildlife sanctuary. It's open daily from 9 am to 5.30 pm and admission is $10 ($5 students).

National Museum of Australia
While progress towards a permanent museum site remains bogged in bureaucracy, the visitor centre (☎ 256 1126) on Lady Denman Drive in Yarralumla displays items from the museum's collection. It's open weekdays from 10 am to 4 pm and weekends from 1 to 4 pm but your time is better spent elsewhere.

Other Attractions
You can do no more than drive by and peek through the gates of the prime minister's

official Canberra residence, **The Lodge**, on Adelaide Ave, Deakin. The same is true of **Government House**, the residence of the governor-general, which is on the south-western corner of Lake Burley Griffin, but there's a lookout beside Scrivener Dam at the end of the lake, giving a good view of the building. The governor-general is the representative of the Australian monarch – who lives in London and also happens to be the British monarch.

The **Australian-American Memorial**, at the eastern end of Kings Ave, is a 79-metre-high pillar topped by an eagle, is a memorial to US support of Australia during WW II.

The **Church of St John the Baptist**, in Reid, just east of Civic, was built between 1841 and 1845. The stained-glass windows were donated by pioneering families of the region. There is an adjoining schoolhouse with some early relics, open on Wednesday morning and on weekend afternoons ($1.50). The **Serbian Orthodox Church** in Forrest is decorated with biblical murals.

The **Royal Military College, Duntroon**, was once a homestead, with parts dating from the 1830s. There are free guided tours on Tuesday and Thursday afternoons at 2.30 pm. Bookings are advised (☎ 275 9408).

The enterprising **Tradesmen's Union Club** on the corner of Badham and Cape Sts, Dickson, has a large collection of 'old and unusual bicycles'. The club also runs the Downer Club nearby on Hawdon St, home to 'the world's largest beer collection'. If that doesn't grab you, there's also an Antarctic igloo on display. Still not interested? Well, what about an observatory with an astronomer on duty nightly from nightfall (or 7 pm, whichever is later) until midnight. Admission to all this is free.

Bushwalking

Tidbinbilla Fauna Reserve has marked trails. For other places see the Around Canberra section. Contact the Canberra Bushwalking Club through the Environment Centre (☎ 247 3064) on Kingsley St in the ANU campus. Here you can buy *Above the Cotter*, which details walks and drives in the area.

Exploring Namadgi and Tidbinbilla is useful for planning day walks. There are also some good rock climbing areas.

Bushwalking information is also available from the ACT Government City Shopfront on City Walk.

Water Sports

In spring and summer Dobel Boat Hire (☎ 249 6861) at the Acton Park Ferry Terminal on the northern shore of Lake Burley Griffin rents aquabikes for $14 per hour and surf skis from $16. Canoeing in the Murrumbidgee River, 20-odd km west of Canberra at its closest point, is also popular.

Swimming pools around the city include the Olympic Pool on Allara St, Civic. Swimming in Lake Burley Griffin is not recommended.

River Runners (☎ 288 5610) offer rafting on the Shoalhaven River, 1½ hours from Canberra, for $115, less if you can meet them there.

Cycling

Canberra has a great series of bicycle tracks – probably the best in Australia. See Getting Around for more information.

Other Activities

Inline skates can be hired from several places, including Mr Spokes near the Acton Park Ferry Terminal and Canberra Blade Centre (which is cheaper) on Allara St in the city, opposite the Parkroyal Hotel.

The New South Wales snowfields are within four hours drive of Canberra and the information centre has the latest news on conditions. There are plenty of equipment hire places. Murrays (☎ 295 3611) offers day-trip ski packages from $66 including ski hire.

Organised Tours

The information centre has details of the many tours of the city and the ACT. Half-day city tours start at around $25. Canberra Cruises (☎ 295 3544) has cruises on Lake Burley Griffin from $10. Taking a flight might be a good way of seeing the grand scale of the city's plan. Several outfits offer flights, such as Canberra Flight Training Centre (☎ 248 6766) with scenic swoops for $34 (minimum two people).

Festivals

The Canberra Festival takes place over 10 days in March and celebrates the city's birthday with fun events, many held in Commonwealth Park. In September and October there's the Floriade, concentrating on Canberra's spectacular spring flowers but with many related events.

Places to Stay

Camping *Canberra Motor Village* (☎ 247 5466), five km north-west of the centre on Kunzea St, O'Connor, has a bush setting and charges $11 for sites, $39 a double for on-site vans and from $65 a double in cabins. There's a restaurant, kitchen, tennis court and swimming pool.

The *Canberra Carotel* (☎ 241 1377) off the Federal Highway in Watson, six km north of the centre, has sites from $10, on-site vans from $40 for four people, and more expensive motel-style cabins.

Hostels Smack bang in the centre of Canberra, the *City Walk Hotel* (☎ 257 0124) upstairs on the corner of City Walk and Mort St has dorm beds for $15 and singles/doubles for $35/40. Most rooms share bathrooms but it's a reasonable option, with a spacious TV lounge and kitchen facilities.

The *Canberra YHA Hostel* (☎ 248 9155) is purpose-built and well designed and equipped. There is a travel desk (☎ 248 0177) which handles domestic and international travel. Nightly charges are $15, plus $3 if you need a sleeping sheet, and there are twin rooms for $19 a person. (Add $5 if you aren't a YHA member.) The office is open from 7 am to 10.30 pm but you can check in up until midnight if you give advance warning. The hostel is on Dryandra St, O'Connor, about six km north-west of Civic. Bus No 380 runs from the city twice an hour on weekdays and hourly on weekends to the Scrivener St stop on Miller St, O'Connor.

From there, follow the signs. From the Jolimont Centre take bus No 381 to the corner of Scrivener and Brigalow Sts, head north-east up Scrivener St to Dryandra St and turn right. Driving, turn west off Northbourne Ave onto Macarthur Ave and after about two km turn right onto Dryandra. You can hire bicycles at the hostel.

On the other side of town in Manuka, a couple of km from Parliament House, the *Kingston Hotel* (☎ 295 6844) on the corner of Canberra Ave and Giles St offers shared accommodation for $12 per person with optional linen hire at $4. There are cooking facilities and, as the Kingston is a large and popular pub, counter meals are available. Bus No 352 from the city runs past.

Guesthouses & Hotels The *Victor Lodge* (☎ 295 7777) is a clean and friendly place at 29 Dawes St, Kingston, half a km from the railway station and a couple of km south-east of Parliament House. Rooms with shared bathrooms are $35/40 a single/double or you can share a room for $15, including a light breakfast. Several travellers have reported enjoying their stay here. To get here from the city take bus No 352 to the nearby Kingston shops, or phone and see if they can pick you up. They also rent bikes here.

Also south of the lake, the *Macquarie Private Hotel* (☎ 273 2325) on National Circuit on the corner of Bourke St has 500 rooms. Singles/doubles are $39/60 or $120/240 per week. Breakfast deals are available but aren't great value. All rooms share bathrooms. Bus No 350 from the city stops at the front door.

Entering Canberra from the north, there's a cluster of guesthouses on the east side of Northbourne Ave in Downer, just south of the junction of the Barton Highway from Yass and the Federal Highway from Goulburn. All are clean and straightforward. It's four km or so into town, but buses run past, and Dickson shopping centre is not far away. At No 524 *Blue & White Lodge* (☎ 248 0498), which also runs the similarly priced *Blue Sky* at No 528, has single rooms for about $40 with doubles starting at $50.

Prices include cooked breakfast and all rooms have TV and a fridge but most bathrooms are shared. They can probably pick you up from the bus station. The *Chelsea Lodge* (☎ 248 0655) at No 526 also does pick-ups and charges $40/50 a single/double including cooked breakfast, or $50/60 with private bathroom. *Northbourne Lodge* (☎ 257 2599) at No 522 is a nice place that is a bit cheaper than the others and they tend to find special rates if you're staying a few nights.

Motels Most motels are expensive and few resemble those seen elsewhere in Australia; many are ex-government guesthouses. Among the cheapest is *Motel Monaro* (☎ 295 2111) at 27 Dawes St, Kingston. Although advertised tariffs are around $65 per person, check for standby rates, which can plummet to less than half price. The *Acacia Motor Lodge* (☎ 249 6955) at 65 Ainslie Ave, Braddon, charges from $66/72 a single/double including a light breakfast. Other places are scattered through the suburbs, with a cluster of mid-range motels about eight km south of the city in Narabundah, most on Jerrabomberra Ave.

Top-end places to stay include *Olim's Canberra Hotel* (☎ 248 5511) on the corner of Ainslie and Limestone Aves in Braddon. Rooms cost from $95 a single or double and it's a pleasant old place.

Colleges The ANU, just west of Civic, is a very pleasant place to stay. *Fenner Hall* (☎ 279 9000) is the only college that offers term-time accommodation. Basic rooms are about $20/30 for students/non-students, with rates decreasing the longer the stay. Otherwise, a selection of colleges rent their rooms during the Easter (one week), June/July, September (two weeks) and late-November to late-February vacations. Try *Toad Hall* (☎ 267 4999), $15 per night, or *Bruce Hall* and *Burton and Garran Hall* (☎ 267 4700), $21 for students ($28 for non-students) with each extra person $5 on a folding bed. Weekly rates begin at $90.

Places to Eat

Canberra has a fine eating scene. Most places are around Civic, with an up-market selection in Manuka, an Asian strip in Dickson, and other possibilities scattered around the suburbs.

City Centre There's a food hall in the lower section of the Canberra Centre where you can fill up on burgers, pasta, croissants and more for under $7. There's a smaller food hall in City Market on Bunda St, but it's hard to go past the excellent *Sizzle City*, at the entrance to City Market, and its cheap Japanese lunch packs.

One of the best places to eat is *Thai Lotus* in the Sydney Building on East Row. It's open nightly for dinner, and for lunch from Tuesday to Friday. Prices are reasonable, with mains for about $10 to $13.

The *Imperial Court Chinese Restaurant*, on the Northbourne Ave side of the Sydney Building, serves decent meals that won't break the bank. It is open late every night and until 1 am on weekends.

Bailey's Corner, at the south end of East Row on the corner of London Circuit, has a couple of places with outdoor tables. *Tosolini's* is an Italian-based bistro which is good for a drink or a meal, including breakfast. Lunchtime specials are about $10 and the evening menu has main courses for about $16. The cakes here are to die for.

Around the corner from Tosolini's, in Petrie Plaza, is *Antigo*, a cafe and bar open daily until late. The menu is interesting and main courses are under $15.

Behind the Westpac Bank, on the corner of London Circuit and Akuna St, the cosy *Anarkali Pakistani Restaurant* has main meals from $10. *Cafe Chaos* is on Ainslie Ave where it meets City Walk. The food, although good, is a bit pricey, but it's a nice place to sit with a coffee and watch the shoppers go by.

Garema Place is full of restaurants and cafes. *Mama's Trattoria* is open from lunchtime until late, serving soups, bruschetta and pasta in a good atmosphere. *Happy's* is a reasonably priced Chinese restaurant with lunchtime specials. Nearby, *Caff della Piazza* is a nice Italian place, open all day for meals and snacks. *Noshes* is in the arcade opposite but tables spill out into the plaza when weather permits. Popular with students, Noshes has decent coffee, great sandwiches and cheap pasta.

Around the corner on Bunda St, *Gus's* has outdoor tables and serves unpretentious cafe food (no sun-dried tomato has ever darkened this door). Soup is about $4 and pasta or goulash about $7.50. Gus's is open until midnight and later on weekends.

Not far away from Gus's, *Sammy's Kitchen* is a Chinese and Malaysian place with a good reputation and many dishes between $7 and $9. Nearby, the wonderful *Asian Noodle House* has many dishes under $7.

Ali Baba, on the corner of Bunda St and Garema Place's southern arm, does Lebanese takeaways, with shwarmas and felafels for about $4 and meals averaging $9. Moving south along Bunda St, the *Chairman & Yip* offers more elegant dining, with tapas and Asian-inspired meals, including a large vegetarian selection. Dinner is from $12 with lunch somewhat cheaper. The *Red Sea Restaurant* at Club Asmara on Bunda St has African dishes, from $12 to $15.

There are a couple of good eating options on Marcus Clarke St north-west of Civic. Up near Barry Drive is the *Barocca Cafe*, which has inventive seafood and meat dishes for about $15. *Psychodeli*, just around the corner on Barry Drive, is open daily for pizza and focaccia.

Manuka South of the lake, not far from Capital Hill, is the Manuka shopping centre, which services the diplomatic corps and well-heeled bureaucrats from surrounding neighbourhoods. There's a cinema centre here and several bars and cafes which stay open late, such as *Metropole* on the corner of Furneaux and Franklin Sts.

Across Franklin St is *My Cafe*, with fabulous breakfasts, a bagel-based menu and main courses between $6 and $9. Upstairs in nearby Style Arcade, *Alanya* is a good Turkish restaurant with main courses

(including vegetarian) from $10. Also up here is *Chez Daniel*, one of Canberra's better restaurants, with creative main courses averaging $20. Through the arcade to Bougainville St, the *Lawn* serves modern bistro meals under $15. *Timmy's Kitchen* on Furneaux St is a very popular Malaysian/Chinese place with main courses starting at about $7. There are plenty of other cafes and restaurants.

Dickson Woolley St in Dickson, a few km north of Civic, is a thriving restaurant district. Although dominated by Asian restaurants, the strip is flanked by a Russian restaurant, *Kalinka*, at the northern end, and a trattoria, *Belluci's* at the southern. As for Asian food, *Dickson Noodle House* is a popular Lao and Thai cafe with dishes for about $8. *Rasa Sayang* is a nice Malaysian place. The Japanese *Sakura* has lunch specials under $10 and dinner banquets under $20. On the other side of the road is the huge Chinese *Foodcourt* buffet, with dinner for $13.50. There are lots of other places, including a pizza bar.

Elsewhere In Lyneham, at 96 Wattle St, is well-known *Tilley's*, a cafe, bar and art gallery. The food is healthy (if you don't count the great cakes) and the clientele diverse. There is often entertainment here.

Cheap food can be found at the student union *Refectory* at the ANU.

Entertainment

Canberra is more lively than its reputation suggests. For one thing, liberal licensing laws allow hotels unlimited opening hours and there are some 24-hour bars. Underage drinking is strictly policed in Canberra; if you don't have ID proving you're over 18 forget it. The *Good Times* section in the Thursday *Canberra Times* has full entertainment listings and the free, monthly *BMA* magazine lists bands and other events.

The *casino* on Constitution Ave is open 24 hours. It's a fairly casual place: men need a shirt with a collar and no-one can wear sports shoes after 7 pm.

If you're tired of Oz leagues clubs and workers' clubs, phone one of the clubs catering to Australians of foreign descent to find out if visitors are welcome – see the Yellow Pages under 'Clubs, Social'.

The *Canberra Theatre Centre*, on Civic Square, has several theatres with a varied range of events. Also check with foreign cultural organisations, such as the Goethe Institute German Cultural Centre (☎ 247 4472), to find out what's on. *Gorman House Community Arts Centre* on Ainslie Ave, Braddon, sometimes has theatre, dance performances or exhibitions. An interesting market is held here on weekends. The *Old Bus Depot Market*, on Wentworth Ave in Kingston, is on every Sunday selling art and craft with a New Age slant, as well as food from around the world.

Dancing & Drinking There's live music two or three nights a week during term at the *ANU union bar*, a good place for a drink even when there's no entertainment. Big touring acts often play the *Refectory* here.

In Civic, *Asylum*, upstairs at 23 East Row (near London Circuit), has live music Wednesday to Saturday and mainly features young bands. Entry costs between $3 and $8, depending on who's playing. Next door is the *Phoenix* bar, a good place to mix with Canberra's student population. Also along here is *Terminus*, which has live bands on Friday and Saturday from 10 pm. *Moosehead's Bar* on the south side of the Sydney Building is popular. Around the corner on Northbourne Ave, the *Private Bin* is a big place popular with younger dancers. Not far away, *Pandora's*, on the corner of Alinga and Mort Sts, has a bar downstairs and a dance club upstairs.

Heaven, on Garema Place, is popular with gays. Nearby, and upstairs from Happy's restaurant, *Dorettes Bistro* is a relaxed and pleasant wine bar with live acoustic music; you can have a meal or just a drink. There's music every night, with a cover charge from Thursday to Saturday. *Club Asmara*, at 128 Bunda St near Garema Place, is home to the Red Sea Restaurant, but operates as a night-club too, with an emphasis on African, Latin and reggae rhythms. Bands play here occasionally, and there is a cover charge on weekends.

Olim's Canberra Hotel, on the corner of Ainslie and Limestone Aves in Braddon, has a piano bar with free jazz on Thursday nights and a popular beer garden. *Tilley's* in Lyneham, on the corner of Wattle and Brigalow Sts, has live music, usually a cut above pub bands, on Tuesday and Saturday nights. There are a few bars in Manuka, including *En Vogue*, a trendy joint on Franklin St, which features funk and hip hop. The *Southern Cross Club* in Woden sometimes has good jazz.

Other places that sometimes have bands include the *Canberra Workers' Club*, on Childers St, and the *Tradesmen's Union Club*, in Dickson.

Cinemas There are several cinemas in the Civic Square and London Circuit area. *Electric Shadows* is an art-house cinema on City Walk near Akuna St. There's a popular bar here, too.

The *National Library* shows free films on Tuesday at lunchtime and on Thursday evenings – phone for details (☎ 262 1156). The *National Gallery* (☎ 240 6411) usually screens free films on Friday afternoons.

Getting There & Away

Air Canberra is not an international airport. Sydney is normally only half an hour away; the standard one-way fare with the two major airlines is $146. Melbourne is about an hour away and costs $205. Direct flights to Adelaide cost $328 and to Brisbane it's $291. These prices drop dramatically when you book in advance, and other special deals are often available. Qantas (☎ 13 1313) and Ansett (☎ 13 1300) are both in the Jolimont Centre on Northbourne Ave.

Fares on Eastern Australia and Ansett Express are the same as those on the main carriers, although they fly more frequently. Other smaller airlines fly to New South Wales country destinations.

ACT

Bus Most bus lines have booking offices and their main stop at the Jolimont Centre. Greyhound Pioneer (☎ 13 2030) has the most frequent Sydney service ($30). It takes four to five hours. They also run to Adelaide ($95) and Melbourne ($55, or $53 on the night run). Services to Cooma ($15) and the New South Wales snowfields ($34, including park entry fees) are frequent in winter, less so at other times. Murrays (☎ 295 3611) has day-trip ski packages.

Murrays also has daily express (under four hours) buses to Sydney for $28 or $19 if you pay in advance. The service also runs to Batemans Bay ($21.75) and connects with buses running up to Nowra ($33).

Transborder Express (☎ 226 1378) runs to Yass ($9). Rendell's (☎ 1800 023 328) goes to Orange ($35) and Dubbo ($45), and Capital Coachlines (book through Greyhound Pioneer) runs to Bathurst ($36). Sid Fogg's (☎ 1800 045 952) travels up to Newcastle ($45) four times a week, or daily in school holidays.

The Countrylink Travel Centre (☎ 13 2232) is in the Jolimont Centre. There's also an office at the railway station. There's a daily service to Adelaide via Albury which costs about $95; it's quicker and no more expensive to go by bus via Melbourne.

Train The railway station is south of the lake on Wentworth Ave in Kingston. To Sydney there are two trains daily, taking about four hours and costing $38/52 in economy/1st class.

There is no direct train to Melbourne. The daily V/Line Canberra Link service involves a train between Melbourne and Albury and a connecting bus to Canberra. This costs $45 in economy and takes about nine hours. A longer but much more interesting train/bus service to Melbourne is the V/Line Capital Link which runs via Cooma and the forests of Victoria's East Gippsland then down the Princes Highway to Sale where you catch a train. This takes over 11 hours and costs $45.

Car Rental Avis (☎ 1800 225 411), Hertz (☎ 257 4877), Budget (☎ 13 2727) and

Thrifty (☎ 1800 652 008) have offices at the airport and in town. Cheaper outfits include Oz Drive (☎ 239 2639) at 13 Yallourn St, Fyshwick (car delivery is available), and Rent a Dent (☎ 257 5947) in Ijong St, Braddon, or phone to be picked up from the Jolimont Centre. Expect to pay $35 to $40 a day with 100 free km; better deals are available on longer rentals.

Getting Around

If you're driving, expect to spend a few hours hopelessly lost in Canberra's wonderful roundabout system. The locals are right when they tell you how logical it all is, but it takes a while to tune in. Traffic just isn't meant to be this organised! You could also spend some time searching for a petrol station. By design, most of them are off the main roads in Canberra – look for signs.

To/From the Airport The airport is seven km from the city centre. Note all the government cars lined up outside waiting to pick up 'pollies' and public servants. Hertz, Budget, Avis and Thrifty have airport car rental desks.

Canberra Shuttle Service (☎ 018 488 901) operates regularly between the airport and Canberra's accommodation and transport hubs. The fare is about $5 depending on the number of passengers. You have to book. The taxi fare from Civic is around $12.

Bus Action (Australian Capital Territory Internal Omnibus Network!) buses run fairly frequently. Phone (☎ 207 7611) for information regarding services or fares. The main interchange is on the corner of Alinga St and East Row in Civic, not far from the Jolimont Centre. The information kiosk here is open daily until about 11 pm. If you plan to use a lot of buses it's worth spending $2 on *The Bus Book*.

The flat 'one route' fare is $2 and you need the exact change. Some express buses (700 series) cost twice the normal fare. You can save money with advance purchase tickets, available from newsagents and elsewhere. Fare Go tickets cost $14 for 10 and a weekly

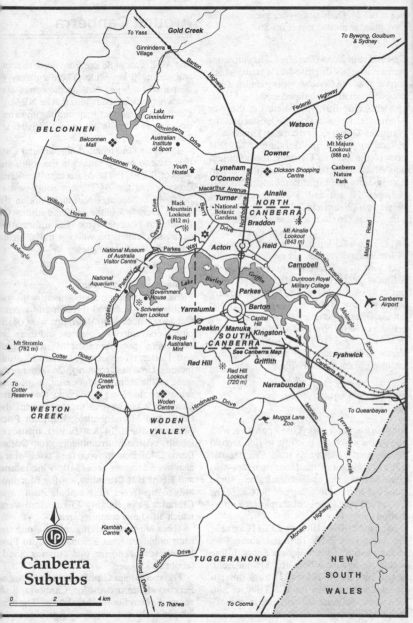

To Yass
Gold Creek
To Bywong, Goulburn & Sydney
Ginninderra Village
Barton Highway
Federal Highway
BELCONNEN
Lake Ginninderra
Watson
Belconnen Mall
Australian Institute of Sport
Mt Majura Lookout (888 m)
Ginninderra Drive
Youth Hostel
Lyneham
Downer
Canberra Nature Park
Belconnen Way
O'Connor
Dickson Shopping Centre
William Hovell Drive
Macarthur Avenue
Turner
Ainslie
Caswell Drive
Black Mountain Lookout (812 m)
National Botanic Gardens
NORTH CANBERRA
Braddon
Mt Ainslie Lookout (843 m)
Molonglo River
National Museum of Australia Visitor Centre
Parkes Way
Acton
Heid
Drive
Campbell
Fairbairn Avenue
Majura Road
National Aquarium
Tuggeranong Parkway
Lake Burley Griffin
Griffin
Parkes
Duntroon Royal Military College
Canberra Airport
Government House
Yarralumia
Barton
Scrivener Dam Lookout
Capital Hill
Kingston
Mt Stromlo (782 m)
Deakin
Manuka
SOUTH CANBERRA
Fyshwick
Cotter Road
Royal Australian Mint
See Canberra Map
Griffith
Molonglo River
To Cotter Reserve
Red Hill
Red Hill Lookout (720 m)
Narrabundah
To Queanbeyan
Weston Creek Centre
Hindmarsh Drive
Monaro Highway
Jerrabomberra Creek
WESTON CREEK
Woden Centre
WODEN VALLEY
Mugga Lane Zoo
Canberra Ave
Canberra Suburbs
Kambah Centre
Erindale Drive
TUGGERANONG
Drakeford Drive
NEW SOUTH WALES
0   2   4 km
To Tharwa
To Cooma

ticket is $24. Daily tickets are great value as they offer unlimited travel for $6.

Special Services The free Downtowner service is a bus disguised as a tram, which runs around the Civic shopping centre, stopping at specially designated stops.

Sightseeing Bus No 901 runs to the War Memorial, Regatta Point, Questacon, the National Gallery, Parliament House and several embassies in Yarralumla; No 904 goes to the Botanic Gardens, the aquarium and Black Mountain. Both services depart hourly from the city interchange, No 901 between 10 am and 3 pm and No 904 between 10.20 am and 3.20 pm. You'll need a day ticket ($6) to ride these services.

Murrays' Canberra Explorer (☎ 295 3611) runs a 25-km route around 19 points of interest and you can get on and off wherever you like. It departs hourly from the Jolimont Centre between 10.15 am and 4.15 pm daily, and tickets ($18, $8 children) are sold on the bus. If you want to make only one circuit without getting off (a good way to orient yourself) buy a one-hour tour ticket ($7, children $5). The youth hostel and Victor Lodge both offer their guests discounted tickets on the Explorer.

Taxi Call ☎ 13 1008.

Bicycle Canberra is a cyclist's paradise, with bike paths making it possible to ride around the city hardly touching a road. One popular track is a circuit of the lake; there are also peaceful stretches of bushland along some suburban routes. Get a copy of the *Canberra Cycleways* map from bookshops or the information centre ($6).

Mr Spokes Bike Hire (☎ 257 1188), near the Acton Park Ferry Terminal, charges $8 an hour and $7 for subsequent hours. Inline skates are available here for $15 an hour. Dial a Bicycle (☎ 286 5463) hires out 10-speed mountain bikes for $25 a day, or $80 for a week, including helmet, bike lock, pick-up and delivery.

Around Canberra

The ACT is about 88 km from north to south and about 30 km wide. There's plenty of unspoiled bush just outside the urban area, and a network of roads into it. The NRMA's *Canberra & District* map and the information centre's guide to tourist drives are helpful.

The plains and isolated hills around Canberra rise to rugged ranges in the south and west of the ACT. The Murrumbidgee River flows across the ACT from south-east to north-west. Namadgi National Park in the south covers 40% of the ACT and adjoins the Kosciusko National Park. The information centre has leaflets on walking trails, swimming spots and camp sites.

Picnic & Walking Areas

Picnic and barbecue spots, many with gas facilities, are scattered through and around Canberra. **Black Mountain**, just west of the city, is convenient for picnics, and there are swimming spots along the Murrumbidgee and Cotter rivers. Other riverside areas include **Uriarra Crossing**, 24 km north-west, on the Murrumbidgee near its meeting with the Molonglo River; **Casuarina Sands**, 19 km west at the meeting of the Cotter and Murrumbidgee; **Kambah Pool Reserve**, about 14 km farther upstream (south) on the Murrumbidgee; the **Cotter Dam**, 23 km from town on the Cotter, which also has a camping area ($10); **Pine Island** and **Point Hut Crossing**, on the Murrumbidgee upstream of Kambah Pool; and **Gibraltar Falls**, roughly 45 km south-west which also has a camping area.

There are good walking tracks along the Murrumbidgee from Kambah Pool to Pine Island (seven km), or to Casuarina Sands (about 14 km).

The spectacular **Ginninderra Falls** are at Parkwood, north-west of Canberra, just across the New South Wales border. The area is open daily and includes gorge scenery, nature trail, canoeing and camping. There's a $5 admission charge ($2 students).

The **Tidbinbilla Nature Reserve** (☎ 237 5120), south-west of the city in the hills beyond the Tidbinbilla Tracking Station, has bushwalking tracks, some leading to interesting rock formations. There are also enclosures where you'll probably see koalas. The reserve is open from 9 am until dusk; the visitor centre from 11 am to 4 pm. South-west of here in the **Corin Forest**, there's a one-km-long metal 'bobsled' run on weekends and during school holidays; a three hour session costs $20 (less if sharing).

Other good walking areas include **Mt Ainslie**, on the north-east side of the city, and **Mt Majura** behind it (the combined area is called Canberra Nature Park), and **Molonglo Gorge** near Queanbeyan.

Namadgi National Park, occupying the whole south-west of the ACT and partly bordering New South Wales' mountainous Kosciusko National Park, has seven peaks over 1600 metres and offers challenging bushwalking. The partly surfaced Boboyan Rd crosses the park, going south from **Tharwa** in the ACT to **Adaminaby** on the eastern edge of the Snowy Mountains in New South Wales. The park visitor centre (☎ 237 5222) is on this road, two km south of Tharwa, and there are picnic and camping facilities in the park at the Orroral River crossing and Mt Clear.

Observatories & Tracking Stations

The ANU's **Mt Stromlo Observatory** is 16 km west of Canberra and has a 188-cm telescope plus a visitor annexe open daily from 9 am to 4.30 pm. **Tidbinbilla Tracking Station**, about 33 km south-west of Canberra, is a joint US-Australian deep-space tracking station. The visitor centre has displays of spacecraft and tracking technology. It's free, and open daily from 9 am to 5 pm (8 pm in summer). The area is popular for bushwalks and barbecues.

Gold Creek

Near the Barton Highway about 15 km north of the city, Gold Creek has a number of attractions. Hard to resist is the **National Dinosaur Museum** (despite the name, this is a private collection) with replica skeletons of 10 dinosaurs and many other bones and fossils. Admission is $7.50 ($5 children) and it's open daily from 10 am to 5 pm. **Ginninderra Village** has a collection of craft workshops and galleries. Next door is **Cockington Green**, a miniature replica of an English village, open daily; admission is $7.50.

Other Attractions

Mugga Lane Zoo, in Red Hill about seven km south of the city centre, has about 80 species of native and exotic animals and is open daily ($7.50). Bus No 352 runs nearby.

Bywong Mining Town, about 30 km north of Canberra, is a re-creation of a mining settlement. It's open daily between 10 am and 4 pm and there are tours at 10.30 am, and 12.30 and 2 pm. Entry is $7.

The beautifully restored **Lanyon Homestead** is about 20 km south of the city centre, on the Murrumbidgee River near Tharwa. The early stone cottage on the site was built by convicts and the grand homestead was completed in 1859. This National Trust homestead, which now documents the life of the region before Canberra existed, is open Tuesday to Sunday from 10 am to 4 pm. A major attraction is a gallery of Sidney Nolan paintings. Admission (including both the homestead and the gallery) is $4 ($2 students).

Cuppacumbalong, also near Tharwa, is another old homestead, now a craft studio and gallery, open Wednesday to Sunday from 11 am to 5 pm.

Day Trips

A popular drive is east into New South Wales, past Bungendore, to pretty **Braidwood** (an hour or so) with its many antique shops, craft stores and restaurants. **Bungendore** has craft galleries such as the Bungendore Wood Works and some old buildings. Another good route takes in **Tharwa**, in hilly grazing lands.

QUEANBEYAN (pop 27,000)

Just across the New South Wales border east

of Canberra is Queanbeyan, now virtually a suburb of the capital it predates. Until 1838 it was known as 'Queen Bean'.

Motel accommodation here is slightly cheaper than in Canberra. There's a history museum in the town and good lookouts on Jerrabomberra Hill five km west and Bungendore Hill four km east. *The School of Arts Cafe* on Monaro St has a 'showbiz' theme, running regular cabaret nights.

New South Wales

PHONE CHANGES

As of July 1996, all Sydney telephone numbers have eight digits, and the area code is (02).

In August 1997, all six-digit numbers outside the Sydney metropolitan telephone area will become eight-digit with the addition of the last two digits of the existing area code, and the area code will change to (02); eg ☎ (063) 123 456 becomes ☎ (02) 6312 3456.

The STD area code for all eight-digit NSW numbers is (02).

HIGHLIGHTS

- Cruising on Sydney Harbour, the best way to view the harbour city
- Bushwalking in the Blue Mountains
- Skiing at Australia's highest mountain, Kosciusko, in the Snowy Mountains
- Catching a wave at Byron Bay, Australia's surfing mecca
- Touring the wineries of the Hunter Valley region
- Visiting the extraordinary archaeological record of Lake Mungo
- Heading into the remote outback 'back of Bourke'

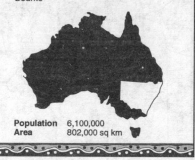

Population	6,100,000
Area	802,000 sq km

New South Wales is the site of Captain Cook's original landing in Australia, and the place where the first permanent European settlement was established. Today it's Australia's most populous state and it has the country's largest city, Sydney. Those expecting NSW to be little more than Sydney's hinterland are in for a real surprise. The state is rich in history, some of it tainted with the brutality of the early penal settlement, but much of it bound up with the gold rush and expansion westward. The state has fabulous coastal and mountain scenery and dry western plains stretching all the way to 'back of Bourke'.

The state capital, with its Opera House, harbour and bridge, is a good place to start your exploration of NSW. It was at Sydney Cove, where the ferries run from Circular Quay today, that the first European settlement was established in 1788, so it's not surprising that Sydney has an air of history which is missing from many Australian cities. That doesn't stop the city being far brasher and more lively than many of it's younger Australian counterparts though.

The Pacific Highway runs north from Sydney and is the gateway to the great beaches, surf and scenery of NSW's northern coastal strip. The Princes Highway heads south from the capital along the state's less-developed southern coast.

GEOGRAPHY & CLIMATE

The state divides neatly into four regions. The narrow coastal strip runs between Queensland and Victoria and has many beaches, national parks, inlets and coastal lakes. The Great Dividing Range also runs the length of the state, about 100 km inland from the coast, and includes the New England tablelands north of Sydney, the spectacular Blue Mountains west of Sydney, and, in the south of the state, the Snowy Mountains, which offer excellent winter skiing and summer bushwalking.

West of the Great Dividing Range is the farming country of the western slopes and the dry western plains, which cover two-

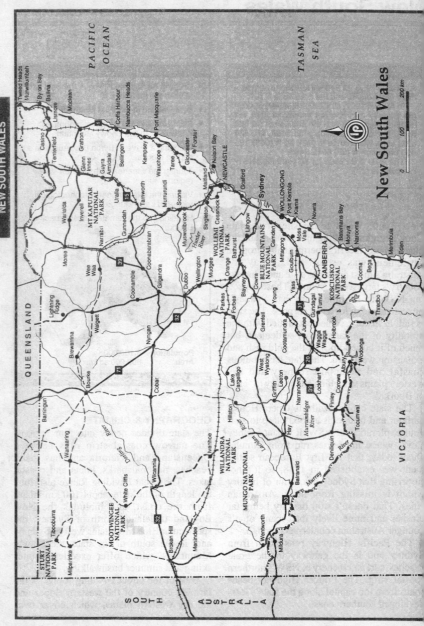

New South Wales

DAVID COLLINS

PAUL STEEL

DAVID COLLINS

JON MURRAY

DAVID COLLINS

New South Wales

A: Courtyard cafe, Sydney Hospital
B: Sydney Opera House
C: Warehouse, the Rocks

D: Strand Arcade, Sydney
E: Justice & Police Museum, Sydney

A		
B	C	D
E		

DAVID COLLINS

JON MURRAY

GREG ALFORD

JON MURRAY

JON MURRAY

New South Wales
A: The Rocks, Sydney
B: Circular Quay, Sydney
C: Royal Hotel, Paddington, Sydney

D: Colo River, near Windsor
E: Blue Mountains

irds of the state. The plains fade into the utback in the far west.

The major rivers are the Murray and the Darling, which meander westward across the plains. As a general rule of thumb, it gets wetter the farther north you go and drier the farther west. In winter, the Snowy Mountains are, not surprisingly, covered with snow.

INFORMATION

There are NSW government travel centres in Sydney and some interstate capitals. There's also a major information centre at Albury, on the Victorian border, and a smaller one at Tweed Heads, on the Queensland border. Most towns have tourist information centres. The interstate NSW government travel centres are:

Queensland
    40 Queen St, Brisbane 4000 (☎ (07) 3229 8833)
South Australia
    Corner King William & Grenfell Sts, Adelaide 5000 (☎ (08) 8231 3167)
Victoria
    388 Bourke St, Melbourne 3000 (☎ (03) 9670 7461)

NATIONAL PARKS

The state's 70-odd national parks include stretches of coast, vast forested inland tracts, the peaks and valleys of the Great Dividing Range, and some epic stretches of outback. Most parks can be reached by conventional vehicles in reasonable weather. Public transport into most parks is scarce, although all the parks surrounding Sydney are accessible by public transport.

Entry to most national parks is $7.50 per car – less for motorbikes and pedestrians. However, entry booths are sometimes unstaffed on weekdays and entry to remoter national parks is often free. The $60 annual pass which gives unlimited entry to the state's parks is worth considering, especially if you plan to visit Mt Kosciusko National Park, where the daily fee is $12. Many parks have camp sites with facilities, costing between $5 and $15 a night for two people. Camp sites at popular parks are often booked out during school holidays. Bush camping is allowed in some parks; call the nearest NSW National Parks & Wildlife Service (NPWS) office for regulations.

The NPWS information line is ☎ (02) 9585 6533. The NPWS has a shop and information centre (open daily) in Cadman's Cottage (☎ (02) 9247 8861), 110 George St, the Rocks, Sydney. Also handy is Gregory's *National Parks NSW* ($18.95).

The state forests – owned by the NSW government and used for logging – have drives, camp sites, picnic areas and walking tracks. The State Forests of NSW head office (☎ (02) 9980 4296) is at Building 2, 423 Pennant Hills Rd, Pennant Hills, Sydney.

ACTIVITIES
Bushwalking

Close to Sydney, there are dramatic cliff-top walks in the Royal National Park, bushwalks around the inlets of Broken Bay in Ku-ring-gai Chase National Park, and all the sandstone bluffs, eucalyptus forests and fresh air you could wish for in the Blue Mountains. Farther south, Kosciusko National Park, in the Snowy Mountains, has excellent alpine walks in summer.

The NSW Confederation of Bushwalking Clubs (☎ (02) 9548 1228), GPO Box 2090, Sydney 2001, and the NPWS have information on bushwalking. The Department of Land & Water Conservation (DLWC; ☎ (02) 9228 6111), 23-33 Bridge St, Sydney, has free brochures and discovery kits ($10) on the 250-km Great North Walk linking Sydney with the Hunter Valley, and the Hume & Hovell Track running through High Country between Yass and Albury.

Lonely Planet's *Bushwalking in Australia* details some walks in NSW. Other useful books are *100 Walks in New South Wales* by Tyrone T Thomas and *Bushwalks in the Sydney Region* edited by Lord & Daniel.

Water Sports

Swimming & Surfing The state's 1900-km coastline is liberally sprinkled with beaches offering excellent swimming. See the Sydney section for surf beaches within the metropolitan area. North of Sydney, surfing spots include Newcastle, Port Macquarie, Seal Rocks, Crescent Head, Nambucca Heads, Coffs Harbour, Angourie, Lennox Head and Byron Bay. South of Sydney, try Wollongong, Jervis Bay, Ulladulla, Merimbula or Eden. Contact the NSW Surfriders Association (☎ (02) 9970 7066), PO Box 330, Manly, NSW 2095, for detailed information.

Surf carnivals start in November and run until May. Contact Surf Life Saving NSW (☎ (02) 9663 4298) for dates and venues.

Diving & Snorkelling North of Sydney, try Terrigal, Port Stephens, Seal Rocks, Coffs Harbour or Byron Bay. On the south coast, head to Jervis Bay, Merimbula or Eden.

Sailing Sydney Harbour and Pittwater both offer exceptional sailing. See the Sydney section for details. Lake Macquarie, south of Newcastle, and Myall Lakes, just to the north, are also good. Contact the Yachting Association of NSW (☎ (02) 9660 1266) for information on sailing clubs and courses.

White-Water Rafting & Canoeing Rafting takes place on the upper Murray and Snowy rivers in the Snowy Mountains, and on the Shoalhaven River, 220 km south of Sydney. In the north, there's rafting on the Nymboida and Gwydir rivers. Albury, Jindabyne and Nowra are the centres for the southern rivers; Coffs Harbour and Nambucca Heads for the northern. A day trip costs around $100.

There's an abundance of canoeing spots in NSW, but you might like to try Port Macquarie, Barrington Tops (for whitewater canoeing), Myall Lakes, Jervis Bay, and the Murrumbidgee River near Canberra. The NSW Canoe Association (☎ (02) 9660 4597) can provide information, and publishes *The Canoeing Guide to NSW* ($24.95).

Cycling
Bicycle NSW Incorporated (☎ (02) 9283 5200), 209 Castlereagh St, Sydney 2000, can provide information on cycling routes throughout the state.

Skiing
See the Snowy Mountains section for skiing information.

GETTING THERE & AWAY
See Getting There & Away in the Sydney section for information on international and interstate air, rail and bus links.

GETTING AROUND
Air
Smaller airlines like Ansett Express and Eastern Australia Airlines operate comprehensive networks within the state, and other airlines serve particular regions. The chart shows some routes and standard economy one-way fares. In many instances, discount return tickets are as cheap as economy one-way fares. Discounted tickets generally require purchase 21 days in advance and carry restrictions.

Bus
Buses are often quicker and cheaper than

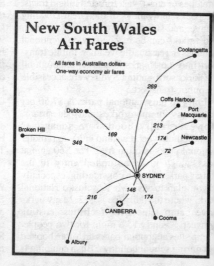

New South Wales Air Fares

All fares in Australian dollars
One-way economy air fares

trains, but not always. If you want to make stops on the way to your ultimate destination, look for cheap stopover deals rather than buying separate tickets. Once you've reached your destination, there are usually local bus lines, though services may not be frequent. In remote areas, school buses may be the only option. They will usually pick you up, but they aren't obliged to do so.

Train

Countrylink has the most comprehensive state rail service in Australia and will, in conjunction with connecting buses, take you quite quickly to most sizeable towns in NSW. The frequency of services and their value for money is variable so compare options with private bus services. Countrylink offers first and economy-class tickets and a quota of discount tickets; return fares are double the single fare. Australian students travel for half the economy fare.

All Countrylink services have to be booked in advance (☎ 13 2232 daily between 6.30 am and 10 pm). You can do this in person at Central Station or the Countrylink Travel Centre, 11-31 York St (both in Sydney). Bicycles and surfboards are carried free but reservations must be made in advance. For lost property ☎ (02) 9211 1176.

Intrastate services and one-way economy fares from Sydney include Albury, 643 km, $67; Armidale, 569 km, $62; Bathurst, 223 km, $26; Bourke, 835 km, $76; Broken Hill, 1125 km, $91; Byron Bay, 883 km, $76; Canberra, 326 km, $38; Coffs Harbour, 608 km, $67; Cooma, 441 km, $51; Dubbo, 462 km, $55; Port Macquarie, 474 km, $61; and Tamworth, 455 km, $55.

Frequent commuter-type trains run between Sydney and Wollongong ($6.20), Katoomba ($9), Lithgow ($14), Newcastle ($14) and, less frequently, Goulburn ($21).

A one-month NSW Discovery Pass offers economy-class travel and unlimited stopovers on the state network for $249 (YHA members get a 10% discount).

Sydney

Population 3,740,000

Australia's oldest and largest settlement is a vibrant city built around one of the most spectacular harbours in the world. Instantly recognisable thanks to its opera house, harbour and bridge, Sydney also boasts lesser-known attractions like the historic Rocks, Victorian-era Paddington, excellent beaches such as Bondi and Manly, and two superb coastal national parks on the city fringe.

The city is built on land once occupied by the Iora tribe, whose presence lingers in the place names of many suburbs and whose artistic legacy can be seen at many Aboriginal engraving sites around the city. After its brutal beginnings, and a long period when it seemed content to be a second-rate facsimile of a British city, Sydney has finally come of age. Selected to host the 2000 Olympic Games, it is undergoing a period of rejuvenation as it strives to bring its cityscape on a level with its natural charms.

An array of ethnic groups contribute to the city's social life – the dynamism of the Chinese community in particular has played an important role in altering the city's Anglo-Mediterranean fabric, and preparing it to become a key player in the Pacific region.

Orientation

The harbour divides Sydney into northern and southern halves, with the Sydney Harbour Bridge and the Harbour Tunnel joining the two shores. The city centre and most places of interest are south of the harbour. The central area is long and narrow, stretching from the Rocks and Circular Quay in the north to Central Station in the south. It is bounded by Darling Harbour to the west and a string of pleasant parks to the east.

East of the city centre are the inner-city suburbs of Darlinghurst, Kings Cross and Paddington. Farther east again are exclusive suburbs such as Double Bay and Vaucluse. To the south-east of these are the ocean-

The 2000 Olympics

Sydney will take its place on the world stage when it hosts the Olympic Games in 2000. There's an almost tangible sense of expectation as energies are harnessed, key areas are given face-lifts, and politicians cat-fight over budget blowouts. There's also a smudge of Sydney fatalism in the air, which reasons that no matter what happens, it will all be worth it in the end, because the major star of the games will, of course, be the city itself.

Facilities are being constructed at Olympic Park on Homebush Bay, where existing sport, aquatic and athletic centres will be supplemented by an 80,000-seat Olympic Stadium, an Olympic Village and a new RAS Show Ground.

Homebush Bay is 12 km west of the Harbour Bridge on the Parramatta River. The Homebush Bay Corporation operates daily guided 35-minute bus tours of the Olympic site. Tours depart from Strathfield railway station at 9.30 and 10.30 am and 12.30 pm on Bus No 401, and cost $5 ($2.50 concession). The Rocket Harbour Express (☎ 9264 7377) cruises up the Parramatta as far as Homebush Bay and plans to stop at the Olympic site (see under Cruises in the Sydney Organised Tours section).

The Olympic Showcase and Information Centre is based in the *SS South Steyne*, an elegant old Manly ferry moored near the eastern end of the Pyrmont Bridge in Darling Harbour. The showcase is a useless piece of sugary propaganda, little more than a poor excuse to start selling souvenirs five years in advance; admission is $2. ■

---

beach suburbs of Bondi and Coogee. Sydney's Kingsford-Smith airport is in Mascot, 10 km south of the city centre, jutting into Botany Bay.

West of the centre is the radically changing suburb of Pyrmont, and the peninsula suburbs of Glebe and Balmain. The inner west includes Newtown and Leichhardt.

Suburbs stretch a good 20 km north and south of the centre, their extent limited by national parks. The suburbs north of the bridge are known collectively as the North Shore and are somewhat loosely considered the territory of Sydney's middle classes. The western suburbs sprawl 50 km to reach the foothills of the Blue Mountains, encompassing the once separate settlements of Parramatta and Penrith.

Information

Tourist Offices The NSW Government Travel Centre (☎ 13 2077), 19 Castlereagh St, is open weekdays from 9 am to 5 pm. The Sydney Visitors Information Booth (☎ 9235 2424) is nearby in Martin Place (sharing a booth with Halftix) and is open the same hours.

The Travellers' Information Service in the international terminal at the airport (☎ 9669 5111) is open daily from 5 am to 11 pm. It can book hotel rooms and allows travellers to make a free local phone call to arrange hostel accommodation.

There's another helpful Travellers' Information Service (☎ 9281 9366) in the Sydney Coach Terminal on the corner of Pitt St and Eddy Ave, outside Central Station. It's open daily from 6 am until 10.30 pm and makes bus and hotel (but not hostel) bookings.

Some areas, like the Rocks, Kings Cross and Manly have their own tourist offices (see those sections for details).

The areas where backpackers stay are excellent for travel tips. Kings Cross hostel notice boards offer everything from flat-shares and job opportunities to cars and unused air tickets.

Money There are six Thomas Cook bureaus in the airport's international terminal which are open daily from around 5.15 am until after the last flight. There's an American Express branch at 92 Pitt St and Thomas Cook branches at 175 Pitt St, in the lower level of the Queen Victoria Building on York St, and in the Kingsgate shopping centre in

ngs Cross, but they are all closed Saturday
ernoon and Sunday.

If you want to change money at an
likely hour, the bureau de change at the
destrian juncture of Springfield Ave and
arlinghurst Rd, Kings Cross, is open daily
om 7.45 am until 1 am.

st & Telecommunications The main
st office (the GPO) is on Martin Place, but
siness is conducted around the corner at
9-171 Pitt St. The poste restante here is
en weekdays and there are computer ter-
inals which show if mail is waiting for you.
ou can have your mail redirected to any
burban post office for $5 a month.

Several travel agencies offer mail-holding
d forwarding services. Try Travellers
ontact Point (☎ 9221 8744), Suite 11-15,
h floor, 428 George St or Travel Active
9357 4477), 3 Orwell St, Kings Cross.

The Telstra Phone Centre, 130 Pitt St, has
nks of coin, phonecard and credit card
ephones and a credit card fax service. It's
en weekdays from 8 am to 10 pm and
eekends from 10 am to 7 pm. The Translat-
g & Interpreting Service (☎ 9221 1111)
n help with language difficulties.

Most major on-line services are represented
Australia, including CompuServe (☎ 1800
5 240) and the Microsoft Network (☎ 9934
00), whose local chapter is called On Aus-
alia. There are also a growing number of
ternet service providers, such as Oz-Email
9391 0480), which can provide access to
our existing POP E-mail account and to other
ternet services.

Net cafes can be found at the Paragon
otel (☎ 9241 3522), on the corner of Alfred
d Loftus Sts, and the Hotel Sweeney
9267 1116), 236 Clarence St.

ther Services The YHA Membership &
avel Centre (☎ 9261 1111) is at 422 Kent St,
tween Market and Druitt Sts. The centre
fers normal travel agency services and
ables travellers to make national and interna-
onal hostel bookings. The National Roads &
otorists Association (NRMA) head office is
151 Clarence St (☎ 9260 9222).

If your backpack needs repairing, try
Custom Luggage, 317 Sussex St. Cameras
can be repaired at Whilton Camera Service,
251 Elizabeth St, opposite Hyde Park.

If you just need a damn good wash, you
can get a shower at Travellers Aid in Central
Station for $3 on weekdays between 7 am
and 4.30 pm.

Bookshops The Travel Bookshop, 20
Bridge St, has the most comprehensive range
of guidebooks and travel literature.
Dymocks Booksellers, 424-426 George St,
claims to be the largest bookshop in the
southern hemisphere. Other good bookshops
are Abbey's Bookshop, 131 York St;
Gleebooks, 49 Glebe Point Rd, Glebe; and
Ariel, 42 Oxford St, Paddington.

Publications *For Backpackers, By Backpackers* is a free monthly booklet-magazine
with brief listings of budget places to stay
and things to see and do. It's available from
hostels and tourist offices.

The *Metro* lift-out in the Friday edition of
the *Sydney Morning Herald* provides a comprehensive listing of what's on in the city
over the coming week. The free music and
entertainment newspapers delivered to pubs,
cafes and record shops have listings and
supply addresses for those clubs that open
and close so fast that you never actually find
out where they are. They include *3D World*,
Drum Media and *Beat*.

The *Sydney Review* is a free monthly
newspaper covering cultural issues. Pick up
a copy at bookshops and galleries.

There are plenty of guidebooks to Sydney.
Lonely Planet's *Sydney city guide* and *New
South Wales & the ACT* are general guides.
Specialised books include the *Sydney Good
Walks Guide* by Joan Lawrence, *Sydney
Bushwalks* by Neil Paton and *Seeing Sydney
by Bicycle* by Julia Thorne.

A great piece of travel literature to read
while visiting the city is *Sydney* by Jan
Morris. For a literary journey through the
mean streets of Sydney, try one of Peter
Corris' Cliff Hardy thrillers.

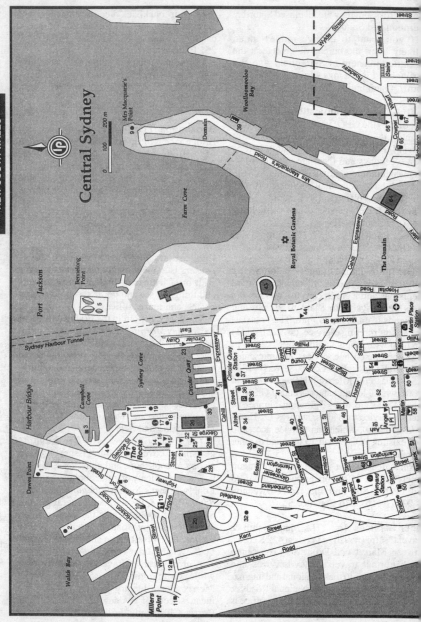

NEW SOUTH WALES

Central Sydney

0   100   200 m

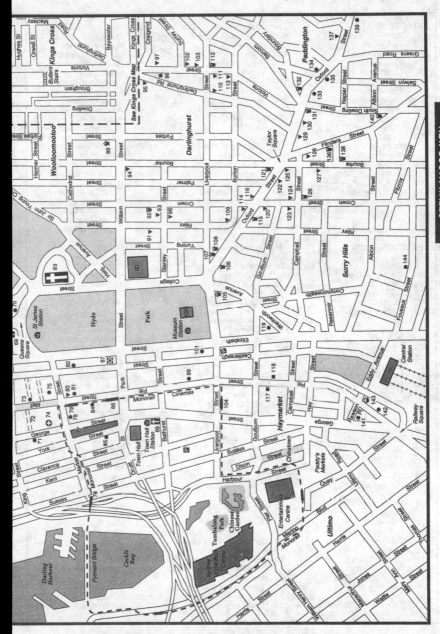

NEW SOUTH WALES

PLACES TO STAY

3   Park Hyatt
6   Harbour View Hotel
11   Palisade Hotel
12   Lord Nelson Hotel
27   The Stafford
29   Russell Hotel
33   Regent Hotel
45   Wynyard Travelodge
46   Grand Hotel
50   Wynyard Hotel
54   Sydney City Centre
     Serviced
     Apartments
88   Forbes Terrace Hostel
96   L'Otel & Govinda's
105 YWCA
117 CB Private Hotel
118 Westend Hotel
119 Sydney Central Private
     Hotel
144 Excelsior Hotel

PLACES TO EAT

8   Bilson's
14   Playfair St Cafe
16   G'Day Cafe
21   Gumnut Cafe
22   Rocks Cafe
23   Sydney Cove Oyster
     Bar
25   Rockpool
31   Rossini's
44   Kiosk on Macquarie
51   Merivales & Metro Bar
61   Carruthers
66   Harry's Cafe de
     Wheels
80   Merivales
91   Atlas
93   Bill and Toni's & Three
     Frogs
94   Cosmos
95   Tum Tum Thai &
     Cauldron
97   La Bussola & Bar
     Coluzzi
98   No Names
102 Burgerman
103 TJ's
109 Metro (Vegetarian
     Cafe)
110 Fishface
111 Fu-Manchu & Oh
     Calcutta!
113 Lauries
114 Open Kitchen
116 Tandoori Palace &
     Remo General Store
120 Roobar
122 Senate
123 Betty's Soup Kitchen

124 Maltese Cafe
125 Courthouse Hotel &
     Kinselas
127 Riberries
128 Bagel House
129 Balkan Seafood
130 Angkor Wat &
     Thai-Nesia
137 Bar Bola

ENTERTAINMENT
& PUBS

1   Pier One (Harbourside
     Brasserie)
2   Pier Four (Sydney
     Theatre Company)
7   Mercantile Hotel
10   Hero of Waterloo
28   Australian Hotel
35   The Basement
60   Dendy Cinema &
     Dendy Bar & Bistro
     (Martin Place)
65   Woolloomooloo Bay
     Hotel
68   Theatre Royal
71   Soup Plus
78   State Theatre
82   Riva
92   Hard Rock Cafe
99   Dendy Cinema
     (George Street)&
     Metro (Music
     Venue)
106 DCM
107 Burdekin Hotel
108 Exchange Hotel & Q
112 Green Park Hotel
115 Midnight Shift
121 Oxford Hotel
126 Bentley Bar
131 Beauchamp Hotel
132 Albury Hotel
133 Academy Twin
     Cinema &
     Goodbar
135 Verona Cinema
136 Flinders Hotel
138 Beresford Hotel
140 Palace Hotel

ATTRACTIONS

4   Earth Exchange
5   Sydney Opera House
9   Mrs Macquarie's Chair
13   Garrison Church
20   Sydney Observatory
24   Government House
26   Museum of
     Contemporary Art
32   National Trust Centre
37   Customs House

38   Justice & Police
     Museum
41   Macquarie Place
42   Museum of Sydney
43   Conservatorium of
     Music
56   Parliament House
62   Sydney Mint Museum
63   Sydney Hospital
64   Art Gallery of NSW
67   Artspace
69   St James Church
70   Hyde Park Barracks
75   Sydney Tower &
     Centrepoint
83   St Mary's Cathedral
84   Marble Bar & Hilton
     Hotel
87   Great Synagogue
89   St Andrew's Cathedral
90   Australian Museum
100 Anzac Memorial
139 Victoria Barracks

OTHER

15   Rocks Centre
17   Rocks Heritage &
     Information Centre
18   Cadman's Cottage
     (NPWS Information
     Centre)
19   Overseas Passenger
     Terminal
30   Commissioners &
     Harbourmaster's
     Steps
34   Australian Wine Centre
36   Paragon Hotel Internet
     Cafe
39   Boy Charlton Pool
40   The Travel Bookshop
47   Countrylink Travel
     Centre
48   Wynyard Park Bus
     Terminal
49   State Library of NSW
52   American Express
53   NSW Government
     Travel Centre
55   Sydney Visitors
     Information Booth &
     Halftix
57   NRMA
58   Main Post Office
59   Telstra Phone
     Centre
72   Strand Arcade
73   Skygarden
74   Traveller's Medical
     Centre, Travellers
     Contact Point &
     Dymocks
     Booksellers

Maps Just about every brochure you pick up includes a map of the city centre, but the *UBD Sydney Tourist* map ($4.50) has good coverage of the city centre and inner suburbs. If you're intending to drive around the city, the *Sydney UBD* street directory ($32) is an invaluable resource. For topographic maps, go to the DLWC (☎ 9228 6111), 23-33 Bridge St.

Medical Services The Traveller's Medical & Vaccination Centre (☎ 9221 7133), Level 7, 428 George St, and the Kings Cross Travellers' Clinic (☎ 9358 3066), Suite 1, 13 Springfield Ave, Kings Cross, are both open weekdays and Saturday mornings. It's best to book.

Emergency Phone ☎ 000 for police, fire or ambulance.

The Wayside Chapel (☎ 9358 6577), 29 Hughes St, Kings Cross, is a crisis centre which can handle personal problems.

Other emergency support services include Lifeline (☎ 13 1114) and the Rape Crisis Centre (☎ 9819 6565, 24 hours).

Dangers & Annoyances Sydney isn't an especially dangerous city but you should remain alert. The usual big-city rules apply: never leave luggage unattended, never flaunt money and never get drunk in the company of strangers. Harassment of gays, lesbians and non-Anglo-Saxons is not rife but it does

happen. Use extra caution in Kings Cross, which attracts shady characters.

Left-Luggage There are cloakrooms at Central and Town Hall train stations, costing $1.50 per item per day for the first day and $4.50 per day for subsequent days. Luggage lockers at the Sydney Coach Terminal on the corner of Pitt St and Eddy Ave, cost $4 a day. Lockers at the airport's international terminal also cost $4 per day; larger articles can be left in storage for $5 per item per day.

Sydney Harbour
The harbour has melded and shaped the Sydney psyche since the first days of settlement, and today it's both a major port and the city's playground. Its waters, beaches, islands and waterside parks offer all the swimming, sailing, picnicking and walking you could wish for.

Officially called **Port Jackson**, the harbour stretches some 20 km inland to join the mouth of the Parramatta River. The headlands at the entrance are known as North Head and South Head. The city centre is about eight km inland and the most scenic area is on the ocean side. **Middle Harbour** is a large inlet which heads north-west a couple of km inside the Heads.

The best way to view the harbour is to persuade someone to take you sailing, to take a day trip on a boat or to catch any one of the numerous ferries that ply its waters. The Manly ferry offers vistas of the harbour east of the bridge, while the Parramatta RiverCats cover the west.

Sydney's **harbour beaches** are generally sheltered, calm coves with little of the frenetic activity associated with the ocean beaches. On the south shore, they include Lady Bay (nude, mainly gay), Camp Cove (mainly locals) and Nielsen Park (families); all accessible by bus No 325 to Watsons Bay.

On the North Shore, there are harbour beaches at Manly Cove (suburban beach), Reef Beach (legal ruling awaited on nudity) Clontarf (families), Chinaman's Beach (quiet hideaway) and Balmoral (popular day trip for North Shore residents). The Manly

NEW SOUTH WALES

Harbour Walks

The 10-km **Manly Scenic Walkway** from Manly Cove to Spit Bridge is one of the best ways for landlubbers to experience the harbour. It passes through native bushland at Dobroyd Head, runs close to several hideaway beaches, passes Aboriginal engravings and a charming lighthouse at Grotto Point, and has panoramic views of Sydney Harbour and Middle Harbour. It can be a complicated walk to follow, so pick up a leaflet at Cadman's Cottage in the Rocks or at the Manly Visitors Information Bureau on South Steyne, Manly. Bus Nos 178, 180 and 182 run from Spit Bridge back to the city centre. The best way to get to Manly Cove is by ferry from Circular Quay.

There's a four-km walking track in **Ashton Park**, south of Taronga Zoo, which passes Bradleys Head and Taylor Bay. Bradleys Head has military fortifications and memorabilia. Take the Taronga Zoo ferry from Circular Quay to get to Ashton Park.

The walking track along the **Hermitage Foreshore** in Nielsen Park has spectacular views back to the city, and you can cool off at netted Shark Beach (known locally by the less scary name of Nielsen Park Beach). Bus No 325 from the city passes Nielsen Park via Kings Cross and terminates at Watsons Bay. **South Head**, near Watsons Bay, is a good spot for a cliff-top stroll. ∎

ferry docks at Manly Cove, and Reef Beach is a couple of km walk along the Manly Scenic Walkway. All the other beaches are accessible, with a bit of walking, by catching bus Nos 178, 180 and 182 which depart from Wynyard Park, travel along Military Rd and cross Spit Bridge.

Sydney Harbour National Park This park protects the scattered pockets of bushland around the harbour and includes several small islands. It offers some great walking tracks, scenic lookouts, Aboriginal carvings and a handful of historic sites. On the south shore, it incorporates South Head and Nielsen Park; on the North Shore, it includes North Head, Dobroyd Head, Middle Head and Ashton Park. Fort Denison, Goat, Clarke and Shark islands are also part of the park. The park headquarters (☎ 9337 5511) is at Greycliffe House in Nielsen Park, and you can also pick up information at Cadman's Cottage in the Rocks.

Previously known as Pinchgut, **Fort Denison** is a small fortified island off Mrs Macquarie's Point, used originally to isolate troublesome convicts. The fort was built during the Crimea War amid fears of a Russian invasion. Hegarty's Ferries (☎ 9206 1166) has daily 1½-hour tours to the island

at noon and 2 pm, and also at 10 am on weekends. They depart from Wharf 6 at Circular Quay and cost $8.50 ($6 concession). There are also three-hour guided tours (☎ 9555 9844) of **Goat Island**, just west of the Harbour Bridge, which has been a shipyard, quarantine station and gunpowder depot. Tours depart on weekends from the Harbourmaster's Steps at Circular Quay West at 10.25 am and 1.25 pm, and cost $12 ($8 concession).

Clarke Island, off Darling Point, and **Shark Island**, off Rose Bay, make great picnic getaways, but you'll need to hire a water taxi or have access to a boat to reach them. It costs $3 per person to visit the islands and bookings should be made several weeks in advance (☎ 9555 9844).

The Rocks

Sydney's first White settlement was on the rocky spur of land on the western side of Sydney Cove, from which the Harbour Bridge now crosses to North Shore. It was a squalid, raucous place of convicts, whalers, prostitutes and street gangs, though in the 1820s the nouveaux riches inexplicably built three-storey houses on the ridges overlooking the slums.

It later became an area of warehouses and

maritime commerce and then fell into decline as modern shipping and storage facilities moved away from Circular Quay. An outbreak of bubonic plague at the turn of this century led to whole streets being razed and the construction of the Harbour Bridge resulted in further demolition.

Since the 1970s, redevelopment has turned the Rocks into a sanitised, historical tourist precinct, full of narrow cobbled streets, fine colonial buildings, converted warehouses, tea rooms and stuffed koalas. If you ignore the kitsch, it's a delightful place to stroll around, especially in the backstreets and in the less developed, tight-knit, contiguous community of Millers Point.

Pick up a self-guided tour map of the area from the Rocks Heritage & Information Centre (☎ 9255 1788) in the old Sailors Home at 106 George St. It's open daily and has exhibits narrating the colourful and shameful history of the Rocks. Guided 75-minute walking tours of the area start at the centre on weekdays at 10.30 am and 12.30 and 2.30 pm, and on weekends at 11.30 am and 2.30 pm. The tours cost $10 ($6.50 concession).

Cadman's Cottage, in the Rocks, is the oldest house in Sydney

Next door to the Heritage Centre, at 110 George St, is **Cadman's Cottage** (1816), the oldest house in Sydney. It once housed longboats and was home to the last Government Coxswain, John Cadman, but it's now some distance from the water and is home to the National Parks & Wildlife Service Information Centre (☎ 9247 8861). The centre is open daily and is a good place for information about national parks near Sydney.

Despite all the helpful tourist infrastructure, the beauty of the Rocks is that it's as much fun to wander aimlessly around as it is

---

City Views

Sydney is an ostentatious city that offers visitors a dramatic spectacle. You can see the complete panorama by whooshing to the top of **Sydney Tower**, a needle-like column which has an observation deck and a 305-metre-high revolving restaurant. The view, extending as far as the Blue Mountains in the west, enables you to grasp an idea of the city's geography. The tower is on top of the Centrepoint complex on Market St, between Pitt and Castlereagh Sts. It's open daily from 9.30 am to 9.30 pm (11.30 pm on Saturday); entry costs $6 ($4 concession).

The Harbour Bridge is another obvious vantage point, but even many locals have never visited the small **Harbour Bridge Museum** and climbed the 200 stairs inside the south-eastern pylon to enjoy the dazzling view. The pylon and museum are open daily between 10 am and 5 pm; admission is $2. Enter from the bridge's pedestrian walkway, accessible from Cumberland St in the Rocks or from near Milsons Point station on the North Shore. There are impressive ground-level views of the city and harbour from **Mrs Macquarie's Point**, and from **Observatory Hill** in Millers Point. **Blues Point Reserve** and **Bradleys Head** are the best vantage points on the North Shore.

The most enjoyable and atmospheric way to view Sydney is by boat. If you can't persuade someone to take you sailing, jump aboard a ferry at Circular Quay. The Manly ferry offers an unforgettable cruise down the length of the harbour east of the bridge for a mere $3.60. If you really want to have your breath taken away, Heli-Scenic (☎ 9317 3402) offers 25-minute helicopter flights over the harbour daily for a cool $140. ■

to see particular attractions. Soak up the atmosphere, sample the frequent entertainment in The Rocks Square on Playfair St, browse around the ever vibrant **Rocks Centre** for that Aussie present you must go home with, dine at an outdoor cafe, admire the views of Circular Quay and **Campbell Cove**, and join the melee at the weekend **Rocks Market**.

A short walk west along Argyle Street, through the convict-excavated **Argyle Cut**, takes you to the other side of the peninsula and **Millers Point**, a delightful district of early colonial homes with a quintessential English village green. Close at hand are the **Garrison Church** and the more secular delights of the Lord Nelson Hotel and the Hero of Waterloo Hotel which vie for the title of Sydney's oldest pub.

Sydney Observatory (☎ 9217 0485) has a commanding position atop Observatory Hill overlooking Millers Point and the harbour, but it's crying out for direction and refurbishment. The observatory is open from 2 to 5 pm (from 10 am on weekends) and admission is free. Night visits and telescope viewing cost $5 ($2 concession) and must be booked in advance.

In the old military hospital building close by, the **National Trust Centre** houses a museum, art gallery, bookshop and tea rooms. It's open daily weekdays except Monday from 11 am to 5 pm, and weekends from 2 to 5 pm. Admission is $6 ($3 concession).

At Dawes Point on Walsh Bay, just west of the Harbour Bridge, are several renovated wharves. **Pier One** is an under-used shopping and leisure complex: **Pier Four** is beautifully utilised as the home of the prestigious Sydney Theatre and Sydney Dance companies.

Sydney Harbour Bridge

The much-loved, imposing 'old coat hanger' crosses the harbour at one of its narrowest points, linking the southern and northern shores and joining central Sydney with the satellite business district in North Sydney.

Sydney's famous icon, the Harbour Bridge, as seen from the Rocks

The bridge was completed in 1932 at a cost of $20 million and has always been a favourite icon, partly because of its sheer size, partly because of its function in uniting the city and partly because it kept a lot of people in work during the Depression.

You can climb inside the south-eastern stone pylon, which houses the Harbour Bridge Museum (see the earlier City View aside).

Cars, trains, cyclists, joggers and pedestrians use the bridge. The cycleway is on the western side and the pedestrian walkway on the eastern; stair access is from Cumberland St in the Rocks and near Milsons Point Station on the North Shore.

The best way to experience the bridge is undoubtedly on foot; don't expect much of a view crossing by car or train. Driving south (only) there's a $2 toll.

The **Harbour Tunnel** now shoulders some of the bridge's workload. It begins about half a km south of the Opera House, crosses under the harbour just to the east of the bridge, and rejoins the highway on the north ern side. There's a southbound (only) toll of $2. If you're heading from the North Shore to the eastern suburbs, it's much easier to use the tunnel.

Sydney Opera House

The Opera House is dramatically situated on the eastern headland of Circular Quay. Its soaring sail-like, shell-like roofs were actually inspired by palm fronds, but may remind you of turtles engaging in sexual congress. It's a memorable experience to see a performance here, and just as fulfilling to sit at one of the outdoor cafes and watch harbour life go by.

The Opera House has four auditoriums and hosts classical music, ballet, theatre and film, as well as seasonal opera performances. On Sunday, there is free music on the building's 'prow' and a bustling craft market in the forecourt.

Popular operas sell out quickly (despite the three-figure sums for the best seats) but there are often 'restricted view' tickets available for $30 for those with a long neck or a good imagination. Decent seats to see a play or hear the Sydney Symphony Orchestra are more affordable at around $35. The box office (☎ 9250 7777) is open Monday to Saturday between 9 am and 8.30 pm and 2½ hours prior to a Sunday performance.

Worthwhile one-hour tours of the building run daily between 9 am and 4 pm (☎ 9250 7250). They depart from the concourse and cost $9 ($6 students). Not all tours can visit all theatres because of rehearsals, but you're more likely to see everything if you take an early tour. There are irregular backstage tours on Sunday for $13.50.

Circular Quay

Circular Quay, built around Sydney Cove, is one of the city's major focal points. The first European settlement grew around the Tank Stream, which now runs underground into the harbour here near Wharf 6. For many years this was the shipping centre of Sydney, but it's now both a commuting hub and a recreational space, combining ferry quays, a railway station and the Overseas Passenger Terminal with harbour walkways, restaurants, buskers, fisherfolk and parks.

The **Museum of Contemporary Art** (MCA) is in the stately Art-Deco building dominating Circular Quay West. It's home to an eclectic array of modern art and is open daily from 11 am to 6 pm; entry is $8 ($5 concession). The grand **Customs House** fronting Circular Quay is awaiting redevelopment, possibly as a performance venue.

Macquarie Place & Surrounds

Narrow lanes lead south from Circular Quay

The Soap Opera House

The hullabaloo surrounding construction of the Sydney Opera House was an operatic blend of personal vision, long delays, bitter feuding, cost blowouts and narrow-minded politicking. Construction began in 1959 after Danish architect Jørn Utzon won an international design competition with his plans for a $7 million building. After political interference, Utzon quit in disgust in 1966, leaving a consortium of Australian architects to design a compromised interior. The parsimonious state government financed the eventual $102 million cost through a series of lotteries. The building was finally completed in 1973, but it was lumbered with an internal design impractical (too small, for one thing) for staging operas.

After all the brawling, the first public performance at the Opera House was, appropriately, Prokofiev's *War & Peace*. The preparations were reported to be a debacle and a possum appeared on stage during one of the dress rehearsals. One of the latest operas to debut here was staged by the resident Australian Opera in late 1995. It was called *The Eighth Wonder* and dramatised the events surrounding the building of the Opera House. ∎

towards the centre of the city. At the corner of Loftus and Bridge Sts, under the shady Moreton Bay figs in Macquarie Place, are a cannon and anchor from the First Fleet flagship, HMS *Sirius*. There is also an **obelisk**, erected in 1818, indicating road distances to various points in the nascent colony. The square has a couple of pleasant outdoor cafes and is overlooked by the rear facade of the imposing 19th-century **Lands Department building** on Bridge St.

The excellent new **Museum of Sydney** is east of here, on the corner of Bridge and Phillip Sts, on the site of the first and infamously fetid Government House built in 1788. The museum uses multiple perspective and installation art to explore the early history of Sydney. It's open daily and admission is $6.

The **Justice & Police Museum** is in the old Water Police Station on the corner of Phillip and Albert Sts. It's set up as a turn-of-the-century police station, and is open Sunday from 10 am to 5 pm; admission is $4 ($2 concession).

City Centre

Central Sydney stretches from Circular Quay in the north to Central Station in the south. The business hub is towards the northern end, but most redevelopment is occurring at the southern end and this is gradually shifting the focus of the city.

Sydney lacks a true civic centre, but **Martin Place** lays claim to the honour, if only by default. This grand pedestrian mall extends from Macquarie St to George St and is impressively lined by the monumental buildings of financial institutions and the colonnaded Victorian post office. The street has a couple of fountains, plenty of public seating, a Cenotaph commemorating Australia's war dead and an amphitheatre which is a popular lunchtime entertainment spot.

The old civic locus used to be the plaza a few blocks south of here containing the Town Hall and St Andrew's Cathedral but traffic flows and insensitive encroachment have diminished the area's authority. The **Town Hall**, on the corner of George and

Old and new architecture lines the streets of Sydney's city centre

Druitt Sts, was built in 1874 and it's outrageously ornate exterior is matched by the elaborate chamber room and concert hall inside. The Anglican **St Andrew's Cathedral** was built around the same time and is the oldest cathedral in Australia. Free organ recitals are held on Thursday lunchtimes.

The city's most sumptuous shopping complex, the Byzantine **Queen Victoria Building** (QVB), is next to the Town Hall and takes up an entire city block bordered by George, Druitt, York and Market Sts. Other interesting shopping centres include the lovingly restored Strand Arcade and the modern Skygarden arcade nearby.

Opposite the QVB, underneath the Royal Arcade linking George and Pitt Sts, is an extravagant piece of Victoriana called the **Marble Bar**. The city's other ostentatious building is the **State Theatre**, just to the north at 49 Market St; it's worth going to see a concert or musical here just to loiter in the lobby and marvel at the pomp-and-ceremony décor.

To the south-west are **Spanish Town** and **Chinatown**, two lively areas in a part of the city that includes an inordinate number of unsightly holes in the ground where development projects in the 1980s fell foul of economic downturn. Chinatown is booming, fuelled by an influx of money from Hong Kong, and it probably won't be long before this dynamic part of the city spreads to breathe life into the dead south-eastern zone, where Central Station lies isolated on the southern periphery.

Darling Harbour

This huge, purpose-built waterfront leisure park on the western edge of the city centre was once a thriving dockland area. Having declined to being an urban eyesore, it was reinvented in the 1980s by a combination of vision, politicking, forbearance and huge amounts of cash. The emphasis is on casual fun of the kind appreciated by families and coach tourists. The supposed centrepiece is the **Harbourside Festival Marketplace** – a graceful structure crammed with shops and tacky food outlets – but the real attractions are the stunning aquarium, state-of-the-art museums, the Chinese Garden and nifty water sculptures.

The **monorail** circles Darling Harbour and links it to the city centre. Harbourside, Convention, Haymarket and Darling Park are convenient stations for access to the complex.

Ferries leave from Circular Quay and stop at Darling Harbour's Aquarium Wharf every 30 minutes ($2.80). The Darling Harbour Rocket ferry departs every 20 minutes from the Harbourmaster's Steps at Circular Quay West ($3). The Sydney Explorer bus (see the Sydney Getting Around section) stops at five points around Darling Harbour every 20 minutes.

The main pedestrian approaches are across footbridges from Market and Liverpool Sts. The one from Market St leads to **Pyrmont Bridge**, now a pedestrian-and-monorail-only route, but once famous as the world's first electrically operated swingspan bridge.

The Darling Harbour Visitors Centre (☎ 9286 0100) is in the centre of the complex, under the highway, and is open daily.

Sydney Aquarium This aquarium, displaying the richness of Australian marine life, should not be missed. Three 'oceanariums'

are moored in the harbour with sharks, rays and big fish in one, and Sydney Harbour marine life and seals in the others. There are also informative and well-presented exhibits of freshwater fish and coral gardens. Transparent underwater tunnels offer spectacular views.

The aquarium is near the eastern end of Pyrmont Bridge and is open daily from 9.30 am to 9 pm; admission costs $14.90 (students $10).

Australian National Maritime Museum This thematic museum tells the story of Australia's relationship with the sea, from Aboriginal canoes and the First Fleet to surf culture and the America's Cup. A naval destroyer, a racing yacht and a Vietnamese refugee boat are moored outside awaiting exploration. Free guided tours take place on the hour between 11 am and 2 pm. The museum is near the western end of Pyrmont Bridge and is open daily from 9.30 am to 5 pm; admission is $7 ($4.50 concession).

Powerhouse Museum Sydney's most spectacular museum covers the decorative arts, social history, science and technology with exhibits covering just about anything from costume jewellery and Australian rock music to locomotives and space capsules. The collections are superbly displayed and the emphasis is on hands-on interaction and education through enjoyment.

The museum is behind the Sydney Exhibition Centre, at 500 Harris St, Ultimo, and is open daily from 10 am to 5 pm; admission is $5 ($2 concession), except on the first Saturday of each month when it's free.

Chinese Garden The exquisite Chinese Garden in the south-eastern corner of Darling Harbour is an oasis of tranquillity. It was designed by landscape architects from NSW's Chinese sister province, Guangdong, and it's worth every cent of the $2 (50c concession) entrance fee. Enter through the Courtyard of Welcoming Fragrance, circle the Lake of Brightness and round off the experience with tea and cake in the Chinese

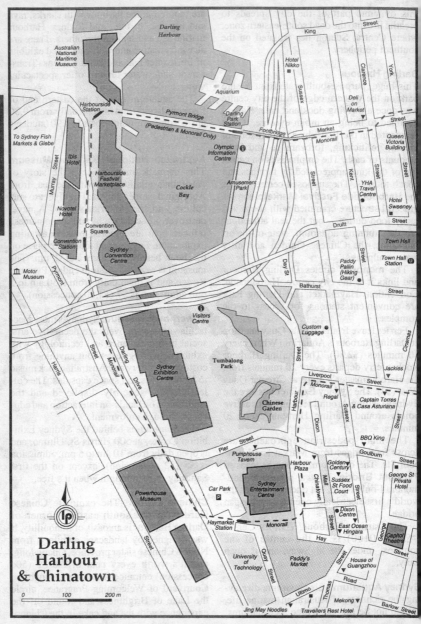

NEW SOUTH WALES

Darling Harbour & Chinatown

0   100   200 m

teahouse. The garden is open daily from 9.30 am to 4.30 pm.

Motor Museum There are over 100 vehicles on display at the Motor Museum, from vintage beauties to Morris Minors. It's at level 1, 320 Harris St, Ultimo – a short walk from the Powerhouse Museum, and is open Wednesday to Sunday and school holidays, from 10 am until 5 pm; admission is $8 ($4 concession).

Sydney Harbour Casino This enormous complex is being built on a waterfront site in Pyrmont on the north-eastern headland of Darling Harbour. It's scheduled to open in 1998. In the meantime, a temporary casino operates at Wharves 12 & 13 at Darling Harbour.

Sydney Fish Markets Fish auctions are held on weekdays at these markets, on the corner of Pyrmont Bridge Rd and Bank St, west of Darling Harbour. They begin at 5.30 am and last from three to six hours, depending on the size of the catch. The complex includes eateries and a couple of fabulous fish shops.

Macquarie St

Sydney's greatest concentration of early public buildings grace Macquarie St, which runs along the eastern edge of the city from Hyde Park to the Opera House. Many of the buildings were commissioned by Lachlan Macquarie, who was the first governor to have a vision of the city beyond that of a convict colony. He enlisted convict forger Francis Greenway as an architect to realise his plans.

Two Greenway gems on Queens Square, at the northern end of Hyde Park, are **St James Church** (1819-24) and the Georgian-style **Hyde Park Barracks** (1819). The barracks were built originally as convict quarters, then became an immigration depot, and later a court. They now house a museum which concentrates on the history of the building and provides an interesting perspective on Sydney's social history. The museum (☎ 9223 8922) is open daily from 10 am to 5 pm; admission is $5 ($3 concession).

Next to the barracks is the lovely **Mint Building** (1814), which was originally the southern wing of the infamous Rum Hospital built by two Sydney merchants in return for a monopoly on the rum trade. It became a branch of the Royal Mint in 1854 and now houses the Sydney Mint Museum, which has exhibits on the gold rush, coins and minting. It's open daily from 10 am to 5 pm; admission is $5 ($2 concession) except on the first Saturday of the month when entry is free.

The Mint's twin is **Parliament House**, which was originally the northern wing of the Rum Hospital. This simple, proud building is now home to the Parliament of NSW. It's open to the public on weekdays between 9.30 am and 4 pm and admission is free. There are free tours of the chambers at 10 and 11 am and 2 pm on non-sitting days. The public gallery is open on sitting days.

Next to Parliament House is the **State Library of NSW**, which is more of a cultural centre than a traditional library. It houses the Australian Research Collections, documenting early life in Australia, and hosts innovative temporary exhibitions in its galleries. The library is open daily, except the Australian Research Collections, which is closed on Sunday.

The **Sydney Conservatorium of Music** was built by Greenway as the stables and servants quarters of Macquarie's planned new government house. Macquarie was replaced as governor before the house could be finished, partly because of the extravagance of this project. The conservatorium is now a centre of musical studies and hosts performances, including free lunchtime concerts on Wednesday and Friday during study terms.

Art Gallery of NSW

This gallery has an excellent permanent display of Australian, Aboriginal, European and Asian art, and some inspired temporary exhibits. It's in the Domain, east of Macquarie St, and is open daily from 10 am to 5 pm. Admission is free but fees may apply to special exhibitions. There are free guided tours on the hour during lunchtime.

Art Gallery of NSW

Australian Museum

This natural history museum has an excellent Australian wildlife collection and a gallery tracing Aboriginal history from the Dreamtime to the present. It's on the eastern flank of Hyde Park, on the corner of College and William Sts. It's open daily from 9.30 am to 5 pm; admission is $5 ($3 concession) but it's free after 4 pm. There are free tours at 10 am, noon and 2 pm.

Parks

The city's favourite picnic spot, jogging route and place to stroll is the enchanting **Royal Botanic Gardens**, which border Farm Cove, east of the Opera House. The gardens were established in 1816 and feature plant life from the South Pacific. They include the site of the colony's first paltry vegetable patch, which has been preserved as the First Farm exhibit.

The tropical plant display in the Arc and Pyramid glasshouses is worth seeing ($5). The visitor centre (☎ 9231 8125) is open daily from 9.30 am to 4.30 pm. Guided walks begin at the centre on Wednesday and Friday at 10 am and on Sunday at 1 pm.

Government House dominates the western headland of Farm Cove. Until early 1996 this was the home of the Governor of NSW, but in the new spirit of republicanism the NSW government has made the governor's post a part-time, live-at-home position. The Government House grounds will be incorporated into the botanic gardens

and there is talk of transforming the house itself into a public art gallery.

The **Domain** is a grassy area east of Macquarie St which was set aside by Governor Phillip for public recreation. Today it's used by city workers for lunchtime sports and as a place to escape the hubbub. On Sunday afternoons, it's the gathering place for soapbox speakers who do their best to entertain or enrage their listeners.

On the eastern edge of the city centre is the formal **Hyde Park**, which was originally the colony's first racetrack and cricket pitch. It has a grand avenue of trees, delightful fountains, and a giant public chess board. It contains the dignified **Anzac Memorial**, which has a free exhibition on the ground floor covering the nine overseas conflicts Australians have fought in. **St Mary's Cathedral** overlooks the park from the east and the **Great Synagogue** from the west.

Sydney's biggest park is **Centennial Park**, which has running, cycling and horse tracks, duck ponds, barbecue sites and sports pitches. It's five km from the centre, just east of Paddington. You can hire bikes from several places on Clovelly Rd near the southeastern edge of the park (see Getting Around), or horses ($20) from Centennial Park Horse Hire (☎ 9361 4513) at the RAS Show Grounds on Lang Rd, just west of Centennial Park.

Neglected **Moore Park** abuts the eastern flank of Centennial Park and contains sports pitches, a golf course, the Sydney Football Stadium (SFS), the Sydney Cricket Ground (SCG) and the Royal Agricultural Society's (RAS) Show Ground. Sportspace (☎ 9380 0383) offers behind-the-scenes guided tours (1¾ - hours) of the SCG and SFS. Tours are held three times a day except Sunday (unless they conflict with a sporting event) and cost $18 ($12 concession). Most of the RAS Show Ground site is destined to become a 20th Century Fox film studio and entertainment complex in 1999.

On the North Shore, **Davidson Park** is an eight-km corridor of bushland stretching north-west from Middle Harbour to Ku-ring-gai Chase National Park. The **Lane Cove**

National Park runs between the suburbs of Ryde and Chatswood, and has extensive walking tracks along the picturesque but polluted Lane Cove River. Entry to the park costs $7.50 per car. The *Reliance* (☎ 9566 2067) departs from Darling Harbour on weekends at 11 am and cruises up the Lane Cove River. The 3¾-hour trip includes a barbecue lunch and costs $35. Swimming in the river is prohibited.

See the Sydney Harbour section for information on the parks and bushland areas which comprise the Sydney Harbour National Park.

Kings Cross

The Cross is a bizarre cocktail of strip joints, prostitution, crime and drugs, shaken and stirred with a handful of classy restaurants, designer cafes, international hotels and backpacker hostels. It attracts an odd mix of low-life, sailors, travellers, Japanese tourists, inner-city trendies and suburbanites looking for a big night out.

The Cross has always been a bit raffish, from its early days as a centre of bohemianism to the Vietnam War era, when it became the vice centre of Australia. While the vice is real and nasty enough, Sydneysiders are quite fond of the Cross. It appeals to the larrikin spirit, which always enjoys a bit of devil-may-care and 24-hour drinking. Many travellers begin and end their Australian adventures in the Cross, and it's a good place to swap information, meet up with friends, pick up work, browse the hostel notice boards and buy or sell a car.

Darlinghurst Rd is the trashy main drag. This doglegs into Macleay St which continues into the more up-market suburb of Potts Point. Most of the hostels are on Victoria St, which diverges from Darlinghurst Rd just north of William St, near the iconic Coca-Cola sign. The thistle-like El Alamein Fountain in Fitzroy Gardens is the psychological centre of the area, and there's a market here every Sunday.

The helpful Kings Cross Tourist Information Service (☎ 9368 0479) operates from a window booth in the Fitzroy Gardens. You can book tours and bus tickets here and the staff know the area well and will recommend places to stay.

In the dip between the Cross and the city is Woolloomooloo, one of Sydney's oldest areas. Sensitive urban restoration has made it a lovely place to stroll around. Its huge disused wharf is awaiting redevelopment. Harry's Cafe de Wheels is next to the wharf and must be one of the few pie carts in the world to be a tourist attraction. It opened in 1945, stays open 18 hours a day and is *the* place to go for a late-night chicken and mushroom fill-up. The innovative Artspace gallery is opposite.

The easiest way to get to the Cross from the city is by train ($1.40 one way). It's the first stop outside the city loop on the line to Bondi Junction. Bus Nos 324, 325 and 327 from Circular Quay pass through the Cross. You can walk from Hyde Park along William St in 15 minutes. A prettier, longer route involves crossing the Domain, descending the hill behind the Art Gallery of NSW, walking past Woolloomooloo's wharf and climbing McElhone Stairs to the northern end of Victoria St.

Inner East

The lifeblood of Darlinghurst, Surry Hills and Paddington, Oxford St is one of the more exciting places for late-night action. It's a strip of shops, cafes, bars and nightclubs where the hip and the oh-so contemporary rub shoulders with the soiled and the so-so. It's flamboyance and spirit are largely attributed to its vibrant and vocal gay community, and the route of the Sydney Gay & Lesbian Mardi Gras parade passes this way.

The main drag of Oxford St runs from the south-eastern corner of Hyde Park to the north-western corner of Centennial Park, though it continues in name into Bondi Junction. Taylor Square is the hub of social life in the area. Oxford St street numbers restart west of the junction with South Dowling and Victoria Sts on the Darlinghurst-Paddington border. Bus Nos 380 and 382 from Circular Quay, and No 378 from Railway Square, run the length of the street.

NEW SOUTH WALES

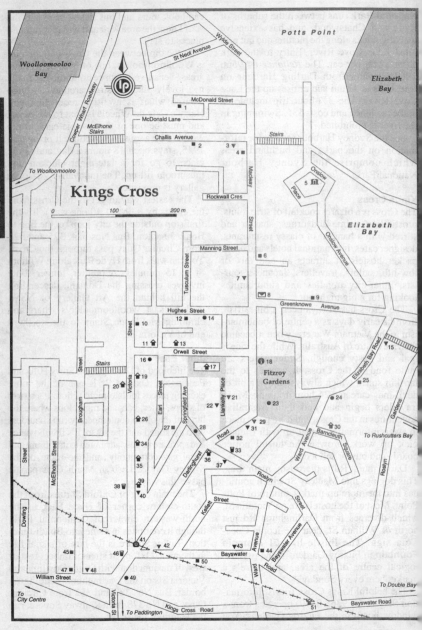

Kings Cross

Woolloomooloo Bay

Potts Point

Elizabeth Bay

St Neot Avenue

Wylde Street

Cowper Wharf Roadway

McDonald Street

McDonald Lane

McElhone Stairs

Challis Avenue

Stairs

Mackeay Street

Onslow Place

Onslow Avenue

To Woolloomooloo

Rockwall Cres

Elizabeth Bay

0   100   200 m

Tusculum Street

Manning Street

Greenknowe Avenue

Hughes Street

Elizabeth Bay Road

Street

Orwell Street

Victoria Street

Earl Street

Springfield Ave

Llankelly Place

Fitzroy Gardens

Stairs

Street

Brougham Street

Elizabeth Bay Road

Ward Avenue

Barncleuth Square

Roslyn Gardens

To Rushcutters Bay

Darlinghurst Road

Roslyn Street

McElhone Street

Dowling Street

Street

Kellett Street

Bayswater Avenue

Bayswater Road

To Double Bay

William Street

Victoria St

To City Centre

To Paddington

Kings Cross Road

Bayswater Road

PLACES TO STAY

1	Rucksack Rest
2	Challis Lodge
4	Macleay Lodge
6	De Vere Hotel
9	Manhattan Hotel
10	Victoria Court Hotel
11	Eva's Backpackers
12	Gala Hotel
13	Jolly Swagman (16 Orwell St)
17	Jolly Swagman (27 Orwell St)
19	Jolly Swagman (Victoria St)
20	Kanga House
25	Sebel Town House
26	Travellers Rest
27	Bernly Private Hotel & Springfield Lodge
30	Pink House
32	Kingsview Motel
34	Original Backpackers
35	Highfield House
36	Dury House Backpackers
39	Plane Tree Lodge
44	Metro Motor Inn
45	Cross Court Tourist Motel
47	O'Malley's Hotel
50	Barclay Hotel
51	Backpackers Headquarters

PLACES TO EAT

3	Cicada
7	Japanese Noodles Shop
15	Arun Thai
21	Yakitori
22	Pad Thai
29	Fountain Cafe
31	Bourbon & Beefsteak
37	Cosmic Cafe & Barrons
40	Roys Famous
42	Waterlily Cafe
43	Bayswater Brasserie & Darley St Thai
48	William's on William & Mamma Marias

PUBS & CLUBS

33	Round Midnight
38	Soho Bar
46	Kings Cross Hotel

OTHER

5	Elizabeth Bay House
8	Post Office
14	Wayside Chapel
16	Travel Active
18	Tourist Information
23	El Alamein Fountain
24	Car Market
28	Bureau de Change
41	Kings Cross Train Station
49	Thomas Cook

The inner-city mecca for bright young things wanting to be close to the action and live on nothing but cafe lattes is **Darlinghurst**. It's a vital area of trendy, self-conscious, urban cool that's fast developing a cafe monoculture, and there's no better way to soak up its studied ambience than to loiter in a few sidewalk cafes and do as the others do. Darlinghurst encompasses the vibrant 'Little Italy' of Stanley St in East Sydney, and is wedged between Oxford and William Sts.

South of Darlinghurst is **Surry Hills**, the centre of Sydney's rag trade and print media, and home to a mishmash of inner-city residents and a swag of good pubs. The Surry Hills Market is held on the first Saturday of the month in Shannon Reserve on the corner of Crown and Foveaux Sts. The Brett Whiteley Studio, 2 Raper St, is in the artist's old home and studio, and is open on weekends between 10 and 4 pm; admission is $6 ($4 concession). Surry Hills is a short walk east of Central Station or south from Oxford St. Catch bus Nos 301, 302 and 303 from Circular Quay.

Next door to Surry Hills is **Paddington**, an attractive residential area of leafy streets and tightly packed Victorian terrace houses. It was built for aspiring artisans, but during the lemming-like rush to the outer suburbs after WW II the area became a slum. A renewed interest in Victorian architecture and the pleasures of inner-city life led to its restoration during the 1960s and today these modest terraces swap hands for a decent portion of a million dollars.

Most facilities, shops, cafes and bars are on Oxford St but the suburb doesn't really have a geographic centre. Most of its streets cascade down the hill north of here towards Edgecliff and Double Bay. It's a lovely place to wander around at any time, but the best time to visit is Saturday when the **Paddington Village Bazaar** is in full swing on the corner of Newcombe and Oxford Sts.

There are over 20 art galleries in Paddington; pick up a copy of *Paddington Galleries & Environs* at the first one you stumble upon. Free tours of the stately Victoria Barracks on Oxford St are held on Thursday between 10 am and 2 pm, including a performance by the military band. The Army Museum is open on Sunday between 10 am and 3 pm; admission is free.

Victorian-era terraces dominate the leafy streets of Paddington

Eastern Suburbs

A short walk north-east of the Cross is the harbour-front apartment suburb of **Elizabeth Bay**. Elizabeth Bay House, 7 Onslow Ave, is one of Sydney's finest colonial homes. It's open daily except Monday from 10 am to 4.30 pm; admission is $5 ($3 concession).

Beautiful, yacht-clogged **Rushcutters Bay** is the next bay east. Its handsome harbourside park is just a five-minute walk from the Cross and is the closest place for cooped up backpackers to stretch their legs. Tennis courts (☎ 9357 1675) can be hired for $16 an hour. This is the yachting centre of Sydney and is one of the best places to learn to sail (see the Sailing & Boating section).

Farther east is the manicured suburb of **Double Bay**, which is over-endowed with smart cafes and designer stores, and reeks with the glamour of money. The views from the harbour-hugging New South Head Rd as it leaves Double Bay, passes **Rose Bay** and climbs east towards wealthy **Vaucluse**, are up there with the best. Vaucluse House, in Vaucluse Park, is an attractive colonial villa

open daily except Monday from 10 am to 4.30 pm; admission is $5.

At the entrance to the harbour is **Watsons Bay**, a snug community composed of harbourside restaurants, a palm-lined park and a couple of nautical churches. It makes a great day trip if you want to forget you're in the middle of a large city. Nearby **Camp Cove** is one of Sydney's best harbour beaches, and there's a nude beach near South Head at **Lady Bay**. South Head has great views across the harbour entrance to North Head and Middle Head. **The Gap** is a dramatic cliff-top lookout on the ocean side (it's also Sydney's favourite suicide spot).

Bus Nos 324 and 325 from Circular Quay service the eastern suburbs via Kings Cross. Sit on the left side heading east to make the most of the views.

Southern Beaches

The grande dame of Sydney's beaches is **Bondi**, which has a majesty all its own. The focus is on the sand 'n' surf, but the suburb has a unique flavour blended from the mix

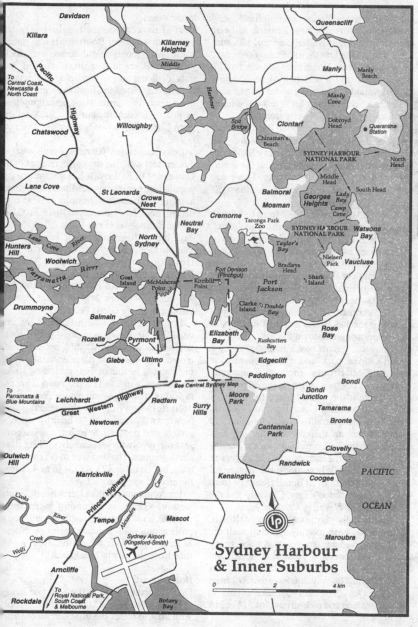

Sydney Harbour & Inner Suburbs

of old Jewish and Italian communities, dyed-in-the-wool Aussies, New Zealand and UK expats, working travellers and surf rats who live here bonded by their love for the beach.

In recent years Bondi has shed much of its tired facade and a new lick of paint, some long-awaited landscaping and a rash of new cafes has been enough for it to be suddenly 'rediscovered' by inner-city trendies.

The ocean road is Campbell Parade, where most of the shops, cafes and hotels are. The Bondi Beach Market is held every Sunday at the Bondi Beach Public School, at the northern end of Campbell Parade. There are Aboriginal rock engravings on the golf course in North Bondi.

Catch bus Nos 380 or 382 from the city to get to the beach or, if you're in a hurry, catch a train to Bondi Junction and pick up one of these buses as they pass through the Bondi Junction bus station.

Just south of Bondi is **Tamarama**, a lovely cove with strong surf that's popular with Sydney's 'beautiful' people. Get off the bus as it kinks off Bondi Rd onto Fletcher St, just before it reaches Bondi Beach. Tamarama is a five-minute walk down the hill.

There's a superb beach hemmed in by a bowl-shaped park and eroded sandstone headlands at **Bronte**, south of Tamarama. Cafes with outdoor tables on the edge of the park make it the perfect place for a day of rest and relaxation. Catch bus No 378 from the city or catch a train to Bondi Junction and pick the bus up there; sit on the left side heading to the beach and wait for the breathtaking view as the bus descends Macpherson St. You can walk here along the wonderful cliff-top footpath from Bondi Beach or from Coogee via Gordon's Bay, Clovelly and the sun-bleached Waverley Cemetery.

Traditionally the poor cousin of Bondi, **Coogee** has been recently sprucing itself up. It has a relaxed air, few graces, a good sweep of sand and a couple of established hostels and hotels. You can reach Coogee by catching bus No 372 from Railway Square or No 373 from Circular Quay. Alternatively, take a train to Bondi Junction and pick up bus Nos 314 or 315 from there.

Inner West

West of the centre is the higgledy-piggledy peninsula suburb of **Balmain**. It was once a notoriously rough neighbourhood of dock yard workers but gentrification ha transformed it into an arty, middle-class are of restored Victoriana flush with pubs. It's great place for a casual stroll, a walking tou or just to fossick for curios. Catch a ferr from Circular Quay or bus No 442 from th QVB.

Cosy, bohemian **Glebe** is south-west o the centre, bordering the northern edge of th University of Sydney. It has a large studer population, a relaxing cafe-lined main stree a tranquil Buddhist temple and severa decent hostels. A market is held at Gleb Public School, on Glebe Point Rd, on Satu day. It's a 10-minute walk from Centra Station along Broadway or you can wal from the city centre across Darlin Harbour's Pyrmont Bridge and alon Pyrmont Bridge Rd (20 minutes). Bus Nc 431 and 434 from Millers Point run vi George St along Glebe Point Rd.

Bordering the southern flank of the un versity is **Newtown**, a melting pot of soci and sexual subcultures, students and hom renovators. King St, its relentlessly urba main drag, is full of funky clothes store bookshops, cafes and far too many Thai res taurants for its own good. While it definitely moving up the social scal Newtown comes with a healthy dose c grunge and political activism, and harbou several of Sydney's fast-dwindling live music venues. The best way to get there is b train, but bus Nos 422, 423, 426 or 428 fro the city all run along King St.

Predominantly Italian **Leichhardt**, soutl west of Glebe, is becoming increasingl popular with students, lesbians and your professionals. Its Italian eateries on Nortc St have a city-wide reputation. Bus No 44 runs from the city to Leichhardt.

North Shore

On the northern side of the Harbour Bridg is **North Sydney**, a high-rise office cent with little to tempt the traveller. **McMahor**

oint is a lovely, forgotten suburb wedged etween the two business districts, on the estern side of the bridge. There's a line of leasant sidewalk cafes on Blues Point Rd, hich runs down to Blues Point Reserve on e western headland of Lavender Bay. The eserve has fine views across to the city.

Luna Park, on the eastern shore of Lavnder Bay, is a gaudy, but charming, musement park. Unfortunately, declining evenue led the renovated park to temporary close as this book was going to press. The ark may re-open, but there is talk of selling e land for hotel or residential development.

At the end of Kirribilli Point, east of the ridge, stand **Admiralty House** and **irribilli House**, the Sydney residences of e governor-general and the prime minister spcctively (Admiralty House is the one arer the bridge).

East of here are the up-market suburbs of **eutral Bay**, **Cremorne** and **Mosman**, all ith pleasant coves and harbourside parks erfect for picnics. Ferries go to all these burbs from Circular Quay.

On the northern side of Mosman is the etty beach suburb of **Balmoral**, which ces Manly across Middle Harbour. There's promenade, picnic areas, three beaches, a uple of waterfront restaurants, and water ort hire facilities (see the Activities ction).

ronga Park Zoo

ronga Park Zoo in Mosman has a superb rbourside setting and more than 4000 critrs, including lots of native Australian. rries leave Wharf 2 at Circular Quay and op at the Taronga Park Wharf. The rear trance to the zoo is near the wharf. owever, the zoo complex is on a steep hill, if you don't want to experience it by nstantly walking uphill, you can catch a s to the main entrance at the top of the hill d walk down. An alternative is catch the ble car (grandly called the Aerial Safari) m the rear (bottom) entrance to the main op) one. The cable car costs $2.50 one way.

The zoo (☎ 9969 2777) is open daily from am to 5 pm, although night visits are

Taronga Park Zoo

planned. Admission is $14.50 ($8.70 concession). A Zoo Pass, sold at the ferry ticket counters at Circular Quay, costs $18 and includes a return ferry ride, zoo admission and either the bus or the Aerial Safari to the top entrance.

Manly

The jewel of the North Shore, Manly is located on a narrow peninsula which ends at the dramatic cliffs of North Head. It boasts harbour and ocean beaches, a ferry wharf, all the trappings of a full-scale holiday resort and a great sense of community identity. It's a sun-soaked place not afraid to show a bit of tack and brashness to attract visitors, and makes a refreshing change from the prim upper-middle class harbour enclaves nearby.

The Manly Visitors Information Bureau (☎ 9977 1088) on the promenade at South Steyne is open daily from 10 am to 4 pm. It has useful, free pamphlets on the 10-km Manly Scenic Walkway and sells Manly Heritage Walk booklets for $3.50. Small lockers are available for $2 a day. There's a bus information booth at the entrance to the wharf.

Both ferries and JetCat catamarans ply

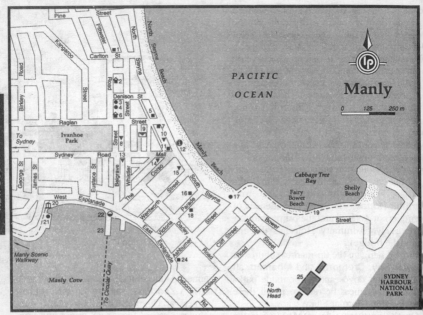

PACIFIC OCEAN

Manly

0   125   250 m

Cabbage Tree Bay

Shelly Beach

Fairy Bower Beach

Manly Beach

SYDNEY HARBOUR NATIONAL PARK

Manly Cove

Manly Scenic Walkway

To Sydney

To North Head

NEW SOUTH WALES

PLACES TO STAY

1 Manly Beach Resort
2 Manly Astra Backpackers
5 Manly Pacific Parkroyal
6 Manly Backpackers Beachside
7 Manly Paradise Motel & Manly Blades
11 Steyne Hotel
16 Eversham Private Hotel
18 Manly Lodge
24 Periwinkle Guesthouse

PLACES TO EAT

8 Cafe Tunis & Candy's Coffeehouse
10 Brazil
13 Malacca Straits
14 Green's Eatery
15 Cafe Nice

OTHER

3 Aloha Surf
4 Manly Cycle Centre
9 Post Office

12 Visitors Information Bureau
17 Surf Lifesaving Club
19 Rock Pool
20 Manly Art Gallery & Museum
21 Oceanworld
22 Bus Interchange
23 Manly Wharf/Ferries
25 St Patrick's College

between Circular Quay and Manly. The JetCats seem to traverse the harbour before you get a chance to blink, so jump on one of the stately Manly ferries. These navigate the length of the harbour in a cool 30 minutes and offer fantastic views of the city.

The ferry wharf is on Manly's harbour shore. A short walk along Manly's pedestrian mall, the Corso, brings you to the ocean beach lined by towering Norfolk Pines. North and South Steyne are the roads running along the foreshore. A footpath follows the shoreline from South Steyne around the small headland to Fairy Bower Beach and the picturesque cove of **Shelly Beach**.

The **Manly Art Gallery & Museum** has local history exhibits focussing on the suburb's special relationship with the beach. The museum is on West Esplanade, on the Manly Cove foreshore, and is open Tuesday to Sunday from 10 am to 5 pm; entry is $2.

The excellent **Oceanworld** is next door. The big drawcards are the sharks and sting-rays, and the best time to visit is 12.15 and 2.30 pm when divers enter the tanks to feed the bigger fish. An underwater perspex tunnel offers dramatic (but dry) close encounters with the fish. If that's still not close enough for your thrill levels, certified Scuba divers can dive with the sharks in the evenings for $65. Oceanworld is open daily from 10 am to 5.30 pm. Entry is $12.50 ($9 concession) which includes a free voucher to visit the Manly Art Gallery & Museum. Behind Oceanworld is the wonderful 10-km-long Manly Scenic Walkway (see the Harbour Walks aside).

North Head, at the entrance to Sydney Harbour, is about three km south of Manly. Most of the dramatic headland is in Sydney Harbour National Park. The **Quarantine Station** represents an interesting slice of Sydney's social history; it housed suspected disease carriers from 1832 right up until 1984. To visit the station you have to book a guided tour (☎ 9977 6522). These depart daily at 1.10 pm, take 1½ hours and cost $6 ($4 concession). Catch bus No 135 from Manly Wharf.

Northern Beaches

A string of ocean-front suburbs stretches north along the coast from Manly, ending some 30 km on at beautiful, well-heeled **Palm Beach** and the spectacular Barrenjoey Heads at the entrance to Broken Bay. There are plenty of beaches along the way, including **Freshwater** (teenagers), **Curl Curl, Dee Why, Collaroy** and **Narrabeen** (families and surfers). The most spectacular are **Whale Beach** and **Bilgola**, near Palm Beach, which both have dramatic steep headlands. Several of the northernmost beach suburbs also back onto **Pittwater**, a lovely inlet off Broken Bay and a favoured sailing spot.

Bus Nos 136 and 139 run from Manly to Freshwater and Curl Curl. Bus No 190 from Wynyard in the city runs to Newport and north to Palm Beach. The Northern Beaches Explorer (☎ 9913 8402) runs hop-on/hop-off buses from Manly to Palm Beach on Thursday and weekends which stop at most of the northern beaches. Tickets cost $20 and are valid all day. Buses depart hourly from Manly Wharf from 9.15 am to 2.15 pm all year, except in winter when the service is radically reduced.

This route is becoming increasingly popular as the first step on the journey to the northern coast of NSW or as a weekend excursion to the Central Coast from Sydney. The thrice daily Palm Beach Ferry Service (☎ 9918 2747) runs between Palm Beach and Patonga on the Central Coast ($6 return).

Activities

Swimming Sydney's harbour beaches offer sheltered water conducive to swimming. But if you just want to frolic, nothing beats being knocked around in the waves that pound the ocean beaches, where swimming is safe if you follow instructions and swim within the 'flagged' areas patrolled by lifeguards. There are some notorious but clearly signposted rips even at Sydney's most popular beaches, so don't underestimate the surf just because it doesn't look threatening. Efforts are made to keep surfers separate from swimmers. If you're worried about sharks, just remind yourself that Sydney has had only one fatal shark attack since 1937.

Outdoor pools in the city include the salt-water Boy Charlton pool in the Domain, on the edge of Woolloomooloo Bay; the Prince Alfred Park pool, near Central Station; the Victoria Park pool on Broadway, next to the University of Sydney; and the North Sydney Olympic Pool in Milsons Point. The Boy Charlton and Alfred Park pools currently close during winter.

Surfing South of the Heads, the best spots are Bondi, Tamarama, Coogee and Maroubra. Cronulla, south of Botany Bay, is also a serious surfing spot. On the North

Shore, there are a dozen surf beaches between Manly and Palm Beach; the best are Manly, Curl Curl, Dee Why, North Narrabeen, Mona Vale, Newport Reef, North Avalon and Palm Beach itself.

Shops such as the Bondi Surf Company, 72 Campbell Parade, Bondi Beach, and Aloha Surf, 44 Pittwater Rd, Manly, hire equipment. Expect to pay $25 for a board and up to $10 for a wetsuit for the day.

Sailing & Boating There are plenty of sailing schools in Sydney and even if you're not serious about learning the ropes, an introductory lesson can be a fun way of getting out on the harbour.

Sydney Sail (☎ 9907 0004) offers a 90-minute introductory hands-on sail for $29 departing daily from the National Maritime Museum in Darling Harbour.

The sociable East Sail Sailing School (☎ 9327 1166) at d'Albora Marina, New Beach Rd, Rushcutters Bay, runs a huge range of courses from introductory to racing level.

Northside Sailing School (☎ 9969 3972), at the southern end of the Spit Bridge in Mosman, also offers courses and rents sailboards and lasers.

Rose Bay Aquatic Centre (☎ 9371 7036) and Balmoral Marine (☎ 9969 6006) offer tuition and rent sailboards ($10), catamarans ($20 to $25) and motor boats by the hour.

The Elizabeth Bay Marina (☎ 9358 2977), close to Kings Cross, hires 17-foot boats with outboards for $55 for a half-day.

Pittwater and Broken Bay offer excellent sailing. Scotland Island Schooners (☎ 9999 3954) at Church Point runs intensive two-day yachting courses and offers generous discounts to travellers and YHA members. It also operates occasional schooner cruises for $24.

Diving The best shore dives in Sydney are the Gordons Bay Underwater Nature Trail, north of Coogee; Shark Point, Clovelly; and Ship Rock, Cronulla. Popular boat dive sites are Wedding Cake Island, off Coogee;

around the Sydney Heads; and off the Royal National Park.

Plenty of outfits will take you diving and many run dive courses, including Pro Dive (☎ 9264 6177) at 428 George St in the city and 27 Alfreda St, Coogee (☎ 9665 6333), and Dive Centre Manly (☎ 9976 3297) at 10 Belgrave St, Manly. Qualified divers can also dive with the sharks at Manly's Oceanworld (see the Manly section).

Canoeing & Kayaking The NSW Canoe Association (☎ 9660 4597) provides information on canoe courses, hire and tours. Canoe Specialists (☎ 9969 4590) at the southern end of Spit Bridge in Mosman rents sea kayaks for $10 for the first hour and $5 for each subsequent hour. Natural Wanders (☎ 9555 9788) has kayak tours of the harbour which go under the bridge and stop in secluded bays. A five-hour tour costs $75 including lunch; no experience is necessary.

Inline Skating The beach promenades at Bondi and Manly are the two most favoured spots for skating. Manly Blades (☎ 9976 3833), 49 North Steyne, hires skates for $10 for the first hour and $5 for each subsequent hour, or $25 per day; Bondi Boards & Blades (☎ 9365 6555), 148 Curlewis St, Bondi Beach, has the same hourly rate and charges $28 a day. Protective gear is free.

Organised Tours

Conventional city and country tour operators include Australian Pacific (☎ 13 1304), Clipper Gray Line (☎ 9241 3983) and Murrays (☎ 9319 1266). A half-day city tour costs around $35, and a one-day tour costs around $70. Tours of the Blue Mountains cost around $60, the Hunter Valley $65 and Canberra $70.

Maureen Fry (☎ 9660 7157) offers a variety of guided walking tours of Sydney for around $12 ($6 concession). World Beyond (☎ 9555 9653) runs cycling day tours of Sydney on weekends for $75, including cycle and helmet hire, ferry transport and lunch. It also arranges custom cycle tours for small groups and has basic two-day

$115) and luxury four-day ($450) cycle ours of the Blue Mountains.

The Wonderbus runs backpacker-friendly ay tours to the Blue Mountains for $48. It's ossible to arrange a one-night stopover in Catoomba and catch the tour back to Sydney he next day, depending on seating availability. Sook at the YHA Travel Centre (☎ 9261 1111) r Quayside Booking Centre (☎ 9247 5151). Oz Trek (☎ 9369 7055) also runs a reportedly ood Blue Mountains day tour for $43.

Cruises There's a wide range of relatively inexpensive cruises on the harbour, from erry boats and cruisers to paddlewheelers nd sailing ships. You can book most at the Quayside Booking Centres (☎ 9247 5151) at Wharves 2 & 6, Circular Quay. Captain 'ook Cruises (☎ 9206 1111) has its own ooking office at Wharf 6.

STA ferries offer some good-value ruises, such as the 2½-hour Ferry Cruise which departs Circular Quay at 1 pm on veekdays and 1.30 pm on weekends and isits Middle Harbour. Tickets cost $16 and an be purchased from the ticket office oppo- te Circular Quay's Wharf 4.

The Sydney Harbour Explorer is a hop- n/hop-off service which stops at Circular Quay, the Opera House, Watsons Bay, aronga Zoo and Darling Harbour. Boats run wo-hourly from 9.30 am until 3.30 pm and he fare is $18 ($13 concession).

The Rocket Harbour Express (☎ 9264 377) operates a hop-on/hop-off service etween Darling Harbour, Luna Park, aronga Zoo and Harbourmaster's Steps at 'ircular Quay West. The service cruises up he Parramatta River as far as the Olympic iames site at Homebush Bay. Boats depart very two hours from 9 am, with the last boat eparting at 3 pm. The fare is $18.

For $39 you can take a two-hour weekday unch cruise on the *Bounty* (☎ 9247 1789), a eplica of the ship lost by Captain Bligh, which departs Campbell Cove in the Rocks : 12.30 pm.

Festivals
he Sydney Festival is the umbrella for a range of events in January, including street theatre around Circular Quay and huge free outdoor concerts in the Domain. Chinese New Year is celebrated in Chinatown with firecrackers in January or February. Surf life-saving carnivals are held at Sydney's ocean beaches from mid-November to May.

The highlight of the month-long Gay & Lesbian Mardi Gras is the outrageous parade along Oxford St which ends in a bacchana-lian party at the RAS Show Ground in Moore Park in late February or early March.

The 12-day Royal Easter Show is an agricultural show and funfair also held at the RAS Show Ground, but scheduled to move to Homebush Bay in 1998. It begins a week before Good Friday with a parade of animals through the city centre.

The 14-day Sydney Film Festival is held in June at the State Theatre and other cinemas. The Biennale of Sydney is an inter-national art festival held between July and September in even-numbered years at the Art Gallery of NSW, the Powerhouse Museum and other venues.

The 14-km City to Surf Run takes place on the second Sunday in August and attracts a mighty 30,000 entrants prepared to run from Hyde Park to Bondi Beach. The Manly Jazz Festival is held over the Labour Day long weekend in early October and the Kings Cross Carnival takes place in late October or early November.

Thousands of backpackers descend on Bondi Beach for a booze fest on Christmas Day, much to the consternation of the powers that be and the overworked lifesavers. Sydney Harbour is a fantastic sight on Boxing Day as boats of all shapes and sizes farewell the competitors in the gruelling Sydney to Hobart Yacht Race. The Rocks, Kings Cross and Bondi Beach are all tradi-tional gathering places for alcohol-sodden celebrations on New Year's Eve.

Places to Stay
Sydney has a huge variety of accommoda-tion, including a large selection of travellers hostels. Prices listed below are winter rates. In summer, prices rise and special deals

vanish. At these times, expect hostel rates to increase by just the odd dollar; hotel rooms at beachside suburbs can increase by as much as 50%.

Bed & Breakfast Sydneyside (☎ 9449 4430), PO Box 555, Turramurra, 2074, arranges accommodation in private homes for about $45 to $65 a night for a single, or $65 to $95 a double. Global Village Accommodation Services (☎ 9211 3145), PO Box 1839, Strawberry Hills, NSW 2012, aims to link visitors with local people offering accommodation. It costs $75 to register and requires a minimum stay of one month.

If you want to find long-stay accommodation, peruse the 'flats to let' and 'share accommodation' ads in the *Sydney Morning Herald*, especially on Wednesday and Saturday. Hostel notice boards are also good sources of information.

Camping Sydney's caravan parks are a long way out of town, but those listed below are within 25 km of the city centre:

East's Lane Cove River Van Village (☎ 9805 0500), Plassey Rd, North Ryde has sites/vans/cabins from $16.50/45/50 a double.
Sheralee Tourist Caravan Park (☎ 9567 7161), 88 Bryant St, Rockdale offers sites/vans from $12/35 a double.
Lakeside Caravan Park (☎ 9913 7845), Lake Park Rd, North Narrabeen has sites/cabins from $15/58 a double.
The Grand Pines Caravan Park (☎ 9529 7329), 289 Grand Parade, San Souci rents vans/cabins from $45/50 a double.

Hostels The largest concentration of hostels is in Kings Cross, but there are others in Glebe, Manly and Coogee. The average price for a dorm bed is $15, but in the peak summer period they can rise to $20. Facilities vary from dorms with en suite, TV, fridge and cooking facilities to just a plain room with a couple of bunks. Some hostels have set hours for checking in and out, although all have 24-hour access once you've paid.

City Centre The *YWCA* hostel (☎ 9264 2451) on Wentworth Ave allows both men and women to stay. A dorm bed costs $22 a night, but the maximum stay is just three nights. Rooms go for $47/65/80 for singles/twins/triples; $65/90/100 with bathroom.

The big *CB Private Hotel* (☎ 9211 5115), 417 Pitt St, has dorms for $12, but it's not really a travellers hostel.

A 500-bed YHA hostel was due to open in January 1997 on the corner of Pitt St and Rawson Place ($20 a night).

Kings Cross & Nearby There are heaps of hostels in the Cross and little to distinguish between many of them. Eva's has the best reputation, followed by Backpackers Headquarters. The Pink House is for those who like their hostels a little more lived-in and cosy. The Jolly Swagman hostels have the best organised social life.

Heading north along Victoria St from Kings Cross Station, the first hostel you come to is *Plane Tree Lodge* (☎ 9356 4551) at No 172. This is an average Kings Cross hostel, with a variety of rooms. Rates start at $14 ($80 weekly) in a six-bed dorm with TV and fridge, $15 ($90 weekly) in a four-bed. Twins cost $16 per person and doubles with en suite $35. Next down the street at No 166 is *Highfield House* (☎ 9358 1552), another average place with three-bed dorms for $15, twins for $16 per person, and singles/doubles for $30/40 ($180/240 weekly).

The *Original Backpackers* (☎ 9356 3232) in the lovely Victorian building at No 162 is the original hostel in this part of the world. It's a reasonably clean, lived-in kind of place with a rear courtyard and a pleasant kitchen-dining area. Dorms cost $15 ($90 weekly) and singles/doubles are $20/32 ($120/195 weekly).

The accommodating *Travellers Rest* (☎ 9358 4606) at No 156 has OK dorms with fridge and TV for $12, twins for $15 per person, singles for $25 ($140 weekly) and doubles with en suite for $34 ($198 weekly).

One of the three busy *Jolly Swagman* (☎ 9357 4733) hostels is at No 144. The others are at 16 Orwell St (☎ 9358 6600) and 27 Orwell St (☎ 9358 6400). They all charge $16 ($96 weekly) for bright dorms with kitchenettes and fridge, and $36 ($216 weekly) for doubles. The 27 Orwell St hostel received a five-backpack rating in the recent Federal government survey. Organised entertainment includes barbecues, tennis matches and trips. Across the road at No 141 is the basic *Kanga House* (☎ 9357 7897), which charges $13 ($80 weekly) for dorms and $15/28 ($90/175 weekly) for singles/doubles.

Eva's Backpackers (☎ 9358 2185) at 6-8 Orwell St is a clean, friendly, well-run place, and with a five-backpack rating. Dorms cost $15 and doubles/triples $34/45. It's so popular that it's often full, even in winter. The secure, squeaky-clean *Backpackers Headquarters* (☎ 9331 6180) at 79 Bayswater Rd has dorms from $14 ($84 weekly) and is also often full.

One of the most popular hostels in the Cross is the mellow, homely *Pink House* (☎ 9358 1689), which has a lovely patio, a rear courtyard and a good travellers' atmosphere. It's east of Darlinghurst Rd at 6 Barncleuth Square. Dorm beds cost $14 ($84 weekly) and twins are $15 per person ($94 weekly). *Dury House Backpackers* (☎ 9358 4844), 2 Roslyn St, is just off Darlinghurst Rd. It has spacious dorm rooms, with modern bathrooms and kitchens, for $15.

Rucksack Rest (☎ 9358 2348), 9 McDonald St, Potts Point, is a quiet hostel for international travellers only. Dorm beds cost $15 ($90 weekly) and singles/doubles $25/30. *Forbes Terrace* (☎ 9358 4327), 153 Forbes St, Woolloomooloo, is four streets east of Victoria St. It's a clean, quiet hostel with a five-backpack rating. It has a courtyard area and rooms equipped with TV and fridge. Dorms cost $16 ($98 weekly), singles/doubles go for $35/45.

South of the Centre *Kangaroo Bakpak* (☎ 9319 5915) at 665 South Dowling St, Surry Hills, has dorm beds for $13 ($80 weekly). Bus Nos 372, 393 and 395 run along Cleveland St from Central Station; bus Nos 301, 302 and 303 run along Bourke St from Circular Quay. *Nomads Backpackers* (☎ 9331 6487) in the renovated Captain Cook Hotel, 162 Flinders St, Surry Hills, has dorms for $16. It's only a few minutes walk from Taylor Square.

The *Excelsior Hotel* (☎ 9211 4945), 64 Foveaux St, Surry Hills, is a small pub only a few blocks from Central Station with dorms for $15 ($85 weekly) and singles for $35 ($190 weekly).

The *Alfred Park Private Hotel* (☎ 9319 4031), 207 Cleveland St, is just a short stroll from Central Station. It has a pleasant courtyard and kitchen, and dorms with en suite, TV and fridge for $16 ($98 weekly). Singles/doubles cost $35/55 and doubles with en suite $65.

Billabong Gardens (☎ 9550 3236), 5 Egan St, Newtown, is a quiet hostel with a pool and spa and a five-backpack rating. Dorms with en suite cost $15 ($100 weekly) and singles/doubles $20/40 ($120/240 weekly). Take a train to Newtown Station, turn right into King St, and Egan St is about four blocks along on the left.

Glebe The YHA has two large, squeaky-clean hostels in Glebe: the *Hereford YHA Lodge* (☎ 9660 5577) at 51 Hereford St, and *Glebe Point YHA Hostel* (☎ 9692 8418) at 262 Glebe Point Rd. Hereford Lodge justly has a five-backpack rating. It has a small rooftop pool, good communal areas and an en suite in every room. It accommodates 260 people, and if it feels about as atmospheric as a becalmed university hall of residence, that's the price you pay for having its exceptional facilities at your disposal. Six-bed dorms cost $17 ($105 weekly), four-bed dorms $19 ($120 weekly) and twin rooms $23 per person. Nonmembers pay $2 more. It's often full, even in winter, so try to arrive around 10 am (check-out time) to be sure of a bed.

Glebe Point is a smaller hostel with shared bathroom facilities. Six-bed dorms cost $16, four-bed $18 and twin rooms $50. Both hostels offer a range of activities, and they both store luggage and deduct the airport bus fare from your bill. The YHA also operates a *summer hostel* at St Andrews College at the

University of Sydney, where dorms cost $16 and twins $19 per person.

The friendly *Glebe Village Backpackers* (☎ 9660 8133), 256 Glebe Point Rd, is a large ramshackle hostel in two big houses suitable for those travellers who place sociability above cleanliness. The dorms and common areas look like a student sharehouse after a bunfight, but it has a lovable, tatty charm. Dorms cost from $16 and doubles $42.

Popular *Wattle House* (☎ 9692 0879), 44 Hereford St, has dorm beds for $18 ($110 weekly) and twin or double rooms from $44 ($240 weekly). The *Alishan International Guesthouse* (☎ 9566 4048) at 100 Glebe Point Rd is a lovely, civilised guesthouse which has a few dorm beds for $18 ($112 weekly).

Bondi Bondi has a range of hostel accommodation, not all of it particularly appealing, but with the consolation of the beach on your doorstep you're unlikely to spend much time staring at the paint peeling in your room. This is a popular base for long-term working travellers so there are plenty of cheap flats available if you plan on sticking around for a while.

The *Lamrock Hostel* (☎ 9365 0221), 7 Lamrock Ave, is a well-worn but bright, uninstitutional and friendly hostel. It's a block back from Campbell Parade on the corner of Lamrock and Jacques Aves. Dorms cost $15, singles/doubles $20/45 and studio flats $70 per person per week.

The *Bondi Beach Guest House* (☎ 9389 8309), 11 Consett Ave, is two blocks from the beach, and has unpromising dorms for $15 ($90 weekly) and singles/doubles $20/40.

Bondi Lodge (☎ 9365 2088), 63 Fletcher St, is a short, sharp walk up the hill from the southern end of the beach, but it's well placed to get to neighbouring Tamarama Beach. It offers dinner, bed and breakfast for $30 in a dorm ($125 weekly) and from $40/60 in singles/doubles.

Coogee It's worth ringing before setting off to Coogee because some hostels have limited office hours. *Surfside Backpackers Coogee* (☎ 9315 7888), on the corner of Arden and Alfreda Sts, is conveniently just across the road from the beach and the main bus stop. It's a fine hostel with a five-backpack rating. Dorms cost $15 ($90 per week) and doubles $34.

The popular *Coogee Beach Backpackers* (☎ 9665 7735), 94 Beach St, is a short but stiff walk up the hill at the northern end of the beach. The hostel is in a summery Federation house and a modern block next door. It's clean, and has good common areas and a deck with great views of the ocean. Spacious dorms cost $16 and doubles $33.

Indy's (☎ 9315 7644), 302 Arden St, is up the hill at the southern end of the beach. Four-bed dorms cost $15, which includes breakfast.

In nearby Clovelly is the *Nomads Clovelly Beach Backpackers* (☎ 9665 1214) at 381 Clovelly Rd. Dorms are $15, doubles $20.

Manly This is the best place to stay if you want to be free of city hassles, experience Sydney's beach culture and still be within commuting distance of the city.

Manly Backpackers Beachside (☎ 9977 3411), 28 Raglan St, has modern dorms costing $15, with a $2 linen fee for the first night. Singles cost $30. The older *Manly Astra Backpackers* (☎ 9977 2092) is nearby at 68-70 Pittwater Rd. Dorms cost $14 ($78 weekly) and singles/doubles $20/28 ($100/156 weekly).

Manly Beach Resort (Backpackers) (☎ 9977 2092), 6 Carlton St, is part of a motel on the corner of Pittwater Rd and Carlton St. A bed in a spartan five-bed dorm with en suite costs $16 for the first night and $14 for each subsequent night ($91 weekly).

The huge *Steyne Hotel* (977 4977) on the Corso has squashy four-bed dorms for $20, which includes what is described as 'a big hearty Australian breakfast'. There are good shared kitchen facilities but with cheap food available in the bar downstairs there's not much point cooking for yourself. *Manly Lodge* (☎ 9977 8655), 22 Victoria Parade,

DAVID COLLINS

JON MURRAY

JON MURRAY

JON MURRAY

JON MURRAY

New South Wales

A: Megalong Valley, Blue Mountains
B: Sunset, Darling River
C: Protesters' Falls near Nimbin
D: Border Ranges National Park
E: Abondoned farmhouse, Cooma

JON MURRAY

JON MURRAY

JON MURRAY

| A |
| B |
| C |

New South Wales
A: Mootwingee National Park
B: Ghost town in the Riverina
C: Mungo National Park

has backpacker dormitories at Tower St and Wood St from $15 per night ($75 weekly).

North Shore *Kirribilli Court Private Hotel* (☎ 9955 4344), 45 Carabella St, Kirribilli, has dorm beds for $15 ($80 weekly) and singles/doubles with shared bathroom and kitchen for $25/40.

The *Harbourside Hotel* (☎ 9953 7977), 41 Cremorne Rd, Cremorne Point, is a large hostel which looks more like a NSW north coast commune. Dorms cost $14 ($90 weekly). It's close to Cremorne Wharf, but a long hike from facilities on Military Rd.

For a break from inner-city life, try the relaxed northern beachside suburb of Avalon, where the purpose-built *Avalon Beach Hostel* (☎ 9918 9709), 59 Avalon Parade, offers the nicest hostel accommodation in Sydney. It has an open-plan common area, couches around a fire, a big balcony, and the atmosphere of a beachside rainforest lodge. There are surfboards and bikes for hire. Dorms cost from $14 a night ($90 weekly) and doubles are $36. Take bus No 190 from Wynyard Park, York St, and ask for Avalon Beach (1¼ hours, $4.40). Make sure you phone in advance because it's often full, even in winter.

Hotels & Guesthouses – bottom end

There are some fine budget hotels and guesthouses, which work out only fractionally more expensive than hostels if you're travelling with friends. A refundable key deposit of around $10 is often required.

City Centre & the Rocks The *George St Private Hotel* (☎ 9211 1800), 700A George St, is the best of the budget inner-city hotels. It's plain, clean, equipped with cooking and laundry facilities, and doesn't have the slightest whiff of seediness. Spartan singles/doubles/triples with shared bathroom cost $30/44/55 ($180/260/330 weekly), doubles with en suite cost $60.

The nearby *CB Private Hotel* (☎ 9211 5115), 417 Pitt St, opened in 1908 and was once the largest hotel in the country. It's fairly well maintained, but gets a lot of wear.

Singles/doubles/triples with shared bathroom are $29/45/55. If you stay a week, you get one night free.

The *Sydney Central Private Hotel* (☎ 9212 1005), 75 Wentworth Ave, is a basic hotel with cooking and laundry facilities, just a short walk from Central Station and Oxford St. Singles/doubles cost $30/40 ($115/195 weekly) with shared bathroom, or $40/50 with en suite.

The small *Harbour View Hotel* (☎ 9252 3769) on the corner of Lower Fort and Cumberland Sts is a community pub on the fringes of the Rocks. There's some noise from trains on the bridge and even more from the awful bands in the bar, but with clean singles/doubles with views for $45/55, it's great value and a great location.

The *Palisade Hotel* (☎ 9247 2272) stands like a sentinel at 35 Bettington St, Millers Point. It has basic pub rooms with shared bathroom, and city, bridge, harbour and dockyard views for $60 a double.

Kings Cross & Nearby One of the accommodation bargains near the Cross is *Challis Lodge* (☎ 9358 5422), 21-23 Challis Ave, which occupies a pair of cavernous terraces in Potts Point. It's a low-key, well-run establishment offering singles/doubles with fridge and TV for $30/38 ($150/190 weekly) or $40/44 ($200/220 weekly) with en suite. Rooms on the upper floors are quieter and get better light. Nearby *Macleay Lodge*, (☎ 9368 0660), 71 Macleay St, Potts Point has good-value, bright singles/doubles with TV, fridge and shared bathroom from $30/38.

Springfield Lodge (☎ 9358 3222), 9 Springfield Ave, has similar rooms but they're a tad depressing and not as well maintained. Singles/doubles with shared bathroom are $32/42 ($160/210 weekly) and, with en suite, $42/49 ($190/245 weekly).

The nearby *Bernly Private Hotel* (☎ 9358 3122), 15 Springfield Ave, has light, modern singles/doubles/triples with TV and shared bathroom for $40/50/60; rates are negotiable.

The *Cross Court Tourist Motel* (☎ 9368 1822) is a terrace house at 203 Brougham St, which offers smart, tasteful singles/doubles with TV, fridge and shared bathroom for $40/50 for the first night and $35/40 for subsequent nights.

The *Gala Hotel* (☎ 9357 1199), 23 Hughes St, is a welcoming guesthouse with a TV lounge and communal kitchen. Singles/doubles with fridge and shared bathroom cost $40/45, doubles with en suite $55.

Newtown The clean, pleasant-looking *Australian Sunrise Lodge* (☎ 9557 4400), 485 King St, has motel-style singles/doubles with TV and fridge for $45/55, or $55/65 with en suite.

Watsons Bay If you want to enjoy the harbour in a quiet locale and still be within a short ferry ride of the city, try the harbourside *Watsons Bay Hotel* (☎ 9337 4299), 1 Military Rd, Watsons Bay, which has singles/doubles for $40/70.

Bondi Bondi's hotels are prone to summer price rises like most other beachside suburbs. Rates below are for the low season. Summer visitors should also expect weekend price hikes and the disappearance of bargain winter weekly rates.

The *Thellelen Beach Inn* (☎ 9130 5333), 2 Campbell Parade, is the brightly painted 1930s landmark drawing attention to itself at the southern end of the beach. It's a well-run place in a great location with clean, acceptable rooms with TV and fridge and shared bathroom facilities. Singles cost $35, small doubles $39 and large doubles $45 ($160/190/220 weekly). Three people can occupy a double for an extra $5.

The *Biltmore Private Hotel* (☎ 9130 4660), 110 Campbell Parade, was a large, depressing place but a recent renovation may have remedied this and it could be OK. Singles/doubles/triples cost $30/40/45 ($130/180/210 weekly).

The *Hotel Bondi* (☎ 9130 3271) is the peach-coloured layer-cake at 178 Campbell Parade. It has OK single rooms for $30 or

$35 with an en suite, and doubles for $55 or $65 with an ocean view.

The *Thellelen Lodge* (☎ 9130 1521), 11a Consett Ave, is run by the same people who manage the Thellelen Beach Inn. It's a modest operation in a renovated suburban house two blocks back from the beach. It's very clean, has a good communal kitchen and double rooms (only) cost $45 ($220 weekly).

Coogee The *Grand Pacific Private Hotel* (☎ 9665 6301), Carr St, overlooks the southern end of the beach. Singles/doubles with TV and fridge cost from $17/30 (from $100/140 weekly). Some rooms have views.

Manly The *Eversham Private Hotel* (☎ 9977 2423), 27-29 Victoria Parade, is a huge, somewhat depressing place more reminiscent of an Edwardian boarding school than accommodation at a beach resort. Acceptable singles/doubles cost $28/46 ($123/150 weekly) and triples $69 ($225 weekly).

North Shore *St Leonards Mansions* (☎ 9439 6999), 7 Park Rd, St Leonards, has singles/doubles with TV, cooking facilities and telephone for $35/45 with shared bathroom or $45/55 with en suite, including breakfast. From St Leonards station, turn left (west) along the Pacific Highway and Park Rd is the second street on the left.

Kirribilli Court Private Hotel (☎ 9955 4344), 45 Carabella St, has dorm beds for $15 ($80 weekly) and singles/doubles with shared bathroom and kitchen for $25/40.

Tremayne Private Hotel (☎ 9955 4155), 89 Carabella St, Kirribilli, is a guesthouse with singles/doubles with shared bathroom for $140/220 weekly (no daily rates).

The *Neutral Bay Motor Lodge* (☎ 9953 4199), on the corner of Karraba Rd and Hayes St in Neutral Bay, has motel-style singles/doubles/triples with en suite, fridge and TV for $50/55/60.

Hotels, Motels, Guesthouses & Serviced Apartments – middle There are some mid-range hotels and guesthouses offering top-value facilities at little more than budget prices.

City Centre & The Rocks The *Sydney City Centre Serviced Apartments* (☎ 9233 6677), 7 Elizabeth St, offers the best-value accommodation in the city. It's in the heart of the financial district, between Martin Place and Hunter St. The apartments are fully equipped with kitchenette, TV, fridge, phone, en suite, washing machine and drier, and cost $60 a double. If you want to chance arriving without a booking, enquire at the travel agent next door.

The *Wynyard Hotel* (☎ 9299 1330), on the corner of Clarence and Erskine Sts, is a pub with singles/doubles with shared bathroom for $50/60. Another city pub, the *Grand Hotel* (☎ 9232 3755), 30 Hunter St, has singles/doubles with TV and fridge for $60/80. In the south of the city, the renovated *Westend Hotel* (☎ 9211 4822), 412 Pitt St, offers doubles for $90.

The *Travellers Rest Hotel* (☎ 1800 023 071), 37 Ultimo Rd, Haymarket, is close to Chinatown and Darling Harbour. It has good singles/doubles from $59/69, or $79/89 with bathroom. A spacious, spartan room with four bunks and shared bathroom costs $69.

The *Lord Nelson Hotel* (☎ 9251 4044), on the corner of Kent and Argyle Sts, Millers Point, is a boutique pub on the edge of the Rocks. It has three doubles with shared bathroom for between $60 and $100.

Kings Cross & Nearby *O'Malley's Hotel* (☎ 9357 2211) is a friendly Irish pub at 228 William St, near the Coca-Cola sign. It has excellent singles/doubles with fridge, TV and en suite from $50/60.

The *Barclay Hotel* (☎ 9358 6133), 17 Bayswater Rd, has a wide range of air-con singles/doubles with TV, telephone and en suite from $55/65. At 40 Bayswater Rd, there's a *Metro Motor Inn* (☎ 9356 3511) charging $79 for doubles with TV, kitchen and en suite.

The *Kingsview Motel* (☎ 9358 5599), 30 Darlinghurst Rd, has air-con rooms with TV

and en suite for $68 on weekends and $90 during the week.

In Potts Point, the *De Vere Hotel* (☎ 9358 1211), 46 Macleay St, has air-con singles/doubles with TV, telephone and en suite from $79/89. The lovely Art-Deco *Manhattan Hotel* (☎ 9358 1288), 8 Greenknowe Ave, has doubles from $85, or $95 with a harbour view. The comfortable *Victoria Court Hotel* (☎ 9357 3200), 122 Victoria St, has doubles with TV, telephone and en suite for $99, including breakfast.

The very hip *L'Otel* (☎ 9360 6868), 114 Darlinghurst Rd, is on the Darlinghurst side of the huge William St-Victoria St-Darlinghurst Rd junction. It's a stylish boutique hotel charging from $80 a double with TV, telephone and en suite.

The *Lodge* (☎ 9327 8511), 38-44 New South Head Rd, Rushcutters Bay, has studio apartments with TV, kitchenette and en suite for $69 a double. Check-in is at the Bayside Motel diagonally opposite.

Glebe The *Alishan International Guesthouse* (☎ 9566 4048), 100 Glebe Point Rd, is a guesthouse and up-market hostel, with good common areas, including kitchen, laundry facilities, jacuzzi and a small garden. Singles/doubles with en suite cost $65/75.

As well as hostel accommodation, the YHA's *Hereford Lodge* (☎ 9660 5577), 51 Wattle St, has good motel-style singles for $65, plus $5 for each extra person, up to four. YHA members get a discount.

The *Rooftop Motel* (☎ 9660 7777), 146-148 Glebe Point Rd, is a pleasant motel charging $75 for air-con rooms with TV, fridge, telephone and en suite.

The *Haven Inn* (☎ 9660 6655), 196 Glebe Point Rd, has excellent rooms with en suite that comfortably sleep three people from $99. There's a heated swimming pool, spa and secure parking.

Bondi The *Bondi Beachside Inn* (☎ 9130 5311), 152 Campbell Parade, is the kind of architectural monstrosity which gave Bondi a bad name, but inside it's a delightful place with spacious apartment-style rooms which have TV, phone, modern kitchen, en suite and balcony. Standard doubles cost $69, or $75 with an ocean view (worth paying for). Renovated rooms are $75, or $88 with a view. There's plenty of room for three people to stay in the room ($10 extra).

Ravesi's, on the corner of Campbell Parade and Hall St, is a classy establishment indicative of the emerging smarter Bondi. Rooms start at $95, or $125 with an ocean view.

Coogee The *Coogee Bay Hotel* (☎ 9665 0000), on the corner of Arden St and Coogee Bay Rd, has air-con singles/doubles with fridge, TV, telephone and en suite for $65/74, and doubles with ocean view from $84.

Manly Like all beach suburbs, Manly is susceptible to price rises in summer and on weekends. The prices below are for midweek rates in winter.

The excellent *Manly Lodge* (☎ 9977 8655), 22 Victoria Parade, offers B&B in good rooms with TV, fridge and en suite for $49/69 for singles/doubles or $79 for a family room which sleeps four. The *Steyne Hotel* (9977 4977) on the Corso has OK singles from $44, and twins and doubles from $69, including breakfast.

Reasonable motel rooms at *Manly Beach Resort* (☎ 9977 2092), 6 Carlton St, cost $70/75 for a single/double, including breakfast. *Periwinkle Guesthouse* (☎ 9977 4668), 18-19 East Esplanade, is an elegant guesthouse on Manly Cove with singles/doubles/triples from $70/80/95. Rooms with en suite or harbour view cost extra.

The *Manly Paradise Motel* (☎ 9977 5799), 54 North Steyne, is on the beachfront. It has a rooftop pool and air-con motel rooms with TV, fridge and en suite for $89, or $95 with an oblique view of the ocean.

Hotels & Serviced Apartments – top end
There are lots of hotels and serviced apartments charging between $100 and $200 a double but many cater to business people so their rates might be lower on weekends. Serviced apartments sometimes sleep more than

two people and with lower weekly rates they can be inexpensive among a group.

The boutique *Russell Hotel* (☎ 9241 3543), 143 George St, the Rocks, has doubles with shared bathroom from $105 and with en suite from $160. The *Stafford* (☎ 9251 6711), 75 Harrington St, the Rocks, has studio apartments from $170.

In the city centre, the *Wynyard Travelodge* (☎ 9299 3000), 7 York St, has rooms from $140. In the Cross, the *Sebel Town House* (☎ 9358 3244), Elizabeth Bay Rd, charges from $155.

Beachside hotels include the *Swiss Grand Hotel* (☎ 9365 5666), Bondi Beach (from $180); the *Holiday Inn* (☎ 9315 7600), Coogee (from $165); and the *Manly Pacific Parkroyal* (☎ 9977 7666), Manly (from $125).

The international hotels with heavyweight reputations include *The Regent* (☎ 9238 0000), 199 George St; the *Park Hyatt* (☎ 9241 1234), 7 Hickson Rd, the Rocks; and the plush *Ritz-Carlton* (☎ 9362 4455), 33 Cross St, Double Bay.

Colleges Many colleges at the University of Sydney (☎ 9692 2222) and the University of NSW (☎ 9385 1000) are eager for casual guests during vacations. Most places quote B&B or full-board rates but it's often possible to negotiate a lower bed-only rate.

University of Sydney This is south-west of the city centre, close to Glebe and Newtown. A sample of colleges offering accommodation includes:

International House (☎ 9950 9800); full board in singles for $35 ($200 weekly) or in twins for $25 ($150 weekly)
St Johns College (☎ 9394 5200); B&B singles for $40 with shared bathroom, and $45 with en suite.
Women's College (☎ 9516 1642); B&B singles/doubles for $40/60.
Sancta Sophia College (☎ 9519 7123); B&B singles for $40, and full board for $55.

University of NSW This is farther from the centre but not far from Oxford St and the southern ocean beaches.

International House (☎ 9663 0418); full-board
singles for $40

New College (☎ 9697 8962); singles from $30, or $25
for students.

Places to Eat

With great local produce, innovative chefs,
inexpensive prices and BYO licensing laws,
it's no surprise that eating out is one of the
great delights of a visit to Sydney.

Modern Australian cuisine mixes Mediterranean, Asian and Californian cooking
practices and emphasises lightness, freshness and healthy eating. In Sydney, this style
has filtered down from sophisticated restaurants to modest corner bistros, so you'll be
able to savour it no matter what your budget.
Cafes tend to serve a ubiquitous diet of
focaccia, sandwiches and filled croissants
and bagels.

If you're going to explore Sydney's food
options, *Cheap Eats in Sydney* ($7.95) lists
affordable places, but it's positive about
every single one of them so learn to read
between the lines. An excellent, critical book
is the Sydney Morning Herald's *Good Food
Guide* ($16.95).

City Centre There's no shortage of places
for a snack or meal in the city, especially on
weekdays. They are clustered around
railway stations, in shopping arcades and
tucked away in the food courts to be found
in just about every office building higher
than 20 storeys.

Bar Paradiso has a lovely aspect and
outdoor tables in the historic precinct of
Macquarie Place. Focaccia, pizza and
Turkish bread go for around $7; soup and
bread for $5.50. The *Customs House Bar*
next door is similar and serves submarine
sandwiches at $1 per inch.

Deli on Market is a large deli-cafe on the
corner of Clarence and Market Sts which
serves a range of breakfasts for between $2
and $4.50, and wholesome lunches for
between $5.50 and $7.

The *Metro Bar* at 123 Pitt St has standard
cafe fare from as cheap as $2.50, plus complimentary views of the bizarre City Golf

driving range. *Merivales Basement Bar* in
the Angel Hotel, 125 Pitt St, has tasty snacks,
and modish lunches and dinner for between
$6 and $10. There's a second, slightly pricier
operation in the basement at 194 Pitt St.

The *Dendy Bar & Bistro* is a funky brasserie in the Dendy Cinema in the MLC
Centre, Martin Place. It has an uncomplicated menu including pastas, burgers and
steaks for between $8 and $15, and it stays
open late. *Carruthers* on Macquarie St,
opposite the Mint, has cheap vegetarian fare,
salads and juices.

Kiosk on Macquarie at the Macquarie St
entrance to the Royal Botanic Gardens is a
nice spot for lunch on a sunny day. Cafe fare
at the outdoor tables costs between $5 and
$10.

Spanish Town consists of a cluster of
seven or eight Spanish restaurants and bars
on Liverpool St between George and Sussex
Sts. *Casa Asturiana*, 77 Liverpool St, is
reputed to have the best tapas in the city, for
which it charges between $4.50 and $6.50.
Captain Torres, at No 73, has good seafood
and a great bar. *Jackies* is the only non-
Spanish place in the strip. It's a relaxing
espresso bar at No 86, which serves honest
cafe fare until midnight.

Planet Hollywood, which is part of the
restaurant chain owned by a consortium of
Hollywood heavyweights, was scheduled to
open at 600 George St as this book was going
to press.

Chinatown Chinatown has expanded well
beyond the confines of the officially designated pedestrian mall on Dixon St. You can
spend a small fortune at some outstanding
Chinese restaurants or eat well for next to
nothing in a food hall.

The best place to start is the *Sussex St
Food Court*, which has counters of Chinese,
Malay, Vietnamese, Thai and Japanese food.
It's the most hectic, bubbly food court in the
city at lunchtime, and during that period it's
one of the best and most atmospheric places
to eat. A full meal costs between $4 and $7.
There are also food courts in the *Dixon
Gourmet Food Centre*, on the corner of

Dixon and Little Hay Sts, and the *Harbour Plaza*, on the corner of Dixon and Goulburn Sts.

Hingara, 82 Dixon St, is a classic low-budget Chinese eatery. *BBQ King*, 18 Goulburn St, is a sociable, high-turnover joint open into the early hours of the morning; expect to pay around $8 for a main. *House of Guangzhou*, on the corner of Thomas St and Ultimo Rd, is a popular, established restaurant with mains around $12. *Jing May* is on the 1st floor of the Prince Centre on the corner of Ultimo Rd and Quay St. It's renowned for its noodle soups, the best of which cost $13, but there are much cheaper dishes on the menu.

If you're looking for quality, expect to pay a little more or choose from the cheaper dishes on the menu. *Marigold Citymark*, 4th & 5th floors, 683 George St, and *East Ocean*, 421 Sussex St, have great yum-cha. The *Golden Century* (☎ 9212 3901), 393 Sussex St, is the king of Sydney's Cantonese restaurants. Seafood mains cost around $18.

The Rocks & Circular Quay Restaurants and cafes in the Rocks are overtly aimed at tourists, but there are still some good deals available, especially in the pubs (and there are lots of them) where most bar meals are still well under $10.

The *G'Day Cafe* at 83 George St, just north of Argyle St, has good-value cooked breakfasts from $3.50, and focaccia for $4. The *Gumnut Cafe* has a rear courtyard and serves breakfast for around $5, and pasta lunches for $7.50. It's on Harrington St, near the junction with Argyle St. There are several restaurants on Playfair St, but the best value is the modest *Playfair St Cafe* where quiches are $3 and a bowl of chilli con carne $4.

The *MCA Cafe*, in the foyer of the Museum of Contemporary Art on Circular Quay West, has a terrace overlooking the ferry wharves and the Opera House. Dine on modern Australian mains for around $12, and pinch yourself as a reminder that you're really there.

There are several average cafes and kiosks amid the ferry wharves; the best is *Rossini's*,

on the Circular Quay Promenade near Wharf 5. Focaccias start at $4 and light meals $7. *The Sydney Cove Oyster Bar* on Circular Quay East has one of the best views in the city. Mains are a tad expensive, but oysters will set you back only $10, so crack open a bottle of wine and toast the spectacular vista.

If you're looking for culinary excellence, the Sydney Opera House's *Bennelong* restaurant has recently been revamped and is expected to become a culinary institution. The *Rockpool* (☎ 9252 1888), at 107 George St, and *Bilson's* (☎ 9251 5600), perched above the Overseas Passenger Terminal at Circular Quay West, have formidable reputations and require a formidable amount of cash.

Kings Cross & Nearby The Cross has a mixture of fast-food joints serving edible fare designed mainly to soak up beer with maximum effect, tiny cafes servicing locals and travellers, and some swanky eateries among the city's best.

The cheapest eats are to be found in the strip of cafes on William St, near the Coca-Cola sign. *William's on William* has eggs, bacon, fries and toast for $3.90 and pasta lunches for $5. *Mamma Marias* offers similar cheap fare. Other bargain eateries include the *Peninsula Cafe* in Highfield House hostel on Victoria St, where an-all-you-can-stomach Asian combo costs $4.50, and *Pad Thai* and *Yakitori* on Llankelly Place, where noodles and rice dishes cost between $4 and $7.

The arty *Cosmic Cafe* at 7 Roslyn St serves brekkies for around $5 and open toasted sandwiches and focaccias for $5 to $7. The *Waterlily Cafe* on Bayswater Rd has a pleasing New Age ambience, and serves the usual cafe fare for $6.50. *Roys Famous* is an innovative vegetarian cafe on Victoria St that's open until midnight. You can lunch for around $7 and fill up in the evening on Asian-influenced mains for around $10.

The two most prominent places in the Cross are the *Fountain Cafe*, a something-for-everyone kind of place that seems intent on taking over Fitzroy Gardens, and the nearby *Bourbon & Beefsteak*, which is just for the tourists unless it's 4 am and you develop the munchies. A better bet are the number of Asian cubby holes punctuating the main drag of Darlinghurst Rd, where you can eat for around $7. There's more sumptuous spicy food at *Arun Thai*, 13/39 Elizabeth Bay Rd, for around $10. Ask to sit on the terrace.

The *Japanese Noodles Shop* on Macleay St is a low-tech forerunner of the current fad for noodle bars. It's a fun place to eat and has a small selection of noodles and soups for between $6 and $9.

If you want to try some of Sydney's best restaurants, and can afford $20 to $25 main courses, the *Bayswater Brasserie* (☎ 9357 2177) on Bayswater Rd is a welcoming institution with great food and impeccable service. The *Darley Street Thai* (☎ 9358 6530), next door, has excellent Thai food. *Cicada* (☎ 9358 1255), 29 Challis Ave, is currently the rage with Sydney's foodies.

Darlinghurst & East Sydney Victoria St is the main cafe and restaurant strip in Darlinghurst. If you're just looking for a caffeine hit, *Bar Coluzzi* at No 322 is a Sydney institution, and *Tropicana*, opposite, is not far behind.

If you can't subsist on caffeine alone, *La Bussola* at No 324 dishes up great pizzas from $7.50. *Burgerman*, 116 Surrey St, near the corner with Victoria St, is a designer burger joint with fabulous combinations from $4.50 to $7.50. Farther south on Victoria St at No 348 is *TJ's*, a pleasant cafe with a rear courtyard and a traveller-friendly menu of cafe fare from $4.20, and Thai food and pasta for $7.

Fu-Manchu at No 249 Victoria St is a hip, gregarious noodle bar where just about everything is under $9. Next door is *Oh Calcutta!*, a quality Indian restaurant with mains from $10 and a balcony for balmy nights.

Lauries, on the corner of Victoria and Burton Sts, has Asian and Italian vegetarian lunches for between $6 and $10.50 and evening mains for around $11.50. There's

more vegetarian food at *Govinda's*, the Hare Krishna restaurant at 112 Darlinghurst Rd, just south of William St and Kings Cross. A $12.50 all-you-can-eat smorgasbord also gives you free admission to the cinema upstairs.

Tum Tum Thai at No 199 Darlinghurst Rd is an eat-in or takeaway Thai place which has curries and stir-fries from $6 and queues out the door. *Fishface* at No 132 is an unlikely place for the best affordable seafood in the city, but it has all manner of marine life seared with a hiss for around $14.

There's a second cluster of restaurants in Stanley St, East Sydney, just south of William St, between Crown and Riley Sts. This strip used to be an Italian monoculture but it's becoming increasingly multicultural. The classic Italian cheapies are *Bill & Toni's* at No 74 and *No Names* above the Arch Coffee Lounge at No 81. *Three Frogs* is a health-food and juice bar with north African and Asian vegetarian mains for around $8. *Atlas*, is just around the corner in a 1st-floor warehouse at No 95 Riley St. It's a local favourite serving modern bistro fare for around $12. If you want to spend a little more and jump in at the deep end, *Cosmos* (☎ 9331 5306), on the corner of William and Bourke Sts, is threatening to give Greek food a good name. Mains are around $20.

Oxford St The strip of restaurants on Oxford St, east of Taylor Square, offer mains for around $10, including the popular *Thai-Nesia* at No 243, and the budget Cambodian *Angkor Wat* at No 227. The *Balkan Seafood* at No 215 is a tad more expensive, but at least you get to watch the chef in operation from the footpath before you go in.

The *Bagel House*, 7 Flinders St, just off Taylor Square, is a friendly cafe above a bakery. It specialises in filled bagels for around $6. The *Courthouse Hotel*, which dominates Taylor Square, has hearty pub fare in the upstairs bar for between $7.50 and $9.50. *Cafe 191*, which also fronts Taylor Square, is the area's main people-watching spot.

The city end of Oxford St has a rash of

NEW SOUTH WALES

nondescript cafes and fast-food Asian eateries, some relying on desperate clubbers and night owls, others on passing trade, so choose selectively. The *Tandoori Palace* at No 86, near the Remo General Store, is a fine budget Indian restaurant with mains for $9.50. *Open Kitchen*, on the corner of Oxford and Crown Sts, is a great cafe with enticing mains for around $10 and snacks for much less. At No 26 Burton St, just to the north, the landmark *Metro* has innovative vegetarian mains for $6, but it's only open Wednesday to Friday evenings and Sunday evening.

There's a concentration of budget restaurants just to the south on Crown St. They include the cosy retro *Roobar* at No 253, which has brekkies for under $4.50, focaccia for $5 and macrobiotic meals under $7. The country-style *Betty's Soup Kitchen* at No 269 has goulash, or soup and damper for $4.80. The modest *Maltese Cafe* at No 310 has pastas for just $3 to $5 and pastizzi snacks for 50c.

If you want to eat Australian flora and fauna, try *Riberries* (☎ 9361 4929), 411 Bourke St, near Taylor Square, where Australian produce is introduced to French cuisine. Although a couple of courses will set you back around $35, it's cheaper than a trip to the outback to see the real thing.

Surry Hills Crown St is the main thoroughfare through Surry Hills but it's a long street and the restaurants occur in fits and starts. *Cafe Crown* at No 355 is a '90s urban cafe where budgeters shouldn't be put off by the designer décor. Smart, light meals are around only $6.50.

Prasits at No 395, near the corner with Foveaux St, is a nifty box-like Thai with a good reputation, where you can get great curries and stir-fries from $8.50. *Meera's Dosa House* at No 567 has a range of dosas for between $7 and $16.

A second smattering of eateries on Devonshire St includes the much-loved *Passion du Fruit* on the corner of Devonshire and Bourke Sts. On the corner of Devonshire and Crown Sts is the *Rustic Cafe*, a hearty

Mediterranean eatery that you need sunglasses to look at; mains are around $11. The elegant *Elephant's Foot* hotel is opposite. It serves unchallenging but pleasant cafe fare for around $9. *Mohr Fish* at No 202 is a designer fish & chip shop; seafood mains are around $12.

At the southern end of Surry Hills, there are half-a-dozen nondescript Lebanese eateries around the corner of Cleveland and Elizabeth Sts, where dishes are between $4 and $6. There's the makings of a 'Little India' on Cleveland St between Crown and Bourke Sts. *Dhaba* at No 466 has good north Indian fare with nothing over $9. *Andy's*, on the corner of Cleveland and Bourke Sts, serves cheap and decent southern Indian meals for $8.50.

Paddington *Bar Bola* at No 100 Oxford St is a likeable cafe where most meals are under $10. *Sloane Ranger* at No 312 is a warm, intimate cafe offering Mediterranean mains for $12 and light meals for $8.

The *Paddington Inn* at No 338 has a reputable bistro with modern Australian mains for around $15. At No 388, the *Golden Dog* has Italian sandwiches for $7.50 and pizza for $12. The lovely *Hot Gossip* deli and cafe at No 438 is one of the nicest hangouts in Paddington.

The *Ritz Hotel* on the corner of Oxford and Jersey Sts is a stylish pub with bar meals for $7.50. The *Centennial Park Cafe*, a five-minute walk inside the park from the Centennial Square entrance off Oxford St, is a good place for those needing a touch of the rural. It's a pleasant open-sided cafe, surrounded by parkland, serving modern Australian mains for around $15 and breakfasts for around $5.

Glebe Glebe Point Rd was Sydney's original 'eat street', and though it has been left behind by the food innovations sweeping the inner east, it has a laid-back, unfaddish atmosphere, good-value food and warm conversation.

IKU Wholefoods at No 25 serves inexpensive macrobiotic dishes and snacks, and is a good culinary introduction to life in Glebe. *Badde Manors* at No 37, on the corner of Francis St, is the mellow neighbourhood favourite. Cafe fare and vegetarian meals are under $10. *Cafe Otto* at No 79 has a lovely front courtyard garden and pasta and salads well under $10.

The *Golden Pie and Pudding Shop*, near the corner of Glebe Point and Bridge Rds, is a budget haven with delicious pies, salads and quiches for under $3. *Craven*, at No 166, next to the Valhalla cinema, is an inexpensive joint with that oh-so Glebe, jumble-sale aura. It's a popular spot for a relaxing coffee, snack or meal.

Lien at No 331 has good value Thai, Vietnamese and Malaysian mains around $7, and *Lilac* at No 333 has Chinese, Malaysian, Indonesian and vegetarian fare mostly under $9. *That's It Thai* at No 381 is another of those popular eat-in/takeaway, closet-sized Thai places popping up all over the city. It serves budget vegetarian and meat dishes for only $6.

The secret gem of Glebe is the *Blackwattle Canteen* in the Blackwattle Studios, a converted wharf at the end of Glebe Point Rd, overlooking Rozelle Bay. It's among the studios of artists, sculptors and picture framers and has nothing over $7 on the menu.

Newtown A swag of funky cafes and restaurants (which include an excess of Thai eateries virtually indistinguishable from one another) lining Newtown's King St offer an interesting introduction to the suburb's community life, despite an . The *Green Iguana Cafe* at No 6 is a lovely down-home vegetarian place with a rear courtyard offering cheap cafe fare. *Le Kilamanjaro* at No 280 is a bustling, high-turnover African eatery with mains around $7.50. *The Old Fish Shop* at No 239 is a wonderful spot for lunch, and *Cafe 381* at No 381 is a great place to pick up on Newtown's distinct inner-city vibes.

If you're down on your luck, the *Hare Krishna Centre* at No 329 serves free food at lunchtime everyday except Sunday, when it's served at 5 pm.

Doyles' on the Beach, at Watsons Bay

Bondi The heap of nondescript restaurants lining Campbell Parade merely rely on passing trade, but there are a couple of decent fish & chip shops, where you can eat well for around $4. The cheapest food is available at the *Hotel Bondi* at No 178, where you can get a steak and salad for just $3.50.

The best value food generally comes without a sea view. Try the lovely *Gusto* delicatessen, a block back from the beach at 16 Hall St, which has affordable salads and frittatas, or the cheap and unpretentious *Hall St Cafe*, two blocks from the beach. The quick turnover *Thai Time* diner at 147 Curlewis St has tasty stir-fries and curries for around $7.

There's a strip of trendy, new wave cafe-bars on Campbell Parade at the southern end of the beach. Most have outdoor seating, ocean views and Mediterranean-influenced bistro fare at around the $12 mark. Try the groovy *Sports Bar* at No 32, the popular *Bondi Tratt* at No 34, or the stripped-bare cool of *Dogs Diner* at No 70. *GPK* at No 80 is a boutique pizza chain with an inventive array of crusts for around $11.

The northern end of the beach is more down-to-earth and here you'll find *Jackie's*, a lovely cafe on the corner of Warners and Wairoa Aves. Brekkies go for around $6 and most mains are under $10. *Diggers Cafe*, 232 Campbell Parade, is another popular spot.

Coogee There are a number of takeaways on Coogee Bay Rd offering cheap eats, but you're better off hitting the cafes which have healthier food, sunnier demeanours and outdoor tables. The exuberant *Congo Cafe* faces the beach at 208 Arden St. Pizzas, focaccias, bagels, melts and salads all cost $7. *La Casa*, next door, has pasta and focaccias for under $5. On a fine day, the outdoor tables across the street at the inexpensive *Sun of a Beach Bar* on the promenade's Beach Plaza are as close as you can eat to the ocean without getting sand in your food.

There are several bright, pleasant places on Coogee Bay Rd serving standard cafe fare costing between $5 and $10. They include *Coogee Cafe* at No 221, *Cafe 242* at No 242, and the *Globe* at No 203. If you want something more substantial, the *Coogee Bay Hotel* has a terrace bistro and a better-than-average pub brasserie with mains between $9 and $13.

Manly The ocean end of the Corso is jam-packed with takeaways and outside tables. Manly Wharf and South Steyne have plenty of eateries, but at most you're paying more for the view than the food.

If you want good value and don't need to see the ocean while you eat, head to Belgrave St where *Candy's Coffeehouse* serves inexpensive food in a cosy, book-lined cafe more reminiscent of Glebe than a beachside suburb. Neighbouring *Cafe Tunis* has the usual pasta, focaccia and salads for around $8, plus more adventurous north African dishes.

Green's Eatery in the mall section of Sydney Rd adjoining the Corso has a sunny atmosphere and serves light meals for around $5. For more spicy food, try *Malacca Straits* on the corner of Sydney Rd and Whistler St, where Malay and Thai dishes cost around $9. If you're in the mood for cheap 'n' cheerful pub food try the *Steyne Hotel* on the Corso.

The best of the stylish cafes peppering the ocean beachfront is *Brazil*, 46 North Steyne. Lunch here will set you back around $10. The South Steyne cafes and restaurants are overpriced, but if you're feeling groovy, *Cafe Nice* is currently the rage. *Armstrong's*

Manly is the best of the restaurants on Manly Wharf. Coffee, cakes and snacks are available in the morning and afternoon.

North Sydney The *North Sydney Noodle Market* (☎ 9417 3256) is a praiseworthy attempt to capture the flavour of Asian street-food markets. It's held on Sunday lunchtimes during autumn and winter, and on Friday nights during spring and summer, in the park on Miller St, between McClaren and Ridge Sts, North Sydney.

Entertainment

The *Sydney Morning Herald* lift-out, *Metro*, is published on Friday and lists events in town for the coming week. Free newspapers, such as *Drum Media* and *Beat*, are available from shops, bars and record stores and also have useful listings.

Halftix sells half-price seats to performances and events from a booth on Martin Place near Elizabeth St. Tickets are available only for shows that night, and Halftix doesn't post lists of which shows are available until noon. There's a $2.20 booking fee. The booth is also a Ticketek agency (☎ 9266 4800), so if you miss out on cheap seats you can always buy full-price ones. Halftix is open weekdays from noon to 5.30 pm and Saturday from 10.30 am to 5 pm. The Ticketek side of the business is open weekdays from 9 am to 5 pm and Saturday from 10.30 am to 4 pm.

Pubs There are plenty of good pubs in Sydney's inner suburbs.

The Rocks Two interesting pubs in this district are the *Lord Nelson*, on the corner of Argyle Place and Kent St, which brews its own ale, and the friendly *Hero of Waterloo*, on the corner of Lower Fort and Windmill Sts.

Molly Bloom's Bar at the *Mercantile Hotel*, 25 George St, is a nice place to sink a Guinness. The *Australian Hotel*, on the corner of Gloucester and Cumberland Sts, is the only place in the city with NSW's most renowned local brews on tap.

Kings Cross The Cross has plenty of hotels, though many are in less than salubrious surroundings. The 24-hour *Kings Cross Hotel*, at the junction of William and Victoria Sts, is a backpacker favourite. It's the spooky-looking building in the shadow of the Coca-Cola sign.

O'Malley's, on the corner of William and Brougham Sts, is a convivial Irish pub which has occasional live music. The *Soho Bar*, 171 Victoria St, is a discreet neighbourhood watering hole.

The *Bourbon & Beefsteak*, on the dogleg of Darlinghurst Rd, is a 24-hour institution still suffering a hangover from the Vietnam War. *Barrons* is a snug, late-night alternative, with awful jukebox, tucked above a restaurant at 5 Roslyn St. There's also a strip of late-night hybrid bar-restaurant-clubs on Kellett St.

A five-minute walk from the Cross is the huge *Woolloomooloo Bay Hotel*, 2 Bourke St, Woolloomooloo. It has weekend free-for-alls with crowd-pleasing live music.

Darlinghurst The *Green Park Hotel*, on the corner of Liverpool and Victoria St, is the haunt of dark-clothed, pool-playing, inner-city groovers. The *Hard Rock Cafe*, 121 Crown St, is for those who feel the need to add to their T-shirt collection.

On Oxford St, the cavernous shell of the *Burdekin Hotel* at No 2 attracts a lively, mixed crowd, especially on Friday and Saturday night. The *Lizard Lounge*, upstairs in the Exchange Hotel at No 34, is a hip melting pot of straights, gays and lesbians. *Q* is a hard-to-find pool hall cum bar at No 46, above Central Station Records.

The *Bentley Bar*, on the corner of Crown and Campbell Sts, is a loud, young pub open till the cock crows. See the Out & About aside for gay pubs and clubs near Oxford St.

Surry Hills There's a batch of decent pubs here, including the *Palace Hotel*, 122 Flinders St; the *Cricketers Arms*, 106 Fitzroy St; the *Hopetoun Hotel* on the corner of Fitzroy and Bourke Sts; and the *Forresters Hotel* on the corner of Foveaux and Riley Sts.

Paddington The *Paddington Inn*, 338 Oxford St, is a sociable local. The *Lord Dudley*, 236 Jersey St, Woollahra, is as close as Sydney gets to English pub atmosphere.

Glebe The *Friend in Hand* at 58 Cowper St has crab racing, live music and pool comps. The legendary *Harold Park Hotel*, 115 Wigram Rd, should win an award for its packed entertainment programme, which includes theatre, comedy, bands, poetry readings and chess competitions.

Clubs Sydney's club scene is thriving, eclectic and tribal. Some of the more established venues are:

Cauldron, 207 Darlinghurst Rd, Darlinghurst (flashy funk-house club-restaurant)

DCM, 33 Oxford St, Darlinghurst (nominally gay, muscly & sweaty)

Goodbar, 11 Oxford St, Paddington (cool basement club with super-strict door policy)

Kinselas, 383 Bourke St, Taylor Square, Darlinghurst (hip, triple-decked funk mecca)

Riva, Sheraton on the Park, Castlereagh St, Sydney (for the glitzy and chintzy city crowd)

Live Music Sydney doesn't have a dynamic pub music scene, but there are still places where you can count on something most nights of the week. For detailed listings of venues and acts, see the listings in the papers mentioned in the Entertainment introduction.

Rock Local talent definitely worth checking out include You Am I, The Cruel Sea, Ed Kuepper and Swoop. There's sometimes no charge for young local bands, a charge of between $5 and $10 for more well-known local acts, around $20 for top Australian bands, and up to $50 for international performers. Venues worth considering are:

Annandale Hotel, corner of Nelson and Parramatta Rds, Annandale (institution showcasing established & talented local bands)

Enmore Theatre, 130 Enmore Rd, Newtown (major Australian & overseas acts)

Excelsior Hotel, 64 Foveaux St, Surry Hills (neighbourhood pub with young bands)

Hordern Pavilion, RAS Show Ground, Moore Park (major Australian & overseas acts)

NEW SOUTH WALES

Out & About in Gay Sydney

Sydney has vibrant, vocal and well-organised gay and lesbian communities, which throw some spectacular parties and provide a range of social support services. There are large gay and lesbian populations in Darlinghurst, Paddington and Surry Hills and growing communities in Newtown, Leichhardt and Alexandria. Light tans and heavy pecs are the rage, so hit the beach and the gym a few weeks before arriving.

Gay social life is predominantly focussed on Oxford St, where many cafes, restaurants and businesses are gay-owned and operated. Major entertainment venues include:

Albury Hotel, 6 Oxford St, Paddington (drag show heaven)
DCM, 33 Oxford St, Darlinghurst (nominally gay, muscles & lycra)
Exchange Hotel, 34 Oxford St, Darlinghurst (groovy basement disco)
Midnight Shift, 85 Oxford St, Darlinghurst (1st-floor disco with trippy light show)
Oxford Hotel, 134 Oxford St, Darlinghurst (boozy bar & 1st-floor cocktail lounge)

Other gay and lesbian haunts include the *Beauchamp Hotel*, 267 Oxford St, Darlinghurst; the *Beresford Hotel*, 354 Bourke St, Surry Hills; and the *Flinders Hotel*, 63 Flinders St, Surry Hills. In Newtown, try the *Bank Hotel*, 342 King St, or the *Newtown Hotel*, 174 King St. Gay beach life is focussed on Lady Bay (nude) and Tamarama (also known as Glamarama).

The major social events of the year are the month-long Sydney Gay & Lesbian Mardi Gras, which culminates in an outrageous parade and party in March, and the Sleaze Ball which takes place in late September or early October. The parties for both events are held at the RAS Show Ground in Moore Park. Tickets are restricted to Mardi Gras members. Gay and lesbian international visitors wishing to attend the parties should contact the Mardi Gras office well in advance (☎ (02) 9557 4332).

The free gay press includes the *Sydney Star Observer* and *Capital Q*, which can be found in shops and cafes in the inner east and west. Both papers have excellent listings of gay and lesbian organisations, services and events.

The Australian Gay & Lesbian Tourism Association publishes a Tourism Services Directory listing all Australian members, including tour operators and accommodation. It's available by writing to PO Box 208, Darlinghurst, NSW 2010. Break Out Tours (☎ (02) 9558 8229) is a gay-operated tour company offering daily trips to the Blue Mountains (from $65) and occasional trips to Hunter Valley vineyards ($89). ■

Lansdowne Hotel, corner of Broadway and City Rd, Darlington (one of the oldest sanctums of Sydney's live music scene, scarily undergoing renovation)

Metro, 624 George St, Sydney (major local & international acts)

Phoenician Club, 173 Broadway, Ultimo (young bands & occasional touring gems)

Rose, Shamrock & Thistle Hotel (aka 'the three weeds'), 139 Evans St, Rozelle (folk, blues & light rock)

Sandringham Hotel, 387 King St, Newtown (breeding ground of Aussie pub rock)

Selinas (in the Coogee Bay Hotel), Coogee Bay Rd, Coogee Bay (touring Aussie bands & occasional headliners)

Sydney Entertainment Centre, Darling Harbour (for the Elton Johns & Neil Diamonds of the world)

Jazz Sydney has a healthy and innovative jazz circuit, with a variety of venues and door prices. Current bands or performers of note include acid-jazz band DIG, pianist Mike Nock, saxophonist Bernie McGann, and vocalist Kate Ceberano.

The Basement, 29 Reiby Place, Circular Quay (good venue with a mix of local and international acts)

Harbourside Brasserie, Pier One, Walsh Bay (established local acts & international bands – high ticket prices)

Kinselas, 383 Bourke St, Taylor Square, Darlinghurst (groove, funk & acid jazz – the hip end of the spectrum)

Round Midnight, 2 Roslyn St, Kings Cross (cocktail jazz venue with stiff drink prices)

Soup Plus, 383 George St, Sydney (comfortable jazz supper club in city centre venue)

Strawberry Hills Hotel, corner of Devonshire and Elizabeth Sts, Surry Hills (wonderful local dedicated to good-time & original jazz)

Classical The best classical music venues are the *Concert Hall* in the Sydney Opera House, the *Sydney Town Hall*, the *Conservatorium of Music* and the ABC's *Eugene Goosens Hall* (☎ 9333 1500), 700 Harris St, Ultimo.

Musica Viva Australia (☎ 9698 1711) presents an ambitious programme of Australian and international chamber music at various city venues.

Theatre The top theatre company is the *Sydney Theatre Company* (☎ 9250 1777), which has its own theatre at Pier Four, Hickson Rd, Walsh Bay. The similarly prestigious *Sydney Dance Company* is also there.

The *Drama Theatre* in the Sydney Opera House (☎ 9250 7777) stages innovative plays.

Mainstream theatres specialising in blockbusters and musicals include the *Capitol Theatre* (☎ 9320 9122), on the corner of George and Campbell Sts; the *Theatre Royal* (☎ 9320 9111), in the MLC Centre, King St; and the *State Theatre* (☎ 9373 6655), 49 Market St.

There are invariably interesting productions at the *Belvoir Theatre* (☎ 9699 3444), 25 Belvoir St, Surry Hills; the *Seymour Centre* (☎ 9364 9400), on the corner of Cleveland St and City Rd, Chippendale; and *The Performance Space* (☎ 9319 5091), 199 Cleveland St, Redfern.

Comedy & Cabaret The heart and home of Sydney comedy is the *Comedy Store* (☎ 9564 3900), on the corner of Parramatta Rd and Crystal St, Petersham. It's open Tuesday to Sunday and has a different show each night.

Best supporting role goes to the *Harold Park Hotel*, which hosts 'Comics in The Park' on Monday and various stand-up gigs throughout the week.

The *State Theatre*, 49 Market St, Sydney, presents international celebrity comics touring Australia.

The *Tilbury Hotel* (☎ 9358 1295), on the corner of Forbes and Nicholson Sts, Woolloomooloo, is the showcase for local cabaret acts.

Cinemas Commercial cinemas line George St between Liverpool and Bathurst Sts. The average ticket price is $11.50 (students around $9). Mainstream prices are cheaper on Tuesdays when all tickets are $8.

For art-house and commercial films, try independent cinemas such as the *Dendy* at 624 George St and in the MLC Centre in Martin Place; the *Academy Twin* at 3 Oxford St, Paddington; the nearby *Verona* at 17 Oxford St, Paddington; and the *Chauvel Cinema* in the Paddington Town Hall, on the corner of Oxford St and Oatley Rd. On the North Shore, try the Art-Deco *Cremorne Hayden*, 180 Military Rd; and the *Manly Twin*, opposite Manly Wharf.

Places to catch independent films or cult re-runs include the *Valhalla Cinema*, 166 Glebe Point Rd, Glebe; and the *Movie Room* above Govinda's, at 112 Darlinghurst Rd.

The *State Movie Theatre* on Market St, between Pitt and George Sts, hosts the Sydney Film Festival in June.

Spectator Sports Sydney is one of the world capitals of rugby league. The main competition is the Winfield Cup and the finals are played at the Sydney Football Stadium (☎ 9360 6601) in Moore Park in September.

The Sydney Cricket Ground (☎ 9360 6601) in Moore Park is the venue for sparsely attended Sheffield Shield matches, well-attended five-day Test matches and sell-out one-day World Series matches. It's also the home ground of the improving Sydney Swans, NSW's only contribution to the Australian Football League. Aussie rules matches are generally played between March or April and September.

A spectator boat leaves the Sydney Flying Squadron (☎ 9955 8350) at McDougall St, Milsons Point, on Saturday at 2 pm to follow

---

The Best Things in Life Are Free

There's plenty of free entertainment in Sydney for those who want fun without having to splash around their hard-earned cash. The Art Gallery of NSW has no admission charge for its permanent exhibitions. Both the Powerhouse Museum and the Sydney Mint Museum have no admission charge on the first Saturday of the month. You can get a one-hour peek around the Australian Museum without paying a cent if you turn up after 4 pm.

Lunchtime offers a feast of free music, from bands who play regularly in the Martin Place amphitheatre to classical music at the Conservatorium of Music (Wednesday and Friday during term). There are plenty of buskers, or free performances on weekends, at Circular Quay, Playfair St in the Rocks, and in Darling Harbour's Tumbalong Park. There's also free music on the 'prow' of the Opera House on Sunday.

The Paddington Village Bazaar is a spectacle in itself, and there are often performers strutting their stuff in Oxford St. 'Speakers Corner' in the Domain attracts the mad, the dangerous and the erudite on Sunday afternoons.

Don't forget the simple pleasures. It costs nothing to stroll across the Harbour Bridge, walk around the Royal Botanic Gardens, lie on the beach or frolic in the surf. ■

---

the spectacular, honed-down 18-foot skiffs that race on the harbour between late September and April ($10).

The sporting year ends with the start of the Sydney to Hobart Yacht Race on Boxing Day. A huge fleet of spectator boats follow the racing yachts to the Heads as they set sail for the three to five-day voyage to Tasmania.

Things to Buy

Shopping complexes in the city include the Queen Victoria Building, Piccadilly, Centrepoint, Skygarden and the Strand Arcade. David Jones and Grace Brothers are the biggest department stores. The hub of shopping is the Pitt St mall. For outdoor gear, head to the corner of Kent & Bathurst Sts, where Paddy Pallin is just one of several outdoor suppliers in the area. Late night shopping is on Thursday night, when most stores stay open until 9 pm.

Aboriginal Art The Aboriginal & Tribal Art Centre (☎ 9247 9625) at Level One, 117 George St, the Rocks, has paintings and crafts. Prices range from $5 to $5000.

At 27 Abercrombie St, Chippendale, the Boomali Aboriginal Artists Co-operative (☎ 9698 2047) is an interesting Aboriginal-run gallery, showroom and resource centre.

Australiana There are plenty of shops selling Australian arts, crafts and souvenirs in the Rocks and in Darling Harbour's Harbourside Festival Marketplace, but you're more likely to pick up bargains at the city's markets (see below).

The Rocks Centre on Playfair St in the Rocks has one of the best selections of goods aimed at tourists. For bush gear, try R M Williams, 389 George St, or Thomas Cook, 790 George St.

Street-smart goods can be found on the upper floors of the Strand Arcade, where several leading Australian designers have shops. Those in the Art Gallery of NSW and the Powerhouse Museum are good places for presents other than stuffed koalas.

The Australian Wine Centre in Goldfields House, 1 Alfred St, stocks wine from every Australian wine-growing region, has tastings on Friday and Saturday afternoon and can send wine overseas.

Markets Sydney has lots of weekend 'flea' markets. The most interesting is the trendy Paddington Village Bazaar, held in the grounds of the church on the corner of Oxford and Newcombe Sts on Saturday.

The weekend Rocks Market in George St in the Rocks is more tourist oriented but it's still a colourful affair. The arty-farty Sunday Tarpeian Market is at a fantastic site, on the concourse of the Opera House.

There are bric-a-brac markets in Glebe (Saturday; Glebe Public School, Glebe Point Rd); Balmain (Saturday; St Andrews Church, Darling St); Kings Cross (Sunday; Fitzroy Gardens); and Bondi Beach (Saturday; Bondi Public School, Campbell Parade).

The biggest inner-city market is the weekend Paddy's Market, at the corner of Hay and Thomas Sts, Haymarket. It's a smorgasbord of tack in a gloomy dungeon, but it has cheap fruit and vegetables and can be an interesting place to stroll around if you're not allergic to fake Calvin Klein T-shirts and fluffy slippers.

Getting There & Away

Air Sydney's Kingsford-Smith airport is Australia's busiest and the most inadequate for handling demand, so expect delays. It's only 10 km south of the city centre making access easy, but this also means that flights cease between 11 pm and 5 am due to noise regulations.

You can fly into Sydney from all the usual international points and from all over Australia. Both Qantas (☎ 13 1313) and Ansett (☎ 13 1300) have frequent flights to other capital cities and major airports. Smaller airlines, such as Ansett Express, Eastern Australia, Hazelton and Kendell, fly within NSW.

Cheap international flights are advertised in the Saturday *Sydney Morning Herald*.

Bus The private bus operators are competitive and service is efficient. Make sure you shop around for discounts – backpackers get 30% concession on Kirklands' (☎ 9281 2233) service to Brisbane, for example. Always compare private operator prices to the government's Countrylink network of trains and buses, which has discounts of up to 40% on economy fares.

The Sydney Coach Terminal (☎ 9281 9366) deals with all companies and can advise you on the best prices. It's on the corner of Pitt St and Eddy Ave, outside Central Station. Coach operators have offices either in the terminal or nearby. Most buses stop in the suburbs on the way in and out of cities.

To/From Brisbane It generally takes about 16 hours to reach Brisbane via the coastal Pacific Highway. The standard fare is around $64 but with discounts it can cost less. This is a popular route, so it's best to book in advance. Companies running the Pacific Highway route include Greyhound Pioneer (☎ 13 2030), McCafferty's (☎ 13 1499), Kirklands and Lindsay's (☎ 1800 027 944).

Greyhound Pioneer and McCafferty's also use the inland New England Highway. McCafferty's operates the fastest service, departing Sydney daily at 6.30 pm and arriving in Brisbane, via the New England Highway, 14 hours later ($65).

Some typical fares from Sydney to towns along the way are Port Macquarie $40 (seven hours), Coffs Harbour $47 (9½ hours), Byron Bay $62 (13 hours) and Surfers Paradise $64 (14½) hours. Not all buses stop in all main towns en route.

The backpacker-friendly Oz Experience (☎ 9907 0522) offers three and four-day trips between Sydney and Brisbane from $99. The Pioneering Spirit (☎ 9368 1504) 'mobile hostel' is a double-decker bus with sleeping quarters on the upper deck which runs from Sydney to Brisbane via the coast, taking a leisurely six days and costing $39 a day, plus $6 food kitty.

Ando's Opal Outback Experience (☎ 9559 2901) travels between Sydney and Byron Bay via a week-long outback detour for $389. Ando is quite a character and his tour gets good reports.

To/From Canberra Murrays (☎ 9252 3590) has three daily express buses to Canberra taking under four hours for $28, or around $22 if you pay in advance. Greyhound

Pioneer has the most frequent Canberra service and costs $30 one way or $54 return.

To/From Melbourne It's a 12 to 13-hour journey to Melbourne if you travel via the Hume Highway. Firefly Express (☎ 9211 1644) charges $45, while most other companies charge around $50. Greyhound Pioneer runs along the Hume and the prettier, but much longer (up to 18 hours), coastal Princes Highway for $61.

If you don't like the idea of just staring at the landscape through the window, Straycat (☎ 1800 800 840) runs a service between Sydney and Melbourne via Canberra and the High Country, taking three days and stopping for activities en route. The standard fare is $149 which includes all meals; accommodation for two nights is an extra $28. The service does not operate during July and August. Straycat also runs two-day 'Funky Coast' trips that explore points of interest along the coast between Sydney and Melbourne. A bus departs Sydney on Wednesday and Saturday year-round and costs $79, plus $13 for overnight accommodation at the Merimbula YHA. Stopovers can be arranged on both these routes at no extra cost.

Alpine Wilderness Adventures (☎ 1800 635 058) runs five-day trips between Sydney and Melbourne via the Snowy Mountains departing every Monday between October and April. The trip includes canoeing, hiking and bush camping, and costs $199, plus $25 food kitty.

To/From Adelaide Sydney to Adelaide takes 22 to 25 hours and costs from about $90. Services run via Mildura ($74) or Broken Hill ($95). The Sydney-Melbourne-Adelaide run with Firefly might be a little cheaper than travelling Sydney-Adelaide with other companies. Countrylink's daily Speedlink service is the fastest option. It takes just under 20 hours and involves catching a train to Albury, then a connecting bus to Adelaide. The fare is $99.

To/From Elsewhere To the Snowy Mountains, Greyhound Pioneer runs to Cooma ($38), Jindabyne ($48), and the ski resorts (about $52). The 52 to 56-hour trip to Perth costs $257. To Alice Springs, it's $214 and takes 42 hours (plus some waiting in Adelaide).

Train The government's Countrylink rail network is complemented by coaches. Discounts of up to 40% on economy tickets are possible, subject to availability, making prices comparable to the private bus lines; Australian students get a 50% discount on economy fares. Discount tickets are operated on a first-come/first-served quota basis. As long as it's not a public or school holiday, you stand a pretty good chance of getting one, even if you purchase your ticket on the day of departure; book in advance to be sure.

Interstate trains can be faster than buses, and on interstate journeys you can arrange free stopovers on economy and student tickets, but not on discounted tickets.

All interstate and principal regional services operate to and from Central Station. Tickets must be booked in advance. Call the Central Reservation Centre (☎ 13 2232).

Three trains run daily to Canberra taking about four hours and costing $37.80/51.80 in economy/1st class.

Two trains run between Sydney and Melbourne, one leaving in the morning and travelling throughout the day, and the other departing in the evening and travelling overnight. The trip takes 10½ hours and the economy/1st-class fare is $97/135; a 1st-class sleeper is $221. Discounted tickets can bring the economy fare down to $58.20

The nightly train to Brisbane takes about 13½ hours. Economy/1st class costs $102/148; a sleeper costs $234. There's also a daily morning train to Murwillumbah in northern NSW with connecting buses to either the Gold Coast or Brisbane (nearly 16 hours).

A daily Speedlink train/bus service between Sydney and Adelaide via Albury costs $99 economy and takes just under 20 hours. You can also travel on the twice-weekly Indian Pacific via Broken Hill, but this takes just over 25 hours. The economy fare is $120, an economy sleeper is $241 and a 1st-class sleeper $376.

See the Perth section in the Western Australia chapter for details of train travel between Sydney and Perth on the Indian Pacific.

There's an extensive rail network within the state – see the NSW introductory Getting Around section for details.

Car Rental There are Avis, Budget, Delta, Hertz and Thrifty branches, and a number of local operators, on William St. The larger companies' daily metropolitan rates are typically about $60 a day for a small car (Holden Barina), about $85 for a medium car (Toyota Corolla), or about $95 for a big car (Holden Commodore), all including insurance and unlimited km. Some places require you to be over 23 years old.

There's no shortage of outfits renting older cars which offer reasonable transport as long as you're expectations are modest. Check for things like bald tyres and bad brakes before you sign, and check the fine print regarding insurance excess. Cut Price Rent-a-Car (☎ 9281 3003) on William St is reputable and has adequate cars. A 15-year-old Toyota costs only $180 per week if you're prepared to risk a $1000 excess.

Buying/Selling a Car or Motorbike Sydney is a good place for this; Parramatta Rd is lined with used car lots. It's illegal to sell cars on the street in Kings Cross but there's a daily car market (☎ 9358 5811) at the Kings Cross Car Park on the corner of Ward Ave and Elizabeth Bay Rd which charges sellers from $35 a week (if the car has a roadworthy certificate known as a pink slip). This place can help with paperwork and arrange third-party property insurance. Although it's a dismal spot, it's becoming something of a travellers' rendezvous. The Flemington Car Market (☎ 0055 21122), near Flemington station on Sunday, charges sellers $60.

Several dealers will sell you a car with an undertaking to buy it back at an agreed price, but make sure you read the small print and don't accept any verbal guarantees – get it in writing. Holiday Wheels Motorcycles (☎ 9718 6668), 587 Canterbury Rd, Belmore, sometimes has buy-back deals on motorbikes and can help arrange insurance.

Before you buy a vehicle, it's worth having it checked by a mechanic. The NRMA (☎ 13 2132) does this for members for $98; nonmembers $125. Some service stations conduct inspections for less. For full details of the steps involved in buying a car, pick up the NRMA's free booklet, *Worry-Free Guide to Buying a Car*, at any NRMA office.

Getting Around

The State Transit Authority of NSW (STA) controls the bus and ferry network in Sydney, while City Rail runs the rail network. The state government plans to amalgamate the two entities to better co-ordinate services, so expect changes to timetables. For information on buses, ferries and trains, phone ☎ 13 1500 between 6 am and 10 pm daily.

To/From the Airport Sydney airport is 10 km south of the city centre. The international and domestic terminals are a four-km bus trip apart on either side of the runway.

The Airport Express is a special STA service operating every 10 minutes from Central Station, with bus No 300 going to the airport via Circular Quay and No 350 going via Kings Cross. Airport Express buses have their own stops, extra-large luggage racks, and are painted green and yellow. The one-way fare is $5 and a return ticket, valid for two months, is $8. Travel between the terminals costs $2.50. It's about 15 minutes from the airport to Central Station; add another 15 minutes to reach Circular Quay or Kings Cross.

Kingsford Smith Transport (KST) (☎ 9667 0663) runs a door-to-door service between the airport and places to stay (including hostels) in the city, Kings Cross, Darling Harbour and Glebe. The fare is $6. When heading to the airport, book at least three hours before you want to be collected.

There are car rental agencies in the terminals, such as Hertz (☎ 9669 2444). A taxi from the airport to Circular Quay should cost between $20 and $25.

Bus Sydney's bus network extends to most suburbs. Fares depend upon the number of 'sections' you pass through, so consult the driver. As a rough guide, short jaunts cost $1.20, and most other fares in the inner suburbs are $2.50. Buses run between 5 am and midnight.

The major starting points for bus routes are Circular Quay, Argyle St in Millers Point, Wynyard Park and the Queen Victoria Building on York St, and Railway Square. Most buses head out of the city on George or Castlereagh Sts, and take George or Elizabeth Sts coming in. Pay the driver as you enter, or dunk your prepaid ticket in the ticket machines by the door.

The bus information kiosk on the corner of Alfred and Loftus Sts at Circular Quay is open daily. There are other information offices on Carrington St and in the Queen Victoria Building on York St.

Special Bus Services The Sydney Explorer is a red STA tourist bus which navigates the inner-city on a route designed to pass most central attractions. A bus departs every 20 minutes from Circular Quay daily between 9 am and 7 pm, but you can board at any of the 29 clearly marked red bus stops on the route. Tickets are sold on board the bus and at STA offices, and entitle you to get on and off the bus as often as you like. They cost $20, so the service is really only worthwhile if you don't want the hassle of catching ordinary buses.

The Bondi & Bay Explorer operates on similar lines, running a much larger circuit from Circular Quay to Kings Cross, Double Bay, Rose Bay, Vaucluse, Watsons Bay, the Gap, Bondi Beach and Coogee, returning to the city along Oxford St. Just riding around the circuit takes two hours, so if you want to get off at many of the 22 places of interest along the way you'll need to start early. The buses depart half-hourly from Circular Quay daily between 9 am and 6 pm; tickets cost $20.

The privately run Northern Beaches Explorer (☎ 9913 8402) operates a similar service from Manly to Palm Beach on Thursday and weekends, stopping at most of the northern beaches. Tickets cost $20 and buses depart hourly from Manly Wharf from 9.15 am to 2.15 pm, except during winter when the service is scaled back.

Nightrider buses provide an hourly service after regular buses and trains stop running. They operate from Town Hall station and service suburban railway stations. Normal bus fares apply.

Train Sydney has a vast suburban rail network and frequent services, making trains much quicker than buses. The underground City Circle comprises seven city centre stations. Lines radiate from the City Circle, but the rail network does not extend to the northern and southern beaches, Balmain or Glebe. All suburban trains stop at Central Station, and usually one or more of the other City Circle stations as well (a ticket to the City will take you to any station on the City Circle). Trains run from around 5 am to midnight.

After 9 am on weekdays and at any time on weekends, you can buy an off-peak return ticket for not much more than a standard one-way fare. A trip anywhere on the City Circle or to a nearby suburb such as Kings Cross is $1.40 single, $1.50 off-peak return and $2.80 day return. A City Hopper costs $2.20 and gives you a day of unlimited rides in the central area after 9 am on weekdays and at any time on weekends. You can go as far north as North Sydney, as far south as Central and as far east as Kings Cross on this ticket. If you buy a City Hopper at a suburban station it costs $1.20 plus the return fare to the city.

Manned ticket booths are supplemented by automatic ticket machines at busy stations. The machines accept 10c, 20c, 50c, $1 and $2 coins. If you have to change trains, it's cheaper to buy a ticket to your ultimate destination: however, don't leave an intermediary station en route to your destination or your ticket will be invalid.

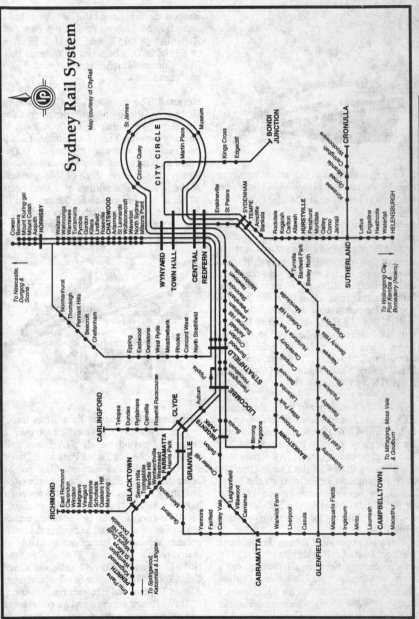

Sydney Rail System

Map courtesy of CityRail

For rail information, ask at any station or drop by the city rail information booth near the ferry ticket office at Circular Quay.

Ferry Sydney's ferries are one of the most enjoyable and sensible ways of getting around. Many people use ferries to commute so there are frequently connecting bus services. Some ferries operate between 6 am and midnight, although ferries servicing tourist attractions operate much shorter hours. Popular places accessible by ferry include Darling Harbour, Balmain, Hunters Hill and Parramatta to the west; McMahons Point, Luna Park, Kirribilli, Neutral Bay, Cremorne, Mosman, Taronga Zoo and Manly on the North Shore; and Double Bay, Rose Bay and Watsons Bay in the eastern suburbs.

There are four types of ferry: the regular STA ferries; fast, modern JetCats which go to Manly ($4.80); RiverCats which traverse the Parramatta River to Parramatta ($4.20); and small private operators. All ferries (and Cats) depart from Circular Quay. There's a ferry information office next to the ticket booths on the concourse behind Wharf 4 (☎ 9256 4670). Most regular harbour ferries cost $2.80, although the longer trip to Manly costs $3.60.

Privately operated ferries include the Darling Harbour Rocket (☎ 9264 7377), which shuttles between Harbourmaster's Steps at Circular Quay West and Darling Harbour every 20 minutes for $3; Hegarty's Ferries (☎ 9247 6606), which run during the day from Wharf 6 at Circular Quay to

wharves directly across the harbour at Lavender Bay, McMahons Point, Luna Park and Kirribilli ($2.25); and Doyles Ferries (☎ 9337 2007), which run to Watsons Bay from Commissioners Steps between 11.30 and 3 pm for $4.

Monorail The monorail circles Darling Harbour and the south-western quarter of the city centre, travelling at 1st-floor level. It operates between 7 am (8 am Sunday) and 9 pm (midnight Thursday to Saturday). The entire loop takes just over 10 minutes, with a train roughly every three or four minutes. A single loop or a portion of a loop costs $2.50; a day pass costs $6. Unless you're heading for Darling Harbour, consider it a novelty rather than a mode of transport.

Fare Deals The Sydney Pass offers three, five or seven-day unlimited travel over a seven-day period on all STA buses and ferries, and the red Travel Pass zone (inner suburbs) of the rail network. The passes cover the Airport Express, the Explorers, the JetCats, RiverCats and three STA-operated harbour cruises. They cost $60 (three days); $80 (five days) and $90 (seven days), which is good value compared to buying the components separately. Passes are available in many places including STA offices, the NSW Government Travel Centre, the Kings Cross Tourist Information Service, and from Airport Express and Explorer bus drivers.

Travel Passes are designed for commuters and offer cheap weekly travel. There are various colour-coded grades offering combinations of distance and service. The Green Travel Pass is valid for extensive train and bus travel and all ferries, except the Manly JetCat during the day. It's a bargain at $26 for a week. Travel Passes are sold at railway stations, STA offices and major newsagents.

If you're just catching buses, get a Metro Ten ticket which gives a sizeable discount on 10 bus trips. There are various colour codes for distances so check which is the most appropriate for your travel patterns. A red Metro Ten costs $17.20 and is suitable to reach most places mentioned in this section. Metro Tens are available from larger newsagents and STA offices. Insert the ticket in the ticket machine as you board the bus.

Ferry Ten tickets are similar and cost $16.40 for 10 inner harbour (ie short) ferry trips, or $24.60 including the Manly ferry. They can be purchased at the Circular Quay ferry ticket office.

Several transport-plus-entry tickets are available which work out cheaper than catching a ferry and paying entry separately. They include the Zoo Pass, Aquarium Pass, Ocean Pass (to Manly's Oceanworld aquarium) and Luna Pass (to Luna Park).

Taxi There are heaps of taxis in Sydney. The four big taxi companies offer a reliable telephone service: Legion (☎ 9289 9000), Premier Radio Cabs (☎ 131 017), RSL Taxis (☎ 9581 1111) and Taxis Combined (☎ 9332 8888).

Water taxis are pricey but fun ways of getting around the harbour. Companies include Taxis Afloat (☎ 9955 3222) and Harbour Taxi Boats (☎ 9555 1155).

Bicycle Bicycle NSW Incorporated (☎ 9283 5200), 209 Castlereagh St, Sydney 2000, publishes a handy book *Cycling Around Sydney* ($10), which details routes and cycle paths. Another guide is *Seeing Sydney by Bicycle* by Julia Thorne.

Bicycle Hire Most cycle hire shops require a hefty deposit (up to $500) or a credit card.
Inner City Cycles (☎ 9660 6605), 31

Glebe Point Rd, Glebe, rents quality mountain bikes for $30 a day, $60 a weekend (Friday afternoon to Monday morning) and $120 a week. The Australian Cycle Company (☎ 9399 3475), 28 Clovelly Rd, Randwick is handy for Centennial Park and rents bikes for $6 an hour, $10 for two hours and $25 a day. Manly Cycle Centre (☎ 9977 1189), 36 Pittwater Rd, Manly, charges $10 for two hours ($5 for each subsequent hour), $25 a day or $60 a week.

Around Sydney

There are superb national parks to the north and south of Sydney, and historic small towns to the west which were established in the early days of European settlement but which survive today as pockets engulfed by urban sprawl.

BOTANY BAY

It's a common misconception that Sydney is built around Botany Bay. But Sydney Harbour is actually Port Jackson and Botany Bay is 10 to 15 km south on the fringe of the city. This area is a major industrial centre so don't expect too many unspoilt vistas. Despite this, the bay has pretty stretches and holds a special place in Australian history. This was Captain Cook's first landing point in Australia, and it was named by Joseph Banks, the expedition's naturalist, for the many botanical specimens he found here.

The **Botany Bay National Park** encompasses both headlands of the bay. At Kurnell, on the southern headland, Cook's landing place is marked by monuments. The 436-hectare park has bushland and coastal walking tracks, picnic areas and an 8-km cycle track. The Discovery Centre (☎ 9668 9923) in the park describes the impact of European arrival, and has information on the surrounding wetlands. It's open weekdays from 9.30 am to 4 pm and weekends from 10 am to 4.30 pm. The park is open from 7 am to 7.30 pm. Entry costs $7.50 per car but pedestrians are not charged so you may as

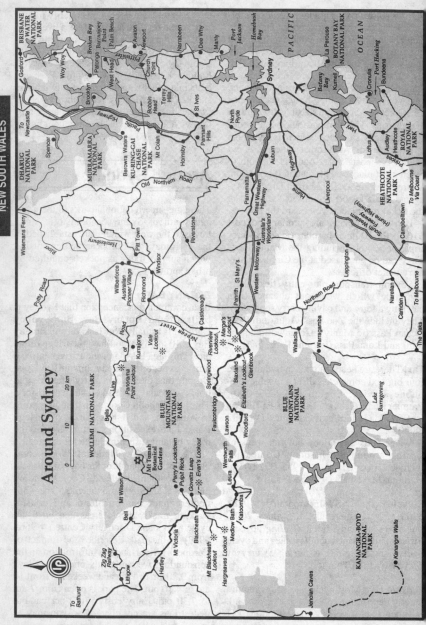

NEW SOUTH WALES

Around Sydney

well park outside as the centre, monuments and most walking tracks are close to the entrance. From Cronulla railway station (10 km away), catch Kurnell Bus Co (☎ 9524 8977) bus No 987 ($2.60). Services are limited on weekends.

La Perouse, on the northern headland, is named after the French explorer who arrived in 1788, just six days after the arrival of the First Fleet. He gave the Poms a good scare because they weren't expecting the French to turn up quite so soon. Although the First Fleet soon sailed to Sydney Harbour, La Perouse camped at Botany Bay for six weeks before sailing off into the Pacific and disappearing. On the headland is a monument built in 1825 by the French explorer Bougainville in honour of La Perouse. The fabulous Laperouse Museum (☎ 9311 3379) in the old cable station charts the history of La Perouse's fateful expedition. It's open daily from 10 am to 4.30 pm, and entry costs $2; guided tours in English or French can be booked for $6.

Just off shore is **Bare Island**, a decaying concrete fort built in 1885 to discourage a feared Russian invasion. Entry is by guided tour only (☎ 9331 3379) which costs $5 on weekends and $7 on weekdays.

There's no entry fee to this northern segment of the national park. Catch bus Nos 394 from Circular Quay or 393 from Railway Square.

ROYAL NATIONAL PARK

This coastal park of dramatic cliffs, secluded beaches, scrub and lush rainforest is the oldest gazetted national park in the world. It begins at Port Hacking just 30 km south of Sydney and stretches 20 km to the south. A road runs through the park with detours to the small township of Bundeena on Port Hacking, to the beautiful beach at Wattamolla, and the more windswept Garie Beach. A spectacular two-day, 26-km coastal trail runs the length of the park and is highly recommended. Garie, Era and Burning Palms are popular surf spots; swimming or surfing at Marley is dangerous (Little Marley is safe). A walking and cycling trail follows the Port Hacking River south from Audley, and other walking tracks pass tranquil, freshwater swimming holes. You can swim in Kangaroo Creek but not the Port Hacking River.

Bushfires in 1994 devastated 95% of the park, but all major picnic areas, beaches and the rainforest canopy in the south-eastern corner were unaffected. The park is rapidly recovering and it's fascinating to see the bush regenerate. All walking tracks are open.

There is a visitor centre (☎ 9542 0648) at Audley, about two km from the park's north-eastern entrance, off the Princes Highway. It's open daily from 9 am to 4 pm (closed between 1 and 2 pm). It's a scenic spot, with picnic grounds on the Port Hacking River, and is the startingpoint of many walks and the cycle track along the river. You can hire rowboats and canoes at the Audley Boat Shed (☎ 9545 4967) for $10 an hour or $20 a day. Bikes cost $6 an hour or $14 for four hours.

Entry to the park costs $7.50 per car; free for pedestrians and cyclists. The road through the park and the offshoot to Bundeena are always open, but the detours to the beaches are closed at sunset.

Places to Stay

The only camp site accessible by car is at Bonnie Vale, near Bundeena, where sites cost from $10 for two people. Free bush camping is allowed in several other areas but permits must be obtained beforehand from the visitor centre. Fires are not permitted except in designated picnic areas. If you camp at Era Beach in the south of the park, beware of deer breaking into your tent and foraging for food. The basic (no electricity or phone) and secluded *Garie Beach YHA* has beds for YHA members only for $6. You need to book and collect a key from the YHA Travel Centre (☎ 9261 1111) at 422 Kent St, Sydney.

The best place to stay on the edge of the park is the *Imperial Hotel*, Clifton (☎ (042) 67 1177), which is dramatically perched on the cliff edge on the coast road from Wollongong. Singles/doubles cost $35/50 including breakfast, and several rooms have views. Doubles are $60 on weekends.

Getting There & Away

You can reach the park from Sydney by taking the Princes Highway and turning off south of Loftus. From Wollongong, the coast road north is a spectacular drive and there are fantastic views of the Illawarra escarpment and the coast from Bald Hill Lookout, just north of Stanwell Park, on the southern boundary of the Royal National Park.

The Sydney-Wollongong railway forms the western boundary of the park. The closest station is at Loftus, four km from the park entrance and another two km from the visitor centre. Bringing a bike on the train is a good idea. Engadine, Heathcote, Waterfall and Otford are on the park boundary and have walking trails leading into the park.

A scenic way to reach the park is to take a train from Sydney to the southern beach suburb of Cronulla ($3.60) then a Cronulla National Park Ferries (☎ 9523 2990) boat to **Bundeena** in the north-eastern corner of the park. Bundeena is the starting-point of the 26-km long coastal walk. Ferries depart from the Cronulla wharf, just below the railway station, hourly on the half-hour (except 12.30 pm) and return from Bundeena hourly on the hour (except 1 pm); the fare is $2.20 one way.

HEATHCOTE NATIONAL PARK

This forgotten 2000-hectare heathland national park adjoins the western boundary of the Royal National Park and is administered from the Audley visitor centre. It has rugged scenery unscarred by the 1994 bushfires, great bushwalking opportunities and plenty of pools suitable for swimming. Bush camping permits are available from the Audley visitor centre. Walking trails enter the park from Heathcote and Waterfall, both on the Princes Highway and the Sydney-Wollongong railway line.

PARRAMATTA

Parramatta, 24 km west of Sydney, was the second European settlement in Australia and contains a number of historic buildings dating from the early days of the colony. When Sydney proved to be a poor area for farming, Parramatta was selected in 1788 for the first farm settlement. Despite its rural beginnings, the settlement has been consumed by Sydney's westward sprawl and is now a thriving but undistinguished commercial centre.

The Parramatta visitor centre (☎ 9630 3703) is on the corner of Church and Market Sts. It's open weekdays from 10 am to 4 pm, Saturday from 9 am to 1 pm, and Sunday from 10.30 am to 3.30 pm. Pick up a free copy of the useful leaflet, *Historic Parramatta: The Cradle City*.

On the western edge of the city, **Parramatta Park** was the site of the area's first farm and contains a number of relics. The elegant **Old Government House** sits atop a rise overlooking the Parramatta River. It was built from 1799 as a country retreat for the early governors of NSW, and is the oldest remaining public building in Australia. It now houses a museum and is open Tuesday to Thursday from 10 am to 4 pm and weekends from 11 am to 4 pm; admission is $5. The park has several other relics from the early days of settlement and is the starting point for a 15-km cycle track that runs east to Putney along the foreshore of the Parramatta River.

St John's Cathedral and the **Town Hall** form a pleasant civic centre near the junction of Church and Macquarie Sts. St John's Cemetery, on O'Connell St between the cathedral and the park, contains the graves of many of the first settlers.

There are more historic buildings east of the city centre. **Elizabeth Farm**, 70 Alice St, is the oldest surviving home in the country. It was built in 1793 by the founders of Australia's wool industry, John and Elizabeth Macarthur, and its deep verandah and simple lines became the prototype for early Australian homesteads. The house is open daily except Monday from 10 am to 4.30 pm; entry is $5 ($3 concession).

Experiment Farm Cottage, 9 Ruse St, is an exquisite colonial bungalow built on the ite of the first land grant issued in Australia. The cottage is open Tuesday to Thursday from 10 am to 4 pm, and on Sunday from 11 am to 4 pm; admission is $4 ($2 concession).

Getting There & Away

The best way to reach Parramatta is by RiverCat from Circular Quay ($4.20), otherwise catch a train from Central Station ($2.60). By car, exit the city via Parramatta Rd and detour onto the Western Motorway tollway ($1.50) at Strathfield.

AROUND PARRAMATTA

There are two mainstream tourist attractions halfway between Parramatta and Penrith, farther west. The **Featherdale Wildlife Park**, 217-229 Kildare Rd, Doonside, has plenty of native fauna. Featherdale is open daily from 9 am to 5 pm and costs $8.50 ($4.25 children). Take a train to Blacktown and bus No 725 from there. **Australia's Wonderland**, Wallgrove Rd, Eastern Creek, is a large amusement park complex with a wildlife park. It's open daily and admission is $29.95 ($21.95 children under 13 years). Admission to the wildlife park only is $9.95 ($6.50 children). Shuttle buses meet trains at Rooty Hill on weekends.

PENRITH

Penrith, on the serene Nepean River, is at the base of the forested foothills of the Blue Mountains. Despite being 50 km west of the city centre, it's virtually an outer suburb of Sydney. The Penrith Tourist Office (☎ (047) 32 7671) is in the car park of the huge Panthers World of Entertainment complex on Mulgoa Rd. It's open daily from 9 am to 4.30 pm.

The **Museum of Fire**, Castlereagh Rd, has fire simulations, bushfire exhibits and old fire engines. It's open daily from 10 am to 3 pm (5 pm on Sunday); admission is $5 ($3 concession). If that's too hot, you can take a cruise through the Nepean Gorge on the *Nepean Belle* paddlewheeler (☎ (047) 33 1274). It operates irregularly, but there are usually cruises (from $12) on Sunday and Wednesday. If you have a car, there are fine views of the **Nepean Gorge** from the Rock Lookout, five km west of the town of Mulgoa. Mulgoa is 10 km south of Penrith on Mulgoa Rd.

You can reach Penrith by train from Central Station ($4.20) or by driving west along Parramatta Rd and taking the Western Motorway tollway at Strathfield ($1.50).

CAMDEN AREA

Camden is promoted as the 'birthplace of the nation's wealth' because it was here that John and Elizabeth Macarthur conducted the sheep-breeding experiments which laid the foundation for Australia's wool industry. Camden is on the urban fringe, 50 km south-west of the city centre via the Hume Highway. The Camden visitor centre (☎ (046) 58 1370), Camden Valley Way, has free walking tour leaflets.

The surrounding countryside has attractions aimed primarily at families and coach tourists, including the **Gledswood** historic homestead at nearby Narellan and the **Australiana Park** tourist complex next door.

The 400-hectare **Mount Annan Botanic Garden** is the native plant garden of Sydney's Royal Botanic Gardens and is midway between Camden and Campbelltown, to the east. It's open daily and admission is $5 per car, $2 for pedestrians. Take a train to Campbelltown station ($4.20) and a Busways bus No 894/5/6 from there.

South of Camden is the small town of **Picton**. The 1839 *George IV Inn* (☎ (046) 77 1415) here is one of the nicest places to stay around Sydney if you need to recharge your batteries. Basic singles/doubles built around a courtyard cost $25/38. In nearby Thirlmere, the **Rail Transport Museum** has a huge collection of steam trains, some in working order. It's open daily; admission is $6.

KU-RING-GAI CHASE NATIONAL PARK

This 15,000-hectare national park (☎ 9457 9322), 24 km north of the city centre, borders the southern edge of Broken Bay and the western shore of Pittwater. It has that classic Sydney mixture of sandstone, bushland and water vistas, plus walking tracks, horse-riding trails, picnic areas, Aboriginal rock engravings and spectacular views of Broken Bay, particularly from West Head at the park's north-eastern tip. There are several roads through the park and four entrances. Entry is $7.50 per car.

The Kalkari visitor centre (☎ 9457 9853) is on Ku-ring-gai Chase Rd, about four km into the park from the Mt Colah entrance. It's open daily from 9 am to 4.15 pm. The road descends from the visitor centre to the picnic area at Bobbin Head on Cowan Creek. Halvorsen (☎ 9457 9011) rents holiday cruisers, but also has row-boats for $10 for the first hour and $4 for subsequent hours; motor boats that seat eight cost $30 for the first hour and $6 for subsequent hours. There are also boats for hire at the Akuna Bay marina on Coal & Candle Creek.

Recommended walks include the America Bay Trail and the Gibberagong and Sphinx tracks. The best places to see Aboriginal engravings are on the Basin Trail and the Garigal Aboriginal Heritage Walk at West Head. It's unwise to swim in Broken Bay because of sharks, but there are safe netted swimming areas at Illawong Bay and the Basin. Large areas of Ku-ring-gai Chase, especially around West Head, were burned in the 1994 bushfires but the area is quickly regenerating. The camping area at the Basin and the Pittwater YHA were not affected.

Places to Stay

Camping is allowed only at the Basin (☎ 9451 8124), on the western side of Pittwater. It's a 2.5-km walk from the West Head road or a ferry ride from Palm Beach. It costs $10 for two people or $15 during school holidays; book in advance and pay at the site. There is safe swimming in the lagoon at the Basin, and basic supplies are brought over by ferry from Palm Beach.

The *Pittwater YHA* (☎ 9999 2196) is on the shore of Pittwater, a couple of km south of the Basin. It's noted for its idyllic setting and friendly wildlife. Dorms cost $14, and twins $18 per person. If you stay for Saturday night only, it's $19 in a dorm and $22 in a twin. Nonmembers pay $2 more. Canoes and sailboats can be hired for just $6. Book in advance and bring food.

Getting There & Away

There are four road entrances to the park: Mt Colah, on the Pacific Highway; Turramurra, in the south-west; and Terrey Hills and Church Point, in the south-east. Hornsby Buses (☎ 9457 8888) bus No 577 runs every 30 minutes from Turramurra station to the nearby park entrance ($2.60) on weekdays; one bus enters the park as far as Bobbin Head. The schedule changes on weekends, with less frequent buses to the entrance but more to Bobbin Head.

The Palm Beach Ferry Service (☎ 9918 2747) runs to the Basin hourly (except 1 pm) from 9 am to 4 pm (5 pm on weekends) for $3 one way. It also departs Palm Beach daily at 11 am for Bobbin Head via Patonga, returning at 3.30 pm. The one-way fare is $10, plus a dollar or two for bikes or big backpacks.

To reach the Pittwater YHA, take a ferry from Church Point to Halls Wharf ($5 return). The hostel is a short walk from here. Bus Nos 155 and 157 run from Manly to Church Point. From the city centre, catch bus No 190 from Wynyard Park as far as Warringah Mall and transfer to No 155 or 159 from there.

HAWKESBURY RIVER

The mighty Hawkesbury River enters the sea 30 km north of Sydney at Broken Bay. It's dotted with coves, beaches and picnic spots, making it one of Australia's most attractive rivers. Before entering the ocean, the river expands into bays and inlets like Berowra Creek, Cowan Creek and Pittwater on the southern side, and Brisbane Water on the northern. The river flows between a succession of national parks – Murramarra and Ku-ring-gai Chase to the south; and Dharug, Brisbane Water and Bouddi to the north. Windsor (see below) is about 120 km upstream.

An excellent way to get a feel for the river is to catch the *Riverboat Postman* (☎ 9985 7566) mail boat, which does a 40-km round trip every weekday, running upstream as far as Marlow, near Spencer. It departs from Brooklyn at 9.30 am and returns at 1.15 pm. A shorter afternoon run on Wednesday and Friday departs at 1.30 pm and returns at 4 pm. It costs $25 ($20 concession). The 8.16 am train from Sydney's Central Station ($4.20) or the 8.17 am from Gosford ($2.60) will get you to Brooklyn's Hawkesbury River Station in time to join the morning boat.

You can hire houseboats in Brooklyn, Berowra Waters and Bobbin Head. These aren't cheap but renting midweek during low season is affordable for a group. Halvorsen (☎ 9457 9011) at Bobbin Head has five berths for $230 for three days during this period. No experience is necessary.

The settlements along the river have their own distinct character. Life in **Brooklyn** revolves totally around boats and the river. The town is on the Sydney-Newcastle railway line, just east of the Pacific Highway. **Berowra Waters** is a quaint community farther upstream, clustered around a free 24-hour winch ferry which crosses Berowra Creek. There are a couple of cafes overlooking the water and a marina which hires outboards for $20 an hour or $45 for a half-day. Berowra Waters is five km west of the Pacific Highway; there's a railway station at Berowra, but it's a six km hike down to the ferry.

Wisemans Ferry is a tranquil settlement overlooking the Hawkesbury River roughly halfway between Windsor and the mouth of the river. A free 24-hour winch ferry is the only means of crossing the river here. The historic *Wisemans Ferry Inn* (☎ (045) 66 4301) has rooms from $50 a double. The *Rosevale Farm Resort* (☎ (045) 66 4207) has tent sites for $4 per person, on-site vans for $30 and motel rooms for $35. It's a couple of km north of the town, on the opposite bank of the river.

The **Yengo National Park**, a rugged sandstone area covering the foothills of the Blue Mountains, stretches from Wisemans Ferry to the Hunter Valley. It's a wilderness area with no facilities and limited road access. A scenic road leads east from Wisemans Ferry to the Central Coast, following the course of the river before veering north through bushland and orange groves. An early convict-built road leads north from Wisemans Ferry to **St Albans**. The friendly *Settlers Arms Inn* (☎ (045) 68 2111) here dates from 1836 and has pleasant rooms from $80 a double. There's a basic camp site opposite the hotel.

Note that it may be unwise to swim in the Hawkesbury River between Windsor and Wisemans Ferry during the summer due to blue-green algae. Call the EPA Pollution Line (☎ 9325 5555) for information.

WINDSOR

Windsor, Richmond, Wilberforce, Castlereagh and Pitt Town are the five 'Macquarie Towns' established on rich agricultural land on the upper Hawkesbury River in the early 19th century, by Governor Lachlan Macquarie. You can see them on the way to or from the Blue Mountains if you cross the range on the Bells Line of Road – an interesting alternative to the Great Western Highway.

The Hawkesbury visitor centre (☎ (045) 88 5895) is on Richmond Rd, between Richmond and Windsor, and is open daily. Windsor has its own tourist information centre (☎ (045) 77 2310) in the 1843 Daniel O'Connell Inn on Thompson Square. Pick up a copy of the *Hawkesbury District Tourist Association Guide to Windsor and Richmond* (50c).

Windsor has some fine old buildings, notably those around the picturesque Thompson Square on the banks of the Hawkesbury River. The Daniel O'Connell Inn houses the **Hawkesbury Museum of Local History** which is open daily from 10 am to 4 pm; admission is $2.50 ($1.50 concession). The **Macquarie Arms Hotel** (1815) has a nice terrace fronting the square and is reckoned to be the oldest pub in Australia, but there are a few 'oldest pubs' around. Other old buildings include the convict-built **St Matthew's Church of England**, completed in 1822 and designed, like the **courthouse**, by the convict architect Francis Greenway. Windsor River Cruises (☎ 9831 6630) offers cruises on the Hawkesbury on Sunday and Wednesday from $12.

If you want to stay overnight in Windsor, the historic *Clifton Cottage* (☎ (045) 87 7135), 22 Richmond Rd, is the best value at $30/55 for a single/double with shared facilities midweek, and $35/58 on weekends.

You can reach Windsor by train from Sydney's Central Station ($4.20) but public transport to the other Macquarie Towns (apart from Richmond) is scarce. By car, exit the city on Parramatta Rd and head north-west on the Windsor Rd from Parramatta.

AROUND WINDSOR

The next largest of the Macquarie Towns is **Richmond**, which has its share of colonial buildings and a pleasant village-green-like park. It's six km west of Windsor, at the end of the metropolitan railway line and at the start of the Bells Line of Road across the Blue Mountains. There's a NPWS office (☎ (045) 88 5247) open on weekdays at 370 Richmond Rd.

The **Australian Pioneer Village** is a theme park which contains Rose Cottage (1811), probably the oldest surviving timber building in the country. It's in Wilberforce, six km north of Windsor, and is open daily; admission is $8. The pretty **Ebenezer Church** (1809), five km north of Wilberforce, is the oldest church in Australia still used as a place of worship.

Wilberforce is the starting point for the Putty Rd, a 160-km isolated back road that runs north to Singleton in the Hunter Valley. The **Colo River**, 15 km north along this road, is a picturesque spot popular for swimming, canoeing and picnicking. There's a caravan park on the river bank where tent sites cost $5 per person, and on-site vans $28 a double. Canoes can be hired for $7 an hour.

Blue Mountains

The Blue Mountains, part of the Great Dividing Range, were an impenetrable barrier to White expansion from Sydney. Despite many attempts to find a route through – and a bizarre belief among many convicts that China, and freedom, was just on the other side – it took 25 years before a successful crossing was made by Europeans. A road was built soon afterwards which opened the western plains to settlement.

The first Whites into the mountains found evidence of Aboriginal occupation but few Aboriginal people. It seems likely that European diseases had travelled from Sydney long before the explorers and wiped out most of the indigenous people.

The Blue Mountains National Park has some truly fantastic scenery, excellent bushwalks and all the gorges, gum trees and cliffs you could ask for. The foothills begin 65 km inland from Sydney and rise as high as 1100 metres. The blue haze which gave the mountains their name is a result of the fine mist of oil given off by eucalyptus trees.

For the past century, the area has been a popular getaway for Sydneysiders seeking to escape the summer heat. Despite the intensive tourist development much of the area is so precipitous that it's still only open to bushwalkers.

Be prepared for the climatic difference between the Blue Mountains and the coast – you can swelter in Sydney but shiver in Katoomba. It usually snows sometime between June and August and the region has a Yuletide Festival during this period, complete with Christmas decorations and dinners.

During the 1994 bushfires, large areas of the Grose Valley were burned but the Blue Gum Forest escaped almost intact. The YHA hostel at North Springwood was destroyed in the fires but there are plans to rebuild it. Contact the YHA Travel Centre in Sydney (☎ (02) 9261 1111) for further information.

Orientation

The Great Western Highway from Sydney follows a ridge running on an east-west axis through the Blue Mountains. Along this less-than-beautiful road, the Blue Mountains towns merge into each other – Glenbrook, Springwood, Woodford, Lawson, Wentworth Falls, Leura, Katoomba (the main accommodation centre), Medlow Bath, Blackheath, Mt Victoria and Hartley. On the western fringe of the mountains is Lithgow – see the Central West section later in this chapter.

To the south and north of the highway's ridge, the country drops away into precipitous valleys, including the Grose Valley to the north, and the Jamison Valley south of Katoomba.

The Bells Line of Road is a much more scenic and less congested alternative to the Great Western Highway. It's the more northerly of the two crossings, beginning in Richmond (see the Around Windsor section) and running north of the Grose Valley to emerge in Lithgow, although you can cut across from Bell to join the Great Western Highway at Mt Victoria.

Information

There are Blue Mountains information centres open daily on the highway at Glenbrook and at Echo Point in Katoomba (☎ (047) 39 6266). The Blue Mountains Heritage Centre (☎ (047) 87 8877) is a NPWS visitor centre on Govetts Leap Rd, Blackheath, about three km off the Great Western Highway. On weekends, another NPWS visitor centre is open on Bruce Rd, Glenbrook (☎ (047) 39 2950).

There are plenty of books on the Blue Mountains. For a general introduction, try *The Blue Mountains of Australia*. Bushwalkers should look at *How to See the Blue Mountains* by Jim Smith. Lonely Planet's *Bushwalking in Australia* by John & Monica Chapman includes walks in the Blue Mountains. Books and maps and individual walking track guides are sold at visitor centres.

You can hire any camping gear you may need from Mountain Designs (☎ (047) 82 5999), 190 Katoomba St, Katoomba.

National Parks

The **Blue Mountains National Park** protects large areas to the north and south of the Great Western Highway. It's the most popular and accessible of the three national parks in the area, and offers great bushwalking, scenic lookouts, breathtaking waterfalls and Aboriginal stencils. **Wollemi National Park**, north of the Bells Line of Road, is the state's largest forested wilderness area and stretches all the way to Denman in the Hunter Valley. It has limited access and the centre of the park is so isolated that a new species of tree, named the Wollemi Pine, was discovered as recently as 1994.

Kanangra-Boyd National Park is southwest of the southern section of the Blue Mountains National Park. It has bushwalking opportunities, limestone caves and grand scenery, and includes the spectacular Kanangra Walls Plateau, which is surrounded by sheer cliffs and can be reached by unsealed road from Oberon or Jenolan Caves.

Entry to these national parks is free unless you enter the Blue Mountains National Park at Bruce Rd, Glenbrook, where it costs $7.50 per car; walkers are not charged.

Bushwalking

The roads across the mountains offer tantalising glimpses of the majesty of the area, but the only way to really experience the Blue Mountains is to start walking. There are walks lasting from a few minutes to several days. The two most popular areas are the Jamison Valley, south of Katoomba, and the Grose Valley, north-east of Katoomba and west of Blackheath. The area south of Glenbrook is another good place.

Visit a NPWS visitor centre for information or, for shorter walks, ask at one of the tourist information centres. It's very rugged country and walkers sometimes get lost, so it's highly advisable to get reliable information, to not go alone, and to tell someone where you're going. Most Blue Mountains watercourses are polluted, so you have to sterilise water or take your own. Be prepared for rapid weather changes.

Adventure Activities

The cliffs and gorges of the Blue Mountains offer excellent abseiling, climbing and canyoning. See the Katoomba Activities section for details.

Places to Stay

Accommodation ranges from camp sites and hostels to guesthouses and luxury hotels. Katoomba is the main centre. Prices are fairly stable throughout the year, but most places charge more on Friday and weekends. Prices listed below are winter rates. If you intend to camp in the national parks, check with the NPWS first.

Getting There & Away

Katoomba is 109 km from Sydney's city centre, but it's still almost a satellite suburb. Trains run roughly hourly from Central Station. The trip takes two hours ($9 single), and there are stops at plenty of Blue Mountains townships on the way.

By car, exit the city via Parramatta Rd and detour onto the Western Motorway tollway ($1.50) at Strathfield. The motorway becomes the Great Western Highway west of Penrith. To reach the Bells Line of Rd, exit the city on Parramatta Rd and from Parramatta head north-west on the Windsor Rd to Windsor. The Richmond Rd from Windsor becomes the Bells Line of Rd west of Richmond.

There are several companies running backpacker-oriented day tours from Sydney, including Wonderbus (☎ 9247 5151) and Oz Trek (☎ 9369 7055). See the Sydney Organised Tours section for details.

Getting Around

The Katoomba Leura Bus Co (☎ (047) 82 3333) runs between Leura, Katoomba, Medlow Bath, Blackheath and (infrequently) Mt Victoria, with some services running down Hat Hill Rd and Govetts Leap Rd which lead respectively to Perrys Look-down and Govetts Leap. The buses take you to within about one km of Govetts Leap but for Perrys Lookdown you have to walk about six km from the last stop. Services are sparse, with only two buses running on Saturday to Hat Hill Rd and Govetts Leap, and none on Sunday. In Katoomba, the bus leaves from the top of Katoomba St, opposite the Carrington Hotel.

The Katoomba-Woodford Bus Company (☎ (047) 82 4213) runs between Katoomba, Leura, Wentworth Falls, and east as far as Woodford. There's roughly one service an hour from Katoomba railway station.

There are railway stations in most Blue Mountains towns along the Great Western Highway. Trains run roughly hourly between stations east of Katoomba and roughly two-hourly between stations to the west.

Cullen Utility Rental (☎ (047) 82 5535), 60 Wilson St, Katoomba, rents cars from $60 a day including insurance and 250 free km per day.

GLENBROOK TO KATOOMBA

From Marge's and Elizabeth's lookouts, just north of Glenbrook, there are good views east to Sydney. The section of the Blue Mountains National Park south of Glenbrook contains **Red Hand Cave**, an old Aboriginal shelter with hand stencils on the walls. It's an easy seven-km return walk, south-west of the NPWS visitor centre.

The artist and author Norman Lindsay lived in **Springwood** from 1912 until he died in 1969. His home at 14 Norman Lindsay Crescent is now a gallery and museum, with exhibits of his paintings, cartoons, illustrations and sculptures. It's open daily from 11 am to 5 pm; admission is $5 ($2.50 concession).

Just south of the town of **Wentworth Falls**, there are great views of the Jamison Valley. You can see the spectacular 300-metre Wentworth Falls from Falls Reserve, which is the starting point for a network of walking tracks.

Leura is a quaint tree-lined centre full of country stores and cafes. Leuralla is an Art-Deco mansion which houses a toy and model ailway museum; admission is $6. Sublime Point, south of Leura, is a great cliff-top lookout. Nearby Gordon Falls Reserve is a popular picnic spot, and from here you can take the cliff-top path or Cliff Drive four km west past Leura Cascades to Katoomba's Echo Point.

Places to Stay & Eat

There are NPWS camping areas accessible by car at Euroka Clearing near Glenbrook, Murphys Glen near Woodford, and Ingar near Wentworth Falls. You need a permit to camp at Euroka Clearing from the NPWS office in Richmond (☎ (045) 88 5247 Monday to Friday) or Glenbrook (☎ (047) 39 2950 weekends and school holidays). The tracks to Ingar and Murphys Glen may be closed after heavy rain.

Leura Village Caravan Park (☎ (047) 84 552), on the corner of the Great Western Highway and Leura Mall, has tent sites (from 17), on-site vans (from $34) and cabins from $42). There are plenty of guesthouses and expensive motel and hotel accommodation; expect to pay from around $40 per person for guesthouse B&B.

Country-style cafes lining Leura Mall serve light meals for around $8. Try *Gracie's on the Mall* at No 174 or the *Original Mountain Deli* at No 134. If you want something a little special, *Le Gobelet* at the top of the mall has beluga caviar for a mere $98.50.

KATOOMBA (pop 8300)

Katoomba and the adjacent centres of Wentworth Falls and Leura form the tourist centre of the Blue Mountains. Katoomba is where the Sydney 'plains-dwellers' escape the summer heat, and has long catered to visitors. Despite the number of tourists and its closeness to Sydney, Katoomba has an uncanny ambience of an another time and place, an atmosphere accentuated by its Art-Deco and Art-Nouveau guesthouses and cafes, its thick mists and occasional snowfalls.

Steep Katoomba St is the main street, and its undistinguished shops belie the town's role as the service centre for the Blue Mountains. The major tourist attraction is at **Echo**

The Three Sisters rock formation near Katoomba

Point, near the southern end of Katoomba St, about a km from the shopping centre. Here you'll find some of the best views of the Jamison Valley and the magnificent **Three Sisters** rock formation.

To the west of Echo Point, at the junction of Cliff Drive and Violet St, are the **Scenic Railway** and **Scenic Skyway** (☎ (047) 82 2699). The railway runs to the bottom of the Jamison Valley (one way $2, return $3.60, extra for backpacks), where the popular six-hour walk to the **Ruined Castle** rock formation begins. The railway was built in the 1880s to transport coal-miners and its 45° incline is one of the steepest in the world. The Scenic Skyway is a cable car which travels some 200 metres above the valley floor, traversing Katoomba Falls gorge ($3.60 return).

If you want to experience the thrills of the Blue Mountains without leaving the comfort of a cushioned seat, The Edge-Blue Mountains Maxvision Cinema (☎ (047) 828900), 235 great Western Highway, is a giant-screen cinema which shows a stunning 38-minute Blue Mountains documentary. It is screened up to 10 times daily and viewings cost $11 ($8.50 concession).

Activities

There are several companies offering rock climbing, abseiling, canyoning and caving adventure activities at similar prices.

NEW SOUTH WALES

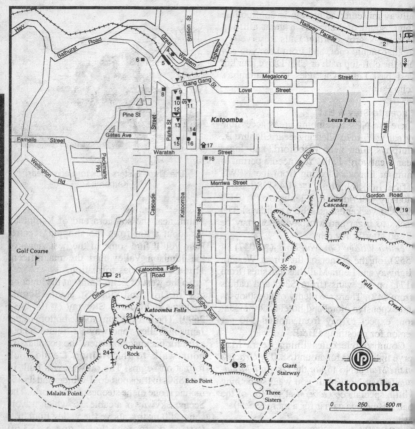

Katoomba

0   250   500 m

PLACES TO STAY

1   Leura Village Caravan
      Park
4   Nomads Gearin's Hotel
6   Blue Mountains
      Backpackers &
      Balmoral House
8   Katoomba Hotel
10   Carrington Hotel
14   Katoomba Mountain
      Lodge
17   Katoomba YHA
18   Clarendon Guesthouse
21   Katoomba Falls
      Caravan Park

22   Three Sisters Motel

PLACES TO EAT

3   Gracie's on the Mall &
      Original Mountain
      Deli
7   The Chilli Pepper
9   Avalon
11   Savoy
13   Paragon & Blues Cafe
15   Pins & Noodles,
      Parakeet

OTHER

2   Leura Train Station
5   Katoomba Train
      Station
12   Post Office
16   Rockcraft &
      Blue Mountains
      Adventure
      Company
19   Leuralla
20   Honeymoon Lookout
23   Scenic Skyway
24   Scenic Railway
25   Information Centre

Rockcraft (☎ (047) 82 2014), 182 Katoomba St, runs the Australian School of Mountaineering and offers, among its huge range of programmes, introductory rock climbing ($80) and abseiling ($69), plus abseiling descents of the Three Sisters ($90) and canyoning ($80). The Blue Mountains Adventure Company (☎ (047) 82 1271), 190 Katoomba St, offers similar activities, plus mountain-bike tours ($75). High 'n Wild (☎ (047) 82 6224) is opposite the railway station, on the corner of Main and Katoomba Sts. It's run by enthusiastic ex-travellers who offer daily introductory abseiling trips for $69.

Places to Stay

Camping *Katoomba Falls Caravan Park* (☎ (047) 82 1835) on Katoomba Falls Rd has tent sites for $7 per person and on-site vans from $35 for two people.

Hostels The *Katoomba YHA* (☎ (047) 82 1416) is in a pleasant old guesthouse on the corner of Lurline and Waratah Sts, near the town centre. Many rooms have attached bathrooms and there are good communal areas. Dorms cost from $11 and twins/doubles are $18/20; nonmembers pay $2 more.

Nearby *Katoomba Mountain Lodge* (☎ (047) 82 3933), 31 Lurline St, is a cosy hostel and guesthouse charging from $11 for dorm beds and $28/42 for singles/doubles with shared bathrooms. Prices rise by about 30% on weekends.

Blue Mountains Backpackers (☎ (047) 82 4226), 190 Bathurst Rd, is a short walk from the railway station. It's a friendly, makeshift hostel reminiscent of a large student house. Dorms cost $13, and twins/doubles $36. *Nomads Gearin's Hotel* and the *Katoomba Hotel* also offer backpacker rooms (see below).

Hotels & Motels The *Katoomba Hotel* (☎ (047) 82 1106), on the corner of Parke and Main Sts, is a smoky Aussie local with uninspiring singles/doubles for $20/30

midweek and $30/40 on weekends. A night in a 12-bed dorm costs $10.

The *Clarendon Guesthouse* (☎ (047) 82 1322), on the corner of Lurline and Waratah Sts, has excellent budget singles/doubles with TV from $30/40 midweek and $50/60 on weekends.

Nomads Gearin's Hotel (☎ (047) 82 6028) is a decent local pub with singles/doubles for $20/40 and dorms for $12. It's at 273 Great Western Highway, next to the railway station.

The *Three Sisters Motel* (☎ (047) 82 2911), 348 Lurline St, is an inexpensive motel, charging from $50/55 for a single/double midweek and $85 for a room on weekends. *Balmoral House* (☎ (047) 82 2264), 196 Bathurst Rd, claims to be the oldest guesthouse in the Blue Mountains. It's certainly in a lovely building, and has log fires and a restaurant. B&B costs $50 per person midweek.

One of the best hotels in the region is the *Hydro Majestic Hotel* (☎ (047) 88 1002), a superb relic of an earlier era. It's a few km west of Katoomba, on the Great Western Highway, at Medlow Bath. Singles/doubles cost from $132/174 including breakfast and dinner. The equally grand *Carrington Hotel* (☎ (047) 82 1111) on Katoomba St should by now have reopened after a major refit.

Places to Eat

The *Savoy* is a calm Art-Deco establishment at 12 Katoomba St serving focaccia, salads and pasta from around $6. The *Carrington Bar & Bistro*, opposite, has pastas and salads for $7 and mains between $11 and $14. The *Blues Cafe* at No 57 is a pleasant spot specialising in vegetarian light meals for around $5 and sandwiches for $3.50. The *Paragon* at No 65 is an Art-Deco masterpiece serving average cafe fare and delicious cakes and sweets. Visitors are welcome to view the closed cocktail bar at the rear which looks like it belongs on a 1930s ocean liner.

For evening or lunch fare, try *Pins & Noodles* at No 189, which serves interesting Asian-inspired noodle dishes from $5.50. *Parakeet* at No 195 is a sociable cafe with hearty breakfasts and meals for around $7. *The Chilli Pepper*, on Main St, right next to the railway station, has south Indian mains around the $10 mark. The relaxed and quaintly eccentric *Avalon* is upstairs at 98 Main St. It's a lovely place for dinner, with tasty mains for between $11 and $16.

Getting Around

You can hire mountain bikes at the YHA hostel for $25 a day or $15 for half a day ($15/10 for guests). Better bikes are available from the Blue Mountains Adventure Company (☎ (047) 82 1271), 190 Katoomba St, for $30 a day (24 hours) or $20 a half-day.

The Katoomba-Woodford Bus Company (☎ (047) 82 4213) runs a service between Katoomba railway station, the Three Sisters Motel (five minutes walk from Echo Point), and the Scenic Railway and Scenic Skyway. There's a bus roughly every 45 minutes. The Katoomba Leura Bus Co (☎ (047) 82 3333) runs a service between Echo Point and Gordon Falls via Katoomba St and Leura Mall. There is roughly one service an hour midweek, less on weekends.

On weekends and public holidays, the hop-on/hop-off Blue Mountains Explorer Bus (☎ (047) 82 1866) does an hourly circuit of 17 attractions in the Katoomba and Leura area. The easiest place to catch the bus is Katoomba railway station; tickets cost $15.

BLACKHEATH AREA

The little town of Blackheath is a good base for visiting the Grose and Megalong valleys. There are superb lookouts a few km east of the town, such as **Govetts Leap** and **Evans Lookout**. To the north-east, via Hat Hill Rd, are **Pulpit Rock**, **Perrys Lookdown** and **Anvil Rock**.

A cliff-top track leads from Govetts Leap to Pulpit Rock, and there are several walks from Govetts Leap down into the Grose Valley. Get details on the walks from the nearby Heritage Centre. Perrys Lookdown is the beginning of the shortest route (four hours return) to the beautiful **Blue Gum Forest** in the valley bottom.

The **Megalong Valley**, south of Black-heath, is largely cleared farmland but it's still a beautiful place with fabulous sandstone escarpments. The road down from Black-heath passes through pockets of rainforest and you can get a taste of the beauty of the Blue Mountains by following the 600-metre Coachwood Glen Nature Trail which is a couple of km before the small valley settlement of Werribee. There are several horse-riding outfits in the valley, such as Werriberri Trail Rides (☎ (047) 87 9171), on Megalong Rd, and Packsaddlers (☎ (047) 87 9150), at the end of the valley in Green Gully. Two-hour rides cost around $30.

Blackheath is on the railway line from Sydney, two stops past Katoomba, or a short drive along the Great Western Highway. From Blackheath, it's a 15-minute winding drive into the Megalong Valley via Shipley and Megalong Rds.

Places to Stay & Eat

The nearest NPWS camp site is Acacia Flat, in the Grose Valley near the Blue Gum Forest. It's a steep walk down from Govetts Leap or Perrys Lookdown. You can also camp at Perrys Lookdown, which has a car park and is a convenient base for walks into the Grose Valley.

The Blackheath Caravan Park (☎ (047) 87 8101) has tent sites from $7 and vans from $35. It's on Prince Edward St, off Govetts Leap Rd, about 500 metres from the Great Western Highway.

The cosy *Gardners Inn* (☎ (047) 87 8347), on the Great Western Highway in Black-heath, is the oldest hotel in the Blue Mountains (1831). It charges $25 per person for B&B midweek and $35 on weekends.

The *Lakeview Holiday Park* (☎ (047) 87 8534), 63 Prince Edward St, has cabins with en suite for $45 a double midweek and $50 on weekends.

The *Wattle Cafe*, on the corner of the Great Western Highway and Govetts Leap Rd, has cooked breakfasts for $5, meals for $7 and a pot-belly stove to warm yourself by. The *Piedmont Inn*, on the highway near Gardners Inn, has pizzas and fettucine for under $9.

MT VICTORIA & HARTLEY

A couple of km west of Blackheath is the pretty National Trust classified town of Mt Victoria. The museum at the railway station is open on weekends and school holidays between 2 and 5 pm. Interesting buildings include the Victoria & Albert guesthouse, the 1849 tollkeeper's cottage and the 1870s church.

Mt Vic Flicks is a lovely little cinema on Harley Ave, near the Victoria & Albert guesthouse. On Saturday night, $10 gets you a double feature plus supper during the interval.

Off the highway at **Mt York** is a memorial to the explorers who first crossed the Blue Mountains. A short stretch of the original road crosses the mountains here.

About 11 km past Mt Victoria, on the western slopes of the range, is the tiny, sandstone ghost town of **Hartley**, which flourished from the 1830s but declined when it was bypassed by the railway in 1887. There are several buildings of historic interest, including the 1837 courthouse and a quaint church and presbytery. There's a NPWS information centre in the Farmers Inn in the centre of town. It's open daily between 10 am and 5 pm (closed between 1 and 2 pm) and tours of the town and courthouse run from here.

Places to Stay

The *Imperial Hotel* (☎ (047) 87 1233) on the Great Western Highway in Mt Victoria is a Blue Mountains institution. It's a fine old hotel, with expensive dorm beds for $27 and singles/doubles from $49/78 midweek. It has a coffee shop with snacks and light meals, and a bistro open on weekends.

Nearby, the *Victoria & Albert* (☎ (047) 87 1241), 19 Station St, is a lovely guesthouse that could be straight out of an Agatha Christie mystery. It offers B&B from $45 per person midweek. The less-atmospheric *Manor House* (☎ (047) 87 1369) on Montgomery St also has B&B from $45 per person midweek. All these establishments offer all-inclusive weekend packages.

JENOLAN CAVES

South-west of Katoomba, on the north-western fringe of Kanangra-Boyd National Park, are the Jenolan Caves (☎ (063) 59 3311), the best-known limestone caves in Australia. One cave has been open to the public since 1867, although parts of the system are still unexplored. Three 'arches' are open for independent viewing, and you can visit nine caves by guided tour. There are about 10 tours a day from 10 am to 4 pm. Tours last between one and two hours, and prices vary from $12 to $20.

The Jenolan Caves are the best-known limestone caves in Australia

Places to Stay

You can camp near Jenolan Caves House for $10 per site. *Binda Bush Cabins* (☎ (063) 59 3311) is on the road from Hartley, about eight km north of the caves, and accommodates six people in bunks for $75 per night midweek and $90 on weekends and school holidays. *Jenolan Caves House* (☎ (063) 59 3304) has singles/doubles from $117/173 midweek, including two meals. There are minimum two-night packages on weekends.

Getting There & Away

The caves are on plenty of tour itineraries from Sydney and Katoomba. By car, turn off the Great Western Highway at Hartley and they're a 45-minute drive along Jenolan Caves Rd. The Six Foot Track from Katoomba to Jenolan Caves is a fairly easy three-day walk, but make sure you get information from an NPWS visitor centre.

BELLS LINE OF ROAD

This back road between Richmond and Lithgow is the most scenic route across the Blue Mountains. It's highly recommended if you have your own transport. There are fine views towards the coast from Kurrajong Heights on the eastern slopes of the range, orchards around Bilpin, and sandstone cliff and bush scenery all the way to Lithgow.

There are grass skiing and karting at **Kurrajong Heights Grass Ski Park** on weekends for $13 for two hours. Roughly midway between Richmond and Lithgow is the exquisite **Mt Tomah Botanic Gardens**, the cool-climate annexe of Sydney's Royal Botanic Gardens. It's open daily and admission is $5 per car and $2 for pedestrians; late October and late April are the most spectacular times to visit.

North of the Bells Line of Road is the quaint town of **Mt Wilson**, which has formal gardens and a nearby remnant of rainforest known as the **Cathedral of Ferns**. The **Zig Zag Railway** is at Clarence, 10 km east of Lithgow. It was built in 1869 and was quite an engineering wonder in its day. Trains used to descend from the Blue Mountains by this route until 1910, when a series of tunnels made the line redundant. A section has been restored and several steam trains run daily. The fare is $10. Call ☎ (063) 53 1795 for timetable information.

North Coast

The popular NSW north coast has excellent beaches, and several national parks offering challenging bushwalks, wildlife and superb scenery.

The Pacific Highway runs north along the narrow coastal strip into Queensland, passing a string of resorts, including Byron Bay – a surfing mecca and an established travellers' haunt. Scenic roads lead inland into the Great Dividing Range and onto the New England tableland.

SYDNEY TO NEWCASTLE

The area between Broken Bay and Newcastle is known as the Central Coast. It's a densely populated area of rampant suburban housing, superb beaches, inland waterways and national parks.

The largest town in the area is **Gosford**, an undistinguished settlement on the shores of Brisbane Water, some 85 km north of Sydney. It's easily accessible by train from Sydney and Newcastle. A visitor information centre (☎ (043) 25 2835) is open daily at 200 Mann St, near the railway station. Gosford makes a sensible base from which to explore the region if you don't have transport because bus services radiate from here. The *Gosford Hotel* (☎ (043) 25 0500), on the corner of Mann and Erina Sts, has singles/doubles from $27/37.

Nine km south-west of Gosford is the **Old Sydney Town** (☎ (043) 40 1104) theatrical heritage park. It's on the Pacific Highway at Somersby, and is open Wednesday to Sunday from 10 am to 4 pm, and daily during school holidays; admission is $15.

Brisbane Water National Park (☎ (043) 24 4911), a few km south-east of Gosford, includes the northern inlets of the Hawkesbury River. It has good bushwalking, Aboriginal engravings, and is renowned for its spring wildflowers. The **Bouddi National Park** extends north along the coast from the mouth of Brisbane Water and offers excellent coastal bushwalking.

There are several beach towns worth exploring. One of the best is the National Trust classified township of **Pearl Beach**, south of Gosford, on the eastern edge of the Brisbane Water National Park. It's a heavenly enclave with a lovely beach and spectacular views. The most attractive of the Central Coast beach resorts is **Terrigal**, 12 km east of Gosford. The *Terrigal Beach Backpackers Lodge* (☎ (043) 85 3330), 10 Campbell Crescent, is one block from the beach and has a five-backpack rating. Dorms cost $14 and doubles $35.

Farther north is a series of large saltwater lakes, including **Tuggerah Lake**, which offer fine boating and fishing opportunities. Farther north again, and just south of Newcastle, is **Lake Macquarie**, Australia's biggest saltwater lake. It's a popular centre for sailing, water-skiing and fishing. The Lake Macquarie visitor centre (☎ (049) 72 1172) is on the Pacific Highway just north of Swansea.

The Sydney to Newcastle freeway is the major road link between the two cities, but it skirts the Central Coast. If you want to explore this area, it's best to take the Pacific Highway between Gosford and Newcastle. You can reach the southern part of the Central Coast from Sydney's Palm Beach by catching the thrice-daily ferry to Patonga. There are four daily Busways (☎ (043) 68 2277) buses from Patonga to Gosford.

NEWCASTLE (pop 265,000)
Newcastle is the state's second-largest city and one of Australia's largest ports, at the mouth of the Hunter River, 167 km north of Sydney. It's a major industrial and commercial centre, with a massive BHP steelworks and other heavy industry. It's also the export port for the Hunter Valley coalfields and for grain from the north-west.

For many, Newcastle conjures up images of belching smokestacks. It's an image that locals resent, and quite rightly. Newcastle is a relaxed and friendly place. The city centre has wide, leafy streets and some fine early colonial buildings. There are clean surf beaches only a few hundred metres away.

Originally named Coal River, the city was founded in 1804 as a place for the most intractable of Sydney's convicts and was known as the 'hell of New South Wales'. The breakwater out to Nobbys Head, with its lighthouse, was built by convicts. The Bogey Hole, a swimming pool cut into the rock on the ocean's edge below the pleasant King Edward Park, was built for Major Morriset, a strict disciplinarian. It's still a great place for a dip.

In late 1989, Newcastle suffered Australia's most destructive recorded earthquake, with 12 people killed and severe property damage. Around town you can still see signs of it – props holding up facades and buildings being restored or demolished.

Orientation
The city centre is a peninsula bordered by the ocean on one side and the Hunter River on the other. It tapers down to the long sandspit leading to Nobbys Head. Hunter St is the three-km-long main street, forming a pedestrian mall between Newcomen and Perkins Sts.

The railway station, the long-distance bus stop, the post office, banks and some fine old buildings are at the north-eastern end of the city centre. Cooks Hill rises steeply behind the centre and offers good views. Apart from checking out the sights, there's not a lot to do in the city centre. Most travellers head for the lively inner western suburb of Hamilton, centred on Beaumont St.

Just across the river from the city centre is Stockton, a modest suburb with beaches and good views back to Newcastle city. It's minutes from the city by ferry but by road you have to wind through the docks and some dramatic industrial landscapes, a trip of about 20 km.

Information
The tourist office (☎ (049) 29 9299) occupies the Old Stationmaster's Cottage (built 1858) at 92 Scott St, just beyond the station. It's open weekdays from 9 am to 5 pm and weekends from 10 am to 3.30 pm. It sells excellent heritage walk maps.

Things to See & Do
The **Newcastle Regional Museum** at 787 Hunter St, Newcastle West, is open daily except Monday (daily in school holidays); admission is $3. It includes the Supernova

NEW SOUTH WALES

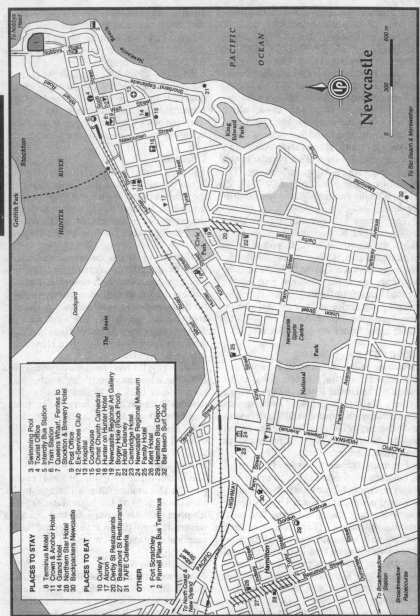

Newcastle

PLACES TO STAY

8 Terminus Motel
11 Crown & Anchor Hotel
14 Grand Hotel
28 Northern Star Hotel
30 Backpackers Newcastle

PLACES TO EAT

10 Curley's
17 Alcron
20 Derby St Restaurants
27 Beaumont St Restaurants
31 TAFE Cafeteria

OTHER

1 Fort Scratchley
2 Parnell Place Bus Terminus
3 Swimming Pool
4 Tourist Office
5 Intercity Bus Station
6 Train Station
7 Queens Wharf, Ferries to
  Stockton & Brewery Hotel
9 Post Office
12 Ex-Services Club
13 Hospital
15 Courthouse
16 Christ Church Cathedral
18 Hunter or Hunter Hotel
19 Newcastle Regional Art Gallery
21 Bogey Hole (Rock Pool)
22 Hotel Delaney
23 Cambridge Hotel
24 Newcastle Regional Museum
25 Family Hotel
26 Kent Hotel
29 Hamilton Bus Depot
32 Bar Beach Surf Club

hands-on science display. The **Fort Scratchley Maritime & Military Museum** is open Tuesday to Sunday from 10 am to 4 pm. Admission is free, but it costs $1 to explore the tunnels under the fort, which are said to run all the way to King Edward Park. Fort Scratchley overlooks Nobbys Head.

The **Newcastle Regional Art Gallery** is on Laman St next to Civic Park. It's free and open weekdays and weekend afternoons. There are several private galleries on nearby Cooks Hill.

Blackbutt Reserve (☎ (049) 52 1449) is a 182-hectare bushland reserve at New Lambton Heights, approximately 10 km south-west of the centre. It has bushwalks and aviaries, wildlife enclosures and fern houses. It has just completed a new koala enclosure. It's open daily from 9 am to 5 pm and admission is free. Bus Nos 232 and 363 run past the upper entrance, Nos 216 and 217 past the lower. The fare is $2.50.

About 10 km west of the centre near Sandgate railway station, the **Shortlands Wetlands Centre** (☎ (049) 51 6466) on the edge of Hexham Swamp has lots of birdlife as well as walks and canoe trails. It's open daily from 9 am to 5 pm and admission is by a $2 donation.

Tours A couple of outfits offer infrequent cruises on the harbour. *Lady Joy* departs from Queens Wharf on Thursday at 2 pm ($12), more often in school holidays, and *William the Fourth*, a replica of an old steamship, leaves Merewether St near Queens Wharf at 11 am and 2 pm on the third Sunday of the month ($11).

Surf Beaches Newcastle's favourite surfing son is former world champ Mark Richards, and many come to seek out the breaks where Richards cut his teeth. The main beach, **Newcastle Beach**, is just a couple of minutes walk from the city centre. It has an ocean pool and good surf. Just north of here is **Nobbys Beach**, more sheltered from the southerlies and often open when other beaches are closed. At the northern end of Nobbys is a fast left-hander known as The

Wedge. The most popular surfing break is about five km south at **Bar Beach**, which is floodlit at night in summer. Nearby **Merewether Beach** has two huge pools. Bus 207 from the Parnell St terminus in the city runs to Merewether Beach every half-hour ($1.20) via Bar Beach.

Places to Stay
Camping Stockton is handy by ferry but it's 20 km by road. *Stockton Beach Caravan Park* (☎ (049) 28 1393) is on the beach at Pitt St. Tent sites are $10 a double and on-site vans start at $50. There are several caravan parks south of Newcastle, around Belmont and on the ocean at Redhead Beach.

Hostels *Backpackers Newcastle* (☎ (049) 69 3436) occupies a couple of fine old weatherboard houses at 42-44 Denison St, Hamilton. It's clean and friendly and in an interesting part of town. Backpacker accommodation at No 42 has dorm beds for $14 and doubles for $28, while No 44 is more up-market with doubles for $36. Each house has a communal lounge and kitchen. There are free surfboards and one of the owners is a keen surfer who gives lessons. The hostel also has lots of information about the region and can organise excursions. Hamilton is several km from the city centre, but you can phone for a free pick-up from town. Otherwise, any bus heading out of town along Hunter St can drop you at the nearby Regional Museum.

Hotels The *Crown & Anchor* (☎ (049) 29 1027) on the corner of Hunter and Perkins Sts has singles/doubles for $25/34. The *Grand Hotel* (☎ (049) 29 3489) is an old pub in the city centre on the corner of Bolton and Church Sts, across from the courthouse. Singles/doubles are $50/52 with bathroom.

Motels The *Terminus Motel* (☎ (049) 26 3244) at 107 Scott St, also known as the Harbourside Motel, has rooms for $50/55. The *Northern Star Hotel* (☎ (049) 61 1087), 112 Beaumont St, has motel-style rooms for $45/55. There's a string of cheaper motels along the Pacific Highway at Belmont, about 15 km south of town.

Places to Eat

During school term, the best deal in town is at *Hunter TAFE College* on Parry St. The cafeteria operated by the college's catering and hospitality school offers main courses for $3.50 and desserts for $1.50. Opening times vary. The owners of Backpackers Newcastle can tell you when it's open.

Beaumont St has the greatest concentration of restaurants. Once known as 'Little Italy' for the profusion of Italian eateries, Beaumont St has now taken on a more international flavour. There are literally dozens of places to choose from. If Italian is what you're after, try *Dolomiti Gelato*, down an alleyway at the corner of Beaumont and Lindsay Sts, or the *Trieste*. The *Anatolia* Turkish restaurant at No 63 offers top value with nothing on the menu over $10. *Gandha's* Indian Restaurant, upstairs at No 54, has a good range of curries and tandoori dishes.

Newcastle's other main restaurant strip is closer to the city on Darby St, south of King St. The choices include Vietnamese *(Lan's)*, Thai *(Al-Oi)*, Malaysian *(Rumah Malaysia)* and Indian *(Taj Takeaway)*. *Splash* claims to have 'the finest fish & chips in the known universe', while *Natural Tucker* has a large selection of vegetarian snacks.

There are several good places for snacks and meals at the eastern end of Hunter St. *Vera's Cafe* on the corner of Pacific and Hunter Sts has footpath tables, and serves breakfast for around $6. *Curley's* (the illuminated sign says Vienna Cafe), just around the corner on Pacific St, is a nice place with focaccia for $4.50 and pasta from $6.50.

If you feel like a blow-out, *Alcron* (☎ (049) 29 2423), at 113 Church St, is perhaps the oldest restaurant in Australia. Main courses are around $20.

Entertainment

Newcastle has a busy home-grown music scene, with live bands playing somewhere every night except Monday and Tuesday. There are gig guides in Thursday's *Newcastle Herald* or the weekly *Newcastle Post*, published on Wednesday. One of the best rock venues is the *Cambridge Hotel* at the corner of Hunter and Denison Sts, home pub of top Aussie bands Screaming Jets and silverchair.

The *Hunter on Hunter Hotel*, at 417 Hunter St, is another pub that promotes local rock talent. The *Family Hotel*, on the corner of Hunter and Steel Sts, has blues, while the *Kent Hotel* and the *Northern Star Hotel*, both on Beaumont St, have jazz.

The *Hotel Delaney* is a relaxed little pub on the corner of Darby and Council Sts, with music most nights. The popular *Brewery*, at the Queens Wharf complex, brews its own.

Getting There & Away

Air Aeropelican flies several times a day between Sydney ($72) and Belmont, just south of Newcastle. Eastern Australia Airlines also has daily flights to Sydney ($89), while Impulse flies between Newcastle and Port Macquarie ($146), Coffs Harbour ($187), Lismore ($235) and Brisbane ($269). Eastern and Impulse use the airport at Williamtown, north of Newcastle.

Bus Between Sydney and Newcastle you're better off taking the train, but heading up the coast from Newcastle buses offer a much better service. Nearly all long-distance buses stop on Watt St near the railway station. Cheapish fares from Newcastle include: Sydney $14.50, Port Macquarie $30, Byron Bay $48, Brisbane $50. Jayes Travel (☎ (049) 26 2000) at 285 Hunter St near Darby St handles most major bus lines.

Sid Fogg's (☎ 1800 045 952) runs to Canberra ($45, four times a week) and up the valley to Dubbo ($46, three times a week). Book at Tower Travel (☎ (049) 26 3199), 245 Hunter St on the corner of Crown St, or phone the depot. Rover Motors (☎ (049) 90 1699) runs to Cessnock ($7). Port Stephens Buses (☎ (049) 81 1207) has nine buses a day to Nelson Bay and Shoal Bay (1½ hours, $6.80).

Train Sydney suburban trains run from Central Station to Newcastle about 25 times a day, taking nearly three hours. The one-way fare is $14; an off-peak return is $17.

Other trains heading north on the lines to Armidale and Murwillumbah bypass central Newcastle, stopping at suburban Broad-meadow – just west of Hamilton. Frequent buses run from here to the city centre. An XPT from Central Station to Broadmeadow takes about 2¼ hours and costs $19.40.

Car Rental As well as the regular places, you can hire used cars from places such as Cheep Heep (☎ (049) 61 3144) at 107 Tudor St, Hamilton, from $29 a day, including insurance.

Getting Around

To/From the Airport Port Stephens Buses (see above) stop at Williamtown airport on the run to Nelson Bay. The trip takes 35 minutes and costs $4.30. Local buses Nos 348, 349, 350 or 358 stop outside Belmont airport (one hour, $3.60).

Bus STA buses cover Newcastle and the eastern side of Lake Macquarie. There are fare deals similar to those on offer in Sydney. An all-day BusTripper pass costs $7.80 and is valid on STA buses and ferries. Most services operate half-hourly. The bus information booth at the west end of the mall, on the corner of Perkins St, has timetables. If it's closed, see the tourist office or phone the Travel Information Centre (☎ (049) 61 8933) between 8.30 am and 4.30 pm. For sightseeing, try route Nos 348, 350 or 358 to Swansea or Nos 306, 307 or 327 to Speers Point.

Ferry There are ferries to Stockton from Queens Wharf approximately half-hourly Monday to Thursday from 5.15 am to 11 pm. On Friday and Saturday they run until midnight and on Sunday they stop at 8.30 pm. The ferry office on Queens Wharf has timetables.

Bicycle Bike-hire places come and go – the tourist office will know if one is operating.

HUNTER VALLEY

The Hunter Valley has two curiously diverse products – coal and wine. The centre of the valley vineyards is the Pokolbin area near Cessnock and some wineries date to the 1860s. You'll find many of Australia's best-known wine names here.

On the southern side of the valley rise the sandstone ranges of the Wollemi and Goulburn river national parks; the northern side is bordered by the high, rugged ranges leading up to Barrington Tops National Park.

The main road through the Hunter Valley is the New England Highway running north-west from Newcastle and climbing up to the New England tablelands near Murrurundi. The 300-km-long Hunter River comes from farther west and doesn't meet the highway until Singleton. The valley is wide in the Lower Hunter area, where you'll find most of the wineries. It narrows upstream from Singleton.

There are more than 50 vineyards in the Lower Hunter, and seven more in the Upper Hunter. Generally they're open daily for tastings and sales, with slightly reduced hours on Sunday. Many have picnic and barbecue facilities.

Organised Tours

Hunter Vineyard Tours (☎ (049) 91 1659) has daily departures from Newcastle and other Hunter centres for $29 ($45 with lunch). Several Sydney companies have day tours of the Lower Hunter wineries. For tours of the Upper Hunter, contact the Scone or Denman information centres.

Getting There & Around

Trains run up the valley en route to Armidale and Moree.

Batterhams Express (☎ (049) 90 5000, 1800 043 339) runs once daily between Sydney and Tamworth via Cessnock ($20) and Scone ($33). Rover Motors (☎ (049) 90 1699) runs between Newcastle and Cessnock ($7.50) six times a day on weekdays, three times on Saturday and not at all on Sunday. Sid Fogg's (☎ 1800 045 952) stops at Denman ($24) three times a week on the Newcastle-Dubbo run.

Between Sydney and the Lower Hunter there's an interesting back route (with some unsealed roads) from Wisemans Ferry, passing through the pretty township of Wollombi. A great drive from Sydney to the Upper Hunter is on the Windsor to Singleton road, known as the Putty Road.

You can hire bicycles from Grapemobile (☎ (049) 98 7639), at the corner of McDonalds and Gillards Rds near Pokolbin. They charge $25 for a day and $15 for a half-day.

Lower Hunter Wineries

The valley's wine-growing heartland is the rolling hill country north-west of Cessnock. The efficient Cessnock Visitor Information Centre (☎ (049) 90 4477) is the place to go for maps and brochures before you set out on a winery tour. It's on Aberdare Rd, on the way into town from Sydney, and is open daily from 9 am to 5 pm.

Several wineries run tours, including McWilliams (weekdays at 11 am and 2 pm); Hunter Estate (daily at 9.30 am); McGuigan Bros (daily at noon); Tyrrells (daily at 1.30 pm) and Rothbury Estate (weekends at 11 am and 2 pm). The Hunter Vintage Walkabout in February and March attracts hordes of wine enthusiasts for wine tasting, and grape-picking and treading contests.

Cessnock This is the main town and accommodation centre for the vineyards, although there is also pub accommodation in nearby towns such as **Neath** and **Bellbird**.

The town's information centre (☎ (049) 90 4477) can book accommodation.

Places to Stay Almost all places offering accommodation charge more at weekends and you might have to take a package (meals included).

There are a couple of caravan parks close to town. The *Valley View* (☎ (049) 90 2573) on Mount View Rd has tent sites for $10, on-site vans from $16 and cabins from $30.

Cessnock Park (☎ (049) 90 5819) off Allandale Rd north of Cessnock has sites for $8, on-site vans from $20 and cabins from $30.

There is no hostel accommodation in town, but there are some good deals at the pubs. The *Black Opal Hotel* (☎ (049) 90 1070) at the southern end of Vincent St, the main shopping street, charges $15 per person Monday to Thursday, and $20 Friday to Sunday. Prices are identical at the *Cessnock Hotel* (☎ (049) 90 1002), on Wollombi Rd opposite the post office. The *Wentworth Hotel* (☎ (049) 90 1364) at 36 Vincent St has singles/doubles for $25/40.

Midweek motel prices include $55 for doubles at the *Cessnock Motel* (☎ (049) 90 2699) and $50 at the *Hunter Valley Motel* (☎ (049) 90 1722), both on Allandale Rd. Prices at these and other motels rise steeply at weekends.

There is a lot of accommodation out among the vineyards. Most is well over $100 a night on weekends, but midweek there are a few places charging around $60 a double, such as the *Hunter Country Lodge* (☎ (049) 38 1744) about 12 km north of Cessnock on Branxton Rd; and *Belford Country Cabins* (☎ (049) 91 2777) on Hermitage Rd north of the Hunter Estate.

Upper Hunter Wineries

The Upper Hunter has only seven wineries, but it's worth visiting because the pace is slower and the scenery more beautiful than the Lower Hunter.

The nearest town to the Upper Hunter wineries is **Denman**, a sleepy little place 25 km south-west of Muswellbrook. The area's information centre (☎ (065) 47 2731) is on Denman's main street at *The Old Carriage Restaurant*, a cafe/restaurant in an old railway carriage. As well as the plentiful accommodation in nearby Muswellbrook and Singleton, there is camping, pub, motel and B&B accommodation in and around Denman.

The New England Highway runs up the Hunter Valley through some old towns and attractive scenery. The **Goulburn River**

National Park at the upper end of the valley follows the river as it cuts through sandstone gorges. This was the route used by Aboriginal people travelling from the plains to the sea and the area is rich in cave art and other sites. You can camp but there are no facilities. Access is from Sandy Hollow (near Denman) or Merriwa (on the Denman to Gulgong road). The Muswellbrook NPWS office (☎ (065) 43 3533), 160 Bridge St, has information.

Maitland An old coal-mining centre, Maitland is now a sprawling town with a population of 50,000. It was established as a convict settlement in 1818 and at one time, along with Sydney and Parramatta, was among Australia's main settlements.

The information centre (☎ (049) 33 2611) is in East Maitland, on the corner of the New England Highway and Banks St. It occupies a 100-year-old slab hut known as Hew Cottage. There are frequent trains between Maitland and Newcastle.

High St follows the winding route of the original track through town and part of it is now the **Heritage Mall**. **Brough House** on Church St houses the art gallery, and its neighbour, **Grossman House**, is the local history museum (open weekends).

The *Hunter River Hotel* (☎ (049) 33 7244) at 10 Melbourne St in East Maitland has singles/doubles for $20/40 and a backpackers' rate of $15 if there is a spare room. There is plenty of other accommodation and a caravan park (☎ (049) 33 2950).

Singleton Founded in 1820, the coal-mining town of Singleton (population 12,000) is one of the oldest towns in the state. The **Singleton Historical Museum** (☎ (049) 77 8536) in Burdekin Park is housed in the old lock-up (jail), built in 1862. It's open on weekends and public holidays from noon to 4 pm and on Tuesday from 10 am to 1 pm. It offers guided walks around the town's historic sites.

The old *Caledonian Hotel* (☎ (065) 72 1356) on the highway near the town centre has accommodation.

Muswellbrook Like other Hunter Valley towns, Muswellbrook (population 10,000) was founded early in Australia's White history and has some interesting old buildings, surrounded by spreading residential areas.

Historic *Eatons Hotel* (☎ (065) 43 2403) on the main street at the northern end of town charges $20/30 a single/double.

Scone With over 40 horse studs in the area, Scone dubs itself 'the horse capital of Australia'. Horse Week is held annually in May. You can arrange to visit studs ($3.50 per person) at the information centre (☎ (065) 45 2907), open daily on the northern side of town, near the Mare & Foal statue.

The friendly *Belmore Hotel* (☎ (065) 45 2078) on Kelly St, not far from the railway station and the information centre, has good rooms for $26/34. The *Golden Fleece Hotel* (☎ (065) 45 1357) on the corner of Kelly and Liverpool Sts charges $15/24. The rural *Scone Youth Hostel* (☎ (065) 45 2072) occupies the old school house at Segenhoe, eight km east of town. Dorm beds in this historic building are $13 and doubles are $28. The owners will pick you up from Scone, or you can catch the school bus (50c) at 3.20 pm.

At **Burning Mountain**, off the highway 20 km north of Scone, a coal seam has been burning for over 5000 years.

NEWCASTLE TO PORT MACQUARIE
Port Stephens
This huge sheltered bay is about an hour's drive north of Newcastle. The bay, which occupies a submerged valley, stretches more than 20 km inland. It's a popular boating and fishing spot, and is well-known for its resident **dolphins**. The bay is surrounded by bushland, and there is a sizeable **koala colony** living at Lemon Tree Passage, on the south side. There is a road to Lemon Tree Passage from the town of Salt Ash.

Development around Port Stephens is confined largely to the Tomaree Peninsula, which forms much of the southern shore. The main town, **Nelson Bay** (population 7000), has an information centre (☎ (049) 81 1579,

1800 808 900) near the marina. Nearby **Shoal Bay** has a long, sheltered beach and is a short walk from surf at Zenith Beach.

Back down the Tomaree Peninsula from Nelson Bay is the small resort town of **Anna Bay**, with good surf beaches nearby. Golf nuts can play 24 hours a day at the floodlit David Graham Golf Complex. Stockton Bight stretches 35 km from Anna Bay to Newcastle, backed by the longest dune in the southern hemisphere.

Opposite Nelson Bay on the northern side of Port Stephens are the small resort settlements of **Tea Gardens** and **Hawks Nest** at the mouth of the Myall River.

Places to Stay There's a YHA hostel in the *Shoal Bay Motel* (☎ (049) 84 2315) on the beachfront road. Dorm beds are $15 and there are doubles for $20 per person (minimum two people); these rates can rise during school holidays.

The *Seabreeze Hotel* (☎ (049) 81 1511), just uphill from the information centre, has beds in comfortable modern dorms for $20. Cooked breakfast is $7.

Samurai Beach Bungalows (☎ (049) 82 1921), just east of Anna Bay at the corner of Frost Rd and Robert Connell Close, offers an opportunity for backpackers to go bush. The bungalows are dotted Asian-style around a covered communal kitchen area. Dorm beds are $12 and doubles $30. Host Mark is a keen surfer and angler who organises frequent outings to surrounding beaches. There's free use of surfboards and bicycles. Buses from Newcastle run past the door.

Hawks Nest Beach Caravan Park (☎ 049) 97 0239) has just a narrow band of bush separating it from a good surf beach. Tent sites are $11 a double and cabins start at $35.

Getting There & Away Port Stephens Buses (☎ 1800 045 949) has a daily service to Sydney ($20) and there are plenty of buses to Newcastle ($6.80). If you're heading north up the coast, it's easiest to backtrack to Newcastle and catch a long-distance bus from there. Great Lakes Coaches (☎ 1800

043 263) has a daily service from Newcastle to Tea Gardens for $12.80.

Getting Around Port Stephens Ferries operates between Nelson Bay and Tea Gardens three times a day (one hour, $15 return).

Barrington Tops National Park

Barrington Tops is a World Heritage wilderness area centred on the rugged Barrington Plateau, which rises to almost 1600 metres around Mt Barrington and Carey's Peak. The lower reaches of the park are covered by rainforest, while the slopes in between are dominated by ancient, moss-covered Antarctic beech forest.

There are good walking trails, but be prepared for snow in winter and cold snaps at any time. Drinking water must be boiled.

The park can be reached from the towns of Dungog, Gloucester and Scone, and camping is permitted at a number of sites. The main one is the Gloucester River Camping Area, 31 km from the Gloucester-Stroud road. The *Barrington Guest House* (☎ (049) 95 3212), 43 km from Dungog on the southern edge of the park, is the nearest accommodation to the park. It has a spectacular setting beneath the plateau escarpment and charges $79 per person with meals.

Myall Lakes National Park

This park is one of the most popular recreation areas in NSW. Its large network of coastal lakes is ideal for water sports. Canoes, windsurfers and runabouts can be hired at **Bombah Point**, the park's main settlement, 11 km from Bulahdelah. A car ferry links Bombah Point to the coastal regions of the park from 8 am to 6 pm. The best beaches are in the north around the township of **Seal Rocks**. There are good walks through coastal rainforest at **Mungo Brush** in the south.

Places to Stay There are several NPWS camp sites around the park, including a good one at Mungo Brush. At Bombah Point, *Myall Shores* (☎ (049) 97 4495) has tent sites from $16, bungalows for $45 and cabins for

$60. There's a shop and a restaurant. The owners can organise a minibus ride from Bulahdelah ($5).

At Seal Rocks a basic caravan park by an excellent beach has tent sites for $9.50 and on-site vans for $30.

Getting There & Away There is road access to the park from Tea Gardens in the south, from Bulahdelah on the Pacific Highway and from Forster-Tuncurry in the north. You can drive from Tea Gardens to Bulahdelah via the Bombah Point ferry.

Seal Rocks is accessible from the Great Lakes Way, a scenic road between Bulahdelah and Forster-Tuncurry. Great Lakes Coaches (☎ 1800 043 263) operates this route.

Forster-Tuncurry (pop 16,200)

Forster-Tuncurry are twin towns on either side of the sea entrance of Wallis Lake. Forster is the larger town and here you'll find the information centre (☎ (065) 54 8799) on Little St, the lakefront road. As well as the lake there are some excellent sea beaches right in town and many others in the area.

Places to Stay *Forster Beach Caravan Park* (☎ (065) 54 6269) is right in the centre of town and a short walk from both the lake and the ocean. It has tent sites from $11 to $17 and on-site vans from $23 ($32 with en suite) to $41 ($57).

The friendly YHA-affiliated *Dolphin Lodge* (☎ (065) 55 8155) is at 43 Head St in Forster. Coming from the town centre it's on the left just before the road makes a right-angle turn to the right. It's clean and spacious and has a surf beach virtually at the back door. Dorm beds are $13 and doubles are $30. Boards and bikes are free.

In the off season there are some good deals on motels, with doubles for $35 or less, but around Christmas/January most are expensive – and booked out.

Getting There & Away Forster-Tuncurry is on the Great Lakes Way, which leaves the Pacific Highway near Bulahdelah and rejoins it south of Taree. Great Lakes Coaches (☎ 1800 043 263) run to Sydney ($35) and Newcastle ($20) daily, while Countrylink operates a combination of bus and train to Sydney twice a day for $37.80. Greyhound Pioneer calls in once a day on its Sydney-Brisbane run.

Manning Valley

From Forster-Tuncurry the highway swings inland to **Taree**, a large town serving the farms of the fertile Manning Valley. Farther up the valley is the timber town of **Wingham**, where you can visit Wingham Brush, a lovely seven-hectare vestige of the dense rainforest which once covered the valley. Small roads run north from Wingham to Wauchope, near Port Macquarie, passing through some interesting towns and great scenery around Comboyne.

On the coast near Taree, **Old Bar** is one of several small resorts. **Crowdy Bay National Park** runs up the coast, and there is camping at **Diamond Head** (named after the quartz crystal found in the area) at the northern end of the park. You need to bring your own water.

North of the national park and accessible from the Pacific Highway at Kew, **Camden Haven** is a collection of small towns clustered around the wide sea entrance of Queens Lake. Just north of here the coast road runs past **Lake Cathie** (pronounced cat-eye), both a town and a shallow lake, and then enters the outer suburbs of Port Macquarie.

PORT MACQUARIE (pop 30,500)

One of the larger resorts on the New South Wales north coast, Port Macquarie makes a good stopping point on the journey from Sydney (430 km south). It was founded in 1821 and was a convict settlement until 1840.

Port, as it is known, has both a river frontage (the Hastings River enters the sea here) and a series of ocean beaches starting right in the town.

Orientation & Information

The city centre is at the mouth of the Hastings

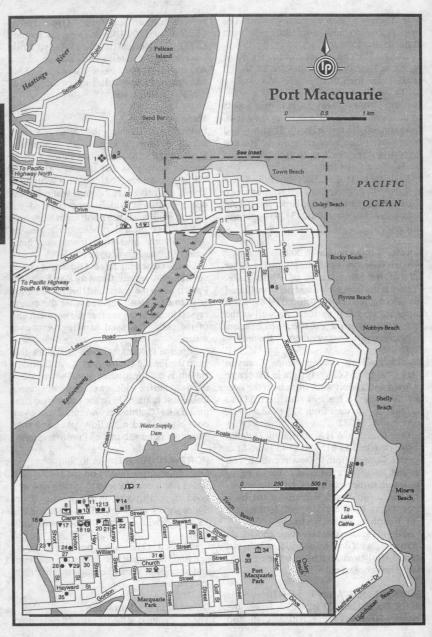

Port Macquarie

0   0.5   1 km

See Inset

PACIFIC

OCEAN

Town Beach

Oxley Beach

Rocky Beach

Flynns Beach

Nobbys Beach

Shelly Beach

Miners Beach

To Lake Cathie

Pelican Island

Sand Bar

Hastings River

To Pacific Highway North

Hastings River Drive

Oxley Highway

To Pacific Highway South & Wauchope

Lake Road

Koolonbung Creek

Water Supply Dam

Koala Street

Savoy St

Grant St

Lord St

Owen St

Pacific Drive

Kennedy Drive

Ocean Drive

0   250   500 m

Town Beach

Clarence Street

Short St

Horton St

Hay St

Murray Street

Munster Street

Stewart Street

Grant Street

Lord Street

Owen Street

Golf St

William Street

Church Street

Hayward St

Gordon St

Macquarie Park

Port Macquarie Park

Oxley Beach

Pacific Drive

To Matthew Flinders Dr

Lighthouse Beach

PLACES TO STAY		11	Dang's	8	Post Office
		14	Toro's Cantina	12	Courthouse
3	Lindel Port Macquarie	17	Macquarie Seafoods	16	Cruises & Fishermen's
	Backpackers	22	Cafe Pacific		Co-Op
7	Sundowner Breakwall	23	Eclipse	18	Lindsay's Buses &
	Caravan Park	29	Yuen Hing		Long-Distance Bus
9	Royal Hotel	30	Sun Hing		Stop
10	Port Macquarie Hotel			19	Information Centre
13	El Paso Motel	**OTHER**		20	Garrison & Cafes
15	River Motel			21	Museum
25	Historic Well Motel	1	Settlement City	24	Jetset Travel
32	Beachside		Shopping Centre &	26	Observatory
	Backpackers (YHA)		RSL Club	27	TC's Nightclub
		2	Port Marina	28	Down Under Nightclub
PLACES TO EAT		5	Koala Hospital & Roto	31	Radio Tower
			Homestead	33	Bowling Club
4	Chiang Mai Thai	6	Sea Acres Rainforest	34	Maritime Museum
	Restaurant		Centre	35	Port Pushbikes

NEW SOUTH WALES

River, and Horton St, the main street, runs down to the water. West of the city centre at the base of the Settlement Point Peninsula is the big Settlement City shopping centre.

The information centre (☎ 1800 025 935) is at the corner of Hay and Clarence Sts and is open daily.

Things to See

The **Koala Hospital** is off Lord St about a km south of the town centre. Convalescent koalas are in outdoor enclosures and you can visit them daily. The hospital is in the grounds of **Roto**, a historic homestead which is open on weekdays from 9 am to 4 pm.

You can meet undamaged koalas and other animals at **Kingfisher Park** (☎ (065) 81 0783), off the Oxley Highway; admission is $6. **Billabong Koala Park** (☎ (065) 85 1060) is farther out, just past the Pacific Highway interchange.

Other than Roto, most surviving old buildings are near the city centre: St Thomas' Church (1828) on William St near Hay St (admission $1); the Garrison (1830) on the corner of Hay and Clarence; the courthouse (1869) across the road; and the **museum** (1830) nearby at 22 Clarence St, open Monday to Saturday from 9.30 am to 4.30 pm and Sunday from 1 pm (admission $3).

An old pilot cottage below Town Beach houses the small **Maritime Museum**, open

daily from 10 am to 4 pm (admission $2). Nearby, a small **observatory** is at the beach end of Lord St. It's open Wednesday and Saturday, at 7.30 pm in winter and 8.15 pm in summer; admission is $2.

Five km south of the town centre, **Sea Acres Rainforest Centre** is a 30-hectare flora and fauna reserve protecting a pocket of coastal rainforest. There's an ecology centre with displays and a 1.3-km boardwalk. Entry is $8.50.

A vehicle ferry ($1) operates 24 hours across the river at Settlement Point, leading to two roads north. One is a very rough dirt road (4WD might be required) running along the coast, past Limeburners Creek Nature Reserve to Point Plomer (good surf) and Crescent Head, from where you can rejoin the highway at Kempsey. The second road – better and gravelled – takes a more inland route to meet the Crescent Head-Kempsey road.

Activities

Water sports are top of the activity list. There are some good surf breaks, particularly at Town Beach and Flynns Beach, which is patrolled on weekends and school holidays.

You can hire watercraft at several places on Settlement Point, such as Hastings River Boat Hire (☎ (065) 83 8811) at Port Marina (powered craft and canoes) and the Settlement Point Boatshed (☎ (065) 83 6300) next to the ferry departure point. Jordans Boating Centre (☎ (065) 83 1005) has yachts and windsurfers. Diving is available with the Port Macquarie Dive Centre (☎ (065) 83 8483).

There are plenty of river cruises. Everglades Tours (book at the information centre) has shallow-draught boats exploring the backwaters and wetlands from $17.

Port Macquarie Camel Safaris(☎ (065) 83 7650) has beach rides for $20. East Coast Mountain Safaris (☎ (065) 84 2366) has 4WD tours of the rainforest hinterland, from $45 for a half-day.

Places to Stay

Camping The most central caravan park is *Sundowner Breakwall* (☎ (065) 83 2755) at 1 Munster St, near the river mouth and Town Beach. It has tent sites at $15 for two people and on-site vans for $37. Prices rise sharply during school holidays. There are cheaper places near Flynns Beach and inland along the river or on the Oxley Highway.

Hostels Backpackers have two good hostels to choose from. *Beachside Backpackers* (☎ (065) 83 5512) is a YHA associate at 40 Church St, near the corner of Grant St. Dorm beds are $13. It's clean, friendly and popular and is a short walk from the town centre and the beach. There's free use of bikes and surfboards. The owners meet the buses.

Lindel Port Macquarie Backpackers (☎ (065) 83 1791) occupies a beautiful old house beside the Oxley Highway on the way into town. It's clean and well run, with dorm beds for $13 and doubles/twins for $30. It's a little way from the town centre, but they meet the buses and there are bikes for hire. There's a small pool, and the owner organises regular canoeing and fishing outings.

Hotels & Motels At the northern end of Horton St are the *Port Macquarie Hotel* and the *Royal Hotel*. The reception desk at the Port Macquarie (☎ (065) 83 1011) handles accommodation for both. The Port Mac-

quarie has motel-style units from $45/55 and there are pub rooms for $20/30 or $25/35 with bathroom. The Royal has motel-style units overlooking the water for just $32/40 and pub rooms with bathroom for $25/30. Singles aren't available at peak times, when prices rise.

There are more than 30 motels. The cheapest, not surprisingly, are the ones farthest from the beaches, with some on Hastings River Drive. In town, the *River Motel* at 5 Clarence St near the corner of School St has off-season doubles for around $40. Several nearby holiday apartments have similar deals.

Places to Eat

There are dozens of restaurants and cafes around the city centre, with something to suit every budget.

The *Fishermen's Co-op* at the western end of Clarence St sells seafood straight off the boats. If you want your seafood cooked, *Macquarie Seafoods*, on the corner of Clarence and Short Sts, does great fish & chips for $3.80.

There's a good choice of Asian food. The *Sun Hing* on William St does Chinese banquets from $7 to $10 per person, while the *Yuen Hing* on Horton St does lunches for as little as $3.50. *Dang's*, opposite the old courthouse on Hay St, has Malaysian and Vietnamese dishes. Fans of Thai food should head for the *Chiang Mai* Thai takeaway, on the way out of town at 153 Gordon St. Most dishes are under $9.

Back in the city centre, *Toro's Cantina* on Murray St is a Mexican place with main courses from $9.50. Opposite the information centre, the *Pancake Place* offers all-you-can-eat meals from $11.90.

For breakfast, try the *Cafe Pacific* on Clarence St, where a cooked breakfast costs $7.50, or *Eclipse*, a small place on Short St near the corner of William St.

Margo's Cafe, in the historic Garrison building on the corner of Hay and Clarence Sts, has tables outside and is a pleasant place for coffee and a snack.

Entertainment

There are three nightclubs in town: *Lachlans*, between the Port Macquarie and Royal hotels, *TC's* on William St and *Down Under* around the corner on Short St. The RSL club's big new complex at Settlement City has live bands on Friday and Saturday nights.

Getting There & Away

The Oxley Highway runs west from Port Macquarie through Wauchope and eventually reaches the New England tablelands near Walcha. It's a spectacular drive.

Air Eastern Australia flies to Sydney at least three times a day for $174 one way. Impulse flies to Sydney for the same fare, as well as to Brisbane ($227 one way) via Coffs Harbour, Lismore and Coolangatta.

Bus Port Macquarie Bus Service (☎ (065) 83 2161) runs to Wauchope several times a day for $6.10. This service stops next to the information centre on Clarence St, as do the long-distance services. Greyhound Pioneer, Lindsay's and McCafferty's all stop in town. Lindsay's (☎ 1800 027 944) runs to Newcastle ($30), Sydney ($37), Byron Bay ($43) and Brisbane ($46). King's (☎ 1800 625 587) runs to Coffs Harbour ($20), Bellingen and Dorrigo ($31), Armidale ($39.60) and Tamworth ($56.90).

Train The nearest station is at Wauchope, 19 km inland. The fare from Sydney is $55. An extra $6.10 will get you into Port Macquarie on the Countrylink bus that meets the train arriving at 5.59 pm.

Getting Around

Port Macquarie Bus Service (☎ (065) 83 2161) runs buses around the town. There are no super-cheap car-rental outfits, only the majors. Budget (☎ (065) 83 5144) is at the corner of William and Short Sts. Port Pushbikes on Hayward St rents ungeared bikes for $8 a half-day, $15 for a day or $25 for a week.

PORT MACQUARIE TO COFFS HARBOUR

Wauchope (pop 4300)

Nineteen km inland from Port Macquarie and on the Hastings River, Wauchope (pronounced 'war hope') is an old timber town – its story is told at **Timbertown** (☎ (065) 85 2322), an interesting working replica of an 1880s town. It's open daily from 9.30 am to 5 pm ($15).

Lilybank Canoe Hire (☎ (065) 85 1600), on the river one km east of the town, has two-person canoes for hire by the hour, day or week, and can advise on camping spots. The **Big Bull**, 'the world's biggest fibreglass bull', is three km east of Wauchope and houses an animal nursery and other displays; entry is $5.

Wauchope has a range of accommodation including *Rainbow Ridge Hostel* (☎ (065) 85 6134), a quiet YHA associate, 10 km west of town on the Oxley Highway. Dorm beds are $10 or you can camp for $5.

Kempsey Area

North along the Pacific Highway from Wauchope is **Kempsey** (population 9150), a large town serving the farms of the Macleay Valley and also the home of the Akubra hat. The information centre (☎ (065) 63 1555) is off the highway at the southern end of town. Next door is the **Macleay River Historical Museum & Cultural Centre** ($2). There is plenty of accommodation in town, but there's no reason to stick around. There are, however, some good spots on the coast.

Crescent Head, a small town 20 km from Kempsey, has a quiet front beach and a surf-washed back beach. The *Crescent Head Caravan Park* (☎ (065) 66 0261) has sites from $9 and cabins from $40, rising to $70 during holiday periods. There are plenty of holiday apartments and some can be cheaper than cabins at the caravan park – contact an estate agent such as Crescent Head Real Estate (☎ (065) 66 0500). South of town, **Limeburners Creek Nature Reserve** (☎ (065) 83 5866) has walking trails and camp sites.

Stretching up the coast from Crescent

Head to Smoky Cape is **Hat Head National Park**. Within the park is the quiet township of **Hat Head**, tucked beneath the headland. It has a beautiful sheltered beach, a shop, a caravan park and holiday flats. There's a basic camp site in the park south of Hat Head and another camp site at the northern end of the park near the **Smoky Cape Lighthouse**. The lighthouse is open to the public on Thursday (and Tuesday in school holidays) from 10 to 11.45 am and 1 to 2.45 pm.

The pleasant resort town of **South West Rocks** is near the mouth of the Macleay River. Fishing and water sports are the main attractions. **Trial Bay Gaol** is on the headland three km east of South West Rocks. This imposing edifice was a prison in the late 19th century and housed German internees during WW I. It's now a museum; open daily ($3.50). Trial Bay is named after the *Trial*, a brig which was stolen from Sydney by convicts in 1816 and wrecked here.

The gaol is part of the **Arakoon State Recreation Area** (☎ (065) 66 6168), which also manages the bayside camping area next to the gaol. There are sites right on the water for $10, rising to $20 in school holidays. The *Costa Rica Motel* (☎ (065) 66 6500) sometimes has share accommodation for about $15.

Getting Around There are buses from Belgrave St in Kempsey to South West Rocks and to Crescent Head, but only on weekdays. Mercury Roadlines (☎ (065) 62 4201) has three buses a day from Kempsey to South West Rocks and Arakoon ($8.20), while Cavanagh's (☎ (065) 62 1228) operates a similar service to Crescent Head ($4.50).

Nambucca Heads (pop 6100)

This quiet resort town has a fine setting overlooking the mouth of the Nambucca (pronounced 'nambucka') River. The name means 'many bends' in the language of the local Gumbaingeri Aboriginal people.

Orientation & Information The town is a couple of km off the Pacific Highway, where you'll find the helpful information centre (☎ (065) 68 6954). The road in, Riverside Drive, runs beside the wide estuary of the Nambucca and then climbs a steep hill to Bowra St, the main shopping street. A right turn onto Ridge St at the top of the hill leads to the beaches.

Main Beach, the patrolled surf beach, is about 1.5 km east of the centre. Follow Ridge St and take the fork left onto Liston St when it splits. The **Headland Museum** ($1) is near the Main Beach car park. A right fork at the end of Ridge St leads along Parkes St to North Head, with stunning views from **Pilot Lookout**.

Places to Stay There are several caravan parks. As usual, prices rise in holidays. *Foreshore Caravan Park* (☎ (065) 68 6014), on Riverside Drive not far from the highway, overlooks the estuary and there is a beach nearby. Outside school holidays tent sites are $10, on-site vans are $22 and cabins are $36.

Nambucca Backpackers Hostel (☎ (065) 68 6360) is a quiet hostel tucked away behind the town at Newman St. It's a one-km walk through bush to the beach. Dorm beds are $13 and doubles are $28, with discounts for longer stays. The friendly managers meet the buses and can arrange outings in the area. They lend snorkel gear and boogie boards.

Scott's Guesthouse (☎ (065) 68 6386), at 4 Wellington Drive, is a stylish old weatherboard guesthouse with large rooms overlooking the river. It charges $60 for a double with breakfast.

Places to Eat The *RSL* has a prime site by the river at the foot of Bowra St and turns out some of the cheapest meals in town. The *Golden Sands Hotel* in Bowra St has pub meals, and *Midnight Express* behind the pub claims a choice of 36 burgers.

Getting There & Away Most long-distance buses stop on the highway at the Shell service station (southbound) or the Aukaka Caravan Park (northbound). The fare to Sydney with Kirklands is $42, to Byron Bay it's $38.

Newman's (☎ (065) 68 1296) has four buses a day to Coffs Harbour ($5), while Jessup's (☎ (066) 53 4552) has a daily bus service on the same route at 7.55 am. Joyce's ☎ (066) 55 6330) runs from Nambucca to Bellingen. These local services leave from outside the police station on Bowra St and run only on weekdays.

Nambucca is on the main railway line north from Sydney ($58). The station is about three km out of town – follow Bowra St north.

Bellingen (pop 2350)

This attractive small town sits on the banks of the Bellinger River just inland from the Pacific Highway about halfway between Nambucca Heads and Coffs Harbour. The turning is north of Urunga. It's a lively country town and a centre for the area's artistic/alternative population. Bellingen Travel (☎ (066) 55 2055), opposite the post office on the main street, has tourist information.

Things to See & Do The main attraction is the setting in the lush Bellinger Valley. If you have your own transport, there are some great swimming holes to be discovered on the **Never Never River** at the aptly named **Promised Land**, about 10 km north of town. **Gambaarri Tours** (see Coffs Harbour Things to Do) has a tour to the area.

A huge colony of flying foxes (grey-headed fruit bats) lives on Bellingen Island, near the caravan park, from December to March. They're an impressive sight when they head off in their thousands at dusk to feed. The island is a small remnant of the subtropical rainforest that once covered the valley. **Ridge to Reef** (☎ (066) 55 2382) includes a guided tour of the island in an interesting range of interpretative walks. Platypuses live in the river nearby.

There are plenty of craft shops, including the **Old Butter Factory** on the eastern approach to town. It houses several workshops, a gallery and a cafe. The Bellingen markets, held at the park on Church St on the third Saturday of the month, have become a major regional event with more than 250 stalls. There's live music and other entertainment.

Places to Stay The *caravan park* (☎ (066) 55 1138) is across the river – turn onto Wharf St from the main street (the post office is on the corner), cross the bridge and follow the road around to the left, then turn left down Dowle St. You can walk from town.

Bellingen Backpackers (☎ (066) 55 1116) (also called Belfry Lodge) is a great place to hang out for a few days. It occupies a beautifully renovated weatherboard house overlooking the river on Short St, behind the Federal Hotel. Dorm beds are $15 and doubles are $32. The owners will pick you up from Urunga by arrangement. There's free use of bikes and the outdoor hot tub.

Places to Eat Bellingen has a surprisingly large choice of restaurants for a town of its size. The *Carriageway Cafe*, on the main street, has meals as well as good coffee and cakes. There are several places on Church St, including the *Good Food Shop* with vegetarian takeaways. As is often the case, the *RSL* restaurant is good value.

Getting There & Away Getting to Bellingen without your own transport can be a bit of a hassle. King's (☎ 1800 625 587) stops at Bellingen on its Port Macquarie-Tamworth run, but is not allowed to offer a service on short sectors such as Coffs Harbour to Bellingen. That route is owned by Jessup's (☎ (066) 53 4552), which operates one service a day – school days only. Buses leave Bellingen at 7.55 am and Coffs Harbour at 3.15 pm. Joyce's (☎ (066) 55 6330) has about four runs a day (fewer in school holidays), weekdays only, between Bellingen and Nambucca Heads ($6.80). There's no public transport between Bellingen and Dorrigo. The bus stop in Bellingen is at the corner of Church St and the main street.

The nearest railway station is at Urunga.

Dorrigo (pop 1120)

It's a spectacular drive from Bellingen up to

the quiet mountain town of Dorrigo. The road climbs 1000 metres through dense rainforest, with occasional breaks in the canopy offering great views down the Bellinger Valley to the coast. Dorrigo was one of the last places to be settled in the eastwards push across the New England tablelands. It's a pleasant base for visiting the area's outstanding national parks.

There is an information centre (☎ (066) 57 2486) at 36 Hickory St, open daily from 10 am to 4 pm.

Things to See & Do The proposed **Steam Railway Museum** appears no closer to opening than it did 10 years ago. There is a long line of steam engines queued up at the old railway station, just out of town on the road to North Dorrigo.

A few km north of town on the road to Leigh are the picturesque **Dangar Falls**. The main attraction though is the magnificent subtropical rainforest of **Dorrigo National Park**, two km east of town. It is the most accessible of Australia's World Heritage rainforests and well worth a visit. The Rainforest Centre (☎ (066) 57 2309), at the entrance, has information about the park's many walks and is open daily from 9 am to 5 pm. Camping is not allowed in the park. The turn-off to the park is clearly signposted on the Dorrigo-Bellingen road. See the New England section for information on other national parks in this area.

Places to Stay *Dorrigo Mountain Resort* (☎ (066) 57 2564), a caravan park with some substantial wooden cabins, is just out of town on the road to Bellingen. Sites cost from $10. There are on-site vans ($28) as well as self-contained cabins $44. The *Commercial Hotel/Motel* (☎ (066) 57 2003) has hotel singles/doubles for $15/20, and motel units for $20/30. It does a hot breakfast for $5.

Getting There & Away The only bus service is provided by King's, which uses Dorrigo as a meal stop on its Port Macquarie-Tamworth run. It operates four times a week, going via Coffs Harbour and Armidale. Aussitel in

Coffs Harbour and the hostels at Bellinger and Nambucca all organise day trips to the park.

Urunga & Mylestom

Urunga, about 20 km north of Nambucca, is a quiet little town at the mouth of the Bellinger and Kalang rivers. The rivers meet just 200 metres from the ocean, forming an impressive estuary that is popular for water sports. There is a surf beach just south of town at **Hungry Head**, but the best beach in the area is about five km south of town a **Third Headland** – signposted off the Pacific Highway along Snapper Beach Rd. The *Ocean View Hotel* (☎ (066) 55 6221) in Urunga has good singles/doubles for $25/35 with breakfast. The rooms at the front have views over the estuary.

North of Urunga is the turn-off to Mylestom, also called **North Beach**. This quiet town is in a great location on the banks of the wide Bellinger River and also has ocean beaches. It has a caravan park (☎ (066) 55 4250) and a backpackers hostel *Caipera Riverside Lodge* (☎ (066) 55 4245) which is on the main street across from the river (the third house on the left as you enter town). The hostel has beds in two-bed 'dorms' for $15 and can organise activities such as white-water rafting and horse riding. There's free use of the lodge's bikes and kayaks. The owners will pick up guests from the train station or bus stop at Urunga; given a day's notice, they can give you a lift from Coffs.

COFFS HARBOUR (pop 56,000)

Coffs Harbour is a busy modern town and one of NSW's most popular tourist destinations. The town appears to have veered away from the Gold Coast-style development i seemed hell-bent upon 10 years ago. A string of good beaches stretches north of town, and Coffs is a good base for exploring the many attractions of the north coast hinterland.

Orientation & Information

The Pacific Highway is called Grafton St on its run through town. The city centre i

NEW SOUTH WALES

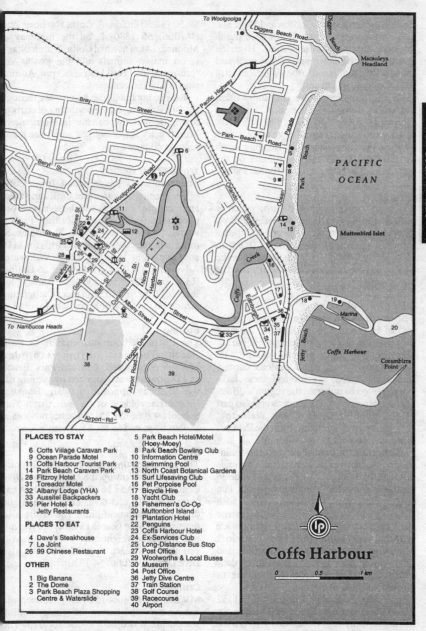

PACIFIC OCEAN

To Woolgoolga

Diggers Beach Road

Macauleys Headland

Muttonbird Islet

Muttonbird Island

Marina

Coffs Harbour

Corambirra Point

To Nambucca Heads

Coffs Harbour

0   0.5   1 km

PLACES TO STAY

6 Coffs Village Caravan Park
9 Ocean Parade Motel
11 Coffs Harbour Tourist Park
14 Park Beach Caravan Park
28 Fitzroy Hotel
31 Toreador Motel
32 Albany Lodge (YHA)
33 Aussitel Backpackers
35 Pier Hotel & Jetty Restaurants

PLACES TO EAT

4 Dave's Steakhouse
7 Le Joint
26 99 Chinese Restaurant

OTHER

1 Big Banana
2 The Dome
3 Park Beach Plaza Shopping Centre & Waterslide

5 Park Beach Hotel/Motel (Hoey-Moey)
8 Park Beach Bowling Club
10 Information Centre
12 Swimming Pool
13 North Coast Botanical Gardens
15 Surf Lifesaving Club
16 Pet Porpoise Pool
17 Bicycle Hire
18 Yacht Club
19 Fishermen's Co-Op
20 Muttonbird Island
21 Plantation Hotel
22 Penguins
23 Coffs Harbour Hotel
24 Ex-Services Club
25 Long-Distance Bus Stop
27 Post Office
29 Woolworths & Local Buses
30 Museum
34 Post Office
36 Jetty Dive Centre
37 Train Station
38 Golf Course
39 Racecourse
40 Airport

around the junction of Grafton and High Sts. East of Grafton St, High St has been transformed into a rainforest mall. High St resumes on the other side of the mall and becomes the main road to the waterfront jetty area, a couple of km east.

The information centre is grandly titled the Coffs Harbour Visitors & Convention Bureau (π (066) 52 1522, 1800 025 650). It's on the northern edge of town at the corner of Rose Ave and Marcia St. Heading north on Grafton St, take the first turning on the right after the Coffs Harbour Tourist Park.

Beaches
The main beach is **Park Beach**, which is patrolled at weekends and school holidays. There is a good beach at **Korora** and then a string of them up to Woolgoolga. Back in town, **Jetty Beach** is more sheltered than the others and can be good for a swim when the surf is rough.

Other Attractions
The **North Coast Botanic Gardens**, at the end of Hardacre St (off High St), are well worth a visit. It's hard to believe that part of the site was once the town tip. The immaculately maintained gardens contain many endangered species and areas have been planted to re-create the region's different rainforest types. The gardens are also part of the popular **Coffs Creek Walk** that follows the creek upstream from the Pet Porpoise Pool to near the town centre.

Muttonbird Island, linked to the mainland by the harbour's northern breakwater, is home to more than 12,000 pairs of mutton birds (wedge-tailed shearwaters) from late August until April. The island is dotted with their nesting burrows. The chicks emerge during December and January. Humpback whales can sometimes be seen off Muttonbird Island during their northbound migration in June and July, and during their southern migration from September to November.

The **Pet Porpoise Pool** (π (066) 52 2164), next to Coffs Creek on Orlando St, has shows daily at 10.30 am and 2.15 pm for

$9.50 ($4.50 children). **Coffs Harbour Zoo** (π (066) 56 1330) is on the highway at Moonee, 14 km north of Coffs. The emphasis is on native animals and the koalas are 'presented' daily at 11 am and 3 pm. Admission is $12 ($6 children).

Fans of big things can talk a walk through the **Big Banana**, on the northern outskirts of town. Behind the banana is Horticulture World; entry is free but you won't see much unless you take a tour.

White-Water Rafting
The Nymboida River inland from Coffs offers excellent white-water thrills and there are a couple of outfits which have received good reports. Whitewater Rafting Professionals (π (066) 51 4066) at 20 Moonee St (next to the bus station) has day trips for $119 and overnight trips for $265. Wildwater Adventures (π (066) 53 4469) at 26 Butlers Rd in Bonville offers much the same, plus four-day trips for $435 and more challenging rafting on the Gwydir River near Inverell.

Surfing
The Coffs Harbour surf club is at **Park Beach**. The best surfing is around Macauleys headland, between Park Beach and **Diggers Beach**, reached by turning off the highway opposite the Big Banana. Helene Enevoldson of the East Coast Surf School (π (066) 51 5515) teaches novices at $14 an hour, or $68 for a six-hour course.

Diving
There's interesting diving at the Solitary Islands, a few km up the coast. Jetty Dive Centre (π (066) 51 1611) at 396 High St has courses ($350) and dives ($25 for a single dive, plus equipment hire). The centre also rents snorkelling gear ($15 a day for the full set, including weights and wetsuit – less if you need less gear). Up in Mullaway is also Dive Quest (π (066) 54 1930).

Cruises
MV *Laura E* (π (066) 51 1434) has deep-sea fishing trips and during the whale-spotting season has a two-hour cruise for $25. The

There are numerous excellent surfing beaches along the New South Wales north coast

Commissioner II (☎ (066) 51 3271) cruises past South Solitary Island daily for $20.

Aboriginal Tours

Gambaarri Tours (☎ (066) 55 4195) has interpretive trips to a number of sites on the coast between Red Rock and Nambucca Heads for $45.

Other Activities

Coffs City Skydivers (☎ (066) 51 1167) offers an introductory first-jump course for $220, captured on video to show your friends.

Outer Limits (☎ (066) 51 4066) at 22 Moonee St offers abseiling. There are a number of places offering horse riding. Valery Trails (☎ (066) 53 4301) is one of the best, with two-hour rides through Pine Creek State Forest for $27. Coffs Harbour Adventures (☎ (066) 58 1871) has 4WD (and 2WD) tours for $55, or $70 including horse riding at Valery.

Places to Stay

Except in the hostels, expect prices to rise by about 50% during school holidays and as much as 100% at Christmas/New Year.

Camping The huge *Park Beach Caravan Park* (☎ (066) 52 3204) on Ocean Parade is right next to the beach and has tent sites from $10, on-site vans from $26 and cabins from $36. There are lower weekly rates but not at peak times.

Coffs Harbour Tourist Park (☎ (066) 52 1694), on the highway a couple of blocks on from the Ex-Services Club, has sites from $10, on-site vans from $23 and cabins from $33. There are plenty of other places along the highway north and south of town.

Hostels There are two good hostels and both can arrange discounts on just about everything in town.

The *Aussitel Backpackers Hostel* (☎ (066) 51 1871) at 312 High St, about 1.5 km from the town centre and 500 metres from the harbour, is a lively place with dorm beds for $14 and doubles for $30. It has all the usual hostel facilities plus a pool. The enthusiastic management will help fix up white-water rafting, diving, surfing and other activities, and will pick you up on arrival and give rides to the beach during the day or to the pub at night. Coffs Creek is over the road and canoes are free.

The town's YHA hostel is *Albany Lodge* (☎ (066) 52 6462), one km from the city centre at 110 Albany St. It's a friendly place with dorm beds for $14 and doubles for $32. Bikes and surfboards are free and there's a spa. The hostel is open all day and someone can usually pick you up – if arriving at night, phone in advance to ask. The hostel also arranges activities and excursions.

Hotels & Motels Officially on Moonee St (although it appears to be on Grafton St), the *Fitzroy Hotel* (☎ (066) 52 3007) is an old-style neighbourhood pub with singles/doubles for $18/25. Down near the harbour on High St, the *Pier Hotel* (☎ (066) 52 2110) has a few large, clean rooms for $20/36.

There's a string of motels on Grafton St on the southern approach to town, such as *Toreador* (☎ (066) 52 3887) and *Golden Glow* (☎ (066) 52 2742). Outside the school holiday periods, prices are around $36 a double.

Another group of motels in the Park Beach area has similar rates. You'll pay around $40 a double at the *Ocean Parade Motel* (☎ (066) 52 6733); in the high season the rates are around $60 a double, and there are no singles.

Apartments There is a huge range of holiday apartments and houses. In the off season the cheapest two-bedroom apartments cost around $45 a night (less by the week) and $90 a night in the high season, although many places are only available by the week at this time. The information centre has a booking service (☎ 1800 025 650).

Places to Eat
Some of the best cheap eats can be found in the clubs, such as the *Ex-Services Club* on the corner of Grafton and Vernon Sts and the *Catholic Club* on High St, about one km inland from Grafton St.

There are snack places on the mall, and the pubs in this area have counter meals. At the *Plantation Hotel* on Grafton St, lunch specials include a meal and a drink for $5.50. The *99 Chinese Restaurant*, upstairs in the

176 Arcade off the mall, offers all you ca
eat for $6.90 at lunchtime and $7.90 a
dinner. *Pancakes All Round*, on High St nea
the corner of Gordon St, has pancakes an
crepes from $6 and pasta from $8.

For choice you can't beat the cluster o
restaurants at the Jetty end of High St, wher
you'll find the excellent *Tahruah Tha
Kitchen*, near the Pier Hotel. Other option
include seafood, Italian, Indian, Chinese an
French.

Le Joint, on Ocean Parade opposite th
Park Beach bowling club, is basically a mil
bar but it has a fine verandah where you ca
eat breakfast and other meals. The nearb
Hoey-Moey has a bistro with good specials
At 99 Park Beach Rd, over York St, *Dave
Steakhouse* has steaks from $14 and seafoo
from $15.

Entertainment
There's something happening every nigh
although the pickings are fairly slim early i
the week. Thursday's edition of the *Coff
Harbour Advocate* has the week's listings.

The *Plantation Hotel* on Grafton St ha
free local bands from Wednesday to Satur
day. Heavy metal heads can check out th
Hoey-Moey at Park Beach. Big-nam
touring bands play at the *Sawtell RSL Clul*
five km south of town. The hostels usuall
organise transport.

The nightclub scene changes constantly
Penguins, in the Bowling Arcade off Grafto
St, is popular. *The Dome* is a new club at th
junction of Bray St and the Pacific Highway

Getting There & Away
Coffs Harbour Coaches & Travel (☎ (066
52 2686), in Moonee St, organises bus, ai
and Countrylink tickets.

Air Coffs has a busy airport, on the sout
edge of town, with direct flights to Sydne
($190) and Brisbane ($165).

Bus All the long-distance lines on th
Sydney to Brisbane route stop at Coffs. Th
long-distance bus stop is in Moonee St jus
west of Grafton St. Nearby, Lindsay'

andles bus bookings (not just for Lindsay's).

Fares from Coffs include: Byron Bay $33, Brisbane $41, Nambucca Heads $14, Port Macquarie $27 and Sydney $47. King's has services to Tamworth via Armidale ($23.80) and Dorrigo ($11.80).

Local buses stop at the car park next to Woolworths on Park Ave. Ryan's (☎ (066) 52 3201) runs several times daily except Sunday to Woolgoolga ($5) via beachside towns off the highway. Bradley's (☎ (066) 53 7300) has a weekday service between Coffs and Grafton, running via Woolgoolga and beachside towns north of there. See the Bellingen and Nambucca Heads sections for other local services.

Train The railway station (☎ (066) 52 2312) is near the harbour at the end of High St. The fare to Sydney is $66.80.

Car Rental As well as the majors there are some local outfits offering cheaper rates, although you should compare the deals carefully. JR's Car & Truck Rental (☎ (066) 52 2480) at 30 Orlando St rents older vehicles.

Boat Cruises Coffs is reportedly a good place to pick up a ride along the coast on a yacht or cruiser. Ask around or put a notice in the yacht club at the harbour. Sometimes the hostels know of boat owners who are looking for crew.

Getting Around
A bus service connects the centre, the Jetty and Park Beach but services are infrequent, with none on Sunday.

The Coffs District Taxi Network (☎ (066) 51 3944) operates a 24-hour service. There's a taxi rank on the corner of High and Gordon Sts.

Bob Wallis World of Wheels (☎ (066) 52 5102), near the harbour at the corner of Collingwood and Orlando Sts, rents bikes.

COFFS HARBOUR TO BYRON BAY
Woolgoolga (pop 4070)
Twenty-six km north of Coffs, Woolgoolga is a small resort with a fine surf beach. It has

a sizeable Indian Sikh population whose *gurdwara* (place of worship), the **Guru Nanak Temple**, is just off the highway at the southern end of town. The 'Indianesque' structure on the northern side of town is the Raj Mahal tourist trap.

The *Woolgoolga Beach Caravan Park* (☎ (066) 54 1373) has tent sites for $9.50, on-site vans from $22 and cabins from $33. For Indian food try the *Koh-I-Nor* at the Raj Mahal or *Temple View* near the temple.

North of Woolgoolga is **Arrawarra**, a quiet seaside town with yet another great beach and a pleasant caravan park close to the water. Sleepy **Red Rock** is on a beautiful little inlet.

Yuraygir National Park
Yuraygir covers the 60 km of coast stretching north from Red Rock to Angourie Point, just south of Yamba. The main attractions are fine beaches and bushwalking in the coastal heath. There are some great camp sites along the coast, including the Illaroo Rest Area at **Minnie Water**. Minnie Water is signposted off the Pacific Highway 10 km south of Grafton.

The Solitary Islands
This island group, strung out along the coast off shore from Yuraygir National Park, is a marine reserve at the meeting place of the warmer tropical currents and the more temperate southern currents, with some interesting varieties of fish attracted by the unusual conditions.

Grafton (pop 17,300)
Grafton is a graceful old country town on the banks of the mighty Clarence River. The town is noted for its fine street trees, particularly the spectacular jacarandas that carpet the streets with their mauve flowers at Jacaranda Festival time in late October. The town lies at the heart of a rich agricultural area. The wide Clarence delta is a patchwork of sugar cane plantations.

On Fitzroy St is **Prentice House** (1880), now an art gallery. The nearby **Schaeffer House** is a historical museum.

The Pacific Highway runs past Grafton and the Clarence River Tourist Centre (☎ (066) 42 4677) is on the highway south of the town. The town centre is north of the river.

Places to Stay The *Rathgar Guesthouse* (☎ (066) 42 3181), next to the Caltex service station on the Pacific Highway south of town, was in the early stages of a much-needed face-lift at the time of writing. It has dorm beds for $15.

There's no shortage of motels and many pubs have accommodation. The *Crown Hotel/Motel* (☎ (066) 42 4000) is a pleasant place overlooking the river on Prince St. Pub rooms are $20/30 for singles/doubles or $30/40 with bathroom. Motel units are $45/55. Another nice old pub in the same area is *Roches* (☎ (066) 44 2866) at 85 Victoria St, where the spotless rooms are $24/30.

Getting There & Away Long-distance buses stop on the highway in South Grafton, not far from the information centre. Fares include Sydney $48 and Byron Bay $25. Countrylink runs up the Gwydir Highway to Glen Innes four times a week for about $17.

Most local-area buses leave from the Market Square shopping centre in the town centre not far from the corner of King and Fitzroy Sts. The bus to Maclean and Yamba (☎ (066) 42 2779) leaves from the Saraton Theatre on Prince St.

The railway station is on the highway side of the river. The fare to Sydney is $66.80.

Grafton to Ballina

From Grafton the highway follows the Clarence River north-east, bypassing the pleasant little river port of **Maclean**. Maclean celebrates its Scottish early settlers with a Highland Gathering each Easter.

The fishing town of **Yamba**, at the river mouth, is a growing resort with good beaches. The *Pacific Hotel* (☎ (066) 46 2466) has a great setting overlooking the main beach on Pilot St. It has backpackers' rooms for $15 per person. The Grafton-

Yamba Bus Service (☎ (066) 46 2019) runs five buses a day (three in school holidays) from Grafton to Yamba via Maclean. There are four ferries a day from Yamba to the town of **Iluka**, on the northern bank of the Clarence, for $3.

Just south of Yamba, **Angourie** is one of the coast's top spots for experienced surfers – but beware of the rips.

Iluka is worth a detour off the highway to visit its World Heritage listed **Nature Reserve**, which contains the largest patch of littoral rainforest in NSW. There's a good camp site at nearby Woody Head. Tent sites cost $10, plus $2 for each extra person, and cabins go for $40/50/60 for two/four/eight people. At peak times you might need to book (☎ (066) 46 6134).

Iluka is at the southern end of **Bundjalung National Park**, which stretches north to Evans Head between the highway and the coast. There are good surfing beaches, plus lots of wildlife. The park's extensive middens and old Aboriginal camp sites indicate it was a popular spot with the local Bundjalung people. The turn-off to Evans Head is at Woodburn.

Ballina (pop 15,250)

This busy town at the mouth of the Richmond River is a popular sailing and fishing spot. There are good beaches north of town.

Orientation & Information The Pacific Highway runs through town, becoming River St, the long main road. The information centre (☎ (066) 86 3484) is at the eastern end of River St, just past the old post office – now the courthouse. It's open daily from 9 am to 5 pm. Ask here about river cruises priced from $9. In the information centre is one of the three balsawood rafts from the La Balsa expedition that drifted across the Pacific from Ecuador to Ballina in 1973, taking 177 days.

Beaches The popular **Shelly Beach** is the closest patrolled beach to town. To get there, head east out of Ballina along River St, cross the bridge over North Creek and take the first ight after the Shaws Hotel turn-off. This road also passes **Lighthouse Beach**. The small beach curving around **Shaws Bay Lagoon** is a quiet place to swim.

Places to Stay *Ballina Lakeside Caravan Park* (☎ (066) 86 3953) has tent sites on the edge of Shaws Bay Lagoon for $11 and cabins from $33. Prices go up sharply during school holidays.

Ballina Travellers Lodge (☎ (066) 86 5737) is a good, modern YHA hostel at 36-38 Tamar St. Dorm beds are $13 and twins are $32. Bikes and boogie boards can be hired for $1 an hour, and there's a pool. The lodge is also a motel and one of the few in town without highway noise. Doubles are $45 in the low season, rising to $75 around Christmas.

The *Flat Rock Camping Ground* (☎ (066) 86 1848), just north of Ballina on the coast road to Lennox Head, has tent sites for $10. At Ballina Quays Marina (☎ (066) 86 4289), off the highway south of the Big Prawn, you can rent houseboats. Prices start at $90 for a week night in the low season ($140 in the high season) for up to four people. Longer hires are cheaper. With over 100 km of navigable river there's plenty of room to move.

Places to Eat *Shellys on the Beach*, above Shelly Beach, has outdoor tables, good food and wonderful views. It's open from 7.30 am. The huge modern *RSL* has a prime position on the riverbank at the corner of Grant and River Sts. The club's downstairs bistro is great value and has seating on a deck overhanging the water. It's a good place to catch the sunset.

The *Cafe Fresco*, at the Henry Rous Hotel in River St, has a large choice of snacks and light meals as well as good coffee. It's open until midnight every night.

Getting There & Away All the major bus lines except Kirklands stop at the Ballina Transit Centre, on the highway just south of town at the Big Prawn. The Kirklands depot (☎ (066) 86 7124) is in Sheather St in the industrial estate. Countrylink stops on River

St near the corner of Cherry St, outside the Jetset Travel agency.

Blanch's (☎ (066) 86 2144) has six buses a day to Lennox Head ($3.40) and Byron Bay ($6.60), departing from outside Jetset Travel on River St. The shop next door has timetables in the window.

Lennox Head (pop 2235)

Lennox Head is a rapidly expanding small town on the coast road halfway between Ballina and Byron Bay. Lennox Head is also the name of the dramatic headland (a prime hang-gliding site) just south of town. Lennox has some of the best surf on the coast, particularly in winter.

Lake Ainsworth, just back from the beach, is popular for sailing and windsurfing. The water is stained brown by the tannin from the surrounding melaleuca trees. It acts as a water softener and is good for the skin and hair. The Lennox Point Hotel often has bands on weekends.

Places to Stay *Lake Ainsworth Caravan Park* (☎ (066) 87 7249) has tent sites from $11 and cabins for $33 ($50 in the high season).

Across the road is *Lennox Beach House Hostel* (☎ (066) 87 7636). It's purpose-built, very clean and very friendly. Both Lake Ainsworth and the beach are nearby and you can have use of a cat and a windsurfer ($5 for as long as you stay). Boards, bikes and other sporting equipment are free. Dorm beds are $16 and there's a double for $35.

BYRON BAY (pop 5100)

Byron Bay is one of the most popular holiday spots on the east coast, and features on almost every backpacker's itinerary. Despite the moans of long-time locals that tourism is over the top, the atmosphere remains pretty laid-back. It's hard to feel otherwise when you're surrounded by superb beaches and enjoy a climate that ranges from warm in winter to hot in summer.

The town is something of a meeting place of alternative cultures: it's almost a pilgrimage destination for surfers thanks to the fame of the breaks below Cape Byron, and is also close to the 'back to the land' lifestyle pursued in the beautiful far north coast hinterland. There are good music venues, wholefood and vegetarian eateries, off-beat people, distinctive craft and clothes shops, a thriving fashion and surf industry, and numerous opportunities to learn yogic dance, take a massage or naturopathic therapy, have your stars read and so on.

Byron Bay market, in Butler St on the first Sunday of each month, is one of a series around the area at which the counterculture (almost establishment up here!) gets a chance to meet and sell its wares.

Orientation & Information

Byron Bay is six km east of the Pacific Highway. Jonson St, which becomes Bangalow Rd, is the main shopping street.

The information centre (☎ (066) 85 8050) is on Jonson St near the railway station. Backpacker Central (☎ 1800 634 951), next to the bus stop, is another good source of information. You can store your pack here for $2 per day. Pick up a copy of the quirky weekly paper *Echo* to get an idea of the way of life around here.

There's a lot to do in and around Byron Bay. Hostels often have the best deals on activities, but it pays to look around.

Cape Byron

Cape Byron was named by Captain Cook after the poet Byron's grandfather, who had sailed round the world in the 1760s. One spur of the cape is the most easterly point of the Australian mainland. You can drive right up to the picturesque 1901 lighthouse, one of the most powerful in the southern hemisphere. There's a 3.5-km walking track right round the cape from the Captain Cook Lookout on Lighthouse Rd. It's circular, so you can leave bikes at the start. You've a good chance of seeing wallabies in the final rainforest stretch.

Humpback whales sometimes pass close by Cape Byron during their northern migration in June/July and the return trip from September to November. Dolphins are fre-

quent visitors all year. The new **Byron Bay Whale Centre**, near the lighthouse, is open every day from 9 am to 4.30 pm.

Beaches

The Byron area has a glorious collection of beaches, ranging from 10-km stretches of empty sand to secluded little coves. **Main Beach**, immediately in front of the town, is a good swimming beach and sometimes has decent surf. The sand stretches 50 km or more, all the way up to the Gold Coast, interrupted only by river or creek entrances and a few small headlands.

The eastern end of Main Beach, curving away towards Cape Byron, is known as **Clarks Beach** and can be good for surfing. The headland at the end of Clarks is called the Pass and the best surf is off here and at the next beach, **Wategos**. **Little Wategos Beach** is farther round, almost at the tip of the cape. Dolphins are quite common, particularly in the surf off Wategos and Little Wategos.

South of Cape Byron, **Tallow Beach** stretches seven km down to rockier shore around Broken Head, where a succession of small beaches (clothes optional) dot the coast before opening on to **Seven Mile Beach** which goes all the way to Lennox Head, a farther 10 km south. You can reach Tallow from various points along the Byron Bay to Lennox Head road.

The turn-off to the 'suburb' of **Suffolk Park** (with more good surf, particularly in winter) is five km from Byron Bay. A farther km down the Byron-Lennox road is the turn-off to the Broken Head caravan park. About 200 metres before the caravan park, the unsealed Seven Mile Beach Rd turns off south and runs behind the rainforest of the **Broken Head Nature Reserve**. Seven Mile Beach Rd ends after five km (at the north end of Seven Mile Beach), but several tracks lead down from it through the forest to the Broken Head beaches – **Kings Beach** (for which there's a car park 750 metres down Seven Mile Beach Rd) and **Whites Beach** (a foot track after about 3.25 km) are just two good ones.

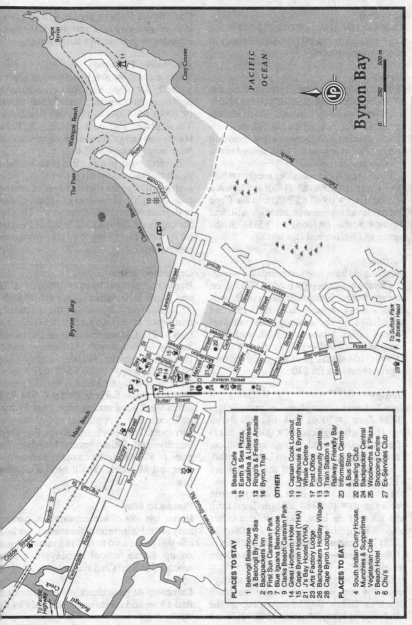

NEW SOUTH WALES

Byron Bay

PACIFIC OCEAN

0   250   500 m

To Suffolk Park
& Broken Head

To Pacific
Highway

PLACES TO STAY
1   Belongil Beachouse
    & Belongil By The Sea
2   Backpackers Inn
3   First Sun Caravan Park
7   Blue Iguana Beachouse
9   Clarks Beach Caravan Park
14 Great Northern Hotel
15 Cape Byron Hostel (YHA)
21 J's Bay Hostel (YHA)
23 Arts Factory Lodge
26 Backpackers Holiday Village
28 Cape Byron Lodge

PLACES TO EAT
4   South Indian Curry House,
    Munchies & Suppertime
    Vegetarian Cafe
5   Beach Hotel
6   Chu's

8   Beach Cafe
12 Earth & Sea Pizza,
    Catalina & Lifestream
13 Ringo's & Feros Arcade
16 Byron Thai

OTHER
10 Captain Cook Lookout
11 Lighthouse & Byron Bay
    Whale Centre
17 Post Office
13 Community Centre
19 Train Station &
    Railway Friendly Bar
20 Information Centre
    & Bus Stop
22 Bowling Club
24 Backpacker Central
25 Woolworths & Plaza
    Shopping Centre
27 Ex-Services Club

Abseiling

Abseiling Byron Bay (☎ 016 283 142) has a range of outings graded from introductory to adventurous, from $59.

Diving

Diving is popular at Julian Rocks, three km off shore, a meeting point of cold southerly and warm northerly currents, which attracts a profusion of marine species. There's cut-throat competition between the growing number of dive operators – ask around to see who has the best deals.

Three operators to consider are Byron Bay Dive Centre (☎ (066) 85 7149), at 9 Lawson St; Sundive (☎ (066) 85 7755), in the Cape Byron Hostel complex on Middleton St; and Bayside Scuba (☎ (066) 85 8333), at the corner of Fletcher and Lawson Sts.

Surfing

Most hostels have free surfboards for guests. The Byron Surf Shop (☎ (066) 85 7536), on Lawson St near Fletcher St, hires surfboards ($20 a day), boogie boards ($15) and wetsuits ($5). The associated Byron Surf School offers lessons for $20, including board and wetsuit. Let's Go Surfing (☎ (066) 85 3991) has similar rates for group lessons, or private lessons for $30.

Flying

Cape Byron is a great place for hang-gliding. Flight Zone (☎ (066) 85 8768) and Byron Bay Hang-gliding School (☎ 066) 85 3917) offer tuition, and tandem flights and tuition. Tandem flights are $65 from Lennox Head. Ring at 10 am to find out if and when there will be flights that day.

Trike flights (ultra-light aircraft) are run by Skylimit (☎ (066) 84 3616) and cost from $50 for half an hour. Skylimit also offers tandem hang-gliding. Skydive (☎ (066) 84 1323) has tandem skydiving. Prices start at $198 for midweek jumps (minimum two people).

Kite-flying is popular and most days around 4 pm you'll see plenty on Main Beach or Tallow Beach, depending on the wind. Byron Kites (☎ (066) 85 5299) in the Cape Byron Hostel complex will sell you kite or you can rent one for $20, which includes tuition and five hours flying.

Alternative Therapies

There are at least two flotation-tank places Samadhi (☎ (066) 85 6905) on Jonson S opposite Woolworths, and Relax Have (☎ (066) 85 8304) at Belongil Beachouse These places also do massage – at Rela Haven you can get an hour in the tank and a hour-long massage for $40.

Several other places offer massage, acu puncture and alternative therapies; othe outfits drift into the fuzzier edges of alterna tive thought. If you need your chakr realigned, contact Quintessence Healin Sanctuary (☎ (066) 85 5533) at 8/11 Fletche St. It offers everything from clairvoyance t sports massage.

Organised Tours

Byron Bay to Bush Tours (☎ (066) 84 0253 and Jim's Alternative Tours (☎ (066) 8 7720) both run day tours of the spectacula north coast hinterland for $20. Jim's also ha trips to The Channon markets on the secon Sunday of each month ($10 return) and t Bangalow on the fourth Sunday ($5 Nimbin Tours (☎ (066) 85 5362) runs t Nimbin Tuesday to Saturday for $15 return

North Coast Surfaris (☎ 1800 634 951 offers week-long surfing trips from Sydne to Byron Bay, stopping at out-of-the-wa surf spots. Their bus leaves Byron Bay ever Sunday, and Sydney every Monday. Th price of $249 includes camping and surfin gear and all meals. You'll need a sleepin bag.

Places to Stay

Byron has lots of accommodation, particu larly at the budget end of the market, but bed can still prove hard to find in summer. Price go up during school holidays and pea around Christmas and Easter.

Camping At peak times you'll be lucky t find a site, and cabins are rented only by th week.

The local council has four caravan parks, all by beaches. *First Sun Caravan Park* (☎ (066) 85 6544) is on Main Beach close to the town centre. Tent sites start at $13, rising in stages to $22 at peak time. There's a range of cabins, the cheapest going for $33 in the low season and $50 at the peak. *Clarks Beach Caravan Park* ☎ (066) 85 6496) is off Lighthouse Rd about a km east of the town centre and has plenty of trees. Sites start at $11 and cabins at $45.

Down at Suffolk Park on Tallow Beach, *Suffolk Park Caravan Park* (☎ (066) 85 3353) is a friendly place with shady sites ($11) and cabins from $32. They can probably squeeze in your tent when everywhere else is full. The small council-run caravan park at Broken Head (☎ (066) 85 3245) has a superb location overlooking Tallow Beach and is marginally cheaper than the others. There's no shop, so you'll need to bring all your supplies.

Belongil by the Sea (☎ (066) 85 8111), next to the Belongil Beachouse hostel, has a clusters of cabins dotted around landscaped gardens with a large swimming pool (heated in winter). Prices start at $45 for two people. *Tallow Beach Resort* (☎ (066) 85 3408, 1800 456 817) is on Tallow Beach and has self-contained cabins from $65.

Hostels The hot competition between the town's numerous hostels is good news for travellers. At the time of writing, there were even hostels. All have their good points, so if you're planning a lengthy stay check them all to see which suits you best. Prices fluctuate depending on demand, peaking around Christmas/January, when you should book. At other times ask about special deals and weekly rates.

The popular *Backpackers Holiday Village Hostel* (☎ (066) 85 7660) at 116 Jonson St, close to the bus stop, is a clean, friendly, well-equipped place with a small pool and spa. Dorm beds cost from $14 and doubles from $36. There's one double with bathroom and TV for $43. Well-maintained bicycles,

surfboards and boogie boards are free and there are plenty of them.

The closest hostel to the beach is *Backpackers Inn* (☎ (066) 85 8231) at 29 Shirley St, about half a km from the town centre. It's a modern hostel with a pool and all the usual features, including free bikes and boogie boards. To get to the beach you just walk across the lawn, cross the railway line (carefully!) and climb a sand dune. Rates start at $14 for dorms and at $38 for doubles.

The *Cape Byron Lodge* (☎ (066) 85 6445) is clean, comfortable and well equipped. It's some way from the town centre at 78 Bangalow Rd (the southern end of Jonson St) but only about 10 minutes walk to Tallow Beach. It has a small pool and bikes are free. This is usually the cheapest hostel in town, with dorm beds starting at $10 and doubles at $30.

Byron Bay has two YHA-affiliated hostels. The impressive *Cape Byron Hostel* (☎ (066) 85 8788) is close to the town centre and Main Beach, at the corner of Byron and Middleton Sts. It's a big new building with its own mini shopping centre and a heated pool. Prices (which might rise in summer) are $13 in a 10-person dorm, $14 in a five-person dorm, $36 in a double or twin and $60 for a double with TV, fridge and bathroom.

The other YHA affiliate is the purpose-built *J's Bay Hostel* (☎ 1800 678 195) on the corner of Carlyle and Middleton Sts.

The *Belongil Beachouse* (☎ (066) 85 7868) is a great place to stay – well-run, relaxed and friendly. It's off Childe St, a quiet road adjacent to Main Beach; bikes, surfboards and boogie boards are free. The cafe here is a big plus, with excellent healthy food served between 8 am and 10 pm. There's a nightly half-price special for guests. You can store gear here for $5 a week. Dorm beds start at $15, rising to $17 around Christmas. Singles/doubles with shared bathroom are $33/38, rising to $37/42. There are some up-market doubles priced from $50, rising to $80.

Those with an alternative bent will enjoy

the atmosphere at the *Arts Factory Lodge* (☎ (066) 85 7709), with its permaculture gardens and creative furnishings. The huge choice of accommodation ranges from tent sites ($8) to teepees and converted double-decker buses ($14). Dorm beds are $15 and doubles start at $36. Ideologically-sound food is available at the co-owned Piggery Cafe. The Arts Factory is about 10 minutes walk from the town centre and beaches. Staff meet buses and there's free use of bikes as well as regular minibuses to town.

The *Blue Iguana Beach House* (☎ (066) 85 5298), opposite the surf club on Bay St, has beds in four-person dorms for $15 during the week, rising to $20 at weekends and more at peak times.

Hotels & Motels The *Great Northern Hotel* (☎ (066) 85 6454) on Jonson St has singles/doubles for $30/40 in the low season, rising to $35/45 in the peak season. There are numerous motels lining the southern and western approaches to town. Doubles are around $60 in the off season.

The *Wheel Resort* (☎ (066) 85 6139), just south of town on Broken Head Rd, is designed and run by wheelchair users for travellers with disabilities. Rates start at $75 for a cabin for up to three people.

Apartments Holiday houses and apartments start from around $300 a week in the off season, $500 during school holidays and $800 over Christmas. Letting agents include Elders (☎ (066) 85 6222) on Jonson St near the train station, which handles bookings for the two old cottages at the lighthouse on Cape Byron. There's a two-bedroom cottage for $450 a week (off season), and a three-bedroom cottage for $550. Rents rocket to $1200 and $1300 a week at Christmas.

Places to Eat
There is a wide choice of restaurants, cafes and takeaways serving good food, and vegetarians are particularly well catered for.

Breakfast is served just about everywhere. Overlooking Clarks Beach, the *Beach Cafe* isn't cheap but the views are superb. *Cafe DOC* at the Cape Byron Hostel complex has breakfast from about $5.50 and good coffee.

The *Beach Hotel* in Bay St has snacks such as burgers from $4.50 and more substantial meals such as satays ($9.50) and steaks (from $12.50). Heading down Jonson St from there, the *South Indian Curry House* is a long-time favourite, with most main courses around $10. It's open nightly for dinner. *Munchies* is a small place with healthy snacks and meals, open during the day. Farther along, *Suppertime Vegetarian Cafe* has similarly healthy food such as vegie-burgers at $4.50 and smoothies from $2.50. Both places stay open until early evening, later in summer.

East of the roundabout on Jonson St, *Ringo's* is one of Byron's older cafes and has a large menu of snacks and drinks, and meals from around $10. It's open from breakfast ($6.50 for bacon & eggs) until about 8.30 pm. Across the road, *Earth & Sea Pizza* is a popular pizza place which also has pasta. *Catalina* is a tapas bar, with live music later in the evening Thursday to Sunday. *Lifestream* is a large health-food cafe with a huge range of goodies. You can put together a decent meal for $5.

At the Railway Friendly Bar, *Annie's Fresco Gusto* opens for lunch and dinner. The food is innovative and not expensive. Farther along Jonson St is the licensed *Mexican Mick's*, open for dinner Tuesday to Saturday. It's an old favourite and is still reasonably priced, with main courses under $14 and lots of snacks on the big menu.

The Feros Arcade dog-legs between Lawson and Jonson Sts and has several options. The *Indian Curry Restaurant* is a small place open Wednesday to Monday for dinner, with vegetarian main courses from $8 and others up to $13. *Annabella's Spaghetti Bar* is open weekdays for lunch and dinner (and occasionally on summer weekends), with main courses from $7 to $10. Next door, the *Raving Prawn* has an interesting modern menu with main courses ranging from $14 to $20.

The Chinese restaurant at the bowling club in Marvell St has various specials and the main courses are all under $8. *Chu's* on Lawson St has no MSG in its Chinese food, with main courses under $10. The *Byron Thai*, at the Bay Beach Motel on Lawson St, has an unusually large vegetarian selection.

Entertainment

The busy nightlife is another of Byron Bay's major drawcards. The *Railway Friendly Bar*, next to the train station, has live music most nights. The *Beach Hotel* and the *Great Northern Hotel* have live bands Thursday to Saturday nights and sometimes on Sunday afternoons. Touring bands play at the *Ex-Services Club* at the southern end of Jonson St. The entertainment lift-out in Friday's *Northern Star* has a gig guide.

It's always worth seeing what's on at the *Epicentre*, on Border St just over the railway line. Whatever it is (and its programmes encompass a wide range of the weird) it's sure to be at least interesting.

Getting There & Away

Bus Numerous buses run through Byron Bay. There are also more-or-less direct buses to Melbourne ($119) and Adelaide ($150). Other approximate fares are Brisbane $20, Sydney $62, Coffs Harbour $31 and Surfers Paradise $18.70.

Kirklands' Lismore-Brisbane route passes through Byron Bay and stops in other useful places such as Murwillumbah, Ballina and Tweed Heads. Blanch's (☎ (066) 86 2144) serves the local area with destinations such as Mullumbimby ($4) and Ballina ($6.60).

Train Byron Bay is on the Sydney to Murwillumbah line, with a daily train in each direction, plus several rail/bus services. From Sydney ($75.60) the quickest service is the 7.05 am XPT, which reaches Byron Bay at 7.30 pm. This train continues to Murwillumbah ($6.20) and connects with a bus to Brisbane ($26.60 from Byron Bay). The southbound train stops in town at 10 am. The fare to Coffs Harbour is $32.60.

Car & Motorbike Rental Earth Car Rentals (☎ (066) 85 7472) has older cars from $35 a day (including 200 free km), more recent vehicles from $45 and new cars from $50. Jetset Travel (☎ (066) 85 6554) rents small current-model cars for $35 a day plus 15c per km.

Ride on Motorcycles (☎ (066) 85 6304), on Jonson St opposite Woolworths, hires motorbikes from $50 a day. You need a motorbike licence, Australian or foreign.

Getting Around

Bicycle The hostels lend bikes of varying quality to guests. Byron Bay Bicycles (☎ (066) 85 6315) in the Plaza shopping centre on Jonson St has good single-speed bikes for $12 a day, including helmet, and geared bikes for $18 a day. Let's Go Bikes (☎ (066) 85 6067), nearby on Jonson St, has single-speed bikes at $15 a day.

BYRON BAY TO TWEED HEADS

The Pacific Highway continues north from the Byron Bay turn-off to the Queensland border at Tweed Heads. Just after the Mullumbimby turn-off is **Brunswick Heads**, a river-mouth town with a small fishing fleet and several caravan parks and motels.

A few km north is the turn-off to the coastal town of **Wooyung**. The coast road from Wooyung to Tweed Heads makes a pleasant alternative to the Pacific Highway. This stretch is known as the Tweed Coast and is much less developed than the Gold Coast to the north.

On the Tweed Coast are the small resorts of **Bogangar-Cabarita** and **Kingscliff**. Cabarita Beach has good surf and there's a good hostel, *Emu Park Backpackers Resort* (☎ (066) 76 1190). It's one of the cleanest hostels around and the rooms are large. Dorm beds are $13 and there's a 'stay two nights, get the third night free' deal outside school holidays. Doubles cost $28, and the en suite double with TV is $38. Bikes and boards are free and the beach is a minute away. The staff will drop you off at Mt Warning and pick you up after your climb for about $45 – not bad among several people.

Guests can be picked up from Coolangatta (Queensland).

Surfside (☎ (07) 5594 0055) has six buses a day from Tweed Heads to Cabarita Beach ($3.50) on weekdays – three on Saturday and two on Sunday, and frequent services to Kingscliff ($2.80).

Murwillumbah (pop 8150)

Murwillumbah is in a banana and sugar-growing area in the broad Tweed Valley. It's also the main town in this part of the north coast hinterland and there are several communes and 'back to the land' centres in the area. You're also within reach of Mt Warning and the spectacular border ranges. You can cross into Queensland by the Numinbah road through the ranges between the Springbrook and Lamington areas (see the Queensland chapter for more details).

The Tweed visitor centre (☎ (066) 72 1340), the main information centre for the Tweed region, is at the junction of the Pacific Highway and the Murwillumbah turning, near the railway station. The excellent **Tweed River Regional Art Gallery** is just up the road from the hostel. The **museum** is on Queensland Rd and is open Wednesday to Sunday from 10 am to 5 pm. Admission is free.

You can hire bikes from Jim's Cycle Centre (☎ (066) 72 3620) at 58 Wollumbin St for $10 a day.

Places to Stay & Eat The associate-YHA *Mt Warning Backpackers of Murwillumbah* (☎ (066) 72 3763) is at 1 Tumbulgum Rd beside the Tweed River – you'll see it on the right as you cross the bridge into town. It's a friendly place with lots of activities, including free canoes and a rowing boat. Dorm beds are $15, singles $20 and twins $34 and the double room is $29.

Several pubs have accommodation, including the solid *Imperial Hotel* (☎ (066) 72 1036) on the main street across from the post office, with rooms from $20/35.

Getting There & Away Murwillumbah is served by most buses on the Sydney (about

$60) to Brisbane ($17) coastal run. Except for Kirklands, which goes into town, the long-distance buses stop at the railway station. Fulton's Bus Service (☎ (066) 21 6231) runs to Uki ($4.50), Nimbin ($12) and Lismore ($14). Surfside runs to Tweed Heads ($3.80).

A daily train from Sydney ($80.80) connects with a bus to the Gold Coast and Brisbane.

TWEED HEADS (pop 45,500)

Sharing a street with the more-developed Queensland resort of Coolangatta, Tweed Heads marks the southern end of the Gold Coast strip. The northern side of Boundary St, which runs along a short peninsula to Point Danger above the mouth of the Tweed River, is in Queensland. This end of the Gold Coast is much quieter than the resorts closer to Surfers Paradise.

The Tweed Heads visitor centre (☎ (07) 5536 4244) is at the northern end of Wharf St (the Pacific Highway), just south of the giant Twin Towns Services Club. It's open daily from 9 am to 5 pm. There's also an information kiosk (☎ (07) 5536 7765) in the Beach House complex at the corner of Marine Parade and McLean St in Coolangatta. It's open Monday to Friday from 8 am to 4 pm, and on Saturday from 10 am to 4 pm.

Things to See

At Point Danger the towering **Captain Cook Memorial** straddles the state border. The 18-metre-high monument was completed in 1970 (the bicentenary of Cook's visit) and is topped by a laser-beam lighthouse visible 35 km out to sea. The replica of the *Endeavour*'s capstan is made from ballast dumped by Cook after the *Endeavour* ran aground on the Great Barrier Reef and recovered along with the ship's cannons in 1968. Point Danger was named by Cook after he nearly ran aground there too. There are views over the Tweed Valley and the Gold Coast from the **Razorback Lookout**, three km from Tweed Heads.

On Kirkwood Rd in South Tweed Heads,

the **Minjungbal Aboriginal Cultural Centre**
(☎ (07) 5524 2109) has exhibits on pre-
contact history and culture. It's open
Monday to Friday from 9 am to 5 pm, and
weekends from 9 am to 3 pm. Entry is $6.

Places to Stay

Accommodation in Tweed Heads spills over
into Coolangatta and up the Gold Coast,
where the choice is more varied. The cheaper
motels along Wharf St are feeling the pinch
as the highway bypasses Tweed Heads and
you'll find doubles advertised for less than
$30.

See the Coolangatta section of the
Queensland chapter for places to stay across
the border.

Places to Eat

The *Tweed Heads Bowls Club* on Wharf St
has specials such as weekday roast lunches
for under $5; the other clubs are also sources
of cheap eats.

The smaller *Rowing & Aquatic Club* on
Coral St has meals for less than $8. Next
door, the *Fishermans Cove Restaurant* is
known for its seafood and has main courses
averaging around $16. At Rainbow Bay, on
the northern side of Point Danger, *Doyle's on
the Beach* has excellent seafood takeaways
and a restaurant.

Getting There & Away

All long-distance buses stop at the
Coolangatta Transit Centre on the corner of
Griffith and Warner Sts. Ticket sales are
handled by Golden Gateway Travel (☎ (07)
5536 6600). Coachtrans offers a same-day
return to Brisbane for $20, $12 one way.
Kirklands goes to Byron Bay for $13.80 and
Coffs Harbour for $40.

Surfside (☎ (07) 5594 0055) has frequent
services to Murwillumbah ($4.20) and to
Kingscliff ($2.80). It also has six buses a day
to Cabarita Beach ($3.50) on weekdays –
three on Saturday and two on Sunday. Buses
leave from outside the Tweed Heads visitor
centre.

There are several car-hire places which
will get you moving for $35 a day, such as

Tweed Auto Rentals (☎ (07) 5536 8000),
which is 100 metres south of the information
centre on Wharf St.

Far North Coast Hinterland

The area stretching 60 km or so inland from the
Pacific Highway in far northern New South
Wales has spectacular forested mountains, and
a high population of alternative lifestylers.
These settlers, the first of whom were attracted
to the area by the Aquarius Festival at Nimbin
in 1973, have become a prominent and colourful part of the community.

The country between Lismore and the
coast was once known as the Big Scrub, an
incredibly inadequate description of a place
that must have been close to paradise at the
time of European incursion. Much of the
'scrub' was cleared for farming, after the
loggers had been through and removed the
prized red cedar. These days the area is mar-
keted as Rainbow Country.

A web of narrow roads covers the hinterland.
If you're planning to explore the area, get the
Forestry Commission's Casino area map ($5)
– the information centres in Byron Bay and
Nimbin are two places which stock it.

Geography

The northern part of the hinterland was
formed by volcanic activity (see the Mt
Warning entry later in this section) and is
essentially a huge bowl almost completely
rimmed by mountain ranges, with the spectacular peak of Mt Warning in the centre. The
escarpments of the McPherson and Tweed
ranges form the north-western rim, with the
Razorback Range to the west and the Nightcap Range to the south-west. National parks,
some of them World Heritage areas, protect
unique and beautiful subtropical rainforests.

The country south of here is a maze of
steep hills and beautiful valleys, some still
harbouring magnificent stands of rainforest,

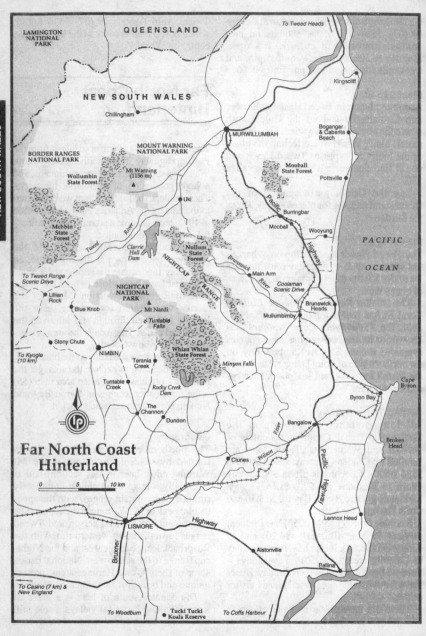

Far North Coast Hinterland

0   5   10 km

others cleared for cattle-grazing and plantations – especially macadamia nuts.

Markets & Music
The alternative community can be seen in
force at the weekend markets listed below.
The biggest market is at The Channon,
between Lismore and Nimbin.

Brunswick Heads
First Saturday of the month, behind the Ampol
service station
Byron Bay
First Sunday, Butler St Reserve
Lismore
First and third Sundays, Lismore Shopping
Square; 5th Sunday, Heritage park
Murwillumbah
First Sunday, Sunnyside Shopping Centre
Lennox Head
Second and fifth Sundays, Lake Ainsworth fore-
shore
The Channon
Second Sunday, Coronation Park
Mullumbimby
Third Saturday, Museum
Ballina
Third Sunday, Fawcett Park
Uki
Third Sunday, Old Buttery
Bangalow
Fourth Sunday, Showground
Nimbin
Fourth Sunday, Showground

Many accomplished musicians live in the
area and they sometimes play at the markets
or in the town pub after the market (notably
at Uki). Friday's edition of the *Northern Star*
includes a guide to the week's gigs and other
activities. The *Brunswick Byron Echo* and
the *Lismore Echo* newspapers give notice of
most musical and cultural events in the area.

LISMORE (pop 41,800)
Thirty-five km inland from Ballina on the
Bruxner Highway to New England, Lismore
is the main town of the state's far north. It's
on the Wilson River, which forms the north
arm of the Richmond River.

The Lismore Information & Heritage
Centre (☎ (066) 22 0122) is on the Bruxner
Highway – known as Ballina St through

town – at the corner of Molesworth St, near
the Wilson River. It has a rainforest display
($1). The Big Scrub Environment Centre
(☎ (066) 21 3278) on Keen St sells topographic maps of the area. The Outdoor &
Disposals shop (☎ (066) 21 3371) on Keen
St rents camping gear: a dome tent, a stove
and a couple of sleeping bags costs about $80
for a week.

The interesting **Richmond River Historical Society Museum** (☎ (066) 21 9993) is
at 165 Molesworth St and is open weekdays
($2). The **regional art gallery** next door is
open Tuesday to Saturday (free). **Rotary
Park** is an interesting six-hectare patch of
remnant rainforest that has survived while
the town has grown around it. The park is
dominated by towering hoop pines and giant
fig trees. It's just off the Bruxner Highway
about three km east of the information
centre. Access is from Rotary Drive.

Tucki Tucki Nature Reserve, 16 km
south of Lismore on the Woodburn road, is
a koala reserve. Initiation ceremonies were
held at the Aboriginal **bora ring** nearby.

The MV *Bennelong* (☎ (066) 21 7729) has
several cruises, ranging from two hours
($10) to a day cruise down to the coast at
Ballina ($50).

Places to Stay
Currendina Travellers Lodge (☎ (066) 21
6118) occupies the old weatherboard
Lismore hospital building at 14 Ewing St –
Currendina means 'place of healing' in the
language of the local Bundjalung Aboriginal
people. It's a cosy place close to the city
centre with dorms for $14, singles from $17
and doubles from $30. Smoking and drink-
ing are not permitted. The friendly managers
can organise trips to places of interest in the
area.

The *Northern Rivers Hotel* (☎ (066) 21
5797), at the junction of Terania and Bridge
Sts on the road out to Nimbin, has good pub
and singles/doubles for $18/25.

Places to Eat
The *Northern Rivers Hotel* (see Places to
Stay) does unbelievably cheap meals, with

roast lunches for $1.99 and dinners for $2.99. Opposite the Northern Rivers, philosophically as well as physically, is the vegan *Gumamilyee Vegetarian Cafe* on Bridge St. In the town centre, *Dr Juice* on Keen St is open during the day for excellent juices and smoothies, plus vegetarian and vegan snacks for around $2. Next door is *Fundamental Health Foods*, a big health-food shop.

Getting There & Away

There are daily flights to Brisbane (Impulse) and Sydney (Hazelton). Kirklands (☎ (066) 22 1499) is based here and runs buses around the immediate area as well as farther afield. Destinations include Byron Bay ($9), Mullumbimby ($9.40), Murwillumbah ($13.20) and Brisbane ($25.90). There's a handy service to Tenterfield in New England ($19.90) on weekdays. The XPT train from Sydney ($75.60) stops here.

NIMBIN (pop 1320)

The Aquarius Festival of 1973 transformed the declining dairy town of Nimbin, 30 km north of Lismore, into a name almost synonymous with Australia's 'back to the land' counterculture movement. It is still a very active alternative centre and there are many communes, also known as multiple occupancy properties, in the area. You're still likely to be asked if you want to buy some 'green' as you walk along the street.

Despite the size of its reputation, Nimbin is a tiny town. Cullen St is the main street. The Nimbin Connection Ecotourist Centre (☎ (066) 89 1764), at the northern end of Cullen St, has tourist information. It can also arrange horse riding and trekking.

The weird and wonderful **Nimbin Museum** is on Cullen St near the Rainbow Cafe. Admission is by donation. It's worth a visit for the conversations you'll have before you get through the door. There's a good market on the fourth Sunday of the month and you may catch a local band playing afterwards.

Nimbin Explorer (☎ (066) 89 1557) has tours of the Nimbin area ($25) and to Border Ranges National Park ($30).

Many people come to the area to visit **Djanbung Gardens** (☎ (066) 89 1755), a permaculture education centre established by Robyn Francis – a disciple of permaculture guru Bill Mollison. Contact the centre for information about courses. The centre, five minutes walk from the town centre on Cecil St, is open for information on Thursday from 10 am to 2 pm, and gives a guided tour on market days at 2 pm.

Places to Stay

The council's basic caravan park (☎ (066) 89 1402) is near the bowling club – go down the road running past the pub. Sites cost $9 and on-site vans are $25.

Granny's Farm (☎ (066) 89 1333), an associate-YHA hostel, is a relaxed place surrounded by farmland, with platypuses in the nearby creek. It also has a swimming pool. Conventional dorm beds are $12 and doubles $30. Other options here are the teepee or 'pleasure dome' (tent) for $10 per person, and creekside camping for $6 per person. The friendly managers will sometimes give rides to places of interest. To get there, go north along Cullen St and turn left just before the bridge over the creek.

The *Rainbow Retreat* (☎ (066) 89 1262) is a new place just outside town with great views from its hilltop setting. The atmosphere is very laid back. There's a good swimming hole on the creek below the guesthouse and plenty of bush to explore. Beds in dorms (or doubles if available) are $10, and there are $5 evening meals for guests. Phone from town for a free pick-up, or call in and see the owner, Doug, at the Nimbin Connection.

Nimbin's up-market option is *Grey Gum Lodge* (☎ (066) 89 1713), a stylishly renovated weatherboard house on the road into town from Lismore. Singles/doubles are $35/50, dropping to $30/45 after three nights.

Places to Eat

The *Rainbow Cafe*, in the centre of town on Cullen St, promotes itself as the place where more than a million joints have been smoked, doubtless leading to some serious assaults on the range of delicious cakes (priced from $2.50). There are vegetarian snacks and meals for around $6. It also does breakfast, as does the nearby *Nimbin Rocks Cafe*, the closest thing you'll find to a standard country town cafe. Across the street, *Choices* has healthy (and not-so-healthy) takeaways and light meals.

At the northern end of Cullen St, *Nimbin Pizza & Trattoria* has pasta from $8.50 and is open daily from 5 pm. The restaurant at *Grey Gum Lodge* gets good reviews for its use of 'bush tucker' ingredients, offering such items as wattle-seed focaccia ($2.50) and emu and mushroom ravioli ($9.50). The restaurant is open for lunch and dinner Tuesday to Sunday.

If you have your own transport, try the delightful *Calurla Tea Garden* (☎ (066) 89 7297), 11 km from town on the edge of Nightcap National Park. To get there, take Blue Knob Rd north out of Nimbin and turn onto Lillian Rock Road after eight km. It's open daily from 10 am to 7 pm, and until late on Friday and Saturday nights.

Entertainment
If there's a dance at the town hall, don't miss the opportunity to meet up with the friendly people from the country around Nimbin. There's an annual *Mardi Grass Festival* at the end of April which culminates with the famous *Marijuana Harvest Ball*.

The *Freemasons Hotel* often has music, and the *Bush Theatre* at the old butter factory, near the bridge at the northern end of town, has films on Friday and Saturday.

Getting There & Away
Goulding's (☎ (066) 89 5144) operates buses between Nimbin and Lismore ($8) daily except Sunday. Fulton's (☎ (066) 79 5267) has a service to and from Murwillumbah on weekdays (leaving Murwillumbah at 7 am, returning at 3.30 pm). It takes two hours and costs $12. Nimbin Tours (☎ (066) 85 5362) charges $10 one way between Nimbin and Byron Bay.

AROUND NIMBIN
The country around Nimbin is superb. The 800-metre-plus Nightcap Range, originally a flank of the huge Mt Warning volcano, rises north-east of the town and a sealed road leads to one of its highest points, **Mt Nardi**. The range is part of **Nightcap National Park**. The Mt Nardi road gives access to a variety of other vehicle and walking tracks along and across the range, including the historic Nightcap Track, a packhorse trail which was once the main route between Lismore and Murwillumbah. The views from **Pholis Gap** on the Googarna road, towards the western end of the range, are particularly spectacular.

The Tuntable Falls commune, one of the biggest, with its own shop and school and some fine houses, is about nine km east of Nimbin and you can reach it by the public Tuntable Falls Rd. You can walk to the 123-metre **Tuntable Falls** themselves, 13 km from Nimbin.

The eastern region of the park covers the Terania Creek catchment area. A stunningly beautiful 700-metre walk leads to **Protesters' Falls**, named after the environmentalists whose 1979 campaign to stop logging was a major factor in the creation of the national park. There is free camping at Terania Creek, but you're supposed to stay only one night. No fires are allowed.

Access to Terania Creek is via **The Channon**, a tiny town off the Nimbin-Lismore road that hosts the biggest of the region's markets on the second Sunday of the month. A dance is sometimes held the night before the market and there's often music afterwards. *The Channon Teahouse & Craftshop* is a pleasant place for a snack or a light meal and has interesting craft to browse through. It's open daily from 10 am to 5 pm, with dinner on Friday and Saturday nights. *The Channon Village Campsite* (☎ (066) 88 6321) is basic but pretty and costs $4 per person. Out of town on the Terania Creek road, *Mimosa Park Holiday Farm* (☎ (066) 88 6230) has cabins for $50 a double.

Nimbin Rocks is an Aboriginal sacred site signposted off along Stony Chute

(Kyogle) Rd, which leads west off the Nimbin-Lismore road just south of Nimbin. **Hanging Rock Creek** has falls and a good swimming hole; take the road through Stony Chute for 14 km, turn right at the Barker's Vale sign, then left onto Williams Rd; the falls are nearby on the right.

MULLUMBIMBY (pop 2750)

This pleasant little town, known locally as Mullum, is in subtropical countryside five km off the Pacific Highway, between Bangalow and Brunswick Heads. Perhaps best known for its marijuana – 'Mullumbimby Madness' – it's a centre for the long-established farming community as well as for the alternative folk from nearby areas, although there's nothing like the cultural frontier mentality of Nimbin here.

West of Mullum in the Whian Whian State Forest, **Minyon Falls** drop 100 metres into a rainforest gorge. There are good walking tracks around the falls and you can get within a couple of minutes walk by conventional vehicle from Repentance Creek on one of the back roads between Mullum and Lismore. The eastern end of the historic Nightcap Track (see Around Nimbin) emerges at the north of Whian Whian State Forest.

Places to Stay & Eat

There are a couple of motels and, 12 km north, *Maca's Main Arm Camping Ground* (☎ (066) 84 5211) is an idyllic place, under the lee of hills lush with rainforest. It's nothing like a commercial caravan park but the facilities are quite good, with a kitchen, hot showers and a laundry. It costs $4 per person and you can hire tents from $5 a day. To get here, take Main Arm Rd and follow the 'camping' signposts.

The *Popular Cafe* on Burringbar St is a popular place to hang out and *Buon Appetito* on Stuart St has inexpensive pasta (from $4.50) and pizzas to eat in or take away. The *Pizza Hive* on Station St has vegetarian meals as well as pizza. *Mullum House* at 103 Stuart St has Chinese mains under $10.

Getting There & Away

Kirklands buses go through Mullum on their Lismore ($9.40) to Brisbane ($20.30) run. The newsagency at the corner of Burringbar and Stuart Sts is the Kirklands agent.

Mullum is on the Sydney ($75.60) to Murwillumbah railway line.

There are two road routes to Mullum from the Pacific Highway: one turns off just south of Brunswick Heads, and the other is the longer but prettier Coolaman Scenic Drive, which leaves the highway north of Brunswick Heads near the Ocean Shores turn-off.

For a scenic drive to Uki and Mt Warning, head out to Upper Main Arm, pass Maca's Camping Ground and follow the unsealed road through the Nullum State Forest. Keep to the main road and watch for signposts at a few ambiguous intersections. Watch out for logging trucks and don't try the road after rain – or you stand a good chance of literally sliding off the mountain.

MT WARNING NATIONAL PARK

The dramatic peak of Mt Warning (1157 metres) dominates the district. It was named by Captain Cook as a landmark for avoiding Point Danger off Tweed Heads. The mountain is the former central magma chamber of a massive volcano formed more than 20 million years ago. It once covered an area of more than 4000 sq km, stretching from Coraki in the south to Beenleigh in the north, and from Kyogle in the west to an eastern rim now covered by the ocean. Erosion has since carved out the deep Tweed and Oxley valleys around Mt Warning, but sections of the flanks survive as the Nightcap Range in the south and parts of the Border Ranges to the north.

The road into the park runs off the Murwillumbah-Uki road. It's about six km to the car park at the base of the track leading to the summit. Much of the 4.5-km walk is through rainforest. The final section is steep (to put it mildly), so allow five hours for the round trip. Take water. If you're on the summit at dawn you'll be the first person on the Australian mainland to see the sun's rays that day! The trail is well marked, but you'll need a torch if you're climbing at night (to reach the summit at dawn).

Even if you don't want to climb Mt Warning it's worth visiting for the superb rainforest in this World Heritage area. There's a short walking track near the car park.

Places to Stay

You can't camp at Mt Warning but the *Wollumbin Wildlife Refuge & Caravan Park* (☎ (066) 79 5120), on the Mt Warning approach road, has tent sites ($10), on-site vans (from $24) and cabins ($35). The vans and cabins cost less if you stay more than one night. There are kitchen facilities and a well-stocked kiosk – and lots of wildlife in the 120-hectare refuge, including koalas. Platypus can be seen at dusk in the adjoining Tweed River.

The *Mt Warning Forest Hideaway* (☎ (066) 79 7139), 12 km south-west of Uki on Byrrill Creek Rd has small units with cooking facilities from $45 to $55, rising to $50 and $60 during school holidays.

Getting There & Away

A Fulton's (☎ (066) 21 6231) school bus runs from Murwillumbah to Uki, Nimbin and Lismore on weekdays. It leaves Knox Park in Murwillumbah at 7 am and can drop you at the start of the six-km Mt Warning approach road. The hostels at Murwillumbah and Cabarita Beach organise trips to the mountain.

BORDER RANGES NATIONAL PARK

The Border Ranges National Park covers the New South Wales side of the McPherson Range along the NSW-Queensland border and some of the range's outlying spurs. The Tweed Range Scenic Drive – gravel but useable in all weathers – loops through the park about 100 km from Lillian Rock (midway between Uki and Kyogle) to Wiangaree (north of Kyogle on the Woodenbong road). It has some breathtaking lookouts over the Tweed Valley to Mt Warning and the coast. The adrenalin charging walk out to the crag called the **Pinnacle**

– about an hour from the road and back – is not for vertigo sufferers! The rainforest along **Brindle Creek** is also breathtaking, and there are several walks from the picnic area here.

There are a couple of camp sites, basic but free, on the Tweed Range Scenic Drive: Forest Tops, high on the range, and Sheepstation Creek, about six km farther west and 15 km from the Wiangaree turn-off. There might be tank water but it's best to bring your own.

New England

New England is the area along the Great Dividing Range stretching north from near Newcastle to the Queensland border. It's a vast tableland of sheep and cattle country with many good bushwalking areas, photogenic scenery and, unlike much of the northern half of Australia, has four distinct seasons. If you're travelling along the eastern seaboard, it's worth diverting inland to New England to get a glimpse of the Australian lifestyle away from the coast. There's a lot less tourist hype, for starters.

A diversion is easy enough thanks to the New England Highway, which runs from Hexham, just north of Newcastle, to Brisbane. This route was developed as an inland alternative to the Pacific Highway. It's an excellent road, with far less traffic than on the coast. There is great scenery on the roads linking the New England Highway with the coast, particularly on the Oxley Highway from Bendemeer (just north of Tamworth) to Port Macquarie, and on the Waterfall Way from Armidale to Bellingen via Dorrigo.

National Parks

The eastern side of the tableland tumbles over an escarpment to the coastal plains below, and along this edge is a string of fine national parks. Gorges and waterfalls are a common feature. The Armidale Visitor's Centre (☎ (067) 73 8527) has information on all the parks listed below.

Werrikimbe This remote, rugged World Heritage listed park straddles the escarpment north of the Oxley Highway between Walcha and Wauchope. There are two main approaches to the park. The easiest is along the Forbes River road, which turns off the highway at Yarras, 45 km west of Wauchope. This leads to the Plateau Beach Rest Area, the launching pad for walks to the gorges of the Forbes and Hastings rivers – recommended for experienced bushwalkers only. The other approach to the park is along the Kangaroo Flat road, 55 km east of Walcha.

Oxley Wild Rivers Consisting of several sections, this park east of Armidale and Walcha is crossed by deep gorges with some spectacular waterfalls – especially after rain. **Wollomombi Falls**, 39 km east of Armidale, are among the highest in Australia with a 220-metre drop; **Apsley Falls** are east of Walcha at the southern end of the park. On the bottom of the gorges is a wilderness area, accessible from Raspberry Rd off the Wollomombi-Kempsey road.

New England & Cathedral Rock New England is a small park with a wide range of ecosystems. There are 20 km of walking tracks and, at the bottom of the escarpment, a wilderness area. Access is from near Ebor and there are cabins and camp sites near the entrance at Point Lookout. Book these through the Dorrigo NPWS office (☎ (066) 57 2309). Cathedral Rock, off the Ebor-Armidale road, has photogenic granite formations.

Dorrigo See the North Coast section for information on this park.

Guy Fawkes River This is gorge country with canoeing and walking. **Ebor Falls**, near the town of Ebor on the road from Armidale to Dorrigo, are spectacular. Access to the park is from Hernani, 15 km north-east of Ebor. From here it's 30 km to the Chaelundi Rest Area, with camp sites and water.

Gibraltar Range & Washpool Dramatic, forested and wild, these parks lie south and north of the Gwydir Highway between Glen Innes and Grafton. Countrylink buses stop at the visitor centre (the start of a 10-km track to the Mulligans Hut camping area in Gibraltar Range) and at the entrance to Washpool (from where it's about three km to camping areas).

Bald Rock & Boonoo Boonoo Bald Rock is about 30 km north of Tenterfield on an unsealed (but deceptively smooth – take it easy) road which continues into Queensland. Bald Rock is a huge granite monolith which has been compared to Uluru. You can walk to the top and camp near the base. Nearby is Boonoo Boonoo, with a 200-metre-drop waterfall and basic camping.

Getting There & Away

There are airports at Armidale and Tamworth, providing daily services to Sydney and Brisbane.

Several bus lines run through New England from Melbourne or Sydney to Brisbane. King's (☎ 1800 625 587) runs between Tamworth and Port Macquarie via Coffs Harbour and Armidale; Kirklands (☎ (066) 22 1499) operates between Lismore and Tenterfield ($19.90); and Batterhams Express (☎ 1800 043 339) runs between Sydney and Tamworth via the Hunter Valley. Trains run from Sydney to Armidale, from where Countrylink buses run up to Tenterfield.

TAMWORTH (pop 35,600)

Spend much time listening to the radio while driving the roads of rural Australia and you'll realise that country music has a big following. Tamworth is the country music centre of the nation, an antipodean Nashville. The town's population doubles during the 10-day country music festival in January which culminates with the Australasian country music awards, Golden Guitars, on the Australia Day long weekend.

Guitar-shaped things are all the rage, starting with the information centre (☎ (067) 66 9422) on the corner of Peel and Murray Sts. Pick up a map of the Heritage Walk or the longer Kamilaroi Walking Track which begins at the Oxley Scenic Lookout at the northern end of White St.

Country music memorabilia around town includes a collection of photos at the Good Companions Hotel, the **Hands of Fame** near the information centre and, at Tattersalls Hotel on Peel St, **Noses of Fame**!

The **Country Collection**, on the New England Highway in South Tamworth, is hard to miss – out the front is the 12-metrehigh **Golden Guitar**. Inside is a wax museum ($4). Also here is the Longyard Hotel, a major venue during the festival. Recording studios, such as Big Wheel (☎ (067) 67 9499) and Hadley Records & Yeldah Music (☎ (067) 65 7813), can be visited by arrangement.

Places to Stay

You'll be lucky to find a bed anywhere during the country music festival.

The *Paradise Caravan Park* (☎ (067) 66 3120), near the information centre at the corner of East and Peel Sts, has tent sites for $10 and on-site vans for $27.

The *Central Hotel* (☎ (067) 66 2160), on the corner of Peel and Brisbane Sts in the city centre, has singles/doubles for $25/37 or $32/42 with bathroom. Other city centre pubs include the *Good Companions* (☎ (067) 66 2850) on Brisbane St, the *Imperial* (☎ (067) 66 2613) on the corner of Brisbane and Marius Sts, and the *Tamworth* (☎ (067) 66 2923) on Marius St.

Many motels are enormous but few are cheap. At slow times you might find some charging $40 or $45 but don't count on it.

Echo Hills Station (☎ 1800 810 243), about 30 km east of town on Mulla Creek Road near Kootingal, offers backpackers a rare opportunity to experience life on a sheep station. It charges $29 per night including meals. Echo Hills also runs week-long courses for would-be jackaroos/jillaroos for about $300. Backpackers can join the activities for $25 a day. The owners will pick you up from Tamworth by appointment. There are also self-contained cottages from $60.

Getting There & Away

Eastern Australia and Tamair have daily flights to Sydney for $168 and Impulse flies to Brisbane for $227. Bus fares include $45 to Sydney and $20 to Armidale.

TAMWORTH TO ARMIDALE

The timber town of **Walcha** (population 1830) is off the New England Highway on the eastern slope of the Great Dividing Range, on the winding and spectacular Oxley Highway route to the coast at Port Macquarie. East of the town is the Apsley Gorge, with magnificent waterfalls; see the National Parks entry earlier in this section.

Back on the highway, the pretty town of **Uralla** (population 2340) is where bushranger Captain Thunderbolt was buried in 1870. Thunderbolt's Rock, by the highway seven km south of town, was one of his hide-outs. There are several craft shops and the big McCrossin's Mill Museum ($2). A fossicking area is about five km north-west of Uralla on the Kingstown road. The town of **Gostwyck**, a little piece of England, is 10 km south-east of Uralla.

ARMIDALE (pop 22,400)

The regional centre of Armidale is a popular stopping point. The 1000-metre altitude means it's pleasantly cool in summer and frosty (but often sunny) in winter. The town is famous for its autumn colours, which are at their best in late March and early April.

The town centre is attractive, with the Beardy St pedestrian mall and some elegant old buildings, and it's a lively place, thanks to the large student population at the University of New England. Education is big business in Armidale. There are also three posh boarding schools, including The Armidale School (TAS), whose imposing buildings and grounds can be seen on the road to Grafton and Dorrigo.

The information centre (☎ (067) 72 4655, 1800 627 736) is just north of the city centre on the corner of Marsh and Dumaresq Sts. It has walking and driving tour brochures. The bus station is in the same building.

The **Armidale Folk Museum** is in the city

centre on the corner of Faulkner and Rusden Sts and is open daily from 1 to 4 pm (admission by donation). The excellent **New England Regional Art Museum** ($5) is south of the centre on Kentucky St.

Saumarez Homestead, on the New England Highway between Armidale and Uralla, is a beautiful old house which still contains the effects of the rich pastoralists who built it.

The Armidale area is noted for its magnificent gorges and waterfalls – best viewed after rain. The best of them are **Wollomombi Falls**, 39 km east of Armidale off the road to Grafton and Dorrigo, and **Dangar's Falls**, 22 km south-east of Armidale off the Dangarsleigh road. Both have basic camp sites.

Places to Stay

The *Pembroke Caravan Park* (☎ (067) 72 6470), about 2.5 km from town on Grafton Rd, has sites from $12, on-site vans from $20/25 a single/double and cabins between $28/32 and $42/45. It is also an associate-YHA hostel, offering beds in a huge partitioned dorm for $13.50. Families might be offered an en suite cabin at YHA rates.

Much more convenient is Armidale's 'Pink Pub', the *Wicklow Hotel* (☎ (067) 72 2421), on the corner of Marsh and Dumaresq Sts, just across from the bus station. It has comfortable pub rooms for $15 per person. *Tattersalls Hotel* (☎ (067) 72 2247) is on the mall so it has little traffic noise. Rooms start at $26/36, costing more with bathroom attached.

There are more than 20 motels but about the only places with doubles for under $50 are *Rose Villa Motel* (☎ (067) 72 3872), which charges from $39/43, and *Hideaway Motor Inn* (☎ (067) 72 5177) which charges from $40/45. Both are on the New England Highway north of town.

Places to Eat

The central streets have a wide variety of eating places. The best place to start is the East Mall. *Tall Paul's*, on the corner of Marsh and Beardy Sts, has roasts ($8.20), steaks ($10) and less expensive eats such as burgers

(from $2.20) and pasta (from $4). *Jean-Pierre's BYO Cafe*, an odd combination of a country town cafe and a French restaurant, has snacks and meals. Nearby, *Minio's Pasta* has takeaway home-made pasta (from $4) with a choice of sauces. *Cafe Midale* farther along Beardy St has breakfast and light meals from $5.50.

Chinese restaurants include *Mekong* on East Mall, which has weekday smorgasbord lunches for $6.50 and a smorgasbord dinner on Thursday for $8.50. *Lee's*, next to Harvey World Travel, on Dangar St, has lunches for $3.90.

Getting There & Away

Eastern Australia and Hazelton fly to Sydney ($193) and Impulse flies to Brisbane ($208).

Countrylink, McCafferty's and Greyhound Pioneer service Armidale, and King's runs down to Coffs Harbour and Port Macquarie, via Dorrigo. Fares from Armidale include Sydney $52, Brisbane $44, Tamworth $20, Glen Innes $23 ($12 with Countrylink), Byron Bay $45, Dorrigo $15.90, Bellingen $22.90, Coffs Harbour $23.80 and Port Macquarie $39.60.

The train fare from Sydney is $62.40.

Realistic Car Rentals (☎ (067) 72 8078) at Armidale Exhaust Centre on the corner of Rusden and Dangar Sts has cars from $45 a day, including insurance and 100 free km.

Getting Around

Armidale Cycle Centre (☎ (067) 72 3718) at 248 Beardy St (near Allingham St) hires bikes for $4 an hour, $15 a day or $35 a week.

NORTH OF ARMIDALE

Guyra (pop 2000)

Guyra is at an altitude of 1300 metres, making it one of the highest towns in the state. The **Guyra & District Historical Society Museum** has filled the old council chambers with its collection of pioneering memorabilia. It's open only on Sunday afternoon, admission $2. **Mother of Ducks** is a waterbird sanctuary on the edge of town. The strange **balancing rock** can be seen by the

highway 12 km before Glen Innes at Stonehenge.

Glen Innes (pop 6500)

You're still at over 1000 metres at Glen
Innes, which was a good place to meet bushrangers a century ago. Buses stop at the new
information centre (☎ (067) 32 2397) on the
New England Highway.

The old hospital on the corner of Ferguson
St and West Ave houses **Land of the Beard-
ies History House**, a big folk museum open
daily from 2 to 5 pm and also from 10 to 11
am on weekdays. Admission is $4. The main
street, Grey St, is worth strolling down for
its old buildings. The area was settled by
Scots, and Glen Innes regards itself as the
Celtic capital of New England – there are
bilingual street signs and the impressive
Standing Stones on a hill above town.

The **Australian Music Festival** is held
over the October long weekend and attracts
about 100 artists; some are big names and an
increasing number are Aboriginal. It's a fun
weekend of singing, dancing and workshops. Some years a special train runs to
Glen Innes from Sydney and you can travel
in antique carriages with many of the performers. For more information contact the
organisers (☎ (067) 32 2397).

Black & White (☎ (067) 32 3687) has a
daily bus to Inverell ($8) Monday to Satur-
day.

Inverell (pop 10,200)

Inverell is a large country town with some
impressive public buildings. The information centre (☎ (067) 22 1693) is in a
converted water tower on Campbell St, a
block back from the main shopping street.
The **mining museum** is here too – silver was
once mined around Inverell and sapphire is
still mined. **Inverell Pioneer Village** is open
from 2 to 4 pm on Sunday and Monday, and
from 10 am to 5 pm the rest of the week.
Admission is $4. The *Empire Hotel* (☎ (067)
22 1411) is an old pub on Byron St with
singles/doubles for $20/35.

You can visit a working sapphire mine at
Dejon Sapphire Centre (☎ (067) 23 2222),

19 km east of Inverell on the Gwydir
Highway. It has tours at 10.30 am and 3 pm.
The Smith Museum of Mining & Natural
History is at **Tingha**, 25 km south of Inverell.

Tenterfield (pop 3350)

At the junction of the New England and
Bruxner highways, Tenterfield is the last
town of any size before the Queensland
border. The information centre (☎ (067) 36
1082) is on Rouse St, the main street, at the
corner of Miles St. The **Sir Henry Parkes
Memorial School of Arts** is where Parkes
launched the national federation movement
in 1889.

Thunderbolt's Hideout, where bushranger Captain Thunderbolt did just that, is
11 km out of town. The main attractions in
the area are the Bald Rock and Boonoo
Boonoo national parks – see the National
Parks entry earlier in this section. The managers of Tenterfield Lodge (see below) can
organise tours of the national parks with
**Woollool Woollool Aboriginal Culture
Tours** for $30, including lunch.

Places to Stay *Tenterfield Lodge* (☎ (067)
36 1477) is a YHA-affiliated hostel/guest-
house at the western end of Manners St, near
the old railway station. The brick and weatherboard house was built in 1870 and is listed
by the National Trust. Shared rooms are $15
per person, doubles are $35 and family
rooms are $45. You can camp out the back
for $10 and there are on-site vans from $22.

Several pubs have accommodation, such
as the *Exchange Hotel* (☎ (067) 36 1054) on
Rouse St with singles/doubles for $10/20.

South Coast

Though much less visited than the coast
north of Sydney, the coast south to the
Victorian border has many beautiful spots
and excellent beaches, good surf and diving,
some attractive little fishing towns and
forests both lovely and spectacularly wild.

The Snowy Mountains are 150 km inland from this southern NSW coast.

The Princes Highway runs along the coast from Sydney through Wollongong to the Victorian border. Although a longer and slower route to Melbourne than the Hume Highway, it's much more interesting.

Getting There & Away

Hazelton flies to Merimbula from Sydney; Kendell flies to the area from Melbourne.

Greyhound Pioneer travels the Princes Highway route. Fares from Sydney include Bega $47 (eight hours), Narooma $40 (seven hours) and Batemans Bay $32 (six hours). Sapphire Coast Express (☎ (044) 73 5517) runs between Batemans Bay and Melbourne ($61) twice a week.

Pioneer Motor Service (a local company) runs buses between Eden and Sydney ($47), and for short hops between coastal towns it's much cheaper than the big lines. There's also a service between Bega and Canberra. Countrylink serves Bega too, on the daily run between Eden and Canberra ($32).

Murrays has daily buses from Canberra to Batemans Bay ($22) and south along the coast to Narooma. Their buses connect with north-bound Pioneer Motor Service buses at Batemans Bay.

The railway from Sydney goes as far south as Bomaderry (Nowra).

WOLLONGONG (pop 182,000)

Only 80 km south of Sydney is the state's third-largest city, an industrial centre which includes the biggest steelworks in Australia at nearby Port Kembla. Wollongong also has some superb surf beaches, and the hills soaring behind provide a fine backdrop, great views over the city and coast, and good walks.

The name Illawarra is often applied to Wollongong and its surrounds – it refers specifically to the hills behind the city (the Illawarra Escarpment) and the coastal Lake Illawarra to the south.

Orientation & Information

The Crown St pedestrian mall is in the centre of town. Through traffic bypasses the city on the Southern Freeway.

Just east of the mall, the information centre (☎ (042) 28 0300) on the corner of Crown and Kembla Sts is open daily.

The post office is in the Gateway on the Mall complex, on Keira St between the mall and Burelli St. The Wollongong East post office is near the tourist information centre. Bushcraft on Stewart St has hiking and camping gear.

Things to See

The fishing fleet is based in the southern part of Wollongong's harbour, **Belmore Basin**, which was cut from solid rock in 1868. On the point are a fish market, a couple of fish restaurants and an 1872 lighthouse.

North Beach, north of the harbour, generally has better surf than the south Wollongong Beach. The harbour itself has beaches which are good for children. Other beaches run north up the coast.

The **City Gallery** on the corner of Kembla and Burelli Sts is open all day Tuesday to Friday, as well as weekend afternoons. The Illawarra Historical Society's **museum** on Market St is open Thursday, Saturday and Sunday afternoons ($2) and includes a reconstruction of the 1902 Mt Kembla town mining disaster.

Port Kembla's industrial area is called **Australia's Industry World** – it sounds like a theme park! The BHP company runs free Friday morning tours (☎ (042) 75 9023) of its steel works.

The enormous **Buddhist Temple** a few km south of the city is open to visitors (☎ (042) 72 0600).

Places to Stay

You have to go a little way out before you can camp. There are camping areas on the beach at Corrimal (☎ (042) 85 5688), near the beach on Farrell Rd in Bulli (☎ (042) 85 5677) and on Fern St in Windang (☎ (042) 97 3166), with beach and lake frontage. Bulli is 11 km north, Corrimal about halfway between Bulli and Wollongong, and Windang is 15 km south, between Lake

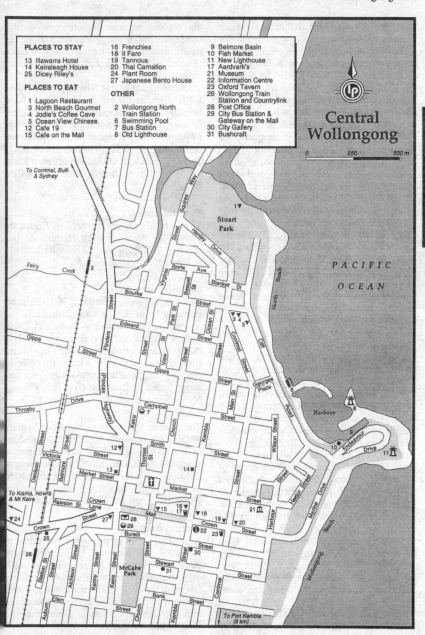

Central Wollongong

NEW SOUTH WALES

PLACES TO STAY

13 Illawarra Hotel
14 Keiraleagh House
25 Dicey Riley's

PLACES TO EAT

1 Lagoon Restaurant
3 North Beach Gourmet
4 Jodie's Coffee Cave
5 Ocean View Chinese
12 Cafe 19
15 Cafe on the Mall

16 Frenchies
18 Il Faro
19 Tannous
20 Thai Carnation
24 Plant Room
27 Japanese Bento House

OTHER

2 Wollongong North Train Station
6 Swimming Pool
7 Bus Station
8 Old Lighthouse

9 Belmore Basin
10 Fish Market
11 New Lighthouse
17 Aardvark's
21 Museum
22 Information Centre
23 Oxford Tavern
26 Wollongong Train Station and Countrylink
28 Post Office
29 City Bus Station & Gateway on the Mall
30 City Gallery
31 Bushcraft

Illawarra and the beach. All charge $11 for camp sites (two people) and from $48 for vans or cabins, with prices rising sharply during school and Christmas holidays.

Keiraleagh House (☎ (042) 28 6765) is at 60 Kembla St, north of Market St. It's a friendly communal place catering mainly to long-term students but they will let you have a bed for $15 a night if there's room.

Several hotels have fairly cheap accommodation. *Dicey Riley's* (☎ (042) 29 1952) at 333 Crown St, near the Wollongong train station, charges $30/35 for singles/doubles and $45 for triples. The *Illawarra Hotel* (☎ (042) 29 5411) on the corner of Keira and Market Sts has singles for $25 and doubles for $40, but it can get rowdy.

About the only inexpensive motel in the area is the *Cabbage Tree Motel* (☎ (042) 84 4000) at 1 Anama St (behind the Cabbage Tree Hotel) in Fairy Meadow, off the Princes Highway 3.5 km north of the city centre. Singles/doubles cost $39/44. Most buses heading north from the Wollongong train station go to Fairy Meadow.

Places to Eat

For good coffee, snacks and meals it's hard to go past *Tannous*, a Lebanese cafe on Crown St on the corner of Corrimal St. Shish kebabs, felafel and other takeaways are $3, or $5 if you eat in. Eat-in meals come with large serves of hummus, tabouli and bread. Just opposite is *Thai Carnation*, the cheapest of the Thai restaurants in the area.

There are plenty of other places in the area. The *Cafe on the Mall* on the corner of Church St is open long hours for snacks and meals. Nearby in Kembla St *Il Faro* serves classic Aussie Italian and across the street is *Frenchies* which has fresh and healthy fare and the strongest coffee in town.

The tiny *Japanese Bento House* on Keira St opposite the Gateway on the Mall has good-value lunch packs. On Keira St north of Market St is a row of mid-priced restaurants including *Cafe 19* which has some great Persian dishes.

The *Plant Room* on Crown St opposite the corner of Gladstone Ave, just up the hill from the Wollongong train station, opens during the day for coffee and snacks and at night for meals; main courses are under $12. It has a relaxed atmosphere and a cosmopolitan menu.

On Bourke St at North Beach, both *Jodie's Coffee Cave* and *North Beach Gourmet* have breakfast and light meals. There are a few swanky restaurants on Cliff Rd. *Ocean View Chinese* is pretty reasonable and has a terrace overlooking the water. The *Lagoon* (☎ (042) 26 1677) is in a great location in Stuart Park. Seafood is the speciality here, with buffets from $25.

Entertainment

Young bands play at the *Oxford Tavern* on Crown St. *Aardvark's* on Kembla St has acoustic entertainment. There's Irish music at *Dicey Riley's* on Crown St.

Getting There & Away

Bus The bus station (☎ (042) 26 1022) is on the corner of Keira and Campbell Sts. Several daily services run to Sydney ($15, sometimes much less) and one to Canberra ($28) via the southern highlands. Greyhound Pioneer's Sydney to Melbourne ($61) coastal route runs through Wollongong and direct buses to Brisbane cost $81. Pioneer Motor Service runs down to Eden ($47).

Train Many trains run to and from Sydney (about 90 minutes, $6.20, off-peak day-return $6.40) and a fair number continue south to Kiama, Gerringong and Bomaderry (Nowra). On weekends a tourist train runs to Moss Vale ($6.40 return), inland near the Hume Highway and Morton National Park.

Getting Around

Almost all buses go through the terminal in Keira St, near the mall. You can ask here about local services. By rail you can reach most of the beaches, and the trains are fairly frequent. A cycle path runs from the city centre north to Bulli and south to Windang and you can hire bikes in Stuart Park on Sunday and holidays.

AROUND WOLLONGONG

The hills rise dramatically behind Wollongong and there are walking tracks and lookouts on Mt Kembla and Mt Keira less than 10 km from the city centre, but no buses go up there. You get spectacular views over the town and coast from the **Bulli Pass** (pronounced: bull-eye) on the Princes Highway, just north of Wollongong.

The country is equally spectacular to the south, inland through the **Macquarie Pass National Park** to Moss Vale or through the Kangaroo Valley. The Fitzroy Falls and other attractions of mountainous Morton National Park can be reached by either route.

North of Wollongong there are several excellent beaches. Those with good surf include **Sandon Point**, **Austinmer**, **Headlands** (only for experienced surfers) and **Sharkies**. The pubs at Clifton and Scarborough both have meals, accommodation and spectacular views.

On the road to Otford and Royal National Park, the **Lawrence Hargrave Lookout** at Bald Hill above Stanwell Park is superb for cliff-top viewing. Hargrave, a pioneer aviator, made his first attempts at flying in the area early this century. Hang-gliders fly there today and Aerial Technics (☎ (042) 94 2545) has courses. Just south of Wollongong, **Lake Illawarra** is popular for water sports.

WOLLONGONG TO NOWRA

South of Lake Illawarra, **Shellharbour** is a popular holiday resort. It's one of the oldest towns along the coast, and back in 1830 was a thriving port but it declined after the coming of the railway. There are good beaches on the Windang Peninsula north of the town and good scuba diving off Bass Point to the south.

Kiama is a pretty seaside town famous for its blowhole: it can spout up to 60 metres high. There is also a heritage museum, good surf beaches, and the scenic Cathedral Rock at Jones Beach. The caravan park (☎ (042) 32 2707) at Blowhole Point is terrific if it's not too windy, with sites for $15.

Just south of Kiama, **Gerringong** has fine beaches and surf. Pioneer aviator Charles Kingsford-Smith took off in 1933 from Seven Mile Beach – immediately south of Gerringong and now a national park – to fly to New Zealand. *Chittick Lodge*, an associate YHA hostel (☎ (042) 34 1249) on Bridges Rd, is a five-minute walk up the hill from Werri Beach. Beds are $12 for members.

The small town of **Berry** was an early settlement, and today it has a number of National Trust classified buildings, a museum and many antique and craft shops. The *Hotel Berry* (☎ (044) 64 1011) is a very pleasant pub charging $40/50 a single/double. There are scenic roads from Berry to pretty **Kangaroo Valley**, where there are more galleries and craft shops, and canoeing.

Coolangatta (no, not the Queensland Coolangatta) has a group of buildings (now a motel, restaurant and exhibition complex) which were constructed by convicts in 1822. The town is also the home of Bigfoot (☎ (044) 48 7131), a strange vehicle which will carry you to the top of Mt Coolangatta for $10 ($5 children).

SHOALHAVEN

The coastal strip south of Gerringong to Durras Lake, just north of Batemans Bay, is a popular holiday destination known as Shoalhaven, which also stretches 50 km inland to include the Morton and Budawang national parks. Inland on Shoalhaven River, the twin towns of **Nowra** and **Bomaderry** form the main population centre. The region is popular for water sports, and white-water rafting is available – phone the information centre (☎ 1800 024 261), on the highway in Bomaderry. There's a NPWS office (☎ (044) 23 9800) at 55 Graham St, Nowra.

Five km east of Nowra on the northern bank of the Shoalhaven River is **Nowra Animal Park** (☎ (044) 21 3949). It's a pleasant place to meet some Australian native animals and you can camp in bushland here for $9. *Riverhaven Backpackers* (☎ (044) 21 2044) is closer to town, just under the bridge on the Nowra side of the river. Dorm beds are $12, double rooms $35. The *White House* (☎ (044) 21 2084) at 30 Junction St is an associate-YHA hostel with modest rooms for $13 per person.

Inland, just north of Kangaroo Valley, Fitzroy Falls is the visitor centre for **Morton National Park** (☎ (048) 87 7270). South of Morton the line of national parks (Budawang, Deua and Wadbilliga) stretches to the Victorian border. These are outstanding mountain wilderness areas which are good for rugged bushwalking.

South of Nowra, **Jervis Bay** is quite suburban but **Huskisson**, one of the oldest towns on the bay, is still a nice place. There is a fascinating wetlands boardwalk (free) near the museum on the Nowra side of Huskisson.

Jervis Bay National Park takes up the south-eastern spit of land on Jervis Bay. It has good swimming, surfing and diving on bay and ocean beaches. There are camp sites at Caves Beach ($8 to $10), where there's surf, and elsewhere. For all camp sites you have to book (☎ (044) 43 0977). Entry to the park costs $5 per car for a week.

Ulladulla is an area of beautiful lakes, lagoons and beaches. There's good swimming and surfing (try Mollymook beach, just north of town). Or you can take the bushwalk to the top of Pigeon House Mountain (719 metres) in the impressive Budawang Range.

South Coast Backpackers (☎ (044) 54 0500) is in Ulladulla at 63 Princes Highway, towards the top of the hill to the north of the shopping centre. It's a small place with spacious five-bed dorms and all the usual facilities. Beds cost $12.50 a night. They'll take guests to Murramarang National Park or Pigeon House for $10.

Fares from Ulladulla with Pioneer Motor Service include Sydney, $23; Nowra, $11; the North Durras turn-off at East Lynne (for Pebbly Beach in Murramarang National Park), $6.80; Batemans Bay, $8.80; and Eden, $29.40.

Murramarang National Park is a beautiful coastal park running from about 20 km south of Ulladulla all the way to Batemans Bay. There is a camp site (☎ (044) 78 6006)

at lovely Pebbly Beach which costs $10 (plus the $7.50 per car entry fee, payable only if you camp). A kiosk operates during school holidays – when tent sites are scarce. Pebbly Beach is about 10 km off the highway and there's no public transport.

There is accommodation at settlements within the park. At **Depot Beach** the basic *Moore's Pioneer Park* (☎ (044) 78 6010) has tent sites for $4 plus $3 per person and a range of on-site vans and cabins from about $45 a night in the off season. As well as the superb beach, **North Durras** is on the inlet to Durras Lake. *Durras Lake North Caravan Park* (☎ (044) 78 6072) has an on-site van set aside for backpackers ($8) – ask at the shop.

BATEMANS BAY TO BEGA
The fishing port of **Batemans Bay** is one of the south coast's largest holiday centres. The visitor centre (☎ 1800 802 528) is on the highway near the town centre. *Batemans Bay Backpackers* (☎ (044) 72 4972) is on the Old Princes Highway just south of the town. *Elaine's* in the Fenning Place arcade in the main street bakes magnificent pies. Beds are $13 a night, climbing to $16 over summer. Buses run to Canberra ($22), Sydney ($29) and Melbourne ($52).

About 60 km inland from Batemans Bay on the scenic road to Canberra is **Braidwood**, with its many old buildings and thriving arts and crafts. From here there's road access to the superb bushwalking country of the Budawang Range.

Moruya is a dairy centre, with oyster farming too. There's some fairly unspoiled coast down the side roads south of Moruya, with a good camp site ($8) at **Congo**, where there are beaches on both sides of a headland. Bring your own supplies; you'll need to boil drinking water.

Narooma is an oyster town popular for serious sport fishing in the nearby inlets and lakes. The information centre (☎ (044) 76 2881) is on the beachfront and the NPWS office (☎ (044) 76 2888) is nearby. About 10 km off shore is **Montague Island**, a nature reserve with a historic lighthouse and many seals and fairy penguins. Tours of the island conducted by NPWS rangers run according to demand ($40). The clear waters around the island are popular with divers.

The delightful wooden town of **Central Tilba**, off the highway 15 km south of Narooma, has undergone little change this century. It perches on the side of **Mt Dromedary** (800 metres) and you can walk to the top from the nearby town of **Tilba Tilba**. The return walk of 11 km takes about five hours, or you could ride up with Mt Dromedary Trail Rides (☎ (044) 76 3376). Umbarra Cultural Tours (☎ (044) 73 7232) runs half-day tours to sites of Aboriginal significance in the area, including Mt Dromedary.

South of the coastal **Wallaga Lake National Park** and off the Princes Highway, **Bermagui** is a fishing centre made famous 50 years ago by American cowboy-novelist Zane Grey. It's a handy base for visits to both Wallaga Lake and Mimosa Rocks national parks, and for Wadbilliga National Park, inland in the ranges. The information centre (☎ (064) 93 4174) is north of the bridge at the BP service station. *Blue Pacific Flats* (☎ (064) 93 4921) at 73 Murrah St has backpacker accommodation for $12 as well as regular holiday flats. Turn into Wattle St south of the bridge, then left into Murrah St at the top of the hill. Bega Valley Coaches (☎ (064) 92 2418) has a weekday service between Bermagui and Bega ($6) and a feeder service connects with Pioneer Motor Service's bus north to Nowra.

The largely unsealed road between Bermagui and Tathra is more interesting than the highway, running through the excellent **Mimosa Rocks National Park**. You can camp at Gillards Beach and Aragunnu Beach ($5 plus $7.50 car entry fee) but bring your own water.

Inland on the Princes Highway is **Cobargo**, another unspoilt old town. The main 2WD access to **Wadbilliga National Park** is near here. It's a rugged park and the thriving animals live in surroundings which haven't changed much in thousands of years.

Bega is a sizeable town near the junction of the Princes and Snowy Mountains high-

ways. The information centre (☎ (064) 92 2045) is in Gipps St near the corner of Carp St, in a craft shop. The *Bega Youth Hostel* (☎ (064) 92 3103) is a modern mud-brick building on Kirkland Crescent (off Kirkland Ave, which departs the highway about a km west of the town centre). It's a friendly place which charges $12 a night.

Countrylink's Eden to Canberra service passes through Bega daily. Pioneer Motor Service runs from Bega to Sydney. Greyhound Pioneer passes through on the coastal run between Sydney and Melbourne, as does Sapphire Coast Express on the run between Batemans Bay and Melbourne.

SOUTH TO THE VICTORIAN BORDER

The coast here is quite undeveloped, and there are many good beaches and some awe-inspiring forests full of wildlife – and loggers.

Merimbula

Merimbula is a big resort with a good 'lake' (actually a large inlet) and ocean beaches. Despite large-scale development, the setting remains beautiful and nearby **Pambula Beach** is quiet in a suburban way.

The information centre (☎ (064) 95 1129) is on the waterfront in Beach St. At the wharf on the eastern point there's a small **aquarium** ($6).

The YHA hostel, *Wandarrah Lodge* (☎ (064) 95 3503), is at 18 Marine Parade. Follow the signs just south of the bridge. Dorm beds are $12 ($15 in summer) with twin rooms available. The hostel is spacious with good facilities. Activities include minibus trips to nearby national parks and rainy day 'mystery tours'.

Eden

At Eden the road bends away from the coast and into Victoria, running through mighty forests. The town is an old whaling port on Twofold Bay, much less touristy than towns farther up the coast. The information centre (☎ (064) 96 1953) is open weekdays and weekend mornings. The NPWS office

(☎ (064) 96 1434) is on the main street at the rear of Twofold Arcade.

At the intriguing **Killer Whale Museum** you can learn about the whaler who, in 1891, was swallowed by a whale and regurgitated, unharmed, 15 hours later. Well, almost unharmed. His hair turned white and fell out due to the whale's digestive juices. There's also the skeleton of a killer whale, Old Tom, which led a pack of other killer whales in herding baleen whales into Twofold Bay where they were killed by whalers. The museum is open weekdays from 10.15 am to 3.45 pm and weekends from 11.15 am to 3.45 pm. Admission is $4.

Whales still swim along the coast in October and November. You can book whale-spotting cruises at the information centre (from $17).

The *Australasia Hotel* (☎ (064) 96 1600) on Imlay St has backpackers' beds for $12 ($15 in summer) and singles/doubles from $25/35 (add $10 in summer).

Boydtown

Boydtown, south of Eden, was founded by Benjamin Boyd, a flamboyant early settler whose landholdings were once second in size only to the Crown's. His grandiose plans included making Boydtown the capital of Australia but his fortune foundered and so did the town – later he did too, disappearing without trace somewhere in the Pacific. Some of his buildings still stand, and the Sea Horse Inn, built by convict labour, is still in use. You can camp nearby for $10.

Ben Boyd National Park

To the north and south of Eden is the Ben Boyd National Park – good for walking, camping, swimming and surfing, especially at Long Beach in the north.

Nadgee Nature Reserve continues down the coast from Ben Boyd National Park but it's much less accessible. **Wonboyn**, a small settlement on Wonboyn Lake at the northern end of the reserve, has a store and *Wonboyn Cabins & Caravan Park* (☎ (064) 96 9131).

Across the lake from Wonboyn but accessed from the road into Ben Boyd

National Park is *Wonboyn Lake Resort* (☎ (064) 96 9162), with self-contained cabins from around $55 for four people.

Snowy Mountains

The first people to ski in Australia were the fur hunters of Tasmania in the 1830s, using three-foot boards. Norwegian miners introduced skiing to Kiandra in the Snowies in the 1860s. Early this century the development of skiing began with lodges like the one at Charlotte Pass and the importing of European skis.

The snowfields straddle the New South Wales-Victoria border. Mt Kosciusko (pronounced 'kozzyosko' and named after a Polish hero of the American War of Independence) is in New South Wales and, at 2228 metres, its summit is Australia's highest. Much of the state's Snowies are within the

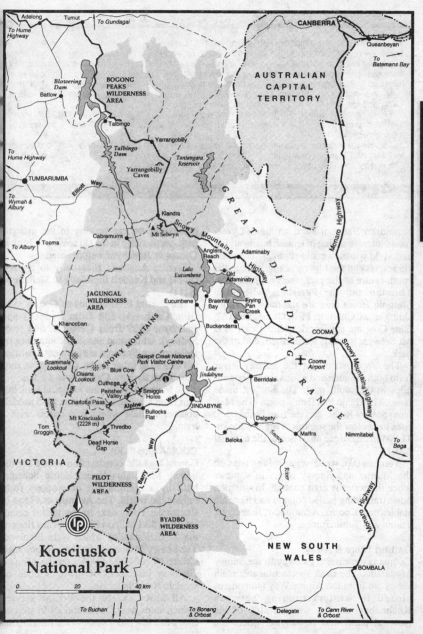

NEW SOUTH WALES

Kosciusko
National Park

0   20   40 km

Snowy Mountains Hydroelectric Scheme

This huge project took more than 25 years to build, largely in mountainous terrain which had been barely explored, much less settled. The scheme was a major source of employment in postwar Australia, and much of the labour was recruited from war-ravaged Europe. Many of those who migrated to Australia to work on the scheme were 'Displaced Persons' from countries which had been over-run by communism. Over 100,000 people worked on the project between 1949 and 1974, and the total cost was a staggering £425 million.

The scheme, however, didn't face environmental concerns – it was begun in the 1950s, when the creation of 16 major dams was seen as an advance of civilisation rather than the drowning of a wilderness.

Two power stations are open to visitors: Murray 1 near Khancoban (tours hourly from 10 am to 2 pm) and Tumut 3 near Talbingo (tours at 10 and 11 am, noon and 1.30 and 2.30 pm). The Snowy Mountains Scheme Information Centre is in Cooma. ■

Kosciusko National Park, an area of year-round interest: skiing in winter, bushwalking and vivid wildflowers in summer. The main ski resorts and the highest country are in the south-centre of the park, west of Jindabyne. Thredbo and the Perisher Valley and Smiggin Holes area are the main downhill skiing areas. Charlotte Pass, Guthega and Mt Blue Cow are smaller downhill areas, as is Mt Selwyn, towards the northern end of the park.

The upper waters of the Murray River form both the state and national park boundaries in the south-west. The Snowy, made famous by Banjo Paterson's poem 'The Man from Snowy River' and the film based on it, rises just below the summit of Mt Kosciusko. The Murrumbidgee also rises in the national park.

You can take white-water rafting trips on the Murray and Snowy rivers in summer when the water is high enough. In summer, horse trail riding is also popular and there are stables near Cooma, Adaminaby, Jindabyne, Tumut and Tumbarumba.

Getting There & Away

Cooma is the eastern gateway to the Snowy Mountains. The most spectacular mountain views are from the Alpine Way (sometimes closed in winter) running between Khancoban, on the western side of the national park, and Jindabyne. There are restrictions on car parking in the national park, particularly in the ski season – check at Cooma or Jindabyne before entering.

Eastern Australia flies daily to Sydney ($114) and Kendell flies daily to Melbourne ($111).

Greyhound Pioneer runs to Cooma ($15 from Canberra, $38 from Sydney) and Jindabyne ($29 from Canberra, $48 from Sydney), with some services continuing on to the resorts. Services are frequent in winter, but less so at other times. Countrylink runs daily from Sydney, Canberra and Eden.

To Melbourne, V/Line's Capital Link bus runs from Canberra via Cooma ($45 to Melbourne) to Sale where it connects with a train.

COOMA (pop 8130)

Cooma was the construction centre for the Snowy Mountains Hydroelectric Scheme, built by a melting pot of workers from around the world. The **Avenue of Flags** in Centennial Park, next to the visitor centre (☎ (064) 50 1742) on Sharp St, flies flags of the 27 nationalities which were involved. The Snowy Mountains Scheme Information Centre (☎ (064) 53 2004), on the Monaro Highway just north of town, is open on weekdays and holidays.

All buses except the V/Line service (which stops near Centennial Park) stop on Sharp St a few blocks east of the information centre, at the Snowstop. Snowliner Travel (☎ (064) 52 1584) handles bus bookings.

If you don't have time to take the town walk (maps at the information centre), at least walk down **Lambie St**, crowded with historic buildings, and also see the imposing granite **courthouse** and nearby **jail** on Vale St. Half a km west is the **Aviation Pioneers Memorial** with the wreckage of the *Southern Cloud*, an aircraft which crashed in the Snowies in 1931 and was only discovered in 1958.

There are several horse-riding outfits in the area, including Reynella (☎ (064) 54 2386) – mainly accommodation packages, and Yarramba (☎ (064) 56 3150) – day rides and longer treks.

Places to Stay

Prices rise in winter, although they are lower here than in Jindabyne or the ski resorts.

The *Mountain View Caravan Park* (☎ (064) 52 4513) is six km out of Cooma towards Jindabyne. It's a nice place with tent sites from $10 and on-site vans from $25. Buses on the way to the resorts will stop here by arrangement.

The *Bunkhouse Motel* (☎ (064) 52 2983) on the corner of Commissioner and Soho Sts has dorm beds for $12 and singles for $20. Each dorm has its own kitchen and en suite. The *Family Motel* (☎ (064) 52 1414) at 32 Massie St has share-rooms from $12 in summer and singles/doubles from $30/40. In winter it would pay to book ahead.

All the pubs have accommodation. The *Australian Hotel* (☎ (064) 52 1844) on the main street has basic rooms for $20 per person, with en suite rooms also available. The *Royal Hotel* (☎ (064) 52 2132) on the corner of Sharp and Lambie Sts is quieter and has clean rooms with shared facilities for $18 per person.

In **Nimmitabel**, a small town on the highway 37 km south-east of Cooma, the delightful *Royal Arms* guesthouse (☎ (064) 54 6422) has singles/doubles for about $36/70 and one small room for $20 per person.

JINDABYNE (pop 1830)

Fifty-six km west of Cooma and a step nearer the mountains, Jindabyne is a new town on the shore of the artificial Lake Jindabyne, which flooded the old town. In summer you can swim or rent boats. A new information centre (☎ (064) 56 2444) is being built on the highway in the centre of town. Paddy Pallin (☎ (064) 56 2922) and Wilderness Sports (☎ (064) 56 2966) run adventure activities in the Snowies, including mountain biking in the summer.

Check the notice board in Nugget's Crossing shopping centre for employment options, cheap accommodation, car shares and second-hand ski gear.

Places to Stay

Winter sees a huge influx of visitors; prices soar and overnight accommodation all but disappears.

The *Snowline Caravan Park* (☎ (064) 56 2099) at the intersection of the Alpine Way and Kosciusko Rd, has tent sites from $10, and cabins from $35 a double. Prices rise in the winter.

Lazy Harry's Lodge (☎ (064) 56 1957), fronting Clyde St but accessible from Kosciusko Rd, is a congenial place with dorm beds for $15 in summer and $25 in winter. Family rooms are also available. Also on Clyde St, *Kookaburra Lodge* (☎ (064) 56 2897, bookings (02) 330 1891) is owned and operated by Sydney's University of Technology Union. B&B rates begin at $40.

There's a fair range of motel-style places, some converting to longer-term accommodation in winter. *Aspen Chalet* (☎ (064) 56 2372), at the eastern edge of town, has doubles from $50 in summer and $120 in the peak season, which is pretty cheap for this town.

Apartments & Lodges Many places offer ski-season accommodation but they fill up – book months in advance if possible. Letting agents include Snow King (☎ (064) 56 2500) and Jindabyne Real Estate (☎ 1800 020 657). Very approximately, apartments sleeping six cost from around $300 a week in the off season and $900 a week in the high winter season.

KOSCIUSKO NATIONAL PARK

The 6900 sq km of the state's largest national park include caves, glacial lakes, forest, ski resorts and the highest mountain in Australia. Most famous for its snow, it's also popular in summer when there are excellent bushwalks and marvellous alpine wildflowers. Outside the snow season you can drive to within nine km of the top of Mt Kosciusko, up Kosciusko Rd from Jindabyne to Charlotte Pass. There are other walking trails from Charlotte Pass, including the 20-km lakes walk which includes Blue, Albina and Club lakes.

Mt Kosciusko and the main ski resorts are in the south-centre of the park. From Jindabyne, Kosciusko Rd leads to the NPWS visitor centre (☎ (064) 56 1700), 14 km north-west at **Sawpit Creek**, then on to Smiggin Holes, Perisher Valley (32 km) and Charlotte Pass, with a turn-off before Perisher Valley to Guthega. The Alpine Way also runs from Jindabyne, to Thredbo (33 km from Jindabyne) and around to Khancoban on the south-western side of the mountains, with accessibility subject to snow conditions.

Entry to the national park (and that includes all the ski resorts) costs $12 per car, *per day*. This makes the $60 annual pass (unlimited entry to all parks in the state and available from NPWS offices) a very good idea. Motorbikes pay $3.50 and bus passengers $4 (usually included in the bus fare).

The CMA's useful *Snowy Kosciusko* map ($4.95) includes maps of the resorts.

Places to Stay

Bush camping is permitted in most of the park but not in ecologically fragile areas. *Kosciusko Mountain Retreat* (☎ (064) 56 2224) is just up the road from the Sawpit Creek visitor centre. It's a pleasant place in bushland with tent sites (from $12 for two people) and cabins (from $53 for two people with no single-night stays around Christmas).

There is plenty of accommodation at the ski resorts, much cheaper in summer, and there is a YHA hostel at Thredbo – see the following sections.

Getting There & Away

Greyhound Pioneer is the main carrier in this area. In winter there are plenty of services from Sydney and Canberra to Cooma and Jindabyne, from where shuttles run to the resorts. It costs $7 from Jindabyne to the Bullocks Flat Skitube terminal (20 minutes) and $10 to Thredbo (about 40 minutes). In summer buses run to Thredbo ($34 from Canberra), but not daily.

In winter you can normally drive as far as Perisher Valley but snow chains must be carried and fitted when directed. The simplest and safest way to get to Perisher/Smiggins in winter is to take the Skitube, a tunnel railway up to Perisher Valley and Blue Cow from below the snow line at Bullocks Flat on the Alpine Way. A return trip from Bullocks Flat to either Blue Cow or Perisher costs $20 and there are deals on combined Skitube and lift tickets. You can hire skis and equipment at Bullocks Flat, and luggage lockers and overnight parking are also available. The Skitube runs a reduced timetable in summer.

SKIING & SKI RESORTS

Snow skiing in Australia can be a marginal activity. The season is short (really only July, August and early September) and good snow is by no means a safe bet. Nor are the mountains ideal for downhill skiing – their gently rounded shapes mean that most long runs are relatively easy and the harder runs tend to be short and sharp. Worse, the short season means the operators have to get their returns quickly and costs can be high.

Having told you the bad, here's the good; when the snow's there and the sun's shining the skiing can be just fine. You will find all the fun (not to mention heart-in-the-mouth fear) you could ask for. Farther, the open slopes of the Australian Alps are a ski tourer's paradise – nordic (cross-country o elemark) skiing is becoming increasingly popular.

The national park includes some famous trails – Kiandra to Kosciusko, the Grey Mare Range, Thredbo or Charlotte Pass to Kosciusko's summit and the Jagungal wilderness. The possibilities for nordic touring are endless, and old cattle-herders' huts may be the only form of accommodation apart from your own tent.

In addition to touring, there is ample scope for cross-country racing (classic or skating) in the Perisher Valley. On the steep slopes of the Main Range near Twynam and Carruthers the cross-country downhill (XCD) fanatics get their adrenalin rushes. In winter, the cliffs near Blue Lake become a practice ground for alpine climbers.

Snowboarding has taken the High Country by storm. Snowboarding gear hire and lessons are widely available and the major resorts are developing purpose-built runs and bowls.

Costs Lift charges vary – see the following information on the various resorts. Class lessons cost from $28 or can be included in a package with lift tickets from about $60 a day, but much less for five days. Boots, skis and stocks can be hired for around $30 a day, but less for longer and less off the mountain. It's a trade-off whether to hire in the towns and risk adjustment problems or at the resort and possibly pay more. There are hire places in towns close to the resorts and many garages hire ski equipment as well as chains. Snow chains must be carried in the mountains during winter even if there is no snow – there are heavy penalties if you haven't got them.

Accommodation The cheapest (and by far the most fun) way to get out on the slopes is to gather a bunch of friends and rent a lodge or an apartment. Costs vary enormously but can be within the bounds of reason. Bring as much food and drink as you can, as supplies in the resorts are expensive. Many agents (including most travel agents) book accommodation and packages on the snowfields.

Specialists include Snow King (☎ (064) 56 2500), the Perisher Smiggins Reservation Centre (☎ 1800 026 356) and the Thredbo Resort Centre (☎ 1800 020 589). The New South Wales Government Travel Centre (☎ 13 2077) also makes bookings.

Accommodation is cheaper in towns like Jindabyne, and particularly in Cooma, which is some distance below the snow line. Buses shuttle from Jindabyne and Cooma to the resorts in the morning and back again late afternoon.

Australian ski resorts are short of the frenetic nightlife of many European resorts, but compensate with lots of partying among the lodges. Nor is there a great variety of alternative activities apart from toboggan runs. Weekends are crowded because the resorts are so convenient, particularly to Canberra.

Snow Reports For snow and road reports ring the various visitor centres. There's a recorded service (☎ 0055 12370). Thredbo has its own number (☎ 0055 34320). For cross-country ski reports phone ☎ 0055 26028.

Thredbo (1365 metres)
Thredbo has the longest runs (the longest is five km through 672 metres of vertical drop) and the best skiing in Australia. A day ticket costs $56, a five-day pass $245 and a five-day lift and lesson package costs $275.

In summer Thredbo is still a good place to visit, unlike the other resorts which become ghost towns. It's a popular bushwalking centre with all sorts of excellent and scenic tracks. The chair lift to the top of Mt Crackenback runs right through the summer ($15 return). From the top of the chair lift it's a two-km walk or cross-country ski to a good lookout point over Mt Kosciusko, or seven km to the top of the mountain itself. Remember to carry adequate clothing and be prepared for all conditions, even in summer.

Places to Stay The *Thredbo YHA Lodge* (☎ (064) 57 6376) costs just $14 a night ($17 per person twin share) outside the ski season and from $36/52 for a weekday/Saturday night or $215 a six-day week during the ski season. A ballot is held for winter places and you have to enter by May. Most people get the nights they want and even if you aren't in the ballot it's worth checking to see if there are cancellations. In June and at the end of September, when snow might be scanty, there is less pressure on places at the lodge. There's plenty of room in the off season. The YHA Travel Centre in Sydney (☎ (02) 9261 1111) is the best place to start making enquiries about Thredbo Lodge.

Although prices do drop over summer, there are no spectacular bargains. *House of Ullr* (☎ (064) 57 6210) is the cheapest with singles/doubles from $48/59.

There's a pretty but basic free camp site, *Thredbo Diggings*, between Jindabyne and Thredbo, near the Skitube at Bullocks Flat.

Perisher Blue (1680 metres)
The Perisher Blue resort, which includes Perisher Valley, Smiggin Holes, Mt Blue Cow and Guthega, has 50 lifts which are accessible with one ticket. It has a great variety of alpine runs, and is a popular cross-country resort with around 1600 hectares of snow-covered terrain. Snowboarding facilities are a high priority here, with purpose-designed snowboarding areas and night boarding sessions on the downhill runs. A day ticket costs $56 ($61 including Skitube), a five-day pass costs $235 ($250 including Skitube), and a five-day lesson, lift and Skitube package costs $280 ($180 for beginners).

Perisher Smiggins Reservations (☎ 1800 026 356) handles all bookings for the resort. *Ben Bullen* is a backpacker-style lodge with shared rooms from $65. Accommodation and ski-lift packages are available.

Charlotte Pass (1780 metres)
At the base of Mt Kosciusko, this is the highest and one of the oldest and most isolated resorts in Australia. In winter you have to snowcat the last eight km from Perisher Valley. Five lifts service rather short but uncrowded runs, and this is good ski touring country.

Mt Selwyn (1492 metres)
Halfway between Tumut and Cooma, this is the only ski resort in the northern end of the national park. It has 12 lifts and is ideal for beginners. One-day lift tickets are $25, five days costs $125 and five days plus lessons $200. It's a day resort – most accommodation is in and around **Adaminaby**. *Lake Eucumbene Units* (☎ (064) 54 2444) offers self-contained accommodation for $50 a double (extra adults $10 each). There are a number of caravan parks in the area. The *Alpine Tourist Park* (☎ (064) 54 2438) has on-site vans from $41 a double. Adaminaby Bus Service (☎ (064) 54 2318) runs between Cooma and Mt Selwyn.

THE ALPINE WAY
From Jindabyne, the Alpine Way runs past Thredbo then loops around the southern end of Kosciusko National Park to the western side of the ranges. Two of the best mountain views are from Olsens Lookout, 10 km off the Alpine Way on the Geehi Dam road, and Scammels Lookout, just off the Alpine Way.

The tiny town of **Khancoban** at the other end of the Alpine Way has backpackers accommodation at the basic *Khancoban Fisherman's Lodge*, where single rooms are $17, groups are $40 for the first two people and each extra adult (up to eight) costs $6. You need to bring your own bedding and cooking utensils. Book and check in at the nearby Khancoban Alpine Inn (☎ (060) 76 9471).

TUMUT AREA
The town of **Tumut** is on the Snowy Mountains Highway on the northern side of the national park. Australia's largest commercial trout farm is at nearby Blowering Dam. The information centre (☎ (069) 47 1849) can tell you about visits to the various centres of the Snowy Mountains Hydroelectric Scheme. For canoeing and rafting, see the friendly people at Adventure Sports (☎ 1800 020 631) in the Old Butter Factory.

Other places to visit are **Talbingo Dam** (40 km south) and the **Yarrangobilly Caves** (70 km south). You can visit a cave by yourself ($4) or take a tour ($8). There's also a thermal pool at a constant 27°C, some beautiful country in the reserve around the caves, and a NPWS information centre (☎ (064) 54 9597).

In a fruit-growing area south of Tumut is **Batlow**. Near the town is **Hume & Hovell's Lookout** where the two explorers did indeed pause for the view in 1824. **Paddy's River Dam** was built by Chinese gold-miners in the 1850s. Continuing south from Batlow you reach **Tumbarumba (NSW)**, site of the early exploits of the bushranger Mad Dog Morgan. Near Tumbarumba, the Pioneer Women's Hut (☎ (069) 48 2635) is an interesting community museum.

South-West & the Murray

This is wide, rolling, sometimes hypnotic country with some of the state's best farming areas and some interesting history. The Murray River forms the boundary between New South Wales and Victoria – most of the larger towns are on the Victorian side. Part of this area is also known as the Riverina because of the meandering Murray and Murrumbidgee rivers and their tributaries.

Getting There & Away

The region is served by a number of airlines, including Ansett, Hazelton and Kendell.

Several roads run through the south-west – the Hume Highway being the obvious one. There are quieter routes like the Olympic Way running through Cowra, Wagga Wagga and Albury. Routes to Adelaide include the Sturt Highway through Hay and Wentworth and you'll also pass through the south-west if travelling between Brisbane and Melbourne on the Newell Highway. The Melbourne to Sydney bus services run on the Hume and trains run close to it. There are regional bus services such as Fearnes Coaches (☎ 1800 029 918) which runs between Sydney and Wagga, Gundagai and

Yass (all $35 from Sydney) and Goulburn and Mittagong (both $20).

Countrylink reaches most other towns in the area. The region is also crisscrossed by major bus routes – from Sydney and Brisbane to both Melbourne and Adelaide.

THE HUME HIGHWAY

The Hume is the main road between Australia's two largest cities. It's the fastest and shortest route and, although it's not the most interesting, there are attractive places and some worthwhile diversions along the way.

One of the simplest diversions is at the Sydney end – take the coastal Princes Highway past Royal National Park to Wollongong. Just after Wollongong take the Illawarra Highway along the picturesque Macquarie Pass to meet the Hume near Moss Vale. Farther south you can leave the Hume to visit Canberra or continue beyond Canberra through the Snowy Mountains on the Alpine Way, rejoining the Hume near Albury.

The Hume is a divided freeway from Sydney to beyond Goulburn, but it will be a long time before the whole road is upgraded. There are long stretches of narrow, two-lane road carrying a lot of traffic.

Sydney to Goulburn

The large towns of **Mittagong** and **Bowral** adjoin each other along the Hume Highway. There is a regional information centre (☎ (048) 71 2888) at Mittagong. Four km south of town, a winding 65-km road leads west to the **Wombeyan Caves** with their spectacular limestone formations. The drive up is through superb mountain scenery and there's a pretty camping ground (☎ (048) 43 5976) at the caves. Bowral was where cricketer Sir Donald Bradman, probably Australia's greatest sporting hero, spent his boyhood. There's a cricket ground and museum dedicated to 'the Don', open daily from 10 am to 4 pm. A little farther south along the Hume is **Berrima**, a tiny town which was founded in 1829 and has changed remarkably little since then.

South of Berrima are the small town of **Bundanoon** and the large **Morton National Park**, with its deep gorges and high sandstone plateaus in the **Budawang Range**. There are several entry points to the park: two of the easiest are Fitzroy Falls (on the road between Moss Vale and Nowra) and Bundanoon. The pleasant *Bundanoon Youth Hostel* (☎ (048) 83 6010) occupies an old Edwardian guesthouse on Railway Ave. It has dorm beds for $13 and doubles for $34. Bundanoon is on the railway line between Sydney ($19.40) and Canberra (and Melbourne). Countrylink buses run daily to Wollongong.

Goulburn (pop 24,400)

Goulburn, founded in 1833, is at the heart of a prosperous sheep-grazing district famous for its fine merino wool – hence the three-storey-high **Big Merino** that towers over the Old Hume Highway in town.

The visitor centre (☎ (048) 21 5343) is on Montague St across from Belmore Park and it has a walking tour map. There are many fine old buildings, including the impressive **courthouse** on Montague St. The **Old Goulburn Brewery** (☎ (048) 21 6071), built in 1836, is a large complex down on the river flats. As well as a working brewery, it has accommodation in renovated mews for $35 a person, including breakfast. There's plenty of other accommodation in town, in pubs, motels and caravan parks.

Yass (pop 4575)

Yass is closely connected with the early explorer Hume, for whom the highway is named. On Comur St, next to the tourist information centre (☎ (06) 226 2557), the **Hamilton Hume Museum** has exhibits relating to him. Near Yass at **Wee Jasper** are Carey's Caves (☎ (06) 227 9622), open on weekend afternoons.

Just east of Yass the Barton Highway branches off the Hume for Canberra. Transborder Express (☎ (06) 226 1378) has several daily buses ($10).

Gundagai (pop 2540)

Gundagai, 386 km from Sydney, is one of the more interesting small towns along the Hume. The long wooden **Prince Alfred Bridge** crosses the flood plain of the Murrumbidgee River. It's now closed to traffic, but you can walk across it. In 1852, Gundagai suffered Australia's worst flood disaster when 89 people were drowned.

Gold rushes and bushrangers were part of the town's colourful early history and the notorious Captain Moonlight was tried in the 1859 **courthouse** in Sheridan St.

The tourist information centre (☎ (069) 44 1341) is open daily on Sheridan St. The building also houses the **Marble Masterpiece**, a 20,000-piece cathedral model. Is it art? Is it lunacy? Is it worth the $1 entry fee? Probably. You at least get to hear a snatch of the tune, *Along the Road to Gundagai*. Other places of interest include the **museum** on Homer St, and the **Gabriel Gallery** of historic photos on Sheridan St.

Places to Stay The *Gundagai River Caravan Park* (☎ (069) 44 1702) is near the

---

Dog on the Tuckerbox

Gundagai features in a number of famous songs, including *Along the Road to Gundagai*, *My Mabel Waits for Me* and *When a Boy from Alabama Meets a Girl from Gundagai*. There, eight km east of town just off the highway is the Dog on the Tuckerbox memorial, a sculpture of the dog who in a 19th-century bush ballad 'sat on the tuckerbox, five miles from Gundagai', and refused to help while its owner's bullock team was bogged in the creek. A popular tale has it that the dog was even less helpful, because in the original version it apparently shat on the tuckerbox. ∎

NEW SOUTH WALES

southern end of the Prince Alfred Bridge, with tent sites from $10. In town, the *Gundagai Caravan Village* (☎ (069) 44 4057) has sites for $15 and on-site vans for $29. The *Criterion Hotel* (☎ (069) 44 1048) and the *Royal Hotel* (☎ (069) 44 1024), both on Sheridan St, have accommodation.

Holbrook (pop 1420)

Holbrook is the halfway point between Sydney and Melbourne, and was known as Germanton until WW I, during which it was renamed after a British war hero. There's a replica of the submarine in which he won a Victoria Cross, in Holbrook Park. The large **Woolpack Inn Museum** (admission $3) has tourist information.

ALBURY (pop 43,200)

Albury is on the Murray River just below the Hume Weir and across the river from the large town of Wodonga, in Victoria. It is a good base for trips and activities in a variety of terrain: the snowfields and High Country of both Victoria and New South Wales, the vineyards around Rutherglen (Victoria), and the tempestuous upper Murray River, which becomes languid below Albury as it starts its journey to South Australia and the sea. It's also a good place to break the journey between Sydney and Melbourne.

Information

The large Gateway Information Centre (☎ (060) 41 3875), with information on both New South Wales and Victoria, is on the highway in Wodonga.

Things to See & Do

In summer there's river swimming from **Noreuil Park** and you can take river cruises on the paddle-steamer *Cumberoona* from $8 (children $4.50). Also in the park is a tree marked by explorer William Hovell when he crossed the Murray on his 1824 expedition with Hume from Sydney to Port Phillip, in Victoria. Charles Sturt departed for his 1838 exploration of the banks of the Murray from here. Murray River Lodge has canoe trips

from around $20 and you don't have to stay there to join in.

The **Ettamogah Wildlife Sanctuary**, 11 km north on the highway and open daily ($5), has a collection of Aussie fauna, most of which arrived sick or injured, so this is a genuine sanctuary. A few km north the grotesque **Ettamogah Pub** looms up near the highway – a real-life re-creation of a famous Aussie cartoon pub and proof that life (of a sort) follows art not vice versa.

The good **Jindera Pioneer Museum** is 16 km north-west of Albury in the town of Jindera and is open daily except Monday ($5, $1 students). Jindera is in an area known as **Morgan Country** because of its association with Mad Dog Morgan. Other pleasant little towns in this area include **Culcairn**, west of Holbrook, where the wonderful *Culcairn Hotel* (☎ (060) 29 8501) has singles/doubles for $30/40.

Places to Stay

The *Albury Central Caravan Park* (☎ (060) 21 8420) is a couple of km north of the centre on North St and has tent sites from $10 and cabins from $30.

The *Murray River Lodge* (☎ (060) 41 1822, 1800 644 459) has dorm beds at $13 and a double room for $32. It's on the corner of David and Smollett Sts. The staff will help you get involved in adventure activities or find a farm where you can work for your board. You can hire bikes here too.

There is a great YHA hostel at the *Albury Motor Village* (☎ (060) 25 3219) on Wagga Rd (the highway) five km from the centre of town. Dorm beds are $14 per person.

Most of the pubs have beds. Try *Soden's* (☎ (060) 21 2400) or the *Termo* (☎ (060) 41 3544), both around $25 per person in basic rooms with shared facilities.

Places to Eat

There are some good places on Dean St west of Kiewa St. *Pappadums* is good for Indian, while *Bazaar*, over the road, has eclectic international cuisine. *Cafe Gryphon* does a good coffee and serves light meals until late. Down the other end of Dean St near the

NEW SOUTH WALES

highway, the *Lone Star Cantina* has hearty snacks under $10. *Matilda's Family Steakhouse* on the corner of David and Hume Sts has all-you-can-eat specials from $8.50 (lunch) and $11.00 (dinner).

Getting There & Away
Kendell Airlines has four flights daily between Albury and Sydney.

The nightly Sydney to Melbourne XPT stops here. If you're travelling between the two capital cities it's much cheaper to stop over in Albury on a through ticket than to buy two separate tickets. The same applies to bus tickets. Buses stop at Vienna World (a service station/diner) on the highway on the corner of Hovell St, across from Noreuil Park. Pyles Coaches (☎ (057) 57 2024) runs to the Victoria's High Country. V/Line runs to Mildura along the Murray.

WAGGA WAGGA (pop 55,000)
Wagga Wagga, on the Murrumbidgee River, is the state's largest inland city. Despite its size, the city retains a relaxed country town feel. The name is pronounced 'wogga' and is usually abbreviated to one word (although there's a literary group called Wagga Wagga Writers Writers).

The long main street is Baylis St which runs north from the railway station, becoming Fitzmaurice St at the northern end. Pick up a driving tour map from the information centre (☎ (069) 23 5402) on Tarcutta St. The excellent **Botanic Gardens** are about 1.5 km south of the railway station. In the gardens is a small zoo with a free-flight aviary of native birds.

The **Murray Cod Hatcheries** (☎ (069) 22 7360) are on the Sturt Highway eight km east of Wagga, just past the small town of **Gumly Gumly**. Here you can see Big Murray (a huge old cod) and a wide range of native animals. It's open daily and admission is $5.

On the Olympic Way, about 40 km north of Wagga, the small town of **Junee** has some historic buildings, including the lovely Monte Cristo Homestead and some splendid pubs. Glass Buslines runs a local service

from Wagga to Junee on weekdays and picks up along Baylis St.

Places to Stay
The *Tourist Caravan Park* (☎ (069) 21 2540) is on the river right next to the swimming beach and a couple of blocks from the town centre. Tent sites are $10, on-site vans are $30 and cabins are $44.

Several pubs have accommodation, including *Romano's Hotel* (☎ (069) 21 2013) on Fitzmaurice St, with good rooms for $30/38, some with attached bathrooms ($65). The *Manor* (☎ (069) 21 5962) is a small, well-restored guesthouse across from the Memorial Gardens on Morrow St, near Baylis St. Singles/doubles range from $35/60 to $70/100 per person, including breakfast. There are plenty of motels, but none of them are cheap.

Places to Eat
Fitzmaurice/Baylis St has a surprisingly diverse range of places to eat. At the top of Fitzmaurice St, the *Kebab Place* is an authentic Lebanese takeaway and restaurant. The *Family Eating House*, in the Huthwaite Centre on Baylis St, offers all-you-can-eat for $8.30 at lunch and $9.30 at dinner. The nearby *Saigon Restaurant* has lunch specials for $4. The plush *Wagga Thai Restaurant* in the Baylis Centre is open in the evenings only. If you don't feel like going anywhere *Pizza Haven* (☎ 13 1241), also on Baylis St, will deliver free.

Getting There & Away
Kendell has flights to Melbourne ($147) and Sydney, and Hazelton flies to Sydney ($170). Ansett (☎ 13 1300) handles bookings for both.

Countrylink buses leave from the railway station but other long-distance services leave from the terminal on Gurwood St, off Fitzmaurice St. You can make bookings here. Wagga is on the railway line between Sydney ($59.40) and Melbourne ($50.80).

NARRANDERA (pop 5180)
Near the junction of the Newell and Sturt

ighways, Narrandera is in the Murrumbidgee Irrigation Area (MIA). The information centre (☎ (069) 59 1766) in Narandera Park has a walking tour map.

Lake Talbot is an excellent water sports reserve, partly a long artificial lake and partly a big swimming complex. Bush (including a koala regeneration area) surrounds the lake and walking trails meander by.

The **John Lake Centre** at the Inland Fisheries Research Station has guided tours (during which you can see a huge Murray cod) on weekdays at 10.30 am ($5); the entre is also open for casual inspection from ? am to 4 pm. Turn off the Sturt Highway our km south-east of Narrandera.

South of Narrandera on the Newell Highway is **Jerilderie**, immortalised by the bushranger Ned Kelly who held up the whole own for two days in 1879. Kelly relics can be seen in the **Telegraph Office Museum** on Powell St.

Places to Stay & Eat

The *Lake Talbot Caravan Park* (☎ (069) 59 302), some way from the town centre at the eastern end of Larmer St, overlooks the Lake Talbot complex. Tent sites are $10, on-site vans cost from $25 and self-contained units re from $35.

The *Star Lodge* (☎ (069) 59 1768), across rom the railway station on Ferrier St (the Newell Highway), has singles/doubles for $25/40. There are kitchen facilities.

Getting There & Away

Greyhound Pioneer has buses to Sydney for 42, stopping at the old railway station.

GRIFFITH (pop 15,000)

Griffith was planned by Walter Burley Griffin, the American architect who designed Canberra. The information centre ☎ (069) 62 4145) is on the corner of Banna Ave (the long main street) and Jondaryan Ave; out the front a Fairy Firefly plane perches on a pole. Ask about taking a school bus for a weekday tour of the district ($1).

High on a hill to the north-east of the town

centre, **Pioneer Park** is a re-creation of an early Riverina village and is worth seeing. It's open daily ($5).

Descendants of the Italian farmers who helped to develop this area make up a large proportion of the population. Although the Hunter Valley is the best-known wine producing area in New South Wales, the Griffith area produces 80% of the state's wine. You can visit eight **wineries** – the information centre has a map.

Fruit-Picking

Many people come to Griffith looking for fruit-picking work. The grape harvest usually begins around mid-February and lasts six to eight weeks, while the citrus harvest begins in November and runs through to March. Few vineyards and almost none of the other farms have accommodation, or even space to camp, so you'll need your own transport. The CES (☎ (069) 69 1100) on Yambil St can help you find work.

Places to Stay

The small *Tourist Caravan Park* (☎ (069) 64 2144) on Willandra Ave, not far from the bus stop, has tent sites from $10, en suite vans for $36 and units from $50. There's a basic camping area at the showgrounds, south of the circular western end of the city centre, which has sites for $5 ($30 per week).

Pioneer Park (☎ (069) 62 4196) has shared accommodation in the old shearers' quarters for $8.50. The rooms are small and basic but there's a good kitchen and lounge. The problem with staying here is that it's a long, steep walk from the city centre and there's no public transport. It's often full at harvest time. The *Area Hotel* (☎ (069) 62 1322) on Banna Ave has rooms for $30/35, including a continental breakfast.

Places to Eat

Italian food is the region's dominant cuisine. For good coffee and cake or pasta (from $5), try *Pasticceria Bassano* at the western end of Banna Ave. It's also open daily for breakfast. A few doors away and down some steps,

NEW SOUTH WALES

the Vico family's *La Scala* is open for dinner Tuesday to Saturday.

Not far away and on the other side of Banna Ave, the *Belvedere Restaurant* has more of a cafe atmosphere and it's also a busy takeaway pizzeria. For pizzas cooked in a wood-fired oven, head out to *La Villa Bianca* at 40 Mackay Ave.

Getting There & Away

Hazelton (☎ (069) 62 6877) flies between Griffith and Sydney daily for $208.

Buses stop at the Griffith Travel & Transit Centre (☎ (069) 62 7199), in Donald's Country Restaurant on Jondaryan Ave. Greyhound Pioneer runs to Canberra ($37), Sydney ($48), Melbourne ($59) and Adelaide ($90). MIA Intercity Coaches (☎ (069) 62 3419) also runs to Melbourne three times a week.

AROUND GRIFFITH

West of Griffith, the last hills of the Great Dividing Range give way to endless plains.

Cocoparra National Park

Cocoparra, just east of Griffith, is not a large park but its hills and gullies provide some contrasts and there is a fair amount of wildlife. The camping area is on Woolshed Flat in the north of the park, not far from Woolshed Falls. Bring your own water. Bush camping is permitted away from the roads. Park entry is $7.50 and camping costs $5.

Leeton (pop 7110)

Leeton is the MIA's oldest town (1913). Like Griffith, Leeton was designed by Walter Burley Griffin and it remains close to the architect's original vision because of restrictions on development.

The visitor centre (☎ (069) 53 2832) is next to the shire offices on Chelmsford Place. Ask here about tours of the rice mill and other food-processing plants. Lillypilly Estate and Toorak Wines are two **wineries** near Leeton, open Monday to Saturday for tastings and for tours on weekdays – 11.30 am at Toorak and 4 pm at Lillypilly.

Willandra National Park

Willandra, on the plains 160 km north-west of Griffith as the crow flies, has been carved from a huge sheep station on a system of lakes, usually dry. The World Heritage listed park's 20,000 hectares represent less than 10% of the area covered by Big Willandra station in its 1870s heyday. The partially restored homestead (1918) was the third to be built on the station.

There are several short walking tracks in the park and the Merton Motor Trail does a loop around the eastern half. The western half has no vehicular access but you can walk here if you are very sure of what you're doing.

There's a camp site ($4) near the homestead and with permission you can bush camp. Shared accommodation in the 'men's quarters' costs $8.

The main access is off the Hillston to Mossgiel road, 40-odd km west of Hillston. It takes very little rain to close roads around here, so phone the NPWS office at Griffith (☎ (069) 67 8159) to check conditions before setting out.

HAY (pop 3050)

In flat, treeless country, Hay is at the junction of the Sturt and Cobb highways and is a substantial town for this part of the world. The information centre (☎ (069) 93 4045) is on Moppett St, just off the main street. There are some fine swimming spots along the Murrumbidgee River, and interesting old buildings like the **Hay Gaol Museum** and **Bishops Lodge**, a corrugated-iron mansion.

Most of the pubs have accommodation but it's not cheap. The *Hay Motel* (☎ (069) 93 1804) has singles/doubles for $38/44 and the *New Crown Hotel/Motel* (☎ (069) 93 1600) charges $35/45. There are several caravan parks. The *Bidgee Beach Primitive Camping Area* (☎ (069) 93 1180), off the Sturt Highway 11 km east of Hay, is a simple camping area on the banks of the Murrumbidgee. Tent sites are $10.

DENILIQUIN (pop 8300)

Deniliquin is an attractive, bustling country

own on a wide bend in the Edward River. Before European settlement, this area was the most densely populated part of Australia.

The information centre (☎ (058) 81 2878) is inside the **Peppin Heritage Centre** building on George St. The heritage centre covers the history of wool-growing in the area; merino sheep breeds developed around here have long been the mainstay of Australia's wool industry. It's open weekdays from 9 am to 4 pm, and weekends from 11 am to 2 pm. Admission is $3. The visitor centre at the **Sun Rice Mill**, the largest rice mill in the southern hemisphere, is open on weekdays from 9 am to noon and 2 to 4 pm. The **Island Sanctuary** has pleasant walks among the river red gums and lots of animals, including a very greedy emu.

You can hire canoes and other boats at Masons' Paringa Caravan & Tourist Park (☎ (058) 81 1131) for about $20 per day.

Places to Stay
There are several caravan parks, such as *McLeans Beach Caravan Park* (☎ (058) 81 2448) by a good river beach at the north-eastern end of Charlotte St. It has a swimming beach. Tent sites are $10, on-site vans are $22 and cabins are $40. The basic but clean *Deniliquin Youth Hostel* (☎ (058) 81 5025) is on the corner of Wood and Macauley Sts about a km south-west of the town centre. YHA members (only) can stay here for $7 a night.

All the hotels have accommodation. The *Globe* (☎ (058) 81 2030) is good value, with rooms at $18 per person, including a cooked breakfast. The *Federal Hotel* (☎ (058) 81 1260) on the corner of Cressy and Napier Sts has rooms for $25/38 with breakfast.

There are plenty of motels. Trucks roll through town all night, so choose one off the highway, such as the *Wendburn Riverside* (☎ (058) 81 2311) at the north-eastern end of Charlotte St. Doubles are $65.

Getting There & Away
Hazelton (☎ 13 1713) has a daily service to Sydney ($304) via Wagga, and Eastern (☎ 13 1313) flies to Canberra ($146).

Long-distances buses stop at the Bus Stop Cafe on Whitelock St. Countrylink runs to Wagga, from where trains run to Sydney and Melbourne. McCafferty's stops here on the run between Melbourne ($27) and Brisbane ($113). Victoria's V/Line (☎ 13 2232) also runs to Melbourne.

ALONG THE MURRAY
Most of the major river towns are on the Victorian side – see the Victoria chapter for more on the river. It's no problem to hop back and forth across the river as in many places roads run along both sides.

The Murray was once an important means of communication, with paddle-steamers splashing upstream and downstream – an antipodean Mississippi. The largest New South Wales town on the river is Albury (see earlier in this section). Downstream from here is **Corowa**, a wine-producing centre – the Lindemans winery has been here since 1860. **Tocumwal** on the Newell Highway is a quiet riverside town with sandy river beaches and a giant fibreglass Murray Cod in the town square. The nearby airport is a gliding centre.

The old river port of **Wentworth** lies at the confluence of the Murray and Darling rivers. The riverboat *Loyalty* (☎ (050) 27 3330) has two-hour cruises to the confluence every day except Saturday, leaving the Wentworth Ex-Services Club at 1.45 pm. The fare is $12. You can see local history in the **Old Gaol** ($3.50) and across the road in the **Pioneer Museum** ($2.50). The **Perry Dunes** are large orange sand dunes six km out of town, off the road to Broken Hill.

Central West

The central west starts inland from the Blue Mountains and continues for about 400 km, gradually fading from rolling agricultural land into the harsh far west. This region has some of the earliest inland towns in Australia. From Sydney, Bathurst is the gateway to the region, and from here you can turn north-west through Orange and Dubbo or south-west through Cowra and West Wyalong.

The Olympic Way, running from Bathurst through Cowra and Wagga to Albury, is an alternative Sydney-Melbourne route. The Newell Highway, the most direct route between Melbourne and Brisbane, also passes through the central west. On long weekends accommodation all along the Newell is booked out.

Getting There & Away

Air The central west is well served by airlines. From Dubbo ($169 from Sydney with Eastern Australia or Hazelton) there are flights to other locations in the centre and far west of the state.

Bus Major lines have services through the region on routes between Sydney and Broken Hill or Adelaide, and from Brisbane to Melbourne or Adelaide. Local companies include Rendell's Coaches (☎ 1800 023 328). Sid Fogg's (☎ 1800 045 952) runs from Newcastle as far as Dubbo ($46).

Train Direct trains run from Sydney to Lithgow ($19.40), Bathurst ($28.20), Orange ($37.80) and Dubbo ($55). There are connecting buses from Lithgow station to Cowra ($40 from Sydney), Forbes ($46) and Mudgee ($35.60).

LITHGOW (pop 20,500)

Lithgow is an industrial town on the western fringe of the Blue Mountains. The Greater Lithgow visitor centre (☎ (063) 53 1859) is on the edge of town in the Old Bowenfels Station, 1 Cooerwull Rd, on the Great Western Highway. Some tourist information is also available at 285 Main St.

The gracious home, **Eskbank House** (☎ (063) 51 3557), is on Bennett St. It was built in 1841 and now houses a museum. It's open Thursday to Monday between 10 am and 4 pm; admission is $2. There are fine views from **Hassan Walls Lookout**, five km south of town. A short drive from Lithgow via Inch and Atkinson Sts brings you to the

Newnes Plateau. There's a five-km walk from here to a disused railway tunnel, now full of glow-worms.

See the Blue Mountains section earlier in this chapter for information on the nearby Zig Zag Railway and the town of Hartley. **Newnes**, about 50 km north of Lithgow, on the edge of the Wollemi National Park, is a ghost town where the pub still functions.

Bent Backs Backpackers (☎ (063) 51 1685), 45 Roy St, has dorms for $15 ($12 if you have a sleeping bag) and doubles for $25. The *Grand Central Hotel* (☎ (063) 51 3050), 69 Main St, has singles for $18.

There are frequent trains between Lithgow and Sydney ($14).

BATHURST (pop 26,420)

Bathurst is Australia's oldest inland city and it was laid out to a grand scale. The streetscape is relatively intact and there are some impressive Victorian-era buildings, such as the 1880 **courthouse** on Russell St, which houses the **historical museum** ($1). The information centre (☎ (063) 32 1444) is on William St.

South-west of the city centre is the 6.2-km **Mt Panorama motor racing circuit**. It's the venue for one of Australia's best-known races, the Tooheys 1000 Touring Car Race, a 1000-km race for production cars held in October. You can drive around the circuit (it's a public road) and there's a small **motor racing museum** ($4) at Murray's Corner. Also on Mt Panorama are the **Sir Joseph Banks Nature Park** ($5), with a koala and other animals, and the **Bathurst Gold Diggings**, a reconstruction of a gold-mining town which is open daily except Saturday. Admission is $6, or $10 for a tour.

Eight km out of town is **Abercrombie House**, a huge Gothic mansion built in the 1870s. Ask about open days at the information centre.

Places to Stay & Eat

There are some good pub rooms at the hotels. The cheapest rooms are at the *Railway Hotel* (☎ (063) 31 2964) on Havana St, where singles/doubles are $20/35 with breakfast.

he *Edinboro Castle Hotel* (☎ (063) 31
020), in William St, has rooms for $25/40.
or pizza from a wood-fired oven or large
ervings of pasta (from $7), try *Uncle Joe's
izza*, opposite the post office on Howick St.
eigler's Cafe on Keppel St has an interest-
ng modern menu and is not too expensive.

ROUND BATHURST

he **Abercrombie Caves** are 72 km south
f Bathurst. There are several guided tours
ach day.

There are some interesting old buildings
t **Sofala**, 37 km north of Bathurst. The
scinating old mining town of **Hill End** is 72
m north-west of Bathurst. It was the scene
f a gold rush in the 1870s and is classified
s a historic site. The visitor centre (☎ (063)
7 8206) is in the old hospital, which also
ouses the **museum** ($2). There are three
PWS camping areas. *The Village* and *Glen-
ora* have facilities and charge $10. *The
rough* is more basic and charges $5. The
oyal Hotel (☎ (063) 37 8261) has
ingles/doubles for $38/60 with breakfast.
he only bus service to Hill End is the Friday
us from Bathurst ($4) at 3.30 pm.

Rockley, 34 km south of Bathurst, is
nother classified historic town. North-east
f Bathurst is **Rylstone**, where there are
andstone buildings and Aboriginal rock
aintings just outside the town (ask at the
hire council).

MUDGEE & AROUND
Mudgee (pop 7620)
Mudgee, about 120 km north of both
ithgow and Bathurst, is a fine example of
n old country town and is a pleasant place
 stay. The information centre (☎ (063) 72
875) is on Market St, near the old police
tation.

Vineries There are many young wineries
un by enthusiastic people, and if you find
he Hunter Valley too commercial, you'll
njoy visiting them. Craigmoor can hardly
e called a newcomer. It has produced a
intage annually since 1858, making it the
econd-oldest continually operating winery

in Australia. Most of the area's 20 wineries
are open daily. In September there's a wine
festival. Despite all the vineyards there isn't
much harvest work available as most is done
by locals.

Places to Stay & Eat Accommodation tends
to fill up on weekends, and several hotels
have above-average pub accommodation.
The *Woolpack Hotel* (☎ (063) 72 1908) on
Market St charges $20/30 for singles/
doubles, while the *Federal Hotel* (☎ (063)
72 2150), on Inglis St near the railway
station, charges $17/32 ($20/36 on weekends).

Near the wineries to the north of town,
Hithergreen Lodge (☎ (063) 72 1022) has
motel units for $50/60. A taxi out here costs
around $6, otherwise it's a pleasant walk of
about five km.

The best place for a coffee or snack is the
The Tramp, through an archway on Market
St near the corner of Church St. Nearby in
the Woolpack Hotel, *Jumbucks* serves good,
standard food (around $10) and local wines.

Getting There & Away Hazelton flies
between Mudgee and Sydney ($150). Coun-
trylink runs from Sydney ($35.60) via
Lithgow; between Mudgee and Gulgong
(see below) the fare is $2. There's also a daily
bus to Bathurst.

Gulgong
Gulgong, 30 km north-west of Mudgee, is an
old gold town once described as 'the hub of
the world'. It was the boyhood home of
author Henry Lawson and the **Henry
Lawson Centre** on Mayne St houses a big
collection of 'Lawsonia', open daily from 10
am to noon ($1).

The information centre (☎ (063) 74 1202)
is in the shire chambers. The huge **Gulgong
Pioneer Museum** on Herbert St is one of the
best country town museums in the state ($4).

Places to Stay The *Centennial Hotel*
(☎ (063) 74 1241) on Mayne St has
singles/doubles with bathroom for $25/35.
The *Heritage Centre* on Red Hill is a field

study centre with a dorm for groups. The information centre can tell you if there's room for individuals. A bed costs $6 (no linen).

Other Towns

At **Nagundie**, 11 km north of Mudgee, there's a rock which is said to hold water year round – it's an old Aboriginal water hole and you can camp there. Farther east, en route to the Goulburn River National Park and the Hunter Valley, **Merriwa** has a number of historic buildings, as has nearby **Cassilis**.

ORANGE (pop 30,500)

This important fruit-growing centre does not grow oranges! Rather, it was named after William of Orange. Pioneer poet Banjo Paterson (who wrote the words of *Waltzing Matilda*) was born here, and the foundations of his birthplace are in Banjo Paterson Park. Orange was considered as a site for the Federal capital before Canberra was eventually selected.

The visitor centre (☎ (063) 61 5226) is on Byng St. The **museum** on McNamara St includes a 300-year-old tree carved with Aboriginal designs. The autumn apple-picking season lasts for about six weeks; contact the CES (☎ (063) 91 2700) on Anson St.

Australia's first real gold rush took place at **Ophir**, 27 km north of Orange. The area is now a nature reserve and it's still popular with fossickers – you can buy a licence and hire a gold pan from the Orange visitor centre. **Mt Canobolas** (1395 metres) is a steep, extinct volcano 20 km south-west of Orange. You can drive to the top or there are a couple of walking tracks.

Places to Stay & Eat

The council's *Colour City Showground Caravan Park* (☎ (063) 62 7254), on Margaret St about two km north-east of the city centre, has tent sites for $7.50, on-site vans for $25 and self-contained units for $40.

The *Hotel Canobolas* (☎ (063) 62 2444), on Summer St at the corner of Lords Place, was once the largest hotel outside Sydney.

Most rooms have bathrooms, steam heat, T and a fridge, and cost $36/57. Rooms wi shared bathrooms are $26/42.

Matilda's Family Steakhouse at the corn of Bathurst Rd and McLachlan St, a fe blocks east of the railway line, has $8 a you-can-eat lunch specials.

Getting There & Away

Rendell's Coaches (☎ 1800 023 328) run Dubbo ($30) and Sydney ($30) dail There's also a service to Canberra ($35 Selwood's Coaches (☎ (063) 62 7963) als run to Sydney daily.

DUBBO (pop 32,520)

North of Orange and 420 km from Sydne Dubbo is a large agricultural town su rounded by sheep and cattle country. Th information centre (☎ (068) 84 1422) is the top end of Macquarie St, the main sho ping street, at the corner of Erskine St. Yo can hire geared bikes for $10 a day at Whee ers (☎ (068) 82 9899) on the corner Darling and Bultje Sts. The YHA hostel hir bikes to guests for $6 a day.

Things to See & Do

The **Old Dubbo Gaol** ($3) on Macquarie S has 'animatronic' characters telling the stor of prison life. Also on Macquarie St is th **museum** ($3).

Five km south-west of town, the **Wester Plains Zoo** (☎ (068) 82 5888) is the large open-range zoo in Australia. The Beng tigers and Asiatic lions alone are worth th price of admission. The zoo's rare black rh noceroses were flown in from Zimbabwe a part of an international programme designe to save these magnificent beasts from extinc tion. You're better off walking around th six-km circuit or hiring a bike ($8 for half day) than joining the crawling line of car The zoo is open daily from 9 am to 5 pm, an admission is $14.50.

The slab homestead **Dundullimal** wa built by a wealthy grazier in the 1830s. It two km beyond the zoo and is open dail ($3).

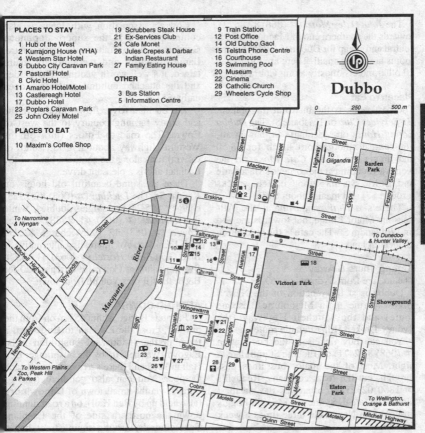

PLACES TO STAY

1 Hub of the West
2 Kurrajong House (YHA)
4 Western Star Hotel
6 Dubbo City Caravan Park
7 Pastoral Hotel
8 Civic Hotel
11 Amaroo Hotel/Motel
13 Castlereagh Hotel
17 Dubbo Hotel
23 Poplars Caravan Park
25 John Oxley Motel

PLACES TO EAT

10 Maxim's Coffee Shop

19 Scrubbers Steak House
21 Ex-Services Club
24 Cafe Monet
26 Jules Crepes & Darbar Indian Restaurant
27 Family Eating House

OTHER

3 Bus Station
5 Information Centre

9 Train Station
12 Post Office
14 Old Dubbo Gaol
15 Telstra Phone Centre
16 Courthouse
18 Swimming Pool
20 Museum
22 Cinema
28 Catholic Church
29 Wheelers Cycle Shop

Dubbo

Places to Stay

The closest caravan park to the town centre is the small *Poplars* (☎ (068) 82 4067), near the river at the western end of Bultje St. *Dubbo City* (☎ (068) 82 4820) is also on the river, but on the western bank and a fair distance by road from the centre.

Kurrajong House (☎ (068) 82 0922) is a pleasant YHA hostel at 87 Brisbane St, north of the railway line. From the bus station head west on Erskine St. Dorm beds are $13 and there are a few twin rooms. Guests get 20% off zoo tickets and the hostel can often arrange a lift out there, or you can hire a bike

and ride ($6 a day). The hostel also organises trips to the huge Dubbo stockyards on sale days – an interesting insight into rural life.

A couple of doors away is the *Hub of the West* (☎ (068) 82 5004), a basic guesthouse where rooms with common bathroom cost from $20/40, plus $5 for linen. Several pubs have accommodation, such as the good *Castlereagh Hotel* (☎ (068) 82 4877) on the corner of Talbragar and Brisbane Sts, which has singles/doubles from $30/50, including a big cooked breakfast. Also good is the *Western Star* (☎ (068) 82 4644) on Erskine St.

The *John Oxley Motel* (☎ (068) 82 4622), towards the southern end of Macquarie St, is central and cheap for Dubbo ($40/45) but the rooms are pretty small. There are more than 20 other motels, mostly along Cobra St.

Places to Eat

The best value is the bistro at the opulent *Ex-Services Club* on Brisbane St. The *Dubbo Eating House* on Macquarie St, has an all-you-can-eat smorgasbord lunch for $8.50 and dinner for $9.50. *Cafe Monet* in the Kemwah building at the corner of Macquarie and Bultje Sts has good coffee, snacks (around $7) and meals (about $15).

There's a *Thai restaurant* at the All-Seasons Motor Lodge, out towards the zoo on Whylandra St. The cafe at the bus station is open 24 hours.

Getting There & Away

The air fare from Sydney is $169.

Dubbo is at the junction of the Newell Highway (the main Melbourne-Brisbane route) and the Mitchell Highway (the Sydney-Broken Hill/Adelaide route).

You can buy tickets at the bus station (☎ (068) 84 2411) on Erskine St until late at night. Most of the major bus lines pass through, but the local company, Rendell's (☎ 1800 023 328), often has the cheapest fares. The fare to Sydney is $45. Sid Fogg's buses run to Newcastle three times a week for $46.

COWRA (pop 8640)

Cowra is a large country town in the fertile Lachlan Valley. The information centre (☎ (063) 42 4333) is on the highway across the bridge from the shopping centre.

It's best known as the scene of a mass break-out by Japanese prisoners of war during WW II. Nearly 250 prisoners died in the failed 1944 attempt, many by suicide. The strange tale of this impossible escape attempt is told in a book and film, both titled *Die Like the Carp*. Australian and Japanese war cemeteries are five km south of the town and a memorial, two km south-east of the cemeteries, marks the site of the break-out.

Cowra's association with Japan is also commemorated in the superb **Japanese Garden** on the hill above the town centre. Large, beautiful and meticulously maintained, it's well worth visiting. The garden and the attached cultural centre are open daily ($5).

The Lachlan River flows through fertile and pretty farming country to the west of Cowra. The road to Forbes (turn off the Western Highway about five km south of Cowra) runs along the southern bank of the Lachlan and is a pleasant drive.

There are some beautiful old hotels on Kendal St. The *Lachlan* (☎ (063) 42 2355) charges $15/25 for singles/doubles, while the *Imperial* (☎ (063) 41 2588) and the *Cowra* (☎ (063) 42 1925) charge $20/30 with breakfast. An interesting alternative is *Blue Gum Farm Hostel* (☎ (063) 41 1352), five km south of Cowra. It charges $20 for B&B; they'll pick you up from town.

AROUND COWRA

At Paynters Bridge, about 45 km on from the turn-off, cross the Lachlan to **Eugowra**, a town in the shadow of bush-clad hills. Eugowra was held up by the bushranger Ben Hall in 1863 and there's a re-enactment each October. You can also get here (and to Forbes) via the small town of **Canowindra** (also held up by Ben Hall), on a road running down the northern side of the Lachlan. Canowindra's curving main street has a number of old buildings and art and craft shops. The town is a centre for ballooning, organised by companies such as Balloon Aloft (☎ (063) 44 1797), which charges $160 for flight and champagne, or $185 with B&B thrown in. There's good accommodation in town at *Poppies & Galah Guesthouse* (☎ (063) 44 1009) in the main street. It charges $35 per person with breakfast.

FORBES (pop 9000)

Forbes is an oddly atmospheric place to wander round. It has wide streets and a number of grand 19th-century buildings reflecting the wealth of its 1860s gold rush. Ben Hall is buried in the town's cemetery –

is death is lamented in a bitter folk song, *he Streets of Forbes*.

The information centre (☎ (068) 52 4155) s in the old railway station, north of the town entre. The **museum**, on Cross St, has Ben Iall relics and other memorabilia and is open aily from 3 to 5 pm (2 to 4 pm in winter). One km south of the centre is the **Lachlan 'intage Village**, a re-creation of a 19th-entury village, open daily.

The old *Vandenberg Hotel* (☎ (068) 52 015) on picturesque Spring St has rooms for 16.50/26 with breakfast. There are other ubs, several caravan parks and plenty of notels.

North-West

'rom Dubbo, roads radiate to various parts f the state. The Newell Highway runs north-ast and is the quickest route between Melbourne and Brisbane. The Castlereagh Highway, forking off the Newell 66 km from Dubbo at Gilgandra, runs north into the ugged opal country towards the Queensland order (its surfaced section ends soon after Lightning Ridge).

The Mitchell Highway heads north-west o Bourke and Queensland via Nyngan. At Nyngan the Barrier Highway forks off west o Broken Hill.

Getting There & Away

Eastern Australia and Ansett fly to several of he main towns. Those on the Newell Highway are served by buses travelling to nd from Brisbane, en route to Melbourne or Adelaide. Countrylink trains and/or buses onnect most other towns in the area with ydney. Fares from Sydney include Gunnedah $55, Coonabarabran $59.40 and Lightning Ridge $75.60.

NEWELL HIGHWAY

Gilgandra is a junction town where the Newell and Castlereagh highways divide, nd a road also cuts across to the Mitchell. It as a small **observatory** with an audiovisual of the moon landing and other space flights, plus a historical display.

Coonabarabran (population 3050) is an access point for the spectacular granite domes and spires of the rugged **Warrumbungle National Park**, which offers great walking and rock climbing (permit required). There is a NPWS visitor centre (☎ (068) 25 4364) at the entrance to the park, about 35 km west of Coonabarabran. Entry costs $7.50 per car. Camping costs $10 for two people on-site. There's also a NPWS office in Coonabarabran (☎ (068) 42 1311).

The largest optical telescope in the southern hemisphere is at **Siding Spring**, on the edge of the national park. There's a visitor centre, open daily from 9.30 am to 4.30 pm. It costs $6 to see the universe display and various hands-on exhibits. If you want to spend $7.50 to look through a telescope, the Skywatch Observatory (☎ (068) 42 2506), on Timor Rd two km from Coonabarabran, is open nightly. Phone first for viewing times.

Coonabarabran has several motels and caravan parks but during school holidays they can fill up. The *Imperial Hotel* (☎ (068) 42 1023) has singles/doubles for $20/28, or $32/45 with bathroom. There's an associate-YHA hostel ($13 a night) at the *Warrumbungles Mountain Motel* (☎ (068) 42 1832), nine km out of town on the road to the national park. The *Jolly Cauli* health-food shop on John St serves salads and snacks.

In the country around the national park are a number of places to stay. *Tibuc* (☎ (068) 42 1740, evenings best), an organic farm, sounds the most interesting.

Narrabri (population 7300) is a cotton-growing centre, with the enormous Australia Telescope (actually five linked radio telescope dishes) 25 km west on the Yarrie Lake road. The interesting visitor centre is open daily. **Mt Kaputar National Park**, good for walking, camping and climbing, is 53 km east of Narrabri by a steep, unsealed road. **Moree** is a large town on the Gwydir River with some reputedly therapeutic hot baths ($2.50).

CASTLEREAGH HIGHWAY

On the edge of the Western Plains is **Coonamble**, 98 km north of Gilgandra. West of here are the extensive **Macquarie Marshes** with their prolific birdlife. The road continues north to **Walgett**, in dry country near the Grawin and Glengarry opal fields.

A few km off the highway near the Queensland border, **Lightning Ridge** is a huge opal field and the world's only reliable source of black opals. Despite the emphasis on tourism, with underground opal showrooms etc, Lightning Ridge remains a mining community where any battler could strike it rich. The **Moozeum** is worth a visit. There are motels (none cheap) and a few caravan parks with on-site vans. The *Tram-o-Tel* (☎ (068) 29 0448), has self-contained accommodation in old trams and caravans for $20/30.

MITCHELL HIGHWAY

From Dubbo the Mitchell Highway passes through the citrus-growing centre of **Narromine**. **Warren**, farther north and off the Mitchell on the Oxley Highway, is an access point for the Macquarie Marshes, as is **Nyngan** where the Mitchell and Barrier highways divide. The huge marshes are breeding grounds for ducks, water hens, swans, pelicans, ibis and herons. Nyngan was the scene of fierce resistance by Aboriginal people to early European encroachment. The highway runs arrow-straight for 206 km from Nyngan to Bourke.

Outback

You don't have to travel to central Australia to experience red-soil country, limitless horizons and vast blue skies. The far west of New South Wales is rough, rugged and sparsely populated. It also produces a fair proportion of the state's wealth, particularly from the mines of Broken Hill.

Always seek local advice before travelling on secondary roads west of the Mitchell Highway. You must carry plenty of wate and if you break down *stay with your vehicl*

BOURKE (pop 3560)

The town of Bourke, about 800 km north west of Sydney, is on the edge of the outbac – hence the expression 'back of Bourke' describe anywhere remote. A glance at th map will show just how outback the are beyond Bourke is – the country is flat an featureless as far as the eye can see. Bourk is a surprisingly pretty town and the sur rounding country can be beautiful – the shee space is exhilarating.

Bourke is on the Darling River as well a the Mitchell Highway and it was once major port. Scores of paddle-steamers plie the river and in the 1880s it was possible fo wool to be in London just six weeks afte leaving Bourke – somewhat quicker than sea-mail parcel today! The courthouse has crown on its spire, signifying that its juris diction includes maritime cases.

The information centre (☎ (068) 72 228C is at the railway station on Anson St. Pick u a 'Mud Maps' leaflet detailing drives places like **Mt Gunderbooka**, which ha Aboriginal cave art and vivid wildflowers i spring, and **Mt Oxley**.

Brewarrina (usually known as Bree) is 9 km east of Bourke. You can see **the Fisher ies**, stone fish traps which the Ngemb Aboriginal people used to catch the fish t feed the inter-tribal gatherings they hostec 'Brewarrina' means 'good fishing'. Nearb is the **Aboriginal Cultural Museum**.

Places to Stay

There are several caravan parks along th river, including the *Paddlewheel* (☎ (068) 7 2277) with tent sites at $10, on-site vans ($2 a double) and cabins ($35).

Back o' Bourke Backpackers (☎ (068) 7 3009) is a good hostel on the corner of Oxle and Sturt Sts, close to the town centre an beside an impressive old bank building Beds in two-bed dorms are $15 per perso or $12 if you have your own linen.

The best of Bourke's hotels is the *Ol Royal* (☎ (068) 72 2544) on Mitchell S between Sturt and Richard Sts. It has singles/doubles for $27/40. The *Central* (☎ (068) 72 2151), at the corner of Anson and Richard Sts, charges $25/35.

Outback Accommodation Several stations in the Bourke area (a very large area) offer accommodation. The information centre has details and can make bookings. One of the best is historic *Urisino Station* (☎ (068) 74 7639), a friendly place which welcomes backpackers (and everyone else). Activities include camel treks and canoeing on the Paroo River. You can stay in the homestead ($45 per person or $70 with meals and activities) or in backpacker accommodation in old mud-brick cottages ($20 per person). Urisino is 230 km west of Bourke, beyond Wanaaring. The owners can arrange transport from Bourke on Tuesday and Friday.

Places to Eat

There are several cafes, such as the *Paddleboat Bistro* on Mitchell St. The dining room at the *Old Royal Hotel* is very popular. There is a Chinese restaurant at the Bowling Club and the Ex-Services Club also does meals.

Getting There & Away

Air Link has five flights a week from Dubbo to Bourke ($172), which connect with Hazelton services from Sydney to Dubbo. Lachlan Travel (☎ (068) 72 2092) on Oxley St sells tickets.

Countrylink buses run to Dubbo four times a week and connect with trains to Sydney ($75.60). It *might* be possible to go along on the bi-weekly mail run to Wanaaring and Brewarrina. The post office (☎ (068) 72 2017) can put you in touch with the contractors.

BACK OF BOURKE – CORNER COUNTRY

There's no sealed road west of Bourke in New South Wales. If you cared to drive the 813 km from Bourke to Broken Hill via Wanaaring and Tibooburra it would be mostly on lonely unsealed roads. The far western corner of the state is a semidesert of red plains, heat, dust and flies, but with interesting physical features and prolific wildlife. Running along the border with Queensland is the Dog Fence, patrolled every day by boundary riders who each look after a 40-km section.

Tibooburra

Tiny Tibooburra, the hottest place in the state, is right in the north-western corner and has a number of stone buildings from the 1880s and '90s. The town was once known as The Granites, after the striking granite formations that surround the town. Sturt National Park starts right on the northern edge of town. You can normally reach Tibooburra from Bourke or Broken Hill in a conventional vehicle, except after rain (which is pretty rare!).

The NPWS office (☎ (080) 91 3308), open daily, also acts as an information centre.

Places to Stay & Eat A basic NPWS camp site is two km north of town at *Dead Horse Gully*. The camping fee is $5 for two people, plus the $7.50 park entry fee. You'll need to bring drinking water. In town, the *Granites Caravan Park* (☎ (080) 91 3305) has sites for $10, on-site vans for $24, cabins for $34 and motel units from $40/50.

The two fine old pubs both have rooms. The *Family Hotel* (☎ (080) 91 3314) has singles/doubles for $20/35, while the *Tibooburra Hotel* (☎ (080) 91 3310) – known as 'the Two-Storey' – has rooms from $25/30. Both bars are worth a beer: the Family's has a mural by Clifton Pugh; the Two-Storey's has more than 60 impressively well-worn hats on the wall, left behind when their owners bought new headgear at the pub.

The hotels do good counter meals and have tables outside where you can sit and watch the occasional 4WD pass by.

Sturt National Park

Sturt National Park occupies the very northwestern corner of the state, bordering both South Australia and Queensland. The park has 300 km of drivable tracks, camping areas and walks, particularly on the **Jump Up**

NEW SOUTH WALES

Loop drive and towards the top of **Mt Wood**. It is recommended that you inform the ranger at Tibooburra where you are heading before venturing into the park. Entry to the park is $7.50 per car and camping costs $5 for two people.

At **Camerons Corner** there's a post to mark the place where Queensland, South Australia and New South Wales meet. It's a favourite goal for visitors and a 4WD is not always necessary to get there. In the Queensland corner, the *Corner Store* (☎ (080) 91 3872) is known for its home-made pies, cakes, damper and ice cream. Everybody coming by the Corner stops here and the staff can advise on road conditions. You can also buy fuel here.

Milparinka

Milparinka, once a gold town, now consists of little more than a solitary hotel and some old sandstone buildings. In 1845 members of Charles Sturt's expedition from Adelaide, searching for an inland sea, were forced to camp near here for six months. The temperatures were high, the conditions terrible and their supplies inadequate. About 14 km north-west of the settlement you can see the grave of James Poole, Sturt's second-in-command, who died of scurvy.

BARRIER HIGHWAY

The Barrier Highway is the main route in the state's west – and just about the only sealed road. It heads west from Nyngan, from where it's 594 km to Broken Hill. This provides an alternative route to Adelaide and it's the most direct route between Sydney and Western Australia.

Cobar (pop 5600)

Cobar has a modern and highly productive copper mine but it also has an earlier history as evidenced by its old buildings, like the Great Western Hotel with its endless stretch of iron lacework ornamenting the verandah. Pick up a town tour map at the information centre (☎ (068) 36 2448), which is in the excellent **museum** ($3) at the eastern end of the main street.

Weather balloons are released at 9 am and 3 pm from the meteorological station on the edge of town, off the Louth road.

There are important Aboriginal cave paintings at **Mt Grenfell**, 40 km west of Cobar, then another 32 km north of the highway. You can't camp here.

The *Cobar Caravan Park* (☎ (068) 36 2425) has sites for $9, on-site vans for $24 and cabins from $30. Several pubs have accommodation. The *New Occidental* (☎ (068) 36 2111) charges $15 per person while the *Great Western* (☎ (068) 36 2503) has motel-style singles/doubles for $34/44 including breakfast.

Wilcannia (pop 1100)

Wilcannia is on the Darling River and was a busy port in the days of paddle-steamers. It's a much quieter place today but you can still see buildings from that era, such as the police station. There are a couple of motels costing around $60 a double. The pubs may provide meals but are best avoided unless you are an experienced bar-room brawler.

White Cliffs (pop 150)

About 100 km north-west of Wilcannia is White Cliffs, an opal-mining settlement. For a taste of life in a small outback community it's worth the drive on a dirt road. You can fossick for opals around the old digging (watch out for unfenced shafts) and there are opal showrooms and underground homes (called dug-outs) open for inspection. The

---

Country Race Meetings

Some country horse-race meetings are real occasions – the one at Louth, on the Darling River about 100 km south-west of Bourke, is particularly revered. One year the population of about 50 recorded 29 planes flying in for the day! The Louth races are held on the first Saturday in August, followed by the Enngonia races on the first Saturday in September. ■

general store has a 'mud map' of the area and information.

As you enter White Cliffs you pass the high-tech dishes of the solar energy research station, where emus often graze out the front. Tours of the station are held daily at 2 pm.

Places to Stay & Eat The *White Cliffs Hotel* (☎ (080) 91 6606) has basic rooms, but they have air-con and are good value at $20/30 for singles/doubles. A big cooked breakfast costs $8. Across the road from the post office is a small camping area (☎ (080) 91 6627) where sites cost just $2 per person and showers are $1. There's also a swimming pool.

PJ's Underground (☎ (080) 91 6626), 1.5 km east of the post office on Turley's Hill, has doubles with breakfast for $55. Up on Smiths Hill is the *White Cliffs Underground Motel* (☎ 1800 021 154). It's surprisingly roomy and the temperature is a constant 22°C, whether there's a heatwave or a frost on the surface. Singles/doubles cost $35/70 and triples $89. There is also an up-market licensed restaurant.

The *Golf Club*, near the solar station, has Sunday roast lunches for $5.

Mootwingee National Park
This park in the Bynguano Range, 131 km north of Broken Hill, teems with wildlife and is a place of exceptional beauty. It is well worth the two-hour drive from Broken Hill on an isolated dirt road. You can also get here from White Cliffs but neither route should be attempted after rain. Entry to the park is $7.50 per car.

In the park is an Aboriginal tribal ground with important rock carvings and cave paintings. The major site is now controlled by the Aboriginal community and is off limits except on ranger-escorted tours on Wednesday and Saturday morning ($4), leaving from the camping area (see below). The tours run from April until the end of November. The NPWS office in Broken Hill (☎ (080) 88 5933) has details.

There are walks through the crumbling sandstone hills to rock pools, which often have enough water for swimming, and rock paintings can be seen in the areas that are not off limits. The *Homestead Creek* camping area ($10) has bore water. You should book sites, especially during school holidays.

BROKEN HILL (pop 24,500)
Out in the far west, Broken Hill is an oasis in the wilderness. It's a fascinating town not only for its comfortable existence in an extremely unwelcoming environment, but also for the fact that it was once a one-company town which spawned one equally strong collective of unions, the Barrier Industrial Council.

History
The Broken Hill Proprietary Company (BHP) was formed in 1885 after Charles Rasp, a boundary rider, discovered a silver lode in the area. Miners working on other finds had failed to notice the real wealth. Other mining claims were staked, but BHP was always the 'big mine' and dominated the town. Charles Rasp amassed a personal fortune and BHP, which later diversified into steel production, became Australia's largest company.

Early conditions in the mine were appalling. Hundreds of miners died and many more suffered from lead poisoning and lung disease. This gave rise to the other great force in Broken Hill, the unions. Many miners were immigrants from various countries but all were united in their efforts to improve conditions.

The town's first 35 years saw a militancy rarely matched in Australian industrial relations. Many campaigns were fought, police were called in to break strikes and, though there was a gradual improvement in conditions, the miners lost many confrontations. The turning point was the Big Strike of 1919 and 1920, which lasted for over 18 months. The miners won a 35-hour week and the end of dry drilling, responsible for the dust that afflicted so many of them.

The concept of 'one big union', which had helped to win the strike, was formalised in 1923 with the formation of

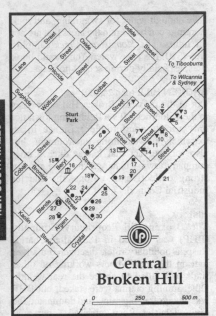

Central Broken Hill

0   250   500 m

To Tibooburra

To Wilcannia & Sydney

NEW SOUTH WALES

PLACES TO STAY

8	Nomads Backpackers
9	Royal Exchange Hotel
15	Mario's Motel
17	Grand Guest House
22	Black Lion Inn
25	Mario's Palace Hotel
28	Tourist Lodge

PLACES TO EAT

1	International Deli
2	West Darling Hotel
3	Oceania Chinese Restaurant
4	Old Capri
5	Alfresco's Cafe
7	Silver City Health Foods
10	Ruby's
14	Stope
18	Champion Pizza & Chinese Takeaway
20	Musician's Club
24	Barrier Social & Democratic Club

OTHER

6	Broken Hill City Art Gallery & Entertainment Centre
11	Theatre Royal Hotel
12	Trades Hall
13	Post Office
16	Railway Museum
19	Royal Automobile Association
21	Train Station
23	Ant Hill Gallery
26	Johnny Windham's Cycles
27	Tourist & Travellers Centre
29	NPWS Office
30	Geocentre

the Barrier Industrial Council, which still largely runs the town.

Today the world's richest deposit of silver, lead and zinc is still being worked, but zinc has assumed a greater importance in the Silver City, as Broken Hill is known. There is enough ore left to ensure at least another 15 years of mining, but new technology has greatly reduced the number of jobs in the mines.

Orientation & Information

The city is laid out in a grid and the central area is easy to get around on foot.

The big Tourist & Travellers Centre (☎ (080) 87 6077) on the corner of Blende and Bromide Sts is open daily. This is where the buses arrive and there's a bus booking agency on the premises, as well as a cafeteria and a car-rental desk. Pick up a heritage tour map ($2).

The NPWS office (☎ (080) 88 5933) is at 183 Argent St. The Royal Automobile Asso-

ciation of South Australia (☎ (080) 88 4999) is at 261 Argent St and provides reciprocal service to other autoclub members. You can buy your South Australian Desert Parks Pass here – see the Outback section of the South Australia chapter.

The swimming pool is north-east of the town centre, on McCulloch St. There's a laundrette on Argent St just east of the West Darling Hotel.

In many ways Broken Hill is closer to South Australia than New South Wales (it is 1170 km from Sydney but only 509 km from Adelaide) and clocks are set on Adelaide (central), half an hour behind Sydney (eastern) time.

Mines

There are two working mines in Broken Hill, the deeper being the North Mine, about 1600 metres deep and incorporating 30 km of winding road. At that depth it can reach 60°C and massive refrigeration plants are needed to control the temperature. You can't visit the working mines but there are tours of old mines.

Delprat's Mine (☎ (080) 88 1604) has an excellent underground tour daily except Sunday, where you don miners' gear and descend 150 metres for a tour lasting nearly two hours. It costs $18 (students $15). Nobody under eight years of age is allowed. To get there, head south-east down Iodide St, cross the railway tracks and follow the signs – it's about a five-minute drive.

Day Dream Mine, begun in 1881, is 33 km from Broken Hill, off the Silverton Rd. A one-hour tour costs $10, or $5 for children (all ages allowed), and sturdy footwear is essential. Contact the tourist centre for bookings.

At **White's Mineral Art Gallery & Mining Museum**, 1 Allendale St, you can walk into a mining stope and see mining memorabilia and minerals. Follow Galena St out to the north-west for two km or so. Admission is $4 (students $3).

Art Galleries

Broken Hill's red earth and harsh light has inspired many artists and there is a plethora of galleries, including the Pro Hart Gallery at 108 Wyman St and Jack Absalom's Gallery at 638 Chapple St. Pro Hart, a former miner, is Broken Hill's best-known artist and a local personality. His kooky gallery is bursting with the fruits of compulsive collecting. Apart from his own work, the gallery displays minor works of major artists (eg, Picasso and Dali) and his collection of Australian art is superb. He charges admission ($2, $1 students) but many others don't.

The Ant Hill Gallery on Bromide St opposite the tourist centre is a commercial gallery featuring local and major Australian artists. In the Broken Hill City Art Gallery (in the Entertainment Centre) is the 'Silver Tree', an intricate silver sculpture commissioned by Charles Rasp. One gallery is devoted to the artists of Broken Hill.

Have a look at the murals inside Mario's Palace Hotel on Argent St.

Royal Flying Doctor Service Base

You can visit the RFDS base at the airport. The tour ($2) includes a film, and you can inspect the headquarters, aircraft and the radio room that handles calls from remote towns and stations. Tour times are Monday to Friday at 10.30 am and 3.30 pm, and weekends at 10.30 am. Bookings are made at the tourist centre.

School of the Air

You can sit in on School of the Air broadcasts to kids in isolated homesteads on weekdays at 8.30 am. The one-hour session costs $2. You can visit during vacations, when a tape-recording is played. Bookings are essential and can be made at the tourist centre.

Other Attractions

The **Sulphide St Station Railway & Historical Museum** is in the Silverton Tramway Company's old station on Sulphide St. The tramway was a private railway running between Cockburn (South Australia) and Broken Hill via Silverton until 1970. It's open daily from 10 am to 3 pm and admission is $2.

The **Geocentre** presents an interactive history of Broken Hill's geology. It's on the corner of Bromide and Crystal Sts and is open daily from 1 to 5 pm. There are rock and mineral samples here, both huge and tiny, and displays on mining and metallurgy.

The **Afghani Mosque** is a corrugated-iron building dating from 1891. Afghani cameleers helped open up the outback and the mosque was built on the site of a camel camp. It's on the corner of William and Buck Sts in North Broken Hill and is open on Sunday between 2.30 and 4.30 pm. It no longer functions as a mosque.

The **Sculpture Symposium** was a project by 12 sculptors from several countries who carved sandstone blocks on a hilltop outside

NEW SOUTH WALES

town. Drive north-west on Kaolin St and keep going on the unsealed road for a couple of km until you get to the signposted turn-off on the right. From here it's another couple of km on a rough road, then a steep walk to the top of the hill. Apart from the sculptures there are excellent views over the plains. This is a good place to watch one of Broken Hill's famous sunsets, as is the **Sundown Nature Trail** 10 km north-east of town off the Silver City Highway.

Organised Tours

Plenty of companies offer tours of the town and nearby attractions, some going farther out to White Cliffs, Mootwingee and other outback destinations. The tourist centre has information and takes bookings.

Tri State Safaris (☎ (080) 88 2389) will tailor a tour to suit your interests in their vehicle or your own. The emphasis is on ecologically responsible touring.

An interesting way to see some of the country beyond Broken Hill is to go along on an outback mail run. Contact Crittenden Air (☎ (080) 88 5702), as far in advance as possible. The mail run departs at 6.30 am on Saturday and calls at about 14 outback stations, stopping in White Cliffs for a tour and lunch. The cost is $210. It also does various air tours.

Places to Stay

Camping The *Broken Hill Caravan Park* (☎ (080) 87 3841) on Rakow St (the Barrier Highway) north-west of the centre has sites ($10), cabins (from $30) and on-site vans ($23). The *Lake View Caravan Park* (☎ (080) 88 2250) on Argent St (the Barrier Highway) to the east has sites ($8) and cabins ($32 a double).

Hostels *Nomads Backpackers* (☎ (080) 87 7788) on the corner of Oxide and Argent Sts is a congenial hostel with dorm beds for $11, singles for $15 and doubles for $24. The owners run tours both locally and farther afield. They can advise you on work opportunities in the area.

The *Tourist Lodge* (☎ (080) 88 2086) at 100 Argent St, not far from the tourist centre, is an associate-YHA hostel with dorms at $14 ($12 YHA members). Singles/twins cost from $20/30, with much cheaper weekly rates. Avoid the seedy men's hostel next door.

Hotels & Motels High ceilings, wide corridors and huge verandahs come as standard equipment on pubs in this hot city. All the places mentioned here also have air-con.

The nice old *Royal Exchange Hotel* (☎ (080) 87 2308) on the corner of Argent and Chloride Sts has rooms for $24/40 or $34/50 with bathroom, fridge and TV. The price drops by about 10% if you stay more than a couple of days. Diagonally opposite, the *Grand Guest House* (☎ (080) 87 5305) has double rooms with shared bathrooms for $49 or $59 with en suite (both tariffs include breakfast).

Farther west on the corner of Sulphide and Argent Sts, *Mario's Palace Hotel* (☎ (080) 88 1699) is an impressive old (1888) pub covered in murals. All rooms have fridges, TVs and tea/coffee-making facilities. Singles/doubles are $27/38 or $38/48 with attached bathroom. The *Black Lion Inn* (☎ (080) 87 4801), on Bromide St across from the tourist centre, isn't on the same scale but has reasonable rooms for $18/28 (no air-con in the single rooms). It's also a party pub so bypass it if you want early nights.

The *Old Vic Guesthouse* (☎ (080) 87 1169) is an airy B&B place on the corner of Oxide and Chapple Sts. Singles/doubles are $25/40.

Mario's Motel (☎ (080) 88 5944) at 172 Beryl St is run-down but likeable. Singles/doubles are $35/50. The *Sturt Motel* (☎ (080) 87 3558), on Rakow St (Barrier Highway) a few km north-west of the centre charges from $37/43. Most of the other motels charge at least $55/65.

Cottages *Beryl Cottage* (☎ (080) 88 3288) at 350 Beryl St is a small house available by the night for $70 for four people, plus $5 for each extra person (up to six). *Budget Cottage* is on the same block and costs $45 for four people.

Places to Eat

The gourmets in Broken Hill are the ones that eat the garnish on their steaks, so don't spend too much time looking for *cuisine minceur* down these dusty streets.

Broken Hill is a club town if ever there was one. The clubs welcome visitors and in most cases you just sign the book at the front door and walk in. Most have reasonably priced, reasonably good and very filling meals. The *Barrier Social & Democratic Club* ('the Demo'), 218 Argent St, has meals including a breakfast (from 6 am, or 7 am weekends) which will keep you going all day. The *Musician's Club* at 267 Crystal St is slightly cheaper, serving steaks and bakes either side of $10.

There are lots of pubs too – this is a mining town – but you'd be lucky to find them cooking after 8.30 pm or at all on a Sunday. The *Black Lion Inn*, Bromide St, has a $5 counter lunch and main courses in the evening for around $10, with curry the speciality. The *West Darling* on the corner of Oxide and Argent Sts has counter meals and you score a free beer if you're staying at Nomads diagonally opposite.

Alfresco's Cafe in Argent St is a pasta and pancake joint which is good for a freshly squeezed fruit juice. Check for specials, but meals here are not particularly good value.

Farther along Argent St to the east are the *Oceania Chinese Restaurant*, with $6.50 lunch specials and main courses from around $7.50, and *Old Capri*, a small Italian place boasting home-made pasta.

Up on Sulphide St, *Champion Pizza & Chinese Takeaway*, dourly holding its own behind the Pizza Hut, stays open late. Also good for late-night supplies is the *International Deli* on Oxide St near Beryl St, open until midnight all week. If you're after a late-night pie, head for the *Camp Oven Pie Cart*, usually parked on Oxide St outside Alfresco's.

Stope, farther west on Argent St, is a bakery cafe with good sandwiches and cakes and the best coffee in Broken Hill. *Silver City Health Foods* is tucked away in an arcade on the other side of Argent St so as not to frighten the miners. They do a neat line in vegie pies and burgers. *Ruby's* near Nomads on Argent St is OK for light meals and usually has a couple of vegetarian items on offer.

Entertainment

Maybe it's because this is a mining town, maybe it's because there are so many nights when it's too hot to sleep, but Broken Hill stays up late. There isn't a lot of formal entertainment but pubs stay open almost until dawn on Thursday, Friday and Saturday nights.

The *Theatre Royal Hotel* on Argent St has a disco, and the *Barrier Social & Democratic Club* runs a nightclub on Friday and Saturday nights. The Demo also has live entertainment, but you'd want to be a country cabaret fan. The *Black Lion Inn* has been recommended as a good pub for a drink. It has a three-page cocktail list and two-for-one deals on some nights.

Two-up (gambling on the fall of two coins) is played at *Burke Ward Hall* on Wills St near the corner of Gypsum St, west of the centre, on Friday and Saturday nights. Broken Hill claims to have retained all the atmosphere of a real two-up 'school' (illegal until recently), unlike the sanitised versions played in casinos.

Getting There & Around

Air Standard one-way fares from Broken Hill include $155 to Adelaide and $199 to Melbourne with Southern Australia (Qantas), and $269 to Sydney with Hazelton.

Bus Greyhound Pioneer runs daily to Adelaide for $53, to Mildura for $35 and to Sydney for $95 (sometimes less). Most buses depart from the tourist centre, where you can book seats.

A Victorian V/Line bus runs to Mildura ($35) and Melbourne ($85) on Wednesday and Friday. Book at the railway station.

Train Broken Hill is on the Sydney to Perth railway line so the Indian Pacific passes through. On Sunday and Wednesday it leaves Broken Hill at 3.20 pm and arrives in Sydney at 9.15 am the next day. The economy fare is $95. To Adelaide ($50) and Perth (from $250), it departs Broken Hill on Tuesday and Friday at 9 am.

There's a slightly faster and marginally cheaper daily service to Sydney called Laser, a Countrylink bus departing Broken Hill daily at 4 am (groan) and connecting with a train at Dubbo, arriving in Sydney at 9 pm ($90).

The Countrylink booking office at the railway station (☎ 13 2232) is open on weekdays.

Car Rental The major companies have offices here but their 'remote region' rates can work out to be expensive. Small cars start at around $70 a day.

Bike Hire You can hire bikes at *Johnny Windham's Cycles* on Argent St between Bromide and Sulphide Sts. The cost is $7 a day including helmet, with cheaper weekly deals.

Taxi For taxi service call ☎ 13 1008.

AROUND BROKEN HILL
Silverton

Silverton, 25 km west of Broken Hill, is an old silver-mining town which peaked in 1885 when it had a population of 3000 and public buildings designed to last for centuries. In 1889 the mines closed and the population (and many of the houses) moved to Broken Hill.

Today it's an interesting little ghost town, which was used as a setting in the movies *Mad Max II* and *A Town Like Alice*. A number of buildings still stand, including the old jail (now the museum) and the Silverton Hotel. There are also a couple of art galleries. The information centre, in the old school, has a walking tour map. The hotel is still operating and it displays photographs taken on the film

sets. Don't leave here without taking the infamous 'Silverton test'; ask at the bar.

The road beyond Silverton becomes bleak and lonely almost immediately. The **Mundi Mundi Plains** lookout five km out of town gives an idea of just how desolate it gets. Farther along, the **Umberumberka Reservoir**, 13 km from Silverton, is a popular picnic spot.

Silverton Camel Farm (☎ (080) 88 5316) runs a variety of camel rides, from 15-minute jaunts ($5) to five-day safaris ($450). The camels are sometimes hitched up in Silverton, but the farm itself is a couple of km back towards Broken Hill.

There's basic camping at Penrose Park (☎ (080) 88 5307), by a creek on the Broken Hill side of town. Bring, or boil, drinking water. Also here are a couple of bunkhouses, with beds for $15 (no power, no kitchen) or $20 (with power and kitchen).

Menindee Lakes

This water storage development on the Darling River, 112 km south-east of Broken Hill, offers a variety of water-sport facilities. **Menindee** is the town for the area. Burke and Wills stayed at Maidens Hotel on their ill-fated trip north in 1860. The hotel was built in 1854 and has been with the same family for nearly 100 years. It still has accommodation (☎ (080) 91 4208) for around $15 per person including breakfast.

Kinchega National Park is close to the town and the lakes, overflowing from the Darling River, are a haven for birdlife. The visitor centre is near the site of the old Kinchega Homestead, about 16 km from the park entrance, and the shearing shed has been preserved. There are plenty of camp sites along the river.

West of Menindee there are some good free camp sites around Lakes Wetherell and Pamamaroo, but bone up on minimal impact camping strategies before you set up: this is a water catchment area.

MUNGO NATIONAL PARK

North-east of Mildura and south of Menindee is **Lake Mungo**, a dry lake which s the site of the oldest archaeological finds n Australia – human skeletons and artefacts dating back 45,000 years, when Aboriginal people settled on the banks of the once fertile lakes and lived on the plentiful fish, mussels, birds and animals. After 25,000 years the climate changed, the lakes dried up and the Aboriginal people adapted to life in a harsh semi-desert, with only periodic floods filling the lakes.

A 25-km semicircle ('lunette') of huge sand dunes has been created by the never-ending west wind, which continually exposes fabulously ancient remains. The park also includes the dry lake-bed and the shimmering white cliffs known as the **Walls of China**. Remember, it is illegal in Australia to remove archaeological objects or to disturb human remains.

Mungo is 110 km from Mildura and 150 km from Balranald on unsealed roads. These towns are the closest places where you can buy fuel. Mallee Outback Experiences (☎ (050) 21 621), which charges $45 for a tour, and Junction Tours (☎ (050) 27 4309) are two Mildura-based companies offering tours.

Information

There's a visitor centre by the old Mungo woolshed. A road leads across the dry lake bed to the Walls of China, and you can drive a complete 60-km loop of the dunes – but not after rain. Park entry costs $7.50 per car.

Places to Stay

Accommodation fills up during school holidays. There are two camp sites – *Main Camp* near the visitor centre and *Belah Camp* on the eastern side of the dunes. Camping costs $5 a night. There is also shared accommodation in the old shearers' quarters for $15 per person. Book through the NPWS office in Buronga (☎ (050) 23 1278), near Mildura.

On the Mildura road about four km from the visitor centre is *Mungo Lodge* (☎ (050) 9 7297). Singles/doubles go for $58/68 and there is a self-contained cottage for $78 for two (add $10 per person, up to six people). There's also a restaurant.

Lord Howe Island

Beautiful Lord Howe is a tiny subtropical island 500 km east of Port Macquarie and 770 km north-east of Sydney. It's not a budget destination. Unless you've got a boat, you'll have to fly there, and both food and accommodation are expensive. Most visitors take flight and accommodation packages.

The island is listed on the World Heritage Register. It's heavily forested and has beautiful walks, a wide lagoon sheltered by a coral reef and some fine beaches. It's small enough at 11 km long and 2.5 km wide for you to get around on foot or by bicycle. The southern end is dominated by towering Mt Lidgbird (777 metres) and Mt Gower (875 metres). You can climb Mt Gower in around six hours (round trip). The lagoon has good snorkelling, and you can also inspect the sea life from glass-bottom boats. On the other side of the island there's surf at Blinky Beach.

Information

The Lord Howe Island Tourist Centre (☎ (02) 9262 6555) is on the 7th floor, 39-41 York St, Sydney.

Places to Stay

Camping is not permitted on the island. There is plenty of accommodation in lodges and self-contained apartments, but the only way to get a decent deal is to buy a package. Prices drop as low as $589 for seven-day packages ex-Sydney, but five nights for $699 is more typical.

Getting There & Away

Eastern Australia has daily flights from Sydney for $762 return, while Sunstate from Brisbane (weekends) is $694 return. Kentia Link operates charters from Coffs Harbour and Port Macquarie.

Getting Around

You can hire bicycles; there are motorbikes and a few rental cars on the island but a bike is all you need. There is a 25 km/h speed limit throughout the island.

Norfolk Island

Norfolk Island is a green speck in the middle of the Pacific Ocean, 1600 km north-east of Sydney and 1000 km north-west of the New Zealand capital, Auckland. It's the largest of a cluster of three islands emerging from the Norfolk Ridge, which stretches from New Zealand to New Caledonia – the closest land-fall almost 700 km to the north.

Norfolk is a popular tourist spot, particularly with older Australians and New Zealanders, and tourism is by far the biggest contributor to the local economy. The cost of air fares means it is not a cheap destination and there is no budget accommodation.

Many visitors enjoy Norfolk Island's lush vegetation. The rich volcanic soil and mild subtropical climate provide perfect growing conditions. There are 40-odd plant species that are unique to the island, including the handsome Norfolk Island pine *(Araucaria heterophylla)* which grows everywhere.

History
Little is known about the island before it was sighted by Captain Cook on 10 October 1774 and named after the wife of the ninth Duke of Norfolk. Fifteen convicts were among the first settlers to reach the island on 6 March 1788, founding a penal colony that survived until 1814. The island was abandoned for 11 years before colonial authorities decided to try again. Governor Darling planned this second penal settlement as 'a place of the extremest punishment short of death'. Under such notorious sadists as commandant John Giles Price, Norfolk became known as 'hell in the Pacific'. The penal colony lasted until 1855, when the prisoners were shipped off to Van Diemen's Land (Tasmania) and the island was handed over to the descendants of the mutineers from the HMS *Bounty*, who had outgrown their adopted Pitcairn Island. About a third of the present population of

2000 are descended from the 194 Pitcairners who arrived on 8 June 1856.

Visas
The island is a self-governing external territory of Australia; this has important ramifications in terms of passports and visas. Travelling to Norfolk Island from Australia means you will pay departure tax, get an exit stamp in your passport and board an international flight. (The same applies from New Zealand.) To return to Australia you will need a re-entry visa, or a valid Australian passport. On arrival at Norfolk Island, you will get a 30-day visa on presentation of a valid passport.

Orientation & Information
The island measures only eight km by five km. Vertical cliffs surround much of the coastline, apart from a small area of coastal plain (formerly swamp) around the historic settlement of Kingston. The only settlement of any consequence is the service town of Burnt Pine, at the centre of the island and near the airport. Most of the northern part of the island is taken up by Norfolk Island National Park.

The Norfolk Islander Visitor Information Centre (☎ 22 147) is next to the post office on the main street in Burnt Pine. The Communications Centre (Norfolk Telstra) is at the edge of town on New Cascade Rd. If you're addressing mail to the island from Australia, the postcode is 2899; the island's international telephone code is 6723.

The Commonwealth Bank and Westpac both have branches in Burnt Pine.

Kingston
The historic settlement of Kingston, built by convicts of the second penal colony, is the island's main attraction. Several of the buildings have been turned into small museums. The finest buildings are those of the colonial administrators along Quality Row, as the settlement's main road is called. The sandstone used for the buildings was quarried from nearby Nepean Island. One place that should not be missed is the convict cemetery,

next to the ocean at the far (eastern) end of Quality Row. There are some very poignant epitaphs on the headstones, such as that of James Saye, who was killed in 1842 during an abortive mutiny:

Stop Christian, stop and meditate
On this man's sad and awful fate
On earth no more he breathes again
He lived in hope but died in pain

Other Attractions
Just south of Kingston is **Emily Bay**, a good sheltered beach, and there are several operators who will take you out in glass-bottom boats to view the corals in the bay.

St Barnabas Chapel, west of Burnt Pine along Douglas Drive, is a magnificent chapel built by the (Anglican) Melanesian Mission, which was based on the island from 1866 to 1920.

There are various walking tracks in **Norfolk Island National Park**, and good views from Mt Pitt (320 metres) and Mt Bates (321 metres). Mt Pitt was the higher of the two before the top was levelled to build a radio transmitter.

Organised Tours
Pinetree Tours (☎ 22 424), in the middle of Burnt Pine, runs a busy schedule of tours around the island. The half-day introductory tour ($18) takes in all the major points of interest.

Places to Stay
Accommodation is expensive, but the cost is often disguised as most visitors come on package deals. There are lots of places to choose from, but few that make the most of the island's natural attributes. Modern motel-style units predominate, priced from $79 a double.

The *Highlands Lodge* (☎ 22 741) is a good place nestled on the hillside below the national park with doubles for $105. *Channer's Corner* (☎ 22 532), on the edge of Burnt Pine, has stylish apartments at $95 for two people.

Places to Eat
There are dozens of restaurants offering everything from humble fish & chips to up-market à la carte. Competition is stiff and prices are quite reasonable, although food in the shops is expensive by Australian standards.

The *Bowling Club* in Burnt Pine has roasts for $8, and the *Workers Club* opposite is equally good value. The *Bounty Inn*, right outside the airport, brews its own beer.

Getting There & Away
Ansett flies four times a week from Sydney ($619 Apex return) and three times a week from Brisbane ($579 Apex return). Air New Zealand flies twice a week from Auckland (from NZ$599 return).

Getting Around
Car hire can be organised at the airport for as little as $9 a day, plus insurance ($3). Petrol is expensive, but you'll struggle to use much. Cows have right of way on the island's roads, and there's a $300 fine for hitting one.

Leaving Norfolk Island
There's a departure tax of $25.

NEW SOUTH WALES

Northern Territory

PHONE CHANGES

As of May 1996, all Northern Territory phone numbers have eight digits.

The STD area code for the Northern Territory is (08).

HIGHLIGHTS

- Taking a boat ride on the wetlands of Kakadu National Park
- Visiting Uluru (Ayers Rock) and Kata Tjuta (the Olgas) at Uluru-Kata Tjuta National Park
- Hiking in the spectacular Kings Canyon, Watarrka National Park
- Fishing for barramundi at Borroloola on the Gulf of Carpentaria
- Paddling a canoe up the Katherine Gorge, Nitmiluk National Park
- Taking an Aboriginal cultural tour at Manyallaluk near Katherine
- Visiting the old gold mines in Tennant Creek
- Trekking the Larapinta Trail in the Western MacDonnell Ranges, near Alice Springs
- Delving into central Australian history at the Old Telegraph Station, Alice Springs

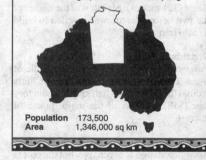

| Population | 173,500 |
| Area | 1,346,000 sq km |

The fascinating Northern Territory is the least populated (with only 1% of the Australian population living in nearly 20% of the country's area) and the most barren area of Australia. The populated parts of Australia are predominantly urban and coastal, but it is in the centre – the Red Heart – that the picture-book, untamed and sometimes surreal Australia exists.

The Centre is not just Uluru (Ayers Rock), bang in the middle of nowhere. There are meteorite craters, eerie canyons, lost valleys of palms, and noisy Alice Springs festivals. Where else is there an annual boat regatta on a dry river bed? The colour red is evident as soon as you arrive – in the soil, the rocks and in Uluru itself. At the other end of the Track – the Stuart Highway, the 1500 km of bitumen that connects Alice Springs to the north coast – is Darwin, probably Australia's most cosmopolitan city.

Even that long, empty road between Alice Springs and Darwin isn't dull – there are plenty of interesting places along the way. As you travel up or down that single link you'll notice another of the Territory's real surprises – the contrast between the Centre's amazing aridity and the humid, tropical wetness of the Top End in the monsoon season. The wetlands and escarpments of Kakadu National Park are a treasure house of wildlife and Aboriginal rock painting.

The Northern Territory has a small population and a more fragile economy than other parts of Australia, and isn't classified as a state. It was formerly administered by New South Wales and then by South Australia, but it has been controlled by the Federal government since 1911. Since 1978 the Territory has been self-governing, although Canberra still has more say over its internal affairs than over those of the states.

ABORIGINAL PEOPLE

Around 22% of the Territory's population is Aboriginal – a higher proportion than in most southern states.

The process of White settlement in the Northern Territory was just as troubled and violent as elsewhere in Australia, with

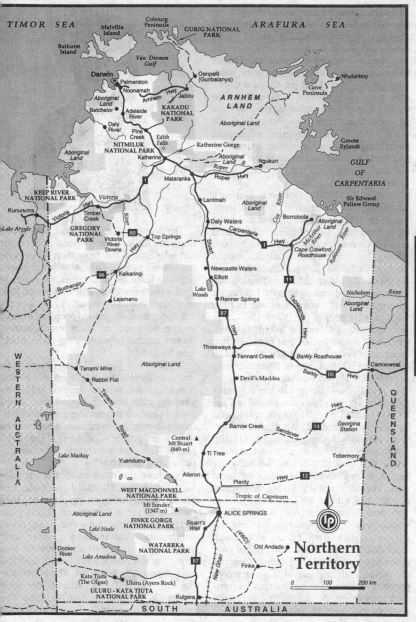

Aboriginal groups vainly trying to resist the takeover of lands on which their way of life depended. By the early 20th century, most Aboriginal people were confined to government reserves or Christian missions. Others lived on cattle stations where they were employed as skilful but poorly paid stockmen or domestic servants, or lived a half-life on the edges of towns, attracted there by food and tobacco and sometimes finding low-paid work, but too often acquiring an alcohol habit. Only a few – some of those on reserves and cattle stations, and those in the remote outback – maintained much of their traditional way of life.

During the 1960s, Northern Territory Aboriginal people began to demand more rights. In 1963 the people of Yirrkala on the Gove Peninsula, part of the Arnhem Land reserve, protested against plans for bauxite mining. The Yirrkala people failed to stop the mining, but the way they presented their case (by producing sacred objects and bark paintings that showed their right to the land under Aboriginal custom) was a milestone. In 1966 the Gurindji people on Wave Hill cattle station went on strike and asked that their tribal land, which formed part of the station, be returned to them. Eventually the Gurindji were given 3238 sq km in a government-negotiated deal with the station owners.

In 1976 the Aboriginal Land Rights (Northern Territory) Act was passed in Canberra. It handed over all reserves and mission lands in the Territory to Aboriginal ownership, and allowed Aboriginal groups to claim government land with which they had traditional ties (unless the land was already leased, or in a town, or set aside for some other special purpose). Today Aboriginal people own almost 50% of the Northern Territory. This includes Uluru National Park, which was handed over to its original Pitjantjatjara owners in 1985 and immediately leased back to the Federal government for use as a national park. Minerals on Aboriginal land are still government property – though the landowners' permission for exploration and mining is usually required and has to be paid for.

The Northern Territory land rights laws improved the lot of many Aboriginal people and encouraged the Outstation Movement that started in the 1970s. Aboriginal people began to leave the settlements and return to a more traditional, nomadic lifestyle on their own land. Ironically, equal-pay laws in the 1960s deprived Aboriginal people of a major source of work, as many cattle station owners reacted by employing white stock men instead.

While White goodwill is on the increase and more Aboriginal people are able to deal effectively with Whites, there are still many yawning gulfs between the cultures. White racism persists, and finding a mode of harmonious coexistence remains a serious and long-term problem, although the 1993 Native Title Act goes some way towards reconciling the two sides.

For these and other reasons it's usually hard for short-term visitors to make real contact with Aboriginal people, who often prefer to be left to themselves. This is gradually changing, however, as more communities feel inclined to share their culture, and are able to do it on their own terms. For this reason tourism on Aboriginal land is generally restricted. The benefits to the communities are twofold: the most obvious is the financial gain, the other that introducing Aboriginal culture and customs

Aboriginal Events & Festivals

There are a number of regular festivals which are well worth attending. Although they are usually held on restricted Aboriginal land, permit requirements are generally waived for the festivals. Be aware also that alcohol is banned in many communities.

Barunga Wugularr Sports & Cultural Festival
For the four days over the Queen's Birthday long weekend in June, Barunga, 80 km south-east of Katherine, becomes a gathering place for Aboriginal people from all over the Territory. There's traditional arts and crafts, as well as dancing and athletics competitions. No accommodation is provided so you'll need your own camping equipment, or visit for the day from Katherine. No permit required.

Merrepen Arts Festival
In June or July, Nauiyu Nambiyu on the banks of the Daly River is the venue for the Merrepen Arts Festival. Several Aboriginal communities from around the district, such as Wadeye, Nauiyu and Peppimenarti, display their arts and crafts. No permit required.

Yuendumu Festival
The Yuendumu community is 270 km north-west of Alice Springs, and Aboriginal people from the central and western desert region meet here over a long weekend in early August. There's a mix of traditional and modern sporting and cultural events. BYO camping gear. No permit required.

Oenpelli Open Day
Oenpelli (Gunbalanya) is in Arnhem Land, across the East Alligator River not far from Jabiru. On the first Saturday in August an open day is held where there's a chance to purchase local artefacts and watch the sports and dancing events. No permit required.

National Aboriginal Art Award
Every Saturday an exhibition of works entered for this award is held at the Museum & Art Gallery of the Northern Territory in Darwin. It attracts entries from all over the country. ■

to non-Aboriginal people helps alleviate the problems caused by the ignorance and misunderstandings of the past. It is important to remember that many Aboriginal people do not appreciate being photographed by strangers, even from a distance.

Permits

You need a permit to enter Aboriginal land, and in general they are only granted if you have friends or relatives working there, or if you're on an organised tour (see entry below) – wandering at random through Aboriginal land to visit the communities is definitely not on. The exception to this rule is travel along public roads through Aboriginal land – though if you want to stop (other than for fuel or provisions) or deviate, you need a permit. If you stick to the main roads, there's no problem.

Three land councils deal with all requests for permits: ask the permits officer of the appropriate council for an application form. The Central Land Council basically deals with all land south of a line drawn between Kununurra and Mt Isa, the Northern Land Council is responsible for land north of that line, and the Tiwi Land Council deals with Bathurst and Melville islands.

Permits take around four to six weeks to be processed.

Northern Land Council
9 Rowling St, (PO Box 42921), Casuarina, Darwin, NT 0820 (☎ 8920 5100; fax 8945-2633)
Tiwi Land Council
Unit 9, Wingate Centre, Winnellie, Darwin, NT 0800 (☎ 8947 1838)
Central Land Council
33 Stuart Highway (PO Box 3321), Alice Springs, NT 0871 (☎ 8962 2343)

Tours on Aboriginal Land

There are a number of tourist operations, some of them Aboriginal owned, running trips to visit Aboriginal land and communities in the Northern Territory. This is the best way to have any meaningful contact with Aboriginal people, even though you may feel that by being on a tour what you're getting is not the 'real thing'. The fact is that this is the way the Aboriginal owners of the land want tourism to work, so that they have some control over who visits what and when.

Arnhem Land offers the most options, mainly because of its proximity to Kakadu. The tours here generally only visit the very western edge of Arnhem Land, and take you to Oenpelli and other places which are normally off limits. Some operators include Umorrduk Safaris, AAT-Kings and Davidson's Arnhem Land Safaris (see the Kakadu and Arnhem Land sections for more details).

Other places in the Top End with similar operations include Tiwi Islands, and the Litchfield and Katherine areas, while in the Centre they are at Kings Canyon and Uluru. See those sections for details.

CLIMATE

The climate of the Top End is best described in terms of the Dry and the Wet, rather than winter and summer. Roughly, the Dry is April to September, and the Wet is October to March, with the heaviest rain falling from January onwards. April, when the rains taper off, and October to December, with their uncomfortably high humidity and that 'waiting for the rains' feeling (known as the 'build-up'), are transition periods. The Top End is the most thundery part of Australia: Darwin has over 90 'thunderdays' a year, all between September and March.

In the Centre the temperatures are much more variable – plummeting below freezing on winter nights (July to August), and soaring into the high 40s on summer days (December to January). Come prepared for both extremes, and for intense sun and the occasional rainstorm at any time of the year. When it rains, dirt roads quickly become quagmires.

Ask any Territorian when the best time to visit the Territory is and invariably they'll say the wet season. The reasons they'll cite will include that everything is green, there's no dust, the barramundi fishing is at its best, prices drop at many places, there are spectacular electrical storms – and all the tourists have gone home! While it's hard to argue with this sort of logic, the Wet does present problems for the visitor – the humidity is often unbearable unless you're acclimatised, dirt roads are often impassable, swimming in the ocean is impossible because of box jellyfish (stingers), and some national parks and reserves are either totally or partially closed.

It's also worth remembering that even though the humidity in the Top End is high

Cyclone Tracy

The statistics of this disaster are frightening. Cyclone Tracy built up over Christmas Eve 1974 and by midnight the winds began to reach their full fury. At 3.05 am the airport's anemometer failed, just after it recorded a speed of 217 km/h. It's thought the peak wind speeds were as high as 280 km/h. Sixty-six lives were lost. Of Darwin's 11,200 houses 50% to 60% were either totally destroyed or so badly damaged that repair was impossible, and only 400 survived relatively intact.

Much criticism was levelled at the design and construction of Darwin's houses, but plenty of places a century or more old, and built as solidly as you could ask for, also toppled before the awesome winds. The new and rebuilt houses have been cyclone-proofed with strong steel reinforcements and roofs which are firmly pinned down.

Most people say that next time a cyclone is forecast, they'll jump straight into their cars and head down the Track – and come back afterwards to find out if their houses really were cyclone-proof! Those who stay will probably take advantage of the official cyclone shelter. ∎

during the Wet, daytime temperatures remain constant at about 30°C to 33°C. In the southern states at this time of year it is often very much hotter, with temperatures into the high 30s and low 40s.

INFORMATION

Surprisingly, the Northern Territory Tourism Commission doesn't have any tourist offices either within the Territory or elsewhere in Australia, although there are regional tourist offices in Darwin, Katherine and Alice Springs.

If you want any predeparture information, contact the Northern Territory Tourism Commission's Information Helpline on ☎ 1800 621 336, or you can find them on the World Wide Web at www.world.net /Travel/Australia/NT_info/NTTC

NATIONAL PARKS

The Northern Territory has some of Australia's best national parks. Most people would be aware of the more famous ones, such as Uluru & Kata Tjuta, Kakadu and Nitmiluk (Katherine Gorge), but there are plenty of others which are equally appealing – parks such as Litchfield, West MacDonnell Ranges and Watarrka (Kings Canyon) are all well worth visiting.

For detailed information on Uluru and Kakadu national parks contact the Australian Nature Conservation Agency (ANCA; formerly the Australian National Parks & Wildlife Service; ☎ 8981 5299; fax 8981 3497) in Smith St, Darwin, which administers the two parks. You will also find excellent information offices in the parks themselves.

Other parks and natural and historic reserves are run by the Parks & Wildlife Commission of the Northern Territory (formerly the Conservation Commission of the Northern Territory; CCNT), which has offices in Alice Springs, Katherine and Darwin, plus information desks in the tourist offices in Darwin and Alice Springs. Parks & Wildlife puts out fact sheets on individual parks, and these are available at the Parks & Wildlife offices or from the parks themselves.

ACTIVITIES

Bushwalking

There are interesting bushwalking trails in the Northern Territory, but take care if you venture off the beaten track. You can climb the ranges surrounding Alice Springs – remember to wear stout shoes, as the spinifex grass and burrs are very sharp. In summer, wear a hat and carry water even on short walks. Walking is best in the Dry, although shorter walks are possible in the Wet when the patches of monsoon rainforest are at their best.

The Larapinta Trail, in the Western MacDonnell Ranges near Alice Springs, is well laid out with camp sites and other basic facilities along the way. Trephina Gorge Nature Park, in the Eastern MacDonnells, has a few marked trails, although they are all day trips or shorter.

Gregory National Park, just off the Victoria Highway, also lends itself to extended bushwalks, although there are no marked trails. The same applies to Kakadu and Watarrka (Kings Canyon).

When undertaking any bushwalks in the Territory parks and reserves it is usually necessary to contact the local ranger for permission.

The Darwin Bushwalking Club (☎ 8985 1484) makes weekend expeditions all year round and welcomes visitors.

Willis's Walkabouts (☎ 8985 2134; fax 8985 2355) is a commercial tour operator in Darwin which offers bushwalks in the Top End, Kimberley and the Centre, ranging from three days to three weeks.

Swimming

Stay out of the sea during the Wet because stings from box jellyfish (stingers) can be fatal. Darwin beaches are popular, however, during the safe months. Beware too, of saltwater crocodiles in both salt and fresh waters in the Top End – though there are quite a few safe, natural swimming holes. Take local advice – and if in doubt, don't take a risk.

NORTHERN TERRITORY

It is a good idea to have vinegar with you when swimming in coastal waters in the Territory, as this is the most effective way to treat box jellyfish weals. Don't try to remove the stings.

Scuba Diving

There are some excellent opportunities for diving in Darwin Harbour, largely thanks to the WW II wrecks which provide a habitat for a variety of marine life.

Cullen Bay Dive (☎ 8981 3049; fax 8981 4913) at the Cullen Bay Marina takes divers out to wrecks in the harbour throughout the year. The cost is $29 per dive, plus $20 for equipment hire, which includes a protective suit to guard against box jellyfish. They also do full-day diving trips at $79.

Other companies which do dives out of Darwin include Coral Divers (☎ 8981 2686) in Stuart Park, and Fathom Five Pro Charters (☎ 8985 4288) in Millner.

Fishing

This is good, particularly for barramundi, a perch that often grows to over a metre long, puts up a great fight and is also great to eat. Barramundi is found both offshore and inland and there are fishing tours out of a number of places for the express purpose of catching it.

Some of the best fishing is found in and around Borroloola in the Gulf country, but Kakadu and Darwin are also OK.

Some of the companies which run fishing tours include Barra Bash (☎ 1800 632 225), Land-a-Barra (☎ 8932 2543) and Top End Sportsfishing Safaris (☎ 8983 1495) in and around Darwin and Kakadu, and Croc Spot (☎ 8975 8721) in Borroloola.

There are size and bag limits on barramundi and mud crabs, so be aware of these. For information contact the Fisheries Management Section (☎ 8999 4321) of the Department of Primary Industry & Fisheries in Darwin.

Fossicking

There are many places for the fossicker –

check with the Northern Territory Department of Mines & Energy for information on the best places and to find out whether permission is required. Good locations for fossicking are around the Harts Range (72 km north-east of Alice Springs) for beryl, garnet and quartz; the Eastern MacDonnell Ranges (east of Alice Springs) for beryl and garnet; Tennant Creek for gold and jasper; Anthony Lagoon (215 km east of the Stuart Highway, north of Tennant Creek) for ribbonstone; Pine Creek for gold; and Brock's Creek (37 km south-west of Adelaide River, south of Darwin) for topaz, tourmaline, garnet and zircon.

The Department of Mines & Energy publishes *A Guide to Fossicking in the Northern Territory*, available for $9 from the department offices in Alice Springs (☎ 8951 5658), Tennant Creek (☎ 8962 1288) and Darwin (☎ 8989 5511). A fossicking permit is required, and these are available for $20 from the same offices.

GETTING THERE & AWAY

See the Alice Springs, Darwin and Uluru (Ayers Rock) sections for transport into the Northern Territory by bus, train, car and air.

GETTING AROUND
Air

Ansett's flight network is more comprehensive than the Qantas service. There's also Airnorth (☎ 1800 627 474), which is a feeder airline affiliated with Ansett and linking Darwin, Katherine, Bathurst Island, Jabiru, Gunbalanya (Oenpelli), Groote Eylandt, Gove, Alice Springs, Tennant Creek, Uluru (Ayers Rock) and Kings Canyon. The chart details regular fares.

Bus

Within the Territory, there's fairly good coverage given by Greyhound Pioneer. See the Getting There & Away sections for the various towns.

Car

Off the beaten track, 'with care' is the thought to bear in mind, and all the usual

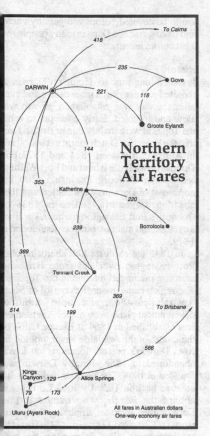

Northern Territory Air Fares

To Cairns
418
235
DARWIN
221
Gove
118
Groote Eylandt
144
353
Katherine
220
239
Borroloola
389
Tennant Creek
369
514
199
To Brisbane
566
Kings Canyon 129 Alice Springs
79 173
Uluru (Ayers Rock)

All fares in Australian dollars
One-way economy air fares

to be found and you'll have shade and some protection from the elements.

Traffic may be fairly light, but a lot of people still manage to run into things, so watch out for the two great Northern Territory road hazards – road trains and animals. Road trains are huge trucks (a prime mover plus two or three trailers), which can only be used on the long outback roads of central and northern Australia – they're not allowed into the southern cities. A road train is very long (around 50 metres) and very big. If you try to overtake one make sure you have plenty of room to complete the manoeuvre – allow about a km. When you see one approaching from the opposite direction on a narrow bitumen road, slow down and pull over – if a road train has to put its wheels off the road to pass you, the shower of stones and rocks that results will not do you or your windscreen any good. On dirt roads it's best to stop altogether, as the dust cloud behind a road train usually blanks your vision completely, if only for a few seconds.

Between sunset and sunrise the Territory's wildlife comes out to play. Hitting a kangaroo is all too easy and the damage to your vehicle, not to mention the kangaroo, can be severe. There are also buffaloes, cattle, wild horses and a number of other driving hazards which you would be wise to avoid. There's really only one sensible way to deal with these road hazards – don't drive at night. If you must drive at night, keep your speed right down, and remember that most animals travel in groups!

An added hazard in the Territory is the fact that there is no speed limit on the open roads, leading to the temptation to travel faster than the road conditions allow.

Hitching

Hitching is generally good, but once away from the main towns lifts can be few and far between. Threeways, where the road to Mt Isa branches off the Darwin to Alice Springs road, is notorious for long waits for lifts.

precautions apply. You can get up-to-date information on road conditions by phoning the Automobile Association of the Northern Territory (☎ 8953 1322 in Alice Springs, or ☎ 8981 3837 in Darwin). They can also advise you on which roads require a 4WD year round or just in the Wet.

It's wise to carry a basic kit of spare parts in case of breakdown. It may not be a matter of life or death, but it can save a lot of time, trouble and expense. Carry spare water, and if you do break down off the main roads, remain with the vehicle; you're more likely

Darwin

Population 78,100

The 'capital' of northern Australia comes as a surprise to many people. Instead of the hard-bitten, rough-and-ready town you might expect, Darwin is a lively, modern place with a young population, an easygoing lifestyle and a cosmopolitan atmosphere.

In part this is thanks to Cyclone Tracy, which did a comprehensive job of flattening Darwin on Christmas Day in 1974. People who were there during the reconstruction say a new spirit grew up with the new buildings, as Darwinites, showing true Top End resilience, took the chance to make their city one of which to be proud. Darwin became a brighter, smarter, sturdier place.

Darwin is still something of a frontier town, with a fairly transient population and a hard-drinking one at that – it's not easy to resist a beer or two after a day in the heat – but it is also becoming increasingly sophisticated. Darwin is extremely ethnically diverse with anywhere between 45 and 60 ethnic groups represented, depending on who you listen to. Asian and European accents are almost as thick in the air as the Aussie drawl.

A lot of people only live here for a year or two – it's surprising how many people you meet elsewhere who used to live in Darwin. It's reckoned you can consider yourself a 'Territorian' if you've stuck the climate and remoteness for five years. There is a constant flow of travellers coming and going from Asia, or making their way around Australia. Backpacks seem part of the everyday scene and people always appear to be heading somewhere else.

Darwin is an obvious base for trips to Kakadu and other Top End natural attractions, such as Litchfield National Park. It's a bit of an oasis too – whether you're travelling south to Alice Springs, west to Western Australia or east to Queensland, there are a lot of

km to be covered before you get anywhere and having reached Darwin many people rest a bit before leaving.

History

It took a long time to decide on Darwin as the site for the region's main centre and even after the city was established growth was slow and troubled. Early attempts to settle the Top End were mainly due to British fears that the French or Dutch might get a foothold in Australia. Between 1824 and 1829 Fort Dundas on Melville Island and Fort Wellington on the Cobourg Peninsula, 200 km north-east of Darwin, were settled and then abandoned. Victoria, settled in 1838 on Cobourg's Port Essington harbour, survived a cyclone and malaria, but was abandoned in 1849.

In 1845 the explorer Leichhardt reached Port Essington overland from Brisbane, arousing prolonged interest in the Top End. The region came under the control of South Australia in 1863, and more ambitious development plans were made. A settlement was established in 1864 at Escape Cliffs on the mouth of the Adelaide River, not too far from Darwin's present location, but it was abandoned in 1866. Finally Darwin was founded in 1869. The harbour had been discovered back in 1839 by John Lort Stokes aboard the *Beagle*, who named it Port Darwin after a former shipmate, the evolutionist Charles Darwin. At first the settlement was called Palmerston, but soon became unofficially known as Port Darwin and in 1911 the name was officially changed.

Darwin's growth was accelerated by the discovery of gold at Pine Creek, about 200 km south, in 1871. But once the gold fever had run its course Darwin's development slowed down, due to the harsh, unpredictable climate (including occasional cyclones) and poor communications with other Australian cities.

WW II put Darwin permanently on the map when the town became an important base for Allied action against the Japanese in the Pacific. The road south to the railhead at Alice Springs was surfaced, finally putting

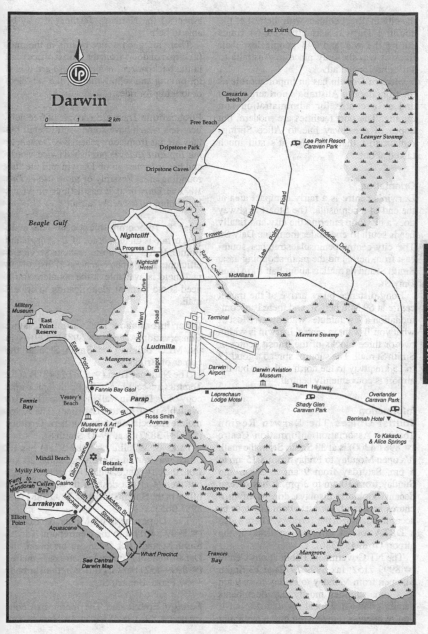

Darwin

0   1   2 km

Beagle Gulf

Lee Point

Casuarina Beach

Free Beach

Dripstone Park

Dripstone Caves

Lee Point Resort Caravan Park

Leanyer Swamp

Nightcliff

Progress Dr

Nightcliff Hotel

Rapid Creek

Trower Road

Rapid Creek Road

McMillans Road

Lee Point Road

Vanderlin Drive

Military Museum

East Point Reserve

East Point Rd

Mangrove

Dick Ward Drive

Bagot Road

Ludmilla

Terminal

Darwin Airport

Marrara Swamp

Darwin Aviation Museum

Fannie Bay

Vestey's Beach

Fannie Bay Gaol

Gregory St

Parap

Ross Smith Avenue

Leprechaun Lodge Motel

Stuart Highway

Shady Glen Caravan Park

Overlander Caravan Park

Berrimah Hotel

To Kakadu & Alice Springs

Mindil Beach

Myilly Point

Museum & Art Gallery of NT

Gilruth Avenue

Gardens Rd

Botanic Gardens

Frances Bay Drive

Casino

Cullen Bay

Ferry to Mandorah

Larrakeyah

Elliott Point

Aquascene

Mitchell Street

South Street

McMinn St

Wharf Precinct

See Central Darwin Map

Frances Bay

Mangrove

Mangrove

the city in direct contact with the rest of the country. Darwin was attacked 64 times during the war and 243 people lost their lives; it was the only place in Australia to suffer prolonged attack.

Modern Darwin has an important role as the front door to Australia's northern region and as a centre for administration and mining. The port facilities are modern, but hopes of a railway line to Alice Springs remain just that, although it's still much talked about.

Orientation

Darwin's centre is a fairly compact area at the end of a peninsula. The Stuart Highway does a big loop entering the city and finally heads south to end under the name Daly St. The city-centre peninsula stretches south-east from here, and the main shopping area, Smith St and its mall, is about half a km from Daly St.

Long-distance buses arrive at the transit centre at 69 Mitchell St, and there is accommodation a few minutes walk away. Most of what you'll want in central Darwin is within two or three blocks of the transit centre or Smith St mall. The suburbs spread a good 12 to 15 km away to the north and east, but the airport is conveniently central.

Information

Tourist Offices The Darwin Region Tourism Association Information Centre (☎ 8981 4300) is at 33 Smith St, in the mall. It's open Monday to Friday from 8.15 am to 5 pm, Saturday from 9 am to 3 pm and Sunday from 10 am to 3 pm. It has several decent booklets, displays dozens of brochures and can book just about any tour or accommodation in the Territory. There's also a DRTA tourist information desk at the airport (☎ 8945 3386).

The NT Government Publications Centre (☎ 8999 7152; fax 8999 7972) at 13 Smith St, open from Monday to Friday from 9 am to 4 pm, supplies mostly dry documents detailing laws and local regulations, but if you're interested in delving into a particular

aspect of the Northern Territory it may be able to help.

There are good notice boards in the mall (a couple of doors from the tourist office) and in the backpacker hostels – these are useful for buying and selling things (like vehicles) or looking for rides.

Publications There are a couple of free publications which have some useful detail but they are far from comprehensive. *Darwin & the Top End Today* is published twice-yearly and has information on Darwin and the surrounding area. Possibly of more use is *This Week in Darwin* as it has listings of what's happening on a weekly basis.

Post & Telecommunications The main post office is on the corner of Cavenagh and Edmunds Sts. The poste restante service is efficient; a computer-generated list of all mail held is available at the counter. You'll need some form of identification to collect mail.

Other Information The Australian Nature Conservation Agency (☎ 8981 5299) is in the MLC building on Smith St near the corner of Briggs St.

The National Trust (☎ 8981 2848) is at 52 Temira Crescent in Myilly Point – pick up a copy of its Darwin walking-tour leaflet (also available from the tourist office). The Automobile Association of the Northern Territory (☎ 8981 3837) is at 79-81 Smith St.

Parks & Wildlife (☎ 8989 5511) has its office way out in Palmerston, some 20 km from the city centre, which is a real nuisance, but there's also a desk in the main tourist office in the Smith St mall (☎ 8999 3881; fax 8981 0653).

The Department of Mines & Energy (☎ 8999 5461) is in the Centrepoint Tower, Smith St mall. For fishing information, the Department of Primary Industry & Fisheries (☎ 8999 4321) has its office in the Harbour View Plaza, Bennett St.

Foreign Embassies The Indonesian consulate (☎ 8941 0048) is at 18 Harry Chan

Ave (PO Box 1953, Darwin 0801) and is open weekdays from 9 am to 1 pm and 2 to 5 pm.

Bookshops Bookworld on Smith St mall is a good bookshop, as is Angus & Robertson in the Galleria shopping centre, also in the Smith St mall; you'll find all the Lonely Planet guides for travel to Asia here.

For maps, the NT General Store on Cavenagh St has a good range. Other places to try include the NT Government Publications Centre or the Ministry of Housing & Lands on Cavenagh St.

Medical & Emergency Services The Department of Health runs an International Vaccination Clinic (☎ 8981 4792) at 43 Cavenagh St. The Traveller's Medical & Vaccination Centre (☎ 8981 2907) is at 4 Westralia St. For emergency medical treatment phone the Royal Darwin Hospital on ☎ 8922 8888.

The Lifeline Crisis Line is ☎ 8981 9227.

Dangers & Annoyances Don't swim in Darwin waters from October to May. Stingers are prevalent, and there are crocodiles along the coast and rivers – any crocodiles found in the harbour are removed, and other beaches near the city are patrolled to minimise the risk. There's a Marine Stinger Emergency Line on ☎ 1800 079 909.

Town Centre
Despite its shaky beginnings and the destruction caused by WW II and Cyclone Tracy, Darwin still has a number of historic buildings. The National Trust produces an interesting booklet titled *A Walk through Historical Darwin*.

Old buildings include the **Victoria Hotel** on Smith St mall, originally built in 1894 and badly damaged by Tracy. On the corner of the mall and Bennett St, the stone **Commercial Bank** dates from 1884. The old **town hall**, a little farther down Smith St, was built in 1883 but was virtually destroyed by Tracy, despite its solid Victorian construction. Today only its walls remain.

Across the road, **Brown's Mart**, a former mining exchange dating from 1885, was badly damaged but now houses a theatre. There's a **Chinese temple**, glossy and new, on the corner of Woods and Bennett Sts.

Christ Church Cathedral, nearer the harbour, was destroyed by the cyclone. It was originally built in 1902, but all that remained after Tracy was the porch, which had been added in 1944. A new cathedral has been built and the old porch retained.

The 1884 **police station** and **old courthouse** at the corner of Smith St and the Esplanade were badly damaged, but have been restored and are now used as government offices. A little farther south along the Esplanade, **Government House**, built in stages from 1870, was known as the Residency until 1911, and has been damaged by just about every cyclone to hit Darwin. It is once again in fine condition.

Opposite Government House is a **monument** commemorating the submarine telegraph cable which once ran from Darwin into the sea on its crossing to Banyuwangi in Java. This cable put Australia into instant communication with Britain for the first time.

Dominating the streetscape in this corner of the city is the hideous new **Parliament Building**. The inside is fortunately much more appealing and is worth a wander around.

Other buildings of interest along the Esplanade include the agreeably tropical **Darwin Hotel**, and **Admiralty House** at the corner of Knuckey St.

Across the road at 74 The Esplanade, in Lyons Cottage, is the **British-Australian Telegraph Residence Museum**. It's free and open daily from 10 am to noon and 12.30 to 5 pm. There are displays on pre-1911 north Australian history. Farther along again is the pink and blue **Beaufort Darwin Centre**, housing a luxury hotel, a couple of up-market cafes, and the Performing Arts Centre (the latter on Mitchell St).

The Esplanade is fronted by the grassy expanse of **Bicentennial Park**, and a pleasant cliff-top pathway runs along from the Hotel Darwin to Daly St.

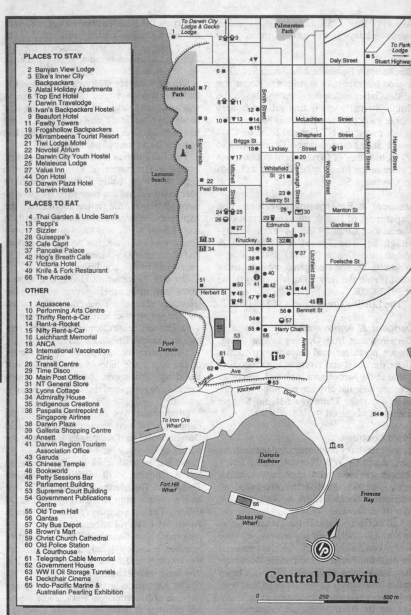

PLACES TO STAY

2 Banyan View Lodge
3 Elke's Inner City
   Backpackers
5 Alatai Holiday Apartments
6 Top End Hotel
7 Darwin Travelodge
8 Ivan's Backpackers Hostel
9 Beaufort Hotel
11 Fawlty Towers
19 Frogshollow Backpackers
20 Mirrambeena Tourist Resort
21 Tiwi Lodge Motel
22 Novotel Atrium
24 Darwin City Youth Hostel
25 Melaleuca Lodge
27 Value Inn
44 Don Hotel
50 Darwin Plaza Hotel
51 Darwin Hotel

PLACES TO EAT

4 Thai Garden & Uncle Sam's
13 Peppi's
17 Sizzler
28 Guiseppe's
32 Cafe Capri
37 Pancake Palace
42 Hog's Breath Cafe
47 Victoria Hotel
49 Knife & Fork Restaurant
66 The Arcade

OTHER

1 Aquascene
10 Performing Arts Centre
12 Thrifty Rent-a-Car
14 Rent-a-Rocket
15 Nifty Rent-a-Car
16 Leichhardt Memorial
18 ANCA
23 International Vaccination
   Clinic
26 Transit Centre
29 Time Disco
30 Main Post Office
31 NT General Store
33 Lyons Cottage
34 Admiralty House
35 Indigenous Creations
36 Paspalis Centrepoint &
   Singapore Airlines
38 Darwin Plaza
39 Galleria Shopping Centre
40 Ansett
41 Darwin Region Tourism
   Association Office
43 Garuda
45 Chinese Temple
46 Bookworld
48 Petty Sessions Bar
52 Parliament Building
53 Supreme Court Building
54 Government Publications
   Centre
55 Old Town Hall
56 Qantas
57 City Bus Depot
58 Brown's Mart
59 Christ Church Cathedral
60 Old Police Station
   & Courthouse
61 Telegraph Cable Memorial
62 Government House
63 WW II Oil Storage Tunnels
64 Deckchair Cinema
65 Indo-Pacific Marine &
   Australian Pearling Exhibition

Central Darwin

0   250   500 m

HUGH FINLAY

HUGH FINLAY

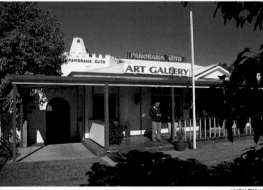

HUGH FINLAY

HUGH FINLAY

HUGH FINLAY

HUGH FINLAY

Northern Territory

A: Memorial to Harold Lasseter, Alice Springs
B: View from MacDonnell Ranges
C: Panorama Guth, Alice Springs
D: Grave of Rev John Flynn, Alice Springs

E: Classic outback road sign
F: Rusting machinery at the old mission, Hermannsburg

PAUL STEEL

NT TOURIST COMMISSION

TONY WHEELER

A
B
C

Northern Territory
A: Kata Tjuta (The Olgas)
B: The Ghan
C: N'Dhala Gorge

Aquascene

At Doctor's Gully, near the corner of Daly St and the Esplanade, fish come in for a feed every day at high tide. Half the stale bread in Darwin gets dispensed to a horde of milkfish, mullet, catfish and batfish. Some are quite big – the milkfish grow to over a metre and will demolish a whole slice of bread in one go. It's a great sight and children love it – the fish will take bread right out of your hand. Feeding times depend on the tides (☎ 8981 7837 for tide times). Admission is $4 ($2.50 children); the bread is free.

Botanic Gardens

The gardens' site north of the city centre was used to grow vegetables during the earliest days of Darwin. Tracy severely damaged the gardens, uprooting three-quarters of the plants. Fortunately, vegetation grows fast in Darwin's climate and the Botanic Gardens, with their noteworthy collection of tropical flora, have been restored. There's a coastal section over the road, between Gilruth Ave and Fannie Bay. It's an easy bicycle ride out to the gardens from the centre.

Indo-Pacific Marine & Australian Pearling Exhibition

This excellent aquarium is a successful attempt to display living coral and its associated life. Each small tank is a complete ecosystem, with only the occasional extra fish introduced as food for some of the carnivores such as stonefish or angler fish. They sometimes have box jellyfish, as well as more attractive creatures like sea horses, clown fish and butterfly fish. The living coral reef display is especially impressive.

Housed in the same building is the pearling exhibition, which deals with the history of the pearling industry in this area. While pearling around Darwin doesn't have the importance it has in places like Broome, quite a bit still goes on. The exhibition has excellent displays and informative videos.

Both displays are housed in the former Port Authority garage, at the Wharf Precinct, which has been completely renovated and air-conditioned. The Indo-Pacific Marine is open daily from 9 am to 5 pm (last entry 4 pm) and costs $10 ($4 children), and the exhibition hours are weekdays from 8 am to 5 pm, and weekends from 10 am to 6 pm. It costs $5.50 ($3).

Wharf Precinct

The Indo-Pacific Marine and Australian Pearling Exhibition are actually part of the Darwin Wharf Precinct. Developed over the past few years, the precinct has turned what was basically the city's ugly port facilities into something attractive.

Right at the outer end of the jetty is an old warehouse, now known as the Arcade, which houses a good food centre. The precinct also features the old **oil-storage tunnels** which were dug into the cliff-face below the city centre during WW II. They are open Tuesday to Sunday from 10 am to 2 pm, and entry is $3.

A shuttle bus operates between the Wharf Precinct sites and the northern end of Smith St mall, or it's a pleasant stroll if you have a morning to spare.

Museum & Art Gallery of the Northern Territory

This excellent museum and art gallery is on Conacher St at Fannie Bay, about four km from the city centre. It's bright, well presented and not too big, but full of interesting displays. A highlight is the Northern Territory Aboriginal art collection, with just the right mix of exhibits and information to introduce visitors to the purpose of this art, and its history and regional differences. It's particularly strong on carvings and bark paintings from Bathurst and Melville islands and from Arnhem Land.

There's also a good collection on the art of the Pacific and Asian nations closest to Australia, including Indonesian *ikat* (woven cloth) and gamelan instruments, and a sea gypsies' *prahu* (floating home) from Sabah in Malaysia.

Pride of place among the stuffed Northern Territory birds and animals undoubtedly goes to 'Sweetheart', a five-metre, 780-kg saltwater crocodile, who became quite a Top

End personality after numerous encounters with fishing dinghies on the Finnis River south of Darwin. Apparently he had a taste for outboard motors. He died when captured in 1979. You can also see a box jellyfish – safely dead – in a jar.

The non-Aboriginal Australian art collection includes works by top names like Nolan, Lindsay and Boyd. The museum has a good little bookshop and outside, but under cover, there is an excellent maritime display with a number of vessels, including an old pearling lugger and a Vietnamese refugee boat.

It's open Monday to Friday from 9 am to 5 pm, and Saturday and Sunday from 10 am to 5 pm. Admission is free. Bus Nos 4 and 6 go close by, or you can get there on the Tour Tub (see Getting Around).

Fannie Bay Gaol Museum
Another interesting museum is a little farther out of town at the corner of East Point Rd and Ross Smith Ave. This was Darwin's main jail from 1883 to 1979, after which a new maximum security lock-up opened at Berrimah. You can look round the old cells and see the gallows used in the Territory's last hanging in 1952. There are also good displays on Cyclone Tracy, transport, technology and industrial archaeology. The museum is open daily from 10 am to 5 pm; admission is free. Bus Nos 4 and 6 from the city centre go very close to the museum, and it's also on the Tour Tub route.

East Point Reserve
This spit of undeveloped land north of Fannie Bay is good to visit in the late afternoon when wallabies come out to feed, cool breezes spring up and you can watch the sunset across the bay. There are some walking and riding trails as well as a road to the tip of the point.

On the northern side of the point is a series of wartime gun emplacements and the **Military Museum**, devoted to Darwin's WW II activities, open daily from 9.30 am to 5 pm ($5). Bus Nos 4 and 6 will take you five km from the city centre to the corner of East Point Rd and Ross Smith Ave; from there it's

three km to the tip of the point, or you can take the Tour Tub.

Darwin Aviation Museum
Darwin's aviation museum would be unspectacular were it not for the American B52 bomber. This truly mammoth aircraft, one of only two displayed outside the USA, dominates the other displays, which include the wreck of a Japanese Zero fighter shot down in 1942. The museum is on the Stuart Highway in Winnellie, about five km from the centre. It is open daily from 10 am to 4 pm; entry is $6. Bus Nos 5 and 8 run along the Stuart Highway.

Beaches
Darwin has plenty of beaches, but you'd be wise to keep out of the water during the October to May wet season because of the deadly box jellyfish. Popular beaches include **Mindil** and **Vestey's** on Fannie Bay, and **Mandorah**, across the bay from the town (see Around Darwin).

In north Darwin, there's a stinger net protecting part of **Nightcliff** beach off Casuarina Drive, and a stretch of the seven-km **Casuarina** beach farther east is an official nude beach. This is a good beach but at low tide it's a long walk to the water's edge.

Organised Tours
There are innumerable tours in and around Darwin offered by a host of companies. The information office in the mall is the best place for information on what's available. Many tours go less frequently (if at all) in the wet season. Some of the longer or more adventurous have only a few departures a year; enquire in advance if you're interested.

Aboriginal Cultural Tours If Darwin is your only chance to delve into Aboriginal culture, there are a few options. The Frontier Darwin Hotel (☎ 1800 891 101; fax 8981 3173) has fairly contrived Aboriginal corroborees three times a week at 7.45 pm. The charge of $38 ($20 children) includes a barbecue.

You may get a more authentic feel for

Aboriginal culture on the four-hour White Crane Dreaming tour operated by Northern Gateway (☎ 8941 1394; fax 8941 2815). This tour includes a 25-minute flight to the homelands of the Kuwuma Djudian people, and a chance to sample bush tucker. The cost is $215 ($175 children aged three to 12).

City Sights Among the Darwin city tours, Darwin Day Tours' (☎ 8981 8696; fax 8981 1777) four-hour trip at 8.15 am daily is pretty comprehensive ($29; $15 children). The same company also does a 4½-hour Sunset Tour for $32 ($16). Keetleys Tours (☎ 8981 4422; fax 8941 1341) does similar tours for slightly less.

The Tour Tub (☎ /fax 8985 4779) is an open-sided minibus which tours the various Darwin sights throughout the day (see Getting Around below), and you can either stay on board and do a full circuit or get on and off at the various stops. The cost is $14 ($7 children).

Harbour Cruises Darwin Hovercraft Tours (☎ 8941 2233; fax 8981 8852) operates one-hour, 35-km hovercraft flights around the harbour from the Frances Bay Drive hoverport for $35 ($25 children), and these can be a lot of fun.

For something a little more sedate Darwin Duchess Cruises (☎ /fax 8978 5094) leaves Stokes Hill Wharf Wednesday to Sunday at 2 pm for a two-hour cruise around the harbour ($22; $12 children), and again at 5.30 pm for a two-hour sunset cruise.

Fishing The Tour Tub (☎ /fax 8985 4779) has a five-metre punt which is available for half-day fishing trips on the harbour, departing daily at 8 am and 1 pm. The cost is $55 ($40 children). Full-day trips cost $100 ($85) including lunch.

Barra Bash (☎ 1800 632 225) and NT Sportsfishing Safaris (☎ 8945 5338) also do one-day fishing trips out of Darwin.

Tours Farther Afield A number of operators do trips to the jumping crocodiles at Adelaide River, to the Crocodile Farm and to the Territory Wildlife Park on the Cox Peninsula road. For Adelaide River try Adelaide River Queen Cruises (☎ 8988 8144; fax 8988 8130), which does half-day trips at 7 am for $55 ($40 children), which includes the two-hour boat ride on the Adelaide River and a visit to Fogg Dam.

Darwin Day Tours (☎ 8981 8696; fax 8981 1777) does a three-hour trip to the Crocodile Farm at 12.30 pm ($25; $13 children), six-hour trips to the Territory Wildlife Park ($30, $16) departing at 7.30 am, and an eight-hour trip which covers the two for $51 ($29).

Festivals

Aside from the Beer Can Regatta in late June or early July, with its sports and contests, there is the Darwin Festival leading up to it, earlier in June. It's a week of concerts, dances, a picnic in the Botanic Gardens and a parade on the final day.

Darwin also goes into festive mood for May Day (International Labour Day), regarded as the start of the 'no-box-jellyfish season' and the occasion of big beach parties, rock concerts the night before, etc. Unfortunately the jellyfish don't always leave on time.

Darwinites are as fond of horse races as other Australians, and two big days at the Fannie Bay track are St Patrick's Day (17 March) and the Darwin Cup (October). The Royal Darwin Show takes place in July, and the Rodeo and Barefoot Mud Crab Tying Competition are in August.

Places to Stay – bottom end

Camping Sadly, Darwin takes no advantage of what could be fine camp sites on its many open spaces. East Point, for instance, would be superb. To camp or get an on-site van you must go to one of the privately run caravan parks in the outer city. A second drawback is that a number of the more conveniently situated caravan parks don't take tent campers. The closest place to the city is the *Leprechaun Lodge Motel* which has a limited number of camp/caravan sites at the rear – enquire at reception.

Shady Glen Caravan Park (☎ 8984 3330), 10 km east of the city, at the corner of Stuart Highway and Farrell Crescent, Winnellie; cramped and with old facilities; camp sites at $12 for two ($16 with power), on-site vans $36 for two.

Lee Point Resort (☎ 8945 0535), 15 km north of the city on Lee Point Rd. This is a new and spacious park close to the beach at Lee Point. The facilities are excellent although the shade trees are still a little small. Unpowered sites cost $14, or with power it's $17, no on-site vans or cabins.

Overlander Caravan Park (☎ 8984 3025), 13 km east of the city at 1064 McMillans Rd, Berrimah; camp sites at $12 for two ($14 powered), on-site vans $30 to $35.

Palms Caravan Park (☎ 8932 2891), 17 km southeast of town on the Stuart Highway at Berrimah; camp sites at $14 for two ($16 powered), or there are on-site vans at $36 and cabins for $68.

Also consider camping at Howard Springs, 26 km out, where there are two caravan parks which take campers (see Around Darwin).

Hostels There's a host of choices in this bracket, with several of the cheapest places on or near Mitchell St, conveniently close to the transit centre. Most places have guest kitchens, and the showers and toilets are almost always communal.

Very popular among travellers is the purpose-built *Frogshollow Backpackers* (☎ 8941 2600) at 27 Lindsay St, about 10 minutes walk from the transit centre but still close to the centre of town. It's a modern, spacious and clean place, and has two spas and a small swimming pool which guests can use. The charge is $13.50 a night in a fan-cooled, eight-bed dorm, and there are double rooms for $30, or $40 with attached bath and air-con. It has a well-appointed kitchen, common area with TV and travel information and, as with other hostels, it does pick-ups from the transit centre (and airport on demand). It also organises free trips for guests out to East Point at sunset.

Ivan's Backpackers Hostel (☎ 1800 800 798) at 97 Mitchell St has a pool, two kitchens and frequent barbecues. A dormitory bunk is $13 in a four to seven-bed air-con self-contained room complete with fridge and TV. Breakfast is included in the price, there's a bar and cheap meals in the evening, and free bicycles for guests to use. Double rooms are available for $45 with attached bath.

Right across the road from Ivan's, at 88 Mitchell St, is *Fawlty Towers* (☎ 1800 068 886), a friendly and informal place with dorm beds for $14, and doubles for $38.

The *Darwin City Youth Hostel* (☎ 8981 6344; fax 8981 6674) is at 69A Mitchell St and is part of the recently remodelled transit centre. Its rooms are all fan-cooled twins and cost $16 per person, or $14 for YHA members. The building has been extensively renovated, so the facilities are as good as any you'll find in the city and the location is great. They also have a comprehensive travel booking service.

Right across the road from the transit centre is the *Melaleuca Lodge* (☎ 1800 623 543), which has recently been transformed from one of Darwin's accommodation low points into a fresh, new backpacker hostel. Dorm beds are $14 (four to 10-bed rooms), or there are doubles with TV and fridge for $40 and triples for $50. All rooms are air-conditioned at night, the kitchen facilities are good and there's a travel desk and swimming pool.

Still on Mitchell St, but just north of Daly St, is *Elke's Inner City Backpackers* (☎ 1800 808 365; fax 8981 4401) at No 112. It's actually in a couple of recently renovated adjacent houses, and it has much more of a garden feel to it than those right in the heart of the city. There's a new pool and spa between the two buildings. Beds are $14.50 in four to six-bed dorms, or twin rooms are $35.

Farther north at 151 Mitchell St, about a 10-minute walk from the centre, is the family-run *Darwin City Lodge* (☎ 1800 808 151; fax 8941 0106). Formerly a family home, this place is one of the Cyclone Tracy survivors and is certainly a bit rough around the edges. However, it's clean, the atmosphere is good, there's a pool and the owners are friendly. It's $14 in a dorm, or there's a separate building nearby which has twin rooms for $35. Some of the rooms are air-conditioned.

In the same area is the *Gecko Lodge* (☎ 1800 811 250) at 146 Mitchell St. This is another smaller hostel in an old house, and there's a pool and a common room. Dorm beds cost $14, or there are twin rooms for $40, and at night all rooms are refreshingly air-conditioned.

The big YWCA *Banyan View Lodge* (☎ 8981 8644; fax 8981 6104) is at 119 Mitchell St. It takes women and men and has no curfew. Rooms have fans and fridges, and are clean and well-kept; there's two TV lounges, a kitchen and an outdoor spa. The charge is $15 per person in a twin share-room, $25/37 for singles/doubles, or $28/40 with air-con.

Places to Stay – middle

Guesthouses Darwin has a number of good small guesthouses, and these can make a pleasant change from the hostel scene, especially if you're planning a longer stay. Among those which aren't too far from the centre is the friendly, quiet and airy *Park Lodge* (☎ 8981 5692; fax 8981 3720) at 42 Coronation Drive in Stuart Park, only a short cycle or bus ride from the city centre. All rooms have fan, air-con and fridge; bathrooms, kitchen, sitting/TV room and laundry are communal. Air-con rooms cost $35/40, and this includes breakfast of toast and jam and tea/coffee. Numerous city buses, including Nos 5 and 8, run to this part of Darwin along the highway; ask the driver where to get off.

Farther out from the centre at 19 Harcus Crt, Malak, close to the airport is *Robyn's Nest* (☎ /fax 8927 7400). Two rooms on the ground floor of this family home are let out to guests, and the cost is $58 per room with attached bath. Both are air-conditioned, with TV, fridge and tea/coffee facilities, and there's a pool and spa.

Hotels Good value in this range is the charming *Darwin Hotel* (☎ 8981 9211; fax 8981 9575), right in the heart of the city on the Esplanade. There's a good range of facilities and a lush garden, which is a rarity in an inner-city hotel. The rooms are comfortable, and all are air-conditioned and have attached bath, TV, phone and fridge. The room rates are $82/105, and this includes taxes and a light breakfast.

Also good is the new *Value Inn* (☎ 8981 4733), in Mitchell St opposite the transit centre. The rooms are comfortable but small, and have fridge, colour TV and bathroom. The price is $55 for up to three people.

The *Don Hotel* (☎ 8981 5311) is also in the centre at 12 Cavenagh St, and air-con rooms with TV and fans cost $60/70 including a light breakfast.

Apartments & Holiday Flats There are plenty of modern places in Darwin, but prices in this range often vary between the Dry and the cheaper Wet. Many give discounts if you stay a week or more – usually of the seventh-night-free variety. Typically these places have air-con and swimming pools.

Good value here and well located is the *Peninsular Apartment Hotel* (☎ 1800 808 564; fax 8941 2547) at 115 Smith St, just a short walk from the city centre. The studios have a double and a single bed, and cost $99 ($84 in the Wet), while the two-bedroom apartments accommodate four people and cost $125 ($94.50).

The *Alatai Holiday Apartments* (☎ 1800 628 833; fax 8981 8887) are modern, self-contained apartments at the northern edge of the city centre on the corner of McMinn and Finniss Sts. Two-bed studio apartments cost $99 ($89 in the Wet), while two-bedroom apartments are $142 ($128) and for three-bedrooms it's $241 ($217). The studios only have a microwave and electric frypan for cooking; the larger apartments also have a stove.

Also in the city centre is the *Mirrambeena Tourist Resort* (☎ 8946 0111) at 64 Cavenagh St. This large place has 90-odd units which cost from $95/103 for a single/double, and $150 with cooking facilities.

Motels Motels in Darwin tend to be expensive. Conveniently central is the *Asti Motel*

(☎ 1800 063 335; fax 8981 8038) on the corner of Smith and Packard Sts just a couple of blocks from the city centre. Rooms cost $54, and there are some four-bed family rooms for $90.

Also in the centre and reasonably priced is the *Tiwi Lodge Motel* (☎ 8981 6471) on Cavenagh St, where rooms cost $61.

The *Tops Boulevard Motel* (☎ 8981 1544) at 38 Gardens Rd, the continuation of Cavenagh St beyond Daly St, is a comfortable modern motel. Double rooms cost $86, or studio rooms with cooking facilities are $115 (these sleep three people). All rooms have private bathroom, fridge and TV. There's also a pool, tennis court and restaurant.

Places to Stay – top end

Darwin's few up-market hotels are on the Esplanade, making best use of the prime views across the bay. The modern *Beaufort Hotel* (☎ 8982 9911) is part of the Performing Arts Complex, and has rooms for $225, and suites from $250.

Close by is the *Novotel Atrium* (☎ 8941 0755), which does indeed have an atrium, complete with lush tropical plants, and rooms for $155 and up. Also on the Esplanade is the *Darwin Travelodge* (☎ 8981 5388) with rooms from $160.

One block back from the Esplanade but still with the fine views is the city's only five-star hotel, the *Darwin Plaza Hotel* (☎ 8982 0000) at 32 Mitchell St. It has all the facilities you'd expect, including some non-smoking floors. Rooms here start at $205 for a single/double.

The new *Holiday Inn* should by now be taking shape on the Esplanade, behind the revamped transit centre.

Places to Eat

Darwin's proximity to Asia is obvious in its large number of fine Asian eateries, but on the whole eating out is expensive. Takeaway places, a growing number of lunch spots in and around the Smith St mall and the excellent Asian-style markets – held two or three times a week at various sites around the city – are the cheapest.

A number of eateries around town, particularly the pubs, offer discount meals for backpackers. Keep an eye out for vouchers at the hostels.

City Centre – cafes, pubs & takeaways

Next to the transit centre on Mitchell St there's the *Banyan food stalls*, which survived the transit centre revamp. A couple of places here offer a range of Asian dishes, and charge $5 for a piled-high plateful – good value. The Mexican *Coyote's* is extremely popular with travellers and has a reputation which spans the Top End.

A host of snack bars and cafes in Smith St mall offer lots of choice during the day – but, except for Thursday, the late shopping night, they're virtually all closed from about 5 pm and on Saturday afternoon and all day Sunday.

There's a good collection of fast-food counters in Darwin Plaza towards the Knuckey St end of the mall – *Omar Khayyam* for Middle Eastern and Indian, *La Veg* for health food, lasagne and light meals, *Ozzy Burgers* for, well, burgers, and *Roseland* for yoghurt, fruit salads and ice cream.

The Galleria shopping centre in the mall has a few good places: *Satay King* specialises in Malaysian food and serves that excellent Nonya dish, curry laksa; *Mamma Bella* serves predictable Italian food; *Al Fresco* has gourmet sandwiches and ice cream; and the *Galleria* is a straightforward burger place. There's a good seating area in the centre, although at lunchtimes it can be difficult to find a spare table.

Farther up the mall is Anthony Plaza where the *French Bakehouse* is one of the few places you can get a coffee and snack every day. For excellent Malay food head for the no-frills *Rendezvous Cafe*, in the Star Village Arcade, also off the Smith St mall. While the ambitious menu covers the full range of cafe dishes, it's the Malay food which stands out in this excellent little place.

Next door to Anthony Plaza is the *Hog's Breath Cafe*, a very popular American-style grill with good food, reasonable prices and occasional live entertainment.

Opposite Anthony Plaza is the Victoria Arcade where the *Victoria Hotel* has lunch or dinner for around $6 in its upstairs Settlers Bar. The barramundi burgers ($9 including chips and salad) are excellent, as are the steaks. In the arcade the *Satay House* has good cheap Indonesian fare.

Simply Foods at 37 Knuckey St is a busy health-food place. It's a good spot with appealing décor, music and friendly service.

At 2 Lindsay St there's the very popular open-air *Lindsay St Cafe* in the garden of a typical elevated tropical house. The menu is varied, with a tendency towards Asian cooking. Main courses are around $15.

Cafe Capri on Knuckey St is a chic new spot which has a good following. Pasta and salads are the go at lunchtime, while in the evening the meals are a bit more sophisticated, featuring dishes such as venison. Main meals are around $18 in the evening, less at lunchtimes.

In the *Green Room* at the Darwin Hotel you can have a barbecue lunch by the pool for $12; it also has menu dishes.

El Toro's is a popular Mexican restaurant in the Saloon Hotel at 21 Cavenagh St.

At the end of Stokes Hill Wharf at the Wharf Precinct, the *Arcade* is a small, Asian-style food centre with a number of different shops offering a variety of cuisines. This is a great spot for an al fresco fish & chips lunch washed down with a cool beer, or a cappuccino and cake.

City Centre – restaurants

The *Pancake Palace* on Cavenagh St near Knuckey St is open daily for lunch and in the evening until 1 am. Conveniently close to many of Darwin's night spots, it has sweet and savoury pancakes from $6.

Also on Cavenagh St is *Guiseppe's*, one of the few good Italian places in Darwin. Main dishes are in the $12 to $15 range, or there's pizza from $12.

An unusual find is the *Swiss Cafe & Restaurant* tucked away in the Harry Chan Arcade off 58 Smith St. For good, solid European food you can't beat this place, and it's reasonably priced with main dishes

around $12 to $15. Offering similar fare is the *Knife & Fork Restaurant*, on Mitchell St. Here the cuisine is mainly German and Russian, and main courses are in the $15 to $23 range.

Other restaurants include steakhouses, seafood specialists, and French, Greek and Italian cuisine. The numerous Chinese places are generally rather up-market. The *Jade Garden* in the Smith St mall (upstairs, roughly opposite the Victoria Arcade) offers a nine-course meal for $15 a head.

The *Sizzler* restaurant on Mitchell St is one of the chain found Australia-wide. It's amazingly popular, with queues out onto the footpath every night. The reason is that it's very good value: for around $15 you can fill your plate from a wide range of dishes, and have a dessert too.

One of the best restaurants in the city centre area is *Peppi's* at 84 Mitchell St. It's fully licensed and a two-course meal for two will set you back around $80 with drinks.

On Smith St, just beyond Daly St, the *Thai Garden Restaurant* serves not only delicious and reasonably priced Thai food but pizzas too! It has a few outdoor tables. There's a takeaway 'Aussie-Chinese' place across the road, and the 24-hour *Uncle Sam's* fast-food joint next door.

Markets

Easily the best all-round eating experience in Darwin is the bustling Asian-style market at Mindil Beach on Thursday nights during the dry season. People begin arriving from 5.30 pm, bringing tables, chairs, rugs, grog and kids to settle under the coconut palms for sunset and decide which of the tantalising food-stall aromas has the greatest allure. It's difficult to know whether to choose Thai, Sri Lankan, Indian, Chinese, Malaysian, Greek or Portuguese. You'll even find Indonesian black rice pudding. All prices are reasonable – around $3 to $5 for a meal. There are cake stalls, fruit-salad bars, arts and crafts stalls – and sometimes entertainment in the form of a band or street theatre.

Similar food stalls can be found at the Parap market on Saturday morning, the one at Rapid Creek on Sunday morning, and in the Smith St mall in the evening (except Thursday), but Mindil Beach is the best for atmosphere and proximity. It's about two km from the city centre, off Gilruth Ave. During the Wet, the market transfers to Rapid Creek. Bus Nos 4 and 6 go past Mindil Beach: No 4 goes on to Rapid Creek, No 6 to Parap.

Entertainment

Darwin is a lively city with bands at several venues and a number of clubs and discos. More sophisticated tastes are also catered for, with theatre, film, concerts and a casino.

The best source of what's on around town is probably the *Avagoodweegend* liftout in the Friday edition of the *NT News*.

Bars & Live Music Live bands play upstairs at the *Victoria Hotel* Wednesday to Saturday from 9 pm. The *Billabong Bar* in the Atrium Hotel, on the corner of the Esplanade and Peel St, has live bands on Friday and Saturday nights until 1 am. Take a look at the hotel's spectacular seven-storey glass-roofed atrium while you're there.

The Darwin Hotel is pleasant in the evening for a quiet drink. There's a patio section by the pool. It's livelier on Friday night when there's a band in the *Green Room*, or on Wednesday to Saturday nights in the *Pickled Parrot Piano Bar*, and there's often bands playing in *The Driveway*, the pub's former drive-in bottle shop which has been turned into a small venue.

The *Jabiru Bar* in the Atrium Hotel is the venue on Wednesday evening for Crab Races. It's all very light-hearted and there are prizes for the winners.

There's also live music in the evenings at *Sweetheart's Bar* at the MGM Grand Darwin casino.

Nightclubs & Discos The *Brewery Bar* in the Top End Hotel on the corner of Mitchell and Daly Sts is a popular evening venue. The *Beachcomber* bar at the rear is a popular disco and nightclub (Wednesday to Saturday), while the down-market *Sportsmens Bar* at the front on Mitchell St offers enter-

tainment of the 'prawns and porn' variety – cheap food and strip-shows to attract the punters.

Petty Sessions on the corner of Mitchell and Bennett Sts is a combination wine bar, nightclub and disco. It's quite a popular place and stays open to 2 am.

On the small street which runs between Smith and Cavenagh Sts one block from Knuckey St is the *Time* disco. It's probably the most popular nightspot in the city, and stays open until the early hours.

Another late night venue is *Caesars* nightclub at the Don Hotel on Cavenagh St.

Folk & Country Music For something a bit more laid back there's the *Top End Folk Club* which meets every second Sunday of the month at the Northern Territory University Social Club, The Breezway, at the Casuarina uni campus. Visitors are welcome. Phone ☎ 8988 1301 for more details.

If you're into Country & Western music, the NT Country Music Association meets every second Wednesday at the Driver Primary School out in Palmerston. This is the place for bootscooters! Contact ☎ 8932 1030 for details.

Jazz On Sunday afternoons at the MGM Grand Darwin casino there's *Jazz on the Lawns*, where you can eat, watch the sunset and listen to some fairly uninspired jazz.

Theatre The *Performing Arts Centre* (☎ 8981 1222) on Mitchell St, opposite McLachlan St, hosts a variety of events, from fashion award nights to plays, rock operas, pantomimes and concerts.

The Darwin Theatre Company (☎ 8981 8424) often has play readings and other performances around the city.

The old Brown's Mart (☎ 8981 5522) on Harry Chan Ave is another venue for live theatre performances.

Cinemas There are several cinemas in town and the *Darwin Film Society* (☎ 8981 2215) has regular showings of off-beat/artistic films at the Museum Theatrette in the

An All-Australian Game

The Alice and Darwin casinos offer plenty of opportunities to watch the Australian gambling mania in full flight. You can also observe a part of Australia's true cultural heritage, the all-Australian game of two-up.

The essential idea of two-up is to toss two coins and obtain two heads. The players stand around a circular playing area and bet on the coins showing either two heads or two tails when they fall. The 'spinner' uses a 'kip' to toss the coins and the house pays out and takes in as the coins fall – except that nothing happens on 'odd' tosses (one head, one tail) unless they're thrown five times in a row. In this case you lose unless you have also bet on this possibility. The spinner continues tossing until they either throw a pair of tails, throw five odds or throw three pairs of heads. If the spinner manages three pairs of heads then they also win at 7½ to one on any bet placed on that possibility, then start tossing all over again. When the spinner finally loses, the next player in the circle takes over as spinner. ■

Museum & Art Gallery of the Northern Territory. The film society also runs the unusual *Deckchair Cinema* (☎ 8981 0700) by the old power station near Stokes Hill Wharf. Here you can watch a movie under the stars while reclining in a deckchair. Screenings are listed in the newspapers, or on fliers around town.

Casino Finally, there's the *MGM Grand Darwin* casino on Mindil Beach off Gilruth Ave – as long as you're 'properly dressed'. That means no thongs, and men wearing shorts will have to conform to the bizarre Aussie predilection for long socks!

Things to Buy

Aboriginal art is generally cheaper in Alice Springs, but Darwin has greater variety. The Raintree Gallery at 29 Knuckey St is one of a number of places offering a range of art work – bark paintings from Arnhem Land, and interesting carvings by the Tiwi people of Bathurst and Melville islands and by the peoples of central Australia. Shades of Ochre in the Smith St mall is another place with quality items.

Another excellent place is Framed, a gallery on the Stuart Highway in Stuart Park which is heavily into Aboriginal art. There are some fine works here, with prices to match.

T-shirts printed with Aboriginal designs are popular but quality and prices vary. Riji Dij at 11 Knuckey St has a large range of T-shirts for $25. They are printed by Tiwi Designs and Territoriana, both local companies using Aboriginal designs and, to a large extent, Aboriginal labour. It stocks Tiwi printed fabric and clothing made from fabric printed by central Australian Aboriginal people. Another place worth trying is Indigenous Creations on Smith St mall.

You can find Balinese and Indian clothing at Darwin's markets – Mindil Beach (Thursday evening, dry season only), Parap (Saturday morning) and Rapid Creek (Sunday morning, and Thursday evening in the wet season). Local arts and crafts (the market at Parap is said to be the best), jewellery and bric-a-brac are on sale too.

Getting There & Away

Air Darwin is becoming increasingly busy as an international and domestic gateway.

International A popular international route is to and from Indonesia with the Indonesian airlines Merpati or Garuda. You can book on Merpati at Natrabu (☎ 8981 3695), an Indonesian government travel agency at 16 Westlane Arcade (behind the Victoria Hotel on Smith St mall). Merpati flies twice a week to and from Kupang in Timor ($198 one way, $330 return), and to Ambon on Monday and Friday ($500 return).

Garuda (☎ 8981 6422), on Cavenagh St,

has direct flights to Denpasar in Bali ($540 one way, $900 return). Ansett (☎ 13 1300) at 14 Smith St mall and Qantas (☎ 13 1313) at 16 Bennett St also fly this route for the same fare.

Royal Brunei Airlines (☎ 8941 1394), also on Cavenagh St, flies twice weekly between Darwin and Bandar Seri Begawan, and on to Manila and Hong Kong.

Singapore Airlines (☎ 8941 1799), in the Paspalis Centrepoint building at the corner of Smith St mall and Knuckey St, also flies to Darwin.

Malaysian Airlines (☎ 8941 3055), on the 2nd floor at 38 Mitchell St, has weekly flights to Kuala Lumpur for $750 one way and $1100 return.

Domestic Within Australia you can fly to Darwin from other states with Qantas and Ansett.

There are often stops or transfers at Alice Springs, Brisbane or Adelaide on longer flights. Some flights from Queensland stop at Gove or Groote Eylandt. One-way fares include Adelaide $536, Alice Springs $353, Perth $628, Broome $320, Cairns $418, Kununurra $158, Mt Isa $352, Brisbane $615 and Sydney $620. In Darwin, Qantas (☎ 13 1313) is at 16 Bennett St, and Ansett (☎ 13 1300) is at 14 Smith St mall.

For air travel within the Northern Territory see the air-fares chart in the introductory Getting Around section to this chapter. Airnorth's office (☎ 1800 627 474) is at Darwin airport.

Bus You can reach Darwin by bus on three routes – the Western Australian route from Broome, Derby and Kununurra; the Queensland route through Mt Isa to Threeways and up the Track; or straight up the Track from Alice Springs. Greyhound Pioneer and McCafferty's both have daily services on all these routes.

On Queensland services you often have to change buses at Threeways or Tennant Creek and Mt Isa. For Western Australia, Greyhound Pioneer and McCafferty's go to and from Perth daily through Kununurra,

Broome and Port Hedland. All buses stop at Katherine.

Fares can vary a bit between the companies, but if one discounts a fare the other tends to follow quite quickly. Although fares vary, travel times are very similar, but beware of services that schedule long waits for connections in Tennant Creek or Mt Isa. For example, you pay around $100 one way to Darwin from Tennant Creek (13 hours), $155 from Mt Isa (21 hours), $250 from Brisbane (51 hours), $90 from Kununurra, $142 from Alice Springs (19 hours), $178 from Broome (22 hours) and $348 from Perth (57 hours). In Darwin both Greyhound Pioneer (☎ 13 2030) and McCafferty's (☎ 13 1499) operate from the transit centre at 69 Mitchell St.

Car Darwin has numerous budget car-rental operators, as well as all the major national and international companies.

Rent-a-Rocket and Nifty Rent-a-Car offer similar deals on their mostly 1970s and early 1980s cars. Costs depend on whether you're staying near Darwin, or going farther afield to Kakadu, Katherine, Litchfield Park and so on. For local trips with Rent-a-Dent you pay around $35 a day, depending on the vehicle, and must stay within 70 km of Darwin. This includes 150 free km, but with these deals you can't go beyond Humpty Doo or Acacia Store (about 70 km down the Track). The prices drop for longer rentals.

Value Rent-a-Car has vehicles from $37, but this doesn't include any free km.

Territory Rent-a-Car is far and away the biggest local operator and is probably the best value. Discount deals to look for include cheaper rates for four or more days hire, weekend specials (three days for roughly the price of two), and one-way hires (to Jabiru, Katherine or Alice Springs). Daily charges start at around $45 daily for a small car, including 100 free km per day.

There are also plenty of 4WD vehicles available in Darwin, but you usually have to book ahead, and fees and deposits can be hefty. The best place to start looking is probably Territory, which has several different models – the cheapest, a Suzuki four-seater, costs around $95 a day including insurance, plus 28c a km over 100 km. Territory also has camping equipment packages at $25 per vehicle per day.

Brits: Australia rents 4WDs and campervans.

Rental companies, including the cut-price ones, generally operate a free towing or replacement service if the vehicle breaks down. But (especially with the cheaper operators) check the paperwork to see exactly what you're covered for in terms of damage to vehicles and injuries to passengers. The usual age and insurance requirements apply in Darwin and there may be restrictions on off-bitumen driving, or on the distance you're allowed to go from the city. Even with the big firms the insurance does not cover you when driving off the bitumen, so make sure you know exactly what your liability is in the event of an accident.

Most rental companies are open every day and have agents in the city centre to save you trekking out to the Stuart Highway. Territory, Budget, Hertz and Thrifty all have offices at the airport. Other addresses are:

Avis
  145 Stuart Highway, Stuart Park (☎ 1800 225 533; fax 8981 3155)
Brits: Australia
  Stuart Highway, Stuart Park (☎ 1800 331 454; fax (03) 9416 2933)
Budget
  69 Mitchell St (☎ 1800 805 627; fax 8981 1777)
Hertz
  Cnr Smith & Daly Sts (☎ 1800 891 112; fax 8981 0288)
Nifty Rent-a-Car
  10 McLachlan St (☎ 8981 2999; fax 8941 0662)
Rent-a-Rocket
  McLachlan St (☎ 8941 3733)
Territory Rent-a-Car
  64 Stuart Highway, Parap (☎ 1800 891 125; fax 8981 5247)
Thrifty Rent-a-Car
  Cnr Smith & McLachlan Sts (☎ 8981 8555; fax 8981 1697)
Value Rent-a-Car
  Mitchell St (☎ 8981 5599)

Getting Around

To/From the Airport Darwin's busy airport, only about six km from the centre of town, handles international flights as well as domestic ones. Hertz, Budget, Thrifty and Territory Rent-a-Car have desks at the airport. The taxi fare into the centre is about $12.

There is an airport shuttle bus (☎ 8941 5000) for $6, which will pick up or drop off almost anywhere in the centre. When leaving Darwin book a day before departure.

Bus Darwin has a fairly good city bus service – Monday to Friday. On Saturday, services cease around lunchtime and on Sunday and holidays they shut down completely. The city services start from the small terminal (☎ 8989 6540) on Harry Chan Ave, near the corner of Smith St. Buses enter the city along Mitchell St and leave along Cavenagh St.

Fares are on a zone system – shorter trips are $1 or $1.40, and the longest cost $1.90. Bus No 4 (to Fannie Bay, Nightcliff, Rapid Creek and Casuarina) and No 6 (Fannie Bay, Parap and Stuart Park) are useful for getting to Aquascene, the Botanic Gardens, Mindil Beach, the Museum of Arts & Sciences, Fannie Bay Gaol Museum and East Point. Bus Nos 5 and 8 go up the Stuart Highway past the airport to Berrimah, from where No 5 goes north to Casuarina and No 8 continues along the highway to Palmerston.

The Tour Tub (☎ 8985 4779) is a private bus which does a circuit of the city, calling at the major places of interest, and you can hop on or off anywhere. In the city centre it leaves from Knuckey St, at the end of the Smith St mall. The set fare is $14, and the buses operate hourly from 9 am to 4 pm. Sites visited include Aquascene (only at fish-feeding times), Indo-Pacific Marine and Wharf Precinct, the MGM Grand Darwin casino, the museum and art gallery, Military Museum, Fannie Bay Gaol, Parap markets (Saturday only) and the Botanic Gardens.

Car See Getting There & Away in this section for details on car rental.

Bicycle Darwin has a fairly extensive network of bike tracks. It's a pleasant ride out from the city to the Botanic Gardens, Fannie Bay, East Point or even, if you're feeling fit, all the way to Nightcliff and Casuarina.

Many of the backpackers hostels have bicycles, and these are often free for guests to use, otherwise there's a small rental charge.

The Top End

There are numerous places of interest close to Darwin, and several of the more remote and spectacular Top End areas are becoming increasingly accessible. The chief glory among the latter is Kakadu National Park. Litchfield National Park, to the south of Darwin, and Melville and Bathurst islands to the north are other places that are worth the effort.

A group of people can hire a vehicle in Darwin and get to most of the mainland places quite economically. There are also tours from Darwin to many of these places (see the Darwin Getting Around section). Some additional places that can be reached from Darwin are covered in the Down the Track section later in this chapter.

AROUND DARWIN

All the places listed here are within a couple of hours travel from the city.

Mandorah

It's only 10 km across the harbour by boat to this popular beach resort on the tip of Cox Peninsula – you can reach it by road, but that's nearly 140 km, about half of it on unsealed roads. The return ferry trip is $15, with the first departure from Darwin at 6.15 am and the last one at 6.05 pm; the crossing takes about 30 minutes. The ferries leave from the Cullen Bay Marina north of the city centre about eight times a day.

Howard Springs Nature Park

The springs, with crocodile-free swimming, are 35 km east of the city. Turn off to the left 24 km down the Stuart Highway, beyond Palmerston. The forest-surrounded swimming hole can get uncomfortably crowded because it's so convenient to the city. Nevertheless on a quiet day it's a pleasant spot for an excursion and there are short walking tracks and lots of birdlife.

Places to Stay There are two nearby caravan parks. The *Howard Springs Caravan Park* (☎ 8983 1169) at Whitewood Rd has unpowered ($12) and powered ($14) caravan sites only.

The *Coolalinga Caravan Park* (☎ 8983 1026) is actually on the Stuart Highway, and is not as close to the springs. Unpowered sites are $10, and with power it's $13.

Arnhem Highway

The Arnhem Highway branches off towards Kakadu, 33 km south of Darwin. Only 10 km along this road you come to the small town of **Humpty Doo**. The *Humpty Doo Hotel* is a colourful pub with some real character, and it does counter lunches and teas all week. Sunday, when local bands usually play, is particularly popular. Graeme Gow's Reptile World has a big collection of Australian snakes and a knowledgeable owner (open daily from 8.30 am to 6 pm).

About 15 km beyond Humpty Doo is the turn-off to **Fogg Dam Conservation Reserve**, a great place for watching water birds. A farther eight km along the Arnhem Highway is **Adelaide River Crossing** where you can take a 1½-hour river cruise and see saltwater crocodiles jump for bits of meat held out on the end of poles. These trips cost $24 and depart at 9 and 11.30 am most days of the year. The whole thing is a bit of a circus really, but it's fun to see crocs doing something other than sunning themselves on a river bank.

The **Window on the Wetlands** centre is an ultra-modern creation atop Beatrice Hill, a small hill by the Arnhem Highway just a few km past the Fogg Dam turn-off. It's the park headquarters for the new **Mary River National Park**, which encompasses import-

Crocodile Wrestling

There are two types of crocodile in Australia – the freshwater or 'freshie' *(Crocodylus johnstoni)* and the saltwater or 'saltie' *(C. porosus)* – and both are present in the Territory. After a century of being hunted, crocodiles are now protected in the Northern Territory – freshies since 1964 and salties since 1971. They are currently thought to number around 100,000.

The smaller freshwater crocodile is endemic to Australia and is found in freshwater rivers and billabongs, while the larger saltwater crocodile can be found in or near almost any body of water, fresh or salt. Freshwater crocodiles, which have narrower snouts and rarely exceed three metres in length, are harmless to people unless provoked, but saltwater crocodiles can definitely be dangerous.

Ask locally before swimming or even paddling in any rivers or billabongs in the Top End – attacks on humans by salties happen more often than you might think. Warning signs are posted alongside many dangerous stretches of water. The beasts are apparently partial to dogs, and even from some distance can be attracted by the sound of dogs barking.

Crocodiles have become a major tourist attraction (eating the odd tourist certainly helps in this respect) and the Northern Territory is very big on crocodile humour. Darwin's shops have a plentiful supply of crocodile T-shirts including the Darwin Crocodile Wrestling Club shirt, complete with gory blood stains and a large hole 'bitten' out of one side. ∎

Saltie   Freshie

ant Mary River wetlands north and south of the Arnhem Highway. The centre has some excellent 'touchy-feely' displays which give some great detail on the wetland ecosystem, as well as the history of the local Aboriginal people and the European pastoral activity which has taken place in the area over the years. There's also great views out over the Mary River system.

Mary River Crossing, 47 km farther on, is popular for barramundi fishing and for camping. A reserve here includes lagoons which are a dry-season home for water birds, and granite outcrops which shelter wallabies.

The *Bark Hut Inn*, two km beyond Mary River Crossing at **Annaburroo**, is another pleasant place for a halt. There's accommodation here but it's no great shakes. Camping costs $10 for a site with or without power, or there's basic accommodation at $20 per person.

The turn-off to Cooinda (in Kakadu) is 19 km beyond the Bark Hut. This is an unsealed road (known as the Old Darwin Rd), often impassable in the Wet, and it's easier to continue along the sealed highway. The entrance to Kakadu National Park is a farther 19 km along the highway. Some Darwin city buses go out as far as Humpty Doo. There are also Greyhound Pioneer and McCafferty's bus services along the Arnhem Highway (see the Kakadu National Park Getting There & Around section).

Darwin Crocodile Farm

On the Stuart Highway, just a little south of the Arnhem Highway turn-off, this crocodile farm has around 7000 saltwater and freshwater crocodiles. This is the residence of many

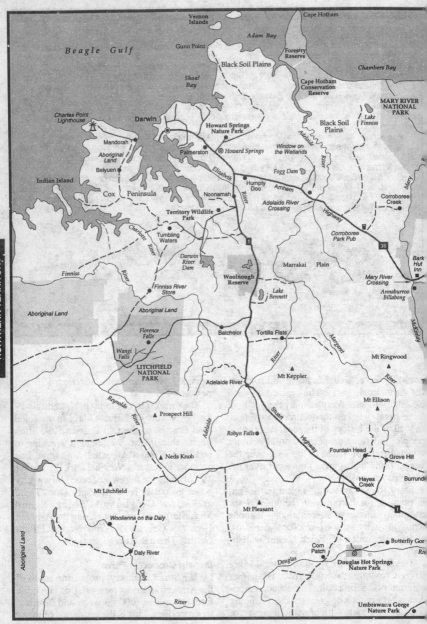

NORTHERN TERRITORY

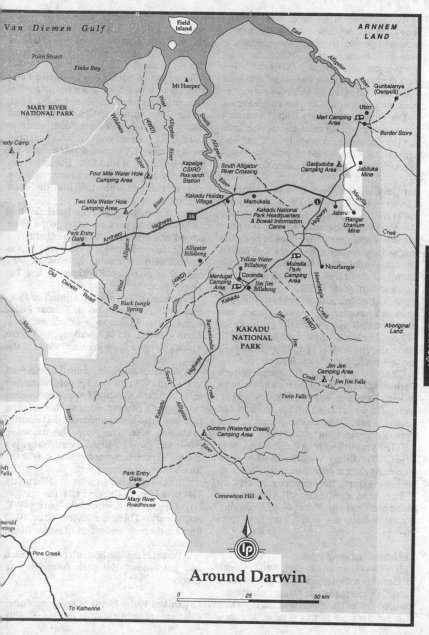

Around Darwin

0   25   50 km

of the crocodiles taken out of Northern Territory waters because they've become a hazard to people. But don't imagine they're here out of human charity. This is a farm, not a rest home, and around 2000 of the beasts are killed each year for their skins and meat – you can find crocodile steaks or even crocodile burgers in a number of Darwin eateries.

The farm is open daily from 10 am to 4 pm. Feedings are the most spectacular times to visit and these occur daily at 2 pm, and again on Monday, Wednesday and weekends at noon. Entry is $9.50 (children $5).

Territory Wildlife Park & Berry Springs

The turn-off to Berry Springs is 48 km down the Track from Darwin, then it's 10 km along the Cox Peninsula road to the **Territory Wildlife Park**. On 400 hectares of bushland this wildlife park (run by Parks & Wildlife) has some excellent exhibits featuring a wide variety of Australian birds, mammals, reptiles and fish, some of which are quite rare. There's a reptile house, superb walk-through aquarium, nocturnal house, aviaries and nature trails. It's well worth the $10 entry fee ($5 children) and you'll need half a day to see it all. The park is open daily from 8.30 am to 4 pm (gates close at 6 pm).

Close by is the **Berry Springs Nature Park** which is a great place for a swim and a picnic. There's a warm thermal waterfall, spring-fed pools ringed with paperbarks and pandanus palms, and abundant birdlife. It is open daily from 8 am to 6.30 pm.

A few km farther along the Cox Peninsula road is **Tumbling Waters**, another good picnic and camping area, although there's no swimming due to the presence of salties.

The road continues all the way to **Mandorah**, the last 30 km or so being dirt. It's much easier just to catch the ferry from Darwin.

Litchfield National Park

This 650-sq-km national park, 140 km south of Darwin, encloses much of the Tabletop Range, a wide sandstone plateau mostly surrounded by cliffs. Four waterfalls, which drop off the edge of this plateau, and their surrounding rainforest patches are the park's main attractions. It's well worth a visit, although it's best to avoid weekends as Litchfield is a very popular day-trip destination for locals.

There are two routes to Litchfield Park, both about a two-hour drive from Darwin. One, from the north, involves turning south off the Berry Springs to Cox Peninsula road onto a well-maintained dirt road, which is suitable for conventional vehicles except in the wet season. A second approach is along a bitumen and dirt road from Batchelor into the east of the park. The two access roads join up so it's possible to do a loop from the Stuart Highway.

If you enter the park from Batchelor it is 18 km from the park boundary to the **Florence Falls** turn-off. The waterfalls lie five km off the road along a good track. This is an excellent swimming hole in the dry season, as is Buley Rockhole, a few km away, where you can also camp.

Eighteen km beyond the turn-off to Florence Falls is the turn-off to **Tolmer Falls**, which are a 400-metre walk off the road. There's also a 1.5-km walking track here which gives you some excellent views of the area.

It's a farther seven km along the main road to the turn-off to the most popular attraction in Litchfield – **Wangi Falls** (pronounced 'wong-gye'), two km along a side road. The falls here flow year round and fill a beautiful swimming hole. There are also extensive picnic and camping areas. From Wangi it's about 16 km to the rangers' station near the park's northern access point.

Bush camping is also allowed at the pretty **Tjaynera (Sandy Creek) Falls**, in a rainforest valley in the south of the park (4WD access only). There are several other 4WD tracks in the park, and plenty of bushwalking possibilities.

As usual in the Top End, it's easier to reach and get around the park from May to October.

Organised Tours Plenty of companies offer day trips to Litchfield from Darwin. Woolly

Butt (☎ 8941 2600), operating out of Frogshollow Backpackers in Darwin, is popular. The price is $65, including morning tea and lunch.

Australian Outback Expeditions (☎ 1800 891 190) offers Aboriginal culture tours to the area. These involve camping at Gurudju on Aboriginal land on the Finniss River north of the park. In addition to the Aboriginal culture aspect of the tour, visits to the park's main attractions are included. The trips cost $360 for 2½ days, or $510 for 3½ days, and you can opt to stay longer at Gurudju.

KAKADU NATIONAL PARK

Kakadu National Park is one of the natural marvels not just of the Northern Territory, but of Australia. The longer you stay, the more rewarding it is.

Kakadu stretches more than 200 km south from the coast and 100 km from east to west, with the main entrance 153 km by bitumen road east of Darwin. It encompasses a variety of superb landscapes, swarms with wildlife and has some of Australia's best Aboriginal rock art.

Kakadu was proclaimed a national park in three stages. Stage One, the eastern and central part of the park including Ubirr, Nourlangie, Jim Jim Falls, Twin Falls and Yellow Water Billabong, was declared in 1979 and is on the World Heritage List for both its natural and cultural importance – a rare distinction. Stage Two, in the north, was declared in 1984 and won World Heritage listing for its natural importance. Stage Three, in the south, was finally listed in 1991, bringing virtually the whole of the South Alligator River system within the park.

The name Kakadu comes from Gagadju, one of the local Aboriginal languages, and much of Kakadu is Aboriginal land, leased to the government for use as a national park. There are several Aboriginal settlements in the park and about one-third of the park rangers are Aboriginal people. Enclosed by the park, but not part of it, are a few tracts of land designated for other purposes – princi-

pally three uranium-mining leases in the east.

Some of the southern areas within the park are subject to a land claim under the Native Title Act by the Jawoyn people of the Katherine region. Should the claim be successful, the land will be leased back to the ANCA for continued use as a national park.

Geography & Vegetation

A straight line on the map separates Kakadu from the Arnhem Land Aboriginal Land to its east, which you can't enter without a permit. The circuitous Arnhem Land escarpment, a dramatic 100 to 200-metre-high sandstone cliff line that provides the natural boundary of the rugged Arnhem Land plateau, winds some 500 km through east and south-east Kakadu.

Creeks cut across the rocky plateau and tumble off the escarpment as thundering waterfalls in the wet season. They then flow across the lowlands to swamp the vast flood plains of Kakadu's four north-flowing rivers, turning the north of the park into a kind of huge, vegetated lake. From west to east the rivers are the Wildman, the West Alligator, the South Alligator and the East Alligator. Such is the difference between dry and wet seasons that areas on river flood plains which are perfectly dry underfoot in September will be under three metres of water a few months later. As the waters recede in the Dry, some loops of wet-season watercourses become cut off, but don't dry up. These are billabongs – and they're often carpeted with water lilies and are a magnet for water birds.

The coastline has long stretches of mangrove swamp, important for halting erosion and as a breeding ground for marine and birdlife. The southern part of the park is dry lowlands with open grassland and eucalypts. Pockets of monsoon rainforest crop up here as well as in most of the park's other landscapes.

In all, Kakadu has over 1000 plant species, and a number are still used by the local Aboriginal people for food, bush medicine and other practical purposes.

Climate

The great change between the Dry and the November-to-March Wet makes a big difference to visitors to Kakadu. Not only is the landscape transformed as the wetlands and waterfalls grow, but Kakadu's lesser roads become impassable in the Wet, cutting off some highlights, such as Jim Jim Falls. The local Aboriginal people recognise six seasons in the annual cycle.

The 'build-up' to the Wet (known as *Gunumeleng*) starts in October. Humidity and the temperatures rise (to 35°C or more) – and the number of mosquitoes, always high near water, rises to near-plague proportions. By November the thunderstorms have started, billabongs start to be replenished and the water birds disperse.

The Wet proper *(Gudjuek)* continues through January, February and March, with violent thunderstorms and an abundance of plant and animal life thriving in the hot, moist conditions. Around 1300 mm of rain falls in Kakadu, most of it during this period.

April is *Banggerreng*, the season when storms (known as 'knock 'em down' storms) flatten the spear grass, which during the course of the Wet has shot up to two metres in height.

Yekke, from May to mid-June, is the season of mists, when the air starts to dry out. It is quite a good time to visit – there aren't too many other visitors, the wetlands and waterfalls still have a lot of water and most of the tracks are open.

The most comfortable time is the late Dry, in July and August – *Wurrgeng* and *Gurrung*. This is when wildlife, especially birds, congregates in big numbers around the shrinking billabongs and watercourses, but it's also when most tourists come to the park.

Wildlife

Kakadu has about 25 species of frog, 60 types of mammal, 51 freshwater fish species, 75 types of reptile, 280 bird species (one-third of all those native to Australia) and at least 4500 kinds of insect. There are frequent additions to the list, and a few of the rarer species are unique to the park. Kakadu's wetlands are on the UN list of Wetlands of International Importance, principally because of their crucial significance to so many types of water bird.

You'll only see a tiny fraction of these creatures in a visit to the park since many are shy, nocturnal or few in numbers. Take advantage of talks and walks led by park rangers – mainly in the Dry – to get to know and see more of the wildlife (details from the park information centre). Cruises are run at South Alligator River and Yellow Water Billabong to enable you to see the water life.

Reptiles The park has both types of Australian crocodile: both Twin and Jim Jim Falls, for instance, have resident freshwater crocodiles, which are considered harmless, while there are about 3500 of the dangerous saltwater variety in the park. You're sure to see a few if you take a South Alligator or Yellow Water cruise.

Kakadu's other reptiles include several types of lizard, such as the frilled lizard, and five freshwater turtle species, of which the most common is the northern snake-necked turtle. There are many snakes, including three highly poisonous types, but you're unlikely to see any. Oenpelli pythons, probably unique to the Kakadu escarpment, were only discovered in 1977.

Kakadu National Park is home to many types of lizard

Birds Kakadu's abundant water birds, and their beautiful wetland setting, make a memorable sight. The park is one of the chief refuges in Australia for several species, among them the magpie goose, green pygmy goose and Burdekin duck.

Other fine water birds include pelicans, darters and the Jabiru stork, with its distinctive red legs and long straight beak.

Herons, egrets, ibis and cormorants are common. You're quite likely to see rainbow bee-eaters and kingfishers (of which there are six types in inland Kakadu). Majestic white-breasted sea eagles are often seen near inland waterways too, and wedge-tailed eagles, whistling kites and black kites are common. At night you might hear barking owls calling – they sound just like dogs. The red-tailed black cockatoos are spectacular, and there are also brolgas and bustards.

Mammals Several types of kangaroo and wallaby inhabit the park, and the shy black wallaroo is more or less unique to Kakadu. You might be lucky enough to see a sugar glider in wooded areas in the daytime. Kakadu is home to 25 bat species and is a key refuge for four endangered varieties.

Water buffalo, which ran wild after being introduced to the Top End from Timor by European settlers in the first half of the 19th century, have been virtually eradicated because they were potential carriers of cattle disease and did much damage to the natural environment.

Fish You can't miss the silver barramundi, which creates a distinctive swirl near the water surface. It can grow to well over a metre long and changes its sex from male to female at the age of five or six years.

Aboriginal Art

Kakadu is an important repository of rock art collections – there are over 5000 sites, which date from 20,000 years old right up to those from the 1960s. Two of the finest collections are the galleries at Ubirr and Nourlangie.

The paintings have been classified into three roughly defined periods: Pre-estuarine, which is from the earliest paintings up to around 6000 years ago; Estuarine, which covers the period from 6000 to around 2000 years ago, when the valleys flooded due to the rising sea levels caused by the melting polar ice caps; and Freshwater, from 2000 years ago until the present.

For the local Aboriginal people the rock-art sites are a major source of traditional knowledge, their historical archives if you like, given that they have no written language. The most recent paintings, some executed as recently as the 1980s, connect the local community with the artists, while the older paintings are believed by many Aboriginal people to have been painted by spirit people, and depict stories which connect the people with creation legends and the development of Aboriginal law.

The majority of rock-art sites open to the public are relatively recent, and some visitors feel somewhat cheated when they learn that the paintings were only done in the 1960s. Many people are also surprised to learn that the old paintings they are seeing have actually been touched up by other Aboriginal people quite recently. In fact this was not uncommon, although the repainting could only be done by a specific person who had knowledge of the story being depicted. What also comes as a surprise to many people is the way the paintings in a particular site are often layered, with newer paintings being placed right over the top of older ones.

The conservation of the Kakadu rock-art sites is a major part of the park management task. As the paintings are all done with natural, water-soluble ochres, they are very susceptible to water damage from drip lines running across the rock. To prevent this sort of damage small ridges of clear silicon rubber have been made on the rocks above the paintings, so the water flowing down the rock is diverted to either side, or actually drips right off. Buffaloes also did their bit to damage the lower paintings as they loved to rub against the walls of the rock shelters. The dust raised by hundreds of tourists tramping past these sites on a daily basis didn't help either. Today most of the accessible sites have boardwalks which not only keep the dust down but also keep people at a suitable distance from the paintings.

Orientation

From where the Arnhem Highway to Kakadu turns east off the Stuart Highway, it's 120 km to the park entrance and another 103 km east across the park to Jabiru; it's sealed all the way. The Kakadu Highway to Nourlangie Rock, Cooinda and Pine Creek turns south off the Arnhem Highway shortly before Jabiru.

A turn-off to the north, 18 km into the park along the Arnhem Highway, leads to camp sites at **Two Mile Water Hole** (eight km) and **Four Mile Water Hole** (38 km) on the Wildman River, which is popular for fishing. The track is not suitable for conventional vehicles except in the Dry, and then only as far as Two Mile Water Hole.

About 35 km farther east along the highway, a turn-off to the south, again impassable to conventional vehicles in the Wet, leads to camp sites at **Alligator** and **Red Lily** billabongs, and on to the Kakadu Highway.

South Alligator River Crossing is on the highway 60 km into the park, about two km past the Kakadu Holiday Village.

Seven km east of South Alligator a short side road to the south leads to **Mamukala**, with views over the South Alligator flood plain, an observation building, a three-km walking trail and birdwatching hides.

The Environment of Uranium Mining

Uranium was discovered in the Kakadu region in 1953, and 12 small deposits in the southern reaches of the park were initially worked in the 1960s. However, these were abandoned following the declaration of the Woolwonga Wildlife Sanctuary. Then, in 1970, huge finds were made at Ranger, Nabarlek and Koongarra. The Nabarlek deposit (in Arnhem Land) was mined in the late 1970s and the Ranger Uranium Mine first started producing ore in 1981. The local Aboriginal people were against the mining of uranium on traditional land, but were enticed with the double lure of land title and royalties. In 1973 one of the world's largest high-grade uranium deposits was found at Jabiluka. Now the favoured site for future exploitation, Jabiluka lies 20 km north of Ranger on the edge of the floodplain of the beautiful Magela Creek, a tributary of the East Alligator River.

When the ore body at Ranger was exhausted, mining giant Energy Resources Australia (ERA) was not able to start mining at Jabiluka as the former Labor government had banned the opening of new mines under its three-mines policy. The policy allowed uranium to be mined from only three sites at any one time – Nabarlek, Ranger, and Roxby Downs in South Australia. Before the policy was introduced, Koongarra (discovered by Noranda Australia Ltd in 1970) was close to development, but in 1983 it was also stalled. Lying outside the national park, 30 km south of Jabiru and only three km east of Nourlangie, Koongarra is one of the major Aboriginal rock-art sites in Kakadu. The three-mines policy was also partly responsible for the scrapping of Coronation Hill (Guratba), a proposed uranium mine in the south of the park, in 1991. Thus, under Labor, ERA was only able to plan for the opening in 1997 of Ranger 3, adjacent to the present Ranger mine.

With Labor's loss to a coalition of the Liberal and National parties in March 1996, uranium mining in Australia is set to undergo a radical expansion. One of the Coalition government's first moves on gaining power was to abolish the three-mines policy and promise the increase of Australian uranium exports. Just weeks after the election, ERA proposed an underground mine at Jabiluka, to include the building of a 22-km road through Kakadu's world-heritage area. Prime Minister John Howard offered his support for the plan, with the qualification that an environmental impact assessment be made.

Green groups have strongly criticised the scrapping of the three-mines policy, pointing out that the contracting world market for uranium will not generate the riches promised and that ERA has a very poor safety record. Since 1977 there have been 30 incidents at Ranger within Kakadu's boundary. Many of these have involved the contamination of Magela Creek with the release of radioactive waste. ∎

nformation

The excellent Bowali Information Centre (☎ 8938 1121; fax 8938 1115), on the Kakadu Highway a couple of km south of the Arnhem Highway turn-off, is open daily from 8 am to 5 pm. Here you'll find informative and interesting displays, including a few to keep the kids happy, a high-tech theatrette showing a 25-minute audio-visual presentation on the park (screened on the hour), plenty of leaflets on various aspects of the park, a cafe, gift shop and excellent resource centre with a comprehensive selection of reference books. There is another dozen or so videos featuring various documentaries made about Kakadu in the last few years, and these are also shown throughout the day (on the half hour).

The recently opened **Warradjan Aboriginal Cultural Centre** near Cooinda gives an excellent insight into the culture of the park's traditional owners. The building itself is circular, symbolic of the way Aboriginal people sit in a circle when meeting or talking; the shape is also reminiscent of the *warradjan* (pig-nosed turtle), hence the name of the centre.

In Darwin you can get information on Kakadu from the Australian Nature Conservation Agency.

Fuel is available at Kakadu Holiday Village, Border Store, Jabiru and Cooinda. Jabiru also has a supermarket, post office and a Westpac bank.

Entry Fees Entry to the park is $15 (children under 16 free). This entitles you to stay in the park for 14 days. The fee is payable at the park gates as you enter. If there's a few of you and you plan camping in the park, it works out cheaper to get a yearly ticket for $60. This covers one vehicle and all its occupants, as well as camping fees at the Mardugal, Muirella Park, Merl and Gunlom camp grounds, which usually cost $7 per person per night.

Walking

Kakadu is excellent but tough bushwalking country. Many people will be satisfied with the marked trails, which range from one km to 12 km long. For the more adventurous there are infinite possibilities, especially in the drier south and east of the park, but take great care and prepare well. Tell people where you're going and don't go alone. You need a permit from the park information centre to camp outside the established camp sites.

The Darwin Bushwalking Club (☎ 8985 1484) welcomes visitors and may be able to help with information. It has walks most weekends, often in Kakadu. Or you could join a Willis's Walkabouts guided bushwalk (see Organised Tours in the Darwin Getting There & Around section).

Kakadu by Foot is a helpful guide to the marked walking trails in Kakadu. It is published by ANCA ($1.95) but seems to be in short supply.

Ubirr

This spectacular rock-art site lies 43 km north of the Arnhem Highway. The turn-off to Ubirr is 95 km from the park entrance and the road is sealed, but there are several creek crossings which make it impassable for a conventional vehicle for most of the wet season – sometimes for 4WD too. The rock-art site is open daily from 8.30 am to sunset from June to November.

Shortly before Ubirr you pass the Border Store. Nearby are a couple of walking trails close to the East Alligator River, which forms the eastern boundary of the park here. There is a backpackers hostel and camp site nearby. Aboriginal-guided **Guluyambi river trips** are held on the East Alligator River here. The tours leave daily from the upstream boat ramp at 9 and 11 am, and at 1 and 3 pm, cost $22.50 ($11 children aged four to 14) and last just under two hours. A free shuttle bus runs between the boat ramp and the Border Store and Merl camping ground. For information and bookings ☎ 1800 089 113.

An easily followed path from the Ubirr car park takes you through the main galleries and up to a lookout with superb views – a 1.5-km round trip. There are paintings on numerous rocks along the path, but the

The Rainbow Serpent

The story of the Rainbow Serpent is a common subject in Aboriginal tradition across Australia, although the story varies from place to place. In Kakadu the serpent is a woman, Kurangali, who painted her image on the rock wall at Ubirr, while on a journey through this area. This journey forms a creation path which links the places she visited: Ubirr, Manngarre, the East Alligator River and various places in Arnhem Land.

To the traditional owners of the park, Kurangali is the most powerful spirit. Although she spends most of her time resting in billabongs, if disturbed she can be very destructive, causing flood and earthquakes, and one local story has it that she even eats people. ■

highlight is the main gallery with a large array of well-executed and preserved x-ray-style wallabies, possums, goannas, tortoises and fish, plus a couple of *balanda* (White men) with hands on hips. Also of major interest is the Rainbow Serpent painting, and the picture of the Namarkan Sisters, shown with string pulled taut between their hands.

The Ubirr paintings are in many different styles. They were painted during the period from over 20,000 years ago right up to the 20th century. Allow plenty of time to seek out and study them.

Jabiru (pop 1750)

The township, built to accommodate the Ranger mine workers, has shops and a public swimming pool. Six km east is Jabiru airport and the **Ranger uranium mine**. Minibus tours of the mine ($10) are available three times a day through Kakadu Parklink (☎ 8979 2411).

Nourlangie

The sight of this looming, mysterious, isolated outlier of the Arnhem Land escarpment makes it easy to understand why it has been important to Aboriginal people for so long. Its long, red, sandstone bulk – striped in places with orange, white and black – slopes up from surrounding woodland to fall away at one end in sheer, stepped cliffs, at the foot of which is Kakadu's best-known collection of rock art.

The name Nourlangie is a corruption of *nawulandja*, an Aboriginal word which refers to an area bigger than the rock itself. The Aboriginal name of the rock is Burrunggui. You reach it at the end of a 12-km sealed road which turns east off the Kakadu Highway, 22 km south of the Arnhem Highway.

Other interesting spots nearby make it worth spending a whole day in this corner of Kakadu. The last few km of the road are closed from around 5 pm daily.

From the main car park a round-trip walk of about two km takes you first to the **Anbangbang shelter**, which was used for 20,000 years as a refuge from heat, rain and frequent wet-season thunderstorms. From the gallery you can walk onto a lookout where you can see the distant Arnhem Land cliff line, which includes Lightning Dreaming (Namarrgon Djadjam), the home of Namarrgon. There's a 12-km marked walk all the way round the rock, for which the park information centre has a leaflet.

Heading back towards the highway you can take three turn-offs to further places of interest. The first, on the left about one km from the main car park, takes you to **Anbangbang Billabong**, with its picnic site and dense carpet of lilies. The second, also on the left, leads to a short walk up to **Nawulandja Lookout** with good views back over Nourlangie Rock.

The third turn-off, a dirt track on the right takes you to another outstanding, although little visited , rock-art gallery, **Nanguluwur**. A farther six km along this road, followed by a three-km walk, will bring you to **Gubara**

(Baroalba Springs), an area of shaded pools set in monsoon forest.

Jim Jim & Twin Falls

These two spectacular waterfalls are along a 4WD dry-season track that turns south off the Kakadu Highway between the Nourlangie Rock and Cooinda turn-offs. It's about 60 km to Jim Jim Falls, with the last km on foot, and 70 km to Twin Falls, where the last few hundred metres are through the water up a snaking, forested gorge – great fun on an inflatable air bed. Jim Jim – a sheer 215-metre drop – is awesome after the rains, but its waters can shrink to nothing at the end of the Dry. Twin Falls doesn't dry up.

Yellow Water & Cooinda

The turn-off to the Cooinda accommodation complex and the superb Yellow Water wetlands, with their big water-bird population, is 48 km down the Kakadu Highway from its junction with the Arnhem Highway. It's then about four km to Cooinda, and a couple more km to the starting point for the boat trips on Yellow Water Billabong. These go three times daily year round and cost $22.50 ($11.50 children) for two hours. There are also three times daily tours of 1½ hours for $19.50 ($10.50). This trip is one of the highlights of most people's visit to Kakadu. Early morning is the best time to go as the birdlife is most active. You're likely to see a saltwater crocodile or two. It's usually advisable to book your cruise the day before at Cooinda (☎ 8979 0111) – particularly for the early departure.

Yellow Water is also an excellent place to watch the sunset, particularly in the dry season when the smoke from the many bushfires which burn in the Top End at this time of year turns bright red in the setting sun. Bring plenty of insect repellent as the mosquitoes are voracious.

Cooinda to Pine Creek

Just south of the Yellow Water and Cooinda turn-off the Kakadu Highway heads south-west out of the park to Pine Creek on the Stuart Highway, about 160 km from Cooinda. About 20 km of this road is unsealed. On the way there is a turn-off to the very scenic falls and plunge pool at **Gunlom (Waterfall Creek)**, which featured in *Crocodile Dundee*. It's 37 km along a good dirt road.

Organised Tours

There are hosts of tours to Kakadu from Darwin and a few that start inside the park. Two-day tours typically take in Jim Jim Falls, Nourlangie Rock and the Yellow Water cruise, and cost from $170. Companies which aim at backpackers and seem to be popular include: Hunter Safaris (☎ 8981 2720); All Terrain (☎ 8941 0070); and Backpacking Australia Tours (☎ 8945 2988; fax 8941 0758). This last company has four-day 4WD trips which cover just about everything, including Jim Jim and Twin Falls, for $380.

A one-day tour to Kakadu from Darwin is really too quick – but if you're short of time it's better than nothing. You could try Australian Kakadu Tours (☎ 8981 5144), which will whiz you to Yellow Water and Nourlangie Rock and back to Darwin for $75 ($85 including lunch), plus the $15 park entry fee.

Longer tours usually cover most of the main sights plus a couple of extras. Some combine Kakadu with the Katherine Gorge.

Katherine Adventure Tours (☎ 1800 808 803; fax 8971 1176) is popular, charging $450 for five days, finishing up in Darwin.

You can take 10-hour 4WD tours to Jim Jim and Twin Falls from Jabiru or Cooinda ($115, $110 for YHA members) with Kakadu Gorge & Waterfall Tours (☎ 8979 0111).

Willis's Walkabouts (☎ 8985 2134) organises bushwalks guided by knowledgeable Top End walkers following your own or preset routes of two days or more. Many of the walks are in Kakadu: prices vary, but $750 for a two-week trip, including evening meals and return transport from Darwin, is fairly typical.

Northern Adventure Safaris (☎ 8981 3833) operates good two-day trips out of

Jabiru for $203 ($160 for Greyhound Pioneer pass holders). Three-day trips also include Jim Jim and Twin Falls, and cost $310 ($265).

Arnhem Land A couple of outfits offer trips into Arnhem Land from Kakadu, although they only nip across the East Alligator River to Oenpelli. Aboriginal-owned Inkiyu Tours (☎ 8979 2474) runs half-day tours from the Border Store.

Lord of Kakadu Tours (☎ 8979 2567) does one-day trips from Jabiru for $135.

Scenic Flights If you can afford it, the view of Kakadu from the air is spectacular. Kakadu Air Services (☎ 8979 2411) at Jabiru runs half-hour flights on the hour throughout the day for $55, or hour-long flights for $100.

Rotor Services (☎ 8945 0944) operates half-hour helicopter rides at $100 per person.

Places to Stay & Eat
Prices for accommodation (other than National Parks camp sites) in Kakadu can vary tremendously depending on the season – dry-season prices (given here) are often as much as 50% above wet-season prices.

Camping There are National Parks sites, and also some (with power) attached to the resorts: *Kakadu Holiday Village*, South Alligator, $20 for two with power, $16 without; *Gagadju Lodge Cooinda*, $13 with power, $7 without; and *Kakadu Frontier Lodge*, Jabiru, $20 with power.

The four main National Parks camp sites are: *Merl*, near the Border Store; *Muirella Park*, six km off the Kakadu Highway a few km south of the Nourlangie Rock turn-off; *Mardugal*, just off the Kakadu Highway 1.5 km south of the Cooinda turn-off; and *Gunlom*, in the south of the park, close to the Gunlom (Waterfall Creek) plunge pool. Only the Mardugal and Gunlom sites are open during the Wet. The camp sites have hot showers, flushing toilets, and drinking water and the fee is $7 per person.

The National Parks provide about 12 more

basic camp sites around the park, and at these there is no fee. To camp away from these you need a permit from the park information centre.

South Alligator Just a couple of km west of the South Alligator River on the Arnhem Highway is the *Kakadu Holiday Village* (☎ 8979 0166; fax 8979 0147), which has singles/doubles from $120, and family rooms at $142. The hotel has a restaurant and a basic shop, as well as a swimming pool, restaurant and bar.

Jabiru The *Gagadju Crocodile Hotel* (☎ 8979 2800) is probably most famous for its design – it's set out in the shape of a crocodile, although this is only really apparent from the air. There's nothing very exotic about the hotel itself, although it is comfortable enough. Prices start at $189 for a double.

The *Kakadu Frontier Lodge* (☎ 8979 2422) has four-bed rooms at $22 per person, or $80 for a whole room. The only cooking facilities are a few barbecues, but the poolside bistro serves reasonable pub-style meals for around $12.

Apart from the restaurants at the two hotels, there's the *Golden Bowl Restaurant* at the sports club. It does a pretty standard range of Chinese food, and you can eat in or take away.

Lastly there's a cafe in the shopping centre, and a bakery near the fire station.

Ubirr The popular *Hostel Kakadu* (☎ 8979 2232) behind the Border Store is the only place in Kakadu that offers budget accommodation and decent facilities. The budget accommodation at the resort hotels is a bit of an afterthought and there's not much in the way of cooking facilities. It's open year round (as long as the road remains open) and has dorm accommodation (one with air-con) at $14 per person. The Border Store has supplies and snack food and is open daily until 5 pm.

Cooinda This is by far the most popular place to stay, mainly because of the proximty of the Yellow Water wetlands and the early-morning boat cruises. It gets mighty crowded at times, mainly with camping tours. The *Gagadju Lodge Cooinda* (☎ 8979 0145; fax 8979 0148) has some comfortable units for $126 single or double, and much cheaper and more basic air-con 'budget rooms', which are just transportable huts of the type found on many building sites and more commonly known in the Territory as 'demountables' or 'dongas'. For $15 per person they are quite adequate, if a little cramped (two beds per room), although there are no cooking facilities.

The restaurant in the bar here serves unexciting but good-value meals at around $11 to $15.

Getting There & Around

Ideally, take your own 4WD. The Arnhem Highway is sealed all the way to Jabiru. The Kakadu Highway is sealed from its junction with the Arnhem Highway, near Jabiru, all the way to Pine Creek, with the exception of a 20-km stretch just inside the park's southern boundary. Sealed roads lead from the Kakadu Highway to Nourlangie Rock, the Muirella Park camping area and to Ubirr. Other roads are mostly dirt and blocked for varying periods during the Wet and early Dry.

Greyhound Pioneer runs daily buses from Darwin to Katherine via Jabiru and Cooinda, and vice versa. This saves backtracking all the way to Darwin. In both directions the buses stop at the Yellow Water wetland in time for the 1 pm cruise, and wait there for 1½ hours until the cruises finish. Southbound the buses leave Darwin at 6.30 am, Jabiru at 9.55 am and Cooinda at 2.30 pm, arriving in Katherine at 5.15 pm. Northbound they leave Katherine at 7.15 am, Cooinda at 2.30 pm, Jabiru at 4.20 pm, arriving in Darwin at 7 pm. The cost is $65, Darwin to Katherine including two stopovers. To travel one way from Darwin to the park costs $25; from Katherine it's $35.

McCafferty's has a daily service from Darwin to Jabiru ($25) and on to Ubirr ($30). The inbound service leaves Darwin at 10 am and Jabiru at 1.40 pm, arriving at the Border Store at 2.20 pm. In the opposite direction it leaves the Border Store at 2.35 pm, Jabiru at 5 pm, arriving in Darwin at 8 pm.

BATHURST & MELVILLE ISLANDS

These two large, flat islands about 80 km north of Darwin are the home of the Tiwi Aboriginal people. You need a permit to visit them and the only realistic option is to take a tour. Tiwi Tours (☎ 8981 5115), a company which employs many Tiwi among its staff, is the only operator, and its tours have been recommended.

The Tiwi people's island homes kept them fairly isolated from mainland developments until this century, and their culture has retained several unique features. Perhaps the best known are the *pukumani* burial poles, carved and painted with symbolic and mythological figures, which are erected around graves. More recently the Tiwi have turned their hand to art for sale – bark painting, textile screen printing, batik and pottery, using traditional designs and motifs.

Figure carved in ironwood, Bathurst Island

The Tiwi had mixed relations with Macassan fisherpeople, who came in search of the trepang, or sea cucumber. A British settlement in the 1820s at Fort Dundas, near Pularumpi on Melville Island, failed partly because of poor relations with the locals. The main settlement on the islands is **Nguiu** in the south-east of Bathurst Island, which was founded in 1911 as a Catholic mission. On Melville Island the settlements are Pularumpi and Milikapiti.

Most Tiwi live on Bathurst Island and follow a nontraditional lifestyle. Some go back to their traditional lands on Melville Island for a few weeks each year. Melville Island also has descendants of the Japanese pearl divers who regularly visited here early this century, and people of mixed Aboriginal and European parentage who were gathered here from around the Territory under government policy half a century ago.

A full-day Tiwi Tours trip costs $210 and includes the necessary permit, a flight from Darwin to Nguiu, visits to the early Catholic mission buildings and craft workshops, a boat crossing of the narrow Apsley Strait to Melville Island, swimming at Turacumbie Falls, a trip to a pukumani burial site and the flight back to Darwin from Melville. This tour is available from April to October. Tiwi Tours also offers two or three-day tours to the islands, staying at a tented camp, for $591 for three days.

COBOURG PENINSULA

This remote wilderness, 200 km north-east of Darwin, includes the Cobourg Marine Park and the Aboriginal-owned Gurig National Park. Entry to the latter is by permit only.

The ruins of the early British settlement at Victoria can be visited on **Port Essington**, a superb 30-km-long natural harbour on the northern side of the peninsula.

At **Black Point** there's a small store open daily except Sunday, but only from 3 to 5 pm. It sells basic provisions, ice, camping gas and fuel (diesel, super, unleaded, outboard mix), and basic mechanical repairs can be under-

taken. Be warned that credit cards are no accepted here.

Permits

The track to Cobourg passes through part o Arnhem Land, and as the Aboriginal owner there severely restrict the number of vehicles going through (15 per week), you're advise to apply up to a year ahead for the necessary permit ($10) from the Northern Territory Parks & Wildlife (☎ 8999 3881; fax 898 0653) desk at the tourist office in Darwin, o write to PO Box 496, Palmerston, NT.

Places to Stay

There are 15 shady camp sites about 10 metres from the shore at the *Smith Poin Camping Ground*. It's run by Parks & Wildlif and facilities include a shower and toilet, an barbecues. There's no electricity and genera tors are banned at night. The charge is $4 pe site for three people, plus $1 for each extr person.

The fully equipped, four-bed *Cobour Cottages* (☎ 8979 0263) at Smith Point cos $100 for the whole cottage, but you need t bring your own supplies.

The only other accommodation option is th *Seven Spirit Bay Resort* (☎ 8979 0277), set i secluded wilderness at Vashon Head and acces sible only by air or boat. It charges $249 pe person for single/double accommodation but this includes three gourmet meals. Accom modation is in individual open-sided hexagonal 'habitats', each with semi-outdoo private bathroom! Activities available (at extr cost) include day trips to Victoria Settlement guided bushwalks and fishing. Return transfe by air from Darwin costs $275 per person.

Getting There & Away

There's an airstrip at Smith Point which i serviced by charter flights from Darwin.

The track to Cobourg starts at Oenpelli. I is recommended for 4WD vehicles only, an only take a trailer if you are prepared to hav it shaken to bits. The track is also closed i the wet season. The 288-km drive to Black Point from the East Alligator River at Ubir crossing takes about six hours and the track

s in reasonable condition, the roughest part
oming in the hour or so after the turn-off
rom Murgenella. The trip must be com-
leted in one day as it's not possible to stop
vernight on Aboriginal land.

Straight after the Wet, the water level at
Cahills Crossing on the East Alligator River
an be high, and you can only drive across
he ford about an hour either side of the low
ide. A tide chart is included with your
ermit, or the Bowali Information Centre in
Kakadu has a list of tide times.

ARNHEM LAND & GOVE

The entire eastern half of the Top End is the
Arnhem Land Aboriginal Land, which is spec-
acular, sparsely populated and the source of
ome good Aboriginal art. It's virtually closed
o independent travellers apart from Gove, the
eninsula at the north-east corner.

At **Nhulunbuy** (population 3550), on the
Gove Peninsula, there is a bauxite-mining
entre with a deep-water export port. The
Aboriginal people of nearby Yirrkala (popu-
ation 590) made an important step in the
and rights movement in 1963 when they
rotested at plans for mining on their tradi-
ional land. They failed to stop it, but forced
government inquiry and won compensa-
ion, and their case caught the public eye.

You don't have to have a permit to fly into
Nhulunbuy and you can fly there direct from
Darwin for $235 or from Cairns for $326
with Qantas or Ansett. Travelling overland
hrough Arnhem Land from Katherine
equires a permit; contact the Gove Regional
Tourist Association (☎ 8987 1985; fax 8987
214) who can get you on the right track.

You can hire vehicles in Nhulunbuy to
xplore the coastline (there are some fine
eaches, but beware of crocodiles) and the
ocal area. You need to get a permit to do this
rom the Northern Land Council in
Nhulunbuy (a formality).

Groote Eylandt, a large island off the east
Arnhem Land coast, is also Aboriginal land,
with a big manganese-mining operation. The
main settlement here is Alyangula (population
70).

Organised Tours

There are a number of tours into Arnhem
Land, but these usually only visit the western
part.

The Aboriginal owned and operated
Umorrduk Safaris (☎ 8948 1306; fax 8948
1305) has a two-day fly-in/fly-out tour from
Darwin to the remote Mudjeegarrdart airstrip in north-western Arnhem Land. The
highlight of the trip is a visit to the 20,000-
year-old Umorrduk rock-art sites. The cost is
$500 per person.

Another operator is Davidson's Arnhem-
land Safaris (☎ 8927 5240). Max Davidson
has been taking people into Arnhem Land for
years and has a concession at Mt Borradaile,
north of Oenpelli, where he has set up his
safari camp. The cost of staying at the camp
is $300 per person per day, which includes
accommodation, all meals, guided tours and
fishing; transfers from Darwin can be
arranged.

AAT-Kings (☎ 1800 334 009) has two-
day coach trips operating out of Darwin
which take you through Kakadu and on to
Davidson's Safari Camp. The cost of these
trips is $499 ($424 children aged three to 14).

From Kakadu you can also visit the
Injalak Arts & Crafts centre in Oenpelli; you
must first get a permit from the Northern
Land Council in Jabiru. Injalak is both a
workplace and shopfront for artists and
craftspeople who produce traditional paintings on bark and paper, dijeridus, pandanus
weavings and baskets, and screenprinted
fabrics. All sales benefit the community.
Both Kakadu Air Services (☎ 8979 2411)
and Lord of Kakadu Tours (☎ 8979 2567)
operate tours to Injalak.

Other trips are available from Jabiru in
Kakadu; see the Kakadu National Park
section for details.

Down the Track

It's just under 1500 km south from Darwin
to Alice Springs, and although at times it can

be dreary there is an amazing variety of things to see or do along the road and nearby.

Until WW II the Track really was just that – a dirt track – connecting the Territory's two main towns, Darwin and 'the Alice'. The need to quickly supply Darwin, which was under attack by Japanese aircraft from Timor, led to a rapid upgrading of the road. Although it is now sealed and well maintained, short, sharp floods during the Wet can cut the road and stop all traffic for days at a time.

The Stuart Highway takes its name from John McDouall Stuart, who made the first crossing of Australia from south to north. Twice he turned back due to lack of supplies, ill health and hostile Aboriginal people, but finally completed his epic trek in 1862. Only 10 years later the telegraph line to Darwin was laid along the route he had followed, and today the Stuart Highway between Darwin and Alice Springs follows roughly the same path.

DARWIN TO KATHERINE

Some places along the Track south of Darwin (Howard Springs, Darwin Crocodile Farm and Litchfield National Park) are covered in the Around Darwin section.

Lake Bennett

This is a popular camping, swimming, sailing and windsurfing spot among Darwinites. It's 80 km down the Track, then seven km east. You can rent small boats. Camping is available for $6, or there are on-site tents for $15/24. If you ring in advance (☎ 8976 0960) staff from the camp site will pick you up from the highway.

Batchelor (pop 660)

This small town, 84 km down the Track from Darwin, then 13 km west, once serviced the now-closed Rum Jungle uranium and copper mine. In recent years it has received a boost from the growing popularity of nearby Litchfield National Park. It has a swimming pool open six days a week and an Aboriginal residential tertiary college.

About an hour's walk away, or a shorter drive, is **Rum Jungle Lake**, where you can canoe or swim.

Places to Stay The *Batchelor Caravillage* (☎ 8976 0166) on Rum Jungle Rd has on-site vans for $42 a double, cabins for $60, or tent sites for $14. The *Rum Jungle Motor Inn* (☎ 8976 0123) has rooms for $88.

Adelaide River (pop 370)

Not to be confused with Adelaide River Crossing on the Arnhem Highway, this small settlement is on the Stuart Highway 111 km south of Darwin. It has a cemetery for those who died in the 1942-43 Japanese air raids. This stretch of the highway is dotted with WW II airstrips.

Adelaide River has a pub, an Aboriginal art shop, the *Shady River View Caravan Park* with tent sites ($12), and the *Adelaide River Motor Inn* with singles/doubles at $35/65.

Old Stuart Highway

South of Adelaide River a sealed section of the old Stuart Highway makes a loop to the south before rejoining the main road 52 km on. It's a scenic trip and leads to a number of pleasant spots, but access to them is often cut in the wet season.

The beautiful 12-metre **Robyn Falls** are a short walk off this road, 17 km along. The falls, set in a monsoon-forested gorge dwindle to a trickle in the dry season, but are spectacular in the Wet.

The turn-off to **Daly River** (see entry below) is 14 km farther on, and to reach **Douglas Hot Springs Nature Park**, turn south off the old highway just before it rejoins the Stuart Highway and continue on for about 35 km. The nature park here includes a section of the Douglas River, a pretty camping area and several hot springs – a bit hot for bathing at 40°C, but there are cooler pools.

Butterfly Gorge National Park is about 15 km beyond Douglas Hot Springs – you'll need a 4WD to get there. True to its name, butterflies sometimes swarm in the gorge. It's safe to swim in these places, although you may well see freshies. There are camp sites with toilets and barbecues.

Daly River

Historic Daly River is 109 km west of the Stuart Highway. Most of the population are part of the Naniyu Nambiyu Aboriginal community, about six km away from the rest of the town. Visitors are welcome without a permit, although note that this is a dry community. Also here is Merrepen Arts, a resource centre which is also an outlet for locally made art and crafts. The associated Merrepen Arts Festival is held each year in June/July.

The main activity for visitors is getting out on the river and dangling a line. Boat hire is available at the Mango Farm and Woolianna tourist outfits. At the Mango Farm you can hire a 3.6-metre dinghy with outboard motor for $16 per hour, $60 for a half day and $90 for a full day, or take a river cruise at $20 per person. Woolianna has two-person boats at $55/80 for a half/full day, as well as three-person ($65/90) and four-person boats ($70/100). Both places also operate guided fishing trips on request.

Places to Stay There are a couple of accommodation options here, including the *Woolianna on the Daly Tourist Park* (☎ 8978 2478), the *Daly River Pub* (☎ 8978 2418) and the *Mango Farm* (☎ 8978 2464).

Pine Creek (pop 450)

This small town, 245 km from Darwin, was the scene of a gold rush in the 1870s and some of the old timber and corrugated iron buildings survive. The Kakadu Highway goes north-east from Pine Creek to Kakadu National Park.

The old **railway station** has been restored and houses a visitor centre and a display on the Darwin to Pine Creek railway, which opened in 1889 but is now closed. **Pine Creek Museum** on Railway Parade near the post office has interesting displays on local history. It is usually open weekdays from 11 am to 3 pm. **Ah Toys General Store** is a reminder of the gold-rush days when the Chinese heavily outnumbered Europeans. In recent years gold mining has returned to Pine Creek with open-cut workings outside the town.

Places to Stay The town has an unattractive caravan park, and there's also the *Pine Creek Hotel* (☎ 8976 1288) with air-con singles/doubles at $63/74.

Around Pine Creek

A well-maintained dirt road follows the line of the old railway line east of the highway between Hayes Creek and Pine Creek. This is in fact the original 'north road', which was in use before the 'new road' (now the Old Stuart Highway!) was built. It's a worthwhile detour to see the 1930s corrugated-iron pub at **Grove Hill**.

About three km along the Stuart Highway south of Pine Creek is the turn-off to **Umbrawarra Gorge Nature Park**, about 30 km west along a dirt road (often impassable in the Wet). There's a camp site with pit toilets and fireplaces, and you can swim in crocodile-free pools one km from the car park.

Edith Falls

At the 293-km mark on the Track you can turn off to the beautiful Edith Falls at the western end of the Nitmiluk (Katherine Gorge) National Park, 19 km east of the road, where there's a camp site with showers, pit toilets and fireplaces. Swimming is possible in a clear, forest-surrounded pool at the bottom of the series of falls. You may see freshwater crocodiles (the inoffensive variety), but be careful. There's a good walk up to rapids and more pools above the falls.

KATHERINE (pop 8500)

Apart from Tennant Creek, this is the only town of any size between Darwin and Alice Springs. It's a bustling little place where the Victoria Highway branches off to the Kimberley and Western Australia. The town's population has grown rapidly in recent years, partly because of the establishment of the large Tindal air-force base just south of town.

Katherine has long been an important stopping point, since the river it's built on and named after is the first permanent running water north of Alice Springs. The town includes some historic old buildings, such as the Sportsman's Arms, featured in *We of the Never Never*, Jeannie Gunn's classic novel of turn-of-the-century outback life. The main interest here, however, is the spectacular Katherine Gorge 30 km to the north-east – a great place to camp, walk, swim, canoe, take a cruise or simply float along on an air mattress.

Orientation & Information

Katherine's main street, Katherine Terrace, is also the Stuart Highway as it runs through town. Coming from the north, you cross the Katherine River Bridge just before the town centre. The Victoria Highway to Western Australia branches off a farther 300 metres on. After another 300 metres Giles St, the road to Katherine Gorge, branches off in the other direction.

At the end of the town centre is the Katherine Region Tourist Association office (☎ 8972 2650; fax 8972 2969) which is open Monday to Friday from 8.45 am to 5 pm, Saturday to 3 pm and Sunday from 9.30 am to 4 pm. The bus station is over the road from the tourist office. There's a Parks & Wildlife office (☎ 8973 8770) on Giles St.

Mimi Arts & Crafts in the Southgate Complex on Lindsay St is an Aboriginal-owned and run shop, selling products made over a wide area – from the deserts in the west to the coast in the east.

Things to See

Katherine's old **railway station**, owned by the National Trust, houses a display on railway history and is open Monday to Friday from 10 am to noon and from 1 to 3 pm in the dry season.

The small **Katherine Museum** is in the old airport terminal building on Gorge Rd, about one km from the centre of town. There's a good selection of old photos and other bits and pieces of interest, including the original Gypsy Moth biplane flown by Dr Clyde Fenton, the first Flying Doctor. It is open weekdays from 10 am to 4 pm, Saturday from 10 am to 2 pm and Sunday from 2 to 5 pm.

The **School of the Air** on Giles St offers an opportunity to see how remote outback kids are taught. There are guided tours on weekdays during the school term.

Katherine has a good public **swimming pool** beside the highway on the way out of town, about 750 metres south of the bus station. There are also some pleasant **thermal pools** beside the river, about three km from town along the Victoria Highway.

The 105-hectare **Katherine Low Level Nature Park** is five km from town, just off the Victoria Highway. It's a great spot on the Katherine River, taking in four km of its shady banks, and the swimming hole by the weir is very popular in the dry season. In the Wet, flash-flooding can make it dangerous. Facilities provided here include picnic tables, toilets and gas barbecues.

Organised Tours

Tours are available from Katherine, taking in various combinations of the town and Springvale Homestead attractions, the Gorge, Cutta Cutta Caves, Mataranka and Kakadu. Most accommodation places can book you on these and you'll be picked up from where you're staying – or ask at the tourist office or Travel North in the bus station.

There are excellent Aboriginal tours at Manyallaluk (see the Around Katherine section for details), and Jankanginya Tours (☎ 1800 089 103) take you out into their land, sometimes referred to as Lightning Brothers country. Here you learn about bush tucker, crafts and medicine, and hear some of the non-secret stories associated with the rock art of the area. Accommodation is in a bush camp. The cost is $99 for a one-day trip, or $240 for two days.

Places to Stay

Camping There are several camping possibilities. One of the nicest is *Springvale Homestead* (☎ 8972 1355), with shady sites or $10. It also has budget units at $39/48 for ingles/doubles, and there is a licensed restaurant, and a kiosk for snacks. It's eight km out of Katherine; turn right off the Victoria Highway after four km and follow the signs.

On the road to Springvale, five km from town, is the *Katherine Low Level Caravan Park* (☎ 8972 3962), a good place close to the river. Tent sites are $12 for two, or $16 with power. On-site vans here cost $36. Closer to town, on the Victoria Highway, is the *Riverview Caravan Park* (☎ 8972 1011), which has reasonably comfortable cabins at $40/45 for singles/doubles and tent sites at $12 ($14 with power). The thermal pools are five minutes walk away.

The *Katherine Frontier Motor Inn* (☎ 8972 1744), four km south of town on the Stuart Highway, has camp sites at $16, plus a pool, barbecue area and restaurant. It also has rooms for $112.

Hostels Kookaburra Lodge Backpackers (☎ 8971 0257), on the corner of Lindsay and Third Sts, is just a few minutes walk from the transit centre. It consists of old motel units with between six and 10 beds and costs $13 night, or there are some twin rooms for $40. With so many people in each unit the bathroom and cooking facilities can get overcrowded at times, but it's a friendly and well-run place, and they also do canoe hire and transport out to Katherine Gorge (see that section for details).

Just around the corner is the *Palm Court Backpackers* (☎ 8972 2722), on the corner of Third and Giles Sts. It's in the most horrendously tasteless building, but the air-con rooms are uncrowded and have their own TV, fridge and bathroom. The problem here is that the communal cooking facilities are inadequate. The cost is $11 per person, or $44 for a double and $52 for a whole room (four beds).

The *Victoria Lodge* (☎ 8972 3464) is at 21 Victoria Highway, not far from the main street. It's a good place with six-bed rooms at $13 per person, doubles at $35 and four-bed rooms for $65.

Motels The *Beagle Motor Inn* (☎ 8972 3998) at the corner of Lindsay and Fourth Sts is probably the cheapest, with 'budget' singles/doubles for $30/40, and rooms with attached bath at $50/60.

Places to Eat

Katherine has one or two of each of the usual types of Aussie eatery. Over the road from the transit centre, which has a 24-hour cafe, there's a *Big Rooster* fast-food place. The *Katherine Hotel Motel*, just up the main street, has counter meals as well as *Aussie's Bistro*, which is open daily for lunch and dinner and is pretty good value with main courses around $8 to $10. Also here is the more formal *Kirby's Restaurant*.

Over the road there's the *Golden Bowl* Chinese restaurant. A block farther up on the corner of Warburton St, the *Crossways Hotel* does good counter meals for around $7.

Alfie's on the main street does good pizzas for $12.50 as well as other meaty main courses for around $10. This place is also open for breakfast from 6 to 10 am.

On the corner of Katherine Terrace and the Victoria Highway is the *Mekhong Thai Cafe & Take-away*. This is an unusual find in an outback country town, and it has an extensive menu with entrees at $3 and main courses from $8 to $11.

Over on First St there's *Annie's Family Restaurant*, a bright little place with main courses (steak/chicken/fish) for $15, including a self-serve salad bar. During the Dry they also do a full roast dinner for $14 or a soup and pasta lunch for $8.

Rusty's Creperie in Katherine Arcade is open from 9 am to 5 pm during the week. Meals here are served in a crepe or on rice, and cost around $6.

Getting There & Away

You can fly to Katherine on weekdays from Darwin ($144) and Alice Springs ($369) with Airnorth. Darfield Travel (☎ 8972 1344), on the main street between Giles and Lindsay Sts, is the agent. Katherine airport is eight km south of town, just off the Stuart Highway. Kakadu Air Services (☎ 1800 089

NORTHERN TERRITORY

113) has daily flights between Katherine and Kakadu for $100, or a full-day tour including park entry and Yellow Water cruise for $250.

All buses between Darwin and Alice Springs, Queensland or Western Australia stop at Katherine, which means two or three daily to and from Western Australia, and usually four to and from Darwin, Alice Springs and Queensland. See the Darwin section for more details. Typical fares from Katherine are Darwin $40, Alice Springs $131, Tennant Creek $65 and Kununurra $50.

Avis (☎ 8971 0520), Hertz (☎ 8941 0944) and Territory Rent-a-Car (☎ 8972 3183) all have car-rental offices in town.

Getting Around

You can rent bicycles at the Kookaburra Lodge, or there's bikes and mopeds for hire at Katherine Moped & Bicycle Hire (☎ 8971 0727), 67 Second St.

Travel North (☎ 8972 1044) has a six-times-daily bus service from the transit centre to the Gorge for $15 return, the first at 8.15 am, the last at 4.15 pm. The first return trip from the Gorge is at 9 am, the last at 5 pm.

AROUND KATHERINE
Springvale Homestead

This homestead, eight km south-west of town (turn right off the Victoria Highway after 3.8 km), claims to be the oldest cattle station in the Northern Territory. Today it's also a tourist accommodation centre, and free half-hour tours around the old homestead are given once or twice daily. From May to September, crocodile-spotting cruises ($33) are run from here in the evenings, and three nights a week there are Aboriginal corroborees with demonstrations by the local Jawoyn people of fire making, traditional dance and spear throwing ($29.50 including barbecue). There's also horse riding and cattle musters by horseback.

NITMILUK (KATHERINE GORGE) NATIONAL PARK

Strictly speaking Katherine Gorge is 13 gorges, separated from each other by rapid of varying length. The gorge walls aren high, but it is a remote, beautiful place. It 12 km long and has been carved out by th Katherine River, which rises in Arnher Land. Farther downstream it becomes th Daly River before flowing into the Tim Sea at a point 80 km south-west of Darwi The difference in water levels between th Wet and Dry is staggering. During the dr season the gorge waters are calm, but fro November to March they can become raging torrent.

Swimming in the gorge is safe exce when it's in flood. The only crocodile around are the freshwater variety and they' more often seen in the cooler months. Th country surrounding the gorge is excelle for walking.

Information

It's 30 km by sealed road from Katherine the visitor centre and the camp site, an nearly one km farther to the car park whe the gorge begins and cruises start. The visit centre (☎ 8972 1886) has displays and info mation on the national park, which spread over 1800 sq km to include extensive bac country and Edith Falls to the north-west, well as Katherine Gorge. There are details a wide range of marked walking tracks star ing here that go through the picturesqu country south of the gorge, descending to th river at various points. Some of the track pass Aboriginal rock paintings up to 700 years old.

You can walk to Edith Falls (76 km, fiv days) or points on the way. For the longer more rugged walks you need a permit fro the visitor centre. The Katherine Gorg Canoe Marathon, organised by the Re Cross, takes place in June.

Activities & Cruises

At the river you can rent canoes for one, tw or three people (☎ 1800 808 211 or call the Kookaburra Lodge Backpackers in Kath erine). These cost $20/28/36 for a half-da or $27/42/57 for a whole day. This is a gre way of exploring the gorge. You can also b

Northern Territory
A: Kings Canyon, Watarrka National Park
B: Nourlangie Rock, Kakadu National Park
C: Billabongs at Kakadu National Park

JOHN CHAPMAN

TONY WHEELER

TONY WHEELER

A
B	C

Northern Territory
A: Ormiston Gorge
B: Garden of Eden, Kings Canyon
C: Palm Valley

adventurous and take the canoes out overnight, but you must book in advance as only a limited number of people are allowed to camp in the gorges. You get a map with your canoe showing things of interest along the gorge sides – Aboriginal rock paintings, waterfalls, plant life, and so on.

The alternative is a cruise. These depart daily: there's the choice of a two-hour run, which goes to the second gorge and includes a visit to some gorge-side rock paintings for $25 ($10 children); a four-hour trip to the third gorge for $38 ($19.50), leaving at 9 and 11 am and at 1 pm. Finally there's an eight-hour trip that takes you up to the fifth gorge, and also involves walking about four km. The cost is $65, and it departs daily at 9 am.

During the Wet, only the four-hour 9 am cruise runs, and this only when the water is not too wild. Tickets for the gorge tours must be pre-booked on ☎ 1800 089 103. You can also take light-aircraft ($47 for 30 minutes) and helicopter flights ($60 for 15 minutes) over the gorge.

Every day at 1.30 pm there's a 2½-hour Aboriginal-guided bush tour which gives you an opportunity to learn a bit about the Jawoyn people and their traditional way of life. The tours leave from the boat ramp, from where you travel by boat to 17 Mile Creek, where the tour itself begins. The cost is $18 ($10 children five to 15), and you can make reservations with Travel North in Katherine (☎ 8972 1044).

Places to Stay

The *Gorge Caravan Park* (☎ 8972 1253) has showers, toilets, fireplaces and a store (open from 7 am to 7 pm) which also serves basic hot meals. Wallabies and goannas frequent the camp site. It costs $13 for a camp site ($17 with power) and there's plenty of grass and shade.

Getting There & Away

The six-times-daily commuter bus costs $15 return, and it operates from the bus station.

CUTTA CUTTA CAVES NATURE PARK

Guided tours of these limestone caverns, 24 km south-east of Katherine along the Stuart Highway, are held six times a day in the dry season, and cost $6.75 ($3.50 children). Orange horseshoe bats, a rare and endangered species, roost in the main cave, about 15 metres below the ground. The rock formations outside the caves are impressive.

MANYALLALUK

Manyallaluk is the former 3000-sq-km Eva Valley cattle station which abuts the eastern edge of the Nitmiluk (Katherine Gorge) National Park. These days it is owned by the Jawoyn Aboriginal people, some of whom now organise and lead very well-regarded tours.

One, two and five-day tours are offered. The one-day trip includes transport to and from Katherine, lunch, billy tea and damper, and you learn about traditional bush tucker and medicine, spear throwing and playing a dijeridu; the two-day trip adds swimming and rock-art sites. The cost is $95 ($63 children) for the day trip, $199 ($147) for the two-day trip, and $825 for the five-day trip, which operates out of Darwin and includes either Litchfield or Kakadu in addition to Manyallaluk and Katherine Gorge. For bookings and enquiries phone ☎ 8975 4727.

The day trip operates on Monday, Wednesday and Saturday from Katherine, or with your own vehicle you can camp at Manyallaluk ($15 for two) and take the day tour from there, which costs $63. It is possible just to camp without taking the tour, but you are restricted to the camping area. No permits are needed to visit the community.

BARUNGA

Barunga is another Aboriginal community, 13 km along the Arnhem Land track beyond the Manyallaluk turn-off. Entry to the community is by permit only, but every year over the Queen's Birthday long weekend in June the settlement really comes alive for the enjoyable Barunga Wugularr Sports & Cultural Festival.

Permits are not required to visit Barunga during the festival, but you will need your own camping gear.

NORTHERN TERRITORY

KATHERINE TO WESTERN AUSTRALIA
It's 513 km on the Victoria Highway from Katherine to Kununurra in Western Australia.

As you approach the Western Australian border you start to see the boab trees found in much of the north-west of Australia. There's a 1½-hour time change when you cross the border. There's also a quarantine inspection post, and all fruit and vegetables must be left here. This only applies when travelling from the Territory to Western Australia.

Victoria River Crossing
The highway is sometimes cut by floods – the wet season here is very wet. In the dry season, if you stand on the Victoria River Bridge by the Victoria River Inn at the crossing, it's hard to imagine that the wide river, flowing far below your feet, can actually flow over the top of the bridge!

Timber Creek
From April to October, daily boat trips are made on the river from Timber Creek, farther west. Max Fogarty, the boat operator, is a local character and you'll be shown fresh and saltwater crocodiles, fish and turtles being fed – try some real billy tea, play the dijeridu and light a fire using fire sticks. Max has good knowledge of the flora and fauna and local history. The cost of a 3½-hour morning tour is $35 ($20 children) and bookings can be made at Max's information centre in Timber Creek (☎ 8975 0850).

You can see a boab marked by an early explorer at Gregory's Tree Historical Reserve, west of Timber Creek.

Gregory National Park
This little-visited national park to the south and west of Timber Creek covers 10,500 sq km and offers good fishing, camping and bushwalking. There's also the 90-km 4WD **Bullita Stock Route** which takes eight hours, although it's better to break the journey at one of the three marked camp sites. For more details contact the Parks &

Wildlife office in Timber Creek (☎ 8975 0888), or the Bullita ranger (☎ 8975 0833).

Keep River National Park
Bordering Western Australia just off the Victoria Highway, this park is noted for its sandstone landforms and has some excellent walking trails. You can reach the main points in the park by conventional vehicle during the dry season. Aboriginal art can be seen near the car park at the end of the road.

There's a rangers' station (☎ (091) 67 8827) three km into the park from the main road, and there are camp sites with pit toilets at Gurrangalng (15 km into the park) and Jarrnarm (28 km).

MATARANKA
Mataranka is 103 km south-east of Katherine on the Stuart Highway. The attraction is **Mataranka Homestead**, seven km off the highway just south of the small town. The crystal-clear thermal pool here, in a pocket of rainforest, is a great place to wind down after a hot day on the road – though it can get crowded. There's no charge.

The pool is just a short walk from the homestead accommodation area, which includes a backpackers hostel, camp site, motel rooms and restaurant – it's more relaxed than it sounds since you're a long way from anywhere else.

A couple of hundred metres away is the **Waterhouse River**, where you can walk along the banks, or rent canoes and rowing boats for $5 an hour. Outside the homestead entrance is a replica of the Elsey Station Homestead which was made for the filming of *We of the Never Never* (whose story is set near Mataranka). There are historical displays inside the replica.

Places to Stay & Eat
The *hostel* at Mataranka Homestead (☎ 8975 4544) is quite comfortable and has some single and twin rooms, though the kitchen is small. It costs $15 per person ($13 with a YHA card). Camping is $14 for a site ($18 with power), and air-con motel rooms with private bathroom are $74 for two. In between

there are self-contained budget cabins which cost $60 for two or three people, $70 for four to five people. There's a store where you can get basic groceries, a bar with snacks and meals (not cheap), or you can use the camp-site barbecues.

In Mataranka town the *Old Elsey Road-side Inn* (☎ 8975 4512) has a couple of rooms at $45/55, and the *Territory Manor Motel* (☎ 8975 4516) is a more luxurious place with a swimming pool, restaurant and motel rooms at $65/72 for singles/doubles; alternatively, you can camp for $18 (with power). Hefty discounts are offered during the Wet.

Getting There & Around
Long-distance buses travelling up and down the Stuart Highway call at Mataranka and the homestead.

MATARANKA TO THREEWAYS
Not far south of the Mataranka Homestead turn-off, the Roper Highway branches east off the Stuart Highway. It leads about 200 km to **Roper Bar**, near the Roper River on the edge of Aboriginal land, where there's a store with a camp site and a few rooms – mainly visited by fishing enthusiasts. All but about 40 km of the road is sealed.

About five km south of the Roper junction is the turn-off to the **Elsey Cemetery**, not far from the highway. Here are the graves of characters like 'the Fizzer' who came to life in *We of the Never Never*.

Larrimah
Continuing south from Mataranka you pass through Larrimah – at one time the railway line from Darwin came as far as here, but it was abandoned after Cyclone Tracy.

There are three camping grounds. The one on the highway at the southern end of town, *Green Park Tourist Complex* (☎ 8975 9937), charges $6 per site ($18 with power). There's a swimming pool and a few crocodiles in fenced-off ponds. You can also camp at the *Larrimah Wayside Inn* (☎ 8975 9931), 100 metres or so off the highway opposite the Green Park. The Wayside has singles/

doubles from $10/20, and camp sites are free, unless you want power, in which case it is $5; it does counter meals and sells petrol several cents cheaper than the places on the highway.

Daly Waters
Farther south again is Daly Waters, three km off the highway, an important staging post in the early days of aviation – Amy Johnson landed here. The historic *Daly Waters Pub* (☎ 8975 9927), with air-con motel-type rooms at $25/35, is not surprisingly the focus of local life. It's an atmospheric place, dating from 1893 and said to be the oldest pub in the Territory, and there's good food available. The pub also has a caravan park with tent sites at $6/10 – and there's another WW II airstrip with a restored hangar. The *Hi-Way Inn & Caravan Park* (☎ 8975 9925), on the Stuart Highway, has singles/doubles from $40/50 and camp sites at $3 per person.

Daly Waters to Threeways
After Daly Waters, there's the fascinating ghost town of **Newcastle Waters**, a few km west of the highway, and then the cattle town of **Elliott**. As you might expect, the land just gets drier and drier. At Elliott, the *Midland Caravan Park* (☎ 8969 2037) has camp sites from $10 for two people, as well as on-site vans ($35) and cabins ($40). There's also the *Elliott Hotel* (☎ 8969 2069) which has singles/doubles from around $25/40.

Lake Woods, on Powell Creek station 14 km west by dirt road, is a great spot for camping, though there are no facilities and you need the permission of the station owners.

Farther south is **Renner Springs**, and this is generally accepted as the dividing line between the seasonally wet Top End and the dry Centre. The actual Renner Springs lie just to the south of the roadhouse, but are hidden in an acacia thicket. These days the water for the roadhouse comes from a bore.

About 50 km before Threeways and four km off the road along the old Stuart Highway is **Churchill's Head**, a large rock said to look like Britain's wartime prime minister, although it's hard to see any resemblance whatsoever. Soon after, there's a memorial to Stuart at **Attack Creek**, where the explorer turned back on one of his attempts to cross Australia from south to north, reputedly after his party was attacked by a group of hostile Aboriginal people.

GULF COUNTRY
Just south of Daly Waters the single-lane, sealed Carpentaria Highway heads east to Borroloola, 378 km away near the Gulf of Carpentaria and one of the best barramundi fishing spots in the Territory. After 267 km the Carpentaria Highway meets the Tablelands Highway, also sealed, at the **Cape Crawford Roadhouse**. The Tablelands Highway runs 404 km south to meet the Barkly Highway at **Barkly Roadhouse**; there's no petrol between these two road-houses.

Borroloola (pop 800)
Borroloola is a small town close to the Gulf of Carpentaria. Tourism, cattle and mining are the mainstays of the economy. The town's colourful past is preserved mainly in the many interesting displays housed in the **old police station**, which dates from 1886 and is open Monday to Friday from 10 am to noon. (At other times the key is available from the Holiday Village.) Here you can learn about the Hermit of Borroloola and the Freshwater Admiral, two of the many colourful eccentrics spawned by the local lifestyle and the subject of a David Attenborough documentary in the 1960s.

Borroloola attracts around 10,000 visitors annually, most of them coming for the fishing – the **Borroloola Fishing Classic** held in June each year draws a large number of enthusiasts. Other annual events include the inevitable Rodeo (August) and the Show (July).

Croc Spot Tours (☎ 8975 8721) offers a choice of several boat tours.

Places to Stay & Eat There is little shade at the *McArthur River Caravan Park* (☎ 8975 8734), in the main street, where powered

sites cost $13.50 per night (add $2.50 if you're using an air-conditioner). Unpowered sites cost $10 for two adults.

The *Borroloola Inn* (☎ 8975 8766) has air-con rooms starting at $40 for a twin. Its bistro restaurant serves a range of sensibly priced and generous meals, and the Sunday night barbecue is excellent value ($12 for all you can eat).

The *Borroloola Holiday Village* (☎ 8975 8742) has air-con units with attached bath, cooking facilities, colour TV and telephone (from $92 for a twin room). There are four economy rooms sleeping just one person each ($50), while budget beds in the bunk-house cost $30.

Getting There & Away Airnorth (☎ 8975 7885) has three flights a week to Darwin ($350) and Katherine ($22), and less frequently to Ngukurr ($135) and Numbulwar ($100) in Arnhem Land.

THREEWAYS
Threeways, 537 km north of the Alice, 988 km south of Darwin and 643 km west of Mt Isa, is basically a bloody long way from anywhere – apart from Tennant Creek, 26 km down the Track. This is a classic 'get stuck' point for hitchhikers.

The *Threeways Roadhouse* (☎ 8962 2744) at the junction has air-con rooms at $42, or you can camp for $8 ($14 with power). The junction is marked by a tasteless memorial to John Flynn, the founder of the Royal Flying Doctor Service.

TENNANT CREEK (pop 3550)
Apart from Katherine, this is the only town of any size between Darwin and Alice Springs. It's 26 km south of Threeways, and 511 km north of Alice Springs. A lot of travellers spend a night here, and there are one or two attractions, mainly related to gold mining, to tempt you to stay a bit longer.

To the Warumungu people, Tennant Creek is Jurnkurakurr, the intersection of a number of dreaming tracks.

There's a tale that Tennant Creek was first settled when a wagonload of beer broke down here in the early 1930s and the drivers decided they might as well make themselves comfortable while they consumed the freight. Tennant Creek had a small gold rush around the same time. One of the major workings was **Nobles Nob**, 16 km east of the town along Peko Rd. It was discovered by a one-eyed man called Jack Noble who formed a surprisingly successful prospecting partnership with the blind William Weaber. This was the biggest open-cut gold mine in the country until mining ceased in 1985. Ore from other local mines is still processed and you can visit the open cut.

Information

The visitor centre (☎ 8962 3388) is in the transit centre in the middle of town.

Anyinginyi Arts & Crafts is an interesting Aboriginal arts and crafts shop on Davidson St. Most of the items on sale are made locally and prices are lower than in Alice Springs.

Things to See

Along Peko Rd you can visit the old **Tennant Creek Battery**, where gold-bearing ore was crushed and treated. The battery is still in working order and guided tours are given twice daily from April to October. Along the same road there is the **One Tank Hill lookout**. Nearby is the Argo mine, the main operation of the Peko company which used to mine at Warrego, north-west of Tennant Creek.

The small **National Trust Museum**, on Schmidt St near the corner of Windley St, houses six rooms of local memorabilia and reconstructed mining scenes. It's open May to October daily from 4 to 6 pm; admission is $2.

Twelve km north of town are the green-roofed stone buildings of the old **telegraph station**. This is one of only four of the original 11 stations remaining in the Territory (the others are at Barrow Creek, Alice Springs and Powell Creek). The station's telegraph functions ceased in 1935 when a new office opened in the town itself. Today it is owned by the government and main-

tained by Parks & Wildlife, and it's worth a wander around.

Organised Tours

An interesting diversion is to take a morning Walala Bush Tucker Tour (☎ 8962 2358). These tours, which are led by local Aboriginal women, operate from March to November and delve into bush tucker and medicine. The cost is $25 ($15 children) for three hours; bookings should be made one day in advance.

Places to Stay

Camping & On-Site Vans The *Outback Caravan Park* (☎ 8962 2459) is one km east of town along Peko Rd. It has a swimming pool, tent sites at $12 a double ($15 with power) and on-site vans or cabins (some air-con) for $25 to $47.50 a double.

The other choice is the *Tennant Creek Caravan Park* (☎ 8962 2325) on Paterson St (Stuart Highway) on the northern edge of town. It has powered sites at $15, twin 'bunkhouse' rooms at $20 per person, and on-site cabins at $40.

Hostels The *Safari Lodge Motel* (☎ 8962 2207; fax 8962 3188) has a wing of back-packer rooms right next to the Anzac Hill lookout, across the road from its main building on Davidson St. A bed in these air-cooled rooms costs $10, and there are communal cooking facilities.

Another budget alternative is the pleasant little *Tennant Creek Youth Hostel* (☎ 8962 2719), in a shady location on the corner of Leichhardt and Windley Sts. Beds in air-con twin rooms cost $12.

Hotels & Motels Tennant Creek's motels aren't cheap. The *Safari Lodge Motel* (☎ 8962 2207) in the centre of town on Davidson St has singles/doubles for $62/72.

The *Goldfields Hotel Motel* (☎ 8962 2030), just around the corner on the highway, has singles/doubles for $55/65.

At the southern end of town the *Bluestone Motor Inn* (☎ 8962 2617) is the only place in this category with a swimming pool. Units range from $55 to $72.

Places to Eat

It comes as something of a surprise to find one of the most highly regarded restaurants in the Territory in the local squash centre! The *Dolly Pot Inn* on Davidson St is open daily from 11 am to midnight and offers good-value meals such as steak and salad, and also features home-made waffles.

On the main street there's *Rocky's Pasta & Pizza* (☎ 8962 2049) with, yep, pizzas and pasta, and they also do deliveries. For takeaway snacks and ice cream there's *Mr Perry's Ice Creamery* near the post office on Paterson St, and the *Transit Centre* also does takeaways.

The Memorial Club on Schmidt St welcomes visitors and has good, straightforward counter meals at its *Memories Bistro*.

The *Bluestone Motor Inn* and the *Eldorado Motor Lodge* both have licensed restaurants.

TENNANT CREEK TO ALICE SPRINGS

About 90 km south of Tennant Creek is the **Devil's Marbles Conservation Reserve**, a haphazard pile of giant spherical boulders scattered on both sides of the road. According to Aboriginal mythology they were laid by the Rainbow Serpent. There's also a Parks & Wildlife camp site here. At **Wauchope**, just to the south of the marbles, there's a pub and caravan park.

After the Devil's Marbles there are only a few places of interest on the trip south to the Alice. Near Barrow Creek the **Stuart Memorial** commemorates John McDouall Stuart. Visible to the east of the highway is Central Mt Stuart.

At **Barrow Creek** itself there is another old post-office telegraph repeater station. It was attacked by Aboriginal people in 1874 and the station master and linesman were killed – their graves are by the road. A great number of Aboriginal people died in the inevitable reprisals. The pub here is a real outback gem, and the Barrow Creek Races in August are a colourful event which draws

people in from all over the area. The *Barrow Creek Hotel & Caravan Park* (☎ 8956 9753) has single/double rooms and cabins for $20/35 and camp sites from $7.

The road continues through **Ti Tree** and finally **Aileron**, which is the last stop before the Alice.

Alice Springs

Population 22,000

The Alice, as it's usually known, was originally founded in the 1870s as a staging point for the overland telegraph line. A telegraph station was built near a permanent water hole in the bed of the dry Todd River. The river was named after Charles Todd, Superintendent of Telegraphs back in Adelaide, and a spring near the water hole was named after Alice, his wife.

A town, named Stuart, was first established in 1888, a few km south of the telegraph station as a railhead for a proposed railway line. Because the railway didn't materialise immediately, the town developed slowly. Not until 1933 did the town come to be known as Alice Springs.

The Overland Telegraph Line through the Centre was built to connect with the undersea line from Darwin to Java, which on its completion put Australia in direct contact with Europe for the first time. It was a monumental task, achieved in a remarkably short time.

Today, Alice Springs is a pleasant, modern town with good shops and restaurants. It is an access point for the many tourist attractions of central Australia. There is also a major and controversial US communications base, Pine Gap, nearby. The Alice Springs Peace Group (☎ 8952 2018) can tell you more about Pine Gap.

Alice Springs' growth to its present size has been recent and rapid. When the name was officially changed in 1933 the population had only just reached 200! Even in the 1950s Alice Springs was still a tiny town with a population in the hundreds. Until WW II

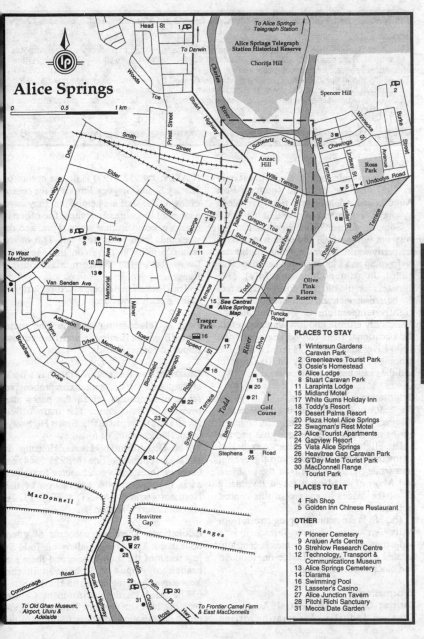

Alice Springs

NORTHERN TERRITORY

PLACES TO STAY

1 Wintersun Gardens
   Caravan Park
2 Greenleaves Tourist Park
3 Ossie's Homestead
6 Alice Lodge
8 Stuart Caravan Park
11 Larapinta Lodge
15 Midland Motel
17 White Gums Holiday Inn
18 Toddy's Resort
19 Desert Palms Resort
20 Plaza Hotel Alice Springs
22 Swagman's Rest Motel
23 Alice Tourist Apartments
24 Gapview Resort
25 Vista Alice Springs
26 Heavitree Gap Caravan Park
29 G'Day Mate Tourist Park
30 MacDonnell Range
   Tourist Park

PLACES TO EAT

4 Fish Shop
5 Golden Inn Chinese Restaurant

OTHER

7 Pioneer Cemetery
9 Araluen Arts Centre
10 Strehlow Research Centre
12 Technology, Transport &
   Communications Museum
13 Alice Springs Cemetery
14 Diarama
16 Swimming Pool
21 Lasseter's Casino
27 Alice Junction Tavern
28 Pitchi Richi Sanctuary
31 Mecca Date Garden

Mparntwe

The Alice Springs area is the traditional home of the Arrernte Aboriginal people, and to them it is Mparntwe. The heart of the area is the junction of the Charles (Anthelke Ulpeye) and Todd (Lhere Mparntwe) rivers, just north of Anzac Hill.

All the topographical features of the town were formed by the creative ancestral beings – the Yeperenye, Ntyarlke and Utnerrengatye caterpillars – as they crawled across the landscape from Emily Gap (Anthwerrke), in the MacDonnell Ranges south-east of town. Alice Springs today still has a sizeable Aboriginal community with strong links to the area. ■

there was no sealed road to it, and it was only in 1987 that the old road south to Port Augusta and Adelaide was finally replaced by a new, shorter and fully sealed highway.

Summer days in Alice Springs can get very hot (up to 45°C) and even winter days are pretty warm. However, winter nights can be freezing and a lot of people get caught off guard. In winter (June and July), five minutes after the sun goes down you can feel the heat disappear, and the average minimum nightly temperature is 4°C. Despite the Alice's dry climate and low annual rainfall, the occasional rains can be heavy and the Todd River may flood – as it did during the running of the 1995 Henley-on-Todd regatta and the races had to be abandoned!

Orientation

The centre of Alice Springs is a conveniently compact area just five streets wide, bounded by the dry Todd River on one side and the Stuart Highway on the other. Anzac Hill forms the northern boundary to the central area while Stuart Terrace is at the southern end. Many of the places to stay and virtually all of the places to eat are in this central rectangle.

Todd St is the main shopping street; from Wills Terrace to Gregory Terrace it is a pedestrian mall. The bus centre is centrally located at the Melanka Lodge on Todd St, one block south of the mall.

Information

Tourist Office The Central Australian Tourism Industry Association office (CATIA; ☎ 8952 5199) is on the corner of Hartley St and Gregory Terrace in the centre of town. The staff are helpful and they have a range of brochures and maps. The office is open weekdays from 9 am to 6 pm, and on weekends from 10 am to 3 pm. This office issues permits to travel on the Mereenie Loop Rd in the Western MacDonnell Ranges.

The *Centralian Advocate* is Alice Springs' twice-weekly newspaper.

Post & Telecommunications The main post office is on Hartley St, and there's a row of public phones outside.

Other Offices Parks & Wildlife has a desk at the tourist office, with a comprehensive range of brochures on all the parks and reserves in the Centre. The main office (☎ 8951 8211) is just off the Stuart Highway, about five km south of town.

The Department of Lands, Housing & Local Government office (☎ 8951 5344) on Gregory Terrace is a good source for maps, as is the Automobile Association of the Northern Territory (AANT; ☎ 8953 1322), also on Gregory Terrace.

Bookshops There are a couple of good bookshops. The Aranta Gallery on Todd St just south of the mall is one, and there's a branch of Angus & Robertson in the Yeperenye shopping centre on Hartley St.

The Arid Lands Environment Centre (☎ 8952 2497) on Gregory Terrace is a non-profit organisation which is full of info on

NORTHERN TERRITORY

both local and national environmental issues. It also sells a range of crafts and souvenirs.

Telegraph Station Historical Reserve

Laying the telegraph line across the dry, harsh centre of Australia was no easy task, as the small museum at the old telegraph station, two km north of the town, shows. The original spring, after which the town is named, is also here. The station, one of 12 built along the Overland Telegraph Line in the 1870s, was constructed of local stone from 1871 to 1872 and continued in operation until 1932.

The station is open daily from 8 am to 7 pm in winter, and until 9 pm in summer; entry is $2.50 ($1 children). From April to October rangers give free guided tours several times daily, and a slide show three evenings a week; at other times you can use the informative self-guided brochure issued to all visitors.

The **Alice Springs** here are a great spot for a cooling dip, and the grassy picnic area by the station has barbecues, tables and some shady gum trees – a popular spot on weekends.

It's easy to walk or ride to the station from the Alice – just follow the path on the western (left hand) side of the riverbed; it takes about half an hour to ride. The main road out to the station is signposted to the right off the Stuart Highway about one km north of the centre of town. There's another pleasant circular walk from the station out by the old cemetery and Trig Hill.

Anzac Hill

At the northern end of Todd St you can make the short, sharp ascent to the top of Anzac Hill (or you can drive there). Aboriginal people call the hill Untyeyetweleye, the site of the Corkwood Dreaming, the story of a woman who lived alone on the hill. The Two Sisters ancestral beings (Arrweketye therre) are also associated with the hill.

From the top you have a fine view over modern Alice Springs and down to the Mac-Donnell Ranges that form a southern

boundary to the town. There are a number of other hills in and around Alice Springs which you can climb, but Anzac Hill is certainly the best-known and most convenient.

Todd St Mall

Todd St is the main shopping street and most of it is a pleasant pedestrian mall. Along the street you can see **Adelaide House**, built in the early 1920s and now preserved as the **John Flynn Memorial Museum**. Originally it was Alice Springs' first hospital. It's open Monday to Friday from 10 am to 4 pm, and Saturday from 10 am to 12.30 pm. Admission is $2.50 (children $1) and includes a cup of tea or coffee. Flynn, who was the founding flying doctor, is also commemorated by the **John Flynn Memorial Church** next door.

Other Old Buildings

There are a number of interesting old buildings along Parsons St including the **Stuart Town Gaol** built from 1907 to 1908. It's open Tuesday and Thursday from 10 am to 12.30 pm, and on Saturday between 9.30 am and noon. The **Old Courthouse**, which was in use until 1980, is on the corner of Parsons and Hartley Sts, and now houses the fledgling **National Pioneer Women's Hall of Fame**. It is open daily from 10 am to 4 pm.

Across the road on Parsons St is the **Residency** which dates from 1926 to 1927. It's now used for historical exhibits and is open weekdays from 9 am to 4 pm and weekends from 10 am to 4 pm. Other old buildings include the **Hartley St School** beyond the post office and **Tuncks Store** on the corner of Hartley St and Stott Terrace.

Near the corner of Parsons St and Leichhardt Terrace, the old **Pioneer Theatre** is a former walk-in (rather than drive-in) cinema dating from 1944. These days it's a YHA hostel.

Museum of Central Australia

Upstairs in the Alice Plaza on the corner of Parsons St and the mall, the Museum of Central Australia has a fascinating collection, including some superb natural history displays. There's an interesting exhibition on

An Aviation Tragedy

In 1929 pioneer aviator Charles Kingsford-Smith went missing in the north-west in his aircraft *Southern Cross*. Two other aviators, Anderson and Hitchcock, set off to search for Kingsford-Smith in their tiny aircraft *Kookaburra*. North of Alice Springs they struck engine trouble and made an emergency landing. Despite not having any tools they managed to fix the fault, but repeated attempts to take off failed due to the sandy, rocky soil. They had foolishly left Alice Springs not only without tools, but with minimal water and food. By the time an aerial search had been organised and their plane located both had died. Their bodies were recovered but the aircraft, intact and undamaged, was left. Kingsford-Smith turned up unharmed a few days later.

The aircraft was accidentally rediscovered by a mining surveyor in 1961, and in the '70s it was decided to collect the remains and exhibit them. They proved strangely elusive, however, and it took several years to find them again. They were finally located in 1978 by Sydney electronics whiz Dick Smith. Fifty years of exposure and bushfires had reduced the aircraft to a crumbled wreck. It is now displayed only a few steps from where the aircraft took off on its ill-fated mission. A short film tells the sad story of this misadventure.

The museum also displays a Wackett, which went missing in 1961 on a flight from Ceduna in South Australia. The pilot strayed no less than 42° off course and put down when he ran out of fuel. An enormous search failed to find him because he was so far from his expected route. The aircraft was discovered, again completely by accident, in 1965. The museum has a small booklet on this bizarre mishap. ■

NORTHERN TERRITORY

meteors and meteorites (Henbury meteorites are on display). There are also exhibits on Aboriginal culture and displays of art of the Centre. It's open from 10 am to 5 pm and admission is $2.

Royal Flying Doctor Service Base

The RFDS base is close to the town centre in Stuart Terrace. It's open Monday to Saturday from 9 am to 4 pm, and Sunday from 1 to 4 pm. The tours last half an hour and cost $2.50 (children 50c). There's a small museum, and a souvenir shop.

School of the Air

The School of the Air, which broadcasts school lessons to children living on remote outback stations, is on Head St, about a km north of the centre. During school terms you can hear a live broadcast (depending on class schedules). The school is open Monday to Friday from 8.30 am to 1 pm and 1.30 to 4.30 pm, and admission is by donation ($2).

Technology, Transport & Communications Museum

Alice Springs has an interesting little museum housed in the former Connellan hangar on Memorial Ave, where the town's airport used to be in the early days. The museum includes a couple of poignant exhibits which pinpoint the dangers of outback aviation.

The museum is not all tragedy – there are exhibits on pioneer aviation in the Territory and, of course, the famous Royal Flying Doctor Service. The museum is open daily from 10 am to 4 pm; admission is free.

Strehlow Research Centre

This centre, on Larapinta Drive, commemorates the work of Professor Ted Strehlow among the Arrernte people of the district (see the Hermannsburg Mission section later in this chapter). The main function of the building is to house the most comprehensive collection of Aboriginal spirit items in the country. These were entrusted to Strehlow for safekeeping by the local Aboriginal people years ago, when they realised their traditional life was under threat. Because the items are so important, and cannot be viewed by an uninitiated male or *any* female, they are kept in a vault in the centre. There is, however, a very good display on the works of Strehlow, and on the Arrernte people.

The building itself is something of a feature – it has the largest rammed-earth wall in the southern hemisphere. The centre is open daily from 10 am to 5 pm (no entry after 4.30 pm); entry is $4.

Araluen Arts Centre

The Araluen Arts Centre on Larapinta Drive has a small gallery full of Albert Namatjira paintings, and often has other displays as well. The stained-glass windows in the foyer are the centrepiece of the centre. It's open weekdays from 10 to 5 pm (4 pm on week-ends). Entry to the Namatjira gallery is $2.

Alice Springs Cemetery

Adjacent to the technology museum is this cemetery which contains a number of inter-esting graves. The most famous is that of the Albert Namatjira – it's the sandstone one on the far side. The headstone features a terra-cotta tile mural of three of Namatjira's dreaming sites in the MacDonnell Ranges. The glazes forming the mural design were painted on by Namatjira's granddaughter, Elaine, and the other work was done by other members of the Hermannsburg Potters.

Other graves in the cemetery include that of Harold Lasseter, who perished in 1931 while trying to relocate the rich gold reef he supposedly found west of Uluru 20 years earlier (see the Lasseter's Lost Reef aside in the Uluru – Kata Tjuta National Park section), and the anthropologist Olive Pink, who spent many years working with the Aboriginal people of the central deserts (see Olive Pink Flora Reserve below).

Pioneer Cemetery

This is the original Alice Springs cemetery, and today it lies almost forgotten and rarely visited in the light industrial area on the western side of the railway line on George Crescent. The gravestones here tell some of the story of the original settlers – including that of the young man who died at Temple Bar of 'foul air'.

Panorama Guth

Panorama Guth, at 65 Hartley St in the town centre, is a huge circular panorama which is viewed from an elevated observation point. It depicts almost all the points of interest around the Centre with uncanny realism. Painted by a Dutch artist, Henk Guth, it measures about 60 metres in circumference and admission is $3 (children $1.50) – whether you think it's worth paying money to see a reproduction of what you may see for real is a different question! It's open from Monday to Saturday from 9 am to 5 pm, Sunday from 2 to 5 pm.

Diarama

On the outskirts of town on Larapinta Drive, the diarama is open daily from 10 am to 5 pm. Admission to this rather quirky collec-tion of three-dimensional illustrations of various Aboriginal legends is $2.50.

Olive Pink Flora Reserve

Just across the Todd River from the centre, off Tuncks Rd, the Olive Pink Flora Reserve has a collection of shrubs and trees which are typical of the 200-km area around Alice Springs. This arid-zone botanic garden is open from 10 am to 6 pm, and there's a visitor centre open between 10 am and 4 pm. There are some short walks in the reserve, includ-ing the climb to the top of Annie Meyer Hill in the Sadadeen Range, from where there's a fine view over the town. The hill is known to the Arrernte people as Tharrarltneme and is a registered sacred site. Looking to the south, in the middle distance is a small ridge running east-west; this is Ntyarlkarle Tyaneme, one of the first sites created by the caterpillar ancestors, and the name relates that this was where the caterpillars crossed the river.

Pitchi Richi Sanctuary

Just south of the Heavitree Gap causeway is Pitchi Richi ('gap in the range'), a miniature folk museum with a collection of sculptures by William Ricketts (you can see more of his interesting work in the William Ricketts Sanc-tuary in the Dandenongs near Melbourne) and

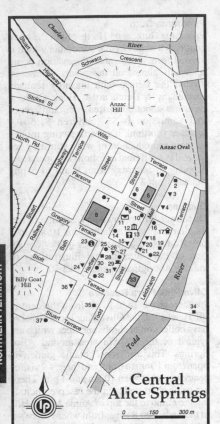

Central Alice Springs

0   150   300 m

an amazing range of various implements and other household items used by early pioneers. There's also billy tea and damper, and an interesting and lively chat on Arrernte Aboriginal lore and traditions.

The sanctuary itself doesn't look too promising, but it's well worth a visit. It's open daily from 9 am to 2 pm; entry is $8 (children $5).

Just a little farther from Pitchi Richi on Palm Circuit is the **Mecca Date Garden**. Entry is free and there are dates and date products for sale.

Frontier Camel Farm

A farther five km south of Pitchi Richi is the Frontier Camel Farm, where you have the chance to ride one of the beasts. These strange 'ships of the desert', guided by their Afghani masters, were the main form of transport before the railways were built. There's a museum with displays about camels, and a guided tour and camel ride is held daily at 10.30 am (and 2 pm from April to October). For more details see Camel Rides under Organised Tours later in this chapter.

Also here is the **Arid Australian Reptile House**, which has an excellent collection of snakes and lizards.

The farm is open daily from 9 am to 5 pm. The cost of the camel tour is $10 (children $5), including a visit to the reptile house.

The Old Ghan Museum & Transport Hall of Fame

At the MacDonnell Siding, off the Stuart Highway 10 km south of Alice Springs, a group of local railway enthusiasts has restored a collection of Ghan locomotives and carriages on a stretch of disused siding from the old narrow-gauge Ghan railway track. You can wander round the equipment, watch the restoration work and learn more about this extraordinary railway line at the information centre.

Also here is the Transport Hall of Fame, with a fine collection of old vehicles, including some very early road trains, and other transport memorabilia.

The area is open daily from 9 am to 5 pm and admission is $6 (children free), or $3 if you just want to visit one or other of the museums.

There are also trips on the old Ghan three days a week out to Mt Ertiva Siding, nine km south of town. The trip starts at 10 am, takes 1½ hours and costs $18 (children $7), and this includes entry to both the museums. Morning tea is available in the dining car. MacDonnell Siding is on the Alice Wanderer bus route (see Getting Around).

Chateau Hornsby

Alice Springs actually has a winery. It's 15 km out of town, five km off the road, before you get to the airport turn-off. The wine produced here (moselle, riesling-semillon and shiraz) is not bad at all, although most of it gets sold to people intrigued by the novelty of a central Australian wine.

The pleasant restaurant here is open for lunchtime barbecues and in the evenings, and is a popular excursion from town. You can pedal out to Chateau Hornsby by bicycle

– after tasting a little free wine the distance back seems much shorter. The easier option is to take the Alice Wanderer. The free Sunday afternoon jazz sessions are very popular, as is the Ted Egan show, which takes place from April to October.

Organised Tours

The tourist office can tell you about all sorts of organised tours from Alice Springs. There are the usual big-name operators and a host of small local operators. There are bus tours, 4WD tours, even balloon tours.

Note that although many of the tours don't operate daily, there is at least one trip a day to one or more of the major attractions – Uluru – Kata Tjuta National Park (Ayers Rock and the Olgas), Kings Canyon, Palm Valley, both the Western and Eastern MacDonnell ranges, Simpson's Gap and Standley Chasm. Tours to less popular places – such as Rainbow Valley and Chambers Pillar – operate less frequently.

Most of the tours follow similar routes and you see much the same on them all, although the level of service and the degree of luxury will determine how much they cost. All the hostels can book tours, and they will also know exactly which company is offering the best deals.

Town Tours Alice Wanderer Express Tours (☎ 8952 2111) can whiz you around five of the town's major sights in about 2 hours for $28 ($15 children) including admission fees. The tours depart daily at 8.30 and 11.30 am, and you are collected from your accommodation.

Aboriginal Culture Tours - Rod Steinert (☎ 8955 5000; fax 8955 5111) operates a variety of tours, including the popular $65 ($42 children) Dreamtime & Bushtucker Tour. It's a half-day trip in which you meet some Warlpiri Aboriginal people and learn a little about their traditional life. You can do the same tour with your own vehicle for $48 ($29).

Oak Valley Day Tours (☎ 8956 0959; fax 8956 0965) is an Aboriginal-owned and run organisation that makes day trips to

Alice Events

The Alice has a string of colourful activities, particularly during the cool tourist months from May to August. The **Camel Cup**, a series of camel races, takes place in mid-July. At around the same time, Chateau Hornsby, the local winery, has a beerfest.

The **Alice Springs Agricultural Show** takes place in early July, and the highlight is a fireworks display.

In August there's the **Alice Springs Rodeo**, when for one week the town is full of bow-legged stockmen, swaggering around in their 10-gallon hats, cowboy shirts, moleskin jeans and R M Williams Cuban-heeled boots.

Finally in late September there's the event which probably draws the biggest crowds of all – the **Henley-on-Todd Regatta**. Having a series of boat races in the Todd River is slightly complicated by the fact that there is hardly ever any water in the river. Nevertheless a whole series of races is held for sailing boats, doubles, racing eights and every boat race class you could think of. The boats are all bottomless, the crews' legs stick out and they simply run down the course!

The **Verdi Club Beerfest** is held early in October, at the end of the regatta. It's held at the Verdi Club on Undoolya Rd and there are many frivolous activities including spit the dummy, tug of war, and stein-lifting competitions. For the beer enthusiast there's a range of local and overseas beers and a range of cuisines.

All through the cooler months there is also a string of country **horse races** at Alice Springs and surrounding outstations like Finke, Barrow Creek, Aileron or the Harts Range. They're colourful events and for the outstations they're the big turnouts of the year. ■

Ewaninga and Rainbow Valley. These trips also go to Mpwellare and Oak Valley, both on the Hugh River Stock Route and both of cultural significance to the Aboriginal people. The cost is $110 ($90 children) and this includes lunch, and morning and afternoon tea.

Camel Rides Camel treks are another central Australian attraction. You can have a short ride for a few dollars at the Frontier Camel Farm (☎ 8953 0444; fax 8955 5015), or take their longer Todd River Ramble, which is a one-hour ride along the bed of the Todd River ($35; $25 children up to 15). They also do extended rides from $300 for a two-day trip.

Noel Fullerton's Camel Outback Safaris (☎ 8956 0925), based at Stuart Well 90 km south of Alice Springs, also operates camel tours.

Ballooning Sunrise balloon trips are also popular and cost from $98 ($50 children), which includes breakfast and the 30-minute flight. One-hour flights cost around $145

($80), or you can just tag along as part of the chase crew for $35 ($25).

Operators include Outback Ballooning (☎ 1800 809 790; fax 8952 3869), Ballooning Downunder (☎ 8952 8816; fax 8952 3869) and Spinifex Ballooning (☎ 1800 677 893; fax 8952 2862), which operates from Chateau Hornsby.

Tours Farther Afield Sahara Tours (☎ 8953 0881; fax 8953 2414) offers very good daily camping trips to Uluru (Ayers Rock) and elsewhere and these are popular with backpackers. It charges $200 for a two-day trip to the Rock and Kata Tjuta (the Olgas), or you can pay an extra $85 and spend an extra day taking in Kings Canyon – well worthwhile if you have the time.

Northern Territory Adventure Tours (☎ 8952 1474; fax 8952 3819) operates the popular Ayers Rock Plus, which has similar two/three-day tours for $195/285. They also offer a two-day trip to the Rock which includes Kings Canyon for $210, but this is cramming an awful lot into a very short time. AKT and Tracks are other cheaper operators.

If your time is really limited you can take a one-day air safari to Uluru and back for around $330 ($245 children), which includes a tour around the Rock and entry fees. Contact Winjeel Airways (☎ 1800 064 141; fax 8953 2322).

Airnorth (☎ 1800 627 474; fax 8945 3559) also do a day air tour which includes climbing the Rock, a trip to Kata Tjuta, buffet lunch and sunset viewing.

Places to Stay – bottom end
Camping Alice Springs's caravan parks and their rates are:

G'Day Mate Tourist Park (☎ 8952 9589), Palm Circuit, near the Mecca Date Garden and Pitchi Richi Sanctuary; camp sites ($14, $16 with power) and self-contained cabins which accommodate up to six people ($46 double, $7 each extra adult).

Greenleaves Tourist Park (☎ 8952 8645), three km north-east on Burke St; camp sites ($15, $17.50 with power) and four-bed on-site vans ($34, plus $8 each extra adult).

Heavitree Gap Caravan Park (☎ 8952 4866), Palm Circuit, four km south of town; camp sites ($12, $15 with power) and on-site vans ($37, plus $7 each extra adult).

MacDonnell Range Tourist Park (☎ 8952 6111), Palm Place, five km from town; camp sites ($13.50, $16.50 with power) and on-site cabins (from $30 to $60).

Stuart Caravan Park (☎ 8952 2547), two km west on Larapinta Drive; camp sites ($12, $15 with power), six-bed on-site vans ($37, plus $6 each extra adult) and four-bed cabins ($47, $7).

Wintersun Gardens Caravan Park (☎ 8952 4080), 2.5 km north on the Stuart Highway; camp sites ($12, $15.50 with power), six-bed on-site vans ($35 double, plus $6.30 each extra adult) and six-bed cabins ($41 to $49 double, $6.30).

Hostels There are plenty of hostels and guesthouses in Alice Springs. All the places catering to backpackers have the usual facilities and services – pool, courtesy bus, travel desk, bicycle hire etc.

Right in the centre of town, on the corner of Leichhardt Terrace and Parsons St in the old Pioneer walk-in cinema, is the YHA *Pioneer Hostel* (☎ 8952 8855; fax 8952 4144). It has 62 beds in air-con dorms, and charges $12 in a four-share room, $14 for a

twin. There's a swimming pool, and bicycles for hire.

Also central is the very popular *Melanka's Backpackers Resort* (☎ 1800 815 066; fax 8952 4587) at 94 Todd St, just a couple of steps from the bus station. This is a huge place with a variety of air-con rooms, ranging from eight-bed dorms at $10 through to twin-shares at $15 per person. There are also singles/doubles for $40/45, or $55/65 with TV, fridge and bathroom. There's a cafeteria, and its Waterhole Bar is the most popular travellers' drinking spot in the Alice.

Over the river and still just a short walk from the centre, is the relaxed *Alice Lodge* (☎ 8953 1975) at 4 Mueller St. This is a small, quiet and friendly hostel with a garden and pool. Nightly rates are $12 in the dorm, $14 in a four-share room, $25 for a single and $16 per person in a double (prices include sheets; quilt hire is $1 with a $9 deposit). There's a small kitchen, and barbecue and laundry facilities.

Also on this side of the river at 18 Warburton St is *Ossie's Homestead* (☎ 8952 2308). B&B in the 12-bed dorm is $12, in a four-bed room $14, and in a double $34. There's a swimming pool and the usual facilities, as well as a pet kangaroo called Thumper. Ossie's also runs horse trail-rides, with various rides ranging in cost from $60 to $205.

Back on the other side of the river, at 41 Gap Rd, is *Toddy's Resort* (☎ 1800 806 240; fax 8952 1767). This complex has laundry facilities and a communal kitchen for those not in the self-contained units. There's a swimming pool, barbecue and small shop on the site. Prices are $10 for six-bed dorms with shared facilities, $12 with TV and bathroom, $34 for doubles ($45 with bathroom). Cheap meals are available at $3 for breakfast and $6.50 for dinner, and there's also bike hire.

Places to Stay – middle
Hotels Right by the river at 1 Todd St mall is the *Todd Tavern* (☎ 8952 1255). This pub gets noisy when there are bands playing on weekends, but it's otherwise quite a reasonable

place to stay. Rates are $38 for singles/doubles (some with bathroom) including a light breakfast.

At the southern end of Gap Rd, just before you go through Heavitree Gap, is the *Gapview Resort Hotel* (☎ 8952 6611; fax 8952 8312). It's about one km from the centre, and charges from $58 to $74 for double room with bathroom, fridge and TV.

Apartments & Holiday Flats There are very few apartments and flats for rent; in most cases the best you can do is a motel-type room with limited cooking facilities, which usually consists of an electric frypan and a microwave oven.

The *Alice Tourist Apartments* (☎ 1800 806 142; fax 8953 2950) are on Gap Rd. There are one and two-room, self-contained, air-con apartments for $63 for a double, $95 for four and $105 for six people, about $10 less in summer. These places consist of a main room with sleeping, cooking and dining facilities, and the larger flats have a second room with two or four beds. These are a good option for families.

The *White Gum Holiday Inn* (☎ 1800 896 131; fax 8953 2092) at 17 Gap Rd, also has rooms with separate kitchen at $78 for up to four people.

On Barrett Drive, next to the Plaza Hotel Alice Springs, the *Desert Palms Resort* (☎ 1800 678 037; fax 8953 4176) has spacious rooms, each with limited cooking facilities, at $68 for two, and $80 for two adults and two children. There's a large island swimming pool, and nicely landscaped gardens.

Conveniently central is *Larapinta Lodge* (☎ 8952 7255; fax 8952 7101), at 3 Larapinta Drive just over the railway line from the town centre. It has singles/doubles for $55/67, with communal kitchen and laundry, and the obligatory swimming pool.

Motels Alice Springs has a rash of motels, and prices range from around $50 to $100 for a double room. There are often lower prices and special deals during the hot summer months.

At 67 Gap Rd there's the *Swagman's Rest Motel* (☎ 8953 1333) with singles/doubles for $52/62. The units are self-contained and there's a swimming pool.

At 4 Traeger Ave is the *Midland Motel* (☎ 8952 1588; fax 8952 8280) which charges from $50/55 for its rooms, and there's also a licensed restaurant.

On Leichhardt Terrace facing the Todd River is the *Territory Motor Inn* (☎ 1800 089 644; fax 8952 7829), with every available mod-con from $90. There's a licensed restaurant here and meals can be served in your unit.

Places to Stay – top end
The top-end accommodation is all on the eastern side of the river where there's more room to spread out.

At the top of the range there's the *Plaza Hotel Alice Springs* (☎ 1800 675 212; fax 8952 3822), on Barrett Drive, with rooms from $205 up to $400. The hotel is very well equipped, with facilities including heated pool, spa/sauna and tennis courts.

Almost next door is the *Lasseters Hotel Casino* (☎ 1800 808 975; fax 8953 1680) with double rooms from $105.

Another top-end option is the *Alice Springs Pacific Resort* (☎ 1800 805 055; fax 8953 0995) at 34 Stott Terrace right by the Todd River, not far from the centre of town. Rooms here go for $140/150, and it includes such luxuries as a heated pool.

Lastly there's the *Vista Alice Springs* (☎ 1800 810 664; fax 8952 1988), stuck in the middle of nowhere at the foot of the MacDonnell Ranges. The 140 units here go for $120.

Places to Eat
Cafes, Snacks & Fast Food There are numerous places for a sandwich or light snack along Todd St mall. Many have tables and chairs outside – ideal for breakfast on a cool morning.

The *Jolly Swagman* in Todd Plaza off the mall is a pleasant place for sandwiches and light snacks. *Le Cafeteriere* is at the southern end of the mall and is open for breakfast, burgers, sandwiches etc. Right next door is the *Red Dog*, a very similar place with tables and umbrellas out on the footpath.

The Alice Plaza has a lunchtime cafeteria-style eating place called *Fawlty's* with snacks, light meals, sandwiches and a salad bar. Also here is *Doctor Lunch*, which is good for pancakes and coffee. Across the mall, the Springs Plaza has *Golly it's Good*, with more sandwiches and snacks.

In the Yeperenye shopping centre on Hartley St there's the *Boomerang Coffee Shop*, the *Bakery*, another *Fawlty's* outlet and a big Woolworths supermarket.

The closest Alice Springs comes to a New Age cafe is the anonymous *Cafe Mediterranean*, tucked away in the small Fan Lane off the mall, opposite the Red Dog cafe. It has an excellent range of health-food dishes, and a very relaxed atmosphere. You can BYO and the front window is a good place to check out the notices for what's happening around town. Dishes here cost around $5 to $10.

The *Swingers Cafe* on Gregory Terrace serves trendy items, such as focaccia, and foreign treats like curry laksa. It's a good spot, despite the silly name.

Another popular place, especially on Friday evenings, is *Uncle's Tavern* on the corner of Gregory Terrace and Hartley St. Here you can have a beer or a cappuccino, as well as light meals and snacks.

Alice Springs also has its share of the well-known fast-food outlets such as *KFC*, *Hungry Jacks* and *Pizza Hut* but, remarkably, no *McDonald's*!

Pub Meals Far and away the most popular place is the *Caf* at the Todd Tavern. The food is tasty and cheap, and there are specials on most nights, when you can get a meal for $5 to $8.

Scotty's Tavern is a small bar in the mall, and it has substantial main courses, such as barramundi or steak, for $18, and other main courses range from $12 to $16.

Restaurants The *Eranova Cafe*, at 70 Todd St, is one of the busiest eating spots in town and it's a comfortable place, with a good

selection of excellent food. It's open for breakfast, lunch and dinner from Monday to Saturday. Meals range from $7 to $15.

Round the corner at 105 Gregory Terrace, *La Casalinga* has been serving up pasta and pizza for many years; it's open from 5 pm to 1 am every night. Meals cost $10 to $15 and it has a bar. You can also get good pasta at the licensed *Al Fresco* at the northern end of the mall. It's open daily from 10 am.

Also in the centre is the licensed *Flynn's on the Mall*, opposite the John Flynn Memorial Museum. It's a popular place, with meals in the $13 to $17 range. Crocodile and kangaroo meat are featured here, and indeed at quite a few restaurants around town. Service can be slow here, however; we waited 10 minutes and still hadn't received a menu.

The *Ristorante Puccini* is also on the mall and serves excellent home-made pasta and char-grilled fish, and has Italian-inspired desserts such as marinated fruit with ricotta zabaglione. Expect to pay around $18 for a main course.

Across the river from the centre, on the corner of Undoolya Rd and Sturt Terrace, the *Casa Nostra* is another pizza and pasta specialist.

Of course the Alice has to have a steak-house, so you can try the *Overlander Steakhouse* at 72 Hartley St. It features 'Territory food' such as beef, buffalo, kangaroo and camel – and the 'Drover's Blowout' ($32.50) is a carnivore's delight! It's quite popular, but not that cheap, with main courses in the $18 to $25 range.

Miss Daisy's at the Diplomat Motor Inn on Hartley St features a variety of exotic Territory flora and fauna on its menu – including emu steaks and desert plum sorbet.

Hidden away at the rear of Fan Lane off the mall is the *Camel's Crossing Mexican Restaurant*, which has a varied menu of both vegetarian and meat dishes. It's open nightly except Sunday, and a two-course meal will set you back about $25.

At the Bath St entrance to the Yeperenye Centre is the *Shanti*, a small Indian restaurant with beef, lamb, chicken, fish and vegetarian main courses for around $12. The dishes are mostly north Indian and are quite good value. You can BYO here, and it's open for lunch and dinner Monday to Saturday.

There are a number of Chinese restaurants around the Alice. The *Oriental Gourmet* is on Hartley St, near the corner of Stott Terrace. *Chopsticks*, on Hartley St at the Yeperenye shopping centre, is said to be good, but it's only open in the evenings. Also good is the bright yellow *Golden Inn* on Undoolya Rd, just over the bridge from the centre. Aside from the usual items you can sample some Malaysian and Szechuan dishes. It's open for lunch on weekdays and for dinner every day.

Out-of-town dining possibilities include a barbecue lunch or dinner at the *Chateau Hornsby* (☎ 8955 5133) winery south of town. At lunchtime, main meals cost from $8.50 to $12, and the dinner menu is more expensive at around $18. In the evenings you can also take in the Ted Egan Show, but you'll need to book in advance for this (see Entertainment).

Dining Tours There are a few interesting alternatives which involve taking a ride out of town. One of these is *Dinner With the Old Ghan* tour at MacDonnell Siding south of town. It operates twice weekly from April to October, and you travel by the old Ghan to a point south of town, where a campfire meal is provided; the cost of the tour is $69. The meal is actually provided by the *Camp Oven Kitchen* (☎ 8953 1411), and consists of soup and damper, and a roast, all cooked in 'camp ovens' – cast-iron pots which are buried in hot coals. It's also possible to have the meal without the train ride for $50 on Monday, Wednesday and Saturday evenings.

Take a Camel to Breakfast/Dinner is another popular dining option. This combines a one-hour camel ride with a meal at the Frontier Camel Farm (☎ 8953 0444). The cost is $49 ($30 children aged six to 12) for breakfast and $75 ($50) for dinner.

Entertainment

There's not much. At the Todd Tavern, by the river on the corner of Wills and Leichhardt terraces, the *Jam Session* has live bands on Monday night, sometimes featuring better-known bands.

Bojangles is a restaurant and nightclub on Todd St, and the *Alice Junction Tavern* on Palm Circuit has a disco on Friday and Saturday nights.

The *Waterhole Bar* at the Melanka on Todd St is the place for a beer and to meet other travellers, and there's occasionally live bands as well.

Outback character and raconteur Ted Egan puts on a performance of tall tales and outback songs three nights a week during winter at *Chateau Hornsby* ($15, or $33 with dinner). Advance booking is essential.

There are all sorts of events at the *Araluen Arts Centre* on Larapinta Drive, including temporary art exhibits, theatre and music performances and regular films. Bookings can be made at the Araluen booking office (☎ 8952 5022).

On Todd St there's a *cinema centre* which shows standard release movies.

If you want to watch the Australian gambling enthusiasm in a central Australian setting head for *Lasseter's Casino* on Barret Drive, but dress up.

Things to Buy

Alice Springs has a number of art galleries and craft centres. If you've got an interest in central Australian art or you're looking for a piece to buy, there are a couple of places where you can buy direct from the artists. The Papunya Tula Artists shop is on Todd St just south of the mall, or there's Jukurrpa Artists at 35 Gap Rd. Both places are owned and run by the art centres which produce the work.

The Central Australian Aboriginal Media Association (CAAMA) shop in the Yeperenye shopping centre is another very good place, and prices are not too unreasonable.

There are plenty of other, generally more commercial outlets for Aboriginal art. Two of the better ones are Gallery Gondwana and the Original Aboriginal Dreamtime Gallery, both on the Todd St mall.

NORTHERN TERRITORY

Getting There & Away

Air You can fly to Alice Springs with Qantas (☎ 13 1313) or Ansett (☎ 13 1300). The two companies face each other across Todd St at the Parsons St intersection.

Alice Springs to Adelaide costs $372, Uluru (Ayers Rock) $179, Darwin $353, Melbourne $517, Perth $484 and Sydney $505. You can also fly direct to Uluru from Adelaide, Sydney, Perth and Cairns. So if you're planning to fly to the Centre and visit Uluru it would be more economical to fly straight to Uluru, then continue to Alice Springs. See Getting There & Away under the Uluru – Kata Tjuta section for more details.

On the regional routes, Airnorth (☎ 1800 627 474) has flights to Uluru (twice daily, $173), Darwin ($389), Katherine ($369) and Tennant Creek ($199, all daily except Saturday) and Kings Canyon (daily, $79).

Bus Greyhound Pioneer (☎ 13 2303) at the Melanka Lodge on Todd St has daily return services from Alice Springs to Uluru ($77), Darwin ($142) and Adelaide ($142). It takes about 20 hours from Alice Springs to Darwin (1476 km) or Alice Springs to Adelaide (1543 km). You can connect to other places at various points up and down the Track – Threeways for Mt Isa and the Queensland coast, Katherine for Western Australia, Erldunda for Uluru, Port Augusta for Perth.

McCafferty's (☎ 13 1499) at 91 Gregory Terrace also has daily departures to Adelaide ($135) and Darwin ($135). To Coober Pedy the fare is $69, and to Katherine $129.

Train The Ghan between Adelaide and Alice Springs costs $140 in coach class (no sleeper and no meals), $309 in holiday class (a sleeper with shared facilities and no meals) and $500 in 1st class (a self-contained sleeper and meals). Low-season (February through June) fares are $140/278/450 respectively. For bookings phone ☎ 13 2232 during office hours.

The train departs from Adelaide on Thursday at 2 pm, arriving in Alice Springs the next morning at 10.30 am. From Alice

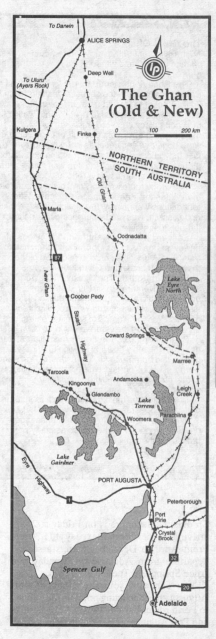

The Ghan
(Old & New)

NORTHERN TERRITORY

The Great Ghan

Australia's great railway adventure would have to be the Ghan. The Ghan went through a major change in 1980 and although it's now a rather more modern and comfortable adventure, it's still a great trip.

The Ghan saga started in 1877 when it was decided to build a railway line from Adelaide to Darwin. It eventually took over 50 years to reach Alice Springs, and they're still thinking about the final 1500 km to Darwin more than a century later. The basic problem was that they made a big mistake right at the start, a mistake that wasn't finally sorted out until 1980. They built the line in the wrong place.

The grand error was a result of concluding that because all the creek beds north of Marree were bone dry, and because nobody had seen rain, there wasn't going to be rain in the future. In fact they laid the initial stretch of line right across a flood plain and when the rain came, even though it soon dried up, the line was simply washed away. In the century or so that the original Ghan line survived it was a regular occurrence for the tracks to be washed away.

The wrong route was only part of the Ghan's problems. At first it was built wide gauge to Marree, then extended narrow gauge to Oodnadatta in 1884. And what a jerry-built line it was – the foundations were flimsy, the sleepers were too light, the grading was too steep and it meandered hopelessly. It was hardly surprising that right up to the end the top speed of the old Ghan was a flat-out 30 km/h!

Early rail travellers went from Adelaide to Marree on the broad-gauge line, changed there to narrow gauge as far as Oodnadatta, then had to make the final journey to Alice Springs by camel train. The Afghani-led camel trains had pioneered transport through the outback and it was from these Afghanis that the Ghan took its name.

Finally in 1929 the line was extended from Oodnadatta to Alice Springs. Though the Ghan was a great adventure, it simply didn't work. At the best of times it was chronically slow and uncomfortable as it bounced and bucked its way down the badly laid line. Worse, it was unreliable and expensive to run. And worst of all, a heavy rainfall could strand it at either end or even in the middle. Parachute drops of supplies to stranded train travellers became part of outback lore and on one occasion the Ghan rolled in 10 days late!

By the early '70s the South Australian state railway system was taken over by the Federal government and a new line to Alice Springs was planned. The $145 million line was to be standard gauge, laid from Tarcoola, north-west of Port Augusta on the transcontinental line, to Alice Springs – and it would be laid where rain would not wash it out. In 1980 the line was completed in circumstances that would be unusual for any major project today, let alone an Australian one – it was ahead of time and on budget.

In the late '80s the old Ghan made its last run and the old line was subsequently torn up. One of its last appearances was in the film *Mad Max III*.

Whereas the old train took 140 passengers and, under ideal conditions, made the trip in 50 hours, the new train takes twice as many passengers and does it in 24 hours. It's still the Ghan, but it's not the trip it once was. ■

Springs the departure is on Friday at 2 pm, arriving in Adelaide the next day at 11.30 am. From April to December there's a second departure from Adelaide on Monday and Alice Springs on Tuesday.

You can also join the Ghan at Port Augusta, the connecting point on the Sydney to Perth route. Fares between Alice Springs and Port Augusta are $106 coach class, $279 holiday class and $464 1st-class sleeper ($106/250/416 low season).

You can transport cars between Alice Springs and Adelaide for $195, or between Alice Springs and Port Augusta for $185. Double-check the times by which you need to have your car at the terminal for loading; they must be there several hours prior to departure for the train to be 'made up'.

Car The basic thing to remember about
getting to Alice Springs is that it's a long way
from anywhere, although at least roads to the
north and south are sealed. Coming in from
Queensland it's 1180 km from Mt Isa to
Alice Springs or 529 km from Threeways,
where the Mt Isa road meets the Darwin to
Alice Springs road (the Stuart Highway).
Darwin to Alice Springs is 1476 km.

These are outback roads, but you're not
yet in the *real* outer-outback, where a breakdown can mean big trouble. Nevertheless,
it's wise to have your vehicle well prepared
since getting someone to come out to fix it is
likely to be very expensive.

Similarly, you are unlikely to die of thirst
waiting for a vehicle to come by if you do
break down, but it's still wise to carry quite
a bit of water. Roads can sometimes be made
impassable by a short, sharp rainfall and
you'll have to wait for the water to recede. It
usually won't take long on a sealed road, but
you could have to wait for a dirt road to dry
out and become passable for rather a long
time.

Fuel is readily available from stops along
the road, but prices tend to be high. Some
fuel stops are notorious for charging well
over the odds, so carrying an extra can of fuel
can save a few dollars by allowing you to go
elsewhere.

Car Rental All the major hire companies
have offices in Alice Springs, and Avis,
Budget, Hertz and Territory Rent-a-Car also
have counters at Alice Springs airport.

Avis, Budget, Hertz and Territory all have
4WDs for hire. You're looking at around $95
per day for a Suzuki, including insurance and
100 km free per day. For a Toyota landcruiser
or similar vehicle the price jumps to around
$165 per day. Discounts apply for longer
rentals (more than four to seven days,
depending on the company).

Brits: Australia has campers and 4WDs
for hire, and with offices in all the major
cities one-way rentals become an option. The
cost is around $120 per day for unlimited km,
including a collision damage waiver, but
there is a seven-day minimum rental period.

Avis
   52 Hartley St (☎ 1800 225 533; fax 8953 0087)
Brits: Australia
   Stuart Highway (☎ 1800 331 454; fax 8941
   62933)
Budget
   10 Gap Rd (☎ 1800 805 627; fax 8952 5308)
Hertz
   Corner Todd St & Wills Terrace (☎ 1800 891
   112; fax 8952 3653)
Koala Camper Rentals
   North Stuart Highway (☎ 1800 998 029; fax
   8952 9133)
Territory Rent-a-Car
   Corner Stott Terrace & Hartley St (☎ 1800 891
   125; fax 8952 9797)
Thrifty
   94 Todd St (☎ 8952 2400; fax 8952 6560)

Hitching Hitching to Alice is not the easiest
trip in Australia since traffic is comparatively
light. For those coming south, Threeways is
a notorious bottleneck where hitchers can
spend a long time. The notice boards in the
various Alice Springs hostels are good places
to look for lifts.

Getting Around
Although there is a limited public bus
system, Alice Springs is compact enough to
get around on foot, and you can reach quite
a few of the closer attractions by bicycle. If
you want to go farther afield you'll have to
take a tour or rent a car.

To/From the Airport The Alice Springs
airport is 14 km south of the town, about $20
by taxi.

There is an airport shuttle bus service
(☎ 8953 0310) which meets flights and takes
passengers to all city accommodation and to
the railway station. It costs $9.

Bus Asbus buses leave from outside the
Yeperenye shopping centre on Hartley St.
The southern route (No 4) runs along Gap Rd
to the southern outskirts of town – useful for
Pitchi Richi and the Mecca Date Garden, or
for hitching. The western route (No 1) goes
out along Larapinta Drive, for the Strehlow
Centre, Araluen Arts Centre and the Technology, Transport & Communications Museum.

Buses run approximately every 1½ hours from 7.45 am to 6 pm on weekdays and Saturday morning only. The fare for a short trip is $1.

The Alice Wanderer bus does a loop around the major sights – Frontier Camel Farm, Mecca Date Garden, the Old Ghan, Flying Doctor Base, the Strehlow Centre, Anzac Hill, School of the Air and the telegraph station. You can get on and off wherever you like, and it runs every 70 minutes from around 9 am to 3 pm. The cost is $18 for a full day, and if you phone ahead (☎ 8952 2111), you can be picked up from your accommodation prior to the 9 am departure. The most convenient pick-up point is the Melanka Lodge.

Car See Getting There & Away in this section for details on car rental.

Bicycle Alice Springs has a number of bicycle tracks and a bike is a great way to get around town and out to the closer attractions, particularly in winter. The best place to rent a bike is from the hostel you're staying at. Typical rates are $10 per day.

Centre Cycles (☎ 8953 2966) at 14 Lindsay Ave east of the town centre has 15-speed mountain bikes for $12 per day, or if you want longer term it's $45 per week and $120 a month.

The MacDonnell Ranges

Outside Alice Springs there are a great number of places within day-trip distance or with overnight stops thrown in. Generally they're found by heading east or west along the roads running parallel to the MacDonnell Ranges, which are directly south of Alice Springs. Places farther south are usually visited on the way to Uluru.

The scenery along the ranges is superb. There are many gorges that cut through the rocky cliffs and their sheer rock walls are spectacular. In the shaded gorges there are rocky water holes, a great deal of wildlife (which can be seen if you're quiet and observant) and wildflowers in the spring.

You can get out to these gorges on group tours or with your own wheels. Some of the closer ones are accessible by bicycle or on foot. By yourself, the Centre's eerie emptiness and peace can get through to you in a way that is impossible in a big group.

Getting There & Away

Unfortunately, and somewhat surprisingly, there is no scheduled transport to either the Eastern or Western Macs, so without your own transport you're stuck with taking a tour. Virtually all places (with the exception of Ruby Gap in the Eastern Macs) are covered by tours from the Alice, so it's a matter of hunting around to find one which suits.

EASTERN MACDONNELL RANGES

Heading south from Alice Springs and just through the Heavitree Gap, a sign points on the road east – the Ross Highway. The highway is sealed all the way to Trephina Gorge, about 75 km from Alice Springs. It's in pretty good condition most of the way to Arltunga, about 100 km from Alice Springs. From here the road bends back north and west to rejoin the Stuart Highway 50 km north of Alice Springs, but this section is a much rougher road and sometimes requires a 4WD.

Emily & Jessie Gaps Nature Park

Emily Gap, 16 km out of town, is the next gap through the ranges east of the Heavitree Gap – it's narrow and often has water running through it. Known to the Arrernte as Anthwerrke, this is one of the most important Aboriginal sites in the Alice Springs area as it was from here that the caterpillar ancestral beings of Mparntwe (Alice Springs) originated. The gap is registered as a sacred site and there are some well-preserved paintings on the eastern wall, although it often involves a swim to get to them.

Jessie Gap is only eight km farther on and, like the previous gap, is a popular picnic and barbecue spot.

The two gaps are important to the Eastern Arrernte people as they are associated with the Caterpillar Dreaming trail.

Corroboree Rock Conservation Reserve

Shortly after Jessie Gap there's the Undoolya Gap, another pass through the range, and the road continues 43 km to Corroboree Rock. There are many strangely shaped outcrops of rocks in the range and this one is said to have been used by Aboriginal people as a storehouse for sacred objects. It is a registered sacred site and is listed on the National Estate. Despite the name, it is doubtful if the rock was ever used as a corroboree area, due to the lack of water in the vicinity.

Trephina Gorge Nature Park

About 60 km out, and a few km north of the road, is Trephina Gorge. It's wider and longer than the other gaps in the range – here you are well north of the main MacDonnell Ranges and in a new ridge. There's a good walk along the edge of the gorge, and the trail then drops down to the sandy creek bed and loops back to the starting point.

Keen walkers can follow a longer trail (about five hours), which continues to the delightful **John Hayes Rockhole**, a few km west of Trephina Gorge. Here a sheltered section of a deep gorge provides a series of water holes which retain water long after the more exposed places have dried up. You can clamber around the rockholes or follow the 90-minute Chain of Ponds marked trail which takes you up to a lookout above the gorge and then back through the gorge – perhaps you'll see why it is also called the Valley of the Eagles.

There's an excellent camp site at the gorge, and a smaller one (only two sites) at John Hayes Rockhole. There's a fee of $1 per adult for camping.

Ross River Homestead

Beyond Trephina Gorge it's another 10 km to the *Ross River Homestead* (☎ 8956 9711). It's much favoured by coach tours, but is equally good for independent visitors. It's a friendly sort of place and there's lots to do,

including walks in the spectacular surrounding countryside, excursions to other attractions, short camel rides or safaris and horseback riding. Or simply lazing around with a cold one.

Units cost $107 for two, and there are four-bed dorms for $12 per person, or you can camp for $15 for two. There's also a restaurant, which has good food, and the bar is very popular.

N'Dhala Gorge Nature Park

N'Dhala Gorge is about 10 km south of Ross River Homestead and has around 6000 ancient Aboriginal rock carvings, although they're generally not easy to spot. You may see rock wallabies. It's possible to turn off before the gorge and loop around it to return to Alice Springs by the Ringwood Homestead road, but this requires a 4WD. The track into N'Dhala from Ross River is marked as 4WD only.

There's a small camp site here with a toilet, but you need to bring your own water and firewood. The flies are friendly, too.

Arltunga Historical Reserve

At the eastern end of the MacDonnell Ranges, 103 km north-east of Alice Springs, Arltunga is a gold-mining ghost town. Gold was discovered here in 1887 and 10 years later reef gold was discovered, but by 1912 the mining activity had petered out. Old buildings, a couple of cemeteries and the many deserted mine sites are all that remain. Alluvial (surface) gold has been completely worked out in the Arltunga Reserve, but there may still be gold farther afield in the area. There are plenty of signs to explain things and some old mine shafts you can safely descend and explore a little way. The reserve has an excellent visitor centre, with many old photographs and some displays, and there's a ranger-guided tour of one of the mines on Sunday afternoon at 2.30 pm.

The 40-km section of road between Arltunga and the turn-off just before Ross River Homestead is unsealed but in good condition, although heavy rain can make the road impassable. You can loop right round

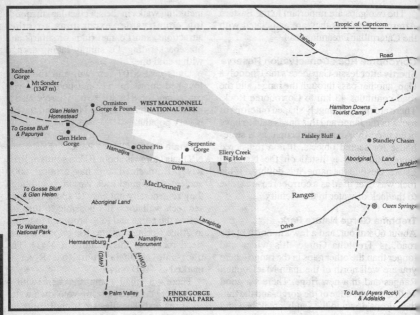

and join the Stuart Highway 50 km north of Alice Springs, but this route is a graded track all the way and can be rough going. With side trips off the road, a complete loop from Alice Springs to Arltunga and back would be something over 300 km.

Places to Stay Camping is not permitted within the historical reserve, but the nearby *Arltunga Hotel & Bush Resort* (☎ 8956 9797) promotes itself as 'the loneliest pub in the scrub' and is a good place to stay. There's camping at $5 and you can hire a swag for $6/8 single/double. There's also an on-site van for $35 (up to four people) and a couple of self-contained family rooms at $35. Meals, snacks and beer are also available.

Ruby Gap Nature Park
Ruby Gap is a farther 44 km to the east, and it's on a rough track which takes a good couple of hours to traverse – definitely 4WD only. The sandy bed of the Hale River is

purple in places due to the thousands of tiny garnets found here. The garnets were the cause of a 'ruby rush' to the area in the 19th century and a few miners did well out of it until the 'rubies' were discovered to be only garnets and virtually worthless. It's a remote and evocative place, and is well worth the effort involved in reaching it.

There's excellent bush camping along the riverbank in the park, and there are some beautiful spots. However, this is a remote area and you need to be well equipped – and bring your own water and collect firewood on the way in.

WESTERN MACDONNELL RANGES
Heading west from the Alice, Larapinta Drive divides just beyond Standley Chasm. Namatjira Drive continues slightly north-west and is sealed all the way to Glen Helen, 132 km from town. Beyond there the road continues to Haasts Bluff and Papunya, in Aboriginal land. From the fork near Standley

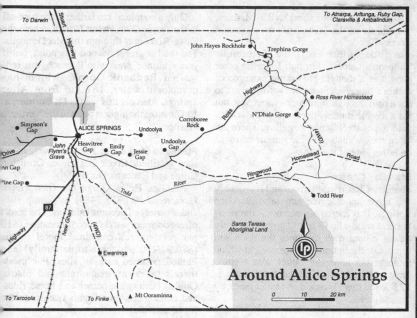

To Darwin

Stuart Highway

To Atnarpa, Arltunga, Ruby Gap, Claraville & Ambalindum

John Hayes Rockhole • ⊕ Trephina Gorge

Ross Highway

⊕ Ross River Homestead

Simpson's Gap

ALICE SPRINGS ⊕ Undoolya

Corroboree Rock

N'Dhala Gorge ⊕

John Flynn's Grave

Heavitree Gap

Emily Gap

Jessie Gap

Undoolya Gap

(4WD)

Drive

an Gap

ine Gap

Todd

River

Ringwood

Homestead

Road

⊕ Todd River

87

New Ghan (4WD)

Highway

⊕ Ewaninga

Santa Teresa Aboriginal Land

Around Alice Springs

0   10   20 km

To Tarcoola

To Finke

▲ Mt Ooraminna

Chasm, Larapinta Drive continues south-west to Hermannsburg and beyond.

There are many spectacular gorges in this direction and also some fine walks. A visit to Palm Valley, one of the prime attractions to the west of Alice Springs, requires a 4WD. See the Alice Springs Getting Around section for tour details.

The whole of the Western MacDonnells is encompassed within the Western MacDonnell Ranges National Park.

Bushwalking

The Larapinta Trail is an extended walking track which, when finally completed in the next few years, will offer a 13-stage, 220-km trail of varying degrees of difficulty along the back-bone of the Western MacDonnells, stretching from the telegraph station in Alice Springs to Mt Razorback, beyond Glen Helen. It will be possible to choose anything from a two-day to a two-week trek, taking in a selection of the attractions in the Western MacDonnells.

At the time of writing, the following sections were open: Section 1, Alice Springs Telegraph Station to Simpson's Gap, 24 km; Section 2, Simpson's Gap to Jay Creek, 23 km; Section 3, Jay Creek to Standley Chasm, 14 km; Section 8, Serpentine Gorge to Ochre Pits, 18 km; Section 10, Ormiston Gorge to Glen Helen Lodge, 12.5 km; and Section 12, out and back from Redbank Gorge to Mt Sonder, 16 km return.

Detailed trail notes and maps ($1 per section) are available from the Parks & Wildlife desk at the tourist office in Alice Springs, or contact the Parks & Wildlife office (☎ 8951 8211) for further details.

Simpson's Gap

Westbound from Alice Springs on Larapinta Drive you start on the northern side of the MacDonnell Ranges. You soon come to the **Desert Wildlife Park & Botanic Gardens** (opening May 1997) and **John Flynn's Grave**; the flying doctor's final resting place is topped by one of the Devil's Marbles, brought down the Track from near Tennant Creek.

A little farther on is the picturesque Simpson's Gap, 22 km out. Like the other gaps it is a thought-provoking example of nature's power and patience – for a river to cut a path through solid rock is amazing, but for a river that rarely ever runs to cut such a path is positively mind-boggling. There are often rock wallabies in the jumble of rocks on either side of the gap.

Standley Chasm

Standley Chasm is 51 km out and is probably the most spectacular gap around Alice Springs. It is incredibly narrow – the near-vertical walls almost meet above you. Only for an instant each day does the noon sun illuminate the bottom of the gorge – at which moment the automatics click and a smile must appear on Mr Kodak's face! Entry is $2.50, and there is a cafe and toilet block by the car park.

Namatjira Drive

Not far beyond Standley Chasm you can choose the northerly Namatjira Drive or the more southerly Larapinta Drive. West along Namatjira Drive another series of gorges and gaps in the range awaits you. **Ellery Creek Big Hole** is 93 km from Alice Springs and has a large permanent water hole – just the place for a cooling dip, and there's a basic camp site close by. It's only 13 km farther to **Serpentine Gorge**, a narrow gorge with a pleasant water hole at the entrance.

The **Ochre Pits**, just off the road 11 km west of Serpentine, were a source of painting material for the Aboriginal people. The various coloured ochres are weathered limestone, and the colouring is actually iron-oxide stains.

The large and rugged **Ormiston Gorge** also has a water hole and it leads to the enclosed valley of the Pound. When the water holes of the Pound dry up, the fish that live there burrow into the sand going into a sort of suspended animation and reappearing after rain.

Only a couple of km farther is the turn-off to the scenic **Glen Helen Gorge**, where the Finke River cuts through the MacDonnells. The road is gravel beyond this point, but if you continue west you'll reach the red-walled **Redbank Gorge**, which has permanent water, 161 km from Alice Springs. Also out this way is **Mt Sonder**, at 1347 metres the highest point in the Northern Territory.

Places to Stay & Eat There are basic camp sites at Ellery Creek Big Hole, Ormiston Gorge and Redbank Gorge.

At Glen Helen Gorge the *Glen Helen Homestead* (☎ 8956 7489) has camp sites and a variety of accommodation. The resort offers dormitory-style accommodation ($10 per person), self-contained motel rooms ($80/92/120 a double/triple/family) and limited powered caravan sites. For meals there's takeaway, restaurant and bistro. Guided bushwalks, camel and horse rides and helicopter scenic flights feature on the list of activities.

Larapinta Drive

Taking the alternative road to the south from Standley Chasm, Larapinta Drive crosses the Hugh River, and then Ellery Creek before reaching the turn-off for **Wallace Rockhole** 17 km off the main road and 117 km from Alice Springs. This is an Arrernte Aboriginal community (☎ 8956 7415) which offers camping and rock-art tours (daily at 9.30 am and 1 pm; $6). Alcohol is prohibited here.

Back on Larapinta Drive, shortly before Hermannsburg, is the **Namatjira Monument**. Today the artistic skills of the central Australian Aboriginal people are widely known and appreciated. This certainly wasn't the case when Albert Namatjira started to paint his central Australian landscapes in 1934.

In 1957 Namatjira was the first Aboriginal person to be granted Australian citizenship. Because of his fame, he was allowed to buy alcohol at a time when this was otherwise illegal for Aboriginal people, but in 1958 he was jailed for six months for supplying alcohol to Aboriginal people. He died the following year, aged only 57. For further information on Namatjira see the Aboriginal art section earlier in this book.

Hermannsburg (pop 420)

Only eight km beyond the Namatjira monument you reach the Hermannsburg Aboriginal settlement, 125 km from Alice Springs. The **Hermannsburg Mission** here was established by German Lutheran missionaries in the middle of the last century. Many of the buildings are intact, and it's well worth a stroll through.

Although the town is restricted Aboriginal land, permits are not required to visit the mission or store, or to travel through. The Kata-Anga Tea Rooms serve excellent home-made pastries, and you can also get fuel (no credit cards) and basic provisions at the settlement store. The staff at the tea rooms also issue permits for travel on the Mereenie Loop Road (see entry below).

Hermannsburg's most famous resident was Professor Ted Strehlow. He was born on the mission and spent more than 40 years studying the Arrernte people, who entrusted him with many items of huge spiritual and symbolic importance when they realised their traditional lifestyle was under threat. These items are now held in a vault in the Strehlow Research Centre in Alice Springs and Strehlow's books about the Arrernte people are still widely read.

Finke Gorge National Park

From Hermannsburg the trail follows the Finke River south to the Finke Gorge National Park, only 12 km farther on.

In the park, **Palm Valley** is a gorge filled with a variety of palm tree unique to this part of the MacDonnell Ranges – the central Australian cabbage palm (*Livistona mariae*). This strangely tropical find in the dry Centre makes Palm Valley a popular day-trip destination.

The track to the park crosses the sandy bed of the Finke a number of times and you need a 4WD to get through, not so much because of the risk of getting bogged, but because of the high ground-clearance needed to negotiate the numerous bars of rock on the track to the gorge.

There's a beautiful shady camping area ($10) with some long-drop toilets, and a couple of signposted walks.

If you are travelling by 4WD there's a track which traverses the full length of the picturesque Finke Gorge, much of the time along the bed of the (usually) dry Finke River. It's a rough but worthwhile trip, and the camp sites at Boggy Hole, about 2½ hours from Hermannsburg, make an excellent overnight stop, although if you are in a hurry you can get from Palm Valley all the way to Watarrka (Kings Canyon) National Park in less than eight hours via this route. Ask the rangers at Palm Valley or Kings Canyon for details.

Ipolera

Continuing west from Hermannsburg along the road to Areyonga, there's a turn-off to the Arrernte Aboriginal community of Ipolera. Here it's usually possible to stay with the Malbunka family who offer excellent two-hour cultural tours. Male and female visitors are taken on separate tours to help preserve and maintain the unique laws which apply to the two sexes. The tours take place from February to November on Monday, Wednesday and Friday at 10 am and cost $25. There's also basic camping at $5 per person.

Permits are not required to visit Ipolera, but bookings for either camping or the tours are obligatory (☎ 8956 7466); alcohol is prohibited. The turn-off for Ipolera is 45 km west of Hermannsburg, and it's then 13 km along a dirt road.

Mereenie Loop Road

From the Ipolera turn-off you can continue west to the Areyonga turn-off (no visitors), and then take the Mereenie Loop Road to Kings Canyon. This dirt road is suitable for robust conventional vehicles and offers an excellent alternative to the Ernest Giles Road as a way of reaching Kings Canyon.

The Mereenie Loop Road was opened in June 1994. You need a permit from the

Central Land Council to travel along it, as it passes through Aboriginal land. The permit includes the informative *Mereenie Tour Pass* booklet, which provides details about the local Aboriginal culture and has a route map. Permits are issued on the spot by the tourist office in Alice Springs, at Glen Helen Homestead and the Kata-Anga Tea Rooms at Hermannsburg.

South to Uluru (Ayers Rock)

You can make some interesting diversions off the road south from Alice Springs to Uluru. The Henbury Meteorite Craters are only a few km off the road, but it's farther to Chambers Pillar, Finke or Kings Canyon.

The Old Ghan Road

Following the 'old south road' which runs close to the old Ghan railway line, it's only 35 km from Alice Springs to **Ewaninga**, with its prehistoric Aboriginal rock carvings. The carvings found here and at N'Dhala Gorge are thought to have been made by Aboriginal tribes who lived here earlier than the current tribes of the Centre.

The eerie, sandstone **Chambers Pillar** is carved with the names and visit dates of early explorers – and, unfortunately, some much less worthy modern-day graffitists. To the Aboriginal people of the area, Chambers Pillar is the remains of Itirkawara, a gecko ancestor of great strength. It's 160 km from Alice Springs and a 4WD is required for the last 44 km from the turn-off at Maryvale station. There's a basic camp site but you need to bring water and firewood.

Back on the main track south, you eventually arrive at **Finke**, a small Apatula Aboriginal settlement 230 km south of Alice Springs. When the old Ghan was running, Finke was a thriving little town; these days it seems to have drifted into a permanent torpor. There's a basic community store, which is also the outlet for the Apatula Arts

Centre, and fuel is available on weekdays. Alcohol is prohibited.

From Finke you can turn west to join the Stuart Highway at Kulgera (150 km), or east to Old Andado station on the edge of the Simpson Desert (120 km). Just 21 km west of Finke, and 12 km north of the road along a signposted track, is the **Lambert Centre**. Here stands a five-metre-high replica of the flagpole found on top of Parliament House in Canberra. The reason? This point has been determined as Australia's centre of gravity!

Rainbow Valley Nature Park

The sandstone bluffs of the James Range are the main attraction of this small park, which lies 22 km off the Stuart Highway along an unsignposted 4WD track 75 km south of Alice Springs. There's a basic camping site but you will need to bring your own firewood and water.

Camel Outback Safaris

This camel farm, 90 km south of Alice at **Stuart's Well**, is run by Noel Fullerton, the 'camel king', who started the annual Camel Cup and has won it four times. For a few dollars you can try your hand at camel riding and there are extended safaris into Rainbow Valley and the outback. The farm exports camels to places around the world, including the Arab nations of the Gulf and the Sahara.

It has been estimated that the central deserts are home to about 15,000 wild camels. (For inspiration read Robyn Davidson's bestselling book *Tracks*, an account of her trek by camel from the Alice to Port Hedland.)

Ernest Giles Road

The Ernest Giles Road heads off to the west of the Stuart Highway about 140 km south of the Alice. This is the route to Kings Canyon, and is an alternative route between Uluru and the Alice. You'll also find the Henbury Meteorite Craters just off it, a few km west of the highway.

The 100-km stretch to the Luritja Road (the turn-off to the south and Uluru) is still unsurfaced and often impassable after heavy

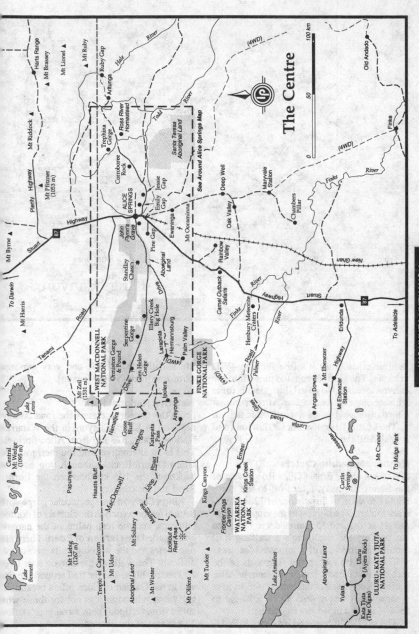

The Centre

NORTHERN TERRITORY

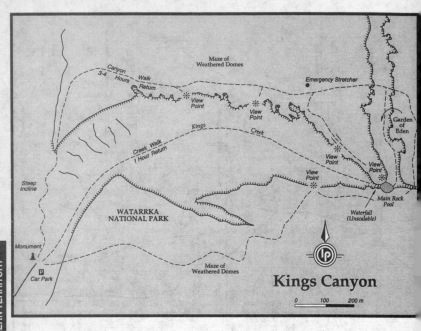

Kings Canyon

0   100   200 m

NORTHERN TERRITORY

rain; at other times it's fine for non-4WD vehicles. The section from the turn-off to the canyon is sealed. To go to Uluru via this route adds about 170 km to the Alice Springs-Uluru distance, but it's a worthwhile detour.

The Luritja Road itself is 100 km long and is sealed all the way.

Henbury Meteorite Craters
A few km along Ernest Giles Road, west of the Stuart Highway, a turn-off to the north leads a few km to this cluster of 12 insignificant craters. The biggest of the craters is 180 metres across and 15 metres deep. From the car park by the site there's a walking trail around the craters with signposted features.

There are no longer any fragments of the meteorites at the site, but the museum in Alice Springs has a small chunk which weighs in at a surprisingly heavy 46.5 kg. It is illegal to fossick for or remove any fragments.

The site is administered by Parks & Wild-

life and there's a basic and very exposed camp site there ($1 per person).

Watarrka National Park
From the meteorite craters the road continues west to Kings Canyon, in the Watarrka National Park, 323 km from Alice Springs. This is an alternative, and rougher, route to Uluru (Ayers Rock) although you have to backtrack the 105 km between the Luritja Road and the canyon.

Kings Canyon is a spectacular gorge with natural features such as the clusters of domed outcrops, and the lush palms of the narrow gorge called the **Garden of Eden**. There are fine views and the walking trails are not too difficult. The walls of the canyon soar over 100 metres high, and the trail around the rim and to the Garden of Eden offers breathtaking views, although it is not for those who suffer from vertigo. There's a rangers' station 22 km east of the canyon.

Organised Tours Kurkara Tours (☎ 8956 865) is an Aboriginal-owned and run tour company which has a variety of trips from he Frontier Resort (see Places to Stay & at). There's the Mungartji (Sunset) Tour $20), the 2½-hour Willy Wagtail Tour ($30) nd the Guided Canyon Walk ($17). All elve into various cultural aspects of the cal Luritja people and are good fun.

Places to Stay & Eat The closest accommo-ation available is at the *Frontier Kings anyon* (☎ 1800 891 101; fax 8956 7410), x km west of the canyon. Camping sites ost $18, or $22 with power. There's a back-ackers bunk house with beds in four-bed ooms at $24 each, or more luxurious motel-pe accommodation for $182. The resort as a swimming pool, bar, cafe, restaurant, hop and (expensive) fuel.

Otherwise, there's the basic but friendly *ings Creek Station Camping Ground* ☎ 8956 7474), on Ernest Giles Road just utside the national park's eastern boundary nd about 35 km from the canyon. The very leasant camping ground is set among large desert oaks and costs start at $6 per person. Fuel, ice and limited stores are available seven days a week at the shop.

Uluru-Kata Tjuta National Park

ULURU (AYERS ROCK)

The world-famous Uluru (Ayers Rock) is 3.6 km long and rises a towering 348 metres from the pancake-flat surrounding scrub. It's believed that two-thirds of the Rock lies beneath the sand. Everybody knows how its colour changes as the setting sun turns it a series of deeper and darker reds before it fades into grey. A performance in reverse, with fewer spectators, is given at dawn each day.

The mighty Rock offers much more than a heavy-breathing scramble to the top and some pretty colours – it has a whole series of strange caves and eroded gullies. The entire area is of deep cultural significance to the

NORTHERN TERRITORY

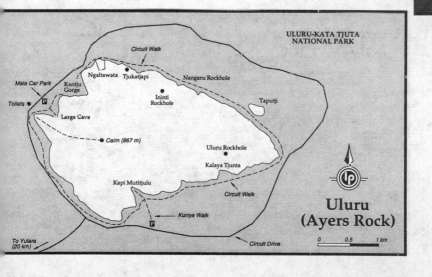

ULURU-KATA TJUTA
NATIONAL PARK

Circuit Walk

Mala Car Park
Kantju Gorge
Ngaltawata   Tjukatjapi
Nangaru Rockhole

Toilets

Large Cave
Ininti Rockhole
Taputji

Cairn (867 m)

Uluru Rockhole

Kalaya Tjunta

Kapi Mutitjulu

Circuit Walk

Kuniya Walk

To Yulara
(20 km)

Circuit Drive

0   0.5   1 km

**Uluru
(Ayers Rock)**

local Anangu Aboriginal people. To them it is known as Uluru – the name given to the Rock and the national park which surrounds it. The Aboriginal people own the national park, although it is leased permanently to, and administered by, the Australian Nature Conservation Agency (ANCA, the Federal government's national parks body) in conjunction with the traditional owners.

There are plenty of walks and other activities around Uluru and the township of Yulara, and it is not at all difficult to spend several days here.

Information

The superb new Uluru-Kata Tjuta National Park Cultural Centre (☎ 8956 3138) is one km before the Rock on the road from Yulara. There are some excellent multi-lingual displays here and it's well worth putting aside an hour or so before visiting Uluru itself. Also here is the Maruku Arts & Crafts outlet where you can see the artists at work (no photos). This is about the cheapest place in the Centre to buy souvenirs (carvings etc) and you're buying direct from the artists. There's also the Aboriginal-run Ininti Store,

which sells snacks and souvenirs, and picnic area with free gas barbecues. Th centre is open daily from 7 am to 5.30 pm (pm in summer).

Entry to the national park costs $10 (fre for children under 16), and this is good for five-day visit. Entry permits can be bough from the visitor centre at Yulara (see below or from the park entry gate on the roa between Yulara and Uluru.

The park is open daily from half an hou before sunrise to sunset.

Walks Around the Base

There are walking trails around Uluru, an guided walks delving into the plants, wild life, geology and mythology of the area. I can take five hours to make the nine-km wal around the base of Uluru, looking at th caves and paintings on the way. Full detai of the Mala and Kuniya walks (see below are given in the self-guided walks brochur available from the rangers' station for $1.

Note that there are several Aborigina sacred sites around the base of Uluru They're clearly fenced off and signposte and to enter these areas is a grave offence

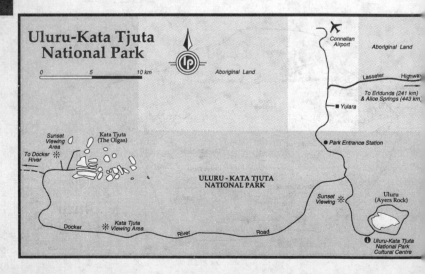

Uluru-Kata Tjuta National Park

not just for non-Aboriginal people but for 'ineligible' Aboriginal people as well.

Mala Walk This walk starts from the base of the climbing point and takes about 1½ hours at a very leisurely pace. The tjukurpa (traditional law) of the Mala (hare-wallaby people) is of great importance to the Anangu. You can do this walk on your own, or there are guided walks daily at 10.30 am from the car park (no booking necessary).

Liru Walk The Liru Walk starts from the Cultural Centre and gives an insight into the way the local Anangu people made use of the area's shrubs and bush materials. It is a two-hour guided walk with Anangu Tours, and it only operates on Tuesday, Thursday, Saturday and Sunday at 9.30 am (8.30 am October to March); the cost is $49 ($36 children) and bookings are essential (☎ 8956 2123).

Kuniya Walk Mutitjulu is a permanent water hole on the southern side of Uluru. The tjukurpa tells of the clash between two ancestral snakes, Kuniya and Liru (see the Rainbow Serpent aside in the Top End section). The water hole is a short walk from the car park on the southern side, and you can either do the walk yourself, or go with Anangu Tours (daily, two hours, 3 pm, 4 pm in summer, $49, children $36, bookings essential), where you'll learn more about the Kuniya tjukurpa, and also about food and medicine plants found here.

Climbing Uluru
Those climbing Uluru should take care – numerous people have met their maker doing so, usually by having a heart attack, but some by taking a fatal tumble. Avoid climbing in the heat of the day during the hot season. There is an emergency phone at the car park at the base of the climb, and another at the top of the chain, about halfway up the climbing route. The climb is actually closed between 10 am and 4 pm on days when the forecast temperature is more than 38°C.

The climb itself is 1.6 km and takes about two hours up and back with a good rest at the

The Anangu People and the Rock
It's important to note that it goes against Aboriginal spiritual beliefs to climb Uluru, and Anangu would prefer you didn't. The reasons for this are that the route taken by visitors is associated closely with the Mala tjukurpa (the traditional law of the hare-wallaby people), and also that Anangu feel responsible for all people on the Rock, and are greatly saddened when a visitor to their land is injured or dies on the Rock. Interestingly, although the number of visitors to Uluru has risen steadily over the years, the number of people actually climbing the Rock is declining. ■

top. The first part of the walk is by far the steepest and most arduous, and there's a chain to hold on to. It's often extremely windy at the top, even when it's not at the base, so make sure hats are well tied on.

KATA TJUTA (THE OLGAS)
Kata Tjuta (the Olgas), a collection of smaller, more rounded rocks, stands 30-odd km to the west of Uluru. Though less well-known, the monoliths are equally impressive – indeed many people find them more captivating. Meaning 'many heads', Kata Tjuta is of Dreaming significance.

The tallest rock, **Mt Olga**, at 546 metres, is about 200 metres higher than Uluru, and here too there are a couple of walking trails, the main one being to the **Valley of the Winds**, a six-km circuit track (2½ to four hours). It's not particularly arduous, but be prepared with water, and sun protection. There is also a short signposted track into the pretty Olga Gorge (Tatintjawiya).

There's a picnic and sunset-viewing area with toilet facilities just off the access road a few km west of the base of Kata Tjuta.

A lonely sign at the western end of the access road points out that there is a hell of a lot of nothing if you travel west – although, if suitably equipped, you can travel all the way to Kalgoorlie and on to Perth in Western Australia. It's 200 km to Docker River, an

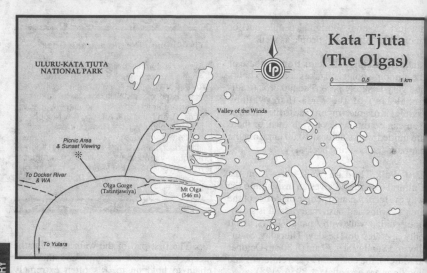

Valley of the Winds

Kata Tjuta
(The Olgas)

ULURU-KATA TJUTA
NATIONAL PARK

Picnic Area
& Sunset Viewing

To Docker River
& WA

Olga Gorge
(Tatintjawiya)

Mt Olga
(546 m)

To Yulara

0   0.5   1 km

NORTHERN TERRITORY

Aboriginal settlement on the road west, and about 1500 km to Kalgoorlie. See the Warburton Road information in the Getting Around chapter.

YULARA (pop 930)

Yulara, the service village for the national park, has effectively turned one of the world's least hospitable regions into an easy and comfortable place for outsiders to visit. Lying just outside the national park, 20 km from Uluru and 53 km from Kata Tjuta, the $260-million complex, administered by the Northern Territory government's Ayers Rock Corporation, makes an excellent and surprisingly democratic base for exploring the area's renowned attractions. Opened in 1984, it supplies the only accommodation, food outlets and other services available in the region. The village incorporates the Ayers Rock Resort, and it combines futuristic flair with low, earth-toned foundations, fitting unobtrusively into the dunes.

By the 1970s it was clear that planning was required for the development of the area. Between 1931 and 1946 only 22 people were known to have climbed Uluru. In 1969 about 23,000 people visited the area. Ten years later the figure was 65,000 and now the annual visitor figure is approaching 500,000!

It was intended when Yulara was built that the ugly cluster of motels, restaurants and other commercial enterprises at the eastern base of Uluru would be demolished, leaving the prime attraction pleasingly alone in its age-old setting. Some of the original buildings are still there because they were turned over to the local Aboriginal people; they are not so obvious now because all access to Uluru is from the west and the Aboriginal community is off-limits to the public.

Orientation & Information

In the spacious village area, where everything is within 15 minutes walk of the centre, there is a visitor centre, four hotels, apartments, a backpackers lodge, two camp sites, a bank, post office, petrol station, newsagency, numerous restaurants, a Royal Flying Doctor Service medical centre, supermarket, craft gallery, pub (of course) and even a pink police station!

The visitor centre (☎ 8956 2240) is open daily from 8 am to 9 pm and contains good displays on the geography, flora, fauna and

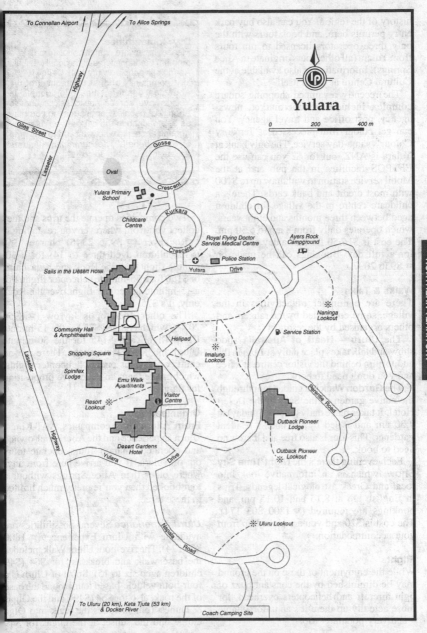

Yulara

NORTHERN TERRITORY

history of the region. You can also buy park entry permits here, and book tours with the only three operators licensed to run tours from Yulara (all other tours originate in Alice Springs). Information is also available at the Cultural Centre at Uluru itself.

The recently revamped shopping square complex includes a supermarket, newsagency, post office and travel agency. You can get colour film processed at Territory Colour's same-day service. The only bank at Yulara is ANZ, but for $2 you can use the EFTPOS facilities in the pub and at the Mobil service station to withdraw up to $100 with most credit and bank cards. There's a childcare centre in the village for children aged between three months and eight years, which operates daily from 8 am to 5.30 pm. The cost is $16.50 for half a day or $27.50 for a full day. Bookings can be made on ☎ 8956 2097.

Walks & Talks
There are a number of activities in the village, some conducted by the rangers and others organised by the resort.

The **Uluru – Heart of Australia** slide show and talk takes place daily at 1 pm in the auditorium behind the visitor centre. It's free and you don't need to book.

The **Garden Walk** is a guided tour through the native garden of the Sails in the Desert Hotel. It takes place daily (except Sunday) at 7.30 am and is led by the hotel's resident gardener. This tour is also free and there's no need to book.

Each evening there's the **Night Time Sky Show**, which is an informative look into local and Greek astrological legends. Trips in English are at 8.15 and 10.15 pm, and bookings are required (☎ 1800 803 174). The cost is $20 and you are picked up from your accommodation.

Flights
While the enjoyment of those on the ground may be diminished by the constant buzz of light aircraft and helicopters overhead, for those actually up there it's an unforgettable – and very popular – trip.

Dry Communities
Please be aware that alcohol (grog) is a problem amongst some of the local Mutitjulu Aboriginal people living near Uluru. It is a 'dry' community and, at the request of the Aboriginal leaders, the liquor outlets in Yulara have agreed not to sell alcohol to Aboriginal people. For this reason you may be approached in the car park at Yulara by Aboriginal people who want you to buy grog on their behalf. The community leaders appeal to you not to do so. ∎

Two companies operate the trips and they collect you from wherever you're staying.

Rockayer (☎ 8956 2345) charges $60 ($45 children aged three to 14) for a 30-minute flight over the Rock and Kata Tjuta, or $150 for a 30-minute helicopter flight. For a 15-minute helicopter flight over the Rock only, it's $75.

The other operator is Jayrow (☎ 8956 2077), which charges $75 for the 15-minute Uluru flight, and $145 for the 30-minute Uluru and Kata Tjuta flight. There are no child concessions on any helicopter flights, which make them an expensive proposition for families.

Organised Tours
From Yulara Three companies, AAT-Kings, Uluru Experience and the Aboriginal-owned and operated Anangu Tours, operate tours out of Yulara. If you arrive here from anywhere other than Alice Springs without a tour booked then you're pretty much limited to these three.

Uluru Experience Several possibilities are available with Uluru Experience (☎ 1800 803 174). The five-hour Uluru Walk includes the base walk and breakfast for $64 ($49 children aged six to 15); Spirit of Uluru is a four-hour vehicle-based tour around the base of the rock, also for $64 ($49); and the Olgas & Dunes Tour includes the walk into Olga Gorge and the sunset at the Olgas for $49

($36). The Uluru Experience Pass lets you choose any two of the above three tours, and includes champagne and sunset at the rock for $102 ($78), and also gives you a discount on the Night Sky Show.

AAT-Kings This company (☎ 8956 2171) has a Rock Pass which includes guided base tour, sunset, climb, sunrise and Kata Tjuta (Olga Gorge only) tours for $122 ($87 children under 15). The pass is valid for three days, and includes the $10 national park entry fee. All these activities are also available in various combinations on a one-off basis: base tour ($33/22 adults/children), sunrise tour ($31/22), climb ($31/22), sunset ($20/16), base and sunset ($44/36), sunrise and climb ($51/33), climb and base ($56/36), sunrise and base ($51/33), sunrise, climb and base ($69/56), Kata Tjuta and Uluru sunset ($54/41). These prices do not include the park entry fee.

AAT-Kings also offers a couple of options which include a barbecue meal, and these can be good fun. The Uluru Sunrise & Breakfast Tour costs $56 ($44 children), or you can combine it with the base tour for $72 ($61). On the Olgas Sunset & Dinner Tour you can do the three-hour Valley of the Winds walk, then enjoy a barbecue with the sunset on the Olgas for $80 ($63).

Anangu Tours This new tour company (☎ 8956 2123) is owned and operated by Anangu from the Muitjulu community. Their tour desk is at the cultural centre inside the park, but they also arrange transfers from Yulara to the cultural centre and Uluru. The Anangu tours are led by two Anangu guides and one interpreter, and they offer a unique chance to meet and talk with Anangu. Two of the three tours currently offered are walks in the Uluru vicinity (see Uluru Walks above for details), while the third, the Lungkata Tour, is a 1½-hour cultural tour where visitors sit in a traditional shade shelter *(wiltja)* and listen to some Anangu storytelling. The cost for the Lungkata Tour is $44 ($33 children six to 15) and it operates on Monday, Wednesday and Friday at 10.30 am (9.30 am

in summer), and bookings are essential for all tours as there is a limit of 25 people. If you book a tour, transfers on the shuttle cost $13 return, and you can return to Yulara at any time on either the Anangu Tours or AAT-Kings bus.

From Alice Springs All-inclusive tours to Uluru by private operators start at about $285 for a three-day camping trip which includes Kings Canyon. Companies such as Sahara Tours (☎ 8953 0881) and Northern Territory Adventure Tours (☎ 1800 063 838) are popular with the budget-conscious.

You have to shop around a bit because the tours run on different days and you may not want to wait for a particular one. Other things to check for include the time it takes to get to the Rock and Kata Tjuta, and whether the return is done early or late in the day. Prices can vary with the season and demand, and sometimes there may be cheaper 'stand-by' fares available. Bus-pass travellers should note that the bus services to the Rock are often heavily booked – if your schedule is tight it's best to plan ahead.

Tours which include accommodation other than camping are generally much more expensive, starting at around $250 for two days.

Another option is the passes offered by Greyhound Pioneer and McCafferty's. These are good value as they give you return transport to Yulara, the base tour, climb, Kata Tjuta and sunrise and sunset tours, and include the park entry fee. See the Getting There & Away section for more details.

Places to Stay
Yulara has something for every budget, from a camping ground up to a five-star hotel. With the rise in visitor numbers over the last few years, it is advisable to book all accommodation in advance, including dorm beds at the *Outback Pioneer Lodge* and tent or van sites at the camping ground, especially during school holidays.

Camping The *Ayers Rock Campground* (☎ 8956 2055) costs $18 for two people on an unpowered site, or $24 with power. There are six-berth on-site vans for $60 for up to four adults, and $9 for each additional adult. Most of the camp sites have beautifully manicured patches of green grass, while the spaces for vans and caravans are gravel. The camping ground is set amongst native gardens, and there's quite a bit of shade. There's also a swimming pool and the reception kiosk sells basic food supplies.

Dormitory & Cheaper Accommodation

For backpackers the place to head for is the well-equipped *Outback Pioneer Lodge* (☎ 8956 2170; fax 8956 2320), on the far side of the village from the shopping centre, about a 10-minute walk by a path across the dunes. Accommodation here consists of beds in 20-bed dorms for $20 for the first night, dropping to $12 on subsequent nights. There's excellent communal cooking facilities, and baggage storage lockers are available for $1. There are also cabin-type rooms with either two bunk beds or a double bed and one bunk, costing $80 for two, and $20 for each extra person up to four people, including bedding. The rooms have fridges and tea/coffee-making facilities, but bathrooms are communal.

All buildings are air-con in summer and heated in winter and there's a swimming pool. Out the back is a good lookout point for sunset views of Uluru.

Part of the same complex is known as the *Outback Pioneer Hotel* and this has expensive units with bathroom for $169.

Next up is the *Spinifex Lodge* (☎ 8956 2131; fax 8956 2163) near the visitor centre. It has 68 one-bedroom units which accommodate from two to four people at a cost of $85 for a double. These are quite good value, the main drawback being that the cooking facilities are pretty limited.

Apartments Probably the best deal at Yulara is offered by the *Emu Walk Apartments* (☎ 8956 2100; fax 8956 2156). There are one and two-bedroom flats which accommodate four and six people respectively. They have a lounge with TV, a fully equipped kitchen

and there's a communal laundry. They are also very central, being right between the visitor centre and the shopping square. The cost is $206 for the small apartments and $256 for the larger ones.

Top-End Hotels The two remaining options are both top-end hotels. The *Desert Gardens Hotel* (☎ 8956 2100; fax 8956 2156) has 100 rooms with TV, phone, minibar and room service, and these cost $226 for a double. The hotel has a pool and a restaurant.

At the top of the range is the *Sails in the Desert Hotel* (☎ 8956 2200; fax 8956 2018), which has all the facilities you'd expect in a top-class hotel, including in-house movies, 24-hour room service, spa and tennis court. Rooms start at $292 for a double.

Places to Eat

The range of eating options is equally varied. At the shopping centre the *Yulara Take-Away* does pretty reasonable fast food which you can take away or eat at the tables in the shopping area. It's open daily from 7.30 am to 9.30 pm. Also in the shopping centre is a *bakery* (open daily from 9 am to 7 pm) and an ice-cream parlour (daily from 11 am to 5 pm).

The *Outback Pioneer Lodge* also has a couple of choices. The kiosk offers light meals and snacks and is open from early morning until early evening. One of the best deals at Yulara is the 'Self-Cook Barbecue' which takes place here every night. For around $12 you get meat (beef, chicken, sausages, hamburger or fish) which you then barbecue yourself, and there's a range of salads. There's also a cheaper vegetarian dish, or you can just have the salads. It's a popular place to eat, probably made more so by the fact that 'exotic' meats such as kangaroo, buffalo and crocodile are often available, and there's often live entertainment. For more conventional dining the hotel also has the *Bough House*, which is open daily from 6 am.

The *Outback Barbecue* at the Tavern in the shopping square is yet another option. In the

Tavern itself you can get good-value buffet meals for around $15.

The Desert Gardens Hotel has the *Rock View* restaurant for casual dining and the more formal *White Gums*, which is open only in the evening. Main courses here are in the $20 to $25 range.

Finally there's the Sails in the Desert Hotel which has the *Rock Pool* outdoor restaurant, the *Desert Rose Brasserie*, which features buffet meals, and the more sophisticated *Kunia Room* for up-market dining.

Entertainment
Each evening at the *Amphitheatre* there's live entertainment. The resident band is Indiginy, and they play an interesting range of music on a variety of instruments, the focus being on the dijeridu – there's some fun audience participation too. The charge is $5.

The *Tavern* has a disco or live bands on Wednesday and Saturday nights, and these go until 2 am.

If you are really bored you could see a movie at the *Auditorium*. Recent releases are screened from Friday to Sunday and cost $5 ($3 children). For listings see the notice board outside the visitor centre.

Getting There & Away
Air Connellan airport is about five km from Yulara. You can fly directly to Uluru from various major centres as well as from Alice Springs, which remains the popular starting point for Uluru. Ansett has at least three flights daily for the 45-minute, $179 hop from Alice to the Rock; Qantas has one.

The numerous flights direct to Uluru can be money-savers. If, for example, you were intending to fly to the Centre from Adelaide, it makes a lot more sense to go Adelaide-Uluru-Alice Springs rather than Adelaide-Alice Springs-Uluru-Alice Springs. You can fly direct between Uluru and Perth ($464 one way), Adelaide ($523), Cairns ($468), Melbourne ($567), Sydney ($505) and Darwin ($490) with Qantas or Ansett, and to Coober Pedy ($206) with the weekly Kendall Airlines flight (Saturday).

Airnorth (☎ 1800 627 474) has daily direct flights between Uluru and Alice Springs ($173) and Kings Canyon ($79).

Day trips to Uluru by air from Alice Springs cost from about $330.

Bus Apart from hitching, the cheapest way to get to the Rock is to take a bus or tour. Greyhound Pioneer and McCafferty's both have daily services between Alice Springs and Uluru. The 441-km trip takes about 6½ hours.

The fare for one-way travel with McCafferty's is $70 from Alice Springs to Yulara, $60 from Erldunda on the Stuart Highway; with Greyhound Pioneer it's $77.

Bus Passes If you don't already have a pass, McCafferty's has its Rock Pass. This is valid for three days and includes return transport from Alice Springs, and then at the Rock itself you join these AAT-Kings tours: Kata Tjuta & Sunset Tour, Uluru Climb, Uluru Sunrise and Uluru Sunset. The pass includes the park entry fee and costs $199. The only condition is that you must stay for two nights, and this is at your own expense.

With Greyhound Pioneer you can either take a two-day accommodated package from Alice Springs (Ayers Rock Experience), which includes the company's own morning Ayers Rock Climb & Base Tour and the afternoon Olgas & Sunset Tour. The price depends on the level of accommodation you want; in the dorms at the Outback Pioneer it's $170, at the Sails in the Desert Hotel it's $291.

If you already have a Greyhound Pioneer pass which gets you to Yulara, you can opt to do the two half-day tours for $50 (normally $38 each).

There are also direct services between Adelaide and Uluru, although this actually means connecting with another bus at Erldunda, the turn-off from the Stuart Highway. Adelaide to Uluru takes about 22 hours for the 1720-km trip and costs $183 ($102 if you can book 15 days in advance).

Car If you haven't got your own vehicle,

NORTHERN TERRITORY

Lasseter's Lost Reef

The gold prospector Lewis Hubert (Harold Bell) Lasseter (1880?-1931) is immortalised as one of Australia's great hopefuls. We still know of him today because of Ion Idriess's romantic account *Lasseter's Last Ride* (1931); otherwise he would probably have faded into the red dust of the Petermann Range. Lasseter claimed to have found, sometime between 1897 and 1911, 'a vast gold bearing reef' in central Australia, some 23 km in length. The diminutive Lasseter had supposedly been looking for rubies when he stumbled upon gold as thick as 'plums in a pudding'. It was in the remote, arid Petermann Range in central Australia on the NT-SA border.

In 1930 the Central Australian Gold Exploration Company was formed, with Lasseter as a guide. The expedition was well equipped with an aeroplane, trucks and wireless. But things started to go wrong: the aircraft crashed near Uluru (Ayers Rock), and Fred Blakeley, the expedition leader, abandoned it at the Rock. Lasseter, after an argument with another hopeful prospector, Paul Johns, headed out alone to look for the reef.

Lasseter died of starvation in January 1931 near Shaws Creek and his body was found by Bob Buck in March; his diaries were retrieved and in them he claimed to have pegged the reef. Idriess used these diaries to write his book.

Subsequent attempts to find Lasseter's lost reef have been unsuccessful. His name is perpetuated in the Lasseter Highway, which runs from the Stuart Highway to Uluru. ■

---

renting a car in Alice Springs to go down to Uluru and back can be expensive. You're looking at $70 to $100 a day for a car from the big operators, and this only includes 100 km a day, each extra km costing 25c. Thrifty and Territory Rent-a-Car in Alice Springs both have deals which include 300 free km per day, and this is a much more realistic option. On one of these deals if you spent three days and covered 1000 km (the bare minimum) you'd be up for around $400, including insurance and petrol costs. Still, between four people that's cheaper than taking a bus there and back.

The road from Alice to Yulara is sealed and there are regular food and petrol stops along the way. Yulara is 443 km from Alice, 244 km west of Erldunda on the Stuart Highway, and the whole journey takes about six to seven hours.

Avis, Budget, Territory and Hertz are all represented at Yulara.

Getting Around

The village sprawls a bit, but it's not too large to get around on foot, and there's a free shuttle bus which runs between all accommodation points daily, every 15 minutes from 10.30 am to 2.30 pm and from 6.30 pm to 12.30 am. Walking trails lead across the dunes to little lookouts overlooking the village and surrounding terrain.

To/From the Airport A free shuttle bus operated by AAT-Kings meets all flights and drops at all accommodation points around the resort. Otherwise you can take a taxi, which costs around $5 one way.

Car See Getting There & Away in this section for details on car rental.

To/From the National Park Several options are available if you want to go from the Yulara resort to Uluru or Kata Tjuta. AAT-Kings and Anangu Tours offer transport from Yulara to the Rock for $12 ($24 return). The Anangu Tours buses run hourly from 7 to 10 am, and from 3 to 7 pm, the AAT-Kings buses run from 10 am to 3 pm from Yulara; the return trips are on the half-hour from 7.30 am to 7.30 pm. You can only buy one-way tickets, which means you can return to Yulara at any time with either operator. The ticket price includes a stop at the cultural centre, and you can then take a later bus to Uluru at no extra charge. The fare does not include the park entry fee.

The taxis at Yulara operate on a multiple-hire basis. Costs include Yulara to Uluru and return for $20 per person, to Kata Tjuta and return $35, sunset $15, sunrise or sunset and climb $20, or to the airport $5. The operator is Sunworth (☎ 8956 2152).

Hertz (☎ 8956 2244) and Avis (☎ 8956 2266) both have desks at the airport, and Territory Rent-a-Car (☎ 8956 2030) is at the Outback Pioneer Hotel.

Queensland

HIGHLIGHTS

- Diving and snorkelling on the incomparable Great Barrier Reef
- Taking a 4WD-trip around beautiful Fraser Island
- Cruising the Whitsunday Islands
- Visiting Australia's northern tip – the rugged Cape York Peninsula
- Partying at the great nightlife centres of Cairns, Surfers Paradise and Brisbane
- Joining a whale-watching tour at Hervey Bay and spotting a wild platypus at the Eungella National Park

Population 3,260,000
Area 1,727,000 sq km

Queensland is Australia's holiday state. You're certain to find something to suit your taste, whether you prefer glossy, neon-lit Surfers Paradise, long deserted beaches, the island resorts and excellent diving of the Great Barrier Reef, or remote national parks.

Brisbane, the state capital, is an increasingly lively city. In the north, Cairns is a busy travellers centre and base for a whole range of side trips and activities. Between Brisbane and Cairns there are strings of towns and islands, offering virtually every pastime you can imagine connected with the sea. Inland, several spectacular national parks are scattered over the ranges and between the isolated towns and cattle stations. In the far south-west corner of the state you'll find one of the most isolated towns of all, Birdsville, on the famous Birdsville Track.

North of Cairns, the Cape York Peninsula remains a wilderness against which people still test themselves. You can get an easy taste of this frontier in Cooktown, Australia's first British settlement and once a riotous goldrush town. Just inland from Cairns is the lush Atherton Tableland with countless beautiful waterfalls and scenic spots. Farther inland, on the main route across Queensland to the Northern Territory, is the outback mining town of Mt Isa and, south-east of here, the town of Longreach with its Stockman's Hall of Fame.

HISTORY

Queensland started as yet another penal colony in 1824. As usual, the free settlers soon followed and Queensland became a separate colony independent of New South Wales in 1859. Its early White settlers indulged in one of the greatest land grabs of all time and encountered fierce Aboriginal opposition. For much of the 19th century, what amounted to a guerrilla war took place along the frontiers of the White advance. For the impact on Aboriginal people, see the entry Aboriginal People & Kanakas below. A good book on the incredible experiences of the Queensland pioneers is *Queensland Frontier* by Glenville Pike.

Traditionally, agriculture and mining have been the backbone of the Queensland economy: the state contains a substantial chunk of Australia's mineral wealth. More recently, vast amounts of money have been invested in tourism, which is on the verge of becoming the state's leading money earner.

For many years, Queensland also had Australia's most controversial state government. The right-wing National Party was led by Sir Johannes Bjelke-Petersen (universally known as Joh) until 1987, when even Joh's own party decided he was a liability and replaced him. Whether it was views on rainforests, on Aboriginal land rights, or even on whether condom machines should be allowed in universities, you could count on the Queensland government to take the opposite stand to just about everybody else. Under the Nationals, the state also had more than its fair share of corruption scandals. After the defeat of the Nationals by the ALP in the 1990 state election, it seemed that everyone from the former Commissioner of Queensland Police to Joh himself appeared in court on charges relating to some sort of shady deal. The National-Liberal coalition is now back in government.

ABORIGINAL PEOPLE & KANAKAS

By the turn of the century, the Aboriginal people of Queensland had been comprehensively run off their lands, and the White authorities had set up reserves around the state for the survivors. A few of these reserves were places where Aboriginal people could live a self-sufficient life with self-respect; others were strife-ridden places with people from different areas and cultures thrown unhappily together under unsympathetic rule.

It wasn't until the 1980s that control of the reserves was transferred to their inhabitants, and that the reserves became known as 'communities'. However, the form of control given to the Aboriginal people, known as the Deed of Grant in Trust, falls well short of the freehold ownership that Aboriginal people have in other parts of Australia, such as the Northern Territory.

Queensland Aboriginal people are quite numerous, but have a lower profile than their NT counterparts. Visitor interest has, however, prompted some opportunities to glimpse their culture – you can visit a number of communities, including the Yarrabah community south of Cairns and the Hope Vale community north of Cooktown. The award-winning Tjapukai Dance Theatre, an Aboriginal dance group based north of Cairns, performs most days for tourists. Perhaps the most exciting event is the Laura Aboriginal Dance and Cultural Festival, held every second year on the Cape York Peninsula in June.

Another people on the fringes of Queensland society – though less so – are the Kanakas, descendants of Pacific Islanders brought in during the 19th century to work, mainly on sugar plantations, under virtual slave conditions. The business of collecting, transporting and delivering them was called blackbirding. The first Kanakas were brought over in 1863 for Robert Towns, the man whose money got Townsville going, and about 60,000 more followed until blackbirding stopped in 1905. You'll come across quite a few Kanakas in the coastal area north of Rockhampton.

GEOGRAPHY

Queensland has a series of distinct regions, generally running parallel to the coast. First there's the coastal strip – the basis for the booming tourist trade. Along this strip there are beaches, bays, islands and, of course, the Great Barrier Reef. Much of the coastal region is green and productive with lush rainforests, endless fields of sugar cane and stunning national parks.

Next comes the Great Dividing Range, the mountain range that continues down through New South Wales and Victoria. The mountains come closest to the coast in Queensland and are most spectacular in the far north, near Cairns, and in the far south.

Then there are the tablelands – areas of flat agricultural land that run to the west. These fertile areas extend farthest west in the south where the Darling Downs have some of the most productive grain-growing land in Australia.

QUEENSLAND

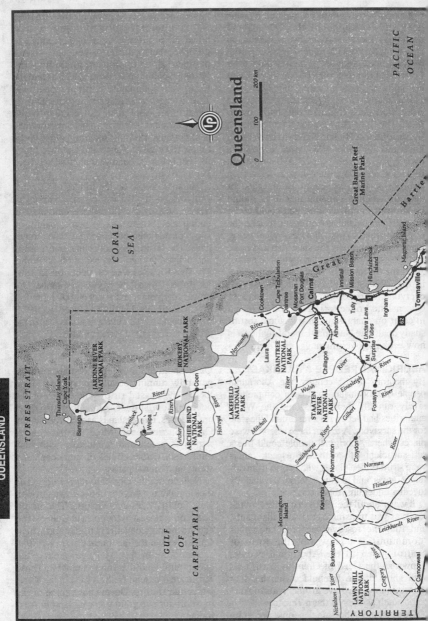

QUEENSLAND

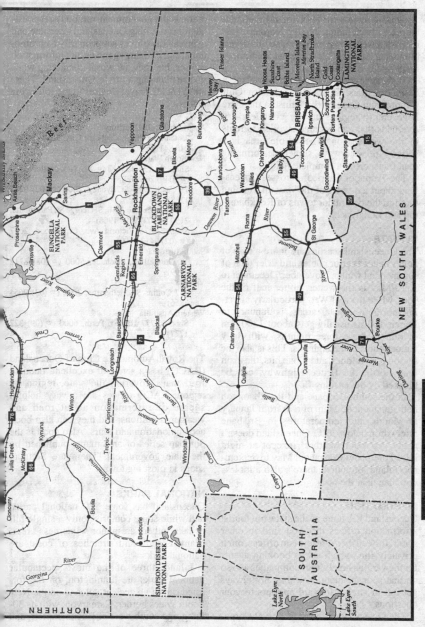

Finally, there's the vast inland area, the barren outback fading into the Northern Territory. Rain can temporarily make this desert bloom but basically it's an area of long empty roads and tiny settlements.

There are a couple of variations from these basic divisions. In the far northern Gulf Country and Cape York Peninsula there are huge empty regions cut by countless dry riverbeds that can become swollen torrents in the wet season. The whole area is a network of waterways, sometimes bringing road transport to a complete halt.

The Tropic of Capricorn crosses Queensland about a quarter of the way up, running through the two major towns of Rockhampton and Longreach.

CLIMATE

The Queensland seasons are more a case of hotter and wetter or cooler and drier than of summer and winter. November/December to April/May is the wetter, hotter half of the year, while the real Wet, particularly affecting northern coastal areas, is January to March. Cairns usually gets about 1300 mm of rain in these three months, with daily temperatures in the high 30s. This is also the season for cyclones, and if one hits, the main road north, the Bruce Highway, can be blocked by the ensuing floods.

In the south, Brisbane and Rockhampton both get about 450 mm of rain from January to March, and temperatures in Brisbane rarely drop below 20°C. Queensland doesn't really get 'cold weather', except at night inland or upland from about May to September. Inland, of course, there's also a lot less rain than near the coast.

INFORMATION

Queensland has none of the state-run tourist information offices that you find in other states. Instead there are tourism offices, often privately run, which act as booking agents for the various hotels, tour companies and so on that sponsor them. You may not always get full or straightforward answers to your questions.

The Queensland Tourist & Travel Corporation is the government-run body responsible for promoting Queensland interstate and overseas. Its offices act primarily as promotional and booking agencies, not information centres, but they are worth contacting when you're planning a trip to Queensland. There are QT&TC Travel Centres in the following places:

Australian Capital Territory
    25 Garema Place, Canberra City, 2601 (☎ (06) 248 8411)
New South Wales
    Shop 3, 133-135 King St, Newcastle, 2300 (☎ (049) 26 2800)
    75 Castlereagh St, Sydney, 2000 (☎ (02) 9232 1788)
    Shop 11, Mayfair Mall, St George St, Parramatta, 2150 (☎ (02) 9891 1966)
    Shop 2, 376 Victoria Ave, Chatswood, 2067 (☎ (02) 9412 3000)
South Australia
    10 Grenfell St, Adelaide, 5000 (☎ (08) 8212 2399)
Victoria
    257 Collins St, Melbourne, 3000 (☎ (03) 9654 3866)
Western Australia
    Shop 6, 777 Hay St, Perth, 6000 (☎ (09) 322 1777)

The Royal Automobile Club of Queensland (RACQ) has a series of excellent, detailed road maps covering the state, region by region. RACQ offices are a very helpful source of information about road and weather conditions, and they can also book accommodation and tours. Also good is the Sunmap series of area maps, published by the state government. There are Sunmap shops in most big towns.

NATIONAL PARKS

Queensland has some 220 national parks, and while some comprise only a single hill or lake, others are major wilderness areas. Many islands and stretches of coast are national parks.

Inland, three of the most spectacular national parks are Lamington, on the forested rim of an ancient volcano on the New South Wales border; Carnarvon, with its 30-km gorge south-west of Rockhampton; and rainforested Eungella, near Mackay, which is swarming with wildlife. Many parks have camping grounds with water, toilets and showers and there are often privately run camping grounds, motels or lodges on the park fringes. Sizeable parks usually have a network of walking tracks.

The Queensland National Parks & Wildlife Service (QNP&WS) operates five main information centres. You can also get information from the QNP&WS offices in most major towns, and from the park rangers. The QNP&WS information centres are at:

Brisbane
    160 Ann St (☎ (07) 3227 8185)
Toowoomba
    158 Hume St (☎ (076) 39 4599)
Rockhampton North
    Yeppoon Rd (☎ (079) 36 0511)
Townsville
    Great Barrier Reef Wonderland (☎ (077) 21 2399)
Cairns
    10 McLeod St (☎ (070) 52 3096)

To camp in a national park – whether in a fixed camping ground or in the bush – you need a permit. You can get permits in advance either by writing to or calling in at the appropriate QNP&WS office, or from a ranger at the park itself. Camping in national parks costs $3 per person per night. Some camping grounds fill up at holiday times, so you may need to book well ahead; you can usually book sites six to 12 weeks ahead by writing to the appropriate office. Lists of camping grounds are available from QNP&WS offices.

The handy *Discover National Parks* booklets ($2.50) also have useful information about Queensland's national parks and state forests, including things to do, camping details and how to get there. These booklets are available from bookshops and QNP&WS offices.

State Forests

There are also camping areas, walking trails and scenic drives in some state forests, which can be just as scenic and wild as national parks. You can get information on camping sites and facilities from tourist offices or from the Forest Services section of the Department of Primary Industry (☎ (07) 3234 0158), on the 5th floor at 160 Mary St, Brisbane. Some other forestry offices are at Fraser Rd, Two Mile, near Gympie; 52 McIlwraith St, Ingham; Gregory St, Cardwell; and at 83 Main St, Atherton.

ACTIVITIES
Bushwalking

This is a popular activity year-round. There are excellent bushwalking possibilities in many parts of the state, including several of the larger coastal islands such as Fraser and Hinchinbrook. There are bushwalking clubs around the state and several useful guidebooks. Lonely Planet's *Bushwalking in Australia* includes three walks in Queensland, which range between two and five days in length.

National parks and state forests often have with marked walking trails. Favourite bushwalkers' national parks on the mainland include Lamington in the southern Border Ranges, Main Range in the Great Divide, Cooloola just north of the Sunshine Coast, and Bellenden Ker south of Cairns, which contains Queensland's highest peak, Mt Bartle Frere (1657 metres). You can get full information from national parks and state forests offices.

Water Sports
Diving & Snorkelling The Great Barrier Reef provides some of the world's best diving and there's ample opportunity to learn and pursue this activity. The Queensland coast is probably the world's cheapest place to learn to scuba dive in tropical water – a five-day course leading to a recognised open water certificate usually costs between $300 and $500 and you almost always do a good part of your learning out on the Barrier Reef itself. These courses are very popular and nearly every town along the coast has one or more dive schools. The three most popular places are Airlie Beach, Townsville and Cairns.

Important factors to consider when choosing a course include the school's reputation, the relative amounts of time spent on pool/classroom training and out in the ocean, and whether your open-water time is spent on the outer reef as opposed to reefs around islands or even just off the mainland (the outer reef is usually more spectacular). Normally you have to show you can tread water for 10 minutes, and swim 200 metres, before you can start a course. Some schools also require a medical, which usually costs extra.

For certified divers, trips and equipment hire are available just about everywhere. You usually have to show evidence of qualifications. You can snorkel almost everywhere too. There are coral reefs off some mainland beaches and around several of the islands, and many day trips out to the Barrier Reef provide snorkelling gear free.

During the wet season, which is usually January to March, floods can wash a lot of mud out into the ocean and visibility for divers and snorkellers is sometimes affected.

White-Water Rafting & Canoeing

The Tully and North Johnstone rivers between Townsville and Cairns are the big ones for white-water rafting. You can do day trips for about $120, or longer expeditions.

Coastal Queensland is full of waterways and lakes so there's no shortage of canoeing territory. You can hire canoes or join canoe tours in several places, including Noosa, Townsville and Cairns.

Swimming & Surfing

Popular surfing and swimming beaches are south of Brisbane on the Gold Coast and north on the Sunshine Coast. North of Fraser Island the beaches are sheltered by the Great Barrier Reef so they're great for swimming but no good for surf. The clear, sheltered waters of the reef hardly need to be mentioned. There are also innumerable, good, freshwater swimming spots around the state.

Other Water Sports

Sailing enthusiasts will find plenty many places that hire out boats, both along the coast and inland. Airlie Beach and the Whitsunday Islands are possibly the biggest centres and you can find almost any type of boating or sailing you want there. Fishing is one of Queensland's most popular sports and you can hire fishing gear or boats in many places. Sailboards can also be hired in many spots along the coast.

Warning From around November to April, avoid swimming on unprotected northern beaches where deadly box jellyfish may lurk. If in any doubt, check with a local person. If you're still in doubt, don't swim – you only get stung once in a lifetime. Great Keppel Island is usually the most northerly safe place in the box jellyfish season. Also in northern waters, saltwater crocodiles are a hazard. They may be found in the open sea or near creeks and rivers – especially tidal ones – sometimes at surprising distances inland.

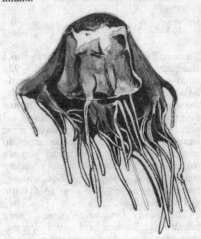

The deadly box jellyfish is most prevalent in northern beaches from November to December

Fossicking

There are lots of good fossicking areas in Queensland; see the *Gem Field* brochure published by the Queensland Tourist & Travel Corporation. It lists the places where you'll have a fair chance of finding gems and the types you might find. You'll need a 'miners right' before you set out.

GETTING THERE & AWAY

See the Brisbane Getting There & Away section for details on transport to Queensland.

GETTING AROUND

The peak tourist seasons are from mid-December to late January, 10 days either side of Easter, and mid-June to mid-October. The low season is February and March.

Air

Ansett (☎ 13 1300) and Qantas (☎ 13 1313) both fly to Queensland's major cities, connecting them to the southern states and across to the Northern Territory. There's also a multitude of smaller airlines operating up and down the coast, across the Cape York Peninsula and into the outback. During the wet season, such flights are often the only means of getting around the Gulf of Carpentaria or the Cape York Peninsula. These smaller airlines include Sunstate (book through Qantas) and Flight West (☎ 13 2392 within Queensland or ☎ 1800 777 879 from elsewhere in Australia, or book through Ansett).

Bus

Greyhound Pioneer Australia (☎ 13 2030) and McCafferty's (☎ 13 1499) have the most comprehensive bus networks throughout Queensland and cover all the major destinations. The busiest route is the coastal run up the Bruce Highway from Brisbane to Cairns – both companies offer a six-month pass for about $155, which gives you unlimited stopovers along this route. The other major routes are the inland routes from Brisbane to Mt Isa (continuing into the Northern Territory); from Townsville to Mt Isa; and from Rockhampton to Longreach (McCafferty's only). Prices are fairly similar, although McCafferty's tends to be a dollar or two cheaper.

There are numerous smaller bus companies that offer more specialised local

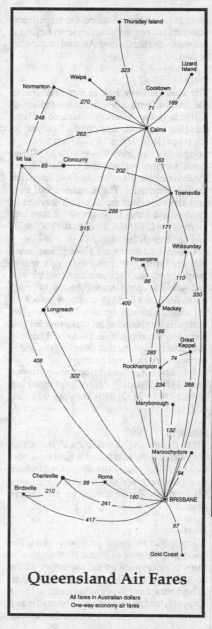

Queensland Air Fares

All fares in Australian dollars
One-way economy air fares

services. A company called Oz Experience offers an interesting alternative to buying a bus pass – see the Getting Around chapter for details.

Train

The main railway line is the Brisbane to Cairns run (with a scenic extension up to Kuranda in the Atherton Tableland). There are also inland services from Brisbane to Charleville, from Rockhampton to Longreach, and from Townsville to Mt Isa. Local services include the *Gulflander* and the *Savannahlander* – see the Gulf Savannah section for details. The Sunshine Rail Pass provides unlimited travel on all services in Queensland. Fares in economy/1st class are: 14 days for $267/388, 21 days for $309/477, and one month for $388/582.

Queensland trains are slower than buses but are similarly priced if you travel economy class. They're almost all air-con and you can get sleeping berths on most trains for $30 a night in economy, or $50 in 1st class. You can break your journey on most services for no extra cost provided you complete the trip within 14 days. The only interstate rail connection from Queensland is between Brisbane and Sydney.

For bookings and information, phone Queensland Rail's centralised booking service (☎ 13 2232) daily between 6 am and 8.30 pm.

Hitching

This is common, but take care: the police sometimes give hitchhikers a hard time, and there are long, lonely stretches of road where strange people are said to pick up unwary hitchhikers. Women should be particularly careful.

Boat

It's possible to make your way along the coast or even over to Papua New Guinea or Darwin by crewing on the numerous yachts and cruisers that sail Queensland waters. Ask at harbours, marinas or sailing clubs. Great Keppel Island, Airlie Beach, Townsville and Cairns are good places to try. Sometimes

you'll get a free ride in exchange for your help, but it's more common for owners to ask $10 to $20 a day for food etc.

Brisbane

Population 1,425,000

When the colony of New South Wales needed a better place to store its more recalcitrant 'cons', the tropical country farther north seemed a good place to drop them. Accordingly, in 1824, a penal settlement was established at Redcliffe on Moreton Bay, but was soon abandoned due to lack of water and hostile Aboriginal people. The settlement was moved south and inland to Brisbane, a town grew up, and although the penal settlement was abandoned in 1839, Brisbane's future was assured when the area was thrown open to free settlers in 1842. As Queensland's huge agricultural potential and mineral riches were developed, Brisbane grew to be a city, and today it is the third-largest in Australia.

For years it was considered to be a bit backward by its larger southern cousins, but since hosting several major international events in the 1980s, including the 1982 Commonwealth Games and Expo 88, Brisbane has developed into a modern and cosmopolitan city.

Although it's close to the coast, Brisbane is very much a river city. It's a scenic place, surrounded by hills and fine lookouts, with several impressive bridges spanning the Brisbane River. It is compact and easy to explore, and enjoys an excellent climate. As in the rest of the state, the city is dominated architecturally by 'Queenslanders' – sprawling, verandahed, timber houses on stilts.

Several of Queensland's major attractions can be reached on day trips from Brisbane. The Gold and Sunshine coasts and their mountainous hinterlands are easy drives from the city, and you can also visit the islands of Moreton Bay or head inland towards the Great Dividing Range and the Darling Downs.

Orientation

Brisbane is built along and between the looping meanders of the Brisbane River, about 25 km upstream from the river mouth. The Brisbane transit centre, where you'll arrive if you're coming by bus or train, is on Roma St about half a km west of the city centre.

You'll find most accommodation and eating options clustered in the suburbs surrounding the city: immediately north is Spring Hill, with some good mid-range options, while west of the centre is Paddington, an attractive residential suburb with good cafes and restaurants. South across the Victoria Bridge is South Brisbane, with the Queensland Cultural Centre and the South Bank Parklands, farther south are Highgate Hill and the arty West End. North-east along Ann St from the city is Fortitude Valley, with lots of nightclubs, cafes and restaurants and a large ethnic population. East of the Valley is New Farm, and farther east across the river from the city is Kangaroo Point.

Information

Tourist Offices The Queen St Mall Information Centre (☎ 3229 5918), on the corner of Queen and Albert Sts, is open Monday to Thursday from 9 am to 5.30 pm, Friday to 9 pm, Saturday to 4 pm and Sunday from 10 am to 4 pm.

At the transit centre, the Greater Brisbane Tourist Association runs a helpful information office (☎ 3236 2020) on level 2 (open weekdays from 8 am to 6 pm and weekends from 9 am to 1 pm) and an accommodation booking office on level 3 (open weekdays from 7 am to 6 pm and weekends from 8 am to 5 pm).

There's also the Tourism Brisbane information desk (☎ 3221 8411) in the City Hall, near King George Square. The Government Travel Centre (☎ 3221 6111), on the corner of Adelaide and Edward Sts is more a booking office than an information centre but they may be able to answer some queries.

At the airport in the international terminal, the Brisbane Visitors & Convention Bureau (☎ 3860 4688) has an information booth that opens to meet most incoming flights.

The Disability Information & Awareness Line (☎ 3224 8031 or ☎ 1800 177 120, Monday to Friday from 9 am to 5 pm) is an information and referral service for people with disabilities.

There are a number of free information guides circulated in Brisbane including *Tourism Brisbane*, which has a useful information directory at the back including a list of foreign consulates.

Post & Telecommunications The main post office is in Queen St. The STD area code for Brisbane is 07.

Other Offices The RACQ (☎ 3361 2444) is beside the main post office at 261 Queen St. For information on national parks, the Naturally Queensland office (☎ 3227 8186) at 160 Ann St is open on weekdays from 8.30 am to 5 pm. The Queensland Conservation Council Environment Centre (☎ 3221 0188) is in the School of Arts building at 166 Ann St.

The YHA Travel Centre (☎ 3236 1680) is at 154 Roma St, opposite the transit centre.

Bookshops Brisbane has several large book chains including Dymocks, with a shop at 235 Albert St, and Angus & Robertson Bookworld, with a shop in Adelaide St under Post Office Square. Good independent booksellers include the American Book Store at 173 Elizabeth St, McGills Technical Books at 201 Elizabeth St, and Folio Books at 80 Albert St. Archives Fine Books at 40-42 Charlotte St has a huge range of second-hand books. World Wide Maps & Guides, at 187 George St, specialises in travel books and maps, as does Travel Books at 66 Boundary St in the West End.

Medical Services The Traveller's Medical & Vaccination Centre (☎ 3221 9066) is on the 6th floor, 247 Adelaide St. The Brisbane Sexual Health Clinic (☎ 3227 7091) is at 484 Adelaide St.

QUEENSLAND

City Hall

Brisbane's City Hall, on the corner of Adelaide and Albert Sts, has gradually been surrounded by skyscrapers but the observation platform still provides a great view across the city – a free lift runs weekdays from 8.30 am to 3.30 pm and Saturday from 10.30 am to 1.30 pm. There's also a free museum and art gallery on the ground floor, open daily from 10 am to 5 pm.

Early Buildings – city centre

The Brisbane City Council publishes a series of *Heritage Trail* brochures that guide you around the city's most interesting old buildings. The National Trust has its headquarters in **Old Government House** (1862), the former state governor's residence at the southern end of George St. Nearby, **Parliament House**, overlooking the City Botanic Gardens, dates from 1868, and was built in French Renaissance style; the roof is made from Mt Isa copper. Free tours are given Monday to Friday four times a day (except when Parliament is sitting).

More of Brisbane's best old buildings line

QUEENSLAND

PLACES TO STAY

7	Globetrekkers Hostel
11	The Homestead Hostel
12	Atoa House Travellers Hostel
13	Edward Lodge
14	Boronia Lodge B&B
15	Waverley B&B
21	Aussie Way Backpackers
23	Banana Benders Backpackers
29	Brisbane City Youth Hostel & City Backpackers Hostel
30	Yellow Submarine Backpackers
37	Swagman's Rest Backpackers
38	Somewhere to Stay Hostel
41	Durham Villa
44	Southern Cross Motel
46	Courtney Place Backpackers

PLACES TO EAT

1	Breakfast Creek Hotel
2	Breakfast Creek Wharf
5	Famish
9	Continental Cafe
16	King Tut's Wa Wa Hut
17	Red Chair Cafe
18	Jakarta Indonesian Restaurant
19	Sultan's Kitchen
24	Meditteraneo Cafe-Bar
33	Qan Heng's Restaurant
34	Caffe Tempo & Wholly Munchies
35	Cafe Babylon
36	King Ahiram's
39	Genji Japanese Kitchen
40	Thai on High

OTHER

3	Newstead House
4	The Valley Swimming Pool

6	Brunswick Hotel
8	New Farm Mountain Bikes
10	Village Twin Cinemas
20	Paddo Tavern
22	Brisbane Arts Theatre
25	Caxton Hotel
26	Crazies Comedy Restaurant & Casablanca
27	Museum of Contemporary Art
28	The Underground Nightclub
31	Castlemaine Perkins XXXX Brewery
32	Travel Books
42	Van Gogh's Earlobe
43	The Cliffs Rock-Climbing Area
45	Brisbane Cricket Ground (The Gabba)

George St – notably the **Mansions** and **Harris Terrace,** Victorian terrace houses on the Margaret St corners, and the **Treasury Buildings** between Queen and Elizabeth Sts, which now house Brisbane's casino.

Next to St Stephen's Cathedral, on Elizabeth St, is the Gothic-style **Old St Stephen's** (1850), which is the oldest church in Brisbane. The **main post office** is an impressive neoclassical edifice dating from the 1870s. Across Queen St and on the corner of Creek St, the **National Bank building** (1885) is one of the finest examples of Italian Renaissance style in Australia. Its front doors were made from a single Queensland cedar log. **St John's Cathedral**, at the top end of Ann St, is still under construction – work started in 1901. Guided tours are conducted Monday to Saturday at 10 am.

The 1828 **Commissariat Stores** building, at 115 William St, was used as a government store until 1962. Today it houses the Royal Historical Society of Queensland's library and museum, and can be visited for $1, Tuesday to Friday from 11 am to 2 pm, and Sunday to 4 pm.

The **Old Windmill & Observatory** (1828) on Wickham Terrace is one of Brisbane's earliest buildings. Built to grind grain for the early convict colony, it was later converted to a signal post and then a meteorological observatory.

Early Buildings – suburbs

There are a number of interesting old houses and period re-creations around Brisbane. **Newstead House** (1846), four km northeast of the centre on Breakfast Creek Rd in Newstead, is the oldest surviving home in Brisbane. It is a stately mansion fitted out with Victorian furnishings. The house and its gardens are open on weekdays from 10 am to 4 pm and on Sunday from 2 to 5 pm; entry costs $3.

Earlystreet Historical Village, four km east of the centre on McIlwraith Ave in Norman Park, is a re-creation of early Queensland colonial life with genuine old buildings in a garden setting. Entry is $6 and it's open daily from 9 am to 4.30 pm.

Miegunyah (1884), at 35 Jordan Terrace, Bowen Hills, is a fine example of

QUEENSLAND

early Brisbane architecture. It's been furnished and decorated in period style as a memorial to the pioneer women of Queensland and is open on Wednesday from 10.30 am to 3 pm and on weekends to 4 pm.

Queensland Cultural Centre

This impressive complex (☎ 3840 7200), just across Victoria Bridge from the city, houses the Queensland Art Gallery, the Queensland Museum, the State Library and the Performing Arts Complex.

You can take a guided tour of the **Performing Arts Complex**, including the Lyric Theatre, the Concert Hall and a small studio theatre, with Behind the Scenes Theatre Tours (☎ 3844 8800).

The **Queensland Museum** is free and well worth a visit, with exhibitions on dinosaurs and whales, photography, natural history, and Melanesian artefacts. The aviation section includes the *Avian Cirrus*, in which Queensland's Bert Hinkler made the first England to Australia solo flight in 1928. It is open daily from 9 am to 5 pm (Wednesday till 8 pm).

The **Queensland Art Gallery's** impressive permanent collection includes works by Sir Sidney Nolan, William Dobell, Margaret Preston and Fred Williams. It's open daily from 10 am to 5 pm (Wednesday until 8 pm). Admission is free, and there are free guided tours on weekdays at 11 am and 1 and 2 pm, and weekends at 11 am and 2 and 3 pm. During special exhibitions hours are extended and a fee is charged.

Other Museums

At 110 George St in the city, the **Sciencentre** is a science museum with interactive displays, optical illusions and a regular 20-minute show in the theatre. It's open daily from 10 am to 5 pm; entry costs $7.

The **Museum of Contemporary Art**, on Petrie Terrace in Paddington, is in a converted grain silo. It's open Monday to Saturday from noon to 6 pm; admission is by $2 donation. Another place at which you can check out the contemporary art scene is the **Institute of Modern Art**, on the corner of

Ann and Gipps Sts in Fortitude Valley. It's well worth a visit, and is open Tuesday to Friday from 11 am to 5 pm and Saturday to 4 pm. Entry is free.

The **Queensland Maritime Museum**, on Sidon St in South Brisbane has an 1881 dry dock, working models, and the WW II frigate HMAS *Diamantina*. It's open daily from 10 am to 5 pm; admission is $4.

Brisbane's trams no longer operate but you can ride some early examples at the **Tramway Museum** on 2 McGinn Rd, Ferny Grove, 11 km north-west of the centre. It is open on Sunday afternoons ($4).

The **Sir Charles Kingsford-Smith Memorial**, featuring his famous *Southern Cross* plane under a giant dome, is beside the airport freeway opposite the new terminal.

The **Archerfield Warbirds Museum** at Archerfield airport 12 km south-west of the centre, is open daily from 10 am to 4 pm.

South Bank Parklands

Brisbane's South Bank, formerly the site of Expo 88, has been extensively redeveloped and is now one of the city's liveliest and most interesting areas. Covering 16 hectares, its attractions include restaurants and cafes, parklands and bike paths, a rainforest sanctuary and butterfly house and market stalls.

The **Gondwana Rainforest Sanctuary** is a quite amazing re-creation of a rainforest environment. Set inside and around a massive synthetic rock, it's populated by native birds, mammals and reptiles including crocodiles, koalas, possums, lorikeets and snakes. An elevated boardwalk winds through the sanctuary. Gondwana is open daily from 8 am to 5 pm; entry costs $9.

The **Butterfly & Insect House** is a glass-enclosed tropical conservatorium that is home to hundreds of Australian butterflies, as well as a large collection of exotic insects and spiders. It's open daily from 10 am to 4 pm and entry costs $6.50.

Our World Environment has a mixed bag of displays loosely relating to the environment. It's open daily from 9 am to 5 pm and admission costs $6. A Discovery Ticket

($18) admits you to all three attractions and includes a ride along the waterway ferries.

South Bank also includes a beautiful **Nepalese Pagoda** that took 160 craftspeople two years to make; **boat trips** on canals through the park; a **sandy beach and swimming lagoon** patrolled by lifesavers; popular **barbecue and picnic areas**; and a large craft and clothing **market** (see Markets below). The South Bank Visitor Information Centre (☎ 3867 2051) is at the main entrance court.

Markets

The popular **Crafts Village markets** at South Bank feature a great range of crafts, clothing, handmade goods, and souvenirs. Stalls are set up in the Stanley St Plaza in rows of colourful tents, and open on Friday night, Saturday and Sunday.

Every Sunday, the carnival-style **Riverside Centre** and **Eagle St Pier Markets** have 150 stalls, including glass blowing, weaving, leather work and children's activities.

On Saturday, the **Fortitude Valley Market**, with a diverse collection of crafts, clothes and junk, is held in the Brunswick St Mall.

City Parks & Gardens

Brisbane's **Botanic Gardens** were established in 1855 on a loop of the Brisbane River, almost in the centre of the city. The gardens occupy 18 hectares, are open 24 hours a day (and lit at night) and are a good spot for strolling, inline skating and bike riding. Free tours (☎ 3221 4528) are run daily (except Monday) at 11 am and 1 pm.

There are good views from **Wickham Park** and **Albert Park** on the hill just north of the city centre. **New Farm Park**, by the river at the southern end of Brunswick St, is noted for its rose displays, jacaranda trees and Devonshire teas.

Mt Coot-tha Park

This large park with a lookout and excellent botanic gardens is just eight km west of the city centre. The views from the top are superb. On a clear day you can see the distant line of Moreton and Stradbroke islands, the Glasshouse Mountains to the north, the mountains behind the Gold Coast to the south, and Brisbane – with the river winding through – at your feet. There's an expensive restaurant and a cafe/kiosk, both with sensational views.

There are some good walks around Mt Coot-tha and its foothills, including the one to J C Slaughter Falls on Simpsons Rd.

The **Mt Coot-tha Botanic Gardens**, at the foot of the mountain, are open daily from 8.30 am to 5 pm. The gardens include an enclosed tropical dome, an arid zone, rainforests and a Japanese garden. There are free guided walks through the gardens daily (except Monday) at 11 am and 1 pm. You'll also find the **Sir Thomas Brisbane Planetarium** here; it's the largest in Australia. There are shows Wednesday to Friday at 3.30 and 7.30 pm; Saturday at 1.30, 3.30 and 7.30 pm; and Sunday at 1.30 and 3.30 pm. Admission is $7.50.

There are limited buses to the lookout and botanic gardens at Mt Coot-tha. Bus No 37A to the gardens leaves from Ann St at King George Square.

Brisbane Forest Park

The Brisbane Forest Park is a 26,500 hectare natural bushland reserve in the D'Aguilar Range. The park starts on the outskirts of Brisbane and stretches for more than 50 km to the north and west. It's a great area for bushwalks, cycling, horse riding, camping and scenic drives.

There's an **information centre** (☎ 3300 4855) in The Gap, at the start of the park. It's open on weekdays from 8.30 am to 4.30 pm and on weekends from 10 am to 5 pm, and the rangers run regular guided bushwalks and tours – ring for details.

In the same spot is **Walk-About Creek**, a freshwater study centre where you can see fish, lizards, pythons and turtles at close quarters. It's open daily from 9 am to 4.30 pm (weekends from 10 am); entry costs $3.50. Upstairs, there's an excellent cafe/restaurant.

QUEENSLAND

To get to the park from the city, follow Musgrave, Waterworks and Mt Nebo roads. By public transport, you can take a bus to The Gap – it's about a 700-metre walk to the information centre. Note that the walking trails start elsewhere in the park and you'll need transport to reach them.

Wildlife Sanctuaries

The **Alma Park Zoo** at Kallangur, 28 km north of the city centre, is an excellent zoo in a spacious garden setting. It has a large collection of Australian wildlife including koalas, kangaroos, emus, dingoes, and exotic animals such as Malaysian sun bears, leopards and monkeys. It's open daily from 9 am to 5 pm; admission costs $14. A daily 'zoo train' departs from the transit centre at 9.05 am (Caboolture line); a courtesy bus runs from Dakabin station to the zoo.

The **Lone Pine Koala Sanctuary** at Fig Tree Pocket, 11 km south-west of the centre, receives much more publicity than Alma Park, but it's somewhat dated and a disappointment in comparison. Set in spacious parklands it has lots of koalas as well as kangaroos, emus, lyrebirds and wombats. It's open daily from 8.45 am to 5 pm and entry costs $11. You can get there on Cityxpress bus No 518 from Queen St, on one of the bus tours, or by river cruise with Mirimar (☎ 3221 0300).

Australian Woolshed

At 148 Stamford Rd, Ferny Hills, 15 km north-west of the centre, the Australian Woolshed has a small fauna park, picnic gardens and a water slide. Their one-hour Ram Shows star trained sheep and dogs and include shearing demonstrations, with shows daily at 10 and 11 am and 2 pm; entry costs $11. They also have dinner dances on Friday and Saturday nights ($30 per person).

Activities

The Cliffs, on the south banks of the Brisbane River in Kangaroo Point, is an excellent rock-climbing venue that is floodlit until midnight or later. Several operators offer climbing and abseiling instruction here,

An inhabitant of the Lone Pine Koala Sanctuary

including Jane Clarkson's Outdoor Adventures (☎ 3830 5044).

For information about bushwalking near Brisbane, contact the Brisbane Bushwalker Club (☎ 3856 4050). Horse-riding schools on the outskirts of Brisbane include Silverado (☎ 3890 2280) and Samford Valley (☎ 3289 1046).

Skatebiz (☎ 3220 0157) in Mary St near the Albert St corner hires out inline skates from $10 for two hours.

The Valley Pool, on the corner of Wickham and East Sts in Fortitude Valley, is open daily from 5.30 am (from 7.30 am on Sunday). Other good swimming pools include the old Spring Hill Baths in Torrington St and the Olympic-sized Centenary Pool, nearby on Gregory Terrace.

Kayak Escapes (☎ 3359 3486) run kayaking trips up the Upper Brisbane River with day trips on Thursday ($75) and two-day expeditions on Tuesday and Saturday ($175 to $225 including meals and camping gear).

Organised Tours & Cruises

City Tours The open-sided City Sights Trambus Tour shuttles around 18 of the city's major sights, leaving every half-hour from Post Office Square in Queen St (daily except Tuesday). All-day tickets cost $12.

Large bus tour operators such as Australian Pacific (☎ 13 1304), Boomerang Baxway (☎ 3236 3614) and Coachtrans (☎ 3236 1000) have city sights tours, visits to wildlife sanctuaries and trips to theme parks and the Gold or Sunshine coasts. Brochures are available everywhere.

From Monday to Wednesday there are free tours of the Castlemaine XXXX (pronounced 'fourex') brewery (☎ 3361 7597) on Milton Rd, Milton, about 1.5 km west of the centre. Most hostels will organise trips to the brewery. The tour lasts about an hour, and is followed by about 40 minutes worth of free beer.

River Cruises The *Kookaburra Queens I* and *II* (☎ 3221 1300) are restored paddle-steamers that cruise the Brisbane River. They offer 1½-hour morning and afternoon tea cruises ($14.90), a 1½-hour lunch cruise ($19.95), and evening dinner cruises (from $19.90 to $49.90). Cruises depart from the Eagle St Pier.

The *Brisbane Star* (☎ 018 190 604) does a four-hour Sunday cruise from the city to the Brisbane River mouth and back, departing at 1 pm from the Edward St Pier ($10).

Other Tours Far Horizons (☎ 3284 5475) runs popular small-group tours to some of the best natural attractions around Brisbane, including the Lamington and Springbrook national parks. Day trips cost $58, including lunch ($52 for backpackers and YHA members).

For a day trip to the Gold Coast, the High Roller bus (☎ 3222 4067) to Jupiter's Casino is good value. It leaves from the transit centre

daily at 9 am and costs $10 return, which includes a $5 meal voucher and a $5 gaming voucher.

Festivals

Brisbane's major festival of the arts, the outdoor Warana Festival, is held over two weeks from mid-September. The Royal National Exhibition (the 'Ekka') is held at the exhibition grounds in mid-August. There's also a 12-day international film festival in August, an international comedy festival in April and a music festival every second June (in odd-numbered years).

Places to Stay

Brisbane has plenty of hostels and backpackers' places, and there are also quite a few well-priced hotels, motels and self-contained apartment blocks within easy reach of the centre.

Camping There are no caravan parks or camping grounds close to the city centre, and in any case many of the caravan parks are full with permanent residents. You could try the following:

Aspley Acres Caravan Park (☎ 3263 2668), 1420 Gympie Rd, Aspley – 13 km north, tent sites from $12, on-site vans from $25

Dress Circle Village (☎ 3341 6133), 10 Holmead Rd, Eight Mile Plain – 14 km south, tent sites from $10, on-site cabins from $50

Gateway Junction Village (☎ 3341 6333), 200 School Rd, Roachdale – 19 km south, powered sites $18, cabins from $50

Sheldon Caravan Park (☎ 3341 6166), also in School Rd, Roachdale – 19 km south, tent sites from $12, on-site vans and cabins from $28

Hostels There are plenty of backpackers hostels, and some excellent mid-range options. The Brisbane Visitors Accommodation Booking Service (☎ 3236 2020) on level three of the transit centre has information on a wide range of accommodation options; if you decide on a hostel, they'll arrange for a courtesy bus to pick you up.

Hostels are concentrated in three main areas: Petrie Terrace and Paddington, just

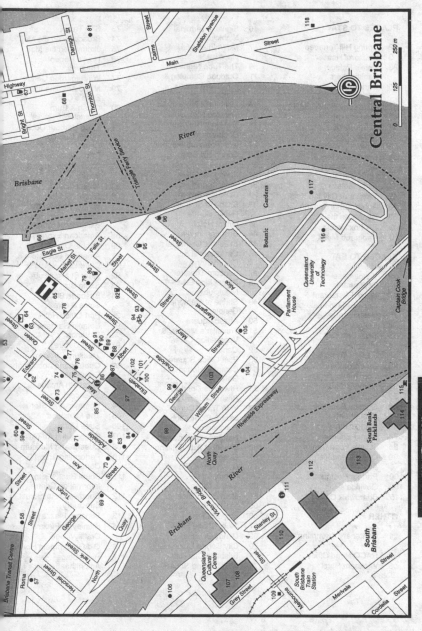

Central Brisbane

PLACES TO STAY

2   Spring Hill Terraces
3   Balmoral House
23 Pete's Palace Backpackers
26 Dahrl Court Apartments
27 Thornbury House B&B
33 Ridge Hotel
37 Marrs Townhouse Motel
38 Soho Club Motel
39 Dorchester Inn Self-Contained Units
41 Astor Motel
42 Yale Inner City Inn
43 Annie's Shandon Inn
68 Ryan's on the River
109 Sly Fox Hotel
118 Kangaroo Motel

PLACES TO EAT

9   Vietnamese Restaurant
10 Seoul Restaurant
12 Universal Noodle Restaurant
13 Enjoy Inn
15 Ric's Cafe-Bar
16 Mellino's
18 Lucky's Trattoria
20 Cafe Europe
21 Giardinetto's
28 Harold's Cafe
29 Papa Mio's
40 Oriental Bangkok Restaurant
62 Shingle Inn
78 Planet Energy
85 Jo Jo's Food Centre
90 Queensland Irish Association
100 Parrots Restaurant
102 Govinda's
115 Boardwalk Cafes

OTHER

1   Centenary Swimming Pool
4   RACQ Head Office
5   Wickham Hotel
6   Signal & Terminal Nightclubs
7   McWhirters Marketplace
8   The Tube Nightclub
11 Outdoor, Camping & Adventure Sports Shops
14 Institute of Modern Art
17 The Zoo Nightclub
19 The Beat Nightclub
22 Dooley's Hotel
24 New Farm Laundromat
25 Spring Hill Baths
30 Options Nightclub
31 Spring Hill Hotel
32 Sportsman's Hotel
34 St Paul's Tavern
35 Brisbane Sexual Health Centre
36 Orient Hotel
44 Brisbane Tavern
45 St John's Cathedral
46 Old Windmill & Observatory
47 Suncorp Theatre
48 Someplace Else Nightclub
49 Shrine of Memories & Cenotaph
50 Anzac Square
51 Traveller's Medical & Vaccination Centre
52 Qantas
53 Post Office Square
54 Customs House Gallery
55 Riverside Centre
56 Brisbane Jazz Club
57 YHA Travel Centre
58 Jazz & Blues Club & Travelodge
59 Naturally Queensland
60 School of Arts Building
61 Queensland Government Travel Centre
63 RACQ Office
64 Main Post Office
65 St Stephen's Cathedral
66 Eagle St Pier
67 Story Bridge Hotel
69 Dendy Cinema
70 City Centre Library
71 Brisbane City Hall
72 King George Square
73 STA Travel
74 Broadway on the Mall
75 Jimmy's on the Mall
76 Hoyt's Regent Theatres
77 Wintergarden Centre
79 Metro Arts Theatre & Zane's Caffe
80 Crash & Burn Nightclub
81 Snug Harbour Dockside & Comedy Cafe
82 CES Job Centre
83 World Wide Maps & Books
84 Ansett
86 Queen St Mall Information Centre
87 Thomas Cook Foreign Exchange Centre
88 American Express
89 Babble On
91 American Bookstore & Caffe Libri
92 Mary St Nightclub
93 Skate Biz
94 Brisbane Bicycle Sales & Hire
95 Port Office Hotel
96 Botanic Gardens Main Entrance
97 Myer Centre
98 Treasury Casino
99 Queensland Aboriginal Creations
101 Elizabeth Arcade
103 Sciencentre
104 Commissariat Stores
105 The Mansions
106 State Library
107 Queensland Art Gallery
108 Queensland Museum
110 Performing Arts Complex
111 South Bank Visitor Information Centre
112 Gondwana Rainforest Sanctuary
113 Suncorp Piazza
114 Stanley St Plaza & Crafts Village
116 Old Government House
117 River Stage Amphitheatre

west of the city centre; Fortitude Valley and New Farm, north-east of the city; and South Brisbane and West End, south of the city. There's another hostel in East Brisbane.

Petrie Terrace & Paddington This isn't the most exciting of areas, but the hostels around Petrie Terrace are the closest to the transit centre, and nearby Paddington has plenty of good cafes, restaurants and bars.

The *Brisbane City Youth Hostel* (☎ 3236 1004), at 392 Upper Roma St, is a stylish new hostel with a good cafe (breakfast, lunch and dinner from $4 to $6, and great coffee) and impressive air-con rooms upstairs, with twins and doubles at $40 ($48 with private bathroom) and triples at $48. In the older section out the back, four to six-bed dorms cost $14, and twins $32. Nonmembers pay $2 extra.

City Backpackers' Hostel (☎ 3211 3221), nearby at 380 Upper Roma St, is another good modern hostel with 76 beds. It's fully air-con and non-smoking, with four to six-bunk dorms at $13 and twins/doubles at $32. The *Roma St Hostel*, between these two places, is not recommended – there are plenty of better options.

Just off Upper Roma St at 66 Quay St, the *Yellow Submarine* (☎ 3211 3424) is a cosy old three-storey house that has been brightly painted with a nautical theme. Three to six-bed dorms cost $12, twins and doubles $28.

Banana Benders Backpackers (☎ 3367 1157), on the corner of Petrie Terrace and Jessie St, is a smallish, older-style hostel with four-share dorms at $13 and doubles at $30. Down the next side street is *Aussie Way Backpackers* (☎ 3369 0711) at 34 Cricket St. It's a 36-bed hostel in a recently renovated two-storey timber house; dorms are $13, and singles/doubles $25/30.

Fortitude Valley & New Farm Known as the Valley', this is one of Brisbane's liveliest inner suburbs. In recent years the Valley has crossed that fine line from seedy to trendy, and it has plenty of good cafes and restaurants and some particularly interesting bars and nightclubs.

At 33 Amelia St in Fortitude Valley, *Balmoral House* (☎ 3252 1397) is clean, modern and quiet, although it isn't really a backpackers' place – it's popular with families and patients from the nearby hospital. A bed in a three or four-bed dorm costs $12, and singles/doubles are $30 ($45 with private bathroom).

Moving east into New Farm, you'll find four more hostels in and around Brunswick St. *Pete's Palace* (☎ 3254 1984) at 515 Brunswick St is in a rambling old timber house with a somewhat chequered history. It has adequate facilities and is quite clean and charges $12 for a dorm bed and $30 for a double.

A bit farther along is the *Globetrekkers Hostel* (☎ 3358 1251) at 35 Balfour St. This is a friendly and quiet hostel in a renovated house, and the good atmosphere and small size make it quite popular. Dorm beds are $12, and doubles $28 or $30 with private bathroom.

The *Homestead* (☎ 3358 3538), at 57 Annie St, is a big modern place with a party attitude and good facilities including a small pool. Six to eight-bed dorms are $12; doubles $30 ($39 with private bathroom). This place offers free pick-ups from the airport.

At 95 Annie St is the long-running *Atoa House Travellers Hostel* (☎ 3358 4507). It's a quiet and laid-back place spread over three old Queenslander houses, with dorms for $14, singles/doubles for $25/30 and self-contained flats at $42 for up to three people or $56 for up to five. You can camp in their big shady backyard for $7.

South Brisbane/West End The *Sly Fox* (☎ 3384 0022), on the corner of Melbourne and Hope Sts in South Brisbane, occupies the top section of an old pub. It's a lively place with bands in the bar downstairs. It's a little shabby, can be noisy and the kitchen is barely adequate, but the location is good. Dorm beds are $14, twins and doubles $32 ($38 with en suite).

Somewhere to Stay (☎ 3846 2858), at 45 Brighton Rd in the West End, is one of

Brisbane's biggest hostels. It has good facilities including a pool, spacious courtyards and a cafe with evening meals for $5, although it can seem a bit impersonal. There are two sections – rooms in the newer section have TV, fridge and private bathroom. Dorms cost from $11 to $15, singles from $20 to $25 and doubles/twins from $28 to $35 ($45 with en suite).

A short distance away is the family-run *Durham Villa* (☎ 3844 6853) at 17 Laura St. It's a small, laid-back hostel with a pool and spacious gardens; dorm beds are $12, and singles/doubles $24/28.

The *Brisbane Backpackers Resort* (☎ 3844 9956) at 110 Vulture St in the West End opposite the old *Swagman's Rest* is a new, 200-bed, purpose-built hostel with excellent facilities, including swimming pool, sauna and tennis court. Beds in four-bed rooms, each with attached bath, TV and fridge, cost $15.

East Brisbane Farther from the centre in a quiet suburban street is *Courtney Place Backpackers* (☎ 3891 5166) at 50 Geelong St. This family-run place is in a two-storey house built many years ago by a dentist with 18 children! A bed in a four or eight-bed dorm costs $12, and singles/doubles are $30. This place has an in-house travel agent. They also have a couple of good self-contained two-bedroom flats down the road, which cost $45 a double or $55 a triple.

Guesthouses & B&Bs *Annie's Shandon Inn* (☎ 3831 8684), a 10-minute walk uphill from the city centre at 405 Upper Edward St, is a charming and friendly small hotel with singles/doubles from $40/50 ($50/60 with private bathroom), including a light breakfast. The hotel has laundry facilities, a TV room and a small car park at the rear.

The *Yale Inner City Inn* (☎ 3832 1663), next to Annie's at 413 Upper Edward St, charges $30/42 with a light breakfast. The rooms and facilities are oldish and uninspiring, but it's clean and has a laundry, TV room and car park.

There are some very good B&Bs near the city centre. *Thornbury House B&B* (☎ 3832 5985), at 1 Thornbury St in Spring Hill, is an 1886 Queenslander house charmingly renovated, with four excellent doubles at $80 and five singles at $45, all with shared facilities. In Paddington, *Waverley B&B* (☎ 3369 8973) at 5 Latrobe Terrace has two excellent guest units downstairs with their own entrance, bathroom and modern kitchen. Singles/doubles are $35/65, and there are good weekly rates.

The *Boronia Lodge B&B* (☎ 3254 1371), is a comfortable 1930s family home at 37 Oxlade Drive in New Farm. It charges $40/60 for singles/doubles. Nearby at 75 Sydney St, *Edward Lodge* (☎ 3254 1078) is an excellent two-storey guesthouse for gay men and lesbian women. Singles/doubles with en suite are $50/60.

Self-Contained Apartments The *Dahrl Court Apartments* (☎ 3832 3458), at 45 Phillips St, Spring Hill, have been recommended by several travellers. These renovated 1930s apartments are comfortable, well-equipped and good value at $65/75 for singles/doubles, or $100 for four people.

Another good option is the *Dorchester Inn Self-Contained Units* (☎ 3831 2967) at 484 Upper Edward St. These renovated spacious units have cooking facilities and private bathrooms and cost $60/70/80 for singles/doubles/triples.

Spring Hill Terraces (☎ 3854 1048) at 260 Water St in Spring Hill, is an attractive and modern place with two-bedroom apartments with all the mod-cons for $69 a double plus $8 for extras. They also have budget rooms at $40 and motel-style units at $56.

Hotels & Motels There are some decent budget motels around Wickham Terrace or the city's edge. The *Astor Motel* (☎ 3831 9522), at No 193, has renovated singles/doubles with air-con from $59/65 and larger units from $79/85. *Marrs Townhouse* (☎ 3831 5388), at No 391 Wickham Terrace, has reasonable units with shared bathroom at $40/55, or from $55/65 with private bathroom, while at No 333, the budget *Soho Club Motel* (☎ 3831 7722) charges $46/49.

The *Sportsman's Hotel* (☎ 3831 2892) at 130 Leichhardt St in Spring Hill has accommodation for gay men, with pub-style rooms upstairs at $25/40.

There's a string of motels along Main St, (the continuation of the Story Bridge), in Kangaroo Point. One of the best is *Ryan's on the River* (☎ 3391 1011) at 269 Main St, which has units from $75. Farther south are a couple of cheaper options: the *Kangaroo Motel* (☎ 3391 1145), at 624 Main St, and the *Southern Cross Motel* (☎ 3391 2881), at 721 Main St; both have budget rooms from $45.

If you're looking to splurge, the *Ridge Hotel* (☎ 3831 5000) on the corner of Leichhardt and Henry Sts in Spring Hill is a well-located mid-range hotel with rooms from $91 and self-contained suites from $120.

Places to Eat

Brisbane's restaurant and cafe scene has blossomed in recent years, and there's no shortage of good eateries in the city and surrounding areas. Many places take advantage of the balmy climate by providing outdoor eating areas.

The *Courier Mail Good Food Guide* ($12.95) is a comprehensive guide to Brisbane's best eateries, although it devotes most of its attention to the more up-market places.

City There's an abundance of daytime eateries in the city centre catering for the hordes of office workers and shoppers. There are also some good restaurants, especially in the Riverside Centre and Eagle St Pier complexes where you can enjoy fine river views while you dine.

The Queen St Mall abounds with possibilities: *Jimmy's on the Mall* has three open-air cafes along the mall serving everything from sandwiches to steak – one of them is open 24 hours a day. There are some good food courts just off the mall, including *Jo Jo's* at 130 Queen St and *Food on Q* in the Broadway on

the Mall complex. The Wintergarden shopping complex also has two food courts, the straightforward *Tastes on the Go* on the 1st level and the more up-market *New Orleans Restaurant* on the 3rd level.

The *Shingle Inn* at 254 Edward St has dishes such as chicken Maryland, grilled cheese on toast, and scones with jam and cream. *Planet Energy* at 171 Edward St has healthy, energy-enhancing drinks made from yoghurt, fresh fruits, honey and other interesting ingredients.

Zane's Cafe, in the basement of the Metro Arts building at 109 Edward St, specialises in modern Italian food and is open for breakfast, lunch and dinner. The *Port Office Hotel* on the corner of Edward and Margaret Sts is popular with office workers at lunchtime with dishes such as T-bone steak or fish & chips with salad for $4.95.

For a good, cheap feed, *Govinda's Restaurant*, upstairs at 99 Elizabeth St, offers filling vegetarian meals for $5 for all you can eat; it's run by the Hare Krishnas. It's open weekdays for lunch and Friday and Sunday for dinner. Nearby is *Parrots*, a stylish, licensed gourmet burger restaurant. McDonald's certainly wouldn't recognise the fare that's dished up in this popular place. The various burgers cost from $8 to $10.50.

The *Queensland Irish Association*, upstairs at 175 Elizabeth St, is a lively Irish club, which welcomes visitors and has a bistro with Irish stew, beef and Guinness pie and the like, with main courses in the $5 to $7 range. Next door, *Caffe Libri* is a good little cafe inside the American Bookstore – you can get a huge bowl of home-made soup with bread for $4.50.

On the Riverfront Two of Brisbane's best and most popular food complexes front the Brisbane River at the north-eastern end of the city. At the Eagle St Pier, *Il Centro* (☎ 3221 6090) is an impressive Italian restaurant. It's licensed, with pasta from $15 to $18 and other main courses from $18 to $21. *Fuddruckers* is a groovy burger joint with chicken, fish and beef burgers in the $5 to $9

QUEENSLAND

range, and *Pier Nine* is a sophisticated oyster bar and seafood restaurant.

At the Riverside Centre, the award-winning restaurant *Michael's* (☎ 3832 5522) specialises in classical cuisine with an emphasis on seafood – main dishes range from $21 to $26. Slightly more affordable are the stalls in the nearby *On The Deck*, a good food court with plenty of choices at reasonable prices.

South Bank There are about a dozen restaurants and cafes in the South Bank Parklands – pick up a copy of the park plan from the information centre at the entrance. *Captain Snapper*, a large seafood and steak restaurant just south of the Stanley St Plaza, has a good selection of meals ranging from $5 to $15 (plus $2.95 for the all-you-can-eat salad and fresh fruit bar), and a takeaway section with tables by the canal.

The Riverside Restaurants building, on the riverfront near the Gondwana Sanctuary, houses three places: *Cafe San Marco*, a stylish open-fronted cafe; the *Wang Dynasty* Asian restaurant, which has a $7.80 lunch special and $16 evening banquet menus on weeknights; and the up-market *Lo Ti Amo* Italian restaurant upstairs.

Sirocco, in the Waterway Cafes complex, is a large Mediterranean cafe/restaurant with Spanish, Italian and Greek food, and main meals are about $15.

Farther south on the Boardwalk, *Ned Kelly's Bush Tucker Restaurant* has outdoor tables and live music on weekends, and specialises in Aussie tucker including witchetty grubs, emu fillets and crocodile satays, with main dishes in the $17 to $25 range. Next door, *Chez Laila* is a Lebanese cafe with a fascinating range of desserts and pastries, and coffee that packs a punch.

Spring Hill The *Spring Hill Hotel*, on the corner of Upper Edward and Leichhardt Sts, has cheap pub food with lunches from $2.95. Try the *Oriental Bangkok* at 454 Upper Edward St for excellent Thai food – mains start from $12.

Papa Mio (☎ 3831 1363), at 48

Leichhardt St, is a stylish Italian bistro set in a wonderfully converted chapel, with main courses ranging from $12 to $16. *Harold' Cafe*, at 466 Boundary St, is a casual court yard bistro with pasta for about $11 and othe mains around $14; they also have a goo gourmet takeaway section.

Fortitude Valley & New Farm The Valley i one of the best eating areas to explore and especially on weekends, it's bustling with crowds of people wandering the streets eating at outdoor tables and spilling out o the many pubs and bars.

Duncan St, between Ann and Wickham Sts, has been transformed into Brisbane' Chinatown and there are lots of Chinese Thai, Vietnamese and Korean restaurants in this area. The excellent *Enjoy Inn*, on th corner of Wickham and Duncan Sts is ope for lunch and dinner every day. It's quit up-market but its banquets ($18.80 o $22.80) are a bargain. A good cheaper optio is the *Universal Noodle Restaurant* at 14 Wickham St. It's not flash but has plenty o dishes between $5 and $8. At 194 Wickham St, the *Vietnamese Restaurant* is also prett basic but very popular, with most main between $6 and $9 and banquet menus fror $12. The *Seoul Restaurant*, at 178 Wickhar St, serves fairly authentic Korean dishe ranging from $6 to $10, and also has se menus from $12.

There's a good produce market and a international foodhall inside *McWhirter Marketplace* on the corner of Brunswick an Wickham Sts. Farther up the Brunswick S Mall, *Mellino's* is a casual bistro that stay open 24 hours and has cooked breakfasts fo $4 and pasta and pizza under $8.

Up the road at 360 Brunswick St, *Caf Europe* is a fun and hectic French cafe/res taurant with good pasta for $10.90 and othe mains from $14 to $16. The popula *Giardinetto's* next door at No 366, is a smal traditional Italian bistro with very good past for about $10 and other mains for about $15

Around the corner at 683 Ann St, th famous *Lucky's Trattoria* is a bustling, nc frills Italian eatery featuring weird loca artwork and hearty meals in the $8 to $16 range. It's BYO and has a separate vegetarian menu.

At 630 Brunswick St in New Farm, the *Baan Thai* has reasonably priced mains between $8 and $12. At *Famish*, at No 640, you can get a filling and very good hot roast meal – pork, chicken, lamb or beef with vegies – for about $10. The *Continental Cafe*, just off Brunswick St at 21 Baker St, is a little gem of a place with pasta and risotto ($10), gourmet pizza ($6 to $9) and main meals from $10 to $16.

Breakfast Creek On the north side of a bend in the Brisbane River, the famous *Breakfast Creek Hotel*, a great rambling building dating from 1889, is a real Brisbane institution. It's long been an ALP and trade union hang-out. In the public bar, the beer is still drawn from a wooden keg. The pub's open-air *Spanish Garden Steak House* is renowned for its steaks and spare ribs, and a huge feed will set you back between $12 and $18; there are daily specials for about $6.

Petrie Terrace & Paddington Both areas have plenty of interesting cafes, restaurants, pubs and bars, most of which are scattered along the winding route of Caxton St/Given Terrace.

On the corner of Petrie Terrace and Caxton St, *Casablanca* is a popular Latin American restaurant, bar and dance club. Down the road at 28 Caxton St, the *Mediterraneo Cafe-Bar* specialises in gourmet-style pizza, pasta and salads, with dishes from $10 to $14.

The *Sultan's Kitchen* (☎ 3368 2194), at 163 Given Terrace, is a very popular BYO Indian restaurant with great curries. They have a lunchtime smorgasbord for $12.95, and at dinner mains are about $14. It's open for lunch and dinner daily (except Saturday lunch) – book on weekends. Nearby at No 215, the *Jakarta Indonesian restaurant* is also popular.

Farther west along Given Terrace, at No 235, the atmospheric *Red Chair Cafe* does excellent gourmet burgers ($9 to $12) as well as breakfasts, pastries, pasta and sandwiches.

At No 267, the very popular *King Tut's Wa Wa Hut* is a great spot for breakfast, lunch or dinner, with an outdoor terrace and good salads, pasta, burgers, juices and sandwiches, all reasonably priced.

West End & Highgate Hill The West End has a couple of good areas for budget eaters to explore. At 181 Boundary St, *Caffe Tempo* is a hip little streetfront eatery with great cooked breakfasts from $6, focaccia and salads for about $6 and pasta and other mains averaging $11. Nearby at No 171 is *Wholly Munchies*, a good wholefoods cafe and takeaway with healthy sandwiches, juices and home-cooked goodies. Across the road at No 142, *Cafe Babylon* has a menu that is half-vegetarian and half-carnivorous, with mains in the $8 to $11 range.

Around the corner at 88 Vulture St, *King Ahiram's* is a cheap and cheerful Lebanese place with takeaway chicken or felafel rolls from $2.50 to $3 and mains from $8 to $11.

Hardgrave Rd in the West End has a cluster of popular and good-value eateries, all within 100 metres of each other. *Kim Thanh* at No 93 has Vietnamese and Chinese dishes from $5 to $7; *Khan's Kitchen* at No 75 serves traditional Pakistani food with all dishes under $7 and a feast menu for $10; and *Chutney Mary's* at No 65 is a more up-market 'Anglo-Indian' restaurant with mains from $13 to $17.

Over in Highgate Hill, try the *Genji Japanese Kitchen* at 9 Gladstone Rd for affordable Japanese food – their banquet menus start from $20. At 36 Gladstone Rd, *Thai on High* is a tiny Thai eatery with only six tables and a roaring takeaway trade. Dishes are all about $8.

Entertainment

The free entertainment papers – *Time Off*, *Rave* and *The Scene* – have comprehensive information on bands, pubs, clubs and theatre, as well as movie listings and reviews.

Ticketworld (☎ 13 1931) is a centralised booking agency for major events and sports. The Queensland Cultural Centre's Dial 'n'

Charge service (☎ 3846 4646) handles bookings for the Performing Arts Complex.

Pubs & Live Music Plenty of pubs, bars and clubs feature live music. Pubs stay open until midnight or 1 am, clubs much later. Cover charges are from $6 for local bands, but much more for touring bands.

At the top of Ann and Queen Sts in the city, the long-running *Orient Hotel* features everything from rock, blues and indie pop to jazz by students from the local conservatorium. *Homebass* in the Brisbane Tavern on the corner of Ann and Wharf Sts has a funk/soul night on Friday and a reggae dance party on Saturday.

In the Valley, there's *Dooley's Hotel* on the corner of Brunswick and McLachlan Sts (free live music in its downstairs Irish Bar Wednesday to Saturday night), *Ric's Cafe-Bar* in the Brunswick St Mall (live bands on weekends) and, on the corner of Wickham and Allen Sts, the *Wickham Hotel* (this is a gay-oriented pub with big crowds, drag shows and great dance music).

Over in Paddington, popular pubs with live music include the up-market *Barracks Hotel*, on the corner of Petrie Terrace and Caxton St, the *Caxton Hotel*, farther along Caxton St, and the *Paddo Tavern*, about one km farther east on Given Terrace (huge western-style saloon with lots of urban cowboys and cowgirls).

Other good rock pubs include the *Port Office Hotel*, on the corner of Edward and Margaret Sts in the city, *St Paul's Tavern*, on the corner of Leichhardt and Wharf Sts in Spring Hill and the *Sly Fox Hotel* in Melbourne St in South Brisbane.

Backpacker Nights Quite a few pubs put on special nights for backpackers, with drinking competitions, giveaways, cheap drinks and music. The *Bomb Shelter* section of the Story Bridge Hotel, at 200 Main St in Kangaroo Point, is big on a Monday with 'Monday Madness', while the *Brunswick Hotel* in Brunswick St in New Farm has backpacker party nights on Friday.

Nightclubs Brisbane has a lively nightclub scene, especially if you know where to look. Mainstream clubs are mostly based in and around the city, and the alternative scene is centred in Fortitude Valley.

Good city nightclubs include *Crash & Burn*, a basement bar on the corner of Mary and Edward Sts; *Babble On* on Elizabeth St; the *Mary St Nightclub & Cafe Sports* in Mary St near the Edward St corner; and the up-market *Someplace Else* in the Sheraton Hotel at 249 Turbot St.

The Underground, on Petrie Terrace in Paddington, is Brisbane's most popular mainstream nightclub, while nearby *Casablanca* is a busy Latin-American dance club bar and restaurant.

The Valley has some fairly wild nightclubs including *The Beat* at 677 Ann St (sweatbox dance club and gay cocktail bar) and *The Tube* at 210 Wickham St (grungy warehouse-style dance club).

Two of the most interesting alternative venues are *The Zoo*, at 711 Ann St in the Valley, and *Van Gogh's Earlobe*, at 588 Stanley St in South Brisbane. Both feature live bands, performance art, dance shows and more – well worth checking out.

Brisbane has a lively gay and lesbian scene. In Spring Hill, the *Sportsman's Hotel* at 130 Leichhardt St has everything from drag shows to talent quests, while *Options* at 18 Little Edward St is a popular nightclub with live shows upstairs and a dance club downstairs. In the Valley, there's *Signal* at 185 Brunswick St and *Terminus* at 249 Brunswick St.

Jazz & Blues The *Jazz & Blues Club*, on the ground floor of the Travelodge (next to the transit centre), is the city's major jazz and soul venue and has good local and international acts. The *Brisbane Jazz Club* (☎ 3391 2006), down by the riverside at 1 Annie St Kangaroo Point, is where the jazz purists head on Saturday and Sunday nights. For a Sunday afternoon jazz fix, check out the *Story Bridge Hotel* or *Snug Harbour Dockside*, both in Kangaroo Point.

Theatre The *Performing Arts Complex* in the Queensland Cultural Centre in South Brisbane features concerts, plays, dance performances and film screenings in its three venues. Brisbane's other main theatres include the *Suncorp Piazza* at South Bank (regular concerts and performances, often free); the *Metro Arts Theatre* at 109 Edward St (community arts and alternative theatre); the *Suncorp Theatre* at 179 Turbot St (performances by the Queensland Ballet and Queensland Theatre companies); and the *Brisbane Arts Theatre* at 210 Petrie Terrace (amateur theatre).

Cinemas In the Queen St Mall, the *Hoyts Regent Theatres* (☎ 3229 5544) screen both art-house and mainstream movies. Specialising in art-house cinema are the *Dendy* (☎ 3211 3244) at 346 George St in the city, the *Classic* (☎ 3393 1066) at 963 Stanley St, East Brisbane, and the Schonell (☎ 3371 1879) at the University of Queensland in St Lucia. The *Village Twin Cinemas* in Brunswick St, New Farm, has $5 nights Tuesday, Wednesday and Thursday.

Casino The *Treasury Casino* is open 24 hours a day with over 100 gaming tables, as well as cafes, bars and restaurants. The dress code is 'smart-casual'. Plenty of pubs and clubs have poker machines.

Comedy *Snug Harbour Dockside* (☎ 3891 6644), at the Dockside complex in Kangaroo Point, is a stylish cabaret-style venue and Brisbane's home of stand-up comedy. *Crazies Comedy Restaurant* (☎ 3369 0555), on the corner of Caxton and Judge Sts in Petrie Terrace, is always a fun night out, with dinner-and-show tickets from $36 to $45.

Sport You can see interstate cricket matches and international Test cricket at the Brisbane Cricket Ground (the Gabba) in Woolloongabba, just south of Kangaroo Point. The cricket season runs from October to March.

During the other half of the year, rugby league is the big spectator sport. Local heroes, the Brisbane Broncos, play their home games at the ANZ/QE2 Stadium in Upper Mt Gravatt. Brisbane also has an Australian Football League club, the Brisbane Bears, now based at the Gabba. Brisbane's major horse-racing tracks are at Doomben and Eagle Farm.

Getting There & Away
Brisbane's transit centre, on Roma St about half a km west of the centre, is the main terminus for all long-distance buses and trains (bookings also). The centre has shops, banks, a post office, plenty of places to eat and drink, an accommodation booking service on level three and an information office on level two. Left-luggage lockers are on level three ($4 a day); there's also a cloakroom where you can store items longer term.

Air Ansett has an office on the corner of George and Queen Sts. Qantas has a domestic travel office at 247 Adelaide St and an international office nearby at No 241 (1st floor). Both have frequent daily flights to the southern capitals and north to the main Queensland centres. Standard one-way fares include Sydney ($274), Melbourne ($399), Adelaide ($494), Darwin ($615) and Perth ($683), and within Queensland, Townsville ($330), Rockhampton ($234), Mackay ($283), Cairns ($400) and Mt Isa (Ansett only – $406).

The little outback airline Flight West goes to Roma ($180 one way), Charleville ($241), Quilpie ($289), Blackall ($283), Longreach ($322), Winton ($362) and Birdsville ($417). Brisbane is also a busy international arrival and departure point with frequent flights to Asia, Europe, the Pacific islands, North America, New Zealand and Papua New Guinea.

Bus The bus companies all have booking desks on level three of the transit centre. If you're shopping around for fare deals, try calling Dial-A-Coach (☎ 3221 2225), a bus-fare broker.

Greyhound Pioneer and McCafferty's both run from Sydney to Brisbane. The coastal run along the Pacific Highway takes about 17 hours; the inland New England Highway trip takes a couple of hours less. The usual fare is about $70, but Kirklands (☎ 3236 4444) and Lindsay's (☎ 1800 027 944) often have cheaper deals.

Between Brisbane and Melbourne, the most direct route is the Newell Highway, which takes about 24 hours. Again, Greyhound Pioneer and McCafferty's travel this route daily. The fare between Brisbane and Melbourne is about $125.

To Adelaide, the shortest route (via Dubbo) takes about 31 hours and costs about $155.

North to Cairns, Greyhound Pioneer and McCafferty's run five buses a day. The approximate fares and journey times to places along the coast are as follows:

Destination	Time	Cost
Noosa Heads	2 hours	$14
Hervey Bay	4 hours	$33
Rockhampton	9 hours	$60
Mackay	13 hours	$87
Townsville	19 hours	$115
Cairns	24 hours	$133

McCafferty's and Greyhound Pioneer also run daily services to the Northern Territory – it's a 46-hour trip to Darwin ($240) via Longreach (17 hours, $80) and Mt Isa (24 hours, $120).

Train Countrylink has a daily XTP service between Brisbane and Sydney. The northbound train runs overnight and the south-bound train runs during the day. The trip takes 13½ hours and costs $98/142 in economy/1st class, and $224.50 in a sleeper.

North from Brisbane, the *Spirit of Capricorn* runs the 639 km to Rockhampton daily (9½ hours, $67 economy only). The *Sunlander* departs three days a week for the 1631-km journey to Cairns (32 hours; $243 1st-class sleeper, $159 economy sleeper, $129 economy seat), via Mackay and Townsville. The *Spirit of the Tropics* is an all-economy 'party train' that covers the same route twice a week.

The luxurious *Queenslander* does the

Brisbane to Cairns run weekly. All passengers travel 1st class, with sleeping berths and all meals included in the fares. Sectors and fares include Brisbane-Mackay (16.5 hours, $377), Brisbane-Townsville (23 hours, $433) and Brisbane-Cairns (32 hours, $433). For another $270, you can take your car with you from Brisbane to Cairns.

The *Westlander* runs on the inland route to Charleville via Roma twice a week; the trip takes 15½ hours and costs $77 for an economy seat, $172 for a 1st-class sleeper.

For reservations, telephone Queensland Rail (☎ 13 2232) or call into its Railway Travel Centre (☎ 3235 1323) beside Central Station, at 305 Edward Sts.

Car, 4WD & Motorbike Rental If you have a car, beware of the two-hour parking limit in the city and inner suburbs – there are no signs, and the parking inspectors are merciless!

The big rental firms have offices in Brisbane and there are a number of smaller operators, including Cut Rate Rentals (☎ 3854 1809), Crown Rent-A-Car (☎ 3854 1848), Dam Cheap (☎ 3252 1177) and National (☎ 3854 1499). Some companies do one-way rentals to Cairns and the southern capitals, depending on availability, the season, and the hire period – it's best to ring around and haggle.

You can hire 4WDs from around $100 a day, usually with a three-day minimum. Operators include Four Wheel Drive Hire Service (☎ 3357 9077) and Allterrain (☎ 3257 1101).

Australian Motorcycle Adventures (☎ 3865 3176) hire on and off-road bikes from $95 a day. They also do motorbike tours and have buy-back deals.

Getting Around
For bus, train and ferry transport information, ring the Trans-Info Service (☎ 13 1230); it operates daily from 6 am to 10 pm. There's a train information office at Central Station, and bus and ferry information is available at the Queen St Information Centre

and in the Bus Station Information Centre under the Queen St Mall.

To/From the Airport Brisbane's airport is north-east of the city, with the new international/domestic terminal about 15 km away. Coachtrans (☎ 3236 1000) runs the Skytrans shuttle bus between the transit centre and the airport, with services about every half-hour between 5 am and 9 pm. The fare is $5.40 ($6.50 for a hotel pick-up). Coachtrans also has direct services from the airport to the Gold Coast, and Suncoast Pacific (☎ 3236 1901) has a direct service to the Sunshine Coast.

A taxi to the centre costs about $18. Avis, Budget, Hertz and Thrifty have car rental desks at the airport.

Bus The red City Circle bus No 333 does a clockwise loop round the area along George, Adelaide, Wharf, Eagle, Mary, Albert and Alice Sts every five minutes on weekdays between 8 am and 5.45 pm; rides are 60c.

In addition to the normal city buses, there are Cityxpress buses that run between the suburbs and the city centre, and Rockets, which are fast peak-hour commuter buses. From the transit centre, you need to walk into the city centre to pick up some buses. Most above-ground bus stops in the city are colour coded to help you find the right one. The underground bus station beneath the Myer Centre is used mainly by Cityxpresses and buses to/from the south of the city. There is a map of the station, above ground in the mall on the corner of Queen and Albert Sts.

In the city centre, buses cost just 60c a trip. Other fares are on a zone system costing $1.20, $1.80, $2.40 and $2.80 for zones 1, 2, 3 and 4 respectively. Special deals include the Day Rover ($5.50 for a day's unlimited travel on buses and ferries) and the RoverLink ($8 for a day's unlimited travel on buses, ferries and trains). There are cheaper off-peak ticket deals.

Buses run every 10 to 20 minutes Monday to Friday till about 6 pm, and on Saturday morning. Services are less frequent on weekday evenings, Saturday afternoon and evening, and Sunday. On Sunday, buses stop at 7 pm, and on other days at 11 pm.

Useful buses from the city centre include Nos 177 or 178 to Fortitude Valley and New Farm (from the brown stops on Adelaide St between King George Square and Edward St). Bardon bus No 144 to Paddington leaves from the red stops opposite the transit centre or from outside the Coles store on Adelaide St.

Bus Nos 160, 180 or 190 to Fortitude Valley and Breakfast Creek leave from the yellow stops on Edward St between Adelaide and Queen Sts. Bus No 177 to West End leaves from the brown stop on Edward St, opposite Anzac Square.

Bayside Buslines (☎ 3245 3333) runs between Brisbane and the southern Bayside, while Hornibrook Bus Lines (☎ 3284 1622) runs between Brisbane and the northern Bayside.

Train The fast Citytrain network has seven lines, out to Ipswich, Beenleigh and Cleveland in the south and Pinkenba, Shorncliffe, Caboolture and Ferny Grove in the north. You can buy Day Rover tickets ($8.50) a day ahead, from any station. These give you unlimited train travel for one day (after 9 am on weekdays).

All trains go through Roma St, Central and Brunswick St stations, and a journey in the city central area is $1.20.

Boat Brisbane has a fast, efficient ferry service along and across the Brisbane River. Cross-river ferries cost $1.20 one way and generally run Monday to Saturday every 10 to 15 minutes from around dawn until after 11 pm; operating hours are shorter on Sunday. You can take a bicycle on the ferry for free. Maps of the ferry routes are available at all the stops, as well as information centres.

Bicycle Brisbane is a good cycling city with some excellent bike tracks, particularly around the Brisbane River. A good way to spend a day is to ride the riverside bicycle track from the city Botanic Gardens out to

QUEENSLAND

Queensland University – it's about seven km one way.

Brisbane Bicycle Sales (☎ 3229 2433) at 87 Albert St and New Farm Mountain Bikes (☎ 3254 0544) at 697 Brunswick St in New Farm both hire out mountain bikes from $20 a day.

Moreton Bay

Moreton Bay, at the mouth of the Brisbane River, is said to have 365 islands. The larger islands shelter a long stretch of coast: South Stradbroke Island is only just north of the Gold Coast, while Bribie Island is only just south of the Sunshine Coast. In between are North Stradbroke and Moreton islands.

THE BAYSIDE

Redcliffe, 35 km north of Brisbane, was the first White settlement in Queensland. The local Aboriginal people called the place Humpybong, or 'Dead Houses', and the name is still applied to the peninsula. Redcliffe is now an outer suburb of Brisbane and a popular retirement place. South of Redcliffe, **Sandgate** is another long-running seaside resort, now also more of an outer suburb.

Coastal towns south of the Brisbane River mouth include **Wynnum, Manly, Cleveland**

and **Redland Bay**. Cleveland is the main access point for North Stradbroke Island. There's an 1864 lighthouse at Cleveland Point and the 1853 Cleveland courthouse is now a restaurant.

Manly is an attractive seaside suburb with boat harbours and yacht clubs along the waterfront. *Nomads Moreton Bay Lodge* (☎ 3396 3020), in the heart of Manly Village on Cambridge Pde, is a well set up backpackers hostel with its own cafe and live acoustic music most nights. Dorms cost from $12 to $14 and doubles from $20 to $25. The hostel can arrange sailing trips ($45) and two-day tours to Moreton Island ($145).

The Redland Bay area is a fertile market garden for Brisbane and the Strawberry Festival is held on the first weekend in September.

Ormiston House in Wellington St, Ormiston, is a very fine home built in 1862 and open for inspection between March and November on Sunday afternoons. The first commercially grown sugar cane in Queensland came from this site.

NORTH STRADBROKE ISLAND (pop 2400)

Until 1896, the two Stradbroke islands were one but in that year a storm cut the sand spit joining the two at Jumpinpin. Today, South Stradbroke is virtually uninhabited but it's a popular day trip from the Gold Coast.

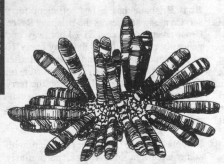

Sea urchins can be found in the shallow waters along the Moreton Bay coastline

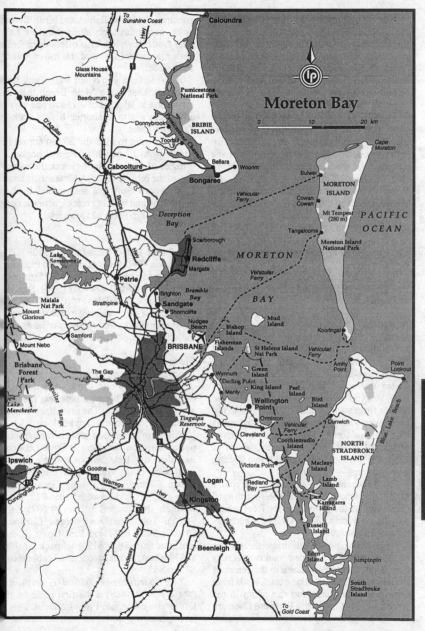

Moreton Bay

To Sunshine Coast
Caloundra
Glass House Mountains
Woodford
Beerburrum
Pumicestone National Park
D'Aguilar Hwy
Donnybrook
BRIBIE ISLAND
Toorbul
Caboolture
Bellara
Woorim
Bongaree
Vehicular Ferry
Deception Bay
Lake Samsonvale
Petrie
Scarborough
Redcliffe
Margate
Bulwer
MORETON ISLAND
Cowan Cowan
Mt Tempest (280 m)
Tangalooma
Moreton Island National Park
Cape Moreton
PACIFIC OCEAN
MORETON
BAY
0 10 20 km
Maiala Nat Park
Mount Glorious
Strathpine
Brighton
Bramble Bay
Sandgate
Shorncliffe
Nudgee Beach
Samford
Mount Nebo
BRISBANE
Bishop Island
Fisherman Islands
Mud Island
St Helena Island Nat Park
Kooringal
Vehicular Ferry
Brisbane Forest Park
The Gap
D'Aguilar Range
Wynnum
Darling Point
Manly
Green Island
King Island
Wellington Point
Ormiston
Peel Island
Bird Island
Amity Point
Point Lookout
Lake Manchester
Cleveland
Vehicular Ferry
Dunwich
Coochiemudlo Island
NORTH STRADBROKE ISLAND
Blue Lake Beach
Ipswich
Goodna
Warrego Hwy
Cunningham Hwy
Logan
Victoria Point
Macleay Island
Kingston
Redland Bay
Lamb Island
Karragarra Island
Russell Island
Beenleigh
Lindesay Hwy
Mount Lindesay Hwy
Pacific Hwy
Eden Island
Jumpinpin
To Gold Coast
South Stradbroke Island

QUEENSLAND

North Stradbroke is a larger island with a permanent population and, although it is a popular escape from Brisbane it's still relatively unspoilt (but the Christmas and Easter holidays can get pretty hectic). 'Straddie' is a sand island and, despite the sand-mining operations in the south, there's plenty of vegetation and beautiful scenery in the north.

In 1828, Dunwich was established on the west coast of the island as a quarantine station for immigrants. In 1850 a ship brought cholera and the cemetery tells the sad story of the 28 victims of the outbreak that followed. Dunwich, Amity Point and Point Lookout, the three small centres on the island, are all in the north and connected by sealed roads. Most of the southern part of the island is closed to visitors due to ongoing sand mining; the only road into this swampier, more remote area is a private mining company road.

The Stradbroke Island Visitor Centre (☎ (07) 3409 9555) is near the ferry terminal in Dunwich.

Activities

Straddie's best beaches are around Point Lookout, where there's a series of points and bays around the headland, and then the endless stretch of white sand at Main Beach. There are some excellent surfing breaks here, and you can hire surfboards and boogie boards from various places. A surf lifesaving club overlooks Main Beach. The island is also famous for its fishing, and the annual Straddie Classic, held in August, is one of Australia's richest and best-known fishing competitions.

On the ocean side you may even spot a humpback whale or two on their northward migration to the Great Barrier Reef where they breed during winter. Dolphins and porpoises are common.

Apart from beach activities, there's the island to explore. A sealed road runs across from Dunwich to Blue Lake in the centre of the island; a 2.7-km walking track leads from the road to the lake. You can swim in the freshwater lake or nearby Tortoise Lagoon, or walk along the track and watch for snakes,

goannas, golden wallabies and birds. Brown Lake, about three km along the Blue Lak road from Dunwich, also offers deep fresh water swimming, and is more easil accessible.

Alternatively, you could walk south from Point Lookout along Main Beach then 2. km inland to Blue Lake – 11 km one way i all. There's also a shorter beach walk t Keyhole Lake.

If you want to hike the 20 km across th island from Dunwich to Point Lookout, number of dirt track loops break the monot ony of the bitumen road. A pleasant diversio is to Myora Springs, surrounded by lus vegetation and walking tracks, near the coas about four km north of Dunwich.

Tours

Stradbroke Island Tours (☎ (07) 3409 8051 runs good 4WD tours of the island includin a fishing trip or half-day tour ($25), a nigh tour ($12) or a full day tour ($50). Straddi Experience Canoe Trips (☎ (07) 3409 8279 offers a half-day canoeing trip to the island' mangrove creeks and freshwater lakes ($3 including transport and lunch).

Places to Stay

Dunwich and Amity Point are mainly resi dential centres. Point Lookout is the mai town and it has the best beaches, facilitie and accommodation. The town itself is quit spread out; it's about three km long.

There are some good council-run campin parks along the foreshore at Point Lookou including the *Adder Rock Camping Groun* at Rocky Point Beach and the *Cylinde Beach Caravan & Camping Ground*. Ten sites are $10, and powered sites $13. Boo through the council office (☎ (07) 340 9025). The *Stradbroke Island Carapar* (☎ (07) 3409 8127) on East Coast Rd ha tent sites from $8 to $13, backpacker cabin at $15 a bed, and self-contained cabins fror $43 to $55.

The *Stradbroke Island Guesthous* (☎ (07) 3409 8888) is the first place on th left as you come into Point Lookout. This i an impressive guesthouse with modern facil ities. A bed in a four-bed dorm costs $15, singles/doubles $35, and tariffs include the use of a surf ski and sandsailer. The guesthouse runs a pick-up bus from Brisbane, which leaves from opposite the transit centre every Monday, Wednesday and Friday at 2.30 pm, and also stops at hostels; you need to book, and it costs $5.

The next place is also on the main road, on the left just after the Stradbroke Hotel (the only pub on the island). The *Straddie Hostel* (☎ (07) 3409 8679) is in a neat two-storey beach-house. The large dorms each have their own kitchen and bathroom, and bunks cost $12 a night.

A little farther up the road on the right-hand side, the *Headland Chalet* (☎ (07) 3409 8252) is an old-style holiday village, with a collection of cabins scattered across a hillside overlooking beautiful Main Beach. It doesn't look much from the outside, but it's an interesting, arty place. The rooms have a fridge, tea and coffee-making gear, great views and a maximum of four beds. The cost is $20 per person for the first night and $15 for subsequent nights. There's a pool, a games and TV room, free washing machines and a small kitchen.

If you're thinking of staying a while, a holiday flat or house can be good value, especially outside the holiday seasons. There are several real estate agents, including the *Accommodation Centre* (☎ (07) 3409 8255).

Places to Eat

There are a couple of general stores selling groceries in Point Lookout, but it's worth bringing basic supplies as the price mark-up on the island is significant.

On the headland, the *Stradbroke Hotel* has a great beer garden with an ocean outlook, and live music on weekends. Its bistro has mains from $9 to $12 and specials for about $5.

Pasta Fino, in the Point Lookout Shopping Village in Endeavour St, is a modern, beachy cafe with pasta and pizzas from $9, Mexican food on Friday nights and Thai food on Sunday. The *Masonic Club* on East Coast Rd has good meals from $3.50 to $9;

it's open for lunch and dinner Wednesday to Sunday.

Getting There & Away

There are numerous ways of getting from central Brisbane to the island: a train or bus and water taxi or ferry; a through-bus; or your own vehicle.

Bus North Stradbroke Coach Service (☎ (07) 3807 4299) runs daily services between Brisbane and the island, combining a bus to Cleveland, a water taxi to the island and another bus to Point Lookout. The trip takes about two hours and the return fare is $24. Buses leave Brisbane from Stop 1 outside the transit centre, and stop at various other places (including hostels if you book).

Bayside Buslines (☎ (07) 245 3333) runs a weekday 40-minute service between Brisbane and Cleveland on the Bayside Bullet, as well as a regular service (Nos 621 and 622), which takes about an hour. Both cost $3.50 and depart about every half hour (less frequently at weekends) from Elizabeth St in central Brisbane. A shuttle bus operates from Cleveland to the ferry terminal.

Train Trains leave Brisbane for Cleveland about every half-hour from 5 am. The journey takes about an hour.

Water Taxi Two water-taxi companies operate between Cleveland and Dunwich. Stradbroke Ferries (☎ (07) 3286 2666) has three boats – the *Spirit*, the *Pride* and the *Gateway* – and charges $9 return. There's also the *Stradbroke Flyer* (☎ (07) 3286 1964), which costs between $7.50 and $10, depending on the season. The trip takes 20 minutes and boats depart hourly on weekdays from 6 am to 7 pm, on Saturday to 6 pm and on Sunday to 6.30 pm.

Car Ferry Stradbroke Ferries also runs the vehicle ferry from Cleveland to Dunwich about 12 times a day. It costs $63 return for a vehicle plus passengers, and $7 return for pedestrians. Last departures from Cleveland

QUEENSLAND

are normally at 6 pm but there are late ferries on Friday at 7.30, 8 and 10 pm.

Getting Around

Stradbroke Island Coaches (☎ (07) 3807 4299) runs 10 services a day between the three main centres; Dunwich to Point Lookout costs $3.50, and short trips around Point Lookout cost 50c to $1.

You can rent a 4WD for $100 a day ($60 a half-day) from Point Lookout Hire (☎ (07) 3409 8353). The Stradbroke Island Guesthouse rents out motor-scooters for $15 an hour or $70 a day (less for guests).

MORETON ISLAND (pop 120)

North of Stradbroke, Moreton Island is less visited and still almost a wilderness. Apart from a few rocky headlands it's all sand, with Mt Tempest – towering to 280 metres – the highest coastal sandhill in the world. It's a strange landscape, alternating between bare sand, forest, lakes and swamps, with a 30-km surf beach along the eastern side. The island's birdlife is prolific, and at its northern tip is a **lighthouse**, built in 1857. Sandmining leases on the island have been cancelled and 96% of the island is now a national park. There are several wrecks off the west coast.

Moreton Island has no sealed roads but 4WD vehicles can travel along beaches and a few cross-island tracks – seek local advice

about tides and creek crossings. The QNP&WS publishes a map of the island, which you can get on the ferry, or from the QNP&WS office at False Patch Wrecks, which is between Cowan Cowan and Tangalooma. The Sunmap Tourist Map, also available on the ferries, is very good.

Tangalooma, halfway down the western side of the island, is a popular tourist resort sited at an old whaling station. The only other settlements, all on the west coast, are **Bulwer** near the north-west tip, **Cowan Cowan** between Bulwer and Tangalooma, and **Kooringal** near the southern tip. The shops at Kooringal and Bulwer are expensive, so bring what you can from the mainland. For a bit of shark-spotting, go to the Tangalooma Resort at 5 pm, when resort staff dump food waste off the end of the jetty.

Without your own vehicle, walking is the only way to get around, and you'll need several days to explore the island. There are some trails around the resort area, and there are quite a few decommissioned 4WD roads with good walks. It's about 14 km from Tangalooma or the Ben-Ewa camping ground on the west side to Eagers Creek camping ground on the east, then seven km up the beach to Blue Lagoon and a farther six to Cape Moreton at the north-eastern tip. There's a strenuous track to the summit of **Mt Tempest**, about three km inland from Eagers Creek; the views at the top are worth the effort.

Shark-spotting is a popular evening pastime at the Toongalooma Resort

About three km south and inland from Tangalooma is an area of bare sand known as the **Desert**, while the **Big Sandhills** and the **Little Sandhills** are towards the narrow southern end of the island. The biggest lakes and some swamps are in the north-east, and the west coast from Cowan Cowan past Bulwer is also swampy.

Tours

Sunrover Expeditions (☎ (07) 3203 4241) has good 4WD day trips ($80 with lunch) from Brisbane on Saturday, Sunday and Monday, and three-day camping trips ($250 all inclusive). The Tangalooma Resort (☎ (07) 3268 6333) runs cruises from Brisbane ($75 with a three-course dinner), departing from the Holt St wharf in Pinkeba every Friday at 5.30 pm.

Places to Stay

QNP&WS *camp sites*, with water, toilets and cold showers are at Ben-Ewa and False Patch Wrecks, both between Cowan Cowan and Tangalooma, and at Eagers Creek and Blue Lagoon on the island's east coast. Sites cost $3 per person per night. For information and camping permits, contact the QNP&WS (☎ (07) 227 8185) at 160 Ann St in Brisbane, or the ranger at False Patch Wrecks (☎ (07) 408 2710).

There are a few holiday flats or houses for rent at Kooringal, Cowan Cowan and Bulwer. A twin room at the *Tangalooma Resort* (☎ (07) 3268 6333) costs from $145 per night.

Getting There & Away

The *Tangalooma Flyer*, a fast catamaran operated by the Tangalooma Resort, leaves from a dock at Holt St, off Kingsford-Smith Drive in Eagle Farm, every day except Monday. You can use it for a day trip or for camping drop-offs; the return fare is $25 and you have to book.

The *Moreton Venture* (☎ (07) 3895 1000) is a vehicular ferry that runs five to six days a week from Whyte Island (at the southern side of the Brisbane River mouth) to Tangalooma or to Short Point. The return fare is

$85 for a 4WD (including passengers); pedestrians are charged $18 return.

Another ferry to the island is the *Combie Trader* (☎ (07) 3203 6399), with daily services between Scarborough and Bulwer (except Tuesday). One-way/return fares are $50/90 for a 4WD and four people, and $13/20 for pedestrians. The ferry also does day trips on Monday, Wednesday, Saturday and Sunday for $20 return.

ST HELENA ISLAND

Little St Helena Island, which is only six km from the mouth of the Brisbane River, was a high-security prison from 1867 to 1932. The island is now a national park. There are remains of several prison buildings, plus the first passenger tramway in Brisbane which, when built in 1884, had horse-drawn cars. Sandy beaches and mangroves alternate around the coast.

St Helena Guided Tours (☎ (07) 3260 7944) runs day trips ($29 including lunch) from the BP Marina on Kingsford-Smith Drive, Breakfast Creek, every Sunday and two or three other days a week, leaving at 9 am and returning at 5 pm. St Helena Ferries (☎ (07) 3393 3726) runs two to three trips a week on its *Cat o' Nine Tails* catamaran, leaving from Manly Harbour. The $23 return fare includes a one-hour tour and entry to the national park. You can reach Manly from central Brisbane in about 35 minutes by train.

OTHER ISLANDS
Coochie Island

Coochiemudlo Island is a 10-minute ferry ride from Victoria Point on the southern Bayside. It's a popular outing from the mainland, having good beaches, but it is more built-up than most other Moreton Bay islands you can visit. You can hire bicycles, boats, catamarans and surf skis on the island. The ferry runs continuously on weekends and holidays from 8 am to 5.30 or 6 pm, less often on other days.

Bay Isles

Russell, **Lamb**, **Karragarra** and **Macleay** islands, known as the Bay Isles, are between

QUEENSLAND

the southern end of North Stradbroke and the mainland. Russell is the largest (about seven km long), and the interesting Green Dragon Museum is in the north-west of the island. Bay Islands Ferries (☎ (07) 3286 2666), operating from the Banana St ramp in Redland Bay, does a loop around the isles three or four times a day; fares are $32 return for a car and passengers, or $2 each way for pedestrians.

Bribie Island

Bribie Island, at the northern end of Moreton Bay, is 31 km long but apart from the southern end, where there are a couple of small towns, the island is largely untouched. There's a bridge across Pumicestone Passage from the mainland to Bellara on the south-west coast. Bongaree, just south of Bellara, is the main town. Buses run there from Caboolture and Brisbane. Bongaree and Bellara, and Woorim on the south-east coast, have a few motels and holiday flats.

Gold Coast

Population 534,000

The Gold Coast is a 35-km strip of beaches running north from the New South Wales-Queensland border. It's the most thoroughly commercialised resort in Australia and is virtually one continuous development culminating in the high-rise splendour of Surfers Paradise.

This coast has been a holiday spot since the 1880s but only after WW II did developers start taking serious notice of Surfers. More than two million visitors a year come to the Gold Coast.

You can stay on the Gold Coast pretty cheaply, and there's quite a range of things to do – good surf beaches, excellent eating and entertainment possibilities and a hinterland with some fine natural features. There's also a huge variety of artificial 'attractions' and theme parks.

Orientation

The whole coast from Tweed Heads in New South Wales up to Main Beach, north of Surfers Paradise, is developed, but most of the real action is around Surfers itself. Tweed Heads and Coolangatta at the southern end are older, quieter, cheaper resorts. Moving north from there you pass through Kirra, Bilinga, Tugun, Currumbin, Palm Beach, Burleigh Heads, Miami, Nobby Beach, Mermaid Beach and Broadbeach – all lower-key resorts.

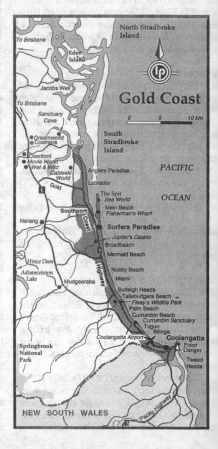

Southport, the oldest town in the area, is north and just inland from Surfers, behind the sheltered expanse of the Broadwater, which is fed by the Nerang and Coomera rivers. The Gold Coast Highway runs right along the coastal strip, leaving the Pacific Highway just north of Coolangatta and rejoining it inland from Southport.

The Gold Coast airport is at Coolangatta. Most buses to the Gold Coast travel the full length of the strip.

Information

The Gold Coast Tourism Bureau (☎ (07) 5538 4419), on the Cavill Ave Mall in Surfers Paradise, is open weekdays from 8 am to 5 pm, Saturday from 9 am to 5 pm and Sunday from 9 am to 3.30 pm.

In Coolangatta, the tourist information booth (☎ (07) 5536 7765) in the Beach House Plaza on the corner of Marine Pde and McLean St is open from Monday to Saturday. Just across the border, the Tweed Heads Visitor Centre (☎ (07) 5536 4244) is open daily.

There are plenty of free glossy booklets available, including *Wot's On*, *Destination Surfers Paradise* and *Point Out* – they have handy maps, as well as entertainment and eating details, although they are mostly full of ads.

Surfers Paradise

The centre of the Gold Coast is a real high-rise jungle; in fact there is such a skyscraper conglomeration that, in the afternoon, much of the beach is in shadow! Still, people pack in for the lights, activities, nightlife, shopping, restaurants, attractions and that strip of ocean sand.

Surfers has come a long way since 1936 when there was just the brand new Surfers Paradise Hotel, a little hideaway nine km from Southport. The hotel has now been swallowed up by a shopping/eating complex called the Paradise Centre.

Yet, despite all the changes and growth, at most times of year you don't usually have to go very far north or south to find a relatively open, quiet and sunny beach.

Cavill Ave, with a pedestrian mall at its beach end, is the heart of Surfers. **Ripley's Believe It Or Not,** just off the Mall, is an 'odditorium' with hundreds of fairly bizarre exhibits; it's open daily and costs $9.

The Gold Coast Highway runs right

QUEENSLAND

High-rise buildings dominate the Surfers Paradise skyline

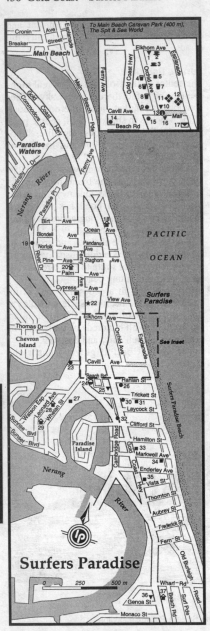

Surfers Paradise

PLACES TO STAY

5	Diamonds Resort
18	Surf & Sun Backpackers
20	Cheers Backpackers
21	Delilah Motel
27	Anchor Inn Holiday Apartments
28	Surfers Central Backpackers
29	Couple O' Days Accommodation
31	Trickett Gardens Holiday Apartments
33	Silver Sands Motel
34	Villas De La Mar
35	Admiral Motor Inn
37	Surfers Paradise Backpackers Resort

PLACES TO EAT

1	The Latin Quarter
2	Beachside Cafe
3	The Artist's Cafe
10	Shell Bar
16	Charlie's, Tamari & Juke Malone's
25	Bunga Raya, La Rustica, La Paella, Maharani & C'Est Paris
36	New Mexico

OTHER

4	The Tunnel Nightclub
6	Fever Nightclub
7	Cocktails & Dreams, The Party Nightclub & Shooters Bar
8	The Penthouse
9	American Express
11	The Mark
12	Raptis Plaza
13	Gold Coast Tourism Bureau
14	Ansett
15	Thomas Cook Foreign Exchange
17	Paradise Centre & Post Office
19	Budd's Beach Water Sportz
22	Police Station
23	Tiki Village Wharf
24	Surfers Paradise Bus Station
26	Surfers Blades
30	Qantas
32	Hoyts Cinema Centre

through Surfers, only a block back from the beach. It takes the southbound traffic, while Remembrance Drive and Ferny Ave, a block farther back from the beach, take the northbound traffic. Another block back is the looping Nerang River. The Surfers rich live around the surrounding canals.

Main Beach & The Spit

North of Surfers is Main Beach, and beyond that the Spit – a narrow, three-km-long tongue of sand dividing the ocean from the Broadwater.

On the Broadwater side of the Spit are three adjacent waterside complexes – **Mariner's Cove**, the **Marina Mirage** and **Fisherman's Wharf**, the departure point for most pleasure cruises. Between them they have a wide range of bars, eateries and shops. Across the road on the ocean side is the Sheraton Mirage Resort, while farther up is **Sea World** (see Theme Parks entry below). The beach at the northern end of the Spit is not developed and is good for relatively secluded sunbathing.

Southport & North

Sheltered from the ocean by the Spit, Southport was the original town on the Gold Coast but it's now modern, residential and rather nondescript. The built-up area continues north of Southport all the way up to Sanctuary Cove, about 10 km north, an up-market resort with a Hyatt hotel, two golf courses, a marina, flats and houses.

Southern Gold Coast

Just south of Surfers is Broadbeach, the **Conrad Jupiter's Casino** is a Gold Coast landmark – it was Queensland's first legal casino. The **Burleigh Head National Park**, on the north side of the mouth of Tallebudgera Creek, is a small but diverse forest reserve with walking trails around and through the rocky headland, a lookout and picnic area – there's a QNP&WS office (☎ (07) 5535 3032) on the Gold Coast Highway near the entrance. On the northern side is one of Australia's most famous surfing point breaks.

There are three excellent wildlife sanctuaries in this area. **Fleay's Wildlife Park**, two km inland along the Tallebudgera Creek in West Burleigh, has an excellent collection of native wildlife and four km of walking tracks through mangroves and rainforest. This was the place where the platypus was first bred

Rainbow lorikeets are a feature of Currumbin Sanctuary

in captivity. It's open daily from 9 am to 5 pm and costs $9.

Back towards the coast, flocks of technicoloured lorikeets and other birds flutter in for morning and afternoon feeds at the **Currumbin Sanctuary**. It's a large bushland park with tree kangaroos, koalas, emus and lots more Australian fauna, plus a two-km miniature railway, an Australian botanical garden and wildlife presentations. The sanctuary is off the Gold Coast Highway half a km south of Currumbin Creek; it is open daily from 8 am to 5 pm, and entry costs $14. If you're travelling by the Surfside bus, get off at stop No 20.

About eight km inland along Currumbin Creek Rd, **Olson's Bird Gardens** have yet more exotic feathered creatures. The gardens are open daily from 9 am to 5 pm ($9).

The 'twin towns' of **Coolangatta** and **Tweed Heads** mark the southern end of the Gold Coast. Tweed Heads is in New South Wales but the two places merge into each other. At **Point Danger**, the headland at the end of the state border, there are good views from the Captain Cook memorial. Coolangatta is a friendly, laid-back little place with good beaches.

Theme Parks
The Gold Coast's theme parks are a major drawcard for tourists. While they are generally quite expensive, the ticket prices usually cover all rides and shows, so for a full day's entertainment they can be worthwhile and good fun.

Sea World, on the Spit in Main Beach, is the longest-running park and one of the most popular, with dolphin and sea lion shows, shark feeding, water-ski shows, and some great rides including a corkscrew rollercoaster, a monorail, water slides, and the 'Bermuda Triangle'. It's open daily from 10 am to 5 pm; admission is $34.

Movie World, otherwise known as 'Hollywood on the Gold Coast', is a re-creation of the Warner Bros film studios. It's on the Pacific Highway at Oxenford, about 16 km north-west of Surfers. Characters from Warner Bros movies and cartoons wander around, and there are stunt shows, western shoot-outs and various rides including 'Batman Adventure – The Ride'. It is open from 9.30 am to 5 pm; entry costs $34.

Just south of Movie World, **Wet 'n' Wild** is a fun water sports park with giant water slides, twisters, theme pools and a wave pool that has one-metre surf; entry costs $17. From September to April, the park screens 'Dive-in Movies' (☎ (07) 5573 2255) on Saturday night.

A couple of km north at Coomera, **Dreamworld** is a Disneyland-style creation with 10 different theme areas, a wildlife sanctuary, and rides such as the Thunderbolt, Gravitron and Wipeout; entry is $34. At **Cableski World**, 12 km north of Surfers near Sanctuary Cove, you can water-ski by being towed around a large network of lakes by overhead cables; day passes are $30, night passes $17.

Water Sports
You can hire water sports equipment from

various places, including Aussie Bob's (☎ (07) 5591 7577) at the Marina Mirage on the Spit, and Budd's Beach Water Sportz (☎ (07) 5592 0644) on River Drive opposite Chevron Island. Both hire out jet skis, fishing boats, sailboards and more, and can take you parasailing or water-skiing.

You can hire motorboats from Popeye Marine & Boat Hire (☎ (07) 5532 5822) at Mariners Cove on the Spit.

Other Activities
Off the Edge (☎ (07) 5530 7699) has two to three-hour mountain bike rides from $25 and can organise speedboat rides, bungy jumping or helicopter rides. The Clifftop Adventures Co (☎ 018 752 510) offers forward abseiling from $40.

Surfers Blades (☎ (07) 5538 3483) at 40 Hanlan St has mountain bikes from $15 a day and in-line skates from $20 a day (as well as surfboards, fishing gear and lots of other stuff).

Numinbah Valley Adventure Trails (☎ (07) 5533 4137) has three-hour horse-riding treks through rainforest and river scenery for $35 ($40 with pick-ups), and the Gold Coast Riding Ranch (☎ (07) 5594 4255) on the Nerang-Broadbeach road next to the Surfers Raceway does trail rides from $20 an hour.

Bungy jumpers are catered for at Bungee Down Under, on the Spit by Sea World. There's another bungy jump at Cableski World.

Organised Tours & Cruises
Hinterland There are plenty of operators offering bus tours to the hinterland, or you can make your own way there with one of the local bus services. Doug Robbins' Off the Beaten Track tours (☎ (07) 5533 5366) offers overnight trips for two to six people to his lodge on the Springbrook Plateau. It's good value at $40 per person, which includes return transport, accommodation, one meal and a half to full-day bushwalk.

Cruises Cruises on offer from Surfers include two-hour harbour and canal trips (about $22), cruises to South Stradbroke Island (about $45 including lunch) and evening dinner cruises (about $50). Boats depart from the Marina Mirage or Fisherman's Wharf on the Spit, or from the Tiki Village Wharf at the river end of Cavill Ave. The *Maranoa* (☎ (07) 5529 5777) is popular with backpackers, with cruises to South Stradbroke Island from $25 (and lunches from $3) – expect to get wet.

Festivals
In March, the three-day international IndyCar Race draws huge crowds. June sees the two-day Gold Coast International Jazz & Blues Festival.

Places to Stay
Apart from the backpackers hostels, all the accommodation places vary their rates with the seasons, with tariffs rising by as much as 50% during the school holidays and up to 100% at Christmas time.

Prices also rise as you get closer to the centre of Surfers Paradise. There are some good-value options along the southern end of the coast at places like Broadbeach, Burleigh Heads, Mermaid Beach and Coolangatta.

Camping There are caravan/camping parks all the way along the Gold Coast from Main Beach to Coolangatta – most of the foreshore parks are run by the local council and are quite good. The closest to the centre is the *Main Beach Caravan Park* (☎ (07) 5581 7722) on Main Beach Pde (near the southern end of the Spit), with tent sites from $12 to $18. The riverside *Broadwater Tourist Park* (☎ (07) 5581 7733), just off the Gold Coast Highway in Southport, has tent sites from $14 to $18.

In Burleigh Heads, the *Burleigh Beach Tourist Park* (☎ (07) 5581 7755) is on Goodwin Terrace, just back from the beach. Sites range from $12 to $18. Farther south in Coolangatta/Tweed Heads, the *Border Caravan Park* (☎ (07) 5536 3134) on Boundary St has tent sites from $11 to $18 and on-site vans from $27 to $60.

Hostels There are several backpackers hostels in Surfers, and others in Southport to the north, and Broadbeach and Coolangatta to the south; those out of the centre all provide regular courtesy buses to/from Surfers.

Southport Southport has one of the most popular hostels on the south coast – the *Trekkers Guest House* (☎ (07) 5591 5616) at 22 White St, about four km north of Surfers. It's in an old house that has been well renovated and furnished. Accommodation is in three or four-bed rooms, most with bathroom. The atmosphere is very appealing and the staff organise trips to nightclubs and other events most evenings. The twice-weekly $5 barbecues are also popular. Nightly cost is $14 and doubles are $30.

The *Gold Coast Backpackers Resort* (☎ (07) 5531 2004) is nearby at 44 Queen St. It's a modern, purpose-built hostel but it lacks atmosphere; dorm beds are $12.

Surfers Paradise The most impressive of the hostels here is the *Surfers Paradise Backpackers Resort* (☎ (07) 5592 4677) at 2835 Gold Coast Highway, about a km south of the centre. It's clean and modern and has good facilities including a pool, a small gym and basement parking. There are two sections, one with four-bed dorms and another with excellent self-contained apartments, mostly accommodating four or five people in two bedrooms. A dorm or unit bed costs $14, and doubles $32. The hostel also runs tours to various places.

At 40 Whelan St, a block south of the bus stop, the friendly *Surfers Central Backpackers* (☎ (07) 5538 4344) has two sections – one with four-bed units with their own bathroom, the other with larger dorms. The communal kitchen is small, but there's a good pool with plenty of space for sunbathing and outdoor eating. Dorm beds cost $14, and doubles $30.

Couple O' Days Accommodation (☎ (07) 5592 4200), at 18 Whelan St, is a converted apartment block that looks a bit worn around the edges these days. Dorm beds are $10.

QUEENSLAND

At 3323 Gold Coast Highway, *Surf & Sun Backpackers* (☎ (07) 5592 2363) is a converted motel with four-bed units with bathrooms, TVs and fridges. It's not flash, but it's a good place if you're in party mode. There's a pool, and this is the closest hostel to the beach. Dorm beds are $14 and there's one double at $30.

Surfers' most recently opened hostel is the 140-bed *Cheers Backpackers* (☎ (07) 5531 6539) at 8 Pine Ave. It's well set up with a good pool, a garden and barbecue courtyard. Four to six-bed dorms are $14, and doubles $30. Cheers is party oriented, with video nights and vouchers for the nightclubs, many of which are within staggering distance.

Broadbeach At 2623 Gold Coast Highway, the *Big Backpackers* (☎ (07) 5538 4633) certainly lives up to its name – even the staff have been known to get lost. This converted nursing home is clean but feels a bit clinical – you expect to see Jack Nicholson walk down the hallway at any moment. Dorms are $14, and doubles $28.

Coolangatta/Bilinga The *Gold Coast Youth Hostel* (☎ (07) 5536 7644) is on Coolangatta Rd, Bilinga, just north of the airport and about three km from central Coolangatta. Six or eight-bed dorms cost $12, doubles $32; nonmembers pay an extra $2. It's a newish building, with good facilities including a pool, but it's really only convenient to the airport.

Motels & Holiday Apartments There are hundreds of motels and holiday apartments up and down the coast. Budget motels line the highway, and advertise cheap deals in flashing neon signs. Holiday apartments can be excellent value, especially for a group of three or four. Many of the apartments have a two-night minimum stay, and a seven-night minimum during the peak holiday seasons.

Surfers Paradise At 2985 Gold Coast Highway, the *Silver Sands Motel* (☎ (07) 5538 6041) has attractively refurbished units and a small pool, with doubles ranging from $50 to $90. Close by at No 2965, the *Admiral Motor Inn* (☎ (07) 5539 8759) has rooms starting from $50, while the *Delilah Motel* (☎ (07) 5538 1722) on the corner of Ferny and Cypress Aves has rooms from $45.

At 24-30 Trickett St, the *Trickett Gardens Holiday Apartments* (☎ (07) 5539 0988) is a low-rise block of good one and two-bedroom apartments that range from $80 to $136 a night. The *Anchor Inn Holiday Apartments* (☎ (07) 5592 0914) at 27 Whelan St is another good option, with units sleeping up to four people from $60 to $90 a night.

Diamonds Resort (☎ (07) 5570 1011) is a small budget resort in the heart of Surfers at 19 Orchid Ave, with motel units and apartments from $55 to $120. For a taste of Gold Coast luxury, the up-market *Villas De La Mar* (☎ (07) 5592 6644) on the corner of Northcliffe Terrace and Markwell Ave has Mediterranean-style units from $120 a night for up to four people or $145 a night for up to six.

Southern Gold Coast In Broadbeach, the old *King Tide Beachfront Apartments* (☎ (07) 5532 7124) are opposite the beach at 136 Old Burleigh Rd. One and two-bedroom units start from $70 and $100 a night respectively.

There are quite a few cheap motels along the Gold Coast Highway at Mermaid Beach. The *Red Emu Motel* (☎ (07) 5575 2748) at No 2583 has doubles from $28, while the *Mermaid Beach Motel* (☎ (07) 5575 1577) at No 2395 has clean units from $25.

In Burleigh Heads, the *Hillhaven Holiday Apartments* (☎ (07) 5535 1055) at 2 Goodwin Terrace have the prime position in Burleigh, with great views along the coast. Oldish but comfy apartments start from $80 for two bedrooms and $115 for three bedrooms.

In Coolangatta, the *Coolangatta Sands Hotel* (☎ (07) 5536 3066), at the corner of Griffith and McLean Sts, has basic pub rooms from $25/35 for singles/doubles. *On The Beach Holiday Units* (☎ (07) 5536 3624), on the beachfront at 118 Marine Pde, has simple older-style flats ranging from $45 to $65 a double, plus $10 for each extra person.

Places to Eat

Surfers Paradise There are plenty of choices in and around the Cavill Ave Mall. In the centre, *Charlie's* is open 24 hours a day and serves reasonably priced breakfasts, lunches and dinners. Next door, *Tamari* is an Italian bistro with pasta from $10 and other mains from $14 to $17. On the other side of Charlie's, *Juke Malone's* is a glitzy American style burger joint with pancakes, seafood gumbo, chilli con carne and more.

On the corner of Cavill and Orchid Aves, the busy *Shell Bar* offers breakfasts for $6 including juice, one of five hot dishes, toast, and tea or coffee. There are some good budget eateries down the Raptis Plaza Arcade (opposite Charlie's) – *Muffin Break* has delicious muffins and coffee, *Sumo* does Japanese takeaways, and *Mr Wong* and *Saigon* have all-you-can-eat Chinese and Vietnamese deals from $3.

In The Mark shopping complex in Orchid Ave, at shop 38, *Sukho Thai* has good mains from $10 to $14, while nearby *Sweethearts* has healthy rolls and sandwiches, juices, burgers etc.

Near the northern end of Orchid Ave, the *Artist's Cafe* is a casual place, with outdoor tables, that serves breakfasts, sandwiches and snacks.

Around the corner in Elkhorn Ave, *The Latin Quarter* is a great little BYO Italian bistro with pasta from $10 and other mains from $15 – good for a splurge. Farther along, the *Beachside Cafe* has breakfast deals at $5.50 for orange juice, cereal, bacon and eggs, tea or coffee – it is open 24 hours.

On the Gold Coast Highway in the block south of Beach Rd are six restaurants side-by-side, and you can choose between Malaysian, French, Spanish, Italian and Indian food: *La Rustica* has pasta and pizza from $9 to $12; *Maharani* has Indian food with mains from $10 to $14; and *Bunga Raya* has Malaysian dishes from $10 upwards; while *La Paella* and *C'est Paris* serve up Spanish and French food respectively.

Farther south, *New Mexico* has all-you-can-eat buffet dinners from $9.90 – it's on the corner of the highway and Genoa St, opposite the Surfers Paradise Backpackers Resort.

Up on the Spit, Fisherman's Wharf, the Marina Mirage and Mariners Cove all have a wide range of eateries.

Southern Gold Coast Broadbeach has a good range of eateries along Victoria St, just off the highway. *Cha Cha*, on the corner of Surf Ave, is a Japanese teppanyaki bar with meals from $6 to $7. Next door, the *Double Eight Chinese Restaurant* has Sichuan cuisine with mains averaging $8.

In Burleigh Heads, the Old Burleigh Theatre Arcade on Goodwin Terrace has the *Bluff Cafe*, with good cooked breakfast deals for $7.50, and *Arlett*, a small French bistro. Upstairs, *Montezuma's* is a licensed Mexican eatery with mains from $8 to $11 and *Tim's Malaysian Hut* has good hawkers-style meals in the $7 to $12 range.

In Coolangatta, the huge *Twin Towers Services Club* has a 'snack bar' on the second floor, which has good meals for $4 to $6 and lunches from $2.50 on weekdays. On the corner of McLean St and Marine Pde, the Beach House Plaza has *Farley's Coffee Lounge*, with breakfast deals for $6.95, *The Jungle*, a Mexican cantina, and *Little Malaya*, with Malaysian and Chinese dishes. The famous *Coolangatta Pie Shop*, at 50 Griffith St, is open on weekends 24 hours and weekdays from 5.30 am to 10.30 pm.

Entertainment

Nightclubs The Gold Coast nightlife is notoriously wild. Orchid Ave is the main nightclub strip in Surfers, and a stroll down here will reveal an abundance of flashing lights, club touts, and beckoning darkened doorways. Fun on tap.

One of the most popular backpackers clubs is *Cocktails & Dreams*, in The Mark complex off Orchid Avenue. It has different themes most nights of the week – toga parties, slave auctions etc. Downstairs, *The Party* is another fairly wild place with live bands and drinks deals. Upstairs in The Mark, the *Shooters Bar* is an American-style saloon with pool tables and big-screen videos.

The Penthouse, near the Cavill Ave corner, is more sophisticated, with a disco, a piano bar and a pool hall. At 18 Orchid Ave, *Fever* is an 'over-25s club' with dress regulations, while farther up, *The Tunnel* is a funky basement club with good dance music; entry costs $5 to $7.

Down in Coolangatta, *The Patch*, in the Queensland Hotel on Hill St, is a popular live music venue. Nearby, the *Hill St Nightclub* in the Greenmount Resort is a more up-market nightclub.

Cinemas & Theatre Cinemas include the *Hoyts Cinema Centre* (☎ (07) 5570 3355) on the corner of the highway and Clifford St in Surfers, and the *Coolangatta Cinema Centre* (☎ (07) 5536 8900) in the Beach Shopping Centre on Griffith St.

Dracula's (☎ (07) 5575 1000), on Hooker Boulevard in Broadbeach, is a popular cabaret restaurant with a three-course meal and an entertaining show for $35 per person ($45 on Saturdays).

The *Gold Coast Arts Centre* (☎ (07) 5581 6500), beside the Nerang River at 135 Bundall Rd, is the main venue for theatre and musical productions, and screens art-house movies. Ring to find out what's on while you're in town.

Casino *Conrad Jupiter's Casino* in Broadbeach is open 24 hours and has live floor shows and the up-market *Fortunes* nightclub; dress regulations apply.

Getting There & Away
Air Coolangatta airport is the seventh busiest in Australia. Ansett and Qantas fly direct from the major cities including Sydney ($269), Melbourne ($393), Adelaide ($436) and Perth ($677). Impulse Airlines (bookings through Ansett) fly from Brisbane to Coolangatta ($97).

Bus The Surfers Paradise Bus Station, on the corner of Beach and Cambridge Rds, is where you'll arrive if you're coming by bus. Inside the terminal are the booking desks of the bus companies, a cafeteria, left-luggage lockers ($4 a day) and the In Transit (☎ (07) 5592 2911) accommodation booking desk – it can book you into one of the five backpackers hostels it represents, or can recommend other types of accommodation.

Greyhound Pioneer and McCafferty's both have frequent services to Brisbane ($12), Byron Bay ($17) and Sydney ($65 to $74); Greyhound also has one service a day to Noosa ($25). Kirklands (☎ (07) 5531 7145) offers discounted services to backpackers and students, including to Brisbane ($8.40) and Byron Bay ($14.25), as well as a special Brisbane-Gold Coast-Byron Bay-Sydney fare of $44.80 with unlimited stopovers (YHA members only).

Coachtrans (☎ (07) 5538 9944) also runs frequent daily buses to Surfers and Coolangatta from Brisbane ($12) and Brisbane airport ($26). The trip takes about 1½ hours to Surfers and just over two hours to Coolangatta.

There are two different bus stops in Coolangatta: Greyhound Pioneer and Lindsay Coaches operate from the Coolangatta transit centre (☎ (07) 5536 6600) on the corner of Griffith and Warner Sts; McCafferty's, Kirklands and Coachtrans operate from Golden Gateway Travel (☎ (07) 5536 1700) on Boundary St, just south of the border.

Train There's no railway station on the Gold Coast but there are connecting bus services once daily to Murwillumbah (one hour) and Casino (three hours) in northern New South Wales; from there you can take a train to Sydney. There's a Queensland Rail booking office (☎ (07) 5539 9088) in the Cavill Park building on the corner of Beach Rd and the Gold Coast Highway in Surfers Paradise.

Getting Around
To/From the Airport Gold Coast Airport Transit (☎ (07) 5536 6841) meets every Qantas flight into Coolangatta and has shuttle buses to Coolangatta ($4) and Surfers

($8), with pick-ups and drop-offs to/from wherever you're staying. Airport & Charter Services (☎ (07) 5576 4000) operates the same service for all Ansett arrivals and departures.

A taxi from the airport costs about $6 to Coolangatta and $20 into Surfers. Avis, Thrifty, Hertz and Budget all have car rental desks at the airport.

Bus Surfside Buslines (☎ (07) 5536 7666) runs a frequent service 24 hours a day up and down the Gold Coast Highway between Southport and Tweed Heads and beyond. You can buy individual fares, get a Day Rover ticket for $8, or a weekly one for $26.

Car, Bicycle & Moped There are dozens of car-rental firms here. Red Back Rentals (☎ (07) 5592 1655) opposite the bus station at 3 Beach Rd has bikes ($20 a day), mopeds (from $35) and cars ($35 to $90). Rent-A-Bomb (☎ (07) 5538 8222) at 8 Beach Rd and Costless (☎ (07) 5592 4499) in the bus terminal are also pretty cheap.

Green Bicycle Rentals (☎ 018 766 880) has good mountain bikes ($18 a day) and will deliver.

GOLD COAST HINTERLAND

The mountains of the **McPherson Range**, about 20 km inland from Coolangatta and stretching about 60 km back along the New South Wales border to meet the Great Dividing Range, are a paradise for walkers. The great views and beautiful natural features are easily accessible if you have a car, and there are plenty of wonderfully scenic drives. Otherwise, there are several places offering tours and day trips from the coast. Expect a lot of rain in the mountains from December to March, and in winter the nights can be cold.

Tamborine Mountain

Just 45 km north-west of the Gold Coast, this 500-metre-high plateau is on a northern spur of the McPherson Range. Patches of the area's original forests remain in nine small national parks. There are gorges, spectacular waterfalls, including Witches Falls and

Cedar Creek Falls, walking tracks and great views inland or over the coast. However, because of its proximity to the coast, this area is more developed and commercialised than the ranges farther south.

The main access roads are from Oxenford on the Pacific Highway or via Nerang from the coast. There's an information centre (☎ (07) 5545 1171) in North Tamborine. Some of the best lookouts are in **Witches Falls National Park**, south-west of North Tamborine, and at **Cameron Falls**, north-west of North Tamborine. **Macrozamia Grove National Park**, near Mt Tamborine township, has some extremely old macrozamia palms.

Springbrook Plateau

This forested 900-metre-high plateau is, like the rest of the McPherson Range, a remnant of the huge volcano that used to be centred on Mt Warning in New South Wales. It's a lovely drive from the Gold Coast, reached by sealed road via Mudgeeraba.

There are three sections of the national park: Springbrook, Mt Cougal and Natural Bridge. The vegetation is cool-temperate rainforest and eucalypt forest, with gorges, cliffs, forests, waterfalls, an extensive network of walking tracks and several picnic areas.

At the **Gwongorella picnic area**, just off the Springbrook road, the lovely Purling Brook Falls drop 109 metres into rainforest. Downstream, Waringa Pool is a beautiful summer swimming hole. There's a good camping ground beside the picnic area.

The **Natural Bridge section**, off the Nerang to Murwillumbah road, has a one-km walking circuit leading to a rock arch spanning a water-formed cave that is home to a huge colony of glow-worms.

There are rangers' offices and information centres at Natural Bridge and Springbrook. Pick up a copy of the national park's walking tracks leaflet. Camping permits for Gwongorella are available from the ranger at Springbrook (☎ (07) 5533 5147, weekdays only, between 3 and 4 pm). Springbrook township itself has a general store, tearooms and craft shops, and several guesthouses. See

QUEENSLAND

the Organised Tours & Cruises earlier in the Gold Coast section for details of trips to Springbrook from the coast.

Lamington National Park
West of Springbrook, this large, 200-sq-km park covers more of the McPherson Range and adjoins the Border Ranges National Park in New South Wales. It includes thickly wooded valleys, 1100-metre-high ranges, plus most of the Lamington Plateau. Much of the vegetation is subtropical rainforest. There are beautiful gorges, caves, superb views, waterfalls and pools, and lots of wildlife. Bower birds are quite common and pademelons, a type of small wallaby, can be seen late in the afternoon.

The two most popular and accessible sections, **Binna Burra** and **Green Mountains**, can both reached via sealed roads from Canungra. The 24-km Border Trail walk links the two.

The park has 160 km of walking tracks ranging from a 'senses trail' for blind people at Binna Burra to a tree-top canopy walk along a series of suspension bridges at Green Mountains. Walking trail maps and brochures are available from QNP&WS offices.

Places to Stay The *Binna Burra Mountain Lodge* (☎ (07) 5533 3622) has a good small camping ground, with sites at $7 per person and on-site tents from $36 a double. It's advisable to book. The lodge has rustic log cabins and costs from $99 per person per night, but that includes all meals, free hiking and climbing gear, and activities such as guided walks, bus trips and abseiling. There's a kiosk and tearooms near the camping ground.

O'Reilly's Guesthouse (☎ (07) 5544 0644), at Green Mountains, has three levels of accommodation from $105 to $140 per person, including meals and activities. There's also a kiosk, and a QNP&WS camping ground about 600 metres away with sites for $3 per person.

You can bush camp in Lamington, but a limited number of permits are issued. You can get information from the QNP&WS offices at Burleigh Heads or Brisbane, but camping permits must be obtained from the ranger at Green Mountains (☎ (07) 5544 0634).

Getting There & Away The Binna Burra bus service (☎ (07) 5533 3622) operates daily between Surfers and Binna Burra (one hour, $16), departing from Surfers at 1.15 pm and from Binna Burra at 10.30 am – book ahead.

Allstate Scenic Tours (☎ (07) 3285 1777) has services daily (except Saturdays) between Brisbane and Green Mountains (three hours, $20 or $35 for a return day trip).

Mountain Coach Company (☎ (07) 5524 4249) has a daily service from the Gold Coast to Green Mountains via Mt Tamborine, costing $30 return.

Mt Lindesay Highway
This road runs south from Brisbane, across

QUEENSLAND

The Crash of the Stinson
On 19 February 1937, a Stinson airliner carrying seven people crashed in the thick, impenetrable forests of the McPherson mountain range. Four passengers were killed instantly, and another died after falling over a cliff when he went for help. The plane had been missing for nine days, and search parties had almost given up, when Bernard O'Reilly, now owner of O'Reilly's Guesthouse, found the wreck and its two survivors. O'Reilly later said that one of the first questions the two men asked was 'What's the cricket score?'. Apparently, they were considerably cheered to hear that Don Bradman was 165 not out.

Parts of the wrecked plane, and photos of the rescue, are on display at O'Reilly's Guesthouse. ■

the Great Dividing Range west of Lamington, and into New South Wales at Woodenbong. **Beaudesert**, in cattle country 66 km from Brisbane, is just 20 km south-west of Tamborine Mountain. It has a pioneer museum and a tourist centre on Jane St.

West of Beaudesert is the stretch of the Great Dividing Range known as the **Scenic Rim** (see the Darling Downs section later in this chapter). Farther south, **Mt Barney National Park** is undeveloped but popular with bushwalkers and climbers. It's in the Great Dividing Range just north of the state border. You reach it from the Rathdowney to Boonah road. There's a tourist office (☎ (07) 5544 1222) on the highway at Rathdowney.

Sunshine Coast

The stretch of coast from the top of Bribie Island to Noosa is known as the Sunshine Coast. It's a popular holiday area, renowned for fine beaches, good surfing and fishing. Although it doesn't have the high-rise jungle and neon-lit strips of the Gold Coast, the coast is still quite commercial and has been heavily developed.

Noosa Heads is the most fashionable and exclusive town on the coast, but it also has a good range of budget accommodation, an excellent national park and great beaches. Maroochydore is also quite popular. North of Noosa is the Cooloola National Park and Rainbow Beach, an access point for Fraser Island. The inland Bruce Highway (the main road north) has a series of artificial tourist attractions.

Getting There & Away
Air The Sunshine Coast airport is on the coast road at Mudjimba, about 10 km north of Maroochydore. Sunstate flies from Brisbane ($97), and Ansett and Qantas fly from Sydney.

Bus Greyhound Pioneer and McCafferty's buses travel along the Bruce Highway, but

not across to the coast (Greyhound has only one bus a day to Noosa and Maroochydore). From Cooroy and Nambour on the highway, Tewantin Bus Services (☎ (074) 49 7422) runs regular buses across to Noosa, continuing to Maroochydore.

Suncoast Pacific (☎ (074) 43 1011) runs frequent direct services from the Brisbane transit centre and Brisbane airport to Noosa (three hours, $17) via Maroochydore (two hours, $14). Sunshine Coast Coaches (☎ (074) 43 4555) has daily services south from Maroochydore and inland across to Landsborough and Nambour.

Train The most convenient stations for the Sunshine Coast are Nambour and Cooroy. There are services daily to these places from Brisbane and from the north.

CABOOLTURE (pop 12,700)
This region, 49 km north of Brisbane, once had a large Aboriginal population. Nowadays, it's a prosperous dairy centre.

It also has two interesting attractions. Seven km east (signposted off the road to Bribie Island), the **Abbey Museum** is a world social history museum with a small but well-presented collection of ancient artefacts, weaponry, pottery and costumes. The collection was previously housed in the UK, Cyprus, Egypt and Sri Lanka. It's open Tuesday, Thursday, Friday and Saturday from 10 am to 4 pm; entry is $4.

The **Caboolture Historical Village** on Beerburrum Rd, two km north of the town, has about 30 early Australian buildings in a bush setting. It is open daily from 10 am to 3 pm and entry is $5.

GLASS HOUSE MOUNTAINS
About 20 km north of Caboolture, the Glass House Mountains are a dramatic visual starting point for the Sunshine Coast. They're a bizarre series of volcanic crags rising abruptly out of the plain to 300 metres, or more, high. They were named by Captain Cook and, depending on whose story you believe, he either noted the reflections of the glass-smooth rock sides of the mountains, or he thought they looked like the glass furnaces in his native Yorkshire.

The mountains are great for scenic drives, bushwalking and rock climbing. The main access is via the Forest Drive, a 22-km-long series of sealed and unsealed roads that wind through the ranges from Beerburrum to the Glass House Mountains township, with several spectacular lookout points en route.

There are four small national parks within the range, and each has walking/climbing trails of varying levels of difficulty: Mt Ngungun is an easy two-hour walk to the summit; Mt Beerwah and Mt Tibrogargan are steep and difficult three-hour climbs; and Mt Coonowrin is popular with experienced rock climbers. Contact the ranger (☎ (074) 94 6630) at Beerwah for more information.

The Glass House Mountains are a series of volcanic crags

Mt Tibrogargan Relaxapark (☎ (074) 96 0151), 1.5 km north of Beerburrum, has a shop, walking trails, and information on walks and wildlife; tent sites are $10, on-site vans $21 and self-contained units from $31.

CALOUNDRA (pop 40,000)

At the southern end of the Sunshine Coast, Caloundra has some decent beaches and excellent fishing but compared with places farther north, it's a bit faded these days. It's still a popular holiday town with families, and has numerous caravan parks and holiday flats, but no backpackers hostel. Bulcock Beach, good for windsurfing, is just down from the main street, overlooking the northern end of Bribie Island.

Points of interest include the **Queensland Air Museum** at Caloundra aerodrome, which is open Wednesday, Saturday and Sunday from 10 am to 4 pm and costs $3, and the **Ettamogah Pub** on the Bruce Highway, just north of the Caloundra turnoff.

There's a tourist office (☎ (074) 91 0202) on Caloundra Rd, just west of the town centre.

Places to Stay

The *Hibiscus Holiday Park* (☎ (074) 91 1564) on the corner of Bowman and Landsborough Park Rds is close to the beach and the centre; tent sites are from $10, and on-site vans and cabins from $25. Opposite the bus terminal, the *Dolphins Motel* (☎ (074) 91 2511) at 6 Cooma Terrace has good units ranging seasonally from $45 to $75.

MOOLOOLABA, ALEXANDRA HEADLAND & MAROOCHYDORE (pop 28,500)

North from Caloundra, the coast is built-up most of the way to the triple towns of Mooloolaba, Alexandra Headland and Maroochydore, which sprawl together to form the Sunshine Coast's biggest and most heavily-developed urban conglomeration.

Maroochydore, the main town, is a busy commercial centre and popular tourist spot,

with both an ocean beach and the Maroochy River, which has lots of pelicans and a few islands. Alexandra Headland has a pleasant beach and good surfing off a rocky point. Mooloolaba has the brightest atmosphere, with a long sandy beach and a strip of shops along the beachfront, including cafes, restaurants and the odd nightspot. Also at Mooloolaba is **The Wharf**, an impressive riverfront development with shops, eateries, a tavern, a marina and the excellent **Underwater World**, a large oceanarium with a transparent tunnel leading underneath and performing seal shows. It's open daily from 9 am to 6 pm; entry costs $15.50.

Information

The Maroochy Tourist Information Centre (☎ (074) 79 1566) is near the corner of Aerodrome Rd (the main road connecting Maroochydore and Mooloolaba) and Sixth Ave.

Activities

As in Caloundra, the main attractions here are the excellent beaches. There are numerous surf shops along the coast where you can hire surf and boogie boards, and inline skates can be hired from Maroochy Skate Biz (☎ (074) 43 6111) on the foreshore in Alexandra Headland.

Places to Stay

There are three hostels in Maroochydore – ring from the bus stop for a pick-up. The friendly *Maroochydore YHA Backpackers' Hostel* (☎ (074) 43 3151) at 24 Schirrmann Drive, a couple of turns off Bradman Ave, is well set up with six to eight-bed dorms from $12 a night and doubles from $30; nonmembers pay $1 more. The hostel has bikes, boards and canoes for hire, and organises various trips and tours. *Cotton Tree Backpackers* (☎ (074) 43 1755), in a rambling old timber guesthouse at 15 The Esplanade, overlooking the river, has dorms at $12 and doubles at $26. At 50 Parker St, the *Suncoast Backpackers Lodge* (☎ (074) 43 7544) is a modern, purpose-built hostel with dorms at $12 and doubles at $30.

QUEENSLAND

The best caravan/camping parks are the foreshore parks run by the local council. They include *Cotton Tree Caravan Park* (☎ (074) 43 1253) on the Esplanade and the *Seabreeze Caravan Park* (☎ (074) 43 1167) behind the information centre. Tent sites are from $10, and powered sites from $12 (no on-site vans).

There are dozens of motels and holiday units, but generally they are rather expensive. *Tallows Lodge Motel* (☎ (074) 43 2981) at 10 Memorial Drive is pretty tacky, but it's close to the beach and has self-contained units from $40 to $70.

Getting There & Around

Long-distance buses stop at the Suncoast Pacific Bus Terminal (☎ (074) 43 1011) on First Ave in Maroochydore, just off Aerodrome Rd (near KFC).

You can hire boats at several places in Maroochydore and Mooloolaba, or take river cruises from The Wharf in Mooloolaba. Motor scooters and Volkswagen Beetles can be hired from Bugs Convertible (☎ (074) 43 7555) on Aerodrome Rd, near the information centre.

NOOSA (pop 19,000)

A surfers' mecca since the early 1960s, Noosa has now become a resort for the fashionable with beaches, good restaurants, the fine coastal Noosa National Park and, just to the north, the walks, waterways and beaches of the Cooloola National Park. Noosa remains a far cry from the hype of the Gold Coast and it has more character than the rest of the Sunshine Coast.

Orientation

Noosa is actually a string of small linked centres – with confusingly similar names – stretching back from the mouth of the Noosa River and along its maze of tributary creeks and lakes. The slickest resort area is Noosa Heads, on the coast between the river mouth and rocky Noosa Head. From Noosa Heads two roads lead back to Noosaville, about three km away. One goes across an island known as Noosa Sound, the other circles

round to the south through Noosa Junction. Noosaville is the departure point for most river cruises.

Farther inland, beyond Noosaville, you reach Tewantin, six km from Noosa Heads. Sunshine Beach, which is about three km south of the centre, has long sandy surf beaches.

Information

The tourist centre (☎ (074) 47 4988) in Hastings St, Noosa Heads, is open daily from 9 am to 5 pm. There are also a number of privately run tour booking agencies in town.

Written Dimension, near the cinemas on Sunshine Beach Rd in Noosa Junction, is a good bookshop.

Noosa National Park

The spectacular cape at Noosa Head marks the northern end of the Sunshine Coast. This small but lovely national park extends for about two km in each direction from the headland, and has fine walks, great coastal scenery and a string of bays on the north side with waves that draw surfers from all over. Alexandria Bay on the eastern side is the best sandy beach.

The main entrance, at the end of Park Rd, has a car park, information centre and picnic areas, and it is also the starting point for five great walking tracks, which range from one to four km in length. You can drive up to the Laguna Lookout from Viewland Drive in Noosa Junction, or walk into the park from McAnally Drive or Parkedge Rd in Sunshine Beach.

Activities

Total Adventures (☎ (074) 49 0943) offers abseiling, rock-climbing, mountain-biking and sea-kayaking trips for $50 a half-day or $85 a full day; they also have two to five-day tours. Noosa Sea Sports (☎ (074) 47 3426) in Noosa Sound hires out surfboards and boogie boards, and fishing and snorkelling gear. Catamarans and surf skis can be hired from the Noosa Main Beach, and most of the surf shops rent boards, including Ozmosis (☎ (074) 47 3300) in Hastings St.

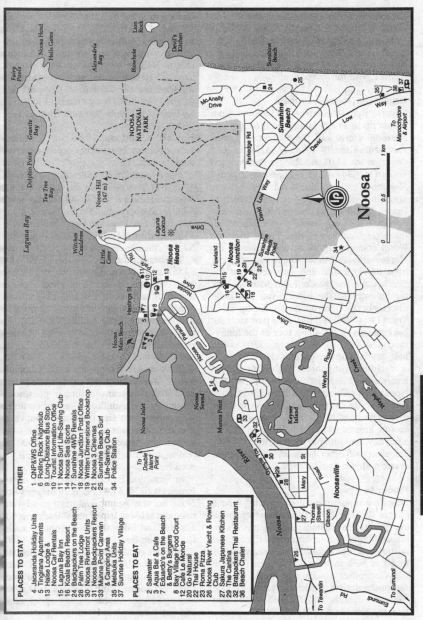

PLACES TO STAY

4 Jacaranda Holiday Units
5 Tingirana Apartments
13 Halse Lodge &
15 Noosa Car Rentals
15 Laguna Bay Inn
16 Koala Beach Resort
24 Backpackers on the Beach
28 Palm Tree Lodge
30 Noosa Riverfront Units
31 Noosa Backpackers Resort
33 Munna Point Caravan
& Camping Area
35 Melaluka Units
37 Sunrise Holiday Village

PLACES TO EAT

2 Saltwater
3 Aqua Bar & Cafe
7 Eduardo's on the Beach
& Betty's Burgers
8 Bay Village Food Court
12 Cafe Le Monde
20 Go Natural
22 Thai House
23 Roma Pizza
26 Noosa River Yacht & Rowing
Club
27 Sakura Japanese Kitchen
29 The Cantina
32 Bratpackers Thai Restaurant
36 Beach Chalet

OTHER

1 QNP&WS Office
6 Rolling Rock Nightclub
9 Long-Distance Bus Stop
10 Tourist Information Office
11 Noosa Surf Life-Saving Club
14 Noosa Sea Sports
17 Sunshine 4WD Rentals
18 Noosa Junction Post Office
19 Written Dimensions Bookshop
21 Noosa 3 Cinemas
25 Sunshine Beach Surf
Life-Saving Club
34 Police Station

Seven different places along the river in Gympie Terrace in Noosaville hire out boats and fishing gear, catamarans and surf skis.

Other activities on offer include horse riding, camel treks, paraflying and joy flights – check with the tourist centre.

Organised Tours & Cruises

Several operators offer 4WD tours from Noosa up to Fraser Island via the Cooloola National Park and the Coloured Sands. Adventure Tours (☎ (074) 47 2411) has good day trips for $110 and Ranger Personalised Tours (☎ (074) 49 9999) has day trips for $95; both include lunch. Adventure Tours also runs good three-day camping safaris to Fraser Island, departing twice weekly and costing $178 per person, which includes all meals and camping gear. These trips are worth considering as an alternative to the Hervey Bay self-drive tours; you get your own driver/guide and can drive up the beaches and see the Cooloola National Park on the way to the island. You can book directly or through your hostel. Kickin' Back Tours (☎ (074) 48 1190) runs two tours for backpackers: a full day's tour of the hinterland and various attractions ($30) and a half-day 'country pubs' tour ($20).

Various companies, including Noosa Everglades Tours (☎ (074) 47 1838) and Noosa River Tours (☎ (074) 49 7362), have cruises up the everglades of the Noosa River to the lakes and the Cooloola National Park, costing around $45 for a half-day or $70 for a full day, including a barbecue lunch. There are plenty of other tours on offer – again, check with the tourist centre.

Places to Stay

Despite a reputation for exclusivity, Noosa covers the accommodation spectrum with everything from backpackers hostels to resort hotels and apartments. Except for hostels, accommodation prices can rise as much as 50% in busy times, even 100% in the December to January peak season. Accommodation booking agents include Accomm Noosa (☎ (074) 47 3444) and Holiday Noosa (☎ (074) 47 4011).

Camping The popular *Sunrise Holiday Village* (☎ (074) 47 3294) on the beachfront in Sunshine Beach has tent sites ($12 to $20), on-site vans ($26 to $50) and good cabins ($30 to $60), plus backpacker beds in on-site vans at $16 (low season only). Also good is the *Munna Point Caravan & Camping Area* (☎ (074) 49 7050) beside the river in Russell St, Noosaville, with tent sites from $13.

Hostels & Lodges All of Noosa's hostels have courtesy buses and do pick-ups from the bus stop.

The *Noosa Backpackers Resort* (☎ (074) 49 8151) at 9 William St, Munna Point, Noosaville, is a friendly and popular hostel with good cooking and sitting areas, a pool and a cafe (see Places to Eat). Dorm beds are $13, and doubles $28; breakfasts start from $2.

The big *Koala Beach Resort* (☎ (074) 47 3355), at 44 Noosa Drive, Noosa Junction, is a converted motel with good facilities including a pool, a cafe, bikes and surf boards. Dorms range from $12 to $15, doubles with shared facilities are $30 and motel units range from $45 to $65. Koala is party-oriented with a bar and nightly entertainment.

In Noosa Heads opposite the bus stop, the friendly *Halse Lodge* (☎ (074) 47 3377) is a beautiful 100-year-old timber guesthouse owned by the Anglican Church, complete with polished wooden floors and great views over the town and sea. Simple two to six-bed rooms with shared bathrooms cost $20 per person, including breakfast – $6 more if you need linen.

In Sunshine Beach, *Backpackers on the Beach* (☎ (074) 47 4739) at 26 Stevens St is close to the beach and has good two bedroom self-contained units. Beds cost $14 a night, and bikes, surfboards and laundry facilities are free.

Another good option in Sunshine Beach is the *Melaluka Units* (☎ (074) 47 3663) at 7 Selene St. It has an assortment of two and three-bedroom holiday units with beds costing $15 per person. There's a pool, sauna and free laundry.

Motels & Holiday Units The best places to stay are those along the beachfront around Hastings St – they're also the most expensive. Cheapest of the bunch are the *Tingirana Apartments* (☎ (074) 47 3274) at 25 Hastings St, with motel units ($65 to $85) and one to three-bedroom holiday units ($85 to $230); and the *Jacaranda Holiday Units* (☎ (074) 47 4011) across the road, with motel-style units ($60 to $90) and one-bedroom units ($80 to $120 for up to five people).

About one km back, the *Laguna Bay Inn* (☎ (074) 49 2873) at 2 Viewland Drive, Noosa Junction, is a good option with four comfortable self-contained units in a shady garden setting, with a pool and barbecue area. The units sleep up to six and range from $60 to $100 a night.

One of the best areas for cheaper accommodation is along Gympie Terrace, the main road through Noosaville. *Noosa Riverfront Units* (☎ (074) 49 7595) at 277 Gympie Terrace has good budget units from $40 for a studio unit or from $80 for two bedrooms. At No 281, *Noosa River Beach* (☎ (074) 49 7873) has old-fashioned budget units from $40 a double. The *Palm Tree Lodge* (☎ (074) 49 7311) at No 233 has a choice of motel rooms or self-contained units.

Places to Eat

Noosa has three main eating centres: Sunshine Beach Rd in Noosa Junction, Gympie Terrace in Noosaville and Hastings St in Noosa Heads. Hastings St has the most glamorous (and most expensive) restaurants and cafes.

In Sunshine Beach Rd, *Roma Pizza*, at the southern end, has pasta and pizzas for about $10 and other mains from $12 to $15. On Monday, Tuesday and Wednesday nights, they have cheap all-you-can-eat pasta or pizza specials. *Thai House*, upstairs at the Sunshine Centre opposite the cinemas, has mains from $12.50. *Go Natural*, a health food shop on the corner of Arcadia St, is a good spot for lunches.

In Noosaville, the BYO *Bratpackers Thai Restaurant* at the front of the Noosa Backpackers Resort is popular with locals and travellers and has good food in the $8 to $14 range. At 247 Gympie Terrace, *The Cantina* is a BYO Mexican eatery with mains from $10 to $14. Up next to the Islander Resort, the small *Sakura Japanese Kitchen* has three-course lunches for $10 – at night, main courses range from $14 to $22. Just before the river crossing, the *Noosa River Yacht & Rowing Club* has river views and good bistro meals from $6.50 to $8.50.

In Noosa Heads, trendy Hastings St is lined with restaurants and cafes, many with candle-lit outdoor tables under umbrellas or canopies. There are some great restaurants here – some very expensive, some quite affordable. *Eduardo's on the Beach* (☎ (074) 47 5875), has excellent food and a great setting right on the beach and serves breakfast, lunch and dinner. In the walkway leading to Eduardo's is *Betty's Burgers*, a tiny takeaway with a huge range of burgers from $1 to $4.50. Set back from the southern side of Hastings St, the *Bay Village Food Court* has a variety of food stalls. At the west end of Hastings St are the Mediterranean-style *Aqua Bar & Cafe* and *Saltwater* (☎ (074) 47 2234), which has great takeaway fish & chips downstairs and a very good seafood restaurant upstairs – you'll need to book. Up the other end past the roundabout, *Cafe Le Monde* is one of the most popular Hastings St restaurants, and has reasonably priced pasta, salads and sandwiches, and sometimes live music.

Entertainment

In Sunshine Beach, the *Beach Chalet* (☎ (074) 47 3944) is a good bar/eatery and live music venue featuring world music, reggae, jazz etc – ring to see what's on. Noosa's most popular nightclub is the *Rolling Rock*, upstairs in the Bay Village Plaza off Hastings St.

The *Noosa 3 Cinemas* (☎ (074) 47 5300) on Sunshine Beach Rd, Noosa Junction, shows mainstream movies. The wonderful old *Majestic Theatre* (☎ (074) 85 2330) in Pomona, 30 km west of Noosa, screens silent films accompanied by a Wurlitzer organ most nights, including Rudy Valentino's last flick *The Son of the Sheik* every Thursday ($7).

Getting Around

Tewantin Bus Services (☎ (074) 49 7422) runs daily services up and down the coast between Noosa and Maroochydore and inland to Tewantin, Cooroy and Nambour. It also runs a local service linking Noosa Heads, Noosaville, Sunshine Beach etc.

Mokes are available from Noosa Car Rental (☎ (074) 47 3777), right opposite the bus stop in Noosa Heads. There are a number of other local operators, plus national firms such as Avis and Thrifty. If you want to drive up the Cooloola Coast beach to the wreck of the *Cherry Venture*, Rainbow Beach or Fraser Island, Sunshine 4WD Rentals (☎ (074) 47 3702) beside the Noosa Junction post office rents 4WDs for $100 to $150 a day (two-day minimum hire).

COOLOOLA COAST

Stretching for 50 km between Noosa and Rainbow Beach, the Cooloola Coast is a remote strip of long sandy beaches backed by the Cooloola National Park. Although this stretch is undeveloped, at times it is so popular with campers you might be excused for thinking otherwise.

The Cooloola Way, a gravel road, runs from Tewantin all the way up to Rainbow Beach (via Boreen Point and the national park). From Tewantin, the Noosa River Ferry operates daily from 6 am to 10 pm (Friday and Saturday until midnight) and costs $4 per car. On the other side are Lake Cooroibah and the beaches of Laguna Bay, and if you have a 4WD you can continue right up the beach to Rainbow Bay, passing the Teewah coloured sand cliffs and the rusting *Cherry Venture*, a 3000-tonne freighter swept ashore by a cyclone in 1973.

Lake Cooroibah

There are several good camping grounds between Lake Cooroibah and the coast, including the low-key *Lake Cooroibah*

Holiday Park (☎ (074) 47 1225), with a bar/restaurant, tennis courts, horse riding, tent sites, on-site tents and cabins. Based here is the *Camel Company Australia* (☎ (074) 42 4402) offering half-day beach rides ($45), overnight safaris ($125) and six-day safaris to Fraser Island ($720 all-inclusive).

Boreen Point

On the western shores of Lake Cootharaba, Boreen Point is a relaxed little place with a caravan park, a motel and a few holiday units. The historic *Apollonian Hotel* (☎ (074) 85 3100) has a garden setting, shady verandahs, meals and simple double rooms from $30. *The Jetty* restaurant (☎ (074) 85 3167), with a lovely setting overlooking the lake, has lunches daily and dinners on Friday and Saturday, with set menus for $36 per person.

Cooloola National Park

North of Noosa, the Cooloola National Park covers over 54,000 hectares, with the Noosa River running through the centre. It's a varied wilderness area with long sandy beaches, mangrove-lined waterways, forest, heaths and lakes, all of it featuring plentiful birdlife and lots of wildflowers in spring.

You can drive through the park, although the best way to see Cooloola is from a boat. Boats can be hired from Tewantin and Noosaville, or there are various operators offering cruises from Noosa.

Five km north of Boreen Point at Elanda Point there's a lakeside camping ground and a rangers' office (☎ (074) 49 7364). Several walking trails start here including the 46-km Cooloola Wilderness Trail and a seven-km trail to the QNP&WS visitor centre (☎ (074) 49 7364) on Kinaba Island.

There are about 10 camping grounds in the park, many of them alongside the river. The main ones are Fig Tree Point at the north of Lake Cootharaba, and Harry's Hut, about four km upstream. Freshwater is the main camp on the coast; it's about six km south of Double Island Point.

SUNSHINE COAST HINTERLAND

The mountains of the **Blackall Range** rise just in from the coast, and this scenic hinterland area has mountain towns, guesthouses and B&Bs, national parks with rainforests and waterfalls, art and craft galleries, and lots of tourists.

Nambour is the main commercial centre for the region. It's an attractive town but it has little of interest for travellers. Six km south, the **Big Pineapple** is one of Queensland's superbly kitsch 'big' creations. You can climb up inside this 15-metre fibreglass wonder then take a combined tour of the plantations, animal nursery and a cane-train ride ($10.50) – all very tacky, but incredibly popular.

Farther north, thousands flock to the **Eumundi Village Markets** every Saturday morning. Eumundi is a charming little rural centre and the original home of Eumundi Lager (now brewed on the Gold Coast). West of town, you can fossick for thunder eggs at **Thunder Egg Farm**.

The scenic Mapleton to Maleny road runs right along the ridge line of the Blackall Range. **Mapleton Falls National Park** is four km west of Mapleton and **Kondalilla National Park** is three km off the Mapleton to Montville stretch of the road. Both have rainforest. At Mapleton Falls, Pencil Creek plunges 120 metres, and the Kondalilla Falls drop 80 metres, into a rainforest valley. This is a great area for exploring – there's lots of birdlife and several walking tracks in the parks.

Midway between Mapleton and Maleny, **Montville** is a very popular tourist spot, with lots of craft shops and restaurants.

The **Maleny Folk Festival**, held annually over the five days leading up to New Year's Eve, is the closest thing Australia has to Woodstock (☎ (074) 76 0600 for information).

SOUTH BURNETT REGION

Farther inland, the South Burnett region includes Australia's most important peanut-growing area. **Kingaroy** almost means 'peanuts' in Australia, not least because the

The mega-kitsch Big Pineapple holds a bizarre fascination for tourists

ex-premier of Queensland, Sir Joh Bjelke-Petersen, hails from here. There's a tourist office (☎ (071) 62 3199) at 128 Haly St, Kingaroy. Next door is the **Heritage Museum & Peanut Exhibition**.

The **Bunya Mountains**, isolated outliers of the Great Dividing Range, rise abruptly to over 1000 metres, and are accessible by sealed road about 50 km south-west of Kingaroy. The mountains are a national park, with a variety of vegetation from rainforest to heathland. There are three camping grounds, plus a network of walking tracks to numerous waterfalls and lookouts. The ranger (☎ (076) 68 3127) is at Dandabah.

Darling Downs

West of the Great Dividing Range in southern Queensland stretch the rolling plains of the Darling Downs, some of the most fertile agricultural land in Australia. In the state's early history, nobody was allowed within an 80-km radius of the penal colony of Brisbane but settlers gradually pushed their way north from New South Wales through the Darling Downs area.

Towns such as Toowoomba and Warwick are among the most historic in the state. South of Warwick, the scenic Granite Belt region has Queensland's only wine-growing district and some fine national parks. Other regional attractions include the historic Jondaryan Woolshed west of Toowoomba and the Miles Historical Village.

West of the Darling Downs, the population becomes more scattered as the crop-producing areas give way to sheep and cattle country centred on towns including Roma, Charleville and Cunnamulla.

Getting There & Away

Air Sabair (☎ (076) 33 1533) has daily flights from Brisbane to Toowoomba ($84), continuing on to St George, Cunnamulla and Thargomindah. Flight West (☎ 13 2392) flies daily from Brisbane to Roma ($180) and Charleville ($241).

Bus Greyhound Pioneer and McCafferty's both operate the following bus services that pass through the Darling Downs (their fares along these routes tend to be similar): from Brisbane to Longreach (17 hours, $77) along the Warrego Highway via Ipswich, Toowoomba (two hours, $15), Miles (5½ hours, $28), Roma (seven hours, $37) and Charleville (10 hours, $44); and inland from Brisbane to Melbourne via Toowoomba and Goondiwindi (five hours, $34).

In addition, McCafferty's has an inland service from Brisbane to Sydney that goes along the New England Highway via Warwick (2¾ hours, $23) and Stanthorpe (3½ hours, $29). There are also McCafferty's buses between Toowoomba and the Gold Coast ($20), and between Brisbane and Rockhampton via Toowoomba and Miles.

Train The *Westlander* runs twice a week from Brisbane to Charleville via Ipswich, Toowoomba and Roma. One-way fares are $77 for an economy seat, $107 for an economy sleeper and $172 for a 1st-class sleeper. There are connecting bus services from Charleville to Quilpie and Cunnamulla.

IPSWICH (pop 77,042)

Virtually an outer suburb of Brisbane now, Ipswich was a convict settlement as early as 1827 and an important early Queensland town. It's the main gateway to the Darling Downs. On the way from Brisbane to Ipswich, **Wolston House** at Grindle Rd, Wacol, 18 km west of Brisbane, is an early colonial country residence, built in 1852 of local materials. It's open Thursday to Monday from 9 am to 5 pm, and costs $3.

Ipswich has many fine old houses and public buildings. If you're interested in Queensland's distinctive architecture, pick up the excellent *Ipswich City Heritage Trails* leaflets, which will guide you around a great diversity of buildings. There's a tourist office (☎ (07) 3281 0555) on the corner of D'Arcy Place and Brisbane St.

IPSWICH TO WARWICK

South-west of Ipswich, the Cunningham Highway to Warwick crosses the Great Dividing Range at **Cunningham's Gap**, with 1100-metre mountains rising either side of the road. **Main Range National Park**, which covers the Great Dividing Range for about 20 km north and south of Cunningham's Gap, is great walking country, with a variety of walks starting from the car park at the crest of the gap. Much of the range is covered in rainforest. There's a camping ground and information office by the road on the western side of the gap; contact the ranger (☎ (076) 66 1133) for permits. **Spicer's Gap**, in the range south of Cunningham's Gap, has excellent views and another camping area. To reach it you turn off the highway five km west of Aratula back towards Ipswich.

WARWICK AREA

Warwick, 162 km south-west of Brisbane, is the oldest town in Queensland after the

MARK ARMSTRONG

PAUL STEEL

PAUL STEEL

Queensland

A: The Greek revivalist cenotaph, Anzac Square, Brisbane
B: Brisbane city by night
C: Aerial view of Surfers Paradise, Gold Coast

MARK ARMSTRONG

JOHN CHAPMAN

MARK ARMSTRONG

A
B
C

Queensland
A: Barron River, near Cairns
B: Mt Warning, Lamington National Park
C: Coloured sands, Fraser Island

capital. It's a busy farming centre noted for its roses, numerous historic buildings built of local sandstone, and its rodeo (held on the last weekend in October).

There's a tourist office (☎ (076) 61 3122) at 49 Albion St, and the **regional art gallery** is next door.

Warwick's major attraction is **Pringle Cottage & Museum** on Dragon St, dating from 1863. It is open daily except Tuesdays; entry costs $3.50. The *Criterion Hotel* (☎ (076) 61 1042) at 84 Palmerin St has B&B for $20 per person and cheap pub meals, and the historic *Aberfoyle B&B* (☎ (076) 61 8334) on the corner of Wood and Albion Sts has good double rooms for $70.

Killarney, 34 km south-east of Warwick near the New South Wales border, is a pretty little town in an area of fine mountain scenery. Among the many lovely waterfalls in the area is **Queen Mary Falls**, tumbling 40 metres into a rainforested gorge 10 km east of Killarney. There's a caravan/camping park (☎ (076) 64 7151) on the road near the falls.

STANTHORPE & THE GRANITE BELT

South of Warwick is the Granite Belt, an elevated plateau of the Great Dividing Range 800 to 950 metres above sea level. It's known for fruit and vegetable production and wine making, and there are more than 20 wineries in the area, most of which are open to visitors.

Stanthorpe is the main centre for the region and it has a good range of accommodation, a historical museum and an art gallery. It celebrates its place as Queensland's coolest town with a Brass Monkey Festival every July, and there's a tourist office (☎ (076) 81 2057) on the corner of Marsh and Lock Sts.

The *Central Hotel* (☎ (076) 81 2044) on the corner of High and Victoria Sts has good singles/doubles from $25/40. Next door, *Il Cavallino* has good-value Italian tucker. Twelve km north at Thulimbah, the *Summit Lodge Backpackers* (☎ (076) 83 2599) on the New England Highway specialises in finding fruit and vegetable-picking work for travellers and has dorm beds for $12.50 a night – ring ahead to see what's available.

From the highway 26 km south of Stanthorpe, a sealed road leads nine km east up to **Girraween National Park**, an area of 1000-metre-high hills, huge granite outcrops, and valleys. The park has a visitor centre (☎ (076) 84 5157), two camping grounds with hot showers, and several walking tracks of varying length. Girraween adjoins Bald Rock National Park over the border in New South Wales. It can fall below freezing on winter nights up here, but summer days are warm.

GOONDIWINDI & FARTHER WEST

West of Warwick, Goondiwindi is on the New South Wales border and the Macintyre River. Known as the home of the great racehorse, Gunsynd, it's a popular stop on the Newell Highway between Melbourne and Brisbane. There's a small museum in the old customs house and a wildlife sanctuary at the Boobera Lagoon. If you continue inland from Goondiwindi you reach **St George**, where cotton is grown on irrigated land.

TOOWOOMBA (pop 88,100)

On the edge of the Great Dividing Range and the Darling Downs, 138 km inland from Brisbane, Toowoomba is a gracious city with pleasant parks, tree-lined streets and many early buildings. The tourist centre (☎ (076) 39 3797) is at 541 Ruthven St; next door is the excellent (and free) **Toowoomba Regional Art Gallery**. The **Cobb & Co Museum** at 27 Lindsay St has a great collection of old carriages and buggies, and nearby the lovely **botanic gardens** occupy the northern section of Queens Park.

The 1859 **Royal Bull's Head Inn** in Drayton, seven km west, can be visited Thursday to Monday from 10 am to 4 pm, for $2.50.

Places to Stay

Near the train station at 70 Russell St, the *Hotel Norville* (☎ (076) 39 2954) has rooms from $20 per person. For a splurge, the magnificent *Vacy Hall Private Hotel* (☎ (076) 39 2055) at 135 Russell St has rooms from $75 to $140 a night.

Cattle farming is the economic mainstay of the Darling Downs

TOOWOOMBA TO ROMA

At **Jondaryan**, 45 km west of Toowoomba, you can visit the 1859 Jondaryan Woolshed (☎ (076) 92 2229), a historic tourist complex with rustic old buildings and daily shearing and blacksmithing demonstrations; entry costs $9. There's also a YHA-associated *youth hostel* here in authentically spartan shearers' quarters, with beds for $9 and camping sites for $8.

At Miles, 167 km farther west, the **Miles Historical Village** is also worth a visit. It's open daily from 8 am to 5 pm; entry costs $8. The *Hotel Australia* (☎ (076) 27 1106) at 55 Murilla St has good pub rooms at $18/30 for singles/doubles.

ROMA (pop 6860)

Early Queensland settlement, and now the centre for a huge sheep and cattle-raising district, Roma also has some curious small industries. There's enough oil in the area to support a small refinery, which produces just enough petroleum for local use. Gas deposits are rather larger, and Roma supplies Brisbane through a 450-km pipeline. There's also the small Bassett's Romavilla Winery, which is open daily. Roma's tourist office (☎ (076) 22 1416) is at the eastern entrance to the town.

Fraser Coast

The focal point of this stretch of coast is the majestic Fraser Island – at 120 km long the world's largest sand island. Hervey Bay, the major access point for the island, has grown into a busy tourist centre, while the southern access point is the sleepy and attractive Rainbow Beach.

Along the Bruce Highway are the rural centres of Gympie, the turn-off for Rainbow Beach, and Maryborough, the turn-off for Hervey Bay. Farther north, Bundaberg is the largest town in the area and mostly famous as the home of the distinctive Bundaberg rum.

GYMPIE (pop 11,700)

Gympie was established with an 1867 gold rush and became one of Queensland's richest goldfields. Gold was mined here right up to 1920. A week-long Gold Rush Festival is held in Gympie every October. The Country Music Muster in August is also pretty big.

There's a tourist office (☎ (074) 82 5444) on the Bruce Highway as you enter Gympie from the south, open daily from 8.30 am to 3.30 pm. In the same building there's a QNP&WS office (☎ (074) 82 4189) where you can get permits and information on Fraser Island and the Cooloola National Park – it is open weekdays only from 8.30 am to 4 pm. Nearby is the interesting and extensive **Gympie Gold Mining & Historical Museum**, which is open daily ($6).

A few km north of the town on Fraser Rd is the **Woodworks Forestry & Timber Museum**, open weekdays from 10 am to 4 pm ($2.50). You can get information here on camping in nearby state forests.

Gympie has several motels and caravan parks, and it's on the main bus and train routes north from Brisbane.

RAINBOW BEACH (pop 730)

This little town on Wide Bay, 70 km northeast of Gympie, is the southern access point for Fraser Island and the northern access point for the Cooloola National Park.

From Rainbow Beach it's a 13-km drive north along the beach to Inskip Point, where ferries leave for Fraser Island. South-east of the town, the beach curves away 13 km to Double Island Point at the top of the Cooloola Coast. One km along this beach is the 120-metre-high **Carlo sand blow**, and beyond it, the coloured sand cliffs after which the town is named. You can walk behind or along the beach all the way from the town and up to the lighthouse on Double Island Point.

The privately run Rainbow Beach Tourist Information Centre (☎ (074) 86 3227) at 8 Rainbow Beach Rd has a list of other walks in the area. In a 4WD it's possible to drive most of the 70 km south to Noosa, along the beach. (See the Cooloola National Park section earlier in this chapter.)

The QNP&WS office (☎ (074) 86 3160), where you can obtain Fraser Island vehicle and camping permits, and northern Cooloola National Park camping permits, is beside the main road as you enter Rainbow Beach; it's open daily from 7 am to 4 pm.

Sun Safari Tours offers day trips to Fraser Island ($58 including lunch) and half-day trips to the Cooloola National Park, Double Island Point and the *Cherry Venture* wreck ($30); book through the information centre.

Places to Stay

The *Rainbow Beach Holiday Village* (☎ (074) 86 3222) on Rainbow Beach Rd has a backpacker section with three-bed tents and basic cooking facilities for $7.50 per person, tent sites from $10 and on-site vans from $25.

Rainbow Beach Backpackers (☎ (074) 86 3288) at 66 Rainbow Beach Rd charges $12 for dorms and $28 for doubles. It's a small, clean place with a kitchenette, pool and restaurant next door (but no laundrette).

The *Rainbow Beach Hotel-Motel* (☎ (074) 86 3125) near the beachfront has rooms from $38/45, and the *Rainbow Sands* (☎ (074) 86 3400) on Rainbow Beach Rd has modern self-contained units from $50 a double.

Getting There & Away

Polley's Coaches (☎ (074) 82 2700) runs three bus services between Gympie and Rainbow Beach every weekday. The one-way fare is $9.25.

Another way to Rainbow Beach is to hitchhike along the beaches up from Noosa or on to Fraser Island. If you have a 4WD vehicle you can drive this way too.

Getting Around

In Rainbow Beach, the tourist centre and Jeep City (☎ (074) 86 3223), at 10 Karounda Court, both rent 4WDs from around $90 a day with a two-day minimum hire.

QUEENSLAND

The *Cherry Venture* wreck on Rainbow Beach

MARYBOROUGH (pop 24,000)

Maryborough's early importance as an industrial centre and port on the Mary River led to the construction of a series of imposing Victorian buildings. The greatest concentration of these is along Wharf St, including the impressive **post office** (1869).

Maryborough's most interesting feature is the National Trust classified **Brennan & Geraghty's Store** at 64 Lennox St. This historic store was run by the same family for 100 years and has been preserved intact with original stock, trading records and other fascinating stuff – well worth a look. It is open daily from 10 am to 3 pm ($3).

There are several motels and caravan parks in the town, plus budget accommodation in some of the old hotels, such as the *Criterion Hotel* (☎ (071) 21 3043) at 98 Wharf St, which has basic rooms for $15 per person.

HERVEY BAY (pop 33,000)

The once-sleepy settlement of Hervey Bay has grown at an astronomical rate in the last decade, and is now a major stopover on the

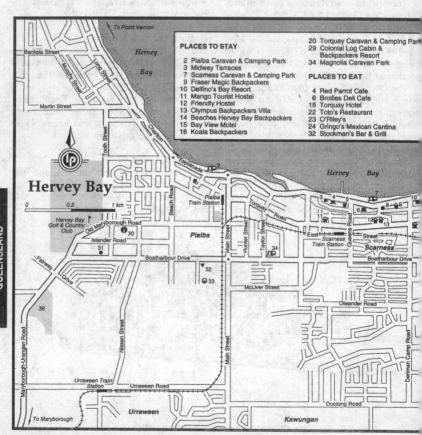

PLACES TO STAY

2 Pialba Caravan & Camping Park
3 Midway Terraces
7 Scarness Caravan & Camping Park
9 Fraser Magic Backpackers
10 Delfino's Bay Resort
11 Mango Tourist Hostel
12 Friendly Hostel
13 Olympus Backpackers Villa
14 Beaches Hervey Bay Backpackers
15 Bay View Motel
16 Koala Backpackers
20 Torquay Caravan & Camping Park
29 Colonial Log Cabin & Backpackers Resort
34 Magnolia Caravan Park

PLACES TO EAT

4 Red Parrot Cafe
6 Brollies Deli Cafe
18 Torquay Hotel
22 Toto's Restaurant
23 O'Riley's
24 Gringo's Mexican Cantina
32 Stockman's Bar & Grill

backpacker circuit. The main attractions are Fraser Island, of which Hervey Bay is the main access point, and whale-watching trips in the bay.

The five small settlements that make up the town are popular family holiday spots with safe beaches and a huge number of caravan parks. There's no surf here – the best beach is at Torquay.

Orientation
The five 'suburbs' of Hervey Bay are strung along a north-facing 10-km stretch of coast.

From west to east they are Point Vernon, Pialba, Scarness, Torquay and Urangan. Pialba is the main business and shopping centre but Torquay is where most of the action is. Fraser Island is 12 km across the Great Sandy Strait from Urangan, with Woody Island in between. River Heads, the departure point for the main Fraser Island ferries, is 15 km south of Urangan.

Information
There are a host of privately run information centres and tour booking offices, including

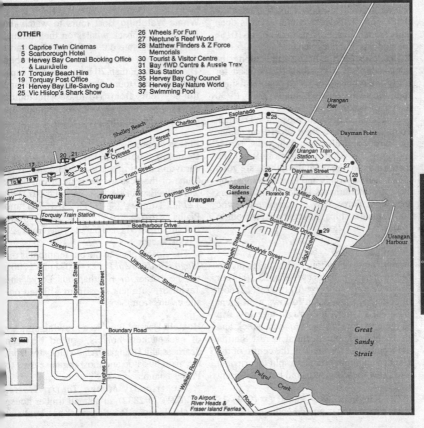

OTHER
1 Caprice Twin Cinemas
5 Scarborough Hotel
8 Hervey Bay Central Booking Office & Laundrette
17 Torquay Beach Hire
19 Torquay Post Office
21 Hervey Bay Life-Saving Club
25 Vic Hislop's Shark Show
26 Wheels For Fun
27 Neptune's Reef World
28 Matthew Flinders & Z Force Memorials
30 Tourist & Visitor Centre
31 Bay 4WD Centre & Aussie Trax
33 Bus Station
35 Hervey Bay City Council
36 Hervey Bay Nature World
37 Swimming Pool

QUEENSLAND

the Hervey Bay Tourist & Visitor Centre (☎ (071) 24 4050) at 63 Old Maryborough Rd in Pialba.

Things to See

Hervey Bay Natureworld, near the corner of Maryborough-Urangan Rd and Fairway Drive, Pialba, has native Australian fauna including wedge-tailed eagles and koalas, as well as introduced species such as camels and water buffalo. Crocodiles are fed at 11.30 am and lorikeets at 3.30 pm, and entry costs $7.

Vic Hislop's Shark Show, on the corner of Charlton Esplanade and Elizabeth St in Urangan, has a gruesome collection of photos, articles, jaw bones and a great white shark, plus shark documentaries. It is open daily from 8.30 am to 6 pm and costs $10 ($8 for students and backpackers).

Urangan Pier, a little farther along the Esplanade, is 1.4 km long. Once used for sugar and oil handling, it's a popular fishing spot, since the far end stands in 25 to 30 metres of water.

Almost one km east of the pier, at Dayman Point, is **Neptune's Reef World,** an aquarium with coral displays, fish, seals, turtles and a croc. It is open daily from 9 am and costs $8. From the point itself there are good views over to Woody and Fraser islands, and there are monuments to Matthew Flinders and the Z Force WW II commandos who sank Japanese ships in Singapore Harbour in 1943.

Organised Tours

Fraser Island Day tours with larger operators such as Top Tours (☎ (071) 25 3933) or Fraser Venture Tours (☎ (071) 27 9122) cost around $55. Each outfit follows a different route but a typical tour might take in a trip up the east coast to the *Maheno* wreck and the Cathedrals, plus Central Forest Station and a couple of the lakes in the centre of the island. You might be able to split the trip and stay a few days on the island before coming back.

The Kingfisher Bay Resort (☎ (071) 25 5511) offers ranger-guided ecotours for $63

including lunch. If you want to fly to the island, Air Fraser Island (☎ (071) 25 3600) offers day trips for $35 per person, or $80 with 4WD hire included.

Self-drive tours organised from the hostels are popular and cost about $95 per person for a three-day trip. This doesn't include food or fuel but all the gear is organised for you. These trips are an affordable and (usually) fun way to see the island, but you'll probably be in a group of up to nine people and you can't choose who you go with. Despite what some of the hostels will tell you, there are plenty of alternative ways to see the island if you'd rather do your own thing.

Whale-Watching Boat tours to watch the majestic humpback whales on their annual migration operate out of Hervey Bay most days between late July and mid-October. There are more than 20 boats offering trips, with half-day tours from $42 to $55 and full-day tours from $40 to $60, including lunch. Book through your accommodation or one of the information centres.

Places to Stay

Camping There are at least a dozen caravan/camping parks in Hervey Bay. Some of the best are the council-run parks along the Esplanade at Scarness (☎ (071) 28 1274), Torquay (☎ (074) 25 1578) and Pialba (☎ (071) 28 1399). These parks have tent sites from $11 and on-site vans from $28 – book ahead.

The closest place to the bus terminal is the *Magnolia Caravan Park* (☎ (071) 28 1700), on the corner of Boatharbour Drive and Taylor St, with tent sites from $13 and on-site cabins from $45.

Hostels Hervey Bay has a growing number of backpackers hostels, spread between Scarness and Urangan. All do pick-ups from the main bus stop and most organise trips to Fraser Island.

The friendly *Mango Tourist Hostel* (☎ (071) 24 2832), in a small timber house at 110 Torquay Rd, Scarness, has bunks at

$12 and one double at $35. It's a very laid-back, alternative hostel run by people who are passionate about Fraser Island, and it's a good place for information about the island and how to get there.

The new *Olympus Backpackers* (☎ (071) 24 5331) at 184 Torquay Rd, Scarness, has eight impressive apartments with their own facilities, plus a pool. Dorm beds are $13, and twins and doubles $28.

Koala Backpackers (☎ (071) 25 3601), at 408 The Esplanade, Torquay, is a large place with good facilities including a pool and a bar. It's fairly party-oriented and has evening meals for $5. There are two-bedroom units with their own kitchen and bathroom at $14, or six-bed dorms with communal facilities at $13; doubles cost $30.

Beaches Hervey Bay Backpackers (☎ (071) 24 1322), at 195 Torquay Terrace in Scarness, has the usual hostel facilities and a pool. There are two sections, one with dorms and the other with rooms with private bathroom and TV; the nightly cost is $13 per person.

At Urangan, the *Colonial Log Cabin & Backpackers Resort* (☎ (071) 25 1844), on the corner of Boatharbour Drive and Pulgul St, is a few km out of the centre but it's quiet and spacious and backs onto bushland. Two and three-bed dorms cost $13, self-contained cabins cost $13 to $15, and doubles are $30. There's a good pool and tennis court, and free bikes.

The *Friendly Hostel* (☎ (071) 24 4107) at 182 Torquay Rd, Scarness, is a small place with three three-bedroom units with their own TV lounge, kitchen and bathroom; beds are $10 per person. *Fraser Magic Backpackers* (☎ (071) 24 3488) at 369 Charlton Esplanade, Scarness, is a converted block of old holiday apartments with dorms at $12 per person and doubles at $30, including breakfast.

Motels & Holiday Units The *Bay View Motel* (☎ (071) 28 1134), at 399 Charlton Esplanade, Torquay, has oldish but clean units from $30/35. *Midway Terraces* (☎ (071) 28 4119) at 335 Charlton Espla-

nade, Scarness, is a small block of straight-forward units that sleep up to five, costing from $35 a double plus $5 for each extra person.

At 383 Charlton Esplanade, Torquay, *Delfino's Bay Resort* (☎ (071) 24 1666) has bright modern motel units from $50 and self-contained units from $60 to $100; there's a pool, sauna and restaurant.

Places to Eat
The majority of the eateries are along the Esplanade. *Brollies Deli Cafe*, at 353 Charlton Esplanade in Scarness, is a good place for breakfast or lunch and has 'real' coffee and excellent sandwiches. Nearby at No 341, the *Red Parrot* is another good daytime cafe.

Gringo's Mexican Cantina, at 449 Charlton Esplanade, has good Mexican tucker with mains from $10 to $15, and nearby at No 446 *O'Riley's* is a casual pizza/pasta joint with crepes and pancakes as well. *Toto's*, at 2 Fraser St, also has good pizza and pasta, and Thai, Malaysian and Italian food – something for everyone! The *China Garden* restaurant has all-you-can-eat deals from $9.50.

The *Torquay Hotel* has a good beer garden. The *Stockman's Bar & Grill*, near the bus stop on Boatharbour Drive, is a popular beer barn with live music and good meals between $5 and $15.

Getting There & Away
Sunstate and Flight West have daily flights between Brisbane and Hervey Bay; the one-way fare is $136. Hervey Bay airport is off Booral Rd, Urangan.

Hervey Bay is on the major bus route. It's about 4½ hours from Brisbane (averaging $30), and about 5½ hours from Rockhampton ($55).

Maryborough-Hervey Bay Coaches (☎ (071) 21 3719) runs a service between the two centres, with nine trips every weekday and three on Saturday.

Buses operate from Geldard's Coach Terminal (☎ (071) 24 4000) in Central Ave, off Boatharbour Drive in Pialba.

Getting Around

There are several good 4WD hire places. The Bay 4WD Centre (☎ (071) 28 2981) at 54 Boatharbour Drive in Pialba, and Allterrain (bookings through Koala Backpackers) have good, reliable vehicles ranging from about $85 a day for a Suzuki Sierra to $125 for a Toyota Landcruiser, usually with a two-day minimum. Aussie Trax (☎ 071) 24 4433) at 56 Boatharbour Drive has ex-army jeeps from $77 a day.

Wheels For Fun (☎ (071) 25 4499), at 3 Florence St, Urangan, hires out trail bikes from $60 a day.

FRASER ISLAND

Fraser Island, the world's largest sand island, was added to the World Heritage List in 1993. The island is 120 km long by about 15 km wide and rises in places to 200 metres above sea level. Apart from three or four small rock outcrops, it's all sand, which is mostly covered in vegetation. Here and there the cover is broken by sand blows – dunes that grow, shrink or move as the wind pushes them. The island also has about 200 lakes, some of them superb for swimming. Nearly all of the northern half forms the Great Sandy National Park.

Fraser Island is a delight for those who love fishing, walking, exploring by 4WD or trail bike, and for those who simply enjoy nature. There are superb beaches (but swimming in the ocean can be dangerous due to severe undertows and the odd shark or 10!), towering dunes, thick forests, walking tracks, clear freshwater lakes and streams for swimming, and interesting wildlife. The island is sparsely populated and although more than 20,000 vehicles a year pile on to it, it remains wild. A network of sandy tracks crisscrosses the island and you can drive along great stretches of beach – but it's 4WD or trail bike only; there are no sealed roads.

The island takes its name from Eliza Fraser, the wife of the captain of a ship that was wrecked farther north in 1836. Making their way south to look for help, a group from the ship fell among Aboriginal people on Fraser Island. Some of the group died during their two-month wait for rescue but with Aboriginal help others, including Eliza Fraser, survived.

The Butchulla Aboriginal people who used Fraser Island as a seasonal home were driven out onto missions when timber cutters arrived in the 1860s. The cutters were after satinay, a rainforest tree almost unique to Fraser Island, which is highly resistant to marine borer; this timber was used to line the Suez Canal. It was not until 1991 that logging on the island ceased.

In the mid-1970s, Fraser Island was the subject of a bitter struggle between conservationists and industry – in this case a sand-mining company. The decision was in favour of the conservationists.

Information

There's a visitor centre on the east coast of the island at Eurong (☎ (071) 27 9128), and rangers' offices at Dundubura and Waddy Point. These places all have plenty of leaflets detailing walking trails and the flora and fauna found on the island.

A good map is essential if you will be spending a few days exploring. The Sunmap 1:140,000 ($6) provides all the detail you need and is widely available in Hervey Bay.

General supplies are available from stores at Eurong, Happy Valley and Cathedral Beach but, as you might expect, prices are high. There are also public telephones at these sites.

At Central Forest Station there's a small display on the history of exploration and logging on the island.

Permits You'll need a permit to take a vehicle onto the island, and to camp. The most convenient place to get permits is the River Heads general store, just half a km from the ferry to Wanggoolba Creek. Vehicle permits cost $15, and camping costs $7.50 per site per night. If you're staying in some of the island's cabin accommodation or camping in one of the private camping grounds, there's no need to pay the $7.50.

Permits can also be obtained from any of the QNP&WS offices in the area or from the Hervey Bay City Council (☎ (071) 25 0222) in Tavistock St.

QUEENSLAND

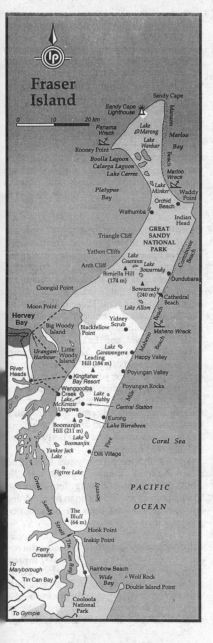

Fraser Island

Driving on the Island The only thing stopping you taking a conventional (non-4WD) vehicle onto the island is the fact that you probably won't get more than half a km before being bogged in sand. Small 4WD sedans are OK, but you may have ground-clearance problems on some of the inland tracks – a 'proper' 4WD gives maximum mobility.

Ask on the mainland about island driving conditions before renting a 4WD vehicle. Sometimes rain and storms can make beaches and tracks very heavy going, if not impassable. The best sources of such information are probably the offices issuing the vehicle permits.

Driving on the island requires a good deal of care to protect not only yourself but the fragile environment. Apart from the beaches, where you are free to drive at will, all tracks are obvious and you should stick to them. Most major junctions are signposted but only the two dedicated 'scenic routes' are signposted along their length. When driving, you should have 4WD engaged at all times, not so much because of the danger of getting stuck, but because your wheels are less likely to spin and damage the sandy tracks.

When driving on the beaches, watch for washouts at the many creek outlets, especially after heavy rain. Use turn indicators to show oncoming vehicles which side you intend passing on. Low tide is the best time to travel as large expanses of smooth hard sand are exposed. At high tide it is much more difficult, and quite slow going. An additional hazard is that the beach directly outside the resorts is used as a landing strip for small aircraft. The speed limit on the beaches is 80 km/h. On the inland tracks it's 35 km/h, although there's little opportunity to reach that speed.

Drive slowly when passing pedestrians and people fishing as they probably won't hear you coming above the roar of the surf.

Driving on the eastern beach is fairly straightforward; the western beach is more treacherous and has swamps and holes – avoid it.

QUEENSLAND

Things to See & Do

Starting from the south at Hook Point, you cross a number of creeks and get to **Dilli Village**, the former sand-mining centre. After the settlements of **Eurong** and **Happy Valley**, you cross Eli Creek, the largest creek on the east coast. About 65 km from Hook Point are the remains of the *Maheno*, a former passenger liner that was wrecked here in 1935 as it was being towed to a Japanese scrap yard.

Four km beyond Eurong is a signposted walking trail to the beautiful **Lake Wabby**, which is being slowly filled by a massive sand blow that advances about three metres a year. It's a 45-minute walk (rewarded by a swim in the lake) or you can drive another 2.6 km north on the beach where a scenic route will take you to a lookout on the inland side of the lake. *Don't* dive into the lake after running down the steep sand dunes – in the last few years, five people have suffered spinal injuries doing exactly that.

A popular inland area for visitors is the south-central lake and rainforest country around Central Forest Station, and lakes McKenzie, Jennings, Birrabeen and Boomanjin. **Lake McKenzie** is unbelievably clear. Known as a 'window' lake, the water here is actually part of the water table, and so has not flowed anywhere over land.

Two marked vehicle tracks lead inland from Happy Valley: one goes to **Lake Garawongera** then south to the beach again at Poyungan Valley (15 km); the other heads to **Yidney Scrub** and a number of lakes before returning to the ocean beach north of the *Maheno* (45 km). The latter route will take you to some fine lakes and good lookout points among the highest dunes on the island.

Not far north of Happy Valley you enter the national park and pass the *Maheno* and the **Cathedrals**, 25 km of coloured sand cliffs. Dundubara has a ranger's hut and probably the best camping ground on the island. Then there's a 20-km stretch of beach before you come to the rock outcrops of Indian Head, Middle Rocks and Waddy Point. Just past here is **Orchid Beach**, and it's a farther 30 km of beach up to **Sandy Cape**, the northern tip, with its lighthouse a few km to the west.

Walking Tracks There are a number of 'walkers-only' tracks ranging from the one-km Wungul Sand Blow Track at Dundubara to the 13-km trail between Wabby and McKenzie lakes. The useful *Fraser Island Recreation Area* leaflet put out by the QNP&WS lists several more.

Places to Stay & Eat

Come well-equipped since supplies on the island are limited and expensive and are only available in a few places. And be prepared for mosquitoes and horseflies.

Camping This is the cheapest way to stay on the island and it gives you the chance to get closer to Fraser Island's unique natural environment. The Queensland forestry department and the QNP&WS operate 11 camping areas on the island, some accessible only by boat or on foot. Those in the north at Dundubara, Waddy Point and Wathumba and in the south at Central Forest Station, Lake Boomanjin and Lake McKenzie all have toilets and showers. You can also camp on some stretches of beach. To camp in any of these public areas you need a permit.

A word of warning: backpackers' tours already have a bad reputation among the rangers here, and they will quite happily throw you off the island and/or fine you if they find you drunk and disorderly or disturbing other campers.

There's also the privately-run *Cathedral Beach Resort & Camping Park* (☎ (071) 28 4988), 34 km north of Eurong. Tent sites cost $14 and cabins are $75 for up to four people, but they're not too keen on backpacker groups here.

Other Accommodation *Dilli Village Recreation Camp* (☎ (071) 27 9130) is 200 metres from the east coast, 24 km from Hook Point and nine km from Eurong. A four-bed cabin with shower and equipped kitchen costs $40 for up to four people ($45 in the holiday season). Cabins without kitchen or bathroom cost $10 per person, or you can camp for $3 per person.

The *Eurong Beach Resort* (☎ (071) 27 9122), 35 km north of Hook Point on the east coast, has several sections ranging from double motel rooms with kitchenettes for $70, to two-bedroom apartments for $160. The resort also has a general store, bar and bistro.

Just south of Happy Valley, the low-key *Yidney Rocks Cabins* (☎ (071) 27 9167) is right on the edge of the beach. They're old but comfortable; the rate is $65 for up to six people or $80 for up to eight.

The *Happy Valley Resort* (☎ (071) 27 9144) has good self-contained timber lodges from $120/150 for doubles/triples, and larger lodges for $170 a night for up to four people. The resort also has a bar, bistro and shop.

The impressive and luxurious *Kingfisher Bay Resort* (☎ 1800 072 555) on the west coast has hotel rooms from $119 per person with breakfast and transfers included. It also has two-bedroom villas from $690 for three nights and three-bedroom villas from $870 for three nights. The resort has restaurants, bars, shops etc, and architecturally, it's worth a look even if you're not staying there. There's also a day-tripper's section near the jetty, with the *Sandbar* bar and brasserie.

Getting There & Around

See the Noosa, Hervey Bay and Rainbow Beach sections for details of tours and 4WD hire from the mainland. On the island, vehicles are available through Kingfisher Bay 4WD Hire (☎ (071) 20 3366), with Lada Nivas from $120 a day and Landrover Defenders from $150 a day; Happy Valley 4WD Hire (☎ (071) 27 9260), with Suzukis from $100 a day and Toyota Landcruisers from $160 a day; and Shorty's Off Road Rentals (☎ (071) 27 9122) at Eurong, with a couple of Suzukis for $90 a day.

On the island you can get fuel at Eurong, Happy Valley, Cathedral Beach and Kingfisher Bay.

Vehicular ferries (known locally as barges) operate to the southern end of Fraser Island from Inskip Point near Rainbow Beach, and to the west coast of the island from River Heads south of Urangan.

The *Rainbow Venture* (☎ (074) 86 3154) operates the 10-minute crossing from Inskip Point to Hook Point on Fraser Island. It makes this crossing daily, regularly from about 7 am to 4.30 pm. The price is $45 return for a vehicle and passengers, and you can get tickets on board the ferry.

The *Fraser Venture* (☎ (071) 25 4444) makes the 30-minute crossing from River Heads to Wanggoolba Creek (also called Woongoolber Creek) on the west coast of Fraser Island. It departs from River Heads at 9 and 10.15 am and 3.30 pm, and returns from the island at 9.30 am, 2.30 and 4 pm. On Saturdays, there's also a 7 am service from River Heads, returning at 7.30 am from the island. The barge takes 27 vehicles but it's still advisable to book. The return fare for vehicle and driver is $55, plus $3 for each extra passenger.

The Kingfisher Bay Resort (☎ (071) 25 5155) also operates two boats: the *Fraser II* does the 25-minute crossing from River Heads to Kingfisher Bay daily. Departures from River Heads are at 7 and 11 am and 2 pm, and from the island at 9.45 am, 12.45 and 4.30 pm. The return fare is $55 for a vehicle and driver, plus $3 for each extra passenger. The *Kingfisher 1* is a passenger catamaran that crosses from the Urangan Boat Harbour to Kingfisher Bay, leaving from Urangan at 8.30 am, noon and 4 pm and returning at 9.30 am, 2 and 5 pm. The return fare is $28, which includes lunch.

The barges also take 'walk-on' passengers for $10 return.

It's quite possible to make your own way around the island, and hitching along the main tracks and beaches is pretty common practice. River Heads is probably the best place to try your luck, as this is where most of the island's traffic starts from.

CHILDERS (pop 1850)

Childers, a historic township on the Bruce Highway, has quite a few Victorian-era buildings. The town is the turn-off for the

QUEENSLAND

lovely **Woodgate Beach** and **Woodgate National Park**.

The *Palace Backpackers Hostel* (☎ (071) 26 2244) is right in the centre of Childers at 72 Churchill St. It's in a restored hotel, and has excellent facilities and four and six-bed dorms for $12 per person. It's mainly a workers' hostel, and the owners can often find harvest work for travellers.

BUNDABERG (pop 32,730)

At the northern end of Hervey Bay, Bundaberg is a major sugar-growing, processing and exporting centre. Some of the sugar ends up in the famous Bundaberg rum. The town is 50 km off the Bruce Highway and 15 km inland from the coast on the Burnett River. It's the southern-most access point for the Great Barrier Reef and it is the departure point for Lady Elliot and Lady Musgrave islands.

Bundaberg attracts a steady stream of travellers looking for harvest work, picking everything from avocados to zucchinis, and the hostels here can often help you find work – but be wary of promises of work that doesn't exist. It's worth ringing a few of the hostel managers and enquiring before you come.

Orientation & Information

Bundaberg Tourist Information Centre (☎ (071) 52 2333) is on the corner of Isis Highway – the main road as you enter the town from the south – and Bourbong St. It's open daily from 9 am to 5 pm. The town centre and post office are about a km east along Bourbong St from the tourist office.

Things to See & Do

You can tour the **Bundaberg Rum Distillery** (☎ (071) 52 4077) on Avenue St in East Bundaberg daily between 10 am and 3 pm; tours cost $4 including a sample drink. While you're here it's worth visiting **Schmeider's Cooperage & Craft Centre**, on nearby Alexandra St, where you can watch coopers hand-make timber barrels and other products.

The **Hinkler House Museum** is dedicated to the life and times of the aviator Bert

Hinkler, who was born in Bundaberg and, in 1928, made the first solo flight from England to Australia. The house in which he lived for his last years was transported from Southhampton, England, to the botanic gardens on the corner of Young St and Perry Rd in North Bundaberg, and is open daily from 10 am to 4 pm ($2). Also in the gardens is the **Bundaberg & District Historical Museum**.

The **Bundaberg Art Gallery** is in the historic School of Arts building in Bourbong St. There's also the **Bundaberg Reptile Reserve**, four km south of the centre.

Moore Park, 20 km north, and **Bargara**, 13 km east, are popular family beaches. Local buses go to Moore Park and Bargara a few times on weekdays from the Bundaberg post office.

Lady Musgrave Barrier Reef Cruises (☎ 1800 072 110) has day trips to Lady Musgrave Island ($96 plus $7 for bus transfers to the port), and whale-watching trips from mid-August to mid-October.

Places to Stay

The clean and modern *Bundaberg Backpackers & Travellers Lodge* (☎ (071) 52 2080) is diagonally opposite the bus terminal, on the corner of Targo and Crofton Sts. Dorm beds are $14 a night. The very well set up *City Centre Backpackers* (☎ (071) 51 3501), in the former Grosvenor Hotel at 216 Bourbong St, has two sections; six-bed motel units cost $15 per person, and dorm beds cost $14. Prices at both places include transport to/from work.

The *Royal Motel* (☎ (071) 51 2201), on the corner of Barolin and Bourbong Sts, has budget doubles from $35. The town also has plenty of other motels and caravan/camping parks.

Getting There & Away

Air services are by Sunstate (daily from Brisbane, Gladstone, Rockhampton, Mackay and Townsville) and Flight West (daily from Brisbane and Gladstone). All the main bus companies serve Bundaberg on the main north-south route. The main stop is Stewart's Coach

Mon Repos Turtle Rookery

Australia's most accessible turtle rookery is at Mon Repos Beach, 15 km north-east of Bundaberg. Four types of turtle – loggerhead, green, flatback and leatherback – have been known to nest here, but it's predominantly the loggerhead that lays its eggs here. The rookery is unusual, since turtles generally prefer sandy islands off the coast. The nesting season runs from early November until the end of March, and you're most likely to see the turtles laying their eggs at about midnight when the tide is high. From mid-January to March, the young begin to emerge and make their way quickly to the sea. Observation of the turtles is controlled by the QNP&WS Information Centre (☎ (071) 59 2628), which is open daily during the season from 7 pm to 6 am; entry costs $4.

During the season, the QNP&WS operates a 24-hour hotline (☎ (071) 59 1652) with recorded information about the turtles. There are no local bus services to Mon Repos, but Lady Musgrave Bus Services (☎ (018) 988 280) runs bus tours from Bundaberg to Mon Repos during the turtle season. The $15 return includes entry to the rookery; the driver will pick you up from wherever you're staying. ■

Terminal (☎ (071) 52 9700) at 66 Targo St. Bundaberg is also a stop for trains between Brisbane and Rockhampton or Cairns.

Capricorn Coast

This central coastal area of Queensland takes its name from its position straddling the Tropic of Capricorn. Rockhampton is the major population centre in the area, and just off the coast lies Great Keppel Island, a popular getaway. Offshore from Gladstone are the Southern Reef Islands, the southernmost part of the Great Barrier Reef, while south of Gladstone are the laid-back townships of Seventeen Seventy and Agnes Water, the state's northernmost surf beach.

Inland, the Capricorn Hinterland has the fascinating gemfields region and the spectacular Carnarvon and Blackdown Tableland national parks.

SOUTHERN REEF ISLANDS

The southernmost part of the Great Barrier Reef, known as the Capricornia section, begins 80 km north-east of Bundaberg around Lady Elliot Island. The coral reefs and cays in this group dot the ocean for about 140 km up to Tryon Island east of Rockhampton.

Several cays in this part of the reef are excellent for snorkelling, diving and just getting back to nature – though reaching them is generally more expensive than reaching islands nearer the coast. Access is from Bundaberg, Gladstone or Rosslyn Bay near Rockhampton. A few islands are important breeding grounds for turtles and sea birds.

On the four national park islands where camping is allowed (Lady Musgrave, Masthead, Tryon and North West) campers must be totally self-sufficient. Numbers of campers are limited so it's advisable to apply well ahead for a camping permit. You can book six months ahead for these islands instead of the usual six to 12 weeks for other Queensland national parks. Contact the QNP&WS (☎ (079) 72 6055) on the corner of Goondoon and Tank Sts in Gladstone. If you get a permit you'll also receive information on any rules, such as restrictions on the use of generators, and on how to avoid harming the wildlife.

Lady Elliot Island

Eighty km north-east of Bundaberg, Lady Elliot Island is a 0.4-sq-km vegetated coral cay. The resort has good diving facilities and you can take certificate courses there. The *Lady Elliot Island Resort* (☎ (071) 56 4444) is the only accommodation. It has simple,

QUEENSLAND

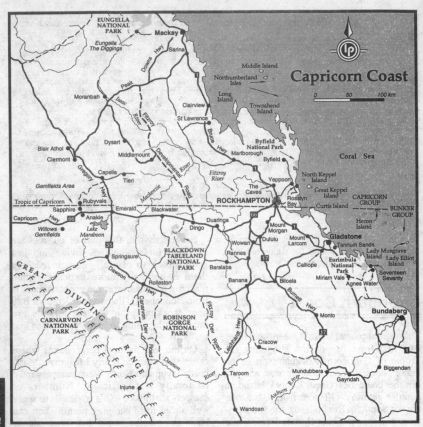

Capricorn Coast

0   50   100 km

no-frills tent-cabins and units ranging from $115 to $170 per person per night, including breakfast and dinner.

Whitaker Air Charters flies resort guests to the resort ($120 return) and offers day trips from Hervey Bay or Bundaberg for $99, or $120 including lunch and snorkelling gear. For resort or day-trip bookings, contact the Sunstate Travel Centre (☎ (079) 51 6077 or 1800 072 200).

Lady Musgrave Island

This 0.15-sq-km cay in the Bunker Group is an uninhabited national park about 100 km north-east of Bundaberg. Lady Musgrave sits at the western end of a huge lagoon and offers excellent diving and snorkelling opportunities. There's a QNP&WS camp site on the western side – there are no facilities apart from bush toilets, so campers must be totally self-sufficient. There's a limit of 50 people.

Lady Musgrave Cruises (☎ (071) 52 9011) operates day trips from Bundaberg four days a week costing $96 (plus $7 for bus transfers to Port Bundaberg), including lunch, snorkelling gear and a glass-bottom boat ride. The MV *Jetty II* (☎ (079) 74 9077) has day trips from Seventeen Seventy for $85 including lunch, snorkelling and fishing gear. You can use either boat as a camping drop-off service for around $190 return.

Heron Island

Only a km long and 0.17 sq km in area, Heron Island is 72 km east of Gladstone. The *Heron Island Resort* (☎ (079) 78 1488) owned by P&O covers the north-eastern third of the island; the rest is national park but you can't camp there. The resort has room for more than 250 people, with nightly tariffs ranging from $140 per person in the bunk rooms to $260 per person in the suites, including all meals – though there are cheaper stand-by rates. There are no day trips – resort guests pay another $136 return in the *Reef Adventurer* fast catamaran from Gladstone.

Although large sections of coral have been killed by silt as a result of dredging for a new, longer jetty at the island, Heron is still something of a mecca for divers. The resort offers lots of dive facilities and trips and has its own dive school – a certificate course for guests is $350, and single dives are available for certified divers.

Wilson Island

North of Heron, Wilson Island is a national park and a popular day trip for Heron guests looking for a break from diving. The island has superb snorkelling and great beaches, and the resort runs day trips for $28 including a barbecue lunch. There is no accommodation.

North West Island

At 0.9 sq km, North West Island is the biggest cay on the Barrier Reef. It's all national park, and it is one of the major nesting sites for green turtles, with nesting occurring between November and February. It's a popular destination for campers, but there's a limit of 150 people and you must be totally self-sufficient.

There are no day trips to the island at the moment, but a couple of operators offer camping drop-offs. From Seventeen

Seventy, the MV *Jetty II* (☎ (070) 74 9077) will do drop-offs for $100 per person each way; they also have camping gear and dinghies available for hire. The *Robert Poulsen* is a charter vessel that costs $1300 for a return trip for 14 people or more – contact P&O Marine Division (☎ (079) 72 5166) for details.

Tryon Island

Immediately north of North West Island, this tiny, beautiful six-hectare national park island is another important nesting area for sea birds and green turtles. There is a camping ground but the island is currently closed to visitors to allow for revegetation. Check with the QNP&WS office in Gladstone (☎ (079) 72 6055) for the latest.

AGNES WATER & SEVENTEEN SEVENTY

These two sleepy coastal townships are among the less commercialised destinations on the Queensland coast. There are no banks, and only a couple of shops and one pub here, plus a couple of caravan parks, some cabins and a B&B. Most people come for the fishing, boating, to kick back on the beaches or to visit the local national parks – apart from Christmas and Easter times, things are very laid back around here.

It's 57 km of mostly unsealed roads from the Bruce Highway across to Agnes Water, then another six km along the coast to Seventeen Seventy. There are no bus or train services to the towns.

Places to Stay & Eat

The *Seventeen Seventy Camping Ground* (☎ (079) 74 9286) is a good camping ground beside the mouth of Round Hill Creek. The excellent *Captain Cook Holiday Village* (☎ (079) 74 9219) one km south has a great bar/bistro, tent sites, on-site vans and cabins, and backpacker bungalows at $15 per person. Seven km inland, the *1770 Holiday Cabin Retreat* (☎ (079) 74 9270) has timber cabins from $50, while another four km west the friendly *Hoban's Hideaway* (☎ (079) 74

9144) has B&B accommodation from
$70/86.

GLADSTONE (pop 25,900)

Twenty km off the highway, Gladstone is one
of the busiest ports in Australia. It handles
agricultural, mineral and coal exports from
central Queensland, plus the alumina which
is processed in Gladstone from bauxite ore
shipped from Weipa on the Cape York Peninsula.

Gladstone's impressive new marina is the
main departure point for boats to Heron,
Masthead and Wilson islands on the Barrier
Reef. Its own harbour, Port Curtis, has many
islands. There's a tourist office (☎ (079) 72
4000) at 56 Goondoon St.

Gladstone has plenty of motels and
caravan parks, and the *Harbour Lodge*
(☎ (079) 72 6463) at 16 Roseberry St is a
very clean and well set up hostel with dorm
beds at $10 and singles/doubles at $15/25.
Don't miss the *Bellowing Bull Char Grill*
steak house on the corner of Goondoon and
William Sts – huge steaks with salads at
$4.50 for lunch or $6 for dinner.

Most coast buses stop at Gladstone and it's
also on the Brisbane to Rockhampton rail
route. You can also fly there with Sunstate or
Flight West.

ROCKHAMPTON (pop 61,600)

Australia's 'beef capital' sits astride the
Tropic of Capricorn. First settled by Europeans in 1855, Rockhampton had a relatively
small, early gold rush but cattle soon became
the big industry.

Rockhampton is now the administrative
and commercial centre of central Queensland. It has a few tourist attractions,
including a good art gallery, an Aboriginal
cultural centre and excellent parks and
gardens, but it is mainly an access point for
Great Keppel and other islands – boats leave
from Rosslyn Bay about 50 km away. Also
near Rocky are the spectacular limestone
caves in the Berserker Range to the north, the
old gold-mining town of Mt Morgan (38 km
south-west), the Koorana Crocodile Farm
near Emu Park, and the very popular Myella

Farm Stay (see the Capricorn Hinterland
section).

Orientation

Rockhampton is about 40 km from the coast,
straddling the Fitzroy River. The long
Fitzroy Bridge connects the old central part
of Rockhampton with the newer suburbs to
the north.

The Bruce Highway skirts the town centre
and crosses the river upstream from the
Fitzroy Bridge. Coming from the south, turn
right up Denham or Fitzroy Sts to reach the
centre of town.

Information

The Capricorn Information Centre (☎ (079)
27 2055) is on the highway three km south
of the centre, beside the Tropic of Capricorn
marker. More convenient is the helpful Riverside Information Centre (☎ (079) 22 5339)
on Quay St, which is open weekdays from
8.30 am to 4.30 pm and weekends from 9 am
to 4 pm. There's a QNP&WS office (☎ (079)
36 0511) seven km north-west of the centre,
near the turn-off to Yeppoon.

Things to See

There are many fine buildings in the town,
particularly on **Quay St**, which has a number
of grand buildings that date to the gold-rush
days. You can pick up tourist leaflets and
magazines that map out town walking trails.

The **Rockhampton City Art Gallery** on
Victoria Pde is open on weekdays from 10
am to 4 pm and on Sunday from 2 to 4 pm;
admission is free. On the Bruce Highway, six
km north of the centre, is the **Dreamtime
Cultural Centre** (☎ (079) 36 1655), an
Aboriginal heritage display centre. It's open
daily from 10 am to 5.30 pm, tours are run
daily at 11 am and 2 pm, and admission costs
$11; its courtesy bus does pick-ups.

The **Botanic Gardens** at the end of
Spencer St, in the south of the city, were
established in 1869 and have an excellent
tropical collection and a small fauna park.
North of the centre the **Cliff Kershaw
Gardens** is an excellent botanical park dedicated to Australian native plants.

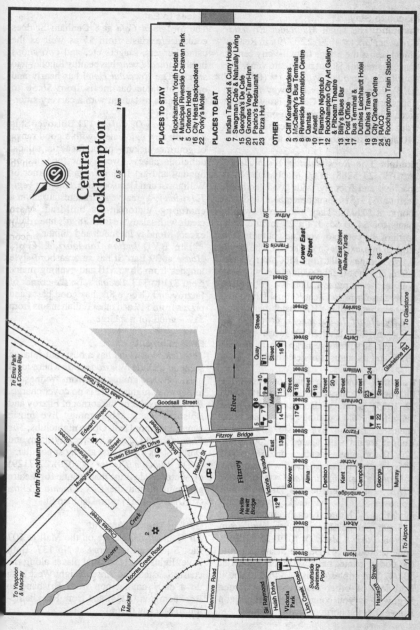

Central Rockhampton

0   0.5   1 km

QUEENSLAND

PLACES TO STAY

1   Rockhampton Youth Hostel
4   Municipal Riverside Caravan Park
5   Criterion Hotel
16 City Heart Backpackers
22 Porky's Motel

PLACES TO EAT

6   Indian Tandoori & Curry House
7   Swagman Cafe & Naturally Living
15 Georgina's De Cafe
20 Gnomes Vegi-Tarri-Inn
21 Pacino's Restaurant
23 Pizza Hut

OTHER

2   Cliff Kershaw Gardens
3   McCafferty's Bus Terminal
8   Riverside Information Centre
9   Qantas
10 Ansett
11 Flamingo Nightclub
12 Rockhampton City Art Gallery
    & Pilbeam Theatre
13 Billy's Blues Bar
14 Post Office
17 Bus Terminal &
    Duthies Leichhardt Hotel
18 Duthies Travel
19 City Cinema Centre
24 RACQ
25 Rockhampton Train Station

Places to Stay

Camping The small *Municipal Riverside Caravan Park* (☎ (079) 22 3779), in Reaney St just across the bridge from the city centre, has tent sites for $9 but no on-site vans. The *Southside Caravan Village* (☎ (079) 27 3013), across the Bruce Highway from the Capricorn Information Centre, is a well-kept place with backpacker beds in on-site vans from $11 to $14 per person, tent sites from $10 and on-site cabins from $38.

Hostels The *Rockhampton Youth Hostel* (☎ (079) 27 5288) at 60 MacFarlane St is spacious and friendly, with good facilities, dorms at $13 ($14 for nonmembers) and twin rooms at $28/32. They also have evening meals for $4 to $5. It's a 20-minute walk north of the centre or you can get there on a High St bus, except on weekends. The hostel is five minutes walk from McCafferty's terminal, and the other bus companies will drop you nearby on request. This is a good place to organise trips to Great Keppel Island and to book the popular YHA hostel there.

City Heart Backpackers (☎ (079) 22 2414) at 170 East St is more central; however, it suffered a large fire in August 1996, and its status is undetermined.

Hotels & Motels On Quay St beside the Fitzroy Bridge, the *Criterion Hotel* (☎ (079) 22 1225) is one of Rockhampton's most magnificent old buildings and it has good cheap meals and live music downstairs. Budget rooms with shared bathrooms are $20/30 for singles/doubles and renovated period-style suites are $40/45 with air-con.

Duthies Leichhardt Hotel (☎ (079) 27 6733), on the corner of Denham and Bolsover Sts, also has backpacker accommodation, with three beds in a motel unit at $15 per person. Motel rooms start from $40/48. *Porky's Motel* (☎ (079) 27 8100) is quite central at 141 George St and, despite the dodgy name, has respectable rooms at $38/42 and triples/quads at $46/49. You'll find lots of other motels on the Bruce Highway as you come into Rockhampton from either the north or south.

Places to Eat

The *Swagman Cafe* at 8 Denham St does cooked breakfasts from $5 as well as the usual burgers, sangers etc, and two shops north *Natural Living* has healthy lunches and salads. The *Criterion Hotel* has hearty and excellent-value bar meals from $6.50 to $7.50 and a restaurant with a carvery smorgasbord for $7.

Georgina's De Cafe at 171 Bolsover St is a trendy new cafe-eatery with a good range of gourmet tucker – pasta, focaccia, salads, delicious cakes... wear your pyjamas on Sunday and get 10% off. On the corner of William St and Denison Lane, *Gnomes Vegi-Tarri-Inn* is a great vegetarian restaurant in a charming Victorian-era building. Main meals with salads are from $8; it's open daily except Monday for lunch and dinner.

The BYO *Indian Tandoori & Curry House* at 39 East St has smorgasbord-style lunches from $6 to $10 and evening mains from $11 to $13. *Pacino's*, on the corner of Fitzroy and George Sts, has good pasta and pizzas from $12 and other Italian mains from $17 – good for a splurge.

Entertainment

The *Criterion Hotel* has a busy but relaxed scene in its little *Newsroom Bar* where local musicians and groups play from Wednesday to Saturday nights; there is no cover charge. *Billy's Blues Bar* on the corner of Fitzroy and Bolsover Sts is a big grungy live music venue and a pool hall. Of the nightclubs, *The Flamingo* on Quay St between William and Derby Sts is the biggest and most popular.

The *Pilbeam Theatre* (☎ (079) 27 7129) on Victoria Pde is the main venue for theatre and music, and the *City Cinema Centre* (☎ (079) 22 1511) is on Denham St.

Getting There & Around

Air Qantas/Sunstate are on the Mall at 107 East St; Ansett is nearby at No 137. Both have flights to all the usual places along the coast. Sunstate and Ansett/Flight West both do a daily coastal hop from Brisbane to Rockhampton ($234) and from Rockhampton to Mackay ($166).

Bus The McCafferty's terminal (☎ (079) 27 2844) is just north of the bridge off Queen Elizabeth Drive; Greyhound Pioneer buses all stop outside Duthies Leichhardt Hotel on the corner of Bolsover and Denham Sts. Both companies stop in Rocky on their major coastal runs. Destinations include Mackay (four hours, $38), Cairns (13 hours, $90) and Brisbane (nine hours, $60). McCafferty's also runs to Emerald ($28) daily, continuing on to Longreach ($51) three times a week.

Young's Bus Service (☎ (079) 22 3813) and Rothery's Coaches (☎ (079) 22 4320) both operate loop services around the Capricorn Coast to Yeppoon and Rosslyn Bay ($6 one way), Emu Park and back, leaving from outside Duthies Leichhardt Hotel. Young's also has buses to Mt Morgan ($6) daily except Sunday.

Opposite the hotel/bus stop, Duthies Travel (☎ (079) 27 6288) handles tickets for most destinations.

Train The Sunlander, Queenslander and Spirit of the Tropics all travel between Brisbane and Cairns via Rockhampton. One-way economy fares are Brisbane-Rockhampton $67 and Rockhampton-Cairns $105. Twice-weekly, the Spirit of the Outback runs between Brisbane, Rockhampton, Emerald and Longreach. For more information, contact the Queensland Rail Travel Centre at the railway station (☎ (079) 32 0242), one km south-east of the centre.

AROUND ROCKHAMPTON
Berserker Range
This rugged mountain range, which starts 26 km north of Rocky, is noted for its spectacular limestone caves and passages. A couple of km from the Caves township, **Olsen's Capricorn Caverns** (☎ (079) 34 2883) has the most impressive caves, and is open daily from 8.30 am with six different tours including a one-hour 'cathedral tour' ($9), an adventure tour ($22) and a night tour ($12). Olsen's also has a pool, walking trails, barbecue areas and self-contained cabins from $60 a night for up to four people. Nearby, the

family-run **Cammoo Caves** has self-guided tours daily from 8.30 am to 4.30 pm ($7).

Rothery's Coaches (☎ (079) 22 4320) has half-day tours from Rockhampton on Monday, Wednesday and Friday ($20 including a cave tour).

Mt Morgan (pop 3200)
The open-cut gold and copper mine at Mt Morgan, 38 km south-west of Rockhampton on the Burnett Highway, was worked (off and on) from the 1880s until 1981. Mt Morgan is a registered heritage town with a well-preserved collection of turn-of-the-century buildings. The tourist office (☎ (079) 38 2312) is housed in a lovely old railway station.

The interesting **Mt Morgan Historical Museum** on the corner of Morgan and East Sts is open daily from 10 am to 1 pm (Sundays until 4 pm); entry is $2. Silver Wattle Tours (☎ (079) 38 1081) runs 2½-hour tours that take in the town sights, the mine, and a cave with dinosaur footprints on its ceiling, departing daily at 9.30 am and 1 pm ($18.50).

There's a good caravan park on the southern outskirts, and a couple of the old pubs have budget accommodation. The *Miners' Rest Motel Units* (☎ (079) 38 2350) one km south of the centre has good cottages from $40 a double.

Young's Bus Service (☎ (079) 22 3813) has regular buses from Rockhampton to Mt Morgan from Monday to Saturday; the fare is $6 one way. McCafferty's also passes through here on its inland Rockhampton-Brisbane run.

YEPPOON (pop 7350)
Yeppoon is a relaxed seaside township 43 km north-east of Rockhampton. It's the main centre on the Capricorn Coast, and although Great Keppel Island is the area's main attraction, Yeppoon itself has quite good beaches and is a reasonably popular holiday town. Boats to Great Keppel leave from Rosslyn Bay, seven km south.

The Capricorn Coast Information Centre

QUEENSLAND

(☎ (079) 39 4888) is at the Ross Creek Roundabout at the entrance to the town.

If you have transport, it's an interesting drive from Yeppoon up to the tiny town of Byfield, 40 km north. The road passes through various state forest parks with good picnic and camping grounds, and you can visit a pottery and a historic homestead en route.

Places to Stay

Up on the hill behind the town, the *Barrier Reef Backpackers* (☎ (079) 39 4702), at 30 Queen St, is a relaxed place in a comfortable old timber house. It has all the usual facilities, a large backyard and good views of the town. Four-bed dorms cost $14, doubles $28, and they offer free pick-ups from Rocky and will drop you at Rosslyn Bay if you're going to Great Keppel.

There are numerous motels and holiday flats. The pleasant *Surfside Motel* (☎ (079) 39 1272) opposite the beach at 30 Anzac Pde has units with kitchenettes from $35/40.

YEPPOON TO EMU PARK

There are beaches dotted all along the 19-km coast from Yeppoon south to Emu Park. At **Cooee Bay**, a couple of km from Yeppoon, the Australian 'Cooee' Championships are held each August.

Rosslyn Bay Boat Harbour, about seven km south of Yeppoon, is the departure point for ferries to Great Keppel Island and other Keppel Bay islands. There's a free day car park at the harbour, or the Kempsea lock-up car park (on the main road near the turn-off) charges $6 a day ($2 for motorbikes).

South of Rosslyn Bay are three fine headlands with good views – **Double Head, Bluff Point** and **Pinnacle Point**. After Pinnacle Point the road crosses **Causeway Lake**, a saltwater inlet where you can rent canoes and sailboards. Farther south at **Emu Park** there are more good views and the 'Singing Ship' – a series of drilled tubes and pipes that emit whistling or moaning sounds when there's a breeze blowing. It's a memorial to Captain Cook.

Koorana Crocodile Farm is five km off the Emu Park to Rockhampton road. The turn-off is 15 km from Emu Park. The farm has hundreds of crocs and is open daily from 11.30 am, with 1½- hour tours daily at 1 pm for $9.

Most towns along this stretch of coast have caravan and camping parks, and there are numerous motels and holiday flats.

GREAT KEPPEL ISLAND

Although it's not actually on the reef, Great Keppel is the equal of most islands up the coast. It's 13 km offshore, and although it's too big for you to see it all in an afternoon, it's small enough to explore over a few days. It covers 14 sq km and boasts 18 km of very fine white-sand beaches.

The Great Keppel Island Resort, owned by Qantas, is beyond the reach of the average shoestring traveller, but the good news about Great Keppel is that, unlike many of the resort islands, there are some good budget accommodation alternatives, and it's also one of the cheapest and easiest Queensland islands to reach. Day-trippers to the resort have access to a pool, bar and restaurant, and they can hire all sorts of water sports gear.

Things to See & Do

Great Keppel's beaches are among the best of any on the resort islands. The main **Fisherman's** and **Putney** beaches are very pleasant, or you can walk around the island and find your own deserted stretch of white sand. The water's clear and war and there is good coral at many points around the island, especially between Great Keppel and Humpy Island to the south. A 30-minute walk around the headland south of the resort brings you to **Monkey Beach** where there's good snorkelling.

There are a number of bushwalking tracks. The longest, and one of the more difficult, goes across to the lighthouse near **Bald Rock Point** on the far side of the island (2½ hours one way). Some beaches, such as **Red Beach** near the lighthouse, are only accessible by boat.

There's a fine **underwater observatory** by Middle Island, close to Great Keppel. A confiscated Taiwanese fishing junk was sunk

next to the observatory to provide a haven for fish.

The Beach Shed on Putney Beach and Keppel Watersports on Fisherman's Beach both hire out water sports gear including sailboards, catamarans, motorboats and snorkelling gear, and can take you water-skiing or paragliding. Keppel Reef Scuba Adventures (☎ (079) 39 5022) on Putney Beach has introductory dives ($60) or, if you're certified, two dives with all gear supplied for $50. Their five-day diving courses cost $385.

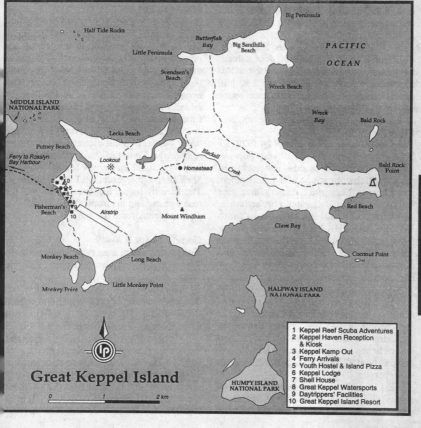

Great Keppel Island

0   1   2 km

1 Keppel Reef Scuba Adventures
2 Keppel Haven Reception
   & Kiosk
3 Keppel Kamp Out
4 Ferry Arrivals
5 Youth Hostel & Island Pizza
6 Keppel Lodge
7 Shell House
8 Great Keppel Watersports
9 Daytrippers' Facilities
10 Great Keppel Island Resort

QUEENSLAND

Organised Cruises

Keppel Tourist Services (☎ (079) 33 6744) runs various cruises aboard the *Reefseeker*. Its island cruise departs daily from Rosslyn Bay at 9.15 am and from Fisherman's Beach at 10 am, and continues on a three-hour cruise around the island. The cruise includes boom netting, snorkelling and an optional visit to the underwater observatory ($10 extra). You then have the afternoon on the island before returning at 4.30 pm; the cruise costs $35 from Rosslyn Bay or $10 if you're already on the island.

The *Reefseeker* also does inner reef trips on Tuesday and Thursday to Barren Island, departing from Rosslyn Bay at 9.15 am. The cost of $90 includes lunch, snorkelling gear and a glass-bottom boat ride; scuba dives are an optional extra.

Every Wednesday, Friday and Sunday, the *Capricat*, a sailing catamaran, does a three-hour sailing and snorkelling cruise for $20 (departing at either 9.30 am or 12.30 pm, depending on the tides), and a sunset 'booze cruise' for $30 from 5 to 7 pm.

Places to Stay

The *Great Keppel YHA Hostel* (☎ (079) 27 5288) is pretty basic but still very popular, with 16-bed dorms at $14 and eight-bed cabins with bathrooms at $16; nonmembers pay $2 extra. They hire out snorkelling gear and organise bushwalks and other activities. Book through the Rockhampton Youth Hostel or the YHA head office in Brisbane (☎ (07) 3236 1680). Their $72 deal is good value – you get one night in Rocky, two nights on the island, bus and boat transfers, plus an island cruise.

Keppel Haven (☎ (079) 39 1907), formerly Wapparaburra Haven, has semi-permanent safari tents that sleep up to four people at $15 per person; communal facilities include fridges, barbecues and basic kitchen equipment. There are also six-bed cabins at $75 a double, plus $15 for each extra person.

Next door to Keppel Haven is *Keppel Kamp Out* (☎ (079) 39 2131), which is geared to the 18 to 35 age bracket, and has organised activities. The cost of $69 per person per day ($49 stand-by) includes twin-share tents, three meals and activities such as water sports, parties and video nights.

Keppel Lodge (☎ (079) 39 4251) has four good motel-style units that sleep up to five and cost from $80 a double plus $25 for extras; there's a large communal lounge and kitchen and a barbecue area.

The *Great Keppel Island Resort* is particularly popular with young people and promotes itself as 'the active resort'. Qantas has package deals from around $1000 per person for seven days, including air fares, meals and activities.

Places to Eat

If you want to cook it's best to bring a few basic supplies. Fruit, vegetables, groceries and dairy foods are sold at the reasonably pricey kiosk at *Keppel Haven*; the kiosk also does breakfasts and takeaways. Next door, the *Wappa Bar & Bistro* does lunches and evening meals. Near the YHA, the friendly *Island Pizza* makes good pizzas, pasta and submarines.

In the day-trippers' area, the *Keppel Cafe* does burgers, sandwiches etc, and the *Anchorage Char Grill* has grilled steak or fish with salad and chips for $10.50. The *Shell House* does excellent Devonshire teas. The friendly owner has lived on Keppel for many years, and his tropical garden offers a pleasant break from the sun.

Getting There & Away

Air Qantas flies at least twice daily between Rockhampton and Great Keppel ($74 one way).

Boat Ferries for Great Keppel leave from Rosslyn Bay Harbour on the Capricorn Coast. Keppel Tourist Services (☎ (079) 33 6744) operates two boats, the *Reefseeker* and the *Spirit of Keppel*. The *Reefseeker* leaves Rosslyn Bay at 9.15 am and returns from Great Keppel at 4.30 pm, and costs $35 return including an island tour ($25 without the tour). The *Spirit of Keppel* leaves Rosslyn Bay at 11.30 am and 3.30 pm, and returns from Great Keppel at 2 and 4.30 pm; it costs $25 return.

Another boat, the *Australis* (☎ (079) 33 6865), leaves Rosslyn Bay at 9 and 11 am and returns from Great Keppel at 9.45 am and 4 pm; it costs $20 return.

The Rockhampton youth hostel has a special deal of $35 for the bus trip, the ferry across and a three-hour island cruise.

OTHER KEPPEL BAY ISLANDS

Great Keppel is only the biggest of the 18 continental islands dotted around Keppel Bay, all within 20 km of the coast. You may get to visit **Middle Island**, with its underwater observatory, or **Halfway** or **Humpy** islands if you're staying on Great Keppel. Most of the islands have clean white beaches and several, notably Halfway, have excellent fringing coral reefs. Some, including Middle and **Miall**, are national parks where you can maroon yourself for a few days' camping. To camp on a national park island, you need to take all your own supplies including water. Numbers of campers on each island are restricted – for example, eight at a time on Middle and six on Miall. You can get information and permits from the QNP&WS regional office in Rockhampton (☎ (079) 36 0511) or the rangers' office at Rosslyn Bay Harbour (☎ (079) 33 6608).

North Keppel is the second-largest of the group and one of the most northerly. It covers six sq km and is a national park. The most popular camping spot is Considine Beach on the north-west coast, which has well water for washing, and toilets. Take insect repellent.

Just south of North Keppel, tiny **Pumpkin Island** has five cabins (☎ (079) 39 2431) that accommodate either five or six people each at a cost of $90 to $110 per cabin. There's water and solar electricity, and each cabin has a stove, fridge and a bathroom with shower. Bedding is provided.

Keppel Tourist Services (☎ (079) 33 6744) has camping drop-off services (by request) from Rosslyn Bay to the islands; prices start from $120 per person return.

CAPRICORN HINTERLAND

The Capricorn Highway runs inland, virtually along the Tropic of Capricorn, across the central Queensland highlands to Barcaldine, from where you can continue west and north-west along the Landsborough Highway to meet the Townsville to Mt Isa road.

The area was first opened up by miners looking for gold and copper around Emerald and sapphires around Anakie, but cattle, grain crops and coal provide its main living today. Carnarvon National Park, south of Emerald, is one of Australia's most spectacular.

Getting There & Away

McCafferty's has a Rockhampton to Longreach service three times a week, which calls at all towns along the Capricorn Highway. The twice-weekly *Spirit of the Outback* train follows the same route.

Baralaba

About 25 km south-west of Rockhampton and 22 km east of Baralaba is *Myella Farm Stay* (☎ (079) 98 1290), a working cattle station. It's owned by a hospitable family and offers the 'City Slickers' experience – horse riding, cattle mustering, helping out with the fence repairs etc – and has received good reports from travellers. You stay in a breezy old timber farmhouse; the cost is around $60 a day, which includes all meals and activities. Ring for directions.

Blackdown Tableland National Park

The Blackdown Tableland is a spectacular 600-metre sandstone plateau that rises suddenly out of the flat plains of central Queensland. It's definitely worth a visit, with stunning panoramas, great bushwalks to waterfalls and lookout points, Aboriginal rock art, plus some unique wildlife and plant species.

There's a camping area at **Mimosa Creek**, about 10 km into the park. Permits are available from the ranger at Dingo (☎ (079) 86 1964). Bring a gas stove for cooking.

The turn-off to the tableland is 11 km west of **Dingo** and 40 km east of the coal-mining

GREAT BARRIER REEF
Facts & Figures
The Great Barrier Reef is 2000 km in length. It starts slightly south of the Tropic of Capricorn, somewhere out from Bundaberg or Gladstone, and ends in Torres Strait, just south of Papua New Guinea. It is not only the most extensive reef system in the world, but the biggest structure made by living organisms. At its southern end the reef is up to 300 km from the mainland, while at the northern end it runs nearer the coast, is much less broken and can be up to 80 km wide. In the 'lagoon' between the outer reef and the coast, the waters are dotted with smaller reefs, cays and islands. Drilling on the reef has indicated that the coral may be more than 500 metres thick. Most of the reef is about two million years old, but there are sections dating back 18 million years.

What is It?
Coral is formed by a small, primitive animal, a marine polyp of the family *Coelenterata*. Some polyps, known as hard corals, form a hard surface by excreting lime. When they die, the hard 'skeletons' remain and these gradually build up the reef. New polyps grow on their dead predecessors and continually add to the reef. The skeletons of hard corals are white; the colours of reefs come from living polyps.

Coral needs a number of preconditions for healthy growth. The water temperature must not drop below 17.5°C – thus the Barrier Reef does not continue farther south into cooler waters. The water must be clear to allow sunlight to penetrate, and it must be salty. Coral will not grow below a depth of 30 metres because sunlight does not penetrate sufficiently. Nor does it grow around river mouths: the Barrier Reef ends near Papua New Guinea because the Fly River's enormous water flow is both fresh and muddy.

One of the most spectacular sights of the Barrier Reef occurs for a few nights after a full moon in late spring or early summer, when vast numbers of corals spawn at the same time. The tiny bundles of sperm and eggs are visible to the naked eye and the event has been likened to a gigantic underwater snowstorm.

Reef Types
What's known as the Great Barrier Reef is not one reef but about 2600 separate ones. Basically, reefs are either fringing or barrier. You will find fringing reefs off sloping sides of islands or the mainland coast. Barrier reefs are farther out to sea: the 'real' Great Barrier Reef, or outer reef, is at the edge of the Australian continental shelf, and the channel between the reef and the coast can be 60 metres deep. In places, the reef rises straight up from that depth. This raises the question of how the reef built up when coral cannot survive below 30 metres. One theory is that it gradually grew as the sea bed subsided. Another theory is that the sea level gradually rose, and the coral growth was able to keep pace.

Reef Inhabitants
There are about 400 different types of coral on the Barrier Reef. Equally colourful are the many clams that appear to be embedded in the coral. Other reef inhabitants include about 1500 species of fish, 4000 types of mollusc (clams, snails etc), 350 echinoderms (sea urchins, starfish, sea cucumbers etc, all with a five-arm body plan), and countless thousands of species of sponge, worm and crustacean (crabs, shrimps etc).

Reef waters are also home to dugong (the sea cows believed to have given rise to the mermaid myth) and are breeding grounds for humpback whales, which migrate every winter from Antarctica. The reef's islands form important nesting colonies for many types of sea bird, and six of the world's seven species of sea turtle lay eggs on the islands' sandy beaches in spring or summer.

Crown-of-Thorns Starfish One reef inhabitant that has enjoyed enormous publicity is the crown-of-thorns starfish, notorious because it appeared to be chewing through large areas of the reef. It's thought that the crown-of-thorns develop a taste for coral when the reef ecology is upset; for example, when the supply of bivalves (oysters, clams), which comprise its normal diet, is diminished.

Dangerous Creatures Hungry sharks are the usual idea of an aquatic nasty, but the Barrier Reef's most unpleasant creatures are generally less dramatic. For a start, there are scorpion fish with highly venomous spines. The butterfly cod is a very beautiful scorpion fish and relies on its colourful, slow-moving appearance to warn off possible enemies. In contrast, the stonefish lies hidden on the bottom, looking just like a rock, and is very dangerous to step on.

Stinging jellyfish are a danger only in coastal waters and only in certain seasons. The deadly 'sea wasp' is, in fact, a box jellyfish (see the Warning at the beginning of this chapter). As for sharks, there has been no recorded case of a visitor to the reef islands meeting a hungry one.

Viewing the Reef

The best way of seeing the reef is by diving or snorkelling in it. Otherwise you can view it through the floor of glass-bottom boats or the windows of semi-submersibles, or descend below the ocean surface inside 'underwater observatories'. You can also see a living coral reef and its accompanying life forms without leaving dry land, at the Great Barrier Reef Wonderland aquarium in Townsville.

Innumerable tour operators run day trips to the outer reef and to coral-fringed islands from towns on the Queensland coast. The cost depends on how much reef-viewing paraphernalia is used, how far the reef is from the coast, how luxurious the vessel is that takes you there, and whether lunch is included. Usually free use of snorkelling gear is part of the package. Some islands also have good reefs and are usually cheaper to reach; you can stay on quite a few of them.

The Great Barrier Reef Marine Park Authority (GBRMPA) is the body looking after the welfare of most of the reef. Its address is PO Box 1379, Townsville, Queensland 4810 (☎ (077) 81 8811). It also has an office in the Great Barrier Reef Wonderland in Townsville.

Islands

There are three types of island off the Queensland coast. In the south, before you reach the Barrier Reef, are several large vegetated sand islands, including North Stradbroke, Moreton and Fraser islands. These are interesting to visit, although not for coral. Strung along the whole coast, mostly close inshore, are continental islands, such as Great Keppel, most of the Whitsundays, Hinchinbrook and Dunk. At one time, these would have been the peaks of coastal ranges, but rising sea levels submerged the mountains. The islands' vegetation is similar to that of the adjacent mainland.

The true coral islands, or cays, are on the outer reef or isolated between it and the mainland. Green Island near Cairns, the Low Isles near Port Douglas, and Heron Island off Gladstone, are all cays. Cays are formed when a reef is above sea level, even at high tide. Dead coral is ground down by water action to form sand and, in some cases, vegetation eventually takes root. Coral cays are low-lying, unlike the often hilly islands closer to the coast. There are about 300 cays on the reef, and 69 are vegetated.

The islands are extremely variable so don't let the catchword 'reef island' suck you in. Most of the popular resort islands are actually continental islands and some are well south of the Barrier Reef. Many continental islands have fringing reefs as well as other attractions for which a tiny dot-on-the-map coral cay is simply too small: there may be hills to climb, bushwalks to explore and secluded beaches.

The islands also vary considerably in their accessibility. For example, Lady Elliot is a $120 return flight, whereas others cost only a few dollars by ferry. If you want to stay on an island rather than make a day trip from the mainland, this too can vary widely in cost. Accommodation is generally in the form of expensive resorts, where most visitors will be on an all-inclusive package holiday. But there are a few exceptions to this rule, and on some islands it's possible to camp. A few islands have proper camping areas with toilets and fresh water on tap, on others you'll even have to bring drinking water with you.

For more information on individual islands, see the Capricorn Coast, Whitsunday Coast, North Coast and Far North Queensland sections of this chapter. Also good is Lonely Planet's *Islands of Australia's Great Barrier Reef*. ■

QUEENSLAND

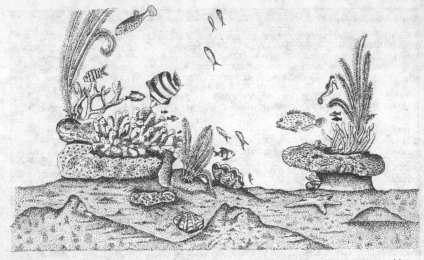

The Great Barrier Reef is home to 1500 fish species, as well as molluscs, crustaceans, echino-derms and other creatures

centre of **Blackwater**. The 20-km gravel road can be unsafe in wet weather and isn't suitable for caravans at any time – the last seven km are incredibly steep and slippery.

Coal Mines
Several of the massive open-cut Queensland coal mines in this region offer free tours lasting about 1½ hours; book ahead. The Blackwater mine tour (☎ (079) 82 5166), 20 km south of Blackwater, leaves the mine office on Wednesday at 10 am. For the Goonyella (☎ (079) 41 3333) and Peak Downs (☎ (079) 41 6233) mines near Moranbah, buses depart Moranbah town square at 10 am on Tuesday and Thursday. Tours of Blair Athol mine (☎ (079) 83 1866) near Clermont start on Tuesday at 9 am.

Gemfields
West of Emerald, about 270 km inland from Rockhampton, the gemfields around Anakie, Sapphire, Rubyvale and Willows Gemfield are known for sapphires, zircons, amethysts, rubies, topaz, jasper, and even diamonds and gold. To go fossicking, you need a 'fossick-

ing licence', sold from the Emerald court-house or on the gemfield. If you're just passing through, you can buy a bucket of 'wash' (dirt) from one of the fossicking parks and hand-sieve and wash it ($4). There are also quite a few tourist mines that you can visit and explore, including the excellent **Silk 'n' Sapphire Mine** 1.5 km north of Rubyvale, with adventurous hands-on underground tours from $30 for two hours.

Anakie, 42 km west of Emerald just off the Capricorn Highway, has a pub, a caravan park and an information centre. **Sapphire** is 10 km north of Anakie on a sealed road, with **Rubyvale**, the main town for the fields, seven km farther north. Rubyvale has a pub, a general store, a post office and a few gem shops and galleries.

At Sapphire, *Sunrise Cabins & Camping* (☎ (079) 85 4281), about a km out of town on the road to Rubyvale, has camp sites at $9 or rustic stone cabins with communal kitchen facilities from $12/25. You can get information, licences and maps, and hire fossicking gear here.

Ramboda Homestead (☎ (079) 85 4154),

on the highway near the turn-off to Sapphire, is a farmstay with dinner, bed and breakfast from \$35/80, and it does pick-ups from Anakie. There are also caravan/camping parks at Anakie, Rubyvale and Willows Gemfield.

Sapphires are found close to the surface at **Willows Gemfield**, 38 km west of Anakie.

Clermont (pop 2800)

North of Emerald is Clermont, with the huge Blair Athol open-cut coal mine. Clermont is Queensland's oldest tropical inland town, founded on copper, gold, sheep and cattle. It was the scene of goldfield race riots in the 1880s, and there was a military takeover of the town in 1891 after a confrontation between striking sheep shearers and non-union labour. The town has a couple of pubs and a caravan park with on-site vans.

Springsure (pop 900)

Springsure, 66 km south of Emerald, has an attractive setting with a backdrop of granite mountains and surrounding sunflower fields. There's a small **historical museum** by the windmill as you enter town from the south. The **Virgin Rock**, an outcrop of Mt Zamia on the northern outskirts, was named for early settlers claimed to have seen the image of the Virgin Mary in the rock face.

Ten km south-west, at Burnside, is the **Old Rainworth Fort**, built following the Wills Massacre of 1861 when Aboriginal people killed 19 Whites on Cullin-La-Ringo Station north-west of Springsure.

For accommodation you have the choice of a motel or a caravan park.

Carnarvon National Park

Rugged Carnarvon National Park, in the middle of the Great Dividing Range, features dramatic gorge scenery and many Aboriginal rock paintings and carvings. The national park has several sections, but the impressive Carnarvon Gorge is all that most people see as the rest is pretty inaccessible.

Carnarvon Gorge is stunning partly because it's an oasis surrounded by drier plains and partly because of the variety of its scenery, which includes sandstone cliffs, moss gardens, deep pools, and rare palms and ferns. There's also lots of wildlife. Aboriginal art can be viewed at three main sites – **Baloon Cave**, the **Art Gallery** and **Cathedral Cave**.

From Rolleston to Carnarvon Gorge, the road is bitumen for 20 km and unsealed for 75 km. From Roma via Injune and Wyseby, the road is good bitumen for about 200 km, then unsealed and fairly rough for the last 45 km. After rain, both roads are impassable.

Three km into the Carnarvon Gorge section, there's an information centre and a scenic camping ground. The main walking track starts beside the information centre and follows Carnarvon Creek through the gorge, with detours to various points of interest such as the Moss Garden (3.6 km from the camping ground), Ward's Canyon (4.8 km), the Art Gallery (5.6 km) and Cathedral Cave (9.3 km). You should allow at least half a day for a visit here, and bring lunch and water with you as there are no shops.

To get into the more westerly and rugged Mt Moffatt section of the park, there are two unsealed roads from Injune: one through Womblebank Station, the other via Westgrove Station. There are no through roads from Mt Moffatt to Carnarvon Gorge or to the third and fourth remote sections of the park – Salvator Rosa and Ka Ka Mundi. Mt Moffatt has some beautiful scenery, diverse vegetation and wildlife, and **Kenniff Cave**, an important Aboriginal archaeological site. It's believed Aboriginal people lived here as long as 19,000 years ago.

Places to Stay The *Oasis Lodge* (☎ (079) 84 4503), near the entrance to the Carnarvon Gorge section of the park, offers 'safari cabins' from \$150 a night per person, including full board and organised activities (\$80 from December to March, without activities). There's a general store with fuel.

You need a permit to camp at the national park camping ground, and it's advisable to book by phoning the Carnarvon Gorge rangers (☎ (079) 84 4505). Sites cost \$3 per person per night or you can bush camp for

$2 per night. Wood for cooking is scarce, so bring your own gas stove.

You can also camp at Big Ben camping area, 500 metres upstream from Cathedral Cave – a 10-km walk up the gorge. Again, permits are required. If you camp here, you can explore the side gorges unhurriedly.

In the Mt Moffatt section, camping with a permit is allowed at six sites but you need to be completely self-sufficient, and a 4WD is advisable; phone the Mt Moffatt rangers for details (☎ (076) 26 3581).

Whitsunday Coast

The Whitsunday Islands, which lie just off the coast between Mackay and Bowen, are famous for their clear aqua-blue waters and forested islands. This is one of the most beautiful parts of the coast, and there's an extensive range of activities to choose from, including dive courses, cruises to and around the islands, snorkelling, fishing and sailing.

Mackay is a major regional centre, while the main access point for the islands is Airlie Beach, which is a very popular travellers' hangout, mainly because many companies offering dive courses and boat trips to the islands operate from here.

MACKAY (pop 23,500)

Mackay is surrounded by sugar cane and processes a third of Australia's sugar crop. The sugar, loaded at the world's largest sugar-loading terminal, at Port Mackay, has been grown here since 1865.

Mackay is nothing special, yet its town centre is attractively planted and there are some good beaches a bus ride away. It's also an access point for the national parks at Eungella and Cape Hillsborough, and for the Great Barrier Reef. There are some interesting islands only an hour or two away.

Orientation

Mackay is split into two halves by the broad Pioneer River, with the compact city centre laid out in a simple grid on the south side of the river. Victoria St, the main street, is an attractive thoroughfare with a central plantation. The bus terminal is a few hundred metres west of the centre on Milton St; the railway station and airport are both about three km south of the centre. The harbour is six km north, and the best beaches are about 15 km north.

Information

Mackay's tourist office (☎ (079) 52 2677), in a replica of the old Richmond Sugar Mill, is about three km south of the centre on Nebo Rd (the Bruce Highway). It's open weekdays from 8.30 am to 5 pm and weekends from 9 am to 4 pm. While you're here, pick up a copy of the very handy *Things to See & Do in Mackay* brochure. The RACQ (☎ (079) 57 2918) is at 214 Victoria St, and the QNP&WS office (☎ (079) 51 8788) is on the corner of Wood and River Sts.

Things to See & Do

Despite the effects of several major cyclones, Mackay still has some interesting old buildings – the tourist office's *A Heritage Walk in Mackay* brochure guides you around 21 historic sites. There are botanic gardens and an orchid house in **Queens Park**, towards the eastern end of Gordon St, and good views over the harbour from **Mt Basset**, and at **Rotary Lookout** on Mt Oscar in North Mackay.

The **Town Beach**, two km from the centre at the eastern end of Shakespeare St, is generally shallow and muddy; **Illawong Beach**, a couple of km farther south, is only slightly better. A better option is the sandy **Harbour Beach**, six km north and just south of the harbour, although the best beaches are about 16 km north of Mackay at Blacks Beach, Eimeo and Bucasia. You turn right at the 'Northern Beaches' sign four km north of town on the Bruce Highway to reach them. Back in town, the **Memorial Swimming Pool** on Milton St is open from August till May.

The **Illawong Fauna Sanctuary**, a small private fauna park on the foreshore two km south of the centre, has kangaroos, birds and

QUEENSLAND

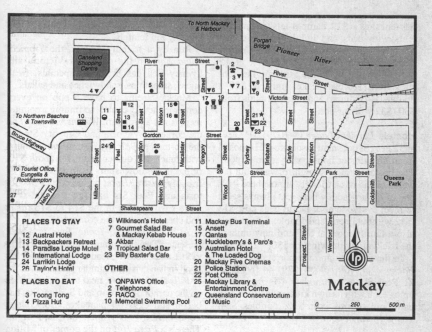

PLACES TO STAY

12 Austral Hotel
13 Backpackers Retreat
14 Paradise Lodge Motel
16 International Lodge
24 Larrikin Lodge
26 Taylor's Hotel

PLACES TO EAT

3 Toong Tong
4 Pizza Hut

6 Wilkinson's Hotel
7 Gourmet Salad Bar
   & Mackay Kebab House
8 Akbar
9 Tropical Salad Bar
23 Billy Baxter's Cafe

OTHER

1 QNP&WS Office
2 Telephones
5 RACQ
10 Memorial Swimming Pool

11 Mackay Bus Terminal
15 Ansett
17 Qantas
18 Huckleberry's & Paro's
19 Australian Hotel
   & The Loaded Dog
20 Mackay Five Cinemas
21 Police Station
22 Post Office
25 Mackay Library &
   Entertainment Centre
27 Queensland Conservatorium
   of Music

Mackay

0   250   500 m

crocodiles, which are fed daily at 3.30 pm; it's open daily ($3).

In the cane-crushing season (July to December), the **Farleigh Sugar Mill** (☎ (079) 57 4727), 12 km north-west of Mackay, has two-hour tours on weekdays at 1 pm ($10); and the **Polstone Sugar Farm**, about six km west, runs 2½-hour tours on weekdays at 1.30 pm ($12.50).

Organised Tours & Cruises

Roylen's Cruises (☎ (079) 55 3066) runs fast catamaran trips from Mackay Harbour to Credlin Reef on the outer reef, where Roylen's has a pontoon with an underwater observatory. Trips depart on Monday, Wednesday and Friday and cost $90, including lunch and a semi-submersible ride; you can hire snorkelling or diving gear. Roylen's also has good cruises to Brampton Island daily, costing $45, which includes lunch at the resort. On weekends only, its catamarans

continue on to Hamilton Island ($36 one way, $40 return) and Lindeman Island ($40 one way, $90 return including lunch) in the Whitsundays.

A couple of local operators, Fredrickson's (☎ (079) 42 3161) and Air Pioneer (☎ (079) 57 6661) offer seaplane flights out to Bushy Atoll on the Barrier Reef (about $150 per person).

Reeforest Tours (☎ (079) 53 1000) has day trips to Eungella National Park for $45. Brigitte's Tropical Tours (☎ 015 632 521) has small group tours to Eungella ($37) on Wednesday and Saturday, to Cape Hillsborough National Park ($33) on Monday and Thursday, and 'sunset' city, harbour and beaches tours ($20) on Sunday.

Places to Stay

Camping The modern *Beach Caravan Park* (☎ (079) 57 4021), on Petrie St at Illawong Beach, about three km south of the centre, has tent sites at $12, camp-o-tels (permanent tents with beds and lighting) at $16 and on-site cabins from $28. The *Central Caravan Park* (☎ (079) 57 6141), at 15 Malcomson St in North Mackay, has tent sites from $8, backpacker units at $20 a double (BYO linen) and on-site cabins from $30 ($32 with air-con).

Hostels *Larrikin Lodge* (☎ (079) 51 3728) at 32 Peel St is a small associate-YHA hostel in an airy timber house, with a small pool. The hostel is fairly straightforward, but it's well-run and has a friendly atmosphere – it's one of those places where you always seem to meet everyone else. Dorm beds cost $13 ($12 without linen), and doubles $30; there's also a family room at $40 and new units in the backyard with twins for $30.

In the street behind the bus station is the *Backpackers Retreat* (☎ (079) 44 0994), at 21 Peel St. Accommodation is in six-bed units, each with its own kitchen facilities and bathroom; dorms cost $12, doubles $34. There's a small pool.

Pubs & Motels *Taylor's Hotel* (☎ (079) 57 2500) on the corner of Wood and Alfred Sts has single rooms for $15, and the *Austral Hotel* (☎ (079) 51 3288) on the corner of Victoria and Peel Sts has singles/doubles with shared bathroom at $20/30 and doubles with bathroom at $35.

The friendly *International Lodge* (☎ (079) 51 1022), at 40 Macalister St, is quite central and has good budget motel rooms from $38/40. The *Paradise Lodge Motel* (☎ (079) 51 3644), in the street behind the bus station at 19 Peel St, has units at $44/48. There are about a thousand motels strung along Nebo Rd (the Bruce Highway) south of the centre. The closest of these, the *Cool Palms Motel* (☎ (079) 57 5477) at 4 Nebo Rd, has budget rooms from $40.

Places to Eat

At 23 Wood St, the narrow and popular *Gourmet Salad Bar* is a lunchtime bargain with rolls and sandwiches from $1.95 as well as very cheap salads and cakes. Nearby, the *Mackay Kebab House* has chicken and lamb kebabs, and felafels.

Run by a friendly couple, the *Tropical Salad Bar*, on the corner of Victoria and Sydney Sts, has breakfast specials, fresh juices, smoothies, sandwiches and salads.

Mackay seems to have a pub on every corner in the city centre, so finding a counter meal is not a problem. *Wilkinson's Hotel* on the corner of Victoria and Gregory Sts has the up-market *Balcony Restaurant* upstairs, with lunch and dinner mains for about $10, or bar meals downstairs from $3 to $5. The friendly *Austral Hotel* on the corner of Victoria and Peel Sts has the tropical-style *Coco's* with mains in the $14 to $18 range and cheap meals in the corner bar.

At 10 Sydney St, *Toong Tong* is a well presented Thai restaurant with mains from $9 to $13, and across the road at No 27, *Akbar* has good Indian curries at similar prices.

Billy Baxter's Cafe, next to the post office on the corner of Gordon and Sydney Sts, has bacon and eggs on pancakes ($6.95) and good coffee – it's open day and night. There's a *Pizza Hut* on the corner of Milton and Victoria Sts with all-you-can-eat pizza and pasta deals from $5.

Mackay's best and most impressive eatery is the *Waterfront Restaurant & Espresso Bar* at 8 River St, with a covered decking area overlooking the river. It's licensed, and mains range from $10 to $17.

Entertainment

The *Blue Moose* nightclub, upstairs at Wilkinson's Hotel, is fairly funky and apparently the best in town. The popular *Loaded Dog*, upstairs in the Australian Hotel on the corner of Wood and Victoria Sts, has pool tables and live bands on weekends. Other nightclubs include *Huckleberry's*, at 99 Victoria St, and *Paro's*, at 85 Victoria St.

The *Austral Hotel* has live music on weekends and a jazz night on the first Thursday of every month. Plenty of other pubs have live bands on the weekends, including the grungy *Prince of Wales* on River St.

The Queensland Conservatorium of Music (☎ (079) 57 3727) at 418 Shakespeare

St has jazz and classical performances – call to find out what's on The *Mackay Five Cinemas* (☎ (079) 57 3515) is at 30 Gordon St.

Getting There & Away

Air Ansett's office is on the corner of Victoria and Macalister Sts; Qantas is at 105 Victoria St. Both airlines have direct flights to/from Brisbane ($283), Townsville ($171) and Rockhampton ($166), and connecting flights to other state capitals.

Flight West flies to/from Cairns ($253), and Sunstate/Qantas flies to/from Brampton Island ($71) and Proserpine ($86). Helijet

---

A Sweet Success

Sugar is easily the most visible crop from Mackay, north past Cairns and up the Queensland coast. Sugar was a success almost from the day it was introduced in the region in 1865, but its early days had a distinctly unsavoury air as the plantations were worked by Pacific Islander people, known as Kanakas, who were often forced from their homes to work on Australian cane fields. 'Blackbirding', as this virtual slave trading was known, was not stamped out until 1905.

Today, cane growing is a highly mechanised business and visitors can inspect crushing plants during the harvesting season (August to December). The most spectacular part of the operation is the firing of the cane fields, when rubbish is burnt off by night fires. Mechanical harvesters cut and gather the cane, which is then transported to the sugar mills, often on narrow-gauge railway lines laid through the cane fields. The cane is shredded and passed through a series of crushers. The extracted juice is heated and cleaned of impurities and then evaporated to form a syrup. Next, the syrup is reduced to molasses and low-grade sugar. Further refining stages end with the sugar loaded into bulk containers for export.

Sugar production is a remarkably efficient process. The crushed fibres, known as bagasse, are burnt as fuel; impurities separated from the juice are used as fertilisers; and the molasses is used either to produce ethanol or as stock feed. ■

QUEENSLAND

(☎ (079) 57 7400) has a range of seaplane and helicopter flights from Mackay to the Whitsundays.

Bus Greyhound Pioneer and McCafferty's buses on the Bruce Highway run stop at the Mackay Bus Terminal (☎ (079) 51 3088) on Milton St. Major stops along the coast include Cairns (10½ hours, $72), Townsville (six hours, $48), Airlie Beach (two hours, $26) and Brisbane (13 hours, $87).

Train The *Sunlander* and *Queenslander* (both from Brisbane to Cairns) stop at Mackay. The Sunlander costs $100 in economy and $199 in a 1st-class sleeper from Brisbane, while the *Queenslander* has only 1st class at $379. All trains now stop at the new station at Paget, about three km south of the centre.

Getting Around
It costs about $8 for a taxi from Mackay airport to the city. Avis, Budget and Hertz have counters at the airport.

Local bus services are operated by Transit Coaches (☎ (079) 57 3330) and Mackay City Buses (☎ (079) 57 8416). The Taxi Transit Service (☎ 008 815 559) takes people to the northern beaches for $5.50 one way.

AROUND MACKAY
Brampton & Carlisle Islands
These two mountainous national park islands are in the Cumberland Group, 32 km north-east of Mackay. Both are about five sq km in area, and are joined by a sand bank which you can walk across at low tide. Carlisle's highest point is 389-metre Skiddaw Peak, and Brampton's is 219-metre Brampton Peak. Both islands have forested slopes, sandy beaches, good walks and fringing coral reefs with good snorkelling.

The Qantas-owned *Brampton Island Resort* (☎ (079) 51 4499) is a good mid-range family resort with singles/doubles from $125/200 a day, including tennis, golf and water sports; there's a restaurant and a cafe. Brampton is also a popular day trip destination, with its good beaches, walking

trails and water sports gear for hire. Carlisle Island is uninhabited, and there's a QNP&WS camp site across from the resort. There are no facilities so you must be totally self-sufficient (although you could always pop across to the resort for a beer or a bite).

Roylen's Cruises (☎ (079) 55 3066) has daily cruises from Mackay Harbour to Brampton; the return fare of $45 includes a smorgasbord lunch at the resort. You can also fly daily from Mackay ($71 one way with Sunstate).

Most other islands in the Cumberland Group and the Sir James Smith Group to the north are also national parks; if you fancy a spot of Robinson Crusoeing and can afford to charter a boat or a seaplane, Goldsmith and Scawfell are good bets. Contact the QNP&WS offices in Mackay (☎ (079) 51 8788) or Seaforth (☎ (079) 59 0410) for all camping permits and information.

Newry & Rabbit Islands
The Newry Island Group is a cluster of rocky, wild-looking continental islands just off the coast about 40 km north-west of Mackay. Newry Island, one km long, has a small and very low-key resort (☎ (079) 59 0214) where camping is $7 per site, a bunk is $12 and cabins, which sleep up to five and have their own bathrooms and cooking facilities, cost $20 per person (maximum charge $60). The resort has a restaurant and bar, and will pick up guests from Victor Creek, four km west of Seaforth, for $15 return.

Rabbit Island, the largest of the group at 4.5 sq km, has a national park camping ground with toilets and a rainwater tank, which might be empty in dry times. It also has the only sandy beaches in the group. From November to January sea turtles nest here. Contact the Mackay (☎ (078) 51 8788) or Seaforth (☎ (079) 59 0410) QNP&WS offices for permits and information.

Eungella National Park
Most days of the year you can be pretty sure of seeing platypuses close to the Broken River bridge and camping ground in this large national park, 84 km west of Mackay

MARK ARMSTRONG

MARK ARMSTRONG

TONY WHEELER

MARK ARMSTRONG

MARK ARMSTRONG

MARK ARMSTRONG

A	B
C	D
E	F

Queensland
A: Masonic lodge, Mackay
B: Old courthouse, Ravenswood
C: Orpheus Island sunset
D: Red sandhill near Windorah

E: Cane fields, near Mackay
F: South Molle Island jetty, Whitsundays

TONY WHEELER

TONY WHEELER

TONY WHEELER

TONY WHEELER

TONY WHEELER

A
B	C	D
E

Queensland
A: Hinchinbrook Island
B: Pisonias, Lady Musgrave Island
C: Heron Island

D: Watson's Bay, Lizard Island
E: South Molle Island

The best times to see the creatures are immediately after dawn and at dusk; you must remain patiently still and silent.

Eungella (pronounced 'young-gulla', meaning 'Land of Clouds') covers nearly 500 sq km of the Clarke Range, climbing to 1280 metres at Mt Dalrymple. The area has been cut off from other rainforest areas for roughly 30,000 years and it has at least six life forms that exist nowhere else: the Eungella honeyeater (a bird), the orange-sided skink (a lizard), the Mackay tulip oak (a tall buttressed rainforest tree) and three species of frog of which one – the Eungella gastric brooding frog – has the unusual ability to incubate its eggs in its stomach and give birth by spitting out the tadpoles!

The main access road from Mackay takes you through the long and narrow **Pioneer Valley**, with a turn-off near the Finch Hatton township to the **Finch Hatton Gorge**. The last section of the 12-km drive to the gorge is quite rough and involves several creek crossings. At the gorge, there's a swimming hole, picnic areas and a 1.6-km walking trail to the spectacular Araluen Falls.

Eungella, 28 km past Finch Hatton, is a sleepy mountain township with a guesthouse and a couple of tearooms. At **Broken River**, five km south of Eungella, there's a rangers' office, a camping ground, picnic area, swimming hole and kiosk. Several excellent walking tracks start from around the Broken River picnic area. There's a platypus-viewing platform near the bridge, and colourful birds are prolific. At night, the rufous bettong, a small kangaroo, is quite common. You might also see two types of brushtail possum and two species of glider. Park rangers sometimes lead wildlife watching sessions, or night spotlighting trips to pick out nocturnal animals.

Places to Stay A couple of km from the Finch Hatton Gorge is the *Platypus Bush Camp* (☎ (079) 58 3204), a simple bush retreat with a lovely forest setting by a creek. You can camp ($5 per person) or sleep in a slab-timber hut ($45 for up to three people); there are communal cooking shelters, hot showers and toilets. Bring your own food and linen. If you phone from Finch Hatton village, someone will pick you up.

In Eungella township, the old *Eungella Chalet* (☎ (079) 58 4509) is an old-fashioned guesthouse perched on the edge of the mountain. It's fairly basic but it has spectacular views, a pool, a bar and restaurant, and a hang-gliding platform. In the guesthouse section, backpacker beds are $15, singles/doubles are $25/39 and rooms with private bathroom are $50. Out the back are timber cabins from $70.

There's a good QNP&WS camping ground ($3 per person per night) at Broken River; for bookings and permits, contact the ranger on ☎ (079) 58 4552 (bookings recommended during school holidays). Also beside the bridge here, the *Broken River Mountain Retreat* (☎ (079) 58 4528) has motel-style timber cabins from $48 and self-contained units from $62.

Getting There & Away There are no buses to Eungella, but two tour operators run day trips from Mackay and will do camping drop-offs – see the Mackay Organised Tours & Cruises section for details.

Cape Hillsborough National Park

This small coastal park, 54 km north of Mackay, takes in the rocky Cape Hillsborough, 300 metres high, and nearby Andrews Point and Wedge Island, which are joined by a causeway at low tide. There are beaches and some good short walking tracks, and the scenery ranges from cliffs, rocky coast, dunes and scrub to rainforest and woodland. Kangaroos hang out on the beaches here and wallabies, sugar gliders and turtles are also quite common. There's a rangers' office and information centre (☎ (079) 59 0410) on the foreshore, and a good picnic and barbecue area nearby.

Places to Stay At the end of the Cape Hillsborough Rd, the *Cape Hillsborough Resort* (☎ (079) 59 0152) has tent sites from $6, on-site vans and cabins from $20, and two-bedroom units from $50.

QUEENSLAND

There's a small QNP&WS camping ground at Smalleys Beach; permits can be booked through the rangers' office.

Getting There & Away There are day trips from Mackay on Monday and Thursday (see the Mackay Organised Tours & Cruises section). Otherwise, there's no public transport, although you might be able to get a lift on the Seaforth-Mackay school bus – check with the tourist office in Mackay.

AIRLIE BEACH (pop 3000)

Airlie Beach, 25 km north-west of Proserpine off the Bruce Highway, is the gateway to the Whitsunday Islands. It's a small but lively centre that has grown phenomenally since the mid-1980s. The whole town now revolves around tourism and pleasure boating, and it attracts a diverse bunch of boaties, backpackers and other tourists, all of whom are here for a good time. It has an excellent range of budget to mid-range accommodation, plenty of good eateries and a lively nightlife.

Airlie Beach also has a reputation as a centre for learning to scuba dive. A wide assortment of travel agents and tour operators are based here, and most boats to the islands leave from Shute Harbour, eight km east of Airlie Beach, or from the Abel Point Marina, one km west. Whale watching boat trips, between July and September, are another attraction. Despite all of the recent development, it's still a small place that has managed to retain its relaxed air.

Information

There's a tourist office (☎ (079) 45 3711) on the Bruce Highway at Proserpine, near the turn-off to Airlie Beach.

In Airlie Beach, nearly everything of importance is on the main road, Shute Harbour Rd. The Whitsunday Visitor Bureau (☎ (079) 46 6673), in an arcade off Airlie Esplanade, is mainly a marketing body but can answer phone enquiries. There are also numerous privately run 'information centres' (ie booking agencies) along Shute Harbour Rd, including Destination Whitsundays (☎ (079) 46 6848) and the Airlie Beach Tourist Information Centre (☎ (079) 46 6665). The notice board outside the newsagency on the main street has notices for work, rooms to rent and boat crews needed.

The QNP&WS office (☎ (079) 46 7022) (signposted as the Whitsunday Information Centre) is two km past Airlie Beach towards Shute Harbour, and is open weekdays from 8 am to 5 pm and at varying weekend hours. This office deals with camping bookings and permits for the Conway and Whitsunday Islands national parks.

Things to See & Do

The **Wildlife Park** has a large collection of Australian animals, birds and reptiles, with various daily shows including crocodile feeding; it's open daily from 8.30 am to 5 pm ($14). The park is eight km west of town – a courtesy bus does pick-ups from Airlie Beach.

The beaches at Airlie aren't great, but there are two places where you can hire catamarans, windsurfers and other water sports gear. There's a good 25-metre pool at the Coral Sea Resort on Ocean View; non-guests can visit for $3.

Brandy Creek Trail Rides (☎ (079) 46 6665) offers half-day 'billy-tea and damper' rides around a nearby forest ($49), and will pick you up from your accommodation. Whitsunday Attractions and Fawlty's 4WD Tropical Tours both offer half-day rainforest tours ($35).

Other possibilities include tandem sky-diving ($239), bungy jumping ($65), abseiling and paintball wars – you can book these through your accommodation or one of the agents in Airlie Beach.

Diving At least four outfits in and around Airlie Beach offer five to seven-day scuba-diving certificate courses. Standard costs vary from $250 to $500; with the cheaper courses you spend most of your time in a pool or classroom, whereas the better courses combine tuition on the mainland with three or four days diving on the Great

Barrier Reef. All the firms also offer diving trips for certified divers. Book where you are staying or at one of the agencies on the main road in Airlie Beach.

The companies include: Oceania Dive (☎ (079) 46 6032), Reef Enterprise Dive Services (☎ (079) 46 7228) and Pro-Dive (☎ (079) 46 6508), all on Shute Harbour Rd; and Kelly Dive (☎ (079) 46 6122) based at the Reef Oceania Village resort.

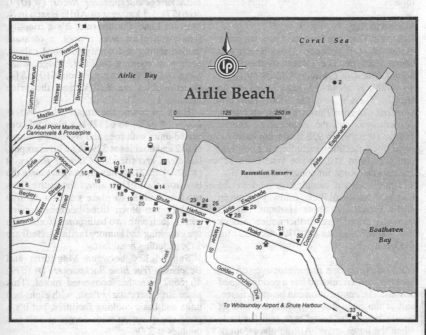

PLACES TO STAY

1 Coral Sea Resort
4 Colonial Court Motel
5 Club 13 Begley Street
6 Sunlit Waters Holiday Flats
8 Airlie Beach Motor Lodge
12 Whitsunday on the Beach
15 Whitsunday Wanderers Resort
16 Blue Waters Lodge
20 Beaches Backpackers
21 True Blue Backpackers
26 Magnum's Whitsunday Village
30 Club Habitat YHA
31 Airlie Beach Hotel
33 Boathaven Lodge
34 Backpackers by the Bay

PLACES TO EAT

11 Happy Gourmet
13 Cafe Le Mignon
19 Beaches Bar & Bistro
22 Magnum's Bar & Grill
24 Cafe Gourmet
27 KC's Char Grill
28 Figaro's
29 Sidewalk Cafe
32 Sports Bar & Cafe

OTHER

2 Whitsunday Sailing Club
3 Long-distance Bus Stop
7 Airlie Beach Rentals
9 Post Office
10 Club Mainstreet
14 Tourist Information Centre
17 Tricks Nightclub
18 Newsagent and Notice Board
23 Thomas Cook
25 Destination Whitsundays

QUEENSLAND

Festivals

Airlie Beach is the centre of activities during the Whitsunday Fun Race (for cruising yachts) each September. The festivities include a Miss Figurehead competition where the contestants traditionally compete topless.

Places to Stay

Camping There are four good caravan parks along the road between Airlie Beach and Shute Harbour. The closest of these, the *Island Gateway Caravan Village* (☎ (079) 46 6228), is about 1.5 km east of Airlie Beach. There's also the *Shute Harbour Gardens Caravan Park* (☎ (079) 46 6483), 2.5 km east, and the *Flame Tree Tourist Village* (☎ (079) 46 9388), six km east. All have good facilities including a pool, and tent sites from $10, on-site vans from $25 and on-site cabins for about $35.

There's also a camping ground in the Conway National Park, midway between Airlie Beach and Shute Harbour, but it's currently closed 'until further notice'. Check the QNP&WS office (☎ (079) 46 7022) for the latest.

Hostels Airlie is a major stopover on the backpackers' circuit and has a good range of hostels. The competition can be quite fierce, and at the main bus stop there's a row of booths where the hostel reps tout for trade when the buses arrive. All the places out of the centre run courtesy buses to and from Airlie Beach.

Right in the centre, *Magnum's Whitsunday Village* (☎ (079) 46 6266) is a huge place, set out in a very pleasant tropical garden with two pools. The emphasis here is on partying – there's a bar/eatery next door with activities each night. The cheapest dorms are the six-share units near the bar at $12 a night; these tend to be noisy and have limited cooking facilities. The four-share timber cabins in the garden are $14. Doubles range from $35 to $50.

Also in the centre is *Beaches Backpackers* (☎ (079) 46 6244), another big place with a party attitude and its own bar and restaurant.

The rooms and facilities in this converted motel are good, with five-bed (not bunk) units with their own bathroom and balcony, TV and air-con, a pool and a good kitchen. Beds cost $14 a night.

If you're after somewhere quieter, try the *Bush Village Backpackers' Resort* (☎ (079) 46 6177), 1.5 km west of Airlie Beach in St Martin's Lane, Cannonvale. It's a friendly, family-run place with a pool, a pleasant garden setting and comfy four-bed cabins, each with cooking facilities, fridge, bathroom and TV. Bunks range from $10 to $14, twins/doubles are $30/32 and the price includes a good breakfast.

Back in town, the small *Blue Waters Lodge* (☎ (079) 46 6182) is a block of converted units with four and five-share dorms at $12 and doubles at $29. It's a bit cramped, but clean and friendly. *Club 13 Begley St* (☎ (079) 46 7376) has great views over the bay from the hill just above the centre. This modern multilevel place consists of five slightly run-down three-bedroom apartments, each with two bathrooms (some with spa), cooking and laundry facilities. Beds are $13, including breakfast.

Sandwiched between Magnums and Beaches is *True Blue Backpackers* (☎ (079) 46 6662), another converted motel. This place isn't particularly flash, with eight-bed units and basic cooking facilities, but it's a good cheap option with dorms at $10 and doubles at $30.

A little farther along Shute Harbour Rd is *Club Habitat YHA* (☎ (079 46 6312), yet another motel converted to backpackers' accommodation. A night in a four to six-bed unit with bathroom costs $14, and twin rooms cost $34; nonmembers pay an extra $2. There's a pool, good communal kitchen and lounge, and the atmosphere is friendly.

A couple of hundred metres out of town towards Shute Harbour is *Backpackers by the Bay* (☎ (079) 46 7267) at Lot 5, Hermitage Drive. It's a small, relaxed hostel with a good atmosphere, and is probably quieter than those in the centre. The nightly cost in a small four-bed dorm is $12 and doubles are $29.

Back the other way from the centre is the *Beach House* (☎ (079) 46 6306), overlooking Shingley Beach. It's about 1.5 km from Airlie Beach – take the Abel Point Marina turn-off and turn left. It's a two-storey block of fan-cooled units costing $25/30/35 a night for twins/triples/quads, plus another $5 for air-con. There's a small pool.

The *Reef Oceania Village* (☎ (079) 46 6137), in Cannonvale three km west of Airlie, has a backpacker section with an eight-share bunk room at $7 and four to six-share cabins at $15.

Pubs & Motels The *Airlie Beach Hotel* (☎ (079) 46 6233) on Shute Harbour Rd has motel units from $49 a double.

Of the motels, the *Colonial Court Motel* (☎ (079) 46 6180) on the corner of Shute Harbour Rd and Broadwater Ave, has doubles from $46 to $55, and the *Airlie Beach Motor Lodge* (☎ (079) 46 6418) on Lamond St has double rooms from $50 and self-contained units from $60.

Holiday Flats & Resorts In the centre at 26 Shute Harbour Rd, *Whitsunday on the Beach* (☎ (079) 46 6359) has small, brightly renovated studio apartments from $75 to $85. Up the hill on the corner of Begley St and Airlie Crescent, *Sunlit Waters* (☎ (079) 46 6352) has budget studio flats at $38 a double plus $8 for extras. *Boathaven Lodge* (☎ (079) 46 6421), a couple of hundred metres east of the centre at 440 Shute Harbour Rd, has neat renovated studio units overlooking Boathaven Bay from $40 for up to three people.

Of the numerous resorts, *Whitsunday Wanderers* (☎ (079) 46 6446) on Shute Harbour Rd has four pools, tennis courts, landscaped gardens, a bar and restaurant, and Melanesian-style units for about $100 a double ($65 standby). *Club Crocodile* (079) 46 7155) at Cannonvale, 2 km west of Airlie Beach, has similar prices and facilities. The *Coral Sea Resort* (☎ (079) 46 6458), at 25 Ocean View Ave, overlooks the ocean from a low headland and has double units from $99 ($125 with ocean views).

Places to Eat

Most of the eating possibilities are on, or just off, Shute Harbour Rd in Airlie Beach. If you're preparing your own food, there's a small supermarket on the main street near the car park entrance.

The two big backpackers' bars have some of the best food deals. *Beaches Bar & Bistro* is almost always crowded with both travellers and locals, and has salads, pasta and burgers ($5 to $6), roasts, chicken and seafood ($6 to $8) and steak ($10 to $12), as well as nightly specials and a Mexican buffet on Tuesdays. *Magnum's Bar & Grill* is equally popular and has a similar set-up, with pool tables and a video screen. Meals range from $4 to $6.

The *Happy Gourmet* at 263 Shute Harbour Rd is a great place for lunch, with delicious filled rolls and sandwiches and home-made cakes. *Cafe Gourmet* at No 289 also has good rolls and sandwiches plus smoothies and juices.

Next to the main car park, *Cafe Le Mignon* has good coffee and muesli, croissants, pancakes etc; if you haven't eaten for a week, go for the Bavarian breakfast ($12). The *Sidewalk Cafe* on Airlie Esplanade has good breakfast deals from $3.75, toasted sandwiches and other cooked meals at good prices.

Figaro's on the corner of Shute Harbour Rd and Airlie Esplanade is a popular BYO pizza/pasta joint with tables on the footpath. Across the road, the rustic *KC's Char Grill* is a bit more up-market, with a lively atmosphere and excellent char-grilled steak and seafood in the $16 to $22 range. Up on the corner of Shute Harbour Rd and Coconut Grove, the *Sports Bar & Cafe* has the ol' sporting memorabilia décor, live music and a diverse menu.

Entertainment

The *Airlie Beach Hotel* has toad races on Tuesday and Thursday nights at 7.30 pm. You can buy a steed for $3 and there are good prizes for the winners (usually boat cruises), and the whole evening is a rowdy, fun event. The pub also has live rock music in the back

QUEENSLAND

bar on weekends. Several of the bars and cafes, including *KC's Char Grill* and the *Sports Bar & Cafe*, have live music most nights.

There are a couple of nightclubs on Shute Harbour Rd: *Tricks*, upstairs next to the newsagency, and *Club Mainstreet* upstairs in an arcade near the post office.

Getting There & Away

Air The closest major airports are at Proserpine and Hamilton Island (Ansett only).

There are half a dozen operators based at the Whitsunday airport, a small airfield about six km past Airlie Beach towards Shute Harbour. Island Air Taxis (☎ (079) 46 9933) flies to Hamilton ($40) and Lindeman ($50) islands. Eagle Air (☎ (079) 46 9176) and Heli Reef (☎ (079) 46 9102) both have a range of flying tours to the reef and islands.

Bus Most Greyhound Pioneer and McCafferty's buses make the detour from the highway to Airlie Beach, stopping in the main car park between the shops and the beach. Buses run to/from all the main centres along the coast, including Brisbane (18 hours, $100), Mackay (two hours, $26), Townsville (four hours, $36) and Cairns (nine hours, $60).

Sampson's (☎ (079) 45 2377) runs local bus services from Proserpine to Airlie Beach ($6.50) and Shute Harbour; buses operate daily from 6 am to 7 pm. Sampson's also meets all flights at Proserpine airport and goes to Airlie Beach ($11) and Shute Harbour ($13).

Boat The sailing club is at the end of Airlie Esplanade. There are notice boards at the newsagency in Airlie Beach and at Abel Point Marina showing when rides or crewing are available. Ask around Airlie Beach or Shute Harbour.

Getting Around

Several car rental agencies operate locally; Avis, Budget and National all have agencies on Shute Harbour Rd. Airlie Beach Rentals (☎ (079) 46 6110), on the corner of Begley St and Waterson Rd, has cars from $45 a day and scooters from $30 a day. Whitsunday Taxis can be booked on ☎ 1800 811 388.

CONWAY NATIONAL PARK

The road between Airlie Beach and Shute Harbour passes through Conway National Park, which stretches away north and south along the coast. The southern end of the park separates the Whitsunday Passage from Repulse Bay, named by Captain Cook who strayed into it thinking it was the main passage.

Most of the park comprises rugged ranges and valleys covered in rainforest, but there are a few walking tracks in the surrounding area. The two-km walk up to **Mt Rooper lookout**, north of the road, gives good views of the Whitsunday Passage and islands. Another pleasant walk is along Mandalay Rd, about three km east of Airlie Beach, up to **Mandalay Point**.

To reach the beautiful **Cedar Creek Falls**, turn-off the Proserpine-Airlie Beach road on to Conway Rd, eight km from Proserpine. It's then about 15 km to the falls – the roads are well signposted. At the end of Conway Rd, 27 km from the turn-off, is the small settlement of **Conway** with a beach and a caravan park.

WHITSUNDAY ISLANDS

The 74 Whitsunday Islands are probably the best-known Queensland islands, and one of Australia's pleasure-boating capitals. The group was named by Captain Cook who sailed through here on 3 July 1770. The islands are scattered on both sides of the Whitsunday Passage and are all within 50 km of Shute Harbour. The Whitsundays are mostly continental islands – the tips of underwater mountains – but many of them have fringing coral reefs. The actual Great Barrier Reef is at least 60 km out from Shute Harbour; Hook Reef is the nearest part of it.

The islands – mostly hilly and wooded – and the passages between them are certainly beautiful, and while a few are developed with tourist resorts, most are uninhabited and several offer the chance of some back-to-nature beach camping and bushwalking. All but four of the Whitsundays are either predominantly or completely national park. The exceptions are Dent Island, and the resort islands of Hamilton, Daydream and Hayman. The other main resorts are on South Molle, Lindeman, Long and Hook islands.

Most people staying in the resorts are on package holidays and, with the exception of the cabins on Hook Island, resort accommodation is beyond the reach of the shoestring traveller. All the resorts offer low-season discounts and standby rates – check with the booking agencies in Airlie Beach.

Camping on the Islands

Although accommodation in the island resorts is mostly expensive, it's possible to camp on several islands. Hook Island has a privately run camping ground, and on North Molle, Whitsunday, Henning, Border, Haslewood, Shaw, Thomas, Repulse and Hook islands you can camp cheaply at QNP&WS sites. Self-sufficiency is the key to camping in these sites; some have toilets, but only a few have drinking water, and then not always year-round. You're advised to take five litres of water per person per day, plus three days extra supply in case you get stuck. You should also have a fuel stove – wood fires are banned on some islands and unwelcome on the others. The QNP&WS office (see the Airlie Beach Information section earlier) publishes a leaflet that describes the various sites, and provides detailed information on what to take and do. You can book sites and get camping permits ($3 per person per night) here, and the rangers can advise you on the best spots and how to get to them.

For information on boat transport to/from the islands, talk to the rangers or contact one of the many booking agencies in Airlie Beach. For $40 to $65 return per person, a number of the regular day-trip boats will drop you off at the end of a cruise and pick you up again on an agreed date. Destination Whitsundays (☎ (079) 46 6848) in Airlie Beach hires out basic camping kits at $12 a night for two people or $15 a night for three people.

Whitsundays

Curiously, the Whitsundays are misnamed – Captain Cook didn't really sail through them on Whit Sunday. When he returned to England, it was found that his meticulously kept log was a day out because he had not allowed for crossing the international date line! As he sailed through the Whitsundays and farther north, Cook was also unaware of the existence of the Great Barrier Reef, although he realised that something to the east of his ship was making the water unusually calm. It wasn't until he ran aground on the Endeavour Reef, near Cooktown, that he finally found out about the reef. ■

The possibilities for camping in national parks in the Whitsundays are summarised in the following table:

Island	Location	People	Drinking Water
Long	Sandy Bay	10	no
North Molle	Cockatoo Beach	36	seasonal
Whitsunday	Whitehaven Beach (southern end)	20	no
	Dugong Beach	40	yes, but may be seasonal
	Sawmill Beach	20	seasonal
	Joe's Beach	10	no
Hook	Stonehaven Beach	6	no
Thomas	Sea Eagle Beach	4	no
Shaw	Neck Bay Beach	12	no
South Repulse	western beach	18	no
Gloucester*	Bona Bay	42	no
Armit*	western beach	18	no
Saddleback*	western side	18	no

* Northern islands such as Armit, Gloucester and Saddleback are harder to reach since the water taxi and cruises from Shute Harbour don't usually go there. Gloucester and Saddleback are best reached from Earlando, Dingo Beach or Bowen.

Long Island

The closest resort island to the coast, Long Island has two active resorts and is nearly all national park. The island is about 11 km long

QUEENSLAND

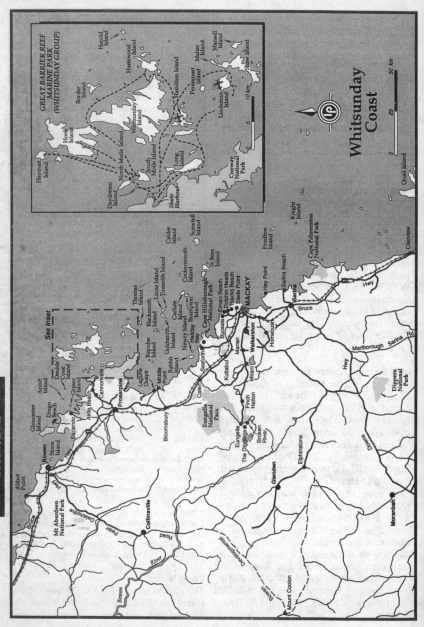

Whitsunday Coast

but no more than 1.5 km wide, and it has lots of rainforest, 13 km of walking tracks and some fine lookouts.

At Happy Bay in the north, the *Whitsunday Long Island Resort* (☎ (079) 46 9400) is a modern mid-range resort fronting a long expanse of genuine tropical island beach. The resort has two pools, a cafe, a restaurant, tennis courts, water sports and so on, as well as the obligatory disco. There are three levels of rooms ranging from $70 a double to $170 a double.

Two km south, the small *Long Island Palm Bay Resort* (☎ (079) 46 9233) is a low-key, old-fashioned resort with Melanesian style cabins and simple units, all with verandahs, kitchenettes and bathrooms. The resort is a pleasant reminder of days gone by, but unfortunately the prices are very contemporary with doubles starting at $200 a night – plus another $50 per person for meals. There's good snorkelling and dinghies, catamarans and sailboards for hire.

Hook Island

Second-largest of the Whitsundays, Hook Island is 53 sq km and rises to 450 metres at Hook Peak. There are a number of beaches dotted around the island. It's mainly national park, with camping areas at Curlew Beach in the southern Macona Inlet and Stonehaven Beach on the western side. The *Hook Island Wilderness Resort* (☎ (079) 46 9380) is the only true budget resort in the Whitsundays. It's a simple and basic lodge with 12 adjoining bunk units; a bunk costs $19 a night, and doubles are $48. They also have tent sites at $8.50 per person, and there's a casual restaurant serving cheap breakfasts, lunches and dinners, as well as communal cooking and bathroom facilities.

The island also has an unimpressive underwater observatory ($8.50). The launch trip to the resort is $20 per person.

The beautiful, fjord-like Nara Inlet on Hook Island is a very popular deep-water anchorage for visiting yachts.

Daydream Island

Tiny Daydream Island, about one km long

and a couple of hundred metres wide, is the nearest resort island to Shute Harbour. At the northern end is the 300-room *Daydream Island Travelodge Resort* (☎ (079) 48 8488), a modern resort catering mainly for families. Rooms start at $180 a double, and children pay $15 a night; rates include use of tennis courts, a gym, pools, water sports gear etc. A classic case of big resort, small island.

Daydream has a good day-trippers' section at the southern end, with a pool, bar and cafe, and water sports gear for hire. The return trip from Shute Harbour costs $22.

South Molle Island

At four sq km, South Molle is the largest of the Molle group of islands and it is virtually joined to Mid Molle and North Molle. It has long stretches of beach and is crisscrossed by walking tracks. The highest point is 198-metre Mt Jeffreys, but the climb up Spion Kop is also worthwhile. You can spend a day walking on the island for the cost of the $25 ferry trip.

Most of South Molle is national park but there's the *South Molle Island Resort* (☎ (079) 46 9433) in the north, where the

QUEENSLAND

boats come in. It's one of the older resorts, with straightforward motel-style rooms, a small golf course, a gym, tennis courts and water sports gear. Nightly costs range from $140 to $175 per person, which includes all meals and activities. Hundreds of rainbow lorikeets fly in to feed every day at 3 pm.

Hamilton Island

The most heavily developed resort island in the Whitsundays, Hamilton is more like a town than a resort. It has its own airport, a 200-boat marina, shops, restaurants and bars, and accommodation for more than 2000 people, including three high-rise tower blocks. Not surprisingly, the range of entertainment, is extensive (and expensive): helicopter joy rides, game fishing, parasailing, cruising, scuba diving, nine restaurants, squash courts and a hill-top fauna reserve with wombats, crocodiles and koalas. The cheapest double room costs $200 a night, ranging up to $1450 a night for your own private villa.

Hamilton is about five sq km and rises to 200 metres at Passage Peak. It can make an interesting day trip from Shute Harbour ($35 return for the launch only), and you can use all of the resort facilities.

The airport is used mainly by people jetting between resort islands, with launches and helicopters laid on to whisk them off to their chosen spots. Ansett flies nonstop to Hamilton from Brisbane ($299 one way), Cairns ($238), Melbourne ($501) and Sydney ($421).

Hayman Island

The most northerly of the Whitsundays, Hayman is four sq km, and rises to 250 metres above sea level. It has forested hills, valleys and beaches. Owned by Ansett, Hayman has become such an exclusive resort that day trips no longer call there. The nearest you'll probably get is some of the reefs or small islands nearby such as Black Island (also called Bali Hai) or Arkhurst, Langford or Bird islands.

The *Hayman Island Resort* (☎ (079) 46 9100), fronted by a wide, shallow reef that emerges from the water at low tide, is a luxurious five-star hotel dripping in style. Rooms range from $375 to $1000 a night.

Lindeman Island

One of the most southerly of the Whitsundays, Lindeman covers eight sq km, most of which is national park. The island has 20 km of walking trails and the highest point is 210-metre Mt Oldfield. Lindeman has plenty of little beaches and secluded bays, and there are also a lot of small islands dotted around, some of which are easy to get across to.

The *Club Med Resort* (☎ (079) 46 9333) in the south has a pool, several restaurants, a bar, a golf course, tennis and lots of water-based activities. Nightly tariffs range from $195 to $250 per person, including all meals and most activities. The internationally famous Club Med style is very evident here, with a heavy emphasis on fun, fun, fun.

Day trips to Lindeman cost about $100 from Shute Harbour. You can also fly here with Island Air Taxis ($50 one way) from Whitsunday airport on the mainland, or with Helijet from Mackay.

Whitsunday Island

The largest of the Whitsundays, this island covers 109 sq km and rises to 438 metres at Whitsunday Peak. There's no resort, but six-km-long Whitehaven Beach on the south-east coast is the longest and finest beach in the group (some say in the country!), with good snorkelling off its southern end. There are QNP&WS camping areas at Whitehaven Beach, Dugong and Sawmill beaches on the west, and Joe's Beach.

Cid Harbour

Between Cid and Whitsunday islands, Cid Harbour was the anchorage for part of the US Navy before the Battle of the Coral Sea, which was the turning point in the Pacific arena of WW II. Today, visiting ocean cruise liners anchor here.

Getting Around

Air Hamilton and Lindeman islands are the only islands with airports. See the Airlie Beach Getting There & Away section for details of flights from the mainland.

Boat There's a bamboozling array of boat trips heading out to the islands. Fantasea Cruises (☎ (079) 46 5111) and Whitsunday Allover (☎ (079) 46 6900) are the two major operators for transfers to the islands – most of their boats depart from Shute Harbour. Island transfers cost between $20 and $35 return, depending on the distance involved; you can also buy tickets that combine visits to two or more islands.

In addition, there are literally dozens of different cruises and pleasure trips heading out to the islands and reefs; these depart from either Shute Harbour or the Abel Point Marina near Airlie Beach.

Depending on how much time and money you have, you can choose from the following: day trips to the islands or reefs from $40 to $60; overnight cruises from $120; two-night/three-day trips from $200; three-night/four-day trips from $225; four-night/five-day trips (camping on the beaches) from $200; or self-skippered charter yachts from about $220 a day for two people or $380 a day for four.

All of the boats and trips are different, so it's worth speaking to a couple of the booking agents to find out which trip will suit you. There are leisurely sailing cruises to uninhabited islands, high-speed diving trips to outer reefs, fishing expeditions, and cruises that take in several destinations. Most trips include activities such as snorkelling and boom netting, with scuba diving as an optional extra. It's worth asking how many people will be on your boat.

Most of the cruise operators do coach pick-ups from Airlie Beach. You can bus to Shute Harbour or you can leave your car in the Shute Harbour car park for $7 for 24 hours. There's a lock-up car park a few hundred metres back along the road by the Shell service station, costing $5 from 8 am to 5 pm or $8 for 24 hours.

Roylen's Cruises has weekend trips from Mackay to Hamilton and Lindeman islands – see the Mackay section for details.

BOWEN (pop 13,500)

Bowen, founded in 1861, was the first coastal settlement north of Rockhampton. Although soon overshadowed by Mackay to the south and Townsville to the north, Bowen survived, and today it is a thriving fruit and vegetable-growing centre. It isn't much of a tourist town, but lots of travellers come here looking for seasonal picking work.

The Bowen Historical Museum, at 22 Gordon St, has displays relating to the town's early history. It's open weekdays and Sunday morning. Just north of Bowen, a string of sandy beaches, some of them quite secluded, dot the coast around the cape.

Places to Stay

There are three 'workers hostels' in Bowen that specialise in finding seasonal picking work for travellers. All three are fairly basic, and have courtesy buses that do pick-ups and run workers to and from work. It's a competitive scene, and it's worth ringing around before you come, to find out what's available.

Barnacles Backpackers (☎ (077) 86 1245), at 16 Gordon St, has a relaxed atmosphere and two sections, with dorm beds at $12 and doubles $28. It can get quite crowded, however. The long-running *Bowen Backpackers* (☎ (077) 86 3433) is nearby at 56 Herbert St (the main road). It has a good reputation for finding fruit-picking work, although the owners will get very annoyed if, after finding you work, you move elsewhere, such as the (cheaper) caravan park. The nightly cost is $12 in four to eight-bed dorms. The latest hostel to open here is *Trinity's Backpackers* (☎ (077) 86 4199), at 93 Horseshoe Bay Rd. It has four to six-share self-contained units at $12 a night.

Getting There & Away

The long-distance bus stop is outside the Traveland travel agency (☎ (077) 86 2835) on William St, near the centre. There are buses along the coast to Rockhampton (6½ hours, $68), Airlie Beach (two hours, $20) and Townsville (2½ hours, $28). The *Sunlander* and *Queenslander* trains also stop at Bowen, three km south of the centre. The economy fare from Brisbane is $109.

North Coast

AYR TO TOWNSVILLE

Ayr (population 8600) is on the delta of one of the biggest rivers in Queensland, the Burdekin, and it is the major commercial centre for the rich farmlands and cane fields of the Burdekin Valley. On Wilmington St, the Ayr Nature Display has exhibits of preserved butterflies, moths and beetles; it's open daily from 8 am to 5 pm ($2.50). *Wilmington House* (☎ (077) 83 5837), at 54 Wilmington St, is a good place to stay if you are looking for fruit-picking work.

South across the Burdekin River is **Home Hill**, where you can visit the bizarre Ashworth's Fantastic Tourist Attraction with its tacky souvenir shop, pottery gallery and collection of fossils, gemstones and rocks ($2). Between Ayr and Townsville is the turn-off to the Australian Institute of Marine Science on Cape Ferguson. You can visit it on weekdays from 9 am to 3 pm, and between March and November there are free guided tours every Friday at 10 am.

Seventy-two km north-west of Ayr there's another turn-off from the Bruce Highway to the **Mt Elliot National Park**. It's six km from the highway to the park, where there's a good camping ground and a ranger station (☎ (077) 78 8203) near Alligator Creek. There are two long walking trails and the creek has good swimming holes. Alligator Creek tumbles down between two rugged ranges that rise steeply from the coastal plains. The taller range peaks in Mt Elliot (1234 metres), whose higher slopes harbour some of Queensland's most southerly tropical rainforest. There's no public transport to the park.

TOWNSVILLE (pop 87,650)

The fourth-largest city in Queensland, Townsville is the port city for the agricultural and mining production of the vast inland region of northern Queensland. Founded in 1864 through the efforts of a Scot, John Melton Black, and the money of Robert Towns, a Sydney-based sea captain and financier, Townsville developed mainly on the back of Chinese and Kanaka labour.

Today Townsville is a working city, a major armed forces base, and the site of James Cook University. It's the start of the main road from Queensland to the Northern Territory. It's the only departure point for Magnetic Island (20 minutes away by ferry), and the Barrier Reef is about 1¾ hours away by fast catamaran.

In the 1990s, millions of dollars have been spent in an effort to attract more visitors to stay in Townsville for a while rather than go straight through to Cairns. A Sheraton hotel-casino and a marina have been built on the ocean front, and the Flinders St East and Palmer St areas on opposite sides of Ross Creek have been redeveloped; yet visitors are still staying away in droves. Apart from a few attractions, such as the excellent aquarium at the Great Barrier Reef Wonderland, and as an access point for Magnetic Island, Townsville still hasn't really got a lot going for it from a budget traveller's point of view.

Orientation

Townsville centres on Ross Creek and is dominated by 290-metre-high Castle Hill, which has a lookout perched on top. The city sprawls a long way, but the centre's a fairly compact area that you can easily get around on foot.

The transit centre, the arrival and departure point for long-distance buses, is on Palmer St, just south of Ross Creek. The city centre is immediately to the north of the creek, over the Dean St bridge. Flinders St Mall stretches to the left from the northern side of the bridge, towards the railway station. To the right of the bridge is the Flinders St East area, which contains many of the town's oldest buildings, plus cafes, restaurants, the Great Barrier Reef Wonderland and the ferry terminal.

Information

Townsville Enterprises' main tourist information office (☎ (077) 78 3555) is on the Bruce Highway, eight km south of the city centre. There's also a more convenient information booth (☎ (077) 21 3660) in the middle of Flinders St Mall, between Stokes and Denham Sts. It's open Monday to Saturday from 9 am to 5 pm and Sunday to 1 pm. The RACQ (☎ (077) 75 3999) is at 202 Ross River Rd, in the suburb of Aitkenvale.

The main post office is on the corner of Flinders St Mall and Denham St and there's a branch in the Great Barrier Reef Wonderland (open weekends). There's also a QNP&WS information office (☎ (077) 21 2399) at the Wonderland, open from Monday to Saturday from 9 am to 5 pm.

Great Barrier Reef Wonderland

Townsville's top attraction is at the end of Flinders St East beside Ross Creek. Although its impressive aquarium is the highlight, there are several other sections including a theatre, a museum, shops, the Great Barrier Reef Marine Park Authority office and a terminal for ferries to Magnetic Island.

A combined ticket to the aquarium, theatre and museum costs $25.50, or you can pay for each individually (see prices below).

Aquarium The huge main tank has a living coral reef and hundreds of reef fish, sharks, rays and other marine life, and you can walk beneath the tank through a clear domed tunnel. To maintain the natural conditions needed to keep this community alive, a wave machine simulates the ebb and flow of the ocean, circular currents keep the water in motion and marine algae are used in the purification system. The aquarium also has several smaller tanks, extensive displays on the history and life of the reef, and a theatrette where slide-shows on the reef are shown, plus regular guided tours. It's open daily from 9 am to 5 pm and admission is $12.

Omnimax Theatre This is a cinema with angled seating and a dome-shaped screen for a 3-D effect. Hour-long films on the reef and various other topics such as outer space alternate through the day from 9.30 am till 4.30 pm. Admission to one film is $10.

Museum of Tropical Queensland This small museum has two sections, with one display focusing on the 'Age of Reptiles' and the other half devoted to the natural history of north Queensland, including wetland birds, other wildlife, rainforest, ocean wrecks and Aboriginal artefacts. The museum is open daily from 9 am to 5 pm and admission is $3.50.

Other Museums & Galleries

The **Townsville Museum**, on the corner of Sturt and Stokes Sts, has a permanent display on early Townsville and the North Queensland independence campaigns. It's open daily from 10 am to 3 pm (to 1 pm on weekends).

The **Jezzine Military Museum** is in an 1890s fort in the grounds of the Jezzine Army Barracks, beyond the northern end of The Strand; it is open Monday, Wednesday and Friday mornings. There's also a **Maritime Museum** on Palmer St beside Ross Creek; it is open weekdays from 10 am to 4 pm and weekends from 1 to 4 pm ($3). The **Perc Tucker Gallery**, at the Denham St end of the Flinders St Mall, is a good regional art gallery that is open daily except Monday (free entry).

Parks, Gardens & Sanctuaries

The **Queens Gardens** on Gregory St, a km from the town centre, contain sports playing fields, tennis courts and Townsville's original **Botanic Gardens**, dating from 1878. The entrance to these lovely gardens is on Paxton St. The new botanic gardens, **Anderson Park**, are six km south-west of the centre on Gulliver St, Mundingburra.

The **Billabong Sanctuary**, 17 km south on the Bruce Highway, is a popular wildlife sanctuary of Australian animals. It's open daily from 8 am to 5 pm, with various shows

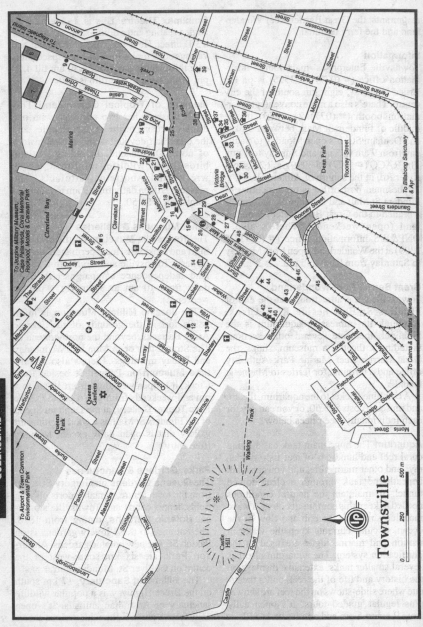

Townsville

PLACES TO STAY		10	Spinnakers on the Breakwater	11	Car Ferry Terminal
5	Historic Yongala Lodge Motel	16	Hog's Breath Cafe	14	Townsville Museum
12	Coral Tree Lodge	18	Thai International Restaurant	15	Perc Tucker Gallery
13	Rex Inn the City Motel	19	Luvits Cafe	17	Hard Blues Bar
22	Reef Lodge	27	Fisherman's Wharf	20	Bank Nightclub
33	Shamrock Hotel	30	Michel's Cafe & Bar	21	Exchange Hotel
35	Andy's Backpackers	31	Australian Hotel	23	Bullwinkle's Cabaret & Bar
36	Southbank Village Backpackers	32	Cactus Jack's Bar & Grill	24	Criterion Tavern
37	Globetrotters Hostel			25	Great Barrier Reef Wonderland & Ferry Terminal
39	YHA Adventurers Resort	**OTHER**		26	Tourist Office & Police Station
40	Central Garden Apartments	2	Seaview Hotel	28	Qantas
41	Civic House Backpackers Inn	4	Hospital	29	Post Office
46	Great Northern Hotel	6	Tobruk Olympic Swimming Pool	34	Transit Centre
		7	Sheraton Breakwater Hotel & Casino	38	Maritime Museum
PLACES TO EAT		8	Townsville Breakwater Entertainment Centre	42	Mike Ball Watersports
1	Norma's, Harold's Seafood & El Charro	9	Magnetic Island Ferry Terminal	43	Townsville Five Cinema Centre
3	C'est Si Bon			44	Police Station
				45	Train Station
				47	STA Travel
				48	Ansett

(including crocodile, koala and giant eel feeding) throughout each day. Admission costs $16. See Organised Tours later in the Townsville section for tours to the sanctuary.

The **Palmetum**, about 15 km south-west of the centre off University Rd, is a 25-hectare botanic garden devoted to native palms, ranging from desert to rainforest species, in their natural environments.

The 32-sq-km **Town Common Reserve**, five km north of the centre off Cape Pallarenda Rd, ranges from mangrove swamps and salt marsh to dry grassland and pockets of woodland and forest. The common isn't particularly attractive but it's a refuge for water birds, such as the magpie geese that herald the start of the wet season, and stately brolgas, which gather in the Dry. Early morning is the best time to see them.

Other Attractions
The **Flinders St Mall** is the retail heart of the city. It's bright and breezy with fountains, plantations and crowds of shoppers. Every Sunday morning, the busy **Cotter's Market** is held in the mall, with a wide range of crafts and local produce on offer.

East of the mall you can stroll along **Flinders St East** beside the creek. Many of the best 19th-century buildings are in this part of town, while farther out, on a breakwater at the mouth of Ross Creek, are the casino, the entertainment centre and a couple of up-market seafood restaurants. A more pleasant walk is north along **The Strand**, a long beachfront drive with a marina, gardens, some awesome banyan trees, the Tobruk swimming pool and a big artificial waterfall. At the top end of The Strand is the **Coral Memorial Rockpool**, a large artificial swimming pool on the edge of the ocean.

Activities
Diving Townsville has four or five diving schools, including one of Australia's best – Mike Ball Watersports (☎ (077) 72 3022), at 252 Walker St. Five-day certificate courses start twice a week and cost either $375 with two separate day trips to the reef or $460 with two days/three nights on the reef, staying on board their boat *Watersport*. You have to take a $50 medical before you start the course.

Pro-Dive (☎ (077) 21 1760), another well-regarded dive school, has an office in

QUEENSLAND

the Great Barrier Reef Wonderland. Pro-Dive's five-day certificate course costs $425, starts twice a week, and includes two nights and three days on the reef, with a total of eight dives.

You can get cheap or free accommodation at some hostels if you book a dive course from that hostel.

For experienced divers, the wreck of the *Yongala*, a passenger liner that sank off Cape Bowling Green in 1911 with 122 lives lost, is more of an attraction than the John Brewer Reef, which is the destination for many day trips. The *Yongala* has huge numbers of fish and other marine life, including turtles and rays. John Brewer Reef has been damaged by the crown-of-thorns starfish and cyclones, and parts of the reef have little live coral. Mike Ball and Pro-Dive both run trips out to the *Yongala*.

Other Activities The Aquatic Adventure Centre (☎ (077) 21 2619) on the Breakwater Marina will take you parasailing (from $40) and has motorboats for hire ($60 a day). Risky Business (☎ (077) 25 4571) has introductory abseiling courses ($49) and full-day training courses ($145), and Tour de Townsville Bicycle Tours (☎ (077) 21 2026) has a variety of cycling tours ($20 to $70) as well as bikes for hire.

Organised Tours
Pure Pleasure Cruises (☎ (077) 21 3555) has daily trips out to Kelso Reef on the outer reef. The cost of $120 includes lunch and snorkelling gear; scuba dives are an optional extra. Detours Coaches (☎ (077) 21 5977) offers a variety of tours in and around Townsville, including a city sights tour ($17), tours to the Billabong Sanctuary ($27), Mt Spec National Park ($57) or Charters Towers ($57), and cruises to Hinchinbrook Island ($95) or Dunk Island ($67).

Places to Stay
Camping There are two caravan parks, which are only about three km from the centre. The best choice is the *Rowes Bay*

Caravan Park (☎ (077) 71 3576), opposite the beach on Heatley Pde in Rowes Bay. Tent sites are $12 and on-site cabins start from $34. The *Showground Caravan Park* (☎ (077) 72 1487), at 16 Kings Rd, West End, has tent sites for $10 and on-site vans for $25.

Hostels Townsville's hostel scene is probably the best example of large operators jumping on the budget accommodation bandwagon. Two huge hostels in Townsville is at least one too many, and the resulting oversupply of beds means that the general standard of hostels here is not as good as in many other towns along the coast.

On the south side of Ross Creek, there are four hostels that are conveniently close to the transit centre but a bit isolated from the town centre. The huge *Adventurers Resort YHA* (☎ (077) 21 1522), at 79 Palmer St, is a multilevel complex with over 300 beds, a shop and a swimming pool. The facilities are quite good, but because of its size it tends to feel impersonal. Accommodation in a four-bunk dorm costs $14 for YHA members, and $15 for nonmembers; singles cost $22/24, and doubles $30/34.

Townsville's other huge offering is *Andy's Backpackers* (☎ (077) 21 2322), which is upstairs on top of the transit centre. It's big, clean and charmless, but if you really want to stay on top of a bus station they have dorm beds for $12 and doubles for $30. Their free evening city tour is popular.

Between these two places is the smaller *Globetrotters Hostel* (☎ (077) 71 3242), behind a house at 45 Palmer St. It's a relaxed, old-style hostel with all the usual facilities – kitchen area, lounge, pool, laundry – and it is clean and well-run. Six-bed dorms cost $13 per night, singles cost $26, and a twin room is $32.

Southbank Village Backpackers (☎ (077) 71 5849), at 33 Plume St, is a rambling old hostel spread over several buildings. It's pretty run-down and disorganised but cheap at $10 a bed.

The other hostels are on the north side of Ross Creek, in and around the city centre.

The pick of this bunch is the *Civic House Backpackers Inn* (☎ (077) 71 5381) at 262 Walker St. This clean and easy-going hostel has three or four-bed dorms for $13, six-bed dorms with bathroom and air-con for $14, and pleasant singles/doubles from $28/30, or $40 with private bathroom. Their courtesy bus does pick-ups and there's a free barbecue on Friday night.

The *Reef Lodge* (☎ (077) 21 1112), at 4 Wickham St, is another small, old-fashioned but fairly clean place with a variety of rooms in several buildings. Dorm beds start at $10 and singles/doubles at $24/28. Most rooms have coin-in-the-slot air-con ($1).

Pubs & Guesthouses The *Great Northern Hotel* (☎ (077) 71 6191), across the road from the railway station at 500 Flinders St, is a good old-fashioned pub with clean, simple rooms at $20/30, and a few doubles with private bathrooms at $35; the food downstairs is good. Opposite the transit centre, the *Shamrock Hotel* (☎ (077) 71 4351) also has singles/twins upstairs at $20/30.

At 32 Hale St, the *Coral Tree Lodge* (☎ (077) 71 5512) is a neat, friendly guesthouse in a renovated Queenslander building, with rooms from $35 and self-contained units from $50, including breakfast.

Motels & Holiday Units Cheaper motels include the *Tropical Hideaway Motel* (☎ (077) 71 4355) at 74 The Strand, with doubles from $45; the central *Rex Inn the City* (☎ (077) 71 6048), at 143 Wills St, with renovated units from $59; and the *Beach House Motel* (☎ (077) 72 1977), at 66 The Strand, with rooms at $50/55.

The *Historic Yongala Lodge Motel* (☎ (070) 72 4633), at 11 Fryer St, has modern motel units and self-contained rooms from $65 and heritage-style units from $79, as well as a good Greek restaurant at the front (see Places to Eat).

The *Townsville Seaside Apartments* (☎ (077) 21 3155) at 105 The Strand has renovated 1960s apartments from $55 a double or $72 for four. At 270-286 Walker St, the *Central Garden Apartments* (☎ (077) 72 2655) has modern one and two-bedroom apartments from $75 and $100 respectively.

Places to Eat
Flinders St East is the main area for eateries, and it offers plenty of choice. The *Thai International Restaurant*, upstairs at No 235, has fine soups for $6, a good range of vegetarian dishes from $5 to $9 and other mains for $10 to $14. At No 205 is the casual and relaxed *Luvits Cafe*. It's a good spot for breakfast or brunch – real coffee, great blueberry pancakes, bacon and eggs, toasted sandwiches etc. It is also open for lunch and dinner. Up past the Exchange Hotel is *A Kabab*, with chicken, beef and lamb kebabs for under $5. The *Hog's Breath Cafe*, one of a chain of saloon-style bar-and-grills, is near the Denham St corner.

Fisherman's Wharf, overlooking Ross Creek from near the west end of Victoria Bridge, has open-air tables and food stalls including Italian, seafood, Mexican and health food. Meals here are reasonably priced, and there's a bar and live entertainment on weekends.

Many of the pubs also do decent counter meals. The *Great Northern Hotel*, on the corner of Flinders and Blackwood Sts, has an excellent bistro with mains from $10 to $12 and good bar meals from $4 to $7. The *Seaview Hotel*, on the corner of The Strand and Gregory St, is another popular pub, and it has a pleasant beer garden. On the corner opposite this pub is a cluster of eateries, including *Norma's*, a small and friendly Lebanese BYO that is good value (cheap takeaways) and great fun – wear your dancing shoes; *Harold's Seafood*, with good burgers and fish & chips; and *El Charro*, a popular Mexican restaurant.

C'est Si Bon, on Eyre St near the Gregory St corner, is a good little gourmet deli with salads, sandwiches and other home-made goodies.

South of the river, Palmer St also has some good pubs and eateries. At No 21 is *Cactus Jack's Bar & Grill* (☎ (077) 21 1478), a lively licensed Mexican place with main courses in the $9 to $13 range; you'll need to book on weekends. At 7 Palmer St, the stylish *Michel's Cafe & Bar* is good for a splurge, while the nearby *Australian Hotel* has a tropical-style courtyard with lunches from $5 and mains in the $10 to $17 range.

The *Historic Yongala Lodge* is fronted by a Greek restaurant in a lovely 19th-century building with period furnishings, memorabilia and finds from the *Yongala* shipwreck. Main meals are in the $16 to $20 range, or there's a banquet menu at $25 a head. *Spinnakers on the Breakwater* (☎ (077) 21 2567), on the breakwater on Sir Leslie Thiess Drive, is an up-market seafood restaurant with two-course lunches at $15 and mains in the $18 to $28 range.

Entertainment
Townsville's lively nightlife also centres on Flinders St East. The *Hard Blues Bar* at No 237 is the main venue for live music, and has a different theme each night including acoustic on Tuesday, jazz on Thursday and rock and blues on weekends. *Portraits Wine Bar*, at the Exchange Hotel at No 151, attracts an older, more sophisticated crowd. Nearby at No 169 is *The Bank*, the city's most up-market nightclub; it's open nightly till late, with a $3 to $5 cover charge and dress regulations. *Bullwinkle's Cabaret & Bar* on the corner of Flinders St East and Wickham St is another popular nightclub.

The big and colourful *Criterion Tavern*, on the corner of The Strand and King St, has a beer garden, nightclub, eatery and several bars. Farther along The Strand, the popular *Seaview Hotel*, on the corner of Gregory St, has the *Arizona Bar* and beer garden downstairs (playing rock & roll with a dash of country) and *Breezes* upstairs (an over-25s nightclub).

The *Townsville Five Cinema Centre* (☎ (077) 71 4101), on the corner of Sturt and Blackwood Sts, shows mainstream current releases. The impressive *Townsville Breakwater Entertainment Centre* (☎ (077) 714000) is the main venue for concerts, the performing arts and other cultural events. If you have the right clothes and fancy trying your luck on the spin of the wheel, the *Sheraton Breakwater Casino* is at the end of Sir Leslie Thiess Drive, beyond Flinders St East.

Getting There & Away
Air Ansett and Qantas have daily flights between Townsville and all the major cities, including Cairns ($163), Brisbane ($330), Sydney, Melbourne, Perth, Darwin and Alice Springs. Ansett and Qantas both have offices in the Flinders St Mall.

Sunstate/Qantas has flights within Queensland to Dunk Island, Mackay, Proserpine, Rockhampton, Gladstone and Bundaberg, while Flight West flies to Mt Isa ($289), often with stops at smaller places on the way, plus Mackay ($171) and Rockhampton ($247).

Bus All long-distance buses operate from the transit centre on Palmer St. Both Greyhound Pioneer and McCafferty's have frequent services up and down the coastal Bruce Highway. Fares and travel times from Townsville include Brisbane (about 19 hours, $115), Rockhampton (11 hours, $73), Mackay (six hours, $48), Airlie Beach (3½ hours, $37), Mission Beach (three hours, $35) and Cairns (five hours, $38). There are also daily services inland to Mt Isa (11 hours, $81) via Charters Towers (1¾ hours, $15), continuing on to the Northern Territory.

Train The Brisbane-Cairns *Sunlander* travels through Townsville three times a week. From Brisbane to Townsville takes 25 hours ($118 for an economy seat, $226 for a 1st-class sleeper). From Townsville, Proserpine is a five-hour journey, Rockhampton is 14½ hours and Cairns is seven hours. The faster and more luxurious *Queenslander* does the Brisbane-Cairns run once a week – the Brisbane-Townsville fare is $433 which includes all meals and a sleeping compartment.

The *Inlander* heads inland twice-weekly from Townsville to Mt Isa (18 hours, $95 in economy or $192 in 1st-class sleeper) via Charters Towers (three hours, $20 in economy only).

Car Rental The larger car-rental agencies are all represented in Townsville. Smaller operators include Rent-a-Rocket (☎ (077) 72 7444), 14 Dean St, South Townsville; Sunrunner Moke Hire (☎ (077) 21 5038) at 11 Anthony St, South Townsville; and Townsville Car Rentals (☎ (077) 72 1093) at 12 Palmer St (near the transit centre).

Getting Around

To/From the Airport Townsville airport is five km north-west of the city at Garbutt; a taxi to the centre costs $9. The Airport Shuttle (☎ (077) 75 5544) services all main arrivals and departures. It costs $5 one way and will drop you off or pick you up almost anywhere fairly central.

Bus Two companies run local bus services around Townsville. Route maps and timetables are available in the Transit Mall (near the Flinders St Mall tourist office).

Taxi For a taxi in Townsville, call Standard White Cabs (☎ (077) 72 1555).

MAGNETIC ISLAND (pop 2500)

Tourists first came to Magnetic Island from the mainland more than 100 years ago, making it one of Queensland's oldest resort islands. Although popular, it's somewhat resort island, with the main attractions being its fine beaches, excellent bushwalks, abundant wildlife and laid-back nature. It's also cheap and easy to get to, being only eight km offshore from Townsville (15 minutes by ferry).

Magnetic Island was named by Captain Cook, who thought his ship's compass went funny when he sailed by in 1770. It's dominated by 494-metre Mt Cook.

Magnetic is one of the larger reef islands (52 sq km) and about 70% of it is national park. There are several small towns along the coast and the island has quite a different atmosphere to the purely resort islands along the reef – it's almost an outer suburb of Townsville, with many of the 2500 residents commuting to the mainland by ferry.

Orientation & Information

Magnetic Island is roughly triangular in shape. Picnic Bay, the main town and ferry pier, is at the southern corner. There's a road up the eastern side of the island to Horseshoe Bay and there's a rough track along the west coast. Along the north coast it's walking only.

The Island Travel Centre (☎ (077) 78 5155) has an information centre and booking office between the end of the pier and the mall in Picnic Bay. You can book local tours and accommodation here, and organise domestic and international travel arrangements. There's a QNP&WS office (☎ (077) 78 5378) on Hurst St in Picnic Bay.

Picnic Bay

Picnic Bay is the main settlement, and the first stop for the ferries. The new mall along the waterfront has a good selection of shops and eateries, and you can hire bikes, cars, scooters and mokes here. Picnic Bay also has quite a few places to stay, and the main beach has a stinger-free enclosure and is patrolled by a life-saving club.

There's a lookout above the town and just to the west of Picnic Bay is **Cockle Bay** with the wreck of the *City of Adelaide*. Heading around the coast in the other direction is **Rocky Bay** where there's a short, steep walk down to its beautiful beach. The popular **Picnic Bay Golf Course** is open to the public.

Nelly Bay

Next up the coast is Nelly Bay, which has a good beach with shade, and a reef at low tide. At the far end of the bay there are some pioneer graves. Also at Nelly Bay is the **Shark World aquarium** in the Magnetic Beach Resort. The aquarium is being upgraded and at the resort you can hire catamarans, canoes, sailboards and snorkelling gear.

Arcadia

Around the headland is **Geoffrey Bay**, a marine park area that has an interesting 400-metre low-tide reef walk over the fringing

QUEENSLAND

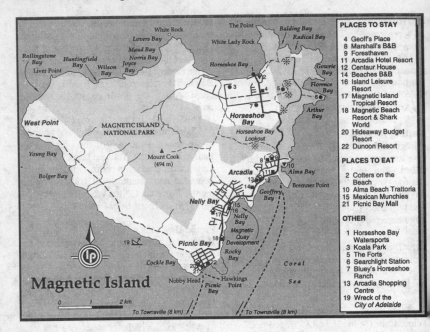

PLACES TO STAY
4 Geoff's Place
8 Marshall's B&B
9 Foresthaven
11 Arcadia Hotel Resort
12 Centaur House
14 Beaches B&B
16 Island Leisure Resort
17 Magnetic Island Tropical Resort
18 Magnetic Beach Resort & Shark World
20 Hideaway Budget Resort
22 Dunoon Resort

PLACES TO EAT
2 Cotters on the Beach
10 Alma Beach Trattoria
15 Mexican Munchies
21 Picnic Bay Mall

OTHER
1 Horseshoe Bay Watersports
3 Koala Park
5 The Forts
6 Searchlight Station
7 Bluey's Horseshoe Ranch
13 Arcadia Shopping Centre
19 Wreck of the City of Adelaide

coral reef from the southern end of the beach; a board indicates the start of the trail. Some of Magnetic Marine's ferries also stop at the jetty on Geoffrey Bay.

Overlooking the bay is the town of Arcadia, with shops, more places to stay and the Arcadia Hotel Resort (where there are live bands at weekends and a pool that is open to the public). Just around the next headland is the very pleasant Alma Bay beach.

Radical Bay & The Forts
The road runs back from the coast until you reach the junction of the road to Radical Bay. You can go straight to Horseshoe Bay, take the central track via the Forts, or turn right to Radical Bay, with tracks leading off it to secluded Arthur and Florence bays, and the old **Searchlight Station** on the headland between the two bays.

From Radical Bay you can walk across the headland to beautiful **Balding Bay** (an unofficial nude bathing beach) and Horseshoe Bay.

Horseshoe Bay
Horseshoe Bay, on the north coast of the island, has a few shops, accommodation and a long stretch of beach. There's a fairly desolate **Koala Park**, which is quite a long drive off the main road, and a **mango plantation**, signposted off the main road, that you can visit. At the beach there are boats, sailboards and canoes for hire. From the beach you can walk to Maud Bay, around to the west, or over to Radical Bay.

Activities
Bushwalks The QNP&WS produces a leaflet for Magnetic Island's excellent bushwalking tracks. Possible walks, with distances and one-way travel times, include Nelly Bay to Arcadia (6 km, 2 hours); Picnic

Bay to West Point (8 km, 2½ hours); Horseshoe Bay Road to Arthur Bay (2 km, 30 minutes); Horseshoe Bay to Florence Bay (2.5 km, 1 hour); Horseshoe Bay to the Forts (2 km, 45 minutes); Horseshoe Bay to Balding Bay (3 km, 45 minutes); Horseshoe Bay to Radical Bay (3 km, 45 minutes); and the Mt Cook ascent (8 km, all day).

Note that the Mt Cook ascent is not for the faint-hearted. Check with the QNP&WS office before attempting this difficult walk.

Other Activities Magnetic Island Pleasure Divers (☎ (077) 78 5788) offers a basic five-day dive course for $249, or a more comprehensive course for $295. (See the Townsville section for details of dive operators based there.) Bluey's Horseshoe Ranch (☎ (077) 78 5109) at Horseshoe Bay offers trail rides at $18 an hour or $45 for a half-day trot.

The Magnetic Island Country Golf Club (☎ (077) 78 5188) in Hurst St, Picnic Bay, is open daily. You can try rap jumping, which is a type of abseiling (☎ 018 450 120), for $55, or go on a half-day sea-kayaking trip ($29) from Horseshoe Bay.

Places to Stay

Hostels There's a good selection of backpackers hostels on the island and it's a competitive scene, with several hostels sending vehicles to meet the ferries at Picnic Bay. There are also package deals on accommodation and transport (see Getting There & Away in this section).

Picnic Bay Only a minute's walk from the Picnic Bay ferry pier, the *Hideaway Budget Resort* (☎ (077) 78 5110) at 32 Picnic St is a clean, renovated place with a small kitchen, pool, a TV room and laundry facilities. A bed in a twin or double room costs $14 per person.

Nelly Bay The *Magnetic Island Tropical Resort* (☎ (077) 78 5955) on Yates St, just off the main road, is a very good budget resort with a swimming pool, an inexpensive restaurant and a pleasant garden setting. A bed in a four to six-bed timber cabin costs $14, or you can rent a whole cabin – they range from $40 to $75 a double plus $10 for each extra adult. This place is good if you're after somewhere quiet and relaxed.

At the southern end of Nelly Bay is the *Magnetic Beach Resort* (☎ (077) 78 5777), attached to the Shark World aquarium. The resort has a snack bar, camp sites at $9 per person, dorm beds in four or eight-bed A-frame cabins at $16, and camp-o-tels at $17 per person.

Arcadia The popular *Centaur House* (☎ (077) 78 5668), at 27 Marine Pde, is a rambling, old-style hostel opposite the beach. The atmosphere is relaxed and friendly, there's a pleasant garden, and a bed in the clean spacious dorms costs $14; double rooms are $30 to $34.

Also in Arcadia is *Foresthaven* (☎ (077) 78 5153) at 11 Cook Rd. This hostel has seen better days and is fairly spartan, although the peaceful bush setting is nice. Accommodation is in old-fashioned two and three-bed units that have their own kitchen; dorm beds cost $14 and twins/doubles cost $34. You can hire mountain bikes ($10 a day), and the owners speak German and French.

Horseshoe Bay *Geoff's Place* (☎ (077) 78 5577) is one of the island's most popular places for young travellers. It has a party atmosphere, nightly activities and a pool. There are extensive grounds, and you can camp for $6 per person, take a bunk in a marquee for $10 or share a four or eight-bed A-frame cedar cabin for $14 (eight-bed cabins have their own bathroom). There's a communal kitchen, a bar and a restaurant with meals from $4 to $7. You can hire mountain bikes for $10 a day. The hostel's courtesy bus shuttles between here and Picnic Bay to meet the ferries.

Other Accommodation There are plenty of pubs, motels, holiday flats and even a couple of B&Bs. Rates for these places vary seasonally, and in the school holiday periods you'll probably need to book.

QUEENSLAND

In Picnic Bay, the *Picnic Bay Hotel* (☎ (077) 78 5166) on the Esplanade has motel rooms from $40. The *Dunoon Resort* (☎ (077) 78 5161) on the corner of Granite St and the Esplanade has self-contained units from $72.

The impressive *Island Leisure Resort* (☎ (077) 78 5511) at 4 Kelly St in Nelly Bay has a pool, tennis court and gym, and units from $89. In Arcadia, the *Arcadia Hotel Resort* (☎ (077) 78 5177) has motel units from $55.

There are also two B&Bs in Arcadia. The friendly *Marshall's B&B* (☎ (077) 78 5112) at 3 Endeavour Rd is a simple beach-house with singles/doubles from $35/45. *Beaches B&B* (☎ (077) 78 5303), a stylish timber cottage with a pool and separate guest wing, is good value at $55 a double.

Places to Eat

Picnic Bay The Picnic Bay Mall, along the waterfront, has a good selection of eating places plus a supermarket. The *Picnic Bay Pub* has decent counter meals. Farther along, *Crusoe's* is a casual little BYO place serving breakfast, lunch and dinner, and the *Green Frog Cafe* is good for breakfasts or light lunches.

The licensed *Max's*, at the far end of the Esplanade, is a bit more up-market and has steaks, and Thai and Malaysian mains from $10 to $17.

Nelly Bay *Mexican Munchies* runs the gamut from enchiladas to tacos, and is open daily from 6 pm. There's a blackboard outside where you can chalk up your reservation during the day. In the small shopping centre on the main road are *Possums Cafe* and a local supermarket.

Arcadia The *Arcadia Hotel Resort* has bistro meals from $10 to $12 and sometimes puts on special deals for backpackers; there's also a more expensive restaurant section. Across the road at Alma Bay, the BYO *Alma Beach Trattoria* has a great setting overlooking a pretty little bay, and does pizzas, pasta and seafood at very reasonable prices.

In the small shopping centre on Hayles Ave, the *Blue Waters Cafe & Restaurant* has a pleasant little courtyard and some of the best food on the island. It's a burger-bar by day; at night mains range from $8 to $14 and they have three-course deals for $13.50. Nearby, the *Bakehouse* is open early and is a good place for a breakfast of coffee and croissants. Next door is *Banister's Seafood*, which is a good fish & chips place with an open-air dining area; it's BYO.

Horseshoe Bay *Cotters on the Beach* is a relaxed licensed restaurant with lunches from $5 to $7 and steak, chicken and seafood dinners from $10 to $17. Next door, the *Bounty Snack Bar* has takeaways and there's a small general store where you can buy groceries.

Getting There & Away

Magnetic Island Ferries (☎ (077) 72 7122) runs what is virtually a shuttle service to the island from its two Townsville terminals – one at the Great Barrier Reef Wonderland, the other at the breakwater on Sir Leslie Thiess Drive near the casino. The first ferry leaves Townsville daily at 6 am; the last service on Sunday, Monday and Wednesday is at 6.45 pm, on Tuesday at 10.40 pm, on Thursday at 9.30 pm, and on Friday and Saturday at about midnight. The trip takes about 15 minutes and the return fare is $19 ($14 for students). All ferries go to Picnic Bay and some continue on to Arcadia.

You can also buy package deals that include return ferry tickets and accommodation; one-night packages start at $29.

The Capricorn Barge Company (☎ (077) 72 5422) runs a vehicular ferry to Arcadia from the south side of Ross Creek four times a day during the week and twice a day on weekends. It's $89 return for a car and up to six passengers.

Getting Around

Bus The Magnetic Island Bus Service operates between Picnic Bay and Horseshoe Bay 12 to 18 times a day, meeting all ferries and dropping off at all accommodation places.

Some bus trips include Radical Bay, others the Koala Park. You can get individual tickets ($1.20 to $3) or a full-day pass ($7).

Car, Moke & Moped Rental Moke Magnetic (☎ (077) 78 5377), in an arcade of the Picnic Bay Mall, and Holiday Moke Hire (☎ (077) 78 5703), based in the Jetty Cafe in the Picnic Bay Mall, have Mokes from $31 a day ($28 if you're over 25) plus 30c per km. Both companies also have Suzuki Sierras, Mazda 121s and other vehicles.

Roadrunner Scooter Hire (☎ (077) 78 5222) has an office in an arcade off the Picnic Bay Mall. Day hire of mopeds is $25, half-day hire $19, and 24-hour hire $30.

Bicycle Magnetic Island is ideal for cycling, and mountain bikes are available for rent at several places, including the Esplanade in Picnic Bay, Foresthaven Resort in Arcadia and Geoff's Place in Horseshoe Bay. Bikes cost $10 for a day, and $6 for half a day.

NORTH COAST HINTERLAND

The Flinders Highway heads inland from Townsville and runs due west for almost 800 km to Cloncurry, via the gold-mining town of Charters Towers.

Ravenswood (pop 200)

At Mingela, 83 km from Townsville, a sealed road leads 40 km south to Ravenswood, a former ghost town from the gold-rush days. Although many of the buildings were demolished or fell down years ago, some interesting **old buildings** linger amid the scattered red-earth hills, including the old post office, two historic pubs and the old courthouse, police station and cell block, which are being restored and will become a mining and historical museum. In recent years a couple of companies have recommenced mining operations here, breathing new life back into the town. The *Imperial Hotel* (☎ (077) 70 2131) has a great public bar, a dining room with home-cooked meals, and B&B from $23/36.

Eighty km on down the road past Ravenswood, the big **Burdekin Falls Dam**, completed in 1987, holds back more than 200 sq km of water.

Charters Towers (pop 9450)

This busy town, 130 km inland from Townsville, was fabulously rich during the gold rush. Many old houses with classic verandahs and lace work, imposing public buildings and mining structures remain. It's possible to make a day trip here from Townsville and get a glimpse of outback Queensland on the way.

The gleam of gold was first spotted in 1871, in a creek bed at the foot of Towers Hill, by an Aboriginal boy, Jupiter Mosman. Within a few years, the surrounding area was peppered with diggings and a large town had grown. In its heyday (around the turn of the century), Charters Towers had almost 100 mines and a population of 30,000, and it even had its own stock exchange. It attracted wealth seekers from far and wide and came to be known as 'The World'. Mosman St, the main street in those days, had 25 pubs.

When the gold ran out in the 1920s, the city shrank, but it survived as a centre for the beef industry. Since the mid-1980s, Charters Towers has seen a bit of a gold revival as modern processes enable companies to work deposits in previously uneconomical areas.

Information The National Trust of Queensland (☎ (077) 87 2374) has an office in the Stock Exchange Arcade on Mosman St, which doubles as a tourist office; it is open daily except Sunday. Pick up the free *Guide to Charters Towers* booklet and a copy of the National Trust's walking tour leaflet.

Things to See & Do On Mosman St a few metres up the hill from the corner of Gill St, is the picturesque **Stock Exchange Arcade**, built in 1887 and restored in 1972. At the end of the arcade opposite the information office is the interesting **Assay Room & Mining Museum** ($1). Farther up Mosman St, the **ABC Bank Building** (1891) is currently being restored and will become a theatre.

At 62 Mosman St, the **Zara Clark Museum** is well worth a visit with an inter-

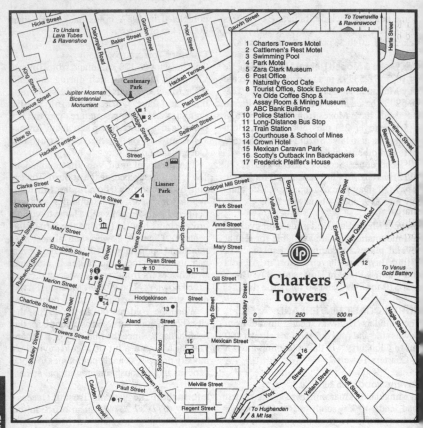

Key to map:
1 Charters Towers Motel
2 Cattlemen's Rest Motel
3 Swimming Pool
4 Park Motel
5 Zara Clark Museum
6 Post Office
7 Naturally Good Cafe
8 Tourist Office, Stock Exchange Arcade,
  Ye Olde Coffee Shop &
  Assay Room & Mining Museum
9 ABC Bank Building
10 Police Station
11 Long-Distance Bus Stop
12 Train Station
13 Courthouse & School of Mines
14 Crown Hotel
15 Mexican Caravan Park
16 Scotty's Outback Inn Backpackers
17 Frederick Pfeiffer's House

esting collection of memorabilia, antiques, photos and a military display. It's open daily from 10 am to 3 pm; entry costs $3.

Probably the finest of the town's old houses is Frederick Pfeiffer's, on Paull St. It's now a Mormon chapel, but you can walk around the outside. Pfeiffer was a gold miner who became Queensland's first millionaire.

Five km from town is the **Venus Battery**, where gold-bearing ore was crushed and processed from 1872 until as recently as 1972. The battery has been restored to working order and is open daily from 9 am to 3 pm, with guided tours at 10 am and 2 pm. Entry is $3.

Gold Nugget Scenic Tours (☎ (077) 87 1568) runs half-day city tours ($15) four days a week.

Festivals During the Australia Day weekend in late January, more than 100 cricket teams and their supporters converge on Charters Towers for a competition known as the Goldfield Ashes. The town also hosts one of Australia's biggest annual country music festivals, on the May Day weekend, and has a major rodeo every Easter.

Places to Stay The *Mexican Caravan Park* (☎ (077) 87 1161) is fairly central, south of Gill St at 75 Church St. It has tent sites at $9 and on-site vans for $24, plus a swimming pool and store.

The excellent *Scotty's Outback Inn Backpackers* (☎ (077) 87 1028) is at 58 York St, 1.4 km south of the town centre. The owners will pick you up from the bus stop if you ring. It's a renovated timber house built in the 1880s, with pleasant breezy verandahs and sitting areas. Four-share dorms cost $12 a night, and you can hire bikes, and get a cheap combined ticket for some of the town's museums and the Venus Battery. The owners run good day trips to Ravenswood ($35), a nearby cattle station ($40) and a half-day trip to Mt Leyshon Gold Mine (Thursday, $10).

The *Park Motel* (☎ (077) 87 1022), at 1 Mosman St, has pleasant grounds and a good restaurant, and units cost from $55/63.

Places to Eat Nearly all the pubs have decent meals. The *Crown Hotel* in Mosman St has all-you-can-eat Chinese smorgasbords at $5.90. *Ye Olde Coffee Shop*, in the Stock Exchange Arcade, has kebabs, sandwiches and cakes, and the *Naturally Good Cafe* on Gill St, opposite the library, is a good gourmet cafe with home-cooked meals, smoothies, burgers and other snacks.

Getting There & Around McCafferty's and Greyhound Pioneer have daily services from Townsville to Charters Towers (1¾ hours, $16), continuing on to Mt Isa (nine hours, $74). Buses arrive and depart at the Goldfield Star service station on the corner of Gill and Church Sts.

The railway station is on Enterprise Rd, 1.5 km east of the centre. The twice-weekly *Inlander* also runs from Townsville to Charters Towers (three hours, $20 economy only) and continues on to Mt Isa (16 hours, $85 in economy, $115 for a sleeper).

TOWNSVILLE TO MISSION BEACH
Mt Spec National Park
This national park, which straddles the 1000-metre-plus Paluma Range, west of the Bruce Highway, has Australia's most southerly pocket of tropical rainforest.

To get there, turn-off the Bruce Highway 61 km north of Townsville. There are two access routes. The southern route is a narrow and spectacular road that winds up along the southern edge of the park, passing **Little Crystal Creek** (with a waterfall and good swimming beside a stone bridge) and **McClelland's Lookout** (three good walking trails) on the way to the sleepy mountain village of **Paluma**. The northern route leads to **Big Crystal Creek**, which has good swimming, a barbecue area, plus a camp site – to book, contact the park ranger (☎ (077) 70 8526). Bower birds are relatively common in the park. Detours runs day trips from Townsville ($57).

Jourama National Park
This small but beautiful park is six unsealed km off the highway, 91 km north of Townsville. It is centred around the Waterview Creek, and has good swimming holes, several lookouts, a picnic area and a camping ground (bookings and permits as for Big Crystal Creek). There are walking trails to the waterfalls (600 metres) and the falls lookout (1.2 km).

Ingham (pop 5100)
Ingham, a major sugar-producing town, celebrates its Italian heritage with the Australian-Italian Festival each May.

There's a good tourist centre (☎ (077) 76 5211) on the corner of Lannercost St and Townsville Rd. The QNP&WS office (☎ (077) 76 1700), at the end of an arcade at 11 Lannercost St, deals with information for Mt Spec, Wallaman Falls, Jourama, and Hinchinbrook and Orpheus islands. The *Hinchinbrook Hotel* (☎ (077) 76 2227), at 83 Lannercost St, offers beds to backpackers at $12 each in a twin room and has good bistro meals with bistro mains from $6 to $9.

There are a number of places to visit

around Ingham including **Wallaman Falls National Park**, 48 km inland, where a tributary of the Herbert River cascades for 305 metres, the longest single drop in Australia. The falls are most spectacular in the wet season. You can usually reach them by conventional vehicle along an unsealed road; there's a QNP&WS camping area with a swimming hole nearby.

Only seven km east of Ingham is the **Victoria Mill**, the largest sugar mill in the southern hemisphere. Free tours are given in the crushing season (about July to December). **Lucinda**, a port town 24 km from Ingham, is the access point for the southern end of Hinchinbrook Island. It also has a six-km jetty used for shipping the sugar.

Orpheus Island

Lying off the coast between Townsville and Ingham, Orpheus is a narrow 14-sq-km granite island surrounded by coral reefs. One of the Palm group, it's a quiet, secluded island that is good for camping, snorkelling and diving. Orpheus is mostly national park and is heavily forested, with lots of birdlife; turtles also nest here. Camping is allowed in two places (permits obtainable from Ingham) but take your own water. Also on the island are a giant clam research station and a small resort with rooms at $400-plus per person.

Campers can get there by charter boat from Dungeness (north of Lucinda) for about $120 return per person – contact the MV *Scuba Doo* (☎ (077) 77 8220) for details.

Cardwell (pop 1300)

Cardwell is one of north Queensland's very earliest towns, dating from 1864, and it is the only town on the highway between Brisbane and Cairns that is actually on the coast. It's more or less a one-street place.

Information The QNP&WS Rainforest & Reef Information Centre (☎ (070) 66 8601, beside the main jetty at 142 Victoria St, has information and permits for Hinchinbrook and other national parks in the area. It's open

weekdays from 8 am to 5 pm and at varying times on weekends.

Things to See & Do Cardwell is mainly the departure point for Hinchinbrook and other islands, but there are also numerous points of interest around town. The **Cardwell Forest Drive** starts from the centre of town and is a 26-km round trip, taking you to some excellent lookouts, swimming holes walking tracks and picnic areas.

Most of the coastal forest north of Cardwell is protected as the **Edmund Kennedy National Park**. There's a camping ground and walking tracks at the southern end of the park. The creeks here are home to estuarine crocodiles, so swimming isn't advised.

The **Murray Falls**, which have fine rock pools for swimming, and a walking track and barbecue area, are 22 km west of the highway – turn-off at the 'Murray Upper Road' sign about 27 km north of Cardwell.

South of Cardwell, the Bruce Highway climbs high above the coast with tremendous views down across the winding, mangrove lined waterways known as the Everglades which separate Hinchinbrook Island from the coast.

Hinchinbrook Adventures (☎ (070) 66 8270) offers reef fishing trips ($100), and Cardwell Fishing Safaris (☎ (070) 66 8176 has daily fishing trips ($55).

Places to Stay The well set up *Kookaburra Holiday Park* (☎ (070) 66 8648), which includes the YHA *Hinchinbrook Hostel*, is 800 metres north of the centre at 175 Bruce Highway. The hostel has dorm beds at $1 and doubles at $25 ($1 extra for nonmembers), camp sites at $6 per person, and on-site vans, cabins and units starting from $26. The facilities include a pool, free mountain bike and fishing gear. This place is a good source of information about Hinchinbrook and other attractions in the area.

Farther north at 178 Bowen St (behind the 'big crab'), the *Cardwell Backpackers Hostel* (☎ (070) 66 8014) has dorm beds at $10 and a few doubles at $25. It specialises in finding fruit-picking work for travellers and has free mountain bikes and hires out camping gear for Hinchinbrook Island. Cardwell also has several other caravan parks, a pub, motels and holiday units.

Getting There & Away All buses between Townsville and Cairns stop at Cardwell. The fare is about $20 from either place. Cardwell is also on the main Brisbane to Cairns railway.

Hinchinbrook Island

This island is a spectacular and unspoiled wilderness area, with granite mountains rising dramatically from the sea and a varied terrain of lush tropical forest on the mainland side and thick mangroves lining the shores, towering mountains in the middle, and long sandy beaches and secluded bays on the eastern side. All 635 sq km of the island is a national park and rugged Mt Bowen, at 1121 metres, is the highest peak. There's plenty of wildlife, especially pretty-faced wallabies and the iridescent blue Ulysses butterfly.

Hinchinbrook is very popular with bushwalkers and naturalists and has some excellent walking tracks. The highlight is the **Thorsborne Trail** (also known as the East Coast Trail), a 32-km walking track from Ramsay Bay to Zoe Bay and on to George Point at the southern tip. It's a three to five-day walk, although you can walk shorter sections if you don't have that much time. Zoe Bay, with its beautiful waterfall, is one of the most scenic spots on the island. Walkers are warned to take plenty of insect repellent; the sandflies and mosquitoes on Hinchinbrook can be a real pest. You'll also have to learn how to protect your food from the native bush rats, and there are estuarine crocodiles in the mangroves!

There's a low-key resort (☎ (070) 66 8585) on the northern peninsula, Cape Richards, with rooms for about 60 people but it's not cheap at $260-plus per person, including meals.

There are seven QNP&WS camping grounds along the Thorsborne Trail, plus others at Macushla and Scraggy Point in the north. There is a limit of 40 people allowed on the main trail at any one time, so it's necessary to book ahead, especially for holiday periods. The QNP&WS produces the informative *Thorsborne Trail* and *Hinchinbrook to Dunk Island* leaflets. To book permits and for detailed trail information, contact the QNP&WS offices in Ingham (☎ (070) 76 1700) or Cardwell (☎ (070) 66 8601).

Getting There & Away There are two ferry services from Cardwell to the northern end of Hinchinbrook Island. Hinchinbrook Travel & Booking Office (☎ (070) 66 8539) at 131 Bruce Highway has ferries departing daily at 9 am and returning at 4 pm. Hinchinbrook Adventures (☎ (070) 66 8270) at 135 Bruce Highway has ferries departing daily at 9 am and returning around 4.30 pm. Both operators charge about $59 for a day trip or $35 one way. Their routes and schedules vary, so ring to find out which one suits you best. Services are less frequent during the wet season.

Hinchinbrook Wilderness Safaris (☎ (077) 77 8307) operates a ferry and coach transfer service between Ingham or Lucinda and the southern end of the island for $37; departure times depend on the tides.

If you're walking the Thorsborne Trail, you can buy a combined ticket ($55) that includes ferry transfers to and from the island and bus transfers back to your starting point.

Tully (pop 2700)

The wettest place in Australia gets a drenching average of over 4000 mm a year, and the Tully River is the setting for white-water rafting trips. There's a tourist office on the highway, and the very basic *Tully Backpackers Hostel* (☎ (070) 68 2820) costs $11 a bed; they sometimes find fruit-picking work for travellers. There's also a caravan park and a motel, although nearby Mission Beach is a much more appealing place to stay.

MISSION BEACH (pop 1000)

This small stretch of coast has become an increasingly popular stopover on the backpacker circuit. The name Mission Beach

QUEENSLAND

actually covers a string of small settlements – Mission, Wongaling and South Mission beaches, Bingil Bay and Garners Beach – dotted along a 14-km coastal strip east of Tully.

This is a good base for visits to Dunk Island and the Barrier Reef, white-water rafting trips on the Tully River, boat trips out to the reef and walks through the rainforest.

Mission Beach is named after an Aboriginal mission that was founded here in 1914 but destroyed by a cyclone in 1918. Tam O'Shanter Point, beyond South Mission Beach, was the starting point for the ill-fated 1848 overland expedition to Cape York led by 30-year-old Edmund Kennedy. All but three of the party's 13 members died, including Kennedy, who was killed by Aboriginal people. There's a memorial to the expedition at Tam O'Shanter Point.

Information
There's a tourist centre (☎ (070) 68 7099) on Porters Promenade in Mission Beach. It's open daily from 9 am to 5 pm (Sunday to 4 pm). Next door is the Wet Tropics Visitor Centre, with information on the local environment and conservation of cassowaries.

Activities
Walks The rainforest around Mission Beach is a haunt of cassowaries but unfortunately the population of these large flightless birds has been depleted by road accidents and the destruction of rainforest by logging and cyclones. The rainforest comes right down to the coast in places, and there are some impressive walks, including the Licuala Walking Track (two hours), Lacey's Creek Walk (30 minutes), the Bicton Hill Lookout (1½ hours) and the Edmund Kennedy Walking Track (three hours).

Mission Beach Rainforest Treks (☎ (070) 68 7152) runs guided walks through the forests. The morning walk costs $28 and the night walk is $18.

White-Water Rafting Raging Thunder (☎ (070) 31 1466) and R'n'R (☎ (070) 51 7777 or 1800 079 039) charge $112 from Mission Beach for trips on the Tully River. These are the same as the trips on offer in Cairns, but you'll save about $10 and several hours travel time by doing them from here.

Both companies also offer three-day sea-kayaking expeditions from Mission Beach for about $370, including meals and equipment.

Other Activities The One Stop Tour Shop (☎ (070) 68 7220) hires out mountain bikes ($15 a day), fishing gear and camping kits for Dunk Island ($30 per person). Girramay Walkabout (☎ (070) 68 8676) has rainforest walking treks ($45) and horseback rides through the forests ($65), and Parachuting Down Under (☎ 1800 638 005) has tandem skydives for $198.

Organised Cruises
There are three cruise companies based at the Clump Point jetty just north of Mission Beach. Friendship Cruises takes day trips out to the reef with snorkelling and a ride in a glass-bottom boat ($55). On the *Quick Cat* you can do a reef trip ($110), or a day trip to Dunk Island ($22). The MV *Lawrence Kavanagh* also does day trips to Dunk ($22) and a combined Dunk-Bedarra trip ($40).

River Rat Wildlife Cruises (☎ (070) 68 7250) runs evening fishing cruises along the Hull River from South Mission Beach ($28)

Places to Stay
Camping In Mission Beach, there's a council-run camping ground on the foreshore with sites for $6, or the excellent *Hideaway Caravan Park* (☎ (070) 68 7104) opposite has tent sites from $11 and on-site cabins from $36. At South Mission Beach the *Beachcomber Coconut Village* (☎ (070) 68 8129) has tent sites from $12, camp-o-tels from $9 per person and on-site cabins from $33.

Hostels All three hostels have courtesy buses and do pick-ups from both bus stops.

The Treehouse (☎ (070) 68 7137), an associate YHA hostel, is at Bingil Bay, six km north of Mission Beach. This popular and very laid-back hostel is in an impressive timber stilt house surrounded by rainforest, with a pool, bikes for hire and good views over the forest and the coast. A bed in a six-bed dorm costs $14, doubles are $35, or you can pitch your tent on the lawns for $9.

The other hostels are both at Wongaling Beach, five km south of Mission Beach. *Scotty's Mission Beach House* (☎ (070) 68 8676), opposite the beach at 167 Reid Rd, is friendly and fun-oriented and has a good pool. There are a couple of dorm beds at $10 and air-con dorms from $14 to $16. Doubles range from $32 to $45, with the more expensive rooms having their own bathrooms and air-con. At the front of the hostel is the new *Scotty's Bar & Grill*, which specialises in steaks and has seafood, roasts, curries and vego dishes from $5 to $20; there are party games and theme nights in the bar most nights.

Mission Beach Backpackers Lodge (☎ (070) 68 8317), at 28 Wongaling Beach Rd, is a modern, well-equipped place with a pool and garden. There are two buildings, one with spacious dorms at $14 a bed, the other with very good double rooms from $30 to $38. This easy-going hostel is a five-minute walk from the beach.

Motels & Holiday Units There's a scattering of motels, holiday units and resorts along the coast. The *Beachside Apartments* (☎ (070) 68 8890), at 32 Reid Rd, Wongaling Beach, has oldish but clean self-contained holiday units on the waterfront that sleep up to eight and cost from $55 a double plus $5 for each extra person.

The *Clump Point Eco Village* (☎ (070) 68 7534), on the foreshore a couple of km north of Mission Beach, has good timber bungalows that sleep up to five and start at $80 a night.

If you're feeling flush, *The Point Resort* (☎ (070) 68 8154) at South Mission Beach is a very stylish resort with rooms from $140 a double.

Places to Eat
Mission Beach proper has a good selection of eateries. The tiny *PC's Cafe*, beside the bus stop, has breakfasts, home-made meals and good coffee. In the arcade just across Campbell St, *The Seafood Place* has good fish & chips and burgers.

There are more eateries across the road: *Butterflies* is a friendly Mexican place with mains from $10 to $15 – by day it becomes *Lama's*, a great breakfast and lunch bar with fresh juices, crepes, muesli etc. *Friends* is a popular open-air BYO with mains for about $17, and farther down David St is an Italian bistro called *Piccolo Paradiso*, with pizzas and pasta from $7 to $10.

The *Mission Beach Hotel* in Wongaling Beach has a huge bistro and cheap bar meals. If you're preparing your own food, there are supermarkets in Mission Beach and Wongaling Beach.

Getting There & Around
McCafferty's buses stop outside Harvey World Travel (☎ (070) 68 7187) in Mission Beach, while Greyhound Pioneer stops at the Mission Beach Resort in Wongaling Beach. The average fare is $13 from Cairns and $35 from Townsville.

Baz's Bus Service (☎ (070) 68 8707) operates daily along the coastal strip.

DUNK ISLAND & THE FAMILY ISLANDS
Dunk Island is an easy and affordable day trip from Mission Beach. It's 4.5 km off the coast, and has walking tracks through rainforest, and good beaches.

The Qantas-owned *Dunk Island Resort* (☎ (070) 68 8199) at Brammo Bay on the northern end of the island, has rooms from $220 per person. There's also a QNP&WS camping ground close to the resort, as well as a takeaway food kiosk and a water sports place that hires out catamarans, sailboards and snorkelling gear. Camping permits ($3 per person) can be booked through the resort's water sports office (☎ (070) 68 8199).

From 1897 to 1923 E J Banfield lived on Dunk and wrote his book *The Confessions of a Beachcomber*; the island is remarkably little changed from his early description. Today it has a small artist colony centred

QUEENSLAND

around the tapestry-maker and former Olympic wrestler, Bruce Arthur. Dunk is noted for prolific birdlife (nearly 150 species) and many butterflies. There are superb views over the entrances to the Hinchinbrook Channel from the top of 271-metre Mt Kootaloo. Thirteen km of walking tracks lead from the camping ground area to headlands and beaches.

South of Dunk are the seven tiny Family Islands. One of them, Bedarra, has a very exclusive resort, where costs start at about $500 a day per person. Five of the other Family Islands are national parks and you can bush camp on Wheeler and Combe (permits available at Cardwell; take your own water).

Getting There & Away

Dowd's Water Taxis (☎ (070) 68 8310) has about six daily services from Wongaling Beach to Dunk and back, and Mission Beach-Dunk Island Water Taxis (☎ (070) 68 8333) has similar services from South Mission Beach. Both companies charge $22 return, although the hostels can usually get you across for less.

You can fly to Dunk with Sunstate/Qantas from Townsville ($118) or Cairns ($108).

MISSION BEACH TO CAIRNS
Mission Beach to Innisfail

Eight km north of **El Arish**, you can turn off the Bruce Highway and take an interesting alternative route to Innisfail via the sugar-cane townships of **Silkwood** and **Mena Creek**, 20 km south-west of Innisfail. At Mena Creek, Paronella Park (☎ (070) 65 3225) is a rambling tropical garden set among the ruins of a Spanish castle built in the 1930s. This place is quite bizarre and well worth a visit – it's open daily from 9 am to 5 pm and costs $6. There's a camping and caravan park next door with sites from $10 and on-site vans from $25.

At **Mourilyan**, seven km south of Innisfail, there's the Australian Sugar Museum, open daily from 9 am to 4.30 pm. An export terminal on the coast east of Mourilyan handles the sugar produced in Innisfail, Tully and Mourilyan.

Innisfail (pop 8500)

At the junction of the North and South Johnstone rivers, this solid and prosperous sugar city has a large Italian population. The Italians arrived early this century to work the cane fields, and in the 1930s there was even a local 'mafia' called the Black Hand.

There's a tourist office (☎ (070) 61 6448) on the highway at the southern edge of town. Points of interest include a **Chinese Joss House** on Owen St, the **Historical Society Museum** at 11 Edith St, and the **Johnstone River Crocodile Farm** four km east on the Flying Fish Point road.

The *River Drive Caravan Park* is opposite the tourist office, and there are numerous pubs and motels. There are also two hostels: *The Endeavour* (☎ (070) 61 6610) at 3 Gladys St and *Backpackers Innisfail* (☎ (070) 61 2284) at 73 Rankin St. Both have dorm beds for $10 and are predominantly workers' hostels – most people who come here are looking for fruit-picking work.

Twenty-eight km west of Innisfail is the **Nerada Tea Plantation** (☎ (070) 64 5177) which is open daily from 9 am to 4.30 pm. The Palmerston Highway winds up to the Atherton Tableland, passing through the rainforest of the **Palmerston National Park** which has a number of creeks, waterfalls, scenic walking tracks and a camping ground at Henrietta Creek just off the road. The ranger's office (☎ (070) 64 5115) is at the eastern entrance to the park, 33 km from Innisfail.

Innisfail to Cairns

About 22 km north of Innisfail there's a turning to **Josephine Falls**, a popular picnic spot eight km inland. There are waterfalls, natural water slides and swimming holes - fun, fun, fun! The falls are at the foot of the Bellenden Ker range, which include Queensland's highest peak, **Mt Bartle Frere** (1657 metres). The Mt Bartle Frere Hiking Track leads from the car park to the Bartle

Frere summit. The ascent is for fit and experienced walkers – it's a 15-km, two-day return trip, and rain and cloud can close in suddenly.

Over on the coast at **Bramston Beach**, the *Plantation Village Resort* (☎ (070) 67 4133) is a good budget resort with camp sites, motel units and self-contained cabins, plus a restaurant, pool and tennis courts.

Back on the highway, **Babinda** is yet another sugar town. It has a quaint old cinema, a pub and the Oolana Gallery, which sells hand-made crafts, dijeridus and boomerangs. Seven km inland, **Babinda Boulders** is a good picnic place with a huge swimming hole, barbecues and walking trails. Nearby, *Bowenia Lodge* (☎ (070) 67 1631) has B&B at $15 per person. From the boulders you can walk the **Goldfield Track**, which leads 10 km to the **Goldsborough Valley State Forest Park**, across a saddle in the Bellenden Ker range.

Gordonvale, 33 km north of Babinda, has two Sikh gurdwaras (places of worship). The winding Gillies Highway leads from here up onto the Atherton Tableland. During the cutting season (July to December), there are tours ($5) of the Mulgrave Sugar Mill ☎ (070) 56 3300).

Four km north is a turn-off to the **Yarrabah Aboriginal Community**, where the Menmuny Museum is open weekdays from 8.30 am to 4.30 pm ($6). On the way you can detour to the Edward River Crocodile Farm.

Far North Queensland

Queensland's far north is one of the most popular tourist destinations in Australia, especially in winter when sun-starved southerners flock here in droves.

Cairns, with its international airport, is the major centre for the region. It's a place where most travellers spend a few days before heading off: north to the superb rainforests of Daintree and Cape Tribulation and the historic town of Cooktown; west to the cool air of the Atherton Tableland; or east to the islands and the Great Barrier Reef.

CAIRNS (pop 93,000)

The 'capital' of the far north, Cairns is now firmly established as one of Australia's top travellers' destinations. It is a centre for a whole host of activities – not only scuba diving but white-water rafting, canoeing, horse riding, bungy jumping and sky diving. On the down side, Cairns' rapid tourist growth has destroyed much of the city's laid-back tropical atmosphere. It also lacks a beach, but there are some good ones not far north.

Cairns marks the end of the Bruce Highway and the railway line from Brisbane, and is at its climatic best – and busiest – from May to October; in summer it gets rather sticky (to put it mildly!).

History

The town began in 1876, a beachhead in the mangroves intended as a port for the Hodgkinson River goldfield 100 km inland. Initially, it struggled under rivalry from Smithfield 12 km north, a rowdy frontier town that was washed away by a flood in 1879 (it's now an outer Cairns suburb), and then there was competition from Port Douglas, founded in 1877 after Christie Palmerston discovered an easier route from there to the goldfield. What saved Cairns was the Atherton Tableland 'tin rush' in 1880. Cairns became the starting point of the railway line to the tableland, which was built a few years later.

Orientation

The centre of Cairns is a relatively compact area running back from the Esplanade. Off Wharf St (the southern continuation of the Esplanade), you'll find Great Adventures Wharf, Marlin Jetty and the Pier – the main departure points for reef trips. Farther around is Trinity Wharf (a cruise-liner dock with shops and cafes) and the transit centre, where long-distance buses arrive and depart.

Back from the waterfront is City Place, a pedestrian mall at the meeting of Shields and Lake Sts.

QUEENSLAND

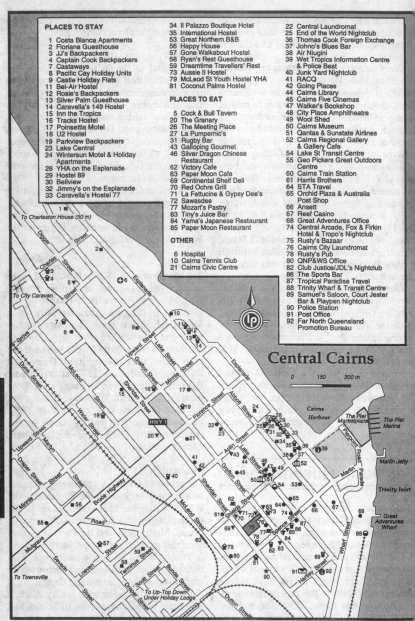

PLACES TO STAY

1 Costa Blanca Apartments
2 Floriana Guesthouse
3 JJ's Backpackers
4 Captain Cook Backpackers
7 Castaways
8 Pacific Cay Holiday Units
9 Castle Holiday Flats
11 Bel-Air Hostel
12 Rosie's Backpackers
13 Silver Palm Guesthouse
14 Caravella's 149 Hostel
15 Inn the Tropics
16 Tracks Hostel
17 Poinsettia Motel
18 U2 Hostel
19 Parkview Backpackers
23 Lake Central
24 Wintersun Motel & Holiday Apartments
28 YHA on the Esplanade
29 Hostel 89
30 Bellview
32 Jimmy's on the Esplanade
33 Caravella's Hostel 77

34 Il Palazzo Boutique Hotel
35 International Hostel
53 Great Northern B&B
56 Happy House
57 Gone Walkabout Hostel
58 Ryan's Rest Guesthouse
59 Dreamtime Travellers' Rest
73 Aussie II Hostel
79 McLeod St Youth Hostel YHA
81 Coconut Palms Hostel

PLACES TO EAT

5 Cock & Bull Tavern
20 The Granary
26 The Meeting Place
27 La Pumpernic's
31 Rugby Bar
43 Galloping Gourmet
46 Silver Dragon Chinese Restaurant
62 Victory Cafe
63 Paper Moon Cafe
69 Continental Shelf Deli
70 Red Ochre Grill
71 La Fettucine & Gypsy Dee's
72 Sawasdee
77 Mozart's Pastry
83 Tiny's Juice Bar
84 Yama's Japanese Restaurant
85 Paper Moon Restaurant

OTHER

6 Hospital
10 Cairns Tennis Club
21 Cairns Civic Centre

22 Central Laundromat
25 End of the World Nightclub
36 Thomas Cook Foreign Exchange
37 Johno's Blues Bar
38 Air Niugini
39 Wet Tropics Information Centre & Police Beat
40 Junk Yard Nightclub
41 RACQ
42 Going Places
44 Cairns Library
45 Cairns Five Cinemas
47 Walker's Bookshop
48 City Place Amphitheatre
49 Wool Shed
50 Cairns Museum
51 Qantas & Sunstate Airlines
52 Cairns Regional Gallery & Gallery Cafe
54 Lake St Transit Centre
55 Geo Pickers Great Outdoors Centre
60 Cairns Train Station
61 Harris Brothers
64 STA Travel
65 Orchid Plaza & Australia Post Shop
66 Ansett
67 Reef Casino
68 Great Adventures Office
74 Central Arcade, Fox & Firkin Hotel & Tropo's Nightclub
75 Rusty's Bazaar
76 Cairns City Laundromat
78 Rusty's Pub
80 QNP&WS Office
86 Club Justice/JDL's Nightclub
86 The Sports Bar
87 Tropical Paradise Travel
88 Trinity Wharf & Transit Centre
89 Samuel's Saloon, Court Jester Bar & Playpen Nightclub
90 Police Station
91 Post Office
92 Far North Queensland Promotion Bureau

Central Cairns

0   150   300 m

Cairns is surrounded by mangrove swamps to the south and north. The sea in front of the town is shallow and at low tide it becomes a long sweep of mud, with lots of interesting water birds.

Information

Tourist Offices There's no shortage of tourist information – if anything, it's the opposite. The Wet Tropics Information Centre, on the Esplanade across from the Shields St corner, combines information with displays on the environment and rainforests of the far north. It's open weekdays from 9.30 am to 5.30 pm and Saturday to 1.30 pm. For phone queries, call the Far North Queensland Promotion Bureau (☎ (070) 51 3588).

There are dozens of privately run 'information centres' in Cairns. These places are basically tour-booking agencies, and include Cairns Eco Tours (☎ (070) 51 1500) on Shields St near the Esplanade, Tropical Paradise Travel (☎ (070) 51 9533) at 51 Spence St, and Going Places (☎ (070) 51 4055) on the corner of Sheridan and Aplin Sts. Most of the backpackers hostels also have helpful tour-booking desks. Note that each booking agent will be pushing different tours, depending on the commission deal they have with the tour companies, so shop around.

The Community Information Service (☎ (070) 51 4953) in Tropical Arcade off Shields St, half a block back from the Esplanade, has more offbeat information like where you can play croquet or do tai chi, details on foreign consulates and health services etc.

Post The main post office, on the corner of Grafton and Hartley Sts, has a poste restante service. For general business (stamps etc), there's also an Australia Post shop in the Orchid Plaza on Lake St.

Other Information The RACQ office (☎ (070) 51 4788), at 112 Sheridan St, is a good place to get maps and information on road conditions, especially if you're driving

up to Cooktown or the Cape York Peninsula, or across to the Gulf.

The QNP&WS office (☎ (070) 52 3096), at 10 McLeod St, is open on weekdays from 8.30 am to 4.30 pm; it deals with camping permits and information for the region's national parks, including islands.

Bookshops Proudmans, in the Pier complex, and Walker's Bookshop, at 96 Lake St, both have a good range. The Green Possum Environmental Bookshop, in an arcade off Grafton St right by Rusty's Bazaar, is also interesting. For maps, check out Sunmap at 15 Lake St.

Things to See

Cairns' main attraction is as a base for getting to the places that surround it, but there are a few places in town worth visiting. The impressive new **Cairns Regional Gallery** is housed in a cleverly restored historic building on the corner of Abbott and Shields Sts, and features theme exhibitions, works by local artists and loans from major galleries. It is open daily from 11 am to 9 pm; entry costs $5 ($2 students). There's also a good cafe (see Places to Eat) and a gallery shop here.

Most of Cairns' older buildings have been engulfed by the booming developments of the 1980s and '90s. The oldest part of town is the **Trinity Wharf** area, but even this has been redeveloped. There are still some imposing neoclassical buildings from the 1920s on Abbott St, and the frontages around the corner of Spence and Lake Sts date from 1909 to 1926. A walk along the **Esplanade Walking Trail**, with views over to rainforested mountains across the estuary and cool breezes in the evening is very agreeable.

Housed in the 1907 School of Arts building on the corner of Lake and Shields Sts, the **Cairns Museum** has some interesting historic displays on the far north including Aboriginal artefacts, a display on the construction of the Cairns to Kuranda railway and exhibits on the old Palmer River and Hodgkinson goldfields. It's open daily (except Sunday) from 10 am to 3 pm ($2).

The colourful markets at **Rusty's Bazaar**, on Sheridan St between Spence and Shields Sts, are great for people-watching and for browsing among the dozens of stalls, which sell fruit and vegies, arts and crafts, clothes and more. The markets are held on Friday night and Saturday and Sunday mornings; Saturday is the busiest and best time.

The **Pier Marketplace** is an impressive shopping plaza with expensive boutiques, souvenir shops, a foodhall, cafes and restaurants. On weekends the **Mud Markets** are held here, with a wide range of stalls selling food and local arts and crafts. Also here is the impressive **Undersea World** aquarium, which is open daily from 9 am to 9 pm; entry is steep at $9.50 (cheaper at night).

Three km north-west of town are the **Flecker Botanic Gardens** on Collins Ave in Edge Hill. Over the road from the gardens, a boardwalk leads through a patch of rainforest to **Saltwater Creek** and the two small **Centenary Lakes**. Collins Ave turns west off Sheridan St (the Cook Highway) three km from the centre of Cairns. The gardens are 700 metres from the turning. Near the gardens is the entrance to the **Whitfield Range Environmental Park**, one of the last remnants of rainforest around Cairns – two long walking tracks give good views over the city and coast. You can get there with Cairns Trans Buses or the Red Explorer.

Also in Edge Hill, the **Royal Flying Doctor Service** regional office, at 1 Junction St, is open to visitors daily from 9 am to 4.30 pm; entry is $5.

The **Tjapukai Dance Theatre**, an award-winning Aboriginal dance troupe, has recently moved from Kuranda to their new theatre complex beside the Skyrail terminal at Smithfield (just off the Captain Cook Highway, about 15 km north of the centre). This multi-million dollar complex incorporates four sections – a cultural village, a 'creation theatre', an audio-visual show, and a traditional dance theatre. Performances include a re-enactment of a traditional corroboree, boomerang and spear-throwing and the telling of Dreamtime stories. The complex is open daily from 9 am to 5 pm; entry costs

$21, or $31 with return bus transfers from Cairns. Allow at least two hours.

Activities
Diving & Snorkelling Cairns is one of the scuba-diving capitals of the Barrier Reef, which is closer to the coast here than it is farther south. The competition is cutthroat – and the company offering the cheapest deal one week may be old news the next.

Most people look for a course that takes them to the outer Barrier Reef rather than the reefs around Green or Fitzroy islands. Some places give you more time on the reef than others but you may prefer an extra day in the pool and classroom before venturing out. A chat with people who have already done a course can tell you some of the pros and cons. A good teacher can make all the difference to your confidence and the amount of fun you have. Another factor is how big the groups are – the smaller the better if you want personal attention.

Two schools with good reputations are Deep Sea Divers Den (☎ (070) 31 2223) at 319 Draper St, and Pro-Dive (☎ (070) 31 5255) at Marlin Jetty. But that's not to dismiss the others, which include Down Under Dive (☎ (070) 31 1288) at 155 Sheridan St and the Cairns Dive Centre (☎ (070) 51 0294) at 135 Abbott St. Most of these places can be booked through the hostels.

Prices differ quite a bit between schools but usually one or other of them has a discount going. Expect to pay about $350 to $450 for a five-day course of two days in the pool and classroom, a day trip to the reef and back, and two more days on the reef with an overnight stay on board.

If you want to learn about the reef before you dive, an entertaining and educational lecture is given at the Cairns Library at 117 Lake St every night (except Sunday) from 6.15 to 8.30 pm. The cost is $10 – for more details phone Paddy at Reef Teach (☎ (070) 51 6882).

White-Water Rafting & Kayaking Three of the rivers flowing down from the Atherton Tableland make for some excellent white-vater rafting. Most popular is a day in the rainforested gorges of the Tully River, 150 km south of Cairns. So many people do this trip that there can be 20 or more craft on the river at once, meaning you may have to queue up to shoot each section of rapids – yet despite this, most people are exhilarated at the end of the day. The Tully day trips leave daily year-round. Two companies running them from Cairns are Raging Thunder ☎ (070) 31 1466) at 111 Spence St, and R n' R (☎ (070) 51 7777 or 1800 079 039) at 74 Abbott St. Day trips on the Tully cost about $122 from Cairns. There are cheaper half-day trips on the Barron River ($65), not far inland from Cairns, or you can make two-day ($360) or five-day ($770) expeditions on the remote North Johnstone River which rises near Malanda and enters the sea at Innisfail.

Foaming Fury (☎ (070) 32 1460) offers white-water rafting for $99 on the Russell River, south of Bellenden Ker National Park, half-day trips on the Barron River for $65 and two-day trips on the North Johnstone River for $210.

Raging Thunder and R'n'R also offer a range of sea-kayaking expeditions from Cairns. Raging Thunder runs a day trip from Fitzroy Island for $85.

Other Activities There are two A J Hackett ☎ (070) 31 1119) bungy jumping sites near Cairns. At Smithfield, 15 km north, you can take the plunge from a steel tower with sensational views ($95), or at the Kuranda markets you can fling yourself from a cage suspended from a crane ($70). A courtesy bus does pick-ups from hostels.

Mulgrave River Horse Adventures ☎ (070) 56 3000) and Springmount Station ☎ (070) 93 4493) both offer half-day horse trail rides for about $55, including pick-ups from Cairns. Airplay (☎ (070) 51 1340) is a hang-gliding school with one-day samplers for $89 and four-day courses for $395. Dan's Tours (☎ (070) 51 8311) has various half-day ($50 to $70) and full-day ($95) mountain bike tours, and two-day expeditions to Port Douglas and Cape Tribulation.

Reef Air Tours (☎ (070) 35 9530) has good joy flights and tours to the reef, ranging from $45 to $175. Cairns Tiger Moth Flights (☎ (070) 35 9400) has joy flights from $70, and Jayrow (☎ (070) 31 4214) has helicopter flights out to the reef starting from $200.

Organised Tours & Cruises

There are literally hundreds of tours available out of Cairns, some of which are specially aimed at backpackers and are very good value. You can make bookings through your accommodation or at one of the many booking agencies in town.

Cairns Half-day trips around the city sights, or two-hour cruises from Marlin Jetty up along Trinity Inlet and around Admiralty Island, start from $20.

Atherton Tableland The 'conventional' bus tour companies run day trips to the Atherton Tableland, which usually include the waterfalls and lakes circuit and the Kuranda markets, and range from $50 to $80. Jungle Tours, KCT Connections and Tropics Explorer have smaller group trips for backpackers for about $45 to $50. Uncle Brian's Fun, Falls & Forest (☎ (070) 50 0615) tours have received good reports from travellers and a day trip is $47 and a two-day trip is $75.

Daintree & Cape Tribulation Cape Trib is one of the most popular day-trip destinations, and there are dozens of operators offering tours.

Jungle Tours, KCT Connections and Tropics Explorer offer fun-oriented trips up to Cape Trib, usually with a cruise on the Daintree River thrown in, for about $70. If you have time, you'd be better off taking one of their overnight or longer packages, which cost about $74 for two days, $86 for three days and $110 for five days, which includes accommodation at Crocodylus Village and/or PK's Jungle Village. Dan's Tours has mountain bike trips to Cape Trib – see Other Activities earlier in this section.

QUEENSLAND

Cooktown Strikie's Safaris (☎ (070) 99 5599) runs good 4WD trips to Cooktown from Cairns and Port Douglas, visiting places such as Black Mountain and the Lion's Den Hotel along the way. A day trip costs $74, two-day trips cost $199 (meals and accommodation not included).

Barrier Reef & Islands There are dozens of options available for day trips to the reef. It's worth asking a few questions before you book, such as how many passengers the boat takes, what's included in the price and how much the 'extras' (such as wetsuit hire and introductory dives) cost, and exactly where the boat is going. Some companies have a dubious definition of 'outer reef'; as a general rule, the farther out you go, the better the diving.

Great Adventures (☎ (070) 51 0455) is the major operator with the biggest boats and a wide range of combination cruises, including a day trip to Norman Reef with a stop on Green Island ($126) and a day trip to Moore Reef with a stop on Fitzroy Island ($88). You get about three hours on the reef itself, lunch, snorkelling gear, and a semi-submersible and glass-bottom boat ride thrown in. Great Adventures has its own wharf.

Compass (☎ (070) 51 5777) and Noah's Ark Cruises (☎ (070) 35 4054) have popular day trips to Hastings Reef and Michaelmas Cay for $40 to $50, including boom netting, snorkelling gear and lunch. Certified divers can take two dives for an extra $40.

Ocean Free (☎ (070) 31 6601), *Falla* (☎ (070) 31 3488), the *Golden Plover* (☎ (070) 31 3513) and *Passions of Paradise* (☎ (070) 31 6465) are all ocean-going yachts that 'sail' out to Upolo Cay, Green Island and Paradise Reef daily for about $45, which includes lunch and snorkelling gear.

There are many, many other boats and operators, so shop around.

Chillagoe & Undara Lava Tubes New Look Adventures (☎ (070) 31 7622) has day trips to the old mining town of Chillagoe ($89). Australian Pacific (☎ 13 1304) and Undara Experience (☎ (070) 31 7933) have

Nautilus shells can be found along the Cairns coast

day trips out to the Undara Lava Tubes ($92) although you'll spend most of the day sitting in the bus. There are also fly/drive tours (about $245), or you could stay overnight or link up with the *Savannahlander* train trip. See the Gulf Savannah section later in this chapter for more details.

Cape York See the Cape York section later in this chapter for details of tours from Cairns to Cape York.

Places to Stay

Cairns has a huge range of tourist accommodation catering for everybody from budget-conscious backpackers to deep-pocketed tourists. There are plenty of hostels, as well as cheap guesthouses and holiday flats. Prices go up and down with the seasons, and lower weekly rates are par for the course. Prices given here for the more expensive places can rise 30% or 40% in the peak season, and some of the hostels will charge a dollar or two less in the quiet times.

Camping There are about a dozen caravan parks in and around Cairns, but none are really central. Almost without exception, they take campers as well as caravans. The closest to the centre is the *City Caravan Park* (☎ (070) 51 1467), about two km north-west on the corner of Little and James Sts, with tent sites from $12, and on-site vans from $30.

Out on the Bruce Highway, about eight km south of the centre, is the huge modern *Cairns Coconut Caravan Village* (☎ (070)

54 6644), with camp sites from $14, on-site cabins from $32 and units from $45. If you want to camp by the beach, the *Yorkeys Knob Beachfront Van Park* (☎ (070) 55 7201), about 20 km north, has tent sites and on-site vans.

Hostels Cairns is the backpacking capital of Queensland, and has more than 20 hostels, ranging from the huge pack-'em-in type to the smaller, quieter owner-operated places. Most have fan-cooled bunk rooms with shared bathrooms, kitchens and laundries, lounge and TV rooms, and a swimming pool, and many also offer private rooms with their own facilities. Nightly costs for dorms range from about $10 to $16. Unfortunately, you still have to beware of theft in some places – use lock-up rooms and safes if they're available.

You have a choice of staying in or around the Esplanade, which has the greatest concentration of hostels, or staying in one of the places farther out. The Esplanade hostels tend to have little outdoor space and to be more cramped, but they are in the thick of the action. The hostels away from the centre offer a bit more breathing space and are generally quieter, and the inconvenience of being out of the centre is minimal as there are courtesy buses that make regular runs into town.

Esplanade Starting from the corner of Shields St and heading along the Esplanade, the *International Hostel* (☎ (070) 31 1424) at No 67 is a big, old multilevel place with about 200 beds. Fan-cooled four, six and eight-bed dorms are $12, twin rooms are $28 and doubles range from $28 to $36 with either air-con and TV or a private bathroom.

Caravella's Hostel 77 (☎ (070) 51 2159) at No 77 is another big, rambling place with about 160 beds. It's one of the longest established Cairns hostels and has old-fashioned but clean rooms, all with air-con. The cost in four to six-bunk dorms is $15 and doubles range from $30 to $32, or $38 with private bathroom.

Jimmy's on the Esplanade (☎ (070) 31 6884) at No 83 is a recently renovated place

with 46 beds in six-bed air-con units with their own bathrooms. There's a new pool and kitchen; dorms cost $15, doubles are $32 to $36, or $45 with your own bathroom.

Next door, the *Bellview* (☎ (070) 31 4377) is a good quiet hostel with clean and comfortable four-bed dorms at $16 and singles/twins from $27/32; all rooms have air-con. The kitchen is good and there's a small pool, a laundry, and a good cafe with continental breakfasts for $5.50. They also have motel-style units from $45 to $55, depending on the size of the room.

Hostel 89 (☎ (070) 31 7477 or 1800 061 712) at No 89 is one of the best-kept hostels on the Esplanade. It's a smallish and helpful place, with twin and double rooms and a few three or four-bed dorms, all air-conditioned. Costs are from $15 per person, with singles/doubles from $27/32. Security is good, with a locked grille at the street entrance.

At No 93 is *YHA on the Esplanade* (☎ (070) 31 1919). There are two blocks, one with spacious, airy five-bed dorms with their own bathroom, the other with small twins and doubles. Some rooms have air-con. Dorm beds cost $14 and doubles $32; nonmembers pay an extra $2.

Three blocks farther along the Esplanade is another cluster of hostels. At No 149 is the large *Caravella's 149* (☎ (070) 31 5680), which can get somewhat crowded. You pay $14 in a 14-bed dorm or $15 in a six-bunk dorm with air-con and bathroom. Doubles cost $30.

Rosie's Backpackers (☎ (070) 51 0235), at No 155, has several buildings with either spacious dorms or six-bed flats; dorm beds are $15 and there are a couple of doubles at $35. This place is helpful, well-run and has a small pool. Next door at No 157, the YHA-associate *Bel-Air Hostel* (☎ (070) 31 4790) is a recently renovated two-storey Queenslander with doubles and twins downstairs for $30 and seven-bunk dorms upstairs at $15; all rooms have air-con.

Around Town Three blocks back from the Esplanade, *Parkview Backpackers* (☎ (070)

QUEENSLAND

51 3700) is at 174 Grafton St. This is a very friendly and laid-back place where you can relax by the pool and listen to reggae music. It's in a rambling old timber building with a large tropical garden; four to eight-bed dorms are $14 and twins and doubles $30.

Tracks Hostel (☎ (070) 31 1474), nearby on the corner of Grafton and Minnie Sts, spans three old timber houses that are starting to look a little run-down. Dorm beds are $13, doubles $26, and you get a voucher for a free dinner at one of the nightclubs.

JJ's Backpackers (☎ (070) 51 7642), at 11 Charles St, is a small block of apartments converted into a hostel with dorm beds for $12 and doubles for $28, plus a small pool. *Captain Cook Backpackers Hostel* (☎ (070) 51 6811) at 204 Sheridan St is a huge and somewhat shabby converted motel with over 300 beds, two pools, a bar and a restaurant. Dorm beds are $12 and doubles are $28; motel units are $30 unserviced or $35 serviced. Prices include a free evening meal.

At 207 Sheridan St is *Castaways* (☎ (070) 51 1238), a quiet and smallish place with double and twin rooms costing $30 ($34 with air-con), five singles at $25 and a few three-bed dorms at $13. All rooms are fan-cooled and have a fridge, and there's a pool and free bike hire.

At 72 Grafton St, the *Aussie II Hostel* (☎ (070) 51 7620) is a basic old-style hostel with about 60 beds. It's a bit of a crash pad, but it's central and cheap at $10 a night.

The YHA *McLeod St Youth Hostel* (☎ (070) 51 0772), opposite the railway station at 20-24 McLeod St, has dorm beds for $14 and singles/doubles for $24/32. Non-members pay $2 extra. The facilities are good and the hostel has car parking spaces.

On the corner of Spence and Sheridan Sts, the *Coconut Palms Hostel* (☎ (070) 51 6946) has dorm beds for $11, twin rooms at $24 and doubles at $26. It's a clean, simple place in an old timber house, with a nice garden and a pool.

Two blocks west of the station at 274 Draper St, *Gone Walkabout Hostel* (☎ (070) 51 6160) is small, popular and well-run with a friendly atmosphere. Set in two breezy old

houses, it has a few four-bed dorms at $12 and mostly twins/doubles at $25, plus a tiny pool. It's not a place for late partying.

The *Up-Top Down Under Holiday Lodge* (☎ (070) 51 3636) at 164-170 Spence St, 1.5 km from the town centre, is a spacious and quiet place with a large, well-equipped kitchen, two TV lounges and a pool. Dorm beds are $14 and singles/doubles $25/30, all with shared bathroom. There's a free barbecue on Sunday nights, with live entertainment.

The new *U2 Hostel* (☎ (070) 31 4077) at 77 McLeod St is a restored Queenslander divided into five flats, and has a pool, dorms at $12 and singles/doubles at $26/28.

Guesthouses A number of guesthouse-type places cater for budget travellers, with an emphasis on rooms rather than dorms. These places are generally quieter, smaller and a bit more personalised than the hostels.

Dreamtime Travellers' Rest (☎ (070) 31 6753), at 4 Terminus St, is a small guesthouse run by a friendly and enthusiastic young couple. It's in a brightly renovated timber Queenslander and has a good pool, double rooms at $30 to $32 and three or four-bed (no bunks) rooms at $14 per person. Another good guesthouse with a similar set-up is *Ryan's Rest* (☎ (070) 51 4734), down the road at 18 Terminus St. It's a cosy and quiet family-run place with three good double rooms upstairs at $30, and two self-contained flats downstairs with twins/doubles at $25 and a four-bed dorm at $15 per person. Cooked and tropical breakfasts are available for $5 and $4.

The Art-Deco *Floriana Guesthouse* (☎ (070) 51 7886) at 183 the Esplanade has four self-contained units with polished timber floors, TVs, en suites and kitchenettes, costing from $46 a double or from $52 for up to four. The old building next door has 24 simple rooms with communal facilities at $28/32 for singles/doubles, or $38 with appealing ocean views (book ahead).

At 8 McKenzie St, *Charleston House* (☎ (070) 51 6317) is an old Queenslander also renovated in Art-Deco style. It's divided into eight comfortable flats and costs $75 a week, or $125 for a room to yourself. The *Happy House* (☎ (070) 31 5898), at 25 Maranoa St, is another restored old Queenslander divided into flats, with a bright, cheerful décor. It also costs $75 a week; you must be working or studying to stay here.

At 153 the Esplanade, the *Silver Palm Guesthouse* (☎ (070) 31 6099) is a quiet little place with singles/doubles from $30/35, including use of a kitchen, laundry, pool and TV room.

Motels & Holiday Flats There are a few budget motels around the centre: the *Wintersun Motel & Holiday Apartments* (☎ (070) 51 2933), at 84 Abbott St, has rooms with immaculate '60s décor and air-con from $45/50, or $50/55 with a kitchenette. The *Poinsettia Motel* (☎ (070) 51 2144), at 169 Lake St, is another cheap option with decent budget rooms from $46/50.

The *Great Northern B&B* (☎ (070) 51 5966), centrally located at 69 Abbott St, has older-style but clean and well-equipped motel-style units from $59/69, including breakfast. *Inn The Tropics* (☎ (070) 31 1088), at 141 Sheridan St, has a good pool and a small guests' kitchen. Motel-style rooms are $34/42 with shared bathroom or $45/52 with private bathroom; the air-con is coin-operated ($1).

Holiday flats are well worth considering, especially for a group of three or four people who are staying a few days or more. Expect pools, air-con and laundry facilities in this category. Holiday flats generally supply all bedding, cooking utensils etc.

At 209 Lake St, the *Castle Holiday Flats* (☎ (070) 31 2229) is an oldish red-brick block of flats with a small pool. There are one-bedroom flats from $50, two-bedroom flats from $60 and singles/doubles with shared bathroom and kitchen facilities from $25/35.

On the waterfront at 241 the Esplanade, the *Costa Blanca Apartments* (☎ (070) 51 3114) aren't particularly flashy, but they're clean and comfy and sleep up to four people, ranging from $45 to $80 a double plus $5 for extras. There's a guest laundry and a big old pool.

Lake Central (☎ (070) 51 4933) at 137 Lake St is a modern complex of air-con units with kitchenettes, ranging from $80 to $92 a double and from $95 to $130 for up to five people. There's a string of motels and holiday units along Sheridan St – these include the *Pacific Cay* (☎ (070) 51 0151) at No 193, with one-bedroom units from $65 and two-bedroom units from $85.

If you're looking to splurge, try the *Il Palazzo Boutique Hotel* (☎ (070) 41 2155) at 62 Abbott St. It has spacious and stylish self-contained apartments, a roof-top pool and a cafe. Costs are $175 a double ($130 standby) plus $20 for extras.

Places to Eat
Cairns has an abundance of eateries, and you shouldn't have too much trouble finding somewhere to satisfy your particular gastronomic craving, and/or your budget.

Cafes & Delis The Esplanade, between Shields and Aplin Sts, has plenty of eateries including Italian and Chinese food, burgers, kebabs, pizzas, seafood and ice cream – open all hours. Around the corner in Aplin St, *The Meeting Place* is a good hawkers-style foodhall with nine different stalls including Japanese, Thai, Chinese, steak and seafood; meals are in the $7 to $14 range.

Mozart's Pastry, on the corner of Grafton and Spence Sts, is good for a breakfast croissant and coffee, and for pastries, cakes and sandwiches. The *Galloping Gourmet*, on Aplin St near the Lake St corner, offers a cooked breakfast deal for $5; the somewhat down-market *John & Diana's Breakfast & Burger House* at 35 Sheridan St also has cooked breakfasts for $5 or less. Across the road is the *Continental Shelf*, an excellent eat-in deli with gourmet meals and snacks.

The very popular *Tiny's Juice Bar*, on Grafton St near the Spence St corner, has a great range of fruit and vegetable juices as well as filled rolls and lentil and tofu burgers at good prices. Over at 113 Sheridan St, *The Granary* is another good choice for lunch with sandwiches and rolls, salads, pastries and more. The *Victory Cafe* at 62 Shields St is an atmospheric BYO cafe that plays good jazz, blues and soul music, and opens for breakfast, lunch and dinner.

In front of the art gallery on the corner of Abbott and Shields Sts, the *Gallery Cafe* is a great open-air street cafe with a diverse menu; main meals are under $7, desserts under $4.

Restaurants *La Fettucini*, a narrow bistro at 43 Shields St, has great home-made pasta at $11.90 and Italian mains for about $16; it's BYO. Next door is the dim and exotic *Gypsy Dee's*, with a bar, live acoustic music nightly and mains in the $11 to $17 range. On the corner of Shields and Sheridan Sts, the *Red Ochre Grill* is a stylish restaurant with innovative Aussie bush tucker; mains range from $15 to $20.

The *Silver Dragon* Chinese restaurant at 102 Lake St has a good three-course lunch deal – soup, a main and ice cream – for $4.90. *La Pumpernic's* on Aplin St near the Esplanade has three-course deals for about $16 and an all-you-can-eat soup, pasta and fruit bar at $7.95.

The friendly *Sawasdee* at 89 Grafton St is a tiny BYO Thai restaurant with lunch specials from $7.50 and dinner mains from $11 to $16. Across the road, the *Paper Moon Cafe* is a narrow and groovy eatery with pasta from $9 to $14 and meat and seafood dishes from $15. For Japanese food, try *Yama* on the corner of Spence and Grafton Sts – it has good-value lunches and dinners. The bright and cheerful *Blue Moon*, nearby at 45 Spence St, specialises in Shanghai cuisine; it's BYO, with mains from $10 to $16.

The Pier Marketplace has a couple of good eating options, including a good international foodhall and *Johnny Rocket's*, an American-style burger joint. On the 1st floor is *Donnini's*, a smart licensed restaurant with some of the best Italian food in town;

gourmet pizzas from $9 to $16, pasta from $12 to $16 and Italian mains about $17.

Nightclubs & Pubs Most of the hostels have giveaway vouchers for cheap meals at various nightclubs, pubs and bars around town. *Samuel's Saloon*, near the corner of Hartley and Lake Sts, is one of the most popular places, with roasts, pasta and stews for $6.50 ($4.50 with a voucher). They even have a bus that picks up hungry travellers from the hostels.

The *End of the World* on the corner of Abbott and Aplin Sts is another popular nightclub with cheap meal deals. Next door on Abbott St is the testosterone-charged *Rugby Bar*, with pool tables, a courtyard and meals from $5 to $8.50. The *Wool Shed*, on Shields St in the mall, has meals in the $5 to $10 range and a Sunday barbecue (50c).

On the corner of Digger and Grove Sts, the *Cock & Bull Tavern* is an excellent English-style tavern with draught beers and hearty, stodgy tucker in the $8 to $12 range – just the spot for homesick Poms! The *Fox & Firkin Hotel* on the corner of Spence and Lake Sts has decent bistro meals at similar prices.

Entertainment
The free and widely available mag *Son of Barfly* covers music gigs, movies, pubs and clubs – and it's quite an entertaining read in itself.

Pubs & Live Music Free lunchtime concerts are held daily at the *City Place Amphitheatre*, in the mall on the corner of Lake and Shields St.

The long-running *Johno's Blues Bar* above McDonald's on the corner of Shields St and the Esplanade, has blues, rock and R&B bands every night until late; the cover charge is about $5. Quite a few pubs in Cairns have regular live bands, including the *Fox & Firkin*, on the corner of Spence and Lake Sts, the *Crown Hotel* on the corner of Shields and Grafton Sts, and the *Pier Tavern* overlooking the bay from the Pier Marketplace – their Sunday arvo sessions are all the go.

In Shields St, *Gypsy Dee's* and the *Victory Cafe* both have live acoustic, jazz and blues music at night (see Places to Eat).

Nightclubs & Bars Cairns' nightclub scene is notoriously wild, especially in the early hours of the morning. The huge complex on the corner of Lake and Hartley Sts houses three places: *Samuel's Saloon*, a backpacker bar and eatery; the *Playpen International*, a huge nightclub that often has big-name bands; and the more up-market *Court Jester Bar*.

The *Junk Yard*, at 82 McLeod St, has a trashy décor, a 'sweat-and-groove' theme, good dance music and live bands.

On Shields St in the mall, the *Wool Shed* is a hectic backpackers' bar with party games, theme nights and other wild and crazy stuff, while the *End of the World* nightclub, on the corner of Abbott and Aplin Sts, has a huge video screen, low lighting, loud music and happy hours.

Rusty's Pub on the corner of Spence and Sheridan Sts has a gay night with a floor show on Saturday nights. At 53 Spence St, *Club Justice* (also known as JDL's) is a gay-oriented dance club.

Cinemas & Theatre The *Cairns Five Cinemas* (☎ (070) 31 1077) at 108 Grafton St screen mainstream releases, or there's the *Coral Twin Drive-in* on the Bruce Highway on the southern edge of town. The *Cairns Civic Centre* (☎ (070) 51 3211) is the main venue for theatre and concerts – ring to see what's on.

Casino Cairns' big *Reef Casino* is on the block bordered by the Esplanade, and Wharf and Spence Sts.

Things to Buy
Many artists live in the Cairns region, so there's a wide range of local handicrafts available at the various markets, including the weekend Mud Markets at the Pier Marketplace, Rusty's Bazaar and the long-running Night Markets on the Esplanade. Sounds Aboriginal, at 83 the Esplanade, is run by the Aboriginal and Torres Strait Islander community and sells hand-made dijeridus and boomerangs.

Harris Brothers, on the corner of Shields and Sheridan Sts, has a good range of Aussie clothing, boots and Akubra hats.

Getting There & Away
Air Qantas and Sunstate have an office on the corner of Shields and Lake Sts; Ansett is at 13 Shields St.

Domestic Flights Ansett and Qantas have daily flights between Cairns and all the major destinations including Melbourne ($596 one way), Sydney ($526), Brisbane ($400), Townsville ($163), Darwin ($418), Alice Springs ($390), Perth ($642) and Adelaide ($599).

Shorter hops within Queensland are shared between a number of smaller airlines. Sunstate flies to Bamaga ($288), Lizard Island ($169) and Thursday Island ($323). Ansett flies to Weipa ($226) and Mt Isa ($263). Flight West flies to Cooktown ($71) and operates a service through the Gulf, the Cape York Peninsula and to Bamaga and the Torres Strait Islands. Hinterland Aviation (☎ (070) 98 9153) have flights to Cow Bay, south of Cape Tribulation, for $60.

International Flights Cairns airport has regular flights to and from North America, Papua New Guinea and Asia. Air Niugini (☎ (070) 51 4177) is at 4 Shields St; the Port Moresby flight costs $378 one way and goes daily except Sunday. Qantas also flies to Port Moresby (daily except Wednesday and Sunday), as well as direct to the US west coast (daily except Tuesday) and to Hong Kong every Thursday.

Bus All the bus companies operate from the transit centre at Trinity Wharf. Most of the backpackers hostels have courtesy buses that meet the arriving buses.

Greyhound Pioneer and McCafferty's (☎ 13 1499) both run at least five buses a day

QUEENSLAND

up the coast from Brisbane and Townsville to Cairns. Journey times and fares are: Brisbane, 23 to 27 hours ($137); Rockhampton, 14 to 16 hours ($91); Mackay, 10 to 12 hours ($72); and Townsville, six hours ($38).

Coral Coaches (☎ (070) 31 7577) has daily buses to Port Douglas ($14.20), Cape Tribulation ($25.30) and Cooktown via either the inland road ($44.90) or the coastal road ($49.60). White Car Coaches (☎ (070) 91 1855) has services to Kuranda and the Atherton Tableland, and Cairns-Karumba Coachline (☎ (070) 35 1853) has services to Karumba in the Gulf, via the Undara Lava Tubes.

Train Three trains run between Cairns and Brisbane – the *Sunlander* (three times a week), the *Queenslander* and the *Spirit of the Tropics* (both weekly). The 1681-km trip from Brisbane takes 32 hours. The luxurious *Queenslander* leaves Brisbane on Sunday and Cairns on Tuesday; the fare is $489 including sleeping berth and all meals (1st class only). For another $270 you can put your car on the train too. The economy fare for the *Sunlander* or *Spirit of the Tropics* is $129. Call Queensland Rail for bookings (☎ 13 2232) and information (☎ (070) 52 6267).

Car, 4WD & Motorbike Rental It's well worth considering renting a vehicle. There's plenty to see and do on land around Cairns, whether it's doing the beach crawl up to Port Douglas and Cape Trib or exploring the Atherton Tableland. The major rental firms have desks at the airport and offices in town, and there are dozens of smaller local operators offering good deals – shop around, but watch out for hidden costs such as insurance and per-km charges. Generally, Mokes are about $45 per day, VW convertibles $55, and regular cars from $50 up. A sizeable deposit is generally required, although this is waived if you're paying with a credit card.

Note that most Cairns rental firms specifically prohibit you from taking their cars, on the road to Cooktown, to Chillagoe or up the Cape Tribulation road. If you ignore this

prohibition and get caught, you'll lose your deposit and/or be up for a hefty fine, so if you're planning to tackle one of these routes you'll need to hire a 4WD. These are widely available, but they cost about $100 a day. See the Cape York section for details of some operators who rent 4WDs for Cape York trips.

Two Wheel Adventures (☎ (070) 31 5707) at 148 Sheridan St rents motorbikes from $60 a day, but has restrictions on where you can go.

Boat The daily *Quicksilver* (☎ (070) 99 5500) fast-catamaran service links Cairns with Port Douglas. The trip takes 1½ hours and costs $20 one way, and $30 return.

Getting Around
To/From the Airport The approach road to the Cairns airport (domestic and international flights) leaves the main highway about 3.5 km north of the centre. The old Cairns airport (local flights) is reached from a second turning about 1.5 km farther north.

The Australia Coach shuttle bus (☎ (070) 35 9555) meets all incoming flights and runs a regular pick-up and drop-off service between the airport and town; the one-way fare is $4. A taxi is about $9.

Bus There are a number of local bus services in and around Cairns. Schedules for most of them are posted at the main city stop (known as the Lake St transit centre) in City Place. Buses on most routes run hourly on weekdays between about 7 am and 6 pm and on Saturday morning. Cairns Trans (☎ (070) 35 2600) operates most of the bus services around town and up to Yorkeys Knob and Holloways Beach. The Beach Bus (No 208), run by Marlin Coast Buslines (☎ (070) 57 7411), goes up to Trinity and Clifton beaches, Wild World, Palm Cove and Ellis Beach. Southern Cross Bus Services (☎ (070) 55 1240) goes to Machans Beach.

The Cairns Red Explorer (☎ (070) 55 1240) is an air-con service that plies a circular route around the city, and you can get on or off at any of the nine stops. It departs daily every hour from 9 am to 4 pm (May to October on Sunday only) from the Lake St transit centre, and a day ticket costs a hefty $20. Stops include the Freshwater Creek swimming hole, Freshwater Connection, the mangrove boardwalk near the airport, the botanic gardens and the Royal Flying Doctor Service complex.

Bicycle Most of the hostels and car-hire firms, plus quite a few other places, have bikes for hire so you'll have no trouble tracking one down. Expect to pay about $10 a day.

ISLANDS OFF CAIRNS

Off the coast from Cairns are Green Island (a coral cay) and Fitzroy Island, which is a continental island. Both attract hordes of day-trippers (some say too many), and both have resorts owned by the cruise company Great Adventures, which in turn is owned by the Japanese corporation Daikyo.

South of Cairns, the Frankland Islands Group is a cluster of undeveloped national park islands. You can do day trips to these islands or camp overnight or longer.

Green Island

Green Island, 27 km north-east of Cairns, is a coral cay 660 metres long by 260 metres wide. The island and its surrounding reef are all national park, although a multi-million dollar tourist resort takes up a substantial proportion of the island. Nevertheless, a 10-minute stroll from the resort to the far end of the island will remind you that the beach is beautiful, the water fine, the snorkelling good and the fish prolific.

The resort has a separate and somewhat crowded section for day-trippers, with impressive facilities, including a pool, a bar, several eateries and water sports gear for hire. Marineland Melanesia is worth a visit ($7), with its aquarium of fish, turtles, stingrays and crocs, and a bizarre collection of Melanesian artefacts.

The five-star *Green Island Reef Resort* (☎ (070) 31 3300) has room for 92 guests who each pay $400-plus a night.

Getting There & Away Great Adventures (☎ (070) 51 0455) has two services to Green Island: by launch ($34 return) or by fast catamaran ($50 return). Other operators include the Big Cat (☎ (070) 51 0444) with a day cruise for $36, or the much faster Reef Jet (☎ (070) 31 5559) has a half-day trip for $35, a full day $38.

Fitzroy Island

Six km off the coast and 26 km east of Cairns, Fitzroy is a continental island with coral-covered beaches, which are good for snorkelling but not ideal for swimming and sunbaking, although Nudey Beach is quite pleasant. Snorkellers will find good coral only 50 metres off the beach in the resort area, and the island has its own dive school. There are some fine walks, including one to the island's high point.

The *Fitzroy Island Resort* (☎ (070) 51 9588) has hostel-style bunk rooms with shared kitchen, bathroom and laundry facilities at $26 per person, and 'villa units' at $229/320 for singles/doubles including activities, breakfast and dinner. There's also a QNP&WS camping ground (permits and bookings through Great Adventures). Sites cost $10 a night, and campers can use most of the resort's facilities. Day-trippers have access to the resort facilities, which include a pool, snack bar, a bar, a couple of shops and a laundrette.

Getting There & Away Great Adventures (☎ (070) 51 0455) has return trips for $27, and Sunlover Cruises (☎ (070) 31 1055) has return trips for $22.

Frankland Islands

Frankland Island Cruise & Dive (☎ (070) 31 6300) has day trips to these untouched national park islands, costing $98 including lunch and snorkelling gear. If you like the idea of camping on a remote tropical island, they also do camping drop-offs for $120 per person.

ATHERTON TABLELAND

Inland from the coast between Innisfail and Cairns, the land rises sharply then rolls

QUEENSLAND

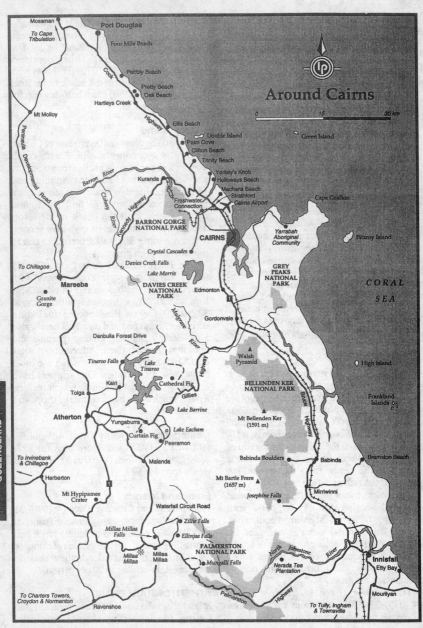

Around Cairns

gently across the lush Atherton Tableland towards the Great Dividing Range. The tableland's altitude, more than 900 metres in places, tempers the tropical heat, and the abundant rainfall and rich volcanic soil combine to make this one of the greenest places in Queensland. In the south are the state's two highest mountains – Bartle Frere (1657 metres) and Bellenden Ker (1591 metres).

Little more than a century ago, this peaceful, pastoral region was still wild jungle. The first pioneers came in the 1870s, looking for a repeat of the Palmer River gold rush, farther north. As elsewhere in Queensland, the Aboriginal population opposed to the intrusion but was soon overrun. Some gold was found and rather more tin, but although mining spurred the development of roads and railways through the rugged, difficult land of the plateau, farming and timber soon became the chief activities.

Getting There & Around

The train ride and the new Skyrail cableway from Cairns to Kuranda are major attractions, and there are bus services to the main towns from Cairns, although hiring a car would be the ideal way to get around. There are also some good tours on offer from Cairns.

From south to north, the three major roads from the coast are: the Palmerston Highway from Innisfail to Millaa Millaa; the Gillies Highway from Gordonvale to Yungaburra and Atherton; and the Kennedy Highway from Cairns to Kuranda and Mareeba. The Peninsula Developmental Road heads north from Mareeba towards Cooktown, with a turning at Mt Molloy to Mossman.

Kuranda (pop 750)

Famed for its markets, this mountain town is surrounded by spectacular tropical scenery. Unfortunately, Kuranda's charms have long since been discovered by the masses, and the place is flooded with tourists on market days. Many of the stalls and shops sell mainly trashy souvenirs, although there are still quite a few good arts, craft and produce stalls.

Things to See & Do The Kuranda Markets are held every Wednesday, Thursday, Friday and Sunday, although things quieten after about 2 pm. On other days, Kuranda reverts to its normal sleepy character.

Within the market area, Birdworld ($7) is a large canopied garden with lake, waterfalls and over 30 species of birds; it's open daily from 9 am to 4 pm. Nearby, the **Australian Butterfly Sanctuary** ($9.50) is open daily from 10 am to 3 pm and has regular guided tours. On Coondoo St, the Kuranda Wildlife Noctarium ($8), where you can see nocturnal rainforest animals such as gliders, fruit bats and echidnas, is open daily from 10 am to 4 pm.

The Tjapukai Dance Theatre, a local Aboriginal dance troupe, have recently moved to a new theatre complex in Smithfield – see the Cairns Things to See section.

Over the footbridge behind the railway station, Kuranda Rainforest Tours runs 45-minute riverboat cruises ($9), and has one-hour guided rainforest walks daily at 10 am ($10). Nearby, Kuranda Glow Shows (☎ (070) 93 7397) runs good-value canoe trips along the Barron River most days, from about $6 an hour.

There are several picturesque walks starting with short signed tracks down through the market. **Jumrum Creek Environmental Park**, off the Barron Falls road, 700 metres from the bottom of Thongon St, has a short walking track and a big population of fruit bats. Farther down, the Barron Falls road divides: the left fork takes you to a lookout over the falls, while a farther 1.5 km along the right fork brings you to Wrights Lookout where you can see back down the Barron Gorge to Cairns.

Places to Stay The leafy *Kuranda Van Park* (☎ (070) 93 7316) is a few km out of town, up the road directly opposite the Kuranda turn-off on the Kennedy Highway. It has camp sites for $12 and on-site cabins at $33.

QUEENSLAND

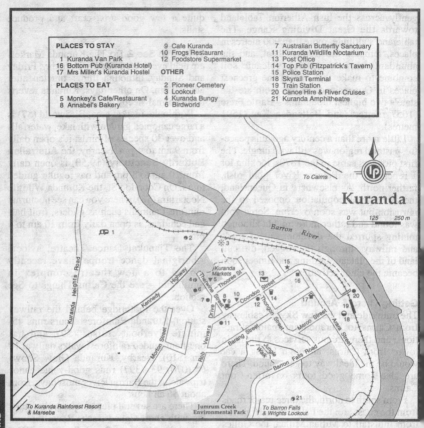

PLACES TO STAY

1   Kuranda Van Park
16 Bottom Pub (Kuranda Hotel)
17 Mrs Miller's Kuranda Hostel

PLACES TO EAT

5   Monkey's Cafe/Restaurant
8   Annabel's Bakery

9   Cafe Kuranda
10 Frogs Restaurant
12 Foodstore Supermarket

OTHER

2   Pioneer Cemetery
3   Lookout
4   Kuranda Bungy
6   Birdworld

7   Australian Butterfly Sanctuary
11 Kuranda Wildlife Noctarium
13 Post Office
14 Top Pub (Fitzpatrick's Tavern)
15 Police Station
18 Skyrail Terminal
19 Train Station
20 Canoe Hire & River Cruises
21 Kuranda Amphitheatre

To Cairns

Kuranda

0   125   250 m

Barron River

Kuranda Markets

Kuranda Heights Road

Kennedy Highway

Morton Street

Rob Veivers Drive

Thooree Street

Arara Street

Coondoo Street

Thorpe Street

Merroo Street

Barang Street

Jungle Walk

Barron Falls Road

To Kuranda Rainforest Resort & Mareeba

Jumrum Creek Environmental Park

To Barron Falls & Wrights Lookout

The *Kuranda Hostel* (☎ (070) 93 7355), also known as *Mrs Miller's*, is at 6 Arara St, near the railway station. It's a big, rambling old timber building with a huge garden, a small saltwater pool, spacious lounge/TV rooms and an enlightening graffiti room. While it's a quiet and relaxing place to stay, it's looking a bit dilapidated nowadays. Dorm beds are $13 and doubles are $32.

The *Bottom Pub/Kuranda Hotel* (☎ (070) 93 7206) at the corner of Coondoo and Arara Sts has a pool and 12 very basic motel-style rooms with ceiling fans from $35/45.

A couple of km out of town, back on the Kennedy Highway towards Mareeba, the up-market *Kuranda Rainforest Resort* (☎ (070) 93 7555) has a bar, restaurant, swimming pool and tennis courts, and rooms from $120.

Places to Eat Some of the best food is found in the market's food stalls – fresh juices, Thai stir-fries, Indian curries etc – just follow your nose! There's a supermarket in Coondoo St if you're self-catering.

Both pubs do counter meals. The Bottom Pub has the very pleasant *Garden Bar &*

Grill in its backyard, with a swimming pool, shady lawns and burgers for $4.50 and other grills for about $8.

Monkey's Cafe/Restaurant, down at the bottom end of Therwine St near the markets, is a good earthy BYO cafe serving breakfast, lunch and dinner. *Frogs Restaurant* on Coondoo St is another good local eatery, with cooked breakfasts for $7, burgers and sandwiches for about $6 and main meals from $10. They have live music here on Sunday nights.

Cafe Kuranda, on the corner of Coondoo and Therwine Sts, does sandwiches, snacks and takeaways, and a few doors up Therwine St, *Annabel's Bakery* has a large range of pies, pastries and more.

Getting There & Away Getting to Kuranda can be just as much fun as actually being there – if not more! You have a choice of a scenic steam-train ride or the new cableway through the rainforests. If you can afford to, take one up and the other back.

The Kuranda Scenic Railway (☎ (070) 52 6249) winds 34 km from Cairns to Kuranda. This line, which took five years to build, was opened in 1891 and goes through 15 tunnels, climbing more than 300 metres in the last 21 km. Kuranda's railway station, decked out in tropical flowers and ferns, is justly famous. The historic steam-trains operate daily and cost $23 one way, $39 return. You can board at the Cairns Railway Station or Freshwater Connection (☎ (070) 55 2222), 10 km out of Cairns.

The new Skyrail Rainforest Cableway (☎ (070) 38 1555) is a 7.5 km gondola cableway that runs from Smithfield, a northern suburb of Cairns, to Kuranda with two stops along the way. It operates daily from 8 am to 5 pm; fares are also $23 one way or $39 return.

White Car Coaches has buses three or four times daily (twice on weekends) from outside Tropical Paradise Travel (☎ (070) 51 9533) at 51 Spence St, Cairns. The fare is $7 one way, $14 return.

Mareeba (pop 17,000)
From Kuranda, the Kennedy Highway runs west across the tableland to Mareeba, the centre of a tobacco and rice-growing area, then continues south to Atherton in the centre of the tableland. From Mareeba, the Peninsula Developmental Road heads 40 km north to Mt Molloy where it forks for Mossman and the coast one way, and Cooktown and Cape York the other. Mareeba has a range of accommodation and in July hosts one of Australia's biggest rodeos.

Chillagoe (pop 450)
From Mareeba, you can continue 140 km west to the old mining township of Chillagoe, and get a glimpse of the outback. All but the last 34 km of the route is along sealed roads, and although the last section is pretty bumpy, it won't present a problem for conventional vehicles during the dry season. At Chillagoe you can visit impressive limestone caves and rock pinnacles, Aboriginal rock-art galleries, ruins of smelters from early this century and a museum.

The rangers run guided tours through the various caves of the **Chillagoe-Mungana Caves National Park**, leaving daily at 9 and 11.30 am and 1.30 pm and costing $2 to $4 – contact the QNP&WS office (☎ (070) 94 7163) on Queen St for more details. The rangers can also tell you about other caves with self-guiding trails, for which you'll need a torch.

Places to Stay There's a camping ground in the national park, and the *Chillagoe Tourist Village* (☎ (070) 94 7177) on Queen St has tent sites, on-site vans and units. The old *Post Office Hotel* (☎ (070) 94 7119) at 37 Queen St has narrow iron beds upstairs for $15, and the *Chillagoe Caves Lodge* (☎ (070) 94 7106) at 7 King St has budget singles/doubles from $20/25 and motel units from $40/45, plus a restaurant.

One km north of town, the *Chillagoe Bush Camp & Ecolodge* (☎ (070) 94 7155) is a former miners' village with beds from $12, doubles from $35 and home-cooked meals.

Getting There & Away White Car Coaches (☎ (070) 91 1855) has bus services from

QUEENSLAND

Cairns to Chillagoe three times a week, with a changeover at Mareeba ($39 one way). There are day tours from Cairns for about $90.

Atherton (pop 9600)

Although it's a pleasant, prosperous town, Atherton has little of interest in its own right. *Atherton Backpackers* (☎ (070) 91 3552) at 37 Alice St, not far from the centre of town, is quite a good place and has dorm beds from $12 and doubles for $27.

Lake Tinaroo

From Atherton or nearby Tolga it's a short drive to this large lake created for the Barron River hydroelectric power scheme. Tinaroo Falls, at the north-western corner of the lake, has a motel and the *Tinaroo Pines Caravan Park* (☎ (070) 95 8232) with tent sites and on-site cabins. Just out of town overlooking the dam, *Cafe Pensini's Deckbar & Bistro* is a good spot for a snack.

The road continues over the dam as a gravel track that does a 31-km circuit of the lake, finally emerging on the Gillies Highway four km north-east of Lake Barrine. This is called the **Danbulla Forest Drive** and it's a pleasant trip – though sometimes impassable for conventional vehicles after heavy rain. It passes several free lakeside camping grounds, run by the Queensland forestry department (there are showers and toilets). **Lake Euramoo**, about halfway along, is in a double volcanic crater; there's a short botanical walk around the lake. There is another crater at **Mobo Creek**, a short walk off the drive. Then, 25 km from the dam, it's a short walk to the **Cathedral Fig**, a truly gigantic strangler fig tree.

Yungaburra (pop 800)

This pretty village is 13 km east of Atherton along the Gillies Highway. It's right in the centre of the tableland, has some good restaurants and accommodation and, if you have transport, it's a good base from which to explore the lakes, waterfalls and national parks nearby. The central streets of the town have been classified by the National Trust and are quite atmospheric. On the main road,

the Collection museum has WW II relics and other memorabilia.

Three km out of Yungaburra on the Malanda road is the strangler fig, known as the **Curtain Fig** for its aerial roots, which form a 15-metre-high hanging screen.

Places to Stay & Eat The excellent *On the Wallaby* (☎ (070) 51 0889), at 37 Eacham Rd, is a small backpackers hostel sleeping 15, with double and twin rooms upstairs and good living areas downstairs. There's a free pick-up bus from Cairns several days a week and the nightly cost is $12 per person, or you can camp in the backyard for $10.

The *Lake Eacham Hotel* (☎ (070) 95 3515) is a fine old timber pub with a magnificent dining room and comfy rooms upstairs at $40/45. Or there's the (non-smoking) *Kookaburra Lodge* (☎ (070) 95 3222) on the corner of Oak St and Eacham Rd, with bright modern units from $45 a double. There's a pool and tiny dining room with three-course meals for $17.

There are three good restaurants: the chalet-style *Nick's Swiss-Italian Restaurant* with its accordion-playing chef; the charming little *Burra Inn* opposite the pub, which has excellent country-style mains for about $18; and *Snibbles BYO* with light lunches from $6, dinner mains from $15 and a three-course roast on Tuesday night for $12.

Lakes Eacham & Barrine

These two lovely crater lakes are off the Gillies Highway east of Yungaburra. Both are reached by sealed roads, and are great swimming spots. There are rainforest walking tracks around their perimeters – 6.5 km around Lake Barrine, and four km around Lake Eacham.

The *Lake Barrine Teahouse* serves Devonshire teas and snacks, and you can take a 45-minute cruise ($7) daily at 10.15 am and 3.15 pm. Lake Eacham is quieter and more beautiful – an excellent place for a picnic or a swim, and there's a small floating kids' pool.

Both lakes are national parks and camping is not allowed. However, there are camp sites at *Lake Eacham Tourist Park* (☎ (070) 95 3730), two km down the Malanda road from Lake Eacham. *Chambers Wildlife Rainforest Holiday Apartments* (☎ (070) 95 3754) has self-contained one-bedroom apartments sleeping one to four people at $240 for three nights.

Malanda (pop 900)
About 15 km south of Lake Eacham, is Malanda, a busy dairy centre that claims to have the longest milk run in Australia, since it supplies milk all the way to Darwin and the north of Western Australia. On the Atherton road on the outskirts, the **Malanda Falls** drop into a big old swimming pool, with picnic facilities and a short walking trail nearby.

Places to Stay There's a caravan park beside the falls, and the huge old *Malanda Hotel* (☎ (070) 96 5101) has pub rooms at $15/30 and good bistro meals – the Friday and Saturday night smorgasbords are particularly popular.

The *Platypus Forest Resort* (☎ (070) 96 5926), about six km north of Malanda off the Lake Eacham road, is a friendly and relaxed lodge that has received good reports from travellers. You might see a Lumholtz's tree-kangaroo in a small patch of rainforest here, and there's a swimming hole, a hot-tub and home-cooked meals. Bunk beds are $15 a night and there's one double at $34. You can get here on a couple of the tours from Cairns.

In the hills between Malanda and Yungaburra, is the *Peeramon Hotel* (☎ (070) 96 5873), a good old country pub with pleasant double rooms for $30 and bunk beds at $15, including breakfast.

Millaa Millaa (pop 330)
The 16-km 'waterfall circuit' road near this small town, 24 km south of Malanda, passes some of the most picturesque falls on the tableland. You enter the circuit by taking Theresa Creek Rd one km east of Millaa Millaa on the Palmerston Highway. **Millaa Millaa Falls**, the first falls you reach, are the most spectacular and have the best swimming hole.

Continuing around the circuit, you reach **Zillie Falls** and then **Ellinjaa Falls** before returning to the Palmerston Highway just 2.5 km out of Millaa Millaa. A farther 5.5 km down the Palmerston Highway there's a turning to **Mungalli Falls**, five km off the highway, where the *Mungalli Falls Outpost* (☎ (070) 31 1144) has self-contained cabins, a teahouse and horse trail rides.

Millaa Millaa itself has a pub and a caravan park, and the Eacham Historical Society Museum is on the main street.

Mt Hypipamee
The Kennedy Highway between Atherton and Ravenshoe passes the eerie Mt Hypipamee crater. It's a scenic 400-metre walk from the picnic area, past **Dinner Falls**, to this narrow, 138-metre-deep crater with its spooky, evil-looking lake far below.

Herberton (pop 950)
On a slightly longer alternative route between Atherton and Ravenshoe, this old tin-mining town holds the colourful Tin Festival each September. On Holdcroft Drive is the Herberton Historical Village, with about 30 old buildings that have been transported here from around the tableland.

Ravenshoe (pop 880)
Ravenshoe is on the western edge of the tableland, at an altitude of 915 metres. It was once a thriving timber town, but things are pretty quiet around here nowadays. It has a caravan park, a couple of pubs and a motel.

On weekends at 2.30 pm, you can take a seven-km ride on the Millstream Express, a historic steam-train ($10). The **Little Millstream Falls** are two km south of Ravenshoe on the Tully Gorge road. Six km past Ravenshoe and one km off the road are the **Millstream Falls**, the widest in Australia although only 13 metres high. You can't camp here, but the swimming is great.

Kennedy Highway
Beyond Ravenshoe, the small mining town of **Mt Garnet**, 47 km west, comes alive one

weekend every May when it hosts one of Queensland's top outback race meetings.

About 60 km past Mt Garnet, the Kennedy Highway passes through **Forty Mile Scrub National Park**, where the semi-evergreen vine thicket is a descendant of the vegetation that covered much of the Gondwana supercontinent 300 million years ago – before Australia, South America, India, Africa and Antarctica drifted apart. Just past the park is the turn-off to Undara and the Gulf region; see the Gulf Savannah section later in this chapter for details of the area west of here.

CAIRNS TO PORT DOUGLAS

The Bruce Highway, which runs nearly 2000 km north from Brisbane, ends in Cairns, but the sealed coastal road continues another 110 km north to Mossman and Daintree. This final stretch, the Cook Highway, is a treat because it often runs right along the shore and there are some superb beaches.

Heading out of Cairns, towards the airport, you'll find an interesting and informative elevated **mangrove boardwalk** 200 metres before you reach the airport. There are explanatory signs at regular intervals, and these give some insight into the surprising ecological complexities of swamp vegetation. There's a small observation platform.

Kamerunga Rd, off the Cook Highway just north of the airport turning, leads inland to the Freshwater Connection, a railway museum complex where you can also catch the Kuranda Scenic Railway. It's 10 km from the centre of town. Just beyond Freshwater is the turning south along Redlynch Intake Rd to Crystal Cascades, a popular outing 22 km from Cairns, with waterfalls and swimming holes.

North along the Cook Highway are the Cairns northern beaches, which are really a string of suburbs. In order, these are Machans, Holloways, Yorkeys Knob, Trinity, Kewarra and Clifton beaches and Palm Cove. **Holloways Beach** has a good foreshore caravan park. **Trinity Beach** is perhaps the best for a short trip from Cairns, with pleasant beaches, a cliff-top pub and a cluster of eateries and up-market resorts along the beachfront. Backpackers can share a four-bed room at the *Sundowner Motel* (☎ (070) 55 6194) on the Esplanade for $15 a night.

Farther north, **Palm Cove** is an exclusive little resort town with fancy hotels, expensive boutiques and restaurants; the very good *Palm Cove Camping Area* on the foreshore has tent sites from $8. On the highway, Wild World has lots of crocodiles and snakes, tame kangaroos and Australian birds; there are shows daily.

Around the headland past Palm Cove and Double Island, **Ellis Beach** is a lovely spot. Its southern end is an unofficial nude bathing beach and in the central part of the beach is the *Ellis Beach Resort* (☎ (070) 55 3538) which has a good camping ground and a new restaurant/bar complex with live music most Sunday afternoons.

Soon after Ellis Beach is Hartleys Creek Crocodile Farm, with a collection of Australian wildlife. Most of the enclosures are a bit shoddy but skill and spectacle makes it one of the most interesting 'animal places' in Australia. When they feed Charlie the crocodile in the 'Crocodile Attack Show' (3 pm) you know for certain why it's not wise to get bitten by one! The park is open daily; entry is $12.

The *Turtle Cove Resort* (☎ (070) 59 1800), 45 km north of Cairns, is a popular resort for gay men and lesbian women. Singles/doubles start from $90/108 a night.

Shortly before Mossman there's a turn-off to fashionable Port Douglas. The turn-off to Cape Tribulation is just before Daintree village. From Cape Tribulation, it's possible to continue up to historic Cooktown by 4WD along the controversial Bloomfield Track (see the aside in the Cape Tribulation Area section). Alternatively, there's the partly surfaced inland road from Cairns, but both roads to Cooktown can be impassable after periods of heavy rain.

PORT DOUGLAS (pop 3800)

In the early days of far north Queensland's development, Port Douglas was a rival for

Cairns, but when Cairns eventually got the upper hand, Port Douglas became a sleepy little backwater. In the mid-1980s, however, people began to realise what a delightful place it was, and up went the multi-million dollar Sheraton Mirage and Radisson Royal Palms resorts. These were quickly followed by a golf course, fast catamaran services from Cairns, a marina and shopping complex, and an avenue of palms lining the road from the Cook Highway to Port Douglas – all the ingredients of a retreat for the rich and fashionable. Yet, despite all this development, Port, as it's known locally, has managed to keep most of its original charm and there is still cheap accommodation. Many travellers arrive here and soon wonder why they spent so long in Cairns – Port is much more relaxed, and there's plenty to do.

The little town has a couple of good central pubs with outdoor sitting areas, and a string of interesting little shops and restaurants to wander around when the beach, the boats and the lookout get dull. You can make trips to the Low Isles, the Great Barrier Reef, the Mossman Gorge and Cape Tribulation.

Orientation & Information

It's six km from the highway along a long, low spit of land to Port Douglas. The Sheraton Mirage resort occupies a long stretch of Four Mile Beach. The main road in, Davidson St, ends in a T-intersection with Macrossan St; the beach is to the right, and to the left, the town centre with most of the shops and restaurants. There's a fine view over the coastline and sea from Flagstaff Hill lookout.

There are several tour booking agents along Macrossan St, including the helpful Port Douglas Tourist Information Centre (☎ (070) 99 5599) at No 23 and the Adventure Centre (☎ (070) 99 4650) at No 8.

Things to See

On the pier off Anzac Park, **Ben Cropp's Shipwreck Museum** is quite interesting and open daily from 9 am to 5 pm; admission is $5. At the **Rainforest Habitat**, where the Port Douglas road leaves the main highway,

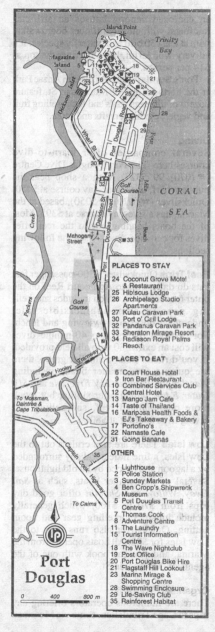

PLACES TO STAY

24 Coconut Grove Motel & Restaurant
25 Hibiscus Lodge
26 Archipelago Studio Apartments
27 Kulau Caravan Park
30 Port o' Call Lodge
32 Pandanus Caravan Park
33 Sheraton Mirage Resort
34 Radisson Royal Palms Resort

PLACES TO EAT

6 Court House Hotel
9 Iron Bar Restaurant
10 Combined Services Club
13 Central Hotel
14 Mango Jam Cafe
14 Taste of Thailand
16 Mariposa Health Foods & EJ's Takeaway & Bakery
17 Portofino's
22 Namaste Cafe
31 Going Bananas

OTHER

1 Lighthouse
2 Police Station
3 Sunday Markets
4 Ben Cropp's Shipwreck Museum
5 Port Douglas Transit Centre
7 Thomas Cook
8 Adventure Centre
11 The Laundry
15 Tourist Information Centre
18 The Wave Nightclub
19 Post Office
20 Port Douglas Bike Hire
21 Flagstaff Hill Lookout
23 Marina Mirage & Shopping Centre
28 Swimming Enclosure
29 Life-Saving Club
35 Rainforest Habitat

Port Douglas

an enclosed canopy houses an artificial rainforest with elevated timber boardwalks, with at least 30 bird and butterfly species. It's all very wonderful, but a bit over the top at $14 per person.

Port's **Sunday Markets**, held in Anzac Park at the northern end of Macrossan St, feature dozens of different stalls and tents, selling fruit and vegies, clothing, crafts and more.

Diving

Several companies offer learn-to-dive courses here. The Port Douglas Dive Centre (☎ (070) 99 5327), with a shop near the public wharf, has a four-day course at $450; Quicksilver (☎ (070) 99 5050), based at the Marina, has a five-day course at $395. Most of the boats heading out to the reef offer dives for certified divers – see the following sections.

Reef Trips Quicksilver's 300-passenger fast cats do daily trips to Agincourt Reef on the outer reef for $118, which includes snorkelling gear, a semi-submersible ride, underwater observatory viewing and lunch. For certified divers, two 40-minute dives will cost an extra $80 with all gear provided. If you'd rather go in a smaller group, there are quite a few smaller boats, including *Wavelength, Impulse, MV Freestyle* and *MV Outer Edge,* which offer similar but much more personalised reef, snorkelling and diving trips starting at $80.

Low Isles There are also cruises out to the Low Isles, a fine little coral cay surrounded by a lagoon and topped by an old lighthouse. Several of the smaller boats, such as *Sail Away, Willow* and *Shaolin* offer good day trips from $70 to $100, which generally include lunch, snorkelling gear and boom netting. Quicksilver also runs trips to the Low Isles for $82. All boats operate from the Marina, and you can book with one of the agents on Macrossan St.

Organised Tours

There are numerous operators offering day trips to Cape Tribulation, some via Mossman Gorge, for about $90. A two-day 4WD Cooktown loop – up via the Bloomfield Track, back via the inland road – with Strikies Safaris (☎ (070) 99 5599) is $199, not including meals and accommodation. Amber Dahlberg's Eco Cruises offers birdwatching tours of the mangroves and wetlands of Dickson's Inlet (two hours, $30). Many of the tours out of Cairns also do pick-ups from Port Douglas. Bookings can be made with any of the agencies in town.

Places to Stay

Port Douglas has three caravan parks. The *Kulau Caravan Park* (☎ (070) 99 5449) at 28 Davidson St is the closest to the centre and a short walk from the beach. It has tent sites from $13 and on-site cabins from $45. About a km farther out, the *Pandanus Van Park* (☎ (070) 99 5944) at 111 Davidson St has tent sites from $12 and on-site units from $42.

The only backpackers' accommodation in Port is the excellent *Port o' Call Lodge* (☎ (070) 99 5422) in Port St, about one km south of the centre, just off Davidson St. It's a YHA-associate and has modern four-bed units with private bathrooms at $16 per person ($17 for nonmembers). They also have air-con motel units that range seasonally from about $60 to $82 a double. There's a pool, cooking facilities, a bar and a good budget restaurant, and a free courtesy coach to and from Cairns every Monday, Wednesday and Saturday. You can also hook up with a couple of the tours that operate between Cairns and Cape Trib from here.

Most of the motels, holiday flats and resorts are fairly expensive, although there are a few affordable exceptions. *Hibiscus Lodge* (☎ (070) 99 5315) on the corner of Mowbray and Owen Sts has a small pool, three comfy older-style units and three newer units. Costs range seasonally from $45 to $95 a double plus $10 for each extra person. The *Archipelago Studio Apartments* (☎ (070) 99 5387) at 72 Macrossan St has new and renovated self-contained studio units ranging from $75 to $100 a double ($110 to $130 with sea views). The *Coconut*

Grove Motel (☎ (070) 98 5124), at 58 Macrossan St, is the cheapest and most central motel with units from $50 to $75 and a popular restaurant.

At the top of the range are the *Sheraton Mirage Resort* (☎ (070) 99 5888), with an amazing swimming pool and five-star hotel rooms from $400 a night, and the *Radisson Royal Palms Resort* (☎ (070) 99 5577), with hotel rooms starting from $155 a night.

Places to Eat

Port Douglas has a great range of cafes and restaurants, mostly along Macrossan St, although not too many places cater for budget travellers.

Namaste Cafe at 43 Macrossan St has good breakfasts, such as muesli with fruit, croissants, or eggs on toast, from $3 to $6, and gourmet sandwiches, salads and burgers from $5. On Grant St just off Macrossan St, the friendly *Mariposa Health Foods* has great smoothies, juices and healthy rolls and sandwiches. Next door are *EJ's Takeaway*, with fish & chips and burgers, and the *Port Douglas Bakery*.

The *Court House Hotel* on the corner of Macrossan and Wharf Sts has an outdoor eating area with meals ranging from $8 to $10, and the *Combined Services Club*, a great old tin and timber building on the waterfront, has bistro meals from $7 to $10.

The *Iron Bar Restaurant* at 5 Macrossan St is decked out like an outback woolshed and specialises in Aussie tucker, and across at No 4 the *Mango Jam Cafe* is a lively and popular bar/restaurant with tasty gourmet pizzas ($12 to $15), pasta, salads and lots more.

On Grant St near the Macrossan St corner, the BYO *Taste of Thailand* has mains from $13, while across at 31 Macrossan St, *Porofinos* is a licensed bistro with good pasta, curries, pizzas and salads from $10 to $15.

Port's best-known restaurant is the bizarre *Going Bananas* (☎ (070) 99 5400) at 87 Davidson St. The décor is almost beyond description – a sort of post-cyclone tropical forest look – and the service is often equally strange. It's quite expensive, with mains from $20 to $26, but well worth the splurge.

Entertainment

On Macrossan St, the *Court House Hotel* has live bands in the beer garden on weekends, the nearby *Iron Bar Restaurant* has live music in the back bar and cane toad races on Wednesday night, and, farther up, the *Mango Jam Cafe* has live music on Tuesday and Friday.

Upstairs in the Marina complex are *FJ's Nightclub* and the *Tide Tavern*, with three bars and live bands three nights a week. There's also the *Wave Bar & Nightclub* on Macrossan St near the Grant St corner.

The bar at *Going Bananas* is a popular watering hole, or you could always pop into the *Sheraton Mirage Resort* for a drink – it's worth a look.

Getting There & Away

Bus The Port Douglas transit centre (☎ (070) 99 5351) is just off Wharf St. Coral Coaches (☎ (070) 98 2600) covers the Cairns to Cooktown coastal route via Port Douglas, Mossman, Daintree, Cape Tribulation and Bloomfield. It has a dozen buses a day between Cairns and Port Douglas (1½ hours, $14.20), about 15 buses a day from Port Douglas to Mossman ($5.20), twice-daily buses to Daintree village ($9.20) and Cape Tribulation (2½ hours, $19), and buses to Cooktown via the (coastal) Bloomfield Track on Tuesday, Thursday and Saturday (about six hours, $41.50). Every Wednesday, Friday and Sunday, they go from Cairns to Cooktown via the inland road (about 5½ hours, $44.90).

Coral Coaches usually lets you stop over as often as you like along the route, so it can be as good as any tour. Owing to the ruggedness of some of the roads, the possibility of delays, and the frequent hopping in and out of the variety of vehicles that cover different sections of the route, riding with Coral Coaches is about as close as you come in Australia to Third World travel – and it's fun.

Boat The daily *Quicksilver* (070) 99 5500) fast catamaran service between Cairns and the Marina at Port Douglas costs $20/30 one way/return.

Getting Around

Avis, National and Budget all have offices on Macrossan St. Cheaper local operators include Network (☎ (070) 99 5111) and Crocodile Car Rentals (☎ (070) 99 555), who specialise in 4WD hire.

Port is very compact, and the best way to get around is by bike. Port Douglas Bike Hire at 40 Macrossan St and the Port o' Call Lodge both hire out good bikes for $10 a day. Call ☎ (070) 99 5345 for a taxi.

MOSSMAN (pop 1800)

Mossman, Australia's most northerly sugar town and a centre for tropical fruit-growing, has a couple of accommodation places but is of little interest. At beautiful **Mossman Gorge**, five km west, there are some excellent swimming holes and rapids and a three-km circuit walking track through rainforest. Coral Coaches runs buses up to the gorge from Mossman and Port Douglas.

Places to Stay & Eat

You can't camp at the Gorge, but there's a creekside caravan park next to the swimming pool in Mossman. The old green and cream *Exchange Hotel* in the centre of town has basic but clean pub rooms at $15/30. The *Demi-View Motel* (☎ (070) 98 1277) at 41 Front St has budget rooms at $50/60, and the *White Cockatoo Cabins* (☎ (070) 98 2222), one km south of the centre, has good self-contained cabins from $65 a double.

The best eatery is the *Mill St Cafe* opposite the Exchange Hotel, with cooked breakfasts for $4.90 and excellent sandwiches and cakes.

DAINTREE

The highway continues 36 km beyond Mossman to the tiny village of Daintree, passing the turn-off to the Daintree River ferry after 24 km.

Originally established as a logging town, with timber cutters concentrating on the prized red cedars that were so common in this area, Daintree is now known as a centre for river cruises along the mighty Daintree River. It's a fairly quiet little backwater, with a couple of shops and cafes and several good B&Bs. The Timber Museum, Gallery & Shop is worth a look, although the pieces for sale carry astronomical price tags.

Daintree River Tours

There are about a dozen operators offering river trips on the Daintree from various points between the ferry and Daintree village. It's certainly a worthwhile activity Birdlife is prolific, and in the cooler months (April-September) croc sightings are common, especially on sunny days when the tide is low, as they love to sun themselves on the exposed banks.

The larger commercial operators include the Daintree Rainforest River Trains (based beside the ferry crossing), with one-hour cruises for $12 and 1½ hour cruises for $20 and the more low-key Daintree River & Cruise Centre (four km beyond the ferry turn-off on the Mossman to Daintree road) with one-hour cruises for $10 and 1½ hour cruises for $15. These operators can take about 50 to 60 passengers in their boats and mainly cater for people on packaged tours but they will also take passing travellers along.

There are several operators that offer more personalised tours for smaller groups. Chris Dahlberg's Specialised River Tours (☎ (070) 98 6169), based at the Red Mill B&B in Daintree village, takes groups of up to 12 people, and Chris is an enthusiastic birdwatcher and knowledgeable guide. His two-hour trips depart at 6.30 am in winter and 6 am in summer and cost $25. Mangrove Adventures (☎ (070) 90 7017), based 300 metres before the ferry crossing, takes up to five people on two-hour tours ($30), half day cruises ($50) and two-hour night tour ($30).

Places to Stay

The *Daintree Riverview Caravan Park* (☎ (070) 98 6119) has tent sites for $12 and on-site vans from $32.

There are several B&Bs in Daintree. The excellent *Red Mill House* (☎ (070) 98 6169) in the centre of town has three comfortable rooms, lovely spacious gardens and a pool. The cost is from $25/60 for singles/doubles, which includes a delicious breakfast on the balcony. *Views of the Daintree* (☎ (070) 98 6118), on Stewart Creek Rd, is a modern homestead with great views over the big river. There are two separate double rooms with en suites at $75, including breakfast.

There's also the impressive *Daintree Eco Lodge* (☎ (070) 98 6100), with classy timber lodges starting at $275/325 for singles/doubles.

Places to Eat
In Daintree village, *Barney's Place* is a casual takeaway cafe with sandwiches, burgers and main meals from $10, while across the road the *Big Barramundi* has an outdoor eating area with light snacks and meals such as tasty barbecued barramundi with salad ($13). There's also the excellent *Baaru House* restaurant at the Daintree Eco Lodge, with buffet breakfasts for $15, light lunches from $5 to $12 and dinner mains in the $17 to $20 range.

CAPE TRIBULATION AREA
After crossing the Daintree River by ferry, there's another 34 km of alternating sealed and unsealed road, with a few hills and creek crossings, to Cape Tribulation. The road is quite good and, unless there has been exceptionally heavy rain, conventional vehicles can make it easily, with care, to Cape Trib.

Cape Tribulation was named by Captain Cook; it was a little north of here that trouble started when his ship ran onto the Endeavour Reef. Mt Sorrow was also named by Cook.

In the 1970s, much of this coast was a seldom-visited hippie outpost, with settlements like Cedar Bay, north of Cape Trib between Bloomfield and Cooktown. These days, Cape Tribulation is much more accessible and there's a steady stream of operators ferrying tourists up from Port Douglas and Cairns. It's no longer quite isolated, but it's still an incredibly beautiful stretch of coast, and it is one of the few places in Australia where tropical rainforest meets the sea.

Remember, however, that this is rainforest – you'll need to bring mosquito repellent. Approaching Cape Trib from the south, the last bank is at Mossman. You can get petrol at two or three places between Mossman and Cooktown along this coastal route.

Note that accommodation at Cape Trib is limited and often booked out during peak holiday periods – ring in advance to make sure there will be a bed for you when you arrive.

Getting There & Away
See the Cairns and Port Douglas sections for details of the buses between those places and Cape Trib. There are also some excellent deals for tours out of Cairns and Port Douglas that include accommodation at the Cape Trib hostels; for example, $74 including one night's accommodation or $86 including two nights. See Organised Tours & Cruises in the Cairns section for more details.

It's quite easy to hitch because, beyond the Daintree ferry, all vehicles have to head to Cape Trib – there's nowhere else to go!

Daintree River to Cape Tribulation
The Daintree River ferry is the gateway to Cape Trib. Ferries operate every few minutes from 6 am to midnight and cost $6 for a car, $3 for a motorbike and $1 for a pedestrian.

Three km beyond the ferry, Cape Kimberley Rd leads down to Cape Kimberley beach, five km away. About nine km from the ferry, just after you cross the spectacular Heights of Alexandra range, is the **Daintree Rainforest Environmental Centre** – an excellent information centre with rainforest displays, a self-guided forest boardwalk and an audio-visual show. It's open daily from 9 am to 5 pm; entry is $8.

About 12 km from the ferry you reach Buchanan Creek Rd, which is the turn-off for **Cow Bay** (5.5 km) and Crocodylus Village.

Farther on, the road strikes the shore at **Thornton Beach**. The **Marrdja Botanical Walk**, at Noah Creek, is an interesting 800-metre boardwalk through rainforest and mangroves. **Noah Beach**, with a QNP&WS

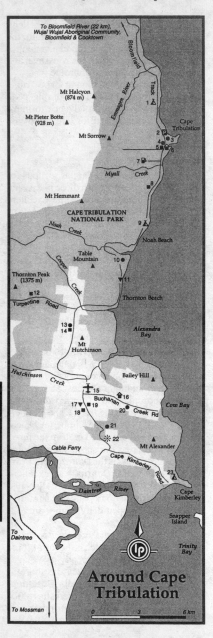

Around Cape Tribulation

camping ground, is eight km before Cape Trib.

Places to Stay & Eat At Cape Kimberley beach, *Club Daintree* (☎ (070) 90 7500) is a beachfront camping park with camp sites for $6 per person, tent-cabins for $8 per person and four-share cabins from $90 a night.

Crocodylus Village (☎ (070) 98 9166) is an associate YHA hostel 2.5 km off the main Cape Trib road, down Buchanan Creek Rd. It's set in the rainforest and has spacious, elevated canvas cabins. There's a pool, a small store, a cafe and a bar. The 16 to 20-bed dorms are $14 ($15 nonmembers). There are also cabins with a double bed, six bunks and bathrooms; these cost $50 a double plus $10 for each extra person. You can hire bikes and the hostel vehicle runs guests to and from Cow Bay beach. The hostel also organises quite a few activities, including informative guided walks through the forests each

Queensland's Wet Tropics World Heritage Area

Nearly all of Australia was covered in rainforest 50 million years ago, but by the time Europeans arrived, only about 1% of the rainforest was left. Today, logging and clearing for farms have reduced that amount to less than 0.3% – about 20,000 sq km of which more than half is in Queensland.

The biggest area of surviving virgin wet tropical rainforest covers the ranges from south of Mossman up to Cooktown. It's called the Greater Daintree.

Throughout the 1980s, a series of battles over the future of the forests was waged between conservationists, the timber industry and the Queensland government. The conservationists argued that apart from the usual reasons for saving rainforests – such as combating the greenhouse effect and preserving species' habitats – this forest region has special value because it's such a diverse genetic storehouse. The timber industry's case, aside from job losses, was that only a small percentage of the rainforest was used for timber – and then not destructively, since cutting is selective and time is left for the forest to regenerate before being logged again.

The 1983 fight over the controversial Bloomfield Track, from Cape Tribulation to the Bloomfield River, drew international attention to the fight to save Queensland's rainforests. The greenies may have lost that battle but the exposure of the blockade indirectly led to a Federal government move in 1987 to nominate Queensland's wet tropical rainforests for World Heritage listing. The area was listed in 1988, with a total ban on commercial logging in the area.

Stretching from Townsville to Cooktown, the Wet Tropics World Heritage Area covers 900,000 hectares of the coast and hinterland, and includes the Atherton Tableland, Mission Beach, Mossman Gorge, Jourama Falls, Mt Spec and the Daintree-Cape Tribulation area. The scenery is diverse and spectacular, ranging from coastal mangroves and eucalypt forest to some of the oldest rainforest in the world.

A 1993 survey found that 80% of north Queenslanders now support the wet tropics area. Part of the reason for the turnaround has been ecotourism – the buzzword of the 1990s and north Queensland's green gold mine. With reef and rainforest-related tourism now easily eclipsing sugar production as the Far North's biggest industry, the rainforests have become a vital part of the area's livelihood. The challenge now is to learn how to manage and minimise the environmental impact of the enormous growth in tourism and population. ■

morning and evening, half-day horse rides ($35), a three-hour sunrise paddletrek ($30) and a two-day sea-kayaking trip to Snapper Island ($139 with everything supplied).

Back on the Cape Trib road near the turn-off, the new *Cow Bay Hotel* (☎ (070) 98 9011) has bistro meals and motel units at $55/60. Across the road there's also the *Rainforest Retreat* (☎ (070) 98 9101), with self-contained motel units from $50/70 and a 20-bed bunkhouse at $15 per person. Next door, *Latitudes 16.12°* is an open-fronted restaurant with everything from burgers and curries to coral trout and barramundi.

About five km north of the Cow Bay turning is *Lync-Haven* (☎ (070) 98 9155), a 16-hectare property with walking trails, plenty of wildlife, a cafe/restaurant, tent sites at $10 and self-contained, six-berth cabins from $65 a double plus $10 for each extra person.

On the Turpentine Rd, which runs inland along the left bank of the Cooper Creek near Thornton Beach, the secluded *Heritage Lodge* (☎ (070) 98 9138) is a small, low-key resort with its own restaurant, a great swimming hole and motel-style units from $109 a double.

At Thornton Beach, the *Thornton Beach Kiosk* is a laid-back beachfront eatery, with takeaways and a bar/cafe with good meals from $5 to $12 and a popular pizza/pasta night on Fridays. You can take a one-hour morning cruise up Cooper Creek from here ($12). Farther north on the beachfront is the self-registration *Noah Beach Camping Area*, with 16 shady sites, toilets and water – permits can be booked through the rangers at Cape Trib (☎ (070) 98 0052).

Cape Tribulation

Cape Tribulation is famed for its superb scenery, with long beaches stretching north and south from the low, forest-covered cape. If you want to do more than relax on the beach, there is a good range of activities, which can be booked directly or through wherever you're staying. Paul Mason's Cape Trib Guided Rainforest Walks (☎ (070) 98 0070) has four-hour daytime walks ($18) and 2½-hour night walks ($20).The boats *H₂O* (☎ (070) 98 9166) and *Taipan Lady* (☎ (070) 98 0040) both offer cruises out to the reef (from $55 including lunch and snorkelling gear), and Wundu Trailrides (☎ (070) 98 9156) offers three-hour horse rides ($35).

The **Bat House**, opposite PK's, is a small rainforest information and education centre, open daily from 10 am to 4 pm.

Places to Stay & Eat

PK's Jungle Village (☎ (070) 98 0040) is a very well set up backpackers hostel, with comfortable log cabins, a pool, a bar, and a restaurant with cheap meals. The nightly cost in an eight-bed cabin is $15 per person, four-share cabins are $46 a double (or $60/76 for triples/quads), or you can camp in the grounds for $7. PK's has a strong party atmosphere, so if you're looking for peace and quiet you'll be better off down at Crocodylus Village.

Across the road from PK's, the *Cape Homestead* (☎ (070) 980034) is a resort complex with 15 safari-tent-cabins at $50 a double plus $10 for each extra person, tent sites at $20 a double and camper-van sites at $25 a double. Facilities include a pool, cafe, shop and laundry. Beside the resort, the *Boardwalk Takeaway* is open from 8 am to 7 pm and serves good breakfasts, burgers and sandwiches at very reasonable prices, and has a limited range of groceries.

Three km north of PK's, the *Pilgrim Sands Holiday Park* (☎ (070) 98 0030) is set in the thick of the forest, with a short walk down to

a secluded beach. Tent sites are $11.50 for two, a four-bed cabin is $46 a double, and two-bedroom units (five beds) with bathroom are $63 a double; extra persons cost $10. This place closes from November until Easter.

Three km south of the cape, the *Coconut Beach Rainforest Resort* (☎ (070) 98 0033) has stylish units with all the mod-cons from $180 a double and villas from $250 a night.

CAPE TRIBULATION TO COOKTOWN

Heading north from Cape Tribulation, the Bloomfield Track (4WD only) continues through the forest as far as the **Wujal Wujal** Aboriginal community 22 km north, on the far side of the Bloomfield River crossing. Even for 4WD vehicles, some sections of the Bloomfield Track can be impassable after heavy rain.

From Wujal Wujal another dirt road – rough but usually passable in a conventional vehicle in the Dry – heads 46 km north through the tiny settlements of **Bloomfield**, **Rossville** and **Helenvale** to meet the main to Cooktown road (also dirt) 28 km before Cooktown.

Places to Stay & Eat

Bloomfield Beach Camping (☎ (070) 60 8207), 11 km north of the Bloomfield River crossing, has a pleasant setting and tent sites for $6 per person and on-site tents at $18 per person (bedding supplied), plus a bar and restaurant. It also offers tours and river cruises. The *Bloomfield Wilderness Lodge* (☎ (070) 35 9166) is close to the mouth of the Bloomfield River and aims to make holes in fat wallets, with package deals from $885/1500 for singles/doubles for three nights, including air transfers, meals and activities.

Signposted 33 km north of the Bloomfield River, the simple *Home Rule Rainforest Lodge* (☎ (070) 60 3925) has a lovely and peaceful setting, with a bar, good cooking facilities and/or cheap meals. They have bunk rooms at $15 per person and camping at $6 per person. There's a two-hour walk to a nearby waterfall, and horse riding is available. Ring from Rossville for a pick-up.

Nine km north at Helenvale, the *Lion's Den Hotel* is a colourful, 1875 bush pub with corrugated tin walls and a slab-timber bar. It has cheap meals and you can camp out the back by the river ($2) or stay in the spartan rooms for $15/20.

CAIRNS TO COOKTOWN – THE INLAND ROAD

The 'main' road up from Cairns loops through Kuranda, Mareeba, Mt Molloy, the tungsten mining town of Mt Carbine, Palmer River and Lakeland, where the road up to Cape York Peninsula splits off. Most of the second half of this 341-km road is unsealed, and often corrugated.

In **Mt Molloy**, the *National Hotel* (☎ (070) 94 1133) has cheap accommodation. James Venture Mulligan, the man who started both the Palmer River and Hodgkinson River gold rushes, is buried in the Mt Molloy cemetery. At the **Palmer River** crossing there's a cafe/petrol station and a camping ground. The 1873 to 1883 Palmer River gold rush occurred in very remote country about 70 km west of here. Its main towns were Palmerville and Maytown, of which very little are left today.

Shortly before Cooktown, the road passes **Black Mountain**, a pile of thousands of granite boulders. It's said that between the huge rocks there are ways that will take you under the hill from one side to the other, but people have died trying to find them. Black Mountain is known to Aboriginal people as Kalcajagga – 'Place of the Spears'. The colour comes not from the rocks, but from lichen growing on them.

COOKTOWN (pop 1300)

Cooktown can claim to have been Australia's first British settlement. From June to August 1770, Captain Cook beached his barque *Endeavour* here, and during that time, Joseph Banks, the chief naturalist, took the chance to study Australian flora and fauna along the banks of the Endeavour River. Banks collected 186 plant species and wrote the first European description of a kangaroo. The north side of the river has scarcely changed since then.

The British explorers had amicable contacts with the local Aboriginal people, but race relations in the area turned sour a century later when Cooktown was founded as the unruly port for the 1873 to 1883 Palmer River gold rush 140 km south-west. Hell's Gate, a narrow pass on the track between Cooktown and the Palmer River, was the scene of frequent ambushes as Aboriginal people tried to stop their lands being overrun. Battle Camp, about 60 km inland from Cooktown, was the site of a major battle between Whites and Cape York Aboriginal people.

In 1874, before Cairns was even thought of, Cooktown was the second-biggest town in Queensland. At its peak there were no less than 94 pubs, almost as many brothels, and the population was over 30,000! As many as half of the inhabitants were Chinese, and their industrious presence led to some wild race riots.

After the gold rush ended, cyclones and a WW II evacuation came close to killing Cooktown. The opening of the excellent James Cook Historical Museum in 1970 started to bring in some visitor dollars although Cooktown's population is still only around 1300 and only three pubs remain.

The effort of getting to Cooktown is rewarded not only by the atmosphere but by some fascinating reminders of the area's past. With a vehicle, you can use the town as a base for visiting the Quinkan rock art near Laura or even Lakefield National Park.

Orientation & Information

Cooktown is on the inland side of a north-pointing headland sheltering the mouth of the Endeavour River. Charlotte St runs south from the wharf, and along it are the three pubs, a post office, a bank, several cafes and a restaurant.

The Cooktown Tourist Information Centre (☎ (070) 69 6100) is in O'Connor Arcade on Charlotte St, between the Cooktown Hotel and Westcoast Hotel.

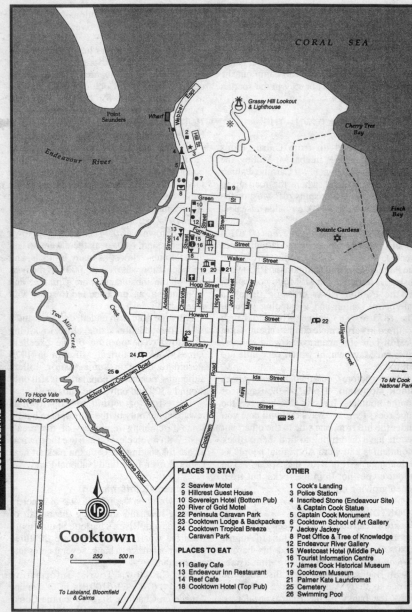

CORAL SEA

Point Saunders

Wharf

Endeavour River

Grassy Hill Lookout & Lighthouse

Cherry Tree Bay

Finch Bay

Botanic Gardens

Chinaman Creek

Two Mile Creek

Green St

Furneaux Street

Walker Street

Hogg Street

Howard Street

Boundary Street

McIvor River-Cooktown Road

Webber Espl

Hill St

Adelaide

Charlotte

Helen

John Street

May Street

Hope

Street

Cooktown Development Road

Ida Street

Mason Street

Racecourse Road

South Road

To Hope Vale
Aboriginal Community

To Mt Cook
National Park

To Lakeland, Bloomfield
& Cairns

QUEENSLAND

Cooktown

0   250   500 m

PLACES TO STAY

2   Seaview Motel
9   Hillcrest Guest House
10 Sovereign Hotel (Bottom Pub)
20 River of Gold Motel
22 Peninsula Caravan Park
23 Cooktown Lodge & Backpackers
24 Cooktown Tropical Breeze
    Caravan Park

PLACES TO EAT

11 Galley Cafe
13 Endeavour Inn Restaurant
14 Reef Cafe
18 Cooktown Hotel (Top Pub)

OTHER

1   Cook's Landing
3   Police Station
4   Inscribed Stone (Endeavour Site)
    & Captain Cook Statue
5   Captain Cook Monument
6   Cooktown School of Art Gallery
7   Jackey Jackey
8   Post Office & Tree of Knowledge
12 Endeavour River Gallery
15 Westcoast Hotel (Middle Pub)
16 Tourist Information Centre
17 James Cook Historical Museum
19 Cooktown Museum
21 Palmer Kate Laundromat
25 Cemetery
26 Swimming Pool

Things to See

Charlotte St has a number of interesting monuments, including one to the tragic Mary Watson (see the Lizard Island section) opposite the Sovereign Hotel. A little farther towards the wharf are memorials to the equally tragic explorer, Edmund Kennedy, and to Captain Cook. Behind these is a cannon, which was sent from Brisbane in 1885 along with three cannonballs, two rifles and one officer in response to Cooktown's plea for defences against a feared Russian invasion! Right by the waterside, a stone with an inscription marks the spot where the *Endeavour* was careened.

The **James Cook Historical Museum** on Helen St, near the corner of Furneaux St, has some fascinating displays relating to all aspects of Cooktown's past: Aboriginal people, Cook's voyages, the Palmer River gold rush and the Chinese community. The museum is open daily from 9.30 am to 4 pm (shorter hours January to March) and costs $5. The **Cooktown Museum** a block away on Walker St isn't really worth the admission price – it's more of a souvenir shop.

On Charlotte St, the **Endeavour River Gallery** houses the Vera Scarth Collection, a series of beautifully detailed colour paintings of local plants. Farther along, the **Jackey Jackey** has a window display of interesting historical photos, and across the road is the **School of Art Gallery**.

The **Cooktown Cemetery** on the McIvor River-Cooktown Rd is worth a visit. There are many interesting graves including those of Mary Watson and the 'Normanby Woman' – thought to have been a north European who survived a shipwreck as a child and lived with Aboriginal people for years until 'rescued' by Whites. She died soon after.

There are spectacular views from the lookout up on **Grassy Hill**. The very pleasant **Botanic Gardens**, off Walker St, were first planted in 1886 and restored in 1984. Walking trails lead from the gardens to the beaches at Cherry Tree and Finch bays.

Organised Tours

An interesting range of tours from Cooktown is on offer; these can be booked directly or through the tourist office.

Cooktown Cruises (☎ (070) 69 5712) has a two-hour scenic cruise up to the head of the Endeavour River and back via a mangrove creek ($18); departing daily at 2 pm.

Cooktown Tours (☎ (070) 69 5301) offers 1½-hour town tours ($16) and half-day trips to Black Mountain and the Lion's Den Hotel ($45); both depart daily at 10 am.

A local botanist, John McLean, takes walking tours around town daily at 9 am and 4 pm ($5), and Reel River Fishing (☎ (070) 69 5346) offers lure-fishing trips on weekends and during school holidays (from $65 per person for a half-day).

Munbah Aboriginal Cultural Tours has day trips to various sights around town including the Coloured Sands and Cape Bedford ($89 including lunch), and you can take an interesting trip on the local bus out to the Hope Vale Aboriginal Community ($20 return, departures on weekdays at 7.30 am and 3 pm).

Places to Stay

There are two good caravan parks: the *Tropical Breeze Caravan Park* (☎ (070) 69 5417) on the McIvor River-Cooktown Rd, and the *Peninsula Caravan Park* (☎ (070) 69 5407) in the bush at the end of Howard St. Both have tent sites, on-site vans and units.

Cooktown Lodge & Backpackers (☎ (070) 69 5166), on the corner of Charlotte and Boundary Sts, is a comfortable, well-equipped hostel with a pool, good kitchen, and TV lounge. Bunks are $13 the first night, then $12 a night, and singles/doubles are $20/30. The *Hillcrest Guest House* (☎ (070) 69 5305) on Hope St is a friendly old place with singles/doubles with shared facilities from $20/40.

The impressive *Sovereign Hotel* (☎ (070) 69 5400), with the Bottom Pub, is on the corner of Charlotte and Green Sts. It has a superb pool and a good range of accommodation, from budget motel rooms from $42/52 to luxury two-bedroom apartments at $132. The *Seaview Motel* (☎ (070) 69 5377) on Webber Esplanade has good units from

$55 a double, and the modern *River of Gold Motel* (☎ (070) 69 5222) on the corner of Hope and Walker Sts has doubles from $64.

Places to Eat

There are two supermarkets and a couple of fairly average cafes, the *Galley* and the *Reef Cafe*, along the main street. The *Cooktown Hotel* (Top Pub) has a good beer garden with decent bistro meals from $6 to $12, or the *Sovereign Hotel* has an excellent balcony restaurant upstairs with tables overlooking the river and mains for about $14 at lunchtime and from $16 to $20 at dinner.

The *Endeavour Inn*, on the corner of Charlotte and Furneaux Sts, is a relaxed colonial-style restaurant with a small bar, a courtyard dining area and live entertainment most weekends. They have a good reputation for their food – mains range from $17 to $19.

Getting There & Away

Air Flight West has daily flights between Cairns and Cooktown for $71, although a discount return fare of $85 is sometimes available. Endeavour Air has charter flights from here to Lizard Island – see the Lizard Island section below.

Bus Coral Coaches (☎ (070) 98 2600) travels from Cairns to Cooktown via the inland road on Wednesday, Friday and Sunday (6½ hours, $44.90) and via the Bloomfield Track on Tuesdays, Thursdays and Saturdays (8½ hours, $49.60).

Getting Around

The Hire Shop (☎ (070) 69 5601), on Charlotte St just north of the Sovereign Hotel, has cars and boats for hire.

LIZARD ISLAND

Lizard Island, the farthest north of the Barrier Reef resort islands, is about 100 km from Cooktown. It was named by Joseph Banks after the numerous lizards he saw there. He and Cook spent a day on the island, trying to find a way out through the reef to the open sea.

A tragedy occurred on the island in 1881

when a settler's wife, Mary Watson, took to sea in a large metal pot with her son and a Chinese servant, after Aboriginal people killed her other servant while her husband was away fishing. The three eventually died of thirst on a barren island to the north, Mary leaving a diary of their terrible last days. Their tragic story is told at the Cooktown museum.

Lizard is dry, rocky and mountainous, with superb beaches, great swimming and snorkelling, the remains of the Watsons' cottage, a pricey resort and a QNP&WS camping ground. There are plenty of bushwalks and birdlife, and great views from Cook's Look, the highest point on the island, from where Captain Cook surveyed the area.

Places to Stay

There's a small QNP&WS camping ground at Watson's Bay. It has a fireplace, pit toilet, picnic table and a hand-pumped water supply 250 metres away. Camping permits are available from the QNP&WS office (☎ (070) 52 3096) in Cairns, and you must take all supplies because the resort won't sell you any. You'll also need charcoal for the barbecues as all timber on the island, including driftwood, is protected.

At the exclusive *Lizard Island Resort* (☎ (070) 60 3999), singles/doubles cost $520/860 per day, including all meals and use of the facilities. Because of its isolation, the resort has been a favourite retreat for celebrities, and a popular stop for yachties, for many years.

Getting There & Away

Sunstate Airlines flies from Cairns for $169 one way, and Aussie Airways (☎ (070) 53 3980) has a good day trip from Cairns for $299 per person including lunch and snorkelling gear. Endeavour Air (☎ (070) 69 5860) has day trips from Cooktown for $130 and does camping drop-offs costing $370 each way for up to five people – well worth considering if you're staying a few days or more.

Cape York Peninsula

The Cape York Peninsula is one of the wildest and least populated parts of Australia. The Tip, as it is called, is the most northerly point on the mainland of Australia, and islands dot the Torres Strait between here and Papua New Guinea, only 150 km away.

Getting up to the Tip along the rough and rugged Peninsula Developmental Road is still one of Australia's great road adventures. It's a trip for the tough and experienced since the roads are all dirt, and even at the height of the Dry there are some difficult river crossings. In the last few years, several tour operators have sprung up to offer this adventure to those who can't or don't want to go it alone.

Of the numerous books on the Cape, Ron and Viv Moon's *Cape York – An Adventurer's Guide* ($20) is the most comprehensive. Lonely Planet's *Outback Australia* and *Queensland* guides have extensive information for travellers to Cape York.

Information & Permits

Visits to the RACQ, the Far North Queensland Promotion Bureau and the QNP&WS offices in Cairns are well worthwhile before you head north. You no longer need a permit to visit Aboriginal or Torres Strait Islander communities, but it's advisable to make contact beforehand by letter or radio phone. Phone the Aboriginal Co-ordinating Council ☎ (070) 31 2623) in Cairns for contact numbers and addresses. Apart from Bamaga, most of the mainland Aboriginal communities are well off the main track north, and do not have any facilities or accommodation for travellers.

Getting There & Away

Air Sunstate/Qantas flies daily from Cairns to Bamaga ($288), Lizard Island ($169) and Thursday Island ($323). Ansett flies to Weipa ($226). Flight West also operates a daily service through the Peninsula and to the Torres Strait Islands.

Cape York Air (☎ (070) 35 9399) operates the Peninsula Mail Run, claimed to be the longest in the world. It flies to remote cattle stations and towns every weekday and will take passengers along, with round trips costing from $155 to $300 depending on the length of the trip.

Bus There are no bus services all the way to the top but, from April to October, Cape York Coaches (☎ (070) 93 0176) operates a weekly service between Cairns and Weipa (13½ hours, $235 return).

Sea Jardine Shipping (☎ (070) 35 1900) operates a weekly barge service from Cairns to Thursday Island and Bamaga ($650 per vehicle and $250 per passenger), while Gulf Freight Services (☎ (070) 69 8619) operates barge services between Weipa and Karumba (about $300 per vehicle and $200 per passenger).

Driving to the Top Every year, more and more hardy travellers equipped with their own 4WD vehicles or trail bikes, make the long haul up to the top of Cape York. Apart from being able to say you have been as far north as you can get in Australia, you also test yourself against some pretty hard going and see some wild and wonderful country into the bargain.

The travelling season is from mid-May to mid-November but the beginning and end of that period are borderline, depending on how late or early the wet season is. The best time is June to September, while during the wet season nothing moves by road at all. Conventional vehicles can usually reach Coen and even, with care and skill, get across to Weipa on the Gulf of Carpentaria but it's *very* rough going. If you want to continue north from the Weipa turn-off to the top, you'll need 4WD, a winch and lots of strong steel wire.

The major problem is the many river crossings; even as late as June or July the rivers will still be swift-flowing and they

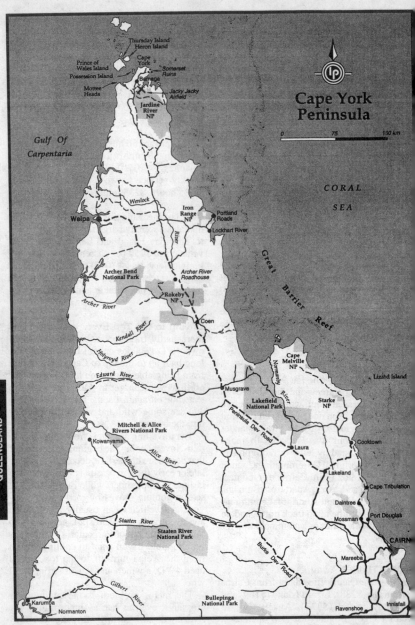

frequently alter their course. The rivers often have very steep banks. The Great Dividing Range runs right up the spine of the peninsula and rivers run east and west off it. Although the rivers in the south of the peninsula flow only in the wet season, those farther north flow year-round.

The ideal set-up for a Cape York expedition is two 4WD vehicles travelling together – one can haul the other out where necessary. You can also make it to the top on motorbikes, floating the machines across the wider rivers. There are usually large truck inner tubes left at the river crossings for this purpose. Beware of crocodiles!

Several Cairns operators hire out 4WDs and equipment for Cape York expeditions, including Marlin Truck & 4WD Rentals (☎ (070) 31 2360) and Brits: Australia (☎ (070) 32 2611) – minimum hire periods apply.

Organised Tours A host of companies operates 4WD tours from Cairns to Cape York. The trips generally range from six to 16 days, and take in Cooktown, Laura, the Quinkan rock-art galleries, Lakefield National Park, Coen, Weipa, Indian Head Falls, Bamaga, Somerset, Cape York itself and Thursday Island.

Travel on standard tours is in 4WDs with five to 12 passengers, accommodation is in tents and all food is supplied. Some of the better-known 4WD tour operators include Oz Tours Safaris (☎ (070) 55 9535), Australian Outback Travel (☎ (070) 31 5833), Heritage 4WD Tours (☎ (070) 38 2186), Kamp Out Safaris (☎ (070) 31 4862), New Look Adventures (☎ (070) 31 7622) and Wild Track Adventure Safaris (☎ (070) 55 2247), the last two being among the most experienced operators and with excellent reputations.

Most of the companies offer a variety of alternatives, such as to fly or sail one way, and travel overland the other. Expect to pay about $1000 to $1300 for a seven-day fly/drive tour, about $1600 for a seven-day sail/drive tour, and anywhere from $1200 to $2000 for a 12 to 14-day safari.

Cape York Motorcycle Adventures (☎ (070) 59 0220) offers a five-day trip for $1550 or a 12-day trip for $3650. Prices include bike hire, all meals and equipment.

The *Kangaroo Explorer* (☎ (070) 55 8188) operates cruises from Cairns to Cape York and Thursday Island, with a choice of a return cruise, or a one-way cruise with a return flight. Four-day cruises range from $1300 to $1700, seven-day cruises range from $1700 to $2400. Costs include all meals, activities and flights.

LAKELAND & LAURA

The Peninsula Developmental Road turns off the Cairns to Cooktown inland road at Lakeland. Facilities here include a general store with food, petrol and diesel, a small caravan/camping park and a hotel-motel. From Lakeland it's 734 km to Bamaga, almost at the top of the peninsula. The first stretch to Laura is not too bad, just some corrugations, potholes, grids and causeways – the creek crossings are bridged. It gets worse.

About 52 km from Lakeland is the turn-off to the **Quinkan Aboriginal rock-art galleries** at Split Rock, located in spectacular sandstone country. The art was executed by Aboriginal tribes whose descendants were decimated during the Palmer River gold rush of the 1870s. The four main galleries at Quinkan – the only ones open to visitors – contain some superb examples of well-preserved rock paintings dating back 14,000 years. Entry to the park costs $3 per person (self-guided) or $5 per person (ranger guided). The rangers also take groups on day tours of the galleries, but you need to book (☎ (070) 60 3214).

Laura, 12 km north of Split Rock, has a general store with food and fuel, a place for minor mechanical repairs, a post office, a Commonwealth Bank agency, a pleasant pub, an airstrip and a museum with Aboriginal art.

At the Jowalbinna Bush Camp (☎ (070) 60 3236), 40 km west of Laura by 4WD, the Trezise Bush Guide Service (☎ (070) 55 1865) offers excellent guided trips to some

QUEENSLAND

of the magnificent rock-art sites in the area ($50 per adult), as well as one, three and four-day safaris to the galleries from Cairns (from $295 to $695). Visitors can stay overnight at the bush camp.

The major event is the Laura Aboriginal Dance and Cultural Festival, held every second year (odd numbers) on the last weekend of June. All the Cape York Aboriginal communities assemble for this festival, which is a great opportunity for outsiders to witness living Aboriginal culture.

Lakefield National Park

The main turn-off to Lakefield National Park is just past Laura and it's only about a 45-minute drive from Laura into the park. Conventional vehicles can get as far as the ranger station at New Laura, and possibly well into the northern section of the park during the dry season.

Lakefield is the second-largest national park in Queensland and the most accessible of those on the Cape York Peninsula. It's best known for its wetlands and associated wildlife. The park's extensive river system drains into Princess Charlotte Bay on its northern perimeter. This is the only national park on the peninsula where fishing is permitted, and a canoe is a good way to investigate the park. Watch out for the crocs! For camping permits see the rangers at New Laura (☎ (070) 60 3260) or Lakefield (☎ (070) 60 3271), farther north in the park.

The wide sweep of Princess Charlotte Bay, which includes the coastal section of Lakefield National Park, is the site of some of Australia's biggest rock-art galleries. Unfortunately, this stretch of coast is extremely hard to reach except from the sea.

LAURA TO ARCHER RIVER ROADHOUSE

North from Laura, there's the Hann River crossing and the *Hann River Roadhouse* (☎ (070) 60 3242) at the 75-km mark. Another 60 km on is **Musgrave** with its historic *Musgrave Telegraph Station* (☎ (070) 60 3229), built in 1887. The station has accommodation at $20/30 for

singles/doubles as well as camp sites, an STD phone, a cafe and an airstrip, and you can get petrol, diesel, food and beer here.

Coen, 245 km north of Laura, is virtually the capital of the peninsula with a pub, two general stores, a hospital, school and police station. You can get mechanical repairs done here. Coen has an airstrip and a racecourse where picnic races are held in August. The whole peninsula closes down for this event. The *Exchange Hotel* (☎ (070) 60 1133) has pub rooms at $25/35 and units at $35/45, and the delightful Mrs Taylor's *Homestead Guest House* (☎ (070) 60 1157) has singles/doubles at $40/50 and home-cooked meals.

Beside the Archer River, 66 km north of Coen, the *Archer River Roadhouse* (☎ (070) 60 3266) has great burgers as well as beer, fuel and groceries, and can handle minor mechanical repairs. There are camp sites, or units at $20 per person.

Northern National Parks

Four national parks can be reached from the main track north of Coen. To stay at any of them you must be totally self-sufficient. Only a few km north of Coen, before Archer River Roadhouse, you can turn west to **Rokeby National Park** and **Archer Bend National Park** – the ranger station is in Rokeby, about 70 km off the main track. Access is for 4WD only.

These little-visited parks cover a large area including the McIlwraith Range in Rokeby and, in the west of very remote Archer Bend, the junction of the Coen and Archer rivers. There are no facilities but bush camping is permitted at a number of river sites in Rokeby. These parks are best explored by bushwalkers. Contact the QNP&WS office in Coen (☎ (070) 60 1137) for more information.

Around 21 km north of the Archer River Roadhouse is the turn-off to Portland Roads, the Lockhart River Aboriginal community and **Iron Range National Park**. The 150-km road into the tiny coastal settlement of Portland Roads passes through the national park. Although still pretty rough, this track has een improved. If you visit the national park, egister with the ranger (☎ (070) 60 7170) on rrival. It has the rugged hills of the Janet and ozer ranges, beautiful coastal scenery and Australia's largest area of lowland rainforest, plus some animals which are also found in New Guinea but no further south in Australia. Bush camping is permitted.

The fourth of the northern national parks s the **Jardine River National Park**.

WEIPA (pop 2500)
Weipa is 135 km from the main track. The outhern turn-off to it is about 20 km north of the Iron Range turn-off, and this road has een realigned and greatly improved – you an cover the distance in only a couple of ours. You can also get to Weipa from Batavia Downs, which is a little farther up he main track and has a 19th-century homestead. The two approaches converge about halfway along.

Weipa is a modern mining town that works he world's largest deposits of bauxite (the ore from which aluminium is processed). The mining company, Comalco, runs regular ours of its operations from May to December. The town has a wide range of facilities ncluding a motel, a hotel and a camping ground.

In the vicinity, there's interesting country o explore, good fishing and some pleasant amping sites.

NORTH TO THE JARDINE
Back on the main track, after Batavia Downs, there are almost 200 km of rough oad and numerous river crossings (the Wenlock and the Dulhunty being the two major ones) before you reach the Jardine River ferry crossing. Between the Wenlock River and the Jardine ferry there are two possible routes: the more direct but rougher old route (116 km), and the more circuitous but quicker new route (159 km), which branches off the old route about one km past he South Alice Creek crossing. Don't miss **Indian Head Falls**, one of the most popular amping and swimming spots on the Cape.

The Jardine River ferry, operated by the Injinoo Community Council, operates daily from 8 am to 5 pm. The ferry fee is a steep $80 return. There's a roadhouse beside the crossing.

Stretching east to the coast from the main track is the **Jardine River National Park** . The Jardine River spills more fresh water into the sea than any other river in Australia. It's wild impenetrable country.

THE TOP
The first settlement north of the Jardine River is **Bamaga**, the Cape's largest Torres Strait Islander community. The town has postal facilities, a hospital, a Commonwealth Bank agency, STD phones, a supermarket, mechanical repairs and fuel. It's only about 40 km from Bamaga to the very northern tip. **Seisia**, on the coast five km north-west, has a good camping ground with units.

North-east of Bamaga, off the Cape York track and about 11 km south-east of the cape, is **Somerset**, which was established in 1863 as a haven for shipwrecked sailors and a signal to the rest of the world that this was British territory. It was hoped at one time that it might become a major trading centre, a sort of Singapore of north Queensland, but it was closed in 1879 when its functions were moved to Thursday Island, which was also thought more suitable for a pearling industry. The story of Somerset is inextricably linked with the adventurous Jardine family, one of whom stayed on after Somerset was officially closed to run his own cattle stations, coconut plantation and pearling business. He married a Samoan princess and entertained passing British dignitaries. He and his wife are buried at Somerset. Sadly, apart from a few of Jardine's coconut trees, there's nothing much left at Somerset now, but the fishing is good and there are lovely views.

At **Cape York** itself are two resorts. *Pajinka Wilderness Lodge* (☎ (070) 31 3988), 400 metres from the Tip, is a luxury resort with cabin-style rooms ranging from $180 to $250 per person, including all meals. It also has a small camping ground with a kiosk, toilets and showers. Sites cost $7 per person. The scenic *Punsand Bay Private*

QUEENSLAND

Reserve (☎ (070) 69 1722) provides more modest accommodation on the western side of the cape. There are cabins and permanent tents or you can pitch your own in the camping ground. Sites cost $7 per person; cabins and permanent tents are from $65 to $95 per person, including meals.

TORRES STRAIT ISLANDS (pop 5000)

The Torres Strait Islands have been a part of Queensland since 1879, the best-known of them being Thursday Island. The 70 other islands are sprinkled from Cape York in the south almost to New Guinea in the north but only 17 are inhabited, and all but three are set aside for islanders. Most visitors to Cape York take a look at Thursday Island or the nearby islands.

Torres Strait Islanders came from Melanesia and Polynesia about 2000 years ago, bringing with them a more material culture than that of the mainland Aboriginal people. The strait saw violence from early days right through to WW II, including head-hunters, marauding pirates, greedy men in pursuit of pearls, 'blackbirders' and Japanese bombs. Christianity, replacing warlike islander cults, has done well this century. **Possession Island**, an uninhabited national park close to Cape York, was where Captain Cook 'claimed' all the east coast of Australia for England in 1770.

The islands' economy is based on fishing but it's hard to compete with the technology used by outfits on Australia's east coast. There is high islander unemployment and economic difficulties have led to cries for compensation, even independence.

It was a claim by a Torres Strait Islander, Eddie Mabo, to traditional ownership of Murray Island that eventually led to the High Court handing down its ground-breaking Mabo ruling. The court's decision in turn became the basis for the Federal government's 1993 Native Title legislation (see Government in the Facts about the Country chapter).

Thursday Island is hilly, just over three sq km in area. At one time, it was a major pearling centre and the cemeteries tell the hard tale of what a dangerous occupation it was. Some pearls are still produced here from seeded 'culture farms', which don't offer much employment to the locals. The island has also lost its importance as a halt for vessels but it's still a popular pause for passing yachties.

Thursday Island is a rough-and-ready but generally easy-going place and its main appeal is its cultural mix – Asians, Europeans and Pacific Islanders have all contributed to its history.

Places to Stay Options include the *Jumula Dubbins Hostel* (☎ (070) 69 2122), at $23 a single, the *Federal Hotel* (☎ (070) 69 1569) at $80 a double, and the *Jardine Motel* (☎ (070) 69 1555), at $150 a double. Accommodation is also available on Horn Island at the *Gateway Torres Strait Resort* (☎ (070) 69 1902) and the *Wongai Tavern* (☎ (070) 69 1683).

Getting There & Around Sunstate/Qantas and Flight West fly between Cairns and Thursday Island. The airport is actually on nearby Horn Island – a ferry links the two islands. Several smaller airlines operate flights around the other islands in the strait.

Peddell's Ferry & Tourist Service (☎ (070) 69 1551) operates ferry services from Seisia, Pajinka and Punsand Bay on the mainland to Thursday Island daily except Sundays. One-way fares range from $35 to $45.

Gulf Savannah

The Gulf Savannah is a vast, flat and sparsely populated landscape of bushland, saltpans and savannah grasslands, all cut by a huge number of tidal creeks and rivers that feed into the Gulf of Carpentaria. During the Wet the dirt roads turn to mud and even the sealed roads can be flooded, so June to September is the safest time to visit this area.

Although Burke and Wills were the first Europeans to pass through the Gulf (see

History in the Facts about the Country chapter), the coast of the Gulf of Carpentaria had been charted by Dutch explorers before Cook's visit to Australia. The actual coastline of the Gulf is mainly mangrove swamps, which is why there is little habitation there.

Two of the settlements in the region, Burketown and Normanton, were founded in the 1860s, before better-known places on the Pacific coast such as Cairns and Cooktown. Europeans settled the area as sheep and cattle country, also in the hope of providing a western port for produce from farther east and south in Queensland.

Today the Gulf is mainly cattle country. It's a remote, hot, tough region with excellent fishing and a large crocodile population. Mornington Island, in the Gulf itself 120 km north of Burketown, is an Aboriginal community.

For tourist information, advice on road conditions and general enquiries, contact the Gulf Local Authorities Development Association, 55 McLeod St, Cairns (☎ (070) 31 1631).

Fishing
A large proportion of visitors to the Gulf come for the fishing – especially the famed barramundi fishing. Karumba and Normanton are the major mainland bases, and there are several fishing resorts in the Gulf of Carpentaria: *Sweers Island Resort* (☎ (077) 48 5544) on Sweers Island charges $160 per person per day, while the *Birri Fishing Resort* (☎ (077) 45 7277) on Mornington Island costs $220 per person per day (open March to October only). Rates include accommodation and all meals, as well as fishing guides, boat hire, fishing equipment, bait and tackle. There are flights to both islands from Cairns, Karumba and Burketown.

Savannah Guides
The Savannah Guides are a network of professionals who staff guide posts at strategic locations throughout the Gulf. They are people with good local knowledge, and they have access to points of interest, many of which are on private property and would be difficult to visit unaccompanied. Contact the Undara Experience office (☎ (070) 31 7933) at 57 McLeod St in Cairns for more information on the guides.

Getting There & Around
Air Flight West Airlines flies a few times a week between Cairns and various places in the Gulf, including Normanton ($270), Karumba ($294), Julia Creek ($341), Burketown ($356) and Mornington Island ($367).

Bus Cairns-Karumba Coachline (☎ (070) 35 1853) has a service three times a week between Cairns and Karumba (12 hours, $116) via Undara ($40), Georgetown ($61), Croydon ($83) and Normanton ($105). Campbell's Coaches (☎ (077) 43 2006) has a weekly bus service from Mt Isa to Normanton ($64) and Karumba ($70).

Train Although there are no train services into the Gulf, there are two very popular short services within the Gulf. The famous *Gulflander* (☎ (077) 45 1391), a weird-looking, snub-nosed vintage train, travels the 153 km between Croydon and Normanton (four hours, $35), leaving Normanton every Wednesday and returning from Croydon every Thursday. The newer *Savannahlander* runs twice-weekly between Mt Surprise and Forsayth (120 km, five hours, $35), leaving Mt Surprise every Monday and Thursday and returning from Forsayth every Tuesday and Friday.

There are bus services from Cairns that connect with both trains.

Car & Motorbike There are two main roads into the Gulf region. The Gulf Developmental Road takes you from the Kennedy Highway, south of the Atherton Tablelands, across to Normanton (450 km, about 300 km of which is sealed), while the Burke Developmental Road runs north from Cloncurry to Normanton (378 km, sealed all the way) via the Burke & Wills Roadhouse. There is also a sealed road between Julia Creek and the Burke & Wills Roadhouse.

QUEENSLAND

Other roads through the region are unsealed. They include the continuation of the Burke Developmental Road from Normanton to Mareeba (710 km, 4WD only), and the Gulf Track, which runs roughly parallel with the coast from Normanton to the Northern Territory (460 km) via Burketown. There's also an unsealed 332-km road from Camooweal, west of Mt Isa, to Burketown, with a turn-off at Gregory Downs to Lawn Hill National Park. If you're driving on any of these roads, make sure you seek advice on road conditions and fuel stops, and carry plenty of water with you.

GULF DEVELOPMENTAL ROAD
Undara Lava Tubes
These massive volcanic tubes were formed around 190,000 years ago after the eruption of a single shield volcano. Huge lava flows drained towards the sea, forming a surface crust as they cooled. Meanwhile, molten lava continued to flow through the centre of the tubes, eventually leaving these hollow basalt chambers.

The *Undara Lava Lodge's* (☎ (070) 97 1411) resident guides run full-day tours ($70) and half-day tours ($52) – both of which include lunch – and 1½-hour introductory tours ($18). The lodge also has three accommodation options: camping/caravan sites ($8 per person); semi-permanent tents ($14 per person or $56 with breakfast, lunch and dinner); and charmingly restored old railway carriages ($96 per person including breakfast, lunch and dinner). There's a restaurant and bar but no shops here so, if you're self-catering, you'll need to bring supplies.

The turn-off to Undara is 17 km past the start of the Gulf Developmental Road and from there it's another 15 km of corrugated dirt road to the lodge. If you're travelling by bus, the lodge will pick you up from the turn-off.

Undara to Croydon
Mt Surprise, 39 km past the Undara turn-off, is the starting point for the *Savannahlander* train. The town has a curiosity museum, a caravan park, two roadhouses and the *Mt*

Surprise Hotel (☎ (070) 62 3118), which has basic rooms for $20.

The **Elizabeth Creek** gemfield, 42 km north-west of Mt Surprise and accessible by conventional vehicle in the Dry, is Australia's best topaz field. Information on the field is available at the Mt Surprise service station (☎ (070) 62 3153).

South and west of Mt Surprise are the old mining townships of Einasleigh and Forsayth, which you can visit on the *Savannahlander*. If you're driving, there's also a (poorly-marked) road off the highway midway between Mt Surprise and Georgetown – it's a slow and bumpy 150-km loop through the towns and back to the highway. **Einasleigh** is a ramshackle little place with a collection of mostly derelict tin buildings. Einasleigh Gorge, good for swimming, is just across the road from the Einasleigh pub. **Forsayth** isn't much bigger, although it is perhaps a little more alive, and the *Goldfields Hotel* (☎ (070) 62 5374) has aircon rooms at $45 per person including breakfast and dinner. Forty-five km south of Forsayth is the scenic **Cobbold Gorge**, where the *Cobbold Camping Village* (☎ (070) 62 5470) offers full-day tours ($75) and half-day tours ($45).

Back on the highway midway between Mt Surprise and Georgetown, you can soak yourself in the **Tallaroo Hot Springs** ($8, April to September only). **Georgetown** is an uninspiring service centre, although the *Latara Resort Motel* (☎ (070) 62 1190) one km west has good singles/doubles at $45/55.

Croydon (pop 220)
Connected to Normanton by the *Gulflander* train, this old gold-mining town was once the biggest in the Gulf. It's reckoned that at one time there were 5000 gold mines in the area and reminders of them are scattered all around the countryside. Such was the prosperity of the town that it had its own aerated water factory, gas street lamps, a foundry and coach builders.

By the end of WW I the gold had run out and the town became little more than a ghost town, but there are still a few interesting istoric buildings here, including the old shire hall, the **courthouse**, the **mining warden's office** and the **Club Hotel**.

The *Club Hotel* (☎ (077) 45 6184) has backpacker beds on the upstairs verandah for $8, pub rooms at $23/33 and motel units at $28/43; meals are available. The publican runs tours of old mining areas in a horse-drawn cart.

Normanton (pop 1200)

Normanton was first set up as a port for the Cloncurry copperfields but then became Croydon's gold-rush port, its population peaking at 3000 in 1891. Today it's the Gulf's major town, a bustling little centre with good barramundi fishing and a handful of historic buildings. These include the railway station, a lovely Victorian-era building that houses the *Gulflander* train when it's not travelling to Croydon and back.

Accommodation includes a caravan park, the *Albion Hotel* (☎ (077) 45 1218) with beds in miners' huts at $15 (often booked out) or motel-style units at $50, and the *Gulfland Motel* (☎ (077) 45 1290), which has good singles/doubles at $50/60.

Karumba (pop 600)

Karumba, 69 km from Normanton by sealed road and actually on the Gulf at the mangrove fringed mouth of the **Norman River**, is a prawn, barramundi and crab-fishing centre. It's possible to hire boats for fishing trips from here, and there's a regular vehicular barge between Karumba and Weipa.

The town has quite an interesting history. At one time it was a refuelling station for the Qantas flying boats that used to connect Sydney and the UK. The RAAF also had Catalina flying boats based here.

Most of the accommodation places cater for fishing enthusiasts. The *Karumba Lodge Motel* (☎ (077) 45 9143) charges $55/65 for singles/doubles, and the *Gulf Country Caravan Park* (☎ (077) 45 9148) has on-site cabins.

NORMANTON TO CLONCURRY

South of Normanton, the flat plains are inter-rupted by a solitary hill beside the road – Bang Bang Jump-up. The *Burke & Wills Roadhouse* (☎ (077) 42 5909), 195 km south of Normanton, has four air-con rooms at $30/40 and a few camping sites at $3.50 per person. **Quamby**, 43 km north of Cloncurry, was originally a Cobb & Co coach stop. The historic *Quamby Hotel* (☎ (077) 42 5952) has air-con rooms at $20 per person, and a pool.

NORMANTON TO THE NORTHERN TERRITORY BORDER

The historic Gulf Track stretches from Normanton across to Roper Bar in the Northern Territory. Although the entire route is along unsealed roads, a 4WD vehicle isn't normally required during the dry season.

Camp 119, the northernmost camp of the Burke & Wills expedition of 1861, is signposted 37 km west of Normanton. Also of interest are the spectacular **Leichhardt Falls** and **Floraville Station**, both about 160 km west of Normanton.

With a population of about 230, **Burketown** is probably best known for its isolation. It's in the centre of a cattle-raising area, and is close to the Albert River and about 25 km south of the Gulf. Some of Nevil Shute's novel *A Town Like Alice* is set here.

Burketown is an excellent place for birdwatching, and is also one of the places where you can view the phenomenon known as 'Morning Glory' – weird tubular cloud formations extending the full length of the horizon, which roll out of the Gulf in the early morning, often in lines of three or four. This only happens from September to November.

The town's focal point is the *Burketown Pub* (☎ (077) 45 5104), a great old pub housed in the former customs house, with pub rooms upstairs from $25/40 and motel-style units from $50/70. Cheaper backpacker beds are sometimes available. There's also a caravan park (no on-site vans).

Escott Lodge (☎ (077) 48 5577), 17 km north-west of Burketown, is a working cattle station and fishing resort with camp sites and singles/doubles from $45/75; meals and tours are available.

QUEENSLAND

The *Hell's Gate Roadhouse* (☎ (077) 45 8258), 175 km west of Burketown, has meals, camp sites, 4WD tours (groups of five or more) and four air-con rooms with B&B from $25 per person.

BURKETOWN TO CAMOOWEAL

This road is the most direct route to Lawn Hill National Park, although for conventional vehicles the mostly sealed route via the Burke & Wills Roadhouse provides much easier access to the park.

The *Gregory Downs Hotel* (☎ (077) 48 5566), 117 km south of Burketown, is the main turn-off to Lawn Hill. The pub sells fuel and has motel units at $46/57 or you can camp out the back on the river bank. There's a great swimming hole here, and every Labour Day in May the pub hosts the Gregory River Canoe Races – great fun if you're in the area.

Lawn Hill National Park

Amid arid country 100 km west of Gregory Downs, the Lawn Hill Gorge is an oasis of gorges, creeks, ponds and tropical vegetation that the Aboriginal people have enjoyed for perhaps 30,000 years. Their paintings and old camping sites abound. Two rock-art sites have been made accessible to visitors. There are freshwater crocodiles – the inoffensive variety – in the creek. Also in the park are extensive and virtually unexplored limestone formations.

Getting there is the problem – it's a beautiful, pristine place that's miles from anywhere or anybody. The last 300 km or so from Mt Isa – after you leave the Barkly Highway – are unsealed and often impassable after rain. A 4WD vehicle is recommended, though it is not always necessary in the dry season. There are 20 km of walking tracks as well as a camping ground with showers and toilets; book sites with the park rangers (☎ (077) 48 5572) or the QNP&WS in Mt Isa (☎ (077) 43 2055). *Adel's Grove Kiosk* (☎ (077) 48 5502), 10 km east of the park entrance, sells fuel and basic food supplies. It also has a camping ground, and canoes for hire ($6 an hour).

Outback

Heading west from the Queensland coast across the Great Dividing Range, the land soon starts to become drier, and the towns smaller and farther apart.

The outback, although sparsely settled, is well serviced by major roads. The Flinders Highway connects northern Queensland with the Northern Territory, meeting the Barkly Highway at Cloncurry; the Capricorn Highway runs along the Tropic of Capricorn from Rockhampton to Longreach; and the Landsborough and Mitchell highways run from the New South Wales border south of Cunnamulla right up to Mt Isa.

Once off these major arteries, however, road conditions deteriorate rapidly, services are virtually nonexistent and you need to be fully self-sufficient, carrying spare parts, fuel and water. With the correct preparation, it's possible to make the great outback journeys down the tracks that connect Queensland with South Australia – the Strzelecki and Birdsville tracks.

Getting There & Away

Air The major towns of the outback are serviced by Flight West Airlines. Ansett also has flights to Mt Isa from Cairns and Brisbane, while Augusta Airways (☎ (086) 42 3100) flies on Saturday from Port Augusta (South Australia) to Birdsville ($205 one way), Bedourie and Boulia.

Bus Greyhound Pioneer and McCafferty's both operate three major bus routes through the outback: from Townsville to Mt Isa, from Rockhampton to Longreach, and from Brisbane to Mt Isa (via Longreach). From Mt Isa you can continue west into the Northern Territory.

Train Similarly, there are three train services heading inland from the coast, all running twice weekly: the *Spirit of the Outback* from Brisbane to Longreach (via Rockhampton), the *Westlander* from Brisbane to Charleville (with connecting buses to Cunnamulla and Quilpie), and the *Inlander* from Townsville to Mt Isa.

CHARTERS TOWERS TO CLONCURRY

As a scenic drive, the Flinders Highway is probably the most boring route in Queensland, although there are a few points of interest along the way to break the monotony. The highway was originally a Cobb & Co coach run, and along its length are a series of small towns that were established as stopovers for the coaches. **Pentland**, 105 km west of Charters Towers, and **Torrens Creek**, 50 km farther on, both have pubs, fuel and camping grounds. At **Prairie**, 200 km west of Charters Towers, the friendly and historic *Prairie Hotel* (☎ (077) 41 5121) has singles/doubles ranging from $15/30 to $30/40, or you can camp out the back for $5.

Hughenden, a busy commercial centre on the banks of the Flinders River, bills itself as 'the home of beauty and the beast'. The 'beast' is imprisoned in the **Dinosaur Display Centre** on Gray St – a replica of the skeleton of *Muttaburrasaurus*, one of the largest and most complete dinosaur skeletons found in Australia.

The 'beauty' is the **Porcupine Gorge National Park**, an oasis in the dry country north of Hughenden. It's about 70 km along the mostly unsealed, often corrugated Kennedy Developmental Road to **Pyramid Lookout**. You can camp here and it's an easy 30-minute walk down into the gorge, with some fine rock formations and a permanent creek. Few people come here and there's a fair bit of wildlife. The Kennedy Developmental Road would eventually take you to the Atherton Tableland, but it would be a pretty rough trip.

Back in town, the *Allan Terry Caravan Park* opposite the railway station has sites for $8 and on-site vans from $20, and the town swimming pool is next door. The *Grand Hotel* (☎ (077) 41 1588), on the corner of Gray and Stanfield Sts, has timber-lined pub rooms at $15/30.

Keep your eyes open for wild emus and brolgas on the Hughenden to Cloncurry stretch.

Richmond, 112 km from Hughenden, and **Julia Creek**, 144 km farther on, are both small towns with motels and caravan/camping parks. From Julia Creek, a sealed road turns off north to Normanton (420 km) and Karumba (494 km) on the Gulf of Carpentaria. You can also reach Burketown (467 km) this way; see the Gulf Savannah section for more information on these towns.

CLONCURRY (pop 3220)

The centre for a copper boom in the last century, Cloncurry was the largest copper producer in the British Empire in 1916. Today it's a pastoral centre, and the town's major claim to fame is as the birthplace of the Royal Flying Doctor Service.

The **John Flynn Place Museum & Art Gallery** in Daintree St houses interesting exhibits on mining, the Royal Flying Doctor Service and the School of the Air. It is open weekdays from 7 am to 4 pm, and from May to October weekends also from 9 am to 3 pm; entry costs $4.

Cloncurry's **Mary Kathleen Park & Museum**, on the east side of town, is partly housed in buildings transported from Mary Kathleen and includes relics of the Burke and Wills expedition and a big collection of local rocks and minerals. The Burke Developmental Road, north from Cloncurry, is sealed all the way to Normanton (375 km) and Karumba (446 km).

Places to Stay

You can camp in the *Cloncurry Caravan Park* opposite the museum, or there's the *Wagon Wheel Motel* (☎ (077) 42 1866) at 54 Ramsay St with budget singles/doubles from $35/45. On the eastern edge of town are the *Gilbert Park Cabins* (☎ (077) 42 2300), with modern self-contained units from $42/48 or $50/55 with linen.

CLONCURRY TO MT ISA

This 124-km stretch of the Flinders Highway has a number of interesting stops. At **Corella River**, 41 km west of Cloncurry, there's a memorial cairn to the Burke and Wills expedition, which passed here in 1861. Another

QUEENSLAND

Last Stand of the Kalkadoons

Before the coming of the Europeans, the arid and rocky hill country to the north-west of Mt Isa was home to the Kalkadoons, one of the fiercest and most warlike of the Aboriginal tribes. They were one of the last tribes to resist White settlement, and from the mid-1870s they conducted a guerilla-type war, frequently ambushing settlers and police.

In 1884 the authorities sent Frederick Urquhart, the Sub-Inspector of Police, to the region to take command. In September of that year, Urquhart gathered his troops and, heavily armed, they rode to the rocky hill that came to be known as Battle Mountain. The Kalkadoons, with only their spears for weapons, stood no chance against the carbines of the troopers and were all but wiped out in a bloody massacre that marked the end of Aboriginal resistance in the region.

A memorial beside the Barkly Highway, 42 km west of Cloncurry, is inscribed with the words: *You who pass by are now entering the ancient tribal lands of the Kalkadoon/Mitakoodi, dispossessed by the European. Honour their name, be brother and sister to their descendants.* ■

km down the road is the **Kalkadoon and Mitakoodi Memorial**, which marks an old Aboriginal tribal boundary (see the aside on the Kalkadoons).

Nine km beyond this is the former site of **Mary Kathleen**, a uranium-mining town from the 1950s to 1982. It has been completely demolished.

The turning to **Lake Julius**, Mt Isa's reserve water supply, is 36 km beyond Mary Kathleen. It's 90 km of unsealed and bumpy road north to the lake, which is a popular spot for fishing, canoeing, sailing and other water sports. The *Lake Julius Recreation Camp* has camp sites ($2.60 per person), dorm beds ($5.50 per person) and there are self-contained units ($32.60 for up to four).

Battle Mountain, north of the Lake Julius dam wall, was the scene of the last stand of the Kalkadoon people in 1884. About 40 km north-east of the lake is the tiny township of **Kajabbi**, where the historic *Kalkadoon Hotel* (☎ (077) 42 5979) has Trevor (the guitar-playing publican), Saturday night barbecues and budget accommodation.

MT ISA (pop 24,250)

The mining town of Mt Isa owes its existence to an immensely rich copper, silver, lead and zinc mine. The skyline is dominated by the massive 270-metre-high exhaust stack from the lead smelter. 'The Isa', as the town is known locally, is a rough and ready but prosperous town, and the job opportunities here have attracted people from about 60 different ethnic groups. There's plenty of low-cost accommodation, and you can tour the mine.

The first Mt Isa deposits were discovered in 1923 by the prospector, John Campbell Miles, who gave Mt Isa its name – a corruption of Mt Ida, a goldfield in Western Australia. Since the ore deposits were large and low-grade, working them required the sort of investment only a company could make. Mt Isa Mines was founded in 1924 but it was during and after WW II that Mt Isa really took off, and today it's the Western world's biggest silver and lead producer. Virtually the whole town is run by Mt Isa Mines, and the ore is transported 900 km to Townsville by rail.

Orientation & Information

The town centre, a fairly compact area, is immediately east of the Leichhardt River which separates it from the mining area.

The Riversleigh Fossils Centre & Tourist Information Office (☎ (077) 49 1555), in Centenary Park on Marian St, is open weekdays from 8.30 am to 4.30 pm, and on weekends (between April and September) from 9 am to 2 pm.

The Crusade Bookshop, at 11 Simpson St is the best bookshop between Townsville and Darwin.

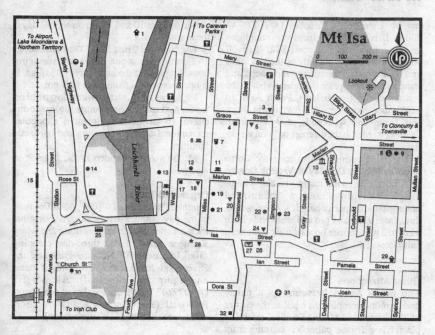

Mt Isa

0   100   200 m

To Airport,
Lake Moondarra &
Northern Territory

To Caravan
Parks

To Cloncurry &
Townsville

To Irish Club

PLACES TO STAY	20	Los Toros Mexican Restaurant	10	Frank Aston Museum
1	Mt Isa Youth Hostel	24	Red Lantern Chinese Restaurant	12	Cinema Mt Isa
4	Burke & Wills Isa Resort Motel	28	Tavern	13	Civic Centre
17	Boyd Hotel			14	Royal Flying Doctor Service
29	Travellers Haven	**OTHER**		15	Train Station
32	Walton's Motel	2	Campbell's Coaches & Long-Distance Bus Terminal	19	Flight West Airlines
PLACES TO EAT			21	Ansett
3	Pizza Hut	7	Switches Nightclub	22	Crusade Bookshop
5	Buffalo Club	8	Tourist Centre & Riversleigh Fossils Interpretive Centre	23	Curly Dan's Outdoor World
6	Bazza's Cafe			25	Swimming Pool
11	Flamenco Cafe	9	Kalkadoon Tribal Centre	26	Police Station
16	Clicks Cafe			27	Post Office
18	Mt Isa Hotel			30	John Middlin Mining Display
				31	Hospital

The Mine

The mine is the major attraction and there are two tours available.

The three-hour underground tour, for which you don a hard hat and miner's suit, takes you down into some of the 4600 km of tunnels. Tours leave Monday to Friday at 8.15 and 11.45 am and cost $25. Book ahead on ☎ (077) 44 2104 – there's a maximum of nine on each tour, and you must be over 16 years of age.

The two-hour surface tours (by bus) are

run by Campbell's Coaches (☎ (077) 43 2006). Drivers pick up from various places on request and the tour costs $12. It's well worth the money, especially as the bus takes you right through the major workshops and mine site, and the price includes a visit to the visitors centre (see below). From April to September, tours depart weekdays at 9 am and 1 pm and weekends at 9 am; from October to March they depart only on weekdays at 9 am.

The mine company also runs the **John Middlin Mining Display & Visitor Centre** on Church St, with audio-visuals, photographic displays and a 'simulated underground experience'. It's open weekdays from 9 am to 4 pm and weekends from 9 am to 2 pm (shorter hours during summer); entry costs $4.

Other Attractions

The **Frank Aston Museum**, is a partly underground complex on a hill at the corner of Shackleton and Marina Sts. This rambling place has a diverse collection ranging from old mining gear to ageing flying doctor radios, and displays on the Lardil Aboriginal people of Mornington Island in the Gulf of Carpentaria and the Kalkadoon people from the Mt Isa area. It's open daily from 10 am to 3 pm and costs $4.

At the tourist office, the **Riversleigh Fossils Interpretive Centre** has a collection of 15-million-year-old fossils that have revealed much about Australia's prehistoric animals. The fossils were found on a station near Lawn Hill National Park, 250 km north-west of Mt Isa.

Next to the tourist office, the **Kalkadoon Tribal Centre & Culture-Keeping Place** has a small collection of artefacts.

You can visit the **Royal Flying Doctor Service** base on the Barkly Highway, weekdays from 9 am to 5 pm and on weekends from 10 am to 2 pm. The $2.50 admission includes a film. The **School of the Air**, which brings education by radio to children in remote places, is at the Kalkadoon High School on Abel Smith Pde. It's open for

public tours at 10 and 11 am on school days; these cost $2.

The National Trust listed **Tent House**, at 16 Fourth Ave, is one of the last surviving houses typical of the early days of Mt Isa. It is open weekdays from 9 am to 3 pm.

Mt Isa has a big, clean **swimming pool** on Isa St, next to the tennis courts. **Lake Moondarra**, 16 km north of town, is a popular recreational area with boating and barbecue facilities.

Mt Isa's August rodeo is the biggest in Australia.

Organised Tours

Campbell's Coaches (☎ (077) 43 2006) runs a one-day outback trip visiting Aboriginal rock-art sites, an old copper mine and Mary Kathleen ($50); and a three-day camping safari to Lawn Hill National Park and the Riversleigh fossil sites ($290 with all meals and equipment supplied). Air Mt Isa (☎ (077) 43 2844), the local mail run operator, will take tourists along on their twice-weekly runs ($180 per person).

Places to Stay

Camping The *Riverside Tourist Park* (☎ (077) 43 3904), at 195 West St, and the *Copper City Caravan Park* (☎ (077) 43 4676), at 185 West St, are both a couple of km north of the centre on the Leichhardt River; both have swimming pools, tent sites from $12 and on-site vans from $30.

The *Moondarra Caravan Park* (☎ (077) 43 9780), about six km north of town on the road to Lake Moondarra, has shady camp sites by the river bank at $10 for two people.

Hostels The *Travellers Haven* (☎ (077) 43 0313), about half a km from the centre on the corner of Spencer and Pamela Sts, is the best of Isa's budget accommodation options. All the rooms are twin-share and have air-con, with bunk beds from $12 and singles/doubles from $24/28. There's a good pool, and bikes for hire ($10 a day), and its courtesy coach does pick-ups.

Mt Isa's 28-bed *Youth Hostel* (☎ (077) 43 5557), in the shadow of the mines at Wellington Park Rd, costs $10 ($11 nonmembers). It's very basic, and unless Travellers Haven is full it's hard to think of any good reason to stay there.

Pubs & Motels The *Boyd Hotel* (☎ (077) 43 3000) on the corner of West and Marina Sts has basic pub rooms at $20 per person.

Just south of the centre at 23 Camooweal St, *Walton's Motel* (☎ (077) 43 2377) is one of the cheapest motels with singles/doubles from $40/50 and a small pool. The *Copper Gate Motel* (☎ (077) 43 3233), near the eastern entrance to town at 97 Marian St (the Barkly Highway), has rooms from $42/54. If you're looking for something more up-market, the three-star *Burke & Wills Isa Resort* (☎ (077) 43 8000) on the corner of Grace and Camooweal Sts is an impressive modern motel with its own restaurant and pool, and rooms ranging from $85 to $100.

Places to Eat

Mt Isa's clubs are among the best places to eat. The *Irish Club*, two km south of the centre on the corner of Buckley and Nineteenth Aves is excellent value, with smorgasbords at $6.50 for lunch and $12.50 for dinner, and bistro meals from $4 to $10. On the corner of Camooweal and Grace Sts, the *Buffalo Club* also has good meals ranging from $7 to $12. Visitors to the clubs sign in as honorary buffaloes or Irish persons, and dress regulations apply.

The *Tavern*, on Isa St, has good pub food with counter meals from $5 to $10 in the public bar, and meals in the bistro from $10. *Clicks* on West St and *Bazza's Cafe* on Miles St both offer a variety of burgers and sandwiches, while the *Flamenco Cafe* on Marian St also has burgers, sandwiches and 20 flavours of ice cream.

If you've just stepped off an early morning bus, the *Mt Isa Hotel*, on the corner of Marian and Miles Sts, serves good breakfasts from 5.30 to 8.30 am, which cost from $5 to $10.

The very popular *Los Toros Mexican Restaurant* (☎ (077) 43 7718) is a lively cantina-style eatery with main courses in the

$10 to $16 range. It's licensed and open every night except Monday.

Entertainment

Switches Nightclub on Miles St is a big up-market nightclub that is open Wednesday to Saturday until 3 am; there's a $5 cover charge and dress regulations apply.

There are live bands in the *Boyd Hotel* most weekends. Also popular are the *Kave* nightclub in the Mt Isa Hotel and the *Buffalo Club* on Grace St. The *Irish Club* (☎ (077) 43 2577) has a good entertainment programme, with free video nights on Monday and Tuesday and a mixture of live music, a disco and karaoke on weekends – ring to find out what's on.

The *Cinema Mt Isa* (☎ (077) 43 2043) on Marian St screens latest releases.

Getting There & Away

Air Ansett has an office at 8 Miles St and Flight West Airlines (☎ (077) 43 9333) is at 14 Miles St.

Ansett has direct flights daily to Brisbane ($406), on Sunday to Alice Springs ($235) and on Saturday and Sunday to Cairns ($263).

Flight West also flies to Cairns, as well as to Normanton ($248), Karumba ($243) and various other places in the Gulf.

Bus The Campbell's Coaches terminal (☎ (077) 43 3685) at 27 Barkly Highway is the main depot for McCafferty's buses, while Greyhound Pioneer buses stop at the Riversleigh Fossil Centre & Tourist Office on Marian St.

Both companies have daily services between Townsville and Mt Isa (11 hours, $81), continuing on from Mt Isa to Tennant Creek in the Northern Territory (7½ hours, $72). From Tennant Creek you can head north to Darwin ($100) or south to Alice Springs ($76). There are also daily buses south to Brisbane (24 hours, $105) by the inland route through Winton ($47) and Longreach ($53).

Campbell's Coaches goes to Normanton ($64) and Karumba ($70) once a week.

Train The air-con *Inlander* operates twice-weekly between Townsville and Mt Isa, via Charters Towers, Hughenden and Cloncurry. The full journey takes about 18 hours and costs $192 in a 1st-class sleeper, $95 in economy.

MT ISA TO THREEWAYS

Camooweal, 188 km from Mt Isa and 13 km east of the Northern Territory border, was established in 1884 as a service centre for the vast cattle stations of the Barkly Tablelands. It has a couple of historic buildings – in particular, **Freckleton's General Store** is worth a visit – as well as a pub and a couple of roadhouses.

From Camooweal, you can head north to the Lawn Hill National Park and Burketown; see the Gulf Savannah section for details. Eight km south of town is the **Camooweal Caves National Park**, where there is a network of unusual caves and caverns with sinkhole openings. This can be a dangerous place to wander around – there are no facilities, and the road in is rough and unsealed.

There's nothing much for the whole 460 km to the Threeways junction in the Northern Territory. The next petrol station west of Camooweal (and the most expensive petrol anywhere between Townsville and Darwin) is 270 km along at *Barkly Homestead* (☎ (089) 64 4549). You can camp here for $3.50 per person. Motel rooms are $62/72.

MT ISA TO LONGREACH

Fourteen km east of Cloncurry, the narrow Landsborough Highway turns off south-east to McKinlay (91 km), Kynuna (165 km), Winton (328 km) and Longreach (501 km).

McKinlay is a tiny settlement that probably would have been doomed to eternal insignificance were it not for the fact that it is the location of the *Walkabout Creek Hotel* (☎ (077) 46 8424), which featured in the amazingly successful movie *Crocodile Dundee*. Photos from the film and other memorabilia clutter the walls of the pub. Greyhound buses between Mt Isa and Brisbane make a refreshment stop here, and if

you want to hang around there are air-con rooms at $35/45 and tent sites from $10.

Kynuna, another 74 km south-east, isn't much bigger than McKinlay. The *Blue Heeler Hotel* (☎ (077) 46 8650) is another renowned old outback pub, which for some reason has its own surf life-saving club! It's a good spot for a feed – meals are served all day every day until 9.30 pm – and there are pub rooms from $30, motel-style units from $45 and tent sites from $6. The nearest beach may be almost 1000 km away, but every year in September the pub hosts a surf life-saving carnival, complete with surfboard relays, a tug of war and a beach party at night.

The turn-off to the **Combo Waterloo**, which Banjo Patterson is said to have visited in 1895 before he wrote *Waltzing Matilda*, is signposted off the highway about 12 km east of Kynuna.

Winton (pop 1750)

Winton is a sheep-raising centre and also the railhead from which cattle are transported after being brought from the Channel Country by road train. It's a friendly, laid-back place with some interesting attractions and characters, and if you're not in a hurry it's a good place for a stopover.

On Elderslie St, beside the post office, is the **Qantilda Museum**, which commemorates two local claims to fame: the founding of Qantas at Winton in 1920 and the poetry of Banjo Patterson. The museum houses an interesting collection of memorabilia and is open daily from 9 am to 4 pm; entry costs $5. Across the road are the *Jolly Swagman* statue – a tribute to Banjo Patterson and the unknown swagmen who lie in unmarked graves in the area – and the **Winton Swimming Pool**.

The **Royal Theatre**, out the back of the Stopover Cafe in the centre of town, is a wonderful open-air theatre with canvas-slung chairs, corrugated tin walls and a star-studded ceiling. Films are screened every Saturday night and, from April to September, on Wednesday night as well. Entry costs $7.

There are a couple of operators offering

tours from Winton – see the following South of Winton section.

The Gift & Gem Centre (☎ (076) 57 1296) on Elderslie St acts as the local information office. Winton's major festival is the nine-day Outback Festival, held every second year (odd numbers) during the September school holidays.

Places to Stay & Eat The *Matilda Country Caravan Park* (☎ (076) 57 1607), at 43 Chirnside St, has tent sites from $10, on-site vans and cabins from $25 to $45, and back-packer beds in on-site vans at $12.50.

At 67 Elderslie St in the centre of town, the *North Gregory Hotel* (☎ (076) 57 1375) has clean budget rooms with air-con at $20 a head. Opposite the Qantilda Museum, the *Matilda Motel* (☎ (076) 57 1433) has units from $42/47.

The *North Gregory Hotel* has good bistro meals and a beer garden with a char-grill out the back. You can also have a meal in the Qantas Board Room Lounge at the *Winton Club*, where the fledgling airline's first meeting was held back in 1921. The club is one block back from the centre on the corner of Oondooroo and Vindex Sts.

Getting There & Away Winton is on the main Brisbane to Mt Isa bus route. There are also connecting bus services between Winton and Longreach that meet up with the *Spirit of the Outback* train.

South of Winton
Carisbrooke Station (☎ (076) 57 3885), 85 km south-west of Winton, has a wildlife sanctuary, Aboriginal paintings and bora rings (circular ceremonial grounds). The station offers day tours from Winton for $60 and has budget accommodation.

At **Lark Quarry Environmental Park**, 115 km south-west of Winton, dinosaur foot-prints 100 million years old have been perfectly preserved in limestone. It takes about two hours to drive from Winton to Lark Quarry in a conventional vehicle but the dirt road is impassable in wet weather – you can get directions at the Winton Shire

Council offices (☎ (076) 57 1188) at 78 Vindex St. Alternatively, Diamantina Outback Tours (☎ (076) 57 1514) runs day trips from Winton to Lark Quarry for $75 per person.

LONGREACH (pop 4130)
This prosperous outback town was the home of Qantas earlier this century, but these days it's just as famous for the Australian Stockman's Hall of Fame & Outback Heritage Centre, one of the biggest attractions in outback Queensland.

Longreach's human population is vastly outnumbered by the sheep population, which numbers over a million; there are a fair few cattle too.

It was here that the Queensland & North-ern Territory Aerial Service, better known as Qantas, was based in its early days in the 1920s. The original Qantas hangar, which still stands at Longreach airport (almost opposite the Hall of Fame), was also the first aircraft 'factory' in Australia – six DH-50 biplanes were assembled here in 1926. The hangar is home to the new **Qantas Founders Outback Museum**, an aviation museum that features the first aircraft owned by the airline, an Avro 504K. It was due to open in August 1996.

Longreach's tourist office (☎ (076) 58 3555), itself a replica of the first Qantas

Captain Starlight
Longreach was the starting point for one of Queensland's most colourful early crimes when, in 1870, Harry Redford and two accomplices stole 1000 head of cattle and trotted them 2400 km to South Australia, where they were sold. Redford's exploit opened up a new stock route south, and when he was finally brought to justice in 1873 he was found not guilty by an adoring public. Ralph Boldrewood's novel *Robbery Under Arms* later immortalised Redford as 'Captain Starlight'. ■

The first Qantas booking office was opened in Longreach

booking office, is on the corner of Duck and Eagle Sts. It is usually open daily from 9 am to 5 pm.

Stockman's Hall of Fame & Outback Heritage Centre

The centre is housed in a beautifully conceived building, two km east of town along the road to Barcaldine. The excellent displays are divided into periods from the first White settlement through to today, and these deal with all aspects of the pioneering pastoral days. The Hall was built as a tribute to the early explorers and stockmen, and also commemorates the crucial roles played by the pioneer women, Aboriginal stockmen and Aboriginal women.

It's well worth visiting the Hall of Fame, as it gives a fascinating insight into this side of the European development of Australia. Allow yourself half a day to take it all in. Admission is $15 ($10 students), and the centre is open daily from 9 am to 5 pm.

The Outback Travel Centre (☎ (076) 58 1776) operates a bus service from the town centre to the Hall of Fame that costs $5 return and will pick you up from wherever you're staying. Otherwise it's a half-hour walk, or a taxi will cost you about $5.50.

Organised Tours

The Outback Travel Centre (☎ (076) 58 1776) at 115 Eagle St offers a variety of tours including a full-day tour that takes in the Hall of Fame, an outback station and a dinner cruise along the Thomson River for $65.

There are also a couple of operators offering popular sunset dinner cruises along the Thomson River for $20. Book with Yellow-belly Express on ☎ (076) 58 1919 or Billabong Boat Cruises on ☎ (076) 58 1776.

Queensland Helicopters offers scenic flights from the Longreach Aerodrome from $20 per person; book through the tourist office.

Places to Stay & Eat

There is no backpackers hostel in Longreach, although this situation may change – check with the tourist office. The *Gunnadoo Caravan Park* (☎ (076) 58 1781), east of town on the corner of the highway and Thrush Rd, has tent sites at $10 as well as self-contained timber cabins from $45.

Hallview Lodge B&B (☎ (076) 58 3777) is a renovated timber house on the corner of Womproo and Thrush Rds. It has singles/doubles with en suite from $45/58 and does pick-ups from the train and bus terminals.

There's a choice of at least four pubs on Eagle St, including the *Welcome Home Hotel* (☎ (076) 58 1361) with basic air-con pub rooms for $20/35.

The *Aussie Beta Cabins* (☎ (076) 58 2322), on the highway out near the Hall of Fame, has modern self-contained cabins from $55 a double plus $5 for extra persons. Closer to the centre, the *Longreach Motor Inn* (☎ (076) 58 2322) at 84 Galah St has good motel rooms from $60/70.

There's a cafe out at the Hall of Fame, and there are also several cafes, takeaways and a bakery on Eagle St in the centre of town. *Starlight's Hideout Tavern*, also on Eagle St, has good bistro meals in the $8 to $12 range. On the corner of Galah and Swan Sts, the *Bush Verandah Restaurant* is a cosy little BYO with rustic décor and country-style cooking.

Getting There & Away

Flight West has daily flights from Longreach to Brisbane ($322), and also flies twice a week to Winton ($91) and Townsville ($230).

Greyhound Pioneer buses stop at the Outback Travel Centre (☎ (076) 58 1776) at 115 Eagle St, and McCafferty's stops out the back of Longreach Travel World (☎ (076) 58 1155) at 113 Eagle St. Both companies have daily services to Winton (two hours, $20), Mt Isa (7½ hours, $53), and Brisbane (17 hours, $77). McCafferty's also operates three times a week to Rockhampton (nine hours, $51).

The *Spirit of the Outback* train runs twice a week between Longreach and Rockhampton (14 hours, $69 in economy, $160 for a 1st-class sleeper): there are connecting bus services between Longreach and Winton.

LONGREACH TO WINDORAH – Longreach to Windorah

The Thomson Developmental Road is the most direct route for people wanting to cut across towards Birdsville from Longreach. The first half of the trip is a narrow sealed road to **Stonehenge**, a tiny settlement in a dry and rocky landscape with half a dozen tin houses and a pub. The *Stonehenge Hotel* (☎ (076) 58 5944) sells fuel and has rooms from $15 a head.

The second half of the route is over unsealed roads of dirt, gravel and sand. **Jundah**, 65 km south of Stonehenge, is a neat little administrative centre with a pub and a general store.

LONGREACH TO CHARLEVILLE
Ilfracombe (pop 340)

This small town 28 km east of Longreach modestly calls itself 'the Hub of the West' and boasts a railway station, a general store, a swimming pool, a golf course and a pub. Along the highway you'll see the **Ilfracombe Folk Museum**, a scattered collection of historic buildings, farming equipment and carts and buggies. The charming little *Wellshot Hotel* (☎ (076) 58 2106) is well worth a visit and has cheap meals and clean rooms from $20/35.

Barcaldine (pop 1750)

Barcaldine (pronounced 'bar-*call*-din'), at the junction of the Landsborough and Capricorn highways 108 km east of Longreach, gained a place in Australian history in 1891 when it became the headquarters of a major shearers' strike. The confrontation saw the troops called in, and led to the formation of the Australian Workers' Party, the forerunner of today's Australian Labor Party. The **Tree of Knowledge**, a ghost gum near the railway station, was the meeting place of the organisers and still stands as a monument to workers and their rights. There's a tourist office (☎ (076) 51 1724) beside the railway station.

Barcaldine's **Australian Workers Heritage Centre**, built to commemorate the role of workers in the formation of Australian social, political and industrial movements, is one of the most impressive attractions in the outback. Set in landscaped gardens, its excellent displays include a circular theatre-tent, an old one-teacher schoolhouse and a replica of Queensland's Legislative Assembly. It's open daily from 9 am to 5 pm (from 10 am on Sunday); entry costs $5.

QUEENSLAND

The **Barcaldine & District Folk Museum** on the corner of Gidyea and Beech Sts has an eclectic collection of memorabilia and is open daily; entry is $2. On the corner of Pine and Bauhinia Sts is the **Beta Farm Outback Heritage & Wildlife Centre**, a ramshackle farmlet with historic buildings, a fauna park, art studios, and billy tea and damper. It's open most days from April to September; entry costs $7.

Places to Stay & Eat The *Homestead Caravan Park* (☎ (076) 51 1308) on Box St has tent sites, on-site vans and cabins, and the owners of this place run a couple of good day trips. The *Commercial Hotel* (☎ (076) 51 1242) at 67 Oak St has singles/doubles from $15/30 and good bistro meals, and *Charley's Coffee Lounge* next door has home-cooked meals. The *Landsborough Lodge Motel* (☎ (076) 51 1100) on the corner of Box and Boree Sts is the best of the four motels, with doubles from $68.

Blackall (pop 2100)
South of Barcaldine is Blackall, supposedly the site of the mythical Black Stump. Four km north-east is the **Blackall Woolscour**, the only steam-driven scour (wool cleaner) left in Queensland. Built in 1908, it operated up until 1978 and is now open for personalised tours daily from 8 am to 4 pm ($5).

In town, the **Jackie Howe Memorial Statue** is a tribute to this legendary shearer who, in 1892, set a world record by shearing 321 sheep in eight hours – with hand shears!

CHARLEVILLE (pop 3500)
At the junction of the Mitchell and Warrego highways, Charleville is a major outback centre. The town was an important centre for early explorers and, being on the Warrego River, it is something of an oasis.

There's a tourist office (☎ (076) 54 3057) on the corner of Wills and Edward Sts. The **Historic House Museum** is housed in the 1880 Queensland National Bank building at 91 Albert St. South-east of the centre on Park St, the QNP&WS operates a captive breeding programme where you can see several endangered species, including the yellow-footed rock wallaby and the bilby. You can also visit the **Royal Flying Doctor Service Base**, the **School of the Air** and the **Skywatch** observatory at the meteorological bureau, which has high-powered telescopes through which you can study the heavens on any cloudless night from March to November ($8). Book through the tourist office.

Places to Stay & Eat There are a couple of caravan parks and three motels, but the best place to stay is at *Corones Hotel* (☎ (076) 54 1022), a grand old country pub on the corner of Wills and Galatea Sts. Basic pub rooms go for $15/22 while restored heritage-style rooms are great value at $30/40. Next to the pub *Poppa's Caffe* has excellent food.

CUNNAMULLA (pop 1650)
The southernmost town in western Queensland, Cunnamulla is on the Warrego River 120 km north of the Queensland-New South Wales border. It's another sheep-raising centre, noted for its wildflowers. Accommodation options include a caravan park, a pub and a motel.

THE CHANNEL COUNTRY
The remote and sparsely populated southwest corner of Queensland, bordering the Northern Territory, South Australia and New South Wales, takes its name from the myriad channels that crisscross the area. In this inhospitable region it hardly ever rains, but water from the summer monsoon farther north pours into the Channel Country along the Georgina, Hamilton and Diamantina rivers and along Cooper Creek. Flooding towards the great depression of Lake Eyre in South Australia, the mass of water arrives or this huge plain, eventually drying up in water holes or salt pans.

Only on rare occasions (the early '70s and 1989 during this century) does the vast amount of water actually reach Lake Eyre and fill it. For a short period after each wet season, however, the Channel Country does become fertile, and cattle are grazed here.

Getting There & Around

Some roads from the east and north to the fringes of the Channel Country are sealed, but during the October to May wet season even these can be cut, and the dirt roads become quagmires. In addition, the summer heat is unbearable, so a visit is best made in the cooler winter from May to September. Visiting this area requires a sturdy vehicle (4WD if you want to get off the beaten track) and some experience of outback driving. Always carry plenty of drinking water and petrol, and if you're heading off the main roads notify the police, so that if you don't turn up at the next town, the necessary steps can be taken.

The main road through the Channel Country is the **Diamantina Developmental Road**. It runs south from Mt Isa through Boulia to Bedourie and then turns east through Windorah and Quilpie to Charleville. In all, it's a long and lonely 1340 km, a little over half of which is sealed.

Mt Isa to Birdsville

It's 295 km south from Mt Isa to Boulia, and the only facilities along the route are at **Dajarra**, which has a pub and a roadhouse.

Boulia, with a population of 540, is the 'capital' of the Channel Country. Burke and Wills passed through here on their long trek, and there's a museum in a restored 1888 stone house in the little town. Near Boulia, the mysterious Min Min Light, a sort of earthbound UFO, is sometimes seen. It's said to resemble the headlights of a car and can hover a metre or two above the ground before vanishing and reappearing in a different place. The *Australian Motel-Hotel* (☎ (077) 46 3144) has singles/doubles at $27/32, or $40/50 with private bathroom. There's also a caravan park (no on-site vans) and a roadhouse.

If you're heading east from Boulia, the sealed Kennedy Developmental Road runs 360 km to Winton. The *Middleton Hotel* (☎ (076) 57 3980), 192 km west, is the only fuel stop along the way.

It's 200 unsealed km south from Boulia to **Bedourie**, the administrative centre for the huge Diamantina Shire Council. The town's *Royal Hotel* hasn't changed much since it was built in 1880; it has budget accommodation. The new *Simpson Desert Roadhouse* (☎ (077) 46 1291) has a general store, a restaurant, motel units for $52/64 and a caravan park.

Twenty-three km south of Bedourie is the intersection of the Diamantina Developmental Road (which turns east towards Windorah, 400 km away) and the Eyre Developmental Road, which takes you 170 km south to Birdsville.

Birdsville (pop 100)

This tiny settlement is the most remote place in Queensland and possesses one of Australia's most famous pubs – the Birdsville Hotel.

Birdsville, only 12 km from the South Australian border, is the northern end of the 481-km Birdsville Track, which leads down to Marree in South Australia. In the late 19th century, Birdsville was quite a busy place as cattle were driven south to South Australia and a customs charge was made on each head of cattle leaving Queensland. With Federation, the charge was abolished and Birdsville became almost ghost-like, although in recent years the growing tourism industry has revitalised the town. Its big moment today is the annual Birdsville Races on the first weekend in September, when as many as 6000 racing and boozing enthusiasts make the trip to Birdsville.

Birdsville gets its water from a 1219-metre-deep artesian well, which delivers the water at over 100°C.

Don't miss the **Birdsville Working Museum**. Inside this big tin shed is one of the most impressive private museums in Australia, with a fascinating collection of drover's gear, shearing equipment, wool presses and much more. It's open daily and private tours cost $5.

Birdsville's facilities include a couple of roadhouses, a general store, a hospital and a caravan park. The *Birdsville Hotel* (☎ (076) 56 3244) dates from 1884 but it has been impressively renovated, and has modern motel-style units out the back at $42/64 for singles/doubles.

Birdsville Track

To the south, the Birdsville Track passes between the Simpson Desert to the west and Sturt's Stony Desert to the east. The first stretch from Birdsville has two alternative routes. Ask for local advice about which is better. The Inner Track – marked 'not recommended' on most maps – crosses the Goyder Lagoon (the 'end' of the Diamantina River) and a big Wet will sometimes cut this route. The longer, more easterly Outside Track crosses sandy country at the edge of the desert where it is sometimes difficult to find the track. You can contact the Birdsville police (☎ (076) 56 3220) for advice on road conditions.

Simpson Desert National Park

West of Birdsville, the waterless Simpson Desert National Park is Queensland's biggest at 5000 sq km. Conventional cars can tackle the Birdsville Track quite easily but the Simpson requires a 4WD and far more preparation. Official advice is that crossings should only be tackled by parties of at least two 4WD vehicles and that you should have a radio to call for help if necessary. Permits are required before you can traverse the park. They are available from the police station in Birdsville (☎ (076) 56 3220) or QNP&WS offices. For more information, contact the QNP&WS offices in Longreach (☎ (076) 58 1761) or Charleville (☎ (076) 54 1255).

Birdsville to Charleville

The Birdsville Developmental Road heads east from Birdsville, meeting up with the Diamantina Developmental Road after 275 km of rough gravel and sand – watch out for cattle grids and sudden dips at the many dry creek crossings. The only 'town' along this route is **Betoota**, with a ramshackle pub, a couple of old tin buildings and a population of one. The pub sells fuel, drinks and potato chips.

Windorah, 384 km east of Birdsville, is either very dry or very wet. The town's general store sells fuel and groceries, the *Western Star Hotel* (☎ (076) 56 3166) has air-con rooms at $25/35, and there's a caravan park (of sorts).

Quilpie is an opal-mining town and the railhead from which cattle are transported to the coast. It has a good range of facilities, including two pubs, a motel and several service stations. From here it's another 210 km to Charleville.

South of Quilpie and west of Cunnamulla are the remote **Yowah Opal Fields** and the town of **Eulo**, which hosts the World Lizard Racing Championships in late August/early September. **Thargomindah**, 130 km west of Eulo, has a pub and a motel. From here camel trains used to cross to Bourke in New South Wales. **Noccundra**, another 145 km farther west, was once a busy little community. It now has only a hotel and a population of eight. If you have a 4WD you can continue west to Innamincka on the Strzelecki Track in South Australia, via the site of the **Dig Tree**, where Burke and Wills camped on their ill-fated 1860-61 expedition (see Innamincka in the Outback section of the South Australia chapter).

South Australia

HIGHLIGHTS

- Soaking up the cosmopolitan atmosphere of Rundle St's lively cafe scene
- Watching southern right whales from the cliffs at Head of Bight
- Canoeing the quiet backwaters of the Murray River National Park
- Sampling the wines on a tour of the Barossa and Clare valleys
- Listening to the night-silence from a lonely sandridge by the Oodnadatta Track
- Experiencing the lunar landscapes and frontier atmosphere of Coober Pedy and Andamooka
- Admiring the vibrant carpets of springtime wildflowers in the arid outback

Population	1,473,000
Area	984,277 sq km

South Australia is the driest of the states – even Western Australia doesn't have such a large proportion of desert. It is also the most urbanised. Adelaide, the capital, once had a reputation as the wowsers' capital and is often referred to as 'the city of churches'. The churches may still be there, but otherwise times have changed.

Today the city's cultural spirit is epitomised by the biennial Adelaide Festival of Arts, while the death of wowserism is nowhere better seen than in the Barossa Valley Vintage Festival, also held every two years. Another example of South Australia's relatively liberal attitude is that it was the first Australian state to have a legal nudist beach – Maslin Beach, just a short drive south of Adelaide.

South Australia is renowned for its vineyards and wineries. The Barossa Valley is probably the best-known wine-producing area, but there are also the fine Clare and Coonawarra valleys and McLaren Vale.

Farther north, the rugged Flinders Ranges offer spectacular scenery and superb bushwalking, while the far north has some of the most inhospitable yet fascinating country in Australia. The long drive west across the Nullarbor Plain runs close to dramatic cliffs along the Great Australian Bight.

That still leaves the mighty Murray River, the wild south-east coast, laid-back Kangaroo Island and the diverse Eyre, Yorke and Fleurieu peninsulas. All have plenty to offer the visitor.

Colonel William Light landed at Holdfast Bay (today Glenelg) in 1836, proclaimed the area a British colony and chose a site about 10 km inland for the capital. Light designed and surveyed the city, and the colony's first governor, Captain John Hindmarsh, named it after the wife of the then British monarch, William IV. At first, progress in the independently managed colony was slow and only British government funds saved it from bankruptcy. The colony was self-supporting by the mid-1840s and self-governing by 1856. Steamers on the Murray River linked the state with the east, and agricultural and pastoral activity became the main industry.

565

South Australia

ABORIGINAL PEOPLE

It is estimated that there were 12,000 Aboriginal people in South Australia at the beginning of the 19th century. In the decades following White settlement, many were killed by settlers or died from starvation and introduced diseases. Except in the northwest, which was unsuitable for pastoral development, they were usually forcibly dispossessed of their traditional lands. As a result, there was a general movement to missions and other centres where they could find safety and food rations.

Today, most of the state's 16,000 Aboriginal people live in urban centres such as Adelaide and Port Augusta. *Survival in Our Own Land* (Hodder & Stoughton, 1992), edited by Christobel Mattingley & Ken Hampton, has been exhaustively researched and has beautifully written individual and historical accounts by Nungas (South Australian Aboriginal people). It is available for $34.95 from good bookshops in Adelaide, such as Imprints in Hindley St.

GEOGRAPHY

South Australia is sparsely settled. Adelaide, the Fleurieu Peninsula to the south, and the area north of the capital with the wine-producing Barossa and Clare valleys, are all green and fairly fertile, but much of the rest of the state is far more barren. As you travel farther north or west the terrain becomes drier and more inhospitable; most of the north is a vast area of semidesert and dry salt lakes with only scattered tiny settlements.

South Australia is also known for its scenic coastline and peninsulas. Starting from the Victorian border, there's the southeast region with Mt Gambier, the wine-producing Coonawarra area and the long, coastal lake of the Coorong. Then there's the Fleurieu Peninsula and nearby Kangaroo Island, the Yorke Peninsula, the remote Eyre Peninsula merging into the Great Australian Bight, and the Nullarbor Plain, which extends into Western Australia.

INFORMATION

The South Australian Tourism Commission (SATC) produces an excellent range of regional brochures, booklets and newspapers. SATC travel centres can also supply leaflets on travel details, accommodation costs and so on. Its travel centres interstate include:

New South Wales
247 Pitt St, Sydney 2000 (☎ (02) 9264 3375)

South Australia
1 King William St, Adelaide 5000 (☎ (08) 8212 1505)

Victoria
455 Bourke St, Melbourne 3000 (☎ (03) 9606 0222)

Western Australia
13/14 Mezzanine floor, Wesley Centre, 93 William St, Perth 6000 (☎ (09) 481 1268)

Heysen Trail

Destined to become one of the world's great long-distance walks, the extraordinary Heysen Trail extends over 1500 km from Cape Jervis at the tip of the Fleurieu Peninsula to Parachilna Gorge in the northern Flinders Ranges. En route it passes over the Mt Lofty Ranges, through the Barossa Valley wine region and the fascinating old copper town of Burra in the mid-north and into the Flinders Ranges, scaling Mt Remarkable and Mt Brown, then on to Wilpena Pound.

For the truly intrepid, the Heysen Trail presents a remarkable challenge, but it is also possible to follow short sections of the trail on day trips or over a few days. Fifteen maps detailing all the sections of the route are available for $5.50 each from the Recreation & Sport Resource Centre (☎ (08) 226 7373), Shop 20, City Centre Arcade, 11 Hindmarsh Square, Adelaide (or write to GPO Box 1865, Adelaide). Due to fire restrictions, the trail is closed between December and April. ■

SOUTH AUSTRALIA

The State Information Centre (☎ 8204 1900), at 77 Grenfell St, Adelaide, is a handy resource centre on features of interest in the state, including cycling and trekking routes. It has brochures and other publications covering a vast range of topics, from museums to industries and legislation. It's open weekdays only from 9 am to 5 pm.

NATIONAL PARKS

For general information on national parks and conservation reserves, contact the Department of Environment & Natural Resources Information Centre (☎ 8204 1910), 77 Grenfell St. It's open weekdays only from 9 am to 5 pm.

ACTIVITIES

Bushwalking

Close to Adelaide there are many walks in the Mt Lofty Ranges, including those at Belair National Park, Cleland, Morialta and Deep Creek conservation parks, Bridgewater-Aldgate, Barossa Reservoir and the Para Wirra recreation park.

In the Flinders Ranges there are excellent walks in the Mt Remarkable and Flinders Ranges national parks, and farther north in the Gammon Ranges National Park and adjoining Arkaroola Wildlife Sanctuary. The 1500-km **Heysen Trail** winds south from near Blinman, in the central Flinders Ranges, to Cape Jervis on the southern tip of the Fleurieu Peninsula.

There are several bushwalking clubs in the Adelaide area which organise weekend walks in the Mt Lofty and Flinders ranges. Information can be obtained from bush-gear shops such as Paddy Pallin and Thor Adventure Equipment (☎ 8232 3155), which share a shop at 228 Rundle St, Adelaide. You can also hire gear there.

Women of the Wilderness (☎ 8340 2422) are at the YWCA, 320 Port Rd, Hindmarsh. They run courses and workshops for women in a range of outdoor activities.

A good general guide to bushwalks in South Australia is Tyrone T Thomas' *Fifty Walks in South Australia*.

Water Sports

Canoeing & Sailing The Murray River and the Coorong are popular for canoeing trips, and visitors can hire equipment and join trips organised by canoeing associations. There is good sailing all along Adelaide's shoreline in the Gulf St Vincent, and there are lots of sailing clubs.

Scuba Diving There are some good diving possibilities around Adelaide. Off Glenelg there's an artificial reef centred on a sunken barge, while at Port Noarlunga (18 km south) you can shore dive on the Marine Reserve or boat dive on the *HA Lum*, a sunken fishing boat.

Despite the effects of stormwater run-off, the reefs off Snapper Point and Aldinga (42 and 43 km south respectively) are still good. You can snorkel at Snapper Point, but the Aldinga Reef is better for scuba diving.

At Second Valley (65 km south of Adelaide) the water is generally clear and the caves are accessible, while 23 km farther on at Rapid Bay you can dive from the jetty and see abundant marine life.

Other good areas include most jetties around the Yorke Peninsula, the reefs off Port Lincoln and the reefs, wrecks and drop-offs around Kangaroo Island.

Any of the scuba gear shops in Adelaide will be able to give you pointers on what there is to do around the state.

Swimming & Surfing There are fine swimming beaches right along the South Australian coast. The Adelaide suburbs of Seacliff, Brighton, Somerton, Glenelg, West Beach, Henley Beach, Grange, West Lakes, Semaphore, Glanville and Largs Bay all have popular city beaches. Farther south there are several beaches with reasonable surf in the right conditions – Seaford and Southport have reliable if small waves. Skinny-dipping is permitted at Maslin Beach, 40 km south of the city.

You have to get over to Pondalowie on the Yorke Peninsula for the state's most reliable strong waves, and there are more powerful breaks nearby. Other worthwhile surfing spots can be found along the Eyre Peninsula between Port Lincoln and the Ceduna area; Cactus Beach, on remote Point Sinclair west of Ceduna, is world-famous for its surf. Closer to Adelaide, and near Victor Harbor on the Fleurieu Peninsula, there's often good surf at Waitpinga Beach, Middleton and Port Elliot.

GETTING THERE & AWAY

See the Adelaide Getting There & Away section for details on transport to South Australia. It is worth noting that if you're travelling to Western Australia you can't take honey, plants, fruit or vegetables past the Norseman checkpoint; travelling into South Australia from Victoria between Mildura and Renmark you'll come across a similar checkpoint. There's another at Oodla-wirra, on the Barrier Highway from Broken Hill.

GETTING AROUND

Air

Kendell Airlines (book through Ansett on ☎ 13 1300) is by far the main regional operator with flights from Adelaide to Mt Gambier, Kangaroo Island, Port Lincoln, Ceduna, Coober Pedy and Broken Hill (in New South Wales). See the South Australian air-fares chart for prices.

Bus

As well as the major interstate companies, services within the state include Stateliner (the main operator) and Premier (☎ 8415 5555 for both) and a number of smaller local companies.

Train

Apart from suburban trains and a couple of tourist steam trains, South Australia does not have any intrastate passenger trains. You can, however, get on and off the *Indian Pacific* (Sydney to Perth), the *Ghan* (Alice Springs to Adelaide) and the *Overland* (Adelaide to Melbourne) at various points along the line.

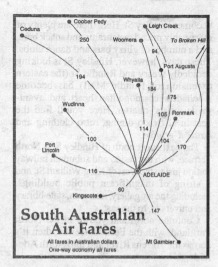

South Australian Air Fares
All fares in Australian dollars
One-way economy air fares

Adelaide

Population 1,070,000

Adelaide is a solid, even gracious, city: when the early colonists built they generally built with stone. The solidity goes further than architecture; Adelaide is still very much an 'old money' place. It's also civilised and calm in a way no other Australian capital city can match. What's more, it has a superb setting, for the city centre is surrounded by green parkland and the metropolitan area is bounded by the hills of the Mt Lofty Ranges, which crowd it against the sea.

Orientation

The city centre is laid out on a clear grid pattern, with several squares. The main street is King William St, with Victoria Square at the geographical centre of the city. Most cross streets change their name at King William St.

Rundle Mall is a colourful hive of activity and most of the big shops are here. Just across King William St, Rundle Mall becomes Hindley St. Here there are plenty of reasonably priced restaurants and snack bars, and a number of glitzy bars and dance clubs. These days, however, Hindley St is looking decidedly weary and Rundle St (the eastern extension of Rundle Mall) has become Adelaide's cosmopolitan heart and avant-garde artists' quarter. Here you'll find the best in al fresco dining, retro clothing and *haute d'grunge*.

The next street north of Hindley St is North Terrace, with the casino and suburban railway station just to the west of King William St, and a string of magnificent public buildings, including the art gallery, museum, state library and university, to the east.

Continue north and you're in the North Parkland, with the Festival Centre; then it's across the Torrens River and into North Adelaide.

Information

Tourist Offices The SATC travel centre (☎ 8212 1505; 1800 882 092) is at 1 King William St, on the corner of North Terrace. It's open weekdays from 8.45 am to 5 pm, and weekends and public holidays from 9 am to 2 pm.

SA-FM, a local radio station, has a 'community switchboard' that provides current information on everything from forthcoming concerts, art shows and festivals, to fire ban days, surfing conditions and beach reports; ☎ 8271 1277 daily between 9 am and 5 pm.

The Women's Information Switchboard (☎ 8223 1244) operates daily from 9 am to 9 pm (except public holidays) and can advise on just about anything, or direct you to someone who can.

Gayline (☎ 8362 3223) operates nightly between 7 and 10 pm and, on weekends only, from 2 to 5 pm. It offers a counselling and information service for gays and lesbians.

Post & Telecommunications The main post office is in the city centre on King William St.

Other Offices The Royal Automobile Association of South Australia (RAA; ☎ 8202 4500) is at 41 Hindmarsh Square. The YHA office (☎ 8231 5583) is at 38 Sturt St, and the Department of Environment & Natural Resources (☎ 8204 1910) is at 77 Grenfell St. The Disability Information Centre (☎ 8223 7522), at 195 Gilles St, can provide advice on tourist destinations and travel agencies that cater for people with disabilities.

Bookshops Adelaide has numerous good new and second-hand bookshops. Open seven days is Imprint Booksellers, at 80 Hindley St, which has quality literature, biographies and a good gay and lesbian section. Mary Martin's Bookshop, an Adelaide institution, is at 12 Pirie St – it boasts a wide range of titles. Try the excellent Europa Bookshop at 16 Pulteney St for its selection of foreign-language and travel books.

The RAA has an excellent little bookshop with a good selection of titles including travel within the state, bushwalking, natural and social history, and Aboriginal culture.

The Conservation Council has a shop at 120 Wakefield St. This is a very good environmental resource centre, and it also has a natural history and environment reference library.

Murphy Sisters Bookshop, at 240 The Parade, Norwood, specialises in feminist and lesbian works, and has an excellent section on Aboriginal studies. The sisters own another shop at Semaphore: Sisters by the Sea, Shop 1, 14 Semaphore Rd.

A good range of second-hand books can be found at the Central and Orange Lane markets (see the Markets section for details).

Maps Mapland (☎ 8226 4946), at the Department of Environment & Natural Resources, 282 Richmond Rd, Netley, has a good range of maps. Maps are also sold at the department's Land Information Centre, in the Colonel Light Centre at 25 Pirie St.

Medical Services The Traveller's Medical & Vaccination Centre (☎ 8212 7522) is at 29 Gilbert Place.

Adelaide

0   250   500 m

PLACES TO STAY

17 Princes Arcade Motel
21 West's Private Hotel
22 Grosvenor Hotel
39 Austral Hotel
42 City Central Motel
44 Hindley Parkroyal
52 YMCA
58 Cannon St Lodge
59 Sydney Backpackers
60 Backpack Australia
61 Metropolitan Hotel
68 New World International Hostel
72 Adelaide Travellers Inn
74 East Park Lodge
77 Moores Brecknock Hotel
79 Adelaide Backpackers Hostel

PLACES TO EAT

7 Union Complex
23 Peyton Hut
24 Parlimento
26 Terrace Eatery
28 Pancake Kitchen
29 Billy Baxter's
30 Amalfi
32 Tapa's Cafe
36 Alfresco Gelateria & Scoozi
37 Boltz Cafe
43 Pancake Kitchen
45 Food for Life
46 Blossom Vegetarian Restaurant
47 Marcellina
48 Taj Tandoor
50 Vinezia
51 Volga
64 Chinatown
66 Rock Lobster Cafe
66 Ming Palace
67 Paul's Cafe
69 Star of Siam
70 Mamma Getta

71 Beijing
76 Hawker's Corner

OTHER

1 Lights Vision
2 Old Adelaide Gaol
3 Elder Park
4 Festival Centre
5 Government House
6 Migration Museum
8 University of Adelaide
9 Royal Adelaide Hospital
10 Art Gallery of South Australia
11 South Australian Museum
12 State Library
13 Parliament House
14 Old Parliament House
15 Adelaide Casino
16 Newmarket Hotel
18 Lion Arts Centre
19 Holy Trinity Church
20 Rave on Hindley
25 SATC Travel Centre
31 Pondon Tavern
33 Paddy Pallin
34 Ayers Historic House
35 East End Market
38 Exeter Hotel
40 Universal Wine Bar
41 State Information Centre & Natural Resources Information Centre
49 Edmund Wright House
53 Tandanya
54 Old Treasury Building
55 Town Hall
57 Main Post Office
60 St Mary's Convent
62 Central Bus Station
    St Francis Xavier Cathedral
63 Central Market
73 Earl of Aberdeen Hotel
75 YHA Office
78 Disability Information Centre

SOUTH AUSTRALIA

Museums

On North Terrace, the **South Australian Museum** is an Adelaide landmark with huge whale skeletons in the front window. Primarily a natural history museum, it also has a very good collection of Aboriginal artefacts, as well as Ngarrindjeri, an Aboriginal Dreamtime exhibition. Open daily between 10 am and 5 pm, it's a fine museum; admission is free.

The excellent **Migration Museum**, at 82 Kintore Ave, tells the story of the groups from over 100 nationalities who have migrated to South Australia. It is open weekdays from 10 am to 5 pm, and weekends and public holidays from 1 to 5 pm; admission is free.

As you're leaving this museum, turn left along the lane, and then right at the double-storey building where the free **Police Museum** can be found on the 1st floor. It's open on weekends and public holidays from 1 to 5 pm.

The **Museum of Classical Archaeology**, on the 1st floor of the Mitchell Building (in the university grounds on North Terrace), has a good collection of antiquities dating from the 3rd millenium BC. It's open from noon to 3 pm during term time; admission is free.

On the corner of King William and Flinders Sts in the old Treasury Building there's the free **Museum of Exploration, Surveying & Land Heritage**, open weekdays from 10 am to 3 pm. For $3 you can do an interesting two-hour tour of this grand old building (it dates from 1839), taking in the museum, cabinet room and underground tunnels. Coffee is included.

The **Maritime Museum**, 126 Lipson St, Port Adelaide, has several old ships, including the *Nelcebee*, the third-oldest ship on Lloyd's register. There's also an old lighthouse and a computer register of early migrants. It's open daily from 10 am to 5 pm; admission is $7. Bus Nos 151 or 153 will get you there from North Terrace, or you can take the train.

Next door is the **Port Dock Station Museum**, which features an extensive collection of railway memorabilia. It's open daily from 10 am to 5 pm and Saturday from noon to 5 pm; admission is $6.

The fascinating **Investigator Science & Technology Museum** is close to the city, at the Wayville Showgrounds off Goodwood Rd. It takes an entertaining look at science and is usually open daily between 10 am and 5 pm (9 am and 6 pm during school holidays); admission is $9. The museum may be closed while exhibitions are changed, so check first on ☎ 8410 1115. To get there, take bus Nos 216, 218 or 296 from King William St.

Also interesting is the **Old Adelaide Gaol** at Gaol Rd, Thebarton; it's open Sunday and public holidays, when guided tours ($6) are conducted between 11.30 am and 3.30 pm. Features include the hanging tower and various depressing gaol artefacts.

Tandanya

Tandanya, at 253 Grenfell St, is an Aboriginal cultural institute containing galleries, art and craft workshops, performance spaces, cafe and a good gift shop. It's open weekdays from 10.30 am to 5 pm and weekends and public holidays from noon to 5 pm; admission is $4.

State Library

Displays at the State Library on North Terrace include Colonel Light's surveying equipment, an 1865 photographic panorama of Adelaide and, in the Mortlock Library in the same complex, memorabilia of cricket legend Sir Donald Bradman. The library is open weekdays from 9.30 am to 8 pm (5 pm Thursday) and weekends from noon to 5 pm. It's closed on public holidays.

Art Galleries

On North Terrace, next to the museum, the **Art Gallery of South Australia** has a good selection of contemporary Australian and overseas work, as well as fine minor work from many periods. It's open daily from 10 am to 5 pm, admission is free and there are daily tours (weekdays from 10 am to 1 pm and weekends from 10 am to 3 pm).

The gallery of the **Royal South Australian Society of Arts**, in the Institute Building on the corner of North Terrace and Kintore Ave, is open weekdays from 11 am to 5 pm and weekends from 2 to 5 pm; admission is free. Other galleries include the free **Union Gallery**, level 6, Union House, at Adelaide University (open weekdays from 10 am to 5 pm) and the **Festival Centre Gallery** near the Playhouse in the Festival Centre.

Grand City Buildings

Close to the city centre, at 288 North Terrace, is **Ayers Historic House**. This grand mansion was constructed in 1846 but was added to over the next 30 years. Now completely restored, it houses a restaurant and is open to visitors Tuesday to Friday between 10 am and 4 pm, and weekends and public holidays between 1 and 4 pm. Admission is $2 and there are tours ($4). The elegant bluestone building serves as the headquarters of the South Australian branch of the National Trust (☎ 8223 1655).

At 59 King William St, **Edmund Wright House** (1876) was originally constructed in an elaborate Renaissance style with intricate decoration for the Bank of South Australia. It's open daily from 9 am to 4.30 pm and admission is free; you can't really see much apart from the old banking chamber. There are lunchtime concerts here on Wednesday from noon to 2 pm.

The imposing **Adelaide Town Hall**, built between 1863 and 1866 in 16th-century Renaissance style, looks out onto King William St between Flinders and Pirie Sts. The faces of Queen Victoria and Prince Albert are carved into the facade. There are free tours on Tuesday and Thursday, but you have to book (☎ 8203 7442). The **main post office** building across the road is almost as impressive.

On North Terrace, **Government House** was built between 1838 and 1840, with further additions in 1855. The earliest section is one of the oldest buildings in Adelaide. **Parliament House** has a facade with 10 marble Corinthian columns. Building

commenced in 1883 but was not completed until 1939.

Holy Trinity Church, also on North Terrace, was the first Anglican church in the state; it was built in 1838. Other early churches are **St Francis Xavier Cathedral** on Wakefield St (around 1856) and **St Peter's Cathedral** in Pennington Terrace, North Adelaide (1869-76).

St Francis Xavier Cathedral is beside Victoria Square, where you will also find a number of other important early buildings: the **Magistrate's Court** (1847-50); the **Supreme Court** (1869); and the old **Treasury building** (1839) – you can do tours of the latter; see Museums (above) for details.

Festival Centre

The Adelaide Festival Centre (☎ 8216 8600), completed in 1977, is close to the Torrens River. Looking vaguely like an ugly squared-off version of the Sydney Opera House, it performs a similar function, with a variety of auditoriums and theatres but a far greater range of entertainment.

While the centre is visually uninspiring, it does have a marvellous riverside setting; people picnic on the grass in front of the theatre and there are several places to eat. You can also hire pedal boats nearby or enjoy free concerts (see the Entertainment section) and exhibitions here.

Botanic Gardens & Other Parks

The central city is completely surrounded by green parkland. The Torrens River, itself bordered by park, separates Adelaide from North Adelaide, also surrounded by parkland.

On North Terrace, the 20-hectare **Adelaide Botanic Garden** has pleasant artificial lakes and is only a short stroll from the city centre. Every Tuesday and Friday at 10.30 am, free guided tours of the gardens, taking about 1½ hours, leave from the kiosk – they're also held at the same time on Sunday in autumn and spring. The gardens are open weekdays from 7 am to sunset, and on weekends and public holidays from 9 am to sunset. A stunning conservatory in the gardens recreates a tropical rainforest environment. It is open between 10 am and 4 pm; admission is $2.50.

Rymill Park in the East Parkland has a boating lake and a 600-metre-long jogging track. The South Parkland contains **Veale Gardens**, with streams and flowerbeds. To the west are a number of sports grounds, while the **North Parkland** borders the Torrens and surrounds North Adelaide. The **Adelaide Oval**, the site of interstate and international cricket matches, is north of the Torrens River in this part of the park.

Light's Vision

On Montefiore Hill, north of the city centre across the Torrens River, stands this statue of Colonel William Light, Adelaide's founder. He's said to have stood here and mapped out his visionary plan. In the afternoon there's a nice view of the city's gleaming office towers rising above the trees, with the Adelaide Hills making a scenic backdrop.

Adelaide Zoo

On Frome Rd, the zoo holds about 1500 exotic and native mammals, birds and reptiles, and also has a children's zoo. It's open daily (including Christmas Day) from 9.30 am to 5 pm; admission is $9. A different way of getting there is to take a cruise on the *Popeye* ($5), which departs daily every 20 minutes (weekends only in winter except school holidays) from Elder Park in front of the Festival Centre. You can also catch bus Nos 272 or 273 from Currie St, or take a pleasant walk along the Torrens from Elder Park.

Markets

Close to the centre of town, the **Central Market** (☎ 8203 7345), off Victoria Square between Grote and Gouger Sts, is a great place for self-catering travellers. You can buy fresh produce direct from the producer, so things are generally quite a bit cheaper than in the shops. It's open Tuesday (7 am to 5.30 pm), Thursday (11 am to 5.30 pm), Friday (7 am to 9 pm) and Saturday (7 am to 1 pm). Many stalls shut down around lunchtime, so get there late in the morning for real bargains.

The very popular and trendy **East End Market** (☎ 8232 5606) off the east end of Rundle St is open Monday, Friday, weekends and public holidays from 9 am to 6 pm. There's a huge market bazaar with about 200 variety stalls and a food court selling everything from Asian fare to French bread and Italian gelati. You can also buy fresh produce here. There are a number of good cafes and restaurants nearby.

The much smaller **Orange Lane Market**, in Norwood, is more casual and will appeal to alternative lifestylers – it's the place to go for Indian fabrics, second-hand clothing, massage, tarot readings, palmistry, remedies, bric-a-brac and junk. You'll find it on the corner of Edward St and Orange Lane (off Norwood Pde) on weekends and public holidays from 10 am to 6 pm. A few steps away on the parade are a couple of good coffee shops and cafes.

Glenelg

Glenelg, with the most popular of Adelaide's beaches, is an excellent place to stay – there are many guesthouses, hotels and holiday flats.

The first South Australian colonists actually landed in Glenelg so there are a number of places of historic interest. Glenelg is exceptionally easy to get to. A vintage tram runs from Victoria Square in the city centre right to Glenelg Beach, taking about 30 minutes (see the Getting Around section for details).

There's a tourist centre behind the town hall, close to the jetty. Next door, Beach Hire (☎ 8294 1477) hires deckchairs, umbrellas, wave skis and body boards. It's open from September to April only; the opening times vary, but if it's sunny, it'll be open.

Holdfast Cycles (☎ 8294 4537), at 768 Anzac Highway, hires well-maintained mountain bikes for the serious touring cyclist. It provides maps for self-guided tours to points of interest, and helmets are included in the rates ($7.50 an hour; $30 a day). The shop is open weekdays from 9 am

5.30 pm and weekends from 10 am to 3
m.

On MacFarlane St, the **Old Gum Tree**
arks the spot where the proclamation of
outh Australia was read in 1836. Governor
lindmarsh and the first colonists landed on
e beach nearby.

The boat harbour shelters a large number
f yachts as well as Glenelg's premier attrac-
on, a reproduction of **HMS Buffalo**, the
riginal settlers' conveyance. The original
uffalo was built in 1813 in India. On board,
ou'll find one of Adelaide's best seafood
estaurants (☎ 8294 7000), as well as a
useum; it's open daily from 10 am to 5 pm
ntry $2.50).

uburban Historic Buildings

Jetty St, Grange (west of the city centre),
Sturt's Cottage, the home of the early
ustralian explorer. It's open Wednesday to
unday and public holidays from noon to 5
m (4 pm in winter); admission is $2.50.
ake bus Nos 130 or 137 from Grenfell St
d get off at stop 29A.

North-west of the city centre, in Sema-
hore, there's **Fort Glanville**, at 359 Military
d, Semaphore Park. The fort was built in
878, when Australia was suffering a phase
f Russophobia as a result of the Crimean
ar. It's open from 1 to 5 pm on the third
unday of each month between September
d May; admission is $3.

In Springfield (south-east of the city),
arrick Hill, at 46 Carrick Hill Drive, is built
the style of an Elizabethan manor house
t in an English-style garden. It's open
ednesday to Sunday and public holidays
om 10 am to 5 pm; admission is $8 and
ere are free guided tours at 11 am, noon, 2
m and 3 pm. Catch bus No 171 from King
illiam St and get off at stop 16.

other Mary MacKillop Sites

he Australian saint-to-be lived in Adelaide
r 16 years and there are a number of sites
sociated with her. They include **St Mary's**
onvent at 253 Franklin St, Adelaide, where
e was excommunicated, and **St Ignatius**
hurch on Queen St, Norwood, where she

assisted at mass during her excommunica-
tion period.

Another is **St Joseph's Convent**, at 286
Portrush Rd, Kensington, where you can find
the **Mary MacKillop Centre** (☎ 8364 5311).
The centre has historic photos and artefacts,
as well as a leaflet describing eight significant pilgrimage sites. It's open weekdays
from 10 am to 4 pm and Sunday from 1 to 4
pm.

Activities

Ice Skating Adelaide's ice-skating rink
(☎ 8352 7977), at 23 East Terrace in Thebarton, is open daily. It also has an artificial
indoor snow-skiing centre, with a 150-
metre-long slope. Take bus Nos 151 or 153
from North Terrace and get off at stop 2.

Organised Tours

There is a huge variety of tours in and around
Adelaide and you can get details from the
SATC. Most of the hostels have travel or tour
agencies specialising in backpackers deals.

Premier (☎ 8415 5555) has a range of
half-day tours including the city sights ($19),
Hahndorf in the Adelaide Hills ($19), or the
Mt Lofty Ranges and the Cleland Wildlife
Park ($22). They also have reasonably priced
day tours.

Tour Delights (☎ 018 845 432) has an
excellent Barossa winery tour ($43), includ-
ing lunch and a visit to six wineries. E&K
Mini-Tours (☎ 8337 8739) has a Barossa day
tour for $30, including lunch, and a two-hour
Adelaide by Night tour for $15.

For $20 you can get a day pass on the
Adelaide Explorer (☎ 8364 1933), a road-
registered tram replica, which does a
continuous circuit of a number of attractions,
including Glenelg. The tour takes 2½ hours
and you can get on and off en route; daily
departures are at 9 am, and 12.20 and 3 pm,
and leave from 14 King William St.

If you're short of time you can take a day
trip to Kangaroo Island with Kendell Airlines (book through Ansett on ☎ 13 1300). It
costs $159, including air fares, a tour, all
entrance fees and a barbecue lunch.

There are numerous trips to the Flinders

Ranges. Stateliner (☎ 8415 5555) has several backpacker specials costing from $120 for a three-day trip, including accommodation; they also have more luxurious, but still reasonably priced tours.

Freewheelin' Cycle Tours (☎ 8232 6860) has a variety of rides, including the McLaren Vale and Barossa wineries (both $39). You can also hire bicycles from Freewheelin' at 237 Hutt St.

Adelaide Festival of the Arts

The Festival of the Arts is one of Australia's premier cultural events and takes place in February and/or March of even-numbered years. The three-week festival attracts culture vultures from all over Australia to drama, dance, music and other live performances. It also includes a writers' week, art exhibitions, poetry readings and other activities with guest speakers and international performers. For information phone the Festival Centre on ☎ 8216 8600.

The Fringe Festival, which takes place at the same time, features alternative contemporary performance art, music and more; phone ☎ 8231 7760 for details.

Places to Stay

Many caravan park, motel and some hotel prices rise between Christmas and the end of January, when accommodation is extremely scarce – some also put their prices up in other school holiday periods. Unless otherwise stated, all prices given here are off-peak.

Places to Stay – bottom end

Camping There are quite a few caravan parks around Adelaide. The following are within 10 km of the city centre – check the tourist office for others. All prices given are for two people.

Adelaide Caravan Park (☎ 8363 1566), two km north-east of the city centre at Bruton St, Hackney; on-site vans from $36, cabins $55 and camp sites $18.

Windsor Gardens Caravan Park (☎ 8261 1091), seven km north-east at 78 Windsor Grove, Windsor Gardens; camp sites $10 and single/double cabins $35/50.

West Beach Caravan Park (☎ 8356 7654), eight km west of the city at Military Rd, West Beach; camp sites $12, on-site vans $32 and cabins $49. The park is close to the beach and only a couple of km from Glenelg.

Marine Land Holiday Village (☎ 8353 2655), also on Military Rd, West Beach; two-bedroom villas for $80 (cheaper after two nights), two-bedroom holiday units for $58, self-contained cabins for $53. There are no camp sites.

Hostels – city There are a couple of hostels near the central bus station. When you leave the terminal, turn left onto Franklin St and on the next corner you'll find the rather run-down *Sunny's Backpackers Hostel* (☎ 8231 2430). Dorm beds are from $12 and twin share/doubles are $14; mountain bikes are for hire for $15 per day, and off-street parking is available. There's a licensed travel agent on the premises (open at 6 am).

At 11 Cannon St, a lane running off Franklin St opposite the bus station, the *Cannon Lodge* (☎ 8410 1218) has bunk beds for $13 and singles/doubles for $21/28. It has cheerful murals and friendly staff, but is otherwise on the shabby side. There's a travel agency and you can hire bicycles for $12 a day. Cheap meals are available.

Backpack Australia (☎ 8231 0639) is at 128 Grote St, opposite the Central Market. Beds cost from $10 to $15 and it has a bar, cheap meals, a tiny camping space on the roof, and a travel agency. However, its facilities (particularly the kitchen) are cramped and it could do with some paint and other repairs. By all accounts it has some memorable parties.

New World International Hostel (☎ 8212 6888; 1800 807 367), at 29-31 Compton St, is handy to the Central Market. This place is very clean (there are even boxes under the bunks to put your smelly shoes in), as well as being light and airy, with ducted heating and cooling. Dorm beds cost $12, and someone will pick you up from the airport, bus station or railway station if you ring. It also has a travel agency.

Nomad's Cumberland Arms Hotel, at 20 Waymouth St in the centre, is a cheap and friendly place with a variety of rooms, from

$11 in an eight-bed room to $16 in a double. Individual security lockers and linen are provided. There are no cooking facilities but good, cheap meals are available in the bar downstairs.

Most of the other hostels are clustered in the south-eastern corner of the city centre. You can get there on bus Nos 191 or 192 from Pulteney St or take any bus going to the South Terrace area (Nos 171 and 172 to Hutt St; 201 to 203 to the King William St and South Terrace corner), although it's not really that far to walk.

The very pleasant *Adelaide YHA Hostel* (☎ 8223 6007) is at 290 Gilles St. Beds for members cost $11, and there's a travel agency on the premises. The reception is closed between 11.30 am and 4 pm daily. It's one of the best – if not *the* best – of Adelaide's hostels.

Nearby is the *Adelaide Backpackers Hostel* (☎ 8223 5680) at 263 Gilles St; its 'other' house at 253 is much nicer than the main one at 263, which is run-down. Dorm beds cost from $11, and double-bed rooms are $25. Bicycle hire is $8 for half a day, and there's a travel agency.

Next door, at 257 Gilles St, *Rucksackers Riders International* (☎ 8232 0823) is very popular with motorbike and bicycle travellers. This lovely 80-year-old house is clean and comfortable, has a reasonably spacious kitchen and its rooms are heated day and night in winter. Dorm beds cost $10, and a twin room with en suite is $12 per person. It doesn't have a travel agency, but tours can be arranged.

Two streets closer to the city centre, at 118 Carrington St, is the small but clean and friendly *Adelaide Travellers Inn* (☎ 8232 5330). Dorm beds are $8 and doubles are $20 in reasonable-size bedrooms, but other facilities are cramped. There's some off-street parking.

Next door at 112 Carrington St, the *Adelaide Backpackers Inn* (☎ 8223 6635) is a converted pub with dorm beds from $13 and doubles from $32. Its facilities are rather weary and somewhat cramped, but the management is dedicated, which makes up for a lot. In contrast,

their annexe across the road at 109 is very pleasant; it has a good kitchen and small but comfortable singles/doubles for $20/36. There's a travel agency on the premises.

At the eastern end of Angas St, *East Park Lodge* (☎ 8223 1228) at No 341 is in a grand old building – it was built 80 years ago as a Salvation Army hostel for young country ladies. It's labyrinthine, but clean and well run, and the management is very friendly; if they spent some money on the place it could be great. Dorm beds cost $12, single rooms $17, twin bunk-bed rooms $13.50 per person, and double-bed rooms $14 per person. It's close to the attractive East Parkland.

The large *YMCA* (☎ 8223 1611) at 76 Flinders St is central and takes guests of either sex. Dorms cost $11 and singles/twins are $18/30, with a 10 per cent discount for members. Office hours are 8.30 am to 8.30 pm daily.

Hostels – Glenelg Both backpacker hostels in Glenelg are a big improvement on most in the city. They're in grand old buildings and are noted for their clean, reasonably spacious facilities and their excellent service.

The *Glenelg Backpackers Resort* (☎ 8376 0007) at 7 Mosely St is around the corner from the tram terminus. It has a pool room, games room and an inexpensive restaurant. Comfortable beds (not bunks) are $14 in dorms and $16 per person in smaller shared rooms. There's a book exchange opposite the hostel.

A little farther south of the tram line but on the sea at 16 South Esplanade is the wonderful *Albert Hall* (☎ 1800 060 488; 8376 0488), a beautifully restored mansion. It's even got marble bathrooms and a spectacular ballroom. Dorm beds cost from $13 and there are some private rooms from $20/30.

Hotels Unless otherwise stated, the following provide basic pub-style accommodation with common facilities. The *Metropolitan Hotel* (☎ 8231 5471), at 46 Grote St, is opposite the Central Market. It has singles/doubles for $20/28 plus a $10 key deposit.

If you want to be handy to Hindley St, you won't get any closer than *West's Private Hotel* (☎ 8231 7575), smack in the middle of the mayhem at 110B Hindley St. It's shabby and basic, but cheap: dorm beds are from $15 ($10 for subsequent nights), and singles/doubles are $20/30. At 205 Rundle St, the *Austral Hotel* (☎ 8223 4660) has rooms for $25/35. There's a trendy bar downstairs.

Moore's Brecknock Hotel (☎ 8231 5467), at 410 King William St, has rooms for $30/45, including a light breakfast. This is a popular Irish pub, and Irish folk groups play on Friday nights. At 44 Flinders St, the *Earl of Zetland Hotel* (☎ 8223 5500) has self-contained rooms for $49/65/75.

The *St Vincent Hotel* (☎ 8294 4377), at 28 Jetty Rd in Glenelg, has single/twin rooms for $30/52, and self-contained singles/doubles for $40/60 – all with a light breakfast.

Holiay Flats & Apartments There are many holiday flats and serviced apartments; most quote weekly rather than daily rates.

The *Glenelg Seaway Apartments* (☎ 8295 8503) at 18 Durham St – about a minute's walk from the tram stop – offers accommodation for backpackers at $15 year round; its self-contained apartments are $50 off-peak ($60 peak) for a couple. It's a very plain and down-to-earth place, but the manager is friendly and makes his guests very welcome.

Colleges At Adelaide University, *St Ann's College* (☎ 8267 1478) operates as a hostel from the second week in December to the end of January; beds are $15 ($18 if you need linen). At other colleges, accommodation generally includes meals and is much more expensive.

Places to Stay – middle
Hotels & Motels The *City Central Motel* (☎ 8231 4049), at 23 Hindley St, has small rooms, but they're clean and comfortable. Singles/doubles cost $49/54.

At 262-266 Hindley St, the *Princes Arcade Motel* (☎ 8231 9524) has motel rooms from $45/50, and off-street parking is available.

The *Clarice Motel* (☎ 8223 3560) is at 220 Hutt St, around the corner from the Gilles St youth hostel. There are budget single rooms with shared facilities for $25, doubles/triples with private toilets for $45/55, and a motel-style double for $59. All tariffs include a light breakfast.

The *Princes Lodge Motel* (☎ 8267 5566), in a grand old mansion at 73 Lefevre Terrace, North Adelaide, has budget singles/doubles with a light breakfast from $30/55. It's within walking distance of the city, and handy to the restaurants and cafes on O'Connell and Melbourne Sts.

Festival Lodge (☎ 8212 7877), at 140 North Terrace, is opposite the casino and has rooms from $69/80. There's no on-site parking, but the motel negotiates reduced rates with a nearby car park.

Although there are motels all over Adelaide, it's worth noting that there's a 'motel alley' along Glen Osmond Rd, leading into the city centre from the south-east. This is quite a busy road so some places are a bit noisy. *Powell's Court* (☎ 8271 7033) is two km out at 2 Glen Osmond Rd, Parkside. Units cost $45/48 for singles/doubles and $55/60 for triples/quads ($15 for each extra person, up to a total of nine) and all have kitchens.

The *Princes Highway* (☎ 8379 9253), at 199 Glen Osmond Rd, Frewville, has rooms from $42/46.

Places to Stay – top end
Hotels These offer various rates depending on such factors as the view; weekend rates are cheaper (these are the one's indicated) so that's the best time to stay if you're going to splurge. All rates are for singles/doubles.

Hindley Parkroyal (☎ 8231 5552), 65 Hindley St, offers luxury accommodation from $130. Opposite the casino, and with panoramic views from above the 7th floor, the *Terrace* (☎ 8217 7552), 150 North Terrace, has luxuriously appointed rooms from $140. With a handsome pile of chips from the casino you could indulge yourself at the *Hyatt Regency Adelaide* (☎ 8231 1234), North Terrace, where rooms start at $195.

Places to Eat

Adelaide has more restaurants – there's about 700 – per head of population than any other city in Australia, and its huge variety of cuisines makes dining here a culinary adventure. Licensing laws are liberal, so a high proportion of restaurants are licensed.

The *Advertiser Good Food Guide* ($12.95) is a useful reference to the constantly changing food scene. It's available from larger newsagencies.

Rundle St At the eastern extension of the Rundle Mall, Rundle St has evolved into Adelaide's bohemian quarter, with shops specialising in Art Deco artefacts and alternative clothing, and a swag of restaurants and cafes.

The *Terrace Eatery* is a large, casual dining area in the basement of the Myer Centre, between Rundle Mall and North Terrace. Its numerous eateries include Mexican, Asian, Italian and English, and there's access through to the evocative *London Tavern* at the North Terrace end. The *City Cross Arcade*, between Rundle Mall and Grenfell St, also has a variety of European and Asian eateries.

Amalfi, at 29 Frome St, just off Rundle St, has excellent Italian cuisine and a great menu. It can be difficult to get into on Friday nights, but it's worth the wait.

Tapas Cafe at 242 Rundle St is a wonderful Spanish bar and restaurant. Imagine tucking into treats such as 'kid goat braised in Moroccan spices with an apricot and walnut infused couscous'.

Just up the street is 'little Italy'. The *Alfresco Gelateria* at No 260 is a good place for a gelato, cappuccino or a variety of sweets. *Scoozi*, at No 272, is a huge cosmopolitan cafe that's popular on Friday and Saturday nights – it's noted for its wood-oven pizzas. In between is *Marconi's*, which sells pasta and pizza. On balmy nights the tables at the front of these three places merge and it's difficult to tell who's eating where.

At 286 is *Boltz Cafe*, another indoor and al fresco place. It specialises in modern Australian fare with a Mediterranean influence – favourites include Caesar salad, and fish & chips in beer batter with a sweet chilli and lemongrass sauce. There's a bar upstairs that has stand-up comics on Thursday nights and live bands on Friday and Sunday nights.

Hindley St Hindley St has become a tad passé, with its glittery bars and discos; however, if you're feeling nostalgic, the old favourites still persevere, and the quality and variety of food is good.

On Gilbert Place, which dog-legs between Hindley and King William Sts, the *Pancake Kitchen* is open 24 hours a day and has main-course specials for under $5. Next door, the *Penang Chinese Restaurant* is open Monday to Saturday from 11 am until 10 pm and is similarly priced.

Cafe Boulevard at 15 Hindley is a pleasant coffee lounge with hot meals for under $7 and cheap and delicious sweets. The *Ceylon Hut*, just off Hindley St at 27 Bank St, has tasty curries from $11.

There are two restaurants at the Hindley Parkroyal: *Cafe Mo* with lunchtime buffets for $23 (evenings are $26); and *Oliphants*, with imaginative main courses from $17.

Abdul and Jamil's friendly *Quiet Waters*, in the basement at No 75, is a pleasant Lebanese coffee lounge serving predominantly vegetarian dishes. Takeaways are also available. Garlic is a favourite ingredient, and there's a belly dancer on Wednesday nights. On the 1st floor at No 79, *Food for Life*, a Hare Krishna restaurant, has vegetarian food (all you can eat) for $4, including dessert. It's open weekdays from noon to 3 pm, and evenings from 5 to 8 pm. *Tung Sing*, at No 147, is open every day except Monday from 6 pm to 2 am. Traditional Chinese dishes are between $8 and $13.

Still on Hindley St but across Morphett St, *Blossom Vegetarian Restaurant* at No 167 serves healthy Asian dishes from $4.50. Walk up Morphett St a little way and you come to *Taj Tandoor* at 76 Light Square. This is one of Adelaide's best Indian restaurants.

At 273 Hindley St, *Marcellina* is a favourite with people from the restaurant trade. This place comes alive after 2 am. It has Italian food, and all-you-can-eat pizza and pasta for $7.90 until 9 pm.

North Terrace The *Pullman Adelaide Casino Restaurant* has a smorgasbord, with lunch at $22 ($24 on weekends) and dinner from $27 ($29 on weekends). *Parlimento*, at No 140 on the corner of Bank St, has chef's specials for under $9 and great coffee.

Just about every Oriental cuisine is represented at *Spices Restaurant* in the Terrace Hotel, 150 North Terrace. Wonderfully aromatic main courses start at about $15.

Food Affair at the Gallerie Shopping Centre, which runs from North Terrace through to Gawler Place and John Martins on Rundle Mall, has numerous international eateries.

Billy Baxters, at No 224 on the corner with Austin St, is said to have the best pancakes in town – mind you, the same is said about the Pancake Kitchen.

Gouger St This is another street of restaurants, many of which have become local institutions.

Tacked on to the western end of Central Market is *Chinatown*, which has a large collection of mainly Asian-style eateries; one group of kitchens shares a communal eating area, which is cheap and extremely popular.

The very popular *Mamma Getta Restaurant* at No 55 is an authentic Italian place and most dishes are around $7. At No 67 is the award-winning *Star of Siam*, serving delicious Thai food; a seven-course luncheon banquet costs $16, and evening banquets start at $20.

Paul's Cafe, at No 79, serves some of the best fish & chips in town, while the *Rock Lobster Cafe*, at No 108, is a great place for fresh rock lobster (in season) and oysters.

The *Red Ochre Grill*, at No 129, is Australian bush tucker gone gourmet. It's open for lunch and dinner, and the menu reads like an internal memo from the National Parks & Wildlife Service (NPWS). Meals are superb, and you may never again get to sample emu or wallaby, followed by wattle-seed pavlova. It's not cheap – an average of $17 for a main course – but it's worth the splurge.

Ming Palace is an unpretentious Chinese restaurant serving good food at No 201. It's open daily and is renowned for its Peking duck.

Around Town There are a number of good restaurants and cafes on O'Connell St in North Adelaide. *Himeiji*, at No 61, is a Japanese restaurant with one of the best sushi bars in town. It's rather expensive, but worth it.

The trendy *Equinox Bistro* at Adelaide University is in the Union Complex, above the Cloisters off Victoria Drive. It's open weekdays from 10 am to 10 pm (8 pm in university holiday periods) and has main courses from just $5. Believe it or not, the *Union Cafeteria* on the ground floor is cheaper.

Also good is *Hawker's Corner*, on the corner of West Terrace and Wright St. It's open daily except Monday for lunch and dinner and has Chinese, Vietnamese, Thai and Indian food. *Hawkers Too*, next door, is a cafe-style eatery with a similar flavour, but main courses start at $6 – it's popular with overseas students.

The *Volga*, upstairs at 116 Flinders St, is Adelaide's only Russian restaurant. It's a friendly place, with Gypsy violinists (Friday and Saturday nights) and beluga caviar for those with expensive palates. Main meals (without the caviar) range from $10 to $20.

Keep heading north a short distance to *Venezia*, a good Italian tavern and restaurant at 121 Pirie St, which has pasta from $9 and steak from $13. There are a couple of other good Italian restaurants next door.

Adelaide is very well supplied with hotels offering counter meals, particularly at lunchtime. Just look for the telltale blackboards outside. You won't have to search for long to find one with meals under $5, particularly now that most have poker machines – many

ffer meals at ridiculous prices to get people
hrough the door.

In North Adelaide, the *British*, at 58
Finniss St, has a pleasant beer garden where
ou can grill the food yourself at the barbe-
ue. Main courses are about $11 ($2 to $3
ess if you cook your own).

En route is the *Festival Bistro*, in the Fes-
ival Centre on King William St, overlooking
he Torrens River. It has sandwiches and
nacks and is open late (closed Sunday
nless there's a performance on).

Entertainment

Bookings for performances at the Festival
Centre and other Adelaide venues can be
nade through Bass on ☎ 13 1246. There are
umerous Bass outlets around town, includ-
ng one at the centre (open Monday to
Saturday from 9 am to 8.30 pm) and another
n the 5th floor of the Myer department store
n Rundle Mall.

Casino The *Adelaide Casino* is housed in
he grand old railway station on North
Terrace. Apart from a wide range of gam-
ling facilities (including a two-up game, of
ourse) there are three bars and two restau-
ants. It's open Monday to Thursday from 10
m to 4 am, and 24 hours a day from Friday
o Sunday and on public holidays. Smart
asual dress is required.

Cinemas Adelaide has several commercial
inemas; ☎ 0055 14632 for a recorded
isting of films showing around town.

The *Mercury Cinema* (☎ 8410 1934), in
he Lion Arts Centre at 13 Morphett St, is
Adelaide's major alternative cinema,
howing a variety of films such as classic,
ult, animation and art-house. It's also the
ome of the biennial Frames Festival of Film
& Video, usually held in September in even-
umbered years, which features recent short
Australian films and videos.

Other cinemas that show alternative films
re the wonderful old *Piccadilly* (☎ 8267
500), 181 O'Connell St in North Adelaide,
nd the *Capri Theatre* (☎ 8272 1177), at 141
Goodwood Rd, Goodwood. The latter occa-

sionally shows foreign-language films; it
often has live performances before a
showing, including an organist on Tuesday,
Friday and Saturday evenings.

Pubs & Music There are lots of pubs with
entertainment. Check *The Guide* in Thursday's *Advertiser* newspaper or phone the
radio station SA-FM (☎ 8272 1990) for a
recorded rundown of who's playing what,
and where, around town. The free music
paper *Rip it Up* is worth picking up for its
listings. For theatre and gallery reviews
check the free monthly *Adelaide Review*.
You'll find both publications at record shops,
hotels, cafes and night spots around town.

Several pubs brewed their own beer until
fairly recently, but it seems the only survivor
is the *Port Dock Brewery Hotel*, at 10 Todd
St in Port Adelaide. It produces four distinctive beers, overseen by a German brew
specialist.

There's the usual rock pub circuit. The
Earl of Aberdeen, on Carrington St at Hurtle
Square, is a very nice, very trendy place with
lots of timber and usually a rock band on
Wednesday, Friday and Saturday nights. It's
handy to the backpackers hostels in the
south-east of the city centre.

On Rundle St, the *Austral* and the *Exeter*,
at Nos 205 and 246 respectively, often have
bands and DJs. They're popular with business folk and office workers during the day
(both pubs have interesting lunchtime
menus), while at night they're university
students' hang-outs. Try them if you're
looking for a place for a drink before heading
out to eat. Nearby, at No 242, *Tapas* has a
jazz band on Friday nights.

Also good for a pre-dinner drink is the
Universal Wine Bar at 285 Rundle St; it's got
a great atmosphere, with plenty of iron fili-
gree, and the doors fold back on summer
nights so you can catch the breeze.

The bar at the *Earl of Zetland* on Flinders
St claims to have the world's largest collection of malt whiskies, with over 275 varieties
available by the nip.

In the old Commercial Hotel on the corner
of Morphett and Hindley Sts is *Rave on*

Hindley, reputedly the most upcoming of the street's nightclubs and popular with teenagers. A couple of huge bouncers (they're twins) keep the riff-raff outside where they belong. It's open between Wednesday and Sunday from 8 pm until late.

Most popular of Adelaide's clubs is the *Heaven Nightclub*, in the grand old Newmarket Hotel on the corner of West and North Terraces. It has DJs between Wednesday and Saturday nights and often has bands on Sunday. The pub also has *Joplins Nightclub*, which is popular with the older set.

The *UniBar* (☎ 8303 5401) in the Union Complex at Adelaide University often features big-name and up-and-coming rock bands during lunchtime, afternoons and evenings – usually Friday. The bar is also an excellent venue for avant-garde performances and social activities. The complex is off Victoria Drive and above the Cloisters, and visitors are welcome.

There are often free concerts in the amphitheatre at the *Festival Centre* on alternate Sundays during summer, and in the centre's foyer every Sunday during winter. On Saturday nights between 10 pm and 1 am, the *Fez Bar*, at the Centre, is a good jazz and rock venue; admission is $7.

Every Friday night the *Irish Club* at 11 Carrington St has live music from 8 pm until late. You don't have to be Irish to get in.

Things to Buy

Rundle St is a good place for retro clothes and boutiques; the East End and Orange Lane markets are worth checking for second-hand and alternative clothing (see the earlier Markets section for details).

Tandanya, run by the Aboriginal Cultural Institute at 253 Grenfell St, includes a craft and souvenir shop; it is open daily. High-quality craftwork is produced and sold at the Jam Factory Craft & Design Centre, in the Lion Arts Centre on the corner of Morphett St and North Terrace. It also has a shop at 74 Gawler Place, in the city centre.

Getting There & Away

Air Many flights from Melbourne and Sydney to the Northern Territory go via Adelaide, and the Darwin route is often heavily booked. Qantas (☎ 13 1313) is at 144 North Terrace and Ansett (☎ 13 1300) is at 142 North Terrace.

Standard one-way fares from Adelaide include: Brisbane $494, Sydney $346, Melbourne $240, Perth $516, Alice Springs $372 and Darwin $536. Remember that there are almost always cheaper fares available.

For air fares within the state, refer to the air-fares chart in the introductory Getting Around section in this chapter.

Bus Most interstate and intrastate services go from Adelaide's central bus station at 101-111 Franklin St. The major carriers – Greyhound Pioneer, Stateliner and McCafferty's – have offices here. Left-luggage lockers are available.

Greyhound Pioneer (☎ 13 2030) has services between Adelaide and all major cities. The fare to Melbourne is $53 (10 hours), Sydney $95 (22 hours), Perth $189 (34 hours) and Alice Springs $142 (20 hours). There's a 10% discount for backpackers.

McCafferty's (☎ 13 1499) also offers backpackers a 10% discount. Fares include Melbourne $45; Sydney $86 via Melbourne and $90 direct; Alice Springs $135; Darwin $243; Brisbane $140; and Cairns $258.

Firefly Express (☎ 8231 1488) is at 185 Victoria Square, near the corner of Franklin St. It runs to Melbourne every evening from Victoria Square at 8.30 pm ($40) and on to Sydney for $50 (day service) and $45 (overnight service).

If you're travelling between Melbourne and Adelaide, a popular alternative to the major bus lines is to spend three days and two nights on the trip with the Wayward Bus Company (☎ 8232 6646; 1800 882 823), which has a 22-seat bus that deviates from the main highways, taking in Victoria's spectacular Great Ocean Road and several national parks, including the Twelve Apostles and the Coorong. The $150 fare includes lunches but not accommodation or other meals. Departures from both ends are two to five times weekly.

Wayward has a similar eight-day Adelaide to Alice Springs trip. Departures are weekly, and take in the Clare Valley, the Flinders Ranges, the Oodnadatta Track, Coober Pedy, Uluru (Ayers Rock) and Kings Canyon. The $560 cost includes admission to all national parks, all meals, and camping or bunk house accommodation en route. It also does a 12-day trip to Perth for $770.

Stateliner, Premier Roadlines (☎ 8415 5555 for both) and other South Australian operators are at the central bus station. Stateliner has services to Wilpena Pound, Port Lincoln, Ceduna, Roxby Downs, Coober Pedy, Clare and the Riverland area. Premier goes to Goolwa, Victor Harbor, Moonta and Murray Bridge. See the appropriate Getting There & Away sections in this chapter for details.

There are at least seven smaller operators providing regional services from Adelaide.

The Yorke Peninsula Passenger Service (☎ 8391 2977) goes to Yorke Peninsula. Hills Transit (☎ 8339 1101) does the Adelaide Hills and Strathalbyn, and ABM Coachlines (☎ 8347 3336) runs through Birdwood, in the Adelaide Hills, to Mannum, on the Murray.

Bute Buses (☎ 8826 2110) goes to Orroroo via Burra, and the Barossa Adelaide Passenger Service (☎ 8564 3022) serves the Barossa. Bonds Mt Gambier Motor Service (☎ 8231 9090) has a daily return service to Mt Gambier. The Murray Bridge Passenger Service (☎ 8415 5555) goes to Murray Bridge and Pinnaroo.

Train There are two stations in Adelaide: the large one on North Terrace, for suburban trains; and the interstate terminal (☎ 8231 7699 for information; 13 2232 for bookings) on Railway Terrace, Keswick, just southwest of the city centre. It's wise to book ahead, particularly on the very popular *Ghan*. You have to ask about discounts, which usually aren't advertised.

Adelaide is connected by rail with Sydney, Melbourne, Perth, Broken Hill, Alice Springs and other centres. To Melbourne the nightly *Overland* takes about 12 hours and

costs $50 economy, $104 in 1st class and $170 with sleeper.

You can travel daily between Sydney and Adelaide via Melbourne on the *Melbourne Express* (Sydney to Melbourne) and *Overland* (Melbourne to Adelaide), and twice weekly via Broken Hill on the *Indian Pacific* (Sydney to Perth). Via Melbourne it's $146 economy, $239 for a 1st-class seat and $391 for a 1st-class sleeper. The connection is poor in Melbourne – you will need to spend the day there. Via Broken Hill it's $120 economy, $241 for a holiday-class economy sleeper and $376 for a 1st-class sleeper.

There's also the Speedlink – a daily bus and train connection that is not only cheaper but five or six hours faster. You travel from Sydney to Albury on the XPT train, and from Albury to Adelaide on a V/Line bus. Travel time is under 20 hours. An economy/1st-class seat is $99/141.

Between Adelaide and Perth there is the *Indian Pacific*, which runs twice weekly (Tuesday and Friday). The trip takes about 36 hours. Fares are $200 for an economy seat, $438 for a holiday-class sleeper (no meals), and $672 for a 1st-class sleeping berth with meals.

The *Ghan* between Adelaide and Alice Springs runs weekly throughout the year (departing Thursday) and twice weekly from April to October (Monday and Thursday). The fare is $140 in economy; $309 in a holiday-class sleeper (no meals); and $500 in a 1st-class sleeper with meals. Low-season (February through June) fares are $140/278/450 respectively.

Boat Kangaroo Island Fast Ferries runs a passenger ferry service from Glenelg to Kingscote; see the Kangaroo Island section for details.

Car & Motorbike Rental The Yellow Pages lists over 20 vehicle rental companies in Adelaide, including all the major national companies.

Those with cheaper rates include Access Rent-a-Car (☎ 8223 7466), Action Rent-a-Car (☎ 8352 7044), Airport Rent-a-Car

(☎ 8343 8855; 1800 631 637), Delta (☎ 13 1390), Rent-a-Bug (☎ 8234 0911) and Smile Rent-a-Car (☎ 8234 0655).

Access and Smile allow their cars to be taken over to Kangaroo Island, but few others do.

Show & Go (☎ 8376 0333), at 236 Brighton Rd, Brighton, has motor scooters for $49 per day (car licence required) and motorbikes from 250 cc ($59) to 1000 cc (from $89 – a full motorcycle licence is required for all bikes).

Getting Around

To/From the Airport Adelaide's international airport is conveniently located seven km west of the city centre. An airport bus service (☎ 8381 5311) operates between hotels at least half-hourly from around 7 am to 9 pm on weekdays, and hourly on weekends and public holidays for $6.

From Victoria Square to the domestic terminal the trip takes about 30 minutes; slightly less to the international terminal. If you're catching a flight on one of the smaller airlines (eg to Kangaroo Island) let the driver know, as the drop-off point is different. A taxi costs about $14. You can travel between the city and the airport entrance on bus Nos 276, 277 and 278 leaving from Grenfell and Currie Sts.

Budget, Hertz, Avis and Thrifty have hire-car desks at the airport.

Some of the hostels will pick you up and drop you off if you're staying with them.

Public Transport Adelaide has an integrated local transport system operated by TransAdelaide (TA; ☎ 8210 1000). The TA Information Bureau, where you can get timetables and buy a transport map for $2, is on the corner of King William and Currie Sts.

The system covers metropolitan buses and trains, as well as Adelaide's vintage tram, which operates to Glenelg, and the O-Bahn Busway, which runs on concrete tracks between the city centre and Tea Tree Plaza, home of the huge Westfield Shopping Centre & Cinema Complex. Tickets purchased on board the buses are $2.70 before 9 am, after 3 pm and on weekends, and $1.60 between

9 am and 3 pm weekdays. They are valid for two hours from the commencement of the first journey. (Tickets cannot be purchased on board trains.) For travellers, the best deal is the day-trip ticket, which permits unlimited travel for the whole day and costs $4.60.

The free Bee Line bus service (No 99B) runs in a loop from the Glenelg tram terminus at Victoria Square, down King William St and around the corner to the railway station. It operates every five to eight minutes weekdays from 8 am to 6 pm, and every 15 minutes on Friday to 7 pm and on Saturday from 8 am to 5 pm.

The airport to city bus service calls into the interstate train station (Keswick) on its regular run between the airport and the city ($3) from the station to the city centre.

There's a solitary vintage tram that rattles its way out to Glenelg from Victoria Square.

Bicycle Adelaide is a relatively cyclist-friendly city, with good cycling tracks and bicycle lanes on many city streets. Linear Park Mountain Bike Hire (☎ 8223 6953) is at Elder Park, next to the Festival Theatre; it's on the Linear Park Bike & Walking Track, a 40-km track that wends its way mainly along the Torrens River from the beach to the foot of the Adelaide Hills. Bicycles are $8 per hour or $20 for the day.

Velodrome Cycles (☎ 8223 6678) at 43 Rundle Mall rents mountain bikes from $15 per day or $70 for a week. Freewheelin' (☎ 8232 6860), at 237 Hutt St, has bicycles from $15 to $20 per day, and offers a pick-up and drop-off service. It also has entire touring outfits, including panniers. Tours from one day to three weeks are available.

Adelaide Hills

Only 30 minutes drive from the city centre, the scenic Adelaide Hills, part of the Mt Lofty Ranges, encompass the region bordered by the towns of Meadows and Strathalbyn to the south, Mt Barker and Nairne to the east, and Mt Pleasant and

Springton to the north. Apart from the beauty of the hills themselves, the opportunities for bushwalking (over 1000 km of trails criss-cross the hills), the range of conservation parks, and historic townships such as Clarendon, Hahndorf and Strathalbyn, make this region a popular day-trip destination from Adelaide.

The RAA produces a touring guide of the Adelaide Hills region ($4 for members and $8 for nonmembers). The Adelaide Hills Information Centre is in Hahndorf.

NATIONAL PARKS & SCENIC DRIVES

To visit the northern hills area, leave the city via Payneham Rd and continue on to Torrens Gorge Rd. This route takes you through Birdwood and north to the Barossa Valley. However, you might prefer to head south at Birdwood and travel through Hahndorf, returning to Adelaide via the South Eastern Freeway.

Alternatively, leave Payneham Rd and take McGill Rd through **Morialta Conservation Park**, near Rostrevor, which has walking trails, barbecues, waterfalls and a

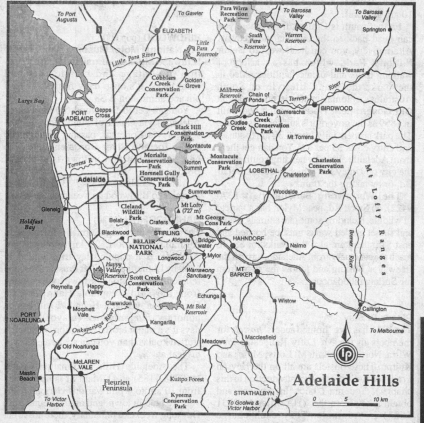

Adelaide Hills

rugged gorge. Continue south via Norton Summit and Summertown to the **Cleland Wildlife Park**. The major attraction here is a wildlife (tamelife?) park with numerous species of Australian fauna. It's open daily from 9.30 am to 5 pm and entry is $7. Buses run to the park; contact the SATC in Adelaide for details. Or you can visit on one of the day tours that operate from the city.

A slight detour will take you to **Mt Lofty Summit** (727 metres), which has impressive views back over the city (particularly at night). From the summit you continue south for about 1.5 km to the large and scenic **Mt Lofty Botanical Gardens** (open weekdays from 8.30 am to 4 pm, and weekends from 10 am to 5 pm).

Farther south is Crafers, from where you can head back to the city via the freeway. Alternatively, you can head west to **Belair National Park**, which has a variety of walking trails and picnic facilities. Also in the park, the grand lifestyle of South Australia's colonial gentry is on display at **Old Government House**, which was built in 1859 as the governor's summer residence. The park is open daily from 8.30 am to sunset and entry costs $3 per car. You can get there from Adelaide either by heading south out of the city on Unley Rd, which becomes Belair Rd, or by taking the train.

The **Warrawong Sanctuary** (☎ 8370 9422), on Stock Rd, near Mylor, has a variety of wildlife, including some rare animals. Dawn and sunset guided walks must be booked and cost $15; there are also day walks for $8. To reach the sanctuary from Adelaide, turn off the freeway at Stirling and follow the signs from the Stirling roundabout.

Places to Stay

The YHA has five 'limited access' *hostels* for members in the Mt Lofty Ranges at Para Wirra, Norton Summit, Mt Lofty, Mylor and Kuitpo. These hostels are all on the Heysen Trail (see Activities in the introduction to this chapter). You must book in advance and obtain a key from the YHA office (☎ 8231 5583) in Adelaide. They each charge between $4 and $7 per night, plus a key deposit ($10).

For something entirely different there's the 17-hectare *Fuzzies Farm* (☎ 8390 1111) at Norton Summit. Set in a scenic valley next to Morialta Conservation Park, this friendly 'eco-village' offers a unique opportunity for some hands-on experience in sharing a cooperative lifestyle. Guests are encouraged to help with activities such as building construction, carpentry, crafts, tending the chooks and shearing the flock of angora goats. A one-night introduction costs $20 with dinner or $15 without. The self-contained cottage accommodation is superb and there are special rates for long stays. This place is very popular, so bookings are essential.

BIRDWOOD (pop 600)

The **National Motor Museum** in the historic Birdwood Mill has Australia's largest collection of vintage and classic cars and motorbikes. It's open daily from 9 am to 5 pm and admission is $8.

You can get to Birdwood (50 km east of Adelaide) via Chain of Ponds and Gumeracha or via Lobethal, passing through the scenic **Torrens River Gorge** en route. The only accommodation in town is at several B&B places.

ABM Coachlines (☎ 8347 3336) runs from Adelaide to Birdwood on weekdays for $7.30.

HAHNDORF (pop 1730)

The oldest surviving German settlement in Australia, Hahndorf, 29 km south-east of Adelaide, is a popular day trip. Settled in 1839 by Lutherans who left Prussia to escape religious persecution, the town took its name from the ship's captain, Hahn; *dorf* is German for 'village'. Hahndorf still has an honorary *Burgermeister* (mayor). These days it's a major tourist attraction, with more stuffed koalas than you can shake a eucalyptus leaf at.

The Adelaide Hills Information Centre (☎ 8388 1185) at 41 Main St is open daily from 10 am to 4 pm. Various German festivals are held in town, and on the Foundation Day long weekend in January, there are street parades and wine tastings, and all the local eateries peddle their wares from tables outside their premises.

The **German Arms Hotel** at 50 Main St dates from 1839. The **Hahndorf Academy**, next to the information centre, was established in 1857 and houses an art gallery, craft shop and museum – it held a valuable collection of the works of 19th-century landscape artist Sir Hans Heysen until early 1995, when thieves made off with it. Guided tours through Sir Hans' studio and house, **The Cedars**, are conducted every Tuesday and Thursday at 11.30 am and 2.30 pm ($5). The **Antique Clock Museum** at 91 Main St has a fine collection of timepieces, including a very large cuckoo clock; admission is $3.

Places to Stay & Eat

Höchstens Convention & Tourist Centre (☎ 8388 7921) has a motel, caravan park and camp sites. It's 1.5 km out of town on Main St. Camp sites start at $10, cabins cost $46 and motel rooms are $79 for singles/doubles. The only other alternatives are a couple of fairly expensive motels.

Hahndorf has many good restaurants and several feature German food. They include the *German Arms Hotel*, the *German Cake Shop* and the *Cottage Kitchen*, all on Main St. *Karl's German Coffee House*, at 17 Main St, is recommended by locals for authentic German cuisine.

A great place to purchase German and continental smallgoods, including bockwurst, bratwurst and other treats, is *Gourmet Foods*, 37 Main St.

Getting There & Away

Hills Transit (☎ 8339 1191) runs several times daily from the central bus station in Adelaide ($4.10).

Getting Around

A pleasant way to amble around the town is in the horse-drawn carriage, which leaves regularly from in front of the Old Mill Motel at 98 Main St. If that's a little too sedate for you, Original Motorbike Tours (☎ 8212

5588) has daily rides on Harley-Davidson motorbikes starting from $10.

Hahndorf Tours (☎ 018 088 225) does two to four-hour minibus tours of the town costing from $15. The other option is Tony's Taxis (☎ 8370 8333). Tony offers half-day tours for $17.50 per person if you're in a group of four.

STRATHALBYN (pop 2700)

On the Angas River, this picturesque town was settled in 1839 by Scottish immigrants. Among the many interesting old buildings in this classified 'heritage town' is **St Andrew's Church**, one of the best-known country churches in Australia.

The tourist office (☎ 8536 3212) is on South Terrace. It's open weekdays from 9.30 am to 4 pm and weekends from 11 am to 4 pm.

You can buy a walking-tour pamphlet ($1.20) that lists historic buildings and other sites of interest in the township. The old courthouse and police station are now a National Trust **museum**; entry costs $2 and it's open from 2 to 5 pm on weekends and school and public holidays.

Places to Stay

The council caravan park (☎ 8536 3681), in the showgrounds on Coronation Rd, has grassed camp sites for $8 and on-site vans from $20.

The *Terminus Hotel* (☎ 8536 2026) on Rankine St has singles/doubles for $25/45, including a light breakfast. The *Robin Hood Hotel* (☎ 8536 2608) on High St charges $29/45, also with breakfast.

Getting There & Away

Hills Transit (☎ 8339 1191) runs from Adelaide to Strathalbyn (changing at Mt Barker) on weekdays for $6.

CLARENDON

Beautiful Clarendon, 28 km south of Adelaide, has inspiring views and heritage buildings.

The **Old Clarendon Winery Complex** (☎ 8383 6166) has cellar-door sales and tastings, as well as two craft shops and a good restaurant. Accommodation in comfortable rooms includes good views over the township and costs $65/70/85, including a light breakfast.

Fleurieu Peninsula

South of Adelaide is the Fleurieu Peninsula, so close that most places can be visited on day trips from the city. The Gulf St Vincent has a series of fine beaches down to Cape Jervis.

The peninsula was named by Frenchman Nicholas Baudin after Napoleon's minister for the navy, who financed Baudin's expedition to Australia. In the early days, settlers on the peninsula ran a smuggling business. In 1837 a whaling station was established at Encounter Bay and this became the colony's first successful industry.

There are good surfing beaches along the rugged southern coastline. Inland there's rolling farmland and the vineyards of the McLaren Vale area.

Getting There & Away

Premier (☎ 8415 5555) has up to three services daily on the two-hour Adelaide to McLaren Vale ($4.70), Port Elliot, Goolwa and Victor Harbor (all $11) route.

Coachlines of Australia (booking centre ☎ 8384 6860) runs once daily to Cape Jervis from Adelaide. The fare to Yankalilla is $8.90 and to Cape Jervis $13.

It's proposed to link Mt Barker (in the Adelaide Hills) with Victor Harbor by the Southern Encounter steam train when the Mt Barker depot is completed. The Cockle Train is a small steam train that travels between Victor Harbor and Goolwa. See the Victor Harbor section for details.

GULF ST VINCENT BEACHES

There is a stretch of fine beaches along the

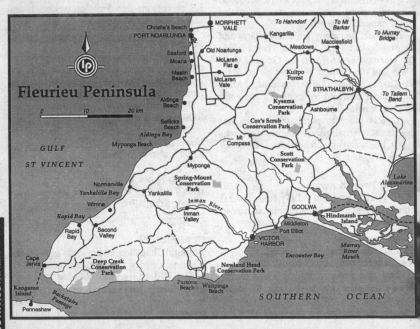

Gulf St Vincent coast of the peninsula. They extend from **Christie's Beach** through **Port Noarlunga**, **Seaford Beach** and **Moana Beach** to **Maslin Beach**.

Farther south, beyond **Aldinga Beach** and **Sellicks Beach**, the coastline is rockier but there are still good swimming beaches at **Carrickalinga** and **Normanville**. The coast road ends at **Cape Jervis** at the tip of the peninsula. From here you can look across the narrow Backstairs Passage to Kangaroo Island, 13 km away. Near Cape Jervis there's a 12-hectare fauna park. The cape is a popular spot for hang-gliding.

The picturesque **Inman Valley** is only 16 km from Victor Harbor and is a prime dairy and grazing area. It is an access point for the Heysen Trail.

Places to Stay

On the main road about two km from Cape Jervis, the friendly *Old Cape Jervis Station Homestead* (☎ 8598 0233) has accommodation starting at $12 per person. This gets you a bed in the historic shearers' quarters, with use of the kitchen. Alternatively, the *Cape Jervis Tavern* (☎ 8598 0276) has rooms for $45/55 and also serves reasonable counter meals from $6.50.

There are caravan parks in Normanville, Second Valley and the Wirrina Resort, all of which have camp sites, on-site vans and cabins. The *Yankalilla Hotel* (☎ 8558 2011), in Yankalilla, four km east of Normanville, has a cottage for a flat rate of $50. It sleeps six and linen is supplied.

The *youth hostel* (☎ 8558 8277), in Inman Valley near Glacier Rock, 16 km west of Victor Harbor, is in a lovely tranquil setting. Beds are $9 for YHA members and $11 for nonmembers; maps of the Heysen Trail are available from the hostel manager.

SOUTHERN VALES

Adelaide has sprawled so far that the small town of **Morphett Vale** is now an outer suburb. Among its historic buildings is St Mary's (1846), the first Roman Catholic church in the state. **Old Noarlunga** is a tiny

old township only 10 minutes drive from McLaren Vale.

Interesting heritage walks are conducted on various days, usually from 2 pm, in Morphett Vale, Old Noarlunga, Port Noarlunga and Reynella. They take from 1½ to two hours and cost $9; phone ☎ 8384 7918 for details.

Wineries

The peninsula has a string of wineries, centred around **McLaren Vale** (population 1520), but also encompassing Reynella, Willunga and Langhorne Creek. The area is particularly well-suited to red wines, but a trend towards white wine consumption in the 1970s prompted growers to diversify.

There's an information centre at the coffee shop in the magnificent Hardy's Tintara complex (open 10 am to 4 pm), in McLaren Vale.

There are over two dozen wineries in the McLaren Vale area alone and about 50 in the whole region. The first winery was established in Reynella in 1838, and some existing wineries date to the last century and have fine old buildings. Most are open to the public from Monday to Saturday, and many are open on Sunday as well. Some have picnic or barbecue areas close to the cellar-door sales area.

Each winery has its own appeal, whether it be a superb setting or just a good full-bodied drop of the home product. The following are suggestions to help with your explorations.

Chapel Hill, Chapel Hill Rd, McLaren Vale south, has a magnificent hill-top location with views over the Gulf St Vincent. This is a small vineyard producing sophisticated whites and reds.

Noon's, Rifle Range Rd, McLaren Vale south, specialises in full-bodied reds. This winery is in a pleasant rural setting beside a small creek, and there are barbecue facilities.

d'Arenberg, Osborne Rd, McLaren Vale, has produced consistently good wines since 1928. There is nothing highbrow about this place – the tasting room is very informal and the staff are friendly and helpful.

Woodstock, Douglas Gully Rd, McLaren Flat, is another small winery in a tranquil garden setting.

The McLaren Vale **Wine Bushing Festival** takes place over a week in late October and/or early November each year. It's a busy time of wine tastings and tours, and the whole thing is topped by a grand feast. During the festival, you can sample offerings from the McLaren Vale wineries on the winery bus service, which picks up and drops off imbibers en route.

A great way to visit a few wineries is on a camel with the Outback Camel Co (☎ 8543 2280). Various tours are available, including a one-day trek for $80. Alternatively, you can see the area from a motorbike with SA Harley Tours (☎ 8378 1415) – a half-hour costs $30 and a half-day $120.

The only other option is to walk or cycle. There's a walking/bicycle track along the old railway line from McLaren Vale to Willunga, six km to the south.

Willunga, in the south of the Southern Vales winery area, has numerous interesting buildings from the colonial era. It's the centre for Australian almond growing, and hosts the Almond Blossom Festival in July.

There are fine views, kangaroos and walks in the **Mt Magnificent Conservation Park**, 12 km east of Willunga. This is also an access point for the Heysen Trail.

Places to Stay & Eat

The friendly *McLaren Vale Lakeside Caravan Park* (☎ 8323 9255), set amid vineyards on Field St, has camp sites ($12), on-site vans (from $31) and luxury cabins ($47). Another nice place is the *Southern Vales B&B* (☎ 8323 8144), on Chalk Hill Rd. It has a colonial authors theme and charges $75 for doubles.

In Willunga, the *Willunga Hotel* (☎ 8556 2135) has rooms from $20/25 for singles/doubles. It's also one of the best places in town for meals.

There are several good restaurants in McLaren Vale. *Magnum's* in the Hotel McLaren is recommended for a top feed, as is *The Barn* bistro. Both are on Main Rd. Perhaps best of all is the historic *Salopian Inn*, just out of town on the Willunga Rd; it has a fascinating menu – imagine seared soy-basted squid, or roasted Tilbaroo calves kidneys – but it is fairly expensive (main courses start at $16). You'll need to book (☎ 8323 8769) as it's small and popular.

The wine-tasters' lunches can be good value: *Brook's Restaurant* in the Middlebrook Winery on Sand Rd is open daily, with main courses from $11. *Haselgrove Wines*, on the corner of Kangarilla and Foggo Rds, has similar prices and is open Wednesday to Sunday. You can get a decent 'picker's platter' for $10 at the rustic *Wirilda Creek Winery*, on McMurtrie Rd.

PORT ELLIOT (pop 1250)

On Horseshoe Bay, a smaller part of Encounter Bay, Port Elliot was established in 1854 as the seaport for the Murray River trade and it was the first town on Encounter Bay. **Horseshoe Bay** has a sheltered, safe swimming beach and a good cliff-top walk. Nearby surf beaches include **Boomer Beach**, on the western edge of town, and **Middleton Beach**, to the east. The Southern Surf Shop, a few doors west from the Royal Family Hotel, hires surfing gear and can provide information on prevailing surfing conditions.

Places to Stay & Eat

You can camp ($11) or stay in on-site vans ($33) or cabins (from $45 for four people) at the *Port Elliot Caravan Park* (☎ 8554 2134) on Horseshoe Bay.

The *Royal Family Hotel* (☎ 8554 2219) at 32 North Terrace has singles/doubles for

$20/25; counter meals start at $7, and there's an excellent bakery across the road.

VICTOR HARBOR (pop 5960)

The main town on the peninsula, and 84 km south of Adelaide, Victor Harbor looks out onto Encounter Bay, where the British explorer, Flinders, and the French explorer, Baudin, had a historic meeting in 1802. Up on the headland known as the Bluff, there's a memorial to the 'encounter'. It's a steep climb up to the Bluff for the fine views.

The town was founded as a sealing and whaling centre. South of the town at Rosetta Bay, below the Bluff, is **Whaler's Haven**, which has many interesting reminders of the whaling days as well as a restaurant and coffee shop. The first whaling station was established here in 1837 and another followed soon after on Granite Island, but operations ceased in 1864.

Information

The tourist office (☎ 8552 5738) is at 10 Railway Terrace, diagonally opposite the railway station. It's open daily from 10 am to 4 pm.

Things to See

Historic buildings include **St Augustine's** **Church of England** (1869), the **Telegraph Station** (1869), the **Fountain Inn** (1840) and the **Old Station Master's Residence** (1866), now administered as a museum by the National Trust (open Sunday, public and school holidays from 11 am to 4 pm). The Telegraph Station houses an art gallery, which often holds exhibitions of the works of well-known Australian artists.

Victor Harbor is protected from the angry Southern Ocean by **Granite Island**, which is connected to the mainland by a causeway and is being developed for tourism. You can ride out there on a double-decker tram pulled by Clydesdale draught horses ($3 return). From the top of the hill there are good views across the bay; it's an easy climb, but if you're feeling lazy you can take the chair lift.

Granite Island is a rookery for little penguins. The NPWS operates one-hour **Little Penguin Sunset Walks** nightly during school holidays and on Wednesday, Friday and Saturday at other times of the year; phone ☎ 8552 3677 for start times and bookings. Walks cost $5 and commence at the end of the causeway on Granite Island.

Between June and October you might be lucky enough to see a **southern right whale** swimming near the causeway. Victor Harbor is on the migratory path of these splendid animals

Southern Right Whales

Southern right whales are so-called because they were considered by whalers to be the 'right' whales to hunt – large quantities of oil and fine whalebone meant a tidy profit from each carcass. The southern rights once roamed the seas in prolific numbers, but unrestrained slaughter last century reduced the population from 100,000 to an estimated 3000 today. Although considered an endangered species, they appear to be fighting back. During recent years, southern right whales have appeared in Encounter Bay, off Victor Harbor, from June to October during their annual breeding migration to warmer coastal waters.

The South Australian Whale Centre operates a whale information network from its information and interpretive centre on Railway Terrace in Victor Harbor. To report a sighting, call ☎ 8552 5644; or for current information on where the whales are, call ☎ 0055 31 223. The centre has an informative booklet ($1) that tells you all about whale-watching, including useful tips on how to avoid damaging the fragile coastal environment. You can write to the centre at PO Box 950, Victor Harbor 5211. ∎

and you can observe them from several lookout points around the bay, including the Bluff. You'll need binoculars with a magnification power of seven or more.

If you want to learn more about whales, the **South Australian Whale Centre**, at the causeway end of Railway Terrace, is the place to go. It operates a 'whale information network' that covers sightings and strandings on the South Australian and Victorian coasts. It is open daily (times vary depending on demand) and entry costs $5; see the aside for further details.

Places to Stay
There are a number of caravan parks, hotels, motels and B&Bs in and around Victor Harbor, and you can get details from the tourist office.

Visitors have recommended the *Victor Harbor Caravan Park* (☎ 8552 1142), on the foreshore at 114 Victoria St, which has camp sites ($10), basic cabins ($35) and self-contained cabins ($45).

The *Warringa Hostel* (☎ 8552 5970) is part of the Anchorage Guest House complex, at 21 Flinders Pde near the railway station. Beds in very basic dorms are $10 for YHA members and $15 for nonmembers. Its guesthouse rooms start from $35/60.

The *Grosvenor Hotel* (☎ 8552 1011), a block away on Ocean St, has basic rooms for $25/35/40/45. The tastefully renovated *Hotel Victor* (☎ 8552 1288) on the Esplanade charges from $65/75/85 for singles/doubles/triples. The most central motel is the *City Motel* (☎ 8552 2455), next to the post office on Ocean St, which has singles/doubles from $45/55.

Places to Eat
The *Original Fish & Chip Shop* in the town centre on Ocean St is popular, but best of the local seafood takeaways is *Pa's Place*, next to the Yilki Store – it's along the coast about three km south of the town centre. Both also have sit-down meals.

The atmosphere at the *Grosvenor* is nothing flash but you can get a decent feed for $5. For more formal dining the *Hotel Victor* is best.

For a different eating experience, *Klaus's Wurst Haus*, run by the ebullient Klaus himself, claims to sell the best German hot dogs in Australia. You'll find his tiny van in the small park on the causeway end of Railway Terrace; it's open weekends only.

Getting There & Away
The depot for the Southern Encounter steam train is being relocated from Adelaide to Mt Barker, and the service to Victor Harbor will then recommence (hopefully). For an update contact the tourist office or SteamRanger (☎ 8231 1707).

The Cockle Train travels daily on the scenic Encounter Coast between Goolwa and Victor Harbor over Easter and during school holidays, with selected Sunday trips at other times. The return fare is $12, and tickets can be purchased at the station in Victor Harbor.

Premier (☎ 8415 5555) has two to three services daily from Adelaide for $11.

Getting Around
Motor scooters can be hired from the Shell service station (☎ 8552 1875) at 165 Hindmarsh Rd for $20 per hour; day rates on application.

GOOLWA (pop 3030)
On Lake Alexandrina near the mouth of the Murray River, Goolwa initially grew with the developing trade along the river. When the Murray mouth silted up and large ships were unable to get up to Goolwa, a railway line, the first in the state, was built from Goolwa to nearby Port Elliot. In the 1880s a new railway line to Adelaide spelt the end for Goolwa as a port town.

The tourist office (☎ 8555 1144), open daily from 10 am to 4 pm, is in the centre of Goolwa near Signal Point. The **Signal Point River Murray Interpretive Centre** (open daily from 10 am to 5 pm) is on the waterfront and contains interesting exhibits on the early history of life on the river ($5). Self-guided walking-tour pamphlets of Goolwa are available from the interpretive centre and the tourist office.

The **museum** on Porter St ($1 admission) is open every afternoon except Monday and Friday and is well worth a visit.

Two km away at the **Malleebaa Woolshed**, you can see 18 breeds of sheep and activities such as shearing and hand-spinning. It's only open by appointment (☎ 8555 3638); entry costs from $4 depending on what you want to see.

The **Sir Richard Peninsula** is a long stretch of beach leading to the mouth of the Murray. You can drive along it (4WD only), but there's no way across to the similar beaches of the Coorong, which begin on the other side of the Murray River mouth.

Milang, on Lake Alexandrina, was a river-trade centre predating Goolwa. In the early days, bullock wagons carried goods overland between here and Adelaide.

There are cruises on Lake Alexandrina on the MV *Aroona* or PS *Mundoo* from $12. More amusing is a trip with the Coorong Pirate (☎ 8552 1221), a large and irredeemably ocker gentleman who runs fun trips from $6. His tours leave on the hour between 10 am and 3 pm.

A free vehicle ferry from Goolwa to **Hindmarsh Island** operates 24 hours a day. A bridge is proposed but its construction is dependent on the outcome of legal challenges arising from claims by local Aboriginal people that construction would damage sacred sites.

Places to Stay

Goolwa has several caravan parks, motels and B&Bs.

Closest to town of the caravan parks is the *Camping & Tourist Park* (☎ 8555 2144) on Kessell Rd, which has camp sites ($8) and on-site vans ($20 to $30).

Right in town, the *Corio Hotel* (☎ 8555 1136) on Railway Terrace has rooms for $25, including a cooked breakfast.

Graham's Castle (☎ 8555 2182), a rambling old home built in 1868, is about two km from the town centre, on Castle St, about 500 metres from the beach. Dormitory accommodation is available for $12 (linen hire extra). There's a pool and games room, and the owners will pick you up from the town centre if you give them a ring on arrival. They also run ecologically oriented boat expeditions into the Coorong National Park from $22.

On Hindmarsh Island, *Narnu Farm* (☎ 8555 2002) has cottages from $64 singles/doubles and $8 for each extra adult. This is a pioneer farm and guests are encouraged to take part in farm activities, such as feeding the animals and hand-milking the cows.

Getting There & Away

Daily buses to Adelaide cost $11. See the earlier Victor Harbor section for details of steam trains that pass through Goolwa.

Kangaroo Island

Separated from the mainland about 9500 years ago, Kangaroo Island is the third-largest island in Australia (after Tasmania, and Melville Island off Darwin). About 150 km long and 30 km wide, the island is sparsely populated and offers superb scenery, pleasant sheltered beaches along the north coast, a rugged and wave-swept south coast, lots of native wildlife and excellent fishing.

It was not until early this century that evidence of Aboriginal habitation on Kangaroo Island was found – prehistoric stone implements have since been discovered, suggesting human occupation more than 11,000 years ago. Archaeologists are uncertain as to what caused the demise of these early inhabitants, but it's thought they disappeared about 2250 years ago. The evidence for this is contained in charcoal deposits that indicate a dramatic decrease in the frequency of bush fires on the island around that time.

Like other islands off the south coast of Australia, Kangaroo Island had a rough-and-ready early European history with sealers, whalers and escaped convicts all playing

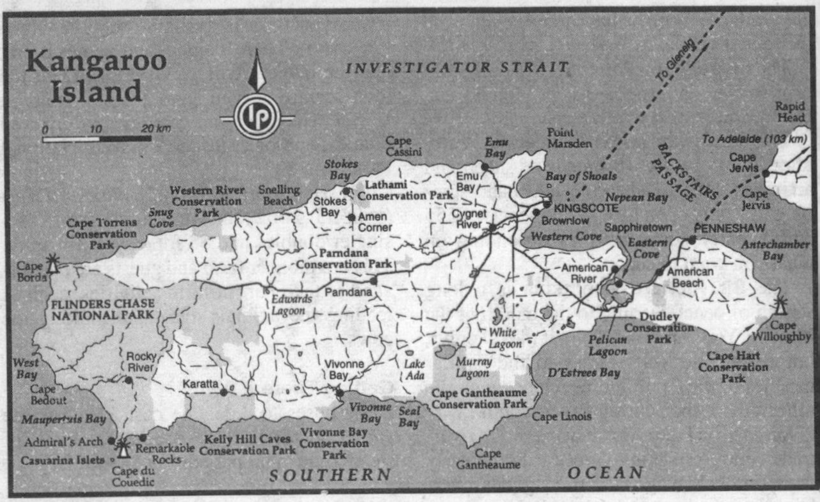

Kangaroo Island

their often ruthless part. Many of the place names on the island have a French flavour, as the first thorough survey of its coast was carried out by the French explorer Nicholas Baudin on two visits in 1802 and 1803. The island was named by Matthew Flinders in 1802 after his crew slaughtered many kangaroos there and enjoyed a welcome feast of fresh meat.

Kangaroo Island's geographical isolation from the mainland has been a boon to the native wildlife: it is free of dingoes, rabbits and foxes. In fact, a number of threatened native Australian animals, such as the koala and platypus, have been introduced to the island where conditions are considered more conducive to their survival. One of the main threats is of the vehicular form, as the number of furry corpses on the roadsides attests. Reducing your driving speed, which is a good idea anyway because the island has many unsealed roads, may help to increase the animals' chances of survival.

Apart from beaches, fishing, surfing, bushwalks and wildlife, there are also a number of shipwrecks off the coast, many of which are of interest to scuba divers.

Information

The main National Parks & Wildlife Service (NPWS) office (which doubles as the tourist office) is at 37 Dauncey St in Kingscote (☎ 8553 2381). It is open from 8.45 am to 5 pm Monday to Friday, but isn't much use for anything other than parks – it's got a good selection of leaflets, however.

The Island Pass ($15), which can be purchased only on the island, is valid for the financial year and covers all NPWS entry and camping fees on the island. The pass also entitles holders to free NPWS tours (see under Organised Tours). Permits and passes can be obtained from any of the island's seven NPWS offices; contact the Kingscote office for details.

A tourist centre was due to open at Penneshaw in either late 1996 or early 1997 and should be a big improvement on the present fragmented situation.

During summer, and into April, fire restrictions are in force. Only gas fires may be lit in national parks, and on days of total fire ban, no fires may be lit (including gas fires). Penalties for lighting a fire illegally are severe. Contact district council offices

SOUTH AUSTRALIA

the Country Fire Service or park rangers for further information.

If you intend walking in remote areas, advise rangers of your plans. It is essential to carry food and water.

Telecommunications The phone numbers listed for Kangaroo Island come into effect from February 1997. Before this time, use the old numbers (preceded by area code 0848 for long-distance calls):

For Kingscote, replace the initial 8553 with 2.

For American River, replace the initial 8553 7 with 33.

For Penneshaw, Western River and Vivonne Bay, leave off the initial 855.

For Flinders Chase National Park, replace the initial 8559 with 3.

Organised Tours

The NPWS operates a range of economical guided tours and walks for visitors to areas of conservation and historical significance, and these are free for Island Pass holders. Note that the Pass does not cover the penguin walks at Kingscote and Penneshaw.

At **Seal Bay**, 55 km south of Kingscote, 45-minute guided tours to the seal colonies are conducted daily between 9 am and 4.30 pm. Tours at the **Kelly Hill Caves Conservation Park**, 79 km from Kingscote, take place daily between 10 am and 4 pm (3 pm in winter).

Rangers also conduct tours of the historic lighthouses at **Cape Borda**, 103 km from Kingscote on the western extremity of the island, and **Cape Willoughby**, 28 km south-east of Penneshaw at the island's eastern end; see the sections on Flinders Chase and Penneshaw for times.

Unless you form part of a large group, bookings are not required.

Package Tours The three island ferry companies (see below under Getting There & Away) and many tour operators on the island offer packages ex-Adelaide. Competition is fierce, so if you shop around you should pick

up a good deal. Don't forget to check the hostels in Adelaide.

Bus Tours Tours designed for backpackers and other budget travellers are run by the Penneshaw Youth Hostel (☎ 8553 1284), Sealink (☎ 13 1301), Kangaroo Island Holiday Tours (☎ 8553 2722), in Kingscote, and Air & Adventure Tours (☎ 8281 0530); you can expect to pay between $65 and $70 for a full-day tour (including lunch) that takes in Seal Bay, Kelly Hill Caves and Flinders Chase National Park.

There are also more personalised 4WD tours, scuba-diving tours, fishing charters and tours, walking tours, and visits to such places as a eucalyptus oil distillery and a sheep's milk dairy.

Places to Stay

Individual establishments are listed under the major towns. The NPWS can arrange budget wilderness accommodation in historic cottages in the national parks, including the lightkeepers' cottages at Cape Willoughby and Cape du Couedic. Contact the office at Flinders Chase (☎ 8559 7235) for details.

The *Valerie Jane* ferry booking office in Penneshaw (☎ 8553 1233; 1800 018 484) has a range of combined accommodation and car-hire packages. Staff can book self-contained properties around the island starting at $50 for a double (car hire extra).

In addition to those at the main townships, small and mainly basic caravan parks are located at Emu Bay, Stokes Bay, Vivonne Bay and near Tandanya.

Getting There & Away

Air Air Kangaroo Island (bookings ☎ 13 1313) has at least twice-daily services from Adelaide to Kingscote ($60); 14-day advance-purchase return fares cost $50. Kendell Airlines (bookings ☎ 13 1300) services Kingscote from Adelaide. Fares are $78 or there's an advance-purchase Saver fare for $45.

Albatross Airlines (☎ 8553 2296), in Kingscote, flies from Adelaide to Kingscote three times daily ($60). Its free courtesy bus transfers passengers between the airport and the town.

Emu Air (☎ 1800 182 353) has a twice-daily service to Penneshaw and Kingscote from Adelaide; the fare is $63 one way.

Ferry Kangaroo Island Fast Ferries (☎ 8295 2688; 1800 626 242), based in Adelaide, runs the passenger ferry MV *Super Flyte* from Glenelg to Kingscote, leaving Glenelg daily at 8 am, plus Friday at 7.30 pm. It carries 500 passengers and does the trip in just over two hours, charging $35 (backpackers $30) one way and $65 ($55) return.

Kangaroo Island Ferry Connections (☎ 8553 1233; 1800 018 484), in Penneshaw, runs the passenger ferry MV *Valerie Jane* from Cape Jervis, at the end of the Fleurieu Peninsula, to Penneshaw. It leaves twice daily for $28, taking 30 minutes – during either July or August the service takes a break. For an extra $10, you can travel by bus from Adelaide to Cape Jervis to connect with the ferry. Contact the *Valerie Jane* booking office for details.

Also departing from Cape Jervis, Kangaroo Island Sealink (☎ 13 1301) operates two vehicular ferries that run all year, taking an hour to Penneshaw. There are at least a couple of sailings each day, with up to 10 in December and January. One-way fares are $30 for passengers, $5 for bicycles, $20 for motorbikes and $60 for cars.

The bus service from Adelaide to Port Jervis, which connects with Sealink ferry departures, costs $13 one way. It departs from the central bus station. Bookings are essential; phone ☎ 13 1301.

Getting Around

To/From the Airport There's an airport bus running from the Kangaroo Island airport to Kingscote for $10. The airport is 14 km from the town centre.

To/From the Ferry Landings The Sealink Shuttle (☎ 13 1301) connects with most ferries and links Penneshaw with Kingscote

($11) and American River ($6.50). You have to book.

Car Rental There are five car hire companies, all based at Kingscote, and more are threatening to open there.

The cheapest starting price is offered by Cut-Price Auto Rental (☎ 8553 2787), which has five-seater cars for $45 a day including unlimited km. Next is Koala Lodge Car Rentals (☎ 8553 9006) at $58 with unlimited km, and then comes Excel (☎ 8553 3255) with $65 – their standby rate is $55. Kangaroo Island Rental Cars (☎ 8553 2390) has rates starting at $69 with 200 free km, while Budget (☎ 8553 3133) charges $70.

Alternatively, you can hire a small 4WD and camper trailer for $165 a day from Island Camp & Drive (☎ 8553 2340) in Kingscote, including insurance and 250 km.

Very few of Adelaide's car-rental outlets will allow their vehicles to be taken across to Kangaroo Island. Two exceptions are Smile Rent-a-Car (☎ 8234 0655) and Access Rent-a-Car (☎ 8223 7466) – with the latter, a $10 per day Kangaroo Island surcharge applies.

Scooter/Motorbike Rental In Kingscote you can hire scooters from: the Country Cottage Shop (☎ 8553 2148) at 6 Centenary Ave; Servo Plus (☎ 8553 2787) at 21 Murray St; and the Kingscote Caravan Park (☎ 8553 2394) at 9 The Esplanade. The Country Cottage Shop also hires 185 cc trail bikes.

The Kingscote Caravan Park is the only one that will let you take scooters on unsealed roads.

Bicycle Hire The number of unsealed roads and the relatively long distances between settlements make cycling hard work and the rigours of the roads prove detrimental to the bicycles themselves.

If you're still game, bicycles (including tandems) can be hired from Servo Plus (☎ 8553 2787) next to the hostel at 21 Murray St in Kingscote.

Boat Hire American River Rendezvous (☎ 8553 7150) and the Kingscote Caravan

Park (☎ 8553 2325) have motorised dinghies, but you need a boat licence.

KINGSCOTE (pop 1450)

Kingscote, the main town on the island, was the first White settlement in South Australia. Although there had been other Europeans on the island many years earlier, Kingscote was only formally settled in 1836 and was all but abandoned just a few years later.

There are branches of the ANZ and BankSA in town, as well as EFTPOS facilities – there's a cash-withdrawal facility at Servo Plus, next to the backpackers hostel at 21 Murray St.

Things to See & Do

The **tidal pool** about 500 metres south of the jetty is the best place in town to swim – most locals head out to **Emu Bay**, 18 km away.

Hope Cottage, on Centenary Ave, was built in 1857. It is now a museum ($2), and it has a variety of old colonial implements and memorabilia. There's an old lighthouse and eucalyptus oil distillery in the grounds.

Every evening at 4 pm there's **bird feeding** at the wharf near the town centre. Around 40 of those wonderful beaked battleships, pelicans, usually turn up for the free tucker, as well as a Pacific gull or two. A 'donation' of $2 is requested.

Each evening at 7.30 and 8.30 pm (8.30 and 9.30 pm during daylight saving) rangers take visitors on a **'Discovering Penguins' walk**. They leave from the reception area of the Ozone Hotel on the Esplanade and cost $5 – wear sturdy footwear and leave your camera flash behind.

Places to Stay & Eat

The *Kingscote Caravan Park* (☎ 8553 2394) is on the foreshore. The *Kangaroo Island Central Backpackers Hostel* (☎ 8553 2787), at 19 Murray St, has dorm beds ($13), twin rooms ($17 per person) and doubles ($18 per person). The facilities are clean, spacious and comfortable, and there's no TV.

On Chapman Terrace there's *Nomads Ellson's Seaview Lodge* (☎ 8553 2030), with it's sweeping verandah. Dorm beds are $14, and singles/doubles $18/32.

The *Queenscliffe Family Hotel* (☎ 8553 2254) has comfortable singles/doubles (some with four-poster beds) for $48/55. It can be a bit rowdy before midnight, when the noise from the public bar downstairs filters up to the rooms. Reasonably priced meals are available in the hotel's restaurant.

The *Ozone Hotel* (☎ 8553 2011), situated on the seafront, has singles/doubles from $52/66, and there's a restaurant in the complex.

AMERICAN RIVER (pop 300)

Between Kingscote and Penneshaw, the small settlement of American River takes its name from the American sealers who built a boat here from 1803 to 1804. The town is on a small peninsula and shelters an inner bay, named **Pelican Lagoon** by Flinders, which is now a bird sanctuary.

Every afternoon at 4.30 pm you can watch the **pelican-feeding** down on the wharf.

Places to Stay & Eat

Linnetts Island Club (☎ 8553 7053) has rooms from $47. It also offers cheap hostel

The Australian pelican is a common sight at Kingscote

beds ($12). The same people manage the *American River Caravan Park* next door.

At *Casuarina Holiday Units* (☎ 8553 7020), next to the post office, basic self-contained units cost from $38.

PENNESHAW (pop 300)

Looking across the narrow Backstairs Passage to the Fleurieu Peninsula, Penneshaw is a quiet little resort town with a pleasant beach at **Hog's Bay** and the tiny inlet of **Christmas Cove**, which is used as a boat harbour. It is also the arrival point for ferries from Cape Jervis.

The council offices on Middle Terrace issue camping permits for Chapmans River, Browns Beach and American River; get them from Sharpys Store outside business hours. There's no bank in town, but Sharpys has an ANZ agency, Servwel has the BankSA agency and the post office is an agent for the Commonwealth Bank. There are EFTPOS cash-withdrawal facilities at Sharpys and Servwel.

Things to See & Do

In the evenings rangers take visitors to view the penguins that nest in the sand dunes and cliffs near the township – you'll generally see more penguins here than at Kingscote. In summer the tours depart at 8.30 and 9.30 pm, in winter at 7 and 8 pm, and the price is $5.

The **Penneshaw Maritime & Folk Museum** has some interesting memorabilia. It's open Monday, Wednesday and Saturday between 3 and 5 pm ($2).

Penneshaw is situated on Dudley Peninsula, a knob of land at the eastern end of the island, and this peninsula has several points of interest outside the town itself: **Pennington Bay** has surf; the sheltered waters of **Chapman River** are popular for canoeing; and the **Cape Willoughby Lighthouse**, the oldest lighthouse in the state – it was first operated in 1852 – has half-hour tours daily every 30 minutes between 10 am and 4 pm.

Adventureland Diving (☎ 8553 1072), 10 km from Penneshaw on the Kingscote road, runs one-day ($85) to five-day ($820) diving tours, with rates fully inclusive except for the

ferry fare from Cape Jervis. It also offers abseiling, canoeing and rock climbing for beginners, as well as dive charters (licensed divers only).

Places to Stay

The *Penneshaw Youth Hostel* (☎ 8553 1284) on North Terrace has dorm rooms for $10, or twin rooms for $12 per person. The *Penguin Walk Hostel* (☎ 8553 1233), operated by Kangaroo Island Ferry Connections, has beds in self-contained units from $12/28.

Coranda Farm (☎ 8553 1019), seven km from Penneshaw on the Cape Willoughby road, has a self-contained 'tent city' and charges $6 per person in two-person tents – it's $4 if you have your own tent or campervan.

The *Sorrento Resort Motel* (☎ 8553 1028) on North Terrace has singles/doubles from $59/78.

NORTH COAST

There are several fine, sheltered beaches along the north coast. Near Kingscote, **Emu Bay** has a beautiful, long sweep of sand. Other good beaches include **Stokes Bay**, **Snelling Beach** and **Western River Cove**.

Kangaroo Island Diving Safaris (☎ 8559 3225) runs a host farm and diving operation at Western River.

FLINDERS CHASE NATIONAL PARK

Occupying the western end of the island, Flinders Chase is one of South Australia's most significant national parks. It has beautiful eucalyptus forests with koalas, echidnas and possums, as well as kangaroos and emus that have become so fearless they'll brazenly badger you for food – the picnic and barbecue area at Rocky River Homestead is fenced off to protect visitors from these freeloaders.

On the north-western corner of the island, **Cape Borda** has a lighthouse built in 1858. There are guided tours weekdays from 10 am to 3.15 pm (2 pm in winter and 4.15 pm in the summer school holidays). There's also an interesting but sad little cemetery nearby at **Harvey's Return**.

In the southern corner of the park, **Cape**

du Couedic is wild and remote. An extremely picturesque lighthouse built in 1906 tops the cape; you can follow the path from the car park down to **Admirals Arch** – a high natural archway formed by pounding seas. You can often see NZ fur seals here.

At Kirkpatrick Point, a couple of km east of Cape du Couedic, the **Remarkable Rocks** are a series of bizarre granite rocks on a huge dome swooping 75 metres down to the sea.

Places to Stay

In Flinders Chase you can camp at the Rocky River park headquarters and in other designated areas with a permit. Watch out for kangaroos; they get into tents looking for food and can cause a lot of damage.

There are only very limited hot showers in the park, but facilities are better at the *Western KI Caravan Park* (☎ 8559 7201), on the South Coast Rd just a few minutes drive from Rocky River. There are plenty of wild koalas here as well.

There are a number of historic cottages available for hire in the park, and these range from $10 to $27.50 per adult; see Places to Stay at the beginning of this section for details on these and other NPWS cottages.

SOUTH COAST

The south coast is rough and wave-swept compared with the north coast. At **Hanson Bay**, close to Cape du Couedic, there's a colony of fairy penguins. A little farther east you come to **Kelly Hill Caves**, a series of limestone caves 'discovered' in the 1880s by a horse named Kelly, which fell into them through a hole in the ground.

Vivonne Bay has a long and beautiful beach. There is excellent fishing but bathers should take great care; the undertows are fierce and swimmers are advised to stick close to the jetty or the river mouth. **Seal Bay** is another sweeping beach, with plenty of resident sea lions. They can only be visited with a park ranger – there are tours daily.

Nearby and close to the south coast road is **Little Sahara**, a series of enormous white sand dunes.

Places to Stay & Eat

Eleanor River Holiday Cabins (☎ 8559 4250) is in Vivonne Bay. *Parndana, Troubridge and Karatta Cottages*, at Cape du Couedic, are administered by the NPWS. See Places to Stay at the beginning of this section for details. The historic *Kaiwarra Cottage* on the south coast road near the Seal Bay turn-off has light meals and Devonshire teas.

Barossa Valley

This famous valley is about 55 km north-east of Adelaide and is Australia's best-known wine-producing area. The gently sloping valley is about 40 km long and five to 11 km wide.

The Barossa still has some of the German flavour from its original settlement in 1842. Fleeing religious persecution in Prussia and Silesia, those first settlers weren't wine makers, but fortunately someone soon came along and recognised the valley's potential. The name is actually a misspelling of Barrosa in Spain, close to where Spanish sherry comes from. Prior to WW I, place names in the Barossa probably sounded even more Germanic, but during the war many German names were patriotically anglicised. When the fervour died down some were changed back.

You must get off the main road to begin to appreciate the Barossa Valley. Take the scenic drive between Angaston and Tanunda or the palm-fringed road to Seppeltsfield and Marananga, or wander through the sleepy historic settlement of Bethany.

Information

The Barossa Valley Visitor Centre (☎ 1800 812 662) is at 66-68 Murray St, Tanunda. It's open weekdays from 9 am to 5 pm and weekends and holidays from 10 am to 4 pm. The complex includes a wine interpretation centre designed to educate visitors in wine making.

Barossa Valley

1	Stockwell Wines	15	Leo Buring	28	Charles Melton Wines
2	Wolf Blass	16	Peter Lehmann	29	Krondorf
3	The Willows Vineyard	17	Veritas	30	Orlando
4	Gnadenfrei Estate	18	Old Barn Wines	31	Rovalley
5	Greenock Creek Vineyard	19	Basedow Wines	32	Jenke Vineyards
6	Seppelts	20	Yalumba	33	Chateau Yaldara
7	Penfolds	21	Lanzerac Country Estate	34	Charles Cimicky Wines
8	Kaesler Farm	22	Turkey Flat Vineyards	35	Kies Estate Cellars
9	Heritage Wines	23	High Wycombe Wines	36	Kellermeister Wines
10	Barossa Cottage Wines	24	St Hallett Wines	37	Liebichwein
11	Saltram Wine Estate	25	Bethany Wines	38	Barossa Settlers
12	Schmidt's Tarchalice	26	Rockford Wines	39	Twin Valley Estate
13	Hardy's Siegersdorf	27	Grant Burge Wines	40	Mountadam Winery
14	Tolley Pedare Wine				

Telecommunications The phone numbers listed here for the Barossa Valley come into effect from February 1997. Before this time, dial the old number by removing the first two digits from the new number (for STD calls add the area code 085).

Wineries

The Barossa has over 50 wineries; almost all are open to the public and offer free wine tastings. Get a copy of SATC's Barossa leaflet for full details of locations and opening hours.

Following are some well-known – and some not so well-known – wineries.

Chateau Yaldara at Lyndoch was established in 1947 in the ruins of a 19th-century winery and flour mill. It has a notable antique collection which can be seen on conducted tours ($2).

St Hallett at Tanunda is a small winery well-known for its top quality wines. There is a keg factory opposite where you can watch kegs being made.

Orlando at Rowland Flat, between Lyndoch and Tanunda, was established in 1847 and is one of the oldest wineries in the valley.

Saltram Wine Estate in Angaston is another old winery. Established in 1859, it has friendly and informative staff, and is set in beautiful gardens.

Seppelts in Seppeltsfield was founded in 1852; the old bluestone buildings are surrounded by gardens and date palms. The extensive complex includes a picnic area with gas barbecues. There is also a family mausoleum. Daily tours cost $3.

Wolf Blass out beyond Nuriootpa was only founded in 1973, but quickly became one of the better known wine labels in Australia. There's an interesting heritage museum at the winery.

Yalumba in Angaston was founded way back in 1849. The blue-marble winery, topped by a clock tower and surrounded by gardens, is the largest family-owned winery in Australia.

Bethany Wines, Bethany Rd, Bethany, is a small family operated winery in a scenic location. Its white port is highly recommended.

Grant Burge Wines, Jacobs Creek, Barossa Valley Highway, Tanunda, is a relative newcomer but has earned a reputation for consistently good wines. The winery boasts a beautifully restored tasting room.

Barossa Events

The colourful **Vintage Festival** is the Barossa's big event, taking place over seven days starting on Easter Monday in odd-num-bered years. It features processions, brass bands, tug-of-war contests between the wineries, maypole dancing and, of course, a lot of wine tasting.

Even more fun is the **Classic Gourmet Weekend** held in August or September. It has a carnival atmosphere and features fine food, wine and music.

Other festive occasions include the **Oom Pah Fest** in January; **Essenfest** in March; the **Hot Air Balloon Regatta** in May; and a **Brass Band Competition** in November.

The main events in the Barossa move with the grape-growing seasons. It takes four to five years for grape vines to reach maturity after they are first planted in September and October. Their useful life is usually around 40 years. The vines are pruned heavily from July to August and grow and produce fruit over summer. The busiest months are from March to early May when the grapes are harvested.

Getting There & Away

There are several routes from Adelaide to the valley; the most direct is via the main north road through Elizabeth and Gawler. More picturesque routes go through the Torrens Gorge, Chain of Ponds and Williamstown or via Chain of Ponds and Birdwood. If you're coming from the east and want to tour the wineries before hitting Adelaide, the scenic route via Springton and Eden Valley to Angaston is the best bet.

The Barossa Adelaide Passenger Service (☎ 8564 3022) has three bus services daily on weekdays and one daily on weekends between the valley and Adelaide. Fares from Adelaide are Lyndoch $7.60, Tanunda $9.30, Nuriootpa $10.10 and Angaston $11. There are no services on public holidays.

Getting Around

Valley Tours (☎ 8562 1524) has a good day tour of the Barossa for $34; a three-course lunch is included. A helicopter flight over the valley costs from $12 for 10 minutes (☎ 8524 4209), while a hot-air balloon flight (☎ 8389 3195) costs $195.

The Zinfandel Tea Rooms in Tanunda and

the Bunkhaus Travellers Cottage in Nuriootpa rent bicycles. There's a bicycle path between Nuriootpa and Tanunda, which runs past the Bunkhaus Travellers Cottage. The Barossa has good potential for cyclists, with many interesting routes and gradients varying from easy to challenging.

LYNDOCH (pop 970)

Coming up from Adelaide, Lyndoch, at the foot of the low Barossa Range, is the first valley town. The fine old **Pewsey Vale Homestead** is near Lyndoch. About one km south of town on the Gawler road is the **Museum of Mechanical Music** (☎ 8524 4014), with some fascinating old pieces and a knowledgeable owner; admission is $5 – less if you're in a group. A few km farther south, the Barossa Reservoir has the famous **Whispering Wall**, a concrete dam wall with amazing acoustics; conversations held at one end can be heard clearly 150 metres away at the other.

Places to Stay & Eat

The *Barossa Caravan Park* (☎ 8524 4262), Barossa Valley Highway, Lyndoch, has camp sites from $10, on-site vans from $25 and cabins from $40.

The *Kersbrook Youth Hostel* (☎ 8389 3185), 20 km south of Lyndoch, is in the grounds of a National Trust property called Roachdale. Beds cost $6 and because of the hostel's distance from the main Barossa towns, you'll need your own transport to get around.

The valley's only true German-style bakery is the *Lyndoch Bakery & Restaurant*. According to locals, *Errigo's Italian Restaurant* makes a mean pizza, but there's nothing mean about the friendly Italian woman behind the counter. Nearby, the *Lyndoch Hotel* has good-value counter meals.

TANUNDA (pop 3130)

In the centre of the valley is Tanunda, the most Germanic of the towns. You can still see early cottages around **Goat Square**, the site of the original Ziegenmarkt.

At 47 Murray St the **Barossa Valley His-**torical Museum has exhibits on the valley's early settlement; it's open daily from 10 am to 5 pm.

Three km from Tanunda on the Gomersal road, trained sheepdogs go through their paces at the **Breezy Gully** property on Monday, Wednesday and Saturday at 2 pm ($6).

There are fine old churches in all the valley towns but Tanunda has some of the most interesting. The Lutheran **Tabor Church** dates from 1849, and the 1868 Lutheran **St John's Church** has life-size wooden statues of Christ, Moses, and the apostles Peter, Paul and John.

From Tanunda, turn off the main road and take the scenic drive through Bethany and via Menglers Hill to Angaston. It runs through beautiful, rural country featuring large gums; the view over the valley from Menglers Hill is superb.

Places to Stay & Eat

The *Tanunda Caravan Park* (☎ 8563 2784), on the Barossa Valley Highway, has camp sites for $11, on-site vans from $27 and air-con cabins from $33.

There's also the reasonable *Tanunda Hotel* (☎ 8563 2030) at 51 Murray St with singles/doubles from $38/44, plus two or three more expensive motels.

Crackers Restaurant has very good meals. The *Zinfandel Tea Rooms* at 58 Murray St specialises in light lunches and continental cakes. *La Buona Vita*, opposite the Barossa Valley Visitor Centre, has reasonably priced Italian food, while the nearby *Happy Garden* specialises in Chinese dishes.

For real value it's hard to beat the *Tanunda Club* at 45 MacDonnell St, which sells hearty dinners for $5.50.

NURIOOTPA (pop 3330)

At the northern end of the valley is its commercial centre, Nuriootpa. There are several pleasant picnic areas along the Para River, as well as some nice river walks close to the town centre.

Places to Stay

The *Barossa Valley Tourist Park* (☎ 8562 1404), on Penrice Rd in Nuriootpa, has camp sites from $10 and cabins from $30.

The *Bunkhaus Travellers Cottage* (☎ 8562 2260) is set on a family vineyard, one km outside Nuriootpa on the main highway between Nuriootpa and Tanunda (look for the keg on the corner). It's a very pleasant and welcoming place with dorm beds for $11 plus a cottage for four people for $30. Mountain bikes can be hired here and Jane Matthew, the proprietor, can help you plan your day.

The *Angas Park Hotel* (☎ 8562 1050) at 22 Murray St has rooms for $15. The nearby *Vine Inn Hotel/Motel* (☎ 8562 2133) has motel units from $45 for singles/doubles and has good-value meals.

ANGASTON (pop 2000)

On the eastern side of the valley, this town was named after George Fife Angas, one of the area's pioneers. **Collingrove Homestead**, built by his son in 1856, is owned by the National Trust; it's open weekdays from 1 to 4.30 pm and weekends and during festivals from 11 am to 4.30 pm (entry $3).

There's a tourist information outlet in the Angaston Galleria, Murray St and in the Saltram winery.

Places to Stay

Angaston has the *Barossa Brauhaus* (☎ 8564 2014) at 41 Murray St, a reasonable hotel with B&B rates of $18 per person. Just down the street at No 59 is the *Angaston Hotel* (☎ 8564 2428). Rooms are $25 per person for B&B.

Good for a splurge is the National Trust's 1856 *Collingrove Homestead* (☎ 8564 1061), about seven km from town on the Adelaide road. The five rooms are part of the old servants' quarters and cost $93/135 including a cooked breakfast.

BETHANY

Near Tanunda, Bethany was the first German settlement in the valley. Old cottages still stand around the Bethany reserve, while the

Landhaus claims to be the world's smallest licensed restaurant – it seats 12 and bookings are usually essential.

Just south-east of the Barossa, in the Eden Valley, is **Springton**, with the Herbig Tree – an enormous hollow gum tree that was home for a pioneer family from 1855 to 1860.

Mid-North

The area between Adelaide and Port Augusta is generally known as the mid-north. Two main routes run north of Adelaide through the area. The first runs to Gawler where you can turn east to the Barossa Valley and the Riverland area, or continue north through Burra to Peterborough. From Peterborough you can turn west to Port Augusta, north-west to the Flinders Ranges or continue on the Barrier Highway to the north-east for the long run to Broken Hill in New South Wales.

The second route heads off slightly north-west through Port Wakefield and then to Port Pirie and Port Augusta on the Spencer Gulf. You can then travel to the Flinders Ranges or the southern Eyre Peninsula, or head west towards the Nullarbor and Western Australia.

The mid-north area includes some of the most fertile land in the state. Sunshine, high rainfall and excellent soil combine to make this a prosperous agricultural region with excellent wine-making areas, such as the Clare Valley.

KAPUNDA (pop 2000)

About 80 km north of Adelaide and a little north of the Barossa Valley, Kapunda is off the main roads that head north, but you can take a pleasant back route from the valley through the town and join the Barrier Highway a little farther north. Copper was found at Kapunda in 1842 and it became the first mining town in Australia. At its peak in 1861 it had 11 hotels and was the colony's major commercial centre outside Adelaide. Large-scale operations ceased in 1878 and the mines closed altogether in 1912.

SOUTH AUSTRALIA

A **lookout** offers views over the old open-cut mines and mine chimneys. In the town there's an interesting **mining interpretive centre** (open Saturday to Thursday from 1 pm to 4 pm) at the rear of the tourist office; entry costs $2. Next door, in the big old church, the **museum** ($2.50) has a large, varied collection of memorabilia.

An eight-metre-high bronze statue of 'Map Kernow' (the 'Son of Cornwall' in old Cornish) stands at the Adelaide end of town as a tribute to pioneer miners.

The *Sir John Franklin Hotel* (☎ 8566 3233) in Main St has counter meals from $4, and rooms costing $25/50 for singles/doubles. There is one family room, sleeping five for $55.

AUBURN (pop 330)

The township of Auburn, 24 km south of Clare, has some beautifully preserved historic buildings, particularly on St Vincent St. Auburn was the birthplace of C J Dennis, one of Australia's best-known colonial authors, but unfortunately the hotel where he was born is no longer standing.

The **Auburn Gallery** has some fine local work and interesting crafts. **Petherick's Antiques**, across from the award-winning Rising Sun Hotel, is considered the best antique shop in the Clare Valley.

CLARE (pop 2600)

At the heart of the Clare Valley wine region, this attractive town 135 km north of Adelaide has eschewed many of the tourist trappings characteristic of the Barossa Valley. It was settled in 1842 and named after County Clare in Ireland.

The first winery was established in 1851 by Jesuit priests, and communion wine is still produced here. The Jesuit **St Aloysius Church** dates from 1875 and the adjoining Sevenhill Cellars produces some fine wines. There are many other wineries in the valley, including the Leasingham Winery (formerly the Stanley Wine Company), dating from 1894. Winery opening times vary, but the *Clare Valley Wine Region Visitor's Guide*,

available at the tourist office, has all the relevant details.

The efficient tourist office (☎ 8842 2131) is in the town hall on the main street and is open daily from 10 am to 4 pm daily. Day tours of the district can be arranged here.

The town has a number of interesting buildings, including an impressive Catholic church, and a police station and courthouse dating from 1850, which are preserved as a **museum**. The **Wolta Wolta Homestead** dates from 1864 and is sometimes open on Sunday from 10 am to 1 pm (admission $3).

Bungaree Station (☎ 8842 2677), a working property 12 km north of Clare, has many historical exhibits. Self-conducted cassette tours are possible between 9 am and sundown ($8 including morning or afternoon tea).

Festivals

The Clare Valley's major event is the **Clare Valley Gourmet Weekend**, a festival of wine, food and music put on by local wineries over the Adelaide Cup weekend in May. Another not to be missed is **Music in the Vines**, featuring big-name musicians and a carnival atmosphere – not to mention fine wine and food, of course. It's held on the first weekend in December.

Places to Stay

The attractive and friendly *Christison Park Caravan Park* (☎ 8842 2724) is the closest camping ground to town. It has sites for $10 (or $5 if you're travelling solo), on-site vans for $30 and cabins from $40.

On Main St, the *Taminga Hotel* (☎ 8842 2808) has basic singles/doubles for $15/30. The *Clare Hotel* (☎ 8842 2816) has single pub rooms for $18 and motel rooms for $35/40.

Bentley's Hotel/Motel (☎ 8842 2815) on the main street has backpacker beds for $15 (very expensive for what you get), hotel singles/doubles/triples for $35/45/55 and motel rooms for $45/55/65.

Bungaree Station (☎ 8842 2677) has accommodation in the shearers' quarters for about $15 a bed, but groups have precedence

Geralka Farm (☎ 8845 8081), 25 km north of Clare, is another working farm that caters for visitors. You can camp ($11 for a powered site) or stay in on-site vans (from $25).

In Mintaro, a small town 18 km south-east of Clare, *Martindale Hall* (☎ 8843 9088) is an imposing mansion that offers accommodation at imposing prices (from $60 per person for B&B).

Getting There & Away
The daily (except Saturday) Stateliner bus to Adelaide (☎ 8415 5555) costs $14.30.

BURRA (pop 1220)
This pretty little town is bursting at the seams with historic sites. It was a copper-mining centre from 1847 to 1877, with various British ethnic groups forming their own communities (the Cornish being the most numerous). The district, Burra Burra, takes its name from the Hindi word for 'great' by one account, and from the Aboriginal name of the creek by another.

Information
The tourist office (☎ 8892 2154) in Market

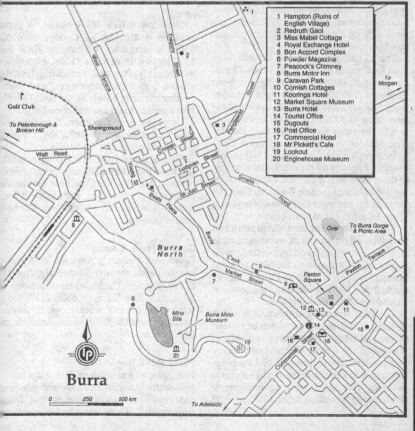

1 Hampton (Ruins of English Village)
2 Redruth Gaol
3 Miss Mabel Cottage
4 Royal Exchange Hotel
5 Bon Accord Complex
6 Powder Magazine
7 Peacock's Chimney
8 Burra Motor Inn
9 Caravan Park
10 Cornish Cottages
11 Kooringa Hotel
12 Market Square Museum
13 Burra Hotel
14 Tourist Office
15 Dugouts
16 Post Office
17 Commercial Hotel
18 Mr Pickett's Cafe
19 Lookout
20 Enginehouse Museum

Burra

0   250   500 km

To Adelaide

Square is open daily from 9 am to 4 pm. Here you can purchase *Discovering Historic Burra* ($5), outlining the town's interesting sites on a 11-km heritage trail. The *Burra Passport* includes this booklet, and a key to some buildings. The basic passport costs $20 for a car containing up to five people and includes half-price entry to the Enginehouse and Bon Accord museums.

Things to See

Burra has many substantial stone buildings, tiny Cornish cottages and numerous other reminders of the mining days. The **Market Square Museum** (admission $2) is across from the tourist office and features a shop, post office and house as they might have looked between 1880 and 1930. Sadly, it's open only on Saturday from 2 to 4 pm and Sunday from 1 to 3 pm.

The 33 cottages at **Paxton Square** were built for Cornish miners in the 1850s. One of the cottages, **Malowen Lowarth**, has been furnished in 1850s style. It's open Saturday from 1 to 3 pm and Sunday and public holidays from 10.30 am to 12.30 pm; admission is $3. The other cottages are available for accommodation (see Places to Stay & Eat).

In Burra's early days nearly 1500 people lived in **dugouts** by the creek and a couple of these have been preserved. Other interesting old buildings include **Redruth Gaol**, on Tregony St, and more **Cornish cottages** on Truro St, north of the town centre.

The **Burra Mine and Enginehouse Museum** are on the site of an original mine and are extremely well presented, with plenty of information – the Enginehouse Museum is open Monday to Friday from 11 am to 2 pm, but you can wander elsewhere around the mine site at any time.

The **Bon Accord Complex** ($3) was a Scottish mining enterprise; however, instead of ore, an underground water source was discovered. Not to be deterred, the canny Scots sold the site to the town, and the property supplied Burra's water until as recently as 1966. The site is now an interpretive centre, open weekdays from 12.30 to 2.30 pm.

There's a lookout over the town at the old mine site, another near the powder magazine and yet another at the Enginehouse Museum.

Places to Stay & Eat

You can stay at the historic *Paxton Square Cottages* (☎ 8892 2622) from $40/50. There are several historic hotels all offering basic pub-style accommodation. Typical is the grand old *Burra Hotel* (☎ 88922 389) or Market Square which has singles/doubles for $26/50 including a cooked breakfast.

The *Burra Motor Inn* (☎ 8892 2777) has large rooms overlooking the creek. Singles/doubles cost $50/55, and the restaurant here has very good, reasonably priced meals.

There are several B&B places. A good example is *Miss Mabel Cottage* (☎ 836? 3306), which offers self-catering B&B for $120 for two. Built in the 1850s, the cottage has homely touches, including freshly ground coffee and fresh eggs, and 19th century romantic novels by the bed! There's also a garden-room spa and open fireplace.

Down by peaceful Burra Creek is the town's *caravan park* (☎ 8892 2442), which has shaded camp sites for $10.

Most of the hotels sell good counter meals and have more formal dining rooms. Alternatively, *Mr Pickett's Cafe* near the tourist office sells great lunches. The nearby *Price's Bakery* is reputed to sell the best Cornish pasties in town.

Getting There & Away

Greyhound Pioneer's Adelaide to Sydney service passes through Burra daily, and it's $17 to Adelaide. The Mobil service station is the agency. Bute Buses (☎ 8826 2110) has a service three times weekly, which passes through Burra ($15.70) on its Adelaide to Orroroo run.

PORT PIRIE (pop 15,100)

Port Pirie, 84 km south of Port Augusta, is an industrial centre with a huge lead smelting complex that handles the output from Broken Hill. There are smelter tours or

Wednesday and Saturday, departing at 10 am contact the tourist office).

The tourist office (☎ 8633 0439) is at the Tourism & Arts Centre in the former railway station on Mary Ellie St. It's open weekdays from 9 am to 5 pm, Saturday from 9 am to 4 pm and Sunday from 10 am to 3 pm. The **Art Centre** itself has an A-class exhibition hall and receives some excellent touring exhibitions; ask to see the exquisite silver tree fern. The centre is open the same hours as the tourist office.

In the town centre on Ellen St, the **National Trust museum** complex (admission $2) includes Port Pirie's first railway station, the old customs house and the old police station. It's open Monday to Saturday from 10 am to 4 pm, and Sunday from 1 to 4 pm.

Carn Brae at 32 Florence St is a historic home with many wonderful features, including stunning stained-glass windows, beautiful antiques and large collections of all sorts of things, from clothes irons to dolls (2500 of them). Mr Young, who is described by locals as 'one of nature's gentlemen', lives here and will take you on an extensive tour, describing the function and history of the exhibits; admission is $5, and is well worth it. It's open daily from 10 am to 4 pm.

Places to Stay & Eat
The tourist office has details of Port Pirie's five motels and four hotels.

The very formal *Port Pirie Caravan Park* (☎ 8632 4275) has camp sites for $8, on-site vans for $25 and cabins from $28.

Beds are $15 per person in the *Family Hotel* (☎ 8632 1382) at 134 Ellen St and the *Central Hotel* (☎ 8632 1031) on Florence St.

The *Abaccy Motel* (☎ 8632 3701) on Florence St is the cheapest (and most basic) of the motels. It charges $40/45 and $5 for extras.

Locals recommend *Annie's Coffee Shop* at 5 Jubilee Place for home-made lunches; *Spud's Chicken & Bread Barn*, at 92 Main Rd, has delicious takeaway chicken and salad. For evening meals there are the pubs and motels, or try the very popular *Port Pirie*

Chinese Restaurant at 34 Main Rd. A pie cart is often parked at night near the post office.

MT REMARKABLE NATIONAL PARK
North of Port Pirie, between Melrose and Wilmington and on the southern edge of the Flinders Ranges, is the Mt Remarkable National Park. From **Wilmington** (population 250) you can drive into the park and walk through colourful **Alligator Gorge**; in places the walls of this picturesque feature are only two metres apart.

The entry fee to the Alligator Gorge area is $3 per car. There's no vehicle-based camping here, but there is a large camping ground at Mambray Creek on the other (western) side of the range. Camping permits ($2 for the site and $2 per adult) can be obtained from the rangers' office (☎ 8634 7068) at Mambray Creek.

The Wilmington Deli is a good place for information on local walks as well as alternative accommodation in the area. Basic rooms are available for $20/35 at the *Wilmington Hotel* (☎ 8667 5154). The town also has two caravan parks.

Hancocks Lookout, just north of the park on the way to Horrocks Pass from Wilmington, offers excellent views of the Spencer Gulf. The seven-km detour (one way) is well worth it.

MELROSE (pop 200)
This tiny town was established in 1853. It's in a beautiful setting at the foot of Mt Remarkable (956 metres). There are a number of fine old buildings, including the police station and courthouse, which now houses a **museum** (open daily from 2 to 5 pm; $2 entry). The **Mt Remarkable Hotel** was built in 1859 and its exterior looks as if it's scarcely changed since.

Places to Stay
The *Melrose Caravan Park* (☎ 8666 2060) has very nice bush camp sites for $8, on-site vans for $24 and cabins for $35. The *Mt Remarkable Hotel* (☎ 8666 2119) has over-priced motel-style accommodation at $30/40/50 for singles/doubles/triples.

PETERBOROUGH (pop 2300)

Peterborough is another mid-north agricultural service town. Steamtown is a working railway museum: on holiday weekends between April and October, narrow-gauge steam trains run between Peterborough and Orroroo ($22 return) or Eurelia ($29 return), both to the north-west; phone ☎ 8651 2106 for details (bookings are sometimes necessary). There are several other worthwhile attractions, most of a historic nature.

For information on the town and district ask at the tourist office (☎ 8651 2708) in the old railway carriage near the town hall. It's open daily from 9 am to 4 pm.

Tiny **Terowie** (population 200), 23 km south of Peterborough, is definitely worth the short detour off the Barrier Highway. The town was originally linked by broad-gauge train line to Adelaide, and narrow-gauge to Peterborough, and the town's railway yards provided hundreds of jobs, as goods had to be transferred from carriages on one line to the other. At its peak, the population exceeded 2000 people. In 1967 the broad-gauge line was extended to Peterborough, sounding the death knell for Terowie. The town is worth a visit as much for its lingering air of a bygone age, as for its wonderful, though sadly deteriorating, historic streetscape.

Places to Stay & Eat

The *Budget Travellers' Hostel* (☎ 8651 2711) in Railway Terrace behind the railway station has beds for $12; its clean, homely facilities and dedicated management make this very good value.

Alternatively, the friendly *Peterborough Caravan Park* (☎ 8651 2545) has grassy camp sites for $9, on-site vans for $22 and cabins from $30.

The tourist office can provide details of pub and motel accommodation in the town.

OTHER MID-NORTH TOWNS

Other towns include **Carrieton**, where a major rodeo is held towards the end of December each year. **Bruce** and **Hammond** are old railheads, which have virtually faded away to ghost towns. **Orroroo**, an agricultural centre, has a fascinating costume museum, a restored settlers cottage and Aboriginal rock carvings at Pekina Creek.

Heading south from Melrose you come to tiny **Murraytown**, where there's a pub and very little else. Continuing on, you can turn west through the scenic **Germein Gorge** to **Port Germein**. Here you will find the *Casuar Affair* (☎ 8634 5242), a coffee shop, gallery and craft centre, with some backpackers accommodation. Dorm beds are in a tranquil Japanese-style room, and cost $9. Cheap meals are available.

Alternatively, go straight ahead from Murraytown to **Wirrabara**. On the outskirt of the nearby Wirrabara Forest is a *yout hostel* (☎ 8668 4158) with beds costing $ for YHA members – $9 if you're a nonmem ber. There are nice walks in the forest, which is on the Heysen Trail.

South-East

The Dukes Highway provides the mos direct route between Adelaide and Mel bourne (729 km), but you wouldn't take it if you wanted to see interesting country · although there are some worthwhile detour to the south.

The Princes Highway runs close to the coast and has greater appeal. You can visi the Coorong (an extensive coastal lagoo system), call in to normally quiet fishing an holiday towns, detour into the Coonawarr wine belt and see the impressive crater lake around Mt Gambier.

Getting There & Away

Air Kendell Airlines and O'Connors Air Ser vices (☎ 8723 0666) have daily return flight from Mt Gambier to Adelaide and Mel bourne. One-way fares are $147 to bot cities.

Bus Bonds Mt Gambier Motor Servic (☎ 8231 9090 in Adelaide; 8725 5037 in M

Gambier) runs from the central bus station in Adelaide to Mt Gambier daily (except Saturday) for $36.90. You can travel either along the coast via the spectacular Coorong, stopping at Meningie ($17.90), Kingston SE ($28.70) and Robe ($32.30); or inland via Bordertown ($27.50), Naracoorte ($35.10) and Penola ($34.30).

The Victorian government's V/Line bus runs to Melbourne from Mt Gambier daily (six hours, $46.20).

THE COORONG NATIONAL PARK

The Coorong is a unique national park – a long, narrow strip curving along the coast for 145 km. The northern end is at Lake Alexandrina where the Murray River reaches the sea; the southern end is at Kingston SE. It's a narrow, shallow lagoon and a complex series of salt pans, separated from the sea by the huge sand dunes of the Younghusband Peninsula, more commonly known as the Hummocks.

This magnificent area is home to vast numbers of water birds. *Storm Boy*, a film about a young boy's friendship with a pelican, and based on a novel of the same name by Colin Thiele, was shot on the Coorong. These wonderful birds are very evident in the park. At Salt Creek you can take the nature trail turn-off from the Princes Highway and follow the old road that runs along the shore of the Coorong for some distance.

Places to Stay

The park has plenty of bush camp sites, but you need a permit ($3 for up to five people per night). You can purchase one from numerous outlets in the area including both roadhouses at Salt Creek and the NPWS office (☎ 8575 1200) on the Princes Highway in Meningie. General park information can also be obtained here.

Camp Coorong (☎ 8575 1557), 10 km south of Meningie on the Princes Highway, is run by the Ngarrindjeri Lands & Progress Association. The Cultural Museum here has information about the Ngarrindjeri Aboriginal people. Visitors can listen to Dreamtime stories about traditional lifestyles and visit a midden site. Self-contained units and bunk house beds are available, but you have to book.

KINGSTON SE (pop 1450)

At the southern end of the Coorong, Kingston is a small beach resort and a good base for visiting the Coorong.

Attractions in town include the **Pioneer Museum** and the nearby **Cape Jaffa Lighthouse**. Kingston is a centre for rock-lobster fishing, and the annual Lobsterfest, held in the second week of January, is celebrated with live bands and exhibitions. This is the only time that the historic lighthouse is activated.

The Australian obsession with gigantic fauna and flora is apparent in **Larry the Big Lobster**, which looms over the highway on the Adelaide approach to town. Larry fronts a tourist centre and cafe. You can buy freshly cooked rock lobster at the jetty during the lobster season.

The **Jip Jip National Park**, 45 km northeast of Kingston, features huge granite outcrops in the bush. From Kingston conventional vehicles can drive 16 km along the beach to the **Granites**, while with 4WD you can often continue right along the beach to the mouth of the Murray River.

Places to Stay & Eat

The *Backpackers Hostel* (☎ 8767 2185) at 21 Holland St has basic dorm beds for $10 including use of the kitchen and lounge. Clean but basic singles/doubles without private facilities are available at the *Crown Inn Hotel* (☎ 8767 2005) on Agnes St for $16/28, and at the *Royal Mail Motel* on Hansen St for $15/25. Both pubs sell counter meals.

Getting There & Away

Bonds Mt Gambier Motor Service operates a daily bus service to Adelaide ($28.70) and Mt Gambier ($19.40). The booking office is at the Big Lobster.

ROBE (pop 750)

Robe, a small port dating from 1845, was one of the state's first settlements. Its citizens made a fortune in the late 1850s when the Victorian government instituted a £10 head tax on Chinese gold miners, and many Chinese circumvented the tax by getting to Victoria via Robe; 10,000 arrived in 1857 alone. The **Chinamen's Wells** in the region are a reminder of that time.

Early buildings include the 1863 **customs house**, on Royal Circus, which is now a nautical museum. The amiable curator has a wealth of knowledge on local history, and will spin you some yarns that you won't find in the history texts.

The tourist office (☎ 8768 2465) is in the public library on the Smillie and Victoria Sts intersection. Nearby **Long Beach** is good for windsurfing and board surfing.

Places to Stay

The *Lakeside Tourist Park* (☎ 8768 2193) is in a beautiful setting with resident ducks and peacocks. Camp sites are $6/12 for singles/doubles and on-site vans are from $28 for singles/doubles.

Bushland Cabins (☎ 8768 2386), about 1.5 km from town on the Nora Creina road, is very peaceful and has lots of wildlife. It has limited backpacker beds for $10, bush camp sites for $10 and basic self-contained cabins at $34 for singles/doubles. The cabins sleep up to six ($6 for each extra person).

The wonderful *Caledonian Inn* (☎ 8768 2029), on Victoria St, has basic rooms for $30/50 with a light breakfast, and self-contained cottages within a stone's throw of the beach for $70/90. Its restaurant is one of the best in Robe.

BEACHPORT (pop 450)

If you have a yen for peace and solitude, you'll love this quiet little seaside town south of Robe with its aquamarine sea and historic buildings. The **Old Wool & Grain Store Museum** ($2) is located in a National Trust building. The interesting **Aboriginal Artefacts Museum**, housed in the former primary school in McCourt St, has an extensive collection. It is open daily from 2 to 4 pm in January, or by appointment (ask at the council office), and admission is $1.

There's good board surfing at the local surf beach, and windsurfing is popular at Lake George, five km north of the township. The town jetty can deliver memorable fishing.

Places to Stay & Eat

The *Beachport Caravan Park* (☎ 8735 8128) is very ordinary but in a great location near the beach. Much nicer is the *Southern Ocean Tourist Park* (☎ 8735 8153), which has camp sites for $11 and cabins from $40.

Pub-style accommodation is available at the *Beachport Hotel* (☎ 8735 8003) at $22/40/45 for singles/doubles/triples.

Bompa's (☎ 8735 8333) near the jetty has backpacker accommodation for $12 (it can be noisy) and delightful guesthouse rooms from $48 a double, with a light breakfast.

MILLICENT (pop 5170)

At Millicent, 50 km north-west of Mt Gambier, the 'Alternative 1' route through Robe and Beachport rejoins the main road. At the Mt Gambier end of George St, the tourist centre (☎ 8733 3205) has a good-quality **craft shop** and an excellent National Trust **museum**. It is open daily from 9.30 am to 4.30 pm; entry is $2.50.

The **Canunda National Park** with its giant sand dunes and rugged coastal scenery is 13 km west of town. It features 4WD tracks (in summer you can drive all the way from Southend to Carpenter's Rocks) and pleasant walks. You can camp near Southend – contact the ranger at Southend (☎ 8735 6053) for details.

In **Tantanoola**, 21 km to the south-east, the stuffed 'Tantanoola Tiger' is on display at the Tantanoola Tiger Hotel. This beast, actually an Assyrian wolf, was shot in 1895 after a lot of publicity. It was presumed to have escaped from a shipwreck, but why a ship would have a wolf on board is not quite clear!

The **Tantanoola Caves** are on the Princes Highway eight km away. The visitor centre (☎ 8734 4153) runs tours ($5) daily every hour from 9.15 am to 4 pm (more often in the summer school holidays and over Easter). They're the only caves in South Australia with wheelchair access.

MT GAMBIER (pop 21,350)

The major town and commercial centre of the south-east, Mt Gambier is 486 km from Adelaide. It is built on the slopes of the extinct volcano from which the town takes its name.

There are three craters, each with its own lake – the beautiful **Blue Lake** is the best-known, although from about March to November the lake is more grey than blue. In November it mysteriously changes back to blue again, just in time for the Blue Lake Festival, which is celebrated with exhibitions and concerts.

Blue Lake is about 85 metres deep at its deepest point and there's a five-km scenic drive around it. The lakes are a popular recreation spot and have been developed with boardwalks (over Valley Lake), a wildlife park, picnic areas, barbecues and signposted walking trails.

Information

For details on local attractions contact the very efficient Lady Nelson Tourist Information & Interpretive Centre (☎ 8724 1730), on Jubilee Highway East. It's open daily from 9 am to 5 pm.

Allow an hour to look through the interpretive centre, which features a replica, with sound effects and taped commentary, of the historic brig *Lady Nelson*, and interesting natural history displays. Admission is $5.

Telecommunications The phone numbers listed here for Mt Gambier come into effect from February 1997. Before this time, dial the old number by removing the first two digits from the new number (for STD calls add the area code 087).

Places to Stay & Eat

Mt Gambier has six caravan parks and all offer camp sites, on-site vans and cabins. You can get details from the tourist office.

The *Blue Lake Motel* (☎ 8725 5211), at 1 Kennedy Ave, just off the highway, has dorm rooms and good facilities, including a kitchen, for $12 per person. The *Mount View Motel* (☎ 8725 8478), on Davison St,

charges $28/35/42 for its standard singles/doubles/triples. Few other motels in town come anywhere near this.

There are a number of grand old hotels in the town's busy centre and all offer good-value accommodation and meals. They include the *Federal Hotel* (☎ 8723 1099) on Commercial St, with singles/doubles for $15/28. Also on Commercial St are the *South Australia Hotel* (☎ 8725 2404) and the *Commercial Hotel* (☎ 8725 3006), which charge $17/25 and $17/28 respectively.

Most sophisticated is the *Mt Gambier Hotel* (☎ 8725 0611), which has large rooms with spas for $55/65.

Other than the pubs, the best value in town for a big feed is the *Barn Steakhouse*, about two km out on Nelson Rd. It serves huge meals. *Squiggles*, a licensed bistro and coffee shop in the old Town Hall building on Commercial St, has a wicked Mississippi mud cake and other tempting offerings.

Getting There & Away

Bonds Mt Gambier Motor Service (☎ 8725 5037) buses depart daily for Adelaide (six hours; $36.90).

PORT MACDONNELL (pop 690)

South of Mt Gambier, this quiet fishing port was once a busy shipping port, hence the surprisingly big 1863 **customs house**. There's a **Maritime Museum**, and the poet Adam Lindsay Gordon's home, **Dingley Dell**, set in a conservation park, is now a museum ($3).

There are some fine walks in the area, including the path to the top of **Mt Schank**, an extinct volcano crater. Closer to town, the rugged coastline to the west is worth a visit.

THE DUKES HIGHWAY

The last town on the South Australian side of the border is **Bordertown** (population 2250). The town is the birthplace of former Australian prime minister Bob Hawke, and there's a bust of Bob outside the town hall. On the left as you enter from Victoria there is a wildlife park, with various species of

Australian fauna, including rare white kangaroos, visible behind a wire fence.

Keith (population 1190) is another farming town; it has a small museum and the **Mt Rescue Conservation Park** 16 km north.

Tintinara (population 320) is the only other town of any size along the highway; it's also an access point to the Mt Rescue park. The tiny township of **Coonalpyn** is an access point to the **Mt Boothby Conservation Park**.

NARACOORTE (pop 4750)

Settled in the 1840s, Naracoorte is one of the oldest towns in the state and one of the largest in the south-east. The tourist office (☎ 8762 1518) is at the award-winning **Sheep's Back Museum** on MacDonnell St. The museum, which is housed in a former flour mill, has interesting displays on the wool industry. It's open daily from 10 am to 4 pm and entry is $3. On Jenkins Terrace, the **Home of a Hundred Collections** museum has an eclectic and interesting collection and a $5 entry fee.

The **Naracoorte Caves Conservation Park** (open daily; ☎ 8762 2340) is 12 km south-east of Naracoorte off the Penola road. Its extraordinary limestone caves featured in David Attenborough's *Life on Earth* series, and have earned World Heritage listing thanks to the significance of the Pleistocene fossil deposits in **Victoria Fossil Cave**.

There are four show caves in the park: the fossil cave; **Alexandra Cave** (the main attraction); **Blanche Cave**; and **Wet Cave**. The Wet Cave can be seen on a self-guided tour. For the others, guided tours run from 9.30 am to 4 pm, with prices from $4.

The **Bat Cave**, from which bats make a spectacular departure on summer evenings, isn't open to the public, but infra-red TV cameras allow you to view the goings on inside ($6).

There are adventure tours involving climbing and crawling to undeveloped caves in the area (wear sneakers or sandshoes and old clothes). These start at $15 for novices and $30 for advanced grade.

Next to the kiosk is a camping area with powered and unpowered sites.

There are some 155 bird species (79 are waterbirds) at the **Bool Lagoon Game Reserve**, 24 km to the south, which, with the adjoining Hacks Lagoon Conservation Park, is the largest wetland in the south-east. Self-guided walks and guided tours are also available, although cost-cutting measures may see the latter disappear. Contact the park office (☎ 8764 7541) for details.

There are two basic but pleasant camping areas near the park office. Sites cost $6 for two people.

Places to Stay & Eat

The classic old *Naracoorte Hotel/Motel* (☎ 8762 2400), 73 Ormerod St, has motel rooms for $47/65 and pub-style singles/doubles for $24/43. It also offers backpacker beds for $10 to holders of YHA or VIP cards.

The *Old Aussie Eatery*, at 190 Smith St, has an interesting menu including a drover's delight ($11) and a swaggy's dream ($12.50). If you haven't yet tried roo steak, camel or crocodile, this is a good place to start. The town's three *hotels* all have good-value meals.

COONAWARRA & PENOLA

The compact (only 12 km by two km) wine-producing area of Coonawarra, which is renowned for its reds, is 10 km north of Penola. Wynn's Estate is the best-known winery, but there are 21 others offering cellar-door sales, most on a daily basis.

The historic town of **Penola** has won recent fame for its association with the Sisters of St Joseph of the Sacred Heart. This was the order that Mother Mary MacKillop, to be canonised as Australia's first saint, co-founded in 1866. Penola has been named as a significant MacKillop pilgrimage site.

The **Woods-MacKillop Schoolhouse**, built in 1867, has memorabilia associated with Mary MacKillop and Father Julian Tenison Woods, who founded the school. It was the first in Australia to welcome children from lower socio-economic backgrounds. It's open daily from 10 am to 4 pm and admission is a gold-coin ($1 or $2) 'donation'.

Places to Stay

Backpacker beds are available for $10 at *Whiskas Woolshed* (☎ 8737 2428; 018 854 505), 12 km south-west of Penola and off the Millicent road. Rooms in the old woolshed sleep up to nine people and each has oil heating. It also has a large recreation room, kitchen and laundry.

Alternatively, over 20 restored historic cottages in the Penola district offer accommodation, with prices starting at $50 for twin share. For more details, or to make a reservation, contact the tourist information centre (☎ 8737 2855) on Arthur St in Penola between 10 am and 4 pm daily.

Penola also has two hotels and a caravan park.

Getting There & Away

Bonds Mt Gambier Motor Service buses depart daily (except Saturday) for Adelaide ($35.10) and Mt Gambier ($7.50) from the tourist centre in Penola.

Murray River

Australia's greatest river starts in the Snowy Mountains in the Australian Alps and for most of its length forms the boundary between New South Wales and Victoria. It meanders for 650 km through South Australia, first heading west to Morgan and then turning south towards the coast, at Lake Alexandrina.

En route, the river is tapped to provide domestic water for Adelaide as well as country towns as far away as Whyalla and Woomera. Between the Victorian border and Morgan, irrigation has turned previously unproductive land into an important wine-making and fruit-growing region. This section is generally known as the Riverland.

The Murray has a fascinating history. Before the advent of the railways, it was the Mississippi of Australia, with paddle-steamers carrying trade from the interior down to the coast. Several of these shallow-draught vessels have been restored and you can relive the past on cruises of a few hours or several days. They include the huge stern-wheeler PS *Murray River Princess*, which regularly makes its stately passage up and down the river from Mannum.

Accommodation

There's plenty of conventional accommodation along the Murray, including a hostel in Berri. Alternatively, you can rent a fully self-contained houseboat and set off to explore the river.

Houseboats can be hired in most towns. However, they're very popular from October through April, and for these months it's wise to book well ahead. Contact the SATC or the Riverland Holiday Booking Centre (☎ 8586 4444; bookings 1800 651 166) in Renmark. Typical prices for the weekly hire of two/four/six/eight-berth houseboats during the high season are around $580/650/850/920. They're usually considerably cheaper in winter.

Getting There & Away

Air Southern Australia Airlines flights can be booked through Qantas (☎ 13 1313). They fly to Renmark from Adelaide ($104) twice daily on weekdays and once daily on weekends.

Bus Stateliner (☎ 8415 5555) has daily services from Adelaide to the Riverland towns. The fare to Berri, Loxton and Renmark is $26.50.

Greyhound Pioneer runs through the Riverland en route to Sydney but can't drop off until past Renmark. Its fare to Sydney from Renmark is $79.

RENMARK (pop 4300)

In the centre of the Riverland irrigation area and 254 km from Adelaide, Renmark was the first of the river towns and a starting point for the great irrigation projects that revolutionised the area.

The tourist office (☎ 8586 6704) is on

Murray Ave, beside the river. It's open weekdays from 9 am to 5 pm, Saturday from 9 am to 4 pm and Sunday from noon to 4 pm. Attached is an interpretive centre ($3) which includes an inspection of the recommissioned 1911 paddle-steamer *Industry*. Ask at the tourist office about 4WD, fishing and dinghy tours in the area.

Renmark River Cruises (☎ 8595 1862) offers cruises from $10 on the MV *River Rambler* departing from the town wharf. There are several art galleries in town, and you may be lucky enough to see koalas and other wildlife on **Goat Island** (also known as Paringa Paddock), which has several walking trails. The Angoves and Renmano **wineries** have cellar-door sales and tastings.

Places to Stay & Eat
Idyllically situated on the river about a km east of town is the *Renmark Caravan Park* (☎ 8586 6315). Camp sites cost $10, on-site vans are $27 and cabins are from $43. It hires canoes for $15 for two hours.

Farther along the river beside the Paringa Bridge, the *Riverbend Caravan Park* (☎ 8585 5131) has camp sites for $9, on-site vans for $24 and cabins from $30. It also hires canoes ($5 per hour).

The tastefully renovated *Renmark Hotel/Motel* (☎ 8586 6755) on Murray Ave has hotel rooms at $35/40 for singles/doubles and motel units at $60/66/71 for singles/doubles/triples. It has counter meals, a bistro and dining room.

There are several restaurants and takeaways in the town. *Sophia's Restaurant*, in the Southern Cross Roadhouse on the Sturt Highway, has good Greek food and takeaway downstairs. For value it's hard to beat the *Renmark Club*, across from the hotel, which has specials on Tuesday and Thursday nights.

BERRI (pop 3700)
At one time a refuelling stop for the wood-burning paddle-steamers, the town takes its name from the Aboriginal *berri berri*, meaning 'big bend in the river'.

The tourist office (☎ 8582 1655) is on Vaughan Terrace. It's open weekdays from 9 am to 5 pm and Saturday to 11.30 am.

The lookout on the corner of Vaughan Terrace and Fiedler St has good views over the town and river. Near the ferry wharf there's a **monument** to Jimmy James, a famous Aboriginal tracker.

The **Willabalangaloo Reserve** ($4) is a flora and fauna reserve with walking trails and a historic homestead. It's open Thursday to Monday from 10 am to 4 pm (daily during school holidays).

Berri Estates winery at Glossop, seven km west of Berri, is one of the biggest in Australia, if not the southern hemisphere. It's open for tastings and cellar-door sales Monday to Saturday from 9 am to 5 pm.

Ferries cross the river to Loxton from opposite the Berri Hotel/Motel on Riverside Ave.

Places to Stay
The *Berri Riverside Caravan Park* (☎ 8582 3723) has camp sites for $9, on-site vans from $29 and cabins from $34. *Berri Backpackers* (☎ 8582 3144), on the Sturt Highway, is one of the best-equipped hostels you'll find anywhere – but it's only for international visitors. It has a pool, sauna, games room, volleyball court, bicycles and canoes for guests' use, and the manager has excellent contacts if you want seasonal work in local orchards and vineyards. Beds are $12 ($80 per week).

At the *Berri Hotel/Motel* (☎ 8582 1411), on Riverview Drive, singles/doubles cost from $34/38 in the pub, and from $62/70 in the motel.

The *Berri Club* across from Berri Backpackers has great-value meals from Thursday to Sunday nights.

LOXTON (pop 3320)
From Berri the Murray makes a large loop south of the Sturt Highway, with Loxton at its base.

The beautiful Katarapko section of the **Murray River National Park** occupies much of the area within the loop; there's great canoeing here and you can camp with a permit ($2 per night per adult). Contact the NPWS office (☎ 8585 2177) in Berri. You can canoe across from Loxton, but road access is through Winkie or Berri on the other side of the river.

The tourist office (☎ 8584 7919) is in front of the Loxton Hotel on East Terrace – ask at the pub if it's closed. Loxton's major attraction is the riverside **Historical Village**. It's open weekdays from 10 am to 4 pm and weekends from 5 pm; admission is $4.

The **Australian Vintage** (formerly Penfolds) winery is open daily except Sunday for tastings.

Riverland Canoeing Adventures (☎ 8584 1494) on Alamein Ave, towards Renmark, rents one-person kayaks for $12 per day and double kayaks and canoes for $20 a day. Transport, maps and camping equipment can be arranged for an extra fee.

Places to Stay & Eat

The *Loxton Riverfront Caravan Park* (☎ 8584 7862) is two km from town and has backpacker beds in a self-contained lodge for $12 per person – if there's four of you the rate drops to $8. It also has camp sites for $9.50, on-site vans for $25 and cabins from $32.

The *Loxton Hotel/Motel* (☎ 8584 7266) on East Terrace has basic pub rooms from $16/24 for singles/doubles and motel units from $50/55. It has a very good bistro plus counter meals. Otherwise there are coffee shops, bakeries and takeaways. The Aussie whopper burgers at *Spring Leaf* takeaway near the pub are just that – whopping.

BARMERA (pop 1900)

On the shores of Lake Bonney, Barmera was once on the overland stock route from New South Wales. The ruins of **Napper's Old Accommodation House**, built in 1850 at the mouth of Chambers Creek, are a reminder of that era, as is the **Overland Corner Hotel** on the Morgan road, 19 km out of town. It takes its name from a bend in the Murray where drovers and travellers once stopped. The hotel (built in 1859) is now owned by the National Trust and has a small

museum. You can also stay here – see Places to Stay.

Lake Bonney, which has sandy beaches, is popular for swimming and water sports. There's a nudist beach at **Pelican Point**.

You'll find a game reserve at **Moorook** and another across the river from **Kingston-on-Murray** – the latter backs onto the Overland Corner Hotel. Both reserves have nature trails and are good spots for birdwatching. For camping permits, contact the Berri NPWS office (☎ 8585 2177).

Riverland Safaris (☎ 8588 3270) offers various guided tours, including winery visits and fishing and yabbying trips, as well as to the Barossa Valley and Flinders Ranges. Contact the tourist office (☎ 8588 2289) for details – it's at the top of the main street next to the roundabout, and is open weekdays from 9 am to 5.30 pm and Saturday until noon.

Places to Stay

There are several caravan parks in the area, including the *Lake Bonney Holiday Park* (☎ 8588 2234), which has camp sites for $10, on-site vans for $26, cabins from $28 to $36 and cottages from $44 to $46.

The comfortable *Barmera Hotel/Motel* (☎ 8588 2111) has budget singles/doubles at $20/30 and has a dining room and counter meals. Out at the *Overland Corner Hotel* (☎ 8588 7021), rooms cost $35/50, including a cooked breakfast.

WAIKERIE (pop 1800)

The town takes its name from the Aboriginal word for 'anything that flies', after the teeming birdlife on the lagoons and river around Waikerie. Curiously, Waikerie also has the most active gliding centre in Australia (☎ 8541 2644).

For tourist information go to **The Orange Tree** (☎ 8541 2332), on the Sturt Highway on the Barmera side of town – you'll know it by the large, green fibreglass sphere with red spots. It sells a comprehensive range of local fruit and nut products and is open daily from 9 am to 5.30 pm.

Places to Stay

The *Waikerie Hotel/Motel* (☎ 8541 2999) has pub rooms at $35/45 for singles/doubles and motel rooms for $40/50. You can eat in the front bar or bistro. Down by the river on the west side of town, the *Waikerie Caravan Park* (☎ 8541 2651) has camp sites for $9.50 and cabins from $30.

Bush camping ($4) is possible at *Eremophila Park*, a private nature park off the Sturt Highway 33 km east of town – there's no power, but other amenities are available; ☎ 8589 3023 for details.

Clydesdales, Carts & Picnics (☎ 8541 9096) is 26 km west of town. It has bush camping (usually with country & western entertainment in the evening) for $85 a day per person including bush trail rides and all meals.

MORGAN (pop 1350)

In its prime this was the busiest river port in Australia, with wharves towering 12 metres high. There's a car ferry across the Murray here. Most businesses around town will sell you a leaflet detailing a historic walk (50c). The **Port of Morgan Historic Museum** has exhibits on the paddle-steamer trade; it opens according to demand.

Places to Stay

The *Morgan Riverside Caravan Park* (☎ 8540 2207) has camp sites for $9, on-site vans for $27 and cabins from $32. It also hires tandem cycles and canoes. The *Commercial Hotel* (☎ 8540 2107) on Railway Terrace has basic rooms for $15 a person. Across the road, the *Terminus Hotel/Motel* (☎ 8540 2006) has pub rooms for $20/34, including a light breakfast, and motel units for $38/43.

SWAN REACH (pop 230)

This sleepy old town, 70 km south-west of Waikerie, has picturesque river scenery but not many swans – there are lots of pelicans, however. Just downstream the Murray makes a tight meander known as Big Bend; the lookout beside the Walker Flat road nine km from town gives you a great view of its high yellow cliffs.

MANNUM (pop 2050)

The *Mary Ann*, Australia's first riverboat, was built here and made the first paddle-steamer trip up the Murray in 1853. There are many relics of the pioneering days, including the 1898 paddle-steamer *Marion*, now a floating museum ($2.50) moored alongside the tourist centre (☎ 8569 1303). Both are open daily from 10 am to 4 pm.

The **Purnong Rd Bird Sanctuary** has a variety of water birds; it starts at the Mannum Caravan Park and you drive along it for several km on the main road to Purnong. The **Cascade Waterfalls**, 9 km from Mannum on Reedy Creek, are worth a visit. Although the falls only flow during winter, the scenery can be enjoyed at any time.

River Cruises

The grand paddle-steamer *Murray River Princess* operates from Mannum. Five-night cruises start at $560 per person. Three-night cruises start at $335, while selected weekend cruises are from $210. Contact Captain Cook Cruises (☎ 1800 804 843) for more details.

Mannum Big River Cruises (☎ 8569 2606) runs morning and afternoon 'coffee' cruises on MV *Wallamba* on weekends and public holidays. Prices start at $10 for one hour.

The MV *Lady Mannum* also does cruises; check times with Lady Mannum Cruises (☎ 8569 1438) in the main street.

Places to Stay

The *Mannum Caravan Park* (☎ 8569 1402) on the town side of the ferry crossing has camp sites ($10) and cabins ($42). You can camp for free on the other side of the river near the ferry and use the shower facilities ($2.50) at the caravan park.

MURRAY BRIDGE (pop 13,500)

South Australia's largest river town, only 82 km south-east of Adelaide, is named for its one-km-long bridge; built in 1879, it was the first to span the Murray. It's a popular area for fishing, swimming, water-skiing and barbecues.

The tourist office (☎ 8532 6660) is on South Terrace, which runs parallel to the main shopping strip.

Things to See & Do
Chocoholics will enjoy viewing **chocolate making** – and eating the result – in the old town pump house, between the vehicle and railway bridges on the town side of the river.

Also of interest is **Butterfly House**, four km out on the Wellington road. Its tropical hot house contains a number of species of gorgeous butterflies that flutter about your ears while you observe and photograph them.

Twenty km to the west of Murray bridge is **Monarto** – the town that never was. A grandiose plan was drawn up to build a second major city for South Australia by the turn of the century. This site was chosen and land purchased in the early 1970s, but nothing further happened and the project was abandoned. The **Monarto Zoological Park** has both Australian and international exhibits, including herds of zebras and giraffes.

River Cruises
The MV *Barrangul* operates irregular day cruises and there's a restaurant on board – check at the tourist office for times. The PS *Proud Mary* departs from Murray Bridge; two-night cruises start at $345 (triple share), and five-night cruises start at $875. Contact Proud Australia Holidays (☎ 8231 9472) in Adelaide.

Places to Stay & Eat
The *Avoca Dell Caravan Park* (☎ 8532 2095) has camp sites and on-site vans. The *Balcony Private Hotel* (☎ 8532 3830) is in the centre of town and has beds for $17.

You can eat at the *Oriental Garden* or the *Murray Bridge Hotel*, which has good counter meals. The *Italian Club* on Lincoln Rd serves dinner from Thursday to Sunday. Thursday is pasta night – all you can eat for $6.

Getting There & Away
Buses to Adelaide cost $10.50 with the Murray Bridge Passenger Service (☎ 8532 6660); they leave daily from outside the tourist office, where tickets can be purchased. If you are travelling from Adelaide, bookings need to be made with Premier on ☎ 8415 5555.

Tickets to Mt Gambier ($36.90) with Bonds Mt Gambier Motor Service (☎ 8231 9090) must be booked at the central bus station in Adelaide.

You can pick up a Greyhound Pioneer bus to Melbourne (from $53) and Sydney (from $98) twice daily.

TAILEM BEND (pop 1600)
At a sharp bend in the river, Tailem Bend is near the mouth of the Murray. **Old Tailem Town** is a fascinating re-creation of a pioneer village; it's open daily and costs $7.50.

You can take a ferry across the river to Jervois from where it's 11 km to the pretty old hamlet of **Wellington**. Here you'll find the Old Wellington Court House Museum (open daily) and the Wellington Hotel, where you can sit on the lawn and watch the river. Aboriginal middens can be seen two km south-east of the township.

After Wellington, the Murray opens into huge **Lake Alexandrina**, but boating is often tricky because of the vagaries of the currents.

Tailem Bend has two hotels, a motel and two caravan parks.

Yorke Peninsula

The Yorke Peninsula is a popular holiday area within easy driving distance of Adelaide. There are pleasant beaches along both sides, the Innes National Park on the tip and plenty of fishing. The area's economy was originally based on the copper mines of Little Cornwall (the name given to the mining areas of the peninsula). As the mines declined, agriculture developed and much of the land now grows barley and other grains.

The **Creative Activities Network** is run

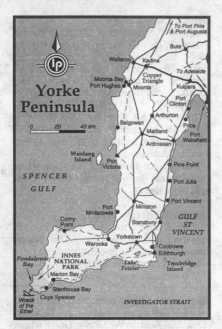

by Yorke Peninsula artisans and residents. It incorporates workshops, bush walks, heritage tours – even farm visits. A range of 'personalised learning experiences' are available, such as spending a day on a sheep farm or attending a bush painting workshop with a local artist. For more details, contact the SATC or the tourist office (☎ 8821 2093) in Kadina.

Copper Mines

In the early 1860s, copper was discovered in the Moonta-Kadina-Wallaroo area (known as the Copper Triangle) and soon a full-scale copper rush was on. Most miners were from Cornwall in England, and the area still has a strong Cornish influence. The boom peaked around the turn of the century, but in the early 1920s a slump in copper prices and rising labour costs closed all the peninsula's mines.

The Kernewek Lowender Festival is held in Little Cornwall over a long weekend in May of odd-numbered years. It's a chance to try Cornish pasties or watch a wheelbarrow race. You may even see a piskey – a mischievous sprite believed by the Cornish people to bring good fortune.

Getting There & Away

Premier (☎ 8415 5555) operates a daily bus from Adelaide to Kadina, Wallaroo, Moonta, Port Hughes and Moonta Bay. It takes about three hours to Moonta and costs $14.50.

The Yorke Peninsula Passenger Service (☎ 8391 2977) runs from Adelaide's central bus station to Yorketown daily. The route alternates daily between the east coast and down the centre of the peninsula. Fares from Adelaide are: Ardrossan $18, Port Vincent $23.20, and Edithburg and Warooka both $24.40.

WEST COAST

The west coast, facing onto the Spencer Gulf, has plenty of beaches, but the road generally runs inland.

Kadina (pop 4500)

The largest town on the peninsula, Kadina was once the centre of copper mining. The interesting **Kadina Museum** ($3) features Matta House (1863), the home of the Matta Matta mine manager. There's also the Matta Matta mine, old farming machinery and a blacksmith's shop, among other displays. It's open Wednesday, weekends and public and school holidays from 2 to 4.30 pm.

The **Wallaroo Mines** are one km west of the town on the Wallaroo road. It takes half an hour to stroll around the complex, which includes numerous deep shafts and the impressive ruins of an enginehouse.

The main tourist office (☎ 8821 2093) for the Copper Triangle is in the town hall. However, it's only open weekdays between 10 am and 2 pm and Saturday from 9.30 am to 1.30 pm.

Places to Stay & Eat The *Kadina Caravan Park* (☎ 8821 2259) has camp sites ($11) and on-site vans ($30).

The *Wombat Hotel* (☎ 8821 1108) on Taylor St charges $19 per person, while the

Kadina Hotel (☎ 8821 1008), a block away, has singles/doubles/triples with private bathroom for $30/47/60. Both include a light breakfast.

Cornish pasties are sold in several shops, but the most popular are those produced by *Prices Bakery*. *Sarah's Place* is good for pancakes, and the *Dynasty Room* is a Chinese place on Goyder St; it has lunch specials, as do the pubs.

Wallaroo (pop 2250)

This port town was a major centre during the copper boom, and it is the second point of the Copper Triangle. The 'big stack', one of the great chimneys from the copper smelters (built in 1861), still stands, but today the port's main function is exporting agricultural products, and the grain terminal dwarfs the town. In the old post office there's the fascinating **Heritage & Nautical Museum**, open on Wednesday, weekends and public and school holidays; admission is $2.50.

A map detailing a town heritage walk can be obtained from the tourist desk (☎ 8823 2020) in the post office, on the corner of Irwin St and Owen Terrace.

Places to Stay & Eat On the beach near the jetty, the *Office Beach Caravan Park* (☎ 8823 2722) has camp sites for $10, on-site vans for $25 and cabins from $30. The *Weerona Hotel* (☎ 8823 2008) on John Terrace has singles/doubles for $22/32, while the charming *Sonbern Lodge* (☎ 8825 6235), a block away, has singles/doubles/triples for $24/38/47.

The town's five hotels have counter meals and there are several takeaways, a bakery and tea rooms.

Moonta (pop 2300)

At Moonta, 18 km south of Wallaroo, the copper mine was the richest in Australia in the late 19th century. The town grew so large that its school once had 1100 students; this wonderful old building houses an excellent museum ($2.50). It's part of the collection of mine-works ruins at the **Moonta Heritage Site**, which you can explore with a self-

guiding map from the museum or from the Kadina tourist office. On weekends, public and school holidays, the tourist train travels around the **Moonta Mines Complex** ($2).

Tandem and standard bicycles can be hired from the BP service station on George St for $7 per hour. The owner will negotiate for day hire.

Places to Stay Right on the beach three km away, the *Moonta Bay Caravan Park* (☎ 8825 2406) has camp sites for $11 and cabins for $46.

The *Cornwall Hotel* (☎ 8825 2304) on Ryan St singles/doubles for $27.50/40; at the *Royal* (☎ 8825 2108) nearby they're $25/40, including a light breakfast.

EAST COAST

The east-coast road from the top of Gulf St Vincent down to Stenhouse Bay near Cape Spencer is generally within a km or two of the sea. En route, tracks and roads lead to many sandy beaches and secluded coves. **Port Clinton** is the northernmost beach resort. A little south is **Price**, where salt is produced at salt pans just outside town. **Ardrossan** is the largest port on this coast. There's a National Trust museum (open Sunday and public holidays from 2.30 to 4 pm) on Fifth St.

Continuing south, in the next 50 km the road runs through **Pine Point**, **Black Point**, **Port Julia** and **Port Vincent** (each has a sandy beach). Port Vincent has the *Tuckerway Youth Hostel* (☎ 8853 7285), with beds from $8, a pub and two caravan parks.

The road continues along the coast through **Stansbury** (with a museum set in a pretty cottage garden), **Wool Bay**, **Port Giles** and **Coobowie** to Edithburgh.

Edithburgh has a tidal swimming pool in a small cove; from the cliff-tops you can look across to **Troubridge Island**. A 2½-hour tour, including a historical commentary, can be taken to the island, and accommodation is also available; (☎ 8852 6290).

Near Marion Bay on the coast road is *Hillocks Drive* (☎ 8854 4002), a large farm where you can enjoy some wonderful coastal scenery, native wildlife and wildflowers (July to November). Bush camping is $5 per car, and on-site vans are $22 to $25. For day visitors there's a $3 entry fee.

Yorketown is the region's business and administrative town. Nearby salt lakes mysteriously turn pink whenever there is going to be a change in the weather, but otherwise they're very uninspiring.

INNES NATIONAL PARK

The southern tip of the peninsula, marked by Cape Spencer, is part of the Innes National Park. There's a $3 entry fee per vehicle. **Stenhouse Bay**, just outside the park, and **Pondalowie Bay**, within the park, are the principal settlements. The park has spectacular coastal scenery as well as good fishing, reef diving and surfing. You'll go a long way to find quieter emus!

Pondalowie Bay is the base for a large lobster-fishing fleet and it also has a fine surf beach. All the other beaches, except for Browns Beach, are dangerous for swimming.

In the park is the wreck of the steel barque *Ethel*, a 711-tonne ship which ran aground in 1904. All that remains are the ribs of the hull rising forlornly from the sands. Her anchor is mounted in a memorial on the cliff top above the beach.

Just past the Cape Spencer turn-off, a sign on the right directs you to the ruins of the **Inneston Historic Site**. Inneston was a gypsum-mining community abandoned in 1930.

Places to Stay

With a permit ($3 per vehicle per night), you can camp in a number of places in the park; phone the NPWS office in Stenhouse Bay (☎ 8854 4040) for more details.

Getting There & Away

There is no public transport to the end of the peninsula. The Yorke Peninsula Passenger Service will take you as far as Warooka or Yorketown (both $24.40) and then you can try to hitch, but traffic is light.

Eyre Peninsula

The wide Eyre Peninsula points south between Spencer Gulf and the Great Australian Bight. It's bordered on the northern side by the Eyre Highway from Port Augusta to Ceduna. The coastal run along the peninsula is in two parts: the Lincoln Highway south-west from Port Augusta to Port Lincoln; and the Flinders Highway north-west to Ceduna. It's 468 km from Port Augusta direct to Ceduna via the Eyre Highway; via the loop south it's 763 km.

The coast is an extremely popular holiday area with many good beaches, sheltered bays and pleasant little port towns. On the wild west coast there are superb surf beaches, spectacular coastal scenery and important breeding grounds for the southern right whale, the Australian sea lion and the great white shark – some scenes for *Jaws* were filmed here.

Eyre Peninsula also has a flourishing agricultural sector, and the iron-ore deposits at Iron Knob and Iron Baron are processed and shipped from the busy port of Whyalla. The peninsula takes its name from Edward John Eyre, the hardy explorer who, in 1841, made the first recorded overland crossing between Adelaide and Albany, WA.

Getting There & Away

Air Kendell Airlines (☎ 13 1300) flies daily to Port Lincoln ($116) and Whyalla ($114), and daily except Saturday to Ceduna ($194) on the Eyre Peninsula. Lincoln Airlines (☎ 1800 018 234) flies between Port Lincoln and Adelaide for $90 four times daily. Whyalla Airlines (☎ 1800 088 858) has daily services to Cleve ($85), Wudinna ($135) and Whyalla ($90).

Bus Stateliner (☎ 8415 5555) has daily services from Adelaide to Port Augusta ($27.20), Whyalla ($31.10), Port Lincoln ($54.70), Ceduna ($64) and Streaky Bay ($57.30).

Boat There are plans to commence a ferry service between Wallaroo, on the Yorke Peninsula, and Cowell, on the east coast of the Eyre Peninsula. Check with the SATC.

PORT AUGUSTA (pop 14,600)

Matthew Flinders was the first European to set foot in the area, but the town of Port Augusta was not established until 1854. Today, this busy port city is the gateway to the outback region of South Australia. It's also a major crossroads for travellers.

From here, roads head west across the Nullarbor to Western Australia, north to Alice Springs and Darwin in the Northern Territory, south to Adelaide and east to Broken Hill and Sydney in New South Wales. The railway line between the east and west coasts and the Adelaide to Alice Springs route both pass through Port Augusta.

Information

The tourist information centre (☎ 8641 0793) is in the Wadlata Outback Centre at 41 Flinders Terrace – it's the major outlet for the Flinders Ranges and the outback, and also has a good selection of material on the Eyre Peninsula. It's open weekdays from 9 am to 5.30 pm and weekends from 10 am to 4 pm.

Open the same times, Wadlata is an interesting interpretive centre ($6), with numerous exhibits tracing the Aboriginal and European history of the Flinders Ranges and the outback.

Telecommunications The phone numbers listed here for Port Augusta come into effect from February 1997. Before this time, dial the old number by removing the first two digits from the new number (for STD calls add the area code 086).

Things to See & Do

There are tours ($2) of the **School of the Air**, at 59 Power Crescent, on weekdays at 10 am. You can also tour the **Royal Flying Doctor Service**, at 4 Vincent St, on weekdays between 10 am and noon, and 1 and 3 pm; admission is by donation.

Another good educational tour takes you around the huge **Northern Power Station** (☎ 8642 0737) – it has the added advantage of being free. Tours of the complex depart at 10 am, 11 am and 1 pm; closed footwear, long trousers and long-sleeved shirts are essential.

Other attractions include the **Curdnatta Art & Pottery Gallery**, in Port Augusta's first railway station, and the **Homestead Park Pioneer Museum**, on Elsie St, open daily from 10 am to 5 pm ($2.50). Pick up brochures from the Wadlata Outback Centre detailing a **heritage walk and drive** around the town.

Places to Stay

There are plenty of places to stay in Port Augusta; the tourist centre has details.

The efficient *Fauna Caravan Park* (☎ 8642 2974) has camp sites for $14, on-site vans for $33 and cabins from $49. It also has a four-bed bunk house for backpackers ($10) with an adjacent campers' kitchen.

Port Augusta Backpackers (☎ 8641 1063), at 17 Trent Rd, is a friendly place with beds for $12. You can arrange Flinders Ranges tours here. The hostel is just off Highway 1, and if you ask the bus drivers, they'll let you off near the hostel.

The *Flinders Hotel/Motel* (☎ 8642 2544), at 39 Commercial Rd, has backpacker accommodation for $14 and self-contained rooms for $39/50.

Getting There & Away

Air Augusta Airways (☎ 8642 3100; bookings ☎ 13 1300) flies weekdays to Adelaide ($105) and Leigh Creek ($94).

On Saturday you can take the mail plane to Boulia ($310) in outback Queensland, stopping at Innamincka ($175) and Birdsville ($255) on the way; for details check with Augusta Airways.

Bus Stateliner's bus station (☎ 8642 5055) is at 23 Mackay St. Buses run to Adelaide ($27.20), Coober Pedy ($59), Wilpena Pound ($23.90), Whyalla ($11), Port Lincoln ($38.50), Ceduna ($50.60) and other places on the Eyre Peninsula.

Greyhound Pioneer (bookings ☎ 13 2030) travels to Perth ($189), Alice Springs ($141) and Sydney ($114).

Train By train Sydney is 32 hours away and a standard economy ticket costs $149. An economy/1st-class sleeper is $287/453. It takes 33 hours to Perth; an economy seat is $197 and an economy/1st-class sleeper is $382/596. It's four hours to Adelaide ($29). In Port Augusta, phone ☎ 8641 8111 for enquiries and bookings.

WHYALLA (pop 25,000)
The largest city in the state after Adelaide, Whyalla is a major steel-producing centre with a busy deep-water port.

Information
The tourist centre (☎ 8645 7900) is on the Lincoln Highway, near BHP. Opening hours are weekdays from 8.45 am to 5.10 pm, Saturday from 9 am to 4 pm and Sunday from 10 am to 4 pm.

Things to See & Do
There are interesting tours of the **BHP steel works** on Monday, Wednesday and Saturday at 9.30 am. They start from the tourist centre and cost $6. Long trousers, long-sleeved shirts and closed footwear are essential.

Next door to the tourist centre is the **Maritime Museum**, featuring the 650-tonne, WW II corvette HMAS *Whyalla*; admission is $5 and it's open daily from 10 am to 4 pm.

Ore comes to Whyalla from the open-cut mines of Iron Knob, Iron Monarch, Iron Baron and Iron Duke. **Iron Knob** was the first iron-ore deposit in Australia to be exploited; there are tours ($3) of the mine on weekdays at 10 am and 2 pm and the Iron Knob tourist office (☎ 8646 2129) can give details. Enclosed footwear is essential.

Whyalla has two fine swimming beaches near town, and a fishing jetty at the marina.

The **Whyalla Wildlife & Reptile Sanctuary** on the Lincoln Highway near the airport is definitely worth a visit; it's open daily at 10 am and admission is $5.

On Ekblom St, there are historical exhibits in the **Mt Laura Homestead Museum**. It's open Sunday, Monday and Wednesday from 2 to 4 pm and Friday from 10 am to noon; admission is $2.

Places to Stay & Eat
The *Whyalla Foreshore Caravan Park* (☎ 8645 7474) on Broadbent Terrace has camp sites for $10, on-site vans for $24 and cabins from $28. Prices for camp sites and on-site vans are similar at the friendly *Hillview Caravan Park* (☎ 8645 9357), off the Lincoln Highway five-km south of town, but cabins cost from $35.

Backpacker accommodation is available at the *Bushman's Rest* (☎ 8644 0620), 46 Aikman Crescent. Beds start from $13.

You can get details of Whyalla's four hotels and six expensive motels from the tourist office. Title of 'cheapest pub' for singles/twin share is shared by the *Hotel Spencer* (☎ 8645 8411) on Playford Ave, and the *Lord Gowrie Hotel* (☎ 8645 1611) on Gowrie Ave. Both charge $25/30.

The *Oriental Inn* on Essington Lewis Ave is said to be the best Chinese restaurant in town. Almost next door is the very popular *Bogart's Caffé*, which offers fancier meals than the pubs but still at a reasonable price.

COWELL (pop 700)
Cowell is a pleasant little town near a large jade deposit. The various mines have closed down as a result of marketing difficulties, but you can purchase a wide range of jade products from the Jade Motel, on the Lincoln Highway at the northern end of town. There's a small **folk museum** in the old post office (next door to the operating post office) and an **agricultural museum** on the Lincoln Highway. Oysters are farmed locally, and you can buy them from several outlets for as little as $5 a dozen.

Places to Stay
Two km north of town, the basic *Harbour View Caravan Park* (☎ 8629 2216) has camp sites ($8), on-site vans ($20) and cabins

(from \$26). Close to the town centre, the *Cowell Foreshore Caravan Park* (☎ 8629 2307) charges \$10 for camp sites and \$27 for on-site vans. Its cabins start at \$32.

Alternatively, the lovely old *Franklin Harbour Hotel* (☎ 8629 2015) has rooms for \$15/25, while the impressive *Commercial Hotel* (☎ 8629 2181) charges \$20/30.

Schultz Farm (☎ 8629 2194), run by kindly Mr and Mrs Schultz, has spacious rooms for \$25 per person including a cooked breakfast. It's about one km from town.

COWELL TO PORT LINCOLN
The first tiny township on the road south from Cowell is **Elbow Hill** (15 km down the Lincoln Highway). There's not much here, but the beaches at nearby **Point Gibbon** (six km) are magnificent – huge white sand dunes and a beautiful coastline.

The very hospitable *Elbow Hill Inn* (☎ 8628 5012) provides morning and afternoon tea, light lunches and evening dining. They also have two rooms with en-suites (\$60 for doubles), and a pool.

Cleve is 43 km inland from Cowell, and although it's just a quiet country town, the drive there is pleasant. It has a fauna park, which needs upgrading, and an interesting agricultural and folk museum in the old council chambers – ask at the council office for a key. The *Cleve Hotel/Motel* (☎ 8628 2011), Fourth St, has pub rooms for \$20/30 and motel rooms for \$45/55.

Back on the coast, **Arno Bay** is another small beach resort with a pub and caravan park.

South again is **Port Neill**, a pleasant seaside town with a vintage vehicle museum. Farther south is **Tumby Bay**, with its long, curving white-sand beach, a National Trust museum and a number of old buildings around the town. Hales Mini Mart (☎ 8688 2584) has tourist information and also hires out tandem bicycles (\$3 per hour).

The **Sir Joseph Banks Islands** are 15 km offshore, and form a marine conservation park. A couple of islands in this group have sea-lion colonies, and there are many attractive bays and reefs plus a wide variety of sea birds, including Cape Barren Geese, which nest on the islands. Cruises and boat hire can be arranged; contact Hales Mini Mart in Tumby Bay or the tourist office in Port Lincoln for details.

PORT LINCOLN (pop 13,000)
Port Lincoln, at the southern end of the Eyre Peninsula, is 662 km from Adelaide by road but only 250 km as the crow flies. The first settlers arrived in 1839 and the town has grown to become the tuna-fishing capital of Australia. The annual **Tunarama Festival**, which runs over the Australia Day weekend in January, signals the start of the tuna-fishing season with boisterous merriment.

Information
The tourist office (☎ 8682 6666) is at the Eyre Travel Centre on Tasman Terrace (the foreshore). It's open weekdays from 9 am to 5.30 pm, Saturday from 9 am to noon and, during school holidays only, on Sunday from 10 am to noon.

Contact the ranger at the NPWS (☎ 8688 3177) for information on Lincoln National Park (see Around Port Lincoln) and Coffin Bay National Park (see Port Lincoln to Streaky Bay).

There are some good surfing and diving spots near the town. For information about the best areas, contact the Port Lincoln Skin-Diving & Surfing Centre (☎ 8682 4428), at 73 Mortlock Terrace. You can also hire scuba-diving equipment, provided you're a licensed diver.

Things to See & Do
Port Lincoln is well situated on Boston Bay. There are a number of historic buildings, including the **Old Mill** on Dorset Place, which has a lookout affording good views over the bay. The **Lincoln Hotel** dates from 1840, making it the oldest hotel on the peninsula. On the Flinders Highway, **Mill Cottage** is a historic homestead built in 1866; it's open daily except Monday from 2 to 4.30 pm.

Thirty-one km offshore is **Dangerous Reef**, a very important breeding area for the white pointer shark. Sightings of sharks are rare, but you'll probably see plenty of sea lions. Cruises to the reef can be arranged through Eyre Travel (☎ 8682 6666) or Westward Ho Holiday Units (☎ 8682 2425). Prices start at $45, which includes a visit to an underwater viewing platform at a tuna farm moored near Boston Island.

Places to Stay & Eat
There are a number of hotels, motels and holiday flats in and around town; the tourist office has details.

The popular *Kirton Point Caravan Park* (☎ 8682 2537) has camp sites for $5 and cabins from $22.

Cheapest of the five hotels is the *Lincoln Hotel* (☎ 8682 1277), which has singles/doubles for $20/35 with shared facilities and $25/40 with private bathroom. Close behind is the *Great Northern Hotel* (☎ 8682 3350) at $20/38.

Westward Ho Holiday Units (☎ 8682 2425) has flats from $50 for doubles. If there's six of you and you have your own bedding, you can get a flat for $58 outside holiday periods.

There are plenty of eating establishments. One of the most popular is *Bugs Restaurant* on Eyre St, which has delicious pasta from $8 to $10. They also make wonderful soups. The pubs all have good-value counter meals and the *Great Northern* is excellent for seafood.

Getting There & Away
Daily Stateliner buses run from Adelaide via Cummins or Tumby Bay for $54.70, but there is no public transport between Port Lincoln and Streaky Bay.

Kendell Airlines and Lincoln Airlines have flights between Adelaide and Port Lincoln, costing $116 and $90 respectively.

Getting Around
There are various tours, including town tours ($15), a day tour of the town and Whalers Way ($45) and a day tour incorporating the lower Eyre Peninsula and Coffin Bay ($45). For details see the tourist office.

AROUND PORT LINCOLN
Cape Carnot, better known as Whalers Way, is 32 km south of Port Lincoln and features beautiful and rugged coastal scenery. Although it is privately owned, it is possible to visit by obtaining a permit ($15 plus key deposit), which is valid for 24 hours and enables you to camp at Redbanks or Groper Bay. Permits can be obtained from most petrol stations or from the tourist office in Port Lincoln.

You can also buy permits ($8) to visit **Mikkira Koala Sanctuary** (closed November to February) from most petrol stations in Port Lincoln or at the tourist office. Don't expect too much!

There are beautiful beaches at **Sleaford Bay**, a three-km detour off the road to Whalers Way. Cabins are available for overnight or weekly stays at the *Sleaford Bay Holiday Park* (☎ 8688 3177).

Also south of Port Lincoln is the **Lincoln National Park**, again with a magnificent coastline. There are camp sites in the park, and caravan access, but you'll need to obtain a camping permit ($4 per car) from the rangers at the park entry station – a day visit costs $3 per car. Over 60% of the park's tracks are suitable for conventional vehicles but you need a 4WD to visit tranquil **Memory Cove**, where the entry fee is $5 per vehicle.

You can visit offshore islands such as **Boston Island**; the tourist office in Port Lincoln will help you find a boat to get you out to them. It is also possible to stay in a historic homestead on Boston Island; ask at the tourist office or phone ☎ 8682 1741.

PORT LINCOLN TO STREAKY BAY
Coffin Bay
Ominous sounding Coffin Bay (it was named by Matthew Flinders to honour Sir Isaac Coffin) is a sheltered stretch of water with many quiet beaches and good fishing. The main centre is the holidayville of Coffin Bay (usual population 200). From here you can visit wild coastal scenery along the ocean side of **Coffin Bay Peninsula**, which is entirely taken up by a national park. Access

for conventional vehicles is limited within the park – you can get to scenic Point Avoid quite easily, but otherwise you need a 4WD. Entry to the park costs $3 per car.

Prolific birdlife, including some unusual species, is a feature of the **Kellidie Bay Conservation Park**, just outside Coffin Bay township.

Places to Stay The *Coffin Bay Caravan Park* (☎ 8685 4170) is the only place in town where you can camp ($8); it also has on-site vans ($25) and cabins ($35). There are motel units at the *Coffin Bay Hotel* (☎ 8685 4111) from $48/55. The pub does counter meals (from $4) and there's a couple of takeaways.

Bush camping (generally with difficult access) is allowed at several places on the peninsula and permits cost $4 per car. Contact the ranger at the park entry station (☎ 8685 4047) near Coffin Bay township.

Coffin Bay to Point Labatt

Just past **Coulta**, 40 km north of Coffin Bay, there's good surfing at **Greenly Beach**. About 15 km south of **Elliston**, a small resort and fishing town on peaceful Waterloo Bay, **Locks Well** is a good area for salmon fishing. Elliston has two caravan parks, a pub and a motel.

Just north of Elliston, take the seven-km detour to **Anxious Bay** and **Salmon Point** for some great ocean scenery – you pass **Blackfellows**, which has some of the strongest waves on the west coast. From here you can see distant **Flinders Island**, where there's a sheep station and tourist accommodation; Flinders Island Holidays (☎ 8626 132) in Streaky Bay can provide details

Talia, farther up the coast, has a colourful granite shore and the limestone **Talia Caves**.

At **Port Kenny** on Venus Bay, there are quiet beaches and plenty of pelicans. There's a caravan park and pub here, and another caravan park at nearby **Venus Bay** township.

Shortly before Streaky Bay, the turn-off to **Point Labatt** takes you to one of the few permanent colonies of sea lions on the Aus-

tralian mainland. You can view them from the cliff top, 50 metres above.

STREAKY BAY (pop 1000)

This attractive little town takes its name from the 'streaky' water, caused by seaweed in the bay. A museum containing the **Kelsh Pioneer Hut** and other exhibits is open on Tuesday and Friday from 2 to 4 pm and at other times by prior arrangement. The **Powerhouse Museum** is open the same hours and contains a large collection of restored engines.

Curious granite outcrops known as inselbergs are found at numerous places around the Eyre Peninsula. You can see a group known as **Murphy's Haystacks** near the highway about 20 km south-east of Streaky Bay – it's not worth a special visit but drop in if you're passing. **Back Beach**, four km west of Streaky Bay, is good for surfing, and there's some grand cliff scenery around the coast here.

Places to Stay

About a km from town, the *Foreshore Tourist Park* (☎ 8626 1666) has camp sites for $11.25 and on-site cabins from $30. The adjoining kiosk does good takeaways.

Dorm-style beds are $10 in *Labatt House* (☎ 8626 1126), in Alfred Terrace across from the Shell Roadhouse – this is the main tourist information outlet. It's said to be quite friendly, and its kitchen, dining room and lounge are spacious and clean.

Just up the road in the centre of town, the comfortable *Streaky Bay Community Hotel/Motel* (☎ 8626 1008) has basic pub rooms for $25/30 and rooms with private bathroom for $44/52/66.

SMOKY BAY (pop 100)

There's not much to do here but fish, or lie on the beach contemplating your navel, and that's what attracts most visitors. The friendly caravan park (☎ 8625 7030) has basic cabins from $16 and camp sites for $7. Smoky Bay has a promising oyster farming industry; you can buy fresh oysters locally for $5 a dozen.

CEDUNA (pop 3600)

Just past the junction of the Flinders and Eyre highways, Ceduna marks the end of the Eyre Peninsula and the start of the long, lonely highway across the Nullarbor Plain into Western Australia. The town was founded in 1896, although a whaling station had existed on St Peter Island, off nearby Cape Thevenard, back in 1850.

The tourist office is in the Ceduna Travel Centre (☎ 8625 2780) in the main street. After a few days fruitlessly waiting for a lift you might find yourself paying it a visit to buy a bus ticket to Western Australia. Greyhound Pioneer charges $146 to Norseman and $189 to Perth.

The **Old Schoolhouse Museum** has pioneer exhibits, but what's really interesting are the artefacts and newspaper clippings from the British atomic weapons program at Maralinga. Entry costs $2 and it's open daily except Sunday – check at the tourist office for times.

There are many beaches and sheltered coves around Ceduna, with good surfing and fishing. **Laura Bay Conservation Park**, off the road to Smoky Bay 20 km south-west of Ceduna, has mangroves and tidal flats that attract many species of seabirds and waders.

Turn off the highway at **Penong**, about 75 km west of Ceduna, and a 20-km dirt track gets you to Point Sinclair. Here you'll find famous (to surfers) **Cactus Beach**, which has some of Australia's best surfing breaks. The area is private property but you can camp for $4 – fees are collected daily. Bring your own drinking water.

Farther west you can go whale-watching at **Head of Bight**, where southern right whales come in close to shore during the breeding season from June to October. Between 20 and 30 calves are born here each year, and most times you'll see several adults swimming along the cliffs. There are excellent lookout points, but it's best if you have binoculars.

You can get permits ($5 per adult or $10 per vehicle) and information from the Yalata Roadhouse and the Nullarbor Hotel/Motel, both on the Eyre Highway. The unmarked turn-off to the viewing area is 78 km past Yalata, heading west.

Places to Stay

The tourist office can give you details on Ceduna's four caravan parks, pub and motels.

Best of the caravan parks is the *Foreshore Caravan Park* (☎ 8625 2290) near the town centre. It's quite attractive and has camp sites for $12 and basic cabins from $33. If the budget is all important, *A1 Cabins* (☎ 8625 2578) on McKenzie St has basic cabins for $22 singles/doubles – they'll sleep five for $31.

The *Ceduna Community Hotel/Motel* (☎ 8625 2008) has pub rooms from $25/29 and motel units from $58/63/71 for singles/doubles/triples. Don't leave any valuables in your car if you're parked in the street overnight.

Farther west there are basic *caravan parks* at the Nundroo Hotel/Motel Inn (☎ 8625 6120), Yalata Roadhouse (☎ 8625 6807), Nullarbor Hotel/Motel Inn (☎ 8625 6271) and Border Village (☎ (090) 39 3474).

Flinders Ranges

Rising from the northern end of Gulf St Vincent and running north for 400 km into the arid outback, the Flinders Ranges offer some of the most spectacular and rugged scenery in South Australia. It's a superb area for bushwalks, wildlife or taking in the ever-changing colours of the outback. In the far north of the Flinders region, the mountains are hemmed in by sand ridges and barren salt lakes.

As in many other dry regions of Australia, the vegetation here is surprisingly diverse and colourful. In the spring, after good winter rains, the country is carpeted with wildflowers. In summer the days can be searingly hot but the nights usually cool down to a pleasant temperature. Winter and early spring are probably the best times to visit

Flinders Ranges

0   25   50 km

To Oodnadatta & Alice Springs

Marree

Birdsville Track to Birdsville

To Innamincka

Mt Hopeless

Strzelecki Track

Talc Mine

Lyndhurst

Mt Painter (790 m)

Paralana Springs

Arkaroola

GAMMON RANGES NATIONAL PARK

Copley

Italowie Gorge

Balcanoona National Park Headquarters

Leigh Creek

Puttapa

Moro Gorge

Sliding Rock

Beltana

Lake Frome (Salt)

Lake Torrens (Salt)

Chambers Gorge

Parachilna Gorge

Glass's Gorge

Eregunda Valley

Blinman

Parachilna

South Blinman

Wirrealpa Homestead

Angorichina Village

Great Wall of China

FLINDERS RANGES NATIONAL PARK

Brachina Gorge

Bunker Hills

Frome Downs (Private Homestead)

Bunyeroo Gorge

Barytes Mine

Oraparinna Homestead

Wilpena

Sacred Canyon

Moralana Scenic Route

Rawnsley Park

Arkaroo Rock Shelter

To Coober Pedy & Alice Springs

Yourambulla Rock Shelter

Hawker

Kanyaka (Ruins)   47

Buckaringa Gorge

Cradock

Warren Gorge

Belton

Quorn

Stuart Highway

87

PORT AUGUSTA

Pichi Richi Pass

Bruce

Carrieton

To Broken Hill (195 km)

To Perth

Alligator Gorge

Hammond

Mannahill

1

Wilmington

56

Willowie

Orroroo

Yunta

32

Hancocks Lookout

Willowie

Barrier Highway

ALT 1

Mambray Creek

MT REMARKABLE NATIONAL PARK

Melrose

Pekina

Black Rock

Port Germein

Mt Remarkable (963 m)

Booleroo Centre

56

WHYALLA

Germein Gorge

Murray Town

Wirrabara

83

Peterborough

To Burra & Adelaide

SPENCER GULF

To Adelaide

1

SOUTH AUSTRALIA

although there are attractions at any time of the year.

In 1802, when Flinders set foot on the coast near Port Augusta, there were a number of Aboriginal tribes in the region. You can visit some of their sites: the rock paintings at Yourambulla (near Hawker) and Arkaroo (near Wilpena); and the rock-cut patterns at Sacred Canyon (near Wilpena) and Chambers Gorge.

Bushwalking is one of the main attractions of the area. Campers can generally find water in rock pools during the winter months, but this is wild, rugged country and care should be taken before setting out. Wilpena Pound, the Arkaroola-Mt Painter Sanctuary and Mt Remarkable National Park all have excellent walks, many of them along marked trails – the Heysen Trail starts in Parachilna Gorge, near Blinman, and winds south through the ranges from there.

In the early mornings and evenings, you've got a good chance of spotting wildlife, including emus, a variety of kangaroos and many different lizards. The birdlife is especially prolific.

Information

The main tourist office for Flinders Ranges & Outback South Australia Tourism (☎ 8373 3430 or 1800 633 060) is at 56B Glen Osmond Rd, Parkside, in Adelaide; it's open weekdays only between 9 am and 5 pm.

The main NPWS office for the northern Flinders Ranges and the far north is at Hawker (☎ 8648 4244), in the same building as the post office; the main office for the southern ranges is at 9 MacKay St, in Port Augusta (☎ 8648 5310). There's another office at Wilpena (☎ 8648 0048) that has information on display 24 hours a day and is usually staffed daily from 8 am to 5.30 pm.

It's definitely worth getting a good map of the area, as there are many back roads and a variety of road surfaces. According to local experts, the most accurate touring map is put out by Westprint; others published by the Flinders Ranges & Outback of South Australia Regional Tourism Association (which

also publishes a useful free tourist guide) and the RAA are also good.

The RAA's comprehensive touring guide *Flinders Ranges* ($4 to members and $8 to nonmembers) is excellent value. Best of all, however, is the glovebox (and rucksack) sized *Guide to the Flinders Ranges*, published by the Royal Geographical Society of Australia (SA branch). It covers a number of bushwalks and driving routes, and includes a swag of general information.

The cheapest walking 'guide' available is the pamphlet *Bushwalking in the Flinders Ranges National Park* ($1), available from NPWS offices. More serious walkers should look for a copy of Adrian Heard's *Walking Guide to the North Flinders Ranges*. Tyrone T Thomas' *Fifty Walks in South Australia* has a good section on the Flinders Ranges. Another good general walking guide is *Flinders Ranges Walks* ($6), published by the Conservation Council of South Australia.

Organised Tours

There are plenty of tours from Adelaide to the Flinders and also tours out from Port Augusta, Wilpena Pound, Arkaroola and other centres. A few cater for backpackers – see hostel notice boards for current fares and itineraries.

The major bus companies also do tours and many companies offer more adventurous 4WD trips, including Treckabout Australia (☎ 8396 2833) and Gawler Outback Tours (☎ 8278 4467), based in Adelaide; Intrepid Tours (☎ 8648 6277), in Quorn; and Range Tours (☎ 8648 4874) in Blinman.

Horse-riding treks are available at the Pichi Richi Holiday Camp (☎ 8648 6075) 14 km south of Quorn in the Pichi Richi Pass. Adnyamathanha stockman Ron Coulthard takes trail rides in the Wilpena area and can go as far as the ABC Range. Ron doesn't have a set program, but he'll certainly teach you something of the bush and Aboriginal culture. You can book through the Wilpena Pound Motel (☎ 1800 805 802); prices range from $20 for one hour to $50 for four hours.

There are camel treks from Blinman

ranging from 1½-hour rides ($25) to eight-day treks ($875); phone ☎ 8648 4874 or ☎ 8543 2280 for details.

At Wilpena you can take a scenic flight for $40 (20 minutes) or $55 (30 minutes). Costs increase if there are less than three people on the flight. Bookings can be made through the Wilpena Pound Motel.

Places to Stay

There are hotels and caravan parks as well as many cottages and farms offering all sorts of accommodation in the Flinders Ranges, but there is no hostel accommodation at Wilpena Pound itself. To stay here, you will need your own camping gear unless you're prepared to fork out for the relatively expensive, but very comfortable, *Wilpena Pound Motel*. The closest budget accommodation is at Rawnsley Park, 10 km south of Wilpena, just outside the walls of the Pound, where on-site vans are available. See under Wilpena Pound. Contact the SATC travel centre in Adelaide (☎ 1800 882 092) for further details.

In Quorn, Quornucopia (☎ 8648 6282), at 17 Railway Terrace, can arrange accommodation. Costs range from $29 per night in a basic cabin to $140 per night in a house.

To camp in the Flinders Ranges National Park (except at the private camping ground at Wilpena Pound) you need a permit from an NPWS office for $2 per person per night.

Getting There & Away

Air Augusta Airways (☎ 8642 3100; bookings 13 1300) flies weekdays from Adelaide to Port Augusta ($105) and Leigh Creek ($175).

Bus Stateliner has daily services to Port Augusta ($27.20) and four services a week to Wilpena Pound ($49) via Quorn ($34.90) and Hawker ($45.80) – two of these go on to Copley ($61) via Blinman ($50.60) and Parachilna ($52.50).

Car There are good sealed roads all the way north to Wilpena Pound. From there the roads are gravel, and although these are quite

good when they're dry, they can be closed by heavy rain. Check with NPWS offices for current information. The Marree road skirting the western edge of the Flinders Ranges is sealed up to Lyndhurst.

Probably the most interesting way to get to Arkaroola is to go to Wilpena Pound and on to South Blinman, then head east to Wirrealpa Homestead, where you head north via Chambers Gorge to meet the Frome Downs road south of Balcanoona. All these roads tend to be difficult after heavy rain.

For recorded information on road conditions in the Flinders Ranges region and other outback regions of South Australia, phone ☎ 11 633.

Getting Around

If you have a vehicle you can make a loop that takes you around an interesting section of the southern part of the ranges. From Port Augusta go through the Pichi Richi Pass to Quorn and Hawker and on up to Wilpena Pound. Continue north through the Flinders Ranges National Park past the Oraparinna Homestead, then veer west through the Brachina Gorge to the main Leigh Creek to Hawker road. From this junction you can either head straight back to Hawker, or make a detour off the main Leigh Creek to Hawker road and travel to Hawker via the Moralana Scenic Route. The section via the Brachina Gorge has a self-guided geology trail, with interpretive signs posted en route. Pick up a leaflet describing the trail from the NPWS office at Wilpena.

From Wilpena Pound, you can also loop north into the Flinders Ranges National Park through Bunyeroo Gorge, meeting up with the Brachina Gorge road. You can then either head back to Wilpena via the Oraparinna Homestead, or head west to the Leigh Creek to Hawker road and travel back to Hawker.

QUORN (pop 1400)

The 'gateway to the Flinders' is about 330 km north of Adelaide and 41 km north-east of Port Augusta. It became an important railway town after the completion of the

Great Northern Railway in 1878, and it still has a strong flavour of the pioneering days.

The railway was closed in 1957, but part of the line to Port Augusta has reopened as a tourist railway. A vintage train – often pulled by a steam engine – makes a 32-km round trip from Quorn to the scenic Pichi Richi Pass for $17. Outside school holiday periods, when it runs fairly frequently, the train operates between early April and mid-November every second weekend and on public holidays (☎ 8276 6232). Ask at the railway station about tours ($4) of the **railway workshop** – usually conducted on train days. Here you'll find a large collection of locomotives, carriages, freight wagons, brake vans and sundry items.

The town, picturesquely sited in a valley, has a couple of art galleries. **Quornucopia** offers a range of unusual crafts and gifts, and the **Studio Gallery** is worth a browse.

From Quorn you can make 4WD trips into the Flinders Ranges and visit the nearby **Warren Gorge** (which has good rock climbing and pleasant picnic sites) and the **Waukarie Creek Trail**, which runs from Woolshed Flat to Waukarie Creek. **Buckaringa Sanctuary**, encompassing the Buckaringa and Middle Gorges, lies 30 km

north of Quorn. An ecotourism venture including self-contained cabins and a restaurant, is planned for the sanctuary. Contact the SATC for details.

The tourist centre next to the council chambers in Seventh St is open Monday to Friday from 9 am to 2 pm and on weekends and public holidays from 9 am to 4 pm.

Places to Stay & Eat

The *Quorn Caravan Park* (☎ 8648 6206) has camp sites from $13 and on-site vans from $26.

The *Transcontinental Hotel* (☎ 8648 6076) on Railway Terrace is the pick of the town's four hotels for accommodation. It's a friendly place with backpacker beds costing $12 and standard rooms at $25/35 for singles/doubles.

The *Pichi Richi Holiday Camp* (☎ 8648 6075), 14 km south of Quorn in the Pichi Richi Pass, has a self-contained cottage for $80 per night (for up to six people; $10 each extra person). It also has horse treks ranging in duration from two hours to six days.

Quorn's four pubs sell counter and dining room meals, usually starting at about $6. There's a very good restaurant in the *Quorn Mill Motel* and another at the old *Willow*

Flinders Ranges Dreaming

The almost palpable 'spirit of place' of the Flinders Ranges has inspired a rich heritage of dreaming stories. Wilpena Pound was an important ceremonial site, known by the Adnyamathanha ('hill people') as Ikara. A lot of the legends – many secret, but some related by Adnyamathanha elders – explain creation, the extraordinary geological features of the pound, and the native birds and animals that inhabit it.

One Adnyamathanha story describes Akurra, a giant snake who carved out gorges in his quest to find water. The rumblings from his giant belly can be heard resounding around the walls of Ikara.

Another story relates that the walls of the pound are the bodies of two Akurra, who coiled around Ikara during an initiation ceremony, creating a whirlwind during which they devoured most of the participants.

In another story the bossy eagle Wildu, seeking revenge on his nephews who had tried to kill him, built a great fire. All the birds were caught in the flames and, originally white, they emerged blackened and burnt. The magpies and willie wagtails were partially blackened, but the crows were entirely blackened and have remained so until this day. ■

Brewery, about 10 km out on the Port Augusta road.

KANYAKA

About 40 km north of Quorn, on the way to Hawker, are the impressive ruins of the old Kanyaka settlement, founded in 1851. Up to 70 families lived here, tending the settlement's 50,000 sheep, but it was finally abandoned in 1888 as a result of drought and overgrazing. The epitaphs on the headstones in the tiny graveyard, which dates from the 1850s, reflect the courage of these early pioneers.

From the homestead ruins, you can take a 10-minute walk to the old woolshed. The track continues about 1.5 km to a picturesque permanent water hole, overlooked by the **Kanyaka Rock**.

If you're coming from Wilpena Pound, don't be confused by the sign that indicates the old Kanyaka town site (surveyed 1863) – the clearly marked turn-off for the ruins is about four km farther on.

HAWKER (pop 450)

Hawker is 55 km south of Wilpena Pound. The NPWS office for the Flinders Ranges and Far North is in the same building as the post office, on the corner of Wilpena Rd and Elder Terrace. For tourist information, chat with the helpful staff at the Mobil service station on the corner of Wilpena Rd and Cradock Rd.

There are Aboriginal rock paintings 12 km south of Hawker at the **Yourambulla Rock Shelter**, a hollow in the rocks high up on the side of Yourambulla Peak, a half-hour walk from the road. The **Jarvis Hill Lookout** is about six km south-west of Hawker and affords good views over Hawker and north to Wilpena Pound.

The **Moralana Scenic Route** is a round-trip drive from Hawker, taking in the magnificent scenery between the Elders and Wilpena ranges. It is 24 km to the Moralana turn-off, and 28 km along an unsealed road that joins up with the sealed Hawker to Leigh Creek road, from where it is 43 km back to Hawker.

Places to Stay & Eat

The *Hawker Caravan Park* in town has lawned camp sites for $9, on-site vans for $25/28, and deluxe cabins for $50. About a km out on the Leigh Creek road, the friendly *Flinders Ranges Caravan Park* (☎ 8648 4266) has camp sites, caravan bays and on-site vans for almost identical prices.

The *Hawker Hotel* (☎ 8648 4102) costs $25/35 for pub-style singles/doubles and $50/60 for motel units. The *Outback Motel* (☎ 8648 4100) charges $50/60.

The *Sight-Seers Cafe* has reasonably priced meals and takeaways, as does the *Hawker Shopping Centre*, which has a well-stocked grocery section. Alternatively, there's the Hawker Hotel/Motel for pub-style meals and the more up-market *Old Ghan Restaurant* in the disused railway station.

Getting There & Away

There are four bus services a week to Wilpena Pound with Stateliner ($9).

WILPENA POUND

The best-known feature of the ranges and the main attraction in the 94,500-hectare **Flinders Ranges National Park**, is the large natural basin known as Wilpena Pound. Covering about 80 sq km, it is ringed by cliffs and is easily accessible only by the narrow opening at Sliding Rock through which Wilpena Creek sometimes flows. On the outside, the Wilpena Wall soars almost sheer for 500 metres; inside, the basin slopes relatively gently away from the peaks.

There is plenty of wildlife in Wilpena Pound, particularly euros (wallaroos) and birds – everything from rosellas, galahs and budgerigars to emus and wedge-tailed eagles. You can make scenic flights over Wilpena Pound and beyond from $40, take a horse ride through the foothills from $20, and explore nearby **Arkaba** station on a 4WD tour for $60 for a full day. All of these can be booked at the Wilpena Pound Motel.

Sacred Canyon, with rock-cut patterns, is to the east. To the north and still within the national park are striking scenic attractions, such as **Bunyeroo Creek**, **Brachina Gorge** and the **Aroona Valley**. There are several fine bush-camping areas, all accessible by conventional vehicle. The 20-km Brachina Gorge Geological Trail (you follow it in your car) features an outstanding geological sequence of exposed sedimentary rock.

Bushwalks

If you're planning to walk for more than about three hours, fill in the log book at the rangers' office – and don't forget to 'sign off' when you return. Searches are no longer initiated by the rangers, so make sure someone responsible knows the details of your walk.

There is a series of bushwalks in the park, clearly marked by blue triangles along the tracks. (Sections that incorporate parts of the Heysen Trail are indicated by red markers.) Pick up a copy of the leaflet *Bushwalking in the Flinders Ranges National Park* issued by the NPWS ($1). Topographical maps (scale 1:50,000) are available for $7.50 from the NPWS office and the store at Wilpena.

Solo walks are not recommended and you must be adequately equipped – particularly with drinking water and sun protection, and especially during the summer months.

Most of the walks start from the camping ground and the walking times indicated are for a reasonably easy pace. The St Marys Peak walk is probably the most interesting, but there are plenty of others worth considering. They vary from short walks, suitable for people with small children, to longer ones taking more than a day.

You can take an excellent day-long walk from the Wilpena camping ground to **St Marys Peak** and back – either as an up-and-down or a round-trip expedition. Up and back, it's faster and more interesting to take the route outside Wilpena Pound and then up to the Tanderra Saddle, as the scenery this way is much more spectacular.

The final climb up to the saddle is fairly steep and the stretch to the top of the peak is a real scramble. The views are superb from the saddle and the peak; the white glimmer of **Lake Torrens** is visible off to the west and

the long Aroona Valley stretches off to the north.

Descending from the peak to the saddle you can then head back down on the same direct route or take the longer round-trip walk through Wilpena Pound via an old homestead and Sliding Rock. This is the same track you take to get to **Edeowie Gorge**. Alternatively, you can take your time and stay at the **Cooinda** bush-camping area within the Pound.

Arkaroo Rock is at the base of the Wilpena Range, about 10 km south of Wilpena off the Hawker road. From the car park it takes about half an hour at a moderate pace to reach the rock shelter, where there are Aboriginal depictions of emu and bird tracks in red ochre.

Places to Stay & Eat

Unless you've got a tent there is no cheap accommodation at Wilpena Pound. There's a *camping ground*, costing $9/14 for unpowered/powered sites, with facilities including a well-stocked store. Permits can be purchased at the store.

Otherwise, the *Wilpena Pound Motel* (☎ 1800 805 802 for bookings) has all mod cons including a swimming pool. Its budget rooms cost $35/45 for singles/doubles while more luxurious rooms are $79/83, including a light breakfast (during December and January, rates are $69/74).

You can get pies, pasties, groceries and last-minute camping requirements at the general store. Counter lunches are available in the motel bar, and there's also a very good restaurant.

Off the Hawker road, about 20 km south of Wilpena and close to the Pound's outer edge, the friendly owners of *Rawnsley Park* (☎ 8648 0030) have camp sites for $8.50 on-site vans for $32 and cabins for $52. There are several good bushwalks on offer and you can also make horse treks and 4WD tours from here.

The Stateliner bus passes four days a week from Adelaide and will drop you at the homestead.

BLINMAN (pop 50)

From the 1860s to the 1890s this was a busy copper town but today it's just a quaint hamlet on the circular route around Wilpena Pound. It's a useful starting point for visits to many of the scenic attractions in the area – the Blinman Deli can arrange 4WD tours and camel treks to out-of-the-way spots. The delightful *Blinman Hotel* (☎ 8648 4867) has a real outback pub flavour – rooms cost $20 per person or $25 with bathroom. Next door, the dusty little *Blinman Caravan Park* (ask at the pub) has camp sites for $5 and powered sites for $8.

About one km to the north is the historic **Blinman copper mine**, which is being developed as a tourist attraction.

AROUND BLINMAN

Dramatic **Mt Chambers Gorge**, 64 km to the north-east of Blinman towards Arkaroola, features a striking gallery of Aboriginal rock carvings. From Mt Chambers you can see over Lake Frome to the east and all the way along the Flinders Ranges from Mt Painter to Wilpena.

The beautiful **Aroona Valley** and the ruins of the **Aroona Homestead** are to the south of Blinman in the Flinders Ranges National Park and are reached from the stunning **Brachina Gorge** farther south. Between Blinman and Wilpena Pound is the **Great Wall of China**, a long ridge capped with ironstone. An inspiring scenic drive along a good dirt road links Blinman with Parachilna, to the west. This route takes you through **Parachilna Gorge**, where there are excellent picnic and camping areas.

Angorichina Tourist Village (☎ 8648 4842), about halfway between Blinman and Parachilna in the Parachilna Gorge, boasts a magnificent setting with steep hills all round. It has camp sites ($8), on-site vans $20/30 for singles/doubles and units (from $42). Stateliner will drop passengers at the front door.

Gum Creek Station (☎ 8648 4883), 15 km south of Blinman, has shearers' quarters for $10 per adult, but there's a minimum of $50 per night.

At tiny Parachilna there's the *Prairie Hotel* (☎ 8648 4895), which has powered sites for $15, basic cabins from $40 for singles/doubles and hotel accommodation for $35/55. The pub has an interesting menu featuring Australian bush tucker, and offers a real gourmet experience in the bush: its emu pâté on damper is delicious. Almost next door, the *Old Schoolhouse* (☎ 8648 4676) has bunks and cooking facilities for $12 per person.

North of Parachilna, on the Marree road, you turn east at the Beltana Roadhouse for access to historic **Old Beltana** (eight km) and the abandoned **Sliding Rock Mine** (31 km). Old Beltana almost became a ghost town but is now inhabited by interesting people seeking to escape the rat race. It's a fascinating spot – just ask local residents for directions. Alternatively, the roadhouse (☎ 8675 2744) is a good source of information about the area.

The tiny *School House* in Old Beltana has bunks and can accommodate up to eight people; the roadhouse will be able to tell you who's looking after the place.

LEIGH CREEK (pop 1420)

North of Beltana, Leigh Creek's huge open-cut coal mine supplies the Port Augusta power station. The present town of Leigh Creek was developed in 1980 when its predecessor was demolished to make way for mining. Landscaping and tree planting have created a very pleasant, leafy environment in dramatic contrast to the stark surroundings.

The Electricity Trust of South Australia (ETSA) (☎ 8675 4214) operates a caravan park with camp sites for $6 – the amenities are good but the ground is like concrete.

ETSA offers a range of free tours of its mining operations. These are very informative and last up to 2½ hours. For an update on schedules and opportunities contact either the ETSA office or the tour guide on ☎ 8675 4216 Monday to Friday between 7.30 am and 4.15 pm. Tours generally leave from the parking bay 200 metres south of the town turn-off on the Marree road.

From Leigh Creek, you can visit the

Aroona Dam (10 km to the south-west), the **Gammon Ranges National Park** and **Arkaroola** (respectively 100 and 130 km to the east). For information on the Gammon Ranges contact the ranger at Balcanoona on ☎ 8648 4829.

ARKAROOLA

The Arkaroola tourist village, in the northern part of the Flinders Ranges, was established in 1968. It's a privately operated wildlife sanctuary in rugged and spectacular country. From the settlement you can take a 4WD trip along the 'ridge top' through wild mountain country, and there are also scenic flights and many walking tracks. The ridge-top tour costs $50 – expensive, but the four-hour trip takes you through amazing scenery and is well worth it. Another excellent tour, which costs $15, allows you to view the heavens through a high-powered telescope at the Arkaroola Astronomical Observatory.

Arkaroola has a garage which has some spare car parts and which can do mechanical repairs.

This was a mining area and old tracks lead to rock pools at the **Barraranna Gorge** and **Echo Camp**, and to water holes at Arkaroola and **Nooldoonooldoona**. Farther on are the **Bolla Bollana Springs** and the ruins of a copper smelter. You can take a guided or tag-along tour, or do your own thing on most of the sanctuary's 100 km of graded tracks. Most places of interest are accessible to conventional vehicles, with some hiking involved.

Mt Painter is a very scenic landmark and you pass close to it on the ridge-top tour. There are fine views from **Freeling Heights** across Yudnamutana Gorge and from **Siller's Lookout** over the salt flats of Lake Frome. This is real red outback country and Arkaroola contains many spectacular examples of that landscape. **Paralana Hot Springs** is the 'last hurrah' of Australia's geyser activity. It's geologically interesting but otherwise not worth a special trip.

Places to Stay & Eat

The resort (☎ 8648 4848) has a good range of accommodation. Camp sites in the caravan park and down along the creek cost $10, as do bunk beds. Cabins are $29 twin share and motel units cost from $39 a double. There's a small shop where you can buy basic supplies, and a good restaurant.

Outback

The area north of the Eyre Peninsula and the Flinders Ranges stretches into the vast, empty area of South Australia's far north. Although sparsely populated and often difficult to travel through, it has much of interest – however, without 4WD or camels it's not possible to stray far from the few main roads. Entry permits are required for large parts of the north-west, which otherwise are prohibited areas (either Aboriginal land or the Woomera restricted area).

National Park Permits

To visit the national parks and conservation reserves up here you need a Desert Parks Permit, which costs $50 per vehicle. It's valid for a year and includes an excellent information book and detailed route and area maps. However, if you just want to visit Cooper Creek in the Innamincka Regional Reserve, Lake Eyre in the Lake Eyre National Park or Dalhousie Springs in the Witjira National Park north of Oodnadatta you need only buy a day/night permit for $15 per vehicle. These are available from Mt Dare Homestead, the Pink Roadhouse in Oodnadatta, the William Creek Hotel, the Oasis Cafe in Marree and the rangers' office in Innamincka.

Desert Parks Passes are available in many towns (although not from most NPWS offices, strangely) including: Adelaide (RAA and others), Alice Springs (Shell Tode service station), Birdsville Track (Mungerannie Roadhouse), Broken Hill (RAA), Coober Pedy (Underground Books), Hawker (Hawker Motors), Innamincka (Trading Post), Marree (Khans General Store, Oasis Cafe), Mt Dare Homestead

Oodnadatta (Pink Roadhouse), Port Augusta (Wadlata Outback Centre) and William Creek (William Creek Hotel).

For an update on outlets and park information contact the Desert Parks HQ, PO Box 102, Hawker 5434 or ring them on ☎ 8648 4244.

ROUTES NORTH

The Stuart Highway is sealed all the way from Port Augusta to Darwin. It's a long, mainly boring drive and the temptation to get it over with quickly has resulted in many high-speed collisions between cars and cattle, sheep, kangaroos and wedge-tailed eagles. Take care, particularly at night.

For those who want to travel to the Northern Territory by a more adventurous route there's the **Oodnadatta Track**. This often lonely road runs from Port Augusta through the Flinders Ranges to Leigh Creek, Lyndhurst, Marree and Oodnadatta before joining the Stuart Highway at Marla, about 180 km south of the Territory border. For most of the way it runs close to the defunct 'Old Ghan' train line.

The 'Track' is sealed as far as Lyndhurst, after which it's a typical rough, dusty outback road all the way to Marla. There are several routes across to the Stuart Highway: from Lake Eyre South via Roxby Downs to Pimba; from William Creek to Coober Pedy; and from Oodnadatta to Coober Pedy and Cadney Homestead (a roadhouse on the Stuart Highway). With a 4WD you can keep going up the old railway line from Oodnadatta to Alice Springs, visiting Witjira National Park and Old Andado on the way.

The two other routes of interest in the far north are the **Birdsville** and **Strzelecki** tracks – see the relevant sections later in this chapter. These days the tracks have been so much improved that during the winter season it's usually quite feasible to do them in any car that's in good condition – a 4WD is generally not necessary.

For more information on these roads check with the state automobile associations. *Outback Central & South Australia*, published by the South Australian Department of Lands, is an excellent tourist map with a lot of interesting information. Westprint does a good *Simpson Desert South-Lake Eyre* map that covers all three tracks. For more detail on outback travel, see Lonely Planet's *Outback Australia*.

The South Australian outback includes much of the **Simpson Desert** and the harsh, rocky landscape of **Sturt Stony Desert**. There are also huge salt lakes that fill with water every once in a long while. **Lake Eyre**, used by Donald Campbell for his attempt on the world's land-speed record in the '60s, filled up for a time in the '70s. It was full again in 1989, only the third occasion since Europeans first reached this area.

When infrequent soaking rains do reach this usually dry land the effect is amazing – flowers bloom and plants grow at a breakneck pace in order to complete their life cycles before the dry returns. There is even a species of frog that goes into a sort of suspended animation, remaining in the ground for years on end, only to pop up when the rains come again.

On a much more mundane level, roads can either be washed out or turned into glue-like mud. Venture into the wrong place after heavy rain and you may be stuck for days – or even weeks.

Note that repair facilities and spare parts are extremely limited in the northern Flinders Ranges, so be prepared in case of breakdown.

WOOMERA (pop 1000)

During the '50s and '60s Woomera was used to launch experimental British rockets and conduct tests in an abortive European project to send a satellite into orbit. The Woomera Prohibited Area occupies a vast stretch of land in the centre of the state. The town of Woomera, in the south-eastern corner of the Prohibited Area, is now an 'open town' but it is just a shadow of its former self. These days its main role is as a service town for the mostly US personnel working at the Joint Facility at Nurrungar, a short distance south of Woomera near Island Lagoon. About 1000 people live here today, as against 7500 in its heyday.

A small **heritage centre** in the centre of town has several interesting displays that tell you about Woomera's past and present roles, and what may happen in the future. Outside is a collection of old military aircraft, rockets and missiles. The centre is open daily from March to November from 9 am to 5 pm, and is closed during the summer.

Woomera Rocket Range Tours (☎ 8671 0788) can take you to the heritage centre, the main firing range at **Koolymilka**, the main operational area at **Range E** and other local attractions. The tours take three hours and cost $26, with a minimum of four passengers.

Places to Stay & Eat
The *Woomera Travellers' Village* (☎ 8673 7800), near the town entrance, has backpacker accommodation ($12/20 singles/ doubles), camp sites ($5 per person), powered sites ($14 for two people), on-site vans (from $25) and self-contained cabins ($50). The camper's kitchen is hardly worthy of the name.

The only alternative is the *Eldo Hotel* (☎ 8673 7867) on Kotara Ave. It has singles/ doubles/triples from $32/45/53.

The small shopping centre has a coffee lounge and snack bar with the usual takeaway fare. For something better you'll have to try the *Eldo Hotel*. It serves counter meals for about $8 and restaurant meals averaging $14 for a main course.

Getting There & Away
Air Kendell Airlines (bookings ☎ 13 1300) flies from Adelaide to Woomera most days of the week for $184.

Bus Woomera is seven km off the Stuart Highway from the scruffy little township of Pimba, 175 km north of Port Augusta. Stateliner and the long-distance bus lines pass through Woomera daily. With Stateliner it's $45.50 to Adelaide and $39.40 to Coober Pedy.

ANDAMOOKA (pop 470)
Off the Stuart Highway, 110 km north of Woomera by sealed road, Andamooka is a rough-and-ready opal-mining town with a strong frontier flavour. However, the local residents are friendly and welcoming as a rule. For general information call in to the Andamooka Opal Showroom in the centre of town and chat to the helpful staff.

Olympic Dam is a huge uranium, gold, silver and copper mine on Roxby Downs Station near Andamooka. Surface tours of the mine cost $16.50. They run daily at 9.45 am from the Olympic Dam Tours Office, next to the BP service station in Roxby Downs township (population 2000). Phone ☎ 8671 0788 for details.

Places to Stay & Eat
Andamooka You can camp ($12) or stay in an on-site van ($27) at the dusty *Andamooka Caravan Park* (☎ 8672 7117). There's not much shade here – not that there is anywhere else, either.

Alternatively, the *Andamooka Opal Hotel/Motel* (☎ 8672 7078) has basic pub-style rooms for $35/45 and motel units for $45/65. Check out *Duke's Guesthouse* (☎ 8672 7007) as it may have backpacker accommodation.

The best place in town to eat at is the *Tuckerbox Restaurant*, which sells hearty meals for reasonable prices.

Roxby Downs The *Roxby Downs Caravan Park* (☎ 8671 1000) has grassed camp sites for $10 and on-site vans for $32, while the *Roxby Downs Motor Inn* (☎ 8671 0311) charges $88 for rooms. You can get reasonably priced bistro and counter meals at the *tavern* across from the motel.

Getting There & Away
Stateliner has three buses a week from Adelaide to Roxby Downs ($69.90) and Andamooka ($88.60).

GLENDAMBO (pop 20)
Glendambo is 113 km north of Pimba and 252 km south of Coober Pedy. It was created

in 1982 as a service centre on the new Stuart Highway to replace the township of Kingoonya, which was bypassed by the new road. Glendambo has a good pub, motel, two roadhouses and a caravan park. The Mobil Roadhouse is the RAA agent and offers 24-hour service. The roadhouses and hotel all sell meals.

The *Glendambo Tourist Centre* (☎ 8672 1030) has bars, a restaurant, a 12-bed bunk house, and 72 motel rooms each sleeping up to five people. Beds in the bunk house cost $12, while motel rooms cost from $49/59 for singles/doubles plus $8 for each extra person.

Right next door is the *Caltex Roadhouse & Caravan Park* (☎ 8672 1035), which has unpowered sites for $7.50 and powered sites from $11.50. Its on-site vans cost $25 for the first person and $5 for each additional person.

COOBER PEDY (pop 3000)

On the Stuart Highway, 535 km north of Port Augusta, Coober Pedy is one of Australia's best-known outback towns. It is very cosmopolitan – about 40 nationalities are represented. The name 'Coober Pedy' is Aboriginal and is said to mean 'white fellow's hole in the ground'. This aptly describes the place, as about half the population lives in dugouts to shelter from the extreme climate: daytime summer temperatures can soar to over 50°C and the winter nights are freezing cold. Apart from the dugouts, there are over 250,000 mine shafts in the area! Keep your eyes open when you're walking around.

Coober Pedy is in an extremely inhospitable area and the town reflects this; even in the middle of winter it looks dried out and dusty, with piles of junk everywhere. This is no attractive little settlement; in fact it's hardly surprising that much of *Mad Max III* was filmed here – the town looks like the end of the world!

There are plenty of opal shops, but banking facilities are limited: there's an EFTPOS cash-withdrawal facility at Fast Photo, a Westpac branch, and a Commonwealth Bank agency in the post office. All are in the main street (Hutchison St).

Coober Pedy has a reputation for being pretty volatile: since 1987 the police station has been bombed twice, the courthouse has been bombed once, the most successful restaurant (the Acropolis) was demolished by a blast and hundreds of thousands of dollars worth of mining equipment has gone the same way.

To state the obvious, while it should be perfectly safe for visitors, it would be unwise for lone females to wander around unaccompanied late at night or accept invitations from unfamiliar men to visit mines or opal collections.

Information

The tourist office (☎ 8672 5298) is in the council offices, opposite the Opal Inn as you enter the town. It's open weekdays. Otherwise the Underground Bookshop (☎ 8672 5558) on Post Office Hill Rd is very good for information on the local area and the outback in general. If there's any work available for backpackers you can find out about it here.

Dugout Homes

Many of the early dugout homes were simply worked-out mines; now, however, they're often cut specifically as residences. Several homes are open to visitors – it seems all you have to do to charge admission is create an eccentric enough abode!

Other Attractions

Coober Pedy has a number of other attractions worth a look. The most prominent is the **Big Winch**, which has a lookout over the town and an extensive display of cut and uncut opal. There are numerous reputable – and some not so reputable – opal outlets in town; it's best to shop around and be wary of anyone offering discounts over 30% (this is a sign that the opal may be overpriced). Some of the best buys are found at the **Opal Cutter** on Post Office Hill Rd.

The **Old Timers Mine** is an old mine and underground home that is well worth the $3 entry fee.

North West Ridge

German Hill Road

To Oodnadatta

Catacomb Road

To Underground
Potteries &
Crocodile
Harry's

Seventeen Mile Road

Post
Office
Hill

Seventeen Mile Road

Umoona Road

Jeweller's
Shop
(Public
Noodling
Area)

Old Water Park Road

Hill Road

Cameron Dr

Paxton Road

Van Brugge Street

Grund Street

Willcox Street

Bean Street

St Nicholas Street

Water
Conservation
Reserve

Stuart Highway

Giles St

Ward Street

Flinders Street

Burke Street

To Wind Generator
& William Creek

32

Stuart Highway

To Riba's Caravan Park

Coober Pedy

SOUTH AUSTRALIA

0   50   100 m

PLACES TO STAY

1 Underground Motel
3 Desert View Motel
4 Lookout Cave Motel
6 Oasis Caravan Park
10 Opal Cave Bedrock
11 Umoona Opal Mine & Museum
15 Desert Cave Motel
18 Tom's Backpackers
19 Budget Motel & Joe's Backpackers
20 Radeka's Motel & Backpackers' Inn
27 Opal Fields Motel
28 Opal Inn Hotel/Motel & Caravan Park
32 Stuart Range Caravan Park

PLACES TO EAT

12 John's Pizza
16 Last Resort Cafe & Underground Books
22 Underground Dugout Restaurant
23 Old Miners Dugout Cafe
25 Traces
26 Tom & Mary's Taverna

OTHER

2 Catacombs Church
5 Hospital
7 Old Timers Mine
8 Big Winch
9 Fast Photo (EFTPOS)
13 Diggers Dream (Underground Home)
14 Doyouwantagoanna (Shop)
17 Opal Cutter (Opal Shop)
21 Post Office
24 Westpac Bank
29 Council Offices (Tourist Information)
30 Bus Station & Ampol Roadhouse
31 Police Station

Opals

Australia is the opal-producing centre of the world and South Australia is where most of the country's opals come from. Opals are hardened from silica suspended in water, and the colour is produced by light being split and reflected by the silica molecules. Valuable opals are cut in three different fashions: solid opals can be cut out of the rough into cabochons (domed-top stones); triplets consist of a layer of opal sandwiched between an opaque backing layer and a transparent cap; and doublets are simply an opal layer with an opaque backing. As well, in Queensland some opals are found embedded in rock; these are sometimes polished while incorporated in the surrounding rock.

An opal's value is determined by its colour and clarity – the brighter and clearer the colour the better. Brilliance of colour is more important than the colour itself. The type of opal is also a determinant of value: black and crystal opals are the most valuable, semiblack and semicrystal are in the middle, and milk opal is the least valuable. The bigger the pattern the better, and visible flaws (such as cracks) also affect the value.

Shape is important: a high dome is better than a flat opal. Finally, given equality of other aspects, the size is important. As with the purchase of any sort of gemstone, don't expect to find great bargains unless you clearly understand what you are buying. ■

The **Umoona Opal Mine & Museum** is ght in the centre of town; opal was still eing pulled out of here until mining within e town limits was banned some years ago. nformative tours of the mine ($5) run roughout the day.

A couple of km north-east of town is **Underground Potteries**, where you can uy some nice pottery. A couple of km arther on is **Crocodile Harry's** ($2), a ugout home that has featured in a number f documentaries, the movies *Mad Max III* nd *Ground Zero*, and the mini-series *Stark*. arry, a Latvian baron, spent 13 years in Far orth Queensland and the Northern Terri- ry hunting crocodiles. The wrecked cars t the front of his dugout make novel veg- able beds!

pal Mining
he town survives on opals, which were first scovered here in 1915. Keen fossickers can ave a go themselves, the safest area being e **Jeweller's Shop** opal field in the orth-east corner of town – fossicking

through the mullock, or waste, dumps is known as noodling.

There are literally hundreds of working mines around Coober Pedy but there are no big operators. When somebody makes a find, dozens of miners home in like bees around a honeypot.

Organised Tours
There are several tours that cover the sights and take you into an opal mine, underground home and a working opal field. Joe's Tours (book at the Budget Motel) include Croco- dile Harry's. Most tours take three hours and cost between $18 and $24.

On Monday and Thursday you can travel with the mail truck along 600 km of dirt roads as it does the round trip from Coober Pedy to Oodnadatta and William Creek. This is a great way to get off the beaten track and visit some small, remote outback communi- ties. The backpackers' special price is $60, which doesn't include lunch. For details, ☎ 1800 069 911 or contact the Underground Bookshop.

Places to Stay

Camping There are three caravan parks in town and another farther out. None are visually inspiring – there's no lawn but plenty of dust, and the ground is as hard as nails. Reasonably central to the action are the brand-new *Opal Inn Caravan Park*(☎ 8672 5054), which has sites for $12, and the *Oasis Caravan Park* (☎ 8672 5169), which has the best shade and shelter, as well as on-site vans and cabins.

The *Stuart Range Caravan Park* (☎ 8672 5179) is the largest and has the best facilities; its cabins are more like motel rooms. The park is about a km from town, near the main entrance off the Stuart Highway.

Friendliest and most basic of all is *Riba's* (☎ 8672 5614), but it's on the William Creek road five km from town. It's also the cheapest, with camp sites costing $3.50 per person – and showers are free.

Hostels The underground *Joe's Backpackers* (☎ 8672 5613) attached to the *Budget Motel* has beds for $12 including linen and showers, or $11 if you produce your YHA card. Although not brilliant, it's considered the best of the local hostel accommodation – it's certainly got a very good kitchen.

The *Backpackers' Inn* at Radeka's Dugout Motel (☎ 8672 5223) on Oliver St offers underground dormitories for $12 including linen and showers.

Tom's Backpackers (☎ 8672 5333) on the main street opposite the Desert Cave Motel has underground accommodation for $12. It also has uninviting above-ground rooms (no air-con) for the same price.

The very basic *Opal Cave Bedrock* (☎ 8672 5028) has a 52-bed dormitory for $8 a bed and more private – if cell-like – four-bunk rooms for $12 a bed. Showers cost 20c for one minute and linen is $6 extra.

Hotels & Motels There are a number of hotels and motels, some underground and some with big air-cons. Most are expensive! Listed here are the cheaper places.

The underground *Umoona Opal Mine* (☎ 8672 5288) on Hutchison St has singles/doubles for $20/25. Bathrooms are communal but there are kitchen facilities.

The *Budget Motel* (☎ 8672 5163) has above-ground rooms with share facilities at $18/30/36 for single/double/triple and rooms with private facilities at $35/45.

The *Opal Inn Hotel/Motel* (☎ 8672 5054) has comfortable pub rooms for $25/35 and motel rooms for $65/70.

Radeka's Dugout Motel (☎ 8672 5223) has an underground family room sleeping six for $90. Singles/doubles in its 'budget' above-ground rooms cost $45/55.

Places to Eat

The *Last Resort Cafe*, next to the Underground Bookshop, has excellent and imaginative food and is easily the best place in town for breakfast – its filling muesl ($6.20) is very popular with Swiss visitors. It makes delicious home-made ice creams, cakes and quiches and you can enjoy them either underground or al fresco. Sadly, it's open only during the day, and not at all on Sunday.

There are a couple of Greek places, *Tom & Mary's Taverna* and *Traces*, and these are both popular in the evenings; Traces stays open until 4 am. You can get a reasonably priced counter meal in the saloon bar of the *Opal Inn*.

The *Old Miner's Dugout Cafe* is indeed underground and it has a nice quiet atmosphere. Its menu is limited but varied, with such things as kangaroo tail soup, sauerkraut cabbage rolls and Mexican chicken enchiladas on offer. It's popular for dinner, but it's not what you'd call cheap – the 'backpacker special' is $7 – and the service can be brusque.

Otherwise there are more expensive restaurants as well as several takeaways and coffee lounges in the main street.

Getting There & Away

Air Kendell Airlines (book through Ansett on ☎ 13 1300) flies from Adelaide to Coober Pedy most days of the week ($250), and from Coober Pedy to Uluru (Ayers Rock) on Saturday only ($206). The Desert Cave Motel

PAUL STEEL

RICHARD NEBESKY

South Australia
Top: Rotunda, Adelaide
Bottom: Sign on the Eyre Highway, Nullarbor Plain

TONY WHEELER

MICHELLE COXALL

MICHELLE COXALL

PAUL STEEL

MATT KING

South Australia

A: Wilpena Pound, Flinders Ranges
B: Local personality, Moonta
C: Widflowers, Flinders Ranges

D: Old farmhouse, Flinders Ranges
E: Dwelling in Coober Pedy

handles reservations and operates the airport shuttle bus ($5 one-way).

Bus It's 413 km from Coober Pedy to Kulgera, just across the border into the Northern Territory, and from there it's another 275 km to Alice Springs.

Stateliner charges $82 from Adelaide to Coober Pedy. With Greyhound Pioneer it's $87 from Adelaide, $70 from Alice Springs and $66 from Yulara near Uluru (Ayers Rock).

AROUND COOBER PEDY
Breakaways

The Breakaway Reserve is a stark yet attractive area of low arid hills and scarps about 30 km from Coober Pedy. You can drive to the lookout in a conventional vehicle and see the colourful mesa known as the **Castle**, which featured in the films *Mad Max III* and *Priscilla, Queen of the Desert*.

You can also make an interesting 70-km loop from Coober Pedy taking in the Breakaways before following the Dog Fence back to the Coober Pedy to Oodnadatta road. (The Dog Fence is supposed to keep dingoes to the north, away from the sheep stations.) The Underground Bookshop has a leaflet and 'mud map' for $1.

MARLA (pop 150)

In the mulga scrub about 180 km south of the Northern Territory border, Marla replaced Oodnadatta as the official regional centre when the Ghan railway line was re-routed in 1980. The rough-and-ready **Mintabie** opal field is on Aboriginal land 35 km west – you need a permit ($5 from the Marla police station) to visit.

Fuel and provisions are available in Marla 24 hours a day – there's also an EFTPOS cash-withdrawal facility.

The *Marla Travellers Rest* (☎ 8670 7001) has camp sites for $5 per person (power $5 extra), backpacker units for $19/28 (in summer check that they're air-con), basic air-con cabins for $27/38 and motel rooms from $49/59. The comfortable and spacious

motel rooms cost $59/65 – it's $10 extra for TV and phone in the room.

On the Stuart Highway 85 km south of Marla, *Cadney Homestead* (☎ 8670 7994) has camp sites for $6 per person, powered sites at $16 for singles/doubles and cabins for $35, or there are motel rooms at $70/77/83 for singles/doubles/triples.

If you're heading for Oodnadatta, turning off the highway at Cadney gives you a shorter run on dirt roads than going via Marla or Coober Pedy. You pass through the aptly named **Painted Desert** on the way, and there are camp sites and cabins at *Copper Hills* homestead, about 32 km east of Cadney. You can visit this interesting area with local identity and artist Hugh Frahn on the Tuesday mail run from Cadney. The tour takes all day and costs $55, lunch included.

MARREE (pop 80)

On the rugged alternative road north through Oodnadatta, sleepy Marree was a staging post for the Afghani-led camel trains of the last century. There are still a couple of old date palms here, and an incongruously large pub. Marree is at the southern end of the Birdsville track. The place fires up in July on odd-numbered years, when they hold the Marree Camel Cup.

Places to Stay

The *Oasis Caravan Park* (☎ 8675 8352) has lawned camp sites for $5 per person, while the somewhat dustier *Marree Tourist Park* (☎ 8675 8371) has camp sites ($6 per person) and on-site vans ($20 for the first person and $10 for extras). Alternatively, the *Great Northern Hotel* (☎ 8675 8344) has twin rooms for $25 per person, or $35 with a cooked breakfast, and family rooms sleeping five persons for $50. The pub also sells counter meals from $10.

OODNADATTA (pop 200)

The tiny town of Oodnadatta (like Marree, it lost much of its population when the Old Ghan Railway closed down) is at the point where the road and the old railway line diverged. It was an important staging post during the construction of the overland telegraph line and later was the railhead for the line from Adelaide, from its original extension to Oodnadatta in 1884 until it finally reached Alice Springs in 1929.

Today the town's most distinctive feature is the **Pink Roadhouse**, which is an excellent place to ask advice about track conditions and attractions in any direction. The owners, Adam and Lynnie Plate, have spent a great deal of time and effort putting in road signs and km pegs over a huge area in this district – even in the Simpson Desert you'll come across signs erected by this dedicated pair! They have no doubt saved many a 4WD traveller hours of searching for the right track. The roadhouse is also the place to buy a permit if you intend camping at Dalhousie Springs.

The old railway station has been converted into an interesting little **museum**. It is kept locked but pick up the key from the pub, store or roadhouse.

The local Aboriginal community owns the town's only pub and the general store.

Places to Stay

The *Oodnadatta Caravan Park* (☎ 8670 7822), attached to the Pink Roadhouse, has camp sites for $13 ($17 with power), an on-site van for $30, cabins sleeping five for $30/35/40 (singles/doubles/triples) and a self-contained backpacker unit sleeping seven for $9 each. There's also the *Transcontinental Hotel* (☎ 8670 7804), which charges $30/55. You can get meals at both the pub (dinner only) and the roadhouse.

BIRDSVILLE TRACK

Years ago cattle from the south-west of Queensland were driven down the Birdsville Track to Marree where they were loaded onto trains. Motor transport took over from the drovers in the 1960s and these days the cattle are trucked out in road trains. It's 520 km between Marree and Birdsville, just across the border.

Although conventional vehicles can usually manage the track without difficulty, it's worth bearing in mind that traffic is anything but heavy – particularly in summer. Petrol, diesel and minor mechanical repair are available at the Mungeranie Roadhouse about 205 km north of Marree and 315 km south of Birdsville.

The track is more or less at the meeting point between the sand dunes of the Simpson Desert to the west and the desolate wastes of Sturt Stony Desert to the east. There are ruins of a couple of homesteads along the track and artesian bores gush out boiling-hot salty water at many places. At Clifton Hill, about 200 km south of Birdsville, the track splits and the main route goes around the eastern side of Goyders Lagoon. The last travellers to die on the track were a family of five. They took a wrong turning, got lost, ran out of petrol and perished from thirst.

STRZELECKI TRACK

These days the Strzelecki Track can be handled by conventional vehicles. It starts at Lyndhurst, about 80 km south of Marree, and runs 460 km to the tiny outpost of Innamincka. The discovery of natural gas deposits near Moomba has brought a great deal of development and improvement to the track, although the amount of heavy transport means the surface is often rough.

The new Moomba-Strzelecki Track is better kept but longer and less interesting than the old track, which follows the Strzelecki Creek. Accommodation, provisions and fuel are available at Lyndhurst and Innamincka, but there's nothing in between.

INNAMINCKA (pop 10)

At the northern end of the Strzelecki Track, Innamincka is on Cooper Creek, where the Burke and Wills expedition of 1860 came to its tragic and hopeless end. Near here is the famous **Dig Tree**, the memorials and markers where Burke and Wills died and where King, the sole survivor, was found. He was cared for by Aboriginal people until his rescue.

There is also a memorial where Howitt, who led the rescue party, set up his depot on the creek. The dig tree is actually across the border in Queensland. The word 'dig' is no longer visible, but the expedition's camp number can still be made out.

Cooper Creek flows only during floods, but there are permanent water holes, so the area was important to Aboriginal people and was a base for European explorers in the 19th century.

Westprint's *Innamincka-Coongie Lakes* map is a good source of information on the Innamincka area. For a moving account of the bumbling, foolhardy and tragic Burke and Wills expedition, read Alan Moorehead's *Cooper's Creek*.

You can get fuel and provisions at the Innamincka Trading Post. The old **Australian Inland Mission hospital** now houses the ranger's office (☎ 8675 9909) and interpretive displays on the surrounding **Innamincka Regional Reserve**.

Places to Stay & Eat

The *Innamincka Hotel* (☎ 8675 9901) has just four motel-style rooms at $40/50. It does reasonable takeaways and has counter meals in the evenings – its Wednesday night 'Beef-and-Reef' and Sunday night roasts are both good value at $10 for all you can eat.

The *Innamincka Trading Post* (☎ 8675 9900) has three very modest two-bedroom cabins for $25 per person.

There are plenty of good places to camp among the coolabahs along Cooper Creek – see the ranger for a permit ($15 per vehicle per night).

THE GHAN

See the Northern Territory chapter for details of the famous Ghan railway line from Adelaide to Alice Springs.

Tasmania

HIGHLIGHTS

- Exploring Tassie's fascinating convict history at Port Arthur
- Strolling past Hobart's exquisite Georgian architecture in Macquarie and Davey Sts
- Enjoying the state's fresh seafood – equally delicious at top restaurants or the local fish & chip shop
- Relaxing in fine country style at a B&B establishment
- Trekking through Cradle Mountain-Lake St Clair – one of the world's last great temperate wilderness areas

Population	473,000
Area	67,800 sq km

Tasmania is Australia's only island state and this has been a major influence on its historical, cultural and geographical development. Being an island, it was considered an ideal location for penal settlements, and convicts who re-offended on the Australian mainland were shipped there. Its isolation has also helped preserve its rich colonial heritage, and ensured that most of the state's wilderness areas (with a few notable exceptions) have remained relatively unspoiled.

The first European to see Tasmania was the Dutch navigator Abel Tasman, who arrived in 1642 and called it Van Diemen's Land, after the governor of the Dutch East Indies. In the 18th century, Tasmania was sighted and visited by a series of European sailors, including captains Tobias Furneaux, James Cook and William Bligh, all of whom believed it to be part of the Australian mainland.

European contact with the Tasmanian coast became more frequent after the soldiers and convicts of the First Fleet settled at Sydney Cove in 1788, mainly because ships heading to the colony of New South Wales from the west had to sail around the island.

In 1798 Lieutenant Matthew Flinders circumnavigated Van Diemen's Land, proving it to be an island. He named the rough stretch of sea between the island and the mainland Bass Strait, after George Bass, the ship's surgeon. The discovery of Bass Strait shortened the journey to Sydney from India or the Cape of Good Hope by a week.

In the late 1790s Governor King of New South Wales decided to establish a second colony in Australia, south of Sydney Cove. Port Phillip Bay in Victoria was considered, but a site on the Derwent River in Tasmania was finally chosen, and in 1804 Hobart Town was established. Although convicts were sent with the first settlers, penal settlements were not built until later: at Macquarie Harbour in 1821, at Maria Island in 1825 and at Port Arthur in 1832. For more than three decades, Van Diemen's Land was the most feared destination for British convicts.

In 1856 transportation to Van Diemen's Land was abolished and its first parliament was elected. Also in 1856, in an effort to escape the stigma of its dreadful penal reputation, Van Diemen's Land became officially known as Tasmania, after its first European visitor.

Reminders of the island's convict days and early colonial history are everywhere. There are the penal settlement ruins at Port

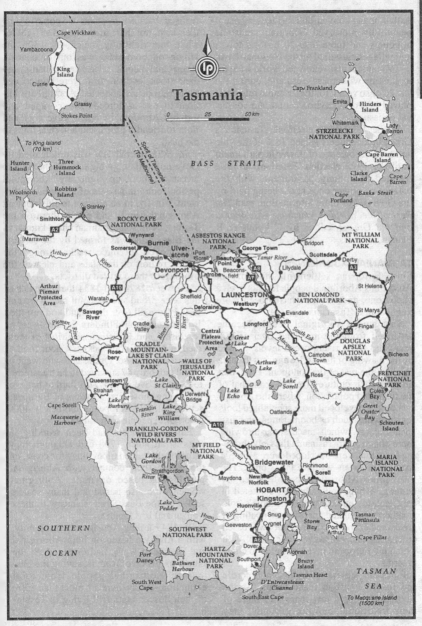

Tasmania

0   25   50 km

Arthur, many convict-built bridges, a host of beautifully preserved Georgian sandstone buildings and more than 20 historic towns and villages classified by the National Trust.

Tasmania is also renowned world wide for its pristine wilderness areas and, during the last 20 or so years, for the essential role it has played in world environmental and conservation issues.

In the 1989 state elections, Tasmania's Green Independents gained 18% of the vote and held the balance of power in parliament until the 1992 election. Elections in 1996 resulted in a hung parliament, with the balance of power once again being held by the Greens. For more information, read *The Rest of the World is Watching – Tasmania and the Greens*, edited by C Pybus & R Flanagan.

TASMANIAN ABORIGINES

Since European settlement, the story of Australia's Aboriginal people has not been a happy one, and nowhere has it been more tragic than in Tasmania.

Tasmania's Aboriginal people became separated from the mainland over 10,000 years ago when rising ocean levels, caused by the thawing of the last ice age, cut the area off from the rest of the continent. From that time on, their culture diverged from that of the mainland population, where the Aboriginal people developed more specialised tools for throwing, such as boomerangs, and also spear-holders, which made spear-throwing more effective. In Tasmania the only throwing tools that were developed were a simple spear, a wooden waddie and stones. The Tasmanian Aboriginal people lived by hunting, fishing and gathering, sheltered in bark lean-tos and, despite Tasmania's cold weather, went naked apart from a coating of grease and charcoal. Their society was based on sharing and exchange – a concept with which the European invaders failed to come to terms.

European settlers found Tasmania fertile and fenced it off to make farms. As the Aboriginal people lost more and more of their traditional hunting grounds, they realised that the Europeans had come to steal their land, not share it, and began to fight for what was rightfully theirs. By 1806 the killing on both sides was out of control. Aboriginal people speared shepherds and their stock, and, in turn, were hunted and shot. Europeans abducted Aboriginal children to use as forced labour, raped and tortured Aboriginal women, gave poisoned flour to friendly tribes, and laid steel traps in the bush.

In 1828 martial law was proclaimed by Governor Arthur, giving soldiers the right to arrest or shoot on sight any Aboriginal person found in an area of European settlement. Finally, in an attempt to flush out all Aboriginal people and corner them on the Tasman Peninsula, a human chain known as the Black Line was formed by the settlers. This moved for three weeks through the settled region of the state and cleared the tribes from these settled districts.

Between 1829 and 1834 the remnants of this once proud and peaceful race were collected from all over the island and resettled in a reserve on Flinders Island – to be 'civilised' and Christianised. Most of them died of despair, homesickness, poor food or respiratory disease. Of the 135 who went to the island, only 47 survived to be transferred to Oyster Cove in 1847. It's hard to believe, but during those first 35 years of European settlement, 183 Europeans and nearly 4000 Aboriginal people were killed.

European sealers had been working in Bass Strait since 1798 and although they occasionally raided tribes along the coast, on the whole their contact with Aboriginal people was based on trade. Aboriginal women were also traded and many sealers settled on the Bass Strait islands with these women and had families.

By 1847 a new Aboriginal community, with a lifestyle based on both Aboriginal and European ways, had emerged on the Furneaux group of islands, saving the Tasmanian Aboriginal people from total extinction. Today there are more than 6500 of their descendants still living in Tasmania.

GEOGRAPHY

Although Tasmania is a small state, its geographical diversity ensures that it has something for everyone.

Tasmania's population is concentrated mainly on the north and south-east coasts, where the undulating countryside is rich and fertile. The coast and its bays are accessible and inviting, with attractive coves and beaches. In winter, the midlands region looks like a re-creation of the green England so beloved of early settlers, and the sparsely populated lakes country in the central highlands is serenely beautiful.

By contrast, the south-west and west coasts are amazingly wild and virtually untouched. For much of the year raging seas batter the length of the west coast and rainfall is high. Inland, the forests and mountains of Tasmania's west and south-west form one of the world's last great wilderness areas, almost all of it made up of national parks which have been listed as World Heritage regions.

INFORMATION
Tourist Offices

There are privately run Tasmanian Travel & Information Centres in Hobart, Launceston, Devonport and Burnie. On the mainland there are government-run branches in:

Australian Capital Territory
165 City Walk, Canberra 2601 (☎ (06) 209 2133)
New South Wales
149 King St, Sydney 2000 (☎ (02) 9202 2022)
Queensland
40 Queen St, Brisbane 4000 (☎ (07) 3405 4122)
South Australia
32 King William St, Adelaide 5000 (☎ (08) 8400 5533)
Victoria
256 Collins St, Melbourne 3000 (☎ (03) 9206 7922)

These travel centres have information on just about everything you need to know about Tasmania and are also able to book accommodation, tours and even airline, boat and bus tickets. The Department of Tourism publishes an invaluable free newspaper called *Tasmanian Travelways* which, along with feature articles, has comprehensive statewide listings of accommodation, activities, public transport, connecting transport facilities and vehicle hire, all with an indication of current costs.

The travel centres also stock a host of free tourist literature, including the monthly magazine *This Week in Tasmania* and the excellent *Let's Talk About...* leaflets, which provide in-depth information about particular towns and regions. The annual free *Tasmania Visitors Guide*, which has a good fold-out touring map of Tasmania, is particularly useful.

For Backpackers By Backpackers has the latest backpacker information for Victoria and Tasmania. It is available from some hostels and travel agencies. While the Tasmania section is brief, it can be useful for discovering new hostel-type accommodation.

One of the best maps of the island is produced by the Royal Automobile Club of Tasmania (RACT) and costs $3. It's available from any Tasmanian Travel & Information Centre or RACT office.

Money

Banks in the smaller centres are often only open one or two days a week. Automatic teller machines (ATMs) are becoming more common; outside Hobart they exist in most major towns across the north coast but are not yet available on the west coast and only in St Helens on the east coast. Many businesses across the state now have EFTPOS, where you can pay for transactions directly from your bank account or credit card, and sometimes make cash withdrawals as well.

Accommodation

There's a good range of accommodation available in Tasmania, including youth hostels in most of the major towns and plenty of caravan parks, most of which have camp sites as well as on-site vans and cabins. Tasmania also has a wide selection of colonial accommodation – that is, places built prior to 1901 which have been decorated in a colonial style. Although a bit pricey ($60 to

$100 for a double B&B), colonial accommodation is a great way to savour Tasmania's history, and can be a real treat for a couple of nights.

Despite the variety of places to stay, Tasmania's major tourist centres are often fully booked in summer, so it's wise to make reservations. Prices at most places are usually fixed all year round.

NATIONAL PARKS

Tasmania has set aside a greater percentage of its land as national park or scenic reserve than any other Australian state. In 1982, Tasmania's three largest national parks, Cradle Mountain-Lake St Clair, Franklin-Gordon Wild Rivers and South-West, along with much of the Central Plateau were placed on the UNESCO World Heritage List. This listing acknowledged that these parks comprise one of the last great temperate wilderness areas left in the world. Today, about 20% of Tasmania is World Heritage Area protected from logging, hydroelectric power schemes and, with a few simple rules, ourselves.

An entry fee is charged for all 14 of Tassie's national parks; a pass is needed whether there is a collection booth or not. There are a number of passes available. A one-day pass to any number of parks costs $8 per car or $2.50 per person. The best value for most will be the holiday pass which costs $25 per vehicle, or for bushwalkers, cyclists and motorcyclists $10 per person. This is valid for two months from the date of issue and provides entry into all parks. An annual pass ($40) for cars only is available at park entrances, from many bus and tour operators and from the national parks head office at 134 Macquarie St, Hobart.

ACTIVITIES
Bushwalking

Tasmania, with its many national parks, has some of the finest bushwalks in Australia, the most well-known of which is the superb Cradle Mountain-Lake St Clair Overland Track. (See the Cradle Mountain-Lake St Clair section for more detail on this walk.)

Good books on the subject include *100 Walks in Tasmania* by Tyrone T Thomas, *South West Tasmania* by John Chapman, *Cradle Mountain Lake St Clair* by John Chapman & John Siseman and Lonely Planet's *Bushwalking in Australia*, which has a large section on some of Tasmania's best walks.

On long walks, it's important to remember that in any season a fine day can quickly become cold and stormy, so warm clothing, waterproof gear, a tent and compass are vital. The Department of Parks, Wildlife & Heritage publishes a booklet called *Welcome to the Wilderness – Bushwalking Trip Planner for Tasmania's World Heritage Area*, which has sections on planning, minimal-impact bushwalking and wilderness survival. Also included is a very useful equipment check list which is essential reading for bushwalkers who are unfamiliar with Tasmania's notoriously changeable weather.

If you write to the department at main post office Box 44A, Hobart, or ring ☎ 6233 6191, you'll be sent this booklet and other leaflets free of charge. You can also pick up all the department's literature from its head office at 134 Macquarie St, Hobart; from its office at Henty House, Civic Square, Launceston; or from any rangers' office in the national parks.

The department also produces and sells an excellent series of maps; again, these can be sent for, or picked up, at outdoor-equipment stores, Wilderness Society shops and newsagencies throughout the state. The Tasmap Centre (☎ 6233 3382) is on the ground floor of the department's head office.

As bushwalking is so popular in Tasmania, there are many excellent shops selling bush gear, as well as several youth hostels which hire out equipment or take bushwalking tours. In the former category, Paddy Pallin in Hobart and Launceston, Allgoods in Launceston and the Backpackers' Barn in Devonport all have a very good range of bushwalking gear and plenty of invaluable advice.

See the sections on individual national parks for more information on Tasmania's walks.

Water Sports

Swimming The north and east coasts have many sheltered white-sand beaches which are excellent for swimming. On the west coast, however, there's some pretty ferocious surf and the beaches are unpatrolled.

Although there are some pleasant beaches near Hobart, such as Bellerive and Sandy Bay, these tend to be polluted so it's better to head towards Kingston, Blackmans Bay or Seven Mile Beach for safe swimming.

Surfing Tasmania has plenty of good surf beaches. Close to Hobart, the best spots are Clifton Beach and the surf beach en route to South Arm. The southern beaches of Bruny Island, particularly Cloudy Bay, are also good. The east coast from Bicheno north to St Helens has good surf when conditions are favourable. The greatest spot of all is Marrawah on the west coast, though you'll need your own transport to get there.

Scuba Diving On the east coast and around King and Flinders islands there are some excellent scuba-diving opportunities. Equipment can be rented in Hobart, Launceston or on the east coast, and dive courses in Tasmania are considerably cheaper than those on the mainland.

Rafting & Canoeing Rafting, rowing and canoeing are all popular pastimes. The most challenging of rivers to raft is the Franklin (see the Franklin-Gordon Wild Rivers National Park section), although rafting trips are also organised on the Picton, upper Huon, Weld and Leven rivers. To book with a tour operator contact a Tasmanian Travel Centre, or to book direct, see the *Tasmanian Travelways* outdoor adventure listings.

Fishing Fishing is another popular activity. Many of the rivers offer superb trout fishing, and the coastal waters are also good. A licence is required to fish in Tasmania's inland waters, and there are bag, season and size limits on a number of fish. Licences cost $38 for the full season, $20 for 14 days, $12 for three days and $7 for one day. They are available from many sports stores, post offices, and Tasmanian Travel & Information Centres.

In general, inland waters open for fishing on the Saturday closest to 1 August and close on the Sunday nearest 30 April. Different dates apply to some places: you can fish at the Great Lake until early June, while around Bradys Lake there is a very short season from November to March. There are many such exceptions and they are detailed in the *Fishing Code* brochure (see below). The lakes in the centre of the state – Arthurs Lake, Great Lake, Little Pine Lagoon (fly-fishing only), Western Lakes (including Lake St Clair), Lake Sorell and Lake Pedder – are the best-known spots for both brown and rainbow trout.

Saltwater fishing is allowed all year without a permit although size restrictions and bag limits apply. For more information contact the Tasmanian Inland Fisheries Commission (☎ 6233 8305), 127 Davey St, Hobart and ask for a current *Fishing Code* brochure.

Caving

Tasmania's caves are regarded as being some of the most impressive in Australia. The caves at Mole Creek and Hastings are open daily to the public but gems such as the Kubla Khan and Croesus caves (near Mole Creek) and the extremely large Exit Cave are only accessible to experienced cavers. Permits are needed to enter any caves; most are locked. Apply through your speleological club or association for permits.

Skiing

There are two minor ski resorts in Tasmania: Ben Lomond, 60 km from Launceston; and Mt Mawson, in Mt Field National Park. Both offer cheaper, although less-developed, ski facilities than the major resorts in Victoria and New South Wales, but despite the state's southerly latitude, snowfalls tend to be fairly light and unreliable. For more information see the sections on the Ben Lomond and Mt Field national parks.

TASMANIA

GETTING THERE & AWAY
Air
The airlines that fly to Tassie are Ansett (☎ 13 1300), Qantas (☎ 13 1313), Kendell (☎ 1800 338 894), Phillip Island Air Services (☎ (03) 5956 7316), King Island Airlines (☎ (03) 9580 3777), Airlines of Tasmania (☎ 1800 030 550), Aus-Air (☎ 1800 331 256) and Hazelton Air Services (☎ (02) 9235 1411).

International flights also operate direct from Christchurch in New Zealand to Hobart. Both Qantas and Air New Zealand

operate this route with return fares ranging from $580 to $1040.

Ansett and Qantas have flights to Tasmania from most Australian state capitals, while the other airlines operate from various airports in Victoria. Most flights are to Hobart, Launceston, Devonport, Wynyard (Burnie), Smithton, Flinders Island or King Island.

Air fares to Tasmania are constantly changing, but because of the number of operators, prices are competitive and you can get some good deals – especially if you book well in advance or if you are planning a trip

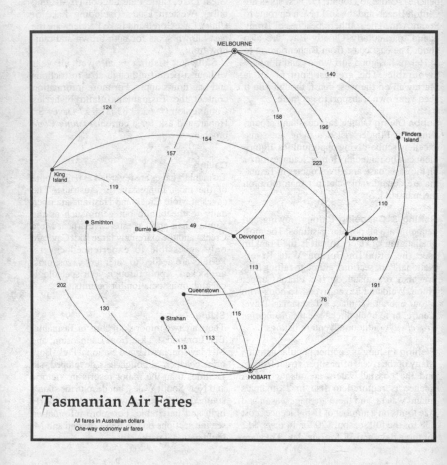

Tasmanian Air Fares

All fares in Australian dollars
One-way economy air fares

in the winter months. In addition, students under 25 years can get some good discounts on fares with the larger airlines.

To/From Hobart The standard one-way economy fare from Melbourne is $223 with Ansett and Qantas, although much cheaper fares are often available (about $240 return, or even less, depending on the flight). From Sydney the standard one-way fare is $322 (rock-bottom return $330) and from Brisbane $430 (rock-bottom return $470).

To/From Launceston Ansett and Qantas fly from Melbourne for $196 one way, but it's around $220 return if you book well in advance. The smaller airlines flying out of Melbourne generally use the city's second-string airports (Essendon and Moorabbin) and have lower base rates but offer fewer discounts.

To/From Devonport & Wynyard (Burnie) There are flights from Melbourne to Devonport and Burnie with Kendell Airlines ($158 and $157 respectively) and Aus-Air ($148 and $142). Airlines of Tasmania flies from Traralgon to Burnie for $154. Phillip Island Air Services flies to Burnie for $105 one way.

To/From Other Destinations Aus-Air, Airlines of Tasmania and Kendell Airlines fly to King Island. Aus-Air and Airlines of Tasmania also fly to Flinders Island. Fewer discounts are available to these destinations and, as you will need accommodation, the best deal is to buy a fly-drive package (which includes accommodation). See the Bass Strait Islands section at the end of this chapter for details.

Boat

The *Spirit of Tasmania*, which operates between Melbourne and Devonport, can accommodate 1300 passengers and over 600 vehicles. It has nine decks and, with its swimming pool, saunas, restaurant, gaming machines and bars, is more like a floating hotel than a ferry. The public areas of the ship

have been designed to cater for wheelchair access, and four cabins have been specially designed for this purpose.

It departs from the TT Line terminal (☎ 1800 030 344) at Melbourne's Station Pier on Monday, Wednesday and Friday at 6 pm and from the terminal on the Esplanade in Devonport on Sunday, Tuesday and Thursday at 6 pm, arriving 14½ hours later, at 8.30 am.

The fares depend on whether you're travelling in the touring or holiday season; the latter roughly corresponds with the school-holiday periods. One-way fares range from $99 ($120 in the holiday season) in hostel-style accommodation (20-bed cabins) up to $325 for suites ($380 in the holiday season). Student discounts apply to cabins but not to hostel-style accommodation. All fares include an evening buffet dinner and continental breakfast, but you can also choose to eat (and pay) at the more formal restaurant.

The cost for accompanied vehicles depends on the size of the vehicle. The minimum one-way rate is $125 ($175 in holiday season) for cars, while motorcycles cost $70 ($100) and bicycles $20 ($25).

GETTING AROUND
Air

Airlines of Tasmania (☎ 1800 030 550) operates a fairly extensive network of flights around the island which can be booked at most travel agencies and any Tasmanian Travel & Information Centre. It's worth noting that the airline also has flights between Melbourne and Launceston via Flinders Island which are only a little more expensive than flying direct; these give you the option of a stopover on Flinders, more or less free.

Bus

Tasmania has a good bus network connecting all major towns and centres, but weekend services are infrequent and this can be inconvenient for the traveller with only a limited amount of time in the state. There are more buses in summer than in winter.

The main bus companies are Tasmanian

Redline Coaches, Hobart Coaches (also trading as Inter-City Coaches) and Tasmanian Wilderness Transport, and they cover most of the state between them. All three have depots in the major centres of Hobart, Launceston and Devonport as well as agents in the stopover towns. Hobart Coaches' fares are sometimes considerably cheaper.

The companies have their own special passes; you can't use a Greyhound Pioneer Aussie Pass in Tasmania, but McCafferty's (☎ 13 1499) has a Tassie Discovery Pass which uses Redline buses. Redline also has the Tassie Bus Pass, for seven, 15 or 31 days, which gives you unrestricted travel on all its routes for $98, $138 or $178 respectively and is also valid for the small east-coast services run by Peakes. Tasmanian Wilderness Transport, with Hobart Coaches, has a Wilderness & Highway Pass available for seven days ($99), 14 days ($140) or 30 days ($179). The pass is valid on all Tasmanian Wilderness Transport and Hobart Coaches routes.

If you are considering buying any of these passes, don't forget to check the weekend timetables. Also, make sure that you buy a pass with a company that has services to the areas that you want to visit; *Tasmanian Travelways* has details of timetables and fares for major routes. These passes can also be bought in advance on the mainland from Greyhound Pioneer, but generally it's cheaper to buy them in Tasmania. To give you some idea of the costs, a one-way trip between Hobart and Launceston costs about $17, between Hobart and Queenstown $30 and between Launceston and Bicheno $18.

Train

There are no longer any passenger rail services in Tasmania, which probably accounts for the number of railway models, displays and exhibitions in the state!

Car & Campervan

Although you can bring cars from the mainland to Tasmania, it might work out cheaper to rent one for your visit, particularly if your stay is a short one. Tasmania has a wide range of national and local car-rental agencies, and the rates (along with parking fines) are considerably lower than they are on the mainland.

Tasmanian Travelways lists many of the rental options, but before you decide on a company, don't forget to ask about any km limitations and find out what the insurance covers. Also ensure that there are no hidden seasonal adjustments. It is, however, quite normal for smaller rental companies to ask for a bond of around $200.

Large national firms such as Budget, Hertz and Avis have standard rates for cars, from $65 to $140 per day. By booking in advance and asking about rates for smaller cars (Corolla, Laser and Pulsar), rates can be as low as $45 per day for one-week hire (outside holiday season). In summer, rates are generally higher at around $50 to $60 for multi-day hire of a small car.

Small local firms such as Advance Car Rentals, which has offices in Hobart, Launceston and Devonport, charge from $37 to $104 a day ($264 a week) for the same type of cars, but with varied conditions. Tasmania also has a number of companies renting older cars like VW beetles for around $20 a day. In this bracket Rent-a-Bug, with offices in Hobart and Devonport, has a good reputation. See the individual Getting There & Away entries for specific locations for more information. The larger firms have offices at the airports and docks; if you book in advance, most smaller companies can arrange for you to collect your car at point of arrival.

Tasmanian Travelways also has a listing of campervan rental companies. All the larger national firms have campervans for around $800 a week, but by far the cheapest and most popular is Touring Motor Homes (☎ 6334 4424), Launceston.

Warning While driving around the state watch out for the wildlife, which all too often ends up flattened on the roadside.

Hitching

Travel by thumb in Tassie is generally good, but wrap up in winter and keep a raincoat handy. A good number of the state's roads are still unsurfaced and the traffic can be very light, so although these roads often lead to interesting places, you normally have to give them a miss if you're hitching.

Bicycle

Tasmania is a good size for exploring by bicycle and you can hire bikes throughout the state. If you plan to cycle between Hobart and Launceston via either coast, count on it taking around 10 to 14 days. For a full circuit of the island, you should allow 14 to 28 days.

Rent-a-Cycle at the Launceston City Youth Hostel has a good variety of touring and mountain bikes plus all the equipment you'll need for short or long trips. You should be able to hire a bike for between $10 and $15 a day or $60 and $95 a week. If you're planning on an extended ride it's worth considering buying a bike and reselling it at the end.

If you bring a bike over on the *Spirit of Tasmania* it will cost you $20 to $25 each way, depending on the season. By air, Ansett charges $15 to carry a bicycle one way to Hobart or Launceston, while Qantas charges $10. It's easier to get your bike over to Tassie on flights to Hobart or Launceston than on those to smaller airports such as Burnie or Devonport.

Hobart

Population 133,000

Hobart is Australia's second-oldest capital city and also the smallest and most southerly. Straddling the mouth of the Derwent River and backed by mountains which offer fine views over the city, Hobart has managed to combine the benefits of a modern city with the rich heritage of its colonial past. The beautiful Georgian buildings, the busy harbour and the easy-going atmosphere all make Hobart one of the most enjoyable and engaging of Australia's cities.

The first inhabitants of the area were the Aboriginal Mouheneer tribe who lived a semi-nomadic lifestyle. The first European colony in Tasmania was founded in 1803 at Risdon Cove, but a year later Lieutenant-Colonel David Collins, governor of the new settlement in Van Diemen's Land, sailed down the Derwent River and decided that a cove about 10 km below Risdon and on the opposite shore was a better place to settle. This became the site of Tasmania's future capital city and began as a village of tents and wattle-and-daub huts with a population of 262 (178 of whom were convicts).

Hobart Town, as it was known until 1881, was proclaimed a city in 1842. Very important to its development was the Derwent River estuary, one of the world's finest deep-water harbours, and many merchants made their fortunes from the whaling trade, ship-building and the export of products like merino wool and corn.

Orientation

Being fairly small and simply laid out, Hobart is an easy city to find your way around. The streets in the city centre, many of which are one way, are arranged in a grid pattern around the Elizabeth St Mall. The Tasmanian Travel & Information Centre, Ansett Airlines, Qantas and the main post office are all in Elizabeth St. The main shopping area extends west from the mall on Elizabeth St.

Salamanca Place, the row of Georgian warehouses, is along the waterfront, while just south of this is Battery Point, Hobart's delightful, well-preserved early colonial district. If you follow the river around from Battery Point you'll come to Sandy Bay, the site of Hobart's university and the Wrest Point Hotel Casino – one of Hobart's main landmarks.

The northern side of the centre is bounded by the recreation area known locally as the Domain (short for the Queen's Domain), which includes the Royal Tasmanian Botanical Gardens and the Derwent River. From here the Tasman Bridge crosses the river to the eastern suburbs and the airport.

TASMANIA

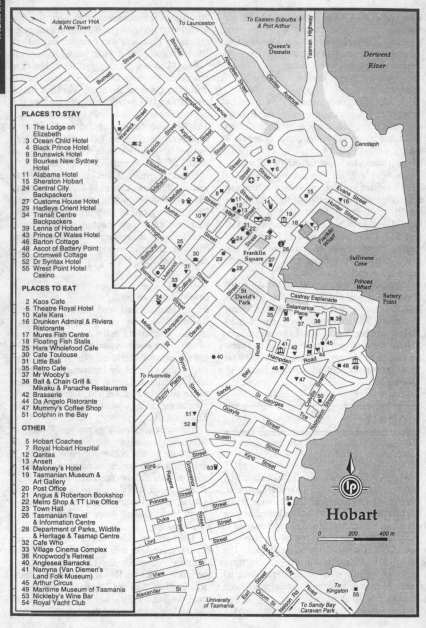

PLACES TO STAY

1 The Lodge on Elizabeth
3 Ocean Child Hotel
4 Black Prince Hotel
8 Brunswick Hotel
9 Bourkes New Sydney Hotel
11 Alabama Hotel
15 Sheraton Hobart
24 Central City Backpackers
27 Customs House Hotel
29 Hadleys Orient Hotel
34 Transit Centre Backpackers
39 Lenna of Hobart
43 Prince Of Wales Hotel
46 Barton Cottage
48 Ascot of Battery Point
50 Cromwell Cottage
52 Dr Syntax Hotel
55 Wrest Point Hotel Casino

PLACES TO EAT

2 Kaos Cafe
6 Theatre Royal Hotel
10 Kafe Kara
16 Drunken Admiral & Riviera Ristorante
17 Mures Fish Centre
18 Floating Fish Stalls
25 Hara Wholefood Cafe
30 Cafe Toulouse
31 Little Bali
35 Retro Cafe
37 Mr Wooby's
38 Ball & Chain Grill & Mikaku & Panache Restaurants
42 Brasserie
44 Da Angelo Ristorante
47 Mummy's Coffee Shop
51 Dolphin in the Bay

OTHER

5 Hobart Coaches
7 Royal Hobart Hospital
12 Qantas
13 Ansett
14 Maloney's Hotel
19 Tasmanian Museum & Art Gallery
20 Post Office
21 Angus & Robertson Bookshop
22 Metro Shop & TT Line Office
23 Town Hall
26 Tasmanian Travel & Information Centre
28 Department of Parks, Wildlife & Heritage & Tasmap Centre
32 Cafe Who
33 Village Cinema Complex
36 Knopwood's Retreat
40 Anglesea Barracks
41 Narryna (Van Diemen's Land Folk Museum)
45 Arthur Circus
49 Maritime Museum of Tasmania
53 Nickleby's Wine Bar
54 Royal Yacht Club

Information

Tourist Office The Tasmanian Travel &
Information Centre (☎ 6230 8233) on the
corner of Davey and Elizabeth Sts is open
weekdays from 8.30 am to 5.15 pm, and from
9 am to 4 pm on weekends and holidays. You
can also get tourist information from the
travel section of Mures Fish Centre, Victoria
Dock and from many accommodation providers.

If you have an FM radio, you can pick up
tourist information broadcast on 88 MHz
within a six-km radius of the city centre.

Post The main post office is in the centre of
the city, on the corner of Elizabeth and Macquarie Sts.

Other Information The Tasmanian YHA
office (☎ 6234 9617) is at 28 Criterion St and
is open Monday to Friday from 10 am to 5
pm. The RACT (☎ 6238 2200) is on the
corner of Murray and Patrick Sts. Paddy
Pallin (☎ 6231 0777) is at 76 Elizabeth St
with the Jolly Swagman opposite. The Wilderness Society's head office (☎ 6234 9366)
is at 130 Davey St and its shop is in the
Galleria, Salamanca Place; the National
Trust shop is in the same arcade.

For information about the Department of
Parks, Wildlife & Heritage and the Tasmap
Centre, see the earlier Bushwalking section
under Activities.

Historic Buildings

One of the things that makes Hobart so
unusual among Australian cities is its wealth
of old and remarkably well-preserved buildings. There are more than 90 buildings in
Hobart that are classified by the National
Trust and 60 of these, featuring some of
Hobart's best Georgian architecture, are in
Macquarie and Davey Sts. An excellent
booklet on both new and old buildings, *An
Architectural Guide to the City of Hobart*, is
available from the National Trust for $3.

Close to the city centre is **St David's Park**,
which has some lovely old trees, and some
gravestones dating from the earliest days of
the colony. In Murray St is the old **Parliament House**, which was originally used as
a customs house. Hobart's prestigious
Theatre Royal, at 29 Campbell St, was built
in 1837 and is the oldest theatre in Australia.

There's a **royal tennis court** in Davey St,
one of only three in the southern hemisphere,
which you can look into on the National
Trust's Saturday-morning tour – see the following Organised Tours & Cruises section
for details. (Royal or 'real' tennis is an
ancient form of tennis played in a four-
walled indoor court.) The historic
Penitentiary Chapel & Criminal Courts
are at 28 Campbell St; the National Trust
runs daily tours of the buildings between
10 am and 2 pm ($4).

Runnymede, at 61 Bay Rd, New Town,
is a gracious colonial residence dating from
the early 1830s. It was built for Robert Pitcairn, the first lawyer to qualify in Tasmania
and a leading advocate for the abolition of
transportation of convicts. Now managed by
the National Trust, it is open daily from
10 am to 4.30 pm; admission is $5. To get
there take bus No 15 or 16 from the corner
of Argyle and Macquarie Sts.

Waterfront

Hobart's busy waterfront area, focusing on
Franklin Wharf, is close to the city centre
and very interesting to walk around. At **Constitution Dock** there are several floating
takeaway seafood stalls and it's a treat to sit
in the sun munching fresh fish & chips while
watching the activity in the harbour. At the
finish of the annual Sydney to Hobart Yacht
Race in early January, and during the Royal
Hobart Regatta in February, Constitution
Dock really comes alive.

Nearby **Hunter St** has a row of fine Georgian warehouses, similar to those of
Salamanca Place, which haven't yet been
developed as a tourist attraction.

Salamanca Place

The row of beautiful sandstone warehouses
on the harbour front at Salamanca Place is a
prime example of Australian colonial architecture. Dating back to the whaling days of
the 1830s, these warehouses were the centre

of Hobart Town's trade and commerce. Today they have been tastefully developed to house galleries, restaurants, nightspots and shops selling everything from vegetables to antiques. Every Saturday morning a popular open-air **craft market** is held at Salamanca Place. To reach Battery Point from Salamanca Place you can climb up the **Kelly Steps**, which are wedged between two of the warehouses.

Battery Point

Behind Princes Wharf is the historic core of Hobart, the old port area known as Battery Point. Its name comes from the gun battery that stood on the promontory by the guardhouse, built in 1818, which is the oldest building in the district.

During colonial times, this area was a colourful maritime village, home to master mariners, shipwrights, sailors, fishermen, coopers and merchants. The houses reflect their varying lifestyles.

Battery Point's pubs, churches, conjoined houses and narrow winding streets have all been lovingly preserved and are a real delight to wander around, especially when you get glimpses of the harbour between the buildings. There is so much to see here; don't miss out on **Arthur Circus** – a small circle of quaint little cottages built around a village green – or **St George's Anglican Church**.

Van Diemen's Land Folk Museum The oldest folk museum in Australia is housed in **Narryna**, a fine Georgian home at 103 Hampden Rd, Battery Point. Dating from 1836, it stands in beautiful grounds and has a large and fascinating collection of relics from Tasmania's early pioneering days. It's open on weekdays from 10 am to 5 pm and at weekends from 2 to 5 pm; admission is $4 (children $2).

Maritime Museum of Tasmania Secheron House, in Secheron Rd, Battery Point, was built in 1831 and is classified by the National Trust. It now houses the fascinating Maritime Museum, which has an extensive collection of photos, paintings, models and

relics depicting Tasmania's, and particularly Hobart's, colourful shipping history. Admission is $2 and it's open daily from 1 to 4.30 pm except Saturday, when it's open from 10 am to 5 pm.

Tasmanian Museum & Art Gallery

The excellent Tasmanian Museum & Art Gallery, at 5 Argyle St (enter via Macquarie St), incorporates Hobart's oldest building, the Commissariat Store, built in 1808. The museum section features a Tasmanian Aboriginal display and relics from the state's colonial heritage, while the gallery has a good collection of Tasmanian colonial art. Entry is free and it's open daily from 10 am to 5 pm.

Anglesea Barracks

Built in 1811, this is the oldest military establishment in Australia still used by the army. There's no admission fee to the museum, which is usually open weekdays from 9 am to 3.30 pm, and there are guided tours of the restored buildings and grounds on Tuesday at 11 am.

Cascade Brewery

Australia's oldest brewery, on Cascade Rd close to the city centre, is still in use and produces some of the finest beer in the country – although no doubt others would argue differently! There are two-hour tours daily ($7) at 9.30 am and 1 pm, and bookings are essential (☎ 6224 1144). The brewery is on the south-western edge of the city centre; bus Nos 44, 46 and 49 go right by it – alight at stop 18.

Risdon Cove

This is the site of the first European settlement in Tasmania and is definitely worth a visit. It's on the eastern shore of the Derwent about 10 km from the city. To get there take a No 68 bus from the Eastlands Shopping Centre; entry is free.

Other Attractions

The **Allport Museum & Library of Fine Arts** is based in the State Library at 91

Murray St. It has a collection of rare books on Australasia and the Pacific region and you can visit on weekdays from 9.30 am to 5 pm; entry is free.

Other museums include the **John Elliott Classics Museum** at the University of Tasmania (free admission) and the **Tasmanian Transport Museum** in Glenorchy ($3). Australia's first public museum, the **Lady Franklin Gallery**, is in Lenah Valley Rd (free admission).

Just by the Tasman Bridge are the **Royal Tasmanian Botanical Gardens**, which are open from 8 am to 4.45 pm daily; admission is free. They are very pleasant and definitely worth a visit, as is the nearby bushland reserve called the **Queen's Domain**.

Hobart is dominated by 1270-metre-high **Mt Wellington** which has many fine views and interesting walking tracks. Buy a copy of the *Mt Wellington Walks* map for all details. There are also good views from the **Old Signal Station** on Mt Nelson, above Sandy Bay.

Organised Tours & Cruises

Several boat cruise companies operate from the Brooke St Pier and Franklin Wharf and offer a variety of cruises in and around the harbour. One of the most popular is the four-hour Cadbury's Cruise, run by the Cruise Company (☎ 6234 9294), which costs $33 (children $16). Leaving at 10 am on weekdays you do a slow return cruise to the Cadbury Schweppes factory in Claremont where you disembark and tour the premises (this is a good place to stock up on chocolate if you are planning any bushwalking).

Cruise timetables are pretty changeable as they depend on tides and seasons so it is best to book. Harbour cruises are also available and vary from one to three hours. The daily lunch cruise includes lunch in the $20 fare and is good value, provided you don't get seasick!

One of the best ways to get a feel for Hobart's colonial history is to take the Saturday morning walking tour organised by the National Trust. The tour concentrates on the historic Battery Point area and departs at 9.30 am from the wishing well in Franklin Square – you don't have to book, just turn up. The walk costs $5 and takes 2½ hours. You could do a similar tour on your own with the help of a *Historic Village Battery Point* leaflet available from the National Trust shop ($1). During summer, twilight walks are held along the waterfront starting at 6.30 pm. You must book earlier in the day at the information centre in Elizabeth St; the walk costs $8.50.

Day and half-day bus tours in and around Hobart are operated by Redline and Hobart Coaches. Typical half-day tours include trips to Richmond ($17), the City Sights and Mt Wellington ($23). Full-day tour destinations include Port Arthur ($40), the Huon Valley ($55) and Bruny Island ($75). Tasmanian Wilderness Transport also runs day and two-day excursions to places like Mt Field National Park, Cradle Mountain and Strahan.

For something different try Harley Tours of Hobart (☎ 6224 1565) offering a ride around Hobart in a Harley Davidson sidecar. They operate from the waterfront and rides start from $15.

Scenic flights are run by Par Avion (☎ 6248 5390) and Tasair (☎ 6248 5088) from Cambridge airport, 15 km from the city. Flight prices start from $60 per person for 30 minutes.

Festivals

From 29 December to 2 January, Hobart's waterfront area is alive with spectators and celebrating yachties at the finish of the annual New Year Sydney to Hobart Yacht Race.

The Royal Hobart Regatta, in early February, is a major four-day aquatic carnival with boat races and other activities. The last day of the carnival, a Monday, is a public holiday and almost the entire town closes down.

Places to Stay

Camping The handiest camping ground is the *Sandy Bay Caravan Park* (☎ 6225 1264), less than three km from the city, at 1 Peel St,

Sandy Bay. It charges $12 a double for a camp site, while on-site vans are $32 a double and cabins $45. To get there, take Metro bus No 54, 55 or 56 from stop D in Elizabeth St near the main post office. There are also parks a little farther out at Elwick and Berriedale (north of the city) and at Mornington (in the eastern suburbs).

Hostels Right in the centre of town is the *Central City Backpackers* (☎ 6224 2404) at 138 Collins St. It's a rambling place with excellent facilities and a friendly couple in charge. There are spacious communal areas, as well as a laundry and individual safe-deposit boxes. The cost is $12 for a bed in a four-bed dorm, or there are twin-share rooms for $17 per person, and singles/doubles for $28/36. Security is good here and it's clean and quiet.

Bourkes New Sydney Hotel (☎ 6234 4516), 87 Bathurst St, charges $12 a night for very basic facilities. It can be difficult to sleep here when a band is playing in the pub as the main dorm is right above the stage.

At the Redline bus depot at 199 Collins St is the *Transit Centre Backpackers* (☎ 6231 2400). It has beds for $11 per night and has all facilities. The communal area is very large and it's a quiet place; the only detraction is that it can be difficult to obtain a room here after hours.

The cheapest place is the *Ocean Child Hotel*, on the corner of Argyle and Melville Sts. For $10 you get a bed in an old hotel with basic facilities close to town.

Hobart also has three YHA hostels. The main one, *Adelphi Court* (☎ 6228 4829), is 2.5 km from the city at 17 Stoke St, New Town. It's an excellent hostel with good facilities and charges $12 for a dorm bed, or $19 each for a twin room. To get there, take Metro bus No 15 or 16 from Argyle St to stop 8A, or any one of bus Nos 25 to 42, 100, or 105 to 128 to stop 13. Redline also provides a drop-off and pick-up service on the airport bus.

The peaceful *Bellerive Hostel* (☎ 6244 2552) is on the other side of the Derwent River at 52 King St, Bellerive, and charges

$10 a night. The lovely old stone building used to be a schoolhouse and dates from 1869. To get there on weekends, when the ferry doesn't run, you can catch any of the Bellerive buses (Nos 83 to 87) from stop C or D near the main post office in Elizabeth St.

The *Woodlands Hostel* (☎ 6228 6720), at 7 Woodlands Ave, New Town, is a superb building and one of New Town's original homes, but it is only used as an overflow hostel when Adelphi Court is full. It's best to turn up at nearby Adelphi first and if there isn't any room you'll be directed here.

Guesthouses In addition to its hostel, *Adelphi Court* (☎ 6228 4829), at 17 Stoke St, New Town, also has guesthouse accommodation at $45/55 including a cooked breakfast.

In Sandy Bay there's *Red Chapel House* (☎ 6225 2273) at 27 Red Chapel Ave, past the casino. Singles/doubles in this smoke-free establishment cost $55/70 including a cooked breakfast, and the place has a friendly, family-run atmosphere.

If you have the money, you can stay in Battery Point in some beautiful colonial guesthouses and cottages. *Barton Cottage* (☎ 6224 1606), at 72 Hampden Rd, is a two-storey building which dates back to 1837 and is classified by the National Trust. B&B accommodation costs $75/95. Another worth considering is *Cromwell Cottage* (☎ 6223 6734) at 6 Cromwell St. This two-storey townhouse dates from the late 1880s and is in a beautiful position overlooking the Derwent River. Each of the five rooms costs $75/95 for B&B. A bit more up-market is *Ascot of Battery Point* (☎ 6224 2434), where comfortable rooms plus cooked breakfast cost $90/115.

A cheaper area for B&B accommodation, and just as close to town as Battery Point, is North Hobart. The *Lodge on Elizabeth* (☎ 6231 3830), at 249 Elizabeth St, is an old mansion full of antiques and charges $85 a double. A bit farther up the road, the *Elms of Hobart* (☎ 6231 3277), at 452 Elizabeth St, is more luxurious. A National Trust classified mansion, the rate here with breakfast is $85/95.

An interesting option is the *Signalman's Cottage* (☎ 6223 1215) on the top of Mt Nelson at 685 Nelson Rd. There's just the single self-contained one-bedroom unit and the cost is $55/65. You'd need your own transport for this place to be convenient.

Hotels At 67 Liverpool St, near the mall, the *Brunswick Hotel* (☎ 6234 4981) is pretty central and has average rooms costing $33/50 with a continental breakfast. Across the road, at 72 Liverpool St, the *Alabama Hotel* (☎ 6234 3737) is a little more comfortable and charges $27/44 for singles/doubles.

Two blocks up from the mall, at 145 Elizabeth St, is the *Black Prince* (☎ 6234 3501), which has large, modern rooms with bathroom and TV for $40/50.

If you want to stay near the docks, the *Customs House Hotel* (☎ 6234 6645), at 1 Murray St, has good views of the waterfront and charges $40/65 with a continental breakfast. The *Prince of Wales Hotel* (☎ 6223 6355) in Hampden Rd, Battery Point provides basic accommodation with private facilities for $50/65 including breakfast.

There are also a couple of moderately priced hotels in Sandy Bay. The *Dr Syntax Hotel* (☎ 6223 6258), at 139 Sandy Bay Rd, is very close to Battery Point. It has comfortable singles/doubles with TV for $35/49. The *Beach House Hotel* (☎ 6225 1161), at 646 Sandy Bay Rd, is two km past the casino and has good rooms with TV and continental breakfast for $42/49.

Hadleys Orient Hotel (☎ 6223 4355), at 34 Murray St, is one of Hobart's best olderstyle hotels. Compared to the large hotel chains, this hotel has a lot more charm and, at $83/93, is a bit cheaper.

Top-end, international-standard accommodation is available at the *Sheraton Hobart* (☎ 6235 4535), the dominating brick block in the heart of the city at 1 Davey St, which charges from $180; or the *Wrest Point Hotel Casino* (☎ 6225 0112) at 410 Sandy Bay Rd, five km south of the city centre. Rooms here start at $100.

If none of these appeal, there's always the wonderful *Lenna of Hobart* (☎ 6232 3900), an old mansion at 20 Runnymede St, Battery Point, which is steeped in history and luxury and charges from $140 for a room.

Motels & Holiday Flats There are plenty of motels in Hobart but some are rather a long way out. The cheapest include the *Shoreline Motor Motel* (☎ 6247 9504) on the corner of Rokeby Rd and Shoreline Drive, Howrah, which charges $55 for a double with continental breakfast; the *Marina Motel* (☎ 6228 4748) at 153 Risdon Rd, New Town, where singles/doubles cost $39/49; and the *Hobart Tower Motel* (☎ 6228 0166) at 300 Park St, New Town which charges $46/55. For a motel closer to the city centre, you could try the *Mayfair Motel* (☎ 6231 1188) at 17 Cavell St, West Hobart, which has rooms for $65/75.

Hobart has a number of self-contained holiday flats with fully equipped kitchens. Fairly close to town, the *Domain View Apartments* (☎ 6234 1181) at 352 Argyle St, North Hobart, charges $55 a double and $5 for each extra person, with a one-night surcharge. The *Knopwood Apartment* (☎ 6223 2290), at 6 Knopwood St, Battery Point, is a threebedroom upstairs flat overlooking Salamanca Place. It costs $60 a double and $14 for each extra person, and has a onenight surcharge.

Places to Eat

Cafes & Light Meals Hobart has plenty of street cafes, such as the *Kafe Kara*, at 119 Liverpool St, which has good food, real cappuccinos (not too common in Hobart) and great décor.

A good lunch-time cafe is *Cafe Toulouse* at 79 Harrington St. There's a good selection of croissants and quiches and you can get a quick, light meal for around $8. A trendy place that serves excellent light meals and is popular with all age groups is the *Kaos Cafe* at 273 Elizabeth St. It's open from noon to midnight daily except Sunday, when it closes at 10 pm.

Another popular place is the *Retro Cafe*,

which is on the corner of Salamanca Place and Montpelier Retreat; it's so popular that you often can't get a table. It opens at 8 am and serves great breakfasts and continues with good food through the day. It closes at 6 pm except Friday, when the doors stay open until midnight.

If you're looking for a snack late at night, you could also try *Mummy's Coffee Shop*, at 38 Waterloo Crescent, just off Hampden Rd, Battery Point. Cakes of various types are the speciality and it's popular for after-theatre snacks. It's open Sunday to Thursday from 10 am to midnight, and Friday and Saturday from 10 am to 2 am.

Another good place for quality snacks is the *Cove* buffet in the Sheraton Hotel. Prices are reasonable with light meals at $5 to $14. For a late-night treat try the dessert and cheese selection; for a bargain $8.50 you can eat all you like from the buffet.

Constitution Dock has a number of floating takeaway seafood stalls such as *Mako Quality Seafoods* and *Flippers*. Close by is *Mures Fish Centre*, where you can get excellent fish & chips and other fishy fare at the bistro on Lower Deck, or an ice cream. Another good fish & chip shop is the *Dolphin in the Bay* at 141 Sandy Bay Rd.

For more exotic takeaways try the tiny *Little Bali* at 84A Harrington St. The dishes are mainly Indonesian and excellent value for around $5. It's open from 11 am to 3 pm weekdays and every evening from 5 to 9.30 pm. If pasta is more to your liking, the *Little Italy*, at 152 Collins St, serves excellent, cheap pasta and is open from 8.30 am to 8 pm or later on weekdays. Both of these places have some tables available for a sit-down meal.

A little more difficult to get to, but well worth the effort, is the historic *Mount Nelson Signal Station Tea House*, on the summit of Mt Nelson, which has spectacular panoramic views of Hobart and the surrounding area.

Pub Meals For $8 you can get a very filling meal at *Bourke's New Sydney Hotel*, 87 Bathurst St. Many other hotels serve good counter meals and those in the $8 to $14 range include the *Shamrock* on the corner of Harrington and Liverpool Sts and the *Aberfeldy Hotel* on the corner of Davey and Molle Sts.

Stoppy's Waterfront Tavern, on Salamanca Place, is a little trendier and has good counter meals for around $10 or more, as well as bands Thursday to Sunday nights.

Restaurants The licensed *Hara Wholefood Cafe* (☎ 6234 1457), at 181 Liverpool St, has an extensive range of mouth-watering vegetarian and vegan dishes and is open Monday to Saturday from 10 am until late evening.

Elizabeth St in North Hobart has a reputation for good-value, interesting places to eat. At 321 Elizabeth St is *Ali Akbar* (☎ 6231 1770), a popular BYO Lebanese restaurant. For good-value pasta and Italian dishes try *Trattoria Casablanca* at 213 Elizabeth St; it's open every evening until after midnight.

North Hobart also has plenty of Asian restaurants. *Vanidols* (☎ 6234 9307), at 353 Elizabeth St, is a comfortable BYO restaurant specialising in Thai, Indian and Indonesian cuisine with main courses for a reasonable $10 to $14; it's open Tuesday to Sunday. Just down the street is another BYO Asian restaurant, *Dede* (☎ 6231 1068), which has good food but can feel a bit cramped on a busy night. Chinese food is also available from *Fortuna Restaurant* at 275 Elizabeth St and the *Golden Bamboo* at 116 Elizabeth St.

On Salamanca Place, *Mr Wooby's* (☎ 6234 3466), tucked away in a side lane, is a pleasant licensed eatery where you can get excellent meals; it's open until quite late. Nearby, at 87 Salamanca Place, is the licensed *Ball & Chain Grill* (☎ 6223 2655), which has a good reputation for grilled steaks; main courses are around $13.

At No 89 there's *Panache* (☎ 6224 2929), a licensed cafe/restaurant which has an outdoor eating area by the adjoining rock walls. For excellent Japanese food, try the licensed *Mikaku* (☎ 6224 0882) at 85 Salamanca Place.

At 31 Campbell St there's the *Theatre Royal Hotel* (☎ 6234 6925), with a highly acclaimed bistro. It's right next door to the

Theatre Royal, Australia's oldest functioning performing-arts theatre.

In Hampden Rd, Battery Point, is the very popular *Brasserie*, which has a reputation for excellent food at moderate prices. Also in Hampden Rd, at No 47, is the popular *Da Angelo Ristorante* (☎ 6223 7011), which serves pasta and pizza for $8. Come early or book as it's often full.

For seafood, the *Upper Deck* (☎ 6231 2121) is licensed, has spectacular harbour views and consistently good seafood. It's at Mures Fish Centre, Victoria Dock. Also on the waterfront, the licensed *Drunken Admiral* (☎ 6234 1903) at 17 Hunter St is open every evening and has good seafood and a great atmosphere. Next door is the popular Italian *Riviera Ristorante* (☎ 6234 3230).

Entertainment

The *Mercury* newspaper has details on most of Hobart's entertainment.

The *New Sydney Hotel* at 87 Bathurst St is Hobart's Irish pub and there is live music there most nights. For jazz, blues and rock & roll, both the *St Ives Hotel* at 86 Sandy Bay Rd and the *Travellers Rest*, 394 Sandy Bay Rd, have bands Wednesday to Sunday nights.

There is always a good scene to be found at *Maloney's Hotel* on the corner of Macquarie and Argyle Sts; there are bands on Friday and Saturday nights and a nightclub upstairs. Another recommended nightclub is *Round Midnight* at 39 Salamanca Place, which is open Tuesday to Saturday until 4 am. Round Midnight is on the top floor of the building which houses the bars *Knopwood's Retreat* and *Cutty's Cafe*.

Nickelby's Wine Bar at 217 Sandy Bay Rd is a popular late-night venue. In the early evening it is a reasonable restaurant and later the live music starts and lasts until the early hours. Another similar place to be seen at is the trendy *Cafe Who*, 251 Liverpool St, which serves meals until 10 pm and has live jazz most nights.

There are 17 bars at the Wrest Point Hotel Casino, and some, like the *Birdcage*, need to be seen to be believed. The casino also has a disco every night with a cover charge on Friday and Saturday only.

At 375 Elizabeth St, North Hobart, you'll find the *State Cinema* (☎ 6234 6318), which screens alternative/off-beat films, while at 181 Collins St there's a large *Village* complex (☎ 6234 7288) which shows mainstream releases.

Getting There & Away

Air For information on international and domestic flights to and from Hobart see the Getting There & Away section at the beginning of this chapter. Ansett (☎ 13 1300) has an office in the Elizabeth St Mall, as does Qantas (☎ 13 1313). Airlines of Tasmania (☎ 6248 5030) has an office at Hobart airport.

Bus The main bus companies operating from Hobart are Tasmanian Redline Coaches (☎ 6231 3233 or 1800 030 033) at the Transit Centre, 199 Collins St; Hobart Coaches (☎ 6234 4077 or 1800 130 620) at 4 Liverpool St; and Tasmanian Wilderness Transport & Tours (☎ 6334 2226), also operating out of the Hobart Coaches office. Hobart Coaches has additional departure points at St David's Cathedral, on the corner of Macquarie and Murray Sts, and outside the Treasury Building in Murray St.

Hobart Coaches' destinations include New Norfolk, Woodbridge, Cygnet, Geeveston, Dover and Port Arthur ($12). Both Redline and Hobart Coaches run to Bicheno ($19), Swansea ($15), St Marys, St Helens ($27), Oatlands, Ross, Campbell Town, Launceston ($17), Deloraine, Devonport ($29) and Burnie ($33). Redline also runs to Wynyard, Stanley, Smithton, Queenstown ($30) and Strahan.

Tasmanian Wilderness Transport fares are usually more expensive (ranging from $20 to $40) but it provides smaller buses, personal service and offers more interesting destinations off the main roads such as Cockle Creek and Scotts Peak Dam in the south-west.

Car Rental There are more than 20 car-rental firms in Hobart. Some of the cheaper ones include Rent-a-Bug (☎ 6231 0300) at 105 Murray St; Advance Car Rentals (☎ 6224 0822) at 277 Macquarie St; Bargain Car Rentals (☎ 6234 6959) at 189A Harrington St; and Statewide Rent-a-Car (☎ 6225 1204) at 388 Sandy Bay Rd, Sandy Bay.

Hitching To start hitching north, first take a Bridgewater or Brighton bus from opposite the main post office in Elizabeth St. To hitch along the east coast, take a bus to Sorell first.

Getting Around

To/From the Airport The airport is in Hobart's eastern suburbs, 16 km from the city centre. Redline runs a pick-up and drop-off shuttle service between the city centre (via Adelphi YHA and some other accommodation places on request) and the airport for $6.60.

Bus The local bus service is run by Metro. The main office (☎ 13 2201) is at 18 Elizabeth St, opposite the main post office. Most buses leave from this area of Elizabeth St, known as the Metro City bus station.

If you're planning to bus around Hobart it's worth buying Metro's user-friendly timetable, which only costs $1.50. For $2.80 you can get a Day Rover ticket which can be used all day at weekends and between 9 am and 4.30 pm and after 6 pm on weekdays.

If you want to go to Mt Wellington without taking a tour, take bus No 48 from Franklin Square in Macquarie St; it will take you to Fern Tree at the base of the mountain, but from there it's a 13-km walk to the top!

Bicycle The Transit Centre Backpackers has mountain bikes for $15 per day, or for $70 per week. Brake Out (☎ 6234 7632) also hires bicycles from the Wrest Point Casino.

Boat On weekdays the ferry MV *Emmalisa* operates between Franklin Wharf and Bellerive Wharf and is a very pleasant way to cross the Derwent River. It departs Franklin Wharf at 7.30 and 8.15 am and 4.35 and 5.15 pm. From

Bellerive there are services at 7.57 and 8.35 am and at 4.50 pm. A one-way ticket costs $1.50. There is no weekend service.

Around Hobart

TAROONA

Ten km from Hobart, on the Channel Highway, is Taroona's **Shot Tower**, completed in 1870. From the top of the 48-metre-high tower there are fine views over the Derwent River estuary. Lead shot was once produced in high towers like this by dropping molten lead from the top which, on its way down, formed a perfect sphere.

The tower, small museum, craft shop and beautiful grounds are open daily from 9 am to 5 pm and admission is $3 (children $1.50). There is also a tearoom which advertises 'convictshire' teas. Take bus No 60 from Franklin Square near Elizabeth St and get off at stop 45.

From Taroona Beach, you can walk around to Kingston Beach (4.5 km) along the **Alum Cliffs Track**; at some points the track runs close to rock cliffs and you get good views of the Derwent across to Opossum Bay.

KINGSTON (pop 12,900)

The town of Kingston, 11 km south of Hobart, is the headquarters of the **Commonwealth Antarctic Division**. The centre is open weekdays from 9 am to 5 pm and admission is free to its fine display. There's a pleasant picnic area beside Browns River at the eastern end of Kingston Beach.

Close by there are also some pleasant beaches, including **Blackmans Bay**, which has a blowhole; **Tinderbox**, where you can go snorkelling along an underwater trail marked with submerged information plates; and **Howden**. There are views across to Bruny Island from Piersons Point, near Tinderbox.

PONTVILLE (pop 1125)

Farther north, on the Midland Highway, is the historic town of Pontville, which has a number of interesting buildings dating from the 1830s. Much of the freestone used in Tasmania's early buildings was supplied from quarries at Pontville. The **barracks** beside the river and **St Marks Anglican Church** on top of the hill are worth a visit.

In nearby Brighton, on Briggs Rd three km off the highway, is the very good **Bonorong Park Wildlife Centre**, which is open daily from 8 am to 5 pm; admission is $5.

NEW NORFOLK (pop 6100)

Set in the lush, rolling countryside of the Derwent Valley, New Norfolk is an interesting historical town. It was first settled in 1803 and became an important hop-growing centre, which is why the area is dotted with old oast houses used for drying hops. Also distinctive are the rows of tall poplars planted to protect crops from the wind.

Originally called Elizabeth Town, New Norfolk was renamed after the arrival of settlers (1807 onwards) from the abandoned Pacific Ocean colony on Norfolk Island.

Things to See & Do

The **Visitors Historical & Information Centre**, next to the council chambers in Circle St, has an interesting display of photographs and other memorabilia. The key to the centre can be obtained from the council office during working hours.

The **Oast House** on Hobart Rd is a museum devoted to the history of the hop industry, with a tearoom and a fine-arts gallery. It's open daily from 10 am to 5 pm and admission is $3.50. The building itself has been classified by the National Trust and is worth seeing from the outside, even if you don't go in.

Also interesting to visit are **St Matthew's Church of England**, built in 1823, which is Tasmania's oldest existing church, and the **Bush Inn**, claimed to be the oldest continuously licensed hotel in Australia. The **Old Colony Inn**, at 21 Montagu St, is a wonderful museum of colonial furnishings and artefacts; there's also a tearoom where you can get some great home-made snacks and sit in the award-winning garden. The inn is open from 9 am to 5 pm and admission is $1.

Australian Newsprint Mills (☎ 6261 0433) is one of the area's major industries and tours can be arranged Tuesday to Friday if you give at least 24 hours notice.

For $40 (children $20) you can also take a **jet-boat ride** on the Derwent River rapids. The 30-minute ride can be booked at the Devil Jet office (☎ 6261 3460), behind the Bush Inn.

In 1864, the first rainbow and brown trout in the southern hemisphere were bred in the **salmon ponds** at Plenty, 11 km west of New Norfolk. The ponds and museum on Lower Bushy Park Rd are open daily; entry is $3.50. You can also sit in the restaurant which serves fine food and watch the fish being fed without paying an entry fee.

Places to Stay

Camp sites ($7), on-site vans ($35) and cabins ($40) are available at *Rosie's Caravan Park* (☎ 6261 1268) on the Esplanade, 1.5 km north of town. It's a great place if you want to fish in the river.

The hotel choices here are pretty limited. The *Bush Inn* (☎ 6261 2011), Montagu St, was built in 1815 and has plain singles/doubles for $28/48 including a cooked breakfast, but there's a one-night surcharge. The *Old Colony Inn* (☎ 6261 2731), also in Montagu St, has just one double room — for short people only — for $70 (watch the doors!). On the other side of the river to the main town, *Rosie's Inn* at 5 Oast St provides B&B from $60 to $75 a double.

The nicest (but most expensive) place is *Tynwald* (☎ 6261 2667), overlooking the river by the Oast House. It's a three-storey house which dates back to the 1830s and is oozing with character. The rooms are well furnished, and it has a heated swimming pool and a tennis court for the energetic. The cost is $116, which includes a light breakfast.

Getting There & Away

Hobart Coaches (☎ 6234 4077) is the main operator between Hobart and New Norfolk and on weekdays there are eight or nine buses in both directions. On weekends there's a limited service: a one-way/return fare costs $4/7. In New Norfolk, the buses leave from Stephen St, beside Arthur Square.

MT FIELD NATIONAL PARK

Mt Field, only 80 km from Hobart, was declared a national park in 1916, which makes it one of Australia's oldest. The park is well known for its spectacular mountain scenery, alpine moorland, dense rainforest, lakes, abundant wildlife and spectacular waterfalls. To get to the magnificent 40-metre **Russell Falls** it's an easy 15-minute walk (the path is suitable for wheelchairs), and there are also easy walks to Lady Barron, Horseshoe and Marriotts falls as well as eight-hour bushwalks. With sufficient snow, there's cross-country and limited downhill skiing at **Mt Mawson**.

Places to Stay

Lake Dobson Cabins, 15 km into the park, has three very basic six-bunk cabins. The cost per cabin is $20 a night, plus $10 for each extra adult, and you must book at the rangers' office. There's also a camping ground run by the rangers; a site (for two) costs $10 and an entry permit is also required.

The *National Park Youth Hostel* (☎ 6288 1369) is 200 metres past the turn off to the park and charges $11 a night; YHA members only. The nearby *Russell Falls Holiday Cottages* (☎ 6288 1198) consists of four one or two-bedroom fully equipped cottages which cost $50 a double, plus $10 for each extra person.

Getting There & Away

On weekdays, the 4 pm Hobart Coaches bus from Hobart to New Norfolk continues on to Mt Field. There is a return service to Hobart on weekdays at 7.55 am. Tasmanian Wilderness Transport also runs one bus to and from Scotts Peak via the park and Maydena on Tuesday, Thursday, Saturday and Sunday during summer. At other times of the year a single service runs on Thursday only.

RICHMOND (pop 780)

Richmond is just 24 km from Hobart and, with more than 50 buildings dating from the 19th century, is Tasmania's premier historic town. Straddling the Coal River, on the old route between Hobart and Port Arthur, Richmond was once a strategic military post and convict station. The much-photographed **Richmond Bridge**, built by convicts in 1823, is the oldest road bridge in Australia.

With the completion of the Sorell Causeway in 1872, traffic travelling to the Tasman Peninsula and the east coast bypassed Richmond. For over 100 years the town lay dormant until the recent tourist boom.

Things to See & Do

The northern wing of **Richmond Gaol** was built in 1825, five years before the settlement at Port Arthur, and is the best preserved convict jail in Australia. It is open daily from 10 am to 5 pm; admission is $3 ($1.50 children).

Other places of interest include **St John's Church** (1836), the oldest Catholic church in Australia; **St Luke's Church of England** (1834); the **courthouse** (1825); the **old post office** (1826); the **Bridge Inn** (1817); the **granary** (1829); and the **Richmond Arms Hotel** (1888). There's also a model village (designed from original plans) of Hobart Town as it was in the 1820s. It's open daily from 9 am to 5 pm and admission is $5 ($2.50 children). The maze, on the main street, is fun but is made of wooden divides, not hedges; admission is $3.50 (children $2.50).

Places to Stay & Eat

Accommodation in Richmond is mostly of the 'colonial cottage' type and is not particularly cheap. Cheapest of all is the *Richmond Cabin & Tourist Park* (☎ 6260 2192), on Middle Tea Tree Rd opposite Prospect House. It has camp sites ($12 for two people), on-site vans ($32) and cabins ($48).

The cheapest B&B is the *Richmond Country Guest House* (☎ 6260 4238), on Prossers Rd, four km north of town, which charges $45/70 for singles/doubles. Everything else is rather expensive, such as the *Red Brier Cottage* (☎ 6260 2349), in Bridge St, which charges $100 for a double.

Prospect House (☎ 6260 2207) is a superb two-storey Georgian country mansion set in 10 hectares of grounds. It's just outside Richmond, on the Hobart road. Accommodation costs $86/96, or $10 more if breakfast is included.

You can get something to eat and drink at the *Richmond Wine Centre* on Bridge Rd. This new building is set back from the street and is a good place for breakfast and lunch. There are also several tearooms with light meals; try *Ma Foosies* in the main street for some country service. The town also has a bakery which is hidden behind the saddlery building.

Getting There & Away

If you have your own car, Richmond is an easy day trip from Hobart. If you don't, both Redline and Hobart Coaches have bus tours most days to Richmond. Hobart Coaches runs four regular buses a day on weekdays to and from Richmond ($6 return); there are no scheduled weekend services.

South-East Coast

South of Hobart are the scenic fruit-growing and timber areas of the Huon Peninsula, D'Entrecasteaux Channel and Esperance, as well as beautiful Bruny Island and the Hartz Mountains National Park. Once mainly an apple-growing region, the area has now diversified and produces a range of other fruits, Atlantic salmon and wines as well as catering to the growing tourism industry. With the abundance of fresh local produce, some of the hotels turn out fabulous meals.

Around the end of February and during March there is fruit-picking work, but competition for jobs is stiff.

KETTERING (pop 310)

The small port of Kettering, on a sheltered bay 34 km south of Hobart, is the terminal for the Bruny Island car ferry. The nearby town of **Snug** has a walking track to Snug Falls (one hour return).

If you are after a good meal try the excellent food at the *Oyster Cove Inn* for a high-standard pub meal. The accommodation upstairs is overpriced at $70 a double.

The nearby *Heron Rise Vineyard* (☎ 6267 4339) has private, luxury accommodation for $80 a double.

On weekdays, Hobart Coaches has four buses a day to Woodbridge via Kingston, Margate, Snug and continuing on to Kettering. A single service runs on Saturday morning from Kettering to Hobart with the return service in the afternoon. There are no Sunday services.

BRUNY ISLAND (pop 440)

Bruny Island is almost two islands, joined by an isthmus where mutton birds and other waterfowl breed. It is a peaceful and beautiful retreat. The sparsely populated island has five state reserves and is renowned for its varied wildlife, including fairy penguins and many reptile species.

The island's coastal scenery is superb and there are plenty of fine swimming and surf beaches, as well as good sea and freshwater fishing. There are a number of signposted walking tracks within the reserves, especially the southern Labillardiere State Reserve and at Fluted Cape.

The island was sighted by Abel Tasman in 1642 and later visited by Furneaux, Cook, Bligh and Cox between 1770 and 1790, but was named after Rear-Admiral Bruni D'Entrecasteaux, who explored and surveyed the area in 1792. Initially the Aboriginal people were friendly towards the Europeans, but relations deteriorated after the sealers and whalers arrived. The island itself remained little changed until the car ferry started in 1954.

Tourism has now become an important part of the island's economy but it is still fairly low-key. There are no massive resorts, just interesting cottages and guesthouses, most of which are self-contained. You'll need to bring all of your food with you unless

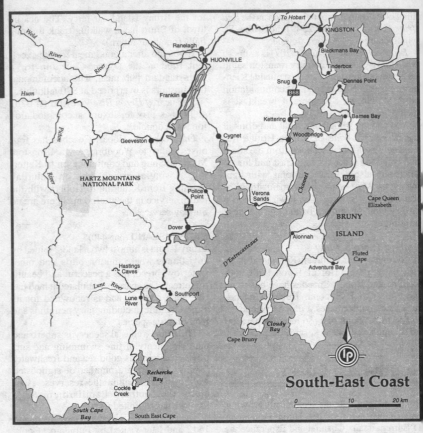

South-East Coast

you're staying at Adventure Bay. Also, it is wise to book accommodation in advance as managers often don't live next door to their rental cottages. A car is necessary to get around the island as there are no buses. Drive slowly as most roads are gravel.

The island's history is recorded in the **Bligh Museum of Pacific Exploration** at Adventure Bay, South Bruny; entry is $2.50. Also of historical interest is South Bruny's **lighthouse**, which was built in 1836 and is the second oldest in Australia. The lighthouse reserve is open to the public.

Places to Stay

Adventure Bay on the southern part of the island is the main accommodation area, but there are places dotted throughout the island. Alonnah is the other main settlement.

The *Adventure Bay Caravan Park* (☎ 6293 1270) has cosy three-bed cabins for $40, on-site vans for $30 and camp sites for $10. The *Captain James Cook Caravan Park* (☎ 6293 1128) is closer to town and has on-site vans for $30 and camp sites for $6.

There are free bush camp sites in a couple of the reserves. The one at Jetty Beach near the lighthouse on the south of the island is on a beautiful sheltered cove. Other sites are near the isthmus and at Cloudy Bay.

The only cheap accommodation is the *Lumeah Hostel* (☎ 6293 1265) in Adventure Bay, which has dormitory beds for $13 ($15 for nonmembers). Cottages can be rented for around $60 a double. Near Adventure Bay are *Rosebud Cottage* (☎ 6293 1325), *Mavista Cottage* (☎ 6293 1347) and *Seaside Cottages* (☎ 6293 1403).

On North Bruny the *Channel View Guest House* (☎ 6260 6266) has good-value singles/doubles for $30/45 including breakfast. If you want your own house then rent the *Christopher Lumsden Cottage* for $55 a double plus $10 for each extra adult. A minimum stay of two nights applies.

Getting There & Away
On weekdays there are nine ferry services daily between Kettering and Roberts Point, on Bruny Island. On Friday there is an extra crossing, and the weekend schedule can vary, so check the times in the Friday edition of the *Mercury* newspaper. There's no charge for foot passengers, but if you have a car it costs $18 return from Monday to Thursday, and $23 on Friday afternoons and weekends. Bicycles cost $3. The Hobart Coaches Kettering bus service normally connects with the ferry.

CYGNET (pop 925)
Named 'Port de Cygne Noir' (Port of the Black Swan) by Rear-Admiral D'Entrecasteaux after the many swans seen on the bay, this town is now known as Cygnet. The surrounding area has many orchards with a wide variety of fruit including apples, stone fruits and berries. The region also offers some excellent fishing, bushwalking and good beaches with safe swimming conditions, particularly at **Verona Sands** on the southern end of the peninsula.

Close to Cygnet is the **Talune Wildlife Park & Koala Garden** ($6 entry fee), the **Hartzview Vineyard** with wine tastings, and the **Deepings wood-turning workshop**.

Places to Stay
Balfes Hill Youth Hostel (☎ 6295 1551) is on the Channel Highway, about five km north of the town. It charges $12 a night ($14 for nonmembers) and can get crowded during the fruit-picking season. From December to April the manager organises walks twice weekly to beautiful South Cape Bay, the most southern beach in Tasmania. A package with two nights accommodation costs around $90. Mountain bikes are available for rent from the hostel for $12 per day.

The *Cygnet Hotel* (☎ 6295 1267) has singles/doubles for $25/50 with a cooked breakfast. There's also a basic camping ground opposite the hotel; it charges a bargain $5 per camp site. If you are fruit picking, many of the hotels in Cygnet will rent you a room at a reasonable weekly rate. Most other accommodation is well out of town on farms and costs $70 to $90 a double.

Getting There & Away
Hobart Coaches has a once-daily, weekday service from Hobart to Cygnet via Snug at 5.15 pm. The return service leaves at 6.55 am.

HUONVILLE (pop 1520)
Named after Huon de Kermadec, who was second in command to D'Entrecasteaux, this small, busy town on the picturesque Huon River is another apple-growing centre. The valuable softwood, Huon pine, was also first discovered here. For the visitor, one of the main attractions these days is a jet-boat ride on the river. You can also hire pedal boats and aqua bikes from the office (☎ 6264 1838) on the esplanade. In the nearby hills are Horseback Wilderness Tours (☎ 018 128 405), and a trout fishery where you are guaranteed a fish.

There is little accommodation in the town. The Huonville Grand Hotel (☎ 6264 1004), near the river, is an old pub with rooms for $25/35. See the following section for information on transport to Huonville.

GEEVESTON (pop 825)
This town was founded by the Geeves family and their descendants still live here. It is an

important base for the timber industry as well as the gateway to the Hartz Mountains National Park.

The town's main attraction is the **Esperance Forest & Heritage Centre**, in the main street, which is open daily from 10 am to 4 pm; admission is $4 ($2 children). It has comprehensive displays on all aspects of forestry. The centre also incorporates the South-West Visitor Centre (☎ 6297 1836).

There are a number of walks in the area, including the Big Tree Walk, which is named after an 87-metre-high swamp gum.

Hobart Coaches runs four buses a day between Hobart and Geeveston via Huonville. Tasmanian Wilderness Transport also runs a service three days a week but it is considerably more expensive at $35.

HARTZ MOUNTAINS NATIONAL PARK

This national park, classified as part of the World Heritage Area, is very popular with weekend walkers and day-trippers as it's only 84 km from Hobart. The park is renowned for its rugged mountains, glacial lakes, gorges, alpine moorlands and dense rainforest. Being on the edge of the South-West National Park, it is subject to vicious changes in weather, so even on a day walk take waterproof gear and warm clothing. The usual park entry fee applies.

There are some great views from the **Waratah Lookout** (24 km from Geeveston) – look for the jagged peaks of the Snowy Range and the Devils Backbone. There are good walks in the park, including tracks to Hartz Peak (five to six hours), and lakes Osborne and Perry (two hours).

DOVER (pop 520)

This picturesque fishing port, 21 km south of Geeveston on the Huon Highway, has some fine beaches and excellent bushwalks. The three small islands in the bay are known as Faith, Hope and Charity. Last century, the processing and exporting of Huon pine was Dover's major industry, and sleepers made here and in the nearby timber towns of Strathblane and Raminea were shipped to China, India and Germany. If you have your own car and are heading farther south, it's a good idea to buy petrol and food supplies here.

Places to Stay

The *Dover Beachside Caravan Park* (☎ 6298 1301), on Kent Beach Rd, has camp sites ($9) and on-site vans ($28). The *Dover Hotel* (☎ 6298 1210), on the Huon Highway, has backpacker accommodation for $10, hotel B&B for $28 per person, or more expensive motel rooms ($55).

The *White Cliffs Lodge* (☎ 6298 1180), on Bay View Rd, has budget accommodation for $12 and also has double rooms for $35 (including linen). Mountain bikes and a rowboat are available for hire. In summer the lodge runs a daily bus service from Adelphi Court YHA in Hobart for $10; bookings are essential.

For something more comfortable try *Annes Old Rectory* (☎ 6298 1222). This is beside the road as you enter the town. It has good old-fashioned service, and charges $55 a double.

Getting There & Away

Hobart Coaches runs one bus a day from Hobart to Dover on weekdays in the late afternoon, returning in the morning (7 am). On school days a second bus operates at similar times.

HASTINGS

Today it's the spectacular **Hastings Cave & Thermal Pool** which attract visitors to the once-thriving logging and wharf town of Hastings, 21 km south of Dover. The cave is found among the lush vegetation of the **Hastings Caves State Reserve**, 10 km inland from Hastings and well signposted from the Huon Highway. Daily tours of the cave ($8; $1 children) leave promptly at 11.15 am and 1.15, 2.15 and 3.15 pm, with up to four extra tours daily from December to April. Allow 10 minutes drive then five minutes walk through rainforest to the cave entrance. For the more energetic a short track continues past the cave to a viewpoint overlooking the forest.

About five km before the cave is a thermal swimming pool ($2.50; $1.50 children), filled daily with warm water from a thermal spring. Near the pool there is a kiosk and a restaurant. The 10-minute sensory walk, suitable for blind people, near the pool is well worth doing.

For those interested in a more adventurous exploration of the caves, Exit Cave Adventure Tours (☎ 6243 0546) runs a trip which is suitable for beginners. It leaves Hobart at 8 am and bookings are essential.

LUNE RIVER

A few km south-west of Hastings is Lune River, a haven for gem collectors and the site of Australia's most southerly post office and youth hostel. From here you can also take a scenic six-km ride on the **Ida Bay Railway** to the lovely beach at Deep Hole Bay. The train runs on Sunday year-round at noon, 1.30 and 3 pm. In the warmer months extra services run on Saturday and Wednesday. The ride costs $10 ($5 children).

The most southerly drive you can make in Australia is along the secondary gravel road from Lune River to **Cockle Creek** and beautiful **Recherche Bay**. This is an area of spectacular mountain peaks and endless beaches – ideal for camping and bushwalking. This is also the start (or end) of the challenging South Coast Track which, with the right preparation and a week or so to spare, will take you all the way to Port Davey in the south-west. See Lonely Planet's *Bushwalking in Australia* for track notes.

Places to Stay

The *Lune River Youth Hostel* (☎ 6298 3163), also known as the Doing Place, charges $10 a night ($12 nonmembers). It's a cosy hostel and there's certainly plenty to do – ask the managers about hiring mountain bikes or kayaks, or about bushwalking, fishing and caving. Don't forget to bring plenty of food with you as the hostel only has basic supplies. The hostel runs a shuttle bus connecting with the Hobart Coaches Dover service; bookings are essential.

Getting There & Away

Apart from the hostel bus, the only other service is that run by Tasmanian Wilderness Transport (☎ 6334 4442). The bus runs on Monday, Wednesday and Friday in summer all the way to the end of the road at Cockle Creek for a flat fee of $35 one way or $65 return.

Tasman Peninsula

The Arthur Highway runs from Hobart through Sorell and Copping to Port Arthur, 100 km away. As there is no bank on the Tasman Peninsula and the supermarkets are quite expensive, it's a good idea to take advantage of both banking and shopping facilities at Sorell. And to get you into the convict mood, at Copping there's an excellent **colonial convict exhibition** ($4 entry) which features many objects once used at Port Arthur.

PORT ARTHUR

In 1830, Governor Arthur chose the Tasman Peninsula as the place to confine prisoners who had committed further crimes in the colony. He called the peninsula a 'natural penitentiary' because it was only connected to the mainland by a narrow strip of land, less than 100 metres wide, called Eaglehawk Neck. To deter convicts from escaping, ferocious guard dogs were chained in a line across the isthmus and a rumour circulated

Convicts at the hellish Port Arthur penal colony wore fetters such as these

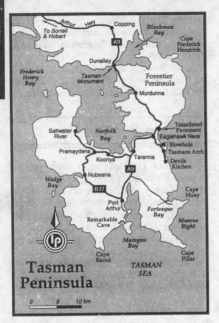

Tasman Peninsula

tables, a boys' prison was built at Point Puer to reform and educate juvenile convicts, and a church (today one of the most readily recognised tourist sights in Tasmania) was erected.

The well-presented historic site of Port Arthur is Tasmania's premier tourist attraction. For a fee of $13 ($6.50 children) you can visit all the restored buildings including the Lunatic Asylum (now a museum) and the Model Prison. The ticket is valid for 24 hours and entitles you to free admission to the museum, a guided tour of the settlement and a free cruise to the **Isle of the Dead**.

The site is open daily from 9 am to 5 pm, but there's nothing to stop you from wandering around outside those hours without paying the entry fee, although the museum and tours are closed.

Tours

The guided tours (included in the site entry fee) are well worthwhile and leave hourly from the car park in front of the information office (☎ 6250 2539) between 9.30 am and 3.30 pm.

Ghostly apparitions, poltergeists and unexplained happenings have been recorded at Port Arthur since the 1870s, and nightly lantern-lit walking 'ghost tours' of the buildings and ruins are fun, but also pretty spooky. Two-hour ghost tours leave from outside the information office at 8.30 pm, or at 9.30 pm during daylight-saving time and are well worth the $10 ($5 for children).

Places to Stay

The *Port Arthur Garden Point Caravan Park* (☎ 6250 2340) is two km before Port Arthur in picturesque surroundings. It costs $10 to camp, $13 each for the hostel and $45 a double for a cabin. You can follow a track around the shoreline from here to Port Arthur.

The *Port Arthur Youth Hostel* (☎ 6250 2311) is very well positioned on the edge of the historic site and charges $10 a night ($12 for nonmembers). To get there, continue half a km past the Port Arthur turn-off and turn left at the sign for the hostel and the Por

that the waters on either side were infested with sharks.

Between 1830 and 1877, about 12,500 convicts served sentences at Port Arthur, and for some of them it was a living hell. In reality, those who behaved often lived in better conditions than they had endured back home in England and Ireland.

The township of Port Arthur became the centre of a network of penal stations on the peninsula and was, itself, much more than just a prison town. It had fine buildings and thriving industries including timber milling, shipbuilding, coal mining, brick and nail production and shoemaking.

Australia's first railway literally 'ran' the seven km between Norfolk Bay and Long Bay: convicts pushed the carriages along the tracks. A semaphore telegraph system allowed instant communication between Port Arthur, the penal outstations and Hobart. Convict farms provided fresh vege-

Tragedy Revisits Port Arthur

Port Arthur was again the scene of tragedy in April 1996. A lone gunman opened fire on visitors and staff at the Port Arthur historic site, and also took hostages at a local guesthouse. After holding siege for many hours and setting fire to the guesthouse, he was finally captured. In all, 35 people were killed and many were injured. ■

Arthur Motor Inn. You can buy your historic-site entry ticket at the hostel.

If you don't mind staying some distance from the town, there are some pleasant farm-style B&Bs. *Anderton's Accommodation* (☎ 6250 2378) and the *Norfolk Bay Convict Station* at Tarrana (☎ 6250 3487) both provide friendly service for around $60 for a double.

Apart from this, most of Port Arthur's accommodation is pricey. The *Port Arthur Motor Inn* (☎ 6250 2101) overlooks the site and has rooms from $90. In this same area, but without views of the ruins, are the *Port Arthur Villas* (☎ 6250 2239). These self-contained units sleep four to six people and cost $70 a double plus $12 for each extra adult.

Places to Eat

The licensed *Frances Langford Tea Rooms*, in the restored policemen's quarters inside the settlement, is a good place for a cuppa or for a light lunch, and is open from 10 am to 5 pm. The *Port Arthur Motor Inn*, next to the youth hostel, offers more formal dining but often has cheap specials on the menu. For fast food, the cafe is next to the information office and is open from 9 am to 6 pm (5 pm in the low season).

Entertainment

There is some unique entertainment at Port Arthur. The classic 1926 silent movie *For the Term of His Natural Life* is screened in the museum daily (there's no extra fee). This film, based on the Marcus Clarke novel about convict life, was filmed on location in Port Arthur. The book was published in 1870 and is Australia's best-known colonial novel. Ask at the information centre about screening times for the film.

Getting There & Away

If you don't have your own transport, the easiest way to visit Port Arthur on a day trip from Hobart is on an organised tour. During the summer season you can often use Hobart Coaches and/or Country Convict Bus Services for a day trip. Check timetables first as they change every year.

Hobart Coaches has a single weekday service which travels via most towns on the Tasman Peninsula for $12. Convict Country Bus Services (☎ 6250 5397) also runs one service a day on weekdays and visits many of the sights on the peninsula ($9 one way). It operates from the Transit Centre in Hobart and will pick you up or drop you off at the youth hostel in Port Arthur.

AROUND THE PENINSULA

The Tasman Peninsula has many bushwalks, superb scenery, delightful stretches of beach and beautiful bays. Near Eaglehawk Neck there are the incredible coastal formations of the **Tessellated Pavement**, the **Blowhole**, the **Devils Kitchen**, **Tasmans Arch** and **Waterfall Bay**.

South of Port Arthur is **Remarkable Cave**, which you can walk through when the tide is out. Around the peninsula are some spectacular walks to Mt Brown (four to five hours), Cape Raoul (1½ hours to the lookout, five hours to the cape) and Cape Huay (five hours). The pocket-sized guide *Tasman Tracks* provides detailed notes. It's available from bookshops and walking shops, such as Paddy Pallin, in Hobart.

You can also visit the remains of the penal outstations at **Koonya**, **Premaydena** and **Saltwater River**, and the ruins of the dreaded **Coal Mines Station**. The **Tasmanian Devil Park** at Taranna is open daily and admission is $8 ($4 children). The **Bush**

TASMANIA

railway and pioneer settlement; admission here is $12 ($6 children).

Organised Tours
Remarkable Tours (☎ 6250 2359) runs one trip a day ($5) to Remarkable Cave as well as twilight tours of the peninsula's other attractions, and bookings are essential. Tours leave from the car park in front of the Port Arthur information office.

If you want to go on a guided walk contact the Storeys at Tasman Trails (☎ 6250 3329). They take bookings up until the walk starts at 9 am and charge $33 for a day's outing including basic gear and lunch.

Places to Stay & Eat
At Eaglehawk Neck, 20 km before the penal settlement, is the *Eaglehawk Neck Backpackers* (☎ 6250 3248), on Old Jetty Rd (the side road heading west from the north side of the isthmus). It's a small and friendly hostel charging $12 a night, and a good base from which to explore the Eaglehawk Neck area.

The pleasant seaside town of Nubeena, 11 km beyond Port Arthur, has the *White Beach Caravan Park* (☎ 6250 2142) has camp sites ($11), on-site vans ($30) and cabins ($45). Also worth checking out is *Parker's Holiday Cottages* (☎ 6250 2138), where self-contained five-bed units cost $45 for a double and $6 for each additional person. The *Nubeena Tavern* does good counter meals.

Near Koonya is the *Seaview Lodge Host Farm* (☎ 6250 2766), which offers bunk beds for $15 or private doubles with breakfast for $50. You can also stay in town at the *Cascades* for $80 a double.

There are also free, but very basic, camping facilities at Lime Bay and White Beach run by the Department of Parks, Wildlife & Heritage. At Fortescue Bay there is a camping ground at Mill Creek run by the Forestry Commission of Tasmania (☎ 6250 2433). There's no power, but cold showers and firewood are available. The charge is $6 per person.

Midlands

Tasmania's midlands region has a definite English feel due to the diligent efforts of early settlers who planted English trees and hedgerows. The agricultural potential of the area contributed to Tasmania's rapid settlement, and coach stations, garrison towns, stone villages and pastoral properties soon sprang up as convict gangs constructed the main road between Hobart and Launceston. Fine wool, beef cattle and timber milling put the midlands on the map and these, along with tourism, are still the main industries.

The course of the Midland Highway has changed slightly from its original route and many of the historic towns are now bypassed, but it's definitely worth making a few detours to see them.

Getting There & Away
Both Redline and Hobart Coaches have several services daily up and down the Midland Highway which can drop you off at any of the towns along the way. Fares from Hobart include Oatlands $9.40, Ross $12.60, Campbell Town $14.20 and Launceston $17.80.

OATLANDS (pop 540)
With the largest collection of Georgian architecture in Australia, and the largest number of buildings dating from before 1837, the town of Oatlands is not to be missed. In the main street alone, there are 87 historic buildings and the oldest is the 1829 convict-built **courthouse**. Much of the sandstone for these early buildings came from the shores of **Lake Dulverton**, now a wildlife sanctuary, which is beside the town.

Today, one of Oatlands' main attractions is **Callington Mill**, the restoration of which was Tasmania's main Bicentennial project. The mill features a faithfully restored cap with a fantail attachment that automatically turns its sails into the wind, and you can climb up the middle. It's open daily and entry is $2.

GLENN BEANLAND

HUGH FINLAY

HUGH FINLAY

PAUL STEEL

PAUL STEEL

A	
C	D
E	

Tasmania

A: Georgian warehouses, Hobart
B: Salamanca Place, Hobart
C: Arts & crafts shop, Richmond

D: Port Arthur, Tasman Peninsula
E: Mt Field National Park

HUGH FINLAY

JOHN CHAPMAN

PAUL STEEL

RAY STAMP

GLENN BEANLAND

A	
B	C	D
E	

Tasmania
A: Eroded hills near Queenstown
B: Mt Hyperion, Cradle Mountain-
    Lake St Clair

C: Cradle Mountain
D: Coastal scenery near Swansea
E: Ross Bridge, Ross

An unusual way of seeing Oatlands's sights is to go on one of Peter Fielding's daily historical tours (☎ 6254 1135). The convict tour leaves at 5 pm, and costs $6 (children $3). The ghost tour starts at 8 pm, costs $8 (children $4) and uses candles for lighting on the tour.

Places to Stay & Eat
There's plenty of accommodation in Oatlands, although much of it is of the more expensive colonial type. The *Oatlands Youth Hostel* (☎ 6254 1320), at 9 Wellington St, is a couple of hundred metres off the main street and charges $10 a night. The *Midlands Hotel* (☎ 6254 1103), at 91 High St, charges $30/40 for singles/doubles with continental breakfast. The *Oatlands Lodge* (☎ 6254 1444), nearby at 92 High St, has four rooms with attached bath at $85 a double including breakfast. *Blossom's of Oatlands*, on the main street, is a good place for meals.

ROSS (pop 290)
This ex-garrison town, 120 km from Hobart, is steeped in colonial charm and history. It was established in 1812 to protect travellers on the main north-south road and was an important coach staging post.

Things to See
The town is known for its convict-built **Ross Bridge**, the third-oldest bridge in Australia. Daniel Herbert, a convict stonemason, was granted a pardon for his detailed work on the 184 panels which decorate the arches.

The town is quite small and walking around is the best way to see it. In the heart of town is a crossroads which can lead you in one of four directions, being: 'temptation' (represented by the Man-O'-Ross Hotel); 'salvation' (the Catholic church); 'recreation' (the town hall); and 'damnation' (the old jail).

Interesting historic buildings include the **Scotch Thistle Inn**; the **old barracks**, restored by the National Trust; the **Uniting Church** (1885); **St John's Church of England** (1868); and the **post office** (1896). The **Tasmanian Wool Centre**, a museum

and craft shop in Church St, is open daily from 9.30 am to 5.30 pm; entry to the museum is $4 ($2 children). Also in Church St is a small **militaria museum**, open Saturday to Thursday.

Places to Stay & Eat
Adjacent to the Ross Bridge is the *Ross Caravan Park* (☎ 6381 5462), which has cheap camp sites ($8) and cheap stone cabins ($20). The *Man-O'-Ross Hotel* (☎ 6381 5240), in Church St, has singles/doubles for $30/48. If you want to treat yourself, then stay at the *Elms Inn* (☎ 6281 5246) in the main street. The cost is $50/79 including breakfast.

For lunch try the bakery next to the Elms Inn. The only place for dinner is the hotel; the counter meals are fairly ordinary.

CAMPBELL TOWN (pop 860)
Twelve km north of Ross is Campbell Town, another former garrison settlement which boasts more examples of early colonial architecture. These include the convict-built **Red Bridge** (1836), the **Grange** (1847), **St Luke's Church of England** (1835), the **Campbell Town Inn** (1840), the building known as the **Fox Hunters Return** (1829), and the **old school** (1878).

There's a secondary road from Campbell Town to Swansea on the east coast, via the excellent fishing and bushwalking area around **Lake Leake** (32 km). The daily Redline bus from Hobart to Bicheno travels this route and can drop you at the Lake Leake turn off, four km from the lake. Another highway, the A4, runs from Conara Junction, 11 km north of Campbell Town, east to St Marys. Buses running from Launceston to Bicheno follow the A4.

LAKE COUNTRY
The sparsely populated Lake Country of Tasmania's Central Plateau is a region of breathtaking scenery with steep mountains, hundreds of glacial lakes, crystal-clear streams, waterfalls and a good variety of wildlife. It's also known for its fine trout fishing, and for its ambitious hydroelectric

schemes which have seen the damming of rivers, the creation of artificial lakes, the building of power stations (both above and below ground) as well as the construction of massive pipelines.

Tasmania has the largest hydroelectric power system in Australia. The first dam was constructed on Great Lake in 1911. Subsequently, the Derwent, Mersey, South Esk, Forth, Gordon, King, Anthony and Pieman rivers were also dammed. If you want to inspect the developments, go along to the Tungatinah, Tarraleah and Liapootah power stations on the extensive Derwent scheme between Queenstown and Hobart.

On the eastern edge of the Central Plateau is the **Walls of Jerusalem National Park**, which is a focal point for mountaineers, bushwalkers and cross-country skiers. There's excellent fishing at **Lake King William**, on the Derwent River, south of the Lyell Highway, as well as at **Lake Sorell**, **Lake Crescent**, **Arthurs Lake** and **Little Pine Lagoon**.

At Waddamana, on the road which loops off the Lake Highway between Bothwell and Great Lake, there's the **Waddamana Power Museum**. It's an interesting display of the state's early hydro history, and is open daily from 10 am to 4 pm; admission is free.

Getting There & Away
Public transport to this area is not good (and neither is hitching). Redline runs a daily service between Bothwell and Hobart. This leaves Bothwell at 7 am and Hobart at 4 pm for the return journey. There is no connecting service between Bothwell and Great Lake.

Tasmanian Wilderness Transport's services between Lake St Clair and Launceston or Devonport go via Bronte Park and Miena. This service runs daily during the summer, and only once a week in autumn and spring. There are no winter services. Booking is essential.

BOTHWELL (pop 420)
Bothwell, in the beautiful Clyde River valley, is a charming and historic town, with 53 buildings recognised or classified by the

National Trust. Places of particular interest include the beautifully restored **Slate Cottage** of 1835; a **bootmaker's shop**, fitted out as it would have been in the 1890s; **Thorpe Mill**, a flour mill from the 1820s; the delightful **St Luke's Church** (1821); and the **Castle Hotel**, first licensed in 1821.

Although Bothwell is probably best known for its great trout fishing, it also has Australia's oldest golf course. This is still in use today and is open to members of any golf club.

Places to Stay
Accommodation in Bothwell can be expensive, but *Mrs Wood's Farmhouse* (☎ 6259 5612), at Dennistoun, eight km from town, is highly recommended at $75 a double. You can also try either *Whites Cottage* (☎ 6259 5651), at $85 a double including a continental breakfast, or *Bothwell Grange* (☎ 6259 5556), at $70 for B&B. Both are in town.

At Swan Bay, near Miena, the *Great Lake Hotel* (☎ 6259 8163) has doubles for $55 to $65 including a continental breakfast, cabins for $15 each and camp sites for $8.

East Coast

Tasmania's scenic east coast, with its long sandy beaches, fine fishing and rare peacefulness, is known as the 'sun coast' because of its mild and often sunny climate.

Exploration and settlement of the region, which was found to be most suitable for grazing, proceeded rapidly after the establishment of Hobart in 1803. Offshore fishing, and particularly whaling, also became important industries, as did tin mining and timber cutting. Many of the convicts who served out their terms in the area stayed on to help the settlers lay the foundations of the fishing, wool, beef and grain industries which are still significant in the region today.

The best features are the major national parks of Maria Island and Freycinet. The spectacular scenery around Coles Bay is not to be missed, and Bicheno and Triabunna are pleasant seaside towns in which to spend a few restful days. Swansea has become very commercial, with generally overpriced services.

Banking facilities on the east coast are limited and in some towns the banks are only open one or two days a week. There are agencies for the Commonwealth Bank at all post offices. There are also EFTPOS facilities along the coast at Coles Bay, Bicheno and St Marys. Petrol can be purchased by EFTPOS from Caltex stations at Orford and Triabunna.

Getting There & Around

Redline and Hobart Coaches are the main bus companies operating, but a couple of smaller companies – Peakes Coach Service (☎ 6372 2390), Bicheno Coach Services (☎ 6257 0293) and Suncoast Bus Service (☎ 6376 1753) – also do runs between Swansea, Coles Bay, Bicheno and St Marys. With all of these you can buy your tickets when boarding. The Redline Tassie Bus Pass can also be used on services run by Peakes.

Bus services are limited at weekends, so it might take a little longer than anticipated to travel between towns.

BUCKLAND

This tiny township, 61 km from Hobart, was once a staging post for coaches. Ye Olde Buckland Inn, at 5 Kent St, welcomed coach drivers and travellers a century ago and today offers a good counter lunch every day and dinner on Friday and Saturday nights. The new roadhouse offers light meals and snacks.

The stone **Church of St John the Baptist**, dating from 1846, is worth a visit. It has a stained-glass window which was rescued from a 14th-century abbey in England just before Cromwell sacked the building.

ORFORD (pop 520)

Orford is a popular little seaside resort on the Prosser River (named after an escaped prisoner who was caught on its banks). The area

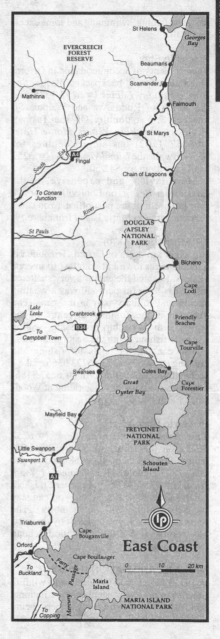

East Coast

has good fishing, swimming and some excellent walks.

Places to Stay

There's plenty of accommodation in Orford, although no real backpacker places. *Sea Breeze Holiday Cabins* (☎ 6257 1375), on the corner of Rudd Ave and Walpole St, charges $35 a double. On the Tasman Highway, the *Blue Waters Motor Hotel* (☎ 6257 1102) has singles/doubles for $35/45, while the *Island View Motel* (☎ 6257 1114) has them for $42/50.

More lavish, and expensive, is the *Eastcoaster Resort*, on Louisville Point Rd, four km north of the post office. (You catch the catamaran to Maria Island from here.)

TRIABUNNA (pop 870)

Just eight km north of Orford, Triabunna is a much larger town but with less to interest visitors. Located the end of a very sheltered inlet, it is a useful port and was a whaling station and military port in the penal era. Today it is the commercial centre of the region with woodchip processing, scallop and cray fishing being the major industries.

You can charter boats for fishing and cruising (☎ 6257 1137 or 6223 6366), take a scenic flight with Salmon Air (☎ 6257 3186) or go bushwalking or horse riding at Woodstock Farm (☎ 6257 3186).

Places to Stay & Eat

The *Triabunna Caravan Park* (☎ 6257 3575), on the corner of Vicary and Melbourne Sts, has camp sites ($8) and on-site vans ($25 double). The *Triabunna Youth Hostel* (☎ 6257 3439), in Spencer St, is in a quiet, farmland setting where you can stay for $10 a night ($12 nonmembers). The *Spring Bay Hotel*, in Charles St by the jetty, has rooms at $30/50 and good, cheap evening meals.

MARIA ISLAND NATIONAL PARK

In 1971 Maria Island was declared a wildlife sanctuary and a year later became a national park. It's popular with birdwatchers, being the only national park in Tasmania where you can see 11 of the state's native bird species. Forester kangaroos, Cape Barren geese and emus are a common sight during the day.

This peaceful island features some magnificent scenery, including fossil-studded sandstone and limestone cliffs; beautiful white, sandy beaches; forests; and fern gullies. There are some lovely walks on the island, including the Bishop & Clerk Mountain Walk and the historical Fossil Cliffs Nature Walk; brochures are available for both. The marine life around the island is also diverse and plentiful, and for those with the equipment, the scuba diving is spectacular.

Historically, Maria Island is also very interesting – from 1825 to 1832, the settlement of **Darlington** was Tasmania's second penal colony (the first was Sarah Island near Strahan). The remains of the penal village, including the commissariat store (1825) and the mill house (1846), are remarkably well preserved and easy to visit; in fact, you'll probably end up staying in one of the old buildings. There are no shops on the island so don't forget to bring your own supplies. A current national park pass is required.

Places to Stay

The rooms in the penitentiary at Darlington and some of the other buildings have been converted into bunkhouses for visitors. These are called the *Parks, Wildlife & Heritage Penitentiary Units* (☎ 6257 1420) and cost $8 a night, but it's wise to book as the beds are sometimes taken by school groups. There is also a camping ground at Darlington for $4 per adult.

Getting There & Away

The Eastcoaster Express (☎ 6257 1589) is operated by the Eastcoaster Resort, Louisville Point Rd, four km north of the Orford post office. It has three services a day between the resort and Maria Island, with an extra service daily during December to April. The return fare is $16 for day visitors ($10 children) and $19 ($12) for campers.

SWANSEA (pop 440)

On the shores of Great Oyster Bay, with superb views across to the Freycinet Peninsula, Swansea is a popular place for camping, boating, fishing and surfing. It was first settled in the 1820s and is the administrative centre for Glamorgan, Australia's oldest rural municipality.

Swansea has a number of interesting historic buildings including the original **council chambers**, which are still in use, and the lovely red-brick **Morris' General Store**, built in 1838. The community centre dates from 1860 and houses a **museum of local history** and the only oversized billiard table in Australia. The museum is open Monday to Saturday and admission is $3 (50 cents children).

The **Swansea Bark Mill & East Coast Museum**, at 96 Tasman Highway, is also worth a look. The restored mill displays working models of equipment used in the processing of black-wattle bark, a basic ingredient used in the tanning of heavy leathers. The adjoining museum features displays of Swansea's early history, including some superb old photographs. It's open daily from 9 am to 5 pm and admission is $5 ($2.75 children).

Places to Stay & Eat

The *Swansea Caravan Park* (☎ 6257 8177) in Shaw St, just by the beach, is very clean and has good services. Camp sites cost $10 and cabins are $35 to $45 double.

The *Swansea Youth Hostel* (☎ 6257 8367), at 5 Franklin St, is in a lovely spot near the sea, although it's not a particularly attractive building. It charges $10 ($12 non-members), and in the busy summer season priority is given to YHA members.

More appealing is the *Central Swansea Backpackers* (☎ 6257 8399), at 20 Franklin St. It's in an attractive old house in the main street, and the charge is $12 per person. It also runs a boat tour across to Freycinet for $15 ($9 child) per person return.

Also in Franklin St, almost opposite the youth hostel, is the *Oyster Bay Guest House* (☎ 6257 8110), which was built in 1836 and offers friendly colonial accommodation at $70 for doubles with a cooked breakfast.

Just Maggies, at 26 Franklin St, has coffee, cakes and light lunches, but for breakfast go to the *Swansea Cafe*, on the corner of Victoria and Franklin Sts. The cafe is also a diner serving counter meals at reasonable prices. For something special try the licensed *Shy Albatross Restaurant* in the Oyster Bay Guest House.

Getting There & Away

Hobart Coaches has a morning service from Hobart to Swansea ($15) on Wednesday, Friday and Sunday and to Bicheno for $19. There's also an afternoon service on weekdays. During January and February, there's an additional morning service on Saturday.

Redline operates an afternoon service on weekdays from Hobart and Launceston to Swansea and Bicheno for under $20. On weekdays, Peakes Coach Service runs a daily bus between Swansea and St Marys for $8 via Bicheno.

COLES BAY & FREYCINET NATIONAL PARK

The small township of Coles Bay is dominated by the spectacular 300-metre-high, pink granite mountains known as the **Hazards**. The town is the gateway to many white-sand beaches, secluded coves, rocky cliffs and excellent bushwalks in the **Freycinet National Park**.

The park, incorporating Freycinet Peninsula, beautiful Schouten Island and the Friendly Beaches (on the east coast north of Coles Bay), is noted for its coastal heaths, orchids and other wildflowers and for its wildlife, including black cockatoos, yellow wattlebirds, honeyeaters and Bennetts wallabies. Walks include a 27-km circuit of the peninsula plus many other shorter tracks, one of the most beautiful being the return walk to **Wineglass Bay**, which takes 2½ to three hours. On any walk remember to sign in (and sign out) at the registration booth at the car park. A current national parks pass is also required.

On the road in to Coles Bay, look for

Moulting Lagoon Game Reserve, which is a breeding ground for black swans and wild ducks.

Information
The post office/store is open daily and sells groceries, basic supplies and petrol. It also has a newsagency and boat hire. The Iluka Holiday Centre has its own mini supermarket, takeaway food and petrol.

Places to Stay
Coles Bay offers a variety of accommodation to suit all travel budgets.

The national park camping ground (☎ 6257 0107) stretches along Richardsons Beach and has sites for $8 for two people. Bookings can be made at the rangers' office, but during peak periods, such as school holidays, it is essential to book well in advance. Facilities are basic – pit toilets and cold water – there are no hot showers!

The *Coles Bay Caravan Park* (☎ 6257 0100) is three km by road from Coles Bay at the western end of Muir's Beach. Sites cost $11 for two and on-site vans are $30.

Freycinet Backpackers (☎ 6257 0115), on Coles Bay Rd, has dormitory-style accommodation for $14 per person. The *Coles Bay Youth Hostel*, actually in the national park, is mainly used by groups and must be booked at the YHA head office in Hobart (☎ 6234 9617). Keys are obtained from the Iluka Holiday Centre.

The *Iluka Holiday Centre* (☎ 6257 0115) on Muir's Beach has the cheapest accommodation in Coles Bay itself. This place is not as well kept as it might be, however it has a variety of on-site vans ($30), cabins ($45) and camp sites ($10).

There are a number of private shacks and cabins for rent, and these are probably the best deal for a group. *Pine Lodge Cabins* (☎ 6257 0113) in Harold St charges $50 per cabin, and *Jessie's Cottage* (☎ 6257 0143), on the Esplanade by the general store, $60 with a one-night surcharge.

Surrounded by the national park is *Freycinet Lodge* (☎ 6257 0101) at the southern end of Richardsons Beach. Rooms cost around $130 a double, and there are some with disabled access. A few rooms also have spas, which unfortunately only exacerbate the town's chronic water problems. Park entry fees are paid by the lodge for guests.

The scenery at the free camp sites of Wineglass Bay (one to 1½ hours), Hazards Beach (two to three hours) and Cooks Beach (about 4½ hours) is well worth the walk. There's little reliable drinking water at any of these sites, and little elsewhere on the peninsula, so you'll normally need to carry your own.

Places to Eat
Eating options are limited. The *Captains Table* restaurant and takeaway has a variety of reasonably priced meals and is open daily for lunch and dinner. More expensive is the *Freycinet* restaurant at the Freycinet Lodge, but the views are superb. Other than that it's a matter of putting your own food together. The general store is pretty well stocked, and the kiosk at Iluka also has some supplies.

Getting There & Away
Redline and Hobart Coaches can drop you at the Coles Bay turn off en route to Bicheno and you can hitch the 28 km from there but, depending on the season, traffic may be light. Bicheno Coach Services (☎ 6257 0293) runs at least two buses each weekday between Coles Bay and Bicheno, and one on Saturday. In Bicheno, buses depart from the newsagency in Foster St, and in Coles Bay from the general store; tickets are $5 per person and $2.50 for a bicycle.

It is more than five km from the town to the national park's car park (where the walking tracks start), and Bicheno Coach Services has a weekday shuttle bus. You must book however. The cost is $2 return. It leaves the general store at 9.40 am, and departs from the car park for the return trip at 10 am.

BICHENO (pop 730)
In the early 1800s, whalers and sealers used Bicheno's narrow harbour, called the Gulch, to shelter their boats. They also built lookouts in the hills to watch for passing whales.

These days, fishing is still one of the town's major occupations, and if you are down at the Gulch around lunchtime, when all the fishing boats return, you can buy fresh crayfish, abalone, oysters or anything else caught that night straight from the boats. Tourism is also very important to Bicheno and it has an information centre in the main street at which you can book tours and hire bikes. Bicheno has beautiful beaches and is a lovely spot to visit for a few days.

Things to See & Do

An interesting three-km **foreshore walkway** from Redbill Point to the blowhole continues south around the beach to Courlands Bay. You can also walk up to the **Whalers Lookout** and the **Freycinet Lookout** for good views.

At nightfall you may be lucky enough to see the fairy penguins at the northern end of Redbill Beach and at low tide you can walk out to **Diamond Island**, opposite the youth hostel.

The Dive Centre (☎ 6375 1138), opposite the Sea Life Centre on the foreshore, runs courses which are more reasonably priced than those in warmer waters, and you can also hire or buy diving equipment from its shop.

The **Sea Life Centre** is open daily from 9 am to 5 pm and features Tasmanian marine life swimming behind glass windows. There's also a restored trading ketch, but at $4.50 for admission, the centre is rather overpriced and a bit depressing. Seven km north of town is the 32-hectare **East Coast Birdlife & Animal Park**, which is open daily from 9 am to 5.30 pm; admission is $6.50.

Just a couple of km north of the animal park is the turn off to the **Douglas-Apsley National Park**. The park was proclaimed in 1989 and protects a large and undisturbed sclerophyll forest. It has a number of waterfalls and gorges, and birds and animals are prolific. There's road access to the **Apsley Gorge** in the south of the park, where there's a water hole with excellent swimming. You can walk the north-south trail through the park in a couple of days.

Places to Stay

The *Bicheno Cabin & Tourist Park* (☎ 6375 1117), in Champ St, has camp sites ($10.50) and expensive on-site vans ($40). The *Bicheno Caravan Park* (☎ 6375 1280), on the corner of Burgess and Tribe Sts, charges $8 a double for a camp site and $28 a double for an on-site van.

A more comfortable option is the *Bicheno Hostel* in Morrison St charging $13 per person. It is centrally located and much newer than the youth hostel. The *Bicheno Youth Hostel* (☎ 6375 1293) is in a lovely location three km north of town on the beach opposite Diamond Island, but this is its only redeeming feature. It's $9.50 a night ($11.50 for nonmembers). Bookings during the summer period are recommended.

The *Silver Sands Resort* (☎ 6375 1266), at the end of Burgess St, has rooms ranging from $50 to $75, the latter with good views of the bay.

Places to Eat

In the main shopping centre, there's the *Galleon Coffee Shop*, which has the usual takeaway meals; pizza is served Thursday to Saturday. Next door is *Rose's Coffee Lounge*, which is open daily from 8.30 am. It serves reasonably priced breakfasts as well as light meals, cake and coffee. The bakery also has a coffee shop.

The *Silver Sands Resort* restaurant has seafood and grills from $10 to $16. Also in Burgess St is *Cyrano* restaurant which specialises in seafood and French cuisine. On the Tasman Highway, the *Longboat Tavern* has good counter meals.

Getting There & Away

For information on the Bicheno services run by Redline, Hobart Coaches and Peakes Coach Service, see the Getting There & Away section for Swansea.

ST MARYS (pop 650)

St Marys is a charming little town, 10 km inland from the coast, near the Mt Nicholas range. There's not much to do except enjoy the peacefulness of the countryside, visit a number of waterfalls in the area, and take walks in the state forest.

Places to Stay & Eat

The *St Marys Youth Hostel* (☎ 6372 2341), on a working sheep farm called Seaview, is surrounded by state forest. It's at the end of a dirt track, eight km from St Marys on German Town Rd, and commands magnificent views of the coast, ocean and mountains. It costs $10 a night ($30 for a double room) and the warden will pick you up from the post office between 10 and 11 am any day, except Sunday, if you phone.

Accommodation is also available in the *St Marys Hotel* (☎ 6372 2181), where singles/doubles cost $28/52. The pub also has counter meals.

Getting There & Away

Peakes operates between St Marys and Swansea for $8 and Bicheno for $4. Redline has one service from Launceston and another from Hobart every day except Saturday – both continue to St Helens.

North-East

The north-east corner of the state is worth a visit as it's off the normal tourist route. It can be very scenic and quiet with long beach and bush walks around St Helens and in the Mt William National Park. There are also some attractions to visit, such as the Tin Mine Centre in Derby and the Lavender Farm in Nabowla. It also has the 'worst little pub in Tassie' and the lovely coastal town of St Helens.

SCAMANDER (pop 410)

Scamander township is stretched along some of the loveliest, white-sand beaches on the east coast and these are protected in a coastal reserve. You can take long walks along the beach or hire a dingy and go fishing in the river.

Places to Stay & Eat

The *Kookaburra Caravan & Camping Ground*, 1.5 km north of the river, is very reasonably priced with sites for $9 for two and cabins at $25. It's only a short walk to the beach. The *Scamander Beach Resort Hotel* (☎ 6372 5255) is an imposing, three-storey building with good views and charges $75 a double.

There are not too many places to eat. Try *Home for Tea* for afternoon teas and snacks, the hotel, or *Bensons* for restaurant meals; otherwise bring your own food.

ST HELENS (pop 1200)

St Helens, on Georges Bay, is the largest town on the east coast. First settled in 1830, this old whaling town has an interesting and varied history which is recorded in the **history room**, at 59 Cecilia St, adjacent to the town's library. It's open weekdays from 9 am to 4 pm and admission is $3.

Today, St Helens is Tasmania's largest fishing port, with a big fleet based in the bay. Visitors can charter boats for offshore game fishing or just take a lazy cruise.

While the beaches in town are not particularly good for swimming, there are excellent scenic beaches at **Binalong Bay** (10 km from St Helens), **Sloop Rock** (12 km) and **Stieglitz** (seven km), as well as at St Helens and Humbug points. You can also visit **St Columba Falls**, near Pyengana, 24 km away.

There are three banks in town and EFTPOS facilities are available at the service stations and supermarkets.

Places to Stay & Eat

The *St Helens Caravan Park* (☎ 6376 1290) is just out of town, south of the bridge on Penelope St. Camp sites are $12, on-site vans $30 and cabins $45 for two persons.

The *St Helens Youth Hostel* (☎ 6376 1661), at 5 Cameron St, is in a lovely, quiet spot by the beach and charges $11 a night. The *Artnor Lodge* (☎ 6376 1234), in Cecilia St, is a comfortable guesthouse charging $35/45 with continental breakfast. For self-catering accommodation, try *Queechy*

Cottages (☎ 6376 1321), on the highway about a km south of the centre. Units for four to six people, with ocean views, cost $50 a double.

In the main street, *Arthur's Hot Bread Kitchen* has good-value pies and cakes and friendly service. You can eat in and enjoy a coffee, or take away. *Trimbole's Pizza*, in Circassian St, has good pizza and pasta.

Getting There & Away
Hobart Coaches runs a winter service on Wednesday, Friday and Sunday from Hobart to St Helens and operates more frequently in summer ($27), but not on Tuesday. Redline has daily (except Saturday) connections to Launceston ($17). The Redline agent in St Helens is the newsagency in Cecilia St. During the week you can get to St Marys or Derby (to connect with the Redline bus to Launceston) with the Suncoast Bus Service.

WELDBOROUGH
The Weldborough Pass, with its mountain scenery and dense rainforests, is quite spectacular. During the tin-mining boom last century, hundreds of Chinese migrated to Tasmania and many made Weldborough their base. The joss house now in Launceston's Queen Victoria Museum & Art Gallery was built in Weldborough.

The *Weldborough Hotel*, the town's only pub, also calls itself the 'worst little pub in Tassie' and has, among other things, 'leprechaun pee soup' and 'leeches and cream' on the menu, but don't be put off – it's quite a nice place to stop for a drink.

GLADSTONE
About 25 km off the Tasman Highway, between St Helens and Scottsdale, is the tiny town of Gladstone. It was one of the last tin-mining centres in north-eastern Tasmania, until the mine closed in 1982. The area also had a number of mining communities and a large Chinese population. Today, many old mining settlements are just ghost towns, and Gladstone shows signs of heading in the same direction.

Twelve km from Gladstone is the popular

Mt William National Park, where you can see many Forester kangaroos. The park also has some excellent beaches – Picnic Rocks is a good surf beach – and there are good bushwalks along beaches and fire trails. The return walk to the summit of Mt William is around three km. It's a gentle climb and takes about 1½ hours. There are several bush camp sites with pit toilets and bore water, but you'll need to carry drinking water. The **Eddystone Lighthouse**, built in 1887, is within the park boundary. For more information, phone the rangers' office (☎ 6357 2108). National park entry fees apply.

DERBY
In 1874, tin was discovered in Derby and, due mainly to the Briseis Tin Mine, this little township flourished throughout the late 19th century. Today Derby is a classified historic town and some of the old mine buildings are now part of the excellent **Tin Mine Centre**, which features a mine museum of old photographs and mining implements, and a re-creation of an old mining shanty town. The centre is open from 10 am to 4 pm and admission is $4 ($1.50 children).

Derby comes alive in late October when several thousand people arrive for the annual Derby River Derby, a five-km course for all sorts of inflatable craft.

Places to Stay & Eat
The *Dorset Hotel* (☎ 6354 2360) has singles/doubles for $28/45 with breakfast, and also does good counter meals. The *Crib Shed Tea Rooms* (part of the mine museum) serves delicious scones.

Six km from Winnaleah, near Derby, is the peaceful *Merlinkei Home Hostel* (☎ 6354 2152), which charges $10 a night ($12 non-members). You can ring from Winnaleah and the manager will pick you up. Being a dairy farm, it has an unlimited supply of fresh milk, and hostellers can help around the farm.

Getting There & Away
On weekdays, Redline has two services daily from Launceston to Derby via Scottsdale

($11). There's only one service on Sunday, and none on Saturday. The Redline agent is the general store in Derby's main street. On weekdays, you can get to St Helens and Winnaleah with the Suncoast Bus Service.

SCOTTSDALE (pop 2090)

Scottsdale, the major town in the north-east, serves some of Tasmania's richest agricultural and forestry country, and its setting is quite beautiful. A camp site at the nearby *Scottsdale Camping Ground* (☎ 6352 2176) charges $5.

Of the two hotels in town, accommodation is cheapest ($20/30 a single/ double) at *Lords Hotel* (☎ 6352 2319), 2 King St. For bus services to Scottsdale, see the Getting There & Away section for Derby.

AROUND SCOTTSDALE

At Nabowla, 21 km west of Scottsdale, is the **Bridestowe Lavender Farm**. It's open daily during the spectacular flowering season from mid-December to late January and admission is $3. At other times it's open weekdays only and entry is free.

Twenty-one km north of Scottsdale is the popular beach resort of **Bridport**, where there's plenty of accommodation. From there, it's another 45 km to the unspoiled beaches and great diving and snorkelling at **Tomahawk**.

To get to Bridport, you can take a local bus from Scottsdale; buses depart twice daily on weekdays from the Redline stop in Scottsdale. You'll need your own transport to visit Tomahawk.

Launceston

Population 69,750

Officially founded by Lieutenant-Colonel William Paterson in 1805, Launceston is Australia's third-oldest city and the commercial centre of northern Tasmania.

The Tamar River estuary was explored in 1798 by Bass and Flinders, who were both attempting to circumnavigate Van Diemen's Land to show that it was not joined to the rest of Australia. Launceston was the third attempt at a settlement on the river and was originally called Patersonia, after its founder. In 1907, the city was renamed in honour of Governor King, who was born in Launceston, England, a town settled 1000 years before on the Tamar River in the county of Cornwall.

Orientation

The city centre is arranged in a grid pattern around the Brisbane St Mall, between Charles and St John Sts. Two blocks north, in Cameron St, there's another pedestrian mall called Civic Square. To the east is Yorktown Square, a charming and lively area of restored buildings which have been turned into shops and restaurants. Launceston's main attractions are all within walking distance of the centre.

Information

The Tasmanian Travel & Information Centre (☎ 6336 3119), on the corner of St John and Paterson Sts, is open weekdays from 9 am to 5 pm, and Saturday and public holidays (and Sunday during the high season) from 9 am to noon. There's a Tasmap Centre, at Henty House in Civic Square, where detailed maps are available. Information is also available on radio by tuning into 99.3 FM.

For camping gear there's Paddy Pallin, at 110 George St, and Allgoods, on the corner of York and St John Sts – both are excellent. If you're in town at the weekend, there's a craft market in Yorktown Square every Sunday.

Cataract Gorge

Only a 10-minute walk from the city centre is the magnificent Cataract Gorge. Here, almost vertical cliffs line the banks of the South Esk River as it enters the Tamar. The area around the gorge has been made a wildlife reserve and is one of Launceston's most popular tourist attractions.

Two walking tracks, one on either side of the gorge, lead up to **First Basin**, which is

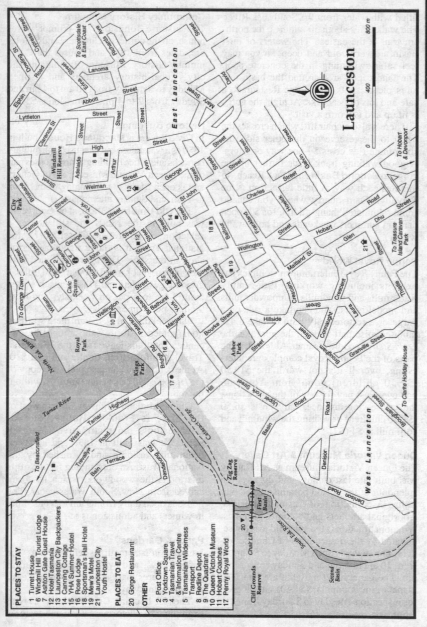

Launceston

PLACES TO STAY

1   Turret House
6   Windmill Hill Tourist Lodge
7   Ashton Gate Guest House
12 Hotel Tasmania
13 Launceston City Backpackers
14 Canning Cottage
15 YHA Summer Hostel
16 Rose Lodge
18 Sportsman's Hall Hotel
19 Mew's Motel
21 Launceston City
    Youth Hostel

PLACES TO EAT

20 Gorge Restaurant

OTHER

2   Post Office
3   Yorktown Square
4   Tasmanian Travel
    & Information Centre
5   Tasmanian Wilderness
    Transport
8   Redline Depot
9   The Quadrant
10 Queen Victoria Museum
11 Hobart Coaches
17 Penny Royal World

filled with water from the South Esk River. The walk takes about 30 minutes; the northern trail is the easiest. The waters of First Basin are very cold and deep, so you may feel safer swimming in the concrete pool. The landscaped area around the basin features picnic spots, the Gorge Restaurant, a cafe and lots of peacocks. At night the gorge is lit up and is worth a visit.

There's also a chair lift, which crosses the basin to the reserve on the other side; the six-minute ride costs $4 one way or return. A good walking track leads farther up the gorge to **Second Basin** and Duck Reach, 45 minutes each way. A little farther on is the Trevallyn Dam quarry where you can do some 'simulated' hang-gliding for $7 (open daily in summer; weekends and holidays in winter).

Penny Royal World

The Penny Royal entertainment complex has exhibits including working 19th-century water mills and windmills, gunpowder mills and model boats. You can take a ride on a barge or a restored city tram or take a 45-minute cruise part-way up the gorge on the *Lady Stelfox* paddle-steamer. Although some parts of the Penny Royal complex are interesting, overall it's not worth the $19.50 ($9.50 children) admission. You can, however, just pay for one of the attractions; the cruise, for instance, only costs $6.50 ($3.50 children) or visiting the windmill and corn mill is $4 ($2).

Queen Victoria Museum & Art Gallery

The Queen Victoria Museum & Art Gallery was built late last century and displays the splendour of the period both inside and out. It has a collection of Tasmanian fauna, Aboriginal artefacts and colonial paintings. A major attraction is the splendid joss house, donated by the descendants of Chinese settlers. The centre is open Monday to Saturday from 10 am to 5 pm and Sunday from 2 to 5 pm. The gallery and museum are free. The planetarium is popular ($1.50) and is open for inspection Tuesday to Saturday from 2 to 3 pm.

Community History Museum

The historic Johnstone & Wilmot warehouse, on the corner of Cimitiere and St John Sts, dates from 1842 and houses the Community History Museum. It contains the city's local-history archives and is open Monday to Saturday from 10 am to 4 pm and Sunday from 2 to 4 pm; admission is $1.

Historic Buildings

In Civic Square is **Macquarie House**, built in 1830 as a warehouse but later used as a military barracks and office building. It now houses part of the Queen Victoria Museum & Art Gallery and is open Monday to Saturday from 10 am to 4 pm, and Sunday afternoons.

The **Old Umbrella Shop**, at 60 George St, was built in the 1860s and still houses a selection of umbrellas. Classified by the National Trust, it is the last genuine period shop in the state. The interior is lined with Tasmanian blackwood timber, and sells a good range of National Trust items. It's open from 9 am to 5 pm on weekdays and from 9 am to noon on Saturday.

On weekdays at 9.45 am there's a one-hour guided historic walk around the city centre. The tours leave from the Tasmanian Travel & Information Centre and cost $10. At the centre you can also pick up a copy of the *Historic Walks* brochure and do it without the tour.

On the Midland Highway, six km west of the city, is **Franklin House**, one of Launceston's most attractive Georgian homes. It was built in 1838 and has been beautifully restored and furnished by the National Trust. An outstanding feature of its interior is the woodwork, which was carved from New South Wales cedar. The house is open daily from 9 am to 5 pm (4 pm in winter) and admission is $5.

Parks & Gardens

Launceston is sometimes referred to as 'the garden city', and with so many beautiful public squares, parks and reserves, it's easy to understand why.

The 13-hectare **City Park** is a fine example of a Victorian garden and features an elegant fountain, a bandstand, a monkey and wallaby enclosure and a conservatory. **Princes Square**, between Charles and St John Sts, features a bronze fountain bought at the 1858 Paris Exhibition.

Other public parks and gardens include **Royal Park**, near the junction between the North Esk and Tamar rivers; the **Punchbowl Reserve**, with its magnificent rhododendron garden; **Windmill Hill Reserve**; the **Trevallyn Recreation Area** and the Cataract Gorge (see earlier).

Other Attractions

The **Design Centre of Tasmania**, on the corner of Brisbane and Tamar Sts, is a retail outlet displaying work by the state's top artists and craftspeople.

The **Waverley Woollen Mills & National Automobile Museum** are on Waverley Rd, five km from the city centre. The mills were established in 1874 and are the oldest operating woollen mills in Australia. Both places are open daily from 9 am to 5 pm; admission to each is $4.

The **Tamar Knitting Mills**, founded in 1926, are at 21 Hobart Rd and can also be inspected. They are open daily from 9 am to 4 pm; admission is $1.

Organised Tours

Tasmanian Redline Coaches (☎ 6331 3233) in George St has half and full-day tours of the Tamar Valley ($39), the north-west coast ($32), the north-east ($40) and Cradle Mountain ($39). Tasmanian Wilderness Transport has tours to Evandale Market on Sunday ($20), Tamar Valley ($35), Cradle Mountain ($40) and the Mole Creek caves ($42). For something unusual try the tour to private country homes and gardens that is organised by Behind the Colonial Gate (☎ 6334 4065). The tour costs $55, including lunch.

Places to Stay

Camping The *Treasure Island Caravan Park* (☎ 6344 2600) is in Glen Dhu St, one km south of the city beside the expressway. It has camp sites ($11) and cabins ($42). As this is the only caravan park in Launceston, it can get crowded at times, and being right next to the highway is quite noisy.

Hostels The smoke-free *Launceston City Backpackers* (☎ 6334 2327), at 173 George St, is in the centre of town. It's an old house which has been thoughtfully renovated, and the cost is $14 per person in four-bed rooms.

The *Launceston City Youth Hostel* (☎ 6344 9779), which is not a YHA hostel, is at 36 Thistle St, two km from the centre of town. It has dorm beds and family rooms for $12 a night. The building dates from the 1940s and used to be the canteen for the Coats Patons woollen mill. The hostel has mountain and touring bikes for hire as well as a comprehensive selection of bushwalking gear.

Other hostels regularly appear and vanish the next season. At present the YHA runs a summer-only hostel (☎ 6334 4505) at 132 Elizabeth St; advance bookings can be made through the Hobart YHA office.

Guesthouses The *Rose Lodge* (☎ 6334 0120), 270 Brisbane St, provides friendly service and small but comfortable rooms with a cooked breakfast for $65 a double.

The *Mews Motel* (☎ 6331 2861), 89 Margaret St, is closer to a guesthouse than a motel and is also reasonably priced at $55 a double.

On the other side of the city, the *Windmill Hill Tourist Lodge* (☎ 6331 9337), at 22 High St, charges $47/57. The lodge also has self-contained holiday flats at $65 a double. A bit closer to town at 32 Brisbane St, the *Maldon* provides good rooms in a grand Victorian building for $70 a double.

If you can afford the extra, there are some great guesthouses offering rather luxurious colonial accommodation, such as the cosy *Ashton Gate Guest House* (☎ 6331 6180) on top of the hill at 32 High St. With a cooked breakfast the cost is $60/80 for singles/doubles or $90 for the best rooms. *Turret House* (☎ 6334 7033), 41 West Tamar Rd, is similar with B&B for $60/90. This is out of town, north of Cataract Gorge.

Another place with a history is the *Old Bakery Inn* (☎ 6331 7900) on the corner of York and Margaret Sts. It dates back to 1870 and charges $62/79.

For something really different, you could try renting your own fully furnished two-bedroom colonial cottage. The *Canning Cottage* (☎ 63314876) is actually two separate cottages at 26-28 Canning St. Both are very cosy and there are lots of steep steps and narrow doorways; these are original cottages. The cost is a very reasonable $75 for a double with breakfast.

Hotels Launceston has a good selection of hotels for a town of its size. One of the cheapest and quietest is the *Sportsman's Hall Hotel* (☎ 6331 3968), at 252 Charles St, where singles/doubles cost $28/40, including breakfast.

Close by, at 191 Charles St, is the *Hotel Tasmania* (☎ 6331 7355), which is better known as the Saloon. The rooms have a fridge and telephone and cost $45/55, including breakfast.

If you really want to be pampered then try the *Country Club Casino* (☎ 6444 8855) at Prospect Vale, five km south of the city. Rooms are $198 a double, plus whatever extra cash you might need for those gaming tables.

Motels & Holiday Flats The *Riverside Motel* (☎ 6327 2522), 407 West Tamar Rd, is a little out of town near Cataract Gorge and charges $60 a double for rooms with breakfast. An attractive but pricey place in town is the *Colonial Motor Inn*, with rooms for $120 a double.

Although a little difficult to find, *Clarke Holiday House* (☎ 6334 2237), at 19 Neika Ave, is about one km out of town and is good value with rooms at $35 a double.

Places to Eat
Banjo's bakes all its own bread, pizza and cakes, and has two shops in town, one in Yorktown Square and one at 98 Brisbane St; both are open daily from 6 am to 6 pm. At Yorktown Square, *Molly York's Coffee Shoppe* is another fine place for breakfast and lunch.

For lunch there are some good-value places around the Quadrant in the city. The best bargain has to be *Pasta Resistance Too* with serves at $4 to $7. Its a tiny place that's packed full of customers. In a side lane the *Muffin Kitchen* is also worth finding and provides some interesting light meals. For somewhere more peaceful try the nearby 1st-floor *Crows Nest Coffee Shoppe*. Meals range from $7 to $10.

The *Konditorei Cafe Manfred* has delicious, inexpensive home-made German rolls and pastries. It's at 95 George St, near the Redline depot, and is a good place to sit while waiting for a bus.

Ripples Restaurant, in the Ritchies Mill Art Centre opposite Penny Royal, specialises in light meals such as crêpes and pancakes, and there's a lovely view of the boats on the Tamar River from the outdoor tables.

Most of Launceston's many hotels have filling, reasonably priced counter meals and the most popular is *Barnaby's* on the corner of Wellington and York Sts. There are over 30 main courses many of which are the same fare offered in different sizes. Prices range from $7 to $14. *O'Keefes Hotel* at 124 George St is another popular pub for meals.

There are a few good restaurants in Launceston charging $10 to $16 for a main course. One of the most popular is *Calabrisella Pizza* (☎ 6331 1958), 56 Wellington St, which serves excellent Italian food and is often packed, so bookings are advisable. It opens daily, except Tuesday, at 5 pm and usually closes at midnight. You can also get takeaway pizza.

La Cantina, in George St beside Yorktown Square, is a popular licensed restaurant with Italian food and pasta dishes from $10 to $18. *Arpar's Thai Restaurant* on the corner of Charles and Paterson Sts is well worth a visit; main courses cost around $12.

For Chinese food try the *Canton*, at 201 Charles St; it's one of the best moderately priced Chinese restaurants in town. The *Golden Sea Dragon*, at 97 Canning St on the edge of town, has an elaborate interior but reasonable prices.

Also good for Tasmanian wines (and excellent meals) is the *Owl's Nest* at 147 Paterson St, next to the Penny Royal complex. The *Gorge Restaurant*, at Cataract Gorge, has fairly good food and undoubtedly the best setting in Launceston with main courses for $15 to $20.

For up-market eating try *Shrimps*, at 72 George St, for seafood and an intimate atmosphere. For French dining try the rather expensive *Elm Cottage* at 168 Charles St. Launceston's Japanese restaurant is the *Tairyo*, on Yorktown Square, where mains are $14 to $22.

Entertainment

There's quite a good range of evening entertainment in Launceston, most of which is advertised either in the free *Launceston Week* newspaper or in *This Week in Tasmania*.

The *Pavilion Tavern* in Yorktown Square has music Tuesday to Saturday nights and a cabaret-style nightclub. The *Saloon* at 191 Charles St provides dancing in a trendy wild-west setting. The *Royal Hotel*, in George St, is another popular venue for live bands Wednesday to Saturday nights. *O'Keefes Hotel* at 124 George St has live bands on Friday, Saturday and Sunday after 10 pm. *Alfresco's* is a wine bar in the Victoria Hotel, 211 Brisbane St, which is also a popular venue.

If you want to risk a few dollars, or just observe how the rich play, check out the *Launceston Federal Country Club Casino* at Prospect, 10 km from the city centre. Most big-name bands touring from the mainland usually perform here. You don't have to pay to get in and about the only article of clothing disapproved of these days is track shoes. The disco at the casino, *Regines*, is free.

Getting There & Away
Air For information on domestic flights to and from Launceston, see the Getting There & Away section at the beginning of this chapter. Ansett Airlines is at 54 Brisbane St, Qantas is based on the corner of Brisbane and

George Sts, and Airlines of Tasmania has an office at the airport.

Bus The main bus companies operating out of Launceston are Redline (☎ 6331 3233), 112 George St; Hobart Coaches (☎ 6334 3600), 174-180 Brisbane St; Tasmanian Wilderness Transport (☎ 6334 4442), 101 George St; and Tamar Valley Coaches (☎ 6334 0828), 26 Wellington St.

Both Redline and Hobart Coaches run buses to Deloraine ($6), Hobart ($17), Devonport ($12) and Burnie ($16) – fares quoted are Redline's. Redline also has services to Wynyard, Stanley, Smithton ($26), George Town ($6), St Marys ($14), St Helens ($17), Bicheno ($18) and Swansea ($15). Tasmanian Wilderness Transport has services to Ben Lomond during the ski season ($25) and to Cradle Mountain ($35) and Cynthia Bay ($45) during summer.

Car Rental There are plenty of car-rental firms in Launceston. Some of the cheaper ones are Apple Car Rentals (☎ 6343 3780), 192 Wellington St; Advance Car Rentals (☎ 6344 2164), 32 Cameron St; and Aberdeen Car Rentals (☎ 6344 5811), 35 Punchbowl Rd. Prices range from $25 to over $100 for a single hire day, less for longer rentals.

Getting Around
To/From the Airport Redline operates an airport shuttle service which meets all incoming flights and picks up passengers an hour or so before all departures. The fare is $6.60. By taxi it costs about $16 to get into the city.

Bus The local bus service is run by Metro, and the main departure points are the two blocks in St John St between Paterson and York Sts. For $2.50 you can buy an unlimited travel Day Rover ticket which can be used all day at weekends and between 9 am and 4.30 pm and after 6 pm on weekdays. Most routes, however, do not operate in the evenings, and Sunday services are limited.

Bicycle Rent-a-Cycle, at the Launceston City Youth Hostel (☎ 6344 9779), has a good range of 10-speed tourers and mountain bikes. The tourers cost $10 a day or $65 a week, including helmet and panniers; and the mountain bikes cost $95 a week. There's a reducing rate for each additional week, and a bond of $50 applies to all rentals.

Around Launceston

HADSPEN (pop 1390)

Eighteen km from Launceston and just west of Hadspen is **Entally House**, one of Tasmania's best-known historic homes. It was built in 1819 by Thomas Haydock Reibey but is now owned by the National Trust. Set in beautiful grounds, it creates a vivid picture of what life must have been like for the well-to-do on an early farming property. The home, its stables, church, coach house and grounds are open daily, admission is $5 ($3 children). The Reibeys have quite an interesting family history which you can read about in a brochure on sale at the property ($1.50).

On the roadside two km west of Hadspen is **Carrick Mill**, a lovely, ivy-covered bluestone mill, which dates from 1810 and has been well restored. On the side road near the mill the **Copper Art Gallery**, beside the dramatic ruins of the burnt-out two-storey Archers Folly, is well worth a visit. The art is unusual, there are no entry fees and all works are for sale.

Places to Stay & Eat

In Hadspen, on the corner of the Bass Highway and Main Rd, is the *Launceston Cabin & Tourist Park* (☎ 6393 6391). The park has good facilities and charges $9 for a camp site, $30 for an on-site van and $45 for well-equipped cabins. The *Red Feather Inn* (☎ 6393 6331), built in 1844, has a good restaurant with main meals for around $14.

LIFFEY VALLEY

The Liffey Valley State Reserve protects the

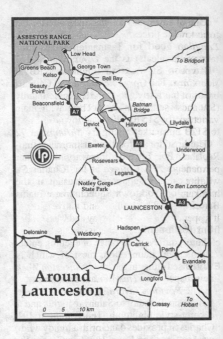

Around Launceston

beautiful rainforested valley at the foot of the Great Western Tiers and features the impressive **Liffey Valley Falls**. It's a popular destination for fishing and bushwalking, and day-trippers are also attracted by an amazing fernery.

The fernery, tearooms and gallery were built from wattle and pine. You can sit in the tearooms, enjoy freshly made scones and take in the view of Drys Bluff which, at 1297 metres, is the highest peak in the Great Western Tiers. The fernery and tearooms are open Wednesday to Sunday between 11 am and 5 pm but are closed during July. Liffey is 34 km south of Carrick, via Bracknell, and is a good day trip from Launceston.

LONGFORD (pop 2720)

Longford, a National Trust classified town, is 27 km from Launceston, in the rich pastoral area watered by the South Esk and Macquarie rivers.

One of the best ways to explore this historic town is to follow the National Trust's *Longford Walkabout* brochure, which will take you past many colonial buildings.

If you want to stay overnight, the *Riverside Caravan Park* (☎ 6391 1470), on the banks of the Macquarie River, has camp sites ($9) and on-site vans ($30). There are also a variety of B&B places around town for $80 to $120 a double.

The **Longford Wildlife Park**, on Pateena Rd, about 14 km from the town, provides a permanent conservation area for Tasmanian wildlife. The 70 hectares of bush and pasture has kangaroos, wallabies, echidnas, Cape Barren geese, wild ducks and native birds. It's open Tuesday to Thursday and weekends from 10 am to 5 pm; admission is $4 ($2 children).

EVANDALE (pop 800)
Evandale, 19 km south of Launceston in the South Esk Valley, is another town classified by the National Trust. Many of its 19th-century buildings are in excellent condition. In keeping with its old-world atmosphere, Evandale hosts the National Penny Farthing Championships in February each year, which attract national and international competitors. A market is held here every Sunday morning.

Eight km south of Evandale is the National Trust property of **Clarendon**, which was completed in 1838 and is one of the grandest Georgian mansions in Australia. The house and its formal gardens are open daily from 10 am to 5 pm (closing an hour earlier in winter) and admission is $5 ($3 children).

The **Clarendon Arms Hotel** has been licensed since 1847 and there are some interesting murals in the hall depicting the area's history. The locals may encourage you to see if you can spot the well-concealed rabbit in the stagecoach mural; have a go – it really is there!

Places to Stay & Eat
The old *Clarendon Arms Hotel* (☎ 6391 8181) has rooms from $25/35. Much more interesting is *Greg & Gill's Place* (☎ 6391

8248), which is in a quiet corner of town in a lovely garden setting. The cost is $65 for a double and includes a light breakfast.

There are a number of the ubiquitous tea-rooms-cum-galleries, such as *Russells Restaurant*, opposite the old bakery in Russell St. Meals here cost $10 to $14. The pubs around town provide the usual counter meals.

BEN LOMOND NATIONAL PARK
This 165-sq-km park, 50 km south-east of Launceston, includes the entire Ben Lomond Range and is best known for its good snow coverage and skiing facilities. During the ski season, a kiosk, tavern and restaurant are open in the alpine village and there's accommodation at the *Creek Inn* (☎ 6372 2444) from $59 upwards for B&B. Lift tickets and equipment hire cost about half what they do on the mainland.

The scenery at Ben Lomond is magnificent all year round and the park is particularly noted for its alpine wildflowers which run riot in spring and summer. The park's highest point is Legges Tor (1573 metres), which is also the second-highest peak in Tasmania. It can be reached via a good walking track from Carr Villa, on the slopes of Ben Lomond.

Getting There & Away
During the ski season, Tasmanian Wilderness Transport (☎ 6343 4442) has a daily return service ($25) between the ski fields and Launceston. It also runs a shuttle service from the bottom of Jacobs Ladder to the alpine village ($6 one way). The ladder is a very steep climb on an unsealed road with six hairpin bends and no safety barriers – parking below it is advised.

Tamar Valley & North Coast

The northern plains are actually gently rolling hills and farmlands which extend from the Tamar Valley north of Launceston west to the Great Western Tiers. There are some interesting towns and scenic spots and the best way to explore this area is to leave the highways and follow the quiet minor roads through the small towns. Most roads in this region are sealed.

The Tamar River separates the east and west Tamar districts and links Launceston with its ocean port of Bell Bay. Crossing the river near Deviot is Batman Bridge, the only bridge on the lower reaches of the Tamar. The river is tidal for the 64 km to Launceston and wends its way through some lovely orchards, pastures, forests and vineyards. Black swans inhabit the area.

The Tamar Valley and nearby Pipers River are among Tasmania's main wine-producing areas and the dry premium wines produced here are starting to achieve recognition.

European history in the region dates from 1798, when Bass and Flinders discovered the estuary and settlement commenced in 1804. Slowly the valley developed, despite resistance from the Aboriginal people, first as a port of call for sailors and sealers from the Bass Strait islands and then as a sanctuary for some of the desperate characters who took to the bush during the convict days. By the 1830s the Aboriginal people had vanished from their former hunting grounds.

In the late 1870s, gold was discovered at Cabbage Tree Hill – now Beaconsfield – and the fortunes of the valley took a new turn. The region boomed and for a time this was the third-largest town in Tasmania, before the mines closed in 1914.

Getting There & Away

On weekdays, Tamar Valley Coaches (☎ 6334 0828) has at least one bus a day along the West Tamar Highway, but there are no weekend services.

On most weekdays Redline has three buses a day up the East Tamar Valley between Launceston and George Town. The service extends to Low Head if advance bookings are made. On Sunday, there is a single service each way in the evenings. There are no Saturday services.

ROSEVEARS

This is a tiny riverside settlement on a side road off the West Tamar Highway. The main attraction is the **Waterbird Haven Trust**, a sanctuary for marine birds ($4). B&B is available beside the haven for $50 a double.

The other feature here is the Strathblynn Wine Centre. This is an outlet for Pipers Brook and tastings are free. Light lunches are also available at the centre.

BEACONSFIELD (pop 1090)

The once-thriving gold-mining town of Beaconsfield is still dominated by the ruins of its three original mine buildings. Two of these house the **Grubb Shaft Museum** complex, which is open daily from 10 am to 4 pm; entry is $3. It is staffed by volunteers and is worth the visit. A free display opposite the mine buildings has a reconstruction of a miner's cottage and old school. Beaconsfield Gold Mines has opened up the old Hart shaft next to the museum, and with today's technology is hoping to strike some of the town's still plentiful gold reserves.

The town has two bakeries and an unusual takeaway counter hidden in the back of the supermarket. The *Club Hotel* offers basic rooms if you need a place to stay.

AROUND BEACONSFIELD

Farther north is picturesque **Beauty Point**, the site of the Australian Maritime College. The *Redbill Point Van Park* provides tent sites for $8 and on-site vans for $25. Hotel and motel rooms are available around the town for $40 to $60.

At the mouth of the Tamar River, the quiet holiday and fishing resorts of **Greens Beach** and **Kelso** have good beaches and caravan parks.

GEORGE TOWN (pop 5025)

George Town is on the eastern shore of the Tamar River close to the heads. It is best known as the site where Colonel Paterson landed in 1804, leading to the settlement of northern Tasmania. Although these days the town gets relatively few visitors, there are some interesting attractions in George Town and the surrounding area.

Just north of the town is Low Head which provides the navigation aids for ships to enter the river. The **pilot station** at Low Head, dating from 1835, is the oldest in Australia and houses an interesting **maritime museum**, and a good cafe which is open daily; admission is $2. There are several navigational lead lights (miniature lighthouses) around town which date from 1881. There is good surf at **East Beach** on Bass Strait, and safe swimming in the river.

In Cimitiere St, the **Grove** is a lovely Georgian stone residence dating from the 1830s which has been classified by the National Trust. It's open daily from 10 am to 5 pm and admission is $3 (children $1). Refreshments are available and lunch is served by staff in period costume.

The **old watch house** in Macquarie St dates from 1843 and has been turned into a museum; it's open on weekdays from 8 am to 5 pm and it costs nothing to look around. Also of interest is the **St Mary Magdalen Anglican Church** in Anne St. On the east side of town you will find a distinctive water tower. The mural is an innovative way of disguising what might otherwise be an eyesore.

Places to Stay

The *Travellers Hostel* (☎ 6382 1399) at 4 Elizabeth St is a YHA hostel in a restored house which dates back to 1891. It has beds for $12 ($14 for nonmembers) and family rooms for $40. The *George Town Hotel-Motel* (☎ 6382 1057) is on the edge of town but has cheap rooms for $35/45.

Other accommodation is pricey, such as *Gray's Hotel* (☎ 6382 2655), 77 Macquarie St, charging $70 a double, and the *Pier Hotel Motel* (☎ 6382 1300), 3 Elizabeth St, with rooms at $75 a double.

If you have transport the *Beach Pines Holiday Park* (☎ 6382 2602), well out of town close to Low Head but right by the sea, has cabins for $50 a double and camp sites for $8.

HILLWOOD

South of Georgetown is the attractive rural area of Hillwood, where you can pick your own strawberries, raspberries and apples in season and sample Tasmanian fruit wines and cheese all year at the **Hillwood Strawberry Farm** (☎ 6394 8180). The village is also noted for its fishing and lovely river views.

LILYDALE

The small town of Lilydale, 27 km from Launceston, stands at the foot of Mt Arthur and is a convenient base for exploring the area. Three km from the town is the **Lilydale Falls Reserve**, which has camping facilities and two easily accessible waterfalls. At the nearby town of Lalla, there's the century-old **rhododendron gardens**, which are spectacular in spring; entry is free.

WESTBURY (pop 1350)

The historic town of Westbury, 28 km west of Launceston, is best known for its **White House**, a property built in 1841 and now managed by the National Trust. The house features colonial furnishings and a collection of 19th-century toys, and is open Tuesday, Thursday and weekends from 10 am to 4 pm; admission is $5.

The **Westbury Gemstone, Mineral & Mural Display**, on the Bass Highway, is open daily; admission is $2.50 ($1 children). Next door is **Pearn's Steam World**, which is open daily; it costs $3 to inspect a wide range of steam engines. The town has a rare village green where a Maypole festival is held every November. See the Deloraine section for bus services to the town.

DELORAINE (pop 2200)

Deloraine is Tasmania's largest inland town and, with its lovely riverside picnic area, superb setting at the foot of the Great Western Tiers and good amenities, makes a great base from which to explore the surrounding area. Being so close to the Cradle Mountain area, and even closer to a number of impressive waterfalls and shorter walking tracks, Deloraine is fast becoming a major bushwalking centre. You'll find the visitor information centre near the roundabout at the top of the main street.

The town itself has a lot of charm, as many of its Georgian and Victorian buildings have been faithfully restored. Places of interest include the **folk museum** ($1 admission) and **St Mark's Church of England**. Two km east of the town is the **Bowerbank Mill**, which is classified by the National Trust; these days it's a gallery and offers accommodation for $95.

Places to Stay & Eat

The *Highview Lodge Youth Hostel* (☎ 6362 2996), perched on the hillside at 8 Blake St, has magnificent views of the Great Western Tiers and charges $12 ($14 nonmembers). The managers organise reasonably priced and well-equipped trips to Cradle Mountain, the Walls of Jerusalem and other destinations, and mountain bikes and touring bikes are available for rent. This hostel receives excellent reports from many travellers.

The *Backpackers Modern Hotel* (☎ 6362 3408), also called Kevs Kumphy Korner, is a backpackers hostel at 24 Bass Highway, across the river from the main part of town. It's clean, modern and charges $10 a night. Almost opposite is the *Bush Inn* (☎ 6362 2365), which also offers good backpackers accommodation at $13 a night with breakfast. There is also the *Apex Caravan Park* (☎ 6362 2345) in West Parade, half a km from the town centre, where camp sites are $6.

Next door to the Deloraine Hotel is *Bonneys Inn* (☎ 6362 2974), which charges $25 per person for B&B in colonial accommodation. This is very good value and one room even has a waterbed!

One of the best places to eat in Deloraine is *Reuben's Restaurant*, in the main street, which is open daily from 8 am onwards. The atmosphere is relaxed and the range of dishes available is excellent.

Getting There & Away

Redline runs at least three services each weekday from Launceston through Westbury to Deloraine. Most buses continue to Devonport and bookings are essential. Hobart Coaches also runs buses along the main highway from Launceston to Devonport. Tasmanian Wilderness Transport runs buses through Deloraine from Launceston, Devonport and also directly from Cynthia Bay at the southern end of the Overland Track. During summer these services operate daily, while in the cooler seasons there are about three services a week.

MOLE CREEK (pop 260)

About 25 km west of Deloraine is Mole Creek, in the vicinity of which you'll find spectacular limestone caves, leatherwood honey and one of Tasmania's best wildlife parks.

Marakoopa Cave, from the Aboriginal word meaning 'handsome', is a wet cave 15 km from Mole Creek which features two underground streams and an incredible glow-worm display. **King Solomon Cave** is a dry cave with amazing calcite crystals that reflect light; it has very few steps in it making it the better cave for the less energetic. There are at least five tours in each cave daily except Christmas Day when they are closed. A visit to one cave costs $8 ($4 children), or you can visit both for $12 ($6 children). Current tour times are prominently displayed on access roads, or ring the ranger (☎ 6363 5182).

The leatherwood tree only grows in the damp western part of Tasmania, so honey made from its flower is unique to this state. From January to April, when the honey is being extracted, you can visit the **Stephens Leatherwood Honey Factory** and learn all about this fascinating industry. The factory is open during weekdays, and admission is free.

Two km from Chudleigh, east of Mole Creek, is the **Tasmanian Wildlife Park & Koala Village**, which is worth a visit. It's open daily from 9 am to 5 pm, and admission is $7.50 ($3.50 children).

Places to Stay

Two km west of town, at the turn-off to the caves and Cradle Mountain, is the *Mol*

Creek Camping Ground (☎ 6363 1150). It has basic facilities and charges $5.

The *Mole Creek Hotel* (☎ 6363 1102), in the main street, has rooms for $20/35 and counter meals daily. The *Mole Creek Guest House* (☎ 6363 1313), also in the main street, is a small place with rooms from $50 a double for B&B.

SHEFFIELD (pop 1030)

Sheffield is either referred to as 'the town of murals' or 'the outdoor art gallery'. Since 1986, 25 murals depicting the history of the area have been painted in and around this little town, with a further 10 in the surrounding district and these have become a major tourist attraction.

At the **Diversity Murals Theatrette**, at the western end of the main street, you can see an interesting documentary explaining the history and meaning of the individual paintings. The theatrette is open all day Monday to Saturday, and Sunday afternoons; admission is free with an optional donation.

The scenery around Sheffield is also impressive, with **Mt Roland** (1231 metres) dominating the peaceful farmlands, thick forests, and rivers brimming with fish. Nearby is beautiful **Lake Barrington**, part of the Mersey-Forth hydroelectric scheme and a major rowing venue and state recreation reserve.

Places to Stay & Eat

The cheapest accommodation in the area is 16 km out of town at Gowrie Park, at the base of Mt Roland. *Mt Roland Accommodation* (☎ 6491 1385) costs only $8.50 a night for bunkhouse-style rooms. Meals are available from the owners but as reports from travellers vary about the food we recommend bringing your own supplies. This is an excellent base for walks to Mt Roland.

In town itself, the *Sheffield Caravan Park* is tucked in behind the town hall. Facilities are basic and it costs $8 to pitch your tent. The *Sheffield Hotel* (☎ 6491 1130) has rooms for $30/40 with a light breakfast. The town also has a motel, and several host farms

and cottages in the surrounding hills with accommodation at higher prices.

For curiosity value alone *Flo's Country Kitchen* in the main street is worth a look. This is run by Flo Bjelke-Peterson, a former senator and wife of the former Queensland premier, Joh Bjelke-Peterson; the speciality is pumpkin scones. Afternoon teas are also available at the *Diversity Theatrette* where the mural films are shown.

DEVONPORT (pop 22,660)

Nestled behind the dramatic lighthouse-topped Mersey Bluff, Devonport is the terminal for the *Spirit of Tasmania*, the vehicular ferry between Victoria and Tasmania.

The Bluff Lighthouse was built in 1889 to direct the colony's rapidly growing sea traffic, and its light can be seen from up to 27 km out to sea. Today, the port is still important and handles much of the export produce from the rich agricultural areas of northern Tasmania.

Devonport tries hard to attract tourists but its visitors are usually arriving or departing rather than actually staying. Indeed, the city is often referred to as the 'gateway to Tasmania'.

Information

For any information about Devonport and Tasmania in general, head for the Backpackers' Barn (☎ 6424 3628) at 12 Edward St. The Barn is open daily from 8 am to 6 pm, and the friendly staff can arrange transport, car rental, help organise itineraries and look after your backpack. It has a cafe, an excellent bushwalking shop, and a rest room with showers which travellers can use for $3.

The Devonport Showcase (☎ 6424 8176), at 5 Best St, also has a complete range of tourist information with displays and workshop demonstrations of arts and crafts. The centre is currently the official information centre and is open daily from 9 am to 5 pm. You can also listen to the tourist radio on 99.3 FM.

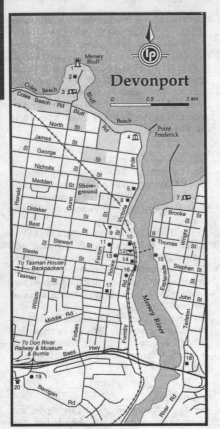

Tiagarra

The **Tasmanian Aboriginal Culture & Art Centre** is at Mersey Bluff, on the road to the lighthouse. It's known as Tiagarra, which is the Tasmanian Aboriginal word for 'keep', and was set up to preserve the art and culture of the Tasmanian Aboriginal people. The centre has a rare collection of more than 250 rock engravings, and is open daily from 9 am to 4 pm, 4.30 in summer; it's well worth the $2.50 admission fee.

Museums

The **Tasmanian Maritime & Folk Museum**, halfway to Mersey Bluff near the foreshore, has a display of model sailing ships based on the vessels which visited Tasmania in the early days. It's open Tuesday to Sunday from 1 to 4 pm and admission is $1.

Taswegia, in the lovely old building at 55-57 Formby Rd, is a commercial printing house with an interesting printing museum. It's open daily from 10 am to 5 pm, and admission is $2.

The **Don River Railway & Museum**, 4 km out of town on the Bass Highway towards Ulverstone, features a collection of steam locomotives and passenger carriages, and you can take a ride on a vintage train along the banks of the Don River. It's open most days from 11 am to 4 pm and a ride costs $6.

Other Attractions

The **Devonport Gallery & Art Centre**, at 45-47 Stewart St, is open Monday to Friday from 10 am to 5 pm, and Sunday afternoons (free).

At 77 Middle Rd, not far from the youth hostel, is **Home Hill**, which used to be the residence of Joseph and Dame Enid Lyons and is now administered by the National Trust. Joseph Lyons is the only Australian to have been both the premier of his state and prime minister of Australia, and Dame Enid Lyons was the first woman to become a member of the House of Representatives. Home Hill is open Tuesday to Thursday and at weekends from 2 to 4 pm; admission is $5.

Organised Tours

Most of the tours operating out of Devonport travel to Tasmania's wilderness areas and they vary from one-day trips to four-day tours. The two main operators are Tasmanian Wilderness Transport and Maxwell's Charter Tour Coach & Taxi Service; book at the Backpackers' Barn.

Places to Stay

East Devonport has two caravan parks, both of which are close to the beach and have good reputations. The *Abel Tasman Caravan Park* (☎ 6427 8794), at 6 Wright St, has camp sites ($7), bunkhouse accommodation $11), on-site vans ($30) and cabins ($46). *Devonport's Vacation Village* (☎ 6427 3886), in North Caroline St (1 km east of Abel Tasman), has camp sites ($15) and cabins ($42).

The *Mersey Bluff Caravan Park* (☎ 6424 3655) is 2.5 km from town, near Tiagarra. It's a pleasant place with some good beaches nearby. It has camp sites ($12), vans ($34) and cabins ($44).

MacWright House (☎ 6424 5696), 400 metres past Home Hill at 155 Middle Rd, is Devonport's YHA hostel; it charges $9 a night ($11 nonmembers) and is a 40-minute walk from the town centre. A Tasmanian Wilderness Transport bus can take you from the ferry terminal or airport to the hostel.

The other budget accommodation is *Tasman House Backpackers* (☎ 6423 2335) at 169 Steele St. Rooms vary from bunk-house to motel style and range from $8 to $12 each. It is a 15-minute walk from town and transport can be arranged when booking.

The friendly *River View Lodge* (☎ 6424 7357), at 18 Victoria Parade on the foreshore,

charges $45/55 for singles/doubles, which includes an excellent cooked breakfast; it's deservedly popular with travellers.

Wenvoe Heights (☎ 6424 1719), at 44 MacFie St, is a beautiful two-storey Federation brick building. Completely renovated, it charges $54/68 for singles/doubles with shared facilities and $15 extra for rooms with private facilities. A cooked breakfast is included in the tariff.

Two good hotels close to the centre of town are the *Alexander Hotel* (☎ 6424 2252), at 78 Formby Rd, which charges $35/50 for a single/double; and the *Formby Hotel* (☎ 6424 1601), at 82 Formby Rd, where rooms cost $35/55 with breakfast.

There are quite a number of motels in the city centre and East Devonport. The *Edgewater Hotel & Motor Inn* (☎ 6427 8441), at 2 Thomas St in East Devonport, is not very attractive from the outside, but is close to the ferry terminal and charges $44/49 for singles/doubles. The *Argosy Motor Inn* (☎ 6427 8872), in Tarleton St, East Devonport, charges $72 a double. North of the city centre at 15 Victoria Parade, the *Elimatta Motor Inn* (☎ 6424 6555) charges $60/72.

Places to Eat

There are plenty of coffee lounges and takeaways in the mall, but for a good atmosphere and great snacks try *Billy 'n Damper*, the cafe at the front of the Backpackers' Barn, 12 Edward St. It's open daily from 8 am to 6 pm, and will take party bookings in the evenings. The *Old Devonport Town Coffee Shop* in the Devonport Showcase is also open daily and is good for a drink or a snack. *Klaas's Bakehouse*, 11 Oldaker St, is only open on weekdays but has excellent cakes and pastries.

Most hotels have good counter meals for around $8 to $15; try the *Tamahere* at 34 Best St, the *Alexander* at 78 Formby Rd, or the *Formby* at 82 Formby Rd. In East Devonport, the *Edgewater Hotel*, at 2 Thomas St, has cheap counter meals.

Devonport has a good selection of moderately priced restaurants. For a bargain lunch at $4.50 a dish try *Dangerous Liaisons* at 28 Forbes St, open Tuesday to Friday for lunch and dinner (dinner only on Saturday). If you prefer pasta try the *Rialto Gallery Restaurant*, 159 Rooke St. While the pasta is not fancy, service is prompt. It's open Monday to Friday for lunch and every evening for dinner until late.

For Chinese food, try the *Silky Apple* at 33 King St, the *Chinese Chef* at 4b Kempling St, or *Laksa House*, shop 1, 5b Edward St. These restaurants are open every evening and also serve takeaway customers if you prefer to eat elsewhere.

Entertainment
Check the *Advocate* newspaper for Devonport's entertainment details. The *Warehouse Nightclub* and *Spurs Saloon* are in King St. The *Elimatta Motor Inn*, at 15 Victoria Parade, occasionally has weekend bands, and on Wednesday, Friday and Saturday nights there's a nightclub called *Steps*. At the Tamahere Hotel is the *Club One* nightclub, while *City Limits*, at 18 King St, is also a popular nightspot.

Getting There & Away
Air For information on domestic flights to and from Devonport, see the Getting There & Away section at the beginning of this chapter.

Bus Redline's agent is the Backpackers' Barn (☎ 6424 3628) at 12 Edward St, although the depot (☎ 6424 5100) is across the road at No 9. All buses also stop at the ferry terminal. Redline has daily buses from Devonport to Hobart ($30), Queenstown ($32), Strahan ($37), Launceston ($12), Burnie ($6) and Smithton ($14).

The Hobart Coaches office (☎ 6424 6599) is at the Devonport Central shopping centre in King St. Hobart Coaches has daily buses to Launceston, Hobart, Burnie and all towns en route.

During the summer, Tasmanian Wilderness Transport buses depart daily from Devonport to Sheffield and to Cradle Mountain ($30) and Lake St Clair. There's a once-weekly service to Strahan ($40) and Zeehan, and a twice-weekly bus to the Walls of Jerusalem. The depot (☎ 6434 4442) is at 14 King St.

If none of the scheduled services suit your particular needs, or you are visiting outside the summer period, you can charter a minibus from either Tasmanian Wilderness Transport or the Backpackers' Barn. For example, a bus from Devonport to Cradle Mountain costs $120, or $30 each if there are five people or more.

Car Rental There are plenty of cheap car rental firms such as Range/Rent-a-Bug (☎ 6427 9034), at 5 Murray St, East Devonport. The major companies all have desks at the *Spirit of Tasmania* terminal or just opposite it.

Boat See the Getting There & Away section at the beginning of this chapter for details on the *Spirit of Tasmania* ferry service between Melbourne and Devonport. The TT Line terminal (☎ 1800 030 344) is on the Esplanade East Devonport. You can't miss seeing the ferry as it dominates the town when it's in port.

Getting Around
There's no shuttle bus to the airport, but most bus services call at the airport. The taxi fare into town is about $10.

South of Best St, local buses are run by Tasmanian Wilderness Transport, while north of Best St and East Devonport is covered by Hobart Coaches. If this is confusing don't worry; most places in Devonport are within easy walking distance.

There's also a Mersey River ferry service linking central Devonport with East Devonport, which operates seven days a week. The one-way adult fare is $1.20 and bicycles cost 50c. You can hire bicycles at the Backpackers' Barn.

AROUND DEVONPORT
Formerly a farm, the **Asbestos Range National Park** was declared a national park in 1976 and named after the mineral once

 found in the area. It's 25 km east of Devonport. Animals and birds are prolific, and there are a number of signed walking tracks through the park. The **Springlawn Nature Walk** takes about an hour from the car park and includes a boardwalk over a wetland to a bird hide.

There are three camp sites in the park with pit toilets, bore water and firewood provided. For more information, contact the park ranger on ☎ 6428 6277.

ULVERSTONE (pop 10,350)
Ulverstone, at the mouth of the Leven River, is a pleasant town with some fine beaches and good amenities; it's a good base from which to explore the surrounding area.

Just 30 km south is the **Gunns Plains Cave Reserve**; daily guided tours of the spectacular wet cave leave hourly from 10 am to 4 pm and cost $6. Nearby is **Leven Canyon**, a magnificent gorge with a number of walking tracks.

If you're driving from Ulverstone to Penguin, consider taking the old Bass Highway, which runs closer to the coast than the new one and offers some fine views of three small islands known as the **Three Sisters**.

Places to Stay & Eat
There are plenty of camping grounds in Ulverstone, including the *Apex Caravan Park* (☎ 6425 2935) in Queen St in West Ulverstone, where camp sites are $8. The *Ulverstone Caravan Park* (☎ 6425 2624), in Water St, is somewhat closer to town and has camp sites ($8.20), on-site vans ($30 for a double), cabins ($41) and units ($51).

For a great location try the *Ocean View Guest House* (☎ 6425 5401), at 1 Victoria St, 100 metres from the beach. It's a lovely old house where singles/doubles with a continental breakfast cost $40/65. If you prefer a motel try the *Bass & Flinders Motor Inn*, just across the river from town, charging $60 a double.

Pedro the Fisherman, down by the wharf, does extremely cheap, but filling, takeaway fish & chips – and if you can't finish the

packet there are plenty of obliging seagulls around!

In Reibey St there's the *Jade Willow* Chinese restaurant, or in West Ulverstone you could try *Midnight Express*, a restaurant in Queen St which combines Chinese, Indian and Italian cuisines.

Getting There & Away
See the Burnie Getting There & Away section for details of transport to and from Ulverstone.

North-West

Tasmania's magnificent north-west coast is a land as rich in history as it is diverse in scenery. Its story goes back 37,000 years to a time when giant kangaroos and wombats roamed the area. Aboriginal tribes once took shelter in the caves along the coast, leaving a legacy of rock engravings and middens.

Europeans quickly realised the potential of the region and settlers moved farther and farther west, building towns along the coast and inland on the many rivers. The area was soon transformed into a vital part of the young colony's developing economy.

BURNIE (pop 21,400)
Although Burnie sits on the shores of Emu Bay and is backed by rich farming land, it is factory smoke, not the views, which usually welcomes the visitor to Tasmania's fourth-largest city. One of Burnie's main assets is its deep-water port, which makes cargo shipping an important industry. Another major employer, Amcor, owns Associated Pulp & Paper Mills, which began producing paper in 1938.

The town (named after William Burnie, a director of the Van Diemen's Land Company) started life quietly, growing mainly potatoes for the first 40 years, until the discovery of tin at Mt Bischoff in Waratah. In 1878, the Van Diemen's Land Company opened a wooden tramway between the mine at Waratah and the port of

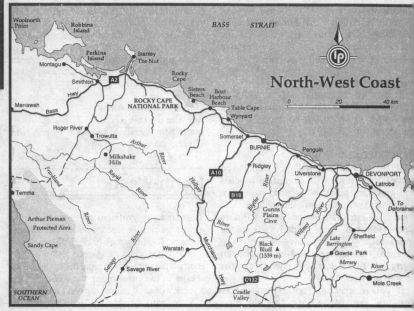

North-West Coast

Burnie. This was the humble beginning of the important Emu Bay Railway which, in the 1900s, linked the port of Burnie to the rich silver fields of Zeehan and Rosebery. The Emu Bay Railway, which travels through some wild and impressive country, still operates today but does not carry passengers.

The Tasmanian Travel & Information Centre, 48 Cattley St, is a good source of information on Tasmania's north-west. Pick up a copy of the *Walk Through Burnie* brochure for a self-guided walking tour of the town centre.

Things to See & Do

The **Pioneer Village Museum**, in High St, next to the Civic Plaza, has an authentic blacksmith's shop, printer and boot shop. This impressive museum is open Monday to Friday from 9 am to 5 pm, and weekends from 1.30 to 4.30 pm; admission is $4 (children $1).

Burnie Park is quite pleasant and feature an animal sanctuary and the oldest buildin in town, the Burnie Inn. The inn was built i 1847 and moved from its original site to th park in 1973. It's classified by the Nationa Trust and is open at weekends.

From Monday to Thursday, at 2 pm, yo can take a free tour of the Amcor complex On weekdays you can also visit the Lacto cheese factory on Old Surrey Rd, where yo can taste and purchase the products. Th **Burnie Regional Art Gallery**, in Wilmot S is open daily and is also worth a look.

There are a number of waterfalls an viewpoints in the Burnie area, includin **Roundhill Lookout** and **Fern Glade**, jus three km from the centre, and the impressiv **Guide Falls** at Ridgley, 16 km away. Th impressive **Emu Valley Rhododendro Gardens**, eight km south of Burnie, are ope daily between September and March; ther is a small entry fee of $2.

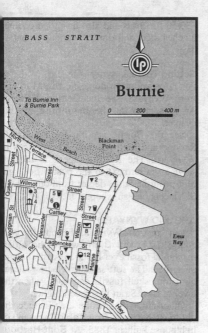

BASS STRAIT

Burnie

0   200   400 m

To Burnie Inn
& Burnie Park

North Terrace

West

Beach

Blackman
Point

Queen Street

Wilmot Street

Street

Hodgman St

Alexander Street

Cattley

Wilson Terrace

Street

Street

View Rd

Ladbrooke St

Mount Street

Marine Terrace

Bass Hwy

Emu
Bay

PLACES TO STAY

1   Regent Hotel
13 Burnie Town House

PLACES TO EAT

2   Beach Hotel
9   Li Yin Chinese Restaurant
10 Renusha's Indian Restaurant
11 Partners Restaurant

OTHER

3   Regional Art Gallery
4   Pioneer Village Museum
5   Club Hotel
6   Tasmanian Travel & Information Centre
7   Bay View Hotel
8   Post Office
12 Redline Depot

Places to Stay

At Cooee, three km west of Burnie on the
Bass Highway, the *Treasure Island Caravan
Park* (☎ 6431 1925) has camp sites ($10),
cabins ($46 double) and on-site vans ($33).
It also has hostel accommodation for $12 per
person.

Cheapest of the hotels is the *Regent*
(☎ 6431 1933), at 26 North Terrace, which
charges $20/30 for singles/doubles. *Glen
Osborne House* (☎ 6431 9866) at 9 Aileen
Crescent, about a km from the town centre,
has en suite rooms for $70/90 including
breakfast. Closer to the town centre is the
Burnie Town House (☎ 6431 4455), at 139
Wilson St, which charges $75/85 for en suite
rooms.

Places to Eat

There are plenty of cafes in the town centre.
For cheap lunches try the *Zodiac* in Cattley
St or the *Napoli* cafe above Fitzgerald's

department store on the corner of Wilson and
Cattley Sts.

Most hotels have reasonably priced
counter meals from Monday to Saturday.
The *Beach Hotel* at 1 Wilson St, on the
waterfront, always has a good spread.

Ladbrooke St, between Mount and Wilson
Sts, is the area to go when you're hungry.
Renusha's Indian Restaurant serves tasty
food and is BYO. Next door is the *Kasbah
Pizza Bar* which is open until late, and oppo-
site is *Li Yin*, which has an all-you-can-eat
Chinese buffet for $12.80.

Not far away, at 104 Wilson St, is the more
up-market *Partners Restaurant* which has
good service and mouth-watering meals for
around $19.

Entertainment

Check the *Advocate* newspaper for entertainment listings. On Friday and Saturday nights
there are discos at the *Bay View Hotel* and
the *Club Hotel*. On Friday nights, the *Beach
Hotel* is a popular place for a drink.

Getting There & Away

Air The nearest airport is at Wynyard, 20 km
from Burnie. North West Travel (☎ 6431
2166), on the corner of Wilmot and Mount

Sts in Burnie, is the agent for Kendell and Ansett Airlines.

Bus Redline has daily services to and from Devonport, Launceston and Hobart. From Monday to Saturday these buses continue to Wynyard and Smithton, with two of these services detouring to Stanley. Redline also has at least one daily service between Burnie and Strahan ($31) via Devonport, Cradle Mountain and Queenstown ($26). The Redline agent in Burnie is at 117 Wilson St.

Hobart Coaches has daily services between Hobart and Burnie via Launceston, Deloraine, Devonport, Ulverstone and Penguin. Its buses leave from outside the Tasmanian Travel & Information Centre in Cattley St.

During the week, Metro Burnie (☎ 6431 3822), at 30 Strahan St, also has regular buses to Ulverstone, Penguin and Wynyard which depart from the bus stops in Cattley St.

WYNYARD (pop 4890)
Sheltered by the impressive Table Cape and geologically fascinating Fossil Bluff, Wynyard sits both on the seafront and on the banks of the Inglis River. The town is surrounded by beautiful patchwork farmland which is best appreciated by flying into Wynyard airport.

Although there's not much to see in the town itself, Wynyard is a good base from which to explore the many attractions in the area. Good sources of tourist information include the council chambers in Saunders St, and most hotels and restaurants.

Places to Stay & Eat
Close to town, on the Esplanade, *Wynyard Caravan Park* (☎ 6442 1998) has camp sites ($10), cabins ($50) and on-site vans ($30).

The *Wynyard Youth Hostel* (☎ 6442 2013) is at 36 Dodgin St, one block south of the main street and has rooms for $11 ($13 non-members). If you've arrived by air, it's only a five-minute walk from the airport.

The *Federal Hotel* (☎ 6442 2056), at 82 Goldie St in the middle of town, charges

$30/50 for B&B and also has good counter lunches daily and dinner Monday to Saturday.

Getting There & Away
For information on domestic flights to and from Wynyard, see the Getting There & Away section at the beginning of this chapter.

See the Burnie section for details on Redline and Metro Burnie bus services to Wynyard. The Redline agent is the BP service station next to the post office, and Metro Burnie buses depart from outside the St Vincent de Paul shop in Jackson St.

AROUND WYNYARD
Seven km from Wynyard, beyond the golf course, is **Fossil Bluff**, where the oldest marsupial fossil ever found in Australia was unearthed. The soft sandstone here features numerous shell fossils deposited when the level of Bass Strait was much higher.

Other attractions in the area include the unforgettable views from **Table Cape** and its lighthouse built in 1885. At **Boat Harbour Beach**, 14 km from Wynyard, there's a beautiful bay with white sand and crystal-blue water – a lovely spot for rock-pool exploring and snorkelling. If you want to stay the night the *Boat Harbour Beach Backpackers* (☎ 6445 1273), in Strawberry Lane not far from the beach, charges $12 per person. The town also has a caravan park, motel and cottage accommodation.

Nearby, in the **Rocky Cape National Park**, is Sisters Beach, an eight-km expanse of glistening white sand with safe swimming and good fishing. Also in the park is the 10-hectare **Birdland Native Gardens**, which has information on more many native bird species. You can also visit a number of waterfalls, including **Detention Falls**, three km south of Myalla, and **Dip Falls**, near Mawbanna.

Unless you have your own transport, you will have to hitch to get to most of these places. Redline Coaches will drop you at the turn-off to Boat Harbour (three km) and Sisters Beach (eight km). Boat Harbour

Beach Backpackers also does pick-ups from the highway.

STANLEY (pop 600)

Nestled at the foot of the extraordinary Circular Head (better known as the Nut), Stanley is a very appealing historic village which has changed little since its early days. In 1826 it became the headquarters of the London-based Van Diemen's Land Company, which was granted a charter to settle and cultivate Circular Head and the north-western tip of Tasmania.

The area prospered when it began shipping large quantities of mutton, beef and potatoes to Victoria's goldfields, and continued to prosper when settlers discovered rich dairying land behind Sisters Hills and tin reserves at Mt Bischoff.

Today, Stanley is a charming fishing village with many historic buildings and great seascapes. To better appreciate Stanley's charm, pick up a walking-tour map from De Jonge's Souvenirs or the Discovery Centre, both in Church St.

The Nut

This striking 152-metre-high volcanic rock formation, thought to be 12.5 million years old, can be seen for many km around Stanley. It's a steep 15-minute climb to the top, but the view is definitely worth it. For the less energetic, a chair lift operates from 9.30 am to 4.30 pm; rides cost $5.50.

Other Attractions

The old bluestone building on the seafront is the **Van Diemen's Land Company Store**, designed by John Lee Archer, a colonial architect; it dates from 1844. The company's actual headquarters were at **Highfield**, two km north of Stanley. This historic site has recently been restored and is open daily ($2 entry).

Near the wharf in Stanley is a particularly fine old bluestone building which used to be a grain store. It was built in 1843 from stones brought to Stanley as ship's ballast.

The **Plough Inn** (1840), in Church St, has been fully restored and furnished with period furniture. Next door is a little folk museum called the **Discovery Centre**, which is open daily from 10 am to 4.30 pm; admission is $2.

Other buildings of historical interest include **Lyons Cottage**, in Church St, which was the birthplace of former prime minister Joseph Lyons (open from 10 am to 4 pm, admission by donation); the **Union Hotel**, also in Church St, which dates from 1849; and the **Presbyterian church**, which was probably Australia's first prefabricated building, bought in England and transported to Stanley in 1853.

Places to Stay

The *Stanley Youth Hostel* (☎ 6458 1266) in Wharf Rd is part of the *Stanley Caravan Park* and charges $12 a night. The caravan park has camp sites ($8.50), on-site vans ($30) and cabins ($45).

Pol & Pen (☎ 6458 1334) are a pair of two-bedroom self-contained cottages, which are good value at $65 a double. The *Union Hotel* (☎ 6458 1161), in Church St, has basic rooms for $25/35 a single/double. There are many B&B cottages dotted around Stanley; prices range from $60 to $120 a double.

Places to Eat

Hursey Seafoods, at 2 Alexander Terrace, sells live fish from the tanks in the shop as well as takeaways, including fish & chips. Next door is *Kermie's Cafe*, where you get to sit down and eat the same food for a higher prices. Upstairs is *Julie & Patrick's Seafood Restaurant* where the best of the fish and crayfish are served in the evenings. All three businesses are run by the same people; the cafe and shop close at 6 pm when the restaurant opens for the evening.

Sullivans, a licensed restaurant at 25 Church St, is open daily and serves light lunches, teas and dinner. The *Union Hotel* has quite good counter meals, and at the Nut there is the *Nut Shop Tearooms*.

Getting There & Away

Redline has two services a day on weekdays which run from Hobart to Smithton via

Stanley, and three running via Stanley in the other direction. The Redline agent is the BP service station on the corner of Wharf Rd and Marine Esplanade.

AROUND STANLEY

Twenty-two km from Stanley, **Smithton** serves one of Tasmania's largest forestry areas and is also the administrative centre for Circular Head. There's not much to see or do in the town itself, but the town's airport makes it an arrival point for some light aircraft flights from the mainland.

Woolnorth, on the north-western tip of Tasmania, near Cape Grim, is a 220-sq-km cattle and sheep property which is the only remaining holding of the Van Diemen's Land Company. Unfortunately, tours of the property are only available to members of bus tours.

Allendale Gardens, on the B22 road to Edith Creek, are a good place to walk around or relax; the two-hectare property includes impressive botanical gardens, a rainforest walk, a wildflower section and a cafe serving Devonshire teas. The centre is open daily from 10 am to 6 pm (closed June to August) and admission is $5 ($2.50 children).

Temperate rainforest and button-grass moorland can be found at **Milkshake Forest Reserve**, 45 km south of Smithton. A farther 26 km south-west of the reserve, set in beautiful rainforest, is tranquil **Lake Chisholm**.

MARRAWAH

Marrawah, at the end of the Bass Highway, is where the wild Indian Ocean occasionally throws up the remains of ships wrecked on the dangerous and rugged west coast. To visit Marrawah, the most westerly town in Tasmania, it is best to have your own vehicle, but from Monday to Saturday you can get a lift with the mail run from Smithton.

The area has seen minimal disturbance due to European development and was once popular with the Tasmanian Aboriginal people. Many signs of these people remain, and particular areas have been proclaimed reserves to protect the remaining relics, including rock carvings, middens and hut

depressions. The main Aboriginal sites are a **Mt Cameron West**, near Green Point, a **West Point** and at **Sundown Point**.

The township of Marrawah consists of hotel, serving daily counter meals, and general store selling petrol and supplies. The hotel has no accommodation, but there is basic camp site at Green Point, two km from Marrawah. This region is good for fishing canoeing, camping and bushwalking, or just for getting away from it all. Marrawah' main attraction, however, is its enormou surf: the state's surfing championships are held here every year around Easter.

ARTHUR RIVER

The sleepy town of Arthur River, 14 kr south of Marrawah, is mainly a collection o holiday houses belonging to people wh come here to fish. There is one kiosk wit basic supplies, no public transport and, apar from a camp site with basic facilities, onl one place to stay. The *Arthur River Holida Units* (☎ 6457 1288), in Gardiner St, ha doubles for $55 to $65.

Apart from the fishing, visitors come her to explore the **Arthur Pieman Protecte Area** and to take a cruise on the Arthur Rive The attractions of the protected area includ magnificent ocean beaches, Rebecc Lagoon, Temma Harbour, waterfalls on th Nelson Bay River, the old mining town o Balfour, the Pieman River and the Norfol Ranges.

Arthur River Cruise

Paddy and Turk Porteous operate scenic da cruises on the Arthur River (☎ 6457 1158 which depart at 10 am and return at 3 pn You sail up the river, feeding sea eagles o the way, to the confluence of the Arthur an Frankland rivers. The cruise runs most day in summer (minimum eight people); book a any Tasmanian Travel & Information Centre The cost is $38 each ($15 children).

HELLYER GORGE

Seven km from Burnie is the small town o Somerset, at the junction of the Murchiso and Bass highways. Hellyer Gorge is abou

40 km south of Somerset on the banks of the Hellyer River. The highway winds its way through the impressive gorge. At the picnic area by the river, there are two very short walks which provide a welcome break from driving. From Burnie to the Waratah area there is an alternative road which is faster but less scenic. It passes through Ridgley and Hampshire on road B18 and avoids the winding road through the Hellyer Gorge. This has diverted some traffic away from the peaceful reserves in the gorge.

About 40 km south of Hellyer Gorge, is the turn off to Cradle Mountain. This road, although classed as a 'C', is actually a major road linking the west coast (via the northern end of Cradle Mountain National Park) with the region south of Devonport.

SAVAGE RIVER

The Mt Bischoff mine, near Waratah, was once the world's richest tin mine, but these days it is the iron ore of Savage River that keeps mining alive in the region. The extracted ore is pumped as a slurry along an 85-km pipeline to Port Latta on the north coast.

There are mine tours on Tuesday and Thursday at 9 am and 2 pm, which must be booked (☎ 6443 4105) but are free.

Accommodation is only available at the *Savage River Motor Inn* (☎ 6446 1177), where rooms cost $40/60.

CORINNA

Corinna, 28 km south-west of Savage River, was once a thriving gold-mining settlement but is now little more than a ghost town. These days it's the scenery and the Pieman River Cruises (☎ 6446 1170) that attract visitors. The cruise passes impressive forests of eucalypts, ferns and Huon pines to Pieman Heads. Costing $30 ($15 children), which includes morning tea, the tours on the MV *Arcadia II* depart daily at 10.30 am and return at 2.30 pm. It's definitely best to book during the summer months.

The only accommodation is at the *Pieman Retreat Cabins* (☎ 6446 1170). Cabins can sleep up to six people and cost $50 a double

and $8 for each extra person. The cabins are self-contained and linen is available at extra cost.

ROSEBERY (pop 1710)

Gold was discovered in Rosebery in the late 1800s and mining began early in the next century with the completion of the Emu Bay Railway between Burnie and Zeehan. However, when the Zeehan lead smelters closed in 1913 operations also closed in Rosebery. The Electrolytic Zinc Company then bought and reopened the mine in 1936 and it has operated ever since.

There's not much to see in Rosebery, but if you want to stay overnight the *Plandome Hotel* (☎ 6473 1351) has accommodation for $38 a double, and there's a caravan park with camping ($8), on-site vans ($28), cabins ($45) and a hostel ($12).

West Coast

Nature at its most awe-inspiring is the attraction of Tasmania's rugged and magnificent west coast. Formidable mountains, button grass plains, ancient rivers, tranquil lakes, dense rainforests and a treacherous coast are all features of this compelling and beautiful region, some of which is now World Heritage Area.

Centuries before the arrival of Europeans, this part of Tasmania was home to many of the state's Aboriginal people, and plenty of archaeological evidence, some of it more than 20,000 years old, has been found of these original inhabitants.

Prior to 1932, when the road from Hobart to Queenstown was built, the only way into the area was by sea, through the dangerously narrow Hells Gates into Macquarie Harbour. Despite such inaccessibility, early European settlement brought explorers, convicts, soldiers, loggers, prospectors, railway gangs and fishermen, while the 20th century has brought outdoor adventurers, naturalists and environmental crusaders.

It was over the wild rivers, beautiful lakes

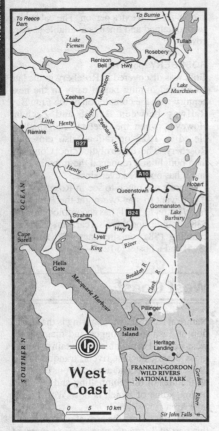

West Coast

0   5   10 km

Sir John Falls

and tranquil valleys of Tasmania's south-west that battles between environmentalists and big business raged. The proposed damming of the Franklin and Lower Gordon rivers caused the greatest and longest-running environmental debate in Australia's history in the 1980s and has subsequently seen the boom of ecotourism in Strahan.

While debate continues on questions of wilderness versus electricity, and World Heritage Area versus woodchipping, nature herself has begun to reclaim what is hers. The barren hills around Queenstown, left from the mining era, are now beginning to show signs of regeneration.

ZEEHAN (pop 1180)

In 1882, rich deposits of silver and lead were discovered in the quiet little town of Zeehan and by the turn of the century, it had become a booming mining centre, known as Silver City, with a population that peaked at nearly 10,000. In its heyday, Zeehan had 26 hotels and its Gaiety Theatre seated 1000 people. In 1908, however, the mines began to fail and the town declined.

With the reopening and expansion of the Renison Tin Mine at Renison Bell, Zeehan experienced a revival in the late 1960s becoming the housing base for Renison Ltd.

Things to See

Buildings that remain from the early boom days include the once-famous **Grand Hotel** the **Gaiety Theatre**, the **post office**, the **bank** and **St Luke's Church**.

For an excellent insight into the working of a mine, visit the **West Coast Pioneers Memorial Museum** in Main St, previously the School of Mines. It's open daily from 8.30 am to 5 pm and admission is free (donations welcome). The museum also features an interesting mineral collection and an exhibit of early west-coast railways.

Places to Stay

At the *Treasure Island West Coast Caravan Park* (☎ 6471 6633) in Hurst St there are camp sites ($11), cabins ($44) and on-site vans ($35). The *Heemskirk Motor Hotel* (☎ 6471 6107), in Main St, has rooms from $60 and a holiday unit for $85 a double.

The old *Hotel Cecil* (☎ 6471 6221), in Main St, has singles/doubles for $30/50 and self-contained holiday units with cooking facilities for $68/70.

Getting There & Away

In summer there is a daily Redline bus from Burnie to Queenstown and another to Strahan via Zeehan. In winter, services run on Tuesday, Thursday and Saturday only. Tasmanian Wilderness Transport's Straha to Devonport service operates on weekends all year and also stops in Zeehan.

QUEENSTOWN (pop 3370)

The final, winding descent into Queenstown from the Lyell Highway is an unforgettable experience. With deep, eroded gullies and naked, multicoloured hills, there is no escaping the fact that this is a mining town and that the destruction of the surrounding area is a direct result of this industry.

The discovery of alluvial gold in the Queen River valley in 1881 first brought prospectors to the area. Two years later, mining began on the rich Mt Lyell deposits, and for nearly a decade miners extracted a few ounces of gold a day and ignored the mountain's rich copper reserves. In 1891, however, the Mt Lyell Mining Company began to concentrate on copper which soon became the most profitable mineral on the west coast.

After 20 years of mining, the rainforested hills around Queenstown had been stripped bare: three million tonnes of timber had been felled to feed the furnaces. By 1900, uncontrolled pollution from the copper smelters was killing any vegetation that had not already been cut down, and bushfires – fuelled by the sulphur-impregnated soils and dead stumps – raged through the hills every summer, until there was no regrowth left at all. The smelters closed in 1969 and in recent years a tinge of green has reappeared across the hills.

The Mt Lyell mine closed temporarily in late 1994, although there is still some small-scale mining in the area. It seems Queenstown's future rests with the tourism industry.

Things to See

The **Galley Museum** started life as the Imperial Hotel and was the first brick hotel in Queenstown. The museum features a good collection of old photographs of the history of Queenstown, as well as a display from the town's pioneering days. The museum is open Monday to Friday from 10 am to 12.30 pm and 1.30 to 4.30 pm, and weekends from 1.30 to 4.30 pm; admission is $2. Opposite the museum, the **Miner's Siding** is a public park featuring a restored ABT steam locomotive and a rock sculpture telling the history of the Queenstown to Strahan railway.

There are good views from **Spion Kop Lookout**, in the centre of town (follow Bowes St). If you look at the football oval you will notice that it is cream instead of green, Queenstown's footy team is tough – they play on gravel, not grass.

Queenstown has a good *Historic Walk* brochure which guides you around the town from the Galley Museum to Spion Kop Lookout. You can pick up the leaflet and map in most shops or hotels and it is an excellent way to see all the sights.

The latest visitor attraction is the **chair lift** which rises 369 metres giving good views of the stark hills. It costs $4 ($2 children) for the ride.

Places to Stay & Eat

The *Queenstown Cabin & Tourist Park* (☎ 6471 1332), at 17 Grafton St, about half a km from the town centre, has below-average bunkhouse accommodation for $20 a double plus $6 for each extra person. There are also on-site vans ($30) and cabins ($43).

At 1 Penghana Rd, just over the bridge on the way to Strahan, is the *Mountain View Holiday Lodge* (☎ 6471 1163), which is the old single men's quarters for the Mt Lyell Mining Company. The hostel section is pretty basic, but for $10 a night you get your own room and there are cooking facilities. Many of the rooms have been renovated as motel-style units and cost $55 a double.

The *Empire Hotel* (☎ 6471 1699), at 2 Orr St, is a lovely old hotel with an imposing staircase classified by the National Trust. Clean and pleasant singles/doubles cost $20/35 and, for a little extra, you can get breakfast. *Hunter's Hotel* (☎ 6471 1531), farther up Orr St, is not as attractive and charges $20 (including breakfast) for singles.

The *Mount Lyell Motor Inn* (☎ 6471 1888), at 1 Orr St, has motel suites for $40/50.

Apart from counter meals, which are pretty good at the *Mount Lyell Motor Inn*, Queenstown has little to offer in the way of places to eat. In Orr St, *Axel's* has good cakes and light snacks, and nearby you'll find the usual takeaways.

Getting There & Away

During summer Redline has daily bus services between Queenstown and Strahan ($5), Hobart ($30), Burnie ($26) and Devonport. During the rest of the year, services run roughly every second day. The Redline agent is in Orr St.

STRAHAN (pop 620)

Strahan, 37 km from Queenstown on Macquarie Harbour, is the only town on this rugged and dangerous coast. Though only a shadow of its former self, the town is rich in convict, logging and mining history.

Treacherous seas, the lack of natural harbours and high rainfall discouraged early settlement of the region until Macquarie Harbour was discovered by sailors searching for the source of the Huon pine that frequently washed up on the southern beaches.

In those days, the area was totally inaccessible by land and very difficult to reach by sea, and in 1821 these dubious assets prompted the establishment of a penal settlement on **Sarah Island**, in the middle of the harbour. Its main function was to isolate the worst of the colony's convicts and to use their muscle to harvest the huge stands of Huon pine. The convicts worked upriver 12 hours a day, often in leg irons, felling the pines and rafting them back to the island's saw-pits where they were used to build ships and furniture.

Sarah Island appeared in Marcus Clarke's graphic novel about convict life *For the Term of his Natural Life*. In 1834, however, after the establishment of the 'escape-proof' penal settlement at Port Arthur, Sarah Island was abandoned.

As the port for Queenstown, Strahan reached its peak of prosperity with the west-coast mining boom, and the completion of the Mt Lyell Mining Company's railway line

in the late 1890s. Steamers operated regularly between Strahan and Hobart, and Launceston and Melbourne carrying copper, gold, silver, lead, timber and passengers. The closure of some of the mines and the opening of the Emu Bay Railway from Zeehan to Burnie led to the decline of Strahan as a port.

These days, Strahan is a charming seaside town which draws visitors in droves for cruises on the Gordon River and scenic flights over the area.

Information

The architecturally innovative **Strahan Wharf Centre** (☎ 6471 7488) is almost a tourist attraction in its own right. The foyer has a river-gravel floor and a superb reception desk built out of Huon pine. Beyond this is the museum section, which presents all aspects of the history of the south-west. The centre is open daily from 10 am to 6 pm (8 pm in summer); entry to the museum section is $4.50.

There is an office of the Department of Parks, Wildlife & Heritage in the old customs house building close to the town centre. This building also houses the post office. There is no bank in Strahan.

Things to See

Probably the finest building on the west coast is Strahan's imposing **customs house**. The walk to **Hogarth Falls** starts east of the town centre at Peoples Park; allow one hour return.

The **lighthouse** at Cape Sorell, on the south head of the harbour, is the third-largest in Tasmania. Opposite the caravan park is a **gemstone & mineral museum**.

Six km from the town is the impressive 33-km **Ocean Beach**, where the sunsets have to be seen to be believed. In October, when the birds return from their winter migration, the beach is also a mutton-bird rookery. About 14 km along the road from Strahan to Zeehan are the **Henty Dunes**, some spectacular sand dunes, many of which are more than 30 metres in height.

Organised Tours & Cruises

Gordon River Cruise The traditional way of experiencing the beauty of the Gordon River is on one of the cruises which operate out of Strahan.

Gordon River Cruises (☎ 6471 7187) has half-day trips (9 am to 1.45 pm) for $44 ($24 children), including morning tea, or full-day trips (9 am to 3.30 pm) for $62 ($30 children), including a smorgasbord lunch.

World Heritage Tours (☎ 6471 7174) has the MV *Heritage Wanderer*, which charges $36 ($16 children) for a trip from 9 am to 4.15 pm; lunch is available on board.

All cruises include a visit to Sarah Island, a Heritage Rainforest Walk and views of Hells Gates (the narrow entrance to Macquarie Harbour).

Seaplane Tour A highly recommended way to see the river and surrounding World Heritage Area is on a seaplane tour with Wilderness Air (☎ 6471 7280). The planes take off from Strahan's wharf about every 1½ hours from 9 am onwards and fly up the river to Sir John Falls, where they land so that you can take a walk in the rainforest before flying back via Sarah Island and Ocean Beach. The 80-minute flight is well worth the $99. Demand for flights is heavy, so book ahead.

Jet-Boat Ride Wild Rivers Jet (☎ 6471 7174), also at the Wilderness Air office on the wharf, offers 50-minute jet-boat rides up the King River for $35 ($22 children); the rides operate daily from 9 am.

Places to Stay

Although Strahan has a range of accommodation, places are often full in the summer, so it's best to book.

There's the *West Strahan Caravan Park* (☎ 6471 7239), which charges $12 for a camp site for two, and there's also a camping ground with basic facilities 15 km away at Macquarie Heads.

At $13 for members ($15 for nonmembers), the *Strahan Youth Hostel* (☎ 6471 7255), in Harvey St, has the cheapest accommodation in town. It is about a 10-minute walk from the town centre.

Three km from town, on Ocean Beach Rd, is the historic *Strahan Wilderness Lodge* (☎ 6471 7142), where doubles, with a continental breakfast, cost $40/45. Unless you have your own transport, it may be a bit inconvenient.

Hamer's Hotel (☎ 6471 7191) is opposite the wharf right in the middle of town and has comfortable rooms for $45/55, including a continental breakfast. It also has a group of somewhat twee, self-contained cottages built in various colonial styles, and these are also on the waterfront. The cost is $95 to $130 for two, and some have a spa.

For a memorable stay you could try the historic *Franklin Manor* (☎ 6471 7311), on the Esplanade just around the bay from the town centre. It costs $130/155 to stay in a self-contained suite including breakfast.

Places to Eat

At the magnificent *Franklin Manor* (☎ 6471 7311) you can get an excellent three-course meal for $26 but it's best to book. *Hamer's Hotel* and *Regatta Point Tavern*, on the Esplanade, and the *Strahan Inn*, in Jolly St, all have good meals.

The *Strahan Bakery* has salad rolls and cakes and at night doubles as a pizza shop. The *Harbour Cafe* has takeaways, but the building now looks a bit drab.

Wild Winds on the Westcoaster

The Westcoaster yacht race, commencing in Melbourne, heads down Tasmania's wild and windy west coast. With few harbours for shelter, it is indeed one of the toughest yachting races around. The race concludes over the same days as its more famous counterpart, the Sydney to Hobart race. Constitution Dock in Hobart is definitely the place to be around New Year, when yachts fill the harbour and much celebrating goes on. ■

Getting There & Away

In summer Redline has daily services to Strahan from Hobart ($34), Burnie ($31) and Devonport ($37). In winter, services are reduced to running roughly every second day. The Redline agent is the newsagency in the main street.

Tasmanian Wilderness Transport also runs buses on weekends all year between Strahan and Hobart ($55) and Devonport ($50); its agent is the Harbour Cafe in the main street.

FRANKLIN-GORDON WILD RIVERS NATIONAL PARK

This World Heritage listed park includes the catchment areas of the Franklin and Olga rivers and part of the Gordon River, as well as the excellent bushwalking region known as **Frenchmans Cap**. It has a number of unique plant species and a major Aboriginal archaeological site at **Kutikina Cave**.

Much of the park is impenetrable rainforest, but the Lyell Highway traverses its northern end and there are a few short walks which start from the road. These include hikes to **Donaghys Hill**, from which you can see the Franklin River and the magnificent white quartzite dome of Frenchmans Cap, and a walk to **Nelson Falls**.

The walk to Frenchmans Cap takes three to five days and is the park's best-known bushwalk. The best way, however, to see this magnificent park is not to cross the Franklin River but to raft down it.

Rafting the Franklin

The Franklin is a very wild river and rafting it can be a hazardous journey. Experienced rafters can tackle it if they are fully equipped and prepared, or there are tour companies which offer complete rafting packages. Whether you go with an independent group or a tour operator, you should contact the Department of Parks, Wildlife & Heritage (☎ 6233 6391) for the latest information on permits and regulations.

All expeditions should register at the booth at the junction between the Lyell Highway and the Collingwood River, 49 km west of Derwent Bridge. The trip, starting at Collingwood River and ending at Heritage Landing on the Franklin, takes about 14 days (you can do a shorter eight-day one). From the exit point (the same for both trips), you can be picked up by a Wilderness Air seaplane, or 22 km farther down the river by a Gordon River cruise boat.

Tour companies that arrange complete rafting packages include Peregrine Adventures (☎ 6231 0977) at 8 Criterion St, Hobart; Rafting Tasmania (☎ 6227 8293), 63 Channel Highway, Taroona; and Tasmanian Expeditions (☎ 6334 3477), 110 George St Launceston. An all-inclusive rafting package, including transport, costs around $150 a day. Departures are mainly from December to March.

Cradle Mountain-Lake St Clair

Tasmania's best-known national park is the superb 1262-sq-km World Heritage Area of Cradle Mountain-Lake St Clair. The spectacular mountain peaks, deep gorges, lakes, tarns, wild open moorlands, and the reserve's incredible variety of wildlife, extend from the Great Western Tiers in Tasmania's north to Derwent Bridge on the Lyell Highway in the south. It is one of the most glaciated areas in Australia and includes Mt Ossa (1617 metres), Tasmania's highest mountain, and Lake St Clair, Australia's deepest natural freshwater lake.

The preservation of this region as a national park is due, in part, to the Austrian Gustav Weindorfer, who fell in love with the area and proclaimed 'This must be a national park for all time. It is magnificent. Everyone should know about it, and come and enjoy it'. In 1912 he built a chalet out of King Billy pine called Waldheim (German for Forest Home), and from 1916 he lived there permanently. Today, eight bushwalkers' huts have been constructed near his original chalet at the northern end of the park, and the area is named Waldheim, after his chalet.

There are plenty of day walks in both the Cradle Valley and Cynthia Bay (Lake St Clair) regions, but it is the spectacular 80-km walk between the two that has turned this park into a bushwalkers' mecca. The Overland Track is one of the finest bushwalks in Australia, and in summer up to 100 people a day can set off on it. The track can be walked in either direction, but most people walk from north to south, from Cradle Valley to Cynthia Bay.

Cradle Valley

At the northern park boundary, and built on the verge of an amazing rainforest, the visitor centre and rangers' station (☎ 6492 1133) is open year-round from 8 am to 5 pm. The centre is staffed by rangers who can advise you about weather conditions, walking gear, maximum and minimum walking groups, bush safety, and bush etiquette.

For visitors in wheelchairs, or with young-sters in prams, the centre also features an easy, but quite spectacular, 500-metre circu-lar boardwalk through the adjacent rainforest called the **Rainforest-Pencil Pine Falls Walking Track**.

Cradle Mountain Scenic Flights (☎ 6492 1132), which operate from the Cradle View Restaurant, offer a much less energetic way to see all the sights. A 25-minute trip costs $130 for two or $55 each for three or more people.

Whatever time of the year you visit, be prepared for cold, wet weather in the Cradle Valley area – on average it rains on seven days out of 10, is cloudy eight days in 10, the sun shines all day only one day in 10, and it snows on 54 days each year!

Cynthia Bay

Cynthia Bay, near the southern park bound-ary, also has an informative rangers' station (☎ 6289 1115) where you register to walk the Overland Track in the opposite direction. At the nearby kiosk (☎ 6289 1137) you can book a seat on the small *Idaclair!* ferry. The boat does a one way ($15) or return ($20) trip to Narcissus Hut at the northern end of Lake St Clair ($25 if you break the trip for a couple

> ### Horizontal Can Be Vertical
> *Anodopetalum biglandulosum* is a real mouthful. Otherwise known as 'horizontal', this scrub is familiar to those who venture off the beaten track. It's found only in Tasmania and sends up thin, vigorous growth when an opening in the forest canopy occurs. The old branches become heavy and fall; it then shoots again. This continual process creates the dense, tangled thickets so typical of Tasmania's native forest. ∎

of hours, $30 if you return on a different day) departing at 9 am and 12.30 and 3 pm. The boat is available for charter. From the same kiosk you can also hire dinghies for a spot of fishing or relaxing on the lake, but don't fall in – it's freezing!

The Overland Track

The best time to walk the Overland Track is during summer, when the flowering plants are most prolific, although spring and autumn also have their attractions. You can walk the track in winter, but only if you're very experienced.

The trail is well marked for its entire length and, at an easy pace, takes around five or six days to walk. En route, however, there are many secondary paths leading up to mountains like Mt Ossa or other natural fea-tures, making it a great temptation to take a few more days to explore the region fully. In fact, the length of time you take is only limited by the amount of supplies you can carry. There are 12 unattended huts along the track which you can use for overnight accommodation, but in summer they can get full so make sure you carry a tent. Camp fires are banned so you must also carry a fuel stove.

The most dangerous part of the walk is the exposed high plateau between Waldheim and Pelion Creek, near Mt Pelion West. The south-west wind that blows across here can be bitterly cold and sometimes strong enough to knock you off your feet.

If you are walking from Cradle Valley to Cynthia Bay, you have the option of radioing from Narcissus Hut for the *Idaclair!* ferry to come and pick you up and save a 5½-hour walk.

A detailed description of the walk is given in Lonely Planet's *Bushwalking in Australia*.

Places to Stay & Eat

Cradle Valley Region The cheapest place in this area is the *Cradle Mountain Camping Ground* (☎ 6492 1395), 2.5 km outside the national park. It costs $14 a double to camp here or $20 per person to stay in the bunkhouse. Bedding is hired out at exorbitant rates so bring a warm sleeping bag.

At Waldheim, five km into the national park, there are eight basic huts, all containing gas stoves, cooking utensils and wood heaters but no bedding. The minimum fees for these cabins are $55 to $75. Check-in and bookings for the huts are handled by the camping ground.

Just on the national park boundary is the luxurious *Cradle Mountain Lodge* (☎ 6492 1303), where doubles in the main chalet cost $85 and basic self-contained cabins are $146 a double. The lodge has good facilities for its guests and anyone is welcome to eat at the excellent restaurant (make sure you book first), visit the Tavern Bar or buy basic groceries and unleaded petrol at the lodge's general store. Expect prices to be higher than in other parts of the state; if that's a problem, bring everything with you.

The *Cradle View Restaurant*, near the camping ground, serves reasonably priced home-made meals; you can also buy leaded petrol and diesel from outside the restaurant.

Cynthia Bay Region At the southern end of Lake St Clair, *Lakeside St Clair Wilderness Holidays* (☎ 6289 1137) has several huts, plenty of camp sites and a kiosk that sells basic food supplies. It costs $8 for two to camp and $6 per person a night to stay in the bunkhouse, *Milligania*. The other huts are designed for groups and cost $8 per person, with a minimum of $30 for the smaller huts.

At Derwent Bridge, five km away, there's accommodation at the wooden chalet-style *Derwent Bridge Hotel* (☎ 6289 1144). Rooms in huts cost $15 per person, and rooms in the hotel are $45/65, including a continental breakfast. The hotel does good, hearty meals at normal prices and, with its open fire and friendly staff, is a good place to spend an evening. You can also buy food, basic supplies and maps, and rent fishing or bushwalking gear here.

If you are after self-contained units, the nearby *Bronte Park Highland Village* (☎ 6289 1126) is just off the highway and has units at $60 and $70 a double. There are also camp sites for a bargain $5, and hostel beds for $12. The hotel there also has good meals at reasonable prices. The only other accommodation is at the *Derwent Bridge Chalets* (☎ 6289 1125), which charges $105 a double in the summer.

Getting There & Away

Cradle Valley Region Transport to/from this area was once a big problem but the construction of the link road to the west coast has meant that the park is now only a short diversion from the Murchison or Midland highways. All the buses coming from the north pass the park, but if coming from Queenstown only the weekend services come this way. During summer, Redline has a service every day from Burnie to the Cradle Mountain Lodge ($26). This bus goes on to Queenstown and Strahan. During winter the bus only runs on Tuesday, Thursday and Saturday.

During summer, Tasmanian Wilderness Transport has buses every day from Launceston ($35) and Devonport ($30); during winter the buses run only three days a week. On Saturday the bus continues to Strahan ($40) and returns from there on Sunday.

Cynthia Bay Region Redline has services five days a week between Hobart and Strahan via Derwent Bridge. One-way fares from Hobart to Derwent Bridge are $20, and from there to Strahan are $16. Redline's agent is the Road House on the Lyell Highway.

Tasmanian Wilderness Transport has return trips to Lake St Clair from Devonport, Launceston and Hobart; its agent is the kiosk at Lake St Clair.

Getting Around
Cradle Valley Region During summer, a Tasmanian Wilderness Transport bus will take you from the camping ground to Lake Dove for $5. Maxwell's (☎ 6492 1400) also runs a shuttle bus on demand for $5 per person.

Cynthia Bay Region Maxwell's also runs an informal taxi to and from Cynthia Bay and Derwent Bridge for $4, and this operates daily on demand (bookings essential). This meets the regular Redline bus along the highway.

South-West

SOUTH-WEST NATIONAL PARK
There are few places left in the world as isolated and untouched as Tasmania's south-west wilderness, the state's largest national park. It is the home of some of the world's last tracts of virgin temperate rainforest, and these contribute much to the grandeur and extraordinary diversity of this ancient area.

The south-west is the habitat of the endemic Huon pine, which lives for more than 3000 years, and of the swamp gum, the world's tallest hardwood and flowering plant. About 300 species of lichen, moss and fern, some rare and endangered, festoon the dense rainforest; superb glacial tarns decorate the jagged mountains; and in summer, the delicate alpine meadows are ablaze with wildflowers and flowering shrubs. Through it all are the wild rivers, with rapids tearing through deep gorges and waterfalls plunging over cliffs. Each year more and more people venture into the heart of this incredible part of Tasmania's World Heritage Area, seeking the peace, isolation and challenge of a region as old as the last Ice age.

The best-known walk in the park is the **South Coast Track** between Port Davey and Cockle Creek, near Recherche Bay. This takes about 10 days and should only be tackled by experienced hikers, well prepared for the often vicious weather conditions. Light planes are used to airlift bushwalkers into the south-west and there is vehicle access to Cockle Creek. Detailed notes to some of the walks in this region are available in Lonely Planet's *Bushwalking in Australia*.

A whole range of escorted wilderness adventures are possible, involving flying, hiking, rafting, canoeing, mountaineering, caving and camping. More information on these can be obtained from the Department of Parks & Wildlife (☎ 6233 6191). Entry fees apply even if you're just driving on the road through the park.

LAKE PEDDER
At the edge of the south-west wilderness lies Lake Pedder, once a spectacularly beautiful natural lake considered the crown jewel of the region. In 1972, however, it was flooded to become part of the Gordon River power development. Together with nearby Lake Gordon, Pedder now holds 27 times the volume of water in Sydney Harbour and is the largest inland freshwater catchment in Australia. The underground Gordon power station is the largest in Tasmania and on most days tours are available for $5. The visitors centre at the dam site has plenty of information about the scheme.

The hydroelectric scheme was built in controversial circumstances, and today many people would like Lake Pedder to be drained and restored to its original condition (see the Pedder 2000 aside in this section).

STRATHGORDON
Built to service HEC employees, the township of Strathgordon is the base from which to visit lakes Pedder and Gordon, the Gordon Dam and the power station. Strathgordon is also becoming a popular bushwalking, trout fishing, boating and water-skiing resort.

Pedder 2000

Tasmania is renowned world-wide for its pristine wilderness areas and, during the last 20 or so years, has gained recognition for the essential role it has played in world environmental issues. The first major conservation issue in Tasmania was the flooding of Lake Pedder in 1972 for a hydroelectric power scheme. This natural lake was the largest of its type in the world. Despite public protest, and claims that the dam was not really necessary for the power scheme, the project went ahead, on the rationale of job creation.

Pedder 2000 is a campaign to reverse this engineering project by draining the lake and restoring it to its former glory. A government enquiry has failed so far to bring about any change, but, even so, conservationists regard the Pedder 2000 campaign as setting a precedent for reversing other such projects. ■

There's a camping ground, and accommodation is available at the *Lake Pedder Motor Inn* (☎ 6280 1166), where singles/doubles cost $45/60. Meals are also available from the restaurant at normal hotel prices.

Bass Strait Islands

Tasmania has two groups of islands, the Hunter and Furneaux groups, at the western and eastern entrances to Bass Strait respectively. Once the transient homes of sealers, sailors and prospectors, today these islands are inhabited by rural communities and are rich in wildlife and natural beauty.

KING ISLAND (pop 2000)

At the western end of Bass Strait in the Hunter Group, this small island has beautiful beaches and quiet lagoons. Discovered in 1798, King Island quickly gained a reputation as a breeding ground for seals and sea elephants. Just as quickly, however, these animals were hunted close to extinction by brutal sealers and sailors known as the Straitsmen.

Over the years, the stormy seas of Bass Strait have claimed many ships and there are several wrecks around the island. The worst occurred in 1845 when the *Cataraqui*, an immigrant ship, went down with 399 people aboard.

King Island is best known for its dairy produce, although kelp and large crayfish are other valuable exports.

Things to See & Do

King Island's four lighthouses guard against its treacherous seas. The one at Currie, built in 1880, is open in the afternoon on weekends, or by appointment, for $3. The Cape Wickham lighthouse is the tallest in the southern hemisphere and is worth visiting for the view of the surrounding great coastal scenery.

Currie Museum, originally the lighthouse keeper's cottage, is open from 2 to 4 pm on weekends. It features many maritime and local history displays and entry is $2. Kelp Industries Pty Ltd is the only kelp processing plant in Australia. From the roadside you can see kelp drying on racks.

The **King Island Dairy** is a must for visitors. It is open all day on weekdays and on Sunday from 12.30 to 4 pm, although times are liable to change. Swimming at deserted beaches or in freshwater lakes, scuba diving amongst exotic marine life and shipwrecks, surfing and fishing are all popular.

If you're interested in a drier pastime, try bushwalking; there is abundant wildlife, including a small colony of fairy penguins at Grassy.

Organised Tours

King Island Coach Tours (☎ 6462 1138) and

Top Tours (☎ 6462 1245) offer half-day trips from $27 and full-day trips from $49.

King Island Dive Charters (☎ 6461 1133) has single dives for $45 or day trips for $90 including equipment hire. It also offers fishing charters for $540 a day for up to six people inclusive.

Places to Stay
Near Currie, the *Bass Caravan Park* (☎ 6462 1260) has on-site vans for $30 and self-contained units for $70 a double. The *Boomerang Motel* (☎ 6462 1288), is moderately priced with single/doubles at $60/70. Rooms have superb ocean views and it's only a short walk into town.

On the other side of the island the *Naracoopa Lodge* (☎ 6461 1294) is close to the beach and has good hostel-style accommodation for $20. *Golden Spoon Chalets* (☎ 6461 1103), in Lovers Lane, charges $72 to $80 a double and is very cosy.

Places to Eat
Currie has many fine eating places within walking distance of most of the accommodation. The *Coffee Shop*, open daily, serves light meals, while the *Bakery* has homemade pies. The *Fishbowl Restaurant* (☎ 6462 1288), at the Boomerang Motel, features local produce and has spectacular ocean views; bookings are essential. The *Cataraqui Restaurant*, at Parers Hotel, offers a similar menu and the hotel also has a bistro.

On the other side of the island in Naracoopa, the *Golden Spoon Restaurant* (☎ 6461 1103) provides lunches and afternoon teas. Booking for dinner is essential.

Getting There & Away
Aus-Air, Airlines of Tasmania and Kendall Airlines all fly to the island. Regular flights are available from Melbourne ($124), Launceston, Hobart and Burnie ($110). Package deals are often the best value with two nights accommodation plus a hire car for $280 a person from Melbourne. Similar deals are available from Launceston.

Getting Around
There is no public transport on the island and most roads are gravel, so drive carefully. Kendall Airlines can arrange airport transfers to Currie for $7 per person each way and to Naracoopa for $28 per person each way. Hire-car companies will meet you at the airport and should be booked.

King Island Auto Rentals (☎ 6462 1297) has cars from $45 a day plus insurance. Howell's Auto Rent (☎ 6462 1282) has cars from around $65 a day with insurance.

FLINDERS ISLAND (pop 1010)
Flinders Island is the largest of the 52 islands which comprise the Furneaux Group. First charted in 1798 by Matthew Flinders, the Furneaux Group became a base for the Straitsmen, who not only slaughtered seals in their tens of thousands but also indulged in piracy.

The most tragic part of Flinders Island's history, however, was its role in the virtual annihilation of Tasmania's Aboriginal people between 1829 and 1834. Of the 135 survivors who were transported to Wybalenna (an Aboriginal word meaning Black Man's House) to be 'civilised', only 47 survived to make their final journey to Oyster Cove near Hobart in 1847.

On a brighter note, Flinders Island has many attractions, including beautiful beaches, good fishing and scuba diving.

The island's main industries are farming, fishing and seasonal mutton-birding. Its administrative centre is Whitemark, and Lady Barron in the south is the main fishing area and deep-water port. Petrol is available in Whitemark and Lady Barron only.

Things to See & Do
Today, all that remains of the unfortunate settlement at **Wybalenna** is the cemetery and the chapel, restored by the National Trust and open to visitors.

Nearby, the **Emita Museum** displays a variety of Aboriginal artefacts as well as old sealing and sailing relics. It's open weekends from 1 to 4 pm and during summer from 1 to

5 pm on weekdays as well. Entry is by dona-tion.

Bushwalking is very popular, and many visitors climb **Mt Strezlecki**. The walk com-mences about 10 km south of Whitemark, is well signposted and takes three to five hours return.

The island supports a wide variety of wild-life, including many bird species, the most well known being the Cape Barren goose (now protected) and the mutton bird. Mutton birds are readily seen at dusk, and Strait Lady Island Adventures (☎ 6359 4507) runs evening tours from December to March from Lady Barron.

Mountain bicycles are available for hire from Flinders Island Bike Hire (☎ 6359 2000) at $10 per day and can be collected at the airport on arrival.

Scuba divers can visit several locations on the northern and western coasts. In many places you can enter from the beach or shelv-ing rocks. There are shipwrecks around the island, some clearly visible from shore.

Rock and beach fishing are popular all year. Fishing tackle and bait can be pur-chased from many stores, however you need to bring your own rod.

A more unusual pastime is fossicking for 'diamonds' (which are actually fragments of topaz) on the beach and creek at Killie-crankie Bay.

Jimmy's Island Tours (☎ 6359 2112) runs day-long coach tours for around $62 per person as well as a three-day package coach tour including accommodation and air fares for around $500.

Places to Stay

Flinders Island Cabin Park (☎ 6359 2188) is five km north of Whitemark, next to the airport. It has self-contained cabins for $25/40 a single/double. Recently renovated, the *Flinders Island Interstate Hotel* (☎ 6359 2114), in the centre of Whitemark, has rooms for $18 to $65.

There are also a variety of holiday homes around the island, including *Echo Hills Holiday Units* (☎ 6359 6509) and *Seaview*

Cottage (☎ 6359 2011), both charging around $60 a double.

The *Furneaux Tavern* (☎ 6359 3521), at Lady Barron overlooking the picturesque Furneaux Sound, costs $60 to $80 a double. Rooms are spacious and the service is friendly. Picnic lunch baskets can be ordered here.

Places to Eat

The *Bakery* at Whitemark sells pies, bread and cold drinks on weekdays. It's also the local pizza place on Friday nights. *Jimmy's Fast Food* store, in Whitemark, is open daily and serves grills and other takeaway meals.

The *Interstate Hotel* (☎ 6359 2114) in Whitemark serves a range of reasonably priced counter meals from Monday to Satur-day. The *Whitemark Sports Club* has a cosy restaurant with a quality menu. Meals are also available in the bistro throughout the week in summer. Bookings for the restaurant are necessary.

Patterson's Store in Lady Barron is open daily and also acts as a post office and a Commonwealth Bank agency. The *Shearwa-ter Restaurant* at the Furneaux Tavern in Lady Barron has a fine selection of bistro meals every day. The *General Store* at Killiecrankie provides snacks and drinks.

Getting There & Away

Aus-Air, Airlines of Tasmania and Promair all fly to the island. There are flights most days from Melbourne ($110) and Smithton ($119). The cheapest way to see the island is using one of the many package deals. These provide return airfares, accommodation for two or more nights and car hire with unlim-ited mileage. Costs vary according to season, but packages start at around $220 from Launceston and $270 from Melbourne.

Getting Around

In Whitemark, Bowman Transport (☎ 6359 2014) has cars from around $45 a day, while both Flinders Island Car Rentals (☎ 6359 2168) and Flinders Island Transport Services (☎ 6359 2060) rent cars for around $50 a day.

Victoria

PHONE CHANGES

As of November 1996, all Victorian phone numbers have eight digits. The STD area code for Victoria is (03).

HIGHLIGHTS

- Driving the spectacular Great Ocean Road from Anglesea to the Port Campbell National Park
- Enjoying adventure activities, including skiing, bushwalking, hang-gliding and fly-fishing, in the High Country
- A leisurely cycling tour around the wineries of the Rutherglen area.
- Visiting the re-created 1860s gold-mining town of Sovereign Hill, Ballarat
- The historic port of Echuca, with its evocative reminders of the paddle-steamer era.
- Bushwalking among the wildflowers, wildlife and mystical beauty of the Grampians (Gariwerd) National Park.
- Melbourne in spring – for the gardens, the Melbourne Cup, the Aussie Rules Grand Final, and the Melbourne International Festival

Population	4,476,000
Area	228,000 sq km

In the early 1800s there was great interest from Europe in the new continent of Australia. The French sent ships to explore the south coast, and in 1803, hoping to forestall a French settlement, Britain hurriedly sent an expedition to establish a colony at Sorrento on Port Phillip Bay. This first settlement on the bay lasted less than a year and, unable to find a permanent supply of fresh water, the settlers broke camp and set sail for Tasmania.

It wasn't until 1835 that the first permanent European settlement was made at the present site of Melbourne, although whalers and sealers had used the Victorian coast for a number of years. The earliest settlers, John Batman and John Pascoe Fawkner, came to Melbourne in search of the land they had been unable to obtain in Tasmania. Not until 1837, by which time several hundred settlers had moved in, was the town named Melbourne and given an official seal of approval.

The new settlement's free-enterprise spirit naturally led to clashes with the staid powers of Sydney. The settlers were not interested in the convict system, for example, and on a number of occasions turned convict ships away. The settlers wanted to form a break-away colony, and their PR efforts included naming it after the Queen and the capital city after her Prime Minister, Lord Melbourne.

Finally, in 1851, the colony of Victoria was formed and separated from New South Wales. At about the same time gold was discovered, and the population doubled in little more than a year. Many diggers made or lost their fortunes and returned to their homelands, but many more stayed on to establish new settlements and work the land. Some of the most interesting historical areas in Victoria are associated with those gold-rush days.

Victoria is Australia's smallest mainland state – it's also the most densely populated and the most industrialised, and features some of the most diverse landscapes and some of the most impressive national parks. Melbourne, as Australia's second-largest city, is one of the state's prime attractions and lays claim to being the fashion, food and cultural capital of Australia. For years it was also considered to be Australia's financial

VICTORIA

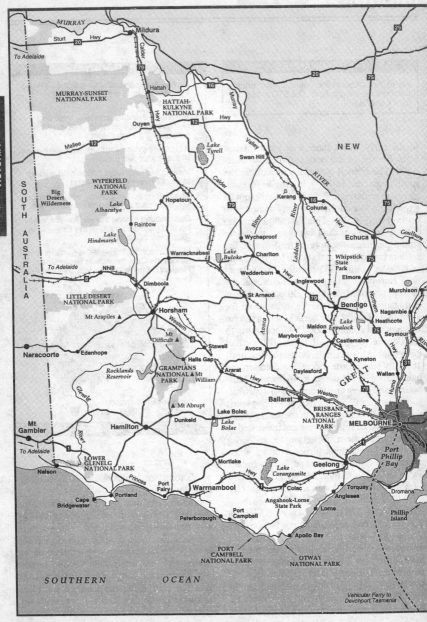

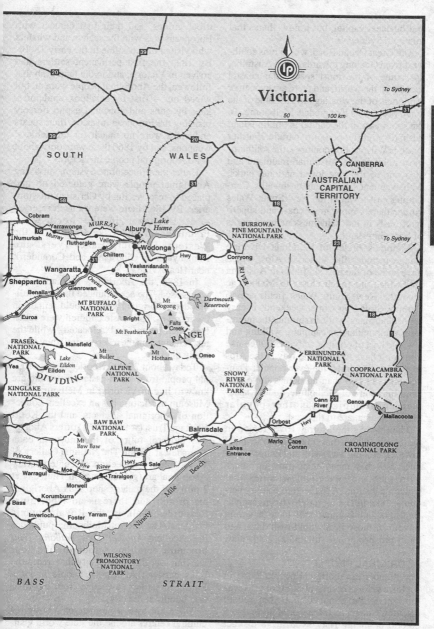

and business capital, but it now shares that role with Sydney.

The Great Ocean Road, which runs south-west from Geelong towards South Australia, has some of the most spectacular coastal scenery in the world, and there are evocative reminders of the whaling days in some of the small port towns that predate Melbourne. To the south-east of the capital is Phillip Island with its nightly penguin parade. Farther south is Wilsons Promontory – the southern-most point on the Australian mainland and also one of the best loved national parks, with excellent scenery and bushwalks. Continuing east towards the New South Wales border there's more great coast and superb rainforests in the wilderness national parks of East Gippsland.

Victoria's stretch of the Great Dividing Range includes the Victorian Alps, which have some of the best ski fields in Australia and which are much closer to Melbourne than the New South Wales fields are to Sydney. Skiing on winter weekends is easy for Melburnians, while in summer the mountains are popular for camping, walking and a whole host of outdoor activities. Of course you don't have to go all the way to the Alps to get into the hills; the ever-popular Dandenongs are less than an hour's drive east from the centre of Melbourne, and the spectacular Grampians, another popular mountain area, are to the west.

Then there's the Murray River region in the north, which has many historic river towns, including Swan Hill and Echuca. Victoria also has many wine-growing areas, with plenty of excellent wineries that welcome visitors. And the gold country certainly shouldn't be forgotten – towns such as Bendigo and Ballarat still have a strong flavour of those heady gold-rush days, and lucky prospectors are still finding gold today.

ABORIGINAL PEOPLE

The number of Aboriginal people living in Victoria before the arrival of Europeans was thought to be about 12,000, but recent research suggests there could have been 50,000 or more. They lived in 38 distinct tribal groups, and their first contact with Europeans was with the sealers and whalers who visited the coastline in the early 1800s. By 1834 the first permanent settlers had arrived in Victoria, and in the land grab that followed, the Aboriginal people were all but wiped out – first by smallpox epidemics, later by guns and poison. Despite fiercely resisting the European invasion, their spears and clubs were no match for the settlers' weapons, and by 1860 there were only about 2000 Aboriginal people in Victoria.

Under the Protectorate System, surviving Aboriginal people were gathered up and placed in reserves run by Christian missionaries. By 1863 there were six such reserves – at Ebenezer in the north-west, Framlingham and Lake Condah in the Western District, Lake Tyers and Ramahyuck in Gippsland, and Coranderrk near Healesville.

In 1886, the Aborigines Protection Act was passed. The act stipulated that only full-blooded Aboriginal people could remain in the reserves. Half-caste children were taken from their parents and 'relocated', while the rest remained on the reserves until they eventually died out.

Today about 20,000 Koories (as Aboriginal people from south-eastern Australia are known) live in Victoria. In Melbourne, the Museum of Victoria has an excellent collection of Aboriginal artefacts, and the Koori Heritage Trust (☎ 9669 9061) offers Aboriginal cultural tours of the museum each Thursday at 10 am. The National Gallery of Victoria has a collection of contemporary Aboriginal art (guided tours on Thursday at 2 pm) and the gallery shop sells Aboriginal art prints, and there is an Aboriginal Resources Walk in the Royal Botanic Gardens. The City of Melbourne publishes the excellent *Another View Walking Trail* brochure detailing a four to five-hour walking tour through the city that traces the links between Aboriginal people and the European settlers (available from information booths in the city).

There are also a number of Aboriginal cultural centres around the state worth visiting, including the Brambuk Living Cultural Centre in the Grampians (Gariwerd) National Park and the Dharnya Centre in the Barmah State Forest north-east of Echuca.

GEOGRAPHY

Victoria's geography is probably more diverse than that of any other Australian state, as it includes both the final stretch of the Great Dividing Range and associated outcrops plus a swath of flatter country to the west. The Great Dividing Range reaches its greatest altitude across the Victoria-New South Wales border. The mountains run south-west from the New South Wales border, then bend around to run more directly west as the range crosses north of Melbourne and finally fades out before the South Australian border.

The Victorian coast is particularly varied. On the eastern side is the mountain-backed Gippsland region while to the west is spectacular coastline running to South Australia.

The north-west of the state, beyond the Great Dividing Range, is flat plains. It is especially dry and empty in the extreme north-west of the state, where you'll find the eerie Sunset Country. For most of the length of the border between New South Wales and Victoria, the mighty Murray River forms the actual boundary.

CLIMATE

Statistically, the weather in Victoria and Melbourne is not too bad; average temperatures in summer or winter is only a few degrees less than Sydney's and Melbourne is certainly far less humid than Sydney or Brisbane. The annual rainfall is also less than in either of those damp cities. The trouble with Melbourne's climate is that it's totally unpredictable; hence the old joke that if you don't like the weather, just wait a minute. Melbourne does have four distinct seasons, although sometimes it seems like they all come on the same day. A good guiding principle is to expect the unexpected.

Although the weather is basically somewhat cooler in Melbourne than elsewhere in continental Australia, you'll rarely need more than a light overcoat or jacket even in the depths of winter. Inland, however, in places like Ballarat or in the Alps, it can get really cold.

INFORMATION

Tourism Victoria operates the following interstate information offices:

New South Wales
    403 George St, Sydney 2000
    (☎ (02) 9299 2288)
South Australia
    16 Grenfell St, Adelaide 5000
    (☎ (08) 8231 4129)

Remarkably, Tourism Victoria doesn't have an office in Melbourne. Tourist information is handled by the RACV's Victorian Information Centre & Booking Service (☎ 9650 1522) in the town hall on the corner of Swanston Walk and Little Collins St in the city.

The government-run bookshop, Information Victoria, is at 318 Little Bourke St. The information desk downstairs supplies free sketch maps of national parks, and the Government Map Shop at the next desk sells maps of Victoria and other parts of Australia.

NATIONAL & STATE PARKS

Victoria has 34 national parks, 40 state parks and a wide range of other protected areas, including coastal and marine reserves and historic areas. These parks are managed by the Department of Conservation & Natural Resources (DC&NR), which has offices in Melbourne and throughout the state and also publishes leaflets about virtually every park in Victoria. At the DC&NR's head office (☎ 9412 4795), at 240 Victoria Pde in East Melbourne, is the very helpful Outdoor Information Centre where you can get maps, leaflets, books and colour posters on the state's parks, animals and native plants.

ACTIVITIES
Bushwalking

Victoria has some great bushwalking areas and a number of very active clubs. Check the

VICTORIA

The Major Mitchell Trail

The Major Mitchell Trail is a 1700-km 'cultural trail' which follows as closely as possible the route taken by the New South Wales surveyor general on his exploratory trip through Victoria in 1836.

Mitchell entered Victoria near present-day Swan Hill, and travelled south to the coast before returning to New South Wales through Hamilton, Castlemaine, Benalla and Wodonga. On his trip he named many places, including the Grampians, Mt Macedon and the Loddon, Glenelg and Wimmera rivers, and explored some previously little-known areas.

Mitchell was so pleasantly surprised by the lushness of the land, in comparison with the dry expanses of New South Wales, that he named the area *Australia Felix* (Australia Fair).

The route today covers many back roads and is well signposted with distinctive small brown and blue signs. An excellent descriptive handbook is available from the DC&NR and local tourist offices for $12.95. ■

outdoor-gear shops around Hardware and Little Bourke Sts in Melbourne for local club news and magazines. For more information about bushwalking in Victoria look for the handy walking guides *50 Bush Walks in Victoria* by Sandra Bardwell and *120 Walks in Victoria* by Tyrone T Thomas. Lonely Planet's *Bushwalking in Australia* is also useful.

Walking areas close to the city include the You Yangs, 56 km to the south-west, with a wide variety of birdlife; and the Dandenongs, right on the eastern edge of the metropolitan area. Wilsons Promontory is to the south-east in Gippsland. 'The Prom' has many marked trails from Tidal River and from Telegraph Bay – walks that can take from a few hours to a couple of days. The Australian Alps Walking Track traverses the High Country from Walhalla, 144 km east of Melbourne, to the outskirts of Canberra. This very long trail is for the experienced walker. There are other popular marked trails in the Bright and Mt Buffalo areas of the Alps.

The Grampians, 250 km to the west, are where Victoria's only remaining red kangaroos hang out. The Croajingalong National Park near Mallacoota in East Gippsland is equally rugged inland but the coastal walks are easier.

You can have backpacks and camping equipment repaired by Remote Repairs at 377 Little Bourke St, above the Mountain Designs shop.

Rock Climbing

Again, the Hardware St outdoor-gear shops are good information sources. Mt Arapiles, in the Western District 330 km north-west of Melbourne near Natimuk, is famous among rock climbers from around the world as it has a huge variety of climbs for all levels of skill.

If you just want to scramble around in rather crowded conditions there is Hanging Rock (of *Picnic at Hanging Rock* fame), 72 km north-west of Melbourne. Sugarloaf and Jawbones are 112 km north-east of Melbourne in the Cathedral Range State Park, a popular weekend spot. The Grampians, 250 km west of Melbourne, have a wide variety of climbs. At Mt Buffalo, 369 km north in the alpine area, the hardest climb is Buffalo Gorge.

Swimming & Surfing

Melbourne's Port Phillip Bay doesn't have great beaches, although there is reasonably good swimming on the eastern side of the bay. Along the Mornington Peninsula you have the choice between sheltered bay beaches on one side and the ocean beaches on the other side.

Outside of the bay, however, the Victorian coastline features some truly spectacular and lovely ocean beaches, many of which have good surf – when the conditions are right, of course. A good surfing reference is the booklet *Where to Look for Surf in Victoria*

($19.95), which covers the coastline from Cape Otway to Wilsons Prom.

The coast along the Great Ocean Rd features dramatic contrasts between sandy beaches at places such as Anglesea, Apollo Bay and Discovery Bay and rugged cliffs and gorges along the Port Campbell National Park. There are also fine beaches all along the eastern coastline, including those at Phillip Island, Wilsons Promontory, Lakes Entrance and Mallacoota.

Scuba Diving

Flinders, Portland, Kilcunda, Torquay, Anglesea, Lorne, Apollo Bay, Mallacoota, Portsea, Sorrento and Wilsons Prom are all popular diving areas. In Melbourne there are clubs and organisations renting equipment. Companies offering courses and diving trips include Diver Instruction Services (☎ 9662 2811); Melbourne Diving School (☎ 9459 4111); Queenscliff Dive Centre (☎ 5258 1188; and Schonberg Diving Services (☎ 5598 6499).

Boating & Sailing

There are many sailing clubs around Port Phillip Bay in Melbourne. Other popular boating areas around the state include the large Gippsland Lakes system, Lake Eildon, and Mallacoota Inlet in East Gippsland. At all of these places you can hire yachts and launches, which work out to be quite economical among a few people.

Houseboat holidays are also popular, and these can be arranged on Lake Eildon and on the Murray River at Echuca and Mildura.

White-Water Rafting

Operators including World Expeditions (☎ 9670 8400), Peregrine Adventures (☎ 9663 8611) and Snowy River Expeditions (☎ 5155 9353) run white-water rafting trips on various rivers in the Victorian Alps. Trips operate all year round, although the best times are during the snow melts from about August to December. Costs range from $115 for one day to $550 for five-day expeditions.

Skiing

See the section on the Alps for details of the Victorian ski fields.

Cycling

Victoria is a great place for cycling. Melbourne has some excellent bike tracks, and in the country you'll find hundreds of km of good roads that carry little traffic. Especially appealing is the fact that in many areas you'll ride a very long way without encountering a hill. Wine regions such as Rutherglen are popular areas for cycling tours and the High Country areas are much favoured by mountain bikers.

Contact the helpful Bicycle Victoria (☎ 9328 3000) at 19 O'Connell St in North Melbourne for more information; ask about their regular tours and events such as the Great Victorian Bike Ride (every November) and the Easter Bike Ride. The book *Bicycling Around Victoria* ($19.95) by Ray Peace details 50 different bike rides around the state.

GETTING THERE & AWAY

Melbourne is the focal point for most transport into Victoria. Many international airlines fly into Melbourne, and Ansett (☎ 13 1300) and Qantas (☎ 13 1313) have flights between Melbourne and the other capital cities.

Greyhound Pioneer Australia (☎ 13 2030), McCafferty's (☎ 13 1499) and several other bus companies have regular services to Sydney and Adelaide, and V/Line (☎ 13 2232) operates the interstate rail links to Adelaide and Sydney.

If you're heading to Tassie, the Tasmanian Travel Centre (☎ 9206 7922) at 256 Collins St in the city can advise on the various ways to get there.

See Getting There & Away in the Melbourne section for more details of transport into Victoria.

GETTING AROUND
Air

Kendell Airlines (bookings through Ansett on ☎ 13 1300) operates the main flights within Victoria, with services between Mel-

VICTORIA

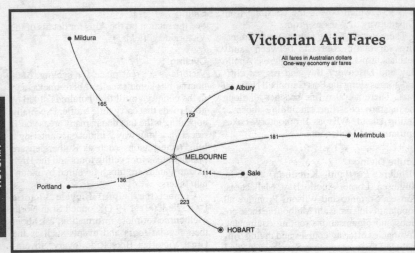

Victorian Air Fares

All fares in Australian dollars
One-way economy air fares

bourne and Mildura, Albury, Portland and Merimbula. Southern Australia Airlines (bookings through Qantas on ☎ 13 1313) also flies between Melbourne and Mildura, and Hazelton (bookings through Ansett) flies from Albury to Traralgon and Sale.

Train & Bus

V/Line (☎ 13 2232 between 7 am and 9 pm) has a fairly comprehensive rail network of country services radiating out of Melbourne – these are supplemented by connecting V/Line buses. The main train routes, and economy fares from Melbourne, are:

West to Geelong ($8) then inland to Warrnambool ($31.80); a bus runs along the Great Ocean Road from Geelong through Lorne ($10.40) and Apollo Bay ($16.80)
North-west to Ballarat ($12.80), Stawell ($29.40), Horsham ($38.60) and to Adelaide ($50) in South Australia; buses connect from Stawell to Halls Gap ($36.40) in the Grampians
North-west through Ballarat to Mildura ($50.60)
North through Bendigo ($19.40) to Swan Hill ($40.60)
North to Shepparton ($21.60) and Cobram ($29.40)
North along the Hume Highway to Albury-Wodonga ($36.40), continuing to Sydney; buses run from Wangaratta to Beechworth and Bright

East through Traralgon ($18.20) and Sale ($25) to Bairnsdale ($31.80); buses connect Bairnsdale to Lakes Entrance, Orbost, Cann River and Merimbula

V/Line has timetables with details of all its services, and these are available from station bookstalls.

The major bus companies, Greyhound Pioneer Australia (☎ 13 2030) and McCafferty's (☎ 13 1499) both operate bus services from Melbourne to Adelaide (via Ballarat and Horsham) and from Melbourne to Sydney (via the Hume Highway). Greyhound Pioneer also operate buses along the coastal Princes Highway between Melbourne and Sydney.

Melbourne

Population 3,300,000

Melbourne is Australia's second-largest city. Its birth and major period of development paralleled Queen Victoria's reign (1837 to 1901), and the city is in many ways a product of its formative era both architecturally and socially. It's a traditionally conservative city of elaborate Victorian-era buildings, gracious parks and gardens, and tree-lined boulevards.

In the years since WW II, Melbourne's social fabric has been radically transformed by the influx of thousands of immigrants, and the city has been greatly enriched by the influence of people and cultures from around the world. Several building booms, most notably that of the 1980s, have altered the city physically so that it is now a striking blend of past and present, with ornate 19th-century buildings sitting alongside towering skyscrapers.

The first European settlement on Port Phillip Bay was established at Sorrento in 1803, although within a year it was abandoned and the settlers moved down to Tasmania. In 1835 a group of Tasmanian entrepreneurs returned and established a permanent settlement near the site of today's city centre.

In 1851 the colony of Victoria became independent of New South Wales and almost immediately the small town of Melbourne became the centre for Australia's biggest and most prolonged gold rush. The immense wealth from the goldfields was used to build a solid and substantial city that came to be known as Marvellous Melbourne. This period of great prosperity lasted until the end of the 1880s, when the property market collapsed and led to a severe depression.

Perhaps best known for its trams, its cafes and restaurants, the diversity of its inner suburbs, and events such as the Melbourne Cup and the International Festival of the Arts, Melbourne today is a vibrant multicultural city that is passionate about the arts, sports, food and wine, and the good life. Melbourne may lack the physical impact of its more flamboyant northern sister and take a little more time to get to know, but it has much to offer.

Orientation

Melbourne's suburbs sprawl around the shores of Port Phillip Bay, with the city centre sited on the north bank of the Yarra River, about five km inland from the bay. The city centre is laid out in a rectangular grid of wide boulevards, interspersed with a network of narrow streets and alleys. The main shopping precinct is in the heart of the city, with the Bourke St Mall as its centrepoint. In the mall you'll find tourist information booths and the large department stores, and on the Bourke and Elizabeth Sts corner is the main post office.

Bus travellers arrive in Melbourne at either the Spencer St Coach Terminal on the west side of the city (V/Line, Skybus, Firefly and McCafferty's buses), or the Melbourne transit centre at 58 Franklin St (Greyhound Pioneer and Skybus buses) on the northern side of the city. Interstate and country trains operate from the Spencer St station, while the Flinders St station on the corner of Swanston and Flinders Sts is the main station for suburban trains.

Swanston St, which runs north-south through the city, is another pedestrian mall. After crossing the Yarra River, Swanston St becomes St Kilda Rd, a tree-lined boulevard that runs all the way south to St Kilda and beyond.

Information

Tourist Offices In the city, the best places for information are the city council's information booths. The Bourke St Mall and City Square booths open on weekdays from 9 am to 5 pm (on Friday until 7 pm), Saturday from 10 am to 4 pm and Sunday from 11 am to 4 pm. The Rialto observation deck booth is open on weekdays from 11 am to 5 pm and on weekends from 10 am to 4 pm.

The Royal Automobile Club of Victoria (RACV; ☎ 9650 1522) has a tourist information office in the town hall on Swanston Walk – plenty of brochures, but it's mainly a booking office for tours and accommodation.

The Federal Airports Corporation has two tourist information booths (☎ 9339 1805) in the international terminal at Melbourne airport (Tullamarine).

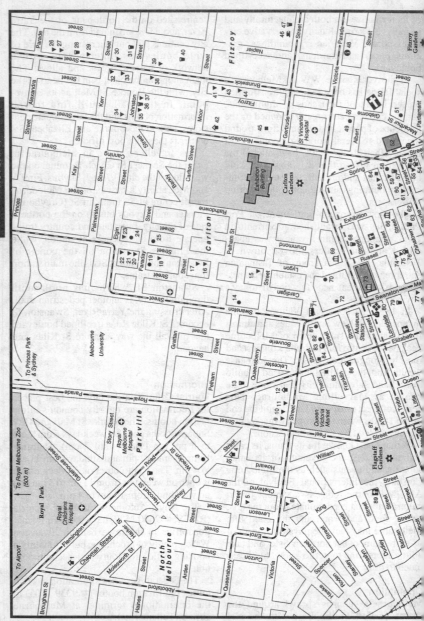

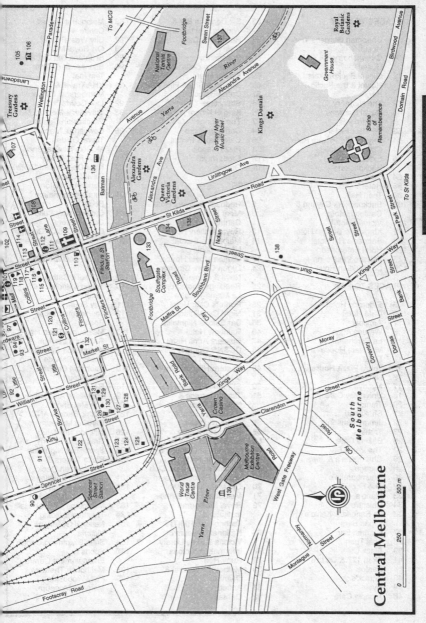

VICTORIA

Central Melbourne

0   250   500 m

VICTORIA

PLACES TO STAY

1 Chapman Gardens YHA Hostel
4 Queensberry Hill YHA Hostel
12 Global Backpackers' Hostel & the Public Bar
42 The Nunnery
45 Royal Gardens Apartments
53 Windsor Hotel
54 City Centre Private Hotel
64 City Limits Motel
76 Exford Hotel Backpackers'
84 Stork Hotel
85 Hotel Y
86 Toad Hall
102 Backpackers City Inn & Carlton Hotel
114 Victoria Hotel
122 Kingsgate Budget Hotel
123 Batman's Hill Hotel
124 Hotel Enterprise
125 Terrace Pacific Inn
129 Le Meridien Hotel

PLACES TO EAT

5 Eldorado Hotel
6 Cafe Hotel
7 Amiconi
8 Warung Agus
9 La Porchetta
10 Viet Nam House
11 Dalat
15 Toto's Pizza House
16 Notturno
17 Nyonya
18 University Cafe
20 Tiamo
21 Shakahari
22 Jimmy Watson's
23 Trotters
26 Bakers Cafe
27 The Vegie Bar
29 Charmaine's & Joe's Garage
30 Rhumbarella's
32 The Fitz
33 Mario's
34 Chishti's
35 La Sangria & Kahlo's Tapas Bars
37 Carmen Bar
38 Thai Thani
39 Black Cat
41 Akari 177 & De Los Santos
43 Annick's
44 Nyala
46 Arcadia Cafe

55 Six Degrees Bar & Waiters' Restaurant
56 Hard Rock Cafe
59 Cafe K
60 Pellegrini's
61 Florentino Cellar Bar
62 Flower Drum
65 Jan Bo & Shark Finn Inn
67 Cafee Baloo
74 Stalactites
75 King of Kings
77 The Lounge
94 Campari Bistro
95 Cafe Max & Panini
103 Pizza Napoli
117 Crossways
118 Gopals

OTHER

2 Redback Brewery Hotel
3 Meat Market Craft Centre
13 Royal Artillery Hotel
14 Melbourne Sexual Health Clinic
19 Carlton Movie House
24 Lygon Court, Cinema Nova & Comedy Club
25 Readings Bookshop & La Mama Theatre
28 Punters Club Hotel
31 Night Cat Nightclub
36 Bar Salona Nightclub
40 Rainbow Hotel
47 Builders Arms Hotel
48 DC&NR Outdoor Information Centre
49 Eastern Hill Fire Station & Museum
50 St Patrick's Cathedral
51 Tasma Terrace & National Trust
52 Parliament House
57 Metro Nightclub
58 Princess Theatre
63 Sadie's Bar
66 Museum of Chinese & Australian History
68 Bennett's Lane Jazz Club
69 Victoria Police Museum
70 Old Melbourne Gaol
71 Melbourne City Baths
72 Royal Melbourne Institute of Technology (RMIT)
73 National Museum of Victoria & State Library
78 Information Victoria
79 Ruby Red
80 Melbourne Central & Daimaru
81 Ansett
82 Qantas

83 Melbourne Transit Centre
87 City West Police
88 Old Royal Mint
89 St James Old Cathedral
90 Spencer St Coach Terminal
91 YHA Travel & Membership Office
92 Law Courts
93 Traveller's Medical & Vaccination Centre
96 Bowyang's Maps & Travel Guides
97 McGill's Newsagency
98 Main Post Office
99 Myer Department Store
100 David Jones Department Store
101 Tourist Information Booth
104 Old Treasury Building
105 Conservatory
106 Captain Cook's Cottage
107 Collins Place & Regent Hotel
108 Hyatt Hotel & Food Court
109 St Paul's Cathedral
110 Young & Jackson's Hotel
111 City Square
112 Tourist Information Booth
113 Melbourne Town Hall & RACV's Victorian Information Centre & Booking Service
115 Sportsgirl Centre & Food Court
116 RACV Office
119 Travellers' Aid Society
120 The Met Shop
121 Gothic Bank & ANZ Banking Museum
126 Inflation Nightclub
127 Grainstore Tavern
128 Sports Bar Nightclub
130 Rialto Towers & Observation Deck
131 Olderfleet Buildings
132 National Mutual Life Association Building
133 Melbourne Concert Hall
134 Theatres Building
135 National Gallery of Victoria
136 State Swimming Centre
137 Sports & Entertainment Centre
138 Malthouse Theatres
139 Polly Woodside Maritime Museum

Post & Telecommunications Melbourne's main post office (the GPO) is on the corner of Bourke and Elizabeth Sts. There's an efficient poste restante section and phones for interstate and international calls. Phone centres can also be found behind the main post office on Little Bourke St and down the road at 94 Elizabeth St.

The STD telephone area code for Melbourne and Victoria is (03).

Other Information The National Trust (☎ 9654 4711) has an office in the historic Tasma Terrace at 4 Parliament Place.

The YHA (☎ 9670 7991) has its helpful Melbourne office at 205 King St, on the corner of Little Bourke St. The Travellers Aid Society (☎ 9654 2600), on the 2nd floor at 169 Swanston St, offers assistance in emergencies.

Bookshops Melbourne's largest bookshops include Angus & Robertson Bookworld, at 107 Elizabeth St; Collins Booksellers, at 115 Elizabeth St; and Dymocks, on the corner of Bourke and Swanston Sts. The agreeably chaotic McGills at 187 Elizabeth St (opposite the main post office) is good for interstate and overseas newspapers.

Bowyangs Maps & Travel Guides at 372 Little Bourke St has the city's most extensive range of travel books and maps, and Information Victoria at 318 Little Bourke St has a wide selection of books on Melbourne and Victoria.

There are also dozens of good specialist bookshops in Melbourne, including Readings at 338 Lygon St, Carlton; Brunswick St Bookstore at 305 Brunswick St, Fitzroy; Cosmos Books & Music at 112 Acland St, St Kilda; and Black Mask Books at 78 Toorak Rd, South Yarra.

The DC&NR's Outdoor Information Centre (☎ 9412 4795), at 240 Victoria Pde in East Melbourne, has an excellent range of maps, books and posters on Victoria's national parks and wilderness areas. The centre is open weekdays from 9 am to 5 pm.

Medical Services The Traveller's Medical & Vaccination Centre (☎ 9602 5788), at Level 2, 393 Little Bourke St in the city, is open weekdays from 9 am to 5 pm (Monday and Thursday till 9 pm) and Saturday from 9 am to 1 pm (appointments necessary). It has excellent up-to-date information on the vaccinations needed for most countries.

The Melbourne Sexual Health Centre (☎ 9347 0244) is at 580 Swanston St in Carlton – visits are free. The Fairfield Infectious Diseases Hospital also has a travellers' advice line (☎ 0055 15676).

Dangers & Annoyances Melbourne trams should be treated with some caution by car drivers. You can only overtake a tram on the left and you must always stop behind one when it halts to drop or collect passengers (except where there are central 'islands' for passengers). In the city centre at most junctions a peculiar left-hand path must be followed to make right-hand turns, in order to accommodate the trams. Note that in rainy weather tram tracks are extremely slippery; motorcyclists should take special care. Cyclists must beware of tram tracks at all times; if you get a wheel into the track you're flat on your face immediately, and painfully.

Tram passengers should be cautious when stepping on and off – a lot of people have been hit by passing cars, so don't step off without looking both ways. Pedestrians in Bourke St Mall and Swanston Walk should watch for passing trams too.

Walking Tour

This walking tour starts at the intersection of Flinders and Swanston Sts, home to three of Melbourne's best-known landmarks. The grand old **Flinders St station** is the main railway station for suburban trains – 'under the clocks' at the station entrance is a favourite Melbourne meeting place. Across the road is one of Melbourne's best-known pubs, **Young & Jackson's**, which is famed mainly for the painting of *Chloe* hanging in the upstairs bar. Judged indecent at the Melbourne Exhibition of 1880, she has gone on to win affection among generations of Melbourne drinkers. The third landmark on this

VICTORIA

corner, **St Paul's Cathedral**, is a master-piece of Gothic revivalist architecture.

Stroll up Swanston St, which has been closed to cars to create the **Swanston Walk**, a tree-lined boulevard that pedestrians share with trams and commercial vehicles. In the block between Flinders Lane and Collins St is the **City Square**, with its fountains and ponds, a statue of the ill-fated explorers Burke and Wills (on the Collins St side), and an information booth nearby. Across Collins St is the **town hall**, built between 1870 and 1880.

Continue up to Bourke St and take a left into the **Bourke St Mall**. Like the Swanston Walk, it's difficult for a pedestrian mall to work with 30-tonne trams barrelling through the middle of it every few minutes, but despite the tram threat the mall has become something of a focus for city shoppers, with its buskers, missionaries and big department stores.

Collect your mail from the main post office at the Elizabeth St end of the mall, then return to Swanston Walk and head north again. Across Little Lonsdale St you'll pass the **State Library** and the **National Museum of Victoria** on your right, and in the next block is the **Royal Melbourne Institute of Technology**, with its rather bizarre architectural facades. Take a right into Franklin St and then another right into Russell St, and head down past the **Old Melbourne Gaol**. When you get to Little Bourke St, turn left and you've entered Melbourne's **China-town**. This narrow lane was a thronging Chinese quarter even back in the gold-rush days and it's now a busy, crowded couple of blocks with excellent Chinese restaurants, Asian supermarkets and shops.

At the top end of Little Bourke St, turn right into Spring St, which has some of Melbourne's most impressive old buildings including the lovely **Princess Theatre**, the gracious **Windsor Hotel**, and the **State Houses of Parliament**. Built with gold-rush wealth, this building served as the national parliament while Canberra was under construction. There are free tours of both houses, when parliament is in recess, every weekday at 10 and 11 am, noon, and 2, 3 and 3.45 pm.

Farther down Spring St, opposite Collins St, the 1853 **Old Treasury Building** is one of the finest 19th-century buildings in the city and houses an interesting exhibition on Melbourne's past and future (open daily from 9 am to 5 pm).

Cross Spring St and you'll enter what's known as the **'Paris End'** of Collins St – mainly because this stretch was once lined with plane trees, grand buildings and street cafes. The plane trees remain and are beautifully lit at night by fairy lights, but sadly quite a few of the historic buildings have been demolished over the years.

On your left you'll see the soaring towers of Collins Place, which house Melbourne's **Regent Hotel**. The hotel's toilets on the 35th floor are well worth a visit – they boast spectacular views over the Melbourne Cricket Ground (MCG), parklands and shimmering suburbs of Melbourne and are one of the city's prime (unofficial) attractions. While you're up here, you could have a drink in the hotel's ritzy Atrium Bar.

Continue down Collins St to Swanston Walk and turn left. Continue past Flinders St station, then turn right just before the river and stroll along the riverside boardwalk. An arched footbridge takes you across the river to the **Southgate** complex, with its excellent restaurants, bars and cafes. South of Southgate is Melbourne's arts precinct, and across St Kilda Rd are the parklands of the **Kings Domain** – a wonderful area to wander through and explore, if you still have the energy.

Other Walking Tours The City of Melbourne publishes a series of *Heritage Walk* brochures to Melbourne, available from the council's information booths, or the Town Hall, Swanston Walk (cnr Little Collins St).

The National Trust's *Walking Melbourne* booklet is particularly useful if you're interested in Melbourne's architectural heritage.

Tram Tours

When you tire of walking, consider buying yourself a Zone 1 daily ticket and continuing your exploration of Melbourne by tram. For

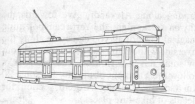

A popular tour of the city can be taken on old W-class trams

$4.10, you can spend the entire day travelling around the city and inner suburbs by tram – a bargain, and a great way to get a feel for Melbourne.

Try a ride on tram No 8. It starts off along Swanston St in the city, rolls down St Kilda Rd beside the Kings Domain and continues up Toorak Rd through South Yarra and Toorak. Another popular tram ride is on No 16, which cruises right down St Kilda Rd to St Kilda.

City Buildings

Melbourne is an intriguing blend of the soaring new and the stately old. Epitomising this blend are buildings such as the **Melbourne Central** shopping complex on the corner of La Trobe and Elizabeth Sts. Opened in 1991, the centrepiece of the complex is the old **shot tower**, which still stands on its original site but is now enclosed within the new building.

The stretch of Collins St between William and King Sts is another embodiment of the old combined with the new. The **Rialto Towers** is an architectural landmark built during the boom of the 1980s. Its semi-reflective glass looks stunningly different under varying light conditions – it's something of a city Ayers Rock! Beside it is the imaginative Le Meridien Hotel, which uses the facades of two old buildings and cleverly incorporates an old stone-paved alleyway that used to run between them. Next to the hotel are the **Olderfleet Buildings**, magnificent monuments to the Gothic revival architecture that dominated during the building boom of the late 19th century.

East along Collins St on the corner of Queen St you'll see three bank buildings that are also fine examples of the extravagance of architecture during Melbourne's land boom period. The 1887 **Gothic Bank** is regarded as the finest Gothic revival building in Melbourne, and the interior has been cleverly restored to highlight the intricate ceiling. Across the road is the impressive **National Mutual Life Association Building** (1891-1903).

Other old buildings in the centre include the 1872 **Old Royal Mint** beside Flagstaff Gardens, the 1842 **St James Old Cathedral** on King St (Melbourne's oldest surviving building), and **St Patrick's Cathedral**, one of the city's most imposing churches, behind the State Houses of Parliament. Victoriana enthusiasts may also find some very small Melbourne buildings of interest – scattered around the city are a number of very fine cast-iron men's **urinals** (like French *pissoirs*). They date mainly from 1903 to 1914, and the one on the corner of Exhibition and Lonsdale Sts is classified by the National Trust.

Rialto Towers Observation Deck

This extremely popular lookout is on the 55th floor of Melbourne's tallest building, the Rialto Towers on Collins St. The lookout platform offers spectacular 360° views of Melbourne's surrounds, and there's a cafe if you want to linger. It's open daily from 11 am to 11.30 pm; entry costs $6, or $8 if you want to watch a 20-minute film on the development of Melbourne.

National Museum & State Library

Extending for a block between Swanston St and Russell St, beside La Trobe St, is the National Museum plus the State Library and La Trobe Library. The State Library has a gracious, octagonal, domed reading room and any book-lover will enjoy its atmosphere. Its collection of more than a million books and other reference material is particularly notable for its coverage of the humanities and social sciences, as well as art,

VICTORIA

music, performing arts, Australiana and rare books.

Exhibits at the museum include artefacts from ancient Egypt, displays on Aboriginal culture, and the stuffed remains of Phar Lap, the legendary racehorse that nearly disrupted Australian-American relations when it died a suspicious death in the USA. The complex also includes a planetarium.

The museum is open every day from 10 am to 5 pm. Admission costs $5.30 for adults and $2.60 for children, or you can buy a combined ticket for the museum and planetarium for $8/4. Towards the end of the century the museum is scheduled to move to a new home in the Carlton Gardens just north of the city centre.

Old Melbourne Gaol

This gruesome old prison and penal museum is a block farther up Russell St. It was built of bluestone in 1841 and was used right up until 1929. In all, 135 prisoners were hanged here. It's a dark, dank, spooky place. The museum displays include death masks of noted bushrangers and convicts, Ned Kelly's armour, the very scaffold from which Ned took his fatal plunge, and some fascinating records of early 'transported' convicts, indicating just what flimsy excuses could be used to pack people off to Australia's unwelcoming shores. It's an unpleasant reminder of the brutality of Australia's early convict days. It is open daily from 9.30 am to 4.30 pm, and admission is $6.50 (children $3.50, family $18, students $4.50). There are also tours of the gaol on Wednesday and Sunday nights at 8.45 pm, costing $15 for adults, $8 for children – book in advance on ☎ 9663 7228.

Yarra River

Melbourne's prime natural feature, the Yarra, is a surprisingly pleasant river, enhanced by the parks, walks and bike tracks that have been built along its banks. Despite the cracks about it 'running upside down', it's just muddy, not particularly dirty.

When the racing rowing boats are gliding down the river on a sunny day, or you're driving along Alexandra Ave towards the city on a clear night, the Yarra can look quite magical. Best of all you can cycle along the riverside without the risk of being wiped out by some nut in a Holden. The bike tracks follow the Yarra out of the city for some 20 km (see the Getting Around section for details of bike-hire places).

A more leisurely way to see the river is on one of the tour boats that operate on the river from Princes Walk beside Princes Bridge (across from Flinders St station).

There are some really beautiful old bridges across the Yarra, and an ultra-modern pedestrian bridge crosses the Yarra from behind Flinders St station, linking the city with Southgate, the Victorian Arts Centre and the National Gallery.

To the north-east of the city, the Yarra is bordered by parkland, much loved by runners, rowers and cyclists. At the **Studley Park Boathouse** in Kew, you can enjoy a meal and/or a drink and hire rowing boats, canoes and kayaks by the hour – good fun, although a fair few people seem to find themselves upside down in the river! In parts of **Studley Park** you could be out in the bush; it's hard to believe the city's all around you. Farther upstream at **Fairfield Park** there is another boathouse, restored to its original Edwardian elegance, offering Devonshire teas and other snacks, and boats and canoes for hire. You might catch a performance in the outdoor amphitheatre next to the boathouse.

Southbank

The area opposite the city centre on the southern side of the Yarra has recently been given a major facelift. This former industrial wasteland has been impressively redeveloped and the Southgate complex features three levels of riverside cafes, restaurants, an international food hall and an up-market shopping galleria with some exclusive and interesting specialty boutiques. There's also an aquarium, the five-star Sheraton Towers Hotel and some specially commissioned sculptures and other art works.

It's a great area for shopping, eating,

drinking or just browsing, and of course the major theatres and galleries are nearby. See Places to Eat for details of some of Southgate's eateries.

Polly Woodside Maritime Museum

Close to Spencer St Bridge, immediately south of the city centre, is the *Polly Woodside*. Built in Belfast, Northern Ireland, in 1885, it's an old iron-hulled sailing ship which carried freight in the dying years of the sailing era. The *Polly Woodside* is the centrepiece of the maritime museum, which is open daily from 10 am to 5 pm; admission is $7 ($4 for children).

Queen Victoria Market

Over on the northern side of the city, the Queen Victoria Market is on the corner of Peel and Victoria Sts. It's the city's main retail produce centre – a popular multicultural scene on Tuesday, Thursday, Friday and Saturday morning, when the stall operators shout, yell and generally go all out to move the goods. On Sunday the fruit and vegies give way to general goods – everything from cut-price jeans to second-hand records. See the Organised Tours section for details of walking tours of the market.

Royal Melbourne Zoo

Three km north of the city centre in Parkville is Melbourne's excellent zoo. There are numerous walk-through enclosures in this well-planned zoo. You can walk through the aviary, around the monkey enclosures and even over the lions' park on a bridge. The butterfly enclosure and the gorilla forest are both excellent. This is the oldest zoo in Australia and one of the oldest in the world.

The zoo is open daily from 9 am to 5 pm (7 pm January and February) and admission is $12 (children $6, family $33). Ring ☎ 0055 33 653 for details on its free summer jazz concerts. The zoo is in **Royal Park**; in the park a marker indicates where Burke and Wills set off on their ill-fated journey in 1860. You can get there on tram No 55 from William St in the city.

Science Works Museum

Opened in mid-1992, this is the science and technology section of the Museum of Victoria, and it has a huge and fascinating array of tactile displays. It's at 2 Booker St, Spotswood, about 15 minutes walk from Spotswood train station, or just over the West Gate Bridge if you're driving. It's open daily from 10 am to 4.30 pm and costs $8 for adults, $4 for children.

Melbourne Cricket Ground

The MCG is Australia's biggest sporting stadium and was the central stadium for the 1956 Melbourne Olympics. Set in Yarra Park, which stretches from the city and East Melbourne to Richmond, the huge stadium can accommodate about 100,000 spectators, and does so at least once a year. The big occasion is the annual Australian Rules football Grand Final in September. This is Australia's biggest sporting event and brings Melbourne, which engages in a winter of Aussie Rules football mania each year, to a fever pitch.

Cricket is, of course, the other major sport played at the MCG. International Test and one-day matches, as well as interstate Sheffield Shield and other local district games, take place here over the summer months and draw big crowds.

On the city side of the stadium there's the **Australian Gallery of Sport & Olympic Museum**, a museum dedicated to Australia's sporting passions. It's open every day from 10 am to 4 pm and admission is $8 (children $5).

Victorian Arts Centre & National Gallery

Melbourne's large arts precinct is just south of the Yarra River and the city centre, alongside St Kilda Rd.

The building closest to the Yarra is the **Melbourne Concert Hall**, the city's main venue for the performing arts. Beside it, the **Theatres Building** houses the State Theatre, the Playhouse, the George Fairfax Studio and the Westpac Gallery. There are one-hour tours of the theatres complex ($8) each weekday at noon and 2.30 pm, as well as each Saturday at 10.30 am and noon. On Sunday, Backstage Tours (☎ 9281 8152) runs 1½-hour backstage tours ($12) at 12.15 and 2.15 pm.

The next building along, the **National Gallery of Victoria**, was the first part of the complex to be completed, back in 1968, and it houses a very fine collection of art. The gallery has outstanding local and overseas collections, an excellent photography collection and many fascinating temporary exhibits from all over the world. There are good displays of Aboriginal art and culture, and the gallery of 19th-century art is really worth a visit. The stained-glass ceiling in the Great Hall is superb – best viewed from a supine position. The gallery is open daily from 10 am to 5 pm and admission is $6.50 (students and children $3). On Monday admission is free, although only the ground and 1st floors are open. There are additional charges for some special exhibits.

The **Performing Arts Museum** is located at ground level in the Concert Hall building, facing the river. The museum has temporary exhibits on all aspects of the performing arts: it might be a display of rock musicians' outfits or an exhibit on horror in the theatre. Opening hours are weekdays from 11 am to 5 pm and weekends from noon to 5 pm; admission is $5 (children $3.50).

Parks & Gardens

Victoria has dubbed itself 'the garden state' and it's certainly true in Melbourne; the city has many swaths of green all around the central area. They're varied and delightful – formal gardens such as the Treasury and Flagstaff gardens; wide empty parklands such as Royal Park; the outstanding Botanic Gardens; and many others.

Royal Botanic Gardens Certainly the finest botanic gardens in Australia and arguably among the finest in the world, this is one of the nicest spots in Melbourne. There's nothing more genteel to do in Melbourne than to have scones and cream by the lake on a Sunday afternoon. The beautifully laid out gardens are right beside the Yarra River;

indeed the river once actually ran through the gardens and the lakes are the remains of curves of the river, cut off when the river was straightened out to lessen the annual flood damage. The garden site was chosen in 1845 but the real development took place when Baron Sir Ferdinand von Mueller took charge in 1852.

There's a surprising amount of fauna as well as flora in the gardens. Apart from the many water fowl and the frequent visits from cockatoos you may also see rabbits and possums if you're lucky. In all, more than 50 varieties of birds can be seen in the gardens. A large contingent of fruit bats, usually found in the warmer climes of north Queensland, has taken up residence in the trees of the fern gully.

You can pick up guide-yourself leaflets at the park entrances; these are changed with the seasons and tell you what to look out for at the different times of year. The gardens are open daily from sunrise to sunset.

Kings Domain The Botanic Gardens form a corner of the Kings Domain, which is flanked by the Yarra River, St Kilda Rd, Domain Rd and Anderson St.

Beside St Kilda Rd stands the massive **Shrine of Remembrance**, a WW I memorial. It's worth climbing up to the top as there are fine views to the city along St Kilda Rd. The shrine's big day of the year is Anzac Day, in April. Back during the Vietnam era some enterprising individuals managed to sneak up to the well-guarded shrine on the night before Anzac Day and paint 'PEACE' across the front in large letters. The shrine is open to visitors daily from 10 am to 5 pm.

Across from the shrine is **Governor La Trobe's Cottage**, the original Victorian government house sent out from the UK in prefabricated form in 1840. Originally sited in Jolimont, near the MCG, it was moved here to preserve this interesting piece of Melbourne's early history. The simple little cottage is open daily except Tuesday and Thursday from 11 am to 4.30 pm; admission is $4 (children $2, family $10).

The cottage is flanked by the **Old Obser-**

vatory and the **National Herbarium**. On some nights the observatory is open to the public for a free view of the heavens between 8 and 10 pm, but it is usually booked out months in advance. Phone the National Museum of Victoria (☎ 9669 9942) for details. Among other things, the herbarium tests suspected marijuana samples to decide if they really are the dreaded weed.

The imposing building overlooking the Botanic Gardens is **Government House**, where Victoria's governor resides. It's a copy of Queen Victoria's palace on England's Isle of Wight. There are guided tours on Monday, Wednesday and Saturday for $6 per person – you need to book on ☎ 9836 7246 (no tours from mid-December to the end of January).

Across the road from the herbarium on Dallas Brooks Drive is the **Australian Centre for Contemporary Art**, which is open Tuesday to Friday from 11 am to 5 pm and weekends from 2 to 5 pm; admission is free. Up at the city end of the park is the **Sidney Myer Music Bowl**, an outdoor performance area in a natural bowl. On Christmas Eve it's the venue for the wonderful Carols by Candlelight; in winter it turns into an ice-skating rink.

Treasury & Fitzroy Gardens These two popular formal parks lie immediately to the east of the city centre – both have a large resident population of possums; you may see them in the early evening or at night.

The Fitzroy Gardens, with its stately avenues lined with English elms, is a popular spot for wedding photographs. The pathways in the park are actually laid out in the form of the Union Jack. The gardens contain several points of interest including **Captain Cook's Cottage**, which was uprooted from its native Yorkshire and reassembled in the park in 1934. Actually it's not certain that the good captain ever did live in this house, but never mind, it looks very picturesque. The house is furnished in period style and has an interesting Captain Cook exhibit. It's open daily from 9 am to 5 pm and admission is $2.50 (children $1.20).

Other City Parks The central **Flagstaff Gardens** were the first public gardens in Melbourne. From a lookout point here, ships arriving at the city were sighted in the early colonial days. A plaque in the gardens describes how the site was used for this purpose.

On the northern side of the city, the **Carlton Gardens** are the site of the Exhibition Building, a wonder of the southern hemisphere when it was built for the Great Exhibition of 1880. Later it was used by the Victorian parliament for 27 years, while the Victorian parliament building was used by the national legislature until the parliament building in Canberra was finally completed. It's still a major exhibition centre today.

Historic Homesteads
Como Overlooking the Yarra River from Como Park in South Yarra, Como was built between 1840 and 1859. Aboriginal rites and feasts were still being held on the banks of the Yarra when the house was first built, and an early occupant writes of seeing a cannibal rite from her bedroom window.

The home has been authentically restored and furnished and, together with its extensive grounds, is operated by the National Trust. It is open from 10 am to 5 pm every day and admission is $7 (students $4.50, children $3.50); you can get there on tram No 8 from the city.

Ripponlea Ripponlea is at 192 Hotham St, Elsternwick, close to St Kilda. It's another fine old mansion with elegant gardens inhabited by peacocks. Ripponlea is open daily (except Monday) from 10 am to 5 pm and admission is $8 (students $5, children $4).

Other Galleries
At 7 Templestowe Rd in the suburb of Bulleen, the **Museum of Modern Art at Heide** is the former home of two prominent art patrons, John and Sunday Reed, and houses an impressive collection of 20th-century Australian art. The sprawling park is an informal combination of deciduous and native trees, with a carefully tended kitchen

garden and scattered sculpture gardens running right down to the banks of the Yarra. Heide is open from Tuesday to Friday between 10 am and 5 pm, and on Saturday and Sunday between noon and 5 pm. Bus No 203 goes to Bulleen, and the Yarra bike path goes close by.

In Eltham, the mud-brick and alternative lifestylers' suburb, **Montsalvat** on Hillcrest Ave (26 km out from the city centre) is Justus Jorgensen's eclectic re-creation of a European artists' colony, which today houses all manner of artists and artisans. It's open daily from dawn to dusk; admission costs $5 for adults and $2.50 for children. In January it's the venue for a major jazz festival. It's a two-km walk from Eltham station.

Other Museums

There are a number of smaller museums around Melbourne. In Chinatown in the city centre the **Museum of Chinese Australian History** is housed in an 1890s warehouse on Cohen Place and traces the history of the Chinese people in Australia. It's open daily from 10 am to 4.30 pm (Saturday from noon); admission is $5 (children $3). The museum also conducts two-hour walking tours around Chinatown every morning, and these cost $15, or $28 including lunch at a Chinatown restaurant. Phone ☎ 9662 2888 for bookings.

Also in the city, the **Postmasters Gallery** at 321 Exhibition St has an outstanding collection of stamps, and is open daily from 8 am to 5 pm (Saturday from 10 am, Sunday from noon). On La Trobe St is the **Victoria Police Museum**, open weekdays from 10 am to 4 pm; admission is free.

The **Jewish Museum of Australia**, at 26 Alma Rd in St Kilda, preserves Jewish culture, art and customs; it's open Tuesday to Thursday from 10 am to 4 pm and Sunday from 11 am to 5 pm. Admission is $5.

At 174-180 Smith St in Collingwood, the **Australian Toy Museum** is open daily from 10 am. The **Melbourne Fire Brigade Museum** at 8 Gisborne St, East Melbourne, is open Friday from 9 am to 3 pm and Sunday from 10 am to 4 pm.

Out at Moorabbin airport, Cheltenham, the **Moorabbin Air Museum** has a collection of old aircraft including a number from WW II. It's open daily from 10 am to 5 pm.

Trams

If Melbourne has a symbol then it's a movable one – trams. The real Melbourne tram – green-and-yellow, ancient-looking and half the weight of an ocean liner – can still be seen. Trams are the standard means of public transport, they work remarkably well and create far less pollution than the car and bus. More than a few cities that once had trams wish they still did today.

The old trams have been joined by a fleet of slick new ones and some of the trams have been turned into mobile works of art, painted from front to back by local artists.

A free city-circle tram has been introduced, designed primarily for tourists and passing many city sights on its route. The trams are the nice older ones, but painted a deep burgundy and gold. They travel on a fixed route along Flinders, Spring and Nicholson Sts to Victoria Pde and then back along La Trobe and Spencer Sts. They run daily every 10 minutes, from 10 am to 6 pm.

Trams are such a part of Melbourne life they've even been used for a play – Act One of *Storming Mont Albert by Tram* took place from Mont Albert to the city, Act Two on the way back. The passengers were the audience, the actors got on and off along the way. It wasn't a bad play! There's even a tram restaurant: the Colonial Tramcar Restaurant cruises Melbourne every night and you can have dinner on the move for $55 to $90 including drinks, depending on the time and the night (☎ 9696 4000 for reservations).

Melbourne Suburbs

The inner suburbs surrounding Melbourne's centre are like a ring of villages, in that each has its own particular character. If you want to get a true feel for Melbourne you'll need to venture beyond the city centre – one of the best ways to explore these inner suburban areas is to jump on a tram or two and just go wherever the tracks take you.

Fitzroy Fitzroy is one of the most fascinating areas in Melbourne. It's probably the most bohemian and alternative of the inner suburbs, with a large ethnic population living alongside lots of musicians, writers, artists and members of various subcultures. **Brunswick St** displays the liveliest array of cafes, restaurants, young designer clothes shops and bookshops to be found in Melbourne – an essential place on any itinerary. **Johnston St** is Melbourne's Spanish quarter and the home of the annual Hispanic Festival, held every November, and **Smith St** is a diverse and multicultural streetscape with plenty of interesting and unusual offerings.

Carlton & North Melbourne Immediately north of the city, Carlton has one of the most attractive collections of Victorian-era architecture. It's also known as the Italian quarter of Melbourne, and busy **Lygon St** has enough Italian restaurants, coffee houses, pizzerias and gelaterias to satisfy the most rabid pasta and cappuccino freak. Carlton is flanked by gracious Parkville, home to the University of Melbourne; consequently, lots of students and members of the 'intelligentsia' live around here.

The Lygon St Festa is held annually in November and always gets a good turn-out. The greasy-pole-climbing competition is popular.

West of Carlton is North Melbourne. a traditionally more working-class suburb that now combines Victorian-era architecture with some semi-industrial areas. It's also home to the YHA hostels (see Places to Stay).

South Yarra & Toorak South (of the) Yarra is a bustling, trendy and style-conscious suburb – the kind of place where avid readers of *Vogue Living* will feel very at home. Nearby, Toorak is the poshest suburb in Melbourne and home to Melbourne's wealthiest (or at least the most ostentatious) homeowners. Toorak doesn't hold much interest for travellers, although it can be interesting to drive around the tree-lined streets looking at the palatial homes.

Running though and linking South Yarra and Toorak is **Toorak Rd**, one of Australia's classiest shopping streets. Apart from expensive boutiques and some of Australia's best (and most expensive) restaurants, Toorak Rd also has a number of very reasonably priced places to eat.

Running south from Toorak Rd in South Yarra is **Chapel St**; if the word for Toorak Rd is 'exclusive' then for Chapel St it's 'trendy'. The strip of Chapel St between Toorak and Commercial Rds is home to some of Melbourne's fashionable clothing and gift shops, bars, and cafes. If you want to check out the latest fashions or some of the coolest people in Melbourne, this is the place to be – especially on a Saturday.

Prahran Chapel St's trendiness fades as it crosses Commercial Rd and heads south into Prahran, although it's still a fascinating multicultural shopping strip all the way down to Dandenong Rd. The delightful Prahran Market is around the corner on Commercial Rd. Farther south you can turn right by the Prahran town hall and wander along Greville St to explore its interesting retro and grunge clothing shops, galleries, junk shops and other offerings.

Prahran is something of a focal point for Melbourne's gay community, with numerous bars, cafes and nightclubs along Commercial Rd.

Richmond As Carlton is to Italy so Richmond is to Greece; this suburb, just to the east of the city centre, is the Greek centre for the third-largest Greek city in the world. That's right, after Athens and Thessaloniki, Melbourne is the next largest city in terms of Greek population. Richmond is, of course, the best place for a souvlaki in Melbourne! More recently Richmond became the centre for a huge influx of Vietnamese people, and colourful **Victoria St** is known as Little Saigon.

The suburb is another centre for Victorian architecture, much of it restored or in the process of restoration. **Bridge Rd** and **Swan St** are Melbourne fashion centres, with shops

VICTORIA

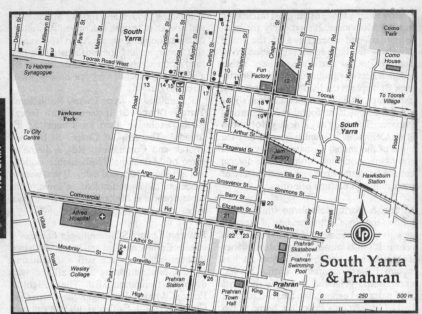

South Yarra & Prahran

PLACES TO STAY	PLACES TO EAT	OTHER
1 Tilba Hotel	8 La Porchetta	7 Longford Cinema
2 Albany Motel	13 Ticino Bistro	9 Readings Bookshop
3 West End Private Hotel	14 Winchell's Deli	10 South Yarra Train
4 Manor House Apart-	15 Frenchy's	Station
ments	17 Tamani	12 Como Centre, Hotel
5 Darling Towers	18 Caffe e Cucina	Como & Cinema
6 Domain Motel	19 Chapelli's & Kanpai	Como
11 Claremont Accommoda-	22 Chinta Ria	16 South Yarra Post Office
tion	23 Blue Elephant	20 Chasers Nightclub
24 Lord's Lodge Back-	25 Feedwell Cafe	21 Prahran Market
packers	26 The Continental	

where many Australian designers sell their seconds and rejects.

St Kilda Seaside St Kilda is Melbourne's most cosmopolitan suburb – it's an exuberant and lively blend of stylish and seedy, alternative and arty, hip and hypnotic. **Fitzroy St** and **Acland St** are the main streets here – both are a constant hive of activity,

especially on weekends and late at night, and both are lined with interesting bars, cafes and restaurants.

St Kilda's foreshore areas have been impressively redeveloped, with several restaurants perfectly positioned along the beachfront. It's also very pleasant to stroll out along the **St Kilda Pier** – there's a cafe at the end, and you can hire boats and bikes or take a **ferry ride** across the bay to Williamstown. There's also a small **penguin colony** here, tours of which operate from the pier.

Every Sunday the **Esplanade Sunday Market** features an excellent collection of art and craft stalls – great if you're looking for souvenirs or gifts. With its famous 'laughing face' entry gates, the **Luna Park** amusement centre is a local icon; a little old-fashioned, it's rides include a roller coaster, ferris wheel and ghost train. Nearby, the huge old **Palais Theatre** is an excellent entertainment venue, while over in Blessington St the lovely **St Kilda Botanic Gardens** are the perfect spot to wind down.

Held each February, the St Kilda Festival features local performing artists, bands and writers, with street stalls and parades, concerts and readings, and a fireworks display over the beach as a finale.

Once notorious as Melbourne's sin centre, St Kilda's image has been given a major facelift in recent years, although it can still be somewhat perilous to wander the streets late at night, particularly for women.

Williamstown At the mouth of the Yarra, this is one of the oldest parts of Melbourne and it has many interesting old buildings and lots of waterside activity. Williamstown remained relatively isolated from developments in the rest of Melbourne until the completion of the West Gate Bridge suddenly brought it to within a few minutes drive of the city centre. On Sunday there are ferries across the bay to Williamstown from St Kilda Pier, Station Pier in Port Melbourne and the World Trade Centre in the city.

Moored in Williamstown is the **HMAS Castlemaine**, a WW II minesweeper, is now preserved as a maritime museum and is open on weekends from noon to 5 pm; admission is $4 (children $2).

The **Railway Museum** on Champion Rd, North Williamstown, has a fine collection of old steam locomotives. It's open weekends and public holidays from noon to 5 pm. Admission is $4 (children $2).

Other Suburbs South of the centre are other inner suburbs with many restored old homes, particularly the bayside suburbs of **South Melbourne**, **Middle Park** and **Albert Park**. Emerald Hill in South Melbourne is a whole section of 1880s Melbourne, still in relatively authentic shape. The parklands around **Albert Park Lake**, which stretch from Albert Park to St Kilda, were controversially redeveloped and as of 1996 are the setting for the Australian Formula One Grand Prix car race. The lake is popular for boating and there's a running track around the perimeter.

Port Melbourne is a traditional working-class suburb that has also been a target for gentrification. Station Pier is the departure point for ferries to Tasmania.

Sandwiched between the city and Richmond is the compact area of **East Melbourne**; like Parkville it's one of the most concentrated areas of old Victorian buildings around the city with numerous excellent examples of early architecture.

Wealthier inner suburbs to the east, which also contain some popular shopping centres, include **Armadale**, **Malvern**, **Hawthorn** and **Camberwell**.

Beaches

Melbourne's bayside beaches are reasonably good considering their proximity to the city. The bay itself tends to look murky, but it's clean enough for swimming, and the beaches have broad strips of sand. Closest to the city are the popular **Albert Park** and **Middle Park** beaches – local meeting places and good spots to observe Aussie beach 'kulcha'. Farther around there's **St Kilda** and then **Elwood**, **Brighton** and **Sandringham**, which are quite pleasant beaches. Beyond Sandringham is the very good **Half Moon Bay** – well worth the half-hour drive from the city.

If you're looking for good surf and spectacular ocean beaches, head for either the Mornington Peninsula or the Great Ocean Road (known as the 'east coast' and the 'west coast' respectively) – both are just over an hour's drive from the city centre.

VICTORIA

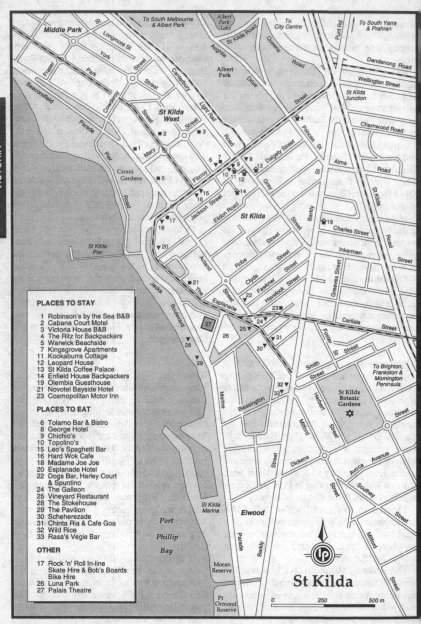

PLACES TO STAY

1 Robinson's by the Sea B&B
2 Cabana Court Motel
3 Victoria House B&B
4 The Ritz for Backpackers
5 Warwick Beachside
7 Kingsgrove Apartments
11 Kookaburra Cottage
12 Leopard House
13 St Kilda Coffee Palace
14 Enfield House Backpackers
19 Olembia Guesthouse
21 Novotel Bayside Hotel
23 Cosmopolitan Motor Inn

PLACES TO EAT

6 Tolarno Bar & Bistro
8 George Hotel
9 Chichio's
10 Topolino's
15 Leo's Spaghetti Bar
16 Hard Wok Cafe
18 Madame Joe Joe
20 Esplanade Hotel
22 Dogs Bar, Harley Court
   & Spuntino
24 The Galleon
25 Vineyard Restaurant
28 The Stokehouse
29 The Pavilion
30 Scheherezade
31 Chinta Ria & Cafe Goa
32 Wild Rice
33 Rasa's Vegie Bar

OTHER

17 Rock 'n' Roll In-line
   Skate Hire & Bob's Boards
   Bike Hire
26 Luna Park
27 Palais Theatre

St Kilda

0   250   500 m

Activities

There are two good indoor **swimming pools** in the city centre – the State Swimming Centre in Batman Ave and the Melbourne City Baths on the corner of Swanston and Victoria Sts (both open all year). Outdoor pools include the Prahran Pool in Essex St and the Carlton Baths in Rathdowne St (both open October to April) and the Harold Holt Swimming Centre in High St, Glen Iris (open all year).

The four-km **jogging** track (popularly known as 'the Tan') around the Kings Domain and the Royal Botanic Gardens is one of the most popular running circuits. Albert Park Lake is also busy.

Inline skating is booming in Melbourne, and the best tracks are those around Port Phillip Bay from Port Melbourne to Brighton. You can hire gear for about $8 an hour from places such as Rock 'n' Roll (☎ 9525 3434), 11 Fitzroy St, St Kilda, and Albert Park In-Line Skates (☎ 9645 9099), 185 Victoria Ave.

There are **sailing** clubs all around Port Phillip Bay, and it's worth contacting them if you're interested in crewing on yachts.

See the section on the Yarra River earlier for details of places where you can hire canoes and rowing boats. See the Getting Around section below for details on cycling in Melbourne.

Organised Tours

Companies such as Melbourne Sightseeing, Australian Pacific and Gray Line run conventional city bus tours, as well as trips to the most popular tourist destinations, including Sovereign Hill, Healesville Sanctuary, Phillip Island and the Great Ocean Road.

Two double-decker buses, the City Explorer and the City Wanderer (☎ 9563 9788), tour the city and inner suburbs. One-day passes cost $15, or you can get on or off wherever you choose.

Queen Victoria Market Walking Tours (☎ 9658 9601) run two-hour tours on Tuesday, Thursday, Friday and Saturday from 9 to 11 am, departing from 513 Elizabeth St and costing $10 to $15.

Autopia Tours (☎ 9326 5536) runs fun-oriented small-group bus tours for backpackers, with day trips along the Great Ocean Rd ($50, or two days for $65), to Hanging Rock and a local winery ($40), to the Phillip Island penguin parade and a fauna park ($40), and to the Grampians National Park (two days, $65).

Mac's Backpacker Tours (☎ 5241 3180) also takes small groups along the Great Ocean Road (one day, $50), to Phillip Island and the Great Ocean Road (two days, $84) and to both the Grampians National Park and the Great Ocean Road (three days, $102).

Melbourne Backpacker Sightseeing (☎ 9663 3388) has a wide range of day trips to Phillip Island, the Great Ocean Road and other destinations around Victoria, and offers special discounts for YHA members.

Some interesting smaller tour operators include Lancefield Bush Rides & Tucker (☎ 5429 1627), which offers a day trip to Hanging Rock with horse riding and bush tucker for $75 ($65 YHA members); and Echidna Walkabout (☎ 9646 8249), which runs day trips with bushwalking, wildlife-watching and an introduction to Aboriginal culture ($75 to $95), as well as two, three and six-day trips to the Grampians, the Great Ocean Rd and the national parks of East Gippsland.

Bogong Jack Adventures (☎ 5727 3382) has a wide range of cycling, bushwalking, skiing and canoeing tours through the Victorian Alps.

Festivals

The Melbourne Music Festival is held during January. In March, Moomba is a popular family festival centred around the Yarra River.

Kicking off on April Fool's Day, Melbourne's month-long International Comedy Festival features a great range of local and international acts at dozens of different venues. The marvellous Melbourne Film Festival is held during the depths of winter in June – the perfect time to be inside a cinema!

In September the Aussie Rules football

VICTORIA

The Melbourne Cup

If you happen to be in Melbourne on the first Tuesday in November you can catch the greatest horse race in Australia, the prestigious Melbourne Cup, the centre of the city's Spring Racing Carnival. Although its position as the bearer of the largest prize for an Australian horse race is constantly under challenge, no other race can bring the country to a standstill.

For about an hour during the lead-up to the race on the first Tuesday in November, a public holiday in the city's metropolitan area, people all over the country get touched by Melbourne's spring racing fever.

Serious punters and fashion-conscious racegoers pack the grandstand and lawns of the Victorian Racing Club's beautiful Flemington Racecourse, those who only bet once a year make their choice or organise Cup syndicates with friends, and the race is watched or listened to on TVs and radios in pubs, clubs and houses across the land. Australia virtually comes to a halt for the three or so minutes when the race is actually run.

The two-mile (3.2 km) flat race attracts horses and owners from Europe and the Middle East, although often it's the New Zealand horses and trainers that leave with the coveted gold cup.

Many people say that to be in Melbourne in November and not go to the Cup is like going to Paris and skipping the Louvre, or turning your back on the bulls in Pamplona. ■

finals dominate, and October features the outstanding Melbourne International Festival of the Arts, a world-class arts festival that incorporates the Melbourne Writer's Festival and the Fringe Arts Festival (highlighted by the wild and crazy street party and parade along Brunswick St).

Places to Stay

In Melbourne you have a choice between backpackers hostels, pubs and motels, B&Bs and guesthouses, serviced apartments and deluxe hotels. Once you've decided what you're looking for, the tricky part is deciding which area to stay in. The city centre is convenient and close to things such as theatres, museums and the train and bus terminals, although it can be a little lifeless at night. The alternative is to stay in one of the inner suburbs that ring the city, each of which has its own distinct flavour and character.

If you decide to stay longer, look in the *Age* classifieds on Wednesday and Saturday under 'share accommodation'. You could try the notice boards in the hostels, and various other places – including the universities, Readings bookshop in Carlton, Cosmos Books & Music and the Galleon cafe in St

Kilda and the Black Cat cafe in Fitzroy – also have 'share accommodation' notice boards.

Camping Melbourne has a few caravan parks and camping grounds in the metropolitan area, although none of them are very close to the centre. The most convenient place is probably the comprehensive Melbourne Caravan & Tourist Park in Coburg East, 10 km north of the city. (From the city take tram No 19 or 20 from Elizabeth St or bus No 526; the bus doesn't run on Sunday. The Footscray site is also convenient but has on-site vans only. The following are some of Melbourne's closer sites:

Melbourne Caravan & Tourist Park (☎ 9354 3533), 10 km north at 265 Elizabeth St, Coburg East; camping $16, on-site vans $37, cabins from $4. to $55.

Footscray Caravan Park (☎ 9314 6646), eight km west at 163 Somerville Rd, West Footscray; no camping, on-site vans from $40.

Bluegum Northside Caravan Park (☎ 9305 3614), 1 km north on the corner of the Hume Highway and Coopers Rd, Campbellfield; camping $15, on-site units from $50.

Crystal Brook Holiday Centre (☎ 9844 3637), 21 km north-east on the corner of Warrandyte and Andersons Creek Rds, Doncaster East; camping $17, on-site vans from $30, on-site cabins from $60.

Hobsons Bay Caravan Park (☎ 9397 2395), 17 km south-west at 158 Kororoit Creek Rd, Williamstown; camping $14, cabins $30/35.

Hostels There are backpackers hostels in the city centre, Fitzroy, North Melbourne, Richmond and South Yarra, although the seaside suburb of St Kilda has the biggest collection of budget accommodation. The hostel scene is fairly competitive, and it can be hard to find a bed in one of the better places over summer. Several of the larger hostels have courtesy buses that do pick-ups from the bus and train terminals.

City Centre The best of the city bunch is *Toad Hall* (☎ 9600 9010) at 441 Elizabeth St, within easy walking distance of the bus terminals. It's a quiet, stylish and well-equipped place with a pleasant courtyard and off-street parking ($5). A bed in a four or six-bed dorm costs from $15; single/double rooms cost from $25/45.

At 199 Russell St, *Exford Hotel Backpackers'* (☎ 9663 2697) is a cheerful and well set-up hostel in the upper section of an old pub. Costs range from $11 in a 10-bed dorm to $15 in a four-bed dorm; twins/doubles are $39 a night.

The *City Centre Private Hotel* (☎ 9654 5401) at 22 Little Collins St is clean and quiet, if somewhat prim. All rooms have a shared bathroom and there's a TV lounge and kitchen on each floor. Backpackers pay $17 in a three or four-bed room and doubles are $35; serviced singles/doubles are $35/50.

The *Backpackers City Inn* (☎ 9650 2734), upstairs in the Carlton Hotel at 197 Bourke St, has dorms at $14 and singles/doubles for $28/35, although both the pub and the accommodation are a bit rough around the edges.

Fitzroy Well located on the fringe of the city at 116 Nicholson St is the *Nunnery* (☎ 9419 8637), one of the best budget accommodation options in Melbourne. It's a converted Victorian building with comfortable lounges, good facilities and a friendly atmosphere. The rooms are small but clean and centrally heated. Costs range from $15 in a 12-bed dorm to $17 in a three-bed dorm; singles are $28 to $34, twins and doubles are $46. Take tram No 96 heading east along Bourke St, and get off at stop No 13.

North Melbourne Melbourne's YHA hostels are both in North Melbourne, north-west of the city centre. Both offer discounts for a four-day or longer stay. From the airport you can ask the Skybus to drop you at the North Melbourne hostels.

The YHA showpiece is the *Queensberry Hill Hostel* (☎ 9329 8599) at 78 Howard St. This huge 348-bed place was completed in 1991 and has excellent facilities. Four or eight-bed dorms cost $17 for YHA members ($3 more for nonmembers); singles/doubles are $37/46, or $47/56 with private bathroom. There's a breakfast and dinner service available, and office hours are 7.30 am to 10.30 pm, although there is 24-hour access once you have checked in. Catch tram No 55 from William St and get off at stop No 14, or any tram north up Elizabeth St to stop No 13.

The *Chapman Gardens YHA Hostel* (☎ 9328 3595), at 76 Chapman St, is smaller and older but can be a bit more intimate than Queensberry Hill. Dorms here cost $15, twin rooms $34 and doubles $38 ($2 more for nonmembers).

Both hostels have good notice boards if you're looking for people to travel or share lifts with, cheap airline tickets or just general information. There are a number of very good tours that operate out of the hostels.

Opposite the Queen Victoria Market at 238 Victoria St, the *Global Backpackers' Hostel* (☎ 9328 3728) is in the top section of an old pub and has dorms ranging from $11 to $14, and singles/doubles for $25/36. The facilities include a good kitchen and an indoor rock-climbing wall. Note that the pub downstairs has bands most nights – great if you're into live music, not so great if you're an early sleeper.

St Kilda St Kilda is one of Melbourne's most interesting and cosmopolitan suburbs, and it has a good range of budget accommodation as well as plenty of restaurants and entertainment venues. From Swanston St in the city, tram No 16 will take you down St Kilda Rd to Fitzroy St, or there's the faster light-rail service (No 96 from Spencer St and Bourke St) to the old St Kilda railway station and along Fitzroy and Acland Sts.

Enfield House Backpackers (☎ 9534 8159), at 2 Enfield St, is the original and probably the most popular of St Kilda's hostels. It's a huge and rambling Victorian-era building with over 100 beds, good facilities and staff who can help organise tours, nights out and activities. Six-bunk dorms are $14, four-bunk dorms $15, singles $20 and twins $34 to $36. Their courtesy bus picks up travellers from the bus terminals, and from Station Pier where the Tasmanian ferries arrive and depart.

The excellent *Olembia Guesthouse* (☎ 9537 1412) at 96 Barkly St is more like a boutique hotel than a hostel. The facilities are very good and include a cosy guest lounge, dining room, a courtyard and off-street parking. The rooms are quite small but clean and comfortable, and all have handbasins and central heating. Dorm beds cost $14, singles are $35, and twins and doubles are $50. Book ahead.

At 169 Fitzroy St, the *Ritz for Backpackers* (☎ 9525 3501) is upstairs from a restaurant/bar and is quite stylish, with comfortable lounges and sitting rooms and a modern and well-equipped kitchen. Four to eight-bunk dorms cost $14, twins and doubles $34. There's a good self-contained flat that sleeps eight people at $14 per person.

The *St Kilda Coffee Palace* (☎ 9534 5283), at 24 Grey St, is another long-running hostel that has recently been renovated and upgraded by its new owners. It's a big, spacious place with its own cafe and a modern kitchen. Dorms range from $12 to $14, twins are $28 and doubles $30. Around the corner at 56 Jackson St is *Kookaburra Cottage* (☎ 9534 5457), a small and laid-back hostel. It's quite comfortable and has all the usual facilities; dorm beds are $13 and there are a couple of good twin rooms for $32.

On the corner of Grey and Jackson Sts is *Leopard House* (☎ 9534 1200), an old and roomy two-storey Edwardian house with four-bed dorms at $13.

South Yarra *Lord's Lodge Backpackers* (☎ 9510 5658) is at 204 Punt Rd, which is a fairly hectic main road. This is a large, two-storey place with a range of accommodation, including six to eight-bed dorms with their own kitchen for $13 and singles/doubles for $25/30.

Richmond The *Richmond Hill Guesthouse* (☎ 9428 6501), well located at 353 Church St, is another big old Victorian-era building with spacious living areas and clean rooms. Dorm beds range from $15 to $18 a night, singles/twins are $35/44, and they have a B&B section with good double rooms for $55.

Also in Richmond, although not as well located, is *Central House* (☎ 9427 9826) at 337 Highett St, with mostly four-bed dorms for $12 a night.

Preston The *Terrace Travellers Hostel* (☎ 9470 1006) is at 418 Murray Rd, Preston – it's not a bad hostel, but unless you've got relatives in Preston it's hard to think of a reason for staying all the way out here.

Hotels, Motels, B&Bs & Serviced Apartments As with cheaper accommodation, you have a choice between the convenience of the city centre and the often more pleasant surroundings of the inner suburbs. You can generally find a reasonable double room from about $40, or from $60 with a private bathroom.

City Centre The hotels along Spencer St are convenient for the bus and train terminals, although this ain't the most salubrious end of town. The *Terrace Pacific Inn* (☎ 9621 3333) at 16 Spencer St is a modern budget hotel with smallish rooms from $49 a double, or from $89 with en suite. The tariff includes a light breakfast. At 44 Spencer St, the *Hotel Enterprise* (☎ 9629 6991) is another refurpished hotel with budget singles/doubles from $35/45, or from $79/89 with en suite. And at No 66, the *Batman's Hill Hotel* (☎ 9614 6344) has doubles from $105, including breakfast.

At 131 King St, the *Kingsgate Budget Hotel* (☎ 9629 4171) is a private hotel that has been renovated. It's a big old place with budget singles/doubles with shared bath-room from $29/45 or with en suite rooms from $60/80.

The *Hotel Y* (☎ 9329 5188), run by the YWCA, is close to the Franklin St bus ter-minal at 489 Elizabeth St. It has basic four-bed bunk rooms for $22, singles/doubles/triples for $58/70/78, and deluxe rooms from $70/82/90. Recently refur-bished, the 'Y' has good facilities including a budget cafe, communal kitchen and laundry, gym and heated pool.

The *Stork Hotel* (☎ 9663 6237), nearby on the corner of Elizabeth and Therry Sts, is an old pub with simple upstairs rooms from $25/30, and a small guest kitchen.

The *Victoria Hotel* (☎ 9653 0441) at 215 Little Collins St is a notch up from the cheap-est city hotels, and a bit of a Melbourne institution. There are 520 rooms in three categories: budget rooms with shared facili-ties at $38/50, standard rooms with en suite and TV at $68/85, and executive rooms at $78/99. The Victoria is one of the best-located hotels in the city centre.

East Melbourne On the fringe of the city, East Melbourne has a pleasant residential feel with its tree-lined streets and grand old Victorian terrace houses.

The *Georgian Court Guesthouse* (☎ 9419 5353), at 21 George St, is an elegant and cosy B&B with singles/doubles at $55/65, or $75/85 with an en suite; prices include a buffet breakfast.

At 2 Hotham St, the *East Melbourne Hotel* (☎ 9419 2040) has clean pub-style rooms upstairs for $35/45. There's a free car park and guest lounge, and their kitchen should be installed by the time you read this – there's also a stylish restaurant and bar downstairs.

At 101 George St the *George Street Apart-ments* (☎ 9419 1333) is a secure and friendly place with serviced apartments from $75 a double, all with bathroom, fridge and cooking facilities. At 25 Hotham St, the *East Melbourne Studio Apartments* (☎ 9412 2555) are also good but a bit more stylish, and accordingly more expensive, ranging from $90 to $130 a night.

Parkville A good option north of the city is the *Royal Park Inn* (☎ 9380 5599) on the corner of Park St and Royal Pde. Close to Melbourne Uni and the zoo, it's an Edward-ian style guesthouse with a guests' kitchen, laundry and lounge, en suite rooms from $75 to $85 and spa rooms at $120.

Fitzroy Well located in Royal Lane, one block back from the Exhibition Gardens, the stylish and spacious *Royal Gardens Apart-ments* (☎ 9419 9888) come in one, two or three-bedroom configurations, costing $165, $195 and $235 respectively.

South Yarra Tram No 8 from Swanston St in the city takes you along Toorak Rd into the heart of the chic suburb of South Yarra.

There are several places opposite the leafy Fawkner Park gardens. The *Tilba* (☎ 9867 8844), on the corner of Toorak Rd West and Domain St, is an elegant boutique hotel with gracious Victorian-era rooms ranging from $130 to $185 a double, depending on size – highly recommended for a splurge. The *West End Private Hotel* (☎ 9866 5375), at 76 Toorak Rd, has B&B with singles/doubles at $35/48 – it's pretty old-fashioned, but has a certain shabby charm. Nearby, the *Albany Motel* (☎ 9866 4485) on the corner of Toorak Rd and Millswyn St has rooms from $60/65.

Farther east at 189 Toorak Rd, the vast *Claremont Accommodation* (☎ 9826 8000) has recently been converted into a B&B. The rooms are bright and freshly painted, with polished-timber floors, heating and modern communal bathroom. Singles/doubles are from $35/45, including breakfast. The *Domain Motel* at 52 Darling St is oldish but well located, and has rooms from $58/65.

South Yarra is the serviced-apartment

capital of Melbourne. Mostly converted blocks of flats, these can be rented overnight, weekly or long-term. Some of the more affordable ones include the *Manor House Apartments* (☎ 9867 1266) at 23 Avoca St, with studio apartments from $75 a night; and *Darling Towers* (☎ 9867 5200) at 32 Darling St, with one-bedroom flats from $85.

St Kilda St Kilda also has some good serviced apartments. One of the best places is *Kingsgrove Apartments* (☎ 9536 3000), right in the heart of the action at 44 Fitzroy St. This place has secure and modern apartments from $78 for a studio, $96 for a one-bedroom apartment (sleeps up to three) and $157 for a two-bedroom apartment (sleeps up to five).

Opposite St Kilda beach at 363 Beaconsfield Pde, *Warwick Beachside* (☎ 9525 4800) has 1950s-style holiday flats. They're not glamorous, but they're quite well equipped, and there's a laundry and off-street parking. Costs range from $55 to $69 for a studio (sleeps up to three) and from $79 to $95 for a two-bedroom apartment (sleeps up to five).

The modern high-rise *Novotel Bayside Hotel* (☎ 9525 5522), overlooking the bay from 14-16 The Esplanade, has rooms ranging from $120 to $470 a night.

St Kilda has plenty of motels, but some of them are fairly dodgy. A couple of more respectable places are the *Cabana Court Motel* (☎ 9534 0771) at 46 Park St, with self-contained units from $80 to $85; and the *Cosmopolitan Motor Inn* (☎ 9534 0781) at 6 Carlisle St, with rooms from $73 and family units with kitchenette from $107.

There are some good B&Bs in St Kilda. Opposite the beach at 335 Beaconsfield Pde, *Robinson's by the Sea* (☎ 9534 2683) is an elegant and impressive Victorian-era terrace house with three double en suite rooms ranging from $100 to $175. *Victoria House* (☎ 9525 4512), at 57 Mary St, has two guest rooms with singles/doubles from $55/85.

Albert Park The *Hotel Victoria* (☎ 9690 3666), with a great position overlooking the bay from 123 Beaconsfield Pde, is a restored 1888 hotel with rooms with shared bathroom from $45 to $60 and doubles with en suite from $80 to $150. Ask for one of the corner suites – the views alone are worth the $135.

The *Avoca* (☎ 9696 1661), at 98 Victoria Ave, is another good B&B in a Victorian-era terrace, with three period-style rooms with private bathroom at $95/125.

Colleges Melbourne has three universities the long-established University of Melbourne and two newer 'bush universities' La Trobe and Monash. Visitors would probably find La Trobe and Monash too far from the centre to be worth considering.

The University of Melbourne is just to the north of the city centre in Parkville. The following colleges have accommodation in the vacation period from late November to mid-February; B&B ranges from $25 to $45 per night, and there's a minimum stay of three nights: *International House* (☎ 9347 6655); *Medley Hall* (☎ 9663 5847); *Ridley College* (☎ 9387 7555); *Ormond College* (☎ 9348 1688); *Queen's College* (☎ 9349 0500); *Trinity College* (☎ 9347 1044); *University College* (☎ 9347 3533); and *Whitley College* (☎ 9347 8388). There are cheaper rates for students at all these colleges.

Places to Eat

Melbourne is a wonderful place to have an appetite – and a terrible place to start a diet. Everywhere you go, there are restaurants, cafes, delis, markets, bistros and brasseries. Gastronomically you can travel the world here – go to Victoria St in Richmond for (very cheap) Vietnamese; Little Bourke St in the city for Chinese; Johnston St in Fitzroy for Spanish food; Swan St in Richmond for Greek; or for sheer variety, Brunswick St in Fitzroy, or Acland and Fitzroy Sts in St Kilda.

The restaurants listed are just a small selection of favourites that are in the main areas where travellers may be staying or visiting. If you want to make a more in-depth study of food in Melbourne, pick up a copy of the *Age Good Food Guide* or the *Age Cheap Eats in Melbourne*.

Most of Melbourne's restaurants are either licensed to sell alcohol and/or BYO. Some BYO places charge a small fee for corkage.

Chinatown The area in and around Chinatown, which follows Little Bourke St from Spring St to Swanston St, is one of the best and most diverse food precincts, with great Chinese restaurants as well as Italian, Malaysian, Thai and others.

Starting from the top end, *Jan Bo* at 40 Little Bourke St has reasonably priced and authentic Chinese food, and serves great yum cha daily from 11 am to 3 pm. At No 50, the *Shark Finn Inn* is also very popular, and stays open until 1.30 am. *Cafe K*, at No 35, is an elegant European-style bistro with mains in the $8 to $15 range.

The highly acclaimed *Flower Drum* (☎ 9662 3655), at 17 Market Lane, is one of Melbourne's best (and most expensive) restaurants, with the best Cantonese food this side of Hong Kong. The low-key *Yamato*, at 28 Corrs Lane, turns out excellent Japanese dishes from $6 to $13 and has banquets from $23.

King of Kings, at 209 Russell St, is a cheap Chinese place that stays open until 2.30 am. *Peony Gardens*, at 283 Little Lonsdale St, is dirt cheap with dishes from $2.50 to $5 – at that price you really can't complain about plastic plates and utensils or having to clear the table after you've eaten.

Other City Centre Areas *Cafee Baloo*, at 260 Russell St, is perhaps the best budget eatery in the city centre. It's a funky little place with Indian/Italian food – great antipasto plates ($3.90), pastas ($4.80) and curries and stir-fries ($3.90 to $5.90). It's open weekdays for lunch and nightly for dinner. Farther south at 122 Russell St, the classy *Pizza Napoli* has some of the best gourmet pizzas ($11.20) in town.

The Lounge, upstairs at 243 Swanston St, is a groovy cafe/club with pool tables, a balcony overlooking Swanston Walk, has snags, stir-fries, satays and salads from $7.

The cheapest place in town is *Gopals* at 139 Swanston St, a vegetarian cafe run by the Hare Krishna sect. It's open for lunch and dinner and has dishes from $1 to $3, three courses for $5.50 or all you can eat for $8.50. The Hares also run nearby *Crossways*, although it's mainly for poor and homeless people.

Stalactites, on the corner of Lonsdale and Russell Sts, is a Greek restaurant best known for its bizarre stalactite décor and the fact that it's open 24 hours.

Off the top end of Bourke St at 20 Myers Place, the *Waiter's Restaurant* serves good, cheap Italian food in unglamorous but cosy surrounds. Back on Bourke St at No 66 is another Melbourne institution – *Pellegrini's*. It's an old Italian bar with great apple strudel, pasta and risotto, and excellent coffee. The *Florentino Cellar Bar*, at No 80, looks expensive but is actually very reasonable. Pastas are $8 and they also serve soup, focaccia and antipasto.

As well as being the home of Melbourne's outdoor adventure shops, Hardware St is lined with cafes with open-air tables. At No 25 *Campari Bistro* is a busy Italian bistro with pastas for about $10 and other mains from $16 to $19. The stylish *Panini* at No 54 has cooked breakfasts for $3.60 and a great selection of sandwiches, salads and hot foods; *Cafe Max* next door is also pretty good.

There are some excellent international food courts around the city, where you have a wide range of cuisines to choose between. They include the *Hyatt Food Court* on the corner of Russell and Collins Sts, and the *Sportsgirl Centre* on Collins St just down from Swanston St. Melbourne's major department stores – Myer, David Jones and Daimaru – also have great food emporiums with a selection of goodies that should satisfy even the most obscure craving.

Southgate Southgate, a stylish development on the south bank of the Yarra River beside the Concert Hall, is one of the best and most popular eating centres in Melbourne.

The setting is great, there's a good range of styles and prices, and you can either eat indoors or outside overlooking the river and the city.

On the ground floor is the *Wharf Food Market*, where you can choose from Japanese, Malaysian or Thai food, fish & chips, a salad and fruit-juice bar, a delicatessen and an ice-cream parlour. On the same level are *E Gusto*, a stylish Italian bistro with main courses from $12 to $16, and *Bistro Vite*, a simple French bistro with excellent food.

On the mid-level, the casual *Blue Train Cafe* serves breakfasts, pastas and risottos, wood-fired pizzas and salads, all at very reasonable prices, and *Bon Bons* specialises in coffee and cakes but also has good breakfasts and sandwiches. *Scusa Mi* is a more up-market Italian bistro and bar with great food and smart service.

St Kilda St Kilda has everything from all-night hamburger joints to stylish cafes, bars and restaurants. Most of the eateries are along Fitzroy and Acland Sts.

Up the beach end at 9 Fitzroy St, the very chic *Madame Joe Joe* is one of the best of the new breed of St Kilda restaurants – pricey, but great for a splurge. More affordable is the tiny and cheerful *Hard Wok Cafe* at No 49, with Asian stir-fries, laksas and curries for $6 to $10. At 55 Fitzroy St, *Leo's Spaghetti Bar* is something of a St Kilda institution, with a coffee bar, bistro and restaurant.

Across at No 42, the wonderful *Tolarno Bar & Bistro* has an excellent restaurant and a small bar/eatery with snacks and meals in the $5 to $10 range, including the best burgers in Melbourne ($5.50). *Topolino's* at 87 Fitzroy St is the place to go for a pizza or a big bowl of pasta – it's usually crowded late at night and stays open until sunrise. *Chichio's*, at No 109, offers meals for two people for $6 each – pizza or pasta, salad, bread and a drink. On the corner of Fitzroy and Grey Sts, the trend-setting *George Hotel* has a popular wine bar with good food, a restaurant and a marvellous bakery.

Farther south at 9 Carlisle St, the *Galleon* is a local favourite with its quirky 1950s concrete-and-laminex décor and everything from toasted sandwiches and apple crumble to chicken and leek pie – all at very reasonable prices. Up Acland St on the Fawkner St corner, you'll find the trendy trilogy of the *Dogs Bar* (an in-vogue bar with good Italian food), *Harley Court* (delicious French pastries), and *Spuntino* (laid-back Italian-style street cafe).

If you're craving a big juicy steak, head for the unassuming *Vineyard Restaurant* at 71a Acland St – the grills are huge and range from $10 to $25. At No 94, *Chinta Ria* (☎ 9525 4664) combines wonderful Malaysian food with jazz and soul music – mains are $7 to $12, and you'll need to book. Next door the quirky and opinionated *Cafe Goa* serves spicy Portuguese-Indian dishes for $6 to $10. *Scheherezade* at No 99 does good Central European food in large quantities.

Acland St is also renowned for it fine delis and cake shops – the window displays emanate so many calories you're in danger of putting on weight just walking past.

Wild Rice, around the corner at 211 Barkly St, is a very good organic/vegan cafe with mains from $5 to $9 and a pleasant rear courtyard – it's open daily from noon to 10 pm. At 5 Blessington St, *Rasa's Vegie Bar* has tofu or lentil burgers for $5.40 and vegetarian stir-fries, curries and pastas for $8 to $11.

The *Pavilion* is a classy seafood restaurant on the foreshore at 40 Jacka Blvd; mains range from $18 to $22, but for those of us without gold Amex cards there's a takeaway section with great fish & chips and outdoor tables. Nearby, the *Stokehouse* also has a great outlook over the bay and is one of the places in St Kilda to see (and be seen). There's a pricey restaurant upstairs, and a big bustling bar/eatery downstairs with great food in the $9 to $14 range (try a number seven gourmet pizza!).

Last but by no means least is the wonderful *Espy Kitchen* way up the back of the Esplanade Hotel. It's always busy, the food is great (mains from $9 to $15), and after you've eaten you can play pool or check out one of the (usually free) live bands.

Fitzroy Brunswick St can't be beaten for sheer variety. It's one of the funkiest and most fascinating streets in Melbourne, and it has just about everything – cafes, bars, Thai, Indian, Turkish, Italian, French, Malaysian, and even Ethiopian and Afghan restaurants.

At the city end at 113 Brunswick St, *Nyala* serves Ethiopian and other African food. The combination plate gives you an interesting variety of dishes to try, and you scoop them up with the spongy bread known as injera. Mains range from $10 to $13. At No 177, *Akari 177* is a Japanese restaurant with good-value set lunches and early dinners for $12 (order before 7 pm). Next door, the Spanish-influenced *De Los Santos* has good tapas, paella and other mains for $6 to $11.

Up at No 252, the famous *Black Cat Cafe* is an arty 1950s-style cafe, ideal for coffee and cake or snacks at late hours. *Thai Thani* at No 293 is an excellent place for lovers of hot and spicy Thai food.

Across Johnston St, the very hip *Mario's* is at No 303. Highly favoured by the locals, it has great Italian food day and night. *Cafe Cappadocia* at No 324 is an unpretentious and cheap Turkish restaurant. Another good option is the *Fitz* at No 347, which has a delicious range of breakfasts ($3 to $7), cakes ($4.90) and meals ($7 to $14), plus tables out on the footpath. Other Brunswick St favourites include the barn-sized *Rhumbarella's*, at No 342, with an art gallery upstairs; *Babka Bakery Cafe* at No 358 (great breakfasts!); and *Joe's Garage* up at No 366. Next to Joe's, *Charmaine's* has simply sensational ice creams. On the corner of Rose St, the *Vegie Bar* exudes delicious aromas and has a great range of vegetarian meals under $8.

Around the corner on Johnston St you'll find Melbourne's small Spanish quarter. At No 74, the popular *Carmen Bar* (☎ 9417 4794) has authentic Spanish food, an outdoor barbecue, and flamenco and Spanish guitar from Wednesday to Saturday nights. There's also a cluster of small Spanish tapas bars along here, including *La Sangria* at No 46 and *Kahlo's* at No 36. At 15 Johnston St, the friendly *Chishti's* has excellent Indian and vegetarian food with mains from $10 to $13.

Gertrude St has an interesting collection of galleries, art suppliers, costume designers and antique shops. At No 193, *Arcadia* is a groovy little cafe, and at No 199 the very straightforward *Macedonia* does grills, goulash and other Balkan specialities. On the corner of Gertrude and Gore Sts, the arty and cosy *Builders Arms Hotel* is a top spot for an ale.

Smith St also has some good eateries. It's an interesting multicultural streetscape, a lot less fashionable than Brunswick St but still worth exploring. *Cafe Birko* at No 123 is a rustic bar/restaurant with burgers, stir-fries, risottos and pastas for about $7.50. At 275 Smith St, the *Soul Food Vegetarian Cafe* is a popular vegan cafe with salads and hot foods for $6.50 to $9 and an organic grocery next door. Farther north at No 354 Smith St, *Cafe Bohemio* (☎ 9417 7627) is a quirky and laid-back Latin-American cafe with mains for $8 to $11 – the chef screens free experimental and classic films upstairs on Sunday at 8.30 pm.

Carlton Lygon St, Melbourne's Italian centre, is all bright lights, big restaurants and flashy boutiques – a local writer calls it an antipodean Via Veneto. A one-time trend-setter in Melbourne's restaurant scene, nowadays Lygon St caters mainly to tourists and out-of-towners, although some of the long-running places are still worth searching out.

Toto's Pizza House at No 101 claims to be the first pizzeria in Australia. Pizzas are cheap and good and it stays open till after midnight. After your pizza, head up to *Notturno* at No 177 for coffee and cake – it's open until 3 am.

Nyonya, at No 191, has excellent Malaysian/Chinese food with main courses from $7 to $12 – try the superb curry laksa. At No 303 *Tiamo* is an old-fashioned Italian bistro with pastas for about $7 and great breakfasts just like mama used to cook ($7.50). Nearby at No 329, *Shakahari* is one of Melbourne's longest running and most popular vegetarian restaurants, with a really interesting menu with main dishes for about $10. Across the road, *Trotters* at No 400 is a popular little bistro serving hearty Italian fare in the $7 to $12 range.

Farther down at 333 Lygon St, *Jimmy Watson's* is a famous Melbourne institution. Wine and talk are the order of the day at this wine bar but the food is good too. It's always been a great spot for a long, leisurely lunch – and nowadays it is also open for evening meals.

North Melbourne North Melbourne has some good eateries if you're prepared to search a little. Opposite the Queen Vic market, *Viet Nam House* at 284 Victoria St and *Dalat* at No 270 both have cheap Vietnamese food with lunches for about $5 and mains from $7 to $12. On the corner of Victoria and Peel Sts, the busy *La Porchetta* is a budget bistro with pizzas and pastas from $4 to $7 and other mains under $10.

Farther along Victoria St is *Warung Agus* at No 305, which has superb Balinese food with mains from $10 to $13. *Amiconi* (☎ 9328 3710), at 359 Victoria St, is a traditional Italian bistro and a local favourite – you may need to book. Across the road, the modern Art Deco-styled *Cafe Hotel* has interesting meals in the $7 to $10 range. The *Eldorado Hotel* at 46 Leveson St also has good pub food and a pleasant courtyard.

Richmond Victoria St in Richmond, known as Little Saigon, is Melbourne's Vietnamese centre and it is lined with dozens of bargain-priced Vietnamese restaurants. Trams No 42 or 109 from Collins St in the city will take you there.

Don't expect vogue décor, but the food will be fresh, cheap and lightning fast. You can have a huge steaming bowl of soup that will be a meal in itself for about $4, and main courses are generally $4 to $8, so you can afford to be adventurous. The very basic *Thy Thy 1* is probably the best-known and most popular place, hidden away upstairs at No 142. *Thy Thy 2* at No 116 is a bit more

up-market – try the pork, chicken, prawn or vegetable spring rolls.

The *Victoria* at No 311 is another good place to try, and also offers Thai and Chinese food. Down the city end at No 66 is the ultra-modern *Tho Tho* – incredibly stylish but still pretty cheap. Farther along at No 397, *Minh Tan III* is also a bit more up-market and specialises in seafood with banquets from $16 to $22 and lunches from $5.

If it's good Greek food you're after, take tram No 70 from Batman Ave, by the river in the city, to the corner of Swan and Church Sts. The tiny *Salona* at 260a Swan St, and *Agapi* next door, both have good traditional Greek food with mains for $8 to $12. *Kaliva* at No 256 is fairly plain, although you can dine to bouzouki music Thursday to Sunday nights.

Bridge Rd (tram No 48 or 75 from Flinders St in the city) also has some great food on offer. Starting at the city end there's the elegant *Chilli Padi* at 18 Bridge Rd, which serves excellent Malaysian dishes. At 78 Bridge Rd, the *Tofu Shop* is definitely one for those on a vegetarian/health kick; the salads, vegetables, filled filo pastries and soyalaki (great invention) are all very tasty.

Rajdoot at 142 Bridge Rd has excellent Indian food including great tandoori dishes; if you've travelled in India you'll remember the name as a popular Indian motorcycle brand! *Que Huong* at No 176 has good $5 lunches and Vietnamese meals under $8.

At the *All Nations Hotel*, between Bridge Rd and Swan St at 64 Lennox St, you can join the locals at the bar for some of the best pub food in Melbourne. It's open for lunch every day and serves dinner on Thursday and Friday; meals range from $6 to $14.

South Yarra & Prahran Take tram No 8 from Swanston St in the city to reach South Yarra. Along Toorak Rd you'll find some of Melbourne's most expensive restaurants – fortunately there are some more affordable places in between.

Tiny *Ticino Bistro*, at No 16, has pizzas and pastas for $6 to $9. *Winchell's Deli* at No

58 offers breakfast specials for $4.50, and if you're feeling indulgent, pop into *Frenchy's* at No 76 for a coffee and one of their sublime French pastries.

Across the road at No 93, *La Porchetta* is one of the best value pizza/pasta joints in town – there are other La Porchettas in North Melbourne and Carlton. At No 156 *Tamani* is a popular, friendly and cheap Italian bistro and something of a Melbourne institution.

Don your designer sunnies and head down Chapel St – you'll find plenty of interesting cafes, bars and restaurants in amongst all the fashion boutiques. *Caffe e Cucina* (9827 6076), at No 581, is one of the smallest, coolest and best cafe/restaurants in town, with great Italian meals in the $14 to $21 range – ring ahead, or expect to queue. Down at No 571 is the friendly *Chapelli's* – the food is pretty good and, most importantly, it's open round the clock. Right next door at No 569 is *Kanpai*, a neat little Japanese restaurant with modestly priced dishes.

The Prahran Market, on Commercial Rd, is a wonderful place to shop or just wander, with fresh fruit and vegies and plenty of little delis to explore. Opposite the market at No 194, the *Blue Elephant* is a funky little cafe with great-value meals including breakfasts from $4.50, pastas and pizzas for $5.50 and other mains under $9. Nearby at No 176, *Chinta Ria* has good Malaysian meals ranging from $7 to $12.

Greville St, which runs off Chapel St beside the Prahran town hall, has an eclectic collection of grungy and groovy clothes boutiques, book and music shops, and a few good eateries. Beside the railway tracks at No 95 is the ever-popular *Feedwell Cafe*, an earthy vegetarian cafe serving interesting and wholesome food in the $5 to $10 range. The *Continental Cafe* at No 132 has wonderful food at affordable prices and a hip, sophisticated atmosphere – it's open from 7 am until midnight.

Entertainment

The best source of 'what's on' info in Melbourne is the *Entertainment Guide (EG)* which comes out every Friday with the *Age*

newspaper. *Beat*, *Inpress* and *Storm* are free music and entertainment magazines that have reviews, interviews, dates of gigs, movie guides and more.

Bass Victoria (☎ 11 500) is the main booking agency for theatre, concerts, sports and other events. If you're looking for cheap tickets, the Half-Tix booth (☎ 9650 9420) in the Bourke St Mall sells half-price tickets on the day of the event.

If you're here during the summer months watch out for the wonderful open-air theatre productions staged in the Royal Botanic Gardens.

Melbourne's major venues include the Victorian Arts Centre, the National Tennis Centre, the outdoor Sidney Myer Music Bowl in the Kings Domain and the Sports & Entertainment Centre.

Pubs & Live Music Melbourne has always enjoyed a thriving pub-rock scene and is widely acknowledged as the country's rock capital. The sweaty grind around Melbourne's pubs has been the proving ground for many of Australia's best outfits. To find out who's playing where, look in the *EG*, *Beat* or *Inpress*, or listen to the gig guides on FM radio stations such as 3RRR (102.7) and 3PBS (106.7) – both of which are excellent independent radio stations. Cover charges at the pubs vary widely: some gigs are free, but generally you'll pay $4 to $10.

In St Kilda is the famed *Esplanade Hotel*, on the Esplanade of course, which has free live bands every night and Sunday afternoon. It's also a great place just to sit with a beer and watch the sun set over the pier, or have a meal in the Espy Kitchen out the back. You can't leave Melbourne without visiting the Espy.

The *Rainbow Hotel*, an old back-street pub at 27 St James St in Fitzroy, has (free) live bands nightly, ranging from jazz, Cajun, and blues to funk and soul. Other good music venues in Fitzroy are the *Punters Club* at 376 Brunswick St and the *Evelyn Hotel* at 351 Brunswick St; the *Builders Arms* at 211 Gertrude St is another good Fitzroy watering hole.

The *Club* at 132 Smith St in Collingwood attracts good bands and stays open until dawn, and the grungy *Great Britain Hotel* at 447 Church St in Richmond is yet another icon of the local music scene. Speaking of grunge, the *Public Bar*, opposite the Queen Vic market at 238 Victoria St, has a nightly line-up of bands playing through until the early hours. Nearby on the corner of Queensberry and Elizabeth Sts, *Arthouse* at the Royal Artillery Hotel is the place to head for if you're into death metal.

The *Continental* (☎ 9510 2788), above the cafe of the same name at 134 Greville St, Prahran, is a sophisticated and popular cabaret-style venue where you have a choice of dinner-and-show deals ($35 to $55) or standing-room ($15 to $20).

The *Limerick Arms*, on the corner of Park and Clarendon St in South Melbourne, is a funky and friendly little pub with jazz bands on Thursday and DJs on Friday and Saturday.

Nightclubs The city centre is home to Melbourne's mainstream clubs. The huge *Metro* at 20 Bourke St is the biggest nightclub in the southern hemisphere – it's worth a visit on a Saturday night. King St is a busy but somewhat sleazy and seedy nightclub strip, with a cluster of places that include *Inflation* at No 60, the *Grainstore Tavern* next door, and the *Sports Bar* at No 14. The *Lounge*, upstairs at 243 Swanston Walk, is a hip, semi-alternative club which features everything from Latin rhythms to techno and hip hop.

Fitzroy has some interesting clubs including *Bar Salona*, a Latin-style dance club at 48 Johnston St, and the very hip *Night Cat* at 141 Johnston St, with 1950s decor and jazz, groove, and soul bands.

Other good clubs include the long-running *Chasers* at 386 Chapel St in Prahran, still one of the hottest dance-music clubs; and *Dream* at 229 Queensberry St in Carlton, which goes gothic on Friday, indie/alternative on Saturday and has gay/S&M nights on

Sunday. Down in St Kilda there's *Joey's*, upstairs at 61 Fitzroy St – it's a seedy dive, but if you're desperate it stays open until sunrise.

Jazz & Blues Hidden down a narrow lane off Little Lonsdale St (between Exhibition and Russell Sts), *Bennett's Lane* is a quintessentially dim, smoke-filled, groovy jazz venue – well worth searching out. Other popular city jazz clubs are *Ruby Red*, a converted warehouse at 11 Drewery Lane, and *Jazz Lane*, a bar/bistro at 390 Lonsdale St.

Quite a few pubs have good jazz and blues sessions on certain nights – check the gig guide in the *EG*. They include the *Limerick Arms* in South Melbourne; the *George Hotel*, on the corner of Fitzroy and Grey Sts in St Kilda; the cosy *Commercial Hotel*, at 238 Whitehall St, Yarraville; the *Rainbow Hotel* in Fitzroy; the *Grace Darling Hotel* on the corner of Smith and Peel Sts, Collingwood; the *Fountain Inn Hotel* in Bay St, Port Melbourne; and the *Emerald Hotel* at 414 Clarendon St, South Melbourne.

Bars Melbourne has a great collection of stylish, ultra-fashionable bars – if you want to rub shoulders with Melbourne's dedicated funksters, the following places are all worth checking out: in the city, the *Six Degrees Bar* in Myers Place (off the top end of Bourke St), and *Sadie's Bar* at 1 Coverlid Place (off Little Bourke St near Russell St); in St Kilda, the *Dogs Bar* at 54 Acland St, and the *George Hotel* on the corner of Grey and Fitzroy Sts; and in Fitzroy, the *Gypsy Bar* at 334 Brunswick St, the *Provincial Hotel* on the corner of Johnston and Brunswick Sts, or any of the tapas bars along Johnston St. Chapel St in South Yarra has the *Tonic Bar* at No 564, the *Kazbar* at No 481, the *Limbo Bar* at No 382, and way down at No 20 is *Cha Chas*, just a short walk from the Astor Cinema.

Comedy Melbourne celebrates its place as Australia's comedy capital with the annual International Comedy Festival in April. At other times of the year, several places feature comedy acts on a fairly regular basis – check the *EG* for specific shows.

The *Last Laugh* (☎ 9419 8600), on the corner of Smith and Gertrude Sts in Collingwood, is the granddaddy of Melbourne's comedy venues. It's an old cinema/dole office, done up in a dazzling mishmash of styles with room for 200 people to have a good time. The food is reasonably good (vegetarians are catered for) and there's a bar. Dinner-and-show tickets cost from $30 to $42, and for the show only it's $15 to $20. *Le Joke*, a smaller stand-up comedy venue upstairs, has dinner and show tickets for $26 to $32 or show only for about $10.

The *Comedy Club* (☎ 9348 1622), at 380 Lygon St in Carlton, is another good cabaret-style comedy venue. Other regular comedy venues include the *Prince Patrick Hotel* at 135 Victoria Pde in Collingwood, the *Waiting Room* at the Esplanade Hotel in St Kilda, and the *Rex Hotel* at 145 Bay St in Port Melbourne.

Cinemas There are plenty of mainstream cinemas in the city, especially around the intersection of Bourke and Russell Sts. Tickets cost $9.50 during the day, $11 at night.

Melbourne also has numerous independent cinemas that feature art-house, classic and alternative films. They include the wonderfully Art Deco *Astor Cinema* on the corner of Chapel St and Dandenong Rd, and the *George* at 133 Fitzroy St, both in St Kilda; the off-beat home of cult films, the *Valhalla* at 89 High St, Northcote; the *Carlton Moviehouse* at 235 Faraday St and *Cinema Nova* at 380 Lygon St, both in Carlton; the *Kino* at 45 Collins St in the city; the *Longford* at 59 Toorak Rd, South Yarra; and the *Trak* at 445 Toorak Rd, Toorak. Check the *EG* or newspapers for screenings and times.

Theatre The *Victorian Arts Centre* (☎ 9281 8000) is Melbourne's major venue for the performing arts. Flanked by the Yarra River on one side and the National Gallery on the other, the centre houses four theatres – the Melbourne Concert Hall, the State Theatre, the Playhouse and the George Fairfax Studio.

The Melbourne Theatre Company is the city's major theatrical company. *La Mama* at 205 Faraday St in Carlton is a tiny, long-running experimental theatre and a great forum for new Australian works. The Playbox company, based at the *Malthouse Theatres* in Sturt St, South Melbourne, also stages predominantly Australian works.

Commercial theatres include the *Athenaeum* at 188 Collins St, the *Comedy Theatre* at 240 Exhibition St, *Her Majesty's Theatre* at 219 Exhibition St, the *Princess Theatre* at 163 Spring St, the *Universal Theatre* at 13 Victoria St in Fitzroy, and the *Gasworks Theatre* in Graham St in Albert Park.

Spectator Sports When it comes to watching sports, Melburnians are about as fanatical as they come. You've probably heard the old expression that Aussie punters would bet on two flies crawling up a wall – well, at times it seems like half of Melbourne would queue up to watch two snails race – and most of them wouldn't mind laying a bet on the outcome either.

Without a doubt, Australian Rules football – otherwise known as the 'Footy' – is the major drawcard, with games at the MCG regularly pulling crowds of 50,000 to 80,000. If you're here between April and September you should try and see a match, as much for the crowds as the game. The sheer energy of the barracking at a big game is exhilarating. Despite the fervour, crowd violence is almost unknown.

During the summer months, the MCG hosts a series of interstate and international one-day and Test cricket matches. The Australian Open tennis championship, one of the four international Grand Slams, is held at the National Tennis Centre each January.

Casino Melbourne's massive *Crown Casino*, which dominates the south bank of the Yarra across King St from the city centre, is open 24 hours a day. Plenty of pubs have poker machines.

VICTORIA

Things to Buy

There are a few places in Melbourne specialising in Aboriginal arts, crafts and souvenirs. The Aboriginal Gallery of Dreamings, at 73-77 Bourke St, the Aboriginal Desert Art Gallery at 31 Flinders Lane and Aboriginal Handcrafts on the 9th floor at 125 Swanston St, all sell a wide range of bark paintings, dijeridus and handicrafts from all over the country.

The best area for outdoor gear is around the intersection of Hardware and Little Bourke Sts in the city, where you'll find a collection of shops specialising in camping, climbing, hiking, skiing and other adventure gear.

If you're in the market for clothing, Chapel St in South Yarra (between Toorak and Commercial Rds) has the grooviest and most fashionable collection of boutiques. Other good areas include Brunswick St in Fitzroy (grunge gear and young designers), Toorak Rd in South Yarra (up-market and pricey), and Swan St and Bridge Rd in Richmond (designer shops and factory 'seconds' outlets). Also good for clothes (and most other stuff) are the city's major department stores – Myer and David Jones in the Bourke St Mall, and the Melbourne Central complex three blocks north, which includes Daimaru.

If you're interested in the local craft scene, head for the Meat Market Craft Centre (☎ 9329 9966) on the corner of Courtney and Blackwood Sts in North Melbourne (open Tuesday to Sunday from 10 am to 5 pm). The previously mentioned Esplanade Sunday Market in St Kilda is another good art and craft outlet, as is the Queen Victoria Market.

Getting There & Away

Air Melbourne airport at Tullamarine services both domestic and international flights. It's more spacious than Sydney's airport and also gets fewer flights, so if you make this your Australian arrival point you may get through immigration and customs a little more speedily.

Ansett (☎ 13 1300) and Qantas (☎ 13 1313) both have frequent connections between Melbourne and other state capitals – Melbourne to Sydney flights depart hourly during the airport's operating hours. Standard one-way economy fares include Adelaide $240, Brisbane $399, Canberra $205, Perth $577 and Sydney $255. Connections to Alice Springs ($517) are via Adelaide or Sydney. See the Getting Around section earlier in the book for details of discounted air fares.

Melbourne is the main departure point from the mainland to Tasmania. Flights to Hobart with Ansett or Qantas cost $223, and to Launceston they cost $193. Flights to Devonport cost $168 and are operated by Kendell Airlines (bookings through Ansett). Aus Air (☎ 9580 6166) also fly to Tassie from Moorabbin airport: destinations include Launceston ($159), Devonport ($148) and King Island ($112).

The Qantas office is at 50 Franklin St. Ansett's is at 501 Swanston St. Both have smaller offices dotted around the city.

Refer to the air fares chart in the introductory Getting Around section in this chapter for details of air fares within Victoria.

Bus Operating from the Melbourne Transit Centre at 58 Franklin St in the city, Greyhound Pioneer (☎ 13 2030) has buses between Melbourne and Adelaide (10 hours, $55), Perth (48 hours, $219), Canberra (nine hours, $55), Brisbane (24 hours, $121), and Sydney (direct, 12 hours, $53; or via the Princes Highway, 15 hours, $61).

McCafferty's (☎ 13 1499), operates out of the Spencer St Coach Terminal, and has similar services but tends to be a few dollars cheaper. Fares include Adelaide ($45), Sydney ($50), Canberra ($45) and Brisbane ($124).

Firefly (☎ 9670 7500) also operate out of the Spencer St Coach Terminal, with services to Adelaide ($45) and Sydney ($50 overnight, $55 during the day).

V/Line buses also depart from the Spencer St Coach Terminal, and go to all parts of Victoria (☎ 13 2232). See the towns in this chapter for the appropriate fares.

There are two fun and scenic alternatives if you're travelling to Sydney or Adelaide.

The Wayward Bus (☎ 1800 882 823) takes three days exploring the Great Ocean Road and coastal route to Adelaide, and costs $150 including three lunches – you pay for accommodation and other meals. Straycat (☎ 1800 800 840) operates between Melbourne and Sydney on a similar principle – it offers a three-day trip via the High Country ($149 including all meals), or a two-day trip around the coastal route ($79 including an evening meal). Both companies offer free stopovers.

Train Rail tickets for travel within Victoria or interstate can be booked by phoning V/Line on ☎ 13 2232 (you may be on hold for 10 or 20 minutes at busy times!), or bought at most suburban stations and at Spencer St railway station in Melbourne, from where the long-distance services depart.

Interstate Melbourne to Sydney takes 10¾ hours by *XPT* train, with the Melbourne-Sydney service operating during the day and the Sydney-Melbourne service overnight. Standard fares are $97 in economy, $135 in 1st class, and $221 for a 1st-class sleeper, although discounts of between 10% and 40% apply for advance bookings.

To get to Canberra by rail you take the daily *Canberra Link*, which involves a train to Wodonga on the Victoria-New South Wales border and then a bus from there. This takes about eight hours and costs $45 in economy or $59 in 1st class.

The *Overland* operates between Melbourne and Adelaide every night of the week. The trip takes 12 hours and costs $50 in economy, $104 in 1st class or $170 for a 1st-class sleeper – you can get a discount of up to 20% off 1st-class fares on advance bookings. You can transport your car on the *Overland* for $80. The *Daylink* to Adelaide involves a train to Bendigo and a bus from there. This trip takes 11 hours and costs $47 in economy, $54.80 in 1st class.

To get to Perth by rail from Melbourne you take the *Overland* to Adelaide and then the *Indian Pacific* (which comes through Adelaide from Sydney). The Melbourne to Perth trip takes two days and three nights, and fares are $250 for an economy seat, $488 for a 'holiday fare' (seat to Adelaide, sleeper to Perth), or $842 for a 1st-class sleeper (all meals included). Between July and January only, you can get a discount of between 10% and 30% off holiday and 1st-class fares for advance bookings. Inclusive of meals, a sleeping berth costs $488 in economy, $715 in 1st class.

Within Victoria For V/Line services within Victoria there are a number of special fares available. Super Saver fares give you a 30% discount for travelling at off-peak times. Basically this means travelling on Tuesday, Wednesday or Thursday, arriving in Melbourne after 9.30 am, and leaving Melbourne at any time except between 4 and 6 pm.

See the introductory Getting Around section at the start of this chapter for details of V/Line's rail network, and see the sections on specific country towns for information on fares and travel from Melbourne.

Car Rental All the big car-rental firms operate in Melbourne. Avis, Budget, Hertz and Thrifty have desks at the airport and you can find plenty of others in the city. The offices tend to be at the northern end of the city or in Carlton or North Melbourne.

Melbourne also has a number of rent-a-wreck-style operators, renting older vehicles at lower rates. Their costs and conditions vary widely so it's worth making a few enquiries before going for one firm over another. You can take the 'from $21 a day' line with a pinch of salt because the rates soon start to rise with insurance, km charges and so on. Beware of distance restrictions; many companies only allow you to travel within a certain distance of the city, typically 100 km.

Some places worth trying are Delta (☎ 13 1390), Dollar (☎ 1800 658 658) and Airport Rent-a-Car (☎ 9335 3355), all of which have branches around Melbourne. Other operators include Rent-a-Bomb (☎ 9428 0088) in Richmond and Y-Not (☎ 9525 5900) in St Kilda. The Yellow Pages lists lots of other firms including some reputable local operators who rent newer cars but don't have the nationwide network (and overheads) of the big operators.

Getting Around

To/From the Airport Melbourne's Tullamarine airport is 22 km north-west of the city centre. It's a modern airport with a single terminal: Qantas at one end, Ansett at the other, international in the middle. There are two information desks at the airport: one on the ground floor in the international departure area and another upstairs next to the duty-free shops.

The Tullamarine Freeway runs from the airport almost into the city centre, finishing in North Melbourne. A taxi between the airport and city centre costs about $25. There's also the regular Skybus (☎ 9662 9275) service, which costs $9 (children $4.50). The Skybus departs from Bay 30 at the Spencer St Coach Terminal and from the Melbourne Transit Centre at 58 Franklin St, with buses about every half-hour between 6 am and 10.30 pm (ring to confirm departure times).

There is also a fairly frequent bus by Gull Airport Services (☎ 5222 4966 between the airport and Geelong. It costs $20 one way. The Geelong terminus is at 45 McKillop St.

Bus, Train & Tram Melbourne's public transport system, the Met, incorporates buses, trains and trams. The trams are the real cornerstone of the system; in all there are about 750 of them and they operate as far as 20 km out from the centre. They're frequent and fun.

Buses are the secondary form of public transport, taking routes where the trams do not go, and replacing them at quiet weekend periods. The trains are the third link in the Met, radiating out from the city centre to the outer suburbs. The fast underground City Loop operates between Spencer St, Flinders St, Flagstaff, Museum and Parliament railway stations.

There's quite an array of tickets, and they are all described in the Met's glossy *Travel Guide* brochure. You can buy tickets on board trams and buses, from railway stations, and from retails outlets including newsagents, milk bars and chemists. The same ticket allows you to travel on trams, trains and buses. The most common tickets are based on a specific period of travelling time – either two hours, one day, one week, one month or one year – and allow you unlimited travel during that period and within the relevant zone.

The metropolitan area is divided into three zones, and the price of tickets depends on which zone/s you will be travelling in and across. Zone 1 covers the city and inner suburban area, and most travellers won't venture beyond that unless they're going right out of town – on a trip to the Healesville Sanctuary, for example, or down to the Mornington Peninsula. The fares are as follows:

Zones	2 Hours	All Day	Weekly
1	$2.10	$4.10	$18.00
2 or 3	$1.50	$2.80	$12.40
1 & 2	$3.60	$6.80	$30.40
1, 2 & 3	$5.00	$9.20	$37.20

Note that if you buy a weekly, monthly or yearly Zone 1 ticket, it also allows you unlimited travel in Zones 1, 2 and 3 on weekends. If you're heading into the city by train from Zone 2 or 3, you can get off-peak tickets for use after 9.30 am which take you into the city and then allow unlimited travel on trams and buses within the city area.

There are also Short Trip tickets ($1.50) which allow you to travel two sections on buses or trams in Zone 1, or you can buy a Short Trip Card ($12) which gives you 10 short trips. There are numerous other deals and you can check these out with the Met.

For information on public transport phone the Met Information Centre (☎ 13 1638), which operates daily from 7 am to 9 pm. The Met Shop at 103 Elizabeth St in the city also has transport information and sells souvenirs and tickets. It also has a 'Discover Melbourne' kit. If you're in the city it's probably a better bet for information than the telephone service, which is usually busy. Railway stations also have some information.

The Met operates an information service for disabled travellers (☎ 9619 2355).

Bicycle Melbourne's a great city for cycling. It's reasonably flat so you're not pushing and panting up hills too often, and there are some excellent cycling routes throughout the metropolitan area. Two of the best are the bike path that runs around the shores of Port Phillip Bay from Port Melbourne to Brighton, and the bike path that follows the Yarra River out of the city for more than 20 km, passing through lovely parklands along the way. There are numerous other bicycle tracks, including those along the Maribyrnong River and Merri Creek.

A new book, *Discovering Melbourne's Bike Paths* ($14.95), has excellent maps and descriptions of the city's bicycle paths. The *Melway Greater Melbourne* street directory is also useful for cyclists. Note that bicycles can be taken on suburban trains for free during off-peak times.

Quite a few bike shops and companies have bikes for hire – the following places are all worth trying: St Kilda Cycles (☎ 9534 3074), 11 Carlisle St, St Kilda; Bob's Boards (☎ 9537 2118), 17 Fitzroy St, St Kilda; Cycle Science (☎ 9826 8877), 320 Toorak Rd, South Yarra; Bicycles for Hire (☎ 018 580 809), below Princes Bridge on the south side of the Yarra; and Borsari Cycles (☎ 9347 4100), 193 Lygon St, Carlton.

Around Melbourne

There are plenty of worthwhile destinations within about an hour's drive of Melbourne, including the fine beaches and seaside towns of the Bellarine and Mornington peninsulas, mysterious Hanging Rock, the scenic Yarra Valley with its wineries and excellent wildlife sanctuary, the verdant Dandenong Ranges, and Phillip Island with its famous penguin parade.

SOUTH-WEST TO GEELONG

It's a quick trip down the Princes Freeway to Geelong. As you leave Melbourne there are fine views of the city from the soaring West Gate Bridge, although the rest of the trip is pretty dull.

Werribee Park & Zoo

Not far out of Melbourne you can turn off to Werribee Park with its free-range zoological park and the huge Italianate **Werribee Park Mansion**, built in 1874. The flamboyant building is surrounded by formal gardens, with good picnic areas. Entrance to the gardens is free, but admission to the mansion costs $8 (children $4). Safari bus tours of the zoo also cost $8/4. Werribee Park is open daily from 10 am to 3.45 pm (to 4.45 pm during summer).

RAAF Aviation Museum

South of Werribee is this aviation museum at the RAAF base at Point Cook, with a collection of 20 antique aircraft as well as aviation memorabilia. It's open daily (except Saturday) from 10 am to 4 pm ($4).

You Yangs

You can also detour to the You Yangs, a picturesque range of volcanic hills just off the freeway. Walks in the You Yangs include the climb up **Flinders Peak**, the highest point in the park, with a plaque commemorating Matthew Flinders' scramble to the top in 1802. There are fine views from the top, down to Geelong and the coast.

Brisbane Ranges National Park

You can make an interesting loop from Melbourne out to the You Yangs and back through the Brisbane Ranges park and Bacchus Marsh. The scenic **Anakie Gorge** in the Brisbane Ranges is a popular short bushwalk and a good spot for barbecues. You may see koalas in the trees near the car park/picnic area.

Fairy Park, on the side of Mt Anakie at the southern edge of the Brisbane Ranges, has 100 clay fairy-tale figures.

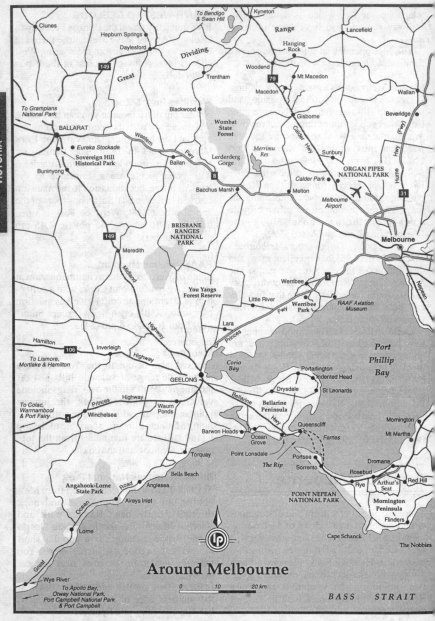

Around Melbourne

0   10   20 km

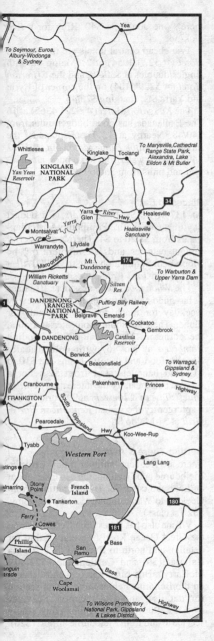

GEELONG (pop 152,200)

The city of Geelong began as a sheep-grazing area when the first White settlers arrived in 1836, and it initially served as a port for the dispatch of wool and wheat from the area. During the gold-rush era it became important as a landing place for immigrants and for the export of gold. Around 1900, Geelong started to become industrialised and that's very much what it is today – an industrial city, and Victoria's second-largest city.

In general there are no real 'not to be missed' attractions in Geelong and it is basically a place people go through on their way to greater attractions, such as the Great Ocean Road or the Otway Ranges.

Information

The Geelong Otway Tourism Centre (☎ 5275 5797), on the corner of the Princes Highway and St George Rd seven km north of Geelong, is open daily from 9 am to 4 pm (from 10 am on Friday). There's another tourist office (☎ 5222 2900) in the National Wool Centre on Moorabool St.

Museums & Art Gallery

The impressive **National Wool Centre**, on the corner of Brougham and Moorabool Sts, is housed in a historic bluestone wool store and has a museum, a number of wool-craft and clothing shops and a restaurant. It is open every day from 10 am to 5 pm and admission to the museum section is $7 ($5.80 students, $3.50 children).

The **Geelong Maritime Museum** at Osborne House in Swinburne St, North Geelong, is open daily, except Tuesday and Thursday, from 10 am to 4 pm. The **Geelong Art Gallery** on Little Malop St is open weekdays from 10 am to 5 pm and weekends from 1 to 5 pm and has an extensive collection of mainly Australian art; entry is $3 (free Monday).

Historic Houses

The city has more than 100 National Trust classified buildings. **Barwon Grange** on Fernleigh St, Newtown, was built in 1856. It's open on Wednesday, Saturday and

Sunday from 2 to 5 pm; entry costs $4. The **Heights**, at 140 Aphrasia St, is open from Wednesday to Sunday from 2 to 5 pm; entry costs $5.50. This 14-room timber mansion is an example of a prefabricated building brought out to the colony in pieces and it features an unusual watchtower.

Another prefabricated building is **Corio Villa**, made from iron sheets in 1856. The bits and pieces were shipped out from Glasgow but nobody claimed them on arrival! It's now a private house, overlooking Eastern Beach. **Osborne House** and **Armytage House** are other fine old private buildings.

Other Attractions

Geelong's attractive botanic gardens (part of Eastern Park) contain the **Customs House**, Victoria's oldest wooden building, which displays telegraph equipment and memorabilia. **Eastern Beach** is Geelong's popular swimming spot and promenade where boats and bicycles can be hired on weekends in summer. There's a restaurant, cafe and kiosk here, as well as swimming/diving platforms, sandy beaches and picnic lawns. There is also a signposted scenic drive along the beachfront.

On hot summer days, **Norlane Waterworld** on the corner of the Princes Highway and Cox St is a good place to head for, with swimming pools and giant waterslides.

Places to Stay

There are four caravan parks along Barrabool Rd on the south side of the Barwon River, including *Billabong Caravan Park* (☎ 5243 6225), with sites from $12 and on-site vans from $30.

The *Geelong YHA Hostel* (☎ 5221 6583), in a small house at 1 Lonsdale St, costs $12 ($14 nonmembers). The colleges at Deakin University (☎ 5227 1158), on the outskirts of Geelong towards Colac, also have cheap accommodation in the summer holidays.

An interesting budget option is *St Albans Backpackers* (☎ 5248 1229), a historic mansion and horse-stud farm on Homestead Driver, Whittington. Bunk beds cost $17 and

there's one double at $40. Ring for a free pick-up.

Two cheap central hotels are the *Carlton Hotel* (☎ 5229 1954) at 21 Malop St, with singles/doubles at $30/40, and the *Criterion Hotel* (☎ 5229 1104) on the corner of Ryrie and Yarra Sts, charging $25/45.

The *Kangaroo Motel* (☎ 5221 4365) at 16 The Esplanade has good budget units from $40/48. Nearby at 13 The Esplanade, the modern *Hamilton Hume Motor Inn* (☎ 5222 3499) on the waterfront has a pool, a restaurant and units from $65/69.

Places to Eat

At 137 Ryrie St, *Cheap Eats* is a budget daytime cafe with 'Philippine-Australian' meals from $1.20 to $4. There's a cluster of budget eateries and late-nighters on the Moorabool St hill, including the *Hill Grill* at No 228 and *Joe's Cafe* opposite.

The *Wholefoods* delicatessan at 10 James St has good natural tucker, and is open every weekday for lunch and on weekends for dinner. There are some good eateries around the corner in Little Malop St, including *Bamboleo* at No 86, with authentically Spanish food and décor – mains are $10 to $12 and banquets start from $22. For a relaxed pub meal, try the interesting *Scottish Chief's Tavern & Brewery* at 99 Corio St. For a splurge, try the stylish *Republican Bar & Grill* at 31 Malop St.

Getting There & Away

There are frequent 'sprinter trains' between Melbourne and Geelong; the trip takes about an hour and costs $8. Trains continue from Geelong to Warrnambool ($22.80 economy, $32 1st class).

V/Line also has buses from Geelong along the Great Ocean Road (see that section for details), and north to Bendigo ($27.20) via Ballarat ($9) and Castlemaine ($22.80). McHarry's Bus Lines services most places on the Bellarine Peninsula (see that section for details), and Gull Airport Services (☎ 5222 4966) at 45 McKillop St runs a daily service to and from Melbourne airport ($20).

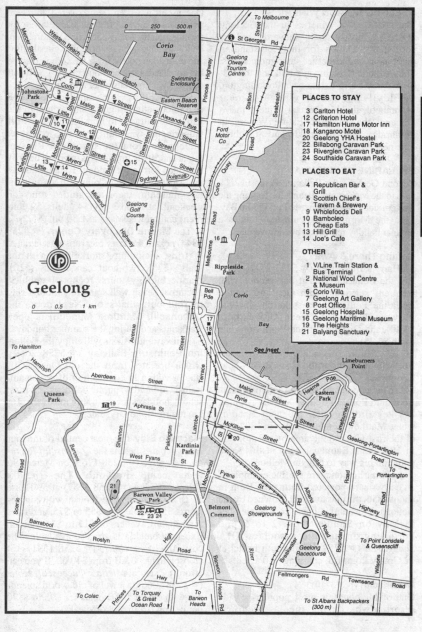

VICTORIA

Geelong

Scale: 0 – 0.5 – 1 km

PLACES TO STAY

3 Carlton Hotel
12 Criterion Hotel
17 Hamilton Hume Motor Inn
18 Kangaroo Motel
20 Geelong YHA Hostel
22 Billabong Caravan Park
23 Riverglen Caravan Park
24 Southside Caravan Park

PLACES TO EAT

4 Republican Bar & Grill
5 Scottish Chief's Tavern & Brewery
9 Wholefoods Deli
10 Bamboleo
11 Cheap Eats
13 Hill Grill
14 Joe's Cafe

OTHER

1 V/Line Train Station & Bus Terminal
2 National Wool Centre & Museum
6 Corio Villa
7 Geelong Art Gallery
8 Post Office
15 Geelong Hospital
16 Geelong Maritime Museum
19 The Heights
21 Balyang Sanctuary

GEELONG REGION WINERIES

The dozen or so wineries in the Geelong region are mostly small vineyards, and are particularly known for their outstanding pinot noir and cabernet-sauvignon wines. They include Scotchman's Hill and the historic Spray Farm Estate near Portarlington, the Idyll and Asher vineyards near Moorabool, the Mt Duneed Winery in Mt Duneed, the Tarcoola Estate Winery in Lethbridge, and Mt Anakie and Staughton Vale near Anakie.

BELLARINE PENINSULA

Beyond Geelong the Bellarine Peninsula is a twin to the Mornington Peninsula, forming the western side of the entrance to Port Phillip Bay. Like the Mornington Peninsula, this is a popular holiday resort and boating venue.

Getting There & Away

McHarry's Bus Lines (☎ 5223 2111) operates the Bellarine Transit bus service with frequent services from Geelong to the Bellarine Peninsula; destinations include Barwon Heads and Ocean Grove (both $3.40), and Queenscliff and Point Lonsdale (both $5.25).

Portarlington, Indented Head & St Leonards

These three towns on the northern peninsula front onto Port Phillip Bay and are popular, low-key little resorts. Indented Head is where Matthew Flinders landed in 1802, one of the first visits to the area by a European. In 1835 John Batman landed at this same point, on his way to buy up Melbourne.

At Portarlington there's a fine example of an early steam-powered **flour mill**. Built in about 1856, the massive mill is owned by the National Trust and is open from September to May on Sunday from 2 to 5 pm. Portarlington has the associate-YHA *Shangri-La* (☎ 5259 2536) youth hostel at 12 Grassy Point Rd, charging $10 a bed.

Queenscliff (pop 3710)

One of Melbourne's most popular seaside resort towns during the last century,

Queenscliff has been 'rediscovered' in recent times and is again a fashionable getaway for the city's gentry. Many of the fine Victorian-era buildings have been restored into guesthouses and up-market hotels; these are complemented by good cafes and restaurants, a great golf course and numerous other attractions.

Queenscliff was established in about 1838 as a pilot station to guide ships through the Rip at the entrance to Port Phillip Bay. **Fort Queenscliff** was built in 1882 to protect Melbourne from the perceived Russian threat and, at the time, it was the most heavily defended fort in the colony. Today it houses the Australian Army Command and a military museum; there are guided tours on weekends at 1 and 3 pm ($4 adults, $2 children) and on weekdays at 1.30 pm ($5/2).

The **Marine Discovery Centre** (☎ 5258 3344) next to the ferry pier runs a great range of trips, including 'snorkelling with the seals' ($35), two-hour canoe trips ($10), marine biology tours, rockpool rambles, nocturnal beach walks and lots more – ring to find out what's on. Next door, the **Queenscliff Maritime Museum** is open weekends and during the summer holidays.

Railway enthusiasts will enjoy the **Bellarine Peninsula Railway** (☎ 5258 2069), which operates from the old Queenscliff station with a fine collection of old steam-trains. On Sunday, public holidays and most school holidays steam-trains make the 16-km return trip to Drysdale.

Places to Stay The most central of the four caravan parks here is the *Queenscliff Recreation Reserve* (☎ 5258 1765) on Mercer St; it has camp sites only. The friendly *Queenscliff Inn* (☎ 5258 3737) at 59 Hesse St is a charming guesthouse with singles from $35, doubles for $55 to $75, and rates for budget travellers of $15 to $25 a night. Excellent breakfasts are also available. The cosy *Athelstane House* (☎ 5258 1591) at 4 Hobson St has B&B from $40/60. If you can afford to, stay at *Mietta's Queenscliff Hotel* (☎ 5258 1066), a jewel of old-world splendour with dinner B&B deals for $95 to $170 per person (from $78 off-peak!).

Getting There & Away Ferries operate between Queenscliff and Sorrento and Portsea. See the Mornington Peninsula Getting There & Away section for details.

Point Lonsdale (pop 3710)

Five km south-west of Queenscliff, Point Lonsdale's **lighthouse and lookout** overlook the turbulent waters of the Rip, which separates the Bellarine and Mornington peninsulas. A fleet of pilot boats guide ships through the narrow opening. Below the lighthouse is **Buckley's Cave** where the 'wild White man', William Buckley, lived with Aboriginal people for 32 years after escaping from the settlement at Sorrento on the Mornington Peninsula in 1803.

The *Royal Park Caravan Park* is open between December and Easter, and the *Terminus B&B & Motel* (☎ 5252 1142) has budget rooms from $15, motel units from $55 and B&B from $75 a double.

Ocean Grove (pop 7020)

This resort on the ocean side of the peninsula has good scuba diving on the rocky ledges of the Bluff, and farther out there are wrecks of ships that failed to get through the tricky entrance to Port Phillip Bay. Some of the wrecks are accessible to divers. The beach at the surf-lifesaving club is very popular with surfers. Ocean Grove is a real-estate agent's paradise and it has grown into the biggest town on the peninsula. Accommodation options include caravan parks, motels and holiday flats.

Barwon Heads

Barwon Heads is a small resort just along from Ocean Grove. It has sheltered river beaches and surf beaches around the headland. The popular *Barwon Heads Park* (☎ 5254 1115) has tent sites from $14 to $21, on-site tents from $28 to $25 and cabins from $40 to $90. The *Barwon Heads Hotel*, overlooking the river, has a few singles/doubles from $35/60.

NORTH-WEST TO BENDIGO

It's about 160 km north-west of Melbourne along the Calder Highway to the old mining town of Bendigo, and there are some interesting stops along the way.

You've hardly left the outskirts of Melbourne when you come to the turn-off to the surprisingly pretty and little-visited **Organ Pipes National Park** on the right, and the amazingly ugly Calder Thunderdome Raceway on the left.

Next is **Gisborne**, at one time a coach stop on the goldfields route. **Mt Macedon**, a 1013-metre-high extinct volcano, soon looms large on the right. The scenic route up Mt Macedon takes you past many impressive country mansions and some lovely gardens to a lookout point at the summit; the road then continues down to Woodend and Hanging Rock.

Hanging Rock

Just north of Mt Macedon is Hanging Rock, a popular picnic spot made famous by the book, *Picnic at Hanging Rock*, and later by the film of the same name. At that mysterious picnic, three schoolgirls on a trip to the rock disappeared without trace; in an equally mysterious way one of the girls reappeared a few days later. The rocks are fun to clamber over and there are superb views from higher up. The Hanging Rock Picnic Races, held on New Year's Day, are a great day out.

To get there, take a train from Melbourne to Woodend ($8) – from there, a taxi to Hanging Rock will cost about $10. See Organised Tours in the Melbourne section for details of day trips to the Hanging Rock area.

Kyneton & Malmsbury

The highway continues through Kyneton, which has fine bluestone buildings. Piper St is a historic precinct, with antique shops, tearooms, and a **historical museum**, housed in a building dating from 1855, which was originally a bank.

Another 11 km brings you to Malmsbury with its historic bluestone **railway viaduct** and a magnificent ruined **grain mill**, which has been converted into a delightful restaurant and gallery.

VICTORIA

YARRA VALLEY & BEYOND

The Yarra Valley, beyond the north-eastern outskirts of Melbourne, is a place of great natural beauty and well worth exploring. It's a good area for bicycle tours or bushwalks, there are dozens of wineries to visit, and the Healesville Wildlife Sanctuary is one of the best places in the country to see Australian wildlife.

Getting There & Away

McKenzie's Bus Lines (☎ 9853 6264) runs a daily bus service from the Spencer St bus terminal through Healesville to Marysville, Alexandra and Lake Eildon.

Wineries

With more than 30 wineries sprinkled through the Yarra Valley, this area is a popular, scenic and very pleasant day trip from Melbourne. Wineries open daily include Domaine Chandon, Lilydale Vineyards, De Bortoli, Fergussons, Kellybrook and Yarra Burn, and about 15 others are open on weekends and holidays.

Gulf Station

Gulf Station, a couple of km north of Yarra Glen, is part of an old grazing run dating from the 1850s. Operated by the National Trust, it's open Wednesday to Sunday and on public holidays from 10 am to 4 pm ($6). There is an interesting collection of rough old timber buildings plus the associated pastures and a homestead garden typical of the period.

Healesville Wildlife Sanctuary

Near the pleasant town of Healesville, 65 km from the centre of Melbourne, is the outstanding Healesville Wildlife Sanctuary (☎ 9728 2000). Most of the enclosures are very natural, and some of the birds just pop in for the day. Some enclosures are only open at certain times so you may want to plan your visit accordingly. The platypus, for example, is only on show in its glass-sided tank from 11.30 am to 1 pm and from 1.30 to 3.30 pm. The nocturnal house, where you can see many of the smaller bush dwellers that come

out only at night, is open from 10 am to 4.30 pm, as is the reptile house. The popular 'birds of prey' show runs daily at noon and 3 pm. The whole park is open daily from 9 am to 5 pm and admission is $12 ($9 students, $6 children). There are barbecue and picnic facilities in the pleasantly wooded park.

Getting There & Away From Melbourne, take a suburban train to Lilydale station, from where McKenzie's Bus Line (☎ 9853 6264) has connecting bus services right to the sanctuary, departing at 9.40 and 11.40 am and leaving for the return trip at 3.40 and 5.30 pm.

Warburton (pop 2510)

Beyond Healesville is Warburton, another pretty little hill town in the Great Dividing Range foothills. There are good views of the mountains along the Acheron Way nearby and you'll sometimes get snow on Mt Donna Buang, seven km from town.

Marysville (pop 670)

This delightful little town is a very popular weekend escape from Melbourne. It has lots of bush tracks that are good for walks: Nicholl's Lookout, Keppel's Lookout, Mt Gordon and Steavenson Falls. **Cumberland Scenic Reserve**, with numerous walks and the Cumberland Falls, is 16 km east of Marysville. The cross-country skiing trails of **Lake Mountain Reserve** are only 10 km beyond Marysville.

The **Cathedral Range State Park** is about 10 km north-west of Marysville, and it offers excellent bushwalks and camping.

Places to Stay The *Marysville Caravan Park* (☎ 5963 3433) is beside the river, and the rambling *Crossways Country Inn* (☎ 5963 3290) has motel-style units from $45/50. There are numerous up-market guesthouses and B&Bs, including *Maryland Country House* (☎ 5963 3204), with dinner B&B for about $200 a double.

About 15 km north of Marysville, the YHA *Australian Bush Settlement* (☎ 5774 7378) is an adventure camp and youth hostel on a farm property; it charges $15 a night ($20 for nonmembers).

THE DANDENONGS

The Dandenong Ranges, just beyond the eastern fringe of Melbourne's suburban sprawl, are a favourite destination for day trips, scenic drives and picnics. Things can get a little hectic up here on weekends – midweek visits are much more relaxed.

The Dandenongs are cool owing to the altitude (Mt Dandenong is all of 633 metres tall) and lushly green because of the heavy rainfall. The area is dotted with fine old houses, old-fashioned tearooms, restaurants, beautiful gardens and some fine short bushwalks. You can see the Dandenongs clearly from central Melbourne (on a smog-free day) and they're only about an hour's drive away.

The small **Ferntree Gully National Park** has pleasant strolls and lots of birdlife. Unfortunately, the lyrebirds for which the Dandenongs were once famous are now very rare. The **Sherbrooke Forest Park** is similarly pleasant for walks and you'll see lots of rosellas. These parks, together with Doongalla Reserve, make up the Dandenong Ranges National Park, proclaimed in 1987.

The **William Ricketts Sanctuary**, on Olinda Rd, is set in fern gardens and features the work of the sculptor William Ricketts, who died in 1993 aged 94. His work was inspired by the Aboriginal people and their affinity with the land – the sculptures rise like spirits out of the ground. The forest sanctuary is open every day from 10 am to 4.30 pm and is well worth the $5 admission.

Puffing Billy

One of the major attractions in the Dandenongs is Puffing Billy (☎ 9754 6800 for bookings; ☎ 9870 8411 for running times), a restored steam-train that runs along a spectacular 13-km track from Belgrave to Lakeside at the Emerald Lake Park. Puffing Billy was originally built in 1900 to bring farm produce to market.

Emerald is a pretty little town with many craft galleries and shops. At **Lakeside**

The golden blooms of the wattle can be seen in Victoria in late winter

there's a whole string of attractions from paddleboats, barbecues and water slides to a huge model railway with more than two km of track! At Menzies Creek station there's a **Steam Museum** with a collection of early steam locomotives (open weekends and public holidays from 11 am to 5 pm).

Puffing Billy runs every day except Christmas day; the round trip takes about 2½ hours and costs $15.50 for adults, $9 for children and $43 for a family. You can get out to Puffing Billy on the regular suburban rail service to Belgrave.

Places to Stay

There are numerous motels, guesthouses and B&Bs in the Dandenongs, but the only budget accommodation in this area is *Emerald Backpackers* (☎ 5968 4086), a comfortable hostel with dorm beds for $12. The people here can often find work for travellers in the local nurseries and gardens.

MORNINGTON PENINSULA

The Mornington Peninsula is the spit of land down the eastern side of Port Phillip Bay, bordered on its eastern side by the waters of Western Port bay. Melbourne's suburban sprawl extends down the peninsula beyond Frankston to Mornington, but from there it's almost a continuous beach strip all the way to Portsea at the end of the peninsula, nearly 100 km from Melbourne.

This is a very popular Melbourne resort area with many holiday homes; in summer the accommodation and camp sites along the peninsula can be packed right out and traffic can be very heavy. In part this popularity arises from the peninsula's excellent beaches and the great variety they offer. On the northern side of the peninsula there is calm water on the bay beaches (the front beaches) looking out onto Port Phillip Bay, and on the southern side there is good surf along the rugged and beautiful ocean beaches (the back beaches), which face Bass Strait.

The peninsula is an acclaimed wine-growing region with some 30 wineries, many of which are open to the public. There are also excellent bushwalking trails along the Cape Schanck Coastal Park. Other attractions include great golf courses, dolphin cruises, horse-riding ranches, craft markets, and the Point Nepean National Park.

There's a tourist information centre in Dromana (☎ 5987 3078) on the Nepean Highway and the DC&NR brochure *Discovering the Peninsula* ($3.50) tells you all you'll want to know about the peninsula's history, early architecture and walking tours.

Markets

The peninsula is an excellent place to check out craft and produce markets. The main markets are: Red Hill (1st Saturday morning each month), Emu Plains and Boneo (3rd Saturday each month), Rosebud (2nd Saturday each month), and Sorrento (from September to April on the 4th Saturday each month).

Getting There & Away

Train/Bus Take a suburban train from Melbourne down to Frankston to connect with the frequent buses of the Peninsula Bus Lines (☎ 5986 5666) along the coastal highway from Frankston to Portsea ($6.45).

Ferry Peninsula Searoad Transport (☎ 5258 3244) operates the car and passenger ferry that links Sorrento with Queenscliff on the Bellarine Peninsula. It runs all year, departing Queenscliff every two hours from 7 am to 5 pm (with a 7 pm high-season service) and returning from Sorrento every two hours

from 8 am to 6 pm (with an 8 pm high-season service). Cars cost $30 to $36 plus $3 per adult; a motorcycle and rider costs $17; and pedestrians cost $7 ($5 for children).

A passenger ferry (☎ 5984 1602) also operates regular daily crossings from Sorrento and Portsea to Queenscliff between Christmas and Easter, and during school holidays; the adult fare is $6 each way.

Frankston to Blairgowrie

Beyond Frankston you reach **Mornington** and **Mt Martha**, both with some old buildings along the Mornington Esplanade and fine, secluded beaches in between. The **Briars** in Mt Martha is an 1840s homestead open to the public.

Dromana is the real start of the resort development and just inland a winding road leads up to **Arthur's Seat** lookout at 305 metres; in summer you can also reach it by a scenic chair lift (weekends and holidays only). On the slopes of Arthur's Seat, in McCrae, the **McCrae Homestead** is a National Trust property, dating from 1843. It is open daily from noon to 4.30 pm. **Coolart** on Sandy Point Rd, Balnarring, on the other side of the peninsula, is another historic homestead, also noted for the wide variety of its birdlife.

After McCrae there's **Rosebud**, **Rye** and **Blairgowrie** before you reach Sorrento.

Sorrento

Just as you enter Sorrento there's a small memorial and pioneer cemetery from the first Victorian settlement at pretty **Sullivan Bay**. The settlement party, consisting of 308 convicts, civil officers, marines and free settlers, arrived from England in October 1803, intending to forestall a feared French settlement on the bay. Less than a year later, in May 1804, the project was abandoned and transferred to Hobart, Tasmania.

The main reason for the settlement's short life was the lack of water. They had simply chosen the wrong place; there was an adequate supply farther around the bay. The settlement's numbers included an 11-year-old boy, John Pascoe Fawkner, who 31 years later would be one of the founders of Melbourne. It also included the convict William Buckley, who escaped soon after the landing in 1803.

Sorrento has a rather damp and cold little aquarium and an interesting small historical museum in the old **Mechanic's Institute** building on the Old Melbourne Rd. In the last century paddle-steamers ran between Melbourne and Sorrento. From 1890 through to 1921 a steam-powered tram operated from the Sorrento pier to the back beach. The magnificent hotels built of local limestone in this period still stand – the Sorrento (1871), Continental (1875) and Koonya (1878).

Moonraker Charters (☎ 5984 4211) and Polperro Dolphin Swims (☎ 5988 8437) both offer the opportunity to swim in the bay with dolphins.

Places to Stay The YHA-affiliated *Bell's Hostel* (☎ 5984 4323) in Sorrento is a very popular place to stay. The owners, Ian and Margaret, are friendly hosts and organise activities including dolphin swims, coastal walks and birdwatching. The nightly charge is $12 ($14 during summer; $2 extra for nonmembers). On Ocean Beach Rd, the *Continental Hotel* (☎ 5984 2201) has basic bunk rooms for $15 ($20 during summer), and *Carmel B&B* (☎ 5984 3512) has B&B from $80 to $120 a double and self-contained units from $80.

Portsea

At the tip of the peninsula, Portsea is where many of Melbourne's wealthier families have built seaside summer mansions, and the small town has an unmistakable but subtle air of privilege. At the Portsea back beach (the surf side) there's the impressive natural rock formation known as **London Bridge**, plus a cliff where hang-gliders make their leap into the void, and fine views across Portsea and back to Melbourne from **Mt Levy Lookout**. Portsea is a popular diving centre, and scuba-diving trips on the bay operate regularly from Portsea Pier. The *Portsea Hotel* (☎ 5984 2213), overlooking

the pier, is particularly popular in summer, and has B&B from $35/60.

Point Nepean National Park

After being off limits to the public for over 100 years, most of the tip of the peninsula was opened up in 1988 as a national park. There's an excellent visitor centre (☎ 5984 4276) where an entrance fee of $7.50 is payable. There are walking tracks through the area, or you can use the tractor-drawn transporter. The booklet *A Guide to Point Nepean's Past* ($5) is available from the visitor centre. Cheviot Beach, at the end of the peninsula, is the place where the Australian prime minister Harold Holt went for a swim in 1967 and was never seen again.

The Ocean Coast

The southern and eastern coasts of the peninsula face Bass Strait and Western Port bay. A connected series of walking tracks has been developed all the way from London Bridge to Cape Schanck and Bushrangers Bay. Some stretches of the **Peninsula Coastal Walk** are along the beach (some are actually cut by the high tide), and in its entirety the walk extends for more than 30 km and takes at least 12 hours to walk from end to end. The walks can be done easily in stages because the park is narrow and accessible at various points.

Cape Schanck is marked by the 1859 lighthouse and there are good walking possibilities around the cape. The rugged coast farther east towards **Flinders** and **West Head** has many natural features including a blowhole. Towns such as Flinders and **Hastings** on this coast are not quite as popular and crowded in the summer as those on Port Phillip Bay. There are dozens of good surf beaches all along this coast – mostly beach breaks along Bass Strait, and mostly reef breaks in Western Port bay.

Off the coast in Western Port is **French Island**, once a prison farm, which is virtually undeveloped, although there are a few camp sites and a lodge. Koalas were introduced some years ago, and the thriving colony provides top-ups for depleted areas elsewhere in

Victoria. The French Island Ferry (☎ 018 553 136) operates daily between Stony Point and Tankerton Jetty on French Island ($15.50 return).

PHILLIP ISLAND

At the entrance to Western Port, 137 km south-east of Melbourne, Phillip Island is a very popular holiday island. Its main attractions are its excellent surf beaches and the incredibly popular and famous (although somewhat commercialised) penguin parade. The island is joined to the mainland by a bridge from San Remo to Newhaven.

Orientation & Information

Cowes, the main town, is on the northern side of the island and has most facilities including banks, plus a good range of eateries and places to stay. The southern side of the island has surf beaches such as Woolamai, Cat Bay and Summerland, which is the home of the famous penguin parade.

There is an excellent information centre (☎ 5956 7447) in Newhaven just after you cross the bridge to the island. It is open daily from 9 am to 5 pm (in summer to 6 pm).

Penguin Parade

Every evening at Summerland Beach in the south-west of the island, the tiny penguins that nest here perform their 'parade', emerging from the sea and waddling resolutely up the beach to their nests – totally oblivious of the thousands of sightseers. The penguins are there year-round but arrive in far larger numbers in the summer when they are rearing their young. It's no easy life being the smallest type of penguin – after a few hours of shut-eye, it's down to the beach again at dawn to start another hard day's fishing.

The parade takes place like clockwork a few minutes after sunset each day and it is a major tourist attraction – Australia's second biggest, in fact. There are huge crowds, especially on weekends and holidays, so advance bookings should be made through either the tourist office, or the Penguin Reserve itself (☎ 5956 8300).

To protect the penguins everything is strictly regimented – keep to the viewing areas, don't get in the penguins' way and no camera flashes. There's a modern visitor centre with a souvenir shop and a walk-through simulated underwater display. The

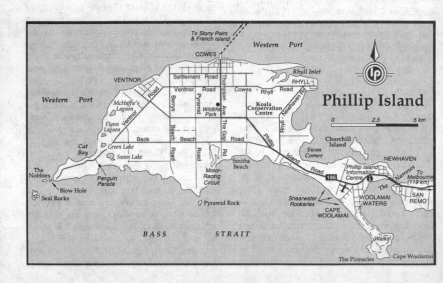

Fairy penguins are a highlight of a trip to Phillip Island

admission charge is $7.50 for adults, $3.50 for children and $21 for a family.

Wildlife Reserves

The **Phillip Island Wildlife Park**, on Thompson Ave about one km south of Cowes, is a well-designed park with wallabies, wombats, emus and other native birds and animals. It's open daily from 9 am to dusk and costs $7 ($4 for children). The **Koala Conservation Centre**, at Fiveways on the Phillip Island Tourist Rd, is open from 10 am to dusk and costs $4/1.50.

Seals & Shearwaters

A colony of fur seals inhabits Seal Rocks, off Point Grant at the south-western tip of the island. There's a timber boardwalk along the foreshore and you can view the seals through coin-in-the-slot binoculars from the kiosk on the headland. The group of rocks closest to the island is called the Nobbies.

Phillip Island also has colonies of shearwaters, particularly in the sand dunes around Cape Woolamai. These birds, also known as mutton birds, are amazingly predictable; they arrive back on the island on exactly the same day each year – 24 September – from their migratory flight from Japan and Alaska.

Other Attractions

The island's old motor-racing circuit was revamped to stage a round of the World Motorcycle Grand Prix back in 1989 and 1990. The event was controversially moved

to Sydney in 1991, but is due to return to Phillip Island in 1997.

There are plenty of impressive walking tracks around the island at places such as rugged **Cape Woolamai**. Maps and brochures are available from the tourist office.

Churchill Island is a small island with a restored house and beautiful gardens. It was here, in 1801, that the first building was constructed by White settlers in Victoria. The island is connected to Phillip Island by a footbridge and the turn-off is well signposted about one km out of Newhaven. It's open daily from 10 am to 4 pm and admission is $5/2.

Organised Tours, Flights & Cruises

Island Scenic Tours (☎ 5952 1042) runs trips most evenings from Cowes out to the penguin parade ($15, which includes entry). They also have three-hour scenic tours ($20) and five-hour tours of the island and various attractions ($35, including entrance fees). Amaroo Park Backpackers Inn (see Places to Stay) also operates an evening service out to the penguin parade.

Phillip Island airport (☎ 5956 7316) operates scenic flights ranging from a 10-minute zip around Cape Woolamai ($30) to a 40-minute loop around Western Port ($75).

Bay Cruises (☎ 5952 3501) runs cruises to Seal Rocks ($30) and French Island ($32) from Cowes' jetty, as well as evening 'shearwater cruises' ($20) from San Remo.

Places to Stay

Camping & Hostels The very friendly *Amaroo Park Backpackers Inn* (☎ 5952 2548), on the corner of Church and Osborne Sts in Cowes, is a good caravan park with an associate YHA hostel. It has six bed dorms costing $12 ($14 for nonmembers), doubles at $28/32 and tent sites for $6/7. It serves breakfasts ($3 to $5) and evening meals ($5), and has a popular bar. It hires out bikes and will organise trips to the penguin parade and Wilsons Prom. The V/Line drivers all know this place and will usually drop you off at the door.

There are another half a dozen caravan parks in the vicinity, including the *Kaloha*

Caravan Park (☎ 5952 2179) on the corner of Chapel and Steele Sts, which is about 200 metres from the beach and close to the centre.

Other Accommodation The *Isle of Wight Hotel* (☎ 5952 2301), on the Esplanade in the centre of Cowes, has hotel rooms from $30/35 or motel units from $42/52. Not quite so central is the *Glen Isla Motel* (☎ 5952 2822) at 234 Church St (about two km from the main street), where double rooms range from $45 to $70. A more up-market option is the central *Continental Resort* (☎ 5952 2316) at 5 The Esplanade, where double rooms range from $55 to $100.

Rhylston Park Historic Homestead (☎ 5952 2730), at 190 Thompson Ave about a km from the centre of Cowes, is a restored 1886 homestead with period-style guestrooms and B&B for about $90 a double.

Places to Eat

Thompson Ave and the Esplanade in Cowes both have a good range of eateries. There are the usual takeaways, and at least three BYO pizza/pasta restaurants. The *Isola de Capri* has a good reputation, and offers a 10% discount to backpackers. *Fish Bizz*, on the Esplanade behind the Isola, has good souvlakis and fish & chips.

The Isle of Wight Hotel has good-value counter meals and a buffet restaurant upstairs. Better again is the *Jetty* on the corner of Thompson Ave and the Esplanade. This place is by no means cheap but the food is very good – especially the seafood.

Entertainment

The Isle of Wight Hotel in Cowes has live bands, including good jam sessions in its intimate cocktail bar. *Banfields Theatre Bar & Bistro* (☎ 5952 2088) at 192 Thompson Ave has live music most Saturday nights, plus a cinema showing latest-release movies.

Getting There & Away

Air Phillip Island Airlines (☎ 9882 9355) has flights to Wynyard in Tasmania costing $132 one way or $189 return – ring for flight details.

Bus Amaroo Park Backpackers runs a free courtesy bus to the island, leaving from the YHA's *Queensberry Hill Hostel* in North Melbourne every Tuesday and Friday at 1 pm.

V/Line has a daily train/bus service to Phillip Island via Dandenong. The trip takes 2¼ hours and costs $12.80.

Getting Around

There is no public transport around the island. Phillip Island Bike Hire (☎ 5952 2381) is at 11 Findlay St in Cowes.

Great Ocean Road

For over 300 km from Torquay (a short distance south of Geelong) to Warrnambool, the Great Ocean Road provides some of the most spectacular coastal scenery in Australia. The road, which took 14 years (1918 to 1932) to complete, was built as a memorial to the soldiers who died in WW I. For most of the distance it hugs the coastline, passing some excellent surf beaches, fine diving centres and even some hills from which hang-gliding enthusiasts launch themselves to catch the strong uplifts coming in from the sea in the evening. Between Anglesea, Lorne and Apollo Bay the road features the beautiful contrast of the ocean beaches on one side and the forests and mountains of the Otway Ranges on the other. Farther west is the famous Port Campbell National Park, with its amazing collection of rock sculptures, such as the Twelve Apostles and the Loch Ard Gorge.

If the seaside activities pall, you can always turn inland to the bushwalks, wildlife, scenery, waterfalls and lookouts of the Otway Ranges.

Organised Tours

Autopia Tours (☎ 9326 5536) runs bus tours along the Great Ocean Road and to Port

Campbell. There is a one-day tour ($50) on Sunday, Wednesday and Friday and a two-day tour ($60) on Monday. Tours leave from the YHA hostels. Mac's Backpacker Tours (☎ 5241 3180) also runs small tours from hostels; they have a one-day tour ($50) on Tuesday, Thursday and Saturday, a two-day tour of Phillip Island and the Great Ocean Road ($79) on Saturday, and a three-day tour of the Great Ocean Road and the Grampians ($98) on Wednesday and Sunday. Melbourne Backpackers Sightseeing (☎ 9663 3388) also has day trips for $50 for YHA members.

Another popular trip with backpackers is the Wayward Bus (☎ 1800 882 823), which does a three-day ramble from Melbourne to Adelaide following the coast all the way. It costs $135, which includes lunches and a T-shirt (but not other meals or accommodation). Kangavic (☎ 5257 1889) offers personalised tours for up to four people along the Great Ocean Road and to the Otways; it too receives good reports from travellers.

Places to Stay

This whole coastal stretch is often heavily booked during the peak summer season and at Easter, when prices also jump dramatically. For budget travellers there are camping grounds and caravan parks all along the coast, as well as backpackers hostels at Lorne, Apollo Bay, Cape Otway and Port Campbell. Other accommodation is generally expensive, although there are a few affordable pubs, guesthouses and B&Bs along the route.

Getting There & Away

V/Line buses operate from Geelong railway station along the Great Ocean Road as far as Apollo Bay ($16.80) via Torquay ($4.20) and Lorne ($14.60) Monday to Friday three times daily, and on weekends twice daily. On Friday (and Monday during summer), a V/Line bus continues from Apollo Bay to Port Campbell and Warrnambool.

McHarry's Bus Lines (☎ 5223 2111) has frequent bus services from Geelong to Torquay ($4.20).

TORQUAY (pop 5000)

On the coast 22 km due south of Geelong, Torquay is a popular holiday town and the capital of Australia's booming surfing industry. There are about a dozen surf shops in town, with the big names like Rip Curl and Quicksilver based at the **Surfworld Plaza** complex on the Surfcoast Highway. Also here is the **Surfworld Australia Surfing Museum** with a wave-making tank, surfing-history displays, board-shaping demos, surf videos and lots more. It's open daily from 9 am to 5 pm (weekends from 10 am) and entry costs $5.

Torquay has a great range of beaches that cater for everyone from paddlers to champion surfers. The protected **Fisherman's Beach** is popular with families, the **Surf Beach** is patrolled by a surf life-saving club, and farther south are the sandy beach breaks of **Jan Juc**, also popular with surfers. A couple more km south-west is the famed **Bells Beach**

You can hire surfing gear or book in for surfing lessons at Surfworld. There's also a good golf course at the western end of town, and **Tiger Moth World** (☎ 5261 5100), 10 km north-east on Blackgate Rd, has an aviation museum and offers joy flights and tours to the Twelve Apostles.

The **Surf Coast Walk** follows the coastline from Jan Juc to Aireys Inlet. The full distance takes about 11 hours, but can be done in stages. The Shire of Barrabool puts out a useful leaflet, available from tourist offices in the area.

Midway between Torquay and Anglesea there's a turn-off to **Point Addis** and the **Ironbark Basin**, a coastal nature reserve with some good walking tracks including the Koori Cultural Walk, an Aboriginal heritage trail.

Places to Stay

Camping is all the go in Torquay. There are four caravan parks here, including the big council-run *Torquay Public Reserve* (☎ 5261 2496) near the Surf Beach, with sites from $17 to $25 and cabins from $45 to $80, and the *Zeally Bay Caravan Park*

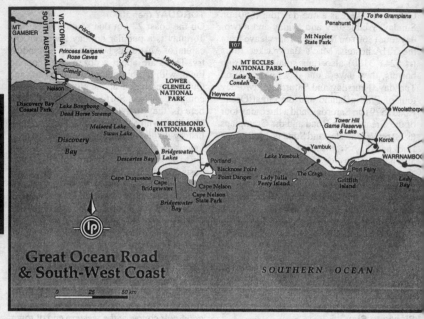

Great Ocean Road & South-West Coast

SOUTHERN OCEAN

0   25   50 km

(☎ 5261 2400) near Fisherman's Beach, with tent sites from $12 to $16 and on-site vans from $35 to $55.

The *Torquay Hotel/Motel* (☎ 5261 6046) at 36 Bell St has motel units ranging from $50 to $65, and at 35 The Esplanade the *Surf City Motel* (☎ 5261 3492) has double units for $68 to $110.

Places to Eat

There are numerous cafes and takeaways along Gilbert St (the main shopping centre). The *Tapas Cafe* at No 14 is good for coffee or a snack, and farther down there's *Yummy Yoghurt*, a health-food cafe with good sandwiches, smoothies, felafels and cakes.

Head to *Micha's* at 23 The Esplanade for Mexican food, or try the *Green Oak* at 45 Surfcoast Highway for good Thai food.

ANGLESEA (pop 2000)

Anglesea, 16 km south-west of Torquay, is another popular family-oriented seaside resort with good beaches and camping grounds. Backed by low hills, it's built around the Anglesea River, which cuts through the hills from the north to the coast.

Anglesea is famous for its scenic **Anglesea Golf Club** (☎ 5263 1582), home to a large population of kangaroos that graze on the fairways; a round costs $20, club hire another $14.

Places to Stay & Eat

Anglesea has three caravan parks. The *Anglesea Family Caravan Park* (☎ 5263 1583), right on the foreshore and beside the river, has tent sites from $16 to $23 and on-site cabins from $43 to $80. There's also a pub and several motels. On the main road, the *Debonair Motel & Guesthouse* (☎ 5263 1440) offers a choice of old-fashioned guesthouse rooms or newer motel units, with tariffs ranging from $54 to $89 a double, including breakfast.

Just south of the river, the *Riverbank Deli*

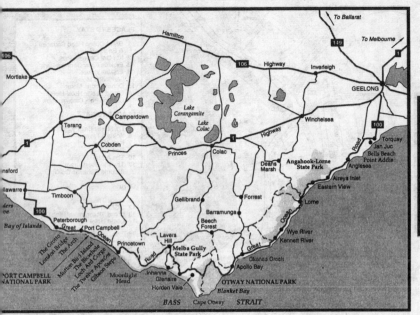

has great sandwiches, rolls, smoothies, cakes and more, while behind the Shell service station is *Diggers,* with cheap pizzas and pastas.

AIREYS INLET (pop 850)
Just south of Anglesea, the Great Ocean Road finally meets the coast and starts its spectacular coastal run. Aireys Inlet, midway between Anglesea and Lorne, is an interesting little town with the **Spit Point Lighthouse**, some fine beaches and walking tracks, a horse-riding ranch, a good pub and a motel.

Accommodation options include the *Aireys Inlet Caravan Park* (☎ 5289 6230), with tent sites from $12 to $15 and on-site vans and cabins from $30 to $50. The *Bush to Beach B&B* (☎ 5289 6538), a two-storey cedar cottage at 43 Anderson St has two en suite guestrooms and singles/doubles for $60/80 and the owner offers guided nature walks. The pub has good bistro meals, and the friendly *Ernie's*

Cantina has a bar and tasty Tex-Mex tucker, with mains mostly $10 to $15.

AIREYS INLET TO LORNE
South of Aireys, the road is wedged between the ocean and steep cliff faces and runs through a series of small townships – **Fairhaven, Moggs Creek** and **Eastern View**. Along this stretch there are some architecturally striking houses that seem to be performing amazing balancing acts on the cliff face.

LORNE (pop 1350)
The small town of Lorne, 73 km from Geelong, was a popular seaside resort even before the Great Ocean Road was built. The mountains behind the town not only provide a spectacular backdrop but also give the town a mild, sheltered climate all year round. Lorne has good beaches and surfing, and there are lovely bushwalks in the vicinity, especially in the Angahook-Lorne State

VICTORIA

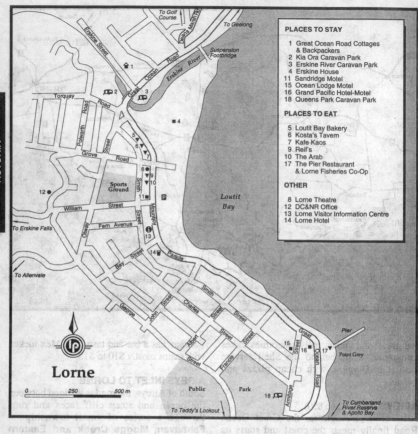

PLACES TO STAY

1 Great Ocean Road Cottages
 & Backpackers
2 Kia Ora Caravan Park
3 Erskine River Caravan Park
4 Erskine House
11 Sandridge Motel
15 Ocean Lodge Motel
16 Grand Pacific Hotel-Motel
18 Queens Park Caravan Park

PLACES TO EAT

5 Loutit Bay Bakery
6 Kosta's Tavern
7 Kafe Kaos
9 Reif's
10 The Arab
17 The Pier Restaurant
 & Lorne Fisheries Co-Op

OTHER

8 Lorne Theatre
12 DC&NR Office
13 Lorne Visitor Information Centre
14 Lorne Theatre

Lorne

0   250   500 m

Park. Lorne is the most fashionable resort on the coast, and it has a wide range of accommodation including camping grounds, a good backpackers hostel, guesthouses, cottages, and even a glossy resort hotel.

Climb up to **Teddy's Lookout** behind the town for fine views along the coast. The beautiful **Erskine Falls** are also close behind Lorne; you can drive there or follow the walking trail beside the river, passing Splitter's Falls and Straw Falls on the way. It's about a three-hour walk each way. There are numerous other short and long walks around Lorne.

The helpful Lorne Visitor Information Centre (☎ 5289 1152) at 144 Mountjoy Pde is open weekdays from 9 am to 5 pm and on weekends from 9.30 am to 4 pm.

Places to Stay

Prices soar and the 'no vacancy' signs go out during the summer school-holiday season when half of Melbourne seems to move down to the coast. Even pitching a tent in one of the camp sites can prove difficult at peak periods.

The Lorne Foreshore Committee (☎ 5289 1382) manages four good camping grounds at Lorne. The *Erskine River Section* is pleasantly sited by the river and is right in the thick of things. The *Queens Park Section* is above it all, on the headland overlooking the pier. Tent sites range from $10 to $19, powered sites from $12 to $23 and on-site cabins from $40 to $70; there are minimum booking requirements at peak periods.

The excellent *Great Ocean Road Cottages & Backpackers* (☎ 5289 1809) is a collection of modern timber cottages in a bushy hillside setting, with lots of wildlife including possums and birds. The backpackers' section has dorm beds at $15 for YHA members and $16 for nonmembers ($23/27 during summer). There are also cosy five-bed self-contained cottages which range seasonally from $75 to $125 a night. The hostel and cottages are up Erskine Ave behind the supermarket, which is where the V/Line bus stops.

The central *Sandridge Motel* (☎ 5289 2722) at 128 Mountjoy Pde has units for $60 to $100, or $80 to $140 with ocean views, and the friendly *Ocean Lodge Motel* (☎ 5289 1330) at 6 Armytage St has cosy units from $65 to $95. The *Grand Pacific Hotel* (☎ 5289 1609) opposite the pier has spacious rooms from $60 to $90 – oldish and a bit shabby, but with great views.

Set in spacious grounds on the waterfront, *Erskine House* (☎ 5289 1209) is a 1930s-style guesthouse with bar, restaurant, tennis, croquet and bowling; B&B for singles/doubles ranges from $59/95 to $110/165 – try negotiating in the low season.

There are some great cottages and cabins for rent in the hills behind Lorne, including the *Erskine Falls Cottages* (☎ 5289 2666), the *Lemonade Creek Cottages* (☎ 5289 2600) and *Allenvale Cottages* (☎ 5289 1450).

Places to Eat

Lorne is the gastronomic capital of the coast and has some fine (if somewhat pricey) cafes and restaurants along Mountjoy Pde. Most of these are open day and night during the holiday seasons, but you'll find the range more limited in the off season.

The *Loutit Bay Bakery* at 46 Mountjoy Pde is crammed with delicious offerings and makes good rolls and sandwiches – it's also a great spot for coffee and pastries. Around the corner at No 50, *Kafe Kaos* is the place for cooked breakfasts, jaffles, focaccias, tofu and vegie burgers and other gourmet goodies.

At No 94, the *Arab* cafe has been a Lorne institution since the mid-50s and serves breakfast, lunch and dinner, while at No 82 *Reif's* restaurant and bar has an affordable range of meals and snacks. Lorne's most popular eatery is the lively *Kosta's Tavern* (☎ 5289 1883) at 48 Mountjoy Pde, serving good Mediterranean food with mains from $16 to $18. For seafood try the *Pier*, with a great setting and mains from $16 to $25, or the fishing co-op next door, which sells fish fresh off the boats.

Entertainment

The old *Lorne Theatre* (☎ 5289 1272) on Mountjoy Pde screens movies during holiday seasons and nightly during summer. Both the *Lorne Hotel* and the grungy *Grand Pacific Hotel* feature live bands, while *Reif's* cafe often has live jazz and acoustic music.

OTWAY RANGES

These beautiful coastal ranges provide a spectacular backdrop to the Great Ocean Road, and if you have time it's worth heading inland to explore the area's rainforests, eucalypt forests, streams, waterfalls and walking trails. There are quite a few small and picturesque settlements scattered throughout the ranges, as well as galleries, tearooms, good picnic areas, and even a winery.

Most of the coastal section of the Otways is protected as part of the 22,000-hectare **Angahook-Lorne State Park**, which stretches from Aireys Inlet to Kennett River. Within the park are well-signposted walking trails, and picnic and camping areas, and there is an abundance of wildlife. For information, walking guides and camping permits, contact the DC&NR (☎ 5289 1732) at 86 Polwarth Rd in Lorne, or the tourist office in Lorne.

As well as the camping areas in the state park, there are numerous cottages, B&Bs, pubs and guesthouses in the Otways. In the town of Forrest is the *Forrest Country Guesthouse* (☎ 5236 6446), where the former Colac Bowling Club has been converted into six quirky, individually themed guestrooms. Singles/doubles cost from $40/70 ($50/85 with en suite) and backpacker beds are $15. For a splurge, try the architect-designed *King Parrot Holiday Cabins* (☎ 5236 3372), overlooking a picture-book valley eight km west of the town of Deans Marsh. Tariffs range from $70 to $100 a double, or from $120 to $160 for four people.

LORNE TO APOLLO BAY

This is one of the most spectacular sections of the Great Ocean Road, a narrow twisting roadway carved into sheer cliffs that drop away into the ocean. Seven km south of Lorne is the *Cumberland River Reserve* (☎ 5289 1382), a scenic camping reserve beside a rocky gorge with good walking trails and fishing. Tent sites cost $10 to $15 and on-site cabins start from $35 (closed during winter).

The small town of **Wye River**, 17 km south-west of Lorne, has a caravan park and the *Rookery Nook Hotel* (☎ 5289 0240), a great little pub overlooking a pretty bay. On a sunny day the front balcony is a top spot for a meal and/or a drink, and there are simple motel units costing $45/60.

Twenty km farther on is **Skenes Creek**, from where Skenes Creek Rd climbs steeply and takes you inland into the Otway Ranges. There's a simple camping reserve on the foreshore here, but if you've got oodles of cash to splash head up to the wonderful *Chris' Restaurant & Villas at Beacon Point* (☎ 5237 6411), a hilltop restaurant/accommodation complex with superb food and splendid views.

APOLLO BAY (pop 1000)

The pretty port of Apollo Bay, 118 km from Geelong, is a fishing town and another popular resort. It's a little more relaxed than Lorne and a lot less trendy, and, as well as all the fishing folk, quite a few artists and musicians live in and around the town.

The long sandy beaches and the surrounding Otway Ranges are the main attractions. There's a small **historical museum** (open weekends and holidays) and the Wingsports Hang-gliding & Paragliding School (☎ 5237 6486) is based nearby. **Mariners Lookout**, a few km from town, provides excellent views along the coast.

The tourist information centre (☎ 5237 6529), at 155 Great Ocean Road, is open daily from 9 am to 5 pm. Enquire here about nearby horse-riding ranches and boats offering cruises and/or fishing expeditions.

Places to Stay

There are five caravan parks here, including the *Pisces Caravan Resort* (☎ 5237 6749) on the Great Ocean Rd two km north of the centre, with a small but comfortable associate-YHA hostel with 10 bunks at $10 a night ($15 nonmembers). Tent sites range from $15 to $28 and on-site cabins from $37 to $70.

On Tuxion Rd, one km back from the coast, is the friendly *Lunabella B&B* (☎ 5237 7059), a bright farmhouse on a lovely hillside farmlet. Doubles cost from $75, which includes a home-cooked breakfast and great views. Lunabella is a member of WWOOF (see Facts for the Visitor).

The *Apollo Bay Hotel* (☎ 5237 6250) in the centre of town has motel units from $55 to $65, and *Bayside Gardens* (☎ 5237 6248) at 219 Great Ocean Road has comfortable self-contained units from $50 a double or from $80 to $100 for up to four.

Places to Eat

The *Bay Leaf Deli*, in the centre of town at 131 Great Ocean Road, is an excellent gourmet deli with great coffee, breakfasts and home-made meals, while farther along at No 61, the *Wholefoods Deli* is a health-food shop with soup, rolls, felafels and more. *Buff's Bistro*, nearby at No 51, is a bustling bistro that is open nightly (except Sunday) and has tasty and interesting mains ranging from $12 to $15.

The *Apollo Bay Hotel* has bistro meals from $11 to $16 and cheaper bar meals. For a splurge, head for the stylish *Beaches Restaurant & Bar* at the Greenacres Country House – there is live jazz or acoustic music most nights in the piano lounge.

CAPE OTWAY

From Apollo Bay the road temporarily leaves the coast to climb up and over Cape Otway. The coast is particularly beautiful and rugged on this stretch, but it is dangerous and there have been many shipwrecks.

The forest-covered cape is still relatively untouched, and the scenic **Otway National Park** has walking trails and picnic areas at Elliot River, Shelly Beach and Blanket Bay; Blanket Bay also has a good camping ground. Although many of the roads through the park are unsurfaced and winding, they present no problems for the average car.

There are a number of scenic lookouts and nature reserves just off the main road. At the **Maits Rest Rainforest Boardwalk**, about 13 km past Apollo Bay, you can stroll along an elevated boardwalk through a spectacular rainforest gully. A little farther on, an unsealed road heads north to the town of Beech Forest via **Hopetoun Falls** and **Beauchamps Falls**, while seven km farther on, another unsealed road heads 15 km south to Cape Otway itself. The 1848 convict-built **Cape Otway Lighthouse** towers nearly 100 metres above a remote and windswept headland. The lighthouse and grounds are open for tours on Tuesday, Thursday and weekends at 9.30, 10.30, 11.30 am and 12.30, 1.30, 2.30 and 3.30 pm ($5 adults, $2 children) – at other times the gates to the grounds are locked.

After passing through the fertile Horden Vale flatlands, the Great Ocean Road meets the coast briefly at **Glenaire** before heading north to the tiny township of **Lavers Hill**, once a thriving timber centre. Six km north of Glenaire is the turn-off to **Johanna**, which has camping and good surfing. Five km south-west of Lavers Hill is the pretty little **Melba Gully State Park**, with its beautiful rainforest ferns, glow-worms and one of

the area's last remaining giant gums – it's over 27 metres in circumference and more than 300 years old.

Farther south is **Moonlight Head**, the starting point of the **Shipwreck Trail** – the treacherous coastline from here to Port Fairy is known as the Shipwreck Coast. Seareach Horse Treks (☎ 5237 5214), based nearby, offer rides along the coastal cliffs and beaches ($25 for two hours, $60 a day). At **Princetown**, the road rejoins the coast and runs along it through the spectacular Port Campbell National Park (see below).

Places to Stay

Bimbi Park (☎ 5237 9246) is a camping ground and horse-riding ranch that offers trail rides through the national park and along the coast ($17 an hour or $30 for 2½ hours). It's also an associate-YHA hostel – beds in on-site vans are $10, or you can sleep in an old army tent for $6. Tent sites range from $9 to $12 and on-site vans start from $25 a double. Bimbi Park is off the Cape Otway lighthouse road, about 7 km after you turn off the Great Ocean Road.

At Blanket Bay, also off the lighthouse road, there's a camping ground with picnic and barbecue facilities; ring the DC&NR (☎ 5237 6889) in Apollo Bay for bookings or information.

At the *Cape Otway Lighthouse* (☎ 5237 9340), the former lighthouse keepers' sandstone cottage sleeps eight people and costs $100 a night or $270 for a weekend, or there's a one-bedroom unit costing from $50 a double (two-night minimum and BYO linen).

The *Shell Roadhouse* (☎ 5237 3251) in Lavers Hill has tent sites from $5 per person and basic bunk rooms at $18 per person or from $45 for four. On the hillside at Glenaire, the simple and secluded *Glenaire Log Cabins* (☎ 5237 9231) sleep up to four and range from $75 to $110 a night. The *Red Johanna Holiday Cabins* (☎ 5237 4238) near Johanna beach start from $35 a double.

PORT CAMPBELL NATIONAL PARK

This narrow coastal park stretches through low heathlands from Moonlight Head to

VICTORIA

Peterborough. It's the most famous section of the Great Ocean Road and features dramatic coastal scenery, including the bizarre rock formations known as the **Twelve Apostles**, huge stone pillars that soar out of the pounding surf (only seven of which can be seen from the lookouts). Nearby you can visit the 1869 **Glenample Homestead** (where the survivors of the famed *Loch Ard* shipwreck recovered) and check out their interesting maritime history displays. The homestead's original owner built **Gibson's Steps**, which lead down to an often treacherous beach.

Loch Ard Gorge has a sad tale to tell: in 1878 the iron-hulled clipper *Loch Ard* was driven onto the rocks offshore. Of the 50 or so on board only two were to survive – an apprentice officer and an Irish immigrant woman, both aged 18. They were swept into the narrow gorge now named after their ship. Although the papers of the time tried to inspire a romance between the two survivors, the woman, the sole survivor of a family of eight, soon made her way back to Ireland's safer climes. This was the last immigrant sailing ship to founder en route to Australia.

A little farther along the coast is **Port Campbell**, the main town in the area and, again, sited on a spectacular gorge. Port Campbell itself is nothing special, but it has a pleasant beach and calm waters, a good range of accommodation, and the **Loch Ard Shipwreck Museum**. Port Campbell Boat Charters (☎ 5598 6463) offers 1½-hour scenic tours to the Twelve Apostles and Bay of Islands ($35), fishing trips (from $40 for four hours), and scuba diving trips ($35 for one dive, $60 for two). There's a dive shop in Lord St where you can hire gear.

Beyond Port Campbell, **London Bridge**, a bridge-like promontory arching across a furious sea, was once a famous landmark along this coast, but in 1990 it collapsed dramatically into the sea, stranding a handful of amazed – and extremely lucky – visitors at the far end. Other formations along here include the **Crown of Thorns** and, eight km past **Peterborough**, the beautiful **Bay of Islands**. After the bay the Great Ocean Road

veers away from the coast and heads inland to Warrnambool, where it joins the Princes Highway.

Places to Stay

At Princetown there's the depressingly spartan *Apostles Camping Park*. You can pitch your tent in the paddock or bed down in one of its cell-like units for $7.

Macka's Farm (☎ 5598 8261), a working dairy farm about five km inland from the Twelve Apostles, offers B&B from $65 to $85 a double, while three km inland from the Twelve Apostles is the friendly *Apostles View Motel* (☎ 5598 8277), with good motel units on a pleasant little farm costing $50 to $70.

In Port Campbell, the *Port Campbell Caravan Park* in Tregea St overlooks the gorge and has tent sites from $8 to $12 and on-site cabins from $35 to $65. Across the road the straightforward associate-YHA *Tregea Hostel* (☎ 5598 6379) has dorm beds for $10 a night – enquiries should be made at the Port Campbell General Store on the main road. There are four motels here to choose from, and the *Port Campbell Hotel* (☎ 5598 6320) has cosy old-fashioned rooms at $25/50 for B&B.

Peterborough has a good riverside caravan park and the *Shomberg Inn Hotel* has motel units out the back.

South-West

The Great Ocean Road ends 12 km east of Warrnambool where it meets the Princes Highway, which continues westwards towards South Australia. This stretch of Victoria's south-west coastline includes some of the earliest settlements in the state.

WARRNAMBOOL (pop 25,700)

Warrnambool is 264 km from Melbourne and has sheltered beaches as well as surf beaches. Gun emplacements intended to repel the Russian invasion that Australia feared in the 1880s can be seen near the ighthouse. This is now the site of the excellent **Flagstaff Hill Maritime Village**, with a museum, restored sailing ships, maritime films, and port buildings of the era. It's open daily from 9 am to 5 pm; entry is $9.50 (students $8, children $4.50).

The **Warrnambool Art Gallery** on Timor St has a good collection of Australian art and is open Tuesday to Friday from 10 am to 4 pm and weekends from noon to 5 pm ($2.50). Other attractions include the attractive **botanic gardens** on the corner of Queen and Cockman Sts; the **Lake Pertobe Adventure Playground** for kids; and the National Trust classified **Proudfoot's Boathouse** on the Hopkins River, with a restaurant and tearooms (serving great scones!). **Hopkins Falls**, known locally as 'mini Niagara', are 13 km north-east of Warrnambool.

The **Mahogany Walking Trail**, which starts at the Thunder Point coastal reserve, is a 22-km coastal walk to Port Fairy, taking you past the possible site of the fabled Mahogany Ship. Historians have speculated that the shipwreck, of which there were numerous reported sightings between 1836 and 1870, could have been part of a secret Portuguese expedition in 1522. The search continues, but if the Mahogany Ship is ever found it would rewrite Australian history.

The tourist information centre (☎ 5564 7837) at 600 Raglan Pde is open daily from 9 am to 5 pm; you can pick up the useful *Warrnambool Visitors Handbook* and the three-km *Heritage Trail* brochure.

Southern Right Whales

The southern coast around Port Fairy and Warrnambool is where the southern right whale *(Eubalagna glacialis)* comes in large numbers every May or June, staying until around October. Whales have been sighted yearly off the Victorian coast since 1970, and at Logan's Beach since 1982. By 1940 it was estimated that there were fewer than 1000 southern right whales left. Although the species has been protected since 1935, today it still numbers only about 1200 to 1500.

Places to Stay

The *Surf Side One Caravan Park* (☎ 5561 2611) on Pertobe Rd is right on the beach, less than a km south of the centre. It has an associate-YHA hostel with dorm beds for $12 ($14 for nonmembers); tent sites range from $12 to $23 and on-site cabins from $40 to $85. Also on Pertobe Rd, the *Lady Bay Hotel* (☎ 5562 1544) has budget motel units from $40 to $50.

The *Stuffed Backpacker* (☎ 5562 2459), above Flaherty's chocolate shop at 52 Kepler St, has spartan bunk rooms and limited cooking facilities, but it's cheap at $10 a night, including a light breakfast. The *Royal Hotel* (☎ 5562 2063), on the corner of Timor and Fairy Sts, is also pretty basic, with B&B at $15 per person.

One of the best of the many motels is the *Olde Maritime Motor Inn* (☎ 5561 1415), on Merri St opposite Flagstaff Hill; standard units are $75, suites range from $85 to $130. There are also numerous B&Bs in and around Warrnambool – check with the tourist office for details.

Places to Eat

Most of the eateries are along Liebig St, including the excellent *Fishtales Cafe* at No 63, with great-value fish & chips, burgers, Asian and vegetarian meals and more. Next door, *Bojangles* is a good Italian bistro with pasta and pizza for about $10. Around the corner at 158 Timor St, *Amarant's* has lunches from $3 to $5 (or three courses for $10!) and is recommended for an evening splurge – try the seafood feast ($40 for two people). For gourmet sandwiches, cakes and great coffee, head for *Dots & Shells Cafe*, near the cinema at 52a Kepler St.

Getting There & Away

V/Line trains run between Melbourne and Warrnambool via Geelong three times daily. The trip takes about three hours and costs $31.80.

Heading west from Warrnambool, daily V/Line buses continue on to Port Fairy ($4), Portland ($11.40) and Mt Gambier ($25). On Friday only (and Monday during summer), a

VICTORIA

The Shipwreck Coast

The Victorian coastline between Cape Otway and Port Fairy was a notoriously dangerous stretch of water in the days when sailing ships were the major form of transport. Navigation of Bass Strait was exceptionally difficult due to numerous barely hidden reefs and frequent heavy fog. More than 80 vessels came to grief on this 120-km stretch in only 40 years.

The most famous wreck was that of the *Loch Ard* (see Port Campbell National Park in this chapter). Another was the *Falls of Halladale*, a Glasgow barque that ran aground in 1908 en route from New York to Melbourne. There were no casualties, but it lay on the reef, fully rigged and with sails set, for a couple of months.

Other vessels that came to grief included the *Newfield* in 1892 and *La Bella* in 1905.

All these wrecks have been investigated by divers, and relics are on display in the Flagstaff Hill Maritime Village in Warrnambool. ∎

bus runs back along the Great Ocean Road to Apollo Bay ($19.40) and on to Geelong ($36.40).

WARRNAMBOOL TO PORT FAIRY

Midway between Warrnambool and Port Fairy is the 614-hectare **Tower Hill State Game Reserve**, based around an extinct volcanic crater. A road circles the central crater lake and takes you through the bushland reserve, home to an abundance of wildlife, including emus, koalas, grey kangaroos, sugar gliders and peregrine falcons. There's also an information centre with natural history displays. Tower Hill is open daily from 9.30 am to 4.30 pm; entry is free.

North of Tower Hill is **Koroit**, a charming little township originally settled by Irish immigrants. Its main street is lined with old verandah-fronted buildings, including a few galleries, craft and antique shops. The old *Koroit Hotel* (☎ 5565 8201), a unique blend of Art Nouveau and Victorian architecture, has B&B for $30 per person and three-course meals on Saturday night for $25.

PORT FAIRY (pop 2600)

This small fishing port 27 km west of Warrnambool was one of the first European settlements in the state, dating back to 1835, although there were temporary visitors from the 1820s. These first arrivals were whalers and sealers seeking shelter along the coast, and Port Fairy is still the home port for one of Victoria's largest fishing fleets. You can watch the boats unload crayfish and abalone at **Fisherman's Wharf**.

Port Fairy was known as Belfast for a time, and although the name was later changed there's still an Irish flavour about the place, including the Belfast Bakery on the main street.

A signposted **history walk** guides you around the many fine old buildings, 50 of which are classified by the National Trust. Also worth a look are the **Port Fairy History Centre** on Gipps St, **Mott's Cottage** at 5 Sackville St, the **old fort and signal station** at the mouth of the river, and **Griffiths Island**, which is reached by a causeway from the town and has a lighthouse and a muttonbird colony.

The **Port Fairy Folk Festival** is held on the Labour Day long weekend in early March. It's Australia's foremost folk festival, with an emphasis on Irish-Australian music, and it attracts top performers and crowds of tens of thousands; apart from camping, accommodation is nonexistent during the festival.

There's an information centre (☎ 5568 2682) on Bank St, and this is also from where the V/Line buses operate.

Places to Stay

The *Gardens Caravan Park* (☎ 5568 1060) on Griffith St is 500 metres north of the town centre and close to the beach; tent sites range from $10 to $13, and timber cabins from $50

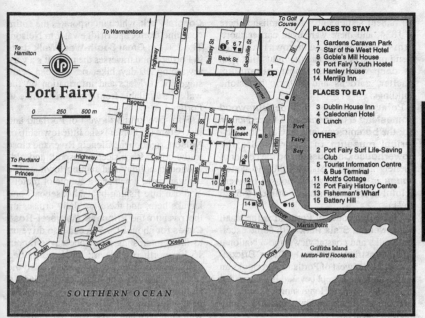

Port Fairy

PLACES TO STAY
1 Gardens Caravan Park
7 Star of the West Hotel
8 Goble's Mill House
9 Port Fairy Youth Hostel
10 Hanley House
14 Merrijig Inn

PLACES TO EAT
3 Dublin House Inn
4 Caledonian Hotel
6 Lunch

OTHER
2 Port Fairy Surf Life-Saving Club
5 Tourist Information Centre & Bus Terminal
11 Mott's Cottage
12 Port Fairy History Centre
13 Fisherman's Wharf
15 Battery Hill

to $70. The YHA's comfortable *Port Fairy Youth Hostel* (☎ 5568 2468), housed in a historic building at 8 Cox St, has a range of bunk rooms and newer units and charges $12 a night. There's also the old *Star of the West Hotel* (☎ 5568 1715) on the corner of Bank and Sackville Sts, with B&B for $20 per person.

Port Fairy has an excellent collection of guesthouses, B&Bs and cottages for rent. They include *Goble's Mill House* (☎ 5568 1118) at 75 Gipps St ($90 to 125 a double), the *Merrijig Inn* (☎ 5568 2324) on Campbell St ($90 to $110 a double), and *Hanley House* (☎ 5568 2709) at 14 Sackville St (about $80 a double). The information centre has a full list of places and can make bookings.

Places to Eat
Lunch, beside the tourist office in Bank St, is an excellent gourmet deli serving breakfasts and lunches – highly recommended. The *Caledonian Hotel* at 41 Bank St has great bar meals, such as roasts and mixed

grills from $3 to $6, and a more expensive bistro. The expensive but well-regarded *Dublin House Inn* restaurant is at 57 Bank St.

Getting There & Away
Daily V/Line buses run between Warrnambool and Port Fairy ($4), continuing on to Mt Gambier.

PORT FAIRY TO PORTLAND
The Crags, signposted off the highway 12 km west of Port Fairy, are the calcified remains of a small coastal forest. Seven km farther on, **Yambuk** has the bluestone *Yambuk Inn Hotel* (☎ 5568 4310), with B&B at $25 per person, and the friendly *Seawinds B&B* (☎ 5568 4206), a restored limestone cottage in a garden setting with B&B at $40/60.

PORTLAND (pop 10,600)
Portland is Victoria's oldest town. Whalers knew this stretch of coast long before the first

permanent settlement was established here in 1834, and there were even earlier short-term visitors. Nowadays the town is a strange blend of the historic and the industrial, with its deep-water tanker port, aluminium smelter, gardens and historic bluestone buildings.

Points of interest include **Burswood Homestead & Gardens**, at 15 Cape Nelson Rd; the **botanic gardens** in Cliff St; a **historical museum** in Charles St; the **Powerhouse Car Museum** on the corner of Glenelg and Percy Sts; and the **old watch house** in Cliff St, which houses the very helpful tourist information office (☎ 5523 2671).

Eleven km south of Portland is the small **Cape Nelson State Park** with some excellent walks and coastal views and a National Trust classified lighthouse. **Cape Bridgewater**, 21 km west of Portland, overlooks an idyllic and windswept bay and has a handful of holiday houses, long sandy beaches, a tearoom with great views and a walking track to a seal colony.

Places to Stay

Portland has caravan parks, pubs, motels and several good B&Bs. *Mac's Hotel* (☎ 5523 2188) at 41 Bentinck St is a reasonable budget option with rooms from $20/30.

At Cape Bridgewater, *Seaview Lodge* (☎ 5526 7276) is an attractive and modern guesthouse on the bay, with B&B at $75 a double and backpacker beds at $18 (BYO bedding) or $25 (bedding supplied). Breakfasts cost from $5 to $8. The owners may be able to pick you up from Portland if you ring in advance.

PORTLAND TO THE SOUTH AUSTRALIAN BORDER

East of Portland, the Princes Highway heads inland. It's the quickest route to Mt Gambier in South Australia, but unless you're in a hurry there is a slower and much more interesting road that runs closer to the coast. This route passes a turn-off to the **Mt Richmond National Park** 20 km west of Portland, and then runs parallel with the **Discovery Bay**

Coastal Park, which incorporates the entire coastline from Cape Bridgewater to Nelson. The 250-km **Great South-West Walk** starts in Portland and traverses the park. It's a very rewarding 10-day hike, or you can walk stages of it. Maps and information on the walk are available from the tourist office in Portland.

Fifty-five km north-west of Portland and just before the border is the little township of **Nelson**, right on the Glenelg River and close to the coast. It's a sleepy, unspoilt and old-fashioned holiday and fishing town with a caravan park, a pub and a couple of motels. You can hire fishing boats, houseboats and kayaks here, and there are daily cruises up the river to the **Princess Margaret Rose Caves** for about $15. You can also drive up to these interesting limestone caves (about 15 km north of Nelson); there are guided tours several times a day. Nelson is also the main access point to the **Lower Glenelg National Park** with its deep gorges and brilliant wildflowers. This park is very popular with canoeists and those who like dangling a line. If you want to paddle the Glenelg River you can hire canoes from South West Canoe Service (☎ 8738 4141) or Nelson Boat Hire (☎ 8738 4048) for about $25 a day; they also do drop-offs and pick-ups.

Places to Stay

There are 15 camp sites in the Discovery Bay Coastal Park along the route of the Great South-West Walk. The Lower Glenelg National Park has a number of very pretty camp sites with minimal facilities; bookings can be made through the information centre (☎ 8738 4051). There are also camp sites and cabins at the Princess Margaret Rose Caves; contact the ranger for bookings (☎ 8738 4171).

In Nelson, the *River Vu Caravan Park* has tent sites and cabins, the *Nelson Hotel* (☎ 8738 4011) has straightforward rooms at $20/30, and the *Pinehaven Motel* (☎ 8738 4041) has double rooms from $45. There's also the *Anchorage B&B* (☎ 8738 4220) west of the river, with one guestroom at

$20/40 and home-cooked Indonesian dinners for $15.

THE WESTERN DISTRICT
The south-west of the state, inland from the coast and stretching to the South Australian border, is particularly affluent sheep-raising and pastoral country. It's also said to be the third-largest volcanic plain in the world, and the area is littered with craters, lakes, lava tubes and other signs of its volcanic past.

Melbourne to Hamilton
On the eastern edge of the Western District is **Colac** (population 9500) and there are many **volcanic lakes** in the vicinity of the town – a couple of lookouts give excellent views. There's also a **botanical garden**, a tourist information office (☎ 5231 3730) and the **Colac Historical Centre**.

You can reach Hamilton, the 'capital' of the Western District, via Ballarat along the Glenelg Highway or via Geelong along the Hamilton Highway. On the Glenelg Highway the **Mooramong Homestead** at Skipton is owned by the National Trust and open by appointment. Farther along the highway the small town of **Lake Bolac** is beside a large freshwater lake popular for water sports. **Inverleigh** is an attractive little town along the Hamilton Highway.

The Princes Highway runs farther south, reaching the coast at Warrnambool. Winchelsea, on the Princes Highway, has **Barwon Park Homestead**, a rambling blue-stone National Trust property. The stone Barwon Bridge dates from 1867. You can reach the Grampians on a scenic route from **Dunkeld** on the Glenelg Highway.

Hamilton (pop 9870)
Hamilton is known locally as the 'Wool Capital of the World'. It is also known for the excellent **Hamilton Art Gallery** on Brown St, which is open from Tuesday to Sunday. There's also the **History Centre** at 43 Gray St, open Sunday to Friday from 2 to 5 pm, and the **Sir Reginald Ansett Transport Museum** on Ballarat Rd, which is open daily.

The **Big Woolbales** on the Coleraine Rd has displays devoted to promoting the wool industry and things woolly; it's open daily and entry costs $2. There's a flora and fauna nature trail at Hamilton's **Institute of Rural Learning**, which is also the last refuge of the endangered eastern barred bandicoot *(Perameles gunnii)*, a small, ground-dwelling marsupial.

The Hamilton Tourist Information Centre (☎ 5572 3746) is on Lonsdale St.

Fifteen km south of Hamilton is the **Mt Napier State Park**, with some fascinating volcanic remnants including the lava tubes of Byaduk Caves and Tunnel Cave.

Places to Stay The *Lake Hamilton Caravan Park* (☎ 5572 3855) on Ballarat Rd has tent sites at $10 and on-site vans from $24. The *Commercial Hotel* (☎ 5572 1078) at 145 Thompson Ave has rooms at $15/25; breakfast is another $5. *Hewlett House* (☎ 5572 2494) at 36 Gray St has B&B from $45/75.

Getting There & Away V/Line has daily buses to Melbourne ($36.40) and also buses to Mt Gambier ($16.80). There are weekday services south to Warrnambool and north to Horsham.

Mt Eccles National Park
About 45 km south of Hamilton, Mt Eccles has numerous volcanic relics including lava caves, vents, craters and the very scenic Lake Surprise. There's a walking trail around the rim of the volcano and several other walks, plus a camping ground – contact the rangers on ☎ 5576 1042.

Lake Condah
Adjoining Mt Eccles, Lake Condah is an important site in the history of local Aboriginal tribes. Part of the legalistic argument behind the concept of *terra nullius*, which the English used to claim Australia as their own, was that as the Aboriginal people were nomads who didn't work the land or have permanent settlements they couldn't be said to have ever 'owned' Australia. The discovery of permanent stone dwellings and a

complex system of stone canals and fish traps at Lake Condah proved that Aboriginal people lived here on a semi-permanent basis.

During the last century when the Western District 'squattocracy' (land-grabbers who became wealthy pastoralists) quickly cleared the land of its people in their hurry to begin intensive sheep farming, Lake Condah became the site of an Aboriginal mission. The site is now run by the Kerrup-jmara community, although the original mission buildings have long since disintegrated and unfortunately, Lake Condah is currently closed to the public.

The Wimmera

The Wimmera region, in Victoria's far west, is mostly endless expanses of wheat fields and sheep farms. In the south is one of Victoria's major attractions, the spectacularly scenic mountains of the Grampians National Park. The region's other main points of interest are the Little Desert National Park and Mt Arapiles, Australia's most famous rock-climbing venue.

The main road through the Wimmera is the Western Highway, which is also the busiest route between Melbourne and Adelaide. It passes through Stawell, which is the turn-off point for the Grampians, and Horsham, the major town and commercial centre of the region.

ARARAT (pop 7800)

After a brief flirtation with gold in 1857, Ararat settled down as a farming centre. Its features include the **Langi Morgala Museum** (open weekends from 2 to 4 pm), the **Alexandra Gardens**, an **art gallery** and some fine old bluestone buildings. Ararat's historic **J Ward**, a former prison for the criminally insane, is open for tours on weekdays at 11 am and on Sunday from 11 am to 4 pm ($5/2). The tourist information centre (☎ 5352 2096) is near the corner of Barkly and Vincent Sts.

Fourteen km east, the **Langi Ghiran State**

Water pumps dot the horizon in the vast Wimmera region

Park has good walking tracks and climbs, plus a winery.

Places to Stay

The *Acacia Caravan Park* (☎ 5352 2994), one km north of the town centre, has tent sites from $9 to $11 and on-site vans and cabins from $25 to $50. On the Western Highway on the northern outskirts, the small *Chalambar Motel* (☎ 5352 2430) is good value with singles/doubles from $32/38.

GREAT WESTERN

Midway between Ararat and Stawell, the small town of Great Western is at the centre of one of Australia's best-known 'champagne' regions. You can tour the old underground cellars at Seppelt's Great Western, and also visit Best's and Garden Gully wineries.

STAWELL (pop 6360)

Stawell, another former gold town, is the turn-off for Halls Gap and the Grampians. The tourist information centre (☎ 5358 2314), on the Western Highway just before the turn-off, is the main information centre for the Grampians and has an accommodation booking service.

The town has a number of National Trust classified buildings, but it's best known as the home of the Stawell Gift, Australia's richest foot race, which attracts up to 20,000 visitors every Easter! The **Stawell Gift Hall of Fame** on Main St details the history of the event.

Bunjil's Cave, with Aboriginal rock paintings, is on the Pomonal road 11 km south.

Places to Stay

There are two caravan parks and plenty of motels in town and along the highway. The *Stawell Holiday Cottages* (☎ 5358 2868) sleep up to six people and cost from $45 to $65 a double plus $7 for each extra person.

Getting There & Away

Stawell is on the Melbourne-Adelaide bus route and train line (although the *Overland* train gets into town at 1.45 am!), and there's a daily V/Line bus between Stawell and Halls Gap ($7). There are also daily train and bus links between Melbourne and the Grampians; see the following section for details.

GRAMPIANS (GARIWERD) NATIONAL PARK

Named after the mountains of the same name in Scotland, the Grampians are the southwest tail end of the Great Dividing Range. The area is a large national park renowned for fine bushwalks, superb mountain lookouts, excellent rock-climbing opportunities,

The wombat is one of the many native animals that make the Grampians their home

prolific wildlife and, in the spring, countless wildflowers.

The Grampians are at their best from August to November when the flowers are most colourful. On a weekend in early spring there's a wildflower exhibition in the Halls Gap Hall, and a jazz festival is held in mid-February. There are also many Aboriginal rock paintings in the Grampians, as well as waterfalls such as the spectacular McKenzie Falls.

There are many fine bushwalks around the Grampians, some of them short strolls you can make from Halls Gap. Keep an eye out for koalas and kangaroos; you sometimes see koalas right in the middle of Halls Gap.

In 1991 the Grampians name was officially changed to include the Aboriginal name, Gariwerd, but it was changed back again when the Kennett government came into office.

Orientation & Information

The Grampians lie immediately west of Ararat and south of the Western Highway between Stawell and Horsham. The small town of Halls Gap, about 250 km from Melbourne, is right in the middle of the region and has a wide range of accommodation. Accommodation is also available in Dunkeld, Glenisla and Wartook.

The DC&NR visitor centre (☎ 5356 4381), three km south of Halls Gap on the Dunkeld road, has excellent information, maps, walking guides and audiovisual displays on the park. Its *Highlights in One Day*

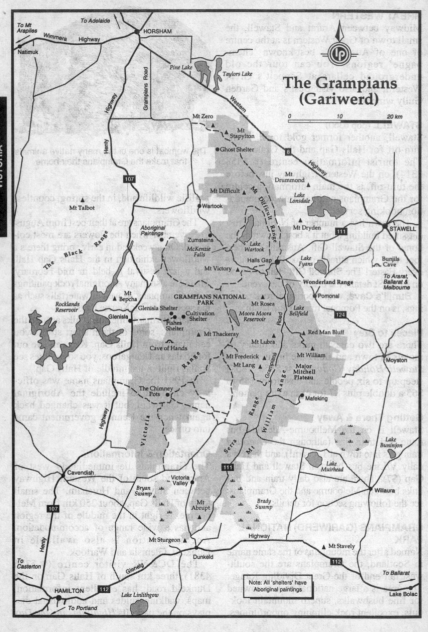

The Grampians (Gariwerd)

0   10   20 km

Note: All 'shelters' have
Aboriginal paintings

brochure is handy for a short stay. The centre is open daily from 9 am to 4.45 pm.

There is no bank in Halls Gap, although the newsagency/general store has an EFTPOS machine and Commonwealth and ANZ bank subagencies, plus a small information section.

Brambuk Living Cultural Centre

Behind the visitor centre is the imaginatively designed Brambuk Living Cultural Centre (☎ 5356 4452), collectively run by five Koori communities. There are displays depicting the history of the Koori people, from customs and lifestyle before White settlement to their persecution by White settlers. Art, clothes, tools and souvenirs are on display and for sale, and there's a bush-tucker cafe – half of the entry fee ($4 adults, $2.50 students) is refundable against anything you buy. Organised tours of the rock-art sites depart from here daily at 2.15 pm ($9.50).

Other Attractions

To the west, the rugged **Victoria Range** is known for its red gums, and there are many Aboriginal rock paintings in the area, including Billimina (Glenisla Shelter) and Wab Manja (Cave of Hands), both near Glenisla on the Henty Highway.

Victoria Valley, in the centre of the Grampians, is a secluded wildlife sanctuary with beautiful bush tracks to drive down.

To the north at **Zumsteins**, 22 km north-west of Halls Gap, kangaroos gather in a paddock in the hope of a free feed, but this is definitely discouraged. Be warned that these are wild animals and they should not be treated like domestic pets.

Activities

The many walks in the Grampians range from well-marked (although often quite arduous) trails to some very rugged walking in the large areas that have been kept free of trails. The best-known established trails are in the Wonderland Range area near Halls Gap, where you can scramble up and down some spectacular scenery on walks ranging

from a half-hour to four hours in duration. Views from the various lookouts down onto the plains far below are well worth the effort. Especially good is the Grand Canyon trail, which leads to the Pinnacle and then on to Boroka Lookout (which has access for the disabled). From here you can walk to the Jaws of Death!

For more detailed information on the various walks available in the Grampians, check out Lonely Planet's *Bushwalking in Australia*, or *50 Walks in the Grampians* by Tyrone T Thomas.

Lake Bellfield, just south of Halls Gap and covering the site of the original town, is a reservoir stocked with brown and rainbow trout.

About 50 minutes drive north-west of Halls Gap, the Grampians Coach House (☎ 5383 9255) offers good horse rides ranging from $30 for an hour to $110 for a day (including lunch). It also has horse-drawn coach tours costing $15 for an hour or $35 for two hours.

There are four or five companies offering rock-climbing courses here – check with the information centre in Stawell for details.

AG Airworks (☎ 5358 2855) in Stawell and Grampians Joyflights (☎ 5356 6294) in Pomonal both offer joy flights over the Grampians, costing anywhere from $35 to $100.

Organised Tours

Grampians National Park Tours (☎ 5356 6221), based at the YHA hostel, runs 4WD tours of the national park costing $70 for a full day or $50 for a three-quarter day; prices includes lunch and afternoon tea. There is also a good package deal: for $58, you get the three-quarter-day tour, two nights dorm accommodation, and return transport from Stawell to Halls Gap.

Places to Stay

Camping There are more than 15 camp sites in the national park, all with toilets, picnic tables and fireplaces, and most with at least limited water. There's no booking system – it's first in, best site. Permits cost $7.50 and you can self-register or pay at the visitor centre.

Bush camping is permitted anywhere outside the designated camp sites except in the Wonderland Range area and around Lake Wartook.

When camping in the park pay close attention to the fire restrictions – apart from the damage you could do to yourself and the bush, you stand a good chance of being arrested if you disobey them. Remember that you can be fined or jailed for lighting *any* fire, including fuel stoves, on days of total fire ban, and the locals will be more than willing to dob you in.

Halls Gap Halls Gap has a gaggle of guesthouses, caravan parks, motels, units and cottages, although during peak periods – especially Easter – it's a good idea to book. The Stawell & Grampians Information Centre (☎ 5358 2314) operates an accommodation booking service.

The *Halls Gap Caravan Park* (☎ 5356 4251), in the centre of town, has tent sites from $12 and on-site vans and cabins from $32 to $58. One km from the centre of Halls Gap on the corner of Buckler St and Grampians Rd is the small *Halls Gap YHA Hostel* (☎ 5356 6221), with dorm beds at $13 ($15 nonmembers) and family rooms at $16 per person.

The *Kingsway Holiday Flats* (☎ 5356 4202) and the *Halls Gap Holiday Flats* (☎ 5356 4304) have good budget flats for about $45 a double or $60 for up to five people. The cosy old *Rocklyn Guesthouse* (☎ 5356 4250) has doubles from $45 to $65, and the stylish *Mountain Grand Guesthouse* (☎ 5356 4232) has B&B for $75 to $85 a double. The half-dozen motels include the central *Halls Gap Kookaburra Lodge* (☎ 5356 4395), with doubles from $65 to $85.

Places to Eat

The general store in Halls Gap has a cafe and takeaway section, and there's a well-stocked supermarket next door. The *Flying Emu Cafe* is good for lunch or a snack, and the *Golden Phoenix* has reasonable Chinese food.

The excellent *Kookaburra Restaurant* (☎ 5356 4222) has a menu based on fresh local produce with mains ranging from $12 to $18. The *Mountain Grand Guesthouse* has an upstairs buffet with meals at $20 a head and a 'jazz cafe' downstairs, and *Suzy's Halls Gap Tavern* is a modern bar/restaurant offering three-course set meals for $15.50.

Getting There & Away

The trip from Melbourne to Halls Gap with V/Line involves a train to Ballarat, a bus to Stawell then another bus to Halls Gap. This service operates every day; the trip takes 4½ hours and the fare is $36.40.

HORSHAM (pop 13,100)

Horsham was first settled in 1842, and has grown to become the main commercial centre of the Wimmera. The **Horsham Art Gallery's** collection includes works by significant Australian artists. The attractive **botanic gardens** are beside the Wimmera River, and **Olde Horsham Village** has antique displays, a gallery and a small fauna park. The **Wimmera Wool Factory**, out on the Golf Course Rd, produces ultrafine wool from merino sheep. There are daily tours and these give an insight into all aspects of the wool industry.

The tourist information centre (☎ 5382 1832) is at 20 O'Callaghans Pde.

Places to Stay

The *Horsham Caravan Park* (☎ 5382 3476) is at the end of Firebrace St by the river, and has on-site vans and cabins from $28 to $36 and tent sites at $10. The *Royal Hotel* (☎ 5382 1255) at 132 Firebrace St has B&B for $20/35, and there are at least a dozen motels in the area as well.

MT ARAPILES

Twelve km west of Natimuk on the Wimmera Highway, Mt Arapiles (more commonly known as 'the Piles') lures rock climbers from around the world. There are more than 2000 climbs for all levels of skill, with colourful names such as Violent Crumble, Punks in the Gym and Cruel

Britannia. It's usually alive with climbers and attracts an eclectic mix of people.

So great is its attraction that the sleepy town of **Natimuk** is now home to quite a few climbers who have moved into the area, bringing with them tastes and attitudes not often associated with small rural towns in Australia – the Natimuk pub must be one of the few to boast vegetarian pancakes on its counter-meal menu and the milkshakes at the local shops are famous.

Despite the mountain's fame as a spot for climbing, there is a sealed road right to the top for those unable to haul themselves up the hard way, and there are excellent views from the lookout. Not far away is the lone rocky outcrop of Mitre Rock, near to its namesake lake, and the Wimmera stretches into the distance.

There are several operators offering climbing and abseiling instruction here, including the Climbing Company (☎ 5387 1329).

Places to Stay

There's a popular camp site (known locally as 'the Pines') in Centenary Park at the base of the mountain – facilities are limited to toilets and a washbasin. There's also a caravan park four km north of Natimuk, and in town the *National Hotel* (☎ 5387 1300) has pub rooms at $20 per person for B&B.

Seven km east of Natimuk and midway between Horsham and Mt Arapiles, *Horsham-Arapiles Backpackers* (☎ 5384 0236) has dorm beds at $13 and two doubles at $30; it also hires out mountain bikes ($10 a day) and can arrange climbing and abseiling instruction.

DIMBOOLA (pop 4300)

The name of this quiet, typically Australian country town on the Wimmera River is a Sinhalese word meaning 'Land of the Figs'. Dimboola is an attractive country town with some fine historic buildings, although its main interest to travellers is as the gateway to the Little Desert National Park, which starts four km south of the town. Accommodation options include a caravan park, motels

and pubs, including the excellent *Victoria Hotel* (☎ 5389 1630) on Wimmera St, with B&B at $26/38.

The **Pink Lake** is a colourful salt lake beside the Western Highway about nine km north-west of Dimboola. The **Ebenezer Aboriginal Mission Station** was established in 1859 in Antwerp, 18 km north of Dimboola. The ruins, complete with its small cemetery, are signposted off the road, close to the banks of the Wimmera River.

LITTLE DESERT NATIONAL PARK

Just south of the Western Highway and reached from Dimboola or Nhill, the Little Desert National Park is noted for its brilliant display of wildflowers in the spring. The name is a bit of a misnomer because it isn't really a desert at all, nor is it that little. In fact with an area of 132,000 hectares it's Victoria's fifth-largest national park, and the 'desert' extends well beyond the national park's boundaries.

There are several introductory walks in the east block of the park: south of Dimboola is the **Pomponderoo Hill Nature Walk**; south of Nhill is the **Stringybark Walk**; and south of Kiata there's the **Sanctuary Nature Walk**.

Places to Stay

You can camp in the park 10 km south of Kiata, just east of Nhill, or on the Wimmera River south of Dimboola. Ring the rangers at Dimboola (☎ 5389 1204) for more information about camping.

The *Little Desert Lodge* (☎ 5391 5232), in the park and 16 km south of Nhill, has units with B&B for $42/56 for singles/doubles, or you can camp for $9.50 per site ($11.50 with power). There's also an environmental study centre and the only aviary in the world housing the fascinating mallee fowl.

The Mallee

North of the Wimmera is the least populated part of Australia's most densely populated state. The Mallee forms a wedge between

South Australia and New South Wales, and this area even includes the one genuinely empty part of Victoria. The contrast between the wide, flat Mallee, with its sand dunes and dry lakes, and the lush alpine forests of East Gippsland is striking – despite being the smallest mainland state, Victoria really does manage to cram in a lot.

The Mallee takes its name from the mallee scrub that once covered the area. Mallee roots are hard, gnarled and slow-burning. Some great Aussie kitsch can still be found – mallee-root egg cups and ashtrays – although they may have crossed that thin line from being kitsch to being collectable.

The Mallee region extends from around the Wyperfeld National Park in the south, all the way up to the irrigated oasis surrounding Mildura. Much of the northern area is encompassed in the recently proclaimed Murray-Sunset National Park.

The main town in the Mallee is **Ouyen**, at the junction of the Sunraysia, Calder and Mallee highways, although Mildura is by far the largest town in the area. The north-west corner of the Mallee is known as 'Sunset Country' – a fine name for the edge of the arid wilderness that stretches right across the continent.

Organised Tours
Based in Ouyen, Sunset 4WD Tours (☎ 5092 1079) runs eight different tours of the national parks in the Mallee region, ranging from half-day to three-day trips.

National Parks & Reserves
Murray-Sunset National Park Covering an area of 633,000 hectares in Victoria's north-west corner, this is the state's second-largest national park after the Alpine National Park.

Murray-Sunset is a largely untouched semi-arid wilderness area. Most of the tracks through the park are accessible only with 4WD, although conventional vehicles can take the 12-km unsealed road leading from the Mallee Highway (60 km west of Ouyen) up to the picnic and camping area at the Pink Lakes. There are no other facilities, but bush camping is allowed elsewhere in the park.

Remember to carry water at all times. Temperatures are extreme here during summer, and visits aren't recommended. Contact the park rangers in Mildura (☎ 5022 3000) for more information.

Wyperfeld National Park Best reached from Albacutya, north of Rainbow, this large park contains a chain of often-dry lakes, including Lake Albacutya. A combination of river gums on the flood plains, sandy mallee scrubland and treed plains supports a wide variety of wildlife, including emus and kangaroos. There are two six-km walking tracks, a 15-km nature drive, and some good longer walks. The park information centre can advise on these and it also has details on the area's flora and fauna, which of course includes the mallee fowl. There are four camping grounds with basic facilities.

Big Desert Wilderness This large wilderness area contains no roads, tracks or any other facilities, which makes it difficult and dangerous to travel in except for those with considerable wilderness experience. It consists of sand dunes and mallee scrub, and wildlife abounds, particularly reptiles.

If you aren't equipped to venture into the wilderness, you can get a tantalising glimpse of the Big Desert along the dry-weather road which runs from Nhill north to Murrayville on the Ouyen Highway. There are camp sites and bore water to be found at **Broken Bucket Reserve**, which is about 55 km north of Nhill.

Hattah-Kulkyne National Park With the near-desert of the mallee country, the woodlands, gum-lined lakes and the Murray River, Hattah-Kulkyne is a diverse and beautiful park.

The Hattah Lakes system fills when the Murray floods and supports many species of water birds. There is a good information centre (☎ 5029 3253) at **Lake Hattah**, a few km into the park from the small town of **Hattah**, on the Sunraysia Highway 35 km north of Ouyen. The park is popular with bushwalkers, cyclists and canoeists. Walking tracks include the 10-km Camel

Pad Walk, which follows the old camel trails that were used to carry salt to riverboats on the Murray River. Check at the information centre on the condition of tracks in the park – many are impassable after rain.

There are camping areas at Lake Hattah and Lake Mournpall with toilets, picnic tables and fireplaces, but you need to bring drinking water. Camping is also possible anywhere along the Murray River frontage in the adjoining Murray-Kulkyne State Park.

Murray River

The mighty Murray River is Australia's most important inland waterway, flowing from the mountains of the Great Dividing Range in north-east Victoria to Encounter Bay in South Australia, a distance of some 2500 km. For much of its route it forms the border between Victoria and New South Wales.

Some of Australia's earliest explorers travelled along the Murray, including Mitchell, Sturt and Eyre. Later, before roads and railways crossed the land, the Murray became a great trade artery and an important means of opening up the interior. Echuca was Australia's leading inland port and the Murray an antipodean Mississippi, with paddle-steamers and riverboats carrying supplies between remote sheep stations, homesteads and the thriving river towns.

Today the Murray is of great economic importance, supplying the vital water for the irrigation schemes that have transformed huge tracts of barren land into prosperous dairy farms, vineyards, market gardens and citrus orchards.

The river is also famous for its magnificent forests of red gums, its plentiful wildlife and as a great place for canoe trips, riverboat cruises, houseboat holidays or river-bank camping. Many of the river towns, particularly Echuca, have reminders of the Murray's colourful past, including preserved paddle-steamers, old buildings and museums.

Getting There & Away

Greyhound Pioneer and McCafferty's both go through Mildura on the Sydney to Adelaide run.

V/Line has bus or combination bus/train

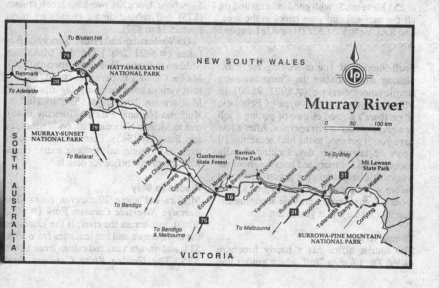

services that connect Melbourne, Bendigo and Ballarat with the Murray River towns, and it also operates bus services running along the Murray between Albury and Mildura.

MILDURA (pop 21,000)

Noted for its exceptional amount of sunshine, Mildura was chosen by the Chaffey brothers as the site of the first Murray River irrigation projects. Today it's something of an oasis in this arid region, and a popular tourist town with quite a few worthwhile attractions.

Mildura's festivals include Country Music Week in September, and the Jazz & Wine Festival in November over the Melbourne Cup weekend.

Information

The Mildura Tourist Information Centre (☎ 1800 039 043), on the corner of Deakin Ave and Twelfth St, is open weekdays from 9 am to 5 pm, Saturday from 9 am to 4 pm and Sunday from 10 am to 4 pm. This place has a good range of information and can also book tours and accommodation.

The DC&NR has an office (☎ 5022 3000) at 253 Eleventh St with good information on all the national and state parks in the area. The RACV (☎ 5021 3272) is at 82a Langtree Ave.

Fruit-Picking If you're looking for fruit-picking work, contact the Commonwealth Employment Service (☎ 5021 9500) in Mildura around the first week of February, when there's a good chance of getting a job as a grape picker or cart operator. After a few days you'll get used to the backbreaking, 10 hours of labour per day. Picking usually starts around February and lasts for about six weeks. It's hard work, but if you've done it before it can mean big bucks (about $350 a week). Some farmers provide accommodation, but take a tent if you're not sure.

Things to See

The tourist office has a handy brochure called *The Chaffey Trail*, which guides you around some of the more interesting sights including the **paddle-steamer wharf**, the **Mildura weir and lock**, **Old Mildura Homestead**, the **Mildara Blass Winery** and the **Old Psyche Bend Pump Station**.

Also on the trail, the **Mildura Arts Centre & Rio Vista** complex is well worth a visit. There's an excellent collection of Australian and European art and a historic homestead with interesting displays. It's on the corner of Chaffey and Curtin Aves, is open weekdays from 9 am to 5 pm and weekends from 2 to 4.30 pm, and costs $2.50.

Orange World, seven km north of town (in New South Wales), has one-hour tours ($5) on tractor trains around the property and is a fascinating introduction to how citrus fruit is produced. The **Golden River Zoo**, four km north-west, is open daily from 9 am to 5 pm and costs $8.50.

Organised Tours & Cruise

Lest you forget that this is riverboat country, you can take **paddle-steamer trips** from the Mildura wharf. The historic steam-powered PS *Melbourne* has two cruises daily ($15), and the PV *Rothbury* does day trips to the zoo ($34) and to Trentham winery ($34). The *Showboat Avoca* has two-hour lunch cruises ($25) and cabaret-dinner cruises by night (from $34 to $37).

On Wednesday and Friday, Sunraysia Bus Lines (☎ 5021 2882) has day trips from Mildura to Broken Hill via Wentworth ($59). Mallee Outback Experiences (☎ 5021 1621) runs various tours including day trips around Mildura on Thursday ($35), to Hattah-Kulkyne National Park on Tuesday ($45), and to Mungo National Park on Wednesday and Saturday ($45). There are also winery trips and Aboriginal heritage tours; check with the tourist office for details.

Places to Stay

Mildura has about 20 caravan parks. The *Buronga Riverside Caravan Park* (☎ 5023 3040), just across the river, is the closest to the town centre and has tent sites from $9 to $11, and on-site vans and cabins from $28 to $35. The *Golden River Caravan Park*

(☎ 5021 2299) is also on the river, five km north-west of the town centre.

The friendly *Rosemont Guest House* (☎ 5023 1535), at 154 Madden Ave, is a cosy old timber guesthouse with simple units out the back. You get your own single, twin or double room for $15 per person for YHA members ($17 for nonmembers), or doubles with en suite and TVs are $40. All rooms have air-con, there's a good pool, and rates include a generous breakfast.

Mildura also has an abundance of motels. The *Riviera Motel* (☎ 5023 3696), opposite the railway station at 157 Seventh St, has singles/doubles from $36/38. The *Commodore Motor Inn* (☎ 5023 0241), well located on the corner of Deakin Ave and Seventh St, has units from $50/55, and on the opposite corner the *Grand Hotel* (☎ 5023 0511) has rooms from $77 to $120 and suites from $140 to $350.

About 20 operators offer houseboats for rent here and costs range upwards from $500 a week for four people, usually with a three-night minimum. Contact the tourist office or the RACV for details.

Places to Eat

Langtree Ave is Mildura's main restaurant precinct. The *Red Brick Cafe* at No 40 has excellent sandwiches, salads and hot foods. *Taco Bill* at No 36 has Mexican food, and next door the *Indian Curry House* has banquets from $18. At No 35 *Siam Palace* has tasty Thai tucker with lunches from $4 and mains from $6.80 to $11.50.

The *Sandbar*, on the corner of Langtree and Eighth Aves, has a pleasant courtyard and meals from $4 to $10. On the corner of Seventh St and Deakin Ave, *Jackie's Corner* is a cheap Chinese takeaway.

The *Mildura Workingman's Club* on Deakin Ave has lunch specials at $3 and other mains from $7 to $11 – this place once boasted the longest bar in the world, but some fool cut it down to fit in more poker machines. The gambling clubs across the river in New South Wales provide cheap meals, free movies and free transport to entice people across the border.

Entertainment

Mildura has a small but lively nightlife scene, with several nightclubs in the town centre. The *Sandbar* on the corner of Langtree and Eighth Aves has live music Wednesday to Saturday nights. The *Deakin Twin Cinema* (☎ 5023 4452) is at 93 Deakin Ave.

Getting There & Away

Air Southern Australia Airlines (☎ 5022 2444) and Kendell Airlines (☎ 13 1300) both fly between Mildura and Melbourne ($165): Southern Australia Airlines also flies between Mildura and Adelaide ($120), Broken Hill ($98) and Renmark ($76).

Bus Between Melbourne and Mildura, V/Line has a direct overnight bus every night except Saturday, as well as several daily train/bus services via Bendigo or Swan Hill. The trip takes about eight hours and costs $50.60. V/Line also has a bus service connecting all the towns along the Murray River four times per week – fares from Mildura include Swan Hill ($27.20), Echuca ($34.80) and Albury ($50.70).

Greyhound Pioneer and McCafferty's both have daily services between Mildura and Adelaide ($37) and Mildura and Sydney ($74); Greyhound Pioneer also has a twice-weekly service to Broken Hill ($35).

AROUND MILDURA

Leaving Mildura you don't have to travel very far before you realise just how desolate the country around here can be. The Sturt Highway runs west arrow-straight and deadly dull to South Australia, about 130 km away.

Going the other way into New South Wales you follow the Murray another 32 km to **Wentworth**, one of the oldest river towns, where you can visit the Old Wentworth Gaol and the Pioneer Museum.

A popular excursion from Mildura is to **Mungo National Park** in New South Wales to see the strange natural formation known as the Walls of China. See the New South Wales chapter for more details.

Red Cliffs, 17 km south, is the home of Big Lizzie, a huge steam-engined tractor – a taped commentary tells her story.

There are also some good wineries to visit around Mildura, such as Lindemans, Mildara Blass and Trentham Estate. At Dareton, 19 km north-west, the **Tulklana Kumbi Gallery** has an excellent collection of locally made Aboriginal arts and crafts on sale.

SWAN HILL (pop 9800)

One of the most interesting and popular towns along the Murray, Swan Hill was named by the early explorer Major Thomas Mitchell, who spent a sleepless night here within earshot of a large contingent of noisy black swans.

Swan Hill is 340 km from Melbourne and has a tourist information centre (☎ 5032 3033) at 306 Campbell St.

Pioneer Settlement

The major attraction is the Swan Hill Pioneer Settlement, a re-creation of a riverside port town of the paddle-steamer era. The settlement has everything from an old locomotive to a working blacksmith's shop and an old newspaper office, plus free rides on horse-drawn vehicles. It's definitely worth a visit and is open daily from 8.30 am to 5 pm; admission is $12 ($6 for children).

Each night at dusk there is a 45-minute sound-and-light show costing $8/4, during which you are driven around the settlement. The paddle-steamer *Pyap* makes short trips from the pioneer settlement for $8/4.

Other Attractions

Swan Hill's **art gallery** is opposite the entrance to the Pioneer Settlement. The town's **military museum**, at 400 Campbell St, has a rather fascinating collection of war memorabilia – fetishists can even have their photo taken in uniform! It's open daily and costs $6.50.

The MV *Kookaburra* (☎ 5032 0003) offers two-hour luncheon cruises daily except Monday, costing $19.

The historic **Tyntynder Homestead**, 16 km north of the town, has a small museum

of pioneering and Aboriginal relics and many reminders of the hardships of colonial life, like the wine cellar! Admission is $7, which includes a tour, and the homestead is open daily from 9 am to 4.30 pm.

There are a couple of wineries worth visiting in the area – Buller's at Beverford (15 km north) and Best's at Lake Boga (17 km south).

Places to Stay

The *Riverside Caravan Park* (☎ 5032 1494) next to the river and the Pioneer Settlement has tent sites from $11 and on-site vans and cabins from $28 to $50.

At 91 Campbell St, the *Commercial Hotel* (☎ 5032 1214) has B&B at $20 per person. The *White Swan Hotel* (☎ 5032 2761) at 182 Campbell St has pub rooms at $22/35, or $30/40 with bathroom. The cheapest central motel is the *Mallee Rest* (☎ 5032 4541) at 369 Campbell St, with doubles ranging from $44 to $52.

Places to Eat

Campbell St has plenty of eateries. One of the better ones is *Teller's Licensed Deli*, on the corner of McCrae St. It has good burgers and sandwiches, steaks, pastas and other meals ranging from $5.50 to $15. *Quo Vadis* at 259 Campbell St is good for pizzas and pastas, and for a pub meal try the White Swan Hotel.

Getting There & Away

V/Line has daily trains between Melbourne and Swan Hill ($40.60) via Bendigo. It also has buses four times weekly between Swan Hill and Mildura ($27.20), Echuca ($21.80) and Albury-Wodonga ($46).

KERANG (pop 4250)

Kerang is on the Murray Valley Highway about 25 km south of the river, and is best known for the huge flocks of ibis that breed on the 50 or so lakes found in the area. Middle Lake, nine km north of Kerang, is the best place to see the colonies, and there's a small hide here. The town itself has a small historical museum, caravan parks and motels.

GUNBOWER STATE FOREST

The superb Gunbower State Forest, which is actually on a long 'island' enclosed by the Murray River and Gunbower Creek, features magnificent river red gums, abundant wildlife and plenty of walking tracks.

Cohuna, 32 km east of Kerang, is the main access point to the forest, although there are numerous marked tracks in from the highway. The tracks within the forest are all on old river mud which becomes impassable for conventional vehicles during wet weather.

Based 16 km north-west of Cohuna, Ganawarra Wetlander Cruises (☎ 5453 3000) runs cruises through these creeks and wetlands from mid-August to mid-May. Its two-hour afternoon cruise operates daily except Thursday ($15), and 3½-hour dinner cruises with live entertainment are offered most Saturday nights ($35).

The DC&NR (☎ 5456 2699) in Cohuna sells maps of the park ($4.50), which detail the various camp sites and picnic areas. There are caravan parks, motels and hotels in Cohuna.

ECHUCA (pop 10,200)

Strategically sited where the Goulburn and Campaspe rivers join the Murray, Echuca, which is an Aboriginal word meaning 'the meeting of the waters', was founded in 1853 by the enterprising ex-convict Henry Hopwood.

In the riverboat days this was the busiest inland port in Australia and the centre of the thriving river trade. In the 1880s the famous red-gum wharf was more than a km long and there were stores and hotels all along the waterfront. At its peak there were more than 300 steamers operating out of the port here.

Today tourism is the main money-spinner. Echuca is the most vibrant and interesting of the towns along the Murray, with numerous worthwhile attractions centred around the old port. There are also paddle-steamer cruises, museums and wineries to visit, and several impressive state forests nearby. In mid-October Echuca hosts its annual Rich River Festival: seven days of entertainment and games.

Information

The Echuca tourist information centre (☎ 5480 7555), by the old port at 2 Leslie St, is open daily from 9 am to 5 pm.

Historic Port of Echuca

The old port area now has numerous attractions along the riverfront. You start at the old Star Hotel (where you buy the tickets) with various old photographs on display, and the 1858 Bridge Hotel nearby, now a licensed restaurant.

Across the road at the wharf, there's a vintage train collection, a cargo shed with audiovisual displays, and the historic paddle-steamers PS *Pevensey* (which featured as the *Philadelphia* in the TV miniseries *All the Rivers Run)* and PS *Adelaide*. The port is open daily from 9.15 am to 5 pm, and tickets cost $6 ($3.50 for children).

Other Attractions

In the same street as the wharf are various other attractions, including the **Red Gum Works**, where wood is still worked using traditional machinery; **Sharp's Magic Movie House** ($7.50), which has old penny-arcade equipment, displays relating to Australia's cinema industry, and classic films projected on authentic equipment; and a **Coach House & Carriage Collection** ($3). You can also take a short ride around the port in a horse-drawn carriage ($4).

The **World in Wax Museum**, at 630 High St, features 60 gruesome and famous characters, and is open daily from 9 am to 5 pm ($5). The **Historical Society Museum** in Dickson St is housed in the old National Trust classified police station and lock-up building (open weekends from 1 to 4 pm). For car buffs, the **National Holden Museum** ($4.50/2) is in Warren St.

Activities

A **paddle-steamer cruise** is almost obligatory, so head down to the river north of the

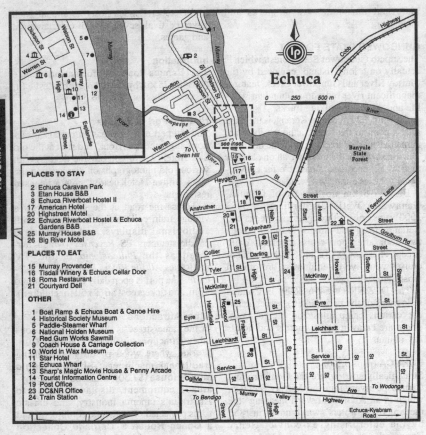

Echuca

0   250   500 m

PLACES TO STAY

2 Echuca Caravan Park
3 Etan House B&B
8 Echuca Riverboat Hostel II
17 American Hotel
20 Highstreet Motel
22 Echuca Riverboat Hostel & Echuca
      Gardens B&B
25 Murray House B&B
26 Big River Motel

PLACES TO EAT

15 Murray Provender
16 Tisdall Winery & Echuca Cellar Door
18 Roma Restaurant
21 Courtyard Deli

OTHER

1 Boat Ramp & Echuca Boat & Canoe Hire
4 Historical Society Museum
5 Paddle-Steamer Wharf
6 National Holden Museum
7 Red Gum Works Sawmill
9 Coach House & Carriage Collection
10 World in Wax Museum
11 Star Hotel
12 Echuca Wharf
13 Sharp's Magic Movie House & Penny Arcade
14 Tourist Information Centre
19 Post Office
23 DC&NR Office
24 Train Station

old port and check out the sailing times. The steam-driven PS *Emmylou* (☎ 5482 3801) does 1½-hour cruises ($12; lunch extra) and overnight trips (from $125 for B&B; dinner extra). PS *Canberra* and PS *Pride of the Murray* also have one-hour cruises ($8), and the MV *Mary Ann* does two-hour lunch cruises ($26) and four-hour dinner cruises ($42).

Based at the boat ramp, Echuca Boat & Canoe Hire (☎ 5480 6208) has motor boats, kayaks and canoes for hire. It also offers canoe cruises – they drive you upstream, you paddle back. A four-hour paddle costs $50

for two people, and three-day trips are $180 per person.

Several operators offer water-skiing trips and classes, and there's a popular go-kart track across the river in Moama.

Places to Stay

The *Echuca Caravan Park* (☎ 5482 2157) on Crofton St is the most central of the town's caravan parks and has on-site vans at $34, cabins from $45 and tent sites at $11.

The YHA *Echuca Riverboat Hostel* (☎ 5480 6522) at 103 Mitchell St is a 10-minute walk from the centre. There are two sections here – a small hostel with dorm beds for $15 ($17 nonmembers), and the pleasant *Echuca Gardens B&B*, with doubles with en suite at $60, including breakfast. There are free bikes, and the owner runs various tours as well as a free courtesy bus between Melbourne and Echuca (see Getting There & Away for details).

The *American Hotel* (☎ 5482 5044) on the corner of Heygarth and Hare Sts has budget rooms at $25/40. There's a stack of motels, the cheapest of which are the *Highstreet Motel* (☎ 5482 1013) at 439 High St and the *Big River Motel* (☎ 5482 2522) at 317 High St, both with singles/doubles for about $40/50.

Etan House B&B (☎ 5480 7477) at 11 Connelly St is a beautifully restored homestead with a guest kitchen, grass tennis court and pool; doubles cost $110. *Murray House B&B* (☎ 5482 4944) at 55 Francis St also has good rooms from $90/130.

There are several operators hiring houseboats that generally sleep between four and 10 people and cost from $600 to $1500 a week. Contact the tourist office for details.

Places to Eat

At 568 High St, the *Murray Provender* is a gourmet deli with good coffee and excellent sandwiches, pies and pastries. For a pub feed, try the *American Hotel*, which has good bar meals from $4 to $6 and a pleasant bistro. The *Roma Restaurant* at 191 Hare St is a cheap pizza/pasta joint.

At the *Courtyard Deli* at 433 High St you can have a 'political sandwich' with salad ($4.80); they also have a good range of hot meals ($4.50 to $7.50). For a night out, head for the atmospheric *Echuca Cellar Door* at Tisdall's Winery on Radcliffe St, with mains from $10 to $16, three-course dinners for $18.50, and wines by the glass.

Getting There & Away

Some long-distance buses operate from the post office or the train station. Others stop at the bus stop near the corner of Heygarth St and Cobb Hwy. V/Line has a daily service from Melbourne to Echuca ($25), changing from train to bus at Bendigo. Four times a week V/Line buses connect Echuca with Albury-Wodonga ($19.50), Swan Hill ($21.80) and Mildura ($34.80).

The owner of the Echuca Riverboat Hostel plans to run free courtesy buses from Melbourne to Echuca. Ring ☎ 5482 2157 for details.

BARMAH STATE PARK

This beautiful wetland area, 34 km northeast of Echuca, centres around the flood plains of the Murray and is forested with old river red gums. The **Dharnya Centre**, a visitor information centre run by the DC&NR, has displays on the heritage and culture of local Aboriginal people, as well as detailed track notes for the park's extensive walking trails. The centre is open daily from 11 am to 3 pm.

Canoeing is also popular through here, and the *Kingfisher* (☎ 5482 6788) cruise boat offers two-hour discovery tours for $15.

You can camp for free anywhere in the park or at the Barmah Lakes camping area. The Dharnya Centre (☎ 5869 3302) has good dorm accommodation at $12 per person (BYO bedding and food), although this is often booked out by school groups.

YARRAWONGA (pop 5900)

About 40 km east of Cobram on the banks of Lake Mulwala, Yarrawonga is known for its fine and sunny weather, for a host of aquatic activities, and as a retirement centre.

Lake Mulwala was formed by the completion in 1939 of Yarrawonga Weir, which was part of the massive Lake Hume project (near Albury) to harness the waters of the Murray for irrigation. The *Lady Murray* and the *Paradise Queen* both offer scenic cruises ($9) and lunch cruises ($14) on the lake; you can also hire canoes and other water sports gear.

There is a tourist information centre (☎ 5744 1989) on the corner of Belmore St and Irvine Pde.

Yarrawonga was first settled by Elizabeth Hume, sister-in-law of the early explorer Hamilton Hume, in about 1842. Her **Byramine Homestead** is 15 km west of the town.

Places to Stay & Eat

The *Yarrawonga Caravan Park* (☎ 5744 3420) on the Murray River has sites and on-site vans. The *Terminus Hotel* (☎ 5744 3025) on Belmore St has budget singles/doubles at $20/40, including breakfast. *Yarrawonga Cottages* (☎ 5748 4265), 11 km west of the town centre, are good value with B&B from $80 a double.

The *Left Bank* in Belmore St is a good cafe, or there's the *Shag's Nest* restaurant next door.

Gold Country

If you have transport, the well-signposted Goldfields Tourist Route takes in all the major centres involved in the rush of last century, and makes for an interesting excursion for a couple of days.

Ballarat and Bendigo are the two major towns on the route, but, in a clockwise direction from Ballarat, it goes through Linton, Beaufort, Ararat, Stawell, Avoca, Maryborough, Dunolly, Tarnagulla, Bendigo, Maldon, Castlemaine, Daylesford and Creswick.

BALLARAT (pop 75,900)

The area around present-day Ballarat, Victoria's largest inland city, was first settled in 1838. When gold was discovered at nearby Bunninyong in 1851 the rush was on and within a couple of years the town that grew out of the Ballarat diggings had a population of 40,000.

Ballarat's fabulously rich quartz reefs were worked by the larger mining companies until 1918. About 28% of the gold unearthed in Victoria came from Ballarat.

Today Ballarat has plenty of reminders of its gold-mining past, including some outstanding Victorian-era architecture. Other attractions include gorgeous gardens, a fine art gallery, good museums, and Sovereign Hill, probably the best attraction of its type in the country.

Information

The helpful Ballarat Tourism Centre (☎ 5332 2694), on the corner of Albert and Sturt Sts, is open weekdays from 9 am to 5 pm and weekends from 10 am to 4 pm. The RACV (☎ 5332 1946) has an office at 20 Doveton St North.

Sovereign Hill

Ballarat's major tourist attraction is Sovereign Hill, a fascinating re-creation of a gold-mining township of the 1860s. It has won numerous awards, and you should allow at least half a day for a visit.

The main street features a hotel, post office, blacksmith's shop, bakery and a Chinese joss house. It's a living history museum with people performing their chores while dressed in costumes of the time. The site was actually mined back in the gold era so much of the equipment is authentic. There's a variety of above-ground and underground mining works, and you can pan for gold in the stream.

Sovereign Hill is open daily from 9.30 am to 5 pm and admission is $16.50 for adults, $12.50 for students, $8.50 for children, or $45 for families, which includes entry into the nearby Gold Museum.

Also at Sovereign Hill is the sound-and-light show 'Blood on the Southern Cross', a simulation of the Eureka Stockade battle. There are two shows nightly from Monday

Gold panning is popular at Sovereign Hill

VICTORIA

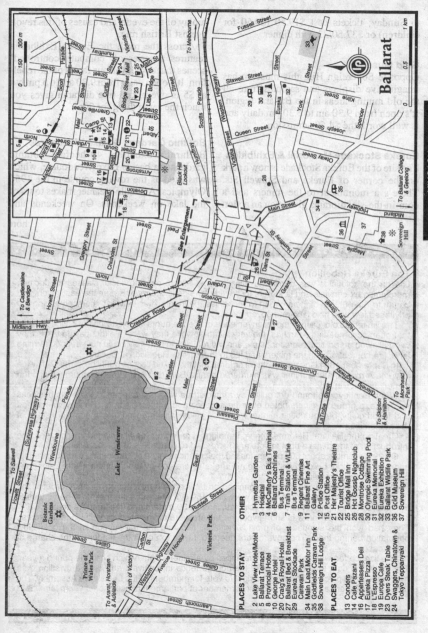

Ballarat

To Melbourne

To Ballarat College & Geelong

To Castlemaine & Bendigo

Midland Hwy

To Sawell

To Ararat, Horsham & Adelaide

To Skipton & Hamilton

To Morshead Park

See Enlargement

Lake Wendouree

Botanic Gardens

Prince of Wales Park

Victoria Park

PLACES TO STAY
2 Lake View Hotel/Motel
5 Ballarat Terrace
8 Provincial Hotel
10 George Hotel
20 Craig's Royal Hotel
27 Ballarat Bed & Breakfast
29 Eureka Stockade
    Caravan Park
34 Mid-City Motor Inn
35 Goldfields Caravan Park
38 Sovereign Hill Lodge

PLACES TO EAT
13 Conders
14 Cafe Pazani
16 Appelteasers Deli
17 Eureka Pizza
18 L'Espresso
19 Europa Cafe
23 Dyers Steak Table
24 Swaggers, Chinatown &
    Tokyo Teppanyaki

OTHER
1 Hymettus Garden
3 Hospital
4 McCafferty's Bus Terminal
6 Ballarat Coachlines
7 Bus Terminal
    Train Station & V/Line
9 Bus Terminal
11 Regent Cinemas
    Ballarat Fine Art
    Gallery
12 Police Station
15 Post Office
21 Her Majesty's Theatre
22 Tourist Office
25 Bridge Mall Inn
26 Hct Gossip Nightclub
28 Montrose Cottage
30 Olympic Swimming Pool
31 Eureka Memorial
32 Eureka Exhibition
33 Ballarat Wildlife Park
36 Gold Museum
37 Sovereign Hill

to Sunday; tickets cost $19.50 ($9.50 for children) or $37.50/23 with dinner.

Gold Museum

Opposite Sovereign Hill, this museum has imaginative displays and samples from all the old mining areas in the Ballarat region. It's open from 9.30 am to 5.30 pm daily and is well worth the $4.50 admission.

Eureka Stockade Memorial & Exhibition

The site of the Eureka Stockade is now a park on the corner of Eureka and Stawell Sts. There's a monument to the miners and a coin-in-the-slot diorama gives you an action replay of the events and causes of this revolt against British rule.

Across the road, the Eureka Exhibition features a series of 'computer-controlled' scenes that depict various facets of the rebellion. It's open daily from 9.30 am to 5 pm but at $5 is overpriced (the diorama gives you much the same thing for 20c).

Botanic Gardens & Lake Wendouree

Ballarat's excellent 40-hectare botanic gardens are beside Lake Wendouree, which was used as the rowing course in the 1956 Olympics. A paddle-steamer makes tours of the lake on weekends. On weekends and

The Eureka Rebellion

Life on the goldfields was a great leveller, erasing all pre-existing social classes as doctors, merchants, ex-convicts and labourers toiled side by side in the mud. But as the easily won gold began to run out, the diggers began to recognise the inequalities between themselves and the privileged few who held land and government.

The limited size of claims, the inconvenience of licence hunts coupled with the police brutality that often accompanied searches, the very fact that while they were in effect paying taxes they were allowed no political representation, and the realisation that they could not get good farming land, fired unrest among the miners and led to the Eureka Rebellion at Ballarat.

In September 1854 Governor Hotham ordered that the hated licence hunts be carried out twice a week. A month later a miner was murdered near a Ballarat hotel after an argument with the owner, James Bentley.

When Bentley was found not guilty, by a magistrate who just happened to be his business associate, a group of miners rioted over the injustice and burned his hotel. Bentley was retried and found guilty, but the rioting miners were also jailed, which fuelled their mounting distrust of the authorities.

Creating the Ballarat Reform League, the diggers called for the abolition of licence fees, the introduction of the miner's right to vote and increased opportunities to purchase land.

On 29 November about 800 miners tossed their licences into a bonfire during a mass meeting, and then set about building a stockade at Eureka where, led by the Irishman, Peter Lalor, they prepared to fight for their rights.

On 3 December, having already organised brutal licence hunts, the government ordered the troopers to attack the stockade. There were only 150 diggers within the makeshift barricades at the time, and the fight lasted only 20 minutes, leaving 30 miners and five troopers dead.

Although the rebellion was short-lived, the miners were ultimately successful in their protest. They had won the sympathy of most Victorians, and had the full support of the goldfields' population behind them. The government deemed it wise to acquit the leaders of the charge of high treason.

The licence fee was abolished and replaced by a miner's right, which cost one pound a year. This gave the right to search for gold; the right to fence in, cultivate and build a dwelling on a moderate-sized piece of land; and the right to vote for members of the Legislative Assembly. The rebel miner Peter Lalor actually became a member of parliament himself some years later. ■

holidays a tourist tramway operates around the gardens from a depot at the southern end.

Kryal Castle

Surprisingly this modern bluestone 'medieval English castle' is a very popular attraction. It's no doubt helped along by the daily hangings (volunteers called for), regular 'whipping of wenches' and a weekly jousting tournament – kids love it. The castle is eight km from Ballarat, towards Melbourne, and is open daily from 9.30 am to 5.30 pm; admission is $11/6 for adults/children ($12.50/7 on weekends).

Other Attractions

Lydiard St is one of the most impressive and intact streetscapes of Victorian architecture in the country, with many fine old buildings including Her Majesty's Theatre, the art gallery and Craig's Royal Hotel. The *Historic Lydiard Precinct* brochure is available from the tourist office.

The **Ballarat Fine Art Gallery**, 40 Lydiard St North, is one of Australia's best provincial galleries and its Australian collection is particularly strong. You can also see the remnants of the original Eureka flag here. The gallery is open daily from 10.30 am to 5 pm; admission is $4.

The **Ballarat Wildlife Park**, on the corner of York and Fussell Sts, is home to wombats, koalas, Tasmanian devils, kangaroos, crocs and others; it is open daily from 9 am to 5.30 pm ($8.50/4.50). The **Ballarat Woolshed**, on the Western Highway on the eastern outskirts, has shearing demonstrations, trained dogs and woolly displays ($8/3.50).

Other attractions include **Montrose Cottage & the Eureka Museum** at 111 Eureka St, an **aviation museum** at the Ballarat airport, and the lovely **Hymettus Garden** at 8 Cardigan St.

Organised Tours

Timeless Tours (☎ 5342 0652) offers half-day guided tours around Ballarat's heritage sites ($20), as well as day trips to destinations farther afield including the Brisbane Ranges and Lerderderg Gorge.

Festivals

In early March Ballarat holds its annual Begonia Festival, which is 10 days of fun, flowers and the arts. Between August and November there's the Royal South Street Competitions, Australia's oldest eisteddfod.

Places to Stay

Camping The *Goldfields Caravan Park* (☎ 5332 7888), 300 metres north of Sovereign Hill at 108 Clayton St, has tent sites at $12, on-site vans at $34 and cabins from $49. Also convenient is the *Eureka Stockade Caravan Park* (☎ 5331 2281) next to the Eureka Stockade Memorial, with tent sites at $9 and on-site vans from $23.

Hostels & Pubs Adjacent to Sovereign Hill, the YHA-associate *Sovereign Hill Lodge* (☎ 5333 3409) has eight to 10-bed bunk rooms at $16 ($18 with linen), singles/doubles from $33/44, and doubles with en suite from $92. The facilities here are excellent (although it's often fully booked) and you get a 10% discount on entry to Sovereign Hill.

The *Provincial Hotel* (☎ 5332 1845), opposite Ballarat railway station at 121 Lydiard St, has basic pub rooms at $10 per person ($15 if you need linen). At 27 Lydiard St, the restored *George Hotel* (☎ 5331 1031) has good singles/doubles from $35/50, or $50/65 with en suite. *Craig's Royal Hotel* (☎ 5331 1377), at 10 Lydiard St South, has been restored to its original grandeur and has budget rooms at $40 (including breakfast), en suite rooms from $60 to $100 and luxury suites from $120.

Motels & B&Bs The *Lake View Hotel/Motel* (☎ 5331 4592), by the lake on Wendouree Pde, has singles/doubles from $49/52. The modern and central *Bakery Hill Motel* (☎ 5333 1363), on the corner of Humffray and Victoria Sts, charges $68/78, and close to Sovereign Hill, the *Main Lead Motor Inn* (☎ 5331 7533) at 312 Main Rd has rooms for $75/85.

At 202 Dawson St, the huge *Ballarat Bed & Breakfast* (☎ 5333 7046) is popular with

VICTORIA

students and travellers, with budget rooms from $25/38. The elegant *Ballarat Terrace* (☎ 5333 2216) at 229 Lydiard St North is highly recommended and has three doubles with B&B from $100 to $130.

Places to Eat

L'Espresso, at 417 Sturt St, is a funky little cafe with good food and coffee. It also sells (and plays) a great selection of jazz, blues and alternative music. A couple of doors south, the *Europa Cafe* serves all-day breakfasts, lunches such as Turkish pita and Spanish omelettes, and Mediterranean-style dinner mains for about $16.

Eureka Pizza, at 316 Sturt St, is a casual BYO with pastas, pizzas and other dishes from $8 to $11, while nearby at No 312 *Apperteasers Deli* serves excellent sandwiches, salads, smoothies and hot foods. Farther down at 102 Sturt St, *Cafe Pazani* is a stylish European bar/restaurant with light lunches from $7 to $9 and mains from $13 to $16. At 12 Sturt St, *Conders* specialises in Middle Eastern cuisine, with good mixed platters ($14) and banquets ($22), and a belly-dancer on weekends.

There's a cluster of eateries in the Bridge St Mall: *Swaggers*, a steak-and-seafood joint, has pastas from $5.80; *Chinatown* has all-you-can-eat deals ($6.90 lunch, $11 dinner); and the *Tokyo Grill House* does sushi and Japanese teppanyaki. For a great steak, head to *Dyer's Steak Stable* in Little Bridge St – it's expensive but very good.

Entertainment

Good live music venues include the *Southern Star Saloon*, on the corner of Sturt and Drummond Sts, and the *Bridge Mall Inn* in Little Bridge St. If you're kicking on to a nightclub, try *21 Arms* at 21 Armstrong St or *Hot Gossip* at 102 Dana St.

The wonderful *Her Majesty's Theatre* (☎ 5333 5800) at 17 Lydiard St South is the main performing arts venue. The *Regent Cinemas* (☎ 5331 1399) are at 49 Lydiard St North.

Getting There & Away

There are frequent daily trains between Melbourne and Ballarat, taking about 1¾ hours and costing $12.80 in economy. On weekdays V/Line buses go from Ballarat to Warrnambool ($16.80), Hamilton ($22.80), and Bendigo ($16.80) via Castlemaine ($12.80). There are also regular buses to Geelong ($9) and trains to Mildura ($44).

Passing through on the Melbourne to Adelaide run, Greyhound Pioneer buses stop at the Ballarat Coachlines terminal near the railway station, while McCafferty's buses stop at the Shell service station on the corner of Sturt and Pleasant Sts. Ballarat Coachlines (☎ 5333 4660) has daily services to Melbourne airport for $20.

Getting Around

Timetables for the local Ballarat Transit bus service are available from the railway station or the tourist office. The two main terminals are in Curtis St and Little Bridge St, on either side of the Bridge St Mall. Take bus No 9 to Sovereign Hill from the northern side of Sturt St, between Armstrong and Lydiard Sts. For the botanic gardens and Lake Wendouree, catch bus No 15 from Little Bridge St. Bus No 2 takes you to the railway station.

CLUNES (pop 820)

In June 1851 Clunes was the site of one of Victoria's very first gold discoveries. Although other finds soon diverted interest, many fine buildings are reminders of the former wealth of this charming little town. The town has a small museum housed in a double-storey bluestone building, but it is open only on Saturday and school holidays ($2).

The small hills around Clunes are extinct volcanoes. Nearby **Mt Beckworth** is noted for its orchids and birdlife; you can visit the old gold diggings of **Jerusalem** and **Ullina** and at **Smeaton**, between Clunes and Daylesford, an impressive bluestone water-driven mill has been restored (open Sunday afternoon only).

Places to Stay

The *Clunes Caravan Park* (☎ 5345 3278) on Purcell St has tent sites and on-site vans, and the excellent *Keebles of Clunes* (☎ 5345 3220) guesthouse has B&B from $110 a double.

MARYBOROUGH (pop 7800)

The district around Charlotte Plains was already an established sheep run, owned by the Simson brothers, when gold was discovered at White Hills and Four Mile Flat in 1854. A police camp established at the diggings was named Maryborough and by 1854 the population had swelled to over 40,000. Gold mining ceased to be economical in 1918 but Maryborough had a strong manufacturing base by then and is still a busy town today.

Built back in 1892, the magnificent and inordinately large Maryborough **railway station** was once described by Mark Twain as 'a railway station with a town attached'. It now houses an impressive tourist complex, which includes the tourist office (☎ 5460 4511), a woodwork gallery, an antique emporium, a cafe and a restaurant. Also of interest is the eclectic **Museum of Creative Arts & Sciences** on High St (open weekdays 10 am to 4 pm, Sunday 1 to 4 pm).

Maryborough's Highland Gathering has been held every year on New Year's Day since 1857 and the annual 16-day Golden Wattle Festival is celebrated in September with literary events, music, the national gumleaf-blowing and bird-call championships, and street parades.

Places to Stay & Eat

The old *Bull & Mouth Hotel* (☎ 5461 1002), at 119 High St, has pub rooms from $18/30, or $25/38 with en suite; there are numerous other pubs, motels and caravan parks.

The Bull & Mouth is good for a pub feed. At the railway station are *La Choo Choo*, a daytime cafe, and the interesting *Twains*, with good-value meals and live (or other) entertainment.

MOLIAGUL, TARNAGULLA & DUNOLLY

The rich alluvial goldfields of the Golden Triangle attracted some 30,000 diggers and produced more gold nuggets than any other area in the country, including the world's largest gold nugget, the 65-kg Welcome Stranger. The Stranger was unearthed in Moliagul in 1869, then taken into Dunolly where it was cut into pieces because it was too big to fit on the scales!

Nowadays things are much quieter. Moliagul is a tiny, tumbledown village with a memorial commemorating the discovery of the Welcome Stranger. Tarnagulla is well worth a visit, with many historic houses and churches, a gemstone and minerals museum and the ghost town of **Wanyarra** nearby. At Dunolly, the largest of the three towns, there's the interesting **Goldfields Historical Arts Museum**, which is open on weekends.

Places to Stay

Dunolly has a caravan park and the *Golden Triangle Motel* (☎ 5368 1166). Tarnagulla also has a caravan park as well as the *Tarnagulla B&B* (☎ 5438 7366), a restored bank building on Commercial Rd, with double rooms from $60 to $80.

DAYLESFORD & HEPBURN SPRINGS (pop 6000)

Set among the scenic hills, lakes and forests of the Central Highlands, the delightful twin towns of Daylesford and Hepburn Springs are enjoying a booming revival as the 'spa centre of Victoria'.

The well-preserved and restored buildings show the prosperity that visited these towns during the gold rush, as well as the lasting influence of the many Swiss-Italian miners who expertly worked the tunnel mines in the surrounding hills.

The health-giving properties of the area's mineral springs were known before gold was discovered here, and by the 1870s Daylesford was a popular health resort, attracting droves of fashionable Melburnians. It was claimed that the waters could cure any complaint, and the spas and relaxed scenic environment could rejuvenate even the most stressed turn-of-the-century city-dweller.

VICTORIA

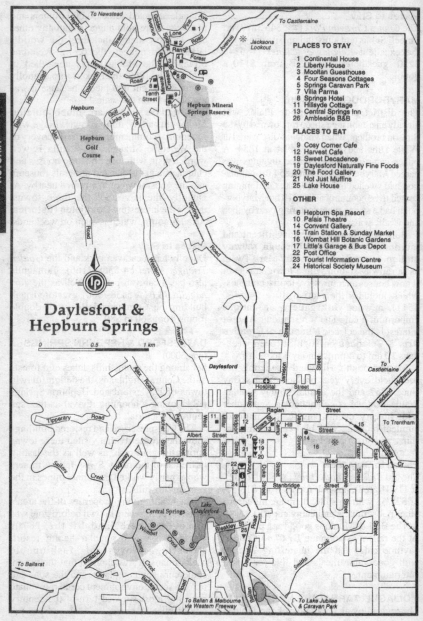

Daylesford & Hepburn Springs

PLACES TO STAY

1 Continental House
2 Liberty House
3 Mooltan Guesthouse
4 Four Seasons Cottages
5 Springs Caravan Park
7 Villa Parma
8 Springs Hotel
11 Hillsyde Cottage
13 Central Springs Inn
26 Ambleside B&B

PLACES TO EAT

9 Cosy Corner Cafe
12 Harvest Cafe
18 Sweet Decadence
19 Daylesford Naturally Fine Foods
20 The Food Gallery
21 Not Just Muffins
25 Lake House

OTHER

6 Hepburn Spa Resort
10 Palais Theatre
14 Convent Gallery
15 Train Station & Sunday Market
16 Wombat Hill Botanic Gardens
17 Little's Garage & Bus Depot
22 Post Office
23 Tourist Information Centre
24 Historical Society Museum

The current trend towards healthy life-styles has prompted a revival of interest in Daylesford and Hepburn Springs. The restored spa complex is again a popular relaxation and rejuvenation centre, and the towns also boast masseurs, craft and antique shops, gardens, galleries, excellent cafes and restaurants, and dozens of charming guest-houses, cottages and B&Bs.

Information
The Daylesford Information Centre (☎ 5348 1339) is next to the post office on Vincent St; it's open daily from 10 am to 4 pm.

Spa Complex
The modern Hepburn Spa Resort (☎ 5348 2034) is open weekdays from 10 am to 8 pm and weekends from 9 am to 8 pm. Among the many services offered are an indoor pool and spa ($8), aero spas with essential oils ($17/26 for singles/doubles), massage ($32 for half an hour), floatation tanks ($45 an hour), and sauna-spa couches ($6).

Other Attractions
The huge 19th-century **Convent Gallery** in Daly St, Daylesford, is a former Catholic convent that has been brilliantly converted into a gallery, with lovely gardens and a great cafe. It's open daily from 10 am to 6 pm and entry costs $3.

Beside the gallery are the lovely **Wombat Hill Botanic Gardens**, with picnic areas and a lookout tower with fine views. The **Historical Society Museum** on Vincent St is open on weekends from 1.30 to 4.30 pm.

In the centre of Daylesford, **Lake Daylesford** is a popular fishing and picnic area, and the scenic **Lake Jubilee** is three km south-east; boats and canoes can be hired at both. There are some great **walking trails** around here; the tourist office has maps.

Most Sundays you can ride the historic **Central Highlands Tourist Railway**, and a **Sunday market** operates at the railway station. The volcanic crater of **Mt Franklin**, 10 km north, has a beautiful camping and picnic area. There are also several horse-riding ranches in the area.

Places to Stay
Accommodation is often heavily booked. The information centre can help with bookings, or try the Daylesford Cottage Directory (☎ 5348 1255), which manages more than 70 privately owned cottages in the area.

Daylesford The *Jubilee Lake Caravan Park* (☎ 5348 2186), three km south-east, has tent sites for $8 and on-site cabins from $35 to $45. The *Central Springs Inn* (☎ 5348 3134) on Wills Square has motel units from $50/65. B&Bs include *Hillsyde Cottage* (☎ 5348 1056) at 26 Millar St, with doubles from $70, and *Ambleside B&B* (☎ 5348 2691) at 15 Leggatt St, with doubles from $95 to $125. The *Lake House* (☎ 5348 3329) has dinner and B&B packages from $230 a double.

Hepburn Springs The *Springs Caravan Park* (☎ 5348 3161) on Forest Ave has camp sites for $8 and a few on-site vans for $25. At 9 Lone Pine Ave, *Continental House* (☎ 5348 2005) is a rambling old timber guesthouse, with a laid-back 'alternative' vibe, a vegan cafe and a strictly vegetarian kitchen. Costs range from $13 to $18 a night (BYO linen) – this isn't a 'party place'.

The *Four Seasons Cottages* (☎ 5348 1221) on Forest Ave range from $140 to $295 for two nights. *Liberty House* (☎ 5348 2809) at 20 Mineral Springs Crescent has B&B from $40/80, and the friendly *Mooltan Guest House* (☎ 5348 3555) at 129 Main Rd has singles from $50 to $70 and doubles from $75 to $130. The evocative *Villa Parma* (☎ 5348 3512) on Main Rd is a rambling Tuscan-style pensione, with B&B from $80/115.

Places to Eat
Daylesford's Vincent St has plenty of good eateries, including *Daylesford Naturally Fine Foods* wholefoods shop at No 59, the *Food Gallery* gourmet deli at No 77, and the aptly named *Sweet Decadence* at No 57, with handmade chocolates and afternoon teas.

On Albert St, *Not Just Muffins* is famous for its home-made muffins and shortcakes, while across the road at No 29 is the laid-

VICTORIA

back *Harvest Cafe*, which specialises in organic foods. Overlooking Lake Daylesford is *Lake House* (☎ 5348 3329), one of country Victoria's best restaurants – highly recommended.

In Hepburn Springs, the very popular *Cosy Corner Cafe* (☎ 5348 3825) is at 3 Tenth Ave.

Getting There & Around

V/Line's trip between Melbourne and Daylesford ($11.40) takes two hours – you change from train to bus at Woodend (four services on weekdays, two on Saturday, one on Sunday). V/Line also has weekday buses to Ballarat ($8), Castlemaine ($4) and Bendigo ($8).

A shuttle bus runs back and forth between Daylesford and Hepburn Springs four times a day (weekdays only).

CASTLEMAINE (pop 7250)

Settlement of this district dates back to the 1830s when most of the land was taken up for farming. The discovery of gold at Specimen Gully in 1851 altered the pastoral landscape radically as 30,000 diggers worked a number of goldfields known, collectively, as the Mt Alexander diggings.

The township that grew up around the Government Camp, at the junction of Barkers and Forest creeks, was named Castlemaine in 1853 and soon became the thriving marketplace for all the goldfields of central Victoria.

Castlemaine's importance was not to last, however, as the district did not have the rich quartz reefs that were found in Bendigo and Ballarat. The centre of the town has been virtually unaltered since the 1860s when the population began to decline as the surface gold was exhausted.

These days Castlemaine is a charming town where the legacy of its rapid rise to prosperity lies in the splendid architecture of its public buildings and private residences and in the design of its streets and many gardens.

The Castlemaine State Festival, one of Victoria's leading celebrations of the arts, is held every second October (even years), alternating with the Castlemaine Garden Festival (odd years).

Information

The tourist office (☎ 5470 6200), in a rotunda on Duke St, is open on weekends, school and public holidays from 10 am to 4 pm.

Buda Historic Home & Gardens

Originally built by a retired Indian army officer in 1857, this is a superb example of Victorian-era colonial architecture. The house and magnificent gardens, extended in the 1890s by a Hungarian gold and silversmith Ernest Leviny, are now open to the public and provide an insight into the town's refined and gracious past. Buda is on the corner of Urquhart and Hunter Sts, and is open daily from 9.30 am to 5 pm; admission is $5.

Castlemaine Art Gallery & Museum

This gallery in Lyttleton St has an excellent collection of colonial and contemporary art and a museum featuring photographs, relics and documents. It's open daily from 10 am to 5 pm ($2).

Other Attractions

Dating back to 1861, the imposing **Old Castlemaine Gaol** looms over the town from a hilltop on Bowden St. The gaol houses a gallery, a restaurant and a coffee shop, and is open daily with hourly tours ($5 adults, $3 children) between 11 am and 5 pm.

The beautiful **botanic gardens** on Walker St were designed in the 1860s by the director of Melbourne's Royal Botanic Gardens, Baron von Mueller, and it's well worth taking the time for a picnic by the lake or just a stroll among the 'significant trees' registered by the National Trust.

Castlemaine's original **market building**, on Mostyn St, is now an art and craft market. Other places of interest include the **Camp Reserve**, the site of the original government camp during the gold rush; the **Burke & Wills Monument**, if you're into statues; a host of **gold-rush buildings**; and the **Kaweka Wildflower Reserve**.

Places to Stay

The *Botanic Gardens Caravan Park* (☎ 5472 1125), beside the gardens, has tent sites from $7.60 and on-site vans from $30.

The *Cumberland Hotel* (☎ 5472 1052) on Barker St has basic singles/doubles for $25/35, and the *Castle Motel* (☎ 5472 2433) at 1 Duke St (opposite the tourist office) has units from $58.

The *Midland Private Hotel* (☎ 5472 1085), opposite the railway station at 2 Templeton St, is a fascinating blend of Victorian and Edwardian architecture with simple rooms at $45/90 (weekends only).

The refined *Ellimatta Guesthouse* (☎ 5472 4454) at 233 Barker St has singles from $50 to $65 and doubles from $85 to $100, including breakfast. Behind the Castlemaine Bookshop at 242 Barker St, charming and self-contained *Bookshop Cottage* (☎ 5472 1557) charges $70 a double with breakfast.

You can also stay in an old cell in the *Old Castlemaine Gaol* (☎ 5470 5311); B&B tariffs are $45 per person, or $65 with dinner.

Places to Eat

Tog's Place at 58 Lyttleton St is a popular and reasonably priced cafe. *Bing's Cafe* at 71 Mostyn St is also good, and the rustic *Capone's* at 50 Hargreaves St is an affordable pizza/pasta joint.

For more up-market dining, try the excellent restaurant at *Ellimatta Guesthouse* on Barker St, or the *Globe Garden* at 81 Forest St.

Entertainment

The historic *Theatre Royal* (☎ 5472 1196), at 30 Hargreaves St, is now a cinema, bar/restaurant, disco and band venue. It's worth ringing to find out what's on.

Getting There & Away

V/Line has daily trains between Melbourne and Castlemaine ($14.20), continuing on to Bendigo ($4), as well as weekday buses to Daylesford ($4), Ballarat ($12.80), Geelong ($21.60) and Maldon ($2.80).

AROUND CASTLEMAINE

The area around Castlemaine holds enough attractions – most of them related to the goldfields – to keep you going for a couple of days. You can visit the **Forest Creek Historic Gold Mine**, the remains of **Garfield's Water Wheel** and the **Dingo Farm**, all near Chewton; the **Heron's Reef Gold Diggings** at Fryerstown; the sombre **Pennyweight Children's Cemetery**, east of Castlemaine; the **Vaughan Springs** mineral springs and swimming hole; and the **Hilltop Cottage Garden** and **Tara Garden**, both at Guildford.

MALDON (pop 3100)

The small township of Maldon is one of the best-preserved relics of Victoria's gold-mining era. In 1966 the National Trust named Maldon the country's first 'notable town', an honour bestowed only on towns where the historic architecture was intact and valuable. Special planning regulations were introduced to preserve the town for posterity. It's a very popular tourist destination: it's flooded with visitors on weekends, and it has its share of trendy (and overpriced) craft and antique shops. Its Spring Folk Festival takes place every November.

The tourist information centre (☎ 5475 2569) on High St is open daily.

Things to See & Do

The tourist office has a handy *Information Guide* (50c) and a *Historic Town Walk* brochure. Interesting buildings around town and along the verandahed main street include **Dabb's General Store** (now the supermarket); the **Maldon**, **Kangaroo** and **Grand** hotels; the 24-metre-high **Beehive Chimney**; the **North British Mine & Kilns**; and the **Eaglehawk Gully Restaurant**.

Carman's Tunnel Goldmine is two km south of town; the 570-metre-long tunnel was excavated in the 1880s. There are candlelight tours through the mine on weekends and school and public holidays from 1.30 to 4 pm ($2.50 adults, $1 children).

Terry & Tangles offers horse-drawn wagon rides around town ($4/2) and picnic tours (from $30 a head). On Sunday you can ride the historic **steam-train** that makes trips along the old Maldon-Castlemaine line ($8/4).

The **historical museum** on High St is open daily from 1.30 to 4 pm. **Porcupine Township**, a re-creation of an 1850s gold-rush town with timber-slab, mud-brick, tin and stone buildings, is open daily from 10 am to 5 pm and costs $7/4.

There are some good bushwalks around the town, and amateur gold hunters still scour the area with some success. There are excellent views from the tops of nearby **Anzac Hill** and **Mt Tarrengower**.

Places to Stay

The *Maldon Caravan Park* (☎ 5475 2344) in Hospital St has tent sites at $10 and vans and cabins from $29 to $37. The *Derby Hill Lodge* (☎ 5475 2033) in Phoenix St has motel-style rooms at $30/60 (weekends and school holidays only).

Most of the other accommodation is in up-market B&Bs and guesthouses. *Palm House* (☎ 5475 2532) at 2 High St is one of the cheapest, with B&B from $35 per person. Other possibilities include the elegant *Calder House B&B* (☎ 5475 2912) at 44 High St, with doubles from $70 to $100, and the historic and charming *Spring Cottage* (☎ 5475 1333), costing from $100 a night.

Places to Eat

The *Kangaroo Hotel* on High St has good meals from $10 to $14. For afternoon tea there's *Berryman's Tearooms* or the elegant *Ruby's at Calder House*, while the quaint *McArthur's Restaurant* has affordable meals ranging from sandwiches to roasts.

Getting There & Away

V/Line has a twice-daily bus service (week-days only) between Castlemaine and Maldon ($2.80).

BENDIGO (pop 71,700)

The solid, imposing and at times extravagant Victorian-era architecture of Bendigo is a testimony to the fact that this was one of Australia's richest gold-mining towns.

In the 1850s thousands upon thousands of diggers converged on the fantastically rich Bendigo diggings to claim the easily obtained surface gold, later turning their pans and cradles to Bendigo Creek and other local waterways in their quest for alluvial gold. The arrival of thousands of Chinese miners from 1854 caused a great deal of racial tension at the time, but today Bendigo is one of the few places with significant reminders of its rich Chinese heritage.

By the 1860s the easily won ore was running out. Reef mining began in earnest and was dominated by the large and powerful mining companies, who poured money back into the town as they extracted enormous wealth from their network of deep mine shafts. Reef mining continued here up until the 1950s.

Today Bendigo is a busy and prosperous provincial city, with an interesting collection of mines, museums, historic buildings and other relics from the gold-mining era. It also has one of the best regional art galleries in Australia, as well as some great wineries in the surrounding district.

Information

The Bendigo Tourist Information Centre (☎ 5447 7788), in the historic former post office on Pall Mall, is open daily from 9 am to 5 pm.

The RACV (☎ 5443 9622) has an office at 112 Mitchell St, and the DC&NR (☎ 5444 6666) is on the corner of Mundy and Hargreaves Sts.

Central Deborah Mine

This 500-metre-deep mine, which was worked on 17 levels and yielded about 1000 kg of gold before it closed in 1954, is a major tourist attraction. There are lots of interesting exhibits and photographs, and you can do a self-guided surface tour ($3.50) or don a hard-hat for the 70-minute underground tour ($12 adults, $6 children), which takes you 61 metres down to inspect newly commenced mining operations. The mine is on Violet St and is open daily from 9 am to 5 pm.

Bendigo Talking Tram & Tram Museum

A vintage tram makes a regular tourist run from the Central Deborah Mine through the centre of the city to the tram museum, with a commentary on the history of Bendigo. It departs daily at 9.30 and 11 am and 12.30, 2 and 3.30 pm from the Central Deborah Mine, or five minutes later from the Alexandra Fountain (more frequently during holidays). The fare is $6.50 for adults, $3.50 for children; you can also buy a combined ticket for the mine and the talking tram tour ($17/9).

Bendigo Art Gallery

Don't judge this gallery by it's bland 1960s facade – it was actually built in the 1880s and has an outstanding collection of Australian colonial and contemporary paintings and 19th-century European art. The gallery is at 42 View St and is open Monday to Saturday from 10 am to 5 pm and on Sunday from 2 to 5 pm; admission is $2/1.

Golden Dragon Museum

On Bridge St, the Golden Dragon Museum houses Loong and Sun Loong, the imperial Chinese dragons that are the centrepieces of the annual Easter Fair parade, plus an impressive collection of Chinese heritage items and costumes. It is open daily from 9.30 am to 5 pm; entry is $5/2.50.

Chinese Joss House

Dating back to the 1860s and classified by the National Trust, this is one of the few remaining practising joss houses in the state, and features figures representing the 12 years of the Chinese solar cycle, commemorative tablets to the deceased, paintings and Chinese lanterns. It's in Finn St in North Bendigo and is open daily from 10 am to 5 pm ($3/1).

Other Attractions

Built in 1897, the magnificent **Shamrock Hotel** on Pall Mall is an outstanding example of the extravagance of late-Victorian architecture. Its size gives some indication of how prosperous the town was in the gold-mining era when, so the story goes, the floors were regularly washed down to collect the gold dust brought in on miners' boots. There are tours of the hotel on Saturday and Sunday at 2.30 pm; the $5 fee includes afternoon tea.

Opposite the Shamrock on Pall Mall are the equally elaborate former **post office** and **law courts** buildings. **Rosalind Park**, just north of Pall Mall, features open lawns and picnic tables, a lookout tower with sensational views, a fernery and the lovely **Conservatory Gardens**.

On High St, the **Sacred Heart Cathedral** is Victoria's largest Gothic-style building outside Melbourne. Work was begun last century and completed in 1977. The **Discovery Science & Technology Centre**, with a wide range of interesting and educational exhibits, is in Railway Place opposite the railway station and is open daily from 10 am to 5 pm.

Dudley House, at 60 View St, is classified by the National Trust. It's a fine old residence with beautiful gardens and is open weekends and during school holidays from 2 to 5 pm. On Chum St the stately mansion **Fortuna Villa**, with its lake and Italian fountain, was once owned by George Lansell, the Quartz King. It's open to the public on Sunday for a three-hour tour ($3) at 1 pm.

North of Bendigo, Eaglehawk also has some impressive historic buildings. The *Eaglehawk Heritage Trail* brochure, available from the information office, guides you around many of them.

Festivals

Bendigo's annual Easter Fair, first held in 1871 to aid local charities, attracts big crowds and features a procession with Chinese dragons, a lantern parade, a jazz night and other entertainment. Bendigo's most curious event is the annual 'swap meet', held in November. It draws thousands

VICTORIA

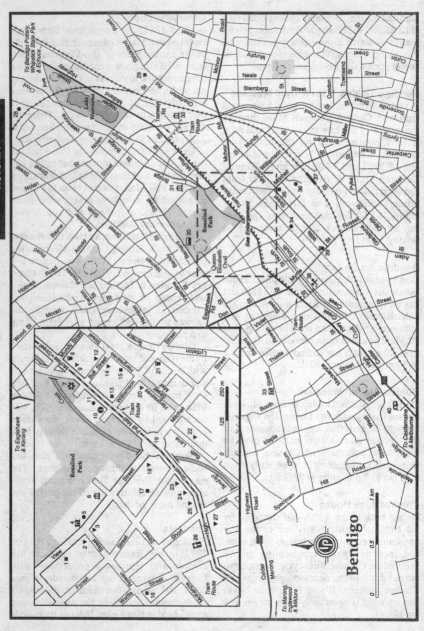

Bendigo

PLACES TO STAY		12	The Match Bar & Bake-	10	Tourist Information
			house		Centre & Old Post
1	Oval Motel	14	Jacquie's Tasteworks		Office
13	Shamrock Hotel	18	The Whirrakee	11	Law Courts
15	Old Crown Hotel	20	Gillies' Pies	19	Alexandra Fountain
16	Marlborough House	22	Green Olive Deli	21	Studio 54 Nightclub
17	City Centre Motel	23	Jo Joe's	26	Sacred Heart Cathedral
29	Fleece Inn	24	Mexican Kitchen	28	Chinese Joss House
35	Hopetoun Hotel	25	Rasoyee	30	Aquatic Centre
40	Central City Caravan	27	Dianne's Deli	31	Golden Dragon
	Park & YHA Hostel				Museum
		OTHER		32	Tram Museum
PLACES TO EAT				33	Fortuna Villa
		4	Dudley House	34	Bendigo Cinemas
2	Turkish Kitchen	5	Bendigo Regional Arts	36	Discovery Science &
3	Rifle Brigade Pub-		Centre		Technology Centre
	Brewery	6	Bendigo Art Gallery	37	Train Station
9	Clogs	7	Conservatory Gardens	38	Central Deborah Mine
		8	Sundance Saloon	39	Golden Vine Hotel

VICTORIA

of motoring enthusiasts from all over the country in search of that elusive vintage-car spare part.

Places to Stay

Hostel & Camping The *Central City Caravan Park* (☎ 5443 6937), at 362 High St, has a basic associate-YHA hostel with beds at $12 ($15 for nonmembers), tent sites from $10 to $12, and on-site vans and cabins from $32 to $50. It's about 2.5 km south of the town centre – you can get there on a Kangaroo Flat bus from Hargreaves St. The *Bendigo Caravan Park* (☎ 5447 1773), seven km south on the Calder Highway, has tent sites from $10 to $14 and on-site vans and cottages from $26 to $62.

Pubs & Motels The *Hopetoun Hotel* (☎ 5443 4871), close to the railway station on the corner of Wills and Mitchell Sts, has singles/doubles for $25/40, although it's pretty grim and shabby. A much better option is the central *Old Crown Hotel* (☎ 5441 6888) at 238 Hargreaves St, with singles/doubles with shared bathroom at $28/44, including breakfast. The *Fleece Inn Hotel* (☎ 5443 3086), opposite the cattle saleyards at 139 Charlston Rd, has B&B at $20/40.

There are plenty of motels in town. Two of the cheaper and more central ones are the *City Centre Motel* (☎ 5443 2077), at 26 Forest St, and the *Oval Motel* (☎ 5443 7211), opposite the Queen Elizabeth Oval at 194 Barnard St. Both have doubles from $47 to $52.

Other Accommodation The *Shamrock Hotel* (☎ 5443 0333) is a nice place for a splurge. Traditional rooms with shared bathroom are $60 a double, en suite rooms are $90, and the two-room suites range from $120 to $150. Also very good is the historic and elegant *Marlborough House* (☎ 5441 4142) on the corner of Rowan and Wattle Sts, with B&B from $55/90 for singles/doubles with private bathroom.

Places to Eat

The small *Jacquie's Tasteworks* at 51 Bull St is crammed with taste sensations: fresh pies and pastries, home-made salads and pastas, cooked breakfasts and more. The *Green Olive Deli* in Bath Lane is the perfect spot for gourmet picnic supplies, with fine cheeses, patés, sandwiches and smallgoods. *Dianne's Deli*, opposite the cathedral in High St, is also pretty good.

In the Hargreaves St Mall, *Gillies'* pies are

VICTORIA

Gold Fever

In May 1851 E H Hargraves discovered gold near Bathurst in New South Wales. Sensational accounts of the potential wealth of the find caused an unprecedented rush as thousands of people dropped everything to try their luck.

News of the discovery reached Melbourne at the same time as the accounts of its influence on the people of New South Wales. Sydney had been virtually denuded of workers and the same misfortune soon threatened Melbourne. Victoria was still being established as a separate colony so the loss of its workforce to the northern goldfields would have been disastrous.

A public meeting was called by the young city's businessmen and a reward was offered to anyone who could find gold within 300 km of Melbourne. In less than a week gold was discovered in the Yarra River but the find was soon eclipsed by a more significant discovery at Clunes. Prospectors began heading to central Victoria and over the next few months the rush north across the Murray was reversed as fresh gold finds and new rushes became an almost weekly occurrence in Victoria.

Gold was found in the Pyrenees, the Loddon and Avoca rivers, at Warrandyte and at Bunninyong. At Ballarat in September 1851, the biggest gold discovery was made, followed by other significant discoveries at Bendigo, Mt Alexander, Beechworth, Walhalla, Omeo and in the hills and creeks of the Great Dividing Range.

By the end of 1851 about 250,000 ounces of gold had been claimed. Farms and businesses lost their workforces and in many cases were abandoned altogether as employers had no choice but to follow their workers to the goldfields. Hopeful miners left England, Ireland, Europe, China and the failing goldfields of California – during 1852 about 1800 people arrived in Melbourne each week.

The government introduced a licence fee of 30 shillings a month for all prospectors, whether or not they found gold. This entitled the miners to a claim, limited to eight feet square, in which to dig for gold, and it provided the means to enforce improvised laws for the goldfields.

The administration of each field was headed by a chief commissioner whose deputies, the state troopers, were empowered to organise licence hunts and to fine or imprison any miner who failed to produce the permit. Although this later caused serious unrest on the diggings, for the most part it successfully averted the lawlessness that had characterised the California rush.

regarded by connoisseurs as among the best in Australia. A Bendigo institution, you queue at the little window, order one of their five or so varieties, then sit in the mall to eat it.

The popular *Rifle Brigade Pub-Brewery* at 137 View St has bar meals for $6 and a good bistro with a courtyard. It also brews its own beers, including Old-fashioned Bitter, Ironbark Dark and Rifle Lager. The Shamrock Hotel has a popular corner bistro. Another pub worth a visit is the restored *Goldmines Hotel*, on the Marong road on the outskirts of town, with elegant dining areas, a courtyard, gardens, and meals in the $10 to $14 range.

At 107 Pall Mall, *Clogs* is a stylish but affordable bar/restaurant with pizzas, pastas and a wide range of other meals – during the week it stays open until 1 am and on weekends until 4 am. *Jo Joe's*, near the corner of High and Forest Sts, is another good pizza/pasta place, and the *Match Bar & Bakehouse* on Bull St specialises in wood-oven pizzas ($8 to $11).

The *Mexican Kitchen* at 28 High St, the *Turkish Kitchen* at 159 View St, and *Rasoyee* Indian restaurant at 40 High St, all have filling main courses for about $10 or less and also do takeaways.

For a splurge, the *Whirrakee* at 17 View St has a small wine bar with cosy sofas, and a restaurant serving excellent 'modern Australian' cuisine with mains in the $16 to $19 range.

Entertainment

For live music one of the best places is the Golden Vine Hotel on the corner of King and

There were, however, the classic features that seem to accompany gold fever: the backbreaking work, the unwholesome food and hard drinking, and the primitive dwellings. There was the amazing wealth that was to be the luck of some, but the elusive dream of others; and for every story of success there were hundreds more of hardship, despair and death.

In *Australia Illustrated* , published in 1873, Edwin Carton Booth wrote of the 1850s goldfields:

...it may be fairly questioned whether in any community in the world there ever existed more of intense suffering, unbridled wickedness and positive want, than in Victoria at [that] time... To look at the thousands of people who in those years crowded Melbourne, and that most miserable adjunct of Melbourne, Canvas Town, induced the belief that sheer and absolute unfitness for a useful life in the colonies... had been deemed the only qualification requisite to make a fortunate digger.

The gold rush had its share of rogues, including the notorious bushrangers who attacked gold shipments being escorted to Melbourne, but it also had its heroes who eventually forced a change in the political fabric of the colony. (See The Eureka Rebellion in the Ballarat section.)

Above all, the gold rush ushered in a fantastic era of growth and material prosperity for Victoria and opened up vast areas of country previously unexplored by Whites.

In the first 12 years of the rush, Australia's population increased from 400,000 to well over a million, and in Victoria alone it rose from 77,000 to 540,000. To cope with the moving population and the tonnes of gold and supplies, the development of roads and railways was accelerated.

The mining companies that followed the independent diggers invested heavily in the region over the next couple of decades. The huge shanty towns of tents, bark huts, raucous bars and police camps were eventually replaced by the timber and stone buildings that were the foundation of many of Victoria's provincial cities, most notably Ballarat, Bendigo, Maldon and Castlemaine.

The gold towns reached the height of splendour in the 1880s. Gold production gradually lost its importance after that time, but by then the towns of the region had stable populations, and agriculture and other activities steadily supplanted gold as the economic mainstay.

Gold also made Melbourne Australia's largest city and financial centre, a position it held for nearly half a century. ■

Myrtle Sts. The *Sundance Saloon*, on the corner of McCrae and Mundy Sts, has pool tables and live bands on weekends, as does the Rifle Brigade Pub-Brewery. Bendigo's nightclubs include *Studio 54*, on the corner of Williamson and Queen Sts, and *TNG*, on the corner of Williamson and Hargreaves Sts.

The *Bendigo Regional Arts Centre* (☎ 5443 9974), in the beautifully restored Capitol Theatre at 50 View St, is the main venue for the performing arts. The *Bendigo Cinemas* (☎ 5442 1666) are at 107 Queen St.

Getting There & Away
There are half a dozen trains between Melbourne and Bendigo on weekdays (fewer on weekends). The trip takes two hours and costs $19.40 in economy or $27.20 in 1st class. Daily trains continue to Swan Hill.

There's also a weekday V/Line bus service between Bendigo and Castlemaine ($4), Ballarat ($16.80) and Geelong ($27.20). Other destinations served by V/Line buses include Swan Hill ($21.60), Mildura ($44) and Echuca ($5.80).

Getting Around
Bendigo and its surrounding area is well served by public buses. Check the route map at the bus stop on Mitchell St, at the end of the mall, or pick up timetables and route maps from the tourist centre or railway station. Tickets cost $1.25 and are valid for two hours.

AROUND BENDIGO
Bendigo Pottery
Established in 1858, the oldest working

pottery in Australia is on the Midland Highway, seven km north of Bendigo. The buildings are classified by the National Trust. There's a cafe, a sales gallery set among historic kilns, and you can watch potters at work in the studio. The pottery is open daily from 9 am to 5 pm; entry is free. Also here is the **Central Victorian Motor Museum**, with a collection of vintage cars, motor cycles and motoring memorabilia; entry costs $4.

Whipstick State Park
Eight km north of Bendigo, this small park was established to conserve the distinctive Whipstick mallee vegetation. There are picnic areas sited on old eucalyptus distilleries, camp sites and walking tracks. Holders of a miner's right can fossick for gold in designated areas. Nearby, **Hartland's Eucalyptus Oil Factory** was established in 1890 and the production process can be inspected on Sunday ($4).

Wineries
The brochure *Wineries of Bendigo & District* details 15 wineries that are open for sales and tastings, all within about half an hour's drive of Bendigo. These include Château Leamon (10 km south of Bendigo), Balgownie (eight km west) and Château Doré (eight km south-west).

Heathcote, a quiet little town 47 km south-east of Bendigo, has a gold-mining past and a wine-making present and is surrounded by some excellent wineries including Jasper Hill, McIvor Creek, Zuber, Heathcote Winery and Huntleigh.

Other Attractions
The large **Lake Eppalock** reservoir, about 30 km south-east of Bendigo, provides the town's water supply and is popular for all sorts of water sports.

The large undercover **Epsom Sunday Market**, nine km north, attracts big crowds. Other popular attractions are the **Bendigo Mohair Farm**, 15 km south-west, and the **Sedgwick Camel Farm**, 20 km south.

ALONG THE CALDER HIGHWAY
From Bendigo it's 45 km north-west to **Inglewood**, another town with its roots firmly planted in the goldfields. Eucalyptus oil has been distilled here for over 100 years, and there's an old distillery in town.

West of Inglewood is the scenic **Kooyoora State Park**, with walking trails, camp sites and the **Melville Caves**, named after the gentleman bushranger Captain Melville who used to hide out there. In 1980 the 27-kg Hand of Faith gold nugget was unearthed in the tiny town of **Kingower**, 11 km west of Inglewood. Kingower also has the Blanche Barkly and Passing Clouds wineries, both well worth a visit. *Passing Clouds* (☎ 5438 8287) has excellent B&B units costing $60/95.

Wedderburn, 35 km north-west of Inglewood, is a faded former gold-mining centre. Small gold nuggets are still being found in the area. The cluttered but interesting **General Store Museum** is at 51 High St, and the **Christmas Reef Gold Mine**, a working mine five km east of town, is open for tours daily ($8).

RUSHWORTH (pop 1010)
This historic town, 100 km north-east of Bendigo and 20 km west of the Goulburn Valley Highway, was once a busy gold-mining centre and now has a National Trust classification. Apparently it was so named because the (gold) rush was worth coming to.

Seven km south of town, in the Rushworth State Forest, is the gold-mining ghost town of **Whroo** (pronounced 'roo'). The small Balaclava open-cut mine here yielded huge amounts of ore. At its peak the town had over 130 buildings, although today ironbark trees and native scrub have largely reclaimed the site.

The old cemetery (also National Trust classified) is an evocative place, and the headstone inscriptions bear testimony to the hard life experienced by those who came in search of gold. There are a couple of signposted nature trails, one leading to a small rock water hole used by the Koories who inhabited this region. There's also a small mud-brick visitor centre and a camp site. Worth the detour.

North-East

LAKE EILDON

About 150 km north-east of Melbourne, via the hill towns of Healesville and Marysville, is Lake Eildon, a massive lake created for hydroelectric power and irrigation purposes. It's a popular holiday area and one of Victoria's favourite water-sports playgrounds – water-skiing, fishing, sailing and houseboat trips are all popular here.

The township of **Eildon** is the main town on the southern end of the lake, and **Bonnie Doon** on one of the lake's northern arms also has some facilities. The main boat harbour is two km north of Eildon township.

The **Snobs Creek Visitor Centre**, six km south-west of Eildon, is a trout farm and hatchery open daily ($5). On the western shores of the lake, the **Fraser National Park** has some good short walks including an excellent guide-yourself nature walk. The 24,000-hectare **Eildon State Park** takes in the south-eastern shore area of the lake. On the eastern side of the lake is the old mining town of **Jamieson**.

Places to Stay

There's a stack of caravan parks in and around Eildon. There are also camp sites in the Fraser National Park and in the Eildon State Park – you'll need to book (☎ 5772 1293) during holiday periods.

In Eildon, the *Golden Trout Hotel/Motel* (☎ 5774 2508) has singles/doubles from $40/45. The *Lakeside Leisure Resort* (☎ 5778 7252) in Bonnie Doon also has an associate-YHA hostel with bunks at $13 ($15 for nonmembers).

For houseboat hire, try *Lake Eildon Holiday Boats* (☎ 5774 2107) in Eildon or *Peppin Point Houseboats* (☎ 5778 7338), nine km south of Bonnie Doon. Costs range

from $600 to $2500 a week for up to 10 people, usually with a three-day minimum.

Getting There & Away

McKenzie's (☎ 9853 6264) runs a daily service from Melbourne to Eildon ($16.80) via Marysville ($10.40) and Alexandra ($14.20).

MANSFIELD (pop 2500)

Mansfield is one of the best base-towns for Victoria's alpine country, with a good range of accommodation and eateries. In winter it offers easy access to the snowfields of Mt Buller and Mt Stirling, and at other times it's a good base for horse riding, bushwalks and water sports on Lake Eildon.

The graves of three police officers killed by Ned Kelly at Tolmie in 1878 are in the Mansfield cemetery, and there's a monument to them in the town.

In late October, the Mansfield Mountain Country Festival features the Great Mountain Race, with the country's best brumbies and riders, and other activities. There's a tourist information centre (☎ 5775 1464) in the old railway station on High St.

Activities

Mountain Adventure Safaris (☎ 5777 3759) offers mountain-bike rides, white-water rafting, trekking, abseiling and more. High Country Camel Treks (☎ 5775 1591), seven km south, offers one-hour rides ($18), as well as one, two and five-day alpine treks. The tourist centre has details of numerous other activities, including horse-riding ranches.

Places to Stay & Eat

The *James Holiday Park* (☎ 5775 2705) on Ultimo St is the most convenient place to camp, with sites at $14 and on-site vans from $35.

The *Mansfield Backpackers Inn* (☎ 5775 1800), in a restored heritage building at 112 High St, has good facilities, and bunks at $15 per person ($20 on winter weekends) and doubles at $35.

The *Mansfield Hotel* (☎ 5775 2101), at 86 High St, and the *Delatite Hotel* (☎ 5775

2004), at 95 High St, have B&B for $20 per person, and there are also a few motels.

On High St, try the *Witches Brew* cafe for breakfast or lunch, or *Mingo's Bar & Grill* for lunch or dinner.

Getting There & Away
V/Line buses operate daily from Melbourne for $25. In the ski season Mansfield-Mt Buller Bus Lines (☎ 5775 2606) has daily buses to Mt Buller ($17/28 one way/return) and Mt Stirling ($13.30/23).

GOULBURN VALLEY
The Goulburn River runs in a wide arc from Lake Eildon north-west across the Hume Highway, joining the Murray River just upstream of Echuca.

The army base of Puckapunyal, nine km west of Seymour, has the **RAAC Tank Museum** with a large collection of tanks and armoured vehicles. It is open daily.

South-west of **Nagambie** are two of the best-known wineries in Victoria: Chateau Tahbilk, with its National Trust classified buildings and cellars, and the ultra-modern Mitchelton, with its observation tower looming above the surrounding countryside.

Shepparton (pop 26,200)
Shepparton and its adjoining centre of Mooroopna are in a prosperous fruit and vegetable-growing area irrigated by the Goulburn River.

The **Shepparton City Historical Museum** on the corner of High and Welsford Sts is open Sunday from 1 to 4 pm and is well worth a visit. There's also an **art gallery** in Welsford St, a fairly tacky **International Village**, and tours of the huge **Shepparton Preserving Company (SPC) cannery** (January to early April).

Most travellers come to Shepparton looking for casual fruit-picking work. The main season is January to April; contact the Department of Employment, Education & Training (☎ 5832 0300) for information.

There's a tourist information office (☎ 5832 9870) by the lake on Wyndham St, just south of the city centre.

Places to Stay & Eat The *Victoria Lake Caravan Park* (☎ 5821 5431) is the most central of the six caravan parks here, and has tent sites and cabins. The *Victoria Hotel* (☎ 5821 9955), situated on the corner of Wyndham and Fryers Sts, charges $25/30 for singles/doubles ($35/44 with en suite).

Getting There & Away V/Line has daily trains and buses between Melbourne and Shepparton ($21.60).

GLENROWAN (pop 350)
In 1880, the Kelly gang's exploits finally came to an end in a bloody shoot-out here, 230 km north of Melbourne. Ned Kelly was captured alive and eventually hanged in Melbourne.

You can't drive through Glenrowan without being confronted by the commercialisation of the Kelly legend. The town

---

Kelly Country

In the north-east of Victoria is 'Kelly Country', where Australia's most famous outlaw, Ned Kelly, had some of his most exciting brushes with the law. Kelly and his gang of bushrangers shot three police officers at Stringybark Creek in 1878, and robbed banks at Euroa and Jerilderie before their lives of crime ended in a siege at Glenrowan. Ned and members of his family were held and tried in Beechworth, and Kelly was hung at the Old Melbourne Gaol.

Not far to the east of the Hume Highway are the Victorian Alps. In winter you'll catch glimpses of their snow-capped peaks from the highway near Glenrowan. ◼

has everything from a giant statue of Ned (complete with armoured helmet), colonial-style tearooms and souvenir shops, to **'Kellyland'**, an impressive animated computerised theatre ($14 adults, $8 children).

The ruins of the Kelly family homestead can be seen a few km off the highway at Greta, though little remains of the slab bush hut.

WANGARATTA (pop 15,600)

'Wang', as it is commonly known, is at the junction of the King and Ovens rivers; it's also the turn-off point for the Ovens Highway to Mt Buffalo, Bright and the northern section of the Victorian Alps. The town has some pleasant parks, and bush-ranger Mad Dog Morgan is buried in the local cemetery.

At Wangaratta airport, four km east off the Hume Highway, **Airworld** has a collection of 40 vintage aircraft. It's open daily from 9 am to 5 pm and entry costs $6.

Wang has a visitor information centre (☎ 5721 5711) on the corner of the Hume Highway and Handley St – don't miss **Mrs Stell's World in Miniature**! The popular Wangaratta Jazz Festival is held on the weekend before the Melbourne Cup horse race.

Places to Stay

The *Painters Island Caravan Park* (☎ 5721 3380), on the Ovens River, has sites and on-site vans. The *Pinsent Hotel* (☎ 5721 2183), at 30 Reid St, has singles/doubles for $25/40, and *Millers Cottage Motel* (☎ 5721 5755), on the highway north of the centre, has units from $45 a double.

Getting There & Away

V/Line has daily trains between Melbourne and Wang ($27.20), continuing on to Albury ($9.20). Wangaratta Coachlines (☎ 5722 1843) runs buses to Albury-Wodonga, Mt Beauty, Beechworth, Bright, Rutherglen etc.

CHILTERN (pop 1200)

Close to Beechworth and only one km west off the Hume Highway between Wangaratta and Wodonga, Chiltern once swarmed with gold-miners in search of their fortunes. It's now a charming and historic town and is worth a visit.

Author Henry Handel Richardson's home, **Lake View**, is preserved by the National Trust and is open on weekends and school and public holidays from 10 am to 4 pm.

RUTHERGLEN (pop 2000)

Close to the Murray River and north of the Hume, Rutherglen is the centre of one of Victoria's major wine-growing areas and has long been famous for its fortified wines. This is a great area for bike-touring – bikes can be hired from Walkabout Cellars (☎ 6032 9784), at 84 Main St. Bogong Jack's Adventures (☎ 5727 3382), in Oxley near Wangaratta, also offers winery tours by bicycle – ring for details.

Rutherglen itself is an attractive little town with a main street lined with old verandah-fronted buildings. There's a small **historical museum** (open Sunday), and the tourist office (☎ 6032 9166), inside the historic Jolimont Wines complex on the corner of Main and Drummond Sts, is open daily from 9 am to 5 pm.

Festivals include the Winery Walkabout Weekend, held on the Queen's Birthday weekend in June, and the Tastes of Rutherglen Weekend, also in June.

Wahgunyah, nine km north-west, was once a busy port for the Ovens Valley gold towns. Its customs house is a relic of that era.

Wineries

An excellent (and free) map and brochure is available from Walkabout Cellars and the wineries. It guides you around the 15 or so wineries in the area, including **All Saints**, which is classified by the National Trust and has a wine museum; **Chamber's Rosewood**, an old family-run winery close to Rutherglen; **Gherig's Winery**, set around the historic Barnawartha Homestead; **Mt Prior**, with luxurious (and expensive) accommodation and a highly regarded restaurant; and **St Leonard's**, with an excellent

Wineries

Some of Australia's best wines are made in Victoria. Grape growing and wine production began with the gold rush of the 1850s and, before the turn of the century, the fine reputation of Victorian fortified wines was established in Europe. Then phylloxera, a disease of grapevines, devastated the Victorian vineyards. Changing tastes in alcohol completed the destruction.

In the 1960s the Victorian wine industry started to recapture its former glory and produce fine table wines, as well as fortified wines.

Victoria's oldest established wine-producing region is in the north-east, particularly around Rutherglen, but extending to Milawa, Glenrowan and beyond. Other fine wine-growing areas include the Yarra Valley and the Mornington Peninsula near Melbourne; the Geelong region; central Victoria around Bendigo and Heathcote; the Goulburn Valley; the Great Western and Pyrenees ranges (between Stawell, Ararat and Avoca); the Macedon ranges north of Melbourne; and the Murray River valley. ■

bistro and a very scenic picnic spot on a billabong by the Murray River.

Places to Stay & Eat

The *Rutherglen Caravan Park* (☎ 6032 8577) has on-site vans from $24 and sites for $9. On Main St, the National Trust classified *Victoria Hotel* (☎ 6032 9610) charges $25/36 for its basic, old-fashioned rooms, or $55 with en suite. The nearby *Star Hotel* (☎ 6032 9625) is just as old (but not quite as charming) and has rooms from $12/25, or motel-style units from $25/35. Rutherglen's half-dozen motels include the modern *Wine Village Motor Inn* (☎ 6032 9900), at 217 Main St, with singles/doubles from $50/60.

There are tearooms and pubs along Main St and several of the wineries have good restaurants, including St Leonards, All Saints and Mt Prior. At 152 Main St the *Shamrock* is open for dinner from Tuesday to Saturday, with mains in the $15 to $19 range. *Mrs Mouse's Pantry* at Wahgunyah is another good place to eat.

Getting There & Away

V/Line has buses between Wangaratta and Rutherglen ($4) on Wednesday, Friday and Sunday.

WODONGA (pop 29,400)

The Victorian half of Albury-Wodonga is on the Murray River, the border between Vic-

toria and New South Wales. The combined cities form the main economic and industrial centre of this region.

For tourist information there's the Gateway Tourist Information Centre (☎ (02) 6041 3875), on the Lincoln Causeway between Wodonga and the Murray. For more information, see the Albury section in the New South Wales chapter.

Places to Stay

The *Herb & Horse* (☎ (02) 6072 9553), on the Murray River 60 km east of Wodonga, is a great place to stay a while. It's an 1890s homestead and farm, with home-cooked meals, excellent horse-riding and canoe trips. There are shared rooms from $18, doubles from $42 and cottages with B&B from $65 per person. The staff can usually arrange free transport from Albury-Wodonga if you ring in advance.

CORRYONG (pop 1300)

Corryong, the Victorian gateway to the Snowy Mountains and Kosciusko National Park, is close to the source of the Murray River, which at this point is merely an alpine stream.

Corryong's main claim to fame, however, is as the last resting place of Jack Riley, 'the Man from Snowy River'. Though some people dispute that Banjo Paterson based his stockman hero on Riley, a tailor turned mountain man who worked this district, the 'man' is nevertheless well remembered in Corryong.

Jack Riley's grave is in the town cemetery and the **Man from Snowy River Museum**, with local history exhibits, is open daily from 10 am to noon and 2 to 4 pm ($2).

Places to Stay

The town has two caravan parks (both with on-site vans and cabins), a pub and a couple of motels.

YACKANDANDAH (pop 700)

There's a saying around these parts that 'all roads lead to Yackandandah'. Indeed, if you were to get lost in the beautiful hills and valleys of this district you would find that most of the signposts do point to this charming little town.

The pretty little 'strawberry capital', 32 km south of Wodonga, 23 km from Beechworth and always on the way to somewhere, has been classified by the National Trust; not just the odd building but the entire town.

Yackandandah was a prosperous gold town and, back then, a welcome stopover on the old main road between Sydney and Melbourne. It has many fine old buildings, including the 1850 **Bank of Victoria**, which is now a museum. The well-preserved buildings along the main street now house a variety of local craft shops, antique stores, cafes and tearooms.

There are tent sites and on-site vans at the *Yackandandah Caravan Park* (☎ 6027 1380), on the Dederang Rd, close to some good bushwalks.

BEECHWORTH (pop 4100)

This picturesque town set amid the rolling countryside of the Ovens Valley has been attracting tourists for a good many years. Way back in 1927 it won the Melbourne *Sun News Pictorial* 'ideal tourist town' competition.

It is still a pleasure to visit Beechworth and spend a few days enjoying its wide tree-lined streets with their fine and dignified gold-rush architecture, or exploring the surrounding forested valleys, waterfalls and rocky gorges. It's a perfect place for walking or cycling.

The town is 35 km east of Wangaratta, and if you're travelling between Wang and Wodonga the detour through Beechworth makes a worthwhile alternative to the frenetic pace of the Hume Highway.

Information

The Beechworth Visitor Information Centre (☎ 5728 3233) is inside the old Shire Hall on Ford St, and is open daily from 9 am to 5 pm.

Things to See

In the 1850s Beechworth was the very prosperous hub of the Ovens River gold-mining region. Signs of the gold wealth are still very much in evidence, reflected in the fact that 32 buildings are classified by the National Trust. They include **Tanswell's Hotel** with its magnificent old lacework, the **post office** with its clock tower, and the **training prison** where Ned Kelly and his mother were imprisoned for a while.

The five-km **Gorge Scenic Drive** takes you past the 1859 **powder magazine**, now a National Trust museum that is open 10 am to noon and 1 to 4 pm daily ($1.30). The National Trust's **Carriage Museum**, on Railway Ave, is open during the same hours ($1.50), and the **Beechworth Stagecoach** offers horse-drawn carriage rides around town ($5).

The very well presented and interesting **Burke Museum**, in Loch St, has an eclectic collection of relics from the gold rush and a replica of the main street a century ago, complete with 16 shopfronts – well worth the $4 entry. The hapless explorer Robert O'Hara Burke was the superintendent of police in Beechworth during the early days of the gold rush before he set off on his historic trek north with William Wills.

Other things of interest in and around Beechworth include the historic **Murray Brewery Cellars**, established in 1872, on the corner of William and Last Sts; the **historic courthouse** on Ford St, site of Ned Kelly's

VICTORIA

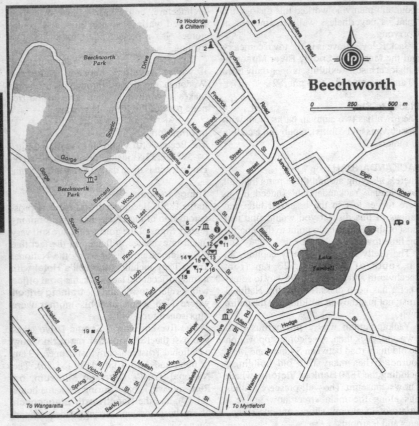

Beechworth

0   250   500 m

PLACES TO STAY

5   Finches of Beechworth
6   Rose Cottage
9   Lake Sambell Caravan Park
18   Tanswell's Commercial Hotel
19   Burnbrae

PLACES TO EAT

12   The Bank
14   Parlour & Pantry
15   Beechworth Bakery
16   Chinese Village

17   Caffe CC

OTHER

1   Beechworth Cemetery
2   Golden Horseshoes Monument
3   Powder Magazine
4   Murray Brewery Cellars
7   Burke Museum
8   Shire Hall & Tourist Office
10   Historic Courthouse
11   DC&NR Office
13   Post Office
20   Carriage Museum

first court appearance; the **Chinese burning towers** and **Beechworth Cemetery**, where the towers, altar and many graves are all that remain of the town's huge Chinese population during the gold rush; and the **Golden Horseshoes Monument** to a local pioneer who made gold horseshoes for his friend who had won a seat in parliament to represent the local miners.

Woolshed Falls, just out of town on the Chiltern road, is a popular picnic area and the site of a major alluvial goldfield that yielded over 85,000 kg of gold in 14 years. Farther west at **Eldorado** a gigantic gold dredge slowly rusts on the lake where it was installed in 1936.

Places to Stay

The *Lake Sambell Caravan Park* (☎ 5728 1421, on McConville Ave, has tent sites from $11, on-site vans from $28 and cabins from $36. At 30 Ford St, *Tanswell's Commercial Hotel* (☎ 5728 1480) has B&B singles/doubles for $25/40 ($35/55 weekends).

Beechworth has a great selection of B&Bs and cottages. One of the best is *Rose Cottage* (☎ 5728 1069), at 42 Camp St, charging $60/85 for B&B. *Burnbrae* (☎ 5728 1091) is a picturesque Victorian cottage on Gorge Rd on the edge of town, and rooms cost from $75/95. For a splurge, *Finches of Beechworth* (☎ 5728 2655), at 3 Finch St, offers B&B at $150 a double ($230 with dinner) in a magnificent Victorian house.

Five km out of town towards Chiltern, the self-contained *Woolshed Cabins* (☎ 5728 1035) sleep up to five people, and cost from $51 for two plus $8 per extra adult.

Places to Eat

At 69 Ford St, the *Parlour & Pantry* is an excellent (if somewhat pricey) gourmet deli and restaurant. *Caffe CC*, across the road at 52 Ford St, is a cosy BYO with good pastas and risottos ($11.50) and other mains ($14); it also does a mean cooked breakfast.

Tanswell's Hotel has bar meals from $4 to $10 and a good bistro, and the *Chinese Village* at 11-15 Camp St has $4 takeaway lunches. The big *Beechworth Bakery* on Camp St has an irresistible selection of hot bread, cakes and home-made pies. On a sunny morning, the tables on the footpath are an excellent place for a coffee and fresh croissant breakfast.

Beechworth's most up-market restaurant is the *Bank*, housed in the historic Bank of Australasia building at 86 Ford St.

Getting There & Around

V/Line has daily services between Melbourne and Beechworth ($31.80), changing from train to bus at Wangaratta. Wangaratta Coachlines (☎ 5722 1843) runs local buses to Albury-Wodonga, Bright and Rutherglen, and Beechworth Bicycle Hire (☎ 5328 2066), at 79 Ford St, has mountain bikes for hire.

BRIGHT (pop 3000)

Deep in the Ovens Valley, Bright has become one of the focal points for adventure activities in the High Country. Renowned for its gorgeous setting, the town celebrates its contrasting seasonal beauty during the Bright Autumn Festival and the Alpine Spring Festival. In 1857 the notorious Buckland Valley riots took place near here; the diligent Chinese gold-miners were forced off their claims and given much less than a fair go. It is about an hour's scenic drive from town to the snowfields of Mt Hotham and Falls Creek, and a half-hour to Mt Buffalo.

The tourist information centre (☎ 5755 2275) in Delany Ave is open daily from 9 am to 5 pm.

Activities

There are plenty of walking trails around here and the tourist office has a *Bright Walking Tracks* brochure, which details eight great walks from 1½ to five km long.

The Bright Sports Centre (☎ 5755 1339) hires out mountain bikes, and Freeburgh Horse Trails (☎ 5755 1370) and Bright High Country Safaris (☎ 5755 1896) both offer horse rides from short trots to overnight treks.

If you want to get airborne, Alpine

Paragliding (☎ 5755 1753) and the Eagle School of Hang-Gliding (☎ 5755 1724) both offer introductory flights and full certificate courses.

Places to Stay

One of about a dozen caravan parks in town, the *Bright Municipal Caravan Park* (☎ 5755 1141) on Cherry Lane also has a very good associate-YHA hostel with beds at $15 ($18 nonmembers). The park's tent sites are $11 to $14 and its on-site cabins $36 to $60.

The modern and well-equipped *Bright Hikers Backpackers' Hostel* (☎ 5750 1244), in the centre of town at 4 Ireland St, has dorm beds at $14 and twins/doubles at $30 – the owners can help with arrangements for numerous activities.

The *Alpine Hotel* (☎ 5755 1366) at 7 Anderson St has motel units from $40 to $45, and the *Elm Lodge Motel* (☎ 5755 1144) at 2 Wood St is one of the best-value motels with singles/doubles from $32/35. There are dozens of other accommodation options here – the tourist centre runs a helpful booking service.

Places to Eat

The *Liquid Am-Bar* on Anderson St is a fun cafe/bar with an interesting and affordable menu. *Alps Pasta & Pizza* on Gavan St has cheap pizzas, pastas and Mexican food.

Getting There & Away

Melbourne to Bright costs $36.40 with V/Line; there are daily trains to Wangaratta and connecting bus services (every day except Saturday) continuing on to Beechworth.

The Alps

The Victorian Alps are the southern end of the Great Dividing Range, which runs all the way down Australia's east coast through Queensland and New South Wales into Victoria's north-east, finishing with a flourish at the Grampians in the state's west.

The Victorian ski fields are at lower altitudes than those in New South Wales, but they receive as much snow and have similar conditions above and below the snow line. The two largest ski resorts are Mt Buller and Falls Creek. Mt Hotham is smaller, but has equally good skiing, while Mt Buffalo and Mt Baw Baw are smaller resorts popular with families and novice to intermediate skiers. Lake Mountain, Mt Stirling and Mt St Gwinear are all mainly cross-country skiing areas with no overnight accommodation. Dinner Plain, near Mt Hotham, is an architect designed village above the snow line (and it has a great pub!).

The roads are fully sealed to all ski resorts except Mt Baw Baw, Mt Stirling and Dinner Plain. In winter, snow chains must be carried to all ski resorts (you may be turned back if you haven't got them) and driving conditions can be hazardous. Other roads that crisscross the Great Dividing Range are unsealed for at least part of their way and only traversable in summer.

The skiing season officially commences on the first weekend of June, and skiable snow usually arrives later in the month. Spring skiing can be good as it is sunny and warm with no crowds, and there's usually enough snow until the end of September.

In the summer months, especially from December to February, the area is ideal for bushwalking, rock climbing, fishing, camping, and observing the native flora and fauna. Other activities include canoeing, rafting, hang-gliding, mountain-biking, horse trekking and paragliding.

Bushwalkers should be self-sufficient, with a tent, a fuel stove, warm clothes and sleeping bag, and plenty of water. In the height of summer, you can walk all day in the heat without finding water, and then face temperatures below freezing at night.

Places to Stay

There are many places to stay, especially in the ski resorts, which have lots of accommodation. Overall, these are very expensive in winter and many people prefer to stay in towns below the snow line and drive up to

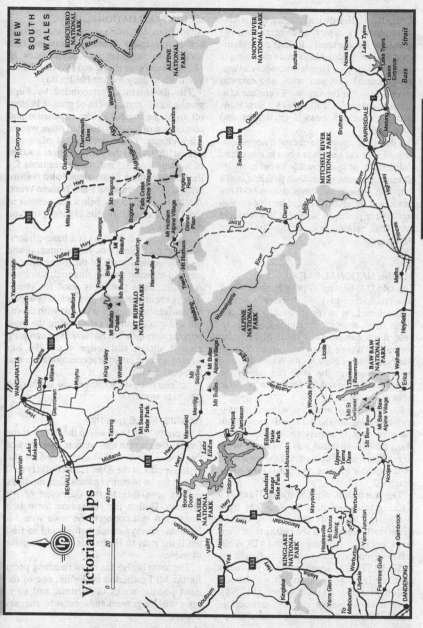

Victorian Alps

0   20   40 km

the ski fields. In July and August it is advisable to book your accommodation, especially for weekends. In June or September it is usually possible to find something if you just turn up. Hotels, motels, chalets, self-contained flats and units, and caravan parks abound in the region. There are also youth hostels at Mt Buller and Mt Baw Baw, plus backpackers hostels in Bright and Mansfield.

Apart from these, the cheapest accommodation in the ski resorts is a bed in one of the club lodges, or it is possible to cut costs by cramming as many people as possible into a flat. The various accommodation-booking services at the resorts should be able to help you find a place. In summer, bushwalkers may find bargain accommodation in the skiing areas.

ALPINE NATIONAL PARK

The 646,000-hectare Alpine National Park was proclaimed in 1989. Victoria's largest national park, it covers most of the state's prime 'high country' stretching from Mansfield north-east to the New South Wales border, and is contiguous with the Kosciusko National Park in New South Wales. Most of the ski resorts in the state fall within the park's boundaries, and access is possible from many points.

Bushwalking and, in winter, cross-country skiing are the main activities within the park as it is largely undeveloped, and plans are to keep it that way. For many years large areas that are now part of the park were used for cattle grazing, but this is now being restricted.

The **Australian Alps Walking Track** is a walking trail that runs for 655 km from Walhalla, near Mt Baw Baw, to the Brindabella Ranges on the outskirts of Canberra. For more information, visit a DC&NR office or contact the rangers in Bright on ☎ 5755 1577. The department also publishes an excellent 70-page colour guidebook called *Into the High Country* ($17.95). Several alpine walks are also covered in Lonely Planet's *Bushwalking in Australia*.

MT BUFFALO NATIONAL PARK

Apart from Mt Buffalo itself, the park is noted for its many pleasant streams and fine walks. The mountain was named back in 1824 by explorers Hume and Hovell on their trek from Sydney to Port Phillip Bay.

The mountain is surrounded by huge granite tors – great blocks of granite broken off from the massif by the expansion and contraction of ice in winter and other weathering effects. There is abundant plant and animal life around the park, and over 140 km of walking tracks. Leaflets are available for the **Gorge Nature Walk**, **View Point Nature Walk** and the **Dicksons Falls Nature Walk**. A road leads up to just below the summit of the 1720-metre Horn, the highest point on the massif.

In summer Mt Buffalo is a hang-gliders' paradise (definitely not for beginners) and the near-vertical walls of the gorge provide some of the most challenging rock climbs in Australia. **Lake Catani** is good for swimming, camping and canoeing, while in winter Mt Buffalo turns into a ski resort with downhill and cross-country skiing being the most popular activities. Mt Buffalo has a camping ground, chalet and lodge – see the Ski Resorts section later for accommodation and transport details.

An entry fee of $6.50 per car is charged ($9.50 in winter).

HARRIETVILLE (pop 100)

This pretty little town sits in the valley at the fork of the eastern and western branches of the Ovens River, and is surrounded by the highest peaks in the Alps. Harrietville is well known for its beautiful natural surroundings and its proximity to the ski resort of Mt Hotham. During the ski season there is a shuttle bus that connects the town with Mt Hotham. Always check beforehand to find out if the road to Hotham is closed because of snow.

The town is also the usual finishing point for the Mt Feathertop bushwalk, one of the most popular walks in Victoria, and so is busy on long weekends outside the ski season.

VICTORIA

Places to Stay

The *Harrietville Caravan Park* (☎ 5759 2523) has sites and on-site vans. The rambling *Bon Accord* (☎ 5759 2530) isn't exactly flash, but it has basic facilities and backpackers' beds for $15. The *Snowline Hotel* (☎ 5759 2524) has motel rooms from $35/50, and the *Alpine Lodge Inn* (☎ 5759 2525) has motel-style B&B from $30/60.

OMEO (pop 270)

This small town is on the Omeo Highway, the southern access route to the snowfields of Mt Hotham during winter. In summer it's a popular departure point for the Bogong High Plains. Rafting trips take place on the nearby Mitta Mitta River.

Omeo still has a handful of interesting old buildings despite the disastrous bushfire and two earthquakes that have occurred since 1885. Omeo's **log jail, courthouse** and **historical museum** are worth searching out. The town also had its own little gold rush.

Places to Stay

The *Holston Tourist Park* (☎ 5159 1351) has tent sites from $9 and on-site vans from $28. *Colonial Bank House* (☎ 5159 1388) has four small self-contained units at $40/55, and the *Golden Age Hotel* (☎ 5159 1344) has B&B for $25 per person.

Getting There & Away

There is a weekday bus between Omeo and Bairnsdale ($22.90) operated by Omeo Buslines (☎ 5159 4231).

SKI RESORTS

Skiing in Victoria goes back to the 1860s when Norwegian gold-miners introduced it in Harrietville. It has grown into a multimillion-dollar industry with three major ski resorts and six minor ski areas. None of these resorts is connected to another by a lift system, but it is possible for the experienced and well-equipped cross-country skier to go from Mt Hotham to Falls Creek across the Bogong High Plains. There is an annual race that covers this route.

The Alpine Resorts Commission (ARC;

☎ 9895 6900) is responsible for managing the ski resorts and on-mountain information centres. Resort entry fees at most resorts are $15 per car per day in winter. For cross-country skiers, there's a $5 trail-use fee at all resorts.

Falls Creek (1780 metres)

This resort sits at the edge of the Bogong High Plains overlooking the Kiewa Valley, a five-hour, 375-km drive from Melbourne. Falls Creek is one of the best resorts in Victoria and the only ski village in Australia where everyone can ski directly from their lodge to the lifts and from the slopes back to their lodge.

The skiing is spread over two bowls with 30 km of trails, 23 lifts and a vertical drop of 267 metres. Runs are divided into 17% beginners, 53% intermediate and 30% advanced. A day ticket costs $52, a seven-day ticket costs $290 and a daily lift and lesson package costs $73. Entry fees are $15 per car, and the ARC (☎ 5758 3224) has an information office in the lower car park.

You'll find some of the best cross-country skiing in Australia here. A trail leads around Rocky Valley pondage to some old huts from the cattle days. The more adventurous can tour to the white summits of Nelse, Cope and Spion Kopjc. You can choose between ski-skating on groomed trails; light touring with day packs; and general touring with heavier packs, usually involving an overnight stay in a tent. Cross-country downhill, the alternative to skiing on crowded, noisy slopes, is also popular.

In summer there are plenty of opportunities for alpine walking to places like Ruined Castle, Ropers Lookout, Wallaces Hut and Mt Nelse, which is part of the Alpine Walking Track.

Places to Stay There is very little cheap accommodation in Falls Creek in winter. Falls Creek Central Reservations (☎ 1800 033 079) can help you find accommodation on the mountain.

A number of ski lodges offer B&B plus dinner packages per week or weekend. One of the best and cheapest is the *Silver Ski Lodge* (☎ 5758 3375), costing from $470 to $820 per person weekly, depending on the season; however, it's normally fully booked during peak seasons. The small *Four Seasons Lodge* (☎ 5758 3254) costs from $55 to $85 per person daily, or $350 to $540 weekly.

In summer, the *Attunga Lodge* (☎ 5758 3255) and the *Pretty Valley Alpine Lodge* (☎ 5758 3210) both cost about $68 per person daily for dinner and B&B.

Cafe Max in the village bowl is a good bistro/bar, and *Winterhaven* is about the best restaurant. The *Frying Pan* and the *Man* are both popular nightspots, with live bands and other entertainment.

Four km below Falls Creek, Sport & Recreation Victoria's *Howman's Gap Alpine Centre* (☎ 5758 3228) is an adventure activity camp that caters mainly for groups. Daily costs range from about $26 per person in summer to $46 in winter, which includes all meals.

Getting There & Around During the ski season, Pyles Coaches (☎ 5754 4024) runs buses to and from Melbourne every day for $49/90 one way/return, and it also has daily services to and from Albury ($23/46) and Mt Beauty ($12/24). There is over-snow transport available from the car park to the lodges and back again.

Mt Baw Baw (1480 metres)

This is a small resort in the Baw Baw National Park, with eight lifts on the edge of the Baw Baw plateau. It is 173 km and an easy three-hour drive from Melbourne, via Noojee. It's popular with novices and families and is more relaxed and less crowded than the main resorts. Runs are 25% beginners, 64% intermediate and 11% advanced, with a vertical drop of 140 metres. There are plenty of cross-country trails, including one that connects to the Mt St Gwinear trails on the southern edge of the plateau.

Car entry fees are $15 and a day ticket costs $38; the ARC (☎ 5165 1136) office is in the village.

Places to Stay The only cheap place is the YHA *Baw Baw Youth Hostel* (☎ 5165 1129), which is in the village and close to all the facilities. It's only open during the ski season, and dorm accommodation costs $32 a night ($34 for nonmembers). Bookings are essential.

The ARC (☎ 5165 1136) can advise you on other accommodation options.

Getting There & Away There are no public transport services between Melbourne and Mt Baw Baw.

Mt Buffalo (1400 metres)

This magnificent national park (also covered earlier in this section) is 333 km from Melbourne and takes about four hours. The winter entry fee is $9.50 per car.

It is another small place more suited to intermediate and beginner skiers, but it has challenging cross-country skiing. Tatra is a picturesque and not overly expensive village, but the downhill skiing is not very good and the snow does not last as long as at some of the other resorts. There are a number of cross-country loops, and one of the trails goes to the base of the Horn, which skiers climb on foot.

The walks are also interesting and take the walker beneath towering granite monoliths.

Places to Stay The *Lake Catani Campground* (☎ 5755 1577) next to the lake has sites from $8 in winter and $12 in summer.

The *Mt Buffalo Chalet* (☎ 5755 1500) was the first place built on the mountain and it still has the charm of the 1920s. Tariffs range from $96 to $150 per person, including all meals.

The modern *Tatra Inn* (☎ 5755 1988) has backpacker bunk rooms from $15 ($17 to $29 in winter), and motel-style units with dinner B&B from $69 per person ($79 to $105 in winter). Both of these places have a restaurant and offer ski hire.

Getting There & Away The closest you can get by public transport is to Bright by bus –

from there, a taxi to Mt Buffalo costs about $35.

Mt Buller (1600 metres)

Less than a three-hour drive from Melbourne and only 246 km away, Mt Buller is the most popular (and crowded) resort in Victoria, especially on the weekends. It has a large lift network with 26 lifts, including a chair lift that begins in the car park and ends in the middle of the ski runs. Runs are 25% beginners, 45% intermediate and 30% advanced, and there's even night skiing until 10 pm on Wednesday, Thursday and Saturday.

In years of light snow cover, Buller is skied out much sooner than Falls Creek or Mt Hotham, though snow-making equipment now extends the season on the main beginners' area. Cross-country skiing is possible around Buller and there is access to Mt Stirling, which has some good trails.

A day ticket costs $52, a seven-day ticket $299, and a daily lift and lesson package costs $72 ($52 for beginners). The entry fee is $15 per car, and the ARC (☎ 5777 6077) office is in the village.

Places to Stay There is plenty of accommodation. The *Mt Buller Youth Hostel* (☎ 5777 6181) is, of course, the cheapest on the mountain. It's only open during the ski season, and the nightly rate is $42 for members, $46 for nonmembers. You'll need to book well in advance; ring or write to PO Box 23, Mt Buller 3723.

Club lodges are the best value, starting at about $32 per person per night, with bunk accommodation and kitchen facilities; contact the Mt Buller Accommodation & Information office (☎ 5777 6280 or ☎ 1800 039 049).

Getting There & Around V/Line has buses twice-daily from Melbourne to Mansfield, costing $25 each way. In winter, Mansfield-Mt Buller Buslines (☎ 5775 2606) runs connecting bus services up to Mt Buller, costing $17/28 one way/return. Mt Buller Snowcaper Day Tours (☎ 1800 033 023) has day trips on weekends ($99) and Monday,

Wednesday and Friday ($85), which includes return transport from Melbourne, lift tickets and a lesson; gear hire is another $17.

In winter, there is an over-snow transport shuttle service that moves people around the village and to and from the car park; fares range from $3.20 to $7.50. Day-trippers can take the quad chair lift from the car park into the skiing area and save time and money by bypassing the village. There are ski rental facilities in the car park. Cross-country skiers turn-off for Mt Stirling at the Mt Buller entrance gate at the base of the mountain. There are day facilities and fast food is available at Telephone Box Junction.

Mt Hotham (1750 metres)

Known as Australia's powder capital, Hotham does get the lightest snow in the country, but don't expect anything like Europe or North America. It's about a 5½-hour drive from Melbourne. You can take either the Hume Highway via Harrietville or the Princes Highway via Omeo – ring the ARC to check road conditions before setting off.

The lift system here is not well integrated and some walking is necessary, even though the 'zoo cart' (see Getting There & Around) along the main road offers some relief. The skiing here is good: there are 10 lifts, and runs are 23% beginners, 37% intermediate and 40% advanced. This is a skiers' mountain with a vertical drop of 428 metres and the nightlife mainly happening in ski lodges. There is some good off-piste skiing in steep and narrow valleys. A day ticket costs $51, a seven-day pass $270, and a lift and lesson package $69. Car entry costs $15. The ARC (☎ 5759 3550) has an information office in the village centre.

Cross-country skiing is good around Hotham and ski touring is very good on the Bogong High Plains, which you can cross to Falls Creek. This is also the starting point for trips across the Razorback to beautiful Mt Feathertop. Below the village, on the eastern side, there is a series of trails that runs as far as Dinner Plain. The biathlon (shooting and skiing) course between Mt Hotham and Dinner Plain is here at Wire Plain.

Places to Stay Most of the accommodation is in private and commercial lodges. It is possible to find beds in these or apartments through the Mt Hotham Accommodation Service (☎ 1800 032 061) or Skicom (☎ 5759 3522).

The *Jack Frost Lodge* (☎ 5759 3586) has one and two-bedroom apartments costing anywhere from $720 to $2600 per week, depending on the season and number of people. The huge *Arlberg Inn* (☎ 9889 0647) also has apartments sleeping from two to eight people; weekly rates start from $600 for two people and from $1340 for eight people. *Zirky's* (☎ 5759 3518) has six double rooms at $100 per person per night for B&B. A couple of places here open during summer – check with the booking services for details.

It is also possible to stay at Dinner Plain, 11 km from Mt Hotham Village, where there are cabins, lodges and B&Bs; ring one of the booking services on ☎ 5159 6426 or ☎ 5159 6451.

Getting There & Around In winter, Trekset Snow Services (☎ 9370 9055) has daily buses from Melbourne to Mt Hotham (twice on Friday), costing $65/90 one way/return. It also has daily services between Hotham and Myrtleford, Bright and Harrietville; fares range from $16 to $25, depending on when you're going.

The village was built on a ridge almost at the top of the mountain and is strung out along the road. Luckily, there are shuttle buses that run frequently all the way along the ridge from 7 am to 1 am (to 3 am on Saturday) at $1 a ride; the free 'zoo cart' takes skiers from their lodges to the lifts between 8.15 am and 5.45 pm. Another shuttle service operates to Dinner Plain.

Other Resorts

There are five other snowfields, although they're mainly for cross-country skiing or sightseeing and have no accommodation. For more information, contact their respec-

tive information offices on the numbers given below.

Lake Mountain (☎ 5963 3288) is 120 km from Melbourne via Marysville. The cross-country facility here is world class, with over 40 km of trails that are groomed daily.

Skiing for the experienced is found around the summit of Victoria's highest peak, **Mt Bogong**. Here, steep gullies tempt the cross-country downhill skier. Accommodation is in tents and in mountain huts. This area is not for beginners.

Mt St Gwinear (☎ 5165 3204) is 171 km from Melbourne via Moe and has connecting cross-country ski trails with Mt Baw Baw.

Mt Stirling (☎ 5777 5624) is a few km from Mt Buller and is another cross-country ski area, with more than 60 km of mostly groomed trails.

Mt Donna Buang is the closest to Melbourne (95 km via Warburton), but is mainly for sightseeing and tobogganing.

Gippsland

The Gippsland region is the south-east slice of Victoria. It stretches from Western Port, near Melbourne, to the New South Wales border on the east coast, with the Great Dividing Range to the north.

Named in 1839 by the Polish explorer Count Paul Strzelecki after Sir George Gipps, the former governor of New South Wales, Gippsland was first settled by prospectors in the 1850s, then by farmers after the completion of the railway from Melbourne in 1887. Extremely fertile, Gippsland is now the focus of the state's dairy industry.

The region can be divided into four distinct sections: West Gippsland, which is dominated by Victoria's industrial heartland, the Latrobe Valley; South Gippsland, which includes the wonderful Wilsons Promontory National Park; the Gippsland Lakes, Australia's largest system of inland waterways; and East Gippsland, an area of often breathtaking beauty known as the Wilderness Coast.

Gippsland

Getting There & Away

The Princes Highway runs from Melbourne to Bairnsdale through the Latrobe Valley, and then follows the coastline into New South Wales. For a slower but more scenic drive you could follow the South Gippsland Highway, which heads south-east from Melbourne towards Phillip Island and the Prom, rejoining the Princes Highway at Sale, 214 km from Melbourne.

V/Line trains between Melbourne and Sale ($25) operate thrice-daily on weekdays and twice-daily on weekends; there are connecting bus services from Sale to Bairnsdale ($7). V/Line also operates a daily bus service around the Princes Highway as far as Narooma in New South Wales via Lakes Entrance ($38.60) and Genoa ($47). Greyhound Pioneer also ply this coastal route.

WEST GIPPSLAND & THE LATROBE VALLEY

The Latrobe Valley contains one of the world's largest deposits of brown coal, and its mines and power stations supply most of Victoria's electricity, while the offshore wells in Bass Strait provide most of Australia's petroleum and natural gas. Although the major towns along the Princes Highway are predominantly residential and industrial centres for the various workforces, the regions surrounding this industrial landscape are surprisingly beautiful. The Princes Highway provides access to a number of very scenic areas, including the idyllic and historic former gold-mining township of Walhalla and the gourmet delights of the Neerim South region.

Warragul (pop 13,000)

A regional centre for the district's dairy farms, which provide most of Melbourne's milk, Warragul is the first major town east of Dandenong. **Darnum Musical Village**, about eight km east of the town centre, is an old church with a collection of musical instruments. It is open daily from 10 am to 4 pm; tours cost $8.

Places to Stay The *Warragul Caravan Park* (☎ 5623 2707) in Burke St has tent sites and on-site vans, and *Warradine* (☎ 5623 1626), in an old pub at 73 Queen St, has B&B at $30/45.

Moe (pop 25,000)

The main attraction of this coal-mining centre is the **Old Gippsland Pioneer Township**, on the Princes Highway, which is open daily from 9 am to 5 pm ($7) with a collection of 30 or more 19th-century buildings. The place has an authentic feel to it, with working displays of old crafts and rides in horse-drawn vehicles. Devonshire teas are served in the historic **Bushy Park Homestead** on Sunday.

You can visit **Yallourn Power Station** from Moe, and the former site of the township of **Yallourn**, which was moved lock, stock and barrel to provide access to the brown-coal deposits underneath. From the hill behind the town site there is a lookout with some information for visitors and views of the vast open-cut mine area.

There's a scenic road from Moe north to Walhalla, the Baw Baw National Park and Mt Erica, from where a secondary road continues north across the Victorian Alps. You can get onto the panoramic Grand Ridge Road across the Strzelecki Ranges easily from either Trafalgar or Moe by turning south via the lovely little townships of Narracan or Thorpdale.

Morwell (pop 15,500)

Founded in the 1880s as a supply centre for diggers heading for the goldfields at Walhalla, these days Morwell is an industrial town servicing the massive open-cut mine, Hazelwood Power Station, Australian Paper's pulp mills and the local briquette works.

Powerworks (☎ 5135 3415), signposted off Commercial Rd, houses models and displays of the Latrobe Valley's coal-mining and power-generating activities. There are also guided tours of the Morwell open-cut mine and Hazelwood Power Station. The small Morwell National Park is 15 km south of town.

Places to Stay *Morwell Caravan Park*
(☎ 5134 3507) is on Maryvale Crescent, and
the *Hazelwood Motor Inn* (☎ 5134 4222) at
259 Princes Highway has good rooms at
$60/66.

Traralgon (pop 20,600)
The original township was a rest stop and
supply base for miners and drovers heading
farther into the gold and farming country of
Gippsland. It is now the centre of the state's
paper and pulp industry and a major Latrobe
Valley electricity centre. Its future is assured
by the colossal Loy Yang Power Station, six
km to the south.

Places to Stay Accommodation is available
at the *Park Lane Caravan Park* (☎ 5174
6749) on Park Lane, and at the *Grand Junction Hotel* (☎ 5174 6011), Franklin St, which
has singles/doubles for $27.50/45.

Walhalla (pop 30)
At the end of 1862 Edward Stringer, one of
a small party of prospectors who had made
it over the mountains, found gold in a creek
running through a deep wooded valley north
of Moe. The Stringer's Creek gold attracted
about 200 miners but it was the later discovery of Cohen's Reef, an outcrop reef almost
two miles long, that put Walhalla on the map.

Work began on the Long Tunnel Mine, the
single most profitable mine in Victoria, in
1865 and continued for 49 years. Walhalla
reached its peak between 1885 and 1890
when there were over 4000 people living in
and around the town.

The railway line from Moe, incorporating
a truly amazing section of tunnels and trestle
bridges between Erica and Walhalla, was
finally completed in 1910, just as the town's
fortunes began to decline.

Although the population is tiny these
days, there's plenty to see in Walhalla and the
area is quite beautiful. There are a number of
old buildings (some of which are classified
by the National Trust), a museum and a very
interesting cemetery. The **Long Tunnel
Extended Gold Mine** is open daily for tours;
entrance is $4.

South of Walhalla, there is a car park and
marked trail to the summit of Mt Erica, the
start of the Australian Alps Walking Track.

Places to Stay There are camp sites along
the creek. The *Old Hospital* (☎ 5165 6246)
is now a guesthouse with B&B at $40/80
(weekends only), and the self-contained *Log
Cabin* (☎ 5176 2741) sleeps up to eight and
costs $70 a night.

Sale (pop 14,050)
At the junction of the Princes and South
Gippsland highways, Sale is a supply centre
for the Bass Strait oil fields. Points of interest
include the **Cobb & Co Stables & Market**,
a craft market and amusement centre, at 199
Raymond St; a **fauna park & bird sanctuary** near Lake Gutheridge; an **art gallery** at
70 Foster St; and the gardens and tearooms
at the historic **Bon Accord Homestead** (see
Places to Stay).

There's a tourist information centre
(☎ 5144 1108) on the Princes Highway, open
daily from 9 am to 5 pm.

Places to Stay The *Thomson River Caravan
Park* (☎ 5144 1102) has all the usual facilities. The *Star Hotel* (☎ 5144 2024) at 173
Raymond St has B&B at $25 per person, and
at 153 Dawson St, *Bon Accord Homestead*
(☎ 5144 5555) has excellent B&B at
$80/100.

SOUTH GIPPSLAND
South Gippsland is an area of great natural
beauty, with rolling hills, forested mountains
and a rugged and spectacular coastline. The
area's major feature is Wilsons Promontory,
one of Victoria's most loved national parks.
The main road through here is the South
Gippsland Highway, but the back roads
through the hills, and the coastal route, are
more scenic and worth exploring if you have
enough time.

The Strzelecki Ranges
Between the Latrobe Valley and South
Gippsland's coastal areas are the beautiful
'blue' rounded hills of the Strzelecki Ranges.

The winding **Grand Ridge Road**, which runs along the ridge of these ranges and past the wonderful Tarra Bulga National Park, is a spectacular but rough scenic route through fertile farmland that was once covered with forests of mountain ash.

A good base for this area is the township of **Mirboo North**, which straddles the Grand Ridge Road south of Trafalgar. The town boasts the **Grand Ridge Brewery & Restaurant** in the old Butter Factory building. The complex not only produces a range of quality beers but also features a cosy bar and a good bistro. There's a caravan park opposite the shire hall, and the *Commercial Hotel* (☎ 5668 1552) has singles/doubles from $35/45.

The **Tarra Bulga National Park**, at the eastern end of the Grand Ridge Road, is one of the last remnants of the magnificent forests that once covered this area. There are several good picnic areas and some lovely nature walks, and there's the 1930s-style *Tarra Bulga Guesthouse* (☎ 5196 6141), with accommodation from $55 per person including three meals a day.

Korumburra (pop 2910)

The **Coal Creek Historical Village**, a very popular re-creation of a coal-mining town of the 19th century, is near Korumburra. Coal was first discovered here in 1872 and the Coal Creek Mine operated from the 1890s right up to 1958. The park is open daily and entry costs $6 for adults and $3 for children.

Port Albert

This quaint little fishing village was one of Victoria's earliest settlements, and it has a large number of historic buildings. It's also a popular fishing spot.

There are two caravan parks, and the *Port Albert Hotel* (☎ 5183 2212) has motel units with B&B for $50 a double and good bistro meals.

WILSONS PROMONTORY

'The Prom' is one of the most popular national parks in Australia. It covers the peninsula that forms the southernmost part of the Australian mainland. The Prom offers more than 80 km of walking tracks and a wide variety of beaches – whether you want surfing, safe swimming or a secluded beach all to yourself, you can find it on the Prom. Finally there's the wildlife, which abounds despite the park's popularity. There are wonderful birds (including emus), kangaroos and, at night, plenty of wombats. The wildlife around Tidal River is very tame and can even become a nuisance.

Information

The DC&NR office (☎ 5680 9555) at Tidal River is open daily from 8.30 am to 4.30 pm. The displays here are excellent. The park office takes reservations for accommodation and issues camping permits. The office is also where you pay your park entry fee ($6.50 per car) if the main gate is not staffed.

Activities

It's probably walkers who get the best value from the Prom, though you don't have to go very far from the car parks to really get away from it all. The park office at Tidal River has free leaflets on walks ranging from 15-minute strolls from Tidal River to overnight and longer hikes. You can also get detailed maps of the park.

The walking tracks take you through ever-changing scenery: swamps, forests, marshes, valleys of tree ferns and long beaches lined with sand dunes. For serious exploration, it's really worth buying a copy of *Discovering the Prom on Foot* ($6.95) from the park office.

Don't miss the **Mt Oberon** walk. It starts from the Mt Oberon car park, takes one hour and is about three km each way. The views from the summit are excellent.

It's a long day walk from the Mt Oberon car park to the south-east point of the Prom, and by prior arrangement (☎ 5680 8529) it's possible to visit the lighthouse. Another popular walk is the Squeaky Beach Nature Walk, a lovely 1½-hour stroll around to the next bay and back.

The northern area of the park is much less visited, simply because all the facilities are

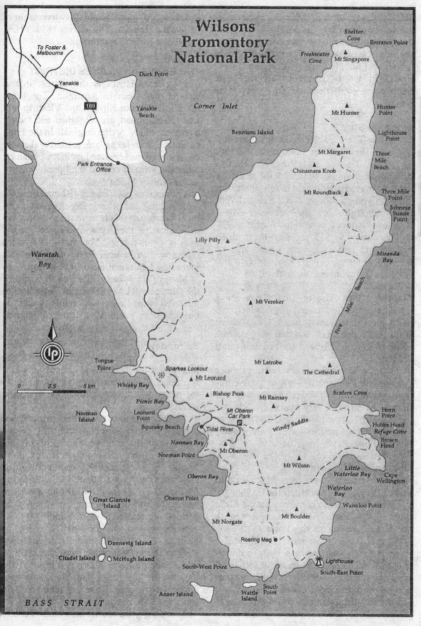

Wilsons Promontory National Park

To Foster & Melbourne

Yanakie

189

Duck Point

Yanakie Beach

Corner Inlet

Bennison Island

Park Entrance Office

Shelter Cove

Entrance Point

Freshwater Cove

Mt Singapore

Mt Hunter

Hunter Point

Lighthouse Point

Three Mile Beach

Mt Margaret

Chinamans Knob

Mt Roundback

Three Mile Point

Johnnie Sussie Point

Waratah Bay

Lilly Pilly

Miranda Bay

Mt Vereker

Five Mile Beach

Tongue Point

Sparkes Lookout

Mt Latrobe

The Cathedral

Whisky Bay

Mt Leonard

Sealers Cove

Picnic Bay

Bishop Peak

Mt Ramsay

Horn Point

Leonard Point

Mt Oberon Car Park

Windy Saddle

Hobbs Head

Refuge Cove

Squeaky Beach

Tidal River

Brown Head

Norman Island

Norman Bay

Mt Oberon

Norman Point

Mt Wilson

Little Waterloo Bay

Cape Wellington

Oberon Bay

Waterloo Bay

Great Glennie Island

Oberon Point

Mt Norgate

Mt Boulder

Waterloo Point

Roaring Meg

Dannevig Island

Citadel Island

McHugh Island

South-West Point

Lighthouse

South-East Point

Anser Island

Wattle Island

South Point

BASS STRAIT

0 2.5 5 km

at Tidal River. Most of the walks in this area are overnight or longer. All the camp sites away from Tidal River have pit toilets but nothing else in the way of facilities. Fires are totally banned (except in designated fire places in Tidal River between May and October) so you'll need to carry some sort of stove.

Places to Stay

Camping The Tidal River camping ground has 500 sites, and at peak times (school holidays, Easter and long weekends) booking is essential. In fact for the real peak at Christmas a ballot is held in July allocating sites, so you can forget about a casual visit then (although a few sites are reserved for overseas visitors for one or two-night stays).

The charge is $13 per site (up to three people and one car), with a surcharge of $2.60 per extra person. For information and booking forms, phone the park office.

Flats & Units Also at Tidal River are a number of self-contained flats, which are available on a weekly basis. Costs range from $215 per week for two people (low season) up to $595 for a six-bed unit (high season).

There are also 'motor huts' and tiny timber cabins with kitchenettes – these share communal bathroom and you must supply all bed linen. The rate is a very reasonable $36 per night for up to four people, and $54 for up to six. The cabins and motor huts are usually heavily booked, so plan ahead.

Getting There & Away

V/Line has daily buses from Melbourne to Foster ($19), 60 km north of the Prom.

If you stay overnight in Foster at the *Little Mud Hut* (☎ 5682 2614), the owners run a postal/bus service to the Prom ($10 each way) at 9.30 am most mornings; they also have camping gear for hire. Beds in dorms cost $15 and there is one double at $30; linen is $2 extra. Ring for details on their transport and accommodation package deals.

From Phillip Island, *Amaroo Park Back-packers* (☎ 5952 2548) runs day trips to the

Prom for $30; you can also stay overnight in their cabin-tents at Tidal River ($12 YHA-members, $14 nonmembers).

THE GIPPSLAND LAKES DISTRICT

The Lakes District is the largest inland waterway system in Australia. The three main lakes, **Lake King**, **Lake Victoria** and **Lake Wellington**, are all joined and fed by a number of rivers that originate in the High Country. The lakes are actually shallow coastal lagoons separated from the ocean by a narrow strip of coastal sand dunes known as the Ninety Mile Beach.

The area is popular for fishing, boating, water-skiing and other water-oriented activities. Obviously, with more than 400 sq km of waterways, the best way to appreciate the area is from a boat. You can join a lakes cruise or hire a boat from various places including Lakes Entrance and Metung.

Most of the **Ninety Mile Beach** is part of the **Gippsland Lakes Coastal Park**. Within this area is the Lakes National Park and the birdwatchers' paradise of **Rotamah Island**.

Bairnsdale (pop 11,500)

Bairnsdale, a large commercial centre at the junction of the Princes and Omeo highways, is a popular base both for the mountains to the north and the lakes immediately to the south.

At 37 Dalmahoy St is the **Krowathunkoo-long Keeping Place**, a cultural centre focusing on the heritage of local Aboriginal people. It is open on weekdays from 9 am to 5 pm ($3). **Howitt Park** is a popular children's playground complete with flying foxes, and **St Mary's Catholic Church**, beside the information centre, has interesting painted murals and is worth a look.

Signposted 42 km north-west of Bairnsdale is the **Mitchell River National Park** with the **Den of Nargun**, a small cave which, according to Aboriginal legend, was haunted by a strange, half-stone creature, known as a *nargun*. There are some excellent short walks in the park.

There's a good tourist information centre

PAUL STEEL

CHRIS KLEP

TOM SMALLMAN

RICHARD STEWART

RICHARD STEWART

Victoria
A: Melbourne skyline
B: Luna Park, St Kilda
C: Swanston Walk, Melbourne
D: A mix of traditional and modern architecture, Melbourne
E: RMIT, Swanston St

RICHARD NEBESKY

RICHARD NEBESKY

GLENN BEANLAND

HUGH FINLAY

CHRIS KLEP

RICHARD NEBESKY

A	B
	D	E
C	F

Victoria

A: Rifle Brigade Hotel, Bendigo
B: Sovereign Hill, Ballarat
C: Moyne River, Port Fairy

D: Grampians (Gariwerd) National Park
E: River red gums, Hattah-Kulkyne National Park
F: Twelve Apostles, Port Campbell National Park

(☎ 5152 3444) at 240 Main St, open daily from 9 am to 5 pm.

Places to Stay & Eat For an on-site van or tent site, try the *Mitchell Gardens Caravan Park* (☎ 5152 4654) on the banks of the Mitchell River. The friendly *Bairnsdale Backpackers Hostel* (☎ 5152 5097), close to the train station at 119 McLeod St, has bunks at $15 including breakfast, while the *Commercial Hotel* (☎ 5152 3031) on the corner of Main and Bailey Sts has basic single rooms for $15 and a good bistro downstairs.

The elegant *Riversleigh Country Hotel* (☎ 5152 6996), at 1 Nicholson St, has excellent heritage-style rooms from $68/75 and one of the best restaurants in country Victoria.

Getting There & Away There's a daily train/bus service between Bairnsdale and Melbourne ($31.80), and daily buses to Lakes Entrance ($7), Orbost ($16.80) and beyond.

Metung (pop 420)

This interesting little fishing village between Bairnsdale and Lakes Entrance is built on a land spit between Lake King and Bancroft Bay. The town offers hot sulphur springs in two outdoor pools, and a wide range of boats can be hired from Riviera Nautica (☎ 5156 2243) to tour the lakes. Two boats, the *Spray* and the *Gypsy*, also offer cruises of the lakes.

There is plenty of accommodation to choose from, including the pub (☎ 5156 2206) right on the water.

Lakes Entrance (pop 4620)

A popular if somewhat old-fashioned tourist town, Lakes Entrance is the main centre of the Lakes District, and also Victoria's largest fishing port.

From the centre of town, a footbridge crosses Cunningham's Arm to the white-sand beaches of the Ninety Mile Beach; from the other side there's a scenic 2.3-km walking track up to the actual 'entrance'. Apart from the beaches, fishing and surfing, the town's attractions include the **Kinkuna**

Country Fun Park, the **Wyanga Park Winery & Bistro**, 10 km north, and **Nyerimilang Park**, a historic homestead and property off the Metung road.

Lots of cruise boats, including the large *Thunderbird*, operate from here to tour the rivers and lakes – the tourist office can advise you and make bookings. Boats can also be hired from Victor Hire Boats (☎ 5155 1888) in Lakes Entrance and Lake Tyers Boat Hire (☎ 5156 5676), six km east of the town.

The Lakes Entrance Fishermen's Co-operative, just off the Princes Highway, provides a viewing platform that puts you in the middle of the boats unloading their fish. Sunday morning is the best time to go. The co-op fish shop is guaranteed to sell the freshest fish in town.

There's a tourist information centre (☎ 5155 1966) on the Princes Highway, as you enter the town from the west.

Places to Stay & Eat Lakes Entrance has a huge array of accommodation, especially caravan parks and motels. The *Lakes Main Caravan Park* (☎ 5155 2365) in Willis St has an associate-YHA hostel with dorm beds for $12 a night ($14 nonmembers), tent sites from $6 per person, and on-site vans and cabins from $18 to $55. The *Glenara Motel* (☎ 5155 1555) at 221 The Esplanade has budget motel rooms from $40 to $80 a double, and *Homlea Cottages* (☎ 5155 1998) at 32 Roadnight St has simple holiday cottages from $25 to $45 a double or from $60 to $90 for six people.

Try *Tres Amigos* at 521 The Esplanade for Mexican meals. The *Kalimna Hotel* has a good bistro overlooking the lakes, and for a seafood splurge try *Skippers Wine Bar & Restaurant* at 481 The Esplanade.

Getting There & Away There are daily V/Line buses between Lakes Entrance and Bairnsdale ($7), with bus/train connections to Melbourne ($38.60). V/Line and Greyhound Pioneer also has daily buses continuing along the Princes Highway into New South Wales.

EAST GIPPSLAND

East Gippsland, also known as the Wilderness Coast, contains some of the most remote and spectacular national parks in the state, ranging from the coastal wilderness areas of Croajingolong to the lush rainforests of the Errinundra Plateau.

Although the area was always considered too remote for agriculture, it has provided a rich harvest for the logging industry since late last century. Today, the logging of these forest areas is a sensitive and controversial issue, with an underlying conflict between the region's history of economic dependence on the logging industry and the current promotion of the area as a wilderness zone.

For those interested in extensive explorations, the DC&NR publishes a very good map/brochure, *East Gippsland: A Guide for Visitors*. The Australian Conservation Foundation publishes the book *Car Touring & Bushwalking in East Gippsland*, although it's information is somewhat outdated.

Orbost (pop 2500)

Orbost is a logging service town with a very pretty location on the Snowy River.

The DC&NR's Rainforest Information Centre (☎ 5161 1375) has excellent information and displays on forests and national parks in East Gippsland. It is open on weekdays from 10 am to 4 pm, and during school holidays on weekends from 10 am to 4 pm.

Orbost's Slab Hut tourist office (☎ 5154 2424) is on Nicholson St.

Places to Stay The *Orbost Caravan Park* (☎ 5154 1097) on Nicholson St has tent sites and on-site vans. The *Commonwealth Hotel* (☎ 5154 1077) at 159 Nicholson St has B&B from $25/35. There are also a couple of motels.

Getting There & Away V/Line has daily buses from Orbost to Bairnsdale ($16.80) and Genoa ($16.80).

Marlo & Cape Conran

On the coast 15 km south of Orbost is the sleepy little settlement of Marlo, at the mouth of the Snowy River. It's a popular fishing spot and the route along the coast to Cape Conran, 18 km to the east, is especially pretty as it winds through stands of banksia trees. The beach at Cape Conran is one long beautiful deserted strip of white sand.

Places to Stay Marlo has a couple of caravan parks, and at Cape Conran the DC&NR (☎ 5154 8438) runs the *Banksia Bluff Camping Area*, with great sites from $6 to $12, and the superb *Cape Conran Cabins*, a set of eight self-contained timber cabins that sleep up to eight and cost from $40 to $80 for four people plus $7 to $12 per extra adult; you'll need to book.

Baldwin Spencer Trail

This is a drive well worth doing: a 265-km route through more superb forest, including Errinundra National Park, north of Orbost on the Bonang Highway.

The route follows the trail of Walter Baldwin Spencer, a noted scientist and explorer who led an expedition through here in 1889. A map/brochure is available from the Rainforest Information Centre in Orbost.

Buchan (pop 400)

There are a number of limestone caves around the tiny and beautiful town of Buchan, 55 km north-west of Orbost. The two major ones, maintained by the DC&NR, are the **Royal Cave** and **Fairy Cave**. There are worthwhile one-hour tours daily at 10 am and 1 and 3.30 pm for the Royal Cave, ($6.50), and 11.15 am and 2.15 pm for the Fairy Cave ($8). The rangers also offer guided tours to more remote and undeveloped caves in the area; phone ☎ 5155 9264.

Places to Stay There's a delightful camping ground at the Buchan Caves (☎ 5155 9264), with sites from $10 and self-contained units from $40.

There's also a pub, motels and cabins in Buchan. Just out of town on Saleyard Rd is the excellent *Buchan Lodge Backpackers* (☎ 5155 9421) is a modern homestead with beds in bunk rooms at $14 a night.

Snowy River National Park

This is one of Victoria's most isolated and spectacular national parks, dominated by deep gorges carved through limestone and sandstone by the mighty Snowy River. The entire park is a smorgasbord of unspoilt and superb bush and mountain scenery.

The two main access routes are the Gelantipy Rd from Buchan and the Bonang Highway from Orbost. These roads are joined by McKillops Rd, which runs across the northern border of the park. Along McKillops Rd you'll come across **McKillops Bridge**, where you can have a dip in the river or camp on its sandy banks. The view from the lookout over **Little River Falls**, about 20 km west of McKillops Bridge, is spectacular.

The classic canoe or raft trip down the Snowy River from Willis or McKillops Bridge to a pull-out point near Buchan offers superb scenery, rugged gorges, raging rapids, tranquil sections and excellent camping spots on broad sand bars. A number of commercial operators organise raft trips on the Snowy, including Snowy River Expeditions (☎ 5155 9353) and Peregrine Adventures (☎ 9663 8611); there are two-day ($240), four-day ($460) and five-day ($550) trips.

Errinundra National Park

This beautiful national park contains Victoria's largest areas of cool-temperate rainforest. The park is on a high granite plateau with a high rainfall, fertile soils and a network of creeks and rivers. There are walking trails throughout, and camp sites with minimal facilities. Access is via the Bonang Highway from Orbost or the Errinundra road from Club Terrace, both of which are unsealed, steep, slow and winding – note that roads through the park are closed from mid-June to the end of October. Contact the rangers at Bendoc (☎ (02) 6458 1456) or in Cann River (☎ 5158 6351) for more information and to check road conditions.

Croajingolong National Park

Croajingolong is a coastal wilderness park that stretches for about 100 km along the easternmost tip of Victoria, and is one of Australia's finest national parks. Magnificent unspoiled beaches, inlets, estuaries and forests make this an ideal area for camping, walking, swimming, surfing or just lazing around. The diverse habitat supports a wide range of plants and animals, with over 250 species of birds recorded in the area.

There are several roads leading from the highway to different parts of the park. Some are quite rough and require 4WD; the DC&NR office at Cann River will give you more information about vehicular access.

There are camp sites within Croajingolong National Park at Wingan Inlet, Thurra River, Mueller River and Shipwreck Creek. Facilities are minimal and it's a good idea to make reservations with the DC&NR office in Cann River (☎ 5158 6351) or Mallacoota (☎ 5158 0219).

Mallacoota (pop 960)

Mallacoota is at the seaward end of a small lake system and is the main service town for this corner of the state. It is a popular and old-fashioned holiday resort, with good fishing, walking trails, boating, and access to the Croajingolong National Park. Abalone and fishing are the town's mainstays, and there are fishing boats and houseboats for hire.

At Christmas and Easter the town becomes packed out with holiday makers, but it's fairly peaceful at other times.

There is no public transport down to Mallacoota from the highway, although some accommodation places do pick-ups.

Organised Tours & Cruises Journey Beyond Eco-Adventures (☎ 5158 0166) offers a range of very good adventure tours, including sea kayaking trips (full day, $95) and mountain bike rides (half-day, $35). They also hire mountain bikes and kayaks.

Wallagaraugh River Wilderness Cruises (☎ 5158 0555) has excellent five-hour cruises through the lakes and river system, costing $35 including lunch. The MV *Loch Ard* (☎ 5158 0144) does a five-hour cruise up to Gypsy Point for $18.

VICTORIA

Places to Stay Accommodation here includes five caravan parks and dozens of holiday flats. The *Mallacoota Camping Park* (☎ 5158 0300) has hundreds of sites on the foreshore, ranging seasonally from $8.50 to $13. The *Beachcomber Caravan Park* (☎ 5158 0233) at 85 Betka Rd has tent sites and cabins. Backpacker beds in on-site vans are $12/22/30 for singles/doubles/triples.

The *Mallacoota Hotel/Motel* (☎ 5158 0455) has motel units from $40/45.

Other places include the excellent *Adobe Mud-brick Flats* (☎ 5158 0329), which cost from $40 to $60 for four people, plus $10 per extra adult; and *Karbeethong Lodge* (☎ 5158 0411), an old-fashioned guesthouse with doubles from $45 to $75 (plus $10 for en suite) and family units from $55 to $90.

Western Australia

HIGHLIGHTS

- Exploring the harsh and beautiful Pilbara, the reefs of Ningaloo and the boom tourist town of Broome, with its fascinating pearling past
- Discovering the 'last frontier' of the wild Kimberley
- Heading out to the mining and ghost towns of the goldfields region
- Relaxing in the laid-back south-west, dotted with beautiful surf and swimming beaches, historic towns, wineries and giant karri forests
- Looking out to sea from the spectacular and rugged coastline of the Great Australian Bight
- Visiting the scenic and historic Avon Valley

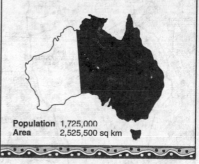

Population 1,725,000
Area 2,525,500 sq km

Western Australia's position near the Indian Ocean trading routes led to very early European contact. The first known Europeans to land near the Western Australian coast were Dutch – Dirk Hartog in 1616, and those previously shipwrecked on its wild shores (whose vessels are still being discovered). Abel Tasman was the first to chart parts of the WA coastline; he charted as far as the Gulf of Carpentaria in 1644.

William Dampier was the first Englishman to comprehensively chart the coast. He visited the area in 1688 on board the *Cygnet*, and his 1697 publication, *New Voyage around the World*, prompted funds for a subsequent trip in 1699 to what was then known as New Holland. On board the HMS *Roebuck*, he charted from the Houtman Abrolhos Islands as far north as Roebuck Bay, near Broome.

Dampier's reports of a dry, barren land discouraged attempts at settlement and it was not until 1829, three years after Britain had formally claimed the land, that the first British settlers arrived in the Swan Valley, later Perth. Their presence was intended to forestall settlement by other European nations, in particular France.

Western Australia's development as a British colony was painfully slow – hardly surprising, given its distance from the main Australian settlements in the east. It was not until the gold rushes of the 1890s that the colony really began to progress. Today, a larger and far more technologically advanced mineral boom forms the basis of the state's prosperity. As a result, Western Australia, more than any other state, is deeply embroiled in the Mabo debate on Aboriginal land rights because of conflicting mining interests (see the Facts about the Country chapter for more on Mabo).

ABORIGINAL PEOPLE

Western Australia has an Aboriginal and Torres Strait Islander population of over 42,000, which represents about 2.6% of the

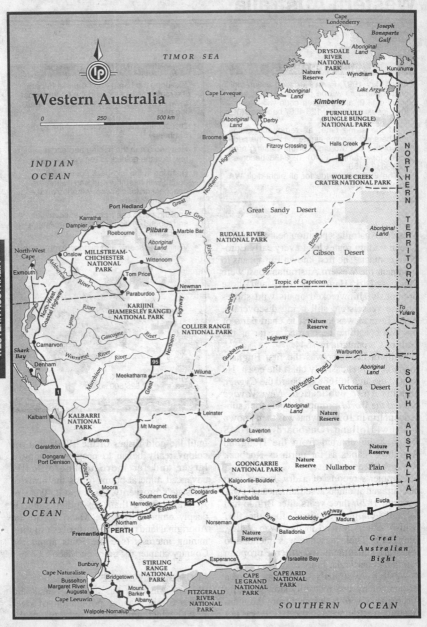

Western Australia

state's population. Roughly a quarter live in the north-west of the state and on its eastern border with the Northern Territory.

Much evidence has been uncovered indicating that Aboriginal people lived as far south as present-day Perth at least 40,000 years ago. The archaeological record is rich, with a 39,500-year-old camp site unearthed at Swan Bridge, stone tools gathered from the Devil's Lair near Cape Leeuwin (30,000 years old) and ochre mined from Wilga Mia in the Murchison (also 30,000 years old), as examples.

The arrival of the Europeans had disastrous consequences for the local Aboriginal people, who lived in harmony with nature, despite the harshness of the environment, by hunting and gathering in small nomadic groups. Pushed off their traditional lands, many of the Aboriginal people who were not killed by the colonisers died of European diseases, against which they had no immunity. Particularly hard hit were the Nyungar people in the south-west.

From the end of WW II many Aboriginal people banded together in protest against their appalling treatment on the cattle stations. These protests were some of the first displays of a re-emerging consciousness.

In June 1992, the High Court of Australia recognised a form of native title which reflected the entitlement of the indigenous inhabitants of Australia to their traditional lands (known as the Mabo ruling). The Western Australian government was quick to pre-empt further legal restriction by rushing through its own Land Bill in December 1993. It also unsuccessfully challenged the validity in the High Court of the Commonwealth Native Title Act. Perhaps the mineral-rich state feels it has the most to lose in the short term.

Aboriginal people in WA have laid claims around Broome, Purnululu and Kununurra, mainly on Crown land as anything on freehold land is well-protected. But injustices continue – Aboriginal people are 29 times more likely to be imprisoned than Whites and many regional prisons, eg Roebourne and Broome, have mainly indigenous prisoners.

Permits

You need a permit to enter Aboriginal land but getting one is only really a problem in the remote communities in the east of the state.

In the Kimberley and Pilbara a permit is usually easily obtained after a courtesy visit to community administration offices. Some insensitive travellers have gone through the gates of communities on the Dampier Peninsula and set up their caravans outside people's houses – imagine if someone set up their tent in your backyard without asking!

Permits can be issued only by the Aboriginal Affairs Department in Perth (☎ (09) 483 1222); individual Aboriginal people apparently can't give permission. Often access is informally allowed, but there can be a problem with control of inconsiderate campers.

Culture

Many tourists come wishing to see Aboriginal culture first-hand and many leave disappointed. Readers are encouraged to make contact with the Aboriginal communities they pass through. Don't, as many White Australians do, ignore these people as if they were passing 'ghosts'.

As yet there are no major Aboriginal events or festivals in the West. Stompem Ground, based in Broome, was a start but seems to have died a quick death as entrepreneurs, who had lost sight of its original purpose, moved in. National Aboriginal Islander Day Observance Committee (NAIDOC) Week, in early July, brings together many groups with displays of indigenous art and cultural performances.

One of the finest collections of traditional and contemporary Aboriginal art and artefacts can be found in the Berndt Museum of Anthropology, in the Social Sciences Building, University of WA, Crawley. There is an interesting indigenous publishing house in Broome – Magabala Books (☎ (091) 92 1991), 28 Saville St.

Tours on Aboriginal Land

There are a number of tours which incorporate aspects of Aboriginal life and culture.

These represent the best opportunity for travellers to have some form of meaningful contact with Aboriginal people.

In the Kimberley, there are a number of options, mostly initiatives of the local Aboriginal people. Operators include Over the Top Tours, Lombadina Tours, Darngku Heritage Cruise (Geikie Gorge), Kooljaman Resort and Wundargoodie Tours (see the Kimberley and Broome sections for more details).

The Purnululu Aboriginal Corporation and CALM (Department of Conservation & Land Management) jointly manage the Purnululu (Bungle Bungle) National Park, one of the first national attempts to balance the needs of local people with the demands of tourism. The traditional owners are looking for opportunities to take tours into the Bungles.

In the Pilbara, Aboriginal people have worked closely with CALM in establishing a cultural centre in the Karijini (Hamersley Range) National Park and a Yinjibarndi visitor centre in Millstream-Chichester National Park. A number of operators take extended trips into Karijini with the Kurrama, Innawonga and Punjima peoples – Karijini Walkabouts has nine-day walking tours.

GEOGRAPHY

Western Australia's geography is a little like a distorted reflection of eastern Australia's except that the west is far drier. The equivalent of the long fertile coastal strip on the east coast is the small south-west corner of WA. As in the east, hills rise behind the coast, but in WA they're much smaller than those of the Great Dividing Range. Farther north it's dry and relatively barren. Fringing the central-west coast is the Great Sandy Desert, a very inhospitable region running right to the sea.

There are a couple of interesting variations, such as the Kimberley, in the extreme north of the state – a wild and rugged area with a convoluted coastline and spectacular inland gorges. It gets good annual rainfall, but all in the 'green' season. Taming the Kimberley has been a long-held dream which has still been only partially realised. It's a spectacular area well worth a visit.

Farther south is the Pilbara, with more magnificent ancient rock and gorge country and the treasure-house from which the state derives its vast mineral wealth. Away from the coast most of WA is simply a vast empty stretch of outback: the Nullarbor Plain in the south, the Great Sandy Desert in the north and the Gibson and Great Victoria deserts in between.

CLIMATE

There are several different climate zones in WA, with the three main ones being tropical in the north, semi-arid in the interior and mild 'Mediterranean' in the south-west. In general the rainfall decreases the farther you get from the coast.

Sandgropers
You will often hear Western Australians colloquially referred to as sandgropers. The sandgroper is actually a subterranean insect known as a cylindrachetid, believed to be a descendant of the grasshopper group. Five species of sandgroper have been found in Australia.

Their bodies are perfectly adapted for 'groping' or burrowing in the sandy soils of the Swan Coastal Plain where they are found. They move through sand in a swimming motion, propelled by their powerful forelegs and with their mid and hind legs tucked away.

Simliar to grasshoppers, sandgropers develop from egg to adult with no larval stage. They appear to be vegetarian although some studies show that at least one species is omnivorous.

Humanoid sandgropers have a diet of Swan Lager, enjoy sunbathing and the footy, eat in Freo's cafe strip, and holiday at the beach. They have yet to perfect the sand swimming technique. ■

In the north the climate is characterised by the Dry and the Wet, rather than winter and summer. As the monsoon develops there is thunderstorm activity (the 'build-up'), followed by the occasional tropical cyclone which develops into rain-bearing depressions as it passes inland. Although many roads are made impassable, the rain is generally welcomed. It is said that Port Hedland receives a cyclone at least every two years.

Farther south, there is little or no rainfall during summer and the winds are generally hot dry easterlies but in the afternoon coastal areas receive sea breezes such as the famed 'Fremantle Doctor'. Cold fronts and accompanying low pressure systems produce most of the rainfall for southern districts and agricultural regions in winter.

INFORMATION

There are no interstate offices of the Western Australian Tourist Centre (WATC). However, some states and territories have agencies:

ACT
    Goddard & Partners, 40 Allara St, Canberra 2600 (☎ (06) 248 9399; 13 1122 for brochures)
New South Wales
    NRMA Travel, 151 Clarence St, Sydney 2000 (☎ 13 1122 for brochures)
Queensland
    Harvey World Travel, 204 Adelaide St, Brisbane 4000 (☎ (07) 3221 5022 – do not post brochures)
South Australia
    RAA Travel (☎ (08) 8202 4589)
Victoria
    RACV, Melbourne 3000 (☎ (03) 9790 2121; 1800 337 743)

WILDFLOWERS

WA is famed for its 8000 species of wildflower, which bloom in greatest number from August to October. Even some of the driest regions put on a technicolour display after just a little rainfall, and at any time of the year.

The south-west alone has over 3000 species, many of which, because of the state's isolation, are unique. Many are known as everlastings because the petals stay attached even after the flowers have died. The flowers seem to spring up almost overnight, and transform vast areas within days.

You can find flowers almost everywhere in the state, but the jarrah forests in the south-west are particularly rich. The coastal national parks, such as Fitzgerald River and Kalbarri, also have brilliant displays. Near Perth, the Badgingarra, Alexander Morrison, Yanchep and John Forrest national parks are excellent choices. There's also a wildflower display in Kings Park, Perth.

The pamphlet *Wildflower Discovery* details the state's wildflower trails. It is available free from the WATC in Perth.

ACTIVITIES
Bushwalking

There are a number of bushwalking clubs in Perth including the Bushwalkers of Western Australia and Perth Bushwalkers; enquire at the WATC for contact numbers. Popular areas for walking in WA include the Stirling Range and Porongurup national parks, both north of Albany. There are also a number of coastal parks in the south and south-west, such as Cape Le Grand, Fitzgerald River, Walpole-Nornalup and Cape Arid, which have good walking tracks. To the north, the Kalbarri, Karijini (Hamersley Range) and Purnululu national parks provide a stimulating hiking environment.

There are interesting walks in the hills around Perth, and if you're a really enthusiastic walker there's the 640-km Bibbulman Track, which runs along old forest tracks between Perth and Walpole on WA's southeast coast. Information on this and many other tracks is available from CALM (☎ (09) 334 0333), 50 Hayman Rd, Como, Perth. Two excellent publications are *Discover Wild Places, Quiet Places* (which covers the south-west) and *North-West Bound* (covering Shark Bay to Wyndham).

Birdwatching can be an integral part of bushwalking, and WA is a fascinating destination for the avifauna addict. It is the only state with two RAOU observatories – at Eyre and Broome, both splendid locations. The diversity of habitats, from the arid central and northern regions to the forests of the south-west, means that a great number of species can be observed.

Water Sports
Swimming People in Perth often claim to have the best surf and swimming beaches of any Australian city. Popular surfing areas around WA include Denmark, near Albany; from Cape Naturaliste to Margaret River in the south-west; Bunbury, 180 km south of Perth; and Geraldton to the north. There are fine swimming beaches all along the WA coast.

Diving Good diving areas include the large stretch of coast from Esperance to Geraldton, and between Carnarvon and Exmouth. You can get to the islands and reefs off the coast in small boats. The more popular diving spots include Esperance, Bremer Bay, Albany, Denmark, Margaret River, Bunbury, Rottnest Island, Shoalwater Islands Marine Park (off Rockingham), Lancelin, the Houtman Abrolhos Islands (off Geraldton), Carnarvon and all around North-West Cape (Exmouth, Ningaloo Reef and Coral Bay).

Fishing The coastal regions of WA offer excellent fishing. Some of the more popular areas include Rottnest Island, Albany, Geraldton and the Houtman Abrolhos Islands, Mackerel Islands, Shark Bay, Carnarvon and the coastline to the north, the North-West Cape and Broome.

Fishing licences are only required if you intend catching marron and rock lobsters, or will be using a fishing net. Licences are available for $10 from the Fisheries Department (☎ (09) 220 5333), 108 Adelaide Terrace, Perth, or country offices.

Heritage Trails Network
The Heritage Trails Network, launched during Australia's Bicentenary in 1988, is an excellent series of road trails covering historical, cultural or natural points of interest throughout the state. A little neglected now, the trails are usually marked with interpretive displays and directional markers. Information on the Heritage Trails Network can be obtained from tourist offices or the WA Heritage Committee (☎ (09) 221 4177), 292 Hay St, East Perth.

GETTING THERE & AWAY
Western Australia is the largest, most lightly populated and most isolated state in the country. Yet despite vast distances, you can drive across the Nullarbor Plain from the eastern states to Perth and then all the way up the Indian Ocean coast and through the Kimberley to Darwin without leaving the bitumen.

Even so, there's absolutely no way of covering all those km cheaply, although the deregulation of the airline industry has certainly helped. Sydney to Perth is 3284 km as the crow flies, and more like 4000 km by road: a one-way economy rail ticket on the route is $320, a discounted air ticket costs $450 return (or even less if you shop around), while a seat on one of the cheaper bus lines costs around $200. (See Getting There & Away in the Perth section for train details.)

Hitching across the Nullarbor is not advisable; waits of several days are not uncommon. Driving yourself is probably the cheapest way of getting to WA from the eastern states – if you have a group. You'll probably spend around $450 to $500 on fuel, travelling coast to coast; shared among four people that's $125 each (see the Eyre Highway section in this chapter).

Another interesting route is from Yulara, near Uluru (Ayers Rock), to Perth via the Warburton Road. There are a number of escorted tours, including Austracks 4WD Outback Adventures (☎ 1800 655 200); their six-day trip is about $625.

GETTING AROUND
Air
Deregulation is just starting to make a difference to flying within WA. Ansett controls most traffic, in league with Skywest, with other operators in spirited competition on some routes. Ansett and Skywest connect

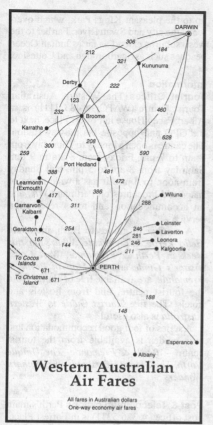

DARWIN

306

212

184

321

Kununurra

Derby

222

123

232

Broome

460

Karratha

628

300

208

259

Port Hedland

590

388

481

Learmonth
(Exmouth)

472

417

386

Carnarvon
Kalbarri

311

Wiluna

288

Geraldton

254

Leinster   246

Laverton   281

Leonora   246

167

144

211

Kalgoorlie

To Cocos
Islands

671

PERTH

To Christmas
Island   671

188

148

Esperance

Albany

Western Australian
Air Fares

All fares in Australian dollars
One-way economy air fares

WESTERN AUSTRALIA

Perth with most regional centres. The frequency of some flights seems ridiculous given the state's small population – until you realise how many mining projects are based in these centres.

Qantas has moved into WA with flights to Broome, Port Hedland, several services to Kalgoorlie (including one from Adelaide thrice weekly) and a Perth to Darwin service.

See the Air Fares Chart for the main Western Australian routes and flight costs.

Bus

Greyhound Pioneer (☎ 13 2030) buses run from Perth along the coast to Darwin ($348), from Perth to Adelaide via Kalgoorlie and the Eyre Highway ($189), and to Melbourne ($219). McCafferty's (☎ 13 1499) has daily Darwin to Perth and Perth to Darwin services (currently their special price is $179 but this is likely to go up). Kalgoorlie Express (☎ (09) 328 9199) goes from Perth via Kalgoorlie to Leonora ($90) and Leinster ($100) on Friday and Sunday.

South-West Coachlines (☎ (09) 322 5173) in the Transperth bus station, Wellington St, Perth, runs services from Perth to centres in the state's south-west such as Bunbury, Busselton, Nannup, Dunsborough, Augusta, Manjimup and Collie. Westrail (☎ 13 2232) runs buses to York, Geraldton, Esperance, Augusta, Pemberton, Hyden, Albany and Meekatharra. Reservations are necessary on all services.

Train

Western Australia's internal rail network, operated by Westrail, is limited to services between Perth and Kalgoorlie (Prospector), and Perth and Bunbury in the south (Australind). Reservations are necessary (☎ 13 2232).

Car

See Getting Around in the Perth section of this chapter for details on car rental.

Backpackers' Transport

A good budget alternative for those who want to see parts of the south-west is Easyrider Backpackers (☎ (09) 383 7848). They do a two-day circuit which includes Perth, Bunbury, Busselton, Margaret River, Augusta, Pemberton, Walpole, Denmark, Albany and Porongurup National Park. The full circuit costs $129 and the ticket is valid for three months; you can join anywhere and return to your starting point and you can organise your accommodation and be dropped off there. It is a fun, relaxed way to travel.

Perth

Population 1,400,000

Perth is a vibrant and modern city, pleasantly sited on the Swan River, with the port of Fremantle a few km downstream and the dormitory cities of Rockingham and Mandurah to the south. It's claimed to be the sunniest state capital in Australia and the most isolated capital city in the world. Of WA's 1.8 million people, around 80% live in and around Perth.

Perth was founded in 1829 as the Swan River Settlement. It grew very slowly until 1850, when convicts were brought in to alleviate the labour shortage. Many of Perth's fine buildings, such as Government House and Perth Town Hall, were built with convict labour. Even then, Perth's development lagged behind that of the eastern cities, until the discovery of gold in the 1890s increased the population fourfold in a decade and initiated a building boom.

More recently, WA's mineral wealth has contributed to Perth's growth, and the resultant construction boom has spread into the outer suburbs. A somewhat hick, squeaky-clean nouveau-riche image has been tainted by political scandals in the 1980s and the crash of entrepreneurs, but it all seems to add to the town's frontier image.

Orientation

The city centre is fairly compact, situated on a sweep of the Swan River, which borders the city centre to the south and east, and links Perth to its port, Fremantle. The main shopping precinct in the city is along the Hay St and Forrest Place malls and the arcades that run between them. St George's Terrace is the centre of the city's business district.

The railway line bounds the city centre on the northern side. Immediately north of the railway line is Northbridge, a popular restaurant and entertainment enclave with a number of hostels and other cheap accommodation. The western end of Perth slopes up to the pleasant Kings Park, which overlooks the city and Swan River. Farther to the west, suburbs extend as far as Indian Ocean beaches such as Scarborough and Cottesloe.

Information

Tourist Offices The Western Australian Tourist Centre (WATC; ☎ 483 1111) is in Albert Facey House in Forrest Place, next to the GPO and opposite the railway station. The centre is open Monday to Thursday from 8 am to 7 pm, Friday from 8 am to 9 pm, Saturday from 8 am to 5 pm, and Sunday from noon to 6 pm. It has a wide range of maps and brochures on Perth and WA, and an accommodation and tours reservation service.

A number of guides to Perth, including *Hello Perth & Fremantle*, *What's on this week in Perth & Fremantle*, *West Coast Visitor's Guide* and the *Map of Perth & Fremantle*, are available free of charge from the tourist centre, and from hostels and hotels. The free *Tourist Guide to Western Australia* is also useful.

A series of four good accommodation and tour guides is available from the tourist centre – *Perth & Fremantle*, *The Unique North*, *The Golden Heartlands* and *Southern Wonders*.

Post & Telecommunications Perth's main post office (☎ 326 5211) is in Forrest Place, which runs between Wellington St and the Murray St Mall. There are phones for international calls in the post office foyer. The STD telephone area code for Perth is 09.

Other Information The Royal Automobile Club of Western Australia (RACWA; ☎ 421 4444) is at 228 Adelaide Terrace. The club's bookshop has an excellent travel section, and detailed regional maps can be obtained at the Road Travel counter. Membership is worth the reduced rate for their excellent *WA Touring & Accommodation Guide* ($3.50).

Disabled visitors can use the services of ACROD (☎ 222 2961), 189 Royal St, East Perth. Paraquad (☎ 381 0173) can advise about accommodation with disabled services.

The YHA (☎ 227 5122) has its office at 236 William St in Northbridge.

Bookshops Some good city bookshops include Angus & Robertson, 199 Murray St and 625 Hay St; Dymocks, Hay St Mall; the Arcane Bookshop, 212 William St, Northbridge; and the Down to Earth Bookshop, 790 Hay St.

Medical Services The Traveller's Vaccination & Medical Clinic (☎ 321 1977) is at Level 5, 1 Mill St, off St George's Terrace.

Kings Park

There are superb views across Perth and the river from this four-sq-km park. It includes a 17-hectare **Botanic Garden** that displays over 2500 different plant species from WA, and a section of natural bushland. In spring, there's a cultivated display of WA's famed wildflowers. In early 1996, fire destroyed large tracts of Kings Park and it will be several years before it returns to its former splendour.

Free guided tours of Kings Park and the Botanic Gardens are available all year. The park also has a number of bike tracks; bikes can be rented from Koala Bicycle Hire (☎ 321 3061) at the western side of the main car park. An information centre, situated next to the car park, is open daily from 9.30 am to 3.30 pm. The park also has a restaurant with a pleasant coffee shop.

Get there on bus No 33 from St George's Terrace, the free Green Clipper bus to Kings Park entrance or walk up Mount St from the city.

City Buildings

Near the corner of King St and St George's Terrace, the **Cloisters** date from 1858 and are noted for their beautiful brickwork. Originally a school, they have now been integrated into a modern office development. On the corner of St George's Terrace and Pier St is the **Deanery**, which was built in 1859 and restored after a public appeal in 1980.

It's one of the few cottage-style houses that have survived from colonial days. The Cloisters and Deanery are not open to the public.

Opposite the Deanery, on St George's Terrace, is **Government House**, a Gothic-looking fantasy built between 1859 and 1864. On the corner of St George's Terrace and William St is the grand and once extravagant **Palace Hotel**; it dates to 1895 and is now a banking chamber.

In the Stirling Gardens off Barrack St is the old **courthouse**, next to the Supreme Court. One of the oldest buildings in Perth, it was built in Georgian style in 1836. Other old buildings include **Perth Town Hall** on the corner of Hay and Barrack Sts (1867-70); the **Central Government Buildings** on the corner of Barrack St and St George's Terrace, recognised by their patterned brick; the restored **His Majesty's Theatre** (originally opened in 1904) on the corner of King and Hay Sts; and the Gothic-style **Old Perth Boys' School**, which was built in 1854 and now houses a National Trust shop.

The distinctive **Barracks Archway**, at the western end of St George's Terrace, is all that remains of a barracks built in 1863 to house the Pensioner Guards of the British Army – discharged soldiers who guarded convicts.

The **Perth Mint** (☎ 421 7223), on the corner of Hill and Hay Sts, which originally opened in 1899, has reopened for public tours. Visitors can mint their own coins and watch gold pours, held on the hour from 10 am to 3 pm weekdays and 10 am to noon on weekends. Entry to the exhibition is $5 (children $3). The Mint is open weekdays from 9 am to 4 pm and weekends 9 am to 1 pm.

Parliament House

Tours of the Parliament buildings on Harvest Terrace can be arranged from Monday to Friday through the Parliamentary Information Officer (☎ 222 7222) – you will of course get a more extensive tour when Parliament is not in session. You can get there on a Purple Clipper bus from St George's Terrace or a Green Clipper to Harvest Terrace.

WESTERN AUSTRALIA

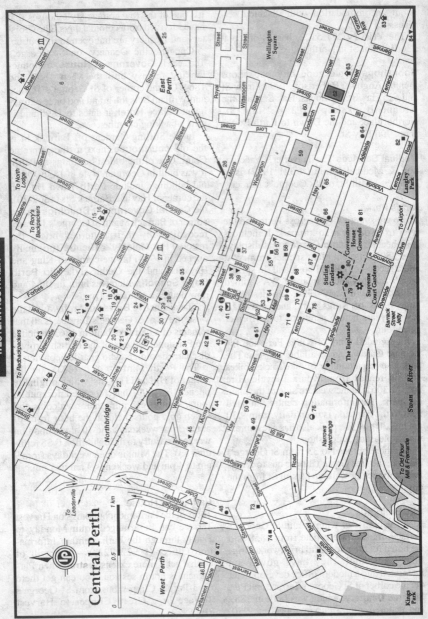

WESTERN AUSTRALIA

WESTERN AUSTRALIA

Museums

On Francis St, north across the railway lines from the city centre, is the **Western Australian Museum**. The museum includes a comprehensive gallery of Aboriginal history, a marine gallery, vintage cars, a 25-metre blue whale skeleton and a good collection of meteorites, the largest of which weighs 11 tonnes (the Australian outback is a rich source of meteorites). The complex also includes Perth's original prison, built in 1856 and used until 1888. Admission is free; it is open weekdays from 10.30 am to 5 pm, and weekends from 1 to 5 pm.

Three other museums close to the city are the **Small World Museum** at 12 Parliament Place, which has the largest collection of miniatures in the country (open daily); the **Army Museum of WA** on the corner of Bulwer and Lord Sts, which has a display of army memorabilia (open Sunday from 1 to 4.30 pm); and the **Fire Safety Education Centre & Museum** on the corner of Irwin and Murray Sts, which has displays on fire safety and fire-fighting equipment (open weekdays from 10 am to 3 pm).

Art Gallery of Western Australia

Housed in a modern building which runs from James St through to Roe St, behind the railway station, the gallery has a fine permanent exhibition of European, Australian and

Asian-Pacific art and a wide variety of temporary exhibitions. It is open daily from 10 am to 5 pm; admission is free.

Perth Zoo

Perth's popular zoo is set in attractive gardens across the river from the city at 20 Labouchere Rd, South Perth. It has a number of interesting collections including a nocturnal house which is open daily from noon to 3 pm, an Australian Wildlife Park, numbat display and Conservation Discovery Centre.

The zoo is open daily from 10 am to 5 pm and admission is $8 (children $4). You can reach the zoo on bus No 110 (or No 108 on weekends), which leaves from stand No 42 on St George's Terrace, or by taking the ferry across the river from the Barrack St jetty.

Underwater World

Underwater World, north of the city, at Hillarys Boat Harbour, West Coast Drive, Hillarys, is certainly not your run-of-the-mill aquarium. There is an underwater tunnel aquarium displaying 2500 examples of 200 marine species including sharks and stingrays. Also in the complex are interactive displays such as a Touch Pool, Microworld and an audiovisual theatre. In season they conduct four-hour whale-watching trips out to see humpbacks ($50). Underwater World is open daily from 9 am to 5 pm and entry costs $13.90 (children $7).

Parks & Gardens

On the Esplanade, between the city and the river, is the **Allan Green Plant Conservatory**. It houses a tropical and semitropical controlled-environment display; admission is free. Also close to the city, on the corner of St George's Terrace and Barrack St, are the **Supreme Court Gardens**, a popular place to eat lunch.

The **Queen's Gardens**, at the eastern end of Hay St, is a pleasant little park with lakes and bridges; get there on a Red Clipper bus. The lake in **Hyde Park**, Highgate, is popular for the water birds it attracts, and the park is the site for the annual Hyde Park Festival – catch bus No 60 from bus stand No 2 in

Barrack St. **Lake Monger** in Wembley is another hang-out for local feathered friends, particularly the famous black swans. Get there on bus Nos 91, 92 or 95 from opposite the Wellington St bus station (stand No 49). **Bold Park**, west of the city centre, is very popular with the locals.

Beaches

There are calm bay beaches on the Swan River at **Crawley**, **Peppermint Grove** and **Como**. Or you can try a whole string of patrolled surf beaches on the Indian Ocean coast including the very popular nude beach at **Swanbourne** – take bus Nos 205 or 207 from stand 32 in St George's Terrace.

Some of the other surf beaches include **Cottesloe**, a safe swimming beach; **Port**; **City**; **Scarborough**, a wide, golden and very popular surf beach which is only for experienced swimmers; **Leighton**; **Floreat**; and **Trigg Island**, another surf beach that is dangerous when rough. Perhaps the best beach of all is on secluded **Carnac Island**, southwest of Fremantle and frequented by the odd marooned human and some sea lions. See also the Rottnest Island section later in this chapter.

Markets

There are many lively markets around Perth – ideal if you're into browsing and buying. The **Subiaco Pavilion**, on the corner of Roberts and Rokeby Rds near Subiaco railway station, is open Thursday to Sunday. The **Wanneroo Markets**, north of Perth at 33 Prindiville Drive, Wangara, feature a large food hall and a variety of stalls; they're open on weekends from 9 am to 6 pm.

Other markets include the well-known and historic **Fremantle Market** (see the Fremantle section in this chapter); the weekend **Stock Rd Markets**, in Bibra Lake south of Perth; **Gosnells Railway Markets**, open Friday to Sunday; and **Scarborough Fair Markets**, the only one by the seaside, open weekends from 9 am to 5.30 pm.

Other Inner-City Attractions

Across Narrows Bridge is one of Perth's

The Old Flour Mill

landmarks: the finely restored **Old Flour Mill**, built in 1835. It's open daily from 10 am to 4 pm; admission is $2 (children $1).

Between Hay St and St George's Terrace is the narrow, touristy **London Court**, a photographer's delight. Although it looks very Tudor English, it dates from just 1937. At one end of this shopping court St George and the dragon do battle above the clock each quarter of an hour, while at the other end knights joust on horseback.

The **Scitech Discovery Centre** on Railway Parade in West Perth has hands-on and large-scale exhibits. It is open weekdays from 10 am to 5 pm and weekends from 10 am to 6 pm. Admission is not cheap at $10 (children $7).

Perth Suburbs

Armadale The **Pioneer World** at Armadale, 27 km south-east of the city, is a working model of a 19th-century colonial village; it's open daily and admission is $3 (children $1.50). You can get to Armadale on a bus from Pier St or a local train from Central Perth railway station.

The **History House Museum**, on Jull St, is a free museum in a 19th-century pioneer's house. It is open weekdays from 10 am to noon and 2 to 4 pm. About six km south of Armadale, **Tumbulgum Farm** has a number of Australian products for sale, and puts on farm shows and displays of Aboriginal culture. It is open Wednesday to Sunday from 9.30 am to 5 pm, and costs $7.50 (children $3.75).

Along the Swan River There are many attractions up the Swan River. On Maylands Peninsula, enclosed by a loop of the river, is the beautifully restored **Tranby House**. Built in 1839, it is one of WA's oldest houses and a fine example of early colonial architecture. It's open Monday to Saturday from 2 to 5 pm, and Sunday from 11 am to 1 pm and 2 to 5 pm; admission is $2.50 (children $1.50).

The **Rail Transport Museum**, Railway Parade, Bassendean, has locomotives and railway memorabilia; it is open Sunday from 1 to 5 pm; entry is $4 (children $1).

Guildford has a number of historic buildings, including the **Mechanics Hall**, in Meadow St, and the **Folk Museum & Gaol** which is open in summer Sunday from 2 to 5 pm. **Woodbridge**, in Third Ave, was built in 1855 and is a fully restored and beautifully furnished colonial mansion overlooking the

The black swan can be seen at Lake Monger in Wembley

river. It's open daily (except Wednesday); entry is $2 (children $1.20).

In West Swan is the **Caversham Wildlife Park & Zoo** which has a large collection of Australian animals and birds; it's open daily from 9 am to 5 pm and entry is $5 (children $1.50).

The Swan Valley **vineyards** are dotted along the river from Guildford to the Upper Swan. Many are open for tastings and cellar sales. Olive Farm Wines, 77 Great Eastern Highway, South Guildford, is the oldest in the region, established in 1829. Houghton Wines on Dale Rd, Middle Swan, was established in 1842 and produced its first vintage in 1859. Lamont's, Bisdee Rd, produces wines in the traditional manner, usually enjoyed with one of their great al fresco lunches.

The river cuts a narrow gorge through the Darling Range at **Walyunga National Park** in Upper Swan, off the Great Northern Highway. There are many walking tracks along the river and it's a popular picnic spot.

Other Suburbs In Subiaco, the **Museum of Childhood**, 160 Hamersley Rd, houses an interesting collection. Across the Canning River towards Jandakot airport, on Bull Creek Drive, there is the excellent **Aviation Museum** with a collection of aviation memorabilia, including a Spitfire and a Lancaster bomber. It is open daily from 11 am to 4 pm and entry costs $5 (children $2). In Melville, off the Canning Highway, is the **Wireless Hill Telecommunications Museum**. It is open on weekends from 1 to 5 pm; entry is $1.40 (children 60c).

In Cannington, on the road to Armadale, is **Woodloes**, a restored colonial home of 1874, open Sunday from 2 to 5 pm. The small **Liddelow Homestead** in Kenwick has also been restored. Yet another early home is the mud-brick and shingle **Stirk Cottage**, Kalamunda, built in 1881. The cottage is open from 1.30 to 4.30 pm; admission is free.

Adventure World, 15 km south of Perth at 179 Progress Drive, Bibra Lake, is a large amusement park open daily ($20; children $18). At **Cables Water Park**, at Troode St in

Spearwood (just off Rockingham Rd, south of the city), cables haul water-skiers along at 20 to 50 km/h. It is open daily; an hour's skiing costs $12.

Bungee West, on Progress Drive in Bibra Lake, is open daily and offers you the chance to throw yourself from a 40-metre tower. The less adventurous can abseil, the downright cowardly can just observe. Go on, jump!

There's a real potpourri of other places to visit in the suburbs; enquire at the WATC.

Tours

The WATC has detailed information about tours around Perth; they can also book them. Half-day city tours of Perth and Fremantle are about $30, and for around $50 you can get tours to the Swan Valley wineries, Cohunu Wildlife Park or Underwater World and the northern beaches.

A favourite is the free tour of the Swan Brewery (☎ 350 0650), 25 Baile Rd, Canning Vale. The tour takes 1½ hours (followed by a beer) and departs Monday to Thursday at 10 am, plus Monday to Wednesday at 2.30 pm. Reservations are essential.

Safari Treks (☎ 271 1271) does a good half-day tour of the Swan Valley wineries and Yanchep Cave; it's not cheap at $67 but you cover a lot of territory.

Cruises

A number of cruise companies operate tours from the Barrack St jetty, including Captain Cook Cruises (☎ 325 3341) and Boat Torque (☎ 221 5844). Tours include scenic cruises of the Swan River, winery visits, trips to Fremantle and lunch and dinner cruises.

From September to May, the Transperth MV *Countess II* departs daily, except Saturday, at 2 pm from the Barrack St jetty on a three-hour cruise towards the Upper Swan River; the cost is $12.

Boat Torque also has a full-day Swan Valley River cruise for $60 (children $40), and Captain Cook Cruises has a three-hour Scenic River Cruise around Perth and Fremantle for $22.50 (one way $12.50). Golden Sun (☎ 325 1616) has a Perth to

Fremantle cruise from Barrack St jetty which is a reasonable $15 return.

Marine Mammal Watching

There are a number of activities that bring you closer to marine mammals in and around Perth, including sea-lion swimming, and dolphin and whale-watching.

One informative, laid-back trip is the *Bellbird* Marine Discovery tour (☎ 335 1521). The small fishing boat takes you out to islands in Cockburn Sound on either a half-day or day trip. You can also swim with Australian sea lions *(Neophoca cinerea)* – these are much larger than fur seals and they range through the Southern and Indian oceans. The sea lions on Carnac Island are nonmating males, barren females and juveniles. The cost is $35 with a healthy lunch; there are discounts for hostellers.

An informative whale-watching trip entitled Sailing with the Whales (☎ 447 7500) is run in conjunction with Underwater World aboard the 18-metre yacht *Dreamtime*. The actual search is for the humpback whale, which returns to Antarctic waters after wintering in the waters of north-western Australia. The trip begins at Hillarys boat harbour from September to November and costs $50 (no discount for children).

Another whale-watching operator is Boat Torque (☎ 221 5844), whose trips cost $22/16.50 for adults and $9/8 for children, from Hillarys/Fremantle, respectively. To get to Hillarys take the train to Warwick and then bus No 423 from there; on the weekend take bus No 929. From Freo there is Rock Island Charters (☎ (336 2060); the cost is $25 (children $15).

Dolphin-watching can be enjoyed on two-hour cruises from Val St jetty (☎ (09) 527 2661), Rockingham. Trips depart in summer on Monday, Wednesday, Friday and Sunday at 9 am.

Festivals

Every year around February/March the Festival of Perth offers music, drama, dance and films. The 'alternative' Northbridge Festival coincides. The Royal Perth Show takes place every September, and the Artrage Festival is in October.

Places to Stay

Perth has a wide variety of accommodation catering for all tastes and price brackets. The main area for budget beds is Northbridge, while hotels, motels and holiday flats are spread throughout Perth.

Camping Perth, like many large cities, is not well-endowed with camp sites convenient to the city centre. However, there are many caravan parks in the suburbs. Some of these include (distances are from the city):

Central Caravan Park (☎ 277 1704), seven km east at 38 Central Ave, Redcliffe; tent/powered sites $14/17, en suite park cabins $50.

Guildford Caravan Park (☎ 274 2828), 19 km north-east at 372 West Swan Rd, Guildford; powered sites from $13 to $16, units from $45.

Karrinyup Waters Resort (☎ 447 6665), 14 km north at 467 North Beach Rd, Gwelup; tent/powered sites $13/16, on-site vans from $29 and cabins $49 to $59.

Kenlorn Tourist Park (☎ 356 2380), nine km south-east at 229 Welshpool Rd, Queens Park; powered sites $15, en suite cabins $40.

Star Haven Caravan Park (☎ 341 1770), 14 km north-west at 18-20 Pearl Parade, Scarborough; sites $12, on-site vans from $23.

Hostels There are over 20 budget hostels around Perth – most are reasonably central.

City Centre & Northbridge The new *Hay Street Backpackers* (☎ 221 9880) at No 286 is the pick of the town's budget accommodation, with modern facilities in a carefully renovated old building. There is a balcony, an outdoor area and modern kitchen. It is well worth the $14 in dorm rooms or $38 for double rooms.

At 195 Hay St is *East Perth Backpackers* (☎ 221 1666) which has dorm beds from $11. Also close to town is *Murray Street International Hostel* (☎ 325 7627), at 119 Murray St; dorm beds are from $13 and it has all the usual facilities as well as an open-air barbecue area.

The *Francis St YHA Hostel* (☎ 328 7794),

at 42-48 Francis St, Northbridge, is in an old guesthouse near the corner of William St, and a little closer to the city. This hostel has friendly hosts, bicycles for hire and a large outdoor area. It has dorm beds for $13 and doubles are $24. Around the corner at 253 William St is the large *Britannia YHA Hostel* (☎ 328 6121) which has recently been tidied up. Dorm beds are from $14 and twins from $32; there is limited parking.

Budget Backpackers International (☎ 328 9468), at 342 Newcastle St, has a comfortable lounge and good kitchen facilities; dorm beds are from $11 per person. Farther along Newcastle St, at No 496, is *Redbackpackers* (☎ 1800 679 969) which has its share of lovers and loathers.

Rory's (☎ 328 9958), also listed as *Backpackers Perth Inn*, at 194 Brisbane St, is farther north of the city centre than other hostels. However, this nice renovated colonial house is very clean and has a pleasant garden and barbecue area. Dorm beds are from $12 and twins are $28.

A good alternative is the *North Lodge* (☎ 227 7588) at 225 Beaufort St. It's clean, friendly, has all the usual facilities and comfortable dorm beds are from $11.

The *Perth Travellers Lodge* (☎ 328 6667) at 156-158 Aberdeen St is actually made up of two recently renovated houses, one for males and one for females. This place takes semipermanent boarders so if you are after international flavour look elsewhere. Otherwise dorm beds are from $10 to $14.

The *Aberdeen Lodge* (☎ 227 6137), at 79 Aberdeen St, East Perth, is central and has four-bed dorms where a bed is $10 or twin rooms are $24. Two other Aberdeen St places are *Backpackers' International* (☎ 227 9977), at the corner of Lake St, and the impressive *12.01 Central* (☎ 227 1201), at the corner of Fitzgerald St. The International has dorms from $10 and twins for $24. In the 12.01 there are dorms from $14, twins for $28 and B&B singles/doubles for $32/44.

Also in the Northbridge area is *Cheviot Lodge* (☎ 227 6817) at 30 Bulwer St. Open 24 hours, it is close to the interstate rail terminal, provides a free pick-up service

from Westrail bus station and hires out bicycles; a bed only is $13 and there are no bunk beds. A little way out of the budget strip, at 235 Vincent St in West Perth, is *Beatty Lodge* (☎ 227 1521) with dorm beds from $12.

At *City Backpackers' HQ* (also known as the Lone Star; ☎ 328 7566), on the corner of Beaufort and Newcastle Sts, most rooms have fridges, fans and balconies; bunk beds are $10, twins and doubles are $12 per person. With the Lone Star Saloon below, you may need earplugs. Next door is the ordinary *Newcastle Lodge* (☎ 328 5186) at 144-148 Newcastle St. Dorm beds are $9 so you get what you pay for!

The *Jewell House YMCA* (☎ 325 8488), at 180 Goderich St (as Murray St becomes after Victoria Square), has over 200 comfortable, clean and modern rooms. It's about a 15-minute walk from the city centre – the Red Clipper bus passes by. Singles/doubles/triples are from $20/37/45 and weekly rates are six times the daily rate.

The *Grand Central YMCA* (☎ 221 2682), at 379 Wellington St, has a great variety of accommodation; bunk beds are $15 and singles/doubles are from $25/40. There is also a restaurant and cafe in the building.

At *St Georges College* (☎ 382 5555), within the University of WA on Mounts Bay Rd, very reasonable B&B singles/doubles are available during university recesses for $20/30. Guests have access to many student facilities.

At 9 Blake St in North Perth there's the *Nomads Knutsford Arms Backpackers* (☎ 443 3499), with dorms for $11, and doubles for $32.

Scarborough This is a good alternative to Northbridge, being close to the surf. The *Mandarin Gardens YHA* (☎ 341 5431), at 20-28 Wheatcroft St, has dorm beds from $12, singles/doubles for $22/28 and units from $50. The hostel is within walking distance of popular Scarborough Beach, and it has friendly hosts, a swimming pool and a recreation area.

The *Sunset Beach* (☎ 341 6655), at 256 West Coast Highway, has dorm beds from

$12 and singles/doubles from $20/32. A 'big' breakfast from the accompanying cafe is $6.

At 6 Westborough St, the *Western Beach Lodge* (☎ 245 1624) has male and female dorms. This small place is clean and airy and singles/doubles are from $13/28. Another place, *Sunset Coast Backpackers* (☎ 245 1161), has opened at 119 Scarborough Beach Rd – their introductory offer is pay for one night, get another free.

Hotels There are several old-fashioned hotels around the centre of Perth. The *Regatta Hotel* (☎ 325 5155), centrally located at 560 Hay St, has friendly staff and simple but clean B&B singles/doubles from $45/64. Also centrally located is the *Downtowner Lodge* (☎ 325 6973), at 63 Hill St, opposite the Perth Mint. The 13 rooms are clean and pleasant, and it's a very quiet, friendly, nonsmoking place with a TV lounge and car park. Beds are $17 in twin rooms and there are weekly rates.

At the back of the Wentworth Plaza Hotel, on the corner of Wellington and William Sts, is the *Royal Hotel* (☎ 481 1000), a renovated Federation-style building in the city centre. It has singles for $30 to $45, and doubles for $45 to $60. The hotel has bars and restaurants.

In Cottesloe, the *Cottesloe Beach Hotel* (☎ 383 1100) is right on the beach on the corner of John St and Marine Parade. Spacious singles/doubles with fridge, tea and coffee facilities and TV cost from $45/65.

Motels & Holiday Flats Perth and the surrounding suburbs have an abundance of motels and holiday flats (see the *Western Australia Accommodation Listing* available from the tourist office for more information).

City Waters Lodge (☎ 325 1566), at 118 Terrace Rd by the river, is conveniently central and good value with cooking facilities, bathroom, TV, laundry and so on. Daily costs are $78 for a one-bedroom family unit.

North of the city centre at 166 Palmerston St are the self-contained *Brownelea Holiday Units* (☎ 328 4840) at $50 a double. The *Adelphi Hotel Apartments* (☎ 322 4666), at 130A Mounts Bay Rd, has well-equipped units for $55/75.

There are a couple of places in Mount St. *Mountway Holiday Units* (☎ 321 8307) at No 36 has singles/doubles from $36/41 and the *Mount Street Inn* (☎ 481 0866) at No 24 has double rooms for $104.

Heading south across the bridge to Applecross, the *Canning Bridge Auto Lodge* (☎ 364 2511) is at 891 Canning Highway, with double rooms from $55. The *Metro Inn Apartments* (☎ 325 1866) at 22 Nile St has double units from $60 to $75. Along the Swan River there is the *Swanview Motel* (☎ 367 5755) at 1 Preston St in Como; units for one or two people are from $64.

There is a host of accommodation between the airport and city on the Great Eastern Highway and many up-market places in the city centre; enquire at the WATC.

Places to Eat

Food Halls This terrific Asian idea has really taken off in Perth, and crowded food halls prove that it's a popular alternative to fast food. You can choose quick meals, desserts and drinks from a range of cuisines to eat in the central eating area.

The *Down Under Food Hall* in the Hay St Mall, downstairs and near the corner of William St, has stalls with Chinese, Mexican, Thai and many other flavours. The food hall is open Monday to Wednesday from 8 am to 7 pm, and Thursday to Saturday from 8 am to 9 pm.

The *Carillon Food Hall*, in the Carillon Arcade on Hay St Mall, is slightly more up-market and has the same international flavour with Italian, Middle Eastern and Chinese food from $5 to $7. It has sandwich shops, a seafood stall and fast-food outlets.

The large *Northbridge Pavilion* on the corner of Lake and James Sts is another good-value international food hall with Japanese, Italian, Indian, Thai, vegetarian and Chinese food. Open from Wednesday to Sunday, it has outdoor seating and bars; the juices at *Naturals* are truly wonderful.

Seafood Perth has excellent seafood restaurants. A number of well-frequented places in Northbridge are *Simon's* at 73 Francis St; *Harry's Seafood Grill* at 94 Aberdeen St; and *The Fishy Affair* at 132 James St. On the Nedlands foreshore, *Jo Jo's* claims to have the freshest seafood in town, and *Jessica's*, in the Hyatt Centre at 99 Adelaide Terrace, is also good.

City The city centre is especially good for lunches and light meals. *Magic Apple Wholefoods*, 447 Hay St, does delicious pita-bread sandwiches and fresh juices. The busy *Bernadi's*, at 528 Hay St, has good sandwiches, quiche, home-made soups and salads. The *Hayashi Japanese BBQ*, at 107 Pier St, has excellent set lunches for around $12. At 117 Murray St, between Pier and Barrack Sts, is the pleasant, reasonably priced Japanese *Jun & Tommy's*, where a sumptuous bento (lunch box) is $12.

Bobby Dazzler's at the Wentworth Plaza, on the corner of William and Hay Sts, prides itself on its Australian menu – a good place for a bite and a drink. The *Granary*, downstairs at 37 Barrack St, has an extensive range of vegetarian dishes. Also on Barrack St, at No 137, is *Ann's Malaysian Food*. Down in Murray St, on the corner of Pier St, is *Miss Maud's*, a Swedish restaurant.

The *Venice Cafe* at the St George's Terrace end of the Trinity Arcade (shop No 201) is a pleasant European-style cafe with tables out the front and light meals such as lasagne, quiche or home-made pies and salad from $4 to $6. They also make excellent coffee.

Perth has the usual selection of counter meals in the city centre area. *Sassella's Tavern*, in the City Arcade, off Hay St, does bistro meals from $8 to $11. The *Savoy Tavern*, under the Savoy Plaza Hotel, at 636 Hay St, has basic pub fare such as roast beef and vegetables and fish & chips for lunch.

Toward the western (Kings Park) end of the city centre, there's a string of places, including the popular *Fast Eddy's* on the corner of Murray and Milligan Sts. Shafto Lane between Murray and Hay Sts has a number of eateries including *Tandoor*

Darbar, the *Manhattan Deli*, and the *Iguana Cafe*, with Wednesday pasta and wine specials for only $10 per person.

Kings Park Restaurant and *Frasers Restaurant* are both good for a splurge, and both have great views over the city and the river.

Northbridge North of the city centre, the area bounded by William, Lake and Newcastle Sts is full of ethnic restaurants. Below are some suggested places to eat, but this list is by no means exhaustive. The best bet is just to walk around and take in the sights and smells – you will soon find something to your liking at an appropriate price.

Kim Anh, at 178 William St near the railway station, is a friendly Vietnamese BYO place with an extensive menu including vegetarian food. At 182 William St is the reasonably priced *Tak Chee*, a favourite amongst the locals – always a good sign. They serve delicious Penang-style rice and noodle dishes. Across the street, at No 175, is the *Linh Phong*. Nearby, at 188 William St, is the cheap and popular *Romany*, one of the city's really long-running Italian places.

Not far away, at No 197, is *Sylvana Pastry*, a comfortable Lebanese coffee bar with an amazing selection of those sticky Middle Eastern pastries which look, and usually taste, delicious. On the corner of Aberdeen and William Sts is the busy *Bar Italia* which serves excellent coffee and light meals including a good selection of pasta; it is open from breakfast until 1 am.

Mamma Maria's, at 105 Aberdeen St on the corner of Lake St, has a pleasant ambience and a reputation as one of Perth's best Italian eateries. Its main courses are priced from $11.50. There are a couple of other places on Lake St which serve tasty food. The reasonably priced *L'Alba Cafe* is on the corner of Newcastle St and the trendy *Lake Street Cafe* is on the corner of Aberdeen St.

At 17 Chinatown (66 Roe St) is the cleverly named *Thai me Down Sport*, open seven days for lunch and dinner for all those spicy Thai favourites. In front of this place is a bewildering array of Asian cuisine squeezed into rambling food halls, exuding aromatic smells reminiscent of Singapore, Canton and Bangkok.

The impecunious can head to *Hare Krishna Food for Life* at 200 William St for cheap food and a good measure of free karma.

Leederville Several restaurants and cafes have recently opened in Leederville, north-west of the city centre. Located on Oxford St, between Vincent and Aberdeen Sts, they include *Villa Bianchi*, *Giardini* and *Palermo*. For Irish food and Guinness stumble to *Molly Malone's* (with O'Reilly's Irish Bar) at 99 Cambridge St; a cockle and mussel chowder is $6 and a prawn and vegetable pie is $13. *Fat Bellies*, 115 Oxford St, serves hearty portions at reasonable prices.

Entertainment

Perth has plenty of pubs, discos and night-clubs. Thursday's *West Australian* has an informative entertainment lift-out called the *Revue*. The *X-press*, a weekly music maga-zine available free at record shops and other outlets, has a gig guide. Northbridge and nearby Oxford St, Leederville, are definitely the places to go after dark – Friday night in Northbridge is witness to frenetic revelry, while the city centre is comparatively 'dead'.

Pubs & Live Music Popular places for inter-esting live music in Northbridge are the *Aberdeen*, at 84 Aberdeen St; and the *Lone Star*, on the corner of Beaufort and Newcas-tle Sts (they have a backpackers' night every Wednesday and live bands on the weekends). For jazz, *The Supper Club* is on the corner of Lake and Francis Sts. For Guinness and a good time, there's *Molly O'Grady's* pub, appropriately plonked on the corner of Milligan (and James) Sts.

Perth has the usual pub-rock circuit, with varying cover charges depending on the gig. Popular venues include *Indi* at 27 Hastings St, Scarborough; *The Loft*, 237 Hay St, East Perth; the *Planet*, 329 Charles St, North Perth; the *Swanbourne*, 141 Claremont Cres-cent, Swanbourne; *Raffs*, corner of Canning Highway and Kintail Rd, Applecross; the

Wembley, 344 Cambridge St, Wembley; and *O'Connors Tavern* at 72 Outram St, West Perth.

Discos & Nightclubs This sort of entertain-ment fits racy Perth to a 'T'. In the city centre is *Mangoes*, a pre-clubbing venue with music and exotic cocktails at 101 Murray St, and the *Loft* nightclub at 237 Hay St. *Havana* is a trendy, up-market venue at 69 Lake St, frequented by Oxo Cuban expats. Those keen on H_2O, filter to the *Aqua Bar* at 232 William St, Northbridge; the 'hungry' go to *Gobbles* at 613 Wellington St; the fit and athletic to the *Racquet Club*, corner of Lord and Aberdeen Sts; the swish and elegant queue up outside *Brannigan's* on the corner of Hay and Irwin Sts; and those looking for an 'outing' go to *Exit* at 187 Stirling St.

The *Kazbah Club* at 298 Hay St, Subiaco, and the *Arcadia* (for techno, house and groove) on the corner of Newcastle and Lake Sts, Northbridge, add to the plethora of pulp. The 'oh so hip' will be seen at the *hip-e-club* on the corner of Newcastle and Oxford Sts in Leederville from 9 pm till late.

Gay and lesbian places include the *Northbridge Hotel*, corner of Lake and Bris-bane Sts; the *Court Hotel*, corner of Beaufort and James Sts; *Connections* (Connies), James St; and *DC's*, Francis St. For venues and activities check in the *Westside Observer*, which is a free publication avail-able from the Arcane Bookshop in Northbridge.

Cinemas, Theatre & Concerts Quality and 'alternative' films are shown at the *Lumiere* in the Perth Entertainment Centre, Welling-ton St; *Luna Cinemas* at 155 Oxford St, Leederville; *Cinema Paradiso* at 166 James St; and the *Astor*, on the corner of Beaufort and Walcott Sts in Mt Lawley. For Oscar-nominated favourites there are huge Hoyts and Greater Union cinema complexes throughout the city and suburbs.

Popular theatres include *His Majesty's* on the corner of King and Hay Sts, the *Regal* at 474 Hay St in Subiaco and the *Hole in the Wall* at the Subiaco Theatre Centre, 180

Hamersley Rd, Subiaco. The *Playhouse* at 3 Pier St is a smaller version of His Majesty's.

For stand-up comedy there is the *Laugh Resort* in Pockets Pool Lounge, 44 Lake St, Northbridge; entry is usually about $5. There are often very interesting, 'touch of the weird' live theatre performances at PICA (Perth Institute of Contemporary Arts) at 51 James St, Northbridge.

The *Perth Concert Hall* in St George's Terrace and the large *Entertainment Centre* in Wellington St are venues for concerts and recitals by local and international acts.

Spectator Sports The people of Perth, like most Australians, are parochial in their support of local sporting teams. These include the West Coast Eagles and the Fremantle Dockers, WA's two representatives in the Australian Football League; the Western Reds in the Australian Rugby League; the WAIS Thundersticks and WAIS Diamonds in the men's and women's national hockey competitions; and the Perth Wildcats and WAIS Breakers in the men's and women's national basketball leagues. All regularly play interstate teams in Perth. See the *West Australian* for details.

Casino On the south bank of the Swan, off the Great Western Highway at Victoria Park, is Perth's glitzy *Burswood Casino*, open daily 24 hours. It has gaming tables, a two-up gallery, Keno, poker machines and extensive off-course betting.

Things to Buy

Perth has a number of excellent outlets for Aboriginal arts and crafts, including the Creative Native Gallery at 32 King St and Indigenart at 115 Hay St, Subiaco. Other local crafts can be found at the many markets – see the Markets section earlier in this chapter.

For camping, backpacking and climbing equipment, there's Paddy Pallin at 915 Hay St and, across the road at No 862, Mountain Designs. Farther down Hay St at No 437 is Off the Edge.

Getting There & Away

Air Both Qantas (☎ 13 1313) and Ansett (☎ 13 1300) have flights to and from Sydney, Melbourne, Brisbane, Cairns, Adelaide, Darwin and Alice Springs. Some Sydney and Melbourne flights go direct, and some via Adelaide or, in the case of Sydney, via Melbourne. Ansett also flies from Perth to Christmas Island and the Cocos Islands twice weekly.

The standard economy fares are $643 to Sydney, $577 Melbourne, $683 Brisbane, $516 Adelaide, $628 Darwin and $484 Alice Springs. As always, check with the airlines for special deals, especially seven-day advance purchase fares; it would be rare that you'd have to pay full economy fare.

Ansett and its subsidiary Skywest (☎ 334 2288) fly to WA centres such as Albany, Broome, Carnarvon, Derby, Esperance, Exmouth, Geraldton, Kalgoorlie, Karratha, Kununurra, Meekatharra, Monkey Mia and Port Hedland.

Bus Greyhound Pioneer (☎ 13 2030) operates daily bus services from Adelaide to Perth ($189 one way/$342 return) from the Westrail Centre on West Parade in East Perth (interstate railway station). The journey from Perth to Darwin along the coast takes around 56 hours by bus and costs $348. Greyhound also operates a thrice-weekly service to Darwin via the more direct, inland route through Newman (it saves five hours and is the same price).

McCafferty's (☎ 13 1499) has a daily service on the Perth-Darwin coastal route which currently costs less than Greyhound. They have a range of economical passes – Darwin to Perth ($275, or $480 with Coral Bay, Monkey Mia and Exmouth), Perth to Monkey Mia ($130) and Perth to Broome ($155, $275 with Monkey Mia, etc).

Westrail operates bus services to a number of WA centres including Albany ($35.10), Augusta ($29.10), Bunbury ($16.30), Busselton ($21.30), Esperance ($52.60), Geraldton ($36.70), Meekatharra ($67.30) and Pemberton ($30.60).

Train Along with the Ghan to Alice Springs, the long Indian Pacific run is one of Australia's great railway journeys – a 65-hour trip between the Pacific Ocean on one side of the continent and the Indian Ocean on the other. Travelling this way you see Australia at ground level and by the end of the journey you either appreciate the immensity of the country or are bored stiff – perhaps both.

From Sydney, you cross New South Wales to Broken Hill and then continue on to Adelaide and across the Nullarbor. From Port Augusta to Kalgoorlie, the seemingly endless crossing of the virtually uninhabited centre takes well over 24 hours, including the 'long straight' on the Nullarbor – at 478 km this is the longest straight stretch of railway line in the world. Unlike the trans-Nullarbor road, which runs south of the Nullarbor along the coast of the Great Australian Bight, the railway line actually crosses the Nullarbor Plain.

To Perth, one-way low/high fares from Adelaide are \$396/438 for a Holiday class sleeper, \$605/672 for a 1st-class sleeper or \$200 in a coach car seat with no meals; and from Sydney \$612/679 Holiday class, \$943/1048 1st class or \$320 seat only. The low season is from 1 February to 30 June; note that a seat-only is the same in all seasons.

A limited number of advance-purchase fares are available in the low season. These offer good reductions (around 30%) if you book at least seven days in advance. Melbourne and Adelaide passengers connect with the Indian Pacific at Port Pirie. Accompanied/unaccompanied cars can be transported between Adelaide and Perth (\$290/440) and most other major cities.

The distance from Sydney to Perth is 3961 km. You can break your journey at any stop along the way and continue later as long as you complete the one-way trip within two months; return tickets are valid for up to six months. Westbound, the Indian Pacific departs Sydney on Monday and Thursday. Heading east, the train departs Perth on Monday and Friday. Book at least a month in advance.

Between Adelaide and Perth you can also travel on the weekly Trans-Australia train. Fares are the same as those on the Indian Pacific, and the trip takes 38 hours.

The only rail services within WA are the *Prospector* from Perth to Kalgoorlie and the *Australind* from Perth to Bunbury – see the Kalgoorlie and Bunbury sections for details. All rail services run to or from the Westrail terminal in East Perth, as do the Westrail buses. Bookings can be made by phoning ☎ 13 2232, or with the WATC, Forrest Place.

Car Rental Carefully read the conditions when you hire a car in WA. Many Perth hire car firms have a pathological fear of their cars being taken into the 'bush' and impose special rates. Hertz (☎ 321 7777), Budget (☎ 322 1100), Avis (☎ 325 7677) and Thrifty (☎ 481 1999) are all represented in Perth, along with cheaper local firms including:

ATC
  126 Adelaide Terrace (☎ 325 1833)
Carousel Rent-a-Car
  318 Charles St, North Perth (☎ 328 8999)
Economic Car Rental
  179 William St (☎ 227 1112)
Network
  253 William St, Northbridge, next to the Britannia YHA (☎ 227 8810)

Hitching Hostel notice boards are worth checking for lifts to points around the country. If you're hitching out of Perth to the north or east, take a train to Midland. For travel south, take a train to Armadale. Trans-Nullarbor hitching is not that easy, and the fierce competition between bus companies and discounted air fares have made those forms of travel much more attractive.

Getting Around

Perth has a central public transport organisation called Transperth which operates buses, trains and ferries. There are Transperth information offices (☎ 13 2213) in the Plaza Arcade (off the Hay St Mall), at the City Bus Port on Mounts Bay Rd at the foot of William St and at the Wellington St bus station. They can all provide advice about getting around

Perth and can also supply a system map and timetables. These offices are open weekdays from 6.30 am to 8 pm, and Saturday from 8 am to 5 pm.

To/From the Airport Perth's airport is busy night and day. The city's isolation from the east coast and the airport's function as an international arrival point mean planes arrive and depart at all hours.

The domestic and international terminals are 10 km apart and taxi fares to the city are around $15 and $20, respectively. The privately run Perth Airport Bus (☎ 479 4131) meets all incoming domestic and international flights and provides transport to the city centre, hotels and hostels. Although the operators claim to meet all flights, some travellers have reported that sometimes it doesn't turn up – if this occurs late at night, a taxi is probably your best option.

The airport bus costs $6 from the domestic terminal and $7 from the international terminal. There are scheduled runs to the terminals every couple of hours from 4.45 am to 10.30 pm. Call them for hotel and hostel pick-ups and timetable information.

Alternatively, you can get into the city for about $2.10 on Transperth bus Nos 200, 201, 202, 208 and 209 to William St on the corner of St George's Terrace. They depart from the domestic terminal every hour or so (more frequently at peak times) from 5.30 am to 10 pm on weekdays and for nearly as long on Saturday; Sunday services are less frequent. Going to the domestic terminal, the bus leaves from stand No 39 on St George's Terrace.

Some of the backpackers' places pick up at the airport (generally only if you are staying in their accommodation that night) and offer reduced fares into the city.

Bus There are five free City Clipper services which operate at least every 15 minutes or so Monday to Friday from 7 am to 6 pm. The Yellow Clipper (No 1), the only Clipper bus operational on Saturday, services the city centre every 15 minutes (there are no Clippers on Sunday). The Yellow, Red and Green

clipper services pass through the Wellington St bus station.

(No 1) Yellow Clipper
    Operates around the central area of the city.
(No 2) Purple Clipper
    Operates from the City Bus Port to West Perth.
(No 3) Green Clipper
    Travels between the Wellington St bus station and West Perth.
(No 4) Blue Clipper
    Runs from the City Bus Port, Mounts Bay Rd, to the Esplanade along Barrack and William Sts, then down Beaufort St.
(No 5) Red Clipper
    Departs Wellington St bus station to East Perth, near the WACA sports ground, and returns.

On regular buses, a short ride of one zone costs $1.50, two zones costs $2.10 and three zones $2.70. Zone 1 includes the city centre and the inner suburbs (including Subiaco and Claremont), and Zone 2 extends all the way to Fremantle, 20 km from the city centre. A Multirider ticket gives you 10 journeys for the price of nine.

The Perth Tram (☎ 367 9404) doesn't run on rails – it's a bus that takes you around some of Perth's main attractions (such as the city, Kings Park, Barrack St jetty and the casino) in 1½ hours for $12. The 'tram' leaves from 124 Murray St (near Barrack St) six times a day, seven days a week.

Train Transperth operates suburban train lines to Armadale, Fremantle, Midland and the northern suburb of Joondalup daily from around 5.20 am to 11.30 pm. All trains leave from the Central Perth station, Wellington St.

Your rail ticket can also be used on Transperth buses and ferries within the ticket's area of validity.

Bicycle Cycling is a great way to explore Perth. There are many bicycle routes along the river all the way to Fremantle and along the Indian Ocean coast. Get the free *Along the Coast Ride* and *Around the Rivers Ride: Recreational Cycle Tour* booklets from the WATC in Forrest Place.

At WA Bike Disposals (☎ 325 1176), in Bennett St, you can buy a bike knowing that you get a guaranteed buy-back price after a certain time. Ride Away (☎ 354 2393), by the city side of the Causeway, also rents cycles.

Boat Transperth ferries cross the river from the Barrack St jetty to the Mends St jetty in South Perth daily, every half an hour (more frequently at peak times) from around 7 am to 7 pm for 80c. The service is extended in summer until 9.30 pm. Take this ferry to get to the zoo.

The Rottnest Island Getting There & Away section has details on ferries from Perth, Hillarys and Fremantle to Rottnest. See the earlier Tours section for river cruises.

Around Perth

FREMANTLE (pop 25,000)

Fremantle ('Freo' to the locals), Perth's port, is at the mouth of the Swan River, 19 km south-west of the city centre. Over the years, Perth has sprawled to engulf Fremantle, which is now more a suburb of the city than a town in its own right. Despite recent development, Freo has a far more laid-back feeling than gleaming, skyscrapered Perth. It's a place with a real sense of history and a very pleasant atmosphere.

Fremantle was founded in 1829 when the HMS *Challenger* landed, captained by Charles Fremantle. Like Perth, the settlement made little progress until it decided to take on convicts. This cheap and hard-worked labour constructed most of the town's earliest buildings, some of them amongst the oldest and most treasured in WA. As a port, Fremantle was abysmal until the brilliant engineer C Y O'Connor built an artificial harbour in the 1890s.

In 1987, the city was the site of the unsuccessful defence of what was, for a brief period, one of Australia's most prized possessions – the America's Cup yachting trophy. Preparations for the influx of tourists associated with the competition certainly transformed Fremantle into a more modern,

colourful and expensive city. Many of the residents protested, however, that their lifestyle and the character of their community were being damaged by development.

The town has numerous interesting old buildings, some excellent museums and galleries, lively produce and craft markets, and a diverse range of pubs, cafes and restaurants. A visit to Freo will be one of the highlights of your trip to WA. Make sure you allow enough time to explore, sip coffee in an outdoor cafe and soak in the atmosphere.

Information

There is an information centre in the Fremantle Town Hall shop (☎ 430 2346), near St John's Square, which is open weekdays from 9 am to 5 pm, and weekends from 10 am to 3 pm. At the time of writing, the out-of-touch civic authorities were closing this office as a cost-cutting measure. It's not clear where the 90,000-plus visitors who make enquiries every year will go. Among their brochures are the informative *Manjaree Track*, *Convict Trail* and *Old Foreshore*.

There is a bookshop, New Editions, in South Terrace.

Fremantle Museum & Arts Centre

The museum, at 1 Finnerty St, is housed in an impressive building constructed as a lunatic asylum in the 1860s by convicts. It has a fine collection, including exhibits on Fremantle's early history, the colonisation of WA and the early whaling industry. It also tells the intriguing story of the Dutch East India Company ships which first discovered the western coast of Australia and in several instances were wrecked on its inhospitable shores. The museum is open Thursday to Sunday from 1 pm to 5 pm; admission is by donation.

The Arts Centre, which occupies one wing of the building, is open daily from 10 am to 5 pm and Wednesday evening from 7 to 9 pm; admission is free.

Maritime Museum

On Cliff St, near the waterfront, is the Maritime Museum, which occupies a building

WESTERN AUSTRALIA

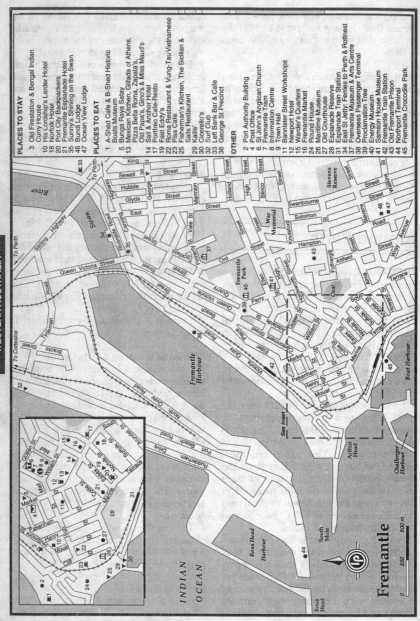

PLACES TO STAY

3 Old Firestation & Bengal Indian
   Curry House
10 His Lordship's Larder Hotel
18 Norfolk Hotel
20 Port City Backpackers
21 Fremantle Esplanade Hotel
35 Sunny's Shining on the Swan
46 Bundi Lodge
47 Ocean View Lodge

PLACES TO EAT

1 A-Shed Cafe & B-Shed Historic
   Boats Museum
5 Bunga Raya Satay
13 Mexican Kitchen, Gilfada of Athens,
   Pizza Bella Roma, Zapata's,
   Old Papa Gino's & Miss Maud's
14 Sail & Anchor Hotel
17 Porfreo Cafe-Resto
19 Fast Eddy's
22 Roma Restaurant & Vung-Tau Vietnamese
23 Pisa Cafe
25 Fisherman's Kitchen, The Sicilian &
   Sails Restaurant
29 Kailis
30 Cicerello's
32 Surf Club
33 Left Bank Bar & Cafe
36 George St Precinct

OTHER

2 Port Authority Building
4 Post Office
6 St John's Anglican Church
7 Fremantle Tram
8 Information Centre
9 Town Hall
11 Bannister Street Workshops
12 Newport Hotel
15 Warder's Quarters
16 Fremantle Market
24 Round House
26 Maritime Museum
27 Old Courthouse
28 Esplanade Reserve
31 Esplanade Train Station
34 East-St Jetty; Ferries to Perth & Rottnest
37 Fremantle Museum & Arts Centre
38 Overseas Passenger Terminal
39 Proclamation Tree
40 Energy Museum
41 Samson House Museum
42 Fremantle Train Station
43 Old Fremantle Prison
44 Northport Terminal
45 Fremantle Crocodile Park

Fremantle

constructed in 1852 as a commissariat store. The museum has a display on WA's maritime history, with particular emphasis on the famous wreck of the *Batavia*. One gallery is used as a working centre where you can see the *Batavia* actually being preserved.

At one end of this gallery is the huge stone facade intended for an entrance to Batavia Castle in modern-day Jakarta, Indonesia. It was being carried by the *Batavia* as ballast when the vessel sank. This intriguing museum is open daily from 10.30 am to 5 pm; admission is free, and a visit is a must.

For boat freaks only, there is a **Historic Boats Museum** displaying boats from the last 100 years in B-Shed at Victoria Quay; admission is by donation. The shed is open weekdays from 10 am to 3 pm, and weekends from 11 am to 5 pm. From late 1997 the building may house *Australia II*, which won the America's Cup in 1983.

Fremantle Market

A prime attraction is the colourful Fremantle Market held on South Terrace at the corner of Henderson St. Originally opened in 1892, the market was reopened in 1975 and draws crowds looking for everything from craft items to vegetables, jewellery and antiques; there is also a great tavern bar where buskers often perform. The market is open Friday from 9 am to 9 pm, Saturday from 9 am to 5 pm, and Sunday from 10 am to 5 pm.

Round House

On Arthur Head at the western end of High St, near the Maritime Museum, is the Round House. Built in 1831, it's the oldest public building in WA. It actually has 12 sides and was originally a local prison (in the days before convicts were brought into WA). It was also the site of the colony's first hanging.

Later, the building was used to hold Aboriginal prisoners before they were taken to prison on Rottnest Island. The site provides good views of Fremantle. The building is open daily from 10 am to 5 pm; admission is free.

Convict-Era Buildings

Many buildings in Fremantle date from the period after 1850, when convict labour was introduced. The *Convict Trail* brochure, available from the Fremantle Town Hall shop, outlines places of interest. They include **Old Fremantle Prison**, one of the first building tasks of the convicts, and a maximum security prison until 1991. The entrance on The Terrace is picturesque. The prison is open daily from 10 am to 6 pm; entry is $10 (children $4). These prices apply also for the eerie candlelight tours, held on Wednesday and Friday at 7.30 pm.

Later Landmarks

Fremantle boomed during the Western Australian gold rush of the 1890s and many buildings were constructed during, or shortly before, this period. They include **Samson House**, a well-preserved 1888 colonial home in Ellen St, which is open Thursday and Sunday from 1 to 5 pm – tours of the house are run by volunteer guides. **St John's Anglican Church** (1882), on the corner of Adelaide and Queen Sts, features a large stained-glass window.

Other buildings of the era include the **Fremantle Town Hall** (1887) in St John's Square; the former **German Consulate** built in 1902 at 5 Mouat St; the **Fremantle railway station** (1907); and the old, Georgian-style **Customs House** on Cliff St. The **water trough** in the park in front of the station has a memorial to two men who died of thirst on an outback expedition. The **Proclamation Tree**, near the corner of Adelaide and Parry Sts, is a Moreton Bay fig that was planted in 1890.

Other Attractions

Fremantle is well-endowed with parks, including the popular **Esplanade Reserve**, beside the picturesque boat harbour off Marine Terrace.

The city is a popular centre for craft workers and one of the best places to find them is at the imaginative **Bannister Street Workshops**. From the observation tower on top of the **Port Authority Building**, at the end of Cliff St, you can enjoy a panoramic view of the harbour. You must take an escorted tour, which are conducted from the foyer weekdays at 1.30 pm only.

The **Energy Museum**, at 12 Parry St, has some entertaining and educational displays tracing the development of gas and electricity. It is open weekdays from 10.30 am to 4.30 pm and weekends from 1 to 4.30 pm; admission is free.

Finally, on the Boat Harbour, there is the **Fremantle Crocodile Park**, where the reptiles have the avarice of entrepreneurs; admission is $8. It is open weekdays from 10 am to 4 pm, and weekends from 10 am to 5 pm. Feeding times are 11.30 am and 2 pm daily, except Monday.

Tours

The Fremantle Tram (☎ 339 8719), very much like the Perth Tram, does a 45-minute historical tour of Fremantle with full commentary for $7. The tram leaves daily from the town hall, near the intersection of High and Adelaide Sts, on the hour between 10 am to 5 pm; a harbour tour is also available for $7 and a Top of the Port tour for $10. You can combine the tour with a cruise to Perth, a tour of Perth on the Perth Tram and a return ticket to Fremantle for $33.

Places to Stay

The *Fremantle Village & Chalet Centre* (☎ 430 4866), on the corner of Cockburn and Rockingham Rds, has tent/powered sites for $12/14, on-site vans for $45 and chalets for $65; all prices are for two. It's about 3.5 km from central Fremantle.

There are three backpackers hostels in Freo. The renovated and central *Port City Backpackers* (☎ 335 6635) at 5 Essex St is the pick of the budget places. It is close to the cafe strip of South Terrace and across the road from the illustrious Esplanade Hotel. It has a courtyard, games room, TV and video lounge, all thrown in for the dorm-bed price of $13; singles/doubles are $20/32.

The *Old Firestation* (☎ 430 5454), at 18 Phillimore St, is only a minute's walk from the Fremantle railway station. It includes a restaurant which has an extensive vegetarian menu, a laundrette, kitchens and passable dorm rooms; a dorm bed is $13 and twins or doubles are $32. On arrival, you receive a box with your name on it, which contains eating utensils and sheets.

The *Bundi Lodge* (☎ 335 3467) is a fine period building at 96 Hampton Rd. Beds in a four-share room are $12, and there's one double at $26.

The *Ocean View Lodge* (☎ 336 2962), 100 Hampton Rd, has twins for $15 per person and singles/doubles for $20/30. This huge complex has a gym, sauna, billiard room, pool, tennis court and barbecue area.

His Lordship's Larder Hotel (☎ 336 1766), on the corner of Mouat and Phillimore Sts, recognisable by the 'skimpy bar' on its corner, is a renovated place with rooms for $25/45. Rooms with facilities in the classier *Norfolk Hotel* (☎ 335 5405), 47 South Terrace, are $60/80 for singles/doubles.

Sunny's Shining on the Swan (☎ 339 1888), 6 Canning Highway, has motel units without/with en suite for $85/120. The ritziest hotel in town is the four-star *Fremantle Esplanade Hotel* (☎ 319 1256) on the corner of Marine Terrace and Collie St; regular/deluxe rooms are from $180/210.

For homestays, contact the information centre (if it still exists) or Fremantle Homestays (☎ 319 1256). They can arrange B&B accommodation in houses around Fremantle from $45 to $60 for a single, or $65 to $80 for a double. Self-contained single and double units are also available from $200 to $700 per week.

You can get a copy of the free *Accommodation Guide to Fremantle* from the Town Hall shop.

Places to Eat

A highlight of Fremantle is its diverse range of cafes, restaurants, food halls and taverns. Many a traveller's day has been whittled away sipping wine, beer or coffee and watching the passing parade from kerbside tables.

Along South Terrace, there's a string of outdoor cafes and restaurants, including the popular *Old Papa's – Ristorante Luigi's*, at

No 17, which has coffee and gelati; the trendy *Gino's* (the place to be seen) at No 1; and the large *Miss Maud's* at No 33. All these places can be crowded on weekends when the weather is fine.

The historic *Sail & Anchor* (formerly the Freemason's Hotel, built in 1854), at 64 South Terrace, has been impressively restored to much of its former glory. It specialises in locally brewed Matilda Bay beers, and on the 1st floor is a brasserie which serves snacks and full meals.

Also on South Terrace is the *Mexican Kitchen*, next door to Old Papa's, with dishes from $10 to $12. Across the road are *Pizza Bella Roma*, the *Glifada of Athens*, with tasty souvlaki, and the popular, licensed Mexican *Zapata's* at Shop 30, South Terrace Piazza. The *Portfreo Cafe-Resto*, on the corner of Parry St and South Terrace, is good for patisseries.

The *Upmarket Food Centre* on Henderson St, opposite the market, has stalls where you can get delicious Thai, Vietnamese, Japanese, Chinese and Italian food from $5 to $7. Open Thursday to Sunday from about noon to 9 pm, it can be very busy, especially on market days. Another cheap place with a good vegetarian menu is the *Bengal Indian Curry House*, part of the Old Firestation in Phillimore St. A plate of soup, choice of at least three dishes and a selection of teas is $6 ($5 for guests of the hostel). The *Bunga Raya Satay* at 8 Cantonment St would win more friends if their serves were larger.

The *Roma*, at 13 High St, is a reliable Freo institution which serves home-made Italian fare including its famous chicken and spaghetti – even the rich and famous queue to eat here. The nearby *Peranakan Place* is good for a cheap breakfast or a quick snack. For Vietnamese food, try the *Vung-Tau*, at 19 High St, with meals (including a vegetarian menu) from $7 to $10. *Fast Eddy's*, a 'satisfy-all' stalwart, is at 13 Essex St.

Fish & chips from *Cicerello's*, *Kailis'* or *Fisherman's Kitchen*, on the Esplanade by the boat harbour, is a Fremantle tradition. The popular *Sicilian*, near McDonald's, is a must – you get a huge plate of fish & chips and a mountain of salad for $10. *Sails*,

upstairs at 47 Mews Rd, has a set-price three-course menu for about $25. Residents describe this harbour area as 'authentic and original Freo'.

The current places to be seen at are the *Left Bank Bar & Cafe* on Riverside Rd down by the East St jetty and the beachy, trendified *Surf Club* (which has both cheap and expensive sections) out at North Fremantle Beach.

Typical pub counter meals are available at the *Newcastle Club Tavern* on Market St and the *National Hotel* on the corner of Market and High Sts; the latter is the best value.

There are also a number of trendy restaurants in the George St precinct, a couple of km north-east of central Fremantle.

Entertainment

There are a number of venues around town with music and/or dancing, the majority concentrated in the High St/South Terrace area.

For Latin, folk and indy music, the *Fly by Night Club*, in Queen St, is frequented by some talented musicians. It's been refurbished and is large and comfortable. The *West End* at 24 High St has a band area in its Club Dread; and the *Go Club* at 80 High St ranges in appeal from dance to less elegant pub sumo wrestling.

Home of the 'big gig' is the *Metropolis* on South Terrace. The *Newport*, also on South Terrace, at No 2, has bands most nights. The *Harbourside*, on the corner of Beach Rd and Parry St, has a regular swathe of thrash bands and is home for ardent moshers.

Getting There & Away

The train between Perth and Fremantle runs every 15 minutes throughout the day ($1.90).

Bus Nos 106 (stand No 35) and 111 (stand No 48) go from St George's Terrace to Fremantle via the Canning Highway; or you can take bus No 105 (stand No 40, St George's Terrace), which takes a longer route south of the river. Bus Nos 103 and 104 also depart from St George's Terrace (southern side) but go to Fremantle via the northern side of the river. Captain Cook Cruises has daily ferries from Perth to Fremantle for around $12.50 one way.

Bell-a-Bike Cycles (☎ 015 978 792) has bikes for hire; they will deliver.

ROTTNEST ISLAND

'Rotto', as it's known to the locals, is a sandy island about 19 km off the coast from Fremantle. It's 11 km long, 4.5 km wide and is very popular with Perth residents and visitors. The island was discovered by the Dutch explorer de Vlamingh in 1696. He named it Rats' Nest because of the numerous king-size 'rats' he saw there (in fact they were small wallabies called quokkas).

The Rottnest settlement was established in 1838 as a prison for Aboriginal people from the mainland – the early colonists had lots of trouble imposing their ideas of private ownership on the nomadic Aborigines. The prison was abandoned in 1903 and the island soon became an escape for Perth society. Only in the last 30 years, however, has it really developed as a popular day trip. The buildings of the original prison settlement are among the oldest in WA.

What do you do on Rotto? Well, you cycle around, laze in the sun on the many superb beaches (the Basin is the most popular, while Parakeet Bay is the place for skinny dipping), climb the low hills, go fishing or boating, ride a glass-bottom boat (the waters off Rotto have some of the world's most southernmost coral), swim in the crystal-clear water or go quokka spotting.

Information

There is a visitor centre (☎ (09) 372 9727) on Rotto, open weekdays from 8.30 am to 5 pm, Saturday from 9 am to 4 pm and Sunday from 10 am to noon and 2.30 to 4 pm. It is just to the left of the jetty at Thomson Bay (the island's largest settlement) as you arrive. There, and at the museum, you can get useful publications, such as a walking tour of the old settlement buildings, heritage trails, information on the various shipwrecks around the island and a cycling guide.

Also grab a copy of the informative paper *Rottnest Islander*. Rottnest is very popular in the summer when the ferries and accommodation are both heavily booked – plan ahead.

Museum

The excellent little museum, open in summer daily from 10 am to 4 pm, has exhibits about the island, its history, wildlife and shipwrecks. You can pick up a walking-tour leaflet here and wander around the old convict-built buildings, including the octagonal 1864 'Quad'. Free guided walking tours depart from the visitor centre daily at 11.15 am and 2 pm.

Other Attractions

Vlamingh's Lookout on View Hill, near Thomson Bay, offers panoramic views of the island. The main lighthouse, built in 1895, is visible 60 km out to sea.

The island has a number of low-lying salt lakes, and it's around these that you are most likely to spot **quokkas**. Bus tours have regular quokka-feeding points where the voracious marsupials appear on demand.

Also of interest is the restored **Oliver Hill Battery**, west of Thomson Bay. You can get to the battery on the Oliver Hill railway line; trains leave Thomson Bay four times daily. The cost of $9/4.50 for adults/children includes entry to the guns and tunnels. Note that the 2.30 pm train ticket doesn't include entry to the guns or tunnels (the trip costs $6/2.50).

The quokka is a native of Rottnest Island

PAUL STEEL

JEFF WILLIAMS

JEFF WILLIAMS

JEFF WILLIAMS

RICHARD NEBESKY

Western Australia

A: Perth skyline
B: Dolphins at Monkey Mia
C: Cape Leeuwin lighthouse

D: Karijini (Hamersley Range) National Park
E: The Pinnacles Desert, Nambung National Park

JEFF WILLIAMS

JEFF WILLIAMS

JEFF WILLIAMS

MATT KING

A
B
C
D

Western Australia
A: Bungle Bungle (Purnululu) National Park
B: Pteroglyphs, near Karratha
C: View from Bluff Knoll, Stirling Range National Park
D: Landscape near Kununurra

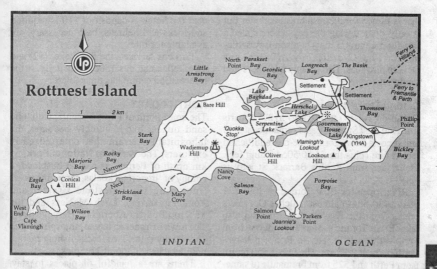

Tours & Cruises

There are two-hour bus tours around the island for $9; they depart from the visitor centre daily at 11.30 am and 1.30 pm – again it is wise to book in the high season.

The *Underwater Explorer* is a boat with windows below the waterline for viewing shipwrecks and marine life. It departs hourly from the jetty at Thomson Bay; an interesting 45-minute trip costs about $15. Some of Rotto's **shipwrecks** are accessible to snorkellers, but getting to most of them requires a boat. There are marker plaques around the island telling the grim tales of how and when the ships sank. Snorkelling equipment, fishing gear and boats can be hired from Dive, Ski & Surf (☎ (09) 292 5167) in Thomson Bay.

Places to Stay

Most visitors to Rotto come only for the day but it's interesting to stay on the island. You can camp for $15 (two people) in hired tents with rubber mattresses or get tent sites for $10 at *Rottnest Camping* (☎ (09) 372 9737). Safari cabins are also available from $25 to $35 a night. Book in advance for a cabin or if you want a tent.

The *Rottnest Island Authority* (☎ (09) 372 9729) has over 260 houses and cottages for rent in Thomson Bay and around Geordie, Fays and Longreach bays, from $50 bungalows to $110 villas (four-bed). Reductions of up to 25% are available in off-peak periods.

The *Kingstown Barracks Hostel* (☎ (09) 372 9780), 1.2 km from the ferry terminal, is in an old barracks built in 1936; the cost per person is from $13 and doubles are $32, linen included.

Units in the *All Seasons Rottnest Lodge* (☎ (09) 292 5161) are from $109.

Places to Eat

Bring your own food if possible because there are slim pickings once you are on the island. *Rottnest Family Restaurant* has a pleasant balcony overlooking Thomson Bay and serves Chinese dishes, dim sum lunches and takeaways. In the same building, coffee and cakes are available from *The Bistro*. There is also a fish & chip outlet and the *Milk Bar* for ice creams.

Brolley's and the *Hampton Chargrill* in the Rottnest Hotel also serve snacks and meals.

The island has a general store and a bakery

that is famed for its fresh bread and pies but is only open during the day. There's also a fast-food centre in the Thomson Bay settlement. The *Geordie Bay Alfresco* has Devonshire teas, fish & chips, burgers and sandwiches.

Getting There & Away

Oceanic Cruises (☎ (09) 430 5127) departs from the East St jetty, East Fremantle, at 9.45 am; it costs $20/6 for a same-day adult/child return fare (plus the $4.50/50c landing fee). Their fare from Perth's Barrack St jetty is $30/11.

Rival operator Boat Torque (☎ (09) 221 5844; 430 5844) almost matches Oceanic's prices from the East St jetty. You can also take Boat Torque's *Star Flyte* ferry from Perth's Barrack St jetty to Rotto; it leaves Perth daily at 9.15 am. The fare is $50 return from Perth and $25 from Fremantle (a same-day return fare). Boat Torque has another service from Hillarys Boat Harbour (north of Perth), which leaves daily at 9.45 am for $37/11, also same-day return.

Another service is Rottnest Express (☎ (09) 335 6406), the fastest ferry on the run, which has about four runs per day from C-Shed, Victoria Quay, directly behind the Fremantle railway station; a same-day return is $20/6. Bookings for all ferry services are essential at peak periods.

You can also fly to Rottnest on the Rottnest Airbus (☎ (09) 478 1322). It leaves Perth airport four times a day, seven days a week for about $80 return; the trip takes just 15 minutes. There's a connecting bus between Rottnest airport and Thomson Bay.

Getting Around

Bicycles are the time-honoured way of getting around the island. The number of motor vehicles is strictly limited, which makes cycling a real pleasure. Furthermore, the island is just big enough to make a day's ride fine exercise. You can bring your own bike over on the ferry (free at present from East St jetty) or rent one of the hundreds available on the island from Rottnest Bike Hire (☎ (09) 372 9722), in Thomson Bay,

near the hotel. A deposit of $10 is required and locks and helmets, both necessary, are available for hire.

Two bus services, the Bayseeker ($2) and the Settlement bus (50c), run daily – the information centre has timetables.

NORTH COAST

The coast north of Perth is scenic, with long sand dunes, but it quickly becomes the inhospitable terrain that deterred early explorers. The **Yanchep National Park**, 51 km north of Perth, has natural bushland, a colony of 'imported' koalas, some fine caves (including the limestone Crystal and Yondemp caves), Loch McNess and the Yaberoo Budjara Aboriginal Heritage Trail. The town of Yanchep has an atmospheric pub and nearby is the Two Rocks fishing marina with attached shopping complex.

There are a handful of places to stay, including the *Lagoon Lodge* (☎ (09) 561 1033), which has dinner, B&B from $70 for two, and a room-only rate of $40 to $60 for two. On weekdays, one bus goes to Yanchep from Perth's Wellington St bus station; check at the WATC for departure times.

Some 43 km north of Yanchep is **Guilderton**, a popular holiday resort beside the mouth of the Moore River. The *Vergulde Draeck* (Gilt Dragon), a Dutch East Indiaman, ran aground near here in 1656. The coast road ends at **Lancelin**, a small fishing port 130 km north of Perth, but coastal tracks continue north and may be passable with a 4WD. Windswept Lancelin is the end of the annual Ledge Point Windsurfing Race.

Pinnacles Desert

The small seaport of **Cervantes**, 257 km north of Perth, is the entry point for the unusual and haunting Pinnacles Desert. Here, in coastal **Nambung National Park**, the flat sandy desert is punctured with peculiar limestone pillars, some only a few cm high, others towering up to five metres. The park is the scene of an impressive wildflower display from August to October.

Try to visit the Pinnacles Desert early in the morning. Not only is the light better for

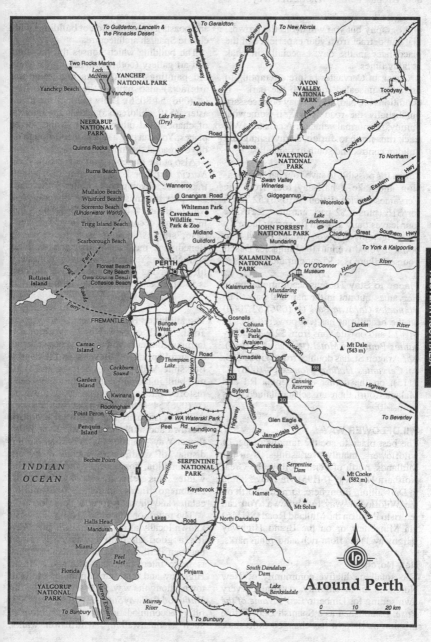

Around Perth

photography but you will avoid the crowds, that can detract from your experience of the place later in the day, especially in peak holiday times.

Check in Cervantes before attempting to drive the unsealed road into the park – if conditions are bad, a 4WD may be necessary but usually the road is OK, if somewhat bumpy, for normal vehicles. A coastal 4WD track runs north to **Jurien**, a crayfishing and holiday centre, and south to Lancelin.

Tours It's possible to save your car's suspension and take a half-day tour from the Cervantes service station (☎ (096) 52 7041) for $16 (plus a $2 park entrance fee). The tour leaves daily at 1 pm (in spring there's a morning tour) and you would be wise to book. If you drive into the Pinnacles Desert yourself, there is a $5 car entrance fee.

Places to Stay There is accommodation in Cervantes but not in the national park. The *Pinnacles Caravan Park* (☎ (096) 52 7060) on the beachfront has tent/powered sites at $10/12 and on-site vans from $25. The *Cervantes Pinnacles Motel* (☎ (096) 52 7145), 227 Aragon St, has doubles from $55 to $75. At *Cervantes Holiday Homes* (☎ (096) 52 7115), on the corner of Valencia Rd and Malaga Court, there are self-contained units from $40.

WILDFLOWER WAY

The best place to see the famous carpet of wildflowers, mainly everlastings, is in the Midlands, north of Perth. Follow the Great Northern Highway (SH95) via New Norcia to Dalwallinu. From here, turn due north on the Wildflower Way to Mullewa. You can return to Perth on the Midland Road (SH116) via Mingenew or on the Brand Highway (Highway 1) via flora-rich sand-plain parks.

New Norcia

The small meditative community of New Norcia is an incongruity, Australia's very own setting for Umberto Eco's *Name of the Rose*. Established as a Spanish Benedictine mission in 1846, it has changed little since

and boasts a fine collection of buildings with classic Spanish architecture.

The building which houses the museum and art gallery (both worth seeing for their old paintings, manuscripts and religious artefacts) also houses the tourist office (☎ (096) 54 8056). Daily tours of the monastery ($10, children $5) take in the interior of chapels and other cloistered and secret places. You can buy a snack of sourdough or olive bread at the museum.

Also at the museum, you can get the *New Norcia Heritage Trail* brochure ($2) which traces the development of the settlement. Just past the museum is the historic *New Norcia Hotel* (☎ (096) 54 8034) which has interesting décor, including a grand staircase; singles/doubles here are $30/45. Benedictine monks still live and work in New Norcia. You can experience monastery life by staying in their guesthouse; the cost is $40 per person for bed and all meals.

The Midlands Roads

To the north of New Norcia is **Moora**, a farming community in an area known for its colourful spring wildflowers. In the nearby Berkshire Valley, an old cottage and flour mill built in the mid-19th century have been restored and now operate as a museum (☎ (096) 54 9040), open most Sundays.

Towns such as **Dalwallinu**, **Perenjori**, **Morawa** and **Mullewa** are part of the Wildflower Way – famous for its brilliant spring display of wildflowers, including wreath leschenaultia, foxgloves, everlastings and wattles. This area is the gateway to the Murchison goldfields; there are gold-mining centres and ghost towns near Perenjori.

The return option is SH116 farther west, known locally as the Midlands Scenic Way. It's a good alternative route for travel between Perth and Geraldton – the scenery is more interesting than along the Brand Highway and there are a number of small towns along the way. At **Watheroo**, the old *Watheroo Railway Station* (☎ (096) 51 7007) offers accommodation, meals and activities such as bushwalking, wildflower walks, tennis and horse riding. It's well worth the detour.

Coorow is 262 km north of Perth and nearby is the **Alexander Morrison National Park**. **Carnamah** is noted for its birdlife. It is near the Yarra Yarra Lakes.

Mingenew has a small historical museum in an old primary school. The tourist centre (☎ (099) 28 1081) is on Midlands Rd.

SOUTH COAST

The coast south of Perth has a softer appearance than the often harsh landscape to the north. This is a very popular beach resort area for Perth residents, many of whom have holiday houses along the coast.

Rockingham (pop 50,000)

Rockingham, just 47 km south of Perth, was founded in 1872 as a port, but that function was taken over by Fremantle. Today, Rockingham is a dormitory city and popular seaside resort with both sheltered and ocean beaches. The beach at Point Peron is safe for young children.

Close by is **Penguin Island**, home to a colony of little blue (fairy) penguins from late October to May, and **Seal Island**. You can get to the islands with Rockingham Sea Tours (☎ (09) 528 2004) which departs from Mersey Point jetty, Arcadia Drive, Shoulwater Bay, daily at 11.15 am and 1.15 pm.

From Rockingham, you can also head inland to the Serpentine Dam and the scenic **Serpentine Falls**, where there are wildflowers and pleasant bushland. You can get to Rockingham on bus No 120 from Fremantle or a No 116 from bus stand No 48 in St George's Terrace, Perth.

The tourist centre (☎ (09) 592 3464), at 43 Kent St, is open weekdays from 9 am to 5 pm, and weekends from 10 am to 4 pm.

Places to Stay & Eat There are five caravan parks in the Rockingham area; enquire at the tourist centre. The *Palm Beach Caravan Park* (☎ (09) 527 1515), at 37 Fisher St, has powered sites for $12 and on-site vans for $35. Another budget place, the *CWA Rockingham* (☎ (09) 527 9560), 108 Parkin St, is operated by a friendly couple. There are two units available, each sleeping six, from $25 per night.

The *Rockingham Lodge Motel* (☎ (09) 527 1230), 20 Lake St, has singles/doubles for $25/38. The *Leisure Inn* (☎ (09) 527 7777), on the corner of Read St and Simpson Avenue, has units/family units for $55/65.

For meals, try the local hotels. Otherwise, there is *Promenade Cafe* at 43 Rockingham Rd for al fresco dining or the *Rockingham Village* at 52 Thorpe St for Chinese food. The *Sub Zero Nightclub*, 26 Kent St, serves lunch and dinner as well as catering for ravers.

Mandurah (pop 32,000)

Situated on the calm Mandurah Estuary, this is yet another popular beach resort, 74 km south of Perth. Dolphins are often seen in the estuary, and the waterways in the area are noted for good fishing, prawning (March and April) and crabbing.

The tourist bureau at 5 Pinjarra Rd (☎ (09) 535 1155) has ferry schedules, maps and other information. To get to Mandurah, catch bus No 116 from stand 48 in St George's Terrace, Perth, or bus No 117 from Fremantle.

Things to see in town include the restored 1830s limestone **Hall's Cottage** on Leighton Rd (open Sunday afternoon) and the **Western Rosella Bird Park** on Old Pinjarra Rd, open daily from 9 am to 6 pm (admission $4). Full-day and short cruises are available on the MV *Peel Princess* from the jetty in town. Prolific birdlife can be seen on Peel Inlet and the narrow coastal salt lakes, Clifton and Preston, to the south.

Places to Stay & Eat There is a string of caravan parks with tent sites and on-site vans, and several B&B places and resorts near town. *Albatross House* (☎ (09) 581 5597), 26 Hall St, has B&B for $35 per person. The *Brighton Hotel* (☎ (09) 535 1242), on Mandurah Terrace, is the best deal in town, with B&B singles/doubles from $25/50; it also serves hearty counter meals.

There are numerous places to eat around town including the excellent BYO *Doddi's* at 115 Mandurah Terrace, open for breakfast, lunch and dinner. A big and tasty serve of fish & chips ($4) is available at *Jetty Fish & Chips* by the estuary near the end of Pinjarra Rd. *Donatelli's*, on the foreshore, is the place for Italian and seafood meals; it is open for lunch and dinner daily, except Tuesday.

Pinjarra (pop 1800)

Pinjarra, 86 km south of Perth, has a number of old buildings picturesquely sited on the banks of the Murray River. The Murray tourist centre (☎ (09) 531 1438) in Pinjarra is in the historic **Edenvale**, on the corner of George and Henry Sts. About four km south of town is **Old Blythewood**, an 1859 colonial farm and a National Trust property. Behind the historic post office is a pleasant picnic area and a suspension bridge – wobbly enough to test your coordination!

The **Hotham Valley Railway** (☎ (09) 221 4444) trains run from Perth to Dwellingup via Pinjarra on Sunday in the 'steam season' (from May to October). These pass through blooming wildflowers and virgin jarrah forests. The Etmilyn Forest Tramway operates from Dwellingup on Tuesday, Thursday and weekends at 2 pm, returning at 3.30 pm; it costs $7 (children $4).

The *Pinjarra Motel* (☎ (09) 531 1811) offers B&B singles/doubles for $40/50. The *Heritage Tearooms* has light meals such as sandwiches and quiche for around $6.

AVON VALLEY

The green and lush Avon Valley, about 100 km north-east of Perth, looks very English and was a delight to homesick early settlers. In the spring, this area is particularly rich in wildflowers. The valley was first settled in 1830, only a year after Perth was founded, so there are many historic buildings. The picturesque Avon River is very popular with canoe enthusiasts.

Getting There & Away

The Avon Valley towns all have bus connections to Perth; contact Westrail (☎ (09) 326 2222) for timetable details. The fare to York

is $9.70. You can take the Prospector train from Perth to Northam ($11.40).

Toodyay (pop 600)

There are numerous old buildings in this charming and historic town, many built by convicts. The tourist centre (☎ (09) 574 2435) is on Stirling Terrace, in the 1870s **Connor's Mill**, which still houses a working flour mill. It is open daily from 9 am to 5 pm.

The **Newcastle Gaol** on Clinton St is open in the afternoon and the **Moondyne Gallery** tells the story of bushranger Joseph Bolitho Johns (Moondyne Joe). Close to town is an old winery, **Coorinja**, which dates from the 1870s; it is open April to December daily from 10 am to 5 pm.

Downriver from Toodyay is the **Avon Valley National Park** and along the Perth road is the popular White Gum Flower farm.

Places to Stay & Eat *Toodyay Caravan Park Avonbanks* (☎ (09) 574 2612), Railway Rd, on the banks of the Avon River, has tent/powered sites for $8/12, air-con on-site vans and chalets. It is noisy and the tent sites are as hard as rock. The *Broadgrounds Park* (☎ (09) 574 2534) has tent sites, on-site vans and a campers' kitchen.

The *Avondown Inn* (☎ (09) 574 2995) at 44 Stirling Terrace has budget accommodation, with dorm beds for $18 and B&B $25 per person. Opposite is the *Freemasons Hotel* (☎ (09) 574 2201) with basic rooms and breakfast for $25 per person. On the same street is the *Victoria Hotel/Motel* (☎ (09) 574 2206) with singles/doubles from $20/40; counter meals are available from $8.

There are eating places on Stirling Terrace including the *Toodyay Bakery*, *Wendouree Tearooms* and the *Cellar Bistro* in O'Meara's Tavern. *Connor's Cottage*, in Piesse St behind Connor's Mill, is open Wednesday to Sunday from 10 am to 5 pm, for lunches and Devonshire teas.

Northam (pop 6600)

Northam, the major town of the Avon Valley, is a farming centre on the railway line to Kalgoorlie. At one time, the line from Perth ended abruptly here and miners had to trek hundreds of km to the goldfields by road. Every year Northam is packed on the first weekend in August for the start of the gruelling 133-km Avon Descent for power boats and canoeists.

The 1836 **Morby Cottage** served as Northam's first church and school It now houses a museum, open on Sunday from 10.30 am to 4 pm; entrance is $1. The **old railway station**, listed by the National Trust, has been restored and turned into a museum; it is open on Sunday from 10 am to 4 pm and admission is $2. Also of interest in town is the colony of **white swans** on the Avon River, descendants of birds introduced from England early this century.

Near Northam, at Irishtown, is elegant **Buckland House**. Credited with being WA's most impressive stately home, it was built in 1874 and has a fine collection of antiques. There is also accommodation here (see Places to Stay).

If your funds are up to it then try **ballooning** over the Avon Valley (April to November); call ☎ (096) 22 3000 for details.

The tourist bureau (☎ (096) 22 2100), 138 Fitzgerald St, is open daily.

Places to Stay The *Northam Guest House* (☎ (096) 22 2301), 51 Wellington St, has cheap accommodation from $15 per person for the first night and $10 for following nights.

The *Avon Bridge Hotel* (☎ (096) 22 1023) is the oldest hotel in Northam, and has singles/twins for $20/30 and counter meals from $5. The only motel in town, aptly named the *Northam* (☎ (096) 22 1755), is at 13 John St; singles/doubles are $48/55. The *Shamrock Hotel*, at 112 Fitzgerald St, is the best in town with elegant en suite bedrooms.

An excellent out-of-town choice is the farmstay *Egoline Reflections* (☎ (096) 22 5811), seven km out on the Toodyay road, which has singles/doubles from $65/100. *Buckland House* (☎ (096) 22 1130), in Irishtown, has B&B singles/doubles for $68/136; children are not welcome.

Places to Eat *Bruno's Pizza Bar* in Fitzgerald St does tasty pizza to eat in or take away. The *Whistling Kettle*, at 48 Broome Terrace overlooking the river, is a great place to enjoy some home-cooked food; it is open daily from 10 am to 5 pm. The Shamrock Hotel has three restaurants and its *Fountain Chargrill* is open Tuesday to Friday for lunch and Tuesday to Saturday for dinner.

York (pop 2500)

The oldest inland town in WA, York was settled in 1831. It is one of the highlights of the Avon Valley even though its efforts to preserve its Englishness are a bit sickly. A stroll down the main street, with its many restored old buildings, is a step back in time. The whole town is classified by the National Trust. The tourist centre (☎ (096) 41 1301), at 105 Avon Terrace, is open daily from 9 am to 5 pm.

York is the state's festival town, with no fewer than a dozen major annual events. The better-patronised ones are the Jazz Festival in October and the Flying 50s Vintage & Veteran car race in August.

There are many places of historic interest in this town. The excellent 1850s **Residency Museum** is open in the afternoons daily (except Monday and Friday). The old **town hall** and Castle Hotel (which dates from the coaching days) are very photogenic, as are the police station, gaol, courthouse and Settlers House. Most people drive their own cars to York so they can enjoy the many heritage drives.

The classy **Motor Museum**, a must for vintage-car enthusiasts, houses Australia's best collection of vintage, classic and racing cars – entrance is $6 (children $2).

Places to Stay The only caravan park around town is *Mt Bakewell Caravan Park* (☎ (096) 41 1421) with tent/powered sites at $10/12 and on-site vans for $30.

The old section of the historic, renovated *Castle Hotel* (☎ (096) 41 1007), on Avon Terrace, is good value with B&B singles/doubles from $30/60. The *Settlers House* (☎ (096) 41 1096), 125 Avon Terrace, has stylish B&B singles/doubles for $80/138.

There are a number of quality B&B and farmstays in the region from about $65 to $90; enquire at the tourist centre.

Places to Eat From the wide selection of places along Avon Terrace, try the *Settlers House* for breakfast, *Cafe Bugatti* for cappuccino and Italian food, *Village Bakehouse* for freshly baked bread and cakes (including delicious vanilla slices) and *Jule's Shoppe* for delicious 'LP-road tested' homemade pasties. The *Castle Hotel* serves good counter meals (from $10) and has an à la carte restaurant.

Beverley (pop 1500)

South of York, also on the Avon River, is Beverley, founded in 1838 and noted for its fine **aeronautical museum**, open daily from 9 am to 4 pm. Exhibits include a locally built biplane, *Silver Centenary*, constructed between 1928 and 1930. The tourist bureau (☎ (096) 46 1555) is housed in this building, impossible to miss as it has a Vampire jet mounted outside the door. There are plenty of opportunities to go **gliding** on the weekend with the Beverley Soaring Society (☎ 015 385 361).

The 706-hectare **Avondale Discovery Farm**, six km west of Beverley, has a large collection of agricultural machinery, a homestead, a workshop and stables.

The **lonely grave**, three km south of town, is the solitary last resting place of a baby who died in January 1883. Why here? There was no town cemetery at the time.

Places to Stay The *Beverley Caravan Park* (☎ (096) 46 1200), on Vincent St, has powered sites for $11. The ordinary *Beverley Hotel* (☎ (096) 46 1190), 137 Vincent St, has singles/doubles for $18/35.

THE DARLING RANGE

The hills that surround Perth are popular for picnics, barbecues and bushwalks. There are also some excellent lookouts from which you can see across Perth and to the coast.

Araluen Botanic Park with its waterfalls and terraced gardens, the **Mt Dale** fire lookout, and **Churchman's Brook** are all off the Brookton Highway. Other places of interest include the hairpin bends of the former **Zig Zag** railway at Gooseberry Hill and the walking trails of **Lake Leschenaultia**.

From **Kalamunda** there are more fine views over Perth. You can get there from Perth on bus Nos 300 or 302, via Maida Vale from stand No 43 in St George's Terrace, or on bus Nos 292 or 305, via Wattle Grove and Lesmurdie, also from stand No 43. Taking one route out and the other back makes an interesting circular tour of the hill suburbs. There's a good walking track at **Sullivan Rock**, 69 km south-east of Perth, on the Albany Highway.

Mundaring Weir

Mundaring, in the Darling Range only 35 km east of Perth, is the site of the Mundaring Weir, built at the turn of the century to supply water to the goldfields over 500 km to the east. The reservoir has an attractive setting and is a popular excursion for Perth residents. There are a number of walking tracks. The **C Y O'Connor Museum** has models and exhibits about the water pipeline to the goldfields – in its time one of the country's most audacious engineering feats.

The **John Forrest National Park** near Mundaring has protected areas of jarrah and marri trees, native fauna, waterfalls, a swimming pool and an old railway tunnel.

Places to Stay The *Mundaring Caravan Park* (☎ (09) 295 1125) is two km west of town on the Great Eastern Highway. The *Djaril-Mari Mundaring Weir YHA Hostel* (☎ (09) 295 1809), on Mundaring Weir Rd, eight km south of town, costs from $11 and meals are available.

The *Mundaring Weir Hotel* (☎ (09) 295 1106) is exceedingly popular with Perth residents for weekend breaks. Its quality rammed-earth units cost from $60 per person.

The Wheatbelt

Stretching north from the Albany coastal region to the areas beyond the Great Eastern Highway (the Perth to Coolgardie road) are the WA wheatlands, commonly referred to as the Wheatbelt. The area is noted for its unusual rock formations (the best known of which is the somewhat overrated Wave Rock near Hyden), for its many Aboriginal sites and *gnamma* (water holes) and magnificent displays of wildflowers in spring.

GREAT EASTERN HIGHWAY

An earthquake in 1968 badly damaged **Meckering**, a small town 24 km west of Cunderdin. The museum in Forrest St, **Cunderdin**, has exhibits relating to that event as well as an interesting collection of farm machinery and equipment. The museum is in an old pumping station formerly used on the goldfields water pipeline.

Merredin (population 3500), the largest centre in the Wheatbelt, is 260 km east of Perth. It has a tourist centre (☎ (090) 41 1666) on Barrack St. The 1920s railway station has been turned into a charming museum with a vintage 1897 locomotive and an old signal box.

There are interesting **rock formations** around Merredin – Kangaroo Rock is 17 km south and Burracoppin Rock is to the north. Sandford Rocks is 11 km east of Westonia.

Although the gold quickly gave out, **Southern Cross**, farther east, was the first gold-rush town on the WA goldfields. The big rush soon moved east to Coolgardie and Kalgoorlie. Like the town itself, the streets of Southern Cross are named after the stars and constellations. The **Yilgarn History Museum** in the courthouse has local displays which are worth a visit. If you follow the continuation of Antares St south for three km, you will see a couple of active open-cut mines. The Yilgarn shire council (☎ (090) 49 1001) provides local information at a pinch.

Southern Cross, some 378 km east of Perth, is really the end of the Wheatbelt and the start of the desert; when travelling by train the change is very noticeable. In the spring, the sandy plains around Southern Cross are carpeted with wildflowers.

Places to Stay & Eat

The *Cunderdin Caravan Park* (☎ (096) 35 1258) in Olympic Avenue has tent/powered sites for $7.50/10. The *Merredin Caravan Park* (☎ (090) 41 1535), on the Great Eastern Highway, has tent/powered sites at $10/12 and on-site vans for $28.

The *Merredin Motel* (☎ (090) 41 1886), on Gamenya Ave, has singles/doubles for $35/50. The *Commercial Hotel* on Barrack St has counter meals, and *Jason's* Chinese, corner of Bates and Mitchell Sts, has takeaway or eat-in meals.

In Southern Cross, there is a caravan park on Coolgardie Rd, two hotels in Antares St and a motel on Canopus St. The *Palace Hotel* (☎ (090) 49 1555), Antares St, has been restored and is a great place to stay, with real country charm, a large bar area and a restaurant; singles/doubles are $30/60.

HYDEN & WAVE ROCK

Wave Rock is 350 km south-east of Perth and three km from the tiny town of Hyden. It's a real surfer's delight – the perfect wave, 15 metres high and frozen in solid rock marked with different colour bands. It hardly justifies the 700-km return trip from Perth, although many people make it.

Other interesting rock formations in the area bear names like the **Breakers**, **Hippo's Yawn** and the **Humps**. **Mulka's Cave** has Aboriginal rock paintings. The information centre (☎ (098) 80 5182) is in the Wave Rock Wildflower Shoppe.

At Wave Rock, the *Wave Rock Caravan Park* (☎ (098) 80 5022) has tent/powered sites for $9/12, and on-site cabins for $52. *Diep's B&B* (☎ (098) 80 5179), on Clayton St in Hyden, has B&B for $26 per person, or there's the recently revamped *Hyden Hotel* (☎ (098) 80 5052), on Lynch St, with singles/doubles for $48/70.

A Westrail bus to Hyden via Bruce Rock leaves Perth on Tuesday and returns on

The 15-metre-high Wave Rock is shaped like a
perfect wave

Thursday; the trip costs $30.60 one way and
takes five hours.

OTHER WHEATBELT TOWNS

Most sizeable Wheatbelt towns have a
caravan park, a pub which serves counter
meals, a motel, a takeaway, a trio of wheat
silos, a pervading ennui and little else.

There is a fine rock formation, known as
Kokerbin (Aboriginal for 'high place'), 45
km west of the town of Bruce Rock.
Corrigin, 68 km south of Bruce Rock, has a
folk museum, a 'Buried Bone' canine cemetery (can you believe it?), a craft cottage and
a miniature railway. **Jilakin Rock** is 18 km
from Kulin, while farther south-east there's
Lake Grace, near the eponymous lake.

Narrogin (population 4970), 192 km
south-east of Perth, is an agricultural centre
with a courthouse museum, a railway heritage park and the **Albert Facey Homestead**,
39 km to the east and close to Wickepin –
well worth a visit, especially if you have read
Facey's popular book *A Fortunate Life*.

Some 26 km north of Narrogin is the
magnificent **Dryandra Forest**, a remnant of
the open eucalypt woodlands which once
covered most of the Wheatbelt. It now supports many species of animal, including the
numbat, and is a good place for birdwatching, bushwalking and, when they're in
season, wildflowers.

Dumbleyung, south-east of Narrogin,
also has a museum. Near the town is the lake
upon which Donald Campbell broke the
world water-speed record (444.66 km/h) in
1964; today it hosts a variety of birdlife.

Wagin, 229 km south-east of Perth, has a
kitsch 15-metre-high fibreglass ram (a
tribute both to the surrounding merino industry and civic bad taste). It is the biggest in the
southern hemisphere – are there actually
more? The historical village, which features
fine restored buildings and a vintage tractor
display, is open daily from 10 am to 4 pm.
The Wagin tourist centre (☎ (098) 61 1232)
quakes beneath the Giant Ram.

There is bushwalking around **Puntapin
Rock** and **Mt Latham** (in Aboriginal known
as Badjarning), both about six km from
Wagin.

Katanning, south of Wagin, has a large
Muslim community, complete with a
mosque built in 1980. The old flour mill on
Clive St houses the tourist centre (☎ (098)
21 2634). You can also visit the ruins of an
old winery.

Eastern Goldfields

Fifty years after its establishment in 1829,
the Western Australia colony was still going
nowhere, so the government in Perth was
delighted when gold was discovered at
Southern Cross in 1887. That first strike
petered out pretty quickly, but there followed
more discoveries and WA profited from the
gold boom for the rest of the century. Gold
finally gave WA the population to make it
viable in its own right, rather than just a
distant offshoot of the east coast colonies.

The major strikes were made in 1892 at
Coolgardie and nearby Kalgoorlie, but in the
whole goldfields area Kalgoorlie is the only

Eastern Goldfields

0   50   100 km

To Meekatharra
Wiluna
Gunbarrel   Highway

Leinster
Agnew

To Warburton, Northern Territory Border,
South Australia Border & Yulara

Lake
Raeside

Windarra
Warburton Road

Laverton

Leonora-Gwalia   Malcolm   Lake
Carey

Lake
Ballard

Kookynie
Niagara   Lake
Raeside

Menzies

Lake Marmion

Lake
Goongarrie   GOONGARRIE
NATIONAL PARK   Lake
Rebecca

Ora Banda
Broad Arrow

Kanowna

Kalgoorlie-Boulder   Lake
Yindarlgooda

Coolgardie

To Perth   Trans-Australia Railway

Kambalda

Lake Lefroy

94

Lake Cowan

To South Australia Border
Norseman   Eyre   Highway
1
To Esperance

large town remaining. Coolgardie's period of prosperity lasted only until 1905 and many other gold towns went from nothing to populations of 10,000 then back to nothing in just 10 years. Nevertheless, the towns capitalised on their prosperity while it lasted, as the many magnificent public buildings grandly attest.

Life on the early goldfields was terribly hard. This area of WA is extremely dry – rainfall is erratic and never high. Even the little rain that does fall quickly disappears into the porous soil. Many early gold seekers, driven more by enthusiasm than by common sense, died of thirst while seeking the elusive mineral. Others succumbed to diseases in the unhygienic shanty towns. The supply of water to the goldfields by pipeline in 1903 was a major breakthrough and ensured the continuation of mining.

Today, Kalgoorlie is the main goldfields centre and mines still operate there. Elsewhere, a string of fascinating ghost and near-ghost towns and modern nickel mines make a visit to WA's gold country a must.

COOLGARDIE (pop 2500)

A popular pause in the long journey across the Nullarbor, and also the turn-off for Kalgoorlie, Coolgardie really is a ghost of its former self. You only have to glance at the huge town hall and post office building to appreciate the size that Coolgardie once was.

Gold was discovered here in 1892, and by the turn of the century the population had boomed to 15,000. The gold then petered out and the town withered away just as quickly. However, there's still plenty to interest the visitor and improved mining techniques have seen a resurgence in the population.

The helpful tourist office (☎ (090) 26 6090), in Bayley St, is open daily from 9 am to 5 pm.

Historical Buildings

The many historical markers scattered in and around Coolgardie describe the past history of its buildings and sites. The **Goldfields Exhibition**, in the same building as the tourist bureau, is open daily between 9 am

WESTERN AUSTRALIA

and 5 pm and has a fascinating display of goldfields memorabilia. You can even find out about US president Herbert Hoover's days on the WA goldfields. It's an interesting museum and worth the $2.50 admission fee, which includes a film shown at the tourist bureau.

The **railway station** also operates as a museum, and there you can learn the incredible story of the miner who was trapped 300 metres underground by floodwater in 1907 and rescued by divers 10 days later.

Warden Finnerty's Residence, restored by the National Trust, is open daily except Tuesday from 1 to 4 pm and Sunday from 10 am to noon ($2; children $1). Nearby is the lightning-dissected **Gaol Tree**, complete with leg irons.

One km west of Coolgardie is the **town cemetery**, which includes many old graves such as that of explorer Ernest Giles (1835-97). Due to the unsanitary conditions and violence in the goldfields, it's said that 'one half of the population buried the other half'.

Other Attractions

The **Camel Farm**, three km west of town, is open daily from 9 am to 5 pm. You can take camel rides or organise longer treks; entry is $2 (rides are $3).

One of Coolgardie's odd sights is **Prior's Open Air Museum**, diagonally opposite the tourist bureau, but its collection seems a little neglected these days.

About 45 km south of Coolgardie is **Queen Victoria Rock Nature Reserve**, which has interesting transitional vegetation types and limited primitive camping.

Places to Stay & Eat

The *Coolgardie Caravan Park* (☎ (090) 26 6009), 99 Bayley St, has excellent tent/powered sites for $9/12 and on-site vans for $29. The atmospheric old *Kurrgordie House* (☎ (090) 26 6051), 56-60 Gnarlbine Rd, has dorm beds from $11 per person. There are a couple of historic hotels in Bayley St with long, shady verandahs.

There is budget accommodation at the *Goldrush Lodge* (☎ (090) 26 6446), 75

Bayley St; it costs $13 for backpackers, and rooms are $30. The *Denver City Hotel* (☎ (090) 26 6031) has double rooms for $30. The *Coolgardie Motor Inne* (☎ (090) 26 6031), Bayley St, has single/double units for $60/65.

Aunt Jeffies is a takeaway place, the *Denver City Pizza Hut* is near the Denver Hotel and there are a couple of roadhouses in town that also serve meals. The *Premier Cafe* has takeaways and excellent meals for $7. All of these places are on Bayley St.

Getting There & Away

Greyhound Pioneer buses pass through Coolgardie on the Perth to Adelaide run; the one-way fare from Perth to Coolgardie is $70, and to Adelaide it's $180. Goldenlines (☎ (090) 21 2655) runs two buses on weekdays from Kalgoorlie to Coolgardie; a ride costs $3.50 (children $1.70).

The *Prospector* from Perth to Kalgoorlie stops at Bonnie Vale railway station, 14 km from Coolgardie, daily except Saturday; the one-way fare from Perth is $56.50, with a meal. For bookings call the tourist bureau or Westrail (☎ (09) 326 2222).

KALGOORLIE-BOULDER (pop 30,000)

Kalgoorlie ('Kal' to the locals) is a real surprise – a prosperous, humming metropolis. It is a raw city, however, exuding all the atmosphere of a frontier mining town. Tattoos, 'skimpys' (scantily-clad bar staff), gambling, brothels, Harley Davidsons and mass consumption of alcohol are *de rigueur*.

The longest-lasting and most successful of WA's gold towns, Kalgoorlie rose to prominence later than Coolgardie. In 1893, Paddy Hannan, a prospector from way back, set out from Coolgardie for another gold strike but stopped at the site of Kal and found enough surface gold to spark another rush.

As in so many places, the surface gold soon petered out, but at Kal the miners went deeper and more and more gold was found. There weren't the story-book chunky nuggets of solid gold – Kal's gold had to be extracted from the rocks by costly and complex processes of grinding, roasting and chemical action – but there was plenty of it.

Kalgoorlie quickly reached fabled heights of prosperity, and the enormous and magnificent public buildings constructed around the turn of the century are evidence of its fabulous wealth. After WW I, however, increasing production costs and static gold prices led to Kalgoorlie's slow but steady decline.

With the substantial increase in gold prices since the mid-1970s, mining of lower-grade deposits has become economical and Kal is again the largest producer of gold in Australia. Large mining conglomerates have been at the forefront of new open-cut mining operations in the Golden Mile – gone are the old headframes and corrugated iron homes. Mining, pastoral development and a busy tourist trade ensure Kal's continuing importance as an outback centre.

Orientation

Although Kalgoorlie sprang up close to Paddy Hannan's original find, the mining emphasis soon shifted a few km away to the Golden Mile, a square mile probably once the wealthiest gold-mining area for its size in the world. The satellite town of Boulder, five km south of Kal, developed to service this area. The two towns amalgamated in 1989 into Kalgoorlie-Boulder city.

Kalgoorlie itself is a grid of broad, tree-lined streets. The main street, Hannan St, flanked by imposing public buildings, is wide enough to turn a camel train – a necessity in turn-of-the-century goldfield towns. You'll find most of the hotels, restaurants and offices on or close to Hannan St.

Information

There's a helpful tourist centre (☎ (090) 21 1966) on the corner of Hannan and Cassidy Sts, where you can get a good free map of Kalgoorlie; a number of other area maps are for sale. The office is open weekdays from 8.30 am to 5 pm, and weekends from 9 am to 5 pm. Kal's daily paper is the *Kalgoorlie Miner*.

Kal can get very hot in December and January; overall the cool winter months are the best time to visit. From late August to the end of September, however, the town is packed because of wildflower tours and the local horse races, and accommodation of any type can be difficult to find.

The RACWA (☎ (090) 21 1511) is on the corner of Porter and Hannan Sts.

Hannan's North Tourist Mine

This mine is one of Kalgoorlie's biggest tourist attractions. You can take the lift-cage down into the bowels of the earth and make a tour around the drives and crosscuts of the mine, guided by an ex-miner.

The $15 (children $7.50) entry fee covers the underground tour, an audiovisual presentation, a tour of the surface workings, and a gold pour. Underground tours are run daily (according to demand and more regularly during high seasons) and the complex is open daily from 9.30 am to 5 pm.

Golden Mile Loopline

You can make an interesting loop around the Golden Mile by catching the 'Rattler', a ramshackle tourist train complete with commentary which makes an hour-long trip daily at 10 am. On Sunday it also leaves at 11.45 am. It departs from Boulder railway station, passing the old mining works. The cost is $9 (children $5).

Museum of the Goldfields

The impressive mine headframe at the north-eastern end of Hannan St marks the entrance to this excellent museum. It is open daily from 10 am to 4.30 pm (by donation) and has a wide range of exhibits including an underground gold vault and historic photographs. The tiny British Arms Hotel (the narrowest hotel in Australia) is part of the museum.

Left to Your Own (De)Vices

Kalgoorlie has a legal **two-up school** in a corrugated-iron amphitheatre; it is five km out along the Menzies road – follow the signs from Hannan St. A lot of money changes hands in this frenetic Australian gambling game, where two coins are tossed and bets

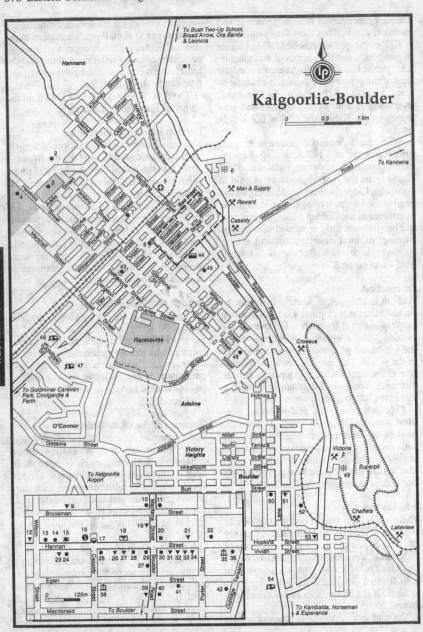

Kalgoorlie-Boulder

PLACES TO STAY

20 Old Australia Hotel
24 York Hotel
28 Windsor House
29 Palace Hotel
30 Exchange Hotel
40 Surrey House
41 Quality Plaza
46 Golden Village Caravan Park
47 Prospector Caravan Park
54 Boulder Village Caravan Park

PLACES TO EAT

9 Food Court
12 Takeaway Food Enclave
15 Basil's
19 Silvio's Pizza
21 Grand Hotel
23 Kalgoorlie Cafe
26 De Bernales

27 Pizza Cantina
31 Matteo's Pizza
32 Criterion Hotel
33 Health Works
34 Top End Thai Restaurant
39 Eagle Boys Pizza
51 Albion Shamrock Hotel
53 Cornwall Hotel

OTHER

1 Hannan's North Tourist Mine
2 Kalgoorlie Cemetery
3 Hammond Park
4 Arboretum
5 Kalgoorlie Hospital
6 Mt Charlotte Lookout
7 Kalgoorlie Train Station
8 Woolworths
10 Hannan's Club
11 Maritana Buildings
13 Town Hall & Paddy Hannan's Statue
14 Ansett

16 Tourist Centre & Goldrush Tours
17 Bus Terminal
18 Post Office
22 RACWA
25 Laslett Buildings
35 Museum of the Goldfields
36 Goldfields Aboriginal Art Gallery
37 Goldrush Tours
38 School of Mines Museum
42 Paddy Hannan's Tree
43 Hay St Brothels
44 Lord Forrest Swimming Pool
45 Goldfields Arts Centre
48 Viewway Drive-In & Cinema
49 Superpit Lookout
50 Boulder Town Hall
52 Golden Mile Loopline

WESTERN AUSTRALIA

are placed on the heads or tails result. It is open from 3.30 to 7 pm.

A few blocks west of Hannan St is Hay St, one of Kal's more famous 'attractions'. Although it's quietly ignored in tourist brochures, this is a block-long strip of **brothels** where working ladies beckon passing men to their true-blue (sometimes pink) galvanised-iron doorways. A blind eye has been turned to this activity for so long that it has become an accepted, historical part of the town.

Other Attractions
The **Mt Charlotte lookout** and the town's reservoir are only a few hundred metres from the north-eastern end of Hannan St. The view over the town is good but there's little to see of the reservoir, which is covered to limit evaporation. The **Super Pit** lookout, just off the Eastern Bypass Rd near Boulder, gives a good insight into modern mining practices; it is open daily from 7.30 am to 4.15 pm (closed when blasting is in progress).

The **School of Mines Museum**, on the corner of Egan and Cassidy Sts, has a geology display including replicas of big

nuggets. It's usually open weekdays from 10 am to 4 pm.

Along Hannan St, you'll find the imposing **town hall** and the equally impressive **post office**. There's an art gallery upstairs in the decorative town hall, while outside is a replica of a statue of Paddy Hannan holding a water bag. The original is inside the town hall, safe from nocturnal spray-painters.

On Outridge Terrace is **Paddy Hannan's tree**, marking the spot where the first gold strike was made. **Hammond Park**, a small fauna reserve with a miniature Bavarian castle, is open daily from 9 am to 5 pm. Not far away is a pleasant, shady **arboretum**.

Tours
Goldrush Tours (☎ (090) 21 2954) is the main tour operator in Kal. They have tours of Kal, Coolgardie and nearby ghost towns. There's also a gold-detector tour for avid fossickers, and August and September wildflower tours. Tours cost $30 for Kal-Boulder (includes admission into Hannan's mine), $40 for Coolgardie and $50 for Ora Banda. Book through the tourist centre or through

Paddy Hannan's statue in the town centre

the Goldrush Tours offices in St Barbara's Square and Boulder Rd.

Geoff Smith's Bush Tours (☎ (090) 21 2180) are good for small groups and include the yarns and lore of the bushies.

You can see Kal's Golden Mile mining operations from above with Goldfields Air Services (☎ (090) 93 2005); flights are from $35 (minimum of two persons).

Places to Stay

There are a number of caravan parks in Kal. The closest to the city centre are the *Golden Village* (☎ (090) 21 4162), on Hay St two km south-west of the railway station, which has tent sites and on-site vans; and the *Prospector* (☎ (090) 21 2524), on the Great Eastern Highway, which has tent sites, on-site vans and cabins. The Prospector has a pool, a grassed area for campers and a kitchen – it's one of the best such parks in WA.

The central *Windsor House* (☎ (090) 21 5483), at the end of the courtyard at 147 Hannan St, is an austere, quiet place with a TV room and kitchen facilities; rooms are $30 for single or twin. At 9 Boulder Rd is the comfortable *Surrey House* (☎ (090) 21

1340), which has backpackers' beds for $15 and singles/doubles for $30/50.

There are several pleasantly old-fashioned hotels right in the centre of Kal, including the *Palace* (☎ (090) 21 2788) on the corner of Maritana and Hannan Sts. Standard singles/doubles cost $30/40. The *York* (☎ (090) 21 2337), 259 Hannan St, has singles/twins for $35/60; it is exceptionally well-located in the heart of town. Perhaps the best value is the *Old Australia* (☎ (090) 21 1320), on the corner of Hannan and Maritana Sts, with its great old verandah and comfortable rooms; singles/twins are $40/60 and include tea and coffee facilities.

There is interesting *homestay* accommodation (☎ (090) 91 1482) at 164 Hay St, a former brothel in the heart of Kal's Rue Pigalle; rooms with a past are $30/50 for B&B singles/doubles and there's a preferred three-night minimum. The tourist centre has a list of other B&B accommodation.

One of the top-end places, the *Quality Plaza* (☎ (090) 21 4544) at 45 Egan St is a monument to 1960s bad taste but it does have a pool; singles/doubles are $113/125.

Places to Eat

There are plenty of pubs serving counter meals, as well as restaurants and cafes in Kal, particularly along Hannan St. For breakfast, join the few early risers reading their papers at *Basil's* at No 268. The *Kalgoorlie Cafe* (No 277) has burger-type fast food. The *York Hotel* (No 259) does solid counter meals from $7 to $10 in its Steak House, and hearty meals for around $6 in the saloon bar. The *Criterion* (No 117) and the *Grand* (No 400) also do counter meals and usually have cheap lunch specials.

For pizza, try *Pizza Cantina* (No 21) or *Matteo's* (No 123), *Silvio's* in Maritana St or *Eagle Boys* in Boulder Rd. The latter has superb multigrain-base pizzas – two large pizzas cost $19.90.

The more up-market *De Bernales* (No 193) serves tasty food from $12 to $16 and has a pleasant verandah opening onto Hannan St – a good place to watch life go by.

The *Health Works* (No 75) has a lunch bar

with an interesting menu – most of it vegetarian. Nearby, the *Top End* Thai restaurant (No 71) is good for a splurge. It has a range of prawn, curry and noodle dishes.

On Wilson St, between Brookman and Hannan Sts, is a small enclave of takeaway places including the *Fu Wah* Chinese. In Egan St is the BYO *Loaded Cactus* Mexican.

The *food court* in Brookman St serves roast meals, fish & chips, curries, and has a Thai and an Italian place.

In Boulder, you can get counter meals at the *Cornwall Hotel* at 25 Hopkins St, and at the *Albion Shamrock* on the corner of Lane and Burt Sts. You can also try *Wah On* Chinese and *Peachy's*, both on Burt St. The *Superpit food hall* in Boulder has six outlets.

Party animals will be well-satisfied at *Sylvesters Dance Club* and *Harry's Bar* at the top end of Hannan St.

Things to Buy

The Goldfields Aboriginal Art Gallery, next to the Museum of the Goldfields, has crafts for sale. Yilba, on Hannan St adjacent to the Palace Hotel, has also been recommended. Kal is the place to buy gold nuggets fashioned into relatively inexpensive jewellery.

Getting There & Away

Air Ansett (or Skywest) and Qantas fly from Perth to Kalgoorlie daily. The Ansett office (☎ 13 1300) is at 314 Hannan St.

Qantas flies from Kalgoorlie to Adelaide on Friday, Saturday and Sunday and returns the same day.

Bus Greyhound Pioneer buses from Perth go through Kal en route to Sydney, Melbourne and Adelaide; the fare from Perth is around $75. Kalgoorlie Express (☎ (09) 328 9199) has a twice-weekly Perth to Kalgoorlie service which then heads north to Laverton ($50 from Kalgoorlie), Leinster ($55) and Leonora ($35). Check timetables carefully – some buses pull into Kal at an ungodly hour when everything is closed, and finding a place to stay can be difficult.

Westrail (☎ (090) 21 2023) runs a bus three times a week from Kal to Esperance – once via Kambalda and Norseman and twice via Coolgardie and Norseman; the trip takes 5½ hours and costs $18 to Norseman and $33.50 to Esperance.

Train The daily Prospector service from Perth takes around 7½ hours and costs $58.80, including a meal. From Perth, you can book seats at the WATC in Forrest Place or at the Westrail terminal (☎ (09) 326 2222). It's wise to book as this service is fairly popular, particularly in the high season. The Indian Pacific and Trans-Australia trains also go through Kalgoorlie.

Getting Around

A regular bus service between Kalgoorlie and Boulder runs on weekdays and on Saturday morning (timetables are at the tourist centre).

If you want to explore very far, you'll have to drive or take a tour, as public transport is limited. You can rent cars from Hertz (☎ (090) 91 2625), Budget (☎ (090) 93 2300) and Avis (☎ (090) 21 1722). Halfpenny (☎ (090) 21 1804) is about the cheapest rental place at $35 per day for two-day hire and 500 km free; they also hire mopeds.

A taxi from the airport costs around $10. You can hire bicycles from Johnston Cycles (☎ (090) 21 1157), 78 Boulder Rd – a deposit is required.

NORTH OF KALGOORLIE

The road north is surfaced from Kalgoorlie all the way to Leonora-Gwalia (240 km) and from there to Laverton (130 km north-east) and Leinster (160 km north). Off the main road, however, traffic is virtually nonexistent and rain can quickly close the dirt roads. Skywest has regular flights from Perth to Leinster, Laverton, Leonora and Wiluna.

Towns of interest include **Kanowna**, just 18 km north-east of Kalgoorlie-Boulder along a dirt road. In 1905, this town had a population of 12,000, 16 hotels, many churches and an hourly train service to Kalgoorlie. Today, apart from the railway station and the odd pile of rubble, absolutely nothing remains!

Broad Arrow farther north has a population of 20, compared with 2400 at the turn of the century. One of the town's original eight hotels operates in a virtually unchanged condition. **Ora Banda** has gone from a population of 2000 to less than 50. There is a tavern for drinks and meals.

Menzies, 132 km north of Kal, has about 110 people today, compared with 5000 in 1900. Many early buildings remain, including the train station with its 120-metre-long platform and the town hall with its clockless clock tower – the ship bringing the clock from England, the SS *Orizaba*, sank en route.

With a population of 1200, **Leonora** serves as the railhead for the nickel from Windarra and Leinster. In adjoining **Gwalia** (a ghost town), the Sons of Gwalia Goldmine, the largest in WA outside Kalgoorlie, closed in 1963 and much of the town closed with it; however due to the increase in gold prices this and other mines in the area have been reopened. At one time, the mine was managed by Herbert Hoover, later to become president of the USA. The Gwalia Historical Society is housed in the 1898 mine office – this fascinating local museum is open daily. Also of interest is the restored State Hotel, originally built in 1903.

South of Leonora-Gwalia, 25 km off the main road, is **Kookynie**, another interesting once-flourishing mining town with just a handful of inhabitants left. The 1894 *Grand Hotel* (☎ (090) 31 3010) has singles/doubles for $30/50. Nearby **Niagara** is also a ghost town; the Niagara Dam was built with cement carried in by a 400-camel train.

From Leonora-Gwalia, you can turn north-east to **Laverton**, where the surfaced road ends. The population here declined from 1000 in 1910 to 200 in 1970, when the Poseidon nickel discovery (beloved of stockmarket speculators in the late '60s and early '70s) revived mining operations in nearby Windarra. The town now has a population of 800, and there are many abandoned mines in the area. From here, it is just 1710 km north-

east to Alice Springs (see the following Warburton Road/Gunbarrel Highway section).

North of Leonora-Gwalia, the road is surfaced to **Leinster** (population 1000), another modern nickel town. Nearby, **Agnew** is another old gold town that has all but disappeared. From here, it's 170 km north to **Wiluna** (population 230) and another 180 km west to Meekatharra on the surfaced Great Northern Highway, which runs 765 km south-west to Perth or 860 km north to Port Hedland. Through the '30s, due to the mining of arsenic, Wiluna had a population of 8000 and was a modern, prosperous town. The ore ran out in 1948 and the town quickly declined. There is a *caravan park*, and the *Club Hotel/Motel* (☎ (099) 81 7012) has single/double units for $80/95.

Warburton Road

For those interested in an outback experience, the unsealed road from Laverton to Yulara (the tourist development near Uluru), via Warburton, provides a rich scenery of red sand, spinifex, mulga and desert oaks. The road, while sandy in places, is suitable for conventional vehicles, although a 4WD would give a much smoother ride. Although this road is often called the Gunbarrel Highway, the genuine article actually runs some distance to the north, but it is rough and not maintained.

You should take precautions relevant to travel in such an isolated area – tell someone reliable of your travel plans and take adequate supplies of water, food, petrol and spare parts. The longest stretch without fuel is between Laverton and Warburton (568 km). Don't even consider doing it from November to March when the heat is extreme. Conditions should not be taken lightly – in 1994 a Japanese motorcyclist, equipped with just four leaky one-litre milk bottles, nearly met his end here. See the Getting Around chapter for more details.

Petrol is available at Laverton, Warburton (where basic supplies are also available), Docker River and Yulara. At **Giles**, about 105 km west of the Northern Territory border, is a weather station with a friendly 'Visitors Welcome' sign and a bar – it is well worth a visit.

As this road passes through Aboriginal land, permits from the Central Land Council in Alice Springs (☎ (08) 8951 6211) and the Aboriginal Affairs Planning Authority in Perth (☎ (09) 483 1333) are required before you can travel along it. These permits take up to two weeks to issue.

KAMBALDA (pop 4460)

Kambalda, south of Kalgoorlie-Boulder, died as a gold-mining town in 1906, but nickel was discovered in 1966 and today it is a major mining centre. There are two town centres, East and West Kambalda, about four km apart. The town is on the shores of **Lake Lefroy**, a large saltpan and a popular spot for land yachting. The view from Red Hill Lookout in Kambalda East is worth checking out.

The tourist bureau (☎ (090) 27 1446), on the corner of Emu Rocks and Marianthius Rds in West Kambalda, can provide information and a map of the region. If you intend to travel on Western Mining Corporation (WMC) private roads you will require permission from the tourist bureau or the WMC reception area. There is a caravan park and motel in Kambalda West.

NORSEMAN (pop 1400)

Norseman is a major crossroads town from where you depart east on the Eyre Highway (Nullarbor) journey. The tourist bureau (☎ (090) 39 0171), at 68 Roberts St, is open daily from 9 am to 5 pm. Nearby is a tourist rest park, open from 8 am to 6 pm.

The **Historical & Geological Collection** in the old School of Mines has items from the gold rush days; it's open weekdays from 10 am to 4 pm and admission is $2. An interesting **gold-mining tour** is conducted by Central Norseman Goldmining weekdays at 10 am and 1 pm. The 2½-hour tour costs $5; book at the tourist bureau.

You can get an excellent view of the town and the surrounding salt lakes from the **Beacon Hill Mararoa Lookout**, down past

the mountainous tailings dumps, one of which contains 4.2 million tonnes of rock.

Also worth a look are the views at sunrise and sunset of the dry, expansive **Lake Cowan**, north of the town. South of Norseman, just under halfway along the road to Esperance, is the small township of **Salmon Gums**, named after the gum trees, prevalent in the area, which acquire a rich, pink bark in late summer and autumn.

Places to Stay & Eat

The *Gateway Caravan Park* (☎ (090) 39 1500) has tent/powered sites for $11/13, vans for $28 and on-site cabins for $36. Both the *Norseman Hotel* (☎ (090) 39 1023) and the *Railway Hotel/Motel* (☎ (090) 39 1115) have rooms; the *Norseman Eyre Motel* (☎ (090) 39 1130) has rooms for $62/69.

Bits & Pizzas has a wide range of eat-in or takeaway meals, including cooked breakfasts with the works for $7.50. The *BP Roadhouse* at the start of the Eyre Highway has a wide range of food, including tasty fish & chips.

Eyre Highway

It's a little over 2700 km between Perth and Adelaide – not much less than the distance from London to Moscow. The long and sometimes lonely Eyre Highway crosses the southern edge of the vast **Nullarbor Plain** – 'Nullarbor' is bad Latin for 'no trees' and indeed there is a small stretch where you see none at all. Surprisingly, the road is flanked by trees most of the way as this coastal fringe receives regular rain, especially in winter.

The road across the Nullarbor takes its name from John Eyre, the explorer who made the first White east-west crossing in 1841. It was a superhuman effort that involved five months of hardship and resulted in the death of Eyre's companion, John Baxter. In 1877, a telegraph line was laid across the Nullarbor, roughly delineating the route the first road would take.

Later in the 19th century, miners en route

WESTERN AUSTRALIA

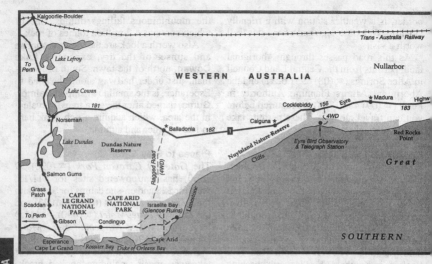

to the goldfields followed this telegraph-line route across the empty plain. In 1896, the first bicycle crossing was made and in 1912 the first car was driven across, but in the next 12 years only three more cars managed to traverse the continent.

In 1941, the war inspired the building of a transcontinental highway, just as it had the Alice Springs to Darwin route. It was a rough-and-ready track when completed, and in the '50s only a few vehicles a day made the crossing. In the '60s, the traffic flow increased to more than 30 vehicles a day and in 1969 the WA state government surfaced the road as far as the South Australian border. Finally, in 1976, the last stretch was surfaced and now the Nullarbor crossing is an easier, but still long, drive.

The surfaced road runs close to the coast on the South Australian side. Here, the Nullarbor region ends dramatically on the coast of the Great Australian Bight, at cliffs that drop steeply into the ocean.

The Indian Pacific Railway runs north of the coast and actually on the Nullarbor Plain – unlike the main road, which only fringes the great plain.

From Norseman, where the Eyre Highway begins, it's 725 km to the WA-SA border, near Eucla, and a farther 480 km to Ceduna (from the Aboriginal, meaning 'a place to sit down and rest') in South Australia. From Ceduna, it's still another 793 km to Adelaide via Port Augusta. It's a bloody long way!

Crossing the Nullarbor
See the Perth Getting There & Away section for air, rail, hitching and bus information on the Nullarbor.

Although the Nullarbor is no longer a torture trail, with cars getting shaken to bits in potholes and travellers facing the real possibility of dying of thirst while waiting for another vehicle if they break down, it's still wise to prepare adequately and to avoid difficulties whenever possible.

The longest distance between fuel stops is about 200 km, so if you're foolish enough to run low on petrol midway, it can be a long trip to get more. Getting help for a mechanical breakdown can be very expensive and equally time-consuming, so make sure your vehicle is in good shape and that you have plenty of petrol, good tyres and at least a basic kit of simple spare parts. Carry some

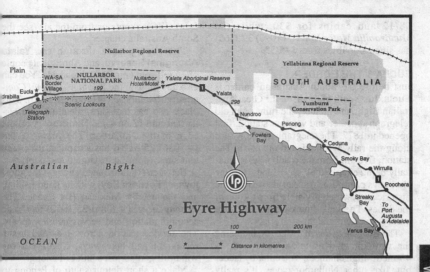

Eyre Highway

0 100 200 km

Distance in kilometres

drinking water just in case you do have to sit it out by the roadside on a hot summer day.

Take it easy on the Nullarbor – plenty of people try to set speed records and plenty more have messed up their cars by hitting kangaroos, particularly at night.

NORSEMAN TO MUNDRABILLA

From Norseman, the first settlement you reach is **Balladonia**, 193 km to the east. After Balladonia, near the old station, you can see the remains of stone fences built to enclose stock. Clay saltpans are also visible in the area. The *Balladonia Hotel/Motel* (☎ (090) 39 3453) has singles/doubles from $58/66 and its dusty caravan park has tent/powered sites for $8/14. The road from Balladonia to Cocklebiddy is one of the loneliest stretches of road across the Nullarbor.

Between Balladonia and Caiguna is one of the longest stretches of straight road in the world – 145 km. At **Caiguna**, the *John Eyre Motel* (☎ (090) 39 3459) has rooms for $50/65, and a caravan park with tent/powered sites from $5/12.

At **Cocklebiddy** are the stone ruins of an Aboriginal mission. Cocklebiddy Cave is the largest of the Nullarbor caves – in 1983 a team

of French explorers set a record there for the deepest cave dive in the world. With a 4WD, you can travel south of Cocklebiddy to Twilight Cove, with its 75-metre-high limestone cliffs. The *Wedgetail Inn* (☎ (090) 39 3462) at Cocklebiddy has a marauding goat, expensive fuel, tent/powered sites for $6/12 and overpriced rooms from $58/66. But it does have wedge-tailed eagles overhead.

The RAOU's Eyre Bird Observatory (☎ (090) 39 3450), housed in the former **Eyre Telegraph Station** 50 km south of Cocklebiddy on the Bight, is a haven for twitchers. Full board is $45 per person per day. Return transport from the Microwave tower on the escarpment costs $25, otherwise you will need to be a competent 4WD driver.

Madura, 91 km east of Cocklebiddy, is close to the Hampton Tablelands. At one time, horses were bred here for the Indian Army. There are good views over the plains from the road. The *Madura Pass Oasis Motel* (☎ (090) 39 3464) has tent/powered sites from $8/15 and rooms (not their 'units of a lesser classification') from $65/75.

Mundrabilla, 116 km to the east, has a caravan park, with tent/powered sites from

$8/12 and cabins for $30, while the *Mundrabilla Motor Hotel* (☎ (090) 39 3465) has singles/doubles from $45/55.

EUCLA & THE BORDER

Just before the South Australian border is **Eucla**. Just south of town, on the Great Australian Bight, are picturesque ruins of an old telegraph repeater and weather station, first opened in 1877. The telegraph line now runs along the railway line, far to the north. The station, five km from the roadhouse, is gradually being engulfed by sand dunes (just the chimneys protrude). You can also inspect the historic jetty, which is visible from the top of the dunes. The sand dunes around Eucla are a truly spectacular sight.

The Eucla area has many caves, including the well-known **Koonalda Cave** with its 45-metre-high chamber. You enter by ladder but, like other Nullarbor caves, it's really only for experienced cave explorers.

Many people have their photo taken at Eucla's famous sign which pinpoints distances to international destinations. For connoisseurs of kitsch there's a ferro-cement sperm whale (a species seldom seen in these parts), and a five-metre-high fibreglass kangaroo nearby.

The *WA-SA Border Village* (☎ (090) 39 3474) has tent/powered sites from $6/12, cabins from $35 a double and single/double motel units from $60/68. The *Eucla Motor Hotel* (☎ (090) 39 3468) has doubles from $68; its Eucla Pass section has tent/powered sites for $4/10 (showers are $1).

EUCLA TO CEDUNA (SA)

Between the WA-SA border and the pit-stop of Nullarbor (184 km to the east in South Australia), the Eyre Highway runs close to the coast and there are fine lookouts over the **Great Australian Bight** – be sure to stop at one or two.

At **Nullarbor**, the *Nullarbor Hotel/Motel* (☎ (086) 25 6271) has a restaurant, budget rooms, tent sites, and single/double units from $55/68. Just look for the diminutive fibreglass southern right whale. There are opportunities to see whales from here, either from cliff lookouts or from the air (see the South Australia chapter).

The road passes through the **Yalata Aboriginal Reserve**, and Aboriginal people often sell souvenirs by the roadside. You can also buy these in the *Yalata Aboriginal Community Roadhouse* (☎ (086) 25 6990). This place also has tent sites, motel units, a restaurant and takeaways. **Nundroo** is on the edge of the Nullarbor. The *Nundroo Inn* (☎ (086) 25 6120) has a caravan park with tent sites, rooms, a restaurant and pool.

Between Nundroo and Penong is the ghost town of **Fowlers Bay**, with its good fishing, and the nearby Mexican Hat Beach. The *Penong Hotel* (☎ (086) 25 1050) has basic accommodation and serves counter meals. The service station across the road has a restaurant and takeaways. Check out the windmill garden just south of Penong.

Make a short detour from Penong to the **Pink Lake, Point Sinclair** and **Cactus Beach** – a surf beach with left and right breaks that is a must for any serious surfer. Although the Point is private property, you can camp there for $5 (bring water).

Eastbound from Penong to Ceduna, there are places with petrol and other facilities. **Ceduna** is effectively the end of the solitary stretch from Norseman, and is equipped with supermarkets, banks and all the comforts (see Ceduna in the South Australia chapter).

The South-West

The southern area of WA, known as the 'Great Southern', has magnificent coastline pounded by huge seas, rugged ranges, national parks, Albany (the oldest settlement in WA) and, in the south-west, the greenest and most fertile areas of the state – a great contrast to the dry and barren country found elsewhere in WA. Here, you will find great karri and jarrah forests, prosperous farming land, wineries and more beautiful wildflowers.

Many travellers between the east and west coasts of Australia take the direct route to or

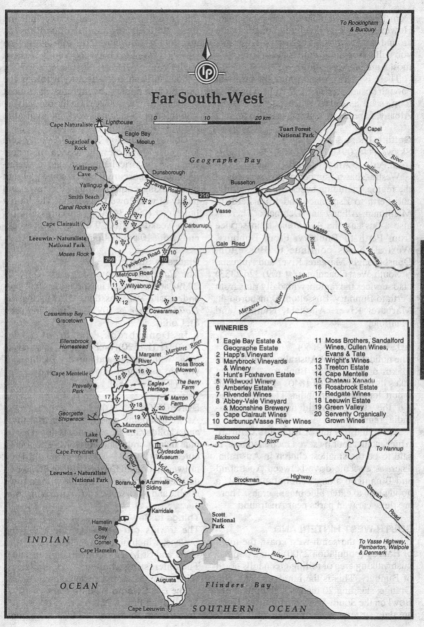

Far South-West

WINERIES

1 Eagle Bay Estate &
  Geographe Estate
2 Happ's Vineyard
3 Marybrook Vineyards
  & Winery
4 Hunt's Foxhaven Estate
5 Wildwood Winery
6 Amberley Estate
7 Rivendell Wines
8 Abbey-Vale Vineyard
  & Moonshine Brewery
9 Cape Clairault Wines
10 Carbunup/Vasse River Wines

11 Moss Brothers, Sandalford
   Wines, Cullen Wines,
   Evans & Tate
12 Wright's Wines
13 Treeton Estate
14 Cape Mentelle
15 Chateau Xanadu
16 Rosabrook Estate
17 Redgate Wines
18 Leeuwin Estate
19 Green Valley
20 Serventy Organically
   Grown Wines

from Perth via Coolgardie and Norseman. However, if you travel the longer route around the south-west corner of Australia, you will be rewarded with some of the state's most stunning scenery.

There is plenty of accommodation, with enough hostels to make a good backpacking loop, such as Perth, Augusta, the forests, Albany, Esperance, and return to Perth.

Getting There & Away

Skywest (☎ (09) 334 2288) has daily flights from Perth to Albany and Esperance.

Westrail has a number of bus services in the region, including buses from Kalgoorlie and Perth to Esperance and from Perth to Manjimup, Albany and Denmark. There is also a bus and the *Australind* train service from Perth to Bunbury. From Bunbury, Westrail buses continue to Busselton, Dunsborough, Margaret River and Augusta.

South-West Coachlines (☎ (09) 324 2333) also services the region, with daily runs from Perth to Bunbury, Busselton, Dunsborough, Margaret River, Augusta, Nannup and Manjimup.

AUSTRALIND (pop 3660)

The holiday resort of Australind is a pleasant 11-km drive north of Bunbury. The town takes its name from an 1840s plan to make it a port for trade with India. The plan failed but the strange hybrid name (Australia-India) remains.

Australind has the **St Nicholas Church**, which, at just four by seven metres square, is said to be the smallest church in Australia. There is a scenic drive between Australind and Binningup along **Leschenault Inlet**, a good place to catch blue manna crabs. There are three caravan parks near Australind.

SOUTH-WEST HINTERLAND

Inland from the south-west coast, the town of **Harvey** (population 2500) is in a popular bushwalking area of rolling green hills north of Bunbury. This is the home of WA's Big Orange, standing 20 metres high at the Fruit Bowl on the South-Western Highway. There are dam systems and some beautiful water-

falls nearby, and the **Yalgorup National Park**, with its peculiar stromatolites, is north-west of town. The tourist bureau (☎ (097) 29 1122) is on the South-Western Highway.

South of Bunbury is **Donnybrook**, in the centre of an apple-growing area. Its tourist centre (☎ (097) 31 1720) is in the old railway station. Apple-picking work is available most of the year.

Collie (population 7660), WA's only coal town, has an interesting replica of a coal mine, an historical museum and a steam-locomotive museum. There is some pleasant bushwalking country around the town and plenty of wildflowers in season. The tourist bureau (☎ (097) 34 2051) on Throssell St is open weekdays from 9 am to 5 pm; weekends from 10 am to 4 pm.

Places to Stay

The *Rainbow Caravan Park* (☎ (097) 29 2239), at 199 King St in Harvey, has tent sites and on-site vans, as does the *Mr Marron Holiday Village* (☎ (097) 34 5088) in Porter St, Collie.

In Donnybrook, the *Brook Lodge* (☎ (097) 31 1520), on Bridge St, is a private lodge with kitchen and laundry facilities. If you are picking fruit you may like to stay here ($70 per week).

BUNBURY (pop 27,000)

As well as being a port, an industrial town and a holiday resort, Bunbury is noted for its blue manna crabs and dolphins. The tourist bureau (☎ (097) 21 7922) is in the old 1904 railway station on Carmody Place. It has two detailed brochures – *Walk About* for a town ramble and *Browse Around* for a driving tour.

Things to See

The town's **old buildings** include King Cottage, which houses a museum, the Rose Hotel and St Mark's Church, built in 1842. The interesting Bunbury Art Galleries, Wittenoom St, are in a restored convent.

The **Big Swamp Wildlife Park** (☎ (097) 21 8380) on Prince Philip Drive, open daily from 10 am to 5 pm, includes kangaroos,

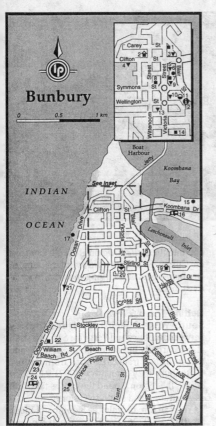

Bunbury

INDIAN OCEAN

PLACES TO STAY

1   Captain Bunbury Hotel
2   Wander Inn - Bunbury Backpackers
7   Trafalgar's Hotel
8   Lord Forrest Hotel
14 Prince of Wales Hotel
16 Koombana Park Caravan Park
19 Backpackers Residency YHA
22 Fawlty Towers
24 Punchbowl Caravan Park

PLACES TO EAT

3   Bakery
4   Louisa's
5   Memories of the Bond Store
9   International Food Hall
10 Rose Hotel
13 Benessé, Gelaré Ice Cream & Henry's on Victoria St
18 Centrepoint: Johanna's & Natural Temptation
21 Back Beach Kiosk

OTHER

6   Entertainment Centre
11 Bus Depot & Old Station Coffee Lounge
12 Tourist Bureau
15 Dolphin Discovery Centre (Koombana Beach)
17 Basaltic Rocks
20 Post Office
23 Arminui Art
25 Big Swamp Wildlife Park

wallabies, fruit bats, snakes and a large walk-in aviary with many native birds.

There is an Aboriginal art shop, Arminui Art (☎ (097) 91 1848), in Beach Rd, for quality purchases, lectures and tours.

Places to Stay

There are four caravan parks in town: *Bunbury Village* on the Bussell Highway; *Glade*, also on the Bussell Highway; the small *Punchbowl* on Ocean Drive and *Koombana Park* on Koombana Drive. There are more outside town.

The efficiently run and friendly *Wander Inn – Bunbury Backpackers* (☎ (097) 21 3242), close to the city centre at 16 Clifton St (two blocks from the Indian Ocean), costs $12 a night in the dorm and $28 for a twin or double. The staff provide free transport to the dolphins, day tours to the Collie region ($25) and trips to the surf beaches ($15).

The *Backpackers Residency YHA* (☎ (097) 91 2621) is on the corner of Stirling and Moore Sts. Good dorm beds in this clean hostel are $15 per night and the one family room is $30.

The *Prince of Wales* (☎ (097) 21 2016) on Stephen St has singles for $25 with breakfast. The *Rose Hotel* (☎ (097) 21 4533), Wellington St, is a clean and lavishly restored place; singles/doubles are $51/64 with breakfast.

The popular *Fawlty Towers* (☎ (097) 21

WESTERN AUSTRALIA

2427), at 205 Ocean Drive, has B&B singles/doubles for $40/55.

For a list of other B&Bs contact the tourist bureau; prices start from $25/50 for singles/doubles. The exquisite *Ellens Cottage* (☎ (097) 21 4626) at 26 Picton Crescent is a good example, with the cottage all to yourself and a hearty breakfast for $100 per couple.

Places to Eat
The *food hall* on Symmons St is a large place with kebabs, roasts, Italian and Chinese dishes and seafood from $5 to $7; it is open Thursday to Sunday from 11 am to 9 pm. *Drooly's*, at 70 Victoria St, has great pizzas at moderate prices. The historic *Rose Hotel* does good counter meals and has a wide range of beers. The Centrepoint shopping centre has good eateries such as *Johanna's* and *Natural Temptation*. The *Back Beach Kiosk*, on Ocean Drive, is worth a visit for the views if not the food.

Along the cafe strip of Victoria St you can sip a coffee in the most 'human-ambient' temperatures in the world. Try *Benessé*, *Henry's on Victoria St* or the *Federation*.

Also in Victoria St are the popular *Memories of the Bond Store*, which has four outlets including a brasserie, and the *China City Garden*. If you are after French cuisine then

hop into the *Little Frog* on Rose St. *Louisa's* on Clifton St is an award winner – one of Bunbury's best and serving modern, innovative cuisine.

Getting There & Away
South-West Coachlines travels daily between Bunbury and Perth for $16. Westrail also has a daily bus (three hours, $16.30) and the *Australind* train ($18) runs from Perth.

Bunbury City Transit (☎ (097) 91 1955) covers the region around the city as far north as Australind and south to Gelorup.

You can hire bicycles at Koombana kiosk (☎ (097) 95 9726) for $7 for a half day and $10 for a full day.

BUSSELTON (pop 9000)
Busselton, on the shores of Geographe Bay, is another popular holiday resort. The town has a two-km jetty which was once reputed to be the longest timber jetty in Australia. Busselton has a tourist bureau (☎ (097) 52 1288) in the civic centre on Southern Drive.

The old **courthouse** has been restored and now houses an impressive arts centre with a gallery, a coffee shop and artists' workshops. **Wonnerup House**, 10 km east of town, is an 1859 colonial-style house lovingly restored by the National Trust.

The best attractions in the region are the

Humpback whale breaching

migrating **whales**, both southern rights and humpbacks. Naturaliste Charters (☎ (097) 55 2276) visits southern rights from June to September near Cape Leeuwin and humpbacks from September to December near Cape Naturaliste. The three-hour cruise costs $35 (children $15).

To get to Busselton you can take a Westrail or South-West Coachlines bus. Geographe Bay Coachlines (☎ (097) 54 2026) conducts two tours: to Cape Naturaliste ($50), and to Augusta, Cape Leeuwin and Margaret River ($50).

Places to Stay
There is a great deal of accommodation along this stretch of coast, with seasonal variation in rates. The most central of the many caravan parks is *Kookaburra* (☎ (097) 52 1516) at 66 Marine Terrace. The *Busselton Caravan Park* (☎ (097) 52 1175), on the Bussell Highway, has powered sites for $14 and on-site vans for $35.

The nearly always full *Motel Busselton* (☎ (097) 52 1908), 90 Bussell Highway, has comfortable units from $30 per double, breakfast included. *Villa Carlotta Private*

Hotel (☎ (097) 54 2026), at 110 Adelaide St, is good, friendly, organises tours and has singles/doubles for $35/50 with breakfast. Another guesthouse, the *Travellers Rest* (☎ (097) 52 2290), 223 Bussell Highway, has B&B for $50.

The *Geographe Bayview Resort* (☎ (097) 55 4166) on the Bussell Highway has air-con guest rooms from $95/105 in the off/high season. The resort, which has tennis courts, pools, practice golf greens, bars and bistro, is typical of others in town.

Places to Eat
There is a stack of places to eat in Busselton including the *Golden Inn* on Albert St for Chinese food, *Beaches Cafe* on the Bussell Highway for lunch and dinner, and hotels such as the *Ship Hotel/Motel* on Albert St and the *Esplanade* on Marine Terrace for counter meals. Enjoy succulent seafood at the BYO *Tails of the Bay*, 42 Adelaide St, and at *Geos at the Resort* in the Geographe Bayview Resort.

DUNSBOROUGH (pop 660)
Dunsborough, just to the west of Busselton, is a pleasant little coastal town dependent on

tourism. The tourist bureau (☎ (097) 55 3517) is in the shopping centre.

North-west of Dunsborough, the Cape Naturaliste Rd leads to excellent beaches such as **Meelup, Eagle Bay** and **Bunker Bay**, some fine coastal lookouts and the tip of **Cape Naturaliste**, which has a lighthouse and some walking trails (the lighthouse is open daily except Wednesday from 9.30 am to 4 pm). In season you can see humpback and southern right whales and dolphins from the lookouts over Geographe Bay. At scenic **Sugarloaf Rock** is the southernmost nesting colony of the rare red-tailed tropicbird.

Both South-West Coachlines and Westrail have daily services from Perth to Dunsborough; the one-way fare is $22.

Places to Stay & Eat

Green Acres Caravan Park (☎ (097) 55 3087), on the beachfront at Dunsborough, has tent/powered sites for $11/12, on-site vans and cabins; prices go up 25% in the high season. Near Dunsborough, in Quindalup, is the *Three Pines Resort YHA* (☎ (097) 55 3107), well-positioned on the beachfront at 285 Geographe Bay Rd; the rate is $14 per person (dorms, twins and family) and you can hire bicycles ($8 per day) and canoes and life jackets ($5 per hour).

The *Forum Food Centre* has a variety of eating places including a fine bakery. *Dunsborough Health Foods* in the shopping centre sells wholemeal salad rolls and delicious smoothies and juices. *Texans*, in Naturaliste Terrace, has introduced Tex/Mex and Cajun food to a former culinary wasteland, and *Cafe Contadino* in Dunn Bay Rd is an Italian place open daily from 10 am.

YALLINGUP

Yallingup, a mecca for surfers, is surrounded by spectacular coastline and some fine beaches. Surfers can get a copy of the free *Down South Surfing Guide* from the Dunsborough tourist centre. Nearby is the stunning **Yallingup Cave** which was discovered, or rather stumbled upon, in 1899. The cave is open daily from 9.30 am to 3.30 pm and you can look around by yourself or take

a guided tour that explores parts of the cave not usually open to visitors.

The *Yallingup Caravan Park* (☎ (097) 55 2164) on the beachfront at Valley Rd has ten sites and on-site vans ($30). On Caves Rd *Caves House* (☎ (097) 55 2131), established in 1903, is an old-world lodge with ocean views and an English garden. As Yallingup means 'place of lovers', the units at Caves House are perfect for honeymooners but are not cheap at $120. There are superb lodges in the area; check with the Margaret River tourist bureau.

The *Yallingup Store* is known for its burgers. There's also the *Surfside* or the more expensive *Wildwood Winery*, eight km south of Yallingup on Caves Rd.

MARGARET RIVER (pop 1700)

Margaret River is a popular holiday spot due to its proximity to fine surf (Margaret River Mouth, Gnarabup, Suicides and Redgate) and swimming beaches (Prevelly and Grace Town), some of Australia's best wineries and spectacular scenery.

You can buy a copy of the *Margaret River Regional Vineyard Guide* at tourist centres ($2.50). It lists wineries from Capes Naturaliste to Leeuwin, including the renowned Leeuwin Estate, Cullens, Sandalford, Chateau Xanadu and Cape Mentelle. In general the wines are expensive but usually worth it. An essential companion is Peter Forrestal's *A Taste of the Margaret River* ($15).

The Augusta-Margaret River tourist bureau (☎ (097) 57 2911) is on the corner of the Bussell Highway and Tunbridge Rd. It has a wad of information on the area, including an extensive vineyard guide and info on the many art and craft places in town. CALM produces an informative, free booklet, *Leeuwin-Naturaliste National Park*.

Ellensbrook, the first home of the Bussell family, eight km north-west of town, is open on weekends. **Eagles Heritage**, five km south of Margaret River on Boodjidup Rd, has an interesting collection of raptors (birds of prey) in a natural setting; it is open daily from 10 am to 5 pm and costs $4.50 (children $2.50).

The **old coast road** between Augusta, Margaret River and Busselton is a good alternative to the direct road which runs slightly inland. The coast here has real variety – cliff faces, long beaches pounded by rolling surf, and calm, sheltered bays.

An interesting two-hour tour, conducted by Bushtucker Tours (☎ (097) 57 2466) at Prevelly Park, takes you on a search for forest secrets. The tour combines walking and canoeing up the Margaret River and teaches Aboriginal culture, bushcraft, flora and fauna; it costs $15 (children $10).

Places to Stay
The *Margaret River Caravan Park* (☎ (097) 57 2180) on Station Rd has tent/powered sites for $11/13 and on-site vans for $30. There's also the *Riverview Caravan Park* (☎ (097) 57 2270) on Willmott Ave (its tent sites are on a bit of an angle).

There are plenty of places to stay around Margaret River but unfortunately most are upwards of $50 per night. One exception is *Margaret River Lodge* (☎ (097) 57 2532), a backpackers hostel about 1.5 km south-west of the town centre at 220 Railway Terrace. It's clean, with facilities including a swimming pool, bicycle hire and an open fireplace. There are dorms at $11, four-bed bunk rooms from $13 per person and doubles from $33.

If you want to splash out, the *Croft* (☎ (097) 57 2845), at 54 Wallcliffe Rd, is a comfortable guesthouse run by a very friendly couple; B&B is $65 per double. Also worth a splurge is the *1885 Inn* (☎ (097) 57 3177) in Farrelly St which has two-person units from $95 to $125.

Places to Eat
Most places to eat in Margaret River are along the Bussell Highway. The *Settler's Tavern* has good counter meals from $10 to $12 – it occasionally has live music. The Margaret River Hotel has seafood meals in its *Rivers* bistro.

Eats Diner and *Mimi's Cafe* are other good

choices on the Bussell Highway. For intimacy and tasty continental fare there is the licensed *1885 Inn*, Farrelly St.

Getting There & Away
There are daily bus services between Perth and Margaret River on South-West Coachlines and Westrail (both about $25); the trip takes around five hours.

Bikes can be rented on a daily or hourly basis from Margaret River Lodge.

AUGUSTA (pop 840)
A popular holiday resort, Augusta is five km north of Cape Leeuwin, which has a rugged coastline, a lighthouse (open daily to the public) with views across two oceans (the Indian and the Southern), and a salt-encrusted 1895 waterwheel. The interesting **Augusta Historical Museum** on Blackwood Ave has exhibits relating to local history. The tourist centre (☎ (097) 58 1695) is in a souvenir shop at 70 Blackwood Ave.

Between Augusta and Margaret River are good beaches such as **Hamelin Bay** and **Cosy Corner**. Scenic flights over the cape are conducted by Leeuwin Aviation; book on ☎ (097) 58 1757 or ☎ 1800 677 757.

'Hidden Wilderness' Caves
There are limestone caves between Naturaliste and Leeuwin capes. These include **Jewel** (the most picturesque), **Lake**, **Mammoth** and **Moondyne**. Fossilised skeletons of Tasmanian tigers have been found in Moondyne (but since removed), and a fossil jawbone of *Zygomaturus trilobus*, a giant wombat-like creature, is on display in the cave. Moondyne is unlit and an experienced guide takes the visitor on a caving adventure; all equipment is provided on this two-hour trip which costs $18. Guided tours, the only way to see these caves, run daily for $7.50.

In all, 120 caves have been discovered between Cape Leeuwin and Cape Naturaliste but only these four, and Yallingup Cave near Busselton, are open to the public. Check opening times with the Augusta-Margaret River tourist bureau (☎ (097) 52 7911).

WESTERN AUSTRALIA

Places to Stay & Eat

Doonbanks (☎ (097) 58 1517) is the most central caravan park, with tent/powered sites for $11/13; it is a well-run place in a good setting. There are a number of basic camp sites in the Leeuwin-Naturaliste National Park including ones on Boranup Drive, Point Rd and Conto's Field, near Lake Cave.

The *Baywatch Manor Resort* (☎ (097) 58 1290), in the town centre at 88 Blackwood Ave, is a purpose-built hostel with beds for $14 a person. It has a fully equipped kitchen, lounge and dining areas, disabled facilities, an outdoor barbecue area and parking. You can book here for many activities in the Augusta region.

The *Augusta Hotel* does counter meals and the *August(a) Moon* is a Chinese place in the Matthew Flinders shopping centre on Ellis St. Between the caves, in the Boranup karri forest, is the quaint *Arumvale Siding Cafe*, which serves a mean nachos, Devonshire teas and a range of juices.

NANNUP (pop 550)

Sixty km east of Margaret River is Nannup, a quiet, historical and picturesque town in the heart of forest and farmland. The tourist centre (☎ (097) 56 1211) at the old 1922 police station in Brockman St (open daily from 9 am to 3 pm) has an excellent booklet (50c) that points out places of interest around town and details a range of scenic drives in the area, including numerous forest drives.

There is a jarrah sawmill, an arboretum, some fine old buildings and several craft shops. The descent of the **Blackwood River**, from the forest to the sea, is one of Australia's great canoe trips.

Places to Stay & Eat

The backpackers lodge is the permaculture-conscious and rustic *Black Cockatoo Eco-Stay* (☎ (097) 56 1035), 27 Grange Rd, with singles/twins for $10/20. The people who run this place are cool and contribute to its laid-back atmosphere. There is a large backyard with a stream as one border.

The centrally located *Dry Brook B&B* (☎ (097) 56 1049), which welcomes YHA members, has singles/doubles for $25/40 with breakfast. There are many cottages in the area which cost from $50; enquire at the tourist centre.

The *Blackwood Cafe* serves light meals such as quiche, soup and sandwiches. It is on Warren Rd, near the *Nannup Hotel*, which has counter meals.

BRIDGETOWN (pop 1520)

This quiet country town on the Blackwood River, about 50 km east of Nannup, is in an area of karri forests and farmland. Bridgetown has some old buildings, including the mud-and-clay **Bridgedale House**, built by the area's first settler in 1862. There is a local history display in the tourist bureau (☎ (097) 61 1740) on Hampton St.

Interesting features of the Blackwood River valley are the burrawangs (grass trees) and large granite boulders. In **Boyup Brook**, 31 km north-east of Bridgetown, there is a flora reserve, a country & western music collection (some 2000 titles) and a large butterfly and beetle display. Nearby is **Norlup Pool** with glacial rock formations, and **Wilga**, an old timber mill with vintage engines.

Places to Stay & Eat

Bridgetown Caravan Park (☎ (097) 61 1053), on the South-Western Highway, has tent/powered sites for $12/14 and on-site vans for $26; backpackers accommodation is $12.50. The *Old Well* (☎ (097) 61 2032) on Gifford St has B&B singles/doubles for $35/65 and *The Nelson House Lodge* (☎ (097) 61 1641) at 38 Hampton St has singles/doubles only, from $35/38 in the off season. Ask at the tourist centre about the many other B&B possibilities.

About 20 km north of town, in Greenbushes, the *Exchange Hotel* (☎ (097) 64 3509) has budget rooms, and units for $38/48.

Good meals are available at *Riverwood House*, the *Pottery* and *Buckley's Bistro*.

MANJIMUP (pop 5000)

Manjimup, the commercial and agricultural

centre of the south-west, is noted (sometimes vilified) for its woodchipping. The **Timber Park Complex** on the corner of Rose and Edwards Sts includes museums, old buildings and the tourist bureau (☎ (097) 71 1831). Very much an apologia for the local timber industry, it defends daily from 9 am to 5 pm. Learn how magnificent trees are felled, stripped, sawn up and sent overseas for pulping.

One Tree Bridge, or what's left of it after the 1966 floods, is 22 km down Graphite Rd. It was constructed from a single karri log. The **Four Aces**, 1.5 km from One Tree Bridge, are four superb karri trees believed to be over 300 years old. **Fonty's Pool**, a cool swimming spot, is 10 km south-west of town along Seven Day Rd.

Nine km south of town, along the South-Western Highway, is the 51-metre-high karri **Diamond Tree** with a wooden lookout tower at the top. You can climb most of the way up to a platform from where there are great views over forest and farmland.

Perup, 50 km east of Manjimup, is the centre of a forest which boasts six rare mammals – the numbat, chuditch, woylie, tammar wallaby, ringtail possum and southern brown bandicoot.

Places to Stay & Eat

The *Manjimup Caravan Park* (☎ (097) 71 2093) has a hostel with dorm beds and cooking facilities for $12 per night – it can get busy in apple-picking season (March to June). It also has tent/powered sites for $10/13 and on-site vans for $25. Two other caravan parks – *Warren Way* (☎ (097) 71 1060), two km north of town, and *Fonty's Pool* (☎ (097) 71 2105), 10 km south-west of town – have tent sites and on-site vans.

The *Manjimup Hotel* (☎ (097) 71 1322) on Giblett St, designed to slake the thirst of raucous timber millers, can be noisy. The staff are friendly and the singles/doubles, most with bathrooms, are worth the $26/48.

If you have transport go to Pemberton for dinner. Otherwise, the *Rose Street Cafe*, a lunch spot at No 31b, boasts a 'gigantic menu' and the *hotel* has counter meals. In Mottram St, across the railway line from the hotel, is a garish, pulsating *takeaway*, usually the last eatery to close.

Getting There & Away

Westrail has a Perth to Manjimup bus service via Bunbury and Collie. South-West Coachlines has a weekday service from Perth; both are about $27 one way.

PEMBERTON (pop 930)

Deep in the karri forests is the delightful township of Pemberton. The child-friendly, well-organised Karri visitors centre (☎ (097) 76 1133), on Brockman St, incorporates the tourist centre, pioneer museum and karri forest discovery centre. You need a day pass to go into the national parks. This is available from the CALM office in Kennedy St and costs $5 per car or $2 for persons in tour groups.

Pemberton has some interesting **craft shops**, the pretty **Pemberton Pool** surrounded by karri trees (ideal on a hot day) and a **trout hatchery** that supplies fish for the state's dams and rivers.

If you are feeling fit, you can make the scary 60-metre climb to the top of the **Gloucester Tree**, reputed to be the highest fire lookout tree in the world. This is not for the faint-hearted and only one visitor in four ascends. The view makes the climb well worthwhile. To get to the tree just follow the signs from town.

Also of interest in the area are the cascading **Cascades** (only so when the water level is high), **Beedelup National Park**, the 100-year-old forest (another apologia for milling) and the **Warren National Park**, where camping is allowed in designated areas.

Tours

The scenic **Pemberton Tramway** is one of the area's main attractions. Trams leave Pemberton railway station for Warren River ($11.50; children $6) daily at 10.45 am and 2 pm, and for Northcliffe ($18/9) at 10.15 am on Tuesday, Thursday and Friday. The route travels through lush marri and karri forests and there are occasional picture stops.

Southern Forest Adventures (☎ (097) 76 1222) has 4WD tours of the forest and coastal areas around Pemberton from $40. Their half-day canoeing trips start from $30.

For diametric views on the forests, the Warren Environment Group takes short walks through beautiful stands of karri, while Pemberton Scenic Bus Tours do forest industry tours; contact both on ☎ (097) 76 1133.

Places to Stay

Camping is permitted in Warren National Park and in some areas of the Pemberton Forest (☎ (097) 76 1200). The picturesque *Pemberton Caravan Park* (☎ (097) 76 1300) has tent sites for $11 and on-site vans for $26.

The *Pimelea Chalets YHA* (☎ (097) 76 1153), in a beautiful forest location at Pimelea, costs $10 a night; doubles in cottages are $35 and two other cottages, Pimelea and Zamia, are $55 each (maximum of five people). It's 10 km north-west of town but the hostel provides a courtesy bus to meet the Westrail bus in Pemberton.

In town, the centrally located *Warren Lodge* (☎ (097) 76 1105), on Brockman St, has backpackers' beds from $12 and B&B at $40 for two. Two km north of town, the *Forest Lodge* (☎ (097) 76 1113) has singles/doubles for $38/45, and chalets from $80 (in the off season). There are many more up-market options.

Places to Eat

Chloe's Kitchen has takeaways, including vegetarian food, while the *Mainstreet Cafe* has good, basic and cheap food such as hamburgers and Lebanese rolls; both are on Brockman St. The *Pemberton Chinese*, next to the supermarket on Dean St, is open Tuesday to Sunday from 5 pm. The *Silver Birch* in Widdeson St has great three-course meals, including trout and marron, for $25.

Getting There & Away

Westrail Perth to Pemberton buses operate daily, via Bunbury, Donnybrook and Manjimup, and cost $30.60; the trip takes about five hours. The Easyrider Backpacker bus will drop you off at the Pimelea Chalets YHA and other accommodation places.

NORTHCLIFFE (pop 800)

Northcliffe, 32 km south of Pemberton, has a **pioneer museum** and a nearby **forest park**, with good walks through stands of grand karri, marri and jarrah trees. The tourist centre (☎ (097) 76 7203) is by the pioneer museum on Wheatley Coast Rd.

Picturesque **Lane Poole Falls** are 19 km south-east of Northcliffe; the 2.5-km track to the falls starts from the 50-metre Boorara lookout tree. The falls slow to a trickle in the summer months.

Windy Harbour, on the coast 29 km south of Northcliffe, has prefab shacks and a sheltered beach; true to its name, it is very windy. The cliffs of magnificent **D'Entrecasteaux National Park** are accessible from here.

Places to Stay

Opposite the school, the *Pine Tree Caravan Park* (☎ (097) 76 7193) has tent sites for $5.50. *Northcliffe Hotel* (☎ (097) 76 7089), the only hotel in town, has basic accommodation for $16/30 and, out of town, *Brook Farm* (☎ (097) 75 1014), Middleton Rd, has B&B singles/doubles for $22/44.

At Windy Harbour, the only place to stay is *Windy Harbour Camping Area* (☎ (097) 76 7056), where basic tent sites are $4.

Getting There & Away

The Perth to Albany Westrail bus goes through Northcliffe twice weekly (Wednesday and Saturday), but you need your own transport to get to Windy Harbour.

WALPOLE-NORNALUP

The heavily forested **Walpole-Nornalup National Park** covers 18,000 hectares around Nornalup Inlet and Walpole; it contains beaches, rugged coastline, inlets and the 'Valley of the Giants', a stand of giant karri and tingle trees, including one that soars 46 metres high. Here, four species of rare eucalypt grow naturally within four km of each other and nowhere else in the world – red, yellow and Rates tingle (*Eucalyptus* *jacksonii, E. guilfoylei, E. cornuta)* and red flowering gum *(E. ficifolia).* Pleasant shady paths lead through the forest and the area is frequented by bushwalkers. The **Frankland River** is popular with canoeists.

Scenic drives include Knoll Drive and the Valley of the Giants Rd. About 13 km from Walpole via Crystal Springs is **Mandalay Beach**, where the wreck of the *Mandalay*, a Norwegian barque wrecked here in 1911, can sometimes be seen. It seems to appear every 10 years out of the sands.

You can get more information from the Walpole tourist bureau (☎ (098) 40 1111), open daily from 10 am to 3 pm; or CALM (☎ (098) 40 1027). Both are on the South Coast Highway.

An informative CALM publication, *Finding the Magic,* costs $1.50 and includes a tree-spotter's guide. It also outlines the Ocean Drive, which takes in the beautiful **Conspicuous Cliffs beach**, not far from the western end of the Valley of the Giants.

Karri to Coast (☎ (098) 40 1170) run day trips around the area for $60, which includes lunch. Both the *Naughty Lass* and *Rainbow Lady* (☎ (098) 40 1036) cruise the inlets and the river systems; enquire at the tourist bureau.

Places to Stay & Eat
There are a number of camping grounds in the Walpole-Nornalup National Park, including tent sites at Peaceful Bay, Crystal Springs and Coalmine Beach, and CALM huts at Fernhook Falls and Mt Frankland. *Rest Point Caravan Park* (☎ (098) 40 1032), perfectly sited on Walpole Inlet, has tent and powered sites, cottages and units.

The *Tingle All Over Backpackers* (☎ (098) 40 1041), on the South Coast Highway in Walpole, has dorm beds for $12 and twins for $30. Walkers and cyclists relax at this laid-back place after doing the Bibbulman Track, which ends in Walpole. There is also the *Dingo Flat Youth Hostel* (☎ (098) 40 8073) on Dingo Flat Rd off the Valley of the Giants Rd, 18 km east of Walpole. You need a car or cycle to get to this hostel, but if you ring ahead they'll pick you up at Bow Bridge

(there is a public phone in the local shop). Beds are $8, and the place has character, with wonderful views over the fields to the forest.

You can get counter meals at the *Walpole Motel/Hotel* but be careful when enquiring about the 'thing' above the bar. There are a couple of street cafes, including *Anne's Pantry* and the *Carragah*.

DENMARK (pop 3500)
Denmark, or Koorabup ('place of the black swan'), has some rare evidence of Aboriginal settlement in Wilson Inlet – 3000-year-old fish traps. Named Denmark by an early explorer to commemorate a friend, the town was first established to supply timber for goldfield developments. About 54 km west of Albany, it has some fine beaches (especially Ocean Beach for surfing) and is a good base for trips into the karri and tingle forests.

The tourist bureau (☎ (098) 48 2055) on Strickland St provides heritage trail brochures. **Trails** include the Mokare Trail (a three-km trail along the Denmark River) and the Wilson Inlet Trail (a six-km trail that starts from the river mouth). There are fine views from **Mt Shadforth**.

The **William Bay National Park**, 15 km west of Denmark, has fine coastal scenery of rocks and reefs. Green's Pool and Elephants Rocks are both calm and safe for swimming.

Places to Stay
Of several caravan parks in town, the closest is the idyllically located *Rivermouth Caravan Park* (☎ (098) 48 1262), one km south of the town centre on Inlet Drive. It has tent and powered sites, on-site vans and cabins.

The *Denmark Youth Hostel* at the Wilson Inlet Holiday Park, over four km south of Denmark, has a dingy dorm in the park's most dilapidated building. It costs $10 per person – four people could band together and get something much better in town.

Edinburgh House (☎ 1800 671 477), on the South Coast Highway in the centre of town, is a friendly place with a TV lounge and clean singles/doubles for $20/40; en suite rooms are from $35/55.

There are many types of chalets and cottages in the Denmark area; the tourist bureau keeps a current list. The *Gum Grove Chalets* (☎ (098) 48 1378), Ocean Beach Rd, and *The Cove* (☎ (098) 48 1770), Payne Rd, have facilities for the disabled. The fully equipped two-bedroom *Karma Chalets* (☎ (098) 48 1568) are good value at $75 per night.

Places to Eat

On North St, the *Mary Rose*, a quaint place with a pleasant balcony, serves tasty light meals. For a quick meal or takeaway food, try *Hugh's Food Haven* on the corner of the highway and Holling Rd.

Beneath Edinburgh House is the *Tiger & Snake*, which serves tasty and hearty Indian and Chinese food ($6 and $8 for small and large servings). Nearby is the small *Blue Wren Cafe*, open for lunch and dinner.

The *Fig Tree Bistro*, in Fig Tree Square, is a pleasant place to sit with a coffee. Beside the river, *Bellini's*, a BYO with blackboard menu, is open until late.

Getting There & Away

Westrail's Perth to Albany service (via the south coast) passes through Denmark daily and costs $41.50 one way. Contact the tourist bureau about local tours and bike hire.

MT BARKER (pop 1520)

Mt Barker, centre of the Plantagenet region, is 50 km north of Albany and about 64 km south of the Stirling Range. There's a tourist bureau at 57 Lowood Rd (☎ (098) 51 1163), open weekdays from 9 am to 5 pm, Saturday from 9 am to 3 pm and Sunday from 10 am to 3 pm.

The town has been settled since the 1830s, with the old police station and gaol building of 1868 preserved as a museum; there is a $2 entry fee. You can get a panoramic view of the area from the Mt Barker Lookout, five km south of town. South-west of the town is the picturesque **St Werburgh's Chapel**, constructed from local materials in 1873.

The region has a good reputation for wine making, and there are many **wineries** with cellar sales and tastings within a few km of

town – see the tourist bureau for locations and opening times. Plantagenet Wines in Mt Barker may show you around their winery.

North of Mt Barker is **Cranbrook**, an access point to the northern Stirling Ranges.

Places to Stay & Eat

The *Mt Barker Caravan Park* (☎ (098) 51 1691), Albany Highway, has tent/powered sites at $8.50/15 and park cabins at $30. The *Plantagenet Hotel* (☎ (098) 51 1008) at 9 Lowood Rd has singles/doubles from $25/40 (in the older section) and good counter meals for around $10. The *Valley Views Motel* (☎ (098) 51 1899) has singles/doubles for $42/54.

The Antique Room in *Sophie's* is the place for a classy meal – a welcome change from bland roadhouse takeaways.

Westrail's Perth to Albany (via Williams) bus service stops daily in Mt Barker.

PORONGURUP & STIRLING RANGES

The beautiful **Porongurup National Park** (2401 hectares) has panoramic views and scenery, large karri trees, 1100-million-year-old granite outcrops and some excellent bushwalks. Walking trails range from the short Tree in the Rock stroll and the intermediate Castle Rock walk (two hours) to the harder Haywards and Nancy Peaks (four hours) and the excellent Devil's Slide and Marmabup Rock (three hours) walks.

A scenic six-km drive along the park's northern edge starts at the ranger's residence.

In the **Stirling Range National Park** (115,650 hectares), Toolbrunup Peak (for views and a good climb), Bluff Knoll (at 1073 metres, the highest peak in the range) and Toll Peak (for the wildflowers) are popular half-day walks. The 96-km range is noted for its spectacular colour changes through blues, reds and purples. The mountains rise abruptly from the surrounding flat and sandy plains, and the area is known for its fine flora and fauna, especially the Stirling Bells, magnificent when in bloom. There are guided walks in September and October (☎ (098) 27 9229); excellent value at $2.

For further information on these parks contact the CALM offices on Bolganup Rd, Mt Barker; on Chester Pass Rd, Stirling Range; or at 44 Serpentine Rd, Albany.

Places to Stay

You can camp in the Stirling Range National Park on Chester Pass Rd, near the Toolbrunup Peak turn-off; call the ranger (☎ (098) 27 9230) for details. Facilities are limited, and tent sites are $5.

Stirling Range Caravan Park (☎ (098) 27 9229), on the north boundary of the park, is also on Chester Pass Rd; park cabins are $30. There is also an associate-YHA hostel, with beds for $12 in self-contained rammed-earth units ($40 for four).

There is no camping in the Porongurups but there's a *caravan park* (☎ (098) 53 1057) in the township. There are backpackers' beds at the friendly *Porongurup Shop & Tea-rooms* (☎ (098) 53 1110) for $11 per person. This place is run by informative, seasoned travellers. The *Karribank Lodge* (☎ (098) 53 1022) has singles/doubles for $25/40, and chalets for $65.

ALBANY (pop 18,800)

The commercial centre of the southern region, Albany is the oldest European settlement in the state, established shortly before Perth in 1826. The area was occupied by Aboriginal people long before and there is much evidence, especially around Oyster Harbour, of their earlier presence.

With its excellent harbour on King George Sound, Albany was until the late 1970s a thriving whaling port. When steamships started travelling between the UK and Australia, Albany was also a coaling station for ships bound for the east coast. During WW I, it was the gathering point for troopships of the 1st Australian Imperial Force (AIF) before they sailed for Egypt, eventually to fight in the Gallipoli campaign.

The coastline around Albany contains some of Australia's most rugged and spectacular scenery. There are a number of pristine beaches in the area where you don't have to compete for space on the sand – try Misery, Ledge and Nanarup beaches.

Information

The impressive tourist bureau (☎ (098) 41 1088), in the old railway station on Proudlove Parade, is open weekdays from 8.30 am to 5.30 pm and weekends from 9 am to 5 pm.

Old Buildings

Albany has some fine colonial buildings – **Stirling Terrace** is noted for its Victorian shopfronts. The 1851 **Old Gaol**, on Lower Stirling Terrace, is now a folk museum and is open daily. The admission of $3 includes entry to the 1832 wattle-and-daub **Patrick Taylor Cottage** in Duke St, the oldest dwelling in WA, also open daily.

The **Albany Residency Museum**, opposite the Old Gaol, was originally built in the 1850s as the home of the resident magistrate; it is open daily from 10 am to 5 pm. Displays include seafaring subjects, flora and fauna and Aboriginal artefacts. Housed in another building is 'Sea & Touch', a great hands-on experience for children and adults.

Next to this museum is a full-scale replica of the brig *Amity*, the ship that brought Albany's founders to the area; there is a $2 entry fee.

The restored **post office** (1870), on Lower Stirling Terrace, houses the Inter-Colonial Museum with its collection of communications equipment from WA's past; it is open daily from 10 am to 4 pm and admission is free.

The farm at **Strawberry Hill**, two km north of the town centre, is one of the oldest in the state, having been established in 1827 as the government farm for Albany. The entry fee is $3.

Other historic buildings include St John's Anglican Church, the elegant home Pyrmont, and the courthouse. A walking-tour of Albany's colonial buildings is available from the tourist bureau.

Views

There are fine views over the coast and inland from the twin peaks, **Mt Clarence** and

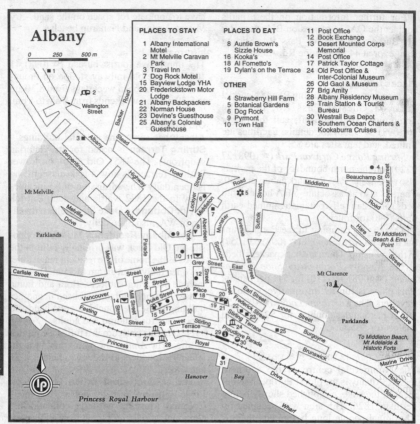

Albany

0   250   500 m

PLACES TO STAY	PLACES TO EAT	11 Post Office
1 Albany International Motel	8 Auntie Brown's Sizzle House	12 Book Exchange
2 Mt Melville Caravan Park	16 Kooka's	13 Desert Mounted Corps Memorial
3 Travel Inn	18 Al Fornetto's	14 Post Office
7 Dog Rock Motel	19 Dylan's on the Terrace	17 Patrick Taylor Cottage
15 Bayview Lodge YHA		24 Old Post Office & Inter-Colonial Museum
20 Frederickstown Motor Lodge	OTHER	26 Old Gaol & Museum
21 Albany Backpackers	4 Strawberry Hill Farm	27 Brig Amity
22 Norman House	5 Botanical Gardens	28 Albany Residency Museum
23 Devine's Guesthouse	6 Dog Rock	29 Train Station & Tourist Bureau
25 Albany's Colonial Guesthouse	9 Pyrmont	30 Westrail Bus Depot
	10 Town Hall	31 Southern Ocean Charters & Kookaburra Cruises

Mt Melville, which overlook the town. On top of Mt Clarence is the Desert Mounted Corps Memorial, originally erected in Port Said as a memorial to the events of Gallipoli. It was moved here when the Suez Crisis (1956) made colonial reminders less than popular in Egypt.

Mt Clarence can be climbed along a track accessible from the end of Grey St East; turn left, take the first street on the right and follow the path by the water tanks. The walk is tough but the views from the top make it worthwhile. The easier way to the top is along Apex Drive. There is a whale-watch walk from Marine Drive on nearby Mt Adelaide to the harbour entrance (45 minutes return).

Panoramic views are also enjoyed from the lookout tower on Mt Melville; the signposted turn-off is off Serpentine Rd.

Other Attractions

Albany's **Princess Royal Fortress**, on Mt Adelaide, was built in 1893 when the strategic port's perceived vulnerability to naval attack was recognised as a potential threat to Australia's security. The restored buildings, gun emplacements and fine views make it

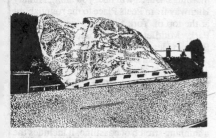

Dog Rock in Albany

well worth a visit. It is open daily from 7.30 am to 5.30 pm and costs $2. **Dog Rock**, a deformed boulder that looks like a dog's head, is on Middleton Rd.

The bizarre **Extravaganza**, a shop with a difference, is at Middleton Beach. All exhibits are for sale; entry is $5.

Whale-Watching

The whale-watching season is from July to September – southern right whales are observed near the bays and coves of King George Sound. Southern Ocean Charters (☎ (098) 41 7176) takes trips out in the *Pamela* to the whales ($25; children $12.50) and also operates diving, fishing, underwater photography and snorkelling tours on demand. Common dolphins, sea lions and fur seals are also often seen.

Two other operators are Albany Whale Tours (☎ (015) 42 3434), aboard the *Avon*, and Silver Star (☎ (098) 41 3333).

Tours & Cruises

The *Silver Star* leaves the town jetty three times a week (outside whale-watching season) for a 2½-hour cruise around King George Sound; the cost is $20 (children $12). Escape Tours operates from the tourist bureau. They have many local half-day and day bus tours around Albany from $27.50 to $55; check at the tourist bureau. Bushed (☎ (098) 42 2127) operates abseiling, rock-climbing, canoeing and bushwalking trips.

Places to Stay

Camping & Hostels There are caravan parks aplenty in Albany. The closest to the city centre, *Mt Melville* (☎ (098) 41 4616), one km north of town on Wellington St, has tent and powered sites, and on-site cabins. The spotless *Middleton Beach* (☎ (098) 41 3593) on Middleton Rd, three km east of town, has park cabins without/with en suite for $35/50.

The *Albany Backpackers* (☎ (098) 41 8848), also centrally located, is on the corner of Stirling Terrace and Spencer St. It's worth stopping by just to check out the murals. A dorm bed is $12, and singles/twins are $20/28. Apart from all the essentials, the hostel hires out mountain bikes.

The *Bayview Lodge YHA* (☎ (098) 41 3949), at 49 Duke St close to the town centre, has had a much needed renovation. It's $11/13 for members/nonmembers. The *London Hotel* (☎ (098) 41 1048) at 160 Stirling Terrace also has budget beds.

Guesthouses & Motels Albany also has a number of reasonably priced guesthouses, many of which offer breakfast with accommodation. *Albany's Colonial Guesthouse* (☎ (098) 41 3704), at 136 Brunswick Rd, charges $25 including breakfast. *Norman House* (☎ (098) 41 5995) at 28 Stirling Terrace, walking distance from the bus station, has B&B at $65 for a double.

The *Middleton Beach Guesthouse* (☎ (098) 41 1295) on Adelaide Crescent has doubles for $32 to $40. The *Coraki Holiday Cottages* (☎ (098) 44 7068) are about a 10-minute drive from Albany, on Lower King River Rd. Self-contained cottages in this pretty setting are $50 for two (minimum of two nights).

The *Frederickstown Motor Lodge* (☎ (098) 41 1600), corner of Frederick and Spencer Sts, has singles/doubles from $58/68; and the *Dog Rock Motel* (☎ (098) 41 4422) on Middleton Rd has singles/doubles from $48/50 (more in the high season) and a Thai restaurant.

Places to Eat

You'll not starve if you wander along Stirling Terrace. *Dylan's on the Terrace* at No 82 has an excellent range of light meals including hamburgers and pancakes; it is open late most nights, and then early for breakfast. Also on the terrace is *Kooka's*, at No 204 in a restored old house, where you can count on paying $30 for an excellent three-course meal. Other sterling choices are the *Penny Post*, the *Harbourfront Steak & Grill*, *Cafe Bizarre* and three pubs with the ubiquitous counter meal, including the *London* with its blackboard menu.

York St is another happy hunting ground for food. The hearty breakfasts at the *Wildflower*, No 187, are recommended; *Eatcha Heart Out*, No 154, is also good for breakfasts; *Al Fornetto's*, No 132, and the *Venice*, No 179, are pizza and pasta places; *Nonna's Brasseria*, No 135, has a range of Australian and Italian cuisine and is a popular place for Albany's smattering of trendies; and *Auntie Brown's Sizzle House*, No 280, has an all-you-can-eat smorgasbord for $20.

At Middleton Beach there's the *Beachside Cafe*, right on the beach, and, close to the Extravaganza, *Middleton Beach Fish & Chips*, which has crisp golden chips and a plethora of fish such as groper, snapper, shark and flounder. *Cravings* at Emu Point has a smorgasbord salad bar and a local fish menu; dinner is from $15.

The tourist bureau has more details, especially on self-catering options.

Entertainment
There is an active art and music scene in Albany. The White Star, Albany and Esplanade hotels all feature live music; a gig guide is printed in *the drum*, available free from most pubs and the tourist bureau.

Getting There & Away
Skywest flies daily from Perth to Albany. Westrail has daily buses from Perth via various Wheatbelt towns for $35.10, and four buses a week via Manjimup and Denmark.

Getting Around
Love's bus service runs around town from Monday to Friday all day, and Saturday mornings. Buses will take you along Albany Highway from Peels Place to the roundabout at the top of York St; others go to Spencer Park, Middleton Beach, Emu Point and Bayonet Head.

You can rent bicycles from Albany Backpackers in Stirling Terrace for $10 per day and at the Emu Beach Caravan Park.

AROUND ALBANY
South of Albany, off Frenchman Bay Rd, is a stunning stretch of coastline. It includes the **Gap** and **Natural Bridge** rock formations; the **Blowholes**, especially interesting in heavy seas when air is blown with great force through the surrounding rock; the **rock-climbing** areas of Peak Head and West Cape Howe; steep, rocky coves such as **Jimmy Newhill's Harbour** and **Salmon Holes** (popular with surfers, although these coves are considered quite dangerous); and **Frenchman Bay**, which has a caravan park, a fine swimming beach and a grassed barbecue area with plenty of shade. This coastline is dangerous; beware of king-size waves.

Whaleworld
Also at Frenchman Bay, 21 km from Albany, is Whaleworld, at the old Cheynes Beach Whaling Station which only ceased operations in 1978. There's a rusting whale-chaser and station impedimenta to inspect after seeing a gore-spattered film on whaling. It is open daily from 9 am to 5 pm, but the $5 admission is considered a bit rich by some. From the beach, listen carefully and you will hear the haunting, mournful songs of the whales at sea. Their presence here in the Sound, in front of the former slaughterhouse, is tinged with irony.

National Parks & Reserves
There are a number of excellent natural areas along the coast both west and east of Albany, and you can explore many different habitats and see a wide variety of coastal scenery.

West Cape Howe National Park is a playground for naturalists, bushwalkers, rock climbers and anglers. **Torndirrup National Park** includes the region's two very popular attractions, the Natural Bridge and the Gap, as well as the Blowholes, Jimmy Newhills Harbour and beach, and Bald Head. Southern right whales can be seen from the cliffs during whale-watching season.

East of Albany is **Two People's Bay**, a nature reserve with a good swimming beach, scenic coastline and a small colony of noisy scrub-birds, a species once thought extinct.

Probably the best of the national parks, but the least visited, is **Waychinicup** which includes Mt Manypeaks and other granite formations. Walking in the area is currently restricted because of dieback, a fungal disease which attacks the roots of plants and causes them to rot. Its spread can be prevented by observing 'no go' road signs and by cleaning soil from your boots where instructed to do so.

ALBANY TO ESPERANCE (476 km)

From Albany, the South Coast Highway runs north-east along the coast before turning inland to skirt the Fitzgerald River National Park and ending in Esperance.

Ongerup & Jerramungup

Ongerup, a small Wheatbelt town, has an annual wildflower show in September/October with hundreds of local species on display. In Jerramungup you can visit the eclectic **Military Museum**.

Bremer Bay

This fishing and holiday town, at the western end of the Great Australian Bight, is 61 km from the South Coast Highway. It is a good spot to observe southern right whales. Information is available from the BP Roadhouse (☎ (098) 37 4093).

The *Bremer Bay Caravan Park* (☎ (098) 37 4018) has powered sites for $14 and on-site vans for $30. A nice place to stay within Fitzgerald River National Park is *Quaalup Homestead* (☎ (098) 37 4124), 18 km east of Bremer Bay; camping is $10, units are from $29 to $44 and chalets are $55; prices are for two.

Ravensthorpe & Hopetoun

Ravensthorpe was once the centre of the Phillips River goldfield. Copper mining followed. Nowadays, the area is dependent on farming. The ruins of a disused smelter and the Cattlin Creek copper mine are near town, and there are drives in the region from which many **wildflowers** can be seen; there is a wildflower show in the first two weeks of September. The Going Bush information centre (☎ (098) 38 1277) is open daily from 8.30 am to 5 pm.

Hopetoun, 50 km south of Ravensthorpe, centres on fine beaches and bays and is the eastern gateway to Fitzgerald River National Park. The information centre (☎ (098) 38 3088) is in the Blue Groper store, Veal St.

About 150 km north of Ravensthorpe, the **Frank Hann National Park** has a range of typical sandplain flora.

Places to Stay & Eat The *Ravensthorpe Caravan Park* (☎ (098) 38 1050) has tent/powered sites at $10/11. The *Palace Motor Hotel* (☎ (098) 38 1005), classified by the National Trust, has B&B singles/doubles for $28/46; the motel rooms are $46/64.

The *Hopetoun Caravan Park* (☎ (098) 38 3096) has tent/powered sites for $9/12 and on-site vans for $25. The *Port Hotel* (☎ (098) 38 3053), Veal St, has singles/doubles for $25/40.

There is a sumptuous cake selection at *Ravy's Country Kitchen* in Ravensthorpe.

Fitzgerald River National Park

This 320,000-hectare park contains beautiful coastline, sand plains, the rugged Barren mountain range and deep, wide river valleys. The bushwalking is excellent and the wilderness route from Fitzgerald Beach to Whalebone Beach is recommended – there is no trail and no water but camping is permitted. Clean your shoes at each end of the walk to discourage the spread of dieback.

The park contains half the orchid species in WA (over 80 species, 70 of which occur nowhere else), 22 mammals, 200 species of birds and 1700 species of plants. It is also the home of those floral marvels, the royal hakea and Quaalup bell, and southern right whales can be seen offshore from August to September.

You can gain access to the park from Bremer Bay and Hopetoun or from the South Coast Highway along Devils Creek, Quiss and Hamersley Rds. There is accommodation in Bremer Bay, Quaalup and Hopetoun.

ESPERANCE (pop 7100)

Esperance, or the Bay of Isles, has become a popular resort due to its temperate climate, magnificent coastal scenery, blue waters, good fishing and dazzling white beaches. Distinctive Norfolk Island pines line the town's foreshore. It is 721 km south-east of Perth and 200 km south of Norseman.

Although the first settlers came to the area in 1863, it was during the gold rush in the 1890s that the town really became established as a port. When the gold fever subsided, Esperance went into a state of suspended animation until after WW II. In the 1950s, it was discovered that adding missing trace elements to the soil around Esperance restored it to fertility, and since then the town has rapidly become an agricultural centre.

Information

The tourist bureau (☎ (090) 71 2330), in Dempster St, is open daily from 8.45 am to 5 pm and can book tours to the islands and the surrounding national parks.

Esperance Museum

The museum contains the tourist bureau and various old buildings, including a gallery, smithy's forge, cafe and craft shop. The museum itself, between the Esplanade and Dempster St, is open daily from 1.30 to 4.30 pm. There's also a Skylab display – a US space station launched in May 1973, which crashed to earth in 1979 and made its fiery re-entry right over Esperance.

Other Attractions

The 36-km scenic **Loop Road** includes vistas from Observatory Point and the Rotary Lookout on Wireless Hill; Twilight Bay and Picnic Cove, popular swimming spots; and the **Pink Lake**, stained by a salt-tolerant algae called *Dunalella salina*.

There are about 100 small islands in the **Recherche Archipelago**, home to colonies of fur seals, penguins and a wide variety of water birds. There are regular trips to Woody Island, a wildlife sanctuary.

Tours & Cruises

Vacation Country Tours (☎ (090) 71 2227) runs a number of tours around Esperance including a town-and-coast tour ($15) and a tour of Cape Le Grand National Park twice a week ($25). More adventurous alternatives are Safari Wheels & Reels (☎ (090) 71 1564), which has 4WD safaris and fishing trips to secluded beaches and bays, and the trips run by the YHA to capes Arid and Le Grand; contact the tourist bureau for prices.

Tours of Esperance Bay are a must. Unfortunately, the tug *Cape Le Grand II* (Mackenzies Marine; ☎ (090) 71 5757) only heads out if the right numbers front up on the jetty, so even though they advertise daily tours these are at the owner's convenience. Mackenzies has a daily ferry to Woody Island in January and February.

The *Dive Master II* (☎ (090) 71 5111) goes out on Tuesday and Thursday. Expect to see seals, sea lions, white-bellied sea eagles, Cape Barren geese, dolphins and a host of other wildlife during the two-hour cruise around the Bay of Isles. Trips are weather-dependent and cost $20 (children $10). The *Dive Master II* is also the flagship for the Esperance Diving Academy.

Places to Stay

Half a dozen caravan parks around Esperance provide camping areas and on-site accommodation. The most central is the *Esperance Bay Caravan Park* (☎ (090) 71 2237), on the corner of the Esplanade and Harbour Rd, with tent/powered sites for $11/13 and cabins from $30, both for two people. The *Esperance Shire Park* (☎ (090) 71 1251), corner of Goldfields and Norseman Rds, has tent/powered sites from $10.50/13. At 817 Harbour Rd, the clean, tidy and well-run *Crokers Holiday Resort*

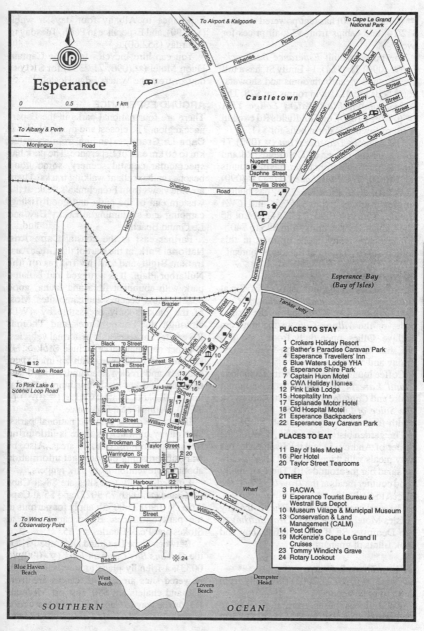

Esperance

0   0.5   1 km

To Airport & Kalgoorlie

To Cape Le Grand National Park

To Albany & Perth

Monjingup Road

Castletown

Esperance Bay
(Bay of Isles)

To Pink Lake & Scenic Loop Road

To Wind Farm & Observatory Point

Blue Haven Beach

West Beach

Lovers Beach

Dempster Head

SOUTHERN   OCEAN

PLACES TO STAY

1 Crokers Holiday Resort
2 Bather's Paradise Caravan Park
4 Esperance Travellers' Inn
5 Blue Waters Lodge YHA
6 Esperance Shire Park
7 Captain Huon Motel
8 CWA Holiday Homes
12 Pink Lake Lodge
15 Hospitality Inn
17 Esplanade Motor Hotel
18 Old Hospital Motel
21 Esperance Backpackers
22 Esperance Bay Caravan Park

PLACES TO EAT

11 Bay of Isles Motel
16 Pier Hotel
20 Taylor Street Tearooms

OTHER

3 RACWA
9 Esperance Tourist Bureau & Westrail Bus Depot
10 Museum Village & Municipal Museum
13 Conservation & Land Management (CALM)
14 Post Office
19 McKenzie's Cape Le Grand II Cruises
23 Tommy Windich's Grave
24 Rotary Lookout

(☎ (090) 71 4100) has tent/powered sites for $12/14, and cabins from $32; all prices for two.

The purpose-built *Esperance Backpackers* (☎ (090) 71 4724), 14 Emily St, has a full kitchen, and clean bathrooms and showers; dorm beds are $13, twin rooms are $28. The large, popular *Blue Waters Lodge YHA* (☎ (090) 71 1040), on Goldfields Rd two km north of town, has dorm beds for $11.

The friendly *Travellers' Inn* (☎ (090) 71 1677), on the corner of Goldfields Rd and Phyllis St two km from town, has clean units for $40/50. The *Pink Lake Lodge* (☎ (090) 71 2075), at 85 Pink Lake Rd, has budget singles/doubles from $25/35, and *CWA Holiday Units* (☎ (090) 71 1364), at Lot 85 The Esplanade, has units from $25 to $40.

There are many more options in this holiday town; enquire at the tourist bureau.

Places to Eat
The town has a good number of cafes. Sip at *Ollies on the Esplanade*, *Beachfront Cafe* and *Taylor Street Tearooms* on the Esplanade, or the *Village Cafe* in the museum enclave. Ollies, open daily from 7 am to 8 pm, has $10.50 specials on Wednesday, Friday and Sunday nights.

Coffee lounges which serve meals include *Island Fare* in the Boulevarde shopping centre and *Captain's Cabin*, at 20 Andrew St. The *Spice of Life*, Andrew St, has a varied health-food menu including tasty pasties.

The garden bistro at the *Pier Hotel*, on the corner of Andrew St and the Esplanade, has tasty meals with a well-stocked all-you-can-eat salad bar for around $10. There are really good counter meals at the *Travellers' Inn* (see Places to Stay).

Up-market choices are *Peaches* in the Bay of Isles Motel and the BYO *Gray Starling* at 126 Dempster St. If you like fish, buy and cook fillets of gnanagi.

Getting There & Away
Skywest (☎ (090) 71 2002) flies daily from Perth to Esperance.

Westrail has buses from Esperance to Kalgoorlie, Tuesday to Saturday ($33.50);

Esperance to Albany four days a week ($45.90); and Esperance to Perth, Tuesday to Saturday ($52.60).

You can hire bicycles from the Captain Huon Motel (☎ (090) 71 2383) for $10 per day, or from the Waters Edge Hostel.

AROUND ESPERANCE
There are four national parks in the Esperance region. The closest and most popular is **Cape Le Grand**, extending from about 20 km to 60 km east of Esperance. The park has spectacular coastal scenery, some good beaches and excellent walking tracks. There are fine views from Frenchman's Peak, at the western end of the park, and good fishing, camping and swimming at Lucky Bay and Le Grand Beach.

Farther east is the coastal **Cape Arid National Park**, at the start of the Great Australian Bight and on the fringes of the Nullarbor Plain. It is a rugged and isolated park with abundant flora and fauna, good bushwalking, beaches and camp sites. Most of the park is only accessible by 4WD, although the Poison Creek and Thomas River sites are accessible in normal vehicles.

Other national parks include **Stokes**, 92 km west of Esperance, with an inlet, long beaches and rocky headlands; and **Peak Charles**, 180 km north. For more information on all parks, contact CALM (☎ (090) 71 3733), Dempster St, Esperance.

If you are going into the national parks, take plenty of water, as there is little or no fresh water in most of these areas. Also, be wary of spreading dieback; get information about its prevention from park rangers.

Limited-facility tent sites are $8 at Cape Le Grand (☎ (090) 75 9022) and $5 at Cape Arid (☎ (090) 75 0055); apply for permits at the park entrances. Basic camp sites at Stokes and Peak Charles are $5.

Between Cape Le Grand and Cape Arid is the *Orleans Bay Caravan Park* (☎ (090) 75 0033), a friendly place to stay; sandy tent/powered sites are $10/12, cabins are from $30 and chalets are $50. Just off Merivale Rd, on the way to Cape Le Grand, tasty food is available at *Merivale Farm*.

Mid-West & Gascoyne

After leaving Perth's north coastal region, the North West Coastal Highway (Highway 1) passes through three interesting regions – the Batavia Coast (evoking memories of the area's many shipwrecks, and including the towns of Geraldton and Kalbarri); the Shark Bay World Heritage region; and the Gascoyne, with Carnarvon and Mt Augustus. Inland are the Murchison goldfields, linked by the Great Northern Highway.

DONGARA & PORT DENISON

The Brand Highway hits the coast at Dongara. This is a pleasant little port with fine beaches, lots of crayfish, a main street lined with Moreton Bay figs, and a tourist centre (☎ (099) 27 1404) housed in the old police station at 5 Waldeck St. **Russ Cottage**, built in 1870, is open on Sunday from 10 am to noon.

Just over the Irwin River is Port Denison. The mouth of the Irwin is a great place to watch birds such as pelicans and cormorants.

Places to Stay

There are a number of places to stay in these coastal towns. There are five caravan parks alone, two recommended ones being *Dongara-Denison Beach* (☎ (099) 27 1131) and the very friendly *Seaspray* (☎ (099) 27 1165). The *Dongara Backpackers Youth Hostel* (☎ (099) 27 1581) at 32 Waldeck St is in an old colonial-style house and has dorm beds for $12, twins for $24 and a volleyball court.

Some 58 km south of Dongara is the *Western Flora Caravan Park* (☎ (099) 55 2030), in the heart of one of the most diverse and dense floral regions in the world. Several tracks branch out from the park into the wonderland of native plant species; a must for visitors. Powered sites are $10, on-site vans are $25 and two-room chalets with TV are $42.

GREENOUGH

Farther north, only about 20 km south of Geraldton, is Greenough, once a busy little mining town but now a quiet farming centre. The excellent **Greenough Historical Hamlet** contains 11 buildings constructed in the 19th century and now restored by the National Trust; guided tours are run daily and it is well worth a visit. The Pioneer Museum, open daily from 10 am to 4 pm, has some fine historical displays. In the local paddocks, look out for flood gums, the 'leaning trees' caused by strong salt winds off the ocean.

The *Greenough Rivermouth Caravan Park* (☎ (099) 21 5845) has tent/powered sites for $10/14 and on-site vans for $25. The *Greenough River Resort* (☎ (099) 21 5888) has singles/doubles for $50/65.

GERALDTON (pop 34,000)

Geraldton, the major town in the mid-west, is on a rugged stretch of coast, with the mystical Houtman Abrolhos Islands offshore. It's 421 km north of Perth and the area has a fine climate, particularly in winter. If you are tempted by fresh lobster or are a windsurfing enthusiast then this is the place to come. But beware, it is bloody windy.

Information

The Geraldton-Greenough tourist bureau (☎ (099) 21 3999), on the corner of Bayly St and Chapman Rd, is almost diagonally across from the railway station. It is open weekdays from 8.30 am to 5 pm, Saturday from 9 am to 4 pm and Sunday from 9.30 am to 4.30 pm.

Geraldton Museum

The town's captivating museum is in two adjacent buildings on Marine Terrace. The Maritime Museum tells the story of the early wrecks and has assorted relics from the doomed Dutch ships, including the *Batavia* and the *Zeewijk*. A feature item is the carved wooden sternpiece from the *Zuytdorp*, found by a stockman in 1927 on top of cliffs near where the ship had grounded.

Geraldton Regional Museum is in the old railway building and has displays on flora, fauna and the settlement of the region by both Aborigines and Europeans. The

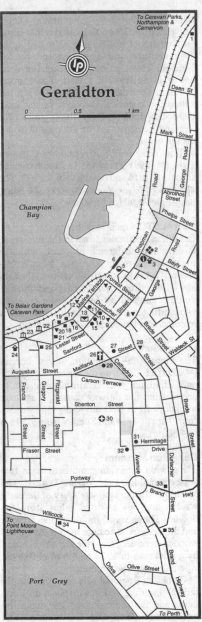

Geraldton

WESTERN AUSTRALIA

PLACES TO STAY

1   Mariner Motor Hotel
3   Batavia Backpackers
17 Grantown Guesthouse
18 Victoria Hotel
19 Sun City Guesthouse
21 Colonial Hotel
24 Peninsula Guesthouse Backpackers
25 Geraldton Hotel
33 Hacienda Motel
34 Ocean West Units
35 Goodwood Lodge

PLACES TO EAT

7   Jade House
8   Skeetas Garden Restaurant
9   Food Hall
12 Cha Cha's
16 Belvedere
20 Koochies & Ugly's Pizza
28 Los Amigos Restaurant

OTHER

2   Northgate Shopping Centre
4   Tourist Bureau & Greyhound Pioneer and
    McCafferty's Bus Depot
5   Westrail Bus Depot
6   Train Station
10 Geraldton Art Gallery
11 RACWA
13 Post Office
14 Murchison Tavern
15 Ansett Australia
22 Regional Museum
23 Maritime Museum
26 St Francis Xavier Cathedral
27 Public Toilets
29 Queen's Park Theatre
30 Hospital
31 St John of God Hospital
32 The Hermitage

museum complex is open Monday to Saturday from 10 am to 5 pm, and Sundays and holidays from 1 to 5 pm; admission is free.

St Francis Xavier Cathedral

Geraldton's cathedral is just one of a number of buildings in Geraldton and the mid-west designed by Monsignor John Hawes, a strange priest-cum-architect who left WA in 1939 and spent the rest of his life as a hermit on an island in the Caribbean (he died in Florida in 1956). Construction of the Byzantine-style cathedral commenced in 1916, a year after Hawes arrived in Geraldton, but his plans were too grandiose and the building was not completed until 1938.

The architecture is a blend of styles. External features include the twin towers of the west front with their arched openings, a large central dome similar to Brunellesci's famous cupola in Florence and a tower with a coned roof which would not be out of place in the Loire Valley. The interior is just as striking, with Romanesque columns, huge arches beneath an octagonal dome and zebra striping on the walls. When completed, Hawes felt that he had 'caught the rhythm of a poem in stone'.

While he was working on the St John of God Hospital in Cathedral Ave, Hawes lived in **The Hermitage** across the road in Onslow St; it is open by appointment only.

Other Attractions

The surprisingly good **Geraldton Art Gallery**, Chapman Rd, is open daily; admission is free. The **Lighthouse Keeper's Cottage** on Chapman Rd, headquarters of the Geraldton Historical Society, is open Thursday from 10 am to 4 pm. You can look out over Geraldton from the Waverley Heights Lookout, on Brede St, or watch the rock lobster boats at Fisherman's Wharf, at the end of Marine Terrace.

Point Moore Lighthouse on Willcock Drive, in operation since 1878, is also worth a visit but visitors can't go inside.

Tours

Batavia Tours (☎ (099) 21 7760) has day tours to Monkey Mia, Greenough and Dongara. Mid West Tours (☎ (099) 64 3929) ranges far wider to Mt Augustus, the inland stations, the wildflower regions and the Murchison goldfields; contact the tourist bureau for prices.

For information on full-blown windsurfing options contact the Sail & Surf Centre

WESTERN AUSTRALIA

Dutch Shipwrecks

During the 17th century, ships of the Dutch East India Company sailing from Europe to Batavia in Java headed due east from the Cape of Good Hope and then beat up the western Australian coast to Indonesia. It took only a small miscalculation for a ship to run aground on the coast and a few did just that, with disastrous results. The west coast of Australia is often decidedly inhospitable, and the chances of rescue at that time were remote.

Four wrecks of Dutch East Indiamen have been located, including the *Batavia*, the earliest and, in many ways, the most interesting wreck.

In 1629, the *Batavia* went aground on the Houtman Abrolhos Islands, off the coast of Geraldton. The survivors set up camp, sent off a rescue party to Batavia (now Jakarta) in the ship's boat and waited. It took three months for a rescue party to arrive and in that time a mutiny had taken place and more than 120 of the survivors had been murdered. The ringleaders were hanged, and two mutineers were unceremoniously dumped on the coast just south of modern-day Kalbarri.

In 1656, the *Vergulde Draeck* (Gilt Dragon) struck a reef about 100 km north of Perth and although a party of seven survivors made its way to Batavia, no trace of the others was found, other than a few scattered coins.

The *Zuytdorp* ran aground beneath the towering cliffs north of Kalbarri in 1712. Wine bottles, other relics and the remains of fires have been found on the cliff-top. The discovery in children of Aboriginal descent of the extremely rare Ellis van Creveld syndrome (rife in Holland at the time the ship ran aground) poses the question: did the *Zuytdorp* survivors pass the gene to Aboriginal people with whom they assimilated 300 years ago?

In 1727, the *Zeewijk* followed the *Batavia* to destruction on the Houtman Abrolhos. Again a small party of survivors made its way to Batavia, but many of the remaining sailors died before they could be rescued. Many relics from these shipwrecks, particularly the *Batavia*, can be seen in the museums in Fremantle and Geraldton. A good account of the wrecks is *Islands of Angry Ghosts* by Hugh Edwards, who led the expedition that discovered the wreck of the *Batavia*. ■

(☎ (099) 21 3159), 176 Chapman Rd; and Sailwest (☎ (099) 64 1722), Willcock Drive, Point Moore.

Places to Stay
Camping & Hostels The closest caravan parks to the city centre are *Separation Point* (☎ (099) 21 2763), Willcock Drive, and *Belair Gardens* (☎ (099) 21 1997) at Point Moore; both have powered sites and on-site vans ($26).

Batavia Backpackers (☎ (099) 64 3001), on Chapman Rd in the Bill Sewell complex, has good facilities and dorm beds from $11; a double is $25. At 305-311 Marine Terrace is the YHA *Peninsula Guesthouse Backpackers* (☎ (099) 21 4770). Backpackers' beds are $12 and double/family rooms are $24/44.

Chapman Valley Farm Backpackers (☎ (099) 20 5160), 25 km to the east, is in an historic homestead; beds are $10. They pick up from the tourist bureau at 11 am.

Guesthouses, Hotels & Motels There are plenty of old-fashioned seaside guesthouses, particularly along Marine Terrace. The *Grantown Guesthouse* (☎ (099) 21 3275) at No 172 has singles/doubles for $25/50, which includes breakfast. The friendly *Sun City Guesthouse* (☎ (099) 21 2205) at No 184 offers quaint rooms for only $15/25; you can observe the sea from a back deck which is slowly falling to meet the waters. There are cheap rooms at older-style hotels – the *Colonial*, *Victoria*, *Freemasons* and *Geraldton*.

The *Hacienda Motel* (☎ (099) 21 2155), on Durlacher St, has rooms at $45/60. The *Mariner Motor Hotel* (☎ 21 2544), at 298 Chapman Rd, is cheaper at $40/50. Family units are available at both places.

Ocean West Units (☎ (099) 21 1047), on the corner of Hadda Way and Willcock Drive at Mahomets Beach, has self-contained cottages from $55 per double. *Goodwood Lodge* (☎ (099) 21 5666), on the corner of the Brand Highway and Durlacher St, also has self-contained doubles for $55.

Places to Eat
The *food hall*, Durlacher St, has Indian, Chinese, Italian and fish & chips outlets. The food is excellent and you should be able to get a good feed for $7.

There are a number of small snack bars and cafes along Marine Terrace including *Ugly's Pizza* at No 205 and *Cha Cha's* at No 98, with Mediterranean cafe food at reasonable prices. *Hardy's*, Chapman Rd in the Bill Sewell complex, has breakfast, lunch and monster burgers.

The *Sail Inn Snack Bar*, near the museum on Marine Terrace, sells burgers and fish & chips. The pick of the breakfast places is the *Belvedere* at No 149. Night owls, on the other hand, will be well satisfied at *Koochies* 24-hour diner on the corner of Fitzgerald St and Marine Terrace.

Chinese restaurants on Marine Terrace include the *Golden Coins* at No 198 and the *Jade House* at No 57. At 105 Durlacher St, *Los Amigos* is a good, straightforward, licensed Mexican place. It's popular, and deservedly so. Fancier restaurants are the *Boatshed* for great seafood and *Skeetas Garden Restaurant* in George Rd for à la carte meals; a four-course set menu is $23. Three km south of town, the *African Reef Resort* has a seafood restaurant and a cafe.

Getting There & Away
Skywest flies from Geraldton to Perth and Port Hedland daily. There are also flights to Exmouth and Carnarvon on Tuesday and Thursday.

Westrail, Greyhound Pioneer and McCafferty's have daily services from Perth to Geraldton. The cost is $38 one way for Greyhound (McCafferty's has a special price of $18). Westrail services continue northeast to Meekatharra (twice a week) or north to Kalbarri (three times a week). Greyhound and McCafferty's continue on Highway 1 through Port Hedland and Broome to Darwin. Westrail stops at the Geraldton railway station; McCafferty's and Greyhound stop at the tourist bureau.

Getting Around
The local bus service (☎ (099) 64 1050) provides access to all the nearby suburbs. Try

Sun City Bike Hire (☎ (099) 21 3999) if you need wheels.

HOUTMAN ABROLHOS ISLANDS

There are more than 100 islands in this group, located about 60 km off the Geraldton coast, and they are a bird-watcher's paradise. The beautiful but treacherous reefs surrounding the islands have claimed many ships over the years. The islands are also the centre of the area's lobster industry. Much of the beauty of the Abrolhos lies beneath the water, where the *Acropora* family of corals abound. Air and diving tours to these protected and spectacular islands can be taken from Geraldton – ask at the tourist bureau.

NORTHAMPTON (pop 900)

Northampton, 50 km north of Geraldton, has a number of historic buildings and provides access to good beaches at **Horrocks** (22 km west) and **Port Gregory** (47 km north-west). The town was founded to exploit the lead and copper deposits discovered in 1848. Today it is an agricultural centre, now embracing embryonic tourism.

An early mining home, **Chiverton House**, is a fine municipal museum ($2 entry). The tourist bureau (☎ (099) 34 1488) is in the Nagle Centre on the main road.

The **Lynton Convict Settlement**, about 40 km from Northampton, was established as a convict-hiring facility in 1853 and abandoned some four years later. Only ruins exist.

Places to Stay

There are *caravan parks* near Northampton (☎ (099) 34 1202), Port Gregory (☎ (099) 35 1052) and Horrocks (☎ (099) 34 3039); all have tent sites, and the Horrocks and Port Gregory caravan parks have on-site vans. The *Killara Holiday Village* at Horrocks has cottages at $35/160 per night/week (these rates vary by season).

There are budget beds in the *Nagle Centre* (☎ (099) 34 1488), formerly the Sacred Heart Convent, for $12 per person in two and four-bed rooms; it has all the usual facilities.

The hotels in town all offer rooms. The *Lynton Homestead B&B* (☎ (099) 35 1040),

next to the convict settlement, costs a very reasonable $25/50 for a single/double.

KALBARRI (pop 1500)

Kalbarri, a popular spot with backpackers, is on the coast at the mouth of the Murchison River, 66 km west of the main highway. The area has an alluring coastline, scenic gorges and haunting Dutch shipwrecks. The *Zuytdorp* was wrecked about 65 km north of Kalbarri in 1712; earlier, in 1629, two *Batavia* mutineers were marooned at Wittecarra Gully, an inlet just south of the town. Although diving around the *Zuytdorp* is very difficult, as a heavy swell and unpredictable currents batter the shoreline, divers from the Geraldton Museum managed to raise artefacts in 1986.

The tourist bureau (☎ (099) 37 1104), Grey St, is open daily from 9 am to 5 pm; it has plenty of information and handles bookings for local activities.

Kalbarri National Park

This park has over 1000 sq km of bushland including some scenic gorges on the **Murchison River**. From Kalbarri, it's about 40 km to the **Loop** and **Z-Bend**, two impressive gorges. Short walking trails lead down into the gorges from road access points but there are also longer walks. It is a two-day walk between Z-Bend and the Loop.

Farther east along the Ajana to Kalbarri road are two lookouts: **Hawk's Head** (a must) and **Ross Graham**. The park has a particularly fine display of wildflowers in spring including everlastings, banksias, grevilleas and kangaroo paws.

Other Attractions

The **Rainbow Jungle** is an interesting rainforest and bird park four km south of town towards Red Bluff ($5; children $2). Boats can be hired (☎ (099) 37 1245) and tours taken on the river aboard the *Kalbarri River Queen* (☎ (099) 37 1104).

South of town is a string of rugged **cliff faces**, including Red Bluff, Rainbow Valley, Pot Alley, Eagle Gorge and Natural Bridge.

WESTERN AUSTRALIA

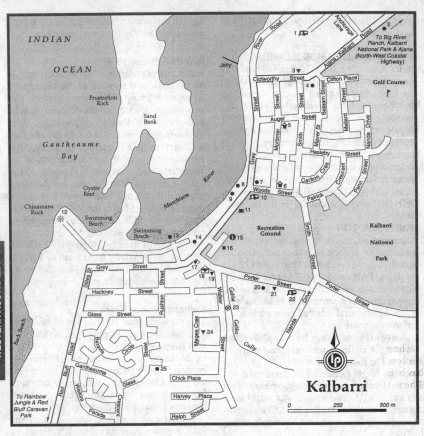

Kalbarri

INDIAN OCEAN

Gantheaume Bay

Frustration Rock

Sand Bank

Oyster Reef

Chinamans Rock

Swimming Beach

Swimming Beach

Murchison River

Jetty

Recreation Ground

Kalbarri National Park

Golf Course

To Big River Ranch, Kalbarri National Park & Ajana (North-West Coastal Highway)

To Rainbow Jungle & Red Bluff Caravan Park

0   250   500 m

PLACES TO STAY		11	Lure 'n' Line Cafe	4	CALM Office
1	Anchorage Caravan Park	17	Seabreeze Coffee Lounge, Kalbarri Hot Bread Shop, Fruit & Vegetable Shop	7	Fantasyland
				8	Pelican Feeding
5	Av-Er-Rest Backpackers			9	Kalbarri Boat Hire
				12	Lookout
6	Kalbarri Backpackers	19	Gilgai Tavern, Kalbarri Cafe & Echoes Restaurant	13	Kalbarri River Queen
10	Murchison Park Caravan Park			14	Children's Playground
		21	Palm Resort	15	Tourist Bureau, Kalbarri Accommodation Service & Jonah's 20
16	Kalbarri Hotel Motel	24	Finlay's Fresh Fish BBQ		
22	Tudor Caravan Park				
25	Courtis Villa			18	Post Office
				20	Entertainment Centre & Bicycle Hire
PLACES TO EAT		**OTHER**		23	Grey's Spring
3	Zuytdorp Restaurant	2	National Park Ranger		

They can all be reached by car but the roads will test car suspensions.

There are some excellent surfing breaks along the coast – **Jakes Corner**, 3.5 km south of town, is amongst the state's best.

Tours

Kalbarri Coachlines (☎ (099) 37 1161) has trips to the Loop, Z-Bend and ocean gorges. The company also runs a canoeing adventure tour into the gorges ($35) which takes in the Fourways gullies. The brave can abseil into the gorges with Gorge-ous Gordon (☎ (099) 37 1564); abseiling trips cost from $35.

The Red Bluff Caravan Park (☎ (099) 37 1080) runs 4WD tours down the coast to Lucky Bay and Wagoe Beach. This recommended tour includes a trip along the sand beach, with views of magnificent sand hills.

There are also 40-minute camel rides conducted from Red Bluff Rd; the cost is $12.

Places to Stay

As Kalbarri is a popular resort, accommodation can be tight at holiday times. There are four caravan parks near town, all with tent sites, on-site vans and cabins.

The clean and modern *Kalbarri Backpackers* (☎ (099) 37 1430), at 2 Mortimer St, has been recommended by many travellers. They have shared rooms from $13, singles/doubles from $20/28 and family and disabled units from $40 ($60 in the high season). They organise snorkelling trips to the Blue Holes, one km south of Kalbarri, and have a barbecue three times a week ($5 a head). Another budget choice is *Av-Er-Rest Backpackers* (☎ (099) 37 1101), Mortimer St, with beds from $10 a night.

The *Kalbarri Hotel Motel* (☎ (099) 37 1000), on Grey St, is central and has comfortable singles/doubles from $40/50. There are a number of private houses for rent. The spacious, three-bedroom *Courtis Villa* (☎ (09) 332 5073) costs from $45 in the off season.

Places to Eat

There are at least four cafes in town: the *Kalbarri Cafe* in the main shopping centre;

the *Seabreeze* in the Kalbarri Arcade (with great prawn rolls); *Rivers* near the jetty; and *Lure 'n' Line* on the riverfront in Grey St. For fish & chips try *Jonah's* in Grey St, and for pizza go to *Kalbarri Pizza*.

Finlay's Fresh Fish BBQ, on Magee Crescent in an old ice works, is a really special place for a meal (most are less than $12). The décor is no frills but the meals and salads are filling – the atmosphere is, in a word, great.

There are three up-market places in town – the *Palm* in the Palm Resort on Porter St, *Echoes* in the main shopping centre (probably the best) and the *Zuytdorp* in the Kalbarri Beach Resort on Clotworthy St.

Getting There & Away

Western Airlines has return flights from Perth on Monday, Wednesday and Friday; the one-way fare is $167.

Westrail buses from Perth ($60) come into Kalbarri on Monday, Wednesday and Friday, returning Tuesday, Thursday and Saturday.

A daily return shuttle into Kalbarri connects with northbound Greyhound Pioneer buses at Ajana on the North-West Coastal Highway; it costs $13/24 one-way/return. Southbound buses are met at the ungodly hour of 12.20 am on Thursday, Friday and Sunday. There are connections with McCafferty's services on Tuesday, Friday and Sunday ($40, ex-Perth).

Bicycles can be rented from Murchison Cycles on Porter St – if no-one is there, ask at the Mini-Putt complex next door.

SHARK BAY

Shark Bay World Heritage & Marine Park has spectacular beaches, important sea-grass beds, the stromatolites at Hamelin Pool and the famous dolphins of Monkey Mia.

The first recorded landing on Australian soil by a European took place at Shark Bay in 1616 when the Dutch explorer Dirk Hartog landed on the island that now bears his name. He nailed an inscribed plate to a post on the beach but a later Dutch visitor collected it. It's now in the Rijksmuseum in Amsterdam, although there's a reproduction in the Geraldton Museum.

Denham, the main population centre of Shark Bay, is 132 km off the North-West Coastal Highway from the Overlander Roadhouse.

Tours & Cruises

There is a wildlife cruise to Steep Point on the MV *Explorer* (subject to weather and demand) for $50; minimum of 10 people. Shark Bay Safari Tours (☎ (099) 48 1247) has various tours around Shark Bay and the World Heritage area. The yacht *Shotover* does daily morning and sunset dolphin cruises for $19. For all tours, enquire at the Shark Bay tourist centre in Denham.

Getting There & Away

Skywest flies to Monkey Mia on Wednesday, Friday and Saturday with flights back to Perth on Monday and Wednesday. Western Airlines flies from Perth to Kalbarri and Denham ($249) on Monday, Wednesday and Friday.

North of Kalbarri, it's a fairly dull, boring and often very hot run to Carnarvon. The Overlander Roadhouse, 290 km north of Geraldton, is the turn-off to Shark Bay. Greyhound Pioneer has a return bus service from Monkey Mia to Overlander connecting with interstate buses on Monday, Wednesday, Thursday and Saturday. The one-way/return fare to Denham from Overlander is $25/45. The fare from Perth to Monkey Mia is $104 if your ticket is booked in advance.

A daily local bus departs Denham (near the tourist centre on Knight Terrace) at 8.45 am and 3 pm for Monkey Mia and returns at 9.15 am and 3.30 pm; the fare is $7 one way. There is an airport bus service; one way to Monkey Mia is $7 and to Denham it is free.

Overlander Roadhouse to Denham

Once off the highway, headed west for Monkey Mia and Denham, the first turn-off (27 km from the highway) is the six-km road to **Hamelin Pool**, a marine reserve which has the world's best-known colony of **stromatolites** (see Stromatolites aside). Information on these unique living-rock formations can be obtained from the 1884 **Telegraph**

Station (☎ (099) 42 5905). The station served as a telephone exchange until 1977. Camping, caravan sites and food are also available.

The 110-km-long stretch of **Shell Beach** consists of solid shells nearly 10 metres deep! In places in Shark Bay, the shells *(Fragum erugatum)* are so tightly packed that they can be cut into blocks and used for building construction. **Nanga Station** has a pioneer museum and at **Eagle Bluff**, halfway between Nanga and Denham, there are superb cliff-top views.

Denham (pop 940)

Denham, the most westerly town in Australia, was once a pearling port. Today, prawns and tourism are the local moneymakers. The Shark Bay tourist centre (☎ (099) 48 1253) at Knight Terrace is open daily from 8 am to 6 pm. The CALM office (☎ (099) 48 1208), also at Knight Terrace, has a great deal of information on the World

Stromatolites

The dolphins at Monkey Mia didn't solely contribute to the listing of Shark Bay as a world heritage region. Perhaps the biggest single contributor were the stromatolites at Hamelin Pool. These structures are thousands of years old, having evolved over 3.5 billion years.

Hamelin Pool is suited to the growth of stromatolites because of the clarity and hypersalinity of the water. In essence, each stromatolite is covered in a form of cyanobacterial microbe shaped like algae which, during daily photosynthesis, wave around. At night the microbe folds over, often trapping calcium and carbonate ions dissolved in the water. The sticky chemicals they exude add to the concretion of another layer on the surface of the stromatolite. Whew, techno-babble rules.

These are the most accessible stromatolites in the world, spectacularly set amidst the turquoise waters of Hamelin Pool. Be careful not to disturb them. ■

Heritage area. There are some buildings in town made of shell blocks.

A couple of km down the road to Monkey Mia is the shallow and picturesque **Little Lagoon**. About four km from Denham on the Monkey Mia Rd is the turn-off to the fascinating, wild **François Peron National Park**. The park is known for its arid scenery, wilderness feel and landlocked salt lakes; entry is $3 for a day visit. There are two artesian bore tanks – one has water at 35°C and the other at a hot 43°C. These are in the grounds of the Peron Homestead, a reminder of the peninsula's grazing days.

Places to Stay & Eat Accommodation in Denham can be very tight and expensive during school holidays. You can camp at Denham or 55 km south at Nanga Station. The *Seaside Caravan Park* (☎ (099) 48 1242), Knight Terrace, is a friendly place on the foreshore with tent/powered sites for $11/13, and cabins from $33. *Shark Bay Caravan Park* (☎ (099) 48 1387) on Spaven Way, and the *Blue Dolphin* (☎ (099) 48 1385) on Hamelin Rd, are similarly priced.

Bay Lodge & Backpackers (☎ (099) 48 1278), an associate-YHA hostel in Knight Terrace, on the Denham foreshore, has a great atmosphere and is the best value in town. Bookings are recommended at this popular hostel. Beds in shared units cost $12, and two bedroom self-contained units are $50.

Shark Bay Holiday Cottages (☎ (099) 48 1206), Knight Terrace, has cottages from $35 to $75. *Shark Bay Accommodation Service* (☎ (099) 48 1323) has private cottages/units, usually rented by the week.

At the well-sited *Nanga Bay Holiday Resort* (☎ (099) 48 3992), a working sheep station, there are tent and powered sites, backpackers' beds for $11, cabins for $45 and motel units for $80.

The *Old Pearler Restaurant* in Knight Terrace has a full à la carte menu with local seafood (crabs and crayfish) in season.

Monkey Mia

This pleasant spot is 26 km north-east of Denham, on the other side of the Peron Pen-insula. The Dolphin Information Centre (☎ (099) 48 1366), near the beach viewing area, has lots of information on dolphins and also screens a 45-minute video on Shark Bay. The high farce begins when the eager 'cross-channel communicators' reach out to get answers, a sign, whatever, from dolphins which venture inshore for a fish handout.

It's believed that bottlenose dolphins have been visiting Monkey Mia since the early 1960s, although it's only in the last 15 years that their visits have become famous.

Monkey Mia's dolphins swim right into knee-deep water, nudge up against you, chuckle and even take a fish if it's offered. The dolphins generally come in every day during the winter months, less frequently during the summer, and more often in the morning. They may arrive alone or in groups of five or more; as many as 13 were recorded on one occasion. The entry fee to the reserve is $3 (children $2). There are essential rules of good behaviour for visitors:

- Stand in knee-deep water and let them approach you – don't chase or try to swim with them.
- Stroke them along their sides with the back of your hand as they swim beside you. Don't touch their fins or their blowhole.
- If you are invited by the ranger to feed them fish (feeding times and quantities are regulated) it should be whole, not gutted or filleted. They take defrosted fish only if it has completely thawed.

Places to Stay & Eat *Monkey Mia Dolphin Resort* has a wide range of accommodation including powered sites for $20.50 (wow, expensive), backpackers' beds in two-tented condos for $11, on-site vans for $30 to $50 and chalets from $40; discounts apply in the off season.

At the *Bough Shed* in Monkey Mia, join the elite and watch the dolphins feed as you do. There is a more economical takeaway and a small grocery shop nearby.

CARNARVON (pop 6900)

Situated at the mouth of the Gascoyne River, Carnarvon is a nondescript place noted for its tropical fruit (particularly bananas) and fine climate – although it can become very

Carnarvon

0   200   400 m

To One Mile Jetty

PLACES TO STAY

2	Fascine Lodge
3	Carnarvon Tourist Centre Caravan Park & Chickenland
9	Port Hotel
13	Backpackers' Paradise & Bus Depot
15	Carnarvon Backpackers
19	Carnarvon Hotel
20	Outcamp
21	Hospitality Inn

PLACES TO EAT

5	Carnarvon Fresh Seafoods
6	Lucki's Asian Takeaway
10	Carnarvon Bakery
12	Gypsy's
16	Northern Heritage Tearooms
17	Dragon Pearl Chinese Restaurant

OTHER

1	Swimming Pool
4	Boulevard Shopping Centre
7	Jolly's Tyrepower Service
8	Post Office
11	Civic Centre
14	Tourist Bureau, Public Toilets & Commonwealth Bank
18	Airport

WESTERN AUSTRALIA

hot in the middle of summer and is periodically subjected to floods and cyclones. Subsurface water, which flows even when the river is dry, is the lifeblood of riverside plantations but anathema to the salt piles produced at nearby Lake Macleod. Prawns and scallops are also harvested in the area.

The main street, Robinson St, is 40 metres wide and a reminder of the days when camel trains used to pass through; it now suits 'hoons' doing 'doughnuts' in hotted-up cars. The Fascine esplanade, lined with palm trees, is a pleasant place to take a stroll and

the 'one mile' jetty is a popular fishing spot, as is the little jetty at the prawning station.

Carnarvon's tourist bureau (☎ (099) 41 1146), Robinson St, is open daily from 8.30 am to 5.30 pm; off season from 9 am to 5 pm.

Tours

Tropical Tripper Tours (conducted by Backpackers Paradise) depart from the tourist bureau and include half-day tours around town for $15 and an all-day tour that takes in Lake Macleod, Cape Cuvier, the wreck of the *Korean Star* and the blowholes for $40.

Places to Stay

Camping You shouldn't have any trouble finding a caravan park as there are seven of them; the closest to the town centre is the *Carnarvon Tourist Centre* (☎ (099) 41 1438), 90 Robinson St, which has powered sites at $13 and on-site vans from $28 to $40. The *Marloo Caravan Park* (☎ (099) 41 1439), on Wise St, is well set up for campers with a kitchen, laundry and great bathroom facilities; tent sites are $11.

Hostels Neither of the hostels are much chop. *Carnarvon Backpackers* (☎ (099) 41 1095), at 46 Olivia Terrace, has dorm beds at $12. *Backpackers Paradise Youth Hostel* (☎ (099) 41 2966), centrally located next to the tourist bureau on Robinson St, has dorm beds from $11, a TV lounge and a large kitchen. The *Carnarvon Accommodation Centre*, 23 Wheelock Way – for single women, no way!

B&B, Hotels & Motels Carnarvon has some old-fashioned hotels with old-fashioned prices. The *Port* (☎ (099) 41 1704) has rooms from $20/40 in the older part of the hotel. The *Carnarvon* (☎ (099) 41 1181), Olivia Terrace, has rooms for $20/35; $35/55 in the newer units.

The *Gateway Motel* (☎ (099) 41 1532), on Robinson St, has rooms at $75. There are self-contained units at the *Carnarvon Beach Holiday Resort* (☎ (099) 41 2226), Pelican Point, at $58. The *Fascine Lodge* (☎ (099) 41 2411) and the *Hospitality Inn* (☎ (099) 41 1600) are both $85.

The top accommodation in Carnarvon is the *Outcamp* (☎ (099) 41 2421) at 16 Olivia Terrace, on the Fascine. This luxurious B&B with all facilities is in the town's best location. It costs from $35 per person, so treat yourself.

Places to Eat

Try *Carnarvon Fresh Seafoods*, on Robinson St, for takeaways. On the same street are *Fascine* and *Kaycee's*, both standard coffee lounges. *Chickenland*, on Robinson St, is a mini food hall with takeaways and pasta at reasonable prices. The *Carnarvon Bakery*, also on Robinson St, has home-made pies and sandwiches.

You can get counter meals at the *Carnarvon* and *Port* hotels. The *Harbourview Cafe* is not as good as it used to be but has a good position by the small boat harbour. *Lucki's Asian Takeaway*, on Robinson St, has

typical Chinese food, as has the *Dragon Pearl* on Francis St.

The recently refurbished *Northern Heritage Tearooms* is the place for lunch and light meals. If you're looking for a more up-market place, try *Gypsy's* on Robinson St; main meals with salads or vegetables are from $16 to $24.

Getting There & Away

Skywest flies to Perth daily, and to Exmouth and Geraldton on Tuesday and Thursday.

Greyhound Pioneer and McCafferty's buses both pass through Carnarvon on their way north and south. The one-way full fare, Perth to Carnarvon, is around $100 for Greyhound Pioneer (currently $50 for McCafferty's).

Bicycles are available for hire from Backpackers Paradise (provide your own helmet). Mopeds can be hired from Jolly's Tyrepower Service in Robinson St.

GASCOYNE AREA

There are daily tours to **banana plantations** (on South River Rd or Robinson St, just out of Carnarvon) which culminate with the almost obligatory eating of a chocolate-coated banana. You can buy a banana cookbook which includes cures for such ills as diarrhoea, ulcers and depression.

Pelican Point, five km to the south-west, is a popular swimming and picnic spot. Other good beaches, also south and off the Geraldton Rd, are **Bush Bay** (turn-off 20 km) and **New Beach** (37 km).

Bibbawarra Bore, 14 km north of Carnarvon, is an artesian well sunk to a depth of 914 metres which is being turned into a spa bath.

The frenzied **blowholes**, 70 km to the north of Carnarvon, are well worth the trip. There's a fine beach about one km south of the blowholes with a primitive camping ground (no fresh water available) and a sort of local shanty town. You can rent a cabin at *Quobba Station* for about $28 – power is limited but water is available. One km south of the homestead is the **HMAS Sydney**

Memorial to the ship sunk here by the German raider *Kormoran* in 1941.

Cape Cuvier, where salt is loaded for Japan, is 30 km north of the blowholes, and nearby is the wreck of the *Korean Star*, grounded in 1988 (do not climb over the wreck as it is dangerous).

Remote **Gascoyne Junction**, 164 km inland (east) of Carnarvon in the gemstone-rich Kennedy Range, has the welcome Junction Hotel. From here, the really adventurous can continue through the outback to **Buringurrah National Park**, 450 km from Carnarvon, to see **Mount Augustus**, the biggest – but certainly not the most memorable – rock (or monadnock) in the world. The rock can be climbed in a day, and Aboriginal rock paintings can be seen.

At *Cobra Station* (☎ (099) 43 0565), 50 km from the rock, singles/doubles are from $35/45; and at *Mt Augustus Resort* (☎ (099) 43 0527) tent sites are $14 and large family rooms are $70.

THE GREAT NORTHERN HIGHWAY

Although most people heading for the Pilbara and the Kimberley travel up the coast, the Great Northern Highway is much more direct. The highway extends from Perth to Newman and then skirts the eastern edge of the Pilbara on its way to Port Hedland; the road is sealed all the way. The total distance is 1636 km – longer if you take the short gravel detour through Marble Bar.

The highway is not the most interesting in Australia, mainly passing through flat and featureless country. The Murchison River goldfields and towns of Mt Magnet, Cue and Meekatharra punctuate the monotony on the way to Newman.

Mount Magnet Area

Gold was found at Mount Magnet in the late 19th century and mining is still the town's lifeblood. Eleven km north of town are the ruins of **Lennonville**, once a busy town. There are some interesting old buildings of solid stone in **Cue**, 80 km north of Mount Magnet, and **Walga Rock**, 48 km to the west, is a large monolith with a gallery of Aborig-

inal art (Walga means 'ochre painting' in the local Warragi language).

Wilgie Mia, 64 km north-west of Cue via Glen Station, is the site of a 30,000-year-old Aboriginal red ochre quarry.

The *Mt Magnet Caravan Park* (☎ (099) 63 4198) has powered sites for $12 and there are a couple of hotels in Mount Magnet's main street. *Cue Caravan Park* (☎ (099) 63 1107) has tent sites at $8 and the *Murchison Club* (☎ (099) 63 1020), Austin St, also in Cue, has doubles from $50.

Meekatharra (pop 1400)

Meekatharra is still a mining centre. At one time it was a railhead for cattle brought down from the Northern Territory and the east Kimberley along the Canning Stock Route. There are ruins of various old gold towns and operations in the area. From Meekatharra, you can travel south via Wiluna and Leonora to the Kalgoorlie goldfields. It's over 700 km to Kal, more than half of it on unsealed road.

The *Meekatharra Caravan Park* (☎ (099) 81 1253) has tent and powered sites at $12.50; and the *Royal Mail Hotel* (☎ (099) 81 1148), on Main St, has singles/doubles for $55/75.

Getting There & Away

Skywest has flights from Perth to Mount Magnet, Cue and Meekatharra. Westrail has a weekly bus service from Perth to Meekatharra ($67.30), stopping at Mount Magnet and Cue.

Coral Coast

North-West Cape, a finger of land jutting north into the Indian Ocean, offers a bewildering array of activities at Coral Bay, Ningaloo Marine Park and Cape Range National Park (all part of the Coral Coast). Whale sharks, humpbacks, manta rays and colourful schools of fish can be seen in and around Ningaloo Reef. In addition there are mammals, marine and land reptiles, and abundant birdlife.

CORAL BAY (pop 730)

This town, 150 km south of Exmouth, is an important access point for Ningaloo Reef and a popular diving centre. The Glass Bottom Boat and Sub-sea Explorer (☎ (099) 42 5955) trips leave from here; 45-minute/two-hour trips cost about $15/20. **Diving** trips with Coral Dive (☎ (099) 42 5940) cost from $55, all gear supplied.

Places to Stay

There are two camping grounds in Coral Bay. The ordinary *People's Park* (☎ (099) 42 5933) has tent/powered sites for $14/16. The friendly *Bayview Holiday Village* (☎ (099) 42 5932) in Robinson St has camping and caravan sites.

Coral Bay Lodge (☎ (09) 387 6383), on the corner of Robinson and French Sts, has double units from $82, and the *Ningaloo Reef Resort* (☎ (099) 42 5934) has units from $80. The resort has backpackers' accommodation for $15 but the dirty kitchen has come in for criticism.

NINGALOO MARINE PARK

Running along the western side of North-West Cape for 260 km is the stunning Ningaloo ('Point of Land') Reef. This miniature, but discontinuous, version of the Great Barrier Reef is actually much more accessible, as in places it is only a few hundred metres offshore. The lagoons enclosed by the reef vary in width from 200 metres to six km. Within the marine park are eight sanctuary zones – no fishing is allowed. Dugongs can be observed, greenback turtles lay their eggs along the cape beach and placid whale sharks, the world's largest fish, can be seen just beyond the reef's waters.

In June and July, humpback whales pass by the coast on the way to calving grounds,

---

Interaction with Marine Life

Visitors to Australia are often morbidly fascinated by sharks, especially the deadly great white shark which frequents the Southern Ocean. The **whale shark** *(Rhiniodon typus)* is the largest of the sharks, but it is a gentle giant. One of the few places in the world where you can come face to face underwater with this enormous leviathan is off Ningaloo Reef, near Exmouth. To swim with these sharks is to experience one of the natural wonders of the world.

The whale shark weighs up to 40,000 kg, is up to 18 metres long and drifts slowly across ocean currents filtering water through its 300 or more bands of minute teeth for the plankton and small fish on which it feeds. These sharks also eat an awful lot of rubbish: a wallet, boot, bucket and part of an oar were found in the stomach of one

The whale shark can be observed from late March, when the coral spawns and the plankton blooms, to the end of May. The largest number of whale sharks are seen off the Tantabiddi and Mangrove Bay areas, and the best way to see them is by licensed charter vessel. The Exmouth Diving Centre (☎ (099) 49 1201) provides all equipment and daily refreshments for $299, and it has a 100% encounter success rate.

Manta rays may be seen from July until about mid-November. The mantas come here for the accumulation of food, and they are seen in pods of 20 to 30. There is no guarantee they will be around on any given day; enquire at the Diving Centre for their whereabouts. You can fly underwater with the mantas as part of a normal dive charter; this costs $25 per dive and daily equipment rental is $50.

The Diving Centre also organises trips to the Muiron Islands, 10 km north-east of the cape, on demand. The islands are a breeding sanctuary for three species of **turtle**: green, loggerhead and hawksbill. During dives you can hand feed the 1.5-metre-long **potato cod** *(Epinephalus tukula)* at the 'cod house'.

When these activities are more widely publicised, Exmouth will probably become an international ecotourism destination. ■

probably near the Monte Bello Islands. In October and November they return to Antarctica. Turtles come onto the beaches when the tide is right to lay their eggs at night, usually from November to January near the top end of the cape.

Exmouth's CALM office (☎ (099) 49 1676), in the old council buildings in Maidstone Crescent, has copies of the *Parks of the Coral Coast* pamphlet, which outlines the area's special fishing regulations.

The semi-submersible Ningaloo Coral Explorer (☎ (099) 49 1101) operates over Bundegi Reef daily at 2 pm for a one-hour viewing ($18). At 3 pm there is a snorkelling trip. Scenic flights with Exmouth Air Charters (☎ (099) 49 2182) allow you to see the reef from the air (from $48 per person).

EXMOUTH (pop 3100)

Exmouth was established in 1967, largely as a service town for a US navy base used to communicate with nuclear-weapons carrying submarines operating in the Indian Ocean. The base has closed but part of North-West Cape is still rendered ugly by 13 very low-frequency transmitter stations. Twelve are higher than the Eiffel Tower, and they all support the 13th, a 396-metre-high structure.

The efficient tourist bureau (☎ (099) 49 1176), temporarily housed in the old council buildings in Maidstone Crescent, has a video display. It is open daily from 9 am to 5 pm.

North of town, apart from the navy base, is the wreck of the cattleship SS *Mildura*, beached in 1907, and **Vlaming Head Lighthouse** from which there are great views.

Places to Stay

Accommodation in and around Exmouth can be quite expensive, although there are several caravan parks. At the *Exmouth Caravan Park* (☎ (099) 49 1331), Lefroy St,

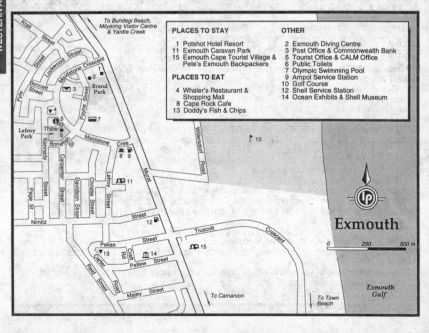

PLACES TO STAY
1 Potshot Hotel Resort
11 Exmouth Caravan Park
15 Exmouth Cape Tourist Village & Pete's Exmouth Backpackers

PLACES TO EAT
4 Whaler's Restaurant & Shopping Mall
8 Cape Rock Cafe
13 Doddy's Fish & Chips

OTHER
2 Exmouth Diving Centre
3 Post Office & Commonwealth Bank
5 Tourist Office & CALM Office
6 Public Toilets
7 Olympic Swimming Pool
9 Ampol Service Station
10 Golf Course
12 Shell Service Station
14 Ocean Exhibits & Shell Museum

Exmouth

powered sites are $17 a double but it is a bit run-down. At Vlaming Head, the *Lighthouse Caravan Park* (☎ (099) 49 1478) has on-site vans for $35.

Exmouth Cape Tourist Village & Pete's Exmouth Backpackers (☎ (099) 49 1101), on the corner of Truscott Crescent and Murat Rd, has powered sites at $17, park cabins for $32 a double and excellent backpackers' rooms for $13 per person; there's also a cold swimming pool. The *Potshot Hotel Resort* (☎ (099) 49 1200), off Payne St, has self-contained units from $95 a double plus more expensive two-bedroom places for $130.

At Minilya Bridge on the North-West Coastal Highway, seven km south of the turn-off to Exmouth, is the *Caravan Facility*. It has typical roadhouse fare and on-site cabins for $35. This place cops flak from travellers; the large 'Backpackers – No Loitering' sign sets the tone.

Places to Eat
Eateries are growing rapidly in response to increased tourism. There are takeaways in the main shopping area, including *Phil's Kitchen*, *Shell's* and *Judy's Fast Food*.

Seafood is a speciality of this region – in town go to *Doddy's* and out of town try *M G Kailis'* prawn palace, 25 km south, open May to November. *Whaler's* in Kennedy St is a tasteful al fresco place with a good selection of chicken, fish and steak dishes; main courses are from $14 to $16.

Getting There & Away
Skywest has flights to Perth daily, to Carnarvon on weekdays and to Karratha on Tuesday, Thursday and Saturday.

A shuttle bus service on Monday, Thursday and Saturday goes from Exmouth to Minilya Roadhouse to meet the Greyhound bus; a one-way/return ticket is $60/108. Three times a week there is a Greyhound service to Exmouth from Perth (Wednesday, Friday and Sunday). Twice a week, the McCafferty's ticket includes the sector from Minilya to Exmouth.

CAPE RANGE NATIONAL PARK
This 510-sq-km park, which runs down the west coast of the cape, includes the modern Milyering visitor centre, a variety of flora and fauna, good swimming beaches, several gorges (the Shothole, Charles Knife and scenic Yardie Creek), Owl's Roost Cave and rugged scenery.

Milyering (☎ (099) 49 2808) is built in rammed-earth style, is solar powered and has environmentally thoughtful waste disposal. A comprehensive display of the area's natural and cultural history can be seen here. It is usually open daily (except Tuesday and Saturday) from 10 am to 4 pm during the high season. There is a fee of $5 per car for entry into Cape Range National Park; the honesty box is near the park entrance.

Equipped (4WD) vehicles can continue south to Coral Bay via the coast and there is a turn-off to Point Cloates lighthouse.

Tent and powered sites are available in the park (☎ (099) 49 1676) at $5 per double.

Tours
Perhaps the most informative land tour in the park is Ningaloo Safaris' (☎ (099) 49 1550) full-day Over the Top safari. The 10-hour trip costs $85 and includes delicious home-made food, a boat trip down Yardie Creek and a crossing of the range. West Coast Safaris (☎ (099) 49 1625) also does this trip for $85.

Pete's Exmouth Backpackers has daily trips from Exmouth to Yardie Creek during the high season. These leave at 8 am (irrespective of numbers) and return at sunset. Snorkelling, lunch and the patter of a knowledgeable guide are all included for $60.

Hour-long boat tours (☎ (099) 49 2659) are conducted up the interesting Yardie Gorge on Monday, Wednesday and Saturday ($15; children $8).

The Pilbara

The Pilbara (meaning 'fish' in a local Aboriginal language) contains some of the hottest country on earth, as well as the iron

WESTERN AUSTRALIA

Station Stays

If you really want to sample a slice of genuine station life out in the red sandy country, then head out to a station stay. On the Bullara-Giralia Rd, 43 km from the North-West Coastal Highway is the 265,000-hectare *Giralia Station* (☎(099) 42 5937). There is a variety of accommodation here, including double B&Bs from $55 (bookings essential), shearers' quarters at $10, and camping and caravan sites for $5; all prices are per person. The homestead is central to many attractions in the Pilbara and Gascoyne regions. If you want to sample activities on the station, which runs 25,000 merino sheep, just ask. The prices are typical of other stations.

There are plenty of other places to stay in the region. Manberry (☎(099) 42 5926), Gnaraloo (☎(09) 388 2881) and Quobba (☎(099) 41 2036) stations are north of Carnarvon; Nallan Station (☎(099) 63 1054) is near Cue; Thundelarra Station (☎(099) 63 6575) is near Yalgoo; Mallina Station (☎(091) 76 4915) is 100 km from Port Hedland; Ninghan Station (☎(099) 63 6517) is south of Paynes Find; Tallering Station (☎(099) 62 3045) is 40 km from Mullewa; Wooleen Station (☎(099) 63 7973) is on the Murchison River; and Cobra Station (☎(099) 43 0565) and Mt Augustus Station (☎(099) 43 0527) are in the true outback at the head of the Gascoyne River. Go outback! ■

ore and natural gas reserves that account for much of WA's prosperity. Gigantic machines are used to tear the dusty red ranges apart. It's isolated, harsh and fabulously wealthy. The Pilbara towns are almost all company towns: either mining centres where the ore is wrenched from the earth, or ports from which it's shipped abroad. Exceptions are the beautiful gorges of Karijini (Hamersley Range) and historic mining centres like Marble Bar. Be careful – the Pilbara is alluring.

If you are driving away from the main coastal highway in this area, always carry a lot of extra water – 20 litres per person is a sensible amount – and adequate fuel. If you're travelling into remote areas, make sure you tell someone reliable of your travel plans, and don't leave your vehicle if you are stranded.

Getting There & Away

Air Ansett flies from Perth to Newman, Paraburdoo and Port Hedland daily. There is a scheduled bus connection to Tom Price for some flights. Karratha on the coast is well served: both Qantas and Ansett have daily flights to and from Perth. Ansett flies to Port Hedland four times weekly and Skywest has three flights weekly to Exmouth and Broome.

Bus Greyhound Pioneer and McCafferty's have daily buses (in both directions) to Karratha ($118) and Port Hedland ($139). On Wednesday, Friday and Sunday there is a service from Perth to Port Hedland via Mount Magnet, Cue, Meekatharra and Newman. There's a once-weekly service from the Nanutarra turn-off to Tom Price, that leaves Perth on Tuesday, and also three services a week to Exmouth from Perth (departing Wednesday, Friday and Sunday).

A Monday and Friday bus service to Wittenoom from Karratha is operated by Snappy Gum Safaris (☎ (091) 85 1278). You can reach Wittenoom directly from Port Hedland (307 km via the Great Northern

Pebble-Mound Mouse

This mouse (*Pseudomys chapmani*), which is unique to the Pilbara, is a recent discovery. It lives between clumps of spinifex in shallow burrows upon which it heaps a relatively flat mound of pebbles.

The carefully selected pebbles are small but the actual mound can be up to 50 cm high. The pebbles are meticulously placed around the entrance of the burrow to provide insulation and moisture. ■

Highway), from near Roebourne (311 km off the North-West Coastal Highway) or from the Nanutarra turn-off (377 km off the North-West Coastal Highway). Many roads in the Pilbara are unsealed or require a permit.

ONSLOW (pop 880)

Onslow has the dubious distinction of being the southernmost Western Australian town to be bombed in WW II and later of being used as a base by the British for nuclear testing in the Monte Bello Islands.

There is good swimming and fishing in the area. The **Old Onslow ruins**, 48 km from town, were abandoned in 1925. They include a gaol and a post office, and are worth a look.

The *Ocean View Caravan Park* (☎ (091) 84 6053) on Second Ave has powered sites at $14 and on-site vans from $30. The *Beadon Bay Hotel* (☎ (091) 84 6002), Second Ave, has rooms for $50/60.

There are expensive resorts on the Direction and Mackerel islands (☎ (09) 388 2020), 11 and 22 km offshore, respectively.

Two taxi services (☎ (091) 84 6298) connect daily with Greyhound Pioneer and McCafferty's buses at the Highway Bus Stop; the cost is $25 (children $22.50).

DAMPIER (pop 2450)

Dampier is on King Bay, across from the 41 islands of the Dampier Archipelago (named after the explorer William Dampier who visited the area in 1699).

Dampier is a Hamersley Iron town, the port for Tom Price and Paraburdoo iron-ore operations. (It will also be the port for the huge Marandoo mineral project.) Gas from the natural-gas fields of the North-West Shelf is piped ashore nearby on the Burrup Peninsula. From there, it is piped to Perth and the Pilbara, or liquefied as part of the Woodside Petroleum project and exported to Japan and South Korea.

An inspection of the port facilities can be arranged (☎ (091) 44 4600). The William Dampier Lookout provides a fine view over the harbour, and the Woodside LNG visitor centre (☎ (091) 83 8100) is open weekdays from 9 am to 4.30 pm during the high season.

WESTERN AUSTRALIA

Montebello Islands

The Montebellos are a group of more than 100 flat limestone islands off the north-west coast of Western Australia between Onslow and Karratha. In 1992 they were gazetted as a conservation park.

In 1622 the survivors of the shipwreck of the *Tryal* camped here before setting off to the East Indies. The islands were named in 1801 after the battle of Monte Bello, by the French explorer Baudin. The pearlers who came next introduced the black rat and the cat, which ensured the extinction of the golden bandicoot and the spectacled hare-wallaby on the island.

In 1952 the British detonated an atomic weapon mounted on HMS *Plym,* anchored in Main Bay off Trimouille Island. Two further atomic tests were carried out in 1956, on Alpha and Trimouille islands.

Some 40 years later we can finally step ashore and get close to a real 'ground zero', the point of detonation of an atomic weapon. It will be interesting to see how long the radiation warning signs last before being souvenired by collectors of the macabre.

Nature is resilient and the islands have thriving populations of both land and marine fauna and more than 100 plant species, including a stand of mangroves. The legless lizard *Aprasia rostrata* is found only on Hermite Island (was it legless before or after 1952?). Two species of marine turtle are known to nest on the islands, as are a number of seabirds. Vignerons will love the names of many of the bays – Hock, Champagne, Burgundy, Claret and Moselle, for example.

'Beautiful mountains' the islands are not. They are, rather, silent witness to the awesome destructive power of the theory that 'energy equals mass times the speed of light squared' and to the miraculous, recuperative powers of nature. ■

Nearby Hearson's Cove is a popular beach and picnic area, as is Dampier Beach. The **Burrup Peninsula** has some 10,000 Aboriginal rock engravings depicting fish, turtles, kangaroos and a Tasmanian tiger. There is a detailed peninsula tour operated by Lynda Gray (☎ (091) 44 1372); the cost is $22.

The **Dampier Archipelago** is renowned as a game-fishing mecca and each year in August it hosts the Dampier Classic.

Places to Stay & Eat

Apart from the *caravan park* (☎ (091) 83 1109) on the Esplanade, there is no budget accommodation in Dampier. The *King Bay Holiday Village* (☎ (091) 83 1440) on the Esplanade has expensive units from $70. Also on the Esplanade is the *Mermaid Hotel* (☎ (091) 83 1222), expensive with single/double units from $60/70.

The *Harbour Lights* restaurant is part of the Holiday Village complex. The *Captain's Galley*, overlooking Hampton Harbour, is good for fish & chips.

KARRATHA (pop 11,300)

Karratha (Aboriginal for 'good country'), the commercial centre of the area, is 20 km from Dampier. The town was developed due to the rapid expansion of the Hamersley Iron and Woodside LNG projects. It's now the hub of the coastal Pilbara.

There are good views from the lookout at the area known as **TV Hill** (because of the television repeater mast). **Miaree Pool**, 35 km to the south-west, is a scenic place to cool off. The area around town is replete with evidence of Aboriginal occupation – carvings, grindstones, etchings and middens are all located on the 3.5-km **Jaburara Heritage Trail** which starts by the information centre. *Terminalia canescens*, the trees which grow in the creek beds here, are a reminder of the area's former tropical climate.

The Karratha & District information centre (☎ (091) 44 4600), on Karratha Rd just before you reach the T-intersection of Karratha and Millstream Rds, has heaps of info on what to see and do in the Pilbara.

The Fe-NaCl-NG Festival is held in August each year. The title combines the chemical abbreviations of the region's main natural resources – iron, salt and natural gas.

Places to Stay & Eat

There are three caravan parks in Karratha: *Balmoral* (☎ (091) 85 3628); *Rosemary Rd* (☎ (091) 85 1855); and the *Karratha* (☎ (091) 85 1012) on Mooligunn Rd. The first two parks have powered sites at $15, and on-site vans at $40. The *International Hotel* and *Quality Inn* are expensive (over $120 for a double).

In Karratha, *Los Amigos*, opposite the BP service station on Balmoral Rd, has Mexican food and 'el cheapo' specials on Wednesday. For a snack, there are cafes and takeaways in the air-conditioned Karratha shopping centre, including *Adrienne's* for muffins. *Trawlers* is a good seafood restaurant.

A little out of town, the oasis-like *Tambrey Community Centre* has a tavern with counter meals; visitors are welcome to use the pool.

ROEBOURNE AREA

The Roebourne area is a busy little enclave of historic towns and modern port facilities. Wickham is the port for the ore produced at Tom Price and Pannawonica, Point Samson is a great fishing spot and Cossack is a very picturesque historic town. European settlement of the north-west began in this area.

Information

Information is available from the tourist bureau (☎ (091) 82 1060), Old Gaol, Queen St, Roebourne. In Cossack, the Heritage Council officials will help. There is a laundrette in the Mt Welcome Motel complex in Roebourne and a good supermarket in Wickham.

Roebourne (pop 1680)

Roebourne is the oldest existing town in the Pilbara. It has a history of grazing, gold and copper mining, and was once the capital of the north-west region. There are still some fine old buildings to be seen, including the **Old Gaol** (which has an excellent Aboriginal art gallery), an 1894 church and the Victoria

Hotel, which is the last of five original pubs. The town was once connected to Cossack, 13 km away, by a horse-drawn tram.

Places to Stay & Eat The *Harding River Caravan Park* (☎ (091) 82 1063) has tent sites at $10. The *Mt Welcome Motel*, in Roe St, is the main accommodation with singles/doubles for $40/60.

The *Roebourne Diner* is good for eat-in and takeaway meals and the *Poinciana Room* in the Mt Welcome Motel serves full meals.

Cossack

Originally known as Tien Tsin Harbour, Cossack, at the mouth of the Harding River, was a bustling town and the main port for the district in the mid to late 19th century. Its boom was short-lived and Point Samson soon supplanted it as the chief port for the area. The sturdy old buildings date from 1870 to 1898, and much of the ghost town has been restored as part of a continuing project.

The town has an **art gallery**, **museum** ($2; children $1) and a budget accommodation house which has boat hire. Beyond town, there's a **pioneer cemetery** with a small Japanese section dating from the old pearl-diving days. In fact, this is where WA pearling actually began; it later moved on to Broome in the 1890s. There are good lookouts and excellent beaches in the area; the cooler, drier months are best for a visit.

The 'staircase to the moon' reflection can be viewed from Reader Head Lookout. It covers an average of 50 km of marsh and lasts for ages.

The *Cossack Backpackers* (☎ (091) 82 1190) is one of those gems of the road. It's housed in the old police barracks administered by the Heritage Council of WA. Dorm rooms are $10, family rooms are $32, and there is a kitchen, refrigerators and hot and cold showers. There is also a small shop nearby. As there are no places to eat, bring your own food from Wickham, six km away. If you ring in advance the proprietors will pick you up from Wickham.

Wickham & Point Samson

Wickham is the Robe River Iron Company town, handling its ore-exporting facilities 10 km away at Cape Lambert, where the jetty is three km long. Ore is railed to the coast from the mining operations inland at Pannawonica.

Point Samson, beyond Wickham, took the place of Cossack when the old port silted up. In turn, it has been replaced by the modern port facilities of Dampier and Cape Lambert. There are good beaches at Point Samson itself and at nearby **Honeymoon Cove**.

Places to Stay & Eat The *Solveig Caravan Park* (☎ (091) 87 1414), on Samson Rd next to the tavern, has tent/powered sites for $12/13. *Samson Holiday Chalets* (☎ (091) 87 1052), Samson Rd, has metered air-con rooms/units from $40/70.

It's worth detouring to Point Samson for the seafood. At *Moby's Kitchen* you can get excellent fish & chips and salad.

Whim Creek

The first significant Pilbara mineral find was at Whim Creek, 80 km east of Roebourne. It once had a copper mine but today all that is left is the *Whim Creek Hotel* (☎ (091) 76 4914) which has accommodation and a restaurant; tent/caravan sites are free, backpackers' beds are $10 and singles/doubles are from $30/40.

MILLSTREAM-CHICHESTER NATIONAL PARK

The impressive 200,000-hectare Millstream-Chichester National Park, in the middle of a semi-arid environment, includes a number of freshwater pools, such as **Python Pool**. This was once an oasis for Afghani camel drivers and is still a good place to pause for a swim. The Millstream Homestead is 150 km south of Roebourne, and 21 km from the turn-off from the Wittenoom road. It has been converted into an information centre with much detail on the Millstream ecosystems and the lifestyle of the Yinjibarndi people.

The **Chinderwarriner Pool**, near the Millstream visitor centre, is a pleasant oasis with pools, palms (including the unique Millstream palm) and lilies; it is well worth a visit. The lush environment is a haven for birds and other fauna such as flying foxes and kangaroos. Over 20 species of dragonfly and damselfly have been recorded around the pool.

The park also has a number of walking/driving trails including Cliff Lookout Drive, the Murlunmunyjurna Trail (6.8 km) and the eight-km Chichester Range Camel Track.

The basic camp sites (☎ (091) 84 5144) at Crossing Pool and Deep Reach have gas barbecues, fire rings and pit toilets; tent sites are $5, and $3 for each extra adult.

WITTENOOM (pop 50)

This ghost town 288 km south-east of Roebourne, a pariah to health officials because of the presence of blue asbestos, is the Hamersley Range's tourist centre. Wittenoom's days as an asbestos-mining town finally ended in 1966; it is the awesome gorges of Karijini (Hamersley Range) which now draw people to the area.

The visage of Charlie Chaplin, slowly peeling off the wall of the abandoned picture theatre, is distinctly mournful. The epitaph 'Died of the Dust' on a grave in the local cemetery reinforces the general air of malaise, and you can almost hear the voices of ghosts shouting above the afternoon wind. Yet to the seasoned traveller there's something irresistible about this place.

The information centre (☎ (091) 89 7096) is in the Gem Shop, Sixth Ave. There are no banking facilities in town, so bring cash.

Places to Stay & Eat

The *Gorges Caravan Park* (☎ (091) 89 7075), on Second Ave, has tent/powered sites from $10/12.50 and on-site vans from $30. *Bungarra Bivouac Hostel* (☎ (091) 89 7026), on Fifth Ave, has beds at $8 per night (incidentally, a bungarra is a big goanna). *Nomad Heights* (☎ (091) 89 7068), on First Ave, is a small arid/tropical permaculture farm where a weekly stay is $44.

At present you have to bring your own food to Wittenoom as there are no restaurants in town. You can get basic supplies at the camping ground or at the local store.

Forty km from Wittenoom, on the Great Northern Highway, is the *Auski Tourist Village Roadhouse* (☎ (091) 76 6988); shady, grassed tent/powered sites are $9/14. Auski? It was set up by Aussies and Kiwis.

Warning

Even after 30 years, there is a health risk from airborne asbestos fibres. Avoid disturbing asbestos tailings in the area and keep your car windows closed on windy days. If you are concerned, seek expert medical advice before going to Wittenoom.

KARIJINI (HAMERSLEY RANGE) NATIONAL PARK

Wittenoom is at the northern end of the Karijini (Hamersley Range) National Park and **Wittenoom Gorge**, infamous because of many asbestos-related deaths, is immediately south of the town. A road runs the 13 km into the gorge, passing old asbestos mines, small gorges and pretty pools.

Like other gorges in central Australia, those of Karijini are spectacular both in their sheer rocky faces and their varied colours. In early spring, the park is often carpeted with colourful wildflowers. Travel down the Roy Hill-Wittenoom road 24 km and there's a turn-off to the **Yampire Gorge** where blue veins of asbestos can be seen in the rock. Fig Tree Soak, in the gorge, was once used by Afghani camel drivers as a watering point. Look carefully at the birdlife around the fig tree – if you are lucky you might see a spotted bower-bird feeding on the ripe figs.

The road continues through Yampire Gorge to **Dales Gorge**. On this same route, you can get to **Circular Pool** and a nearby lookout, and by a footpath to the bottom of the **Fortescue Falls**. The walk from Circular Pool along Dales Gorge to the falls is recommended; you will be surprised by the supply of permanent water in the gorge.

The Joffre Falls road leads to **Knox Gorge**; nearby is a 1.5-km return walk to Red Gorge lookout. From the Joffre Falls

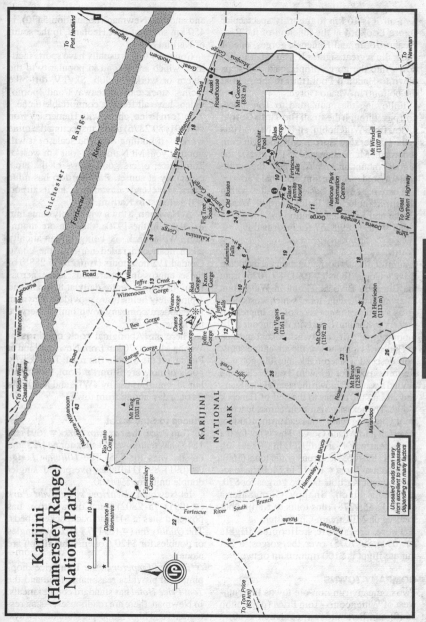

Karijini (Hamersley Range) National Park

WESTERN AUSTRALIA

turn-off it is 16 km to the truly spectacular **Oxers Lookout** at the junction of the Red, Weano, Joffre and Hancock gorges, one of Australia's great sights. If you wish to get down into the gorge proper, take the steps down to Handrail Pool (turn to the right at the bottom) in Weano Gorge.

Following the main road to Tom Price, you pass through the small **Rio Tinto Gorge**, 43 km from Wittenoom, and just beyond this is the **Hamersley Gorge**, only four km from the road. Mt Meharry (1251 metres), the highest mountain in WA, is near the south-eastern border of Karijini National Park.

There are several basic camp sites within Karijini, including Dales Gorge, Weano Gorge and Joffre intersection ($5 for a site) – call ☎ (091) 89 8157 for information.

Tours

A number of tours operate in the area, including Dave's Gorge Tours (☎ (091) 89 7026) from the Bungarra Bivouac Hostel in Wittenoom. The one-day circuit tour, which costs $50, gives a different impression of the impressive scenery in Karijini. It starts in Wittenoom in the morning, going first to Oxers Lookout and then to Hancock Gorge where the adventure starts. You descend a steep track into the gorge to Kermit's Pool for a swim before climbing around a waterfall, down the steep Hades Stairs and around the corner to the end of Hancock Gorge. The next stage is a swim across Junction Pool. Climbing again, you head up the 100-foot waterfall into Weano Gorge. This is not for the faint-hearted. Nomad Heights Trekking (☎ (091) 89 7068) also runs gorge tours ($60).

Design-a-Tour (☎ (091) 44 1460) has one-day tours of Karijini and the gorges for $70, including lunch. Snappy Gum Safaris (☎ (091) 85 1278) runs tours to Karijini but focuses on Millstream-Chichester.

There are scenic helicopter flights (☎ (091) 89 7075) over the gorges; a 25-minute flight is $100 (minimum of two).

COMPANY TOWNS

Two company-run iron-ore towns lie south-west of Wittenoom – Tom Price (population 3540) and Paraburdoo (population 2360) –

and another, Newman (population 5470), is 450 km south of Port Hedland, to the south of Karijini.

Company towns usually have sports facilities, which are second in popularity to the tavern or worker's club. SkyTV, dirt-bike racing, stock cars, takeaways and 'porno' videos have all found a comfortable niche.

In **Tom Price**, check with Hamersley Iron (☎ (091) 89 2375) about inspecting the mine works – if nothing else, the scale of it will impress you. Mt Nameless, four km west of Tom Price, offers good views of the area, especially at sunset. **Paraburdoo** has mine tours, a hotel and caravan park, and its airport is the closest to Karijini.

At **Newman**, a town which only came into existence in the 1970s, the iron-ore mountain, Whaleback, is being systematically taken apart and railed north to the coast. Guided 1½-hour tours (☎ (091) 75 2888) of these engrossing operations leave across from the tourist centre daily at 8.30 am and 1 pm; safety helmets are provided. Newman is a modern company town built to service the mine.

There are Aboriginal **rock carvings** at Wanna Munna, 70 km from Newman, and at Punda, off the Marble Bar road. Two nearby pools of note are **Stuart's Pool**, a difficult but adventurous trip by 4WD, and **Kalgan's Pool**, a day outing from town.

Places to Stay & Eat

In Tom Price, the *caravan park* (☎ (091) 89 1515) has tent/powered sites for $11/13 and on-site vans for $35. The *Hillview Lodge* (☎ (091) 89 1110) has overpriced single/double units for $90/100.

In Newman, *Dearlove's Caravan Park* (☎ (091) 75 2802), on Cowra Drive, has powered sites at $15 and backpackers' beds. The *Quality Inn* (☎ (091) 75 1101) has singles or doubles for $120 (rotten value if you are alone).

The *Red Emperor* in the Tom Price shopping mall provides reasonable food and the *Tom Price Hotel* has standard counter meals. In Newman, there are roadhouses, Asian restaurants and high blood-pressure takeaways.

WESTERN AUSTRALIA

MARBLE BAR (pop 380)

Reputed to be the hottest place in Australia, Marble Bar had a period in the 1920s when for 160 consecutive days the temperature topped 37°C. On one occasion, in 1905, the mercury soared to 49.1°C. From October to March, days over 40°C are common.

The town, 203 km south-east of Port Hedland, is the centre of a 377,000-sq-km shire (larger than New Zealand). It takes its name from the red jasper bar across the Coongan River, five km to the west. The tourist centre (☎ (091) 76 1166) is on Halse Rd.

In town, the 1895 government buildings, made of local stone, are still in use. In late winter, as the spring wildflowers begin to bloom, Marble Bar is actually quite a pretty place and one of the most popular towns in the Pilbara to visit. The **Comet Gold Mine**, 10 km south of Marble Bar, still in operation and with a mining museum, is open daily.

Coppins Gap/Doolena Gorge, about 70 km north-east of Marble Bar, is a deep canyon with impressive views, twisted bands of rock and an ideal swimming hole.

Places to Stay The *Marble Bar Caravan Park* (☎ (091) 76 1067), Contest St, has tent/powered sites for $10/15 and on-site vans from $28. There's a range of rooms at the *Iron Clad Hotel* (☎ (091) 76 1066), one of the area's colourful drinking spots – backpackers' beds are from $15.

PORT HEDLAND (pop 12,500)

This port handles a massive tonnage as it is the place from where the Pilbara's iron ore is shipped overseas. The iron-ore trains are up to 2.8 km long. The town itself is built on an island connected to the mainland by causeways, and the main highway into Port Hedland enters along a three-km causeway.

Even before the Marble Bar gold rush of the 1880s, the town had been important. It became a grazing centre in 1864 and during the 1870s a fleet of 150 pearling luggers was based here. By 1946, however, the population had dwindled to a mere 150.

The port is on a mangrove-fringed inlet – there are plenty of fish, crabs, oysters and birds around. The port and iron-ore eyesores are feted at the expense of the prolific natural wonders in the area.

Information

The sleepy tourist bureau (☎ (091) 73 1711) at 13 Wedge St, across from the post office, is open weekdays from 8.30 am to 5 pm, and weekends from 8.30 am to 4.30 pm. It has a good map of the town, and public showers for $1.50.

Whale & Turtle-Watching

The flatback turtle nests between September and April on some of the nearby beaches, including Munda, Cooke Point, Cemetery and Pretty Pool. At Munda up to 20 turtles may nest in a night.

Humpback whale-watching trips are operated by Big Blue Dive (☎ (091) 73 3202), 5 Wedge St. These take more than six hours, leave on weekends only, cost $65 per person, and are dependent on tides.

Other Attractions

Eight km east of the town centre on the waterfront is **Pretty Pool**, a safe tidal pool where shell collectors will have fun – beware of stonefish. Visits can also be made to the **Royal Flying Doctor Service base**, Richardson St, at 11.15 am on weekdays.

You can visit the wharf area or view it from the 26-metre observation **tower** behind the tourist bureau (you have to sign a waiver to climb it and you'll need closed shoes). From the tower you will see huge ore carriers, stockpiles of ore and a town encrusted in red Pilbara dust. From Monday to Friday, at 9 and 11 am, there is a mind-numbing 1½-hour BHP Iron Ore & Port Tour which leaves from the tourist bureau ($8; children $2).

At Two Mile Ridge, just off Wilson St, there is an Aboriginal **rock engraving** site. A stingray (*jingkiri* in the local Aboriginal language), turtle (*jajarruka*) and a five-metre long whale (*kartarrapuka*) – or is it a dugong (*kurlpanarri*)? – have all been intricately carved into the limestone.

WESTERN AUSTRALIA

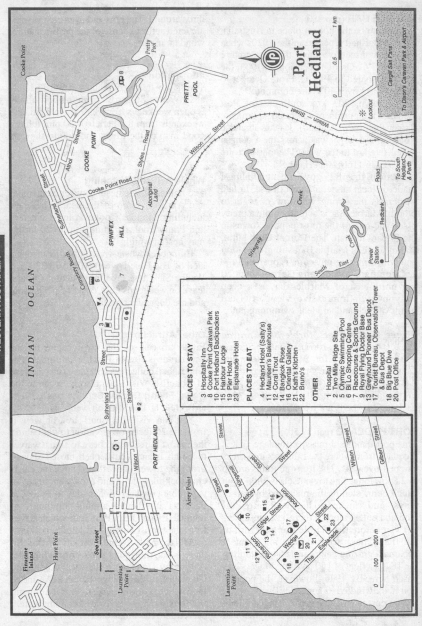

WESTERN AUSTRALIA

PLACES TO STAY

3 Hospitality Inn
8 Cooke Point Caravan Park
10 Port Hedland Backpackers
15 Harbour Lodge
19 Pier Hotel
23 Esplanade Hotel

PLACES TO EAT

4 Hedland Hotel (Salty's)
11 Maureen's Bakehouse
12 Coral Trout
14 Bangkok Rose
16 Oriental Gallery
21 Kath's Kitchen
22 Bruno's

OTHER

1 Hospital
2 Two Mile Ridge Site
5 Olympic Swimming Pool
6 Bi Lo Shopping Centre
7 Racecourse & Sports Ground
9 Royal Flying Doctor Base
13 Greyhound Pioneer Bus Depot
      & Bus Depot
17 Tourist Bureau, Observation Tower
20 Big Blue Dive
20 Post Office

Port Hedland

PORT HEDLAND

Places to Stay

Camping You can camp by the airport at *Dixon's Caravan Park* (☎ (091) 72 2525). Tent/powered sites are $12/15 and backpackers' rooms are $12 per person. The park has a pool and a great recreation room with cooking facilities, tape deck and TV. More convenient, but looking somewhat bereft, is the *Cooke Point Caravan Park* (☎ (091) 73 1271), on Athol St, which is also adjacent to Pretty Pool – dusty tent/powered sites are $12/15.

Hostels The *Port Hedland Backpackers* (☎ (091) 73 3282) is at 20 Richardson St, between Edgar and McKay Sts. The homely atmosphere and friendly hosts make up for the lack of luxuries. Dorm beds cost $11 and the place has kitchen and laundry facilities.

The *Pier Hotel* (☎ (091) 73 1488), on the Esplanade, has $15 beds for backpackers. Similar in price is the *Harbour Lodge* (☎ (091) 73 2996), at 11 Edgar St, with full kitchen, air-con and ceiling fans.

Hotels & Motels On the corner of Anderson St, there's the *Esplanade Hotel* (☎ (091) 73 1798) which has singles/doubles from $40/50. Also on the Esplanade, the *Pier* has singles/doubles for $55/80. The *Hospitality Inn* (☎ (091) 73 1044), on the corner of Webster and Sutherland Sts, provides respite from the omnipresent red dust but such luxury is not cheap, starting from $108.

Places to Eat

The *Pier*, *Esplanade* and *Hedland* hotels serve counter meals; dinners are only available Friday and Saturday nights, until 8 pm.

There are plenty of supermarkets if you want to fix your own food and also a number of coffee bars and other places where you can get a pie or pastie. *Maureen's Bakehouse*, on Richardson St, and *Kath's Kitchen*, Wedge St, are recommended for homestyle cooking; *Bruno's* in Anderson St for pizza. The *Coral Trout*, on the waterfront, has a restaurant and a takeaway section where you can get fish & chips – the mackerel is superb.

The *Oriental Gallery*, on the corner of Edgar and Anderson Sts, does a good-value weekday lunch. There are three other Asian restaurants in town – the *Bangkok Rose* (Thai), *Dynasty Gardens* and *Golden Crown*.

Getting There & Away

Air Ansett has direct flights, Friday and Saturday, from Port Hedland to Darwin. There are a number of daily connections to Perth and also frequent flights to and from Broome, Karratha, the mining towns of the Pilbara and other northern centres. Qantas has a daily service to Perth. Garuda and Qantas operate flights every Saturday between Port Hedland and Bali.

Bus It's 230 km from Karratha to Port Hedland and 604 km more to Broome. Greyhound Pioneer and McCafferty's have services from Perth to Port Hedland, and north on to Broome and Darwin. The Greyhound office is in the Homestead Centre in Throssell St, South Hedland.

As well as the coastal route, Greyhound Pioneer has a service that takes the inland route from Perth to Port Hedland via Newman four times weekly. Fares from Port Hedland are $144 to Perth, $78 to Broome, $46 to Karratha and $242 to Darwin.

Getting Around

The airport is 13 km from town – the only way to get there is by taxi, which costs $15. There's a Hedland Bus Lines service (☎ (091) 72 1394) between Port Hedland and South Hedland; it takes between 40 minutes and an hour and operates Monday to Saturday ($2). You can hire cars at the airport from the usual operators. The backpackers hostel lends its bikes to responsible users.

PORT HEDLAND TO BROOME

The Great Northern Highway continues on from Port Hedland to Broome. Unfortunately, this 604-km stretch is a contender for the most boring length of road in Australia.

About 84 km from Port Hedland is the **De Grey River**, where several bird species can be spotted. *Pardoo Station* (133 km; ☎ (091) 76 4930) has station stays; tent/powered sites are $14/16, budget beds are $15 and self-contained cottages are $60. Near the Pardoo Roadhouse (154 km) is the turn-off to **Cape Keraudren**, where there is great fishing; caravan sites are $5.

At **Eighty Mile Beach**, 245 km from Port Hedland, there is a caravan park with tent and powered sites and fully equipped cabins ($55). The *Sandfire Roadhouse* (295 km) is very much an enforced fuel stop for most – pack your own sandwiches rather than eat the dull, expensive food sold here (there is accommodation if you are desperate). On the other hand, **Port Smith** (477 km) comes recommended; unpowered sites are $5 per person.

COLLIER RANGE & RUDALL RIVER

Two of the most isolated and, perhaps for that reason alone, interesting, of the state's national parks are found in the Pilbara.

The **Collier Range** is the more accessible as the Great Northern Highway bisects it near the Kumarina Roadhouse, 256 km north of Meekatharra. Here, at the upper reaches of the Ashburton and Gascoyne rivers, the ranges vary from low hills to high ridges bounded by cliffs.

Even more remote is the **Rudall River (Karlamilyi)**, a breathtakingly beautiful desert region of 1.5 million hectares, 300 km east of Newman. Visit in July and August when daytime temperatures are tolerable – although nights can be exceptionally cold. The Martu Aboriginal people still live in the park.

At least two vehicles, equipped with RFDS radios, are needed for off-road trips into these parks and visitors must be *totally* self-sufficient. There are no facilities.

The Kimberley

The rugged Kimberley, at the northern end of WA, is one of Australia's last frontiers. Despite enormous advances in the past decade this is still a little-travelled and very remote area of great rivers and magnificent scenery. The Kimberley suffers from climatic extremes – heavy rains in the Wet followed by searing heat in the Dry – but the irrigation projects in its north-east have made great changes to the region.

Rivers and creeks can rise rapidly following heavy rain and become impassable torrents within 15 minutes. Unless it's a very brief storm, it's quite likely that watercourses will remain impassable for some days. After two or three days of rain the Fitzroy River can swell from its normal 100-metre width to over 10 km. River and creek crossings on the Great Northern Highway on both sides of Halls Creek become impassable every Wet. Highway 1 through the Kimberley is sealed all the way, but there are several notorious crossings, which are still only fords and not all-weather bridges.

The best time to visit is between April and September. By October it's already getting hot (35°C), and later in the year daily temperatures of more than 40°C are common until it starts to rain. On the other hand, the Wet is a spectacular time to visit – ethereal thunderstorms, lightning, flowing waterfalls close to the towns and the magic carpet of the green rejuvenated landscape.

Kimberley attractions include idyllic Broome, the spectacular Fitzroy River gorges, the Wolfe Creek meteorite crater, the Gibb River Rd and the Bungle Bungles.

BROOME (pop 10,200)

For many travellers, Broome is Australia's true getaway, with its palm-fringed beaches and cosmopolitan atmosphere. This small, dusty old port is noted for its Chinatown and the Japanese influences of early pearlers. Although still isolated, Broome has certainly been discovered. Today it is something of a travellers' centre with the attendant good and bad characteristics.

Pearling in the sea off Broome started in the 1880s and peaked in the early 1900s when the town's 400 pearling luggers, worked by 3000 men, supplied 80% of the world's mother-of-pearl. Today only a handful of boats operate. Pearl diving was very unsafe, as Broome's Japanese cemetery

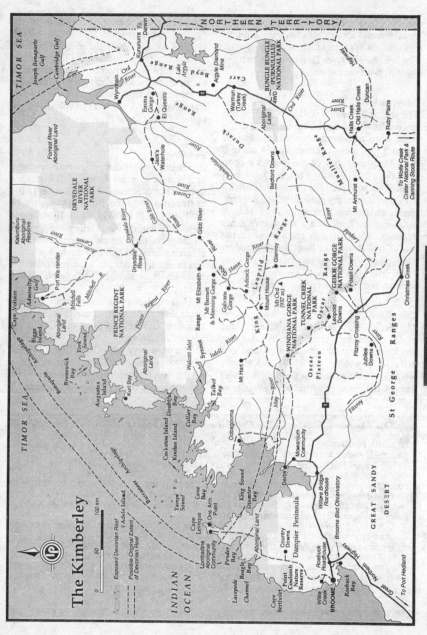

The Kimberley

attests. The divers were from various Asian countries and rivalry between the nationalities was always intense and sometimes ugly. The *Broome Heritage Trail* pamphlet merges the past with the present.

Information

The tourist bureau (☎ (091) 92 2222) is just across the sports field from Chinatown. It's open April to November weekdays from 8 am to 5 pm, and weekends from 9 am to 5 pm. At other times of the year it's open weekdays from 9 am to 5 pm, and weekends from 9 am to 1 pm. The bureau publishes a very useful monthly guide to what's happening in and around Broome, a *Town Map & Information Guide* and a *Broome Holiday Planner*. You can also get a copy of the useful, free *Broome or Bust!* aimed at budget tourists or the more commercial *Broome Time*. The post office is on the corner of Stewart and Hamersley Sts.

Chinatown

The term 'Chinatown' refers to the old part of town, although there is really only one block or so that is truly multicultural and historic. Some of the plain and simple wooden buildings that line Carnarvon St still house Chinese merchants, but most are now restaurants and tourist shops. One of the original general stores here is Mr Wing's General Store – he has the best cure in town for sandfly bites. The bars on the windows of the shops aren't there to deter outlaws but to minimise cyclone damage.

There is a street statue of three men in Carnarvon St – all were involved in the cultured pearl industry.

Pearling

A pearling lugger can occasionally be seen at Streeters jetty off Dampier Terrace, and there are cruises from May to October ($40).

Broome Historical Society Museum, on Saville St, has exhibits both on Broome and its history and on the pearling industry and its dangers. It's in the old customs house and is open weekdays from 10 am to 4 pm, and weekends from 10 am to 1 pm (April to November); reduced hours from November to May.

Mother-of-pearl has long been a Broome speciality. There are pearl shops along Dampier Terrace, and Short and Carnarvon Sts in Chinatown.

The **cemetery**, near Cable Beach Rd, testifies to the dangers that accompanied pearl diving when equipment was primitive and knowledge of diving techniques limited. In

---

Broome Festivals

Broome is something of a festival centre. There are many excuses to party.

The **Shinju Matsuri (Festival of the Pearl)** commemorates the early pearling years and the town's multicultural heritage. During the festival (usually around August and September), the population swells and accommodation is hard to find, so book ahead. It's well worth trying to juggle your itinerary to be in Broome at this time. Many traditional Japanese ceremonies are featured, including the O Bon Festival (Festival of the Dead). It concludes with a beach concert and a huge fireworks display. Don't miss the dragon-boat races.

In late November the town celebrates the **Mango Festival**, commemorating that sticky sweet fruit loved by some, but deplored by parents of small children.

The **Broome Fringe Arts Festival**, where the alternative lifestylers have their day, is in early June. There are markets, Aboriginal art exhibitions and impromptu jamming sessions. There is also the **Broome Sailfish Tournament** (a tag and release event) in July; a Chinatown Street Party in March; a **Dragon Boat Classic** in early April; and evening markets on the many nights of the Staircase to the Moon. ■

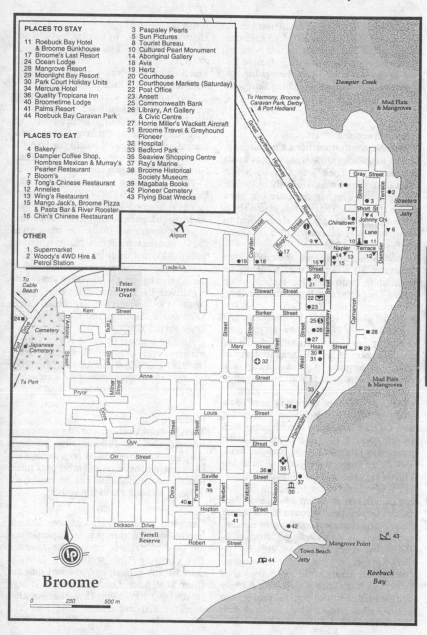

PLACES TO STAY

- 11 Roebuck Bay Hotel & Broome Bunkhouse
- 17 Broome's Last Resort
- 24 Ocean Lodge
- 28 Mangrove Resort
- 29 Moonlight Bay Resort
- 30 Park Court Holiday Units
- 34 Mercure Hotel
- 36 Quality Tropicana Inn
- 40 Broometime Lodge
- 41 Palms Resort
- 44 Roebuck Bay Caravan Park

PLACES TO EAT

- 4 Bakery
- 6 Dampier Coffee Shop, Hombres Mexican & Murray's Pearler Restaurant
- 7 Bloom's
- 9 Tong's Chinese Restaurant
- 12 Annelies
- 13 Wing's Restaurant
- 15 Mango Jack's, Broome Pizza & Pasta Bar & River Rooster
- 16 Chin's Chinese Restaurant

OTHER

- 1 Supermarket
- 2 Woody's 4WD Hire & Petrol Station

- 3 Paspaley Pearls
- 5 Sun Pictures
- 8 Tourist Bureau
- 10 Cultured Pearl Monument
- 14 Aboriginal Gallery
- 18 Avis
- 19 Hertz
- 20 Courthouse
- 21 Courthouse Markets (Saturday)
- 22 Post Office
- 23 Ansett
- 25 Commonwealth Bank
- 26 Library, Art Gallery & Civic Centre
- 27 Horrie Miller's Wackett Aircraft Pioneer
- 31 Broome Travel & Greyhound Pioneer
- 32 Hospital
- 33 Bedford Park
- 35 Seaview Shopping Centre
- 37 Ray's Marine
- 38 Broome Historical Society Museum
- 39 Magabala Books
- 42 Pioneer Cemetery
- 43 Flying Boat Wrecks

Broome

WESTERN AUSTRALIA

1914 alone, 33 divers died of the bends, while in 1908 a cyclone killed 150 seamen caught at sea. The Japanese section is one of the largest and most interesting. Behind the neat Japanese section is the interesting but now run-down section containing European and Aboriginal graves.

Other Attractions

Across Napier Terrace from Chinatown is Wing's Restaurant with a magnificent **boab tree** beside it. There's another boab tree behind, outside what used to be the old police lock-up, with a rather sad little tale on a plaque at its base. The tree was planted by a police officer when his son (later killed in France in WW I) was born in 1898. The boab tree is still doing fine.

The 1888 **courthouse** (entrance from Hamersley St) was once used to house the transmitting equipment for the old cable station. The cable ran to Banyuwangi in Java, the ferry port across from Bali.

Farther along Weld St, by the library and civic centre, is a **Wackett aircraft** that used to belong to Horrie Miller, founder of MacRobertson Miller Airlines (now part of Ansett). The plane is hidden away in a modern, absurdly designed building that most people pass without a second glance.

There's a **pioneer cemetery** near Town Beach at the end of Robinson St. Nearby, there's a park and also a small beach which is worth a visit at high tide. In the bay, at the entrance to Dampier Creek, there's a landmark called **Buccaneer Rock**, dedicated to William Dampier and his ship, the *Roebuck*.

If you're lucky enough to be in Broome on a cloudless night when a full moon rises you can witness the **Staircase to the Moon**. The reflections of the moon from the rippling mud flats create a wonderful golden stairway effect, best seen from Town Beach. The effect is in fact most dramatic about two days after the full moon, as the moon rises after the sky has had a chance to darken. A lively evening market is held on this evening, and the town takes on a carnival air. Check with the tourist bureau for dates and times.

Tours & Cruises

There are a number of tours to make in and around Broome. The *Spirit of Broome* (☎ (091) 93 5025) is a small hovercraft which makes daily one-hour flights around Roebuck Bay ($45) and points of interest.

Also out on the water, you can twilight cruise on a pearling lugger, the *Cornelius* (for $55 they provide drinks and nibbles); go for a full day sail on the magnificent yacht, *Sans Souci* ($135 with lunch); or take the *Tropic Rover* cruise to Willie Creek Pearl Farm ($110, including cost of entry).

There are also good guided bushwalks. Paul Foulkes (☎ (091) 92 1371) concentrates on environmental features close to Broome, such as the palaeontologically important dinosaur footprints ($12), the mangroves ($25), remnant rainforest ($20), a hidden valley ($25) and wildlife exploring ($35).

For those who want to safely venture into the Kimberley on a cycle there are safaris organised by Broome Adventure Tours (☎ (091) 93 7997). A two-day coastal tour is $175 and a three-day trip along the Gibb River Rd is $325.

Another unusual option is Harley Davidson motorcycle tours with Broome by Harley (☎ (018) 93 0500). There are many fly-drive options to the remote areas of the Kimberley; enquire at the tourist bureau.

Places to Stay

Theft by outsiders seems to be a problem in Broome. Get into Broome Time but keep alert and keep your hand on your wallet. During school holidays and other peak times finding accommodation can be extremely difficult, so book ahead if possible.

Camping Even camping sites can become impossible to find in popular Broome, nor are they particularly cheap. The *Roebuck Bay Caravan Park* (☎ (091) 92 1366) is conveniently central; tent/powered sites are from $14/16.50. *Lamb's Vacation Village* (☎ (091) 92 1057), Port Drive, has powered sites for $20 and chalets from $40. The *Broome Caravan Park* (☎ (091) 92 1776), on the Great Northern Highway four km from town, has tent sites and on-site vans.

Hostels Cheap beds in Broome are scarce but there are two hostel choices. On Bagot St, close to the centre and just a short stagger from the airport, is *Broome's Last Resort* (☎ (091) 93 5000), also an associate-YHA hostel. It's adequate and has a rock pool, large kitchen and courtesy bus. The accommodation is not cheap – dorm beds are $14 and twins or doubles are $36, all with shared facilities.

Also close to the centre is the *Broome Bunkhouse* (☎ (091) 92 1221), part of the Roebuck Bay Hotel, on Napier Terrace. Accommodation is rock-bottom, with beds in large dorms for $12 and four-bed units for $48. We dislike checking this place as it seems to get dirtier each time – our last visit was no exception, with the showers leaking on to very musty floors.

One new place is the *Ocean Lodge* (☎ (091) 93 7700), on Cable Beach Rd near the Port Drive turn-off. It has backpackers' rooms for $13 per person and units from $55.

Hotels, Motels & Resorts The *Broometime Lodge* (☎ (091) 93 5067) at 59 Forrest St has singles/doubles for $35/60 in the high season. This is good value for what you get; off-season discounts apply. The *Moonlight Bay Resort* (☎ (091) 93 7888), Carnarvon St extension, has one/two-bedroom units for $150/190 in the high season (off-peak rates are $110/140).

Park Court (☎ (091) 93 5887) in Haas St has small, tidy self-contained apartments, central and close to public telephones, the bus terminal, bank and civic centre. They are well worth the $50 in the off season.

The once legendary *Roebuck Bay Hotel*, the 'Roey' (☎ (091) 92 1221), on the corner of Carnarvon St and Napier Terrace in Chinatown, has single/double units from $55/65. The pool is the hotel's saving grace.

The *Mercure Hotel* (☎ (091) 92 1002) is a modern place on Weld St, at the corner of Louis St, with rooms from $88 a double. The *Mangrove Resort* (☎ (091) 92 1303) is down

near the water, about halfway between the Mercure and Chinatown (entrance off Carnarvon St); units are from $95 to $130.

The *Palms Resort* (☎ (091) 92 1898), on Hopton St, has studio units; those of a 'lesser classification' are from $85.

There are a couple of new places in town. A fabulous B&B option is *Harmony* (☎ (091) 93 7439) on Broome Rd four km from town; and *Tabitta Court* (☎ (091) 93 6026), Anne St, has units from $90.

Places to Eat

Light Meals & Fast Food Finding a place to stay in Broome may be a hassle but eating out is no sweat at all. *Bloom's*, Carnarvon St, serves a very generous cappuccino and has excellent croissants. *Mango Jack's*, on Hamersley St, has hamburgers, sandwiches, fish & chips and tasty kebabs. In the same little shopping centre as Mango Jack's there's *River Rooster* and *Broome Pizza & Pasta Bar*, which turns out good pizzas.

The Jekyll & Hyde *Dampier Coffee Shop*, Dampier Terrace, turns into *Hombres Mexican* at night. This will please any discerning lover of hot and spicy tacos, chicken enchiladas and burritos.

There's an average, pricey *bakery* in Chinatown, on the corner of Carnarvon and Short Sts. The Seaview shopping centre also has a bakery, as well as Broome's biggest supermarket, Charlie Carters. Get your fresh organically grown produce from the Saturday courthouse markets. There are two new supermarkets, one in Chinatown and one near the airport.

Pubs & Restaurants The Roey has the *Oasis Bar Pearlers*, an al fresco dining area with a seafood barbecue ($12) on Saturday night and an Italian banquet on Sunday ($19).

Chin's Chinese on Hamersley St has a variety of dishes from all over Asia. Prices range from $7 for a nasi goreng to $12 for other dishes. The takeaway is popular. Other Chinese specialists are *Wing's*, on Napier Terrace; *Tong's*, just around the corner; *Son*

Ming on Carnarvon St; and *Murray's Pearler's*, on Dampier Terrace.

In Johnny Chi Lane are *Fez*, a Mediterranean place, and *Noodle Fish*, which is a great place for economical lunches ($6 to $7 including delectable local fish). In the original gaol is the *Broome Lock-up*, a cafe in the real sense of the word, with friendly owners and great atmosphere.

Annelies is a Swiss restaurant on Napier Terrace near the Roebuck, and according to the locals it's quite a good place. The *Tea House*, situated at the end of Saville St in a mud-brick building with an outdoor dining area, has a great variety of Thai seafood dishes.

Other more expensive places include the restaurants in the resorts and motels. The Mercure Hotel has both a good bistro and a decent restaurant, the *Port Light*, and the Palms has the popular *Beer & Satay Hut*.

Entertainment

In Chinatown, *Sun Pictures*, the open-air cinema dating from 1916, is near Short St and has a programme of surprisingly recent releases. It is probably the longest-running picture garden in the world.

Despite an attempt to improve its appearance the *Roebuck Bay Hotel* still rocks along – just stand clear of the occasional fight both in the bar area and outside.

Nightclubs in town include the *Nippon Inn* in Dampier Terrace and the weekend band venue *Tokyo Joe's* in Napier Terrace.

Getting There & Away

Air Ansett's Darwin to Perth service passes through Broome daily. The flights then proceed to Perth via Port Hedland. On Saturday and Sunday there is a direct service from Broome to Alice Springs. Qantas has daily flights to Perth, a flight to Alice Springs on Saturday and to Darwin on Sunday, and a Darwin to Broome service Friday and Sunday. Skywest flies to Derby, Karratha and Kununurra.

Ansett's office (☎ (091) 93 5444) is on the corner of Barker and Weld Sts.

Bus Greyhound Pioneer goes through Broome on its Perth to Darwin route. Typical fares from Broome are $201 to Perth, $78 to Port Hedland, $27 to Derby and $176 to Darwin; there are many concessions. Its office (☎ (091) 92 1561) is at Broome Travel on Hamersley St.

McCafferty's also passes through Broome daily; their agent is the Broome tourist bureau. Their services are much cheaper as they are attempting to break into the west coast market. Broome to Darwin is $85, and Broome to Perth is $99.

Car Rental Hertz and Avis have offices near the entrance to the airport but there are better deals available if you just want something for bopping around town or out to the beach. Suzuki jeeps are popular. Local operators are Topless Rentals (☎ (091) 93 5017) on Hunter St; Woody's (☎ (091) 92 1791) on Napier Terrace; Broome *Broome* (☎ 1800 67 6725), in the Roey; and ATC (☎ (091) 93 7788).

Getting Around

To/From the Airport There are taxis to take you from the airport to your hotel (about $5 to Chinatown, considerably more to Cable Beach). However, the airport is so close to the centre that backpackers staying at the Last Resort, or elsewhere, can easily walk.

Bus There's an hourly Broome Coachlines bus (☎ (091) 92 1068) between the town, Seaview shopping centre and Cable Beach. The one-way fare is $2 (or 10 fares for $15). They also do a half-day tour ($32) which takes in the Deep Water jetty, Japanese cemetery, Gantheaume Point and Cable Beach.

Bicycle Cycling is the best way to see the area. There are at least three places that hire bicycles for $8 to $10 a day, including the backpackers places. The Broome Cycle Centre, on the corner of Hamersley and Frederick Sts, hires bikes, does repairs and gives good advice. Pedals of Broome (☎ (015) 241 815) includes a picnic hamper in the price of tandem hire – $35. Broome is an easy area to ride around; it's flat and you'll have no problem riding out to Cable Beach (about seven km) as long as it's not too windy. Stay on the roads or your tyres might be punctured by predatory thorns.

AROUND BROOME
Cable Beach

Six km from town is Cable Beach, the most popular swimming beach in Broome. It's a classic – white sand and turquoise water as far as the eye can see. You can hire surf boards and other beach and water equipment on the beach – parasailing ($50) is always popular. The northern side beyond the rock is a popular nude-bathing area. You can also take vehicles (other than motorbikes) onto this part of the beach, although at high tide access is limited because of the rocks, so take care not to get stranded.

Tandem skydiving is really popular at Cable Beach and the WA Skydiving Academy has tandem freefall jumps for $285 with video and a T-shirt ($190 without freefall); contact the tourist bureau.

Red Sun, and Ships of the Desert, are two companies operating camel rides along the beach; the best time is at sunset. The cost is $25 per hour; again, book at the tourist bureau.

Also on Cable Beach Rd is the **Broome**

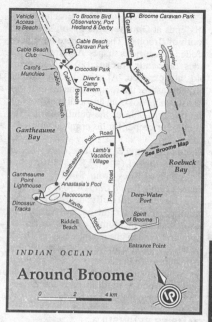

Around Broome

Vehicle Access to Beach
To Broome Bird Observatory, Port Hedland & Derby
Broome Caravan Park
Cable Beach Caravan Park
Cable Beach Club
Carol's Munchies
Crocodile Park
Diver's Camp Tavern
Great Northern Highway
Dampier Creek
Gantheaume Bay
Cable Beach
Cable Beach Road
Gantheaume Point Road
Gantheaume Point
Lamb's Vacation Village
See Broome Map
Roebuck Bay
Gantheaume Point Lighthouse
Anastasia's Pool
Racecourse
Port Road
Deep-Water Port
Dinosaur Tracks
Kavite Road
Spirit of Broome
Riddell Beach
Entrance Point
INDIAN OCEAN
0   2   4 km

Crocodile Park. It's open May to November daily from 10 am to 5 pm; reduced hours for the rest of the year. There are guided tours; check on ☎ (091) 92 1489. Admission is $10 (children $5).

Birdwatching at Roebuck Bay

Roebuck Bay is the most significant site in Australia for observing migratory waders, and it is believed that some 800,000 birds migrate here annually. The wide variety of habitats encourages a vast range of species. Only some of these are migratory, and over 270 species have been recorded, which is about one-third of Australia's total number of species. Furthermore, the 48 species of waders is nearly a quarter of all wader species in the world, and 22 of the 24 raptor (birds of prey) species found in Australia can be observed here.

The Royal Australian Ornithological Union has established an observatory (☎(091) 93 5600) on Crab Creek Rd, not far from the shores of Roebuck Bay. You can stay here and organise economical tours with the observatory staff. The Shorebird, Mangrove Bird and Bush Bird tours are $35 if taken from Broome, or $20 if you leave from the observatory. Tent/powered sites are $12/14, single/double bunk rooms are $22/28 and chalets are $50.

George Swann of Kimberley Birdwatching (☎(091) 92 1246) has a number of excellent birdwatching tours. Happy twitching! ■

The long sweep of Cable Beach eventually ends at **Gantheaume Point**, seven km south of Broome. The cliffs here have been eroded into curious shapes. At extremely low tides **dinosaur tracks**, 120 million years old, are exposed. At other times you can inspect casts of the footprints on the cliff top. Anastasia's Pool is an artificial rock pool on the northern side of the point, built by the lighthouse keeper for his crippled wife.

Places to Stay & Eat The *Cable Beach Caravan Park* (☎ (091) 92 2066) has tent/powered sites from $14/17. The upmarket *Cable Beach Club* (☎ (091) 92 2505) is a large, beautifully designed place, although it's not right on the beach. The resort has an incredibly expensive *restaurant*, and a much cheaper place, *Lord Mac's*, which is a good vantage point at sunset. For a great intimate breakfast try *Carol's Munchies*, which overlooks beautiful Cable Beach and for a boozy night there is the *Diver's Camp Tavern*, Cable Beach Rd.

DAMPIER PENINSULA
The **Willie Creek Pearl Farm** is 35 km north of Broome, off the Cape Leveque Rd. It offers a rare chance to see a working pearl farm and is worth the trip (cost of entrance is $15). During the Wet the road is open only to 4WD vehicles. Broome Coachlines (☎ (091) 92 1068) has daily tours ($45).

It's about 200 km from the turn-off nine km out of Broome to the Cape Leveque Lighthouse at the tip of the Dampier Peninsula. This flora and fauna paradise is a great spot for free humpback whale-watching. On the west coast of the peninsula is **Coulomb Point Nature Reserve**, established to protect unique pindan vegetation.

About halfway (120 km) is a diversion to the **Beagle Bay Aboriginal Community** (☎ (091) 92 4913) which has a beautiful church in the middle of a green. Inside is an altar stunningly decorated with mother-of-pearl. A fee of $5 is charged for entry into the community; fuel is available every day.

Just before Cape Leveque is **Lombadina Aboriginal Community** (☎ (091) 92 4942)

which has a church built from mangrove wood. One-day and overnight mud-crabbing and traditional fishing tours are available with the Bardi people; the tourist bureau has details on the tours and accommodation. Petrol and diesel are available every day except Sunday. A $5 per car permit is required from the office.

Cape Leveque itself, about 200 km from Broome, has a lighthouse and wonderful beaches. Sunset here is truly memorable and a great photo opportunity.

Take note that the communities won't want you to stay on their land, but if you want to see their churches or buy something from their shops they will be helpful. Permission to visit other areas must be obtained in advance. Check with the tourist bureau about road conditions and permits.

Organised Tours
Over the Top Adventure Tours (☎ (091) 93 7700) has an interesting trip which includes Beagle and Pender bays, Lombadina and its beautiful beach, and mystical Cape Leveque. Flaktrak (☎ (091) 92 1487) and Pearl Coast 4WD (☎ (091) 93 5786) also operate tours to the peninsula. Kimberley Detours (☎ (091) 92 1276) has a great one-day tour along the coast north of Broome, from Sunday to Wednesday. It costs $90.

Places to Stay
There is accommodation at *Kooljaman* (☎ (091) 92 4970). In the high season, tent/powered sites are $11/15, exotic beach shelters are $30, cabins without/with en suite are $80/90 and family units are $50; all prices, except for camping, drop in the off season. Bush-tucker and mud-crabbing tours are available, as are all types of vehicle fuel except LPG.

DERBY (pop 4000)
Derby, only 220 km from Broome, is a major administrative centre for the west Kimberley and a good point from which to travel to the spectacular gorges in the region. The road beyond Derby continues inland to Fitzroy Crossing (256 km) and Halls Creek (288 km

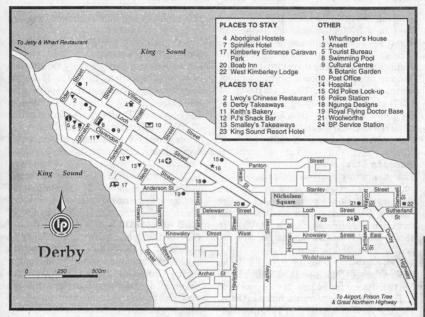

To Jetty & Wharf Restaurant

King Sound

PLACES TO STAY
4 Aboriginal Hostels
7 Spinifex Hotel
17 Kimberley Entrance Caravan Park
20 Boab Inn
22 West Kimberley Lodge

PLACES TO EAT
2 Lwoy's Chinese Restaurant
6 Derby Takeaways
11 Keith's Bakery
12 PJ's Snack Bar
13 Smalley's Takeaways
23 King Sound Resort Hotel

OTHER
1 Wharfinger's House
3 Ansett
5 Tourist Bureau
8 Swimming Pool
9 Cultural Centre & Botanic Garden
10 Post Office
14 Hospital
15 Old Police Lock-up
16 Police Station
18 Ngunga Designs
19 Royal Flying Doctor Base
21 Woolworths
24 BP Service Station

King Sound

Derby

0   250   500m

To Airport, Prison Tree & Great Northern Highway

WESTERN AUSTRALIA

farther on). Alternatively, there's the much wilder Gibb River Rd. Derby is on King Sound, north of the mouth of the mighty Fitzroy, which drains the west Kimberley region.

Information

The tourist bureau (☎ (091) 91 1426), at 1 Clarendon St, is open weekdays from 8.30 am to 4.30 pm and Saturday from 8 to 11.30 am. In the high season it is open daily. Get the *Welcome to Derby* and *Derby & Fitzroy Crossing* leaflets.

Things to See

Derby's cultural centre and botanic garden are just off Clarendon St. There's a small museum and art gallery in **Wharfinger's House**, at the end of Loch St. This has been restored as an example of early housing in the area. Derby's lofty **wharf** has not been used since 1983 for shipping, but it provides a handy fishing spot for the locals. The whole

town is surrounded by huge expanses of mud flats, baked hard in the Dry and occasionally flooded by king tides.

The **Prison Tree**, near the airport, seven km south of town, is a huge boab tree with a hollow trunk 14 metres around. It is said to have been used as a temporary lock-up years ago. Nearby is **Myall's Bore**, a 120-metre-long cattle trough.

Tours & Cruises

From Derby there are flights over King Sound to the BHP-owned **Koolan** and **Cockatoo islands**. You can't land there unless invited by a resident, but scenic flights are available to some of the 800 adjoining islands of the **Buccaneer Archipelago**. Aerial Enterprises (☎ (091) 91 1132) and Derby Air Services (☎ (091) 93 1375) provide two-hour flights for about $110 to the Buccaneer Archipelago; minimum of four. Buccaneer Sea Safaris (☎ (091) 91 1991) does extended tours up the Kimberley coast (including the horizontal falls of Talbot Bay) in a 30-foot aluminium mono-hull (about $195 per day, minimum of four).

Bush Track Safaris (☎ (091) 91 4644) operates four to 10-day tours into the remote Walcott Inlet area. Other land-based tour companies are Boab Tours (☎ (091) 91 1237) which has one-day fishing and rainforest tours ($80) and Hot Land Safaris (☎ (091) 93 1312) which operates a two-day Fitzroy River delta safari ($200).

Places to Stay

The *Kimberley Entrance Caravan Park* (☎ (091) 93 1055), Rowan St, has tent/powered sites for $12/15 and on-site vans for $40. It is a nice place with free barbecues. *Aboriginal Hostels* (☎ (091) 91 1867), at 233 Villiers St, charges $10 per person; a two-course meal is $7.

West Kimberley Lodge (☎ (091) 91 1031), on the corner of Sutherland and Stanwell Sts, has twin rooms for $45.

There are a couple of regular hotels in Derby. The *Spinifex Hotel* (☎ (091) 91 1233), on Clarendon St, has standard singles/doubles at $35/45; there are basic backpackers' rooms for $15 per person. The *Boab Inn* (☎ (091) 91 1044), Loch St, is more motel-like with singles/doubles for $55/65.

Places to Eat

The *Spinifex Hotel*, *Boab Inn* and the *King Sound Resort* all do counter meals. At the Boab there's a wide choice of good food from $10 to $15. The specials at the Spinifex are $5.50. *Keith's Bakery*, just down from the tourist bureau, is good for lunch and has excellent sandwiches. *Albert's Kitchen* in the Clarendon St Arcade is another place for a quick meal, as are *Derby Takeaways* and *Jabiru Cafe*, both in Clarendon St.

At the end of Loch St there's *Lwoy's Chinese Restaurant*. Out at the jetty is the *Wharf*, which has a BYO section; local seafood is their speciality.

Five km from town on the highway is the *Boab Tea Garden*.

Bands can usually be heard at the local hotels on Thursday, Friday and Saturday. If you are lucky you may be invited to one of the legendary marsh parties.

Getting There & Away

Skywest flies to Broome daily from where there are connections to Perth. There are daily services to Kununurra (except Tuesday and Thursday) and a flight to Karratha on Tuesday and Thursday. Ansett's office (☎ (091) 91 1266) is at 14 Loch St.

Greyhound Pioneer and McCafferty's stop in Derby at the tourist bureau. Typical fares are $27 to Broome, $108 to Kununurra, $220 to Perth and $151 to Darwin. Currently McCafferty's is about half these prices, but for how long no one knows.

GIBB RIVER ROAD

This is the 'back road' from Derby to Wyndham or Kununurra. At 667 km it's more direct by several hundred km than the Fitzroy Crossing to Halls Creek route. It's almost all dirt, although it doesn't require a 4WD when it has been recently graded (which is not always the case) but in the Wet the road is impassable. You can also reach many of the Kimberley gorges from this road without a 4WD. Fuel is available at the Mt House, Mt Barnett, El Questro, Durack River and Home Valley stations.

The Kimberley gorges are the major reason for taking this route. You could also make a day trip south to the Windjana and Tunnel Creek gorges (see Devonian Reef National Parks later in this section). Get a copy of *The Gibb River and Kalumburu Roads* from information centres. There's no public transport along the Gibb River Rd – in fact, there's little traffic of any sort, so don't bother trying to hitch.

Derby to Mt Barnett

From Derby the bitumen extends only 62 km. It's 119 km to the Windjana Gorge (21 km) and Tunnel Creek (51 km) turn-off and you can continue down that turn-off to Highway 1 near Fitzroy Crossing.

The Lennard River bridge is crossed at 122 km. At 184 km there is a turn-off to *Mt Hart Homestead* (☎ (091) 91 4645), which is 50 km down a rough dirt road. This is the CALM centre for a new national park which has been established to conserve the Leopold Ranges and gorges. Dinner, B&B is $60 per person; you must book in advance and there is no camping.

Two km farther (190 km) is the turn-off to the **Lennard River Gorge**, eight km off the road along a 4WD track. At 246 km there's the signposted turn-off to *Mt House Station* (☎ (091) 91 4649), where there's fuel, stores, tent sites are $5 and singles/doubles (by prior arrangement) are $35/50.

The turn-off to **Adcock Gorge** is at 267 km. This gorge is five km off the road and is good for swimming, with some fine rocks for jumping or diving off, although you should check for rocks beneath the water before doing so. If the waterfall is not flowing too fiercely, climb up above it for a good view of the surrounding country. You can camp at Adcock Gorge although the site is rocky and there's little shade.

Galvans Gorge is 700 metres off the road, at 286 km. The camp site has good shade, and in the gorge is a swimming hole.

Mt Barnett & Manning Gorge

The Aboriginal-owned and run *Mt Barnett Station* (☎ (091) 91 7007) is at the 306-km point. There's a roadhouse (ice is available) and a small store. It's also the access point for Manning Gorge, which lies seven km off the road along an easy dirt track. There's an entry fee of $4 per person, and this covers you for camping.

The camp site is right by the water hole, but the best part of the gorge is about a 1¼-hour walk along the far bank – walk around the right of the water hole to pick up the track, which is marked with empty drink cans strung up in the trees. It's a strenuous walk and, because the track runs inland from the gorge, you should carry drinking water.

After the hot and sweaty walk, you are rewarded with this most beautiful gorge. It has a waterfall and high rocks for daredevils.

Mt Barnett to Kununurra

First up after Mt Barnett, at 328 km, is the turn-off to the **Barnett River Gorge**, three km down the road. This is a good swimming spot, and if you scan the lower level of the cliff face on the far side you should be able to spot a number of Aboriginal paintings.

The *Mt Elizabeth Station* (☎ (091) 91 4644) lies 30 km off the road at the 338-km mark. Homestead accommodation is available but this must be arranged in advance; dinner, bed and breakfast is $70 per person.

At 419 km you come to the turn-off to the spectacular **Mitchell Falls** and **Kalumburu Aboriginal Reserve**. From the turn-off, it is 162 km to the Mitchell Plateau track and 267 km to the reserve. This is remote, 4WD territory and should not be travelled without adequate preparation; you need an entry permit (☎ (091) 61 4317) prior to arrival. At *Drysdale River cattle station* (☎ (091) 61 4326), B&B costs $30 per person.

There's some magnificent scenery between the Kalumburu turn-off and Jack's Waterhole on the Durack River Station (☎ (091) 61 4324) at 542 km. Apart from fuel, there's also accommodation ($75 for dinner, B&B) or camping for $5. The owners run tours from the station.

At 599 km you get some excellent views of the **Cockburn Ranges** off to the south, and shortly after is the turn-off to *Home Valley Station* (☎ (091) 61 4322), which has camping ($5) and homestead accommodation ($75 per person dinner, B&B).

The large **Pentecost River** is forded at 610 km, but this crossing can be dodgy if there's any amount of water in the river. During the Dry it poses no problems.

El Questro (☎ (091) 69 1777) is another station offering a variety of accommodation, including riverside camping ($5); it lies 16 km off the road at the 634-km mark. This is also the access point for the **Chamberlain Gorge**, 16 km from the turn-off, and Zebedee springs.

The last attraction on the road to Kununurra is **Emma Gorge** at 645 km. A pleasant camping area lies two km off the road, and from here it's about a 40-minute walk to the spectacular gorge. This gorge is close enough to Kununurra to make it a popular weekend escape.

At 667 km you reach bitumen road – Wyndham is to the north, Kununurra is east.

Organised Tours

Kununurra's Desert Inn runs four-day camping trips along the road for $350; these are excellent value.

There are guided trips to the Mitchell Plateau; enquire at the Broome, Derby and Kununurra tourist bureaus. Highlights include waterfalls, Surveyor's Pool, the *Livistonia eastonii* palm and ancient Wandjina art sites, with unique headdress paintings which are typical of Kimberley-style art. Kimberley Air Safari & Eco Tours (☎ (091) 69 1326) has a full-day air and 4WD trip to the Mitchell Plateau; the cost is from $320 per person (minimum of four).

DEVONIAN REEF NATIONAL PARKS

The west Kimberley boasts three national parks, based on gorges which were once part of a western coral 'great barrier reef' in the Devonian era, 350 million years ago. The magnificent **Geikie Gorge** is just 18 km north of Fitzroy Crossing. Part of the gorge, on the Fitzroy River, is in a small national park. During the Wet the river rises nearly 17 metres and in the Dry it stops flowing, leaving only a series of water holes.

The vegetation around this beautiful gorge is dense and there is also much wildlife, including freshwater crocodiles, wallaroos and the rare black-footed wallaby. Sawfish and stingrays, usually only found in or close to the sea, can also be seen in the river. Visitors must at all times stick to the pre-scribed 1.5-km walking track along the west bank.

During the April to November Dry there's a 1½-hour boat trip up the river daily at 9 am and 3 pm. It costs $15 (children $2) and covers 16 km of the gorge. There's a weekday bus (☎ (091) 91 5155) to Geikie from Fitzroy Crossing at 8 am which connects with the morning trip. It is $15 return (children $5).

You can go to the gorge with Darngku Heritage Cruise (☎ (091) 91 5355), who show you a lot more than just rocks and water. These Bunuba people reveal secrets of bush tucker, and tell stories of the region and Aboriginal culture. The cost of $95 includes the ride from Fitzroy Crossing, the river trip and lunch beside the river (it is $75 from Geikie).

You can visit the spectacular formations of Windjana Gorge and Tunnel Creek from the Gibb River Rd, or make a detour off the main highway between Fitzroy Crossing and Derby onto Leopold Station Rd, which only adds about 40 km to the distance.

The walls at the **Windjana Gorge** soar 90 metres above the Lennard River, which rushes through in the Wet but becomes just a series of pools in the Dry. More than likely the deafening screech of corellas and the persistent horseflies will keep you out of the gorge during the middle of the day. Three km from the river are the ruins of **Lillimilura**, an early homestead and, from 1893, a police station. Nightly camping fees for this gorge are $5 (children $1).

Tunnel Creek is a 750-metre-long tunnel which the creek has cut right through a spur of the Napier Range. The tunnel is generally from three to 15 metres wide and you can walk all the way along it. You'll need a good light and sturdy shoes; be prepared to wade through cold chest-deep water in places. Don't attempt it during the Wet, as the creek may flood suddenly. Halfway through, a collapse has created a shaft to the range's top.

Over the Top Tours (☎ (091) 93 7700) operates popular two-day trips combining Windjana and Tunnel Creek with Geikie Gorge, a good way of seeing three sites in one trip; the cost is about $180. West Kimberley Tours (☎ (091) 93 1442) in Derby has day trips out to Tunnel Creek and Windjana; the cost is $75 per person. From Broome, Kimberley Detours (☎ (091) 92 1276) has a two-day tour into the Kimberley, taking in the gorges, Derby and Fitzroy Crossing. It includes an overnight bush camp; cost is $190.

FITZROY CROSSING (pop 1100)

A tiny settlement where the Great Northern Highway crosses the Fitzroy River, this is

Jandamarra ('Pigeon')

Windjana Gorge, Tunnel Creek and Lillimilura were the scene of the adventures of an Aboriginal tracker, Jandamarra, nicknamed 'Pigeon'. In November 1894 Pigeon shot two police colleagues and then led a band of dissident Aboriginal people which skilfully evaded search parties for more than two years. During this time Pigeon killed another four men, but in early 1897 he was trapped and killed at Tunnel Creek. He and his small band had hidden in the seemingly inaccessible gullies of the adjoining Napier Range.

For the full story, get a copy of the *Pigeon Heritage Trail* from the Derby or Broome tourist bureaus ($1.50), or *Jandamarra and the Bunuba Resistance* by Howard Pedersen and Banjo Woorunmurra. ■

another place from which you can get to the gorges and water holes of the area. The old town site is on Russ St, north-east of the present town. The Crossing Inn, near Brooking Creek, is the oldest pub in the Kimberley.

The new, large Fitzroy Crossing tourist office (☎ (091) 91 5355) is on the highway next to the service station. It is open daily, April to November (for less time in the Wet).

Places to Stay & Eat

The *Tarunda Caravan Park* (☎ (091) 91 5330), in town, is a reasonable if dusty place, where powered camp sites cost $15. The *Fitzroy River Lodge* (☎ (091) 91 5141), two km east of town on the banks of the Fitzroy River, is the pick of the bunch. A tent/powered site is $15/16 and you are allowed to use the motel pool for free. Single/double air-con safari tents cost $65/80, while motel units cost $85/100.

In the Old Post Office on Geikie Gorge Rd, about four km from town, you'll find *Darlngunaya Backpackers* (☎ (091) 91 5140); dorm beds are $12. All backpackers get picked up and returned to the bus stop at the roadhouse.

The *Crossing Inn* (☎ (091) 91 5080) has B&B singles/twins for $60/73. It can get pretty noisy as there is a rather colourful, if a little unsavoury, bar next door. If you stay here, there's a good chance you will meet the friendly Bunuba people. They may even invite you to a barbecue or on a fishing trip.

It is cheaper to prepare food for yourself in this town. If your margarine is runny and

the cheese you bought yesterday stinks then the *Homestead* in the Fitzroy River Lodge does reasonable meals.

HALLS CREEK (pop 1300)

Halls Creek, in the centre of the Kimberley and on the edge of the Great Sandy Desert, was traditionally the land of the Jaru and Kija people. Graziers took over in the 1870s and virtually turned these people into slave labourers on the stations. When the stations were sold, about 100 years later, the Aboriginal people drifted to the nearby town and its associated boredom and alcohol. The region was the site of the 1885 gold rush, the first in WA. The gold soon petered out and today the town is a cattle centre, 14 km from the original site where some crumbling remains can still be seen.

Five km east of Halls Creek and then about 1.5 km off the road there's the natural **China Wall** – so called because it resembles the Great Wall of China. This subvertical quartz vein is short but very picturesquely situated.

Halls Creek **Old Town** is a great place for fossicking. All that remains of the once bustling mining town are the ant bed and spinifex walls of the old post office, the cemetery and a huge bottle pile where a pub once stood. 'Old Town' is in fact the general term for the hilly area behind Halls Creek and gold might be found anywhere there. There are tent and powered sites available (☎ (091) 68 8999). You can swim in Caroline Pool, Sawpit Gorge and Palm Springs.

Although Halls Creek is a comfortable

enough little place it's as well to remember that it sits on the edge of a distinctly inhospitable stretch of country. The Halls Creek tourist centre (☎ (091) 68 6262) on the Great Northern Highway has lots of information and handles bookings for tours.

Places to Stay & Eat

The *Halls Creek Caravan Park* (☎ (091) 68 6169), on Roberta Ave towards the airport, has tent/powered sites for $12/14 and on-site vans for $38.

Opposite is the *Kimberley Hotel* (☎ (091) 68 6101). It has a variety of rooms from $65/80 for singles/doubles and currently offers backpackers' accommodation at $20. This hotel, with its 'segregated' bars, best exhibits both the rough and smooth sides of this frontier town. On the Great Northern Highway there is the *Shell Roadhouse* (☎ (091) 68 6060) with cabins from $55 and the *Halls Creek Motel* (☎ (091) 68 6001) with single/double units from $50/65.

The Kimberley Hotel has a pleasant casual bar with standard counter meals at $10. You can eat out at the tables on the grass. Inside there's a surprisingly swish restaurant with smorgasbord meals at $16. The *Poinciana* roadhouse has takeaways and a restaurant.

Getting There & Away

Greyhound Pioneer buses pass through Halls Creek early in the morning (northbound) and late at night (southbound). McCafferty's gets in at a much more reasonable time – 10.10 am (southbound) and 3.50 pm (northbound).

WOLFE CREEK METEORITE CRATER

The 835-metre-wide and 50-metre-deep Wolfe Creek meteorite crater is the second-largest in the world where meteorite fragments have been found. To the local Jaru Aboriginal people, the crater, which they call Kandimalal, marks the spot where a snake emerged from the desert.

The turn-off to the Wolfe Creek Crater National Park is 16 km out of Halls Creek towards Fitzroy Crossing and from there it's 130 km by unsealed road to the south. It's accessible without 4WD (with care), but

you'll need to carry enough fuel, food and water for a return trip, as there are no supplies available at the park. If you can't handle one more outback road you can fly over the crater from Halls Creek for $95 with the local operators – Oasis Air (☎ (091) 68 6462), Kingfisher Aviation (☎ (091) 68 6162) and Crocodile Air (☎ (091) 68 6250).

From Carranya the road, known as the Tanami Track, goes all the way to Alice Springs nearly 900 km away.

BUNGLE BUNGLE (PURNULULU) NATIONAL PARK

The Bungle Bungle (Purnululu) National Park is an amazing spectacle which shouldn't be missed, with its spectacular rounded rock towers, striped like tigers in alternate bands of orange (silica) and black (lichen). The only catch is that the range is hard to get to. Because the rock formations are very fragile you are not allowed to climb them. The name *purnululu* is sandstone in the local Kija language and bungle bungle is thought to be a misspelling of bundle bundle, a common Kimberley grass.

Echidna Chasm in the north or **Cathedral Gorge** in the south are only about a one-hour walk from the car park at the road's end. However, the soaring **Piccaninny Gorge** is an 18-km round trip that takes eight to 10 hours return to walk. Access to the park costs $11 per adult and $1 for a child; this entitles you to seven nights in the park and fuel for campfires. The restricted gorges in the northern part of the park can only be seen from the air, but they are a memorable sight.

From the main highway it's 55 km to a track junction known as Three Ways where there is a rangers' station. From here it's seven km north to *Kurrajong Camp* and 13 km south to *Walardi Camp*. Fire sites and firewood are supplied. Kurrajong and Walardi have toilets, water and individual camp sites. There is no rubbish disposal at either camp so take out what you bring in.

Scenic Flights

As the range is so vast, flights and helicopter rides over the Bungles are popular – it's money well spent. The chopper rides cost $120 for a 45-minute flight from Walardi camp site, or $130 in a faster helicopter from Warmun (Turkey Creek) Roadhouse, on the main highway. This latter flight is a popular option for people without a 4WD. The chopper rides, operated by Heliwork WA (part of Slingair), are most impressive because they fly right in, among and over the deep, narrow gorges, while light planes have to remain above 700 metres.

Flights from Kununurra are $140 and they fly over Lake Argyle and the Argyle Diamond Mine. Out of Halls Creek, the flights to the Bungles only are $110.

Getting There & Away
The 55-km-track from Highway 1 to Three Ways requires a 4WD and takes two hours. From Three Ways it's 20 km north to Echidna Chasm, and 30 km south to Picca-ninny Creek.

The best option if you don't have a 4WD is to take a tour from Kununurra or Halls Creek. Kimberley Wilderness Adventures (☎ (091) 68 1253) and Desert Inn 4WD Adventures (☎ (091) 68 2702) have two-day tours to the Bungles from $220.

WYNDHAM (pop 860)
Wyndham, a sprawling town, is suffering from Kununurra's boom in popularity but its **Five Rivers Lookout** on top of Mt Bastion is still a must. From there you can see the King, Pentecost, Durack, Forrest and Ord rivers enter the Cambridge Gulf. The view is particularly good at sunrise and sunset.

When the tide is right you can observe (from a distance) large saltwater **crocodiles** near the water. A hideous 20-metre ferro-concrete croc greets you as you arrive in town if you happen to miss the real ones.

The **Moochalabra Dam** is a popular fishing and picnic spot about 25 km away. Near the dam are some Aboriginal paintings and another prison boab tree.

Not far from Wyndham is the **Marlgu Billabong** of Parry Lagoons Reserve, a wet-lands which hosts many bird species.

Highly recommended by a number of readers is Wundargoodie Aboriginal Safaris (☎ (091) 61 1054) in O'Donnell St, Wyndham Port. Half-day/one-day tours cost $60/100, ex-Wyndham, and include bush medicine, bush tucker and Aboriginal rock art.

There is a bus service (☎ (091) 61 1201) between Kununurra and Wyndham; the cost is $20 (children $10).

Places to Stay
The *Three Mile Caravan Park* (☎ (091) 61 1064) has tent and powered sites, and shade trees for campers. At the *Wyndham Town Hotel* (☎ (091) 61 1003), on O'Donnell St, rooms cost from $60, and you can try the *Wyndham Community Club* (☎ (091) 61 1130) for cheaper but more basic rooms; singles/doubles are from $40/50.

KUNUNURRA (pop 5000)
In the Miriwoong language, this region is known as 'gananoorrang' – Kununurra is the European version of this word. Founded in the 1960s, Kununurra is in the centre of the Ord River irrigation scheme and is quite a modern and bustling little town. In the past it was just a stopover on the main highway and there was little incentive to linger. That has all changed in recent years with the increase in tourism and there are now enough recreational activities, most of them water-based, to keep you busy for a week.

The town is also a popular place to look for work. The main picking season starts in May and ends about September. Ask at the Desert Inn, Kununurra Backpackers or CES.

Information
The tourist bureau (☎ (091) 68 1177) on Coolibah Drive has information on the town and the Kimberley. It's open weekdays from 8 am to 5 pm, and weekends from 8.30 am to 4 pm. There's a 1½-hour time difference between Kununurra and Katherine in the Northern Territory. Strict quarantine restrictions apply when entering WA.

Lake Kununurra (Diversion Dam)
Lily Creek Lagoon is a mini-wetlands

WESTERN AUSTRALIA

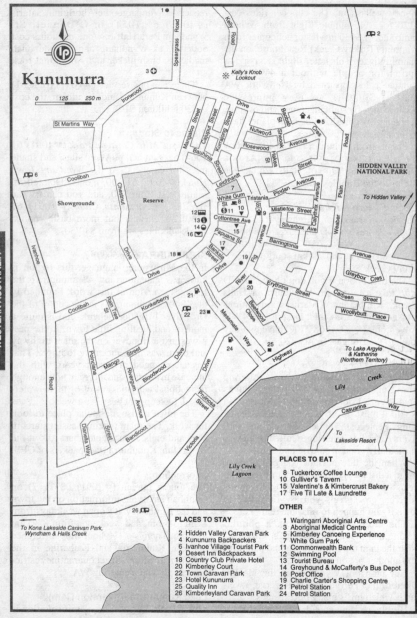

Kununurra

0   125   250 m

St Martins Way

Ironwood Street

Speargrass Road

Kelly Road

Kelly's Knob Lookout

Baobab Street

Nutwood Avenue

Rosewood

Hakea Street

Mangako Street

Cajuput Street

Kurrajong Street

Bauhinia Street

Coolibah

Chestnut Drive

Ivanhoe Drive

Showgrounds

Reserve

Leichhardt

White Gum St

Cottontree Ave

Papuana St

Banksia Street

Drive

Tristania St

Pindan Avenue

Mistletoe Street

Silverbox Ave

Barringtonia

River

Erythrina Street

Fig Avenue

Avenue

Plain

Weaber Road

HIDDEN VALLEY NATIONAL PARK

To Hidden Valley

Calytrix Avenue

Greybox Cres

Carbeen Street

Woollybutt Place

Coolibah

Palm Tree St

Konkerberry Drive

Messmate Way

Beachwood Close

Poinciana Street

Mango Street

Rivergum Avenue

Bloodwood Drive

Bandicoot

Primrose Street

Victoria Highway

Dianella Way

Road

To Kona Lakeside Caravan Park, Wyndham & Halls Creek

Lily Creek Lagoon

To Lake Argyle & Katherine (Northern Territory)

Lily Creek

Casuarina Way

To Lakeside Resort

WESTERN AUSTRALIA

PLACES TO EAT

8 Tuckerbox Coffee Lounge
10 Gulliver's Tavern
15 Valentine's & Kimbercrust Bakery
17 Five Til Late & Laundrette

OTHER

1 Waringarri Aboriginal Arts Centre
3 Aboriginal Medical Centre
5 Kimberley Canoeing Experience
7 White Gum Park
11 Commonwealth Bank
12 Swimming Pool
13 Tourist Bureau
14 Greyhound & McCafferty's Bus Depot
16 Post Office
19 Charlie Carter's Shopping Centre
21 Petrol Station
24 Petrol Station

PLACES TO STAY

2 Hidden Valley Caravan Park
4 Kununurra Backpackers
6 Ivanhoe Village Tourist Park
9 Desert Inn Backpackers
18 Country Club Private Hotel
20 Kimberley Court
22 Town Caravan Park
23 Hotel Kununurra
25 Quality Inn
26 Kimberleyland Caravan Park

beside the town and has plenty of birdlife. Lake Kununurra, also called the Diversion Dam, has picnic spots and is popular with water-skiers and boating enthusiasts. There's good fishing below the Lower Dam (watch for crocodiles) and also on the Ord River at **Ivanhoe Crossing**. If you dare to swim there, be careful.

Other Attractions

There are good views of the irrigated fields from **Kelly's Knob Lookout**, close to the centre of town. During the Wet, distant thunderstorms are spectacular when viewed from the lookout, although caution is needed as the Knob itself is frequently struck by lightning.

Hidden Valley, in **Mirima National Park** and only a couple of km from the centre of town, is a wonderful little park with a steep gorge, some great views and short walking tracks. The banded formations in the park are reminiscent of the Bungle Bungles and are of great spiritual importance to the Miriwoong people.

The **Packsaddle Plains**, six km out of town, has the touristy Zebra Rock Gallery. Farther along this road you will find produce farms (bananas and mangos) which are open to the public. On Ivanhoe Plains look out for the Melon Farm, the Wilf Ord Plantation, Bara Bara Bananas and the dairy farm.

About 250 km south of Kununurra is the huge **Argyle Diamond Mine** which produces around 35% of the world's diamonds, although most are only of industrial quality. There is no public access to the mine and tours, which must be booked through Belray Diamond Tours (☎ (091) 68 1014), cost from $130.

Tours & Flights

Canoe trips on the Ord River, between Lake Argyle and the Diversion Dam, are very popular amongst travellers. A recommended operation, Kimberley Canoeing Experience (☎ (091) 69 1257), has three-day self-guided tours for $90, with all gear supplied and transport to the dam included. They also run half-day wildlife and birdwatching trips.

The highly recommended Kimberley Ecotours Australia (☎ (091) 68 2116) has an informative sunset, wildlife and croc spotting tour ($30) on Tuesday, Thursday and Saturday evenings.

Duncan's Ord River Tours (☎ (091) 68 1823) visits places of interest on the lake and out on the Packsaddle Plains, including the Zebra Rock Gallery and a banana plantation; the trips are from $24. Triple J (☎ (091) 68 2682) operates high-speed boats along the beautiful section of the Ord between Lake Argyle and Kununurra; the cost is $70 to $95, including lunch.

Flights over the Bungle Bungles are popular and cost $145 a person (discounts apply). They take about two hours and also fly over Lake Argyle, the Argyle and Bow River diamond projects and the irrigation area north of the town. Contact Alligator Airways (☎ (091) 68 1333), Slingair (☎ (091) 69 1300), or Kimberley Air Safaris & Eco-Tours (☎ (091) 69 1326) in Kununurra, or Heliwork WA (☎ (091) 68 1811) in Warmun (Turkey Creek).

Barramundi is the major fishing attraction, but other fish are also caught. Half-day boat trips operated by Ultimate Adventures (☎ (091) 68 2310) and Kimberley Sport Fishing (☎ (091) 68 2752) cost from $70.

Places to Stay

During the Dry (high season) accommodation is scarce in this town, so book well ahead. The standard reaction, if you arrive in town and find no place to stay, is 'Stiff luck!'

Camping Kununurra has five caravan parks with tent/powered sites from $12/14. The *Town Caravan Park* (☎ (091) 68 1763) on Bloodwood Drive has on-site vans for $45; the *Ivanhoe Village Tourist Park* (☎ (091) 69 1995) is on the corner of Ivanhoe Rd and Coolibah Drive; the *Hidden Valley Caravan Park* (☎ (091) 68 1790) is on Weaber Plain Rd; *Kimberleyland* (☎ (091) 68 1280) is on the edge of the lagoon near town; and the *Kona Lakeside* (☎ (091) 68 1031), Lake View Drive, has comfy park homes for $85.

Hostels The *Desert Inn Backpackers* (☎ (091) 68 2702) is on Tristania St, opposite Gulliver's Tavern in the centre of town. This friendly and popular purpose-built complex has full facilities, including a spa pool; dorm beds are from $13 and doubles from $30.

At 112 Nutwood Crescent is *Kununurra Backpackers* (☎ (091) 69 1998). It's in a couple of adjacent houses about five minutes walk from the centre of town. The shaded pool is a big drawcard, but kids aren't welcome; dorm beds are from $13 and twins from $30.

Hotels Hotel accommodation is expensive. The *Country Club Private Hotel* (☎ (091) 68 1024) on Coolibah Drive has shabby, cell-like budget twin rooms for $50; up-market rooms are from $120 and it has a functional pool.

Kimberley Court (☎ (091) 68 1411), on the corner of River Fig Ave and Erythrina St, has singles/doubles for $84/94. The *Hotel Kununurra* (☎ (091) 68 1344), Messmate Way, is the town's main hotel and in its motel section rooms are from $78/96; budget cells are $25.

The *Quality Inn* (☎ (091) 68 1455) is on the main highway and has rooms available from $115. The *Lakeside Resort* (☎ (091) 69 1092), by Lily Creek Lagoon on Casuarina Way, has a restaurant and pool.

Places to Eat
The *Five Til Late Cafe*, on Banksia St, offers takeaway tucker and light meals; *Valentine's Pizzeria* and the *Kimbercrust Bakery*, both on Cottontree Ave, are open daily. Just off Coolibah Drive, the *Tuckerbox Coffee Lounge* serves good salads and excellent salad rolls ($2.50), and its small lunch-of-the-day servings at $3.50 are unbeatable value.

Gulliver's Tavern, on Konkerberry Drive, is a popular drinking hole and has good meals (fish & chips for $6.50). The Country Club has the Chinese *Chopsticks* (mains $17.50) and at its *Kelly's Bar & Grill*, in a beautiful tropical setting, you can get excellent steaks with potato and salad for $16.50.

The Quality Inn's *Ivanhoe's Gallery* is the best restaurant in town; a three-course buffet costs $24.

Things to Buy
The Waringarri Aboriginal Arts Centre is on Speargrass Rd, at the turn-off to Kelly's Knob, and the Ochre Gallery is in the town centre. Both are good places to purchase authentic Kimberley Aboriginal art.

Also of interest is Nina's Jewellery, in Konkerberry Drive. Here you can see the famous champagne diamonds from the Argyle mine. The friendly staff explain carat weight, cut, clarity and colour.

Getting There & Away
Air Ansett flies to Darwin and Perth daily, either Ansett or Skywest go to Broome daily (except Tuesday) and Skywest flies to Derby daily except Tuesday and Thursday. There is currently a cheap one-way fare from Darwin to Kununurra on Wednesday ($102 all seasons).

Ansett's office (☎ (091) 68 1622) is in the Charlie Carter shopping complex.

Bus Greyhound Pioneer and McCafferty's travel through Kununurra on the Darwin to Perth route. Greyhound fares are $121 to Broome, $55 to Halls Creek, $50 to Katherine and $100 to Darwin. McCafferty's prices are cheaper on all these routes.

LAKE ARGYLE
Created by the Ord River Dam, Lake Argyle is the second biggest storage reservoir in Australia, holding nine times as much water as Sydney Harbour. Prior to its construction, there was too much water in the Wet and not enough in the Dry. By providing a regular water supply the dam has encouraged agriculture on a massive scale.

At the lake there's a **pioneer museum** in the old Argyle Homestead, moved here when its original site was flooded. The *Lake Argyle Village* has expensive rooms (for what they are) and camp sites. Boats depart from here for lake cruises each morning and afternoon. Downstream of the lake there is now green

Christmas & Cocos (Keeling) Islands

Often forgotten are Australia's Indian Ocean protectorates, Christmas Island and the Cocos (Keeling) Islands, about 2300 and 2750 km north-west of Perth respectively. Both places are wildlife havens and are island paradises.

The average temperature around Christmas is 27°C, but being near the equator it is humid; rain falls between December and April. In the Cocos group temperatures are similar with two distinct periods: the hot and sultry 'doldrums' from October to March and the cooler 'trades' from April to September.

Christmas Island is some 137 sq km in area and over 60% of this has been declared national park. It was named on Christmas Day 1643, but the first recorded landing, by William Dampier, did not occur until 1688. Phosphate was mined from 1897 until 1987 and there is limited mining today. Tourism now plays a large part in the island's prosperity and one great attractor is the spectacular annual migration at the end of the dry season (December/January) of millions of red crabs, from the rainforest to the ocean, to spawn.

The first recorded sighting of the Cocos Islands was in 1609 but the islands were not settled until the 1820s when the Clunies-Ross family established an estate on Home Island. The Cocos Islanders are mostly descendants of Malay workers brought here by the Clunies-Rosses. They speak a Malay dialect and practice Islam.

Travellers are only just waking up to this idyllic island group and there is limited tourist accommodation on West Island (but don't miss a chance to enjoy local seafood cooked in the Malay style). There is a casino/resort at Waterfall Bay.

On all these islands you can see tropical rainforest and orchids, masses of land crabs (18 species on Christmas alone), reptiles, bats and rare seabirds. Diving, snorkelling, surfing, fishing and beachcombing are all popular activities. Contact Coatoc Wildlife Tours (☎(00) 324 2552) or Island Bound Holidays (☎(09) 381 3644) for information. ∎

WESTERN AUSTRALIA

farmland. Encircling these flat lands are the reddish mountains typical of the region.

There are two lake cruises: the *Bowerbird* does a two-hour cruise ($25; children $12.50) and the *Silver Cobbler* a half-day cruise ($80; children $50). These lake cruises are thoroughly recommended as the immensity of this inland sea is not fully appreciated until you are out in the middle of it all.

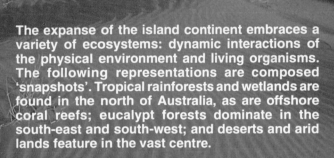

Australian Ecosystems

The expanse of the island continent embraces a variety of ecosystems: dynamic interactions of the physical environment and living organisms. The following representations are composed 'snapshots'. Tropical rainforests and wetlands are found in the north of Australia, as are offshore coral reefs; eucalypt forests dominate in the south-east and south-west; and deserts and arid lands feature in the vast centre.

The typical image of Australia, of a mostly dry and harsh landscape, is largely true; but it wasn't always this way. The familiar arid-land flora and fauna had rainforest-dwelling ancestors – their fossil remains are imprinted in the rocks of the outback. Living and recognisable descendants of this wetter past flourish in the wet tropics of the north and the temperate rainforests of the south-east; a few reside in the deep gorges of central Australia. Contemporary ecosystems reflect this Gondwanan ancestry, the effects of continental drift and a gradually drying climate, the influence of Ice-age events, and, more recently, migrations of other animals (including humans) and plants from the Eurasian continent.

nankeen
night heron

paperbark swamp

magnetic
termite mound

agile wallaby

pied heron

glossy ibis

red lotus lily

magpie goose

Tropical

The tropical wetlands of northern
Australia witness remarkable
seasonal change. Growing,
flowering, feeding and breeding
are all governed by the annual
cycle of Wet and Dry. Towards the
end of the Dry, the receding
swamps and lagoons attract
thousands of water birds; noisy
flocks of whistling ducks and
magpie geese are joined by fish-
hunting jabiru and pied heron. A
series of spectacular storms
precedes the Wet. By the end of

pig-nosed turtle

pandanus

jabiru

brolga

plumed
whistling duck

swamphen

waterlily

Wetland

December heavy rains have arrived, signalling the estuarine
crocodile to nest and forcing the
antilopine wallaroos to higher
ground. In the warm, wet environment, plant growth is rapid. Many
water birds now nest among the
rushes and wild rice. Further
storms flatten the tall grasses,
and by about May, the Wet is over.
As the land dries, natural fires
and Aboriginal hunting fires continue to shape this environment.

salt-water crocodile

Tropical

There is scarcely a niche in the warm, damp environment that is not occupied by lush, green vegetation. The tree canopy filters sunlight and resounds to the calls of birds and fruit bats. The trunks of trees support lichens, ferns and orchids, and the understorey and forest floor are a profusion of palms, more ferns and the essential fungi and micro-organisms that decompose the rich forest litter. Pythons, bandicoots, cassowaries and native mice are the largest inhabitants of the forest floor, while among the tree branches clamber possums, clumsy tree kangaroos and the

little red flying fox

double-eyed fig parrot

fan palm

atlas moth

cassowary

giant tree frog

Alexandra palm

fawn-footed melomys

bracket fungi

Rainforest

monkey-like cuscus. Interrupting the almost uniform green are brightly coloured birds and butterflies, often seen near water or displaying themselves in patches of sunlight.

Most of Australia's tropical rainforest is restricted to a few mountain ranges and along river courses on the north-east coast. The wet tropic region supports many endemic species of plants and animals, some of which closely resemble the inhabitants of the cool rainforest that once covered much of Australia. These remnant rainforests are highly regarded for their beauty and biodiversity.

Herbert River ringtail possum

green python

bird's-nest fern

buff-breasted
paradise kingfisher

Cairns
birdwing
butterfly

maidenhair fern

Cooktown orchid

flat fork
fern

Coral

Unlike other ecosystems of great diversity, coral reefs do not have a conspicuous flora. There are, however, symbiotic algae living within coral, encrusting coralline algae which help to hold the reefs together, and a thin algal turf covering most of the reef. Close to the mainland, in shallows protected from ocean swells by the reef, are seagrass meadows, home to dugongs and a nursery for many fish. Six of the world's seven species of sea turtle feed

green sea turtle

plate coral

gorgonia

whaler shark

feather star

bearded
trigger
fish

long-sp
sea urc

moray eel

sponge

hermit crab

Reef

and breed in these waters. Among the coral swim and crawl a not yet fully recorded variety of fish, crustaceans, echinoderms and molluscs. Above and along the reef edge prowl barracuda, sharks and sailfish. Overhead, gannets, terns, shearwaters, gulls and frigatebirds search for a feed of fish; the isolated coral cays provide a relatively safe nesting ground for thousands of seabirds.

sooty tern

mangrove tree

box jellyfish

Spanish dancer

dugong

sea star

brain coral

giant clam

lionfish

coral cod

seahorse

sea pen

clown fish

ve sea snake

anenome

spider shell

Eucalypt

The eucalypt tree is typically Australian but there is no typical eucalypt forest. Depending on climate and soil, you may find mountain ash (the world's tallest flowering plant), stunted alpine gum, hardy arid land ironbark or desert gum. Understorey ranges from moist ferns to dry acacias, sedges and grasses. Eucalypt-associated faunas reveal similar variety. Although there are over 600 species of eucalypt, only a handful of species in the south-east of the continent are eaten by the koala. Less particular are the common possums, the brushtail and the ringtail, who both supplement their diets of eucalypt leaves with fruits and insects.

koala

laughing
kookaburra

manna gum

sugar
glider

common
wallaroo

common wombat

short-beaked
echidna

blue-breasted
wren

Forest

Scratching around on the forest floor, the superb lyrebird is an excellent mimic – various bush sounds, including other bird calls, accompany the male's impressive courtship display. Announcing its presence with a familiar laugh, the kookaburra is a daytime hunter of lizards, snakes, frogs and small mammals. Grey kangaroos and wallabies may be seen moving into open forest in the evenings to browse shrubs and graze native grasses. Also out for a nightly forage, the common wombat, a relative of the koala, grazes its home range before returning to one of its large and conspicuous burrows.

common brushtail possum

St Andrew's cross spider

superb lyrebird

Tasmanian devil

crimson rosella

satin bowerbird

great barred frog

platypus

eastern brown snake

Central

In the arid centre of Australia life is most conspicuous in shaded gorges and along dry river courses where river red gums, home to colourful and noisy parrots, are able to tap deep reserves of water. On this ancient, eroded landscape, sparse vegetation and red sandy soils are infrequently and temporarily transformed by rain into a carpet of wildflowers. Tell-tale tracks in the sand lead to clumps of spinifex grass and burrows. Small marsupials and mice are mostly nocturnal; the rare and endangered bilby was once common to much of Australia but is now only found in the deserts of

galah

sulphur-crested cockatoo

desert oak

spinifex

dingo

red kangaroo

bilby

thorny devil

Desert

central Australia. A few of the lizards, such as the thorny devil, will venture out into the heat of the day for a feed of ants. Among the scattered mulga and desert oak, mobs of kangaroos, the males brick-red and over two metres tall, seek shelter from the sun; but seemingly impervious to the heat, emus, with an insulating double layer of feathers, continue the search for seeds and fruit. In the evenings rock-wallabies emerge from rocky outcrops to browse on nearby vegetation. Most animals breed in the cooler winter – their eggs and young attracting the attention of dingoes, eagles and perenties.

cabbage palm

ghost gum

cycad

wedge-tailed eagle

emu

black-footed rock-wallaby

perentie

Sturt's desert pea

death adder

HUGH FINLAY

JOHN TURBILL

RICHARD NEBESKY

Top: Sandstone cliffs, Rainbow Valley, NT
Middle: A bangalow palm, Qld
Bottom: Loch Ard Gorge, the Great Ocean Road, Vic

Fauna & Flora

The Australian landmass is one of the most ancient on earth. The sea has kept it cut off from other continents for more than 50 million years, and its various indigenous plants and animals have experienced an unusually long, uninterrupted period of evolution in isolation.

Australia's characteristic vegetation began to take shape about 55 million years ago when Australia broke from the supercontinent of Gondwanaland. At this time, Australia was completely covered by cool-climate rainforest, but as the continent drifted towards warmer climes, it gradually dried out, the rainforests retreated, plants like eucalypts and wattles (acacias) took over and grasslands expanded, resulting in the distinctive habitats found today.

FAUNA

Australia is blessed with a fascinating mix of native fauna, which ranges from the primitive to the highly evolved – some creatures are unique survivors from a previous age, while others have adapted so acutely to the natural environment that they can survive in areas which other animals would find uninhabitable.

Since the European colonisation of Australia, 17 species of mammal have become extinct and at least 30 more are endangered. Many introduced non-native animals have been allowed to run wild, causing a great deal of damage to native species and to Australian vegetation. Introduced animals include the fox, cat, pig, goat, camel, donkey, water buffalo, horse, starling, blackbird, cane toad and the notorious rabbit. Foxes and cats kill small native mammals and birds, rabbits denude vast areas of land, pigs carry disease and introduced birds take over the habitat of the local species.

MONOTREMES

The monotremes are often regarded as living fossils, and although they display some intriguing features from their reptile ancestors, such as laying eggs, they are now recognised as a distinct mammalian lineage rather than a primitive stage in mammalian evolution. It's an exclusive little club with just two members – the platypus, found solely in Australia, and the echidna, which is also found in the highlands of Papua New Guinea. The newly hatched young are suckled on milk. They are both superbly adapted and consequently fairly common within their distributions.

Platypus

The platypus *(Ornithorhynchus anatinus)* is certainly well equipped for its semi-aquatic lifestyle. It has a duck-like bill, which is actually quite soft, short legs, webbed feet and a short but thick, beaver-like tail. Adult males are about 50 cm long, not including the 10 to 13-cm tail, and weigh around two kg; the females are slightly smaller.

A platypus spends most of its time in the extensive burrows which it digs along the river banks; it spends the rest of its time in the water foraging for food with its electrosensitive bill or sunning itself in the open. Its diet is mainly small crustaceans, worms and tadpoles.

The platypus is confined to eastern, mainland Australia and Tasmania.

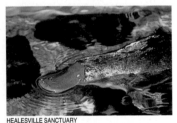

HEALESVILLE SANCTUARY

Platypus, as seen at Healesville Sanctuary's 'Sidney Myer World of the Platypus' exhibit

Echidna

The short-beaked echidna (or spiny anteater; *Tachyglossus aculeatus*) is a small monotreme which is covered on the back with long, sharp spines and on the underside with fur. When fully grown it weighs around 4.5 kg and measures around 45 cm long. The elongated, beak-like snout is around 7.5 cm long and it has a long, sticky tongue which it can whip out some 15 cm beyond the snout – perfect for catching ants and termites, which comprise the major portion of its diet. At the first sign of danger, the echidna rapidly buries its body in the dirt, leaving only its formidable spines exposed.

Short-beaked echidnas are found in a great range of habitats, from hot, dry deserts to altitudes of 1800 metres in the Alps.

CHRIS KLEP

Echidna

MARSUPIALS

Marsupials are mammals which raise their young inside a pouch, or *marsupium*. Marsupials are largely confined to Australia, and included in this group of around 120 species are some of the country's most distinctive and well-known animals – kangaroos, wallabies, koalas, wombats and possums – as well as others less well-known, such as the numerous bandicoots, the predatory quoll and the now-extinct thylacine (or Tasmanian tiger).

Marsupial young are usually very tiny at birth and need to spend a good deal of time in the pouch before being sufficiently developed to live independently of their mothers.

Kangaroos & Wallabies

Kangaroos are probably the most instantly recognisable Australian mammal and hardly need a description, although the name is applied to dozens of species.

There are now greater numbers of kangaroos in Australia than there were when Europeans arrived, a result of the better availability of water and the creation of grasslands for sheep and cattle. Certain species, however, are threatened with extinction through habitat destruction and predation from feral cats and foxes. About three million kangaroos are culled legally each year but many more are killed for sport or by those farmers who believe the cull is insufficient to protect their paddocks from overgrazing by the animals. Kangaroo meat has been exported for some time but it is only in recent years that it has started to appear on Australian menus.

Red Kangaroo The distinctive red kangaroo *(Macropus rufus)* is the largest and most widespread of the kangaroos. A fully grown male can be 2.4 metres long and up to two metres high It's usually only the male that are brick-red; females are often a blue-grey colour. They range over most of arid Australia.

Grey Kangaroo The eastern grey kangaroo *(M. giganteus)* is about the same size as the red, and is found throughout the dry sclerophyll forests of south-eastern Australia, from Queensland to Tasmania. The western grey *(M. fuliginosus)* is very similar, although slightly darker in colour, and is common in the southern regions of Western Australia and South Australia, central and western New South Wales and western Victoria. Mixed populations of eastern and western greys occur in Victoria and New South Wales but there have been no recordings of natural hybrids.

Wallaby Wallabies come in a variety of shapes and sizes. The most commonly seen are the red-necked *(M. rufogriseus)*, agile *(M. agilis)* and the swamp wallaby *(Wallabia bicolor)*, all of which are about 1.7 metres long when fully grown.

Red kangaroo

DENIS O'BYRNE

Eastern grey kangaroo

TONY WHEELER

Agile wallaby

DAVID CURL

DAVID CURL

Bilby

JOHN TURBILL

Common brushtail possum

DAVID CURL

Sugar glider

The various rock-wallabies are small (around one metre long) and are confined to cliffs and rocky habitats around the country. One of the most widespread is the brush-tailed rock-wallaby *(Petrogale penicillata)*, which is found along the Great Dividing Range in eastern Australia.

Quokka The quokka *(Setonix brachyurus)* is a small, nocturnal mammal found only in the south-western corner of Western Australia, including Rottnest Island, where it is found in large numbers. They are gregarious creatures and move in groups which can number more than 100.

Tree Kangaroo The two Australian species of tree kangaroo, Bennett's *(Dendrolagus bennettianus)* and Lumholtz's *(D. lumholtzi)*, are about the size of a cat and, as the name suggests, have given up life on the ground for life in the trees. Unlike other kangaroos they have strong forelimbs, but are rather ungainly climbers.

Both species are restricted to the north Queensland rainforest, and their habitat has come under extreme pressure from logging activities.

Bandicoots & Bilbies

The small, rat-like bandicoots and bilbies have been among the principal victims of domestic and feral cats.

Bandicoots are largely nocturnal, but can occasionally be seen scampering through the bush. They are mainly insect eaters but also eat some plant material.

One of the most common varieties is the southern brown bandicoot *(Isoodon obesulus)*, which is found in eastern and western Australia. Others, such as the eastern barred bandicoot *(Perameles gunnii)*, are these days found in very limited areas. The rare bilby *(Macrotis lagotis)* is found mainly in the Northern Territory and major efforts have been made to ensure its survival. Its rabbit-like ears have recently caused it to be promoted as Australia's own Easter animal: the Easter bilby versus the Easter bunny!

Possums

There is an enormous range of possums (or phalangers) in Australia – they have adapted to all sorts of habitats, including that of the city, where you'll often find them in parks. Some large species are found living in suburban roofs and will eat garden plants and food scraps. Possums are also common visitors at camp sites in heavily treed country, and will often help themselves to any food left out.

Probably the most familiar of all possums is the common brushtail (or grey) possum *(Trichosurus vulpecula)*, which occurs widely throughout the mainland and Tasmania.

The sugar glider *(Petaurus breviceps)* has membranes between its front and rear legs, which when spread out are used for gliding from the tip of one tree to the base of the next, covering up to 100 metres in one swoop – quite a remarkable sight.

Koala

Australia's other instantly recognisable mammal is the much-loved koala *(Phascolarctos cinereus)*. The name is an Aboriginal word meaning 'no water', which refers to the koala's alleged ability to meet all its moisture requirements from gum leaves, although it does drink water from pools.

Although they are protected today and their survival assured, large numbers of females are infertile due to chlamydia, a sexually transmitted disease. Their cuddly appearance also belies an irritable nature, and they will scratch and bite if sufficiently provoked.

When fully grown a koala measures about 70 cm and weighs around 10 kg. Their most distinctive features are their tufted ears and hard, black nose.

Koalas feed only on the leaves of certain types of eucalypt and are particularly sensitive to changes to their habitat. They are found along the east coast from around Townsville down to Melbourne, and have been reintroduced in South Australia, where they had previously been driven to extinction.

Wombats

Wombats are slow, solid, powerfully built marsupials with broad heads and short, stumpy legs. These fairly placid and easily tamed creatures are legally killed by farmers, who object to the damage done by wombats digging large burrows and tunnelling under fences.

Adult wombats are about one metre long and weigh up to 35 kg. Their strong front legs are excellent burrowing tools, and the rear legs are used for pushing the earth away. Their diet consists of grasses, roots and tree barks.

There are three species of wombat, the most prevalent being the common wombat *(Vombatus ursinus)*, which is distributed throughout the forested areas of south-eastern Australia. The other species are the rare and endangered northern hairy-nosed wombat *(Lasiorhinus krefftii)*, and the southern hairy-nosed wombat *(Lasiorhinus latifrons)*, which is also vulnerable and lives inland of the Great Australian Bight.

Koala   CHRIS KLEP

Common wombat

DAVID CURL

DAVID CURL

Northern quoll

DAVID CURL

Tasmanian devil

Dasyuroids

Members of the Dasyuroidea are predatory marsupials, such as quolls, numbats and the Tasmanian devil. The main distinguishing feature of Dasyuroids is a pointy, elongated snout.

Quoll Australia's spotted quolls, or native cats, are about the size of domestic cats and are probably even more efficient killers. Being nocturnal creatures which spend most of their time in trees, they are not often seen.

The native cats include the eastern quoll *(Dasyurus viverrinus)*, western quoll *(D. geoffroii)* and the northern quoll *(D. hallucatus)*. The eastern is now largely extinct on the mainland but is still found in numbers in Tasmania. The spotted-tailed quoll *(D. maculatus)*, also known as the tiger cat, is one of the most ferocious hunters in the Australian bush.

Tasmanian Devil The carnivorous Tasmanian devil *(Sarcophilus harrisii)* is the largest of the dasyuroids, and is as fierce as it looks. It's solitary and nocturnal and has a fierce whining growl. The body is black with a white stripe across the chest, and measures around 60 cm long, while the tail is around 25 cm long. Its diet consists of small birds and mammals, insects and carrion.

Numbat The attractive numbat *(Myrmecobius fasciatus)*, is a pouchless marsupial and is unusual in that it is most active during the day rather than at night. It has striking rust-red fur with six or seven white stripes across the rump. Adult numbats are about the size of a rat and weigh around half a kg.

Numbats live in hollow, fallen wandoo trees *(Eucalyptus reducna)* found in the forests of south-western Australia; their numbers are dwindling.

DAVID CURL

Numbat

EUTHERIANS

The largest mammalian group on earth is the placental mammals or eutherians. Australia's native eutherians include the marine mammals and the 'recent' invaders, having arrived no more than 15 million years ago, which include numerous species of bats, rodents and the native dog or dingo.

Dingo

The dingo *(Canis familiaris dingo)*, is Australia's native dog. It's thought to have arrived in Australia around 6000 years ago, and was domesticated by Aboriginal people. It differs from the domestic dog in that it howls rather than barks and breeds only once a year (rather than twice), although the two can interbreed.

Dingoes prey on rabbits, rats and mice, although when other food is scarce they sometimes attack livestock (usually unattended sheep or calves), and for this reason are considered vermin by many farmers. Efforts to control dingo numbers have been largely unsuccessful.

JOHN TURBILL
Grey headed flying fox

Marine Mammals

Humpback Whale Now a regular visitor to the east and west coasts of Australia, this massive marine mammal *(Megaptera novaeangliae)* is a joy to behold. It migrates northwards from feeding grounds in the polar seas to breed in subtropical waters in winter. Adult humpbacks range from 14 to 19 metres in length and can live for over 30 years.

Southern Right Whale The southern right whale *(Eubalaena australis)*, so-called because it was the 'right' whale to kill, was hunted almost to the point of

JOHN CHAPMAN

WESTERN AUSTRALIAN TOURISM COMMISSION
Humpback whale

RICHARD I'ANSON

Emu

extinction but, since the cessation of whaling, has started to return to Australian waters. It can be seen in the Great Australian Bight, and is easily recognised by its strongly down-turned mouth with long baleen plates (these filter water for planktonic krill).

Dugong This is a herbivorous aquatic mammal *(Dugong dugon)*, often known as the 'sea cow', found along the northern Australian coast, from Shark Bay in Western Australia to the Great Barrier Reef in Queensland. The Shark Bay population is estimated to be over 10,000, about 10% of the world's dugong population. The dugong is found in shallow tropical waters where it feeds on seagrasses, supplemented by algae.

BIRDS

Australia's birdlife is as beautiful as it is varied, with over 750 recorded species, many of them endemic.

The Royal Australasian Ornithologists Union runs bird observatories in New South Wales, Victoria and Western Australia, which provide accommodation and guides. Contact the RAOU (☎ (03) 9882 2622) at 415 Riversdale Rd, Hawthorn East, Victoria 3123.

Emu

The emu *(Dromaius novaehollandiae)* is a shaggy feathered bird that stands two metres high. The only bird larger than the emu is the African ostrich, also flightless. Emus are found across the country, but only in areas away from human habitation. After the female lays her six to 12 large, dark green eggs the male hatches them and raises the young.

Kookaburra

DAVID CURL

Laughing kookaburra

The laughing kookaburra *(Dacelo novaeguinae)* is common throughout coastal Australia, but particularly in the east and south-west of the country. The blue-winged kookaburra *(D. leachii)* is found in northern coastal woodlands. Kookaburras are the largest members of the kingfisher family. The kookaburra is heard as much as it is seen – you can't miss its loud, cackling laugh. Kookaburras can become quite tame and pay regular visits to friendly households, but only if the food is excellent.

Bowerbird

DAVID CURL

Blue-winged kookaburra

The stocky, stout-billed bowerbird, of which there are at least half a dozen species, is best known for its unique mating practice. The brightly coloured male builds a bower which he decorates with various coloured objects to attract the less showy female. The female is impressed by the male's neatly built bower and attractively displayed treasures, but once they've mated all the hard work is left to her.

The three most common species are the great *(Chlamydera nuchalis)*, the spotted *(C. maculata)* and the satin *(Ptilonorhynchus violaceus)*.

Magpie

The black and white magpie (*Gymnorhina* spp) is one of the most widespread birds in Australia, being found virtually throughout the country. One of the most distinctive sounds of the Australian bush is the melodious song of the magpie, which is heard at any time of day, but especially at dawn. One of the magpie's less endearing traits is the way it swoops at people who approach its nest too closely in spring. The several geographic species of magpie all look much alike to the untrained eye but differ in the arrangement of their black and white markings.

Wedge-Tailed Eagle

The wedge-tailed eagle *(Aquila audax)* is Australia's largest bird of prey. It has a wing span of up to two metres, and is easily identified in flight by its distinctive wedge-shaped tail. 'Wedgies' are often seen in outback Australia, either soaring to great heights, or feeding on road-kill carcasses.

Parrots, Rosellas, Lorikeets & Cockatoos

There is an amazing variety of these birds throughout Australia. Some, such as the galah, are fairly plain, while others have vivid colouring.

Rosella There are a number of species of rosella (*Platycercus* spp), most of them brilliantly coloured and not at all backward about taking a free feed from humans. The mainly red, yellow and blue eastern rosella *(P. eximius)* is the most widespread and is found throughout rural south-eastern Australia.

Galah The pink and grey galah *(Cacatua roseicapilla)* is amongst the most common, and is often sighted scratching for seeds on the roadside.

Rainbow Lorikeet The rainbow lorikeet *(Trichoglossus haematodus)* is so extravagantly colourful that it is hard to imagine until you've seen one, with its blue head, orange breast and green body. Lorikeets have a brush-like tongue for extracting nectar from flowers.

CHRIS KLEP

Wedge-tailed eagle

JOHN TURBILL

Galah at nest hollow

DAVID CURL

Rainbow lorikeets

DAVID CURL
Jabiru

DAVID CURL
Magpie goose

DAVID CURL
Brolga

WESTERN AUSTRALIAN TOURISM COMMISSION
Black swan

Budgerigar Budgies *(Melopsittacus undulatus)* are widespread over inland Australia where they can be seen in flocks of thousands flying in tight formation. Budgies are probably the most widely kept cage bird in the world.

Black Cockatoo There are six species of black cockatoo, the most widespread being the large red-tailed black cockatoo *(Calyptorhynchus magnificus)* and the yellow-tailed black cockatoo *(C. funereus)*.

Sulphur-Crested Cockatoo This noisy cocky *(Cacatua galerita)*, often seen in loud, raucous flocks, is found throughout eastern and northern Australia. When the flock is feeding on the ground, several individuals will fly to a high vantage point to watch over the flock and signal if there is any danger.

Lyrebird
The shy superb lyrebird *(Menura novaehollandiae)* is a ground-dwelling rainforest bird found in south-eastern Australia. The male has tail feathers which form a lyre shape when displayed to attract a mate. The similar Albert lyrebird *(M. alberti)* is found in the rainforests of southern Queensland and northern New South Wales. Lyrebirds have a beautiful song and are also clever mimics.

Jabiru
The jabiru (or black-necked stork, *Xenorhynchus asiaticus*) is found throughout northern and eastern Australia, although it is not often seen. It stands over one metre high, and has an almost iridescent green-black neck, black and white body, and orange legs.

Magpie Goose
The magpie (or pied) goose *(Anseranas semipalmata)* is commonly seen in the tropical wetlands of northern Australia – indeed when water becomes scarce towards the end of the dry season (October) they often gather in huge numbers on the retreating wetlands.

Brolga
Another bird commonly seen in wetland areas of northern and, to a lesser extent, eastern Australia, is the tall crane known as the brolga *(Grus rubicundus)*. They stand over one metre high, are grey in colour and have a distinctive red head colouring.

Black Swan
Commonly seen on stretches of water from the Top End to Tasmania are black swans *(Cygnus atratus)*. They are usually seen in large flocks near fresh or brackish water. Black swans nest among reeds or on islands in lakes and both parents take on nesting duties.

REPTILES

Snakes

Australian snakes are generally shy and avoid confrontations with humans. A few, however, are deadly. The most dangerous are the taipan and tiger snake, although death adders, copperheads, brown snakes and red-bellied black snakes should also be avoided. Tiger snakes will actually attack.

Crocodiles

There are two types of crocodile in Australia: the extremely dangerous saltwater crocodile *(Crocodylus porosus)*, or 'saltie' as it's known, and the less aggressive freshwater crocodile *(C. johnstoni)*, or 'freshie'. It is important to be able to tell the difference between them, as both are prolific in northern Australia.

Saltwater Crocodile Salties are not confined to salt water. They inhabit estuaries, and following floods may be found many km from the coast. They may even be found in permanent fresh water more than 100 km inland. Salties, which can grow to seven metres, will attack and kill humans.

Freshwater Crocodile Freshies are smaller than salties anything over four metres should be regarded as a saltie. Freshies are also more finely constructed and have much narrower snouts and smaller teeth. Freshies, though unlikely to seek human prey, have been known to bite, and children in particular should be kept away from them.

Lizards

Goanna Goannas are large and sometimes aggressive lizards, up to two metres long. With their forked tongues and loud hiss they can be quite formidable, and are best left undisturbed as they will stand their ground. The largest goanna is the carnivorous perentie *(Varanus giganteus)*, found in central Australia.

Frilled Lizard The frilled lizard *(Chlamydosaurus kingii)* is Australia's most famous lizard, and is commonly seen in bushland in eastern and northern Australia. The frill is a loose flap of skin which normally hangs flat around the neck. When alarmed or threatened, the lizard raises its frill and opens its mouth to give a more ferocious appearance.

SPIDERS

The redback *(Latrodectus hasselti)* is Australia's most notorious spider. It is generally glossy black with a red streak down its back. Woodheaps and garden sheds are favourite hang-outs, and its bite can be lethal. The funnel-web (Dipluridae family) is a large, aggressive ground-dwelling spider found mainly in New South Wales. Funnel-webs from around Sydney are particularly venomous; their bite can be fatal.

DAVID CURL
Saltwater crocodile

WESTERN AUSTRALIAN TOURISM COMMISSION
Freshwater crocodile

DAVID CURL
Perentie

DAVID CURL
Frilled lizard

FLORA

Despite vast tracts of dry and barren land, much of Australia is well vegetated. Forests cover 5%. or 410,000 sq km. Plants can be found even in the arid centre, though many of them grow and flower erratically.

The arrival of Europeans 200 years ago saw the introduction of new flora, fauna and tools. Rainforests were logged, new crops and pasture grasses spread, hoofed animals such as cows, sheep and goats damaged the soil, and watercourses were altered. Irrigation, combined with excessive tree clearing, gradually resulted in salination of the soil. Human activities seriously threaten Australian flora but to date most species have survived.

JEFF WILLIAMS
Spinifex country, the Kimberley, WA

DAVID CURL
Spear grass *(Sorghum intrans)*, Kakadu NP, NT

NATIVE GRASSES

There are more than 700 native Australian grasses found in a variety of habitats across the country.

Spinifex

The hardiest and most common desert plants belong to the group of desert grasses called spinifex. They are a dense, dome-shaped mass of long, needle-like leaves found on sandy soils and rocky areas. Spinifex grasslands are very difficult to walk through – the explorer Ernest Giles called the prickly spinifex 'that abominable vegetable production'. They cover vast areas of central Australia and support large populations of reptiles.

The resin from spinifex was used by Aboriginal people to fasten spear heads and as a general adhesive.

Mitchell Grass

Mitchell grass covers huge areas of arid land in northern Australia, and is the saviour of the cattle industry in the Top End. It has a well-developed root system and is therefore very drought resistant. The grass usually grows in tussocks on clay soils which develop huge cracks when dry and become quagmires when wet.

SHRUBS & FLOWERS

Callistemons

Callistemons, or bottlebrushes (after the brush-like flowers), are found across the country, but especially in New South Wales. They are attractive, hardy and draw many native birds. There are about 25 different species, which grow from one to 10 metres high. Some of the most common are the crimson bottlebrush *(C. citrinus)*, the weeping bottlebrush *(C. viminalis)* and the prickly bottlebrush *(C. brachycandrus)*.

Grevilleas

Grevilleas are another major family of shrubs. Of the 250 or so varieties, all but 20 are native to Australia. Like bottlebrushes, they come in a variety of sizes and flower colours. Most grevilleas are small to medium shrubs, such as Banks grevillea *(G. banksii)*, which has beautiful red flower spikes. When in flower, the silky oak *(G. robusta)*, which can grow to a height of 30 metres, is one of Australia's most spectacular trees.

Kangaroo Paw

Kangaroo paw (*Anigozanthos* spp) grows wild only in the south-western corner of Western Australia; Mangle's kangaroo paw *(A. manglesii)* is that state's floral emblem. Because they are unusual and attractive they are commonly seen in gardens in the eastern states. The plant takes its name from the distinctive, tubular flowers which are covered in velvet-like hair and come in a variety of colours – from black through to red, green and yellow. The plants were used for medicinal purposes by Aboriginal people.

Sturt's Desert Pea

Sturt's desert pea *(Clianthus formosus)* is a small, annual flower which flourishes in the drier areas of inland Australia, particularly after heavy rain soaks the ground. The plant is the floral emblem of South Australia, and has distinctive red flowers with black centres.

Saltbush

Millions of sheep and cattle living in the arid zone owe their survival to dry shrubby plants called saltbush, named for their tolerance to saline conditions. Saltbush is extremely widespread and can be dominant over vast areas. There are 30 different species.

CYCADS & FERNS

MacDonnell Ranges Cycad

The MacDonnell Ranges cycad *(Macrozamia macdonnelli)* is one of 18 species in Australia belonging to the ancient cycad family. It is a very slow-growing plant, often seen high up on rocky hillsides and gorges. Seed cones grow at the tip of the short trunk on female plants, while male cones carry the pollen. The seeds are poisonous but were eaten by Aboriginal people after the toxins had been leached out.

WESTERN AUSTRALIAN TOURISM COMMISSION

Mangle's kangaroo paw

WESTERN AUSTRALIAN TOURISM COMMISSION

Sturt's desert pea

JOHN TURBILL

MacDonnell Ranges cycad

Cabbage palms

Cootamundra wattle

Scarlet banksia

Tree Ferns

The beautifully ornate rough tree fern (*Cyathea* spp) and the soft tree fern *(Dicksonia antarctica)* are found in the temperate rainforests of eastern Australia. Some varieties can be as much as 20 metres high, and all are topped by a crown of green fronds.

TREES
Cabbage Palms

The most well-known of Australia's 40 palm species is the cabbage palm *(Livistona mariae)* of Palm Valley in the Finke Gorge National Park near Alice Springs. The tree grows up to 30 metres high, and is unique to this area. The growing tip of the tree consists of tender green leaves, and these were a source of bush tucker to Aboriginal people. The mature leaves were also woven into hats by early European inhabitants of the Centre.

Acacias

The Australian species of the genus *Acacia* are commonly known as wattle – and they are common indeed, with over 660 species known to exist in Australia. They vary from small shrubs to towering blackwoods.

Most species flower during late winter and spring. At this time the countryside is often ablaze with yellow flowers, and it's easy to see why a wattle is Australia's floral emblem.

Blackwood The largest of the acacias, the blackwood *(A. melanoxylon)* can grow up to 30 or more metres high in good soil and is generally found on the ranges of eastern and southern Australia.

Mulga The mulga *(A. aneura)* is the dominant species in huge areas of inland Australia. It is very drought tolerant, and the hard wood was preferred by Aboriginal people for making spears and other implements.

Golden Wattle The golden wattle *(A. pycnantha)* is Australia's floral emblem, and is one of the most widespread acacias. It grows best in hot and arid areas, but is common throughout south-eastern Australia.

Banksias

Banksias (*Banksia* spp) take their name from Sir Joseph Banks, the botanist who accompanied Captain James Cook on his exploratory voyage of eastern Australia. There are about 60 species in Australia, and they are often found in poor soils unsuitable for most other plants. Most of them sport upright flower spikes covered with brilliant orange, red or yellow flowers, one of the most spectacular being the scarlet banksia *(B. coccinea)*. These flowers were a favourite source of nectar for Aboriginal people, who would dip the spikes in water to make a sweet drink.

Casuarinas

Also known as sheoaks, these hardy trees are almost as much a part of the Australian landscape as eucalypts. They grow in a variety of habitats, and are characterised by feather-like 'leaves', which are actually branchlets; the true leaves are small scales at the joints of the branchlets.

Desert Oak Its height, broad shady crown, dark weeping foliage and the sighing music of the wind in its leaves make the desert oak *(Allocasuarina decaisneana)* an inspiring feature of its sand-plain habitat. These magnificent trees are confined to the western arid zone of central Australia and are common around Uluru and Kings Canyon, near Alice Springs. Young desert oaks resemble tall hairy broomsticks; they don't look anything like the adult trees and many people think that they're a different species altogether.

River Sheoak The river sheoak *(Casuarina cunninghamania)* is a tall tree, highly valued for its ability to bind river banks, which greatly reduces erosion.

Eucalypts

The eucalypt *(Eucalyptus spp)*, or gum tree, is ubiquitous in Australia except in the deepest rainforests and the most arid regions. Of the 700 species of the genus eucalyptus, 95% occur naturally in Australia, the rest in New Guinea, the Philippines and Indonesia.

Gum trees vary in form and height from the tall, straight hardwoods such as jarrah, karri and mountain ash to the stunted, twisted, shrub-like Mallee gum.

River Red Gum River red gums *(E. camaldulensis)* are generally confined to watercourses where their roots have access to a reliable water source. They are massive trees which can grow up to 40 metres high and can live for up to 1000 years.

Coolabah Coolabah trees *(E. Microtheca)* are widespread throughout inland and northern Australia. They grow to about 20 metres high, and are not the prettiest tree around, usually having an uneven, spreading form and a twisted trunk. The coolabah was Immortalised in Banjo Paterson's poem, *Waltzing Matilda*.

Ghost Gum The ghost gum *(E. papuana)* is one of the most attractive eucalypts and is found throughout central and northern Australia. Its bright green leaves and smooth white bark contrast with the red rocks and soil of the Centre; and, not surprisingly, it is a common subject for artists.

Melaleucas

The paperbarks, or *Melaleucas*, are generally easily recognised by the loose, papery bark which hangs in thin sheets around the trunk. This is actually dead bark which stays on the tree, insulating the trunk from extreme temperature and moisture loss. The trees

Desert oak

DAVID CURL

LINDSAY BROWN

Snow gum *(Eucalyptus pauciflora)*

JOHN TURBILL

Ghost gum

TOURISM NEW SOUTH WALES

Waratah

DENIS O'BYRNE

Boab

LINDSAY BROWN

King William pine

have for centuries been put to many uses by Aboriginal people – drinkable water is obtainable from the trunk, and the bark has been used for water carriers, rafts, shelters and food coverings.

Some of the most common varieties are the swamp paperbark *(M. ericifolia)*, the bracelet honey-myrtle *(M. armillaris)* and the long-leaved paperbark *(M. leucadendron)*.

Waratah

The waratah *(Telopea Speciosissima)* has a spectacular red flower. The scientific name, *Telopea*, means 'seen from afar', which gives some idea of the impact it makes in the bush. The small tree is limited to New South Wales and Victoria and is the floral emblem of NSW. Genera other than *Telopea* are also given the name waratah, such as the waratah tree *(Oreocallis pinnata)* of Queensland and NSW.

Boab

The boab *(Adansonia gregorii)* is Australia's most grotesque tree and is found only from the south-western Kimberley to the Northern Territory's Victoria River, where it grows on flood plains and rocky areas. Its huge, grey, swollen trunk topped by a mass of contorted branches makes it a fascinating sight, particularly during the dry season when it loses its leaves and becomes 'the tree that God planted upside-down'. Although boabs rarely grow higher than 20 metres, their moisture-storing trunks can be over 25 metres in girth.

Conifers

There are several families of native Australian conifers; however, conifers rarely dominate the vegetation in the way some pines and spruces do in parts of the northern hemisphere.

Bunya Pine One of the most unusual pines is the bunya pine *(Araucaria bidwillii)*, which is often found in older botanic gardens. The huge cones can weigh up to seven kg, so take care before taking a rest under one! The seeds found inside these cones were a favourite food of Aboriginal people.

Norfolk Island Pine The Norfolk Island pine *(A. heterophylla)* is native to Norfolk Island, an external territory of Australia about 1600 km north-east of Sydney. These tall, straight trees were first noted by Captain Cook in 1774, and he suggested they would make excellent masts. Their very symmetrical form has made them a popular tree for streets and parks, particularly close to the seashore.

King William Pine The King William pine *(Athrotaxis selaginoides)* is endemic to Tasmania where it is found in high altitude rainforests. It has a characteristic conical shape and can grow to about 40 metres.

Index

MAPS

TEXT

NATIONAL PARKS

THANKS
Thanks to following readers whose letters from all over the world helped with this update:

Tony Abbott & Linda Mylins, Sara Adamson, Robert Arnold, Silvia & Stefan Arvigo, Joanne Ashburn, Melissa Kate Ashwell, Jan Bailey, Amanda Baker, Jan Balodis, Craig Barbour, N Barbour, Danny Barnes, Todd & Kerri Barnsley, Tricia Bathen, Annette Baumann, Jacob Bax, Roberto Bederucci, David Beeuert, Gary & Cheryl Beemer, Malia Bell, Andrea Berner, Julian Best, Dr Thomas Betz, G Biggs & S Wright, G Binks, Belinda Bird, Saskia Bjuhr, Martina Blauth, Carla Blekkink, Amy Boardman, A Bockelmann, Marian Bolt, Stephane Borella, Jane Boyle, Roland Brandenburg, Val Braun, T Brennan, Peter Brereton, Rachel Brew & Co, L B Brighton, Christopher Broad, Angela Brown, Karl Brown, Jurgen Brummeler, Mitch Buchman, Neil Buhrich, Wilma Burgess, Eleanor & Vince Burke, Michael Burles, Ian Burton, Adrian Butcher, Guy Canessa, C J P Cass, Rebecca Charles, M J Chilman, Brian Coad, Chris Cole, Natalie Conway, Karen Cooper & Marc Dyer, B T Cousins, Marvyn Crawshaw, Heather Crookes, Simon Crunden, Michael Cummins, Ake Dahllof, Rupert Dean, Wayne De Currier, Daryl Diamond, Sue Dickery, Michael Donovan, Amy Drapeau, Mindy Dubin, Margaret Dudley, George Dundas, Jim Dunn, Peter Durand, Kate Duryea, Steve Dyer, William Dyson, Kathryn Earle, A R Eddy, Matthew Egan, C Elmetri, Rob & Margaret Elvidge, Andrew Fearon, Mick Feldon, Jan Howard Finder, Hanne Finholt, Dawn Finnie, Calvin Fish, Stuart Forder, P J Forner, R Fournier & M Michelet, Sonia Forster, Anne Frodcen, Fabri Gadoni, Lisa Gagyi, Tim Galvin, Kieran Gartlan, Andrew Gee, John Giba, Geoff Gill, Iris Glatthaar, Dominic Goh, Leigh Goldstein, Christine & Dan Goncalves, Bill Goodchild, David Green, Justine Greeson, Neil Griffiths, John Griffin, A Groeneveld & E van de Velde, Susan Grose, Doug & Cindy Gross, E J Grove, Maxi Gruchot, Ossy Halachmy, Neville Hallam, Niklas Hallberg, Teresa Hannon, Harold Hardwick, Jillian Hardy, Saslua Hardyzer, Inga Hellings, C Helps, L Heng, Hilary Herdman, Jane Hill, P Hiscock, Sara Hogg, Julie Holmes, Jack Holmes, Emma Hoskins, Sarah Hudson, John & Monica Hudson, Teena Hughes, Andrew Hutter, Mary Jackson, Anna James, Amanda Jelowicki, Penelope Johns, Gregory Jones, Ilene F Joyce, Helen Jukes, Miquel Jutte, Marc Kammerer, Wolf Peter Katz, Christopher Kelk, Harry & Ruth Kellerman, Klaus & Petra Kenneth, Jane Kernot, Karen, Sue & John Kerr, Ken & Carolyn Kimpton, Rita Kipfer, Anne Kley, Bep Kruit, Isabelle Laliberte, Gordon Lang, Scott Lang, Remke & Nienke Lasance, J Laycock, Simon Le Fort, Stella Lee, Marianne Leimert, George & Ann Levinger, Cate Lewis, Ruth Lippiatt, Roy Lister, Christian Loffler, Henrik Lorentzen, Jason Lunden, Paul MacEachern, Rainer Mack, Rodney Maier, Mary Mansfield, Nigel Marsden, Audrey Martin, Ricky Lee Martin, Susan Mather, L & K Mazok, Melanie McLaren, Shannon McConnell, Margaret McHugh, Russell McNally, J M Meheux, Joanne Meszoly, Barb Metcalfe, Michael Meyden, John Michael, Josephine Middleton & Co, Susan Milligan, Jeremy Milln, Rod & Yvonne Mills, Franz Miltenburg, I M Milton, Jorg & Grit Moller, Elwyn Morris, Michael Mowry, Michelle Mullens, Miklos Muller, S L Munro, Geraldine Murray, Jaqueline Nanning, Sally Nathan, R E Ness, J & P Netter, Heike Neumann, Lena Newton, Hans Nijssen, Seren Nordvig, Greg O'Brien, Liz O'Donnell, Eileen O'Meara, Alisa & Aluf Orell, J A Osten, Garry Palmer, Sarah Parfitt, Greg Parker, Neville Peck, Ruth Penhall, Roger Perras, Simon Oliver Peter, Roland Phillips, Carlos Pierce, J Pieters, Trent Pingenot, Alex S Pinto, Jason Phillips, David Plaisted, Jeremy Polmear, A F Pooley, Sue Popesku, Mark, Susan & Ashley Pridgeon, Emma Quinn, Peter Quirke, Denise Radomile, R V Rakcowski, P A Ratcliffe, O Raynor, A Reddaway & R Arthur, M & R Renner, Hanjoerg Resa, Rachel Robertson, Jason Rodgers, Doris Rossy, Susan Ruben, Gou Ryan, Bernard Sarosi, Dr Ulrike Schnepf, Helena & Brian Schyberg, Fiona Scott, Donald Scott-Orr, Lucie Seaton, Malcolm Senior, Gail Shaw, Shirley Sheehan, Mandy Sherwood, P G Simmons, Robert Simons-Smith, Sarah Skerp, Gitte Skovsen & Henrik Serensen, D Smith, Heather Smith, Simon Smith, Frank John Snelling, Sam Soppitt, Dana Spanierman, Paul Stang, Daniela & Wolf Starke, Neil Stead, Charlotte Steiner, Mark Stone, James Supaibulpipat, Colin Taylor, Simon Thomas, Patricia Thompson, Bill & Paula Thomson, Sherry Lynn Tischler, Philip Tomasello, Christine Treloar, Teresa Tsang, Kylie Turner, Colin Twomey, Frank van den Heuvel, Nico van der Byl, Jasper van der Zwaan, Fred & Marianne van Kolck, Sandy & Sidney Van Zandt, I Van S'Chaik, Laura Vates, Michael Venter, Des Victory, Gila Vin, Joan Vlahovic, Jean Luc Voisard, Donnie Waful, Gordon Wardrope, Drew Warne-Smith, Margot Warnett, M Warwick, John Waugh, Carla Weemaes, R G Wells, Lisa Whitworth, Marc Wieter, Tim Wilkins, Sarah Williams, Angela Wilson, Marilyn & Terry Wilson, Miriam Wolkenfelt, Jim Wolper, P J Wood, Sarah Wood, Paul & Fiona Woodhouse, Martin Worswick, Janis Worthington, Megan Yorke, Thomas & Rocio Zeiler, Iris & Eyal Zigler, Andrea Zimmerman

Update – March 1997

Recent archaeological findings of ancient rock-art in Australia suggest that humans have been here for up to 176,000 years, which is 100,000 years earlier than previously thought.

COMMUNICATIONS

Since 1995 a new telephone numbering system has been gradually introduced throughout Australia. Most of the new numbers are now in use, and all should be in use by November 1997. This book lists the new numbers for most areas, except Western Australia, the ACT and some regions of Queensland and New South Wales. See the Telephone Number Changes box on page 82, and the Phone Changes boxes at the start of each state chapter, for more information.

HEALTH

As fears rise that the potentially fatal lyssavirus may have spread to Western Australia's northern half, authorities are warning people to stay away from all fruit bats, but particularly those which look unwell or are uncoordinated. The virus has been detected in fruit bats in Queensland and the Northern Territory and has possibly spread to Western Australia.

GETTING THERE & AWAY

Britannia Airlines, owned by British Airways, runs charter flights to and from Australia and New Zealand between November and March. They are the cheapest flights available to these destinations – only £499 (just under A$1000) to Melbourne, Sydney and Adelaide, and £599 to New Zealand. You can stay eight weeks maximum, or buy a one-way ticket and return months later with another airline. However, going to Britain from Australia isn't quite as cheap – during the high season in 1996 the ticket was A$1600, though that's still less than other airlines were offering for that time of year. The flight stops only for

Dear traveller

Prices go up, good places go bad, bad places go bankrupt...and every guidebook is inevitably outdated in places. Fortunately, many travellers write to us about their experiences, telling us when things have changed. If we reprint a book between editions, we try to include the best of this information in an Update section. We also make travellers' tips immediately available on our award-winning World Wide Web Internet site (http://www.lonelyplanet.com) and in a free quarterly newsletter, *Planet Talk*.

Although much of this information has not been verified by our own first-hand research, we believe it can be very useful. We cannot vouch for its accuracy, however, so bear in mind that it could be wrong.

We really enjoy hearing from people out on the road, and apart from guaranteeing that others will benefit from your good and bad experiences, we're prepared to bribe you with an offer of a free book for sending us substantial useful information.

I hope you do find this book useful – and that you let us know when it isn't. Thank you to everyone who has written.

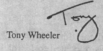

Tony Wheeler

refueling, and you have to cough up all the money when you book.

GETTING AROUND

McCafferty's stopped their bus service between Darwin and Perth, leaving Greyhound coaches as the only bus line operating the route, and you can feel the missing competition. There is only one bus a day running between Coral Bay and Monkey Mia.

Bernhard Brendel

NSW

A new national park has been opened in the south-east of the state. The South East Forest National Park extends from Nimmitabel in the north to the NSW/Victorian border. The creation of the 90,000-hectare park comes after a long battle between loggers and environmentalists.

Sydney

Following the violent brawls in 1995, the

NSW government has announced plans for the control of Christmas Day and New Years Eve celebrations on Sydney's Bondi Beach. As well as an increase in the number of police on the beach, all glass has been banned and sections of the beach will be closed off to revellers.

The new *Sydney Central YHA* (☎ 9281 9111) on the corner of Pitt St and Rawson Place, opposite the Central Railway, is now open. Facilities include a roof-top pool, sauna, sundeck and BBQ area. There is also a mini-mart, tavern, licensed café, travel agency and a day tours desk. The *Hereford YHA Lodge* in Glebe is now closed.

Narooma
The family run *Bluewater YHA Lodge* (☎ (044) 764 440) at 11 Riverside Dr is close to the shores of the beautiful Wagonga Inlet. Dorms cost $15 and twins/doubles are $18. BBQ facilities are available.

QUEENSLAND
Brisbane
The Travellers Medical Service (☎ 3221 8083, 3221 8645) has relocated to Level 1, 245 Albert St (on the corner with Adelaide St – above McDonalds). Opening hours are Monday to Friday from 7.30 am to 7 pm and Saturday from 8 am to 3 pm.

Mt Isa
The *Mt Isa YHA* at Wellington Park Rd closed in January 1997. For alternative accommodation in Mt Isa, contact YHA Queensland on ☎ (07) 3236 1680.

VICTORIA
Melbourne
The Melbourne Passport Office has moved to the 13th Floor, Casselden Place, 2 Lons-dale Street, 3000, (GPO Box 1588P, 3001), ☎ (03) 9221 5555, fax (03) 9221 5467; Passport Information Service ☎ 131 232.

The National Museum will be closing in mid-1997 for about two years due to renovations.

The Valhalla Cinema in Northcote which ran cult and classic films was renamed Westgarth Cinema in 1996.

There is no longer a *YHA Youth Hostel* in Geelong.

Bright
The Alpine High Country Visitor Centre (☎ 1800 500 117) has opened in Bright. They offer information and a booking service.

INTERNET INFO
For the latest travel information, check out the Lonely Planet web site:

 http://www.lonelyplanet.com

This award-winning site contains updates, recent travellers' letters and a useful travellers' bulletin board.

Charles Sturt University's *Guide to Australia* is a bid to build an on-line encyclopedia of information about Australia. Headings include travel, tourism, culture, history and communications:

 http://www.csu.edu.au/education/austral ia.html

Another site, the *Eventnet*, has what's-on information from opera to sport, throughout Australia:

 http://www.eventnet.aust.com

ACKNOWLEDGMENTS
The information in this Update was compiled by Richard Nebesky from various sources including reports by the following travellers: Liz Filleul and Nigel Foster.

LONELY PLANET JOURNEYS

JOURNEYS is a unique collection of travellers' tales – published by the company that understands travel better than anyone else. It is a series for anyone who has ever experienced – or dreamed of – the magical moment when they encountered a strange culture or saw a place for the first time. They are tales to read while you're planning a trip, while you're on the road or while you're in an armchair, in front of a fire.

JOURNEYS books will catch the spirit of a place, illuminate a culture, recount a crazy adventure, or introduce a fascinating way of life. They will always entertain, and always enrich the experience of travel.

ISLANDS IN THE CLOUDS
Travels in the Highlands of New Guinea
Isabella Tree

This is the fascinating account of a journey to the remote and beautiful Highlands of Papua New Guinea and Irian Jaya. The author travels with a PNG Highlander who introduces her to his intriguing and complex world. *Islands in the Clouds* is a thoughtful, moving book, full of insights into a region that is rarely noticed by the rest of the world.

'One of the most accomplished travel writers to appear on the horizon for many years . . . the dialogue is brilliant' – Eric Newby

LOST JAPAN
Alex Kerr

Lost Japan draws on the author's personal experiences of Japan over a period of 30 years. Alex Kerr takes his readers on a backstage tour: friendships with Kabuki actors, buying and selling art, studying calligraphy, exploring rarely visited temples and shrines . . . The Japanese edition of this book was awarded the 1994 Shincho Gakugei Literature Prize for the best work of non-fiction.

'This deeply personal witness to Japan's wilful loss of its traditional culture is at the same time an immensely valuable evaluation of just what that culture was'
– Donald Richie of the Japan Times

THE GATES OF DAMASCUS
Lieve Joris
Translated by Sam Garrett

This best-selling book is a beautifully drawn portrait of day-to-day life in modern Syria. Through her intimate contact with local people, Lieve Joris draws us into the fascinating world that lies behind the gates of Damascus.

'A brilliant book . . . Not since Naguib Mahfouz has the everyday life of the modern Arab world been so intimately described' – William Dalrymple

SEAN & DAVID'S LONG DRIVE
Sean Condon

Sean and David are young townies who have rarely strayed beyond city limits. One day, for no good reason, they set out to discover their homeland, and what follows is a wildly entertaining adventure that covers half of Australia. Sean Condon has written a hilarious, offbeat road book that mixes sharp insights with deadpan humour and outright lies.

'Funny, pithy, kitsch and surreal . . . This book will do for Australia what Chernobyl did for Kiev, but hey you'll laugh as the stereotypes go boom' – Andrew Tuck, Time Out

LONELY PLANET TRAVEL ATLASES

Lonely Planet has long been famous for the number and quality of its guidebook maps. Now we've gone one step further and in conjunction with Steinhart Katzir Publishers produced a handy companion series: Lonely Planet travel atlases – maps of a country produced in book form.

Unlike other maps, which look good but lead travellers astray, our travel atlases have been researched on the road by Lonely Planet's experienced team of writers. All details are carefully checked to ensure the atlas corresponds with the equivalent Lonely Planet guidebook.

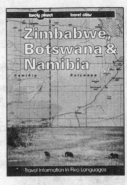

The handy atlas format means no holes, wrinkles, torn sections or constant folding and unfolding. These atlases can survive long periods on the road, unlike cumbersome fold-out maps. The comprehensive index ensures easy reference.

- full-colour throughout
- maps researched and checked by Lonely Planet authors
- place names correspond with Lonely Planet guidebooks
  – no confusing spelling differences
- legend and travelling information in English, French, German, Japanese and Spanish
- size: 230 x 160 mm

Available now:
Thailand; India & Bangladesh; Vietnam; Zimbabwe, Botswana & Namibia

Coming soon:
Chile; Egypt; Israel; Laos; Turkey

LONELY PLANET TV SERIES & VIDEOS

Lonely Planet travel guides have been brought to life on television screens around the world. Like our guides, the programmes are based on the joy of independent travel, and look honestly at some of the most exciting, picturesque and frustrating places in the world. Each show is presented by one of three travellers from Australia, England or the USA and combines an innovative mixture of video, Super-8 film, atmospheric soundscapes and original music.

Videos of each episode – containing additional footage not shown on television – are available from good book and video shops, but the availability of individual videos varies with regional screening schedules.

Video destinations include: Alaska; Australia (Southeast); Brazil; Ecuador & the Galápagos Islands; Indonesia; Israel & the Sinai Desert; Japan; La Ruta Maya (Yucatán, Guatemala & Belize); Morocco; North India (Varanasi to the Himalaya); Pacific Islands; Vietnam; Zimbabwe, Botswana & Namibia.

Coming soon: The Arctic (Norway & Finland); Baja California; Chile & Easter Island; China (Southeast); Costa Rica; East Africa (Tanzania & Zanzibar); Great Barrier Reef (Australia); Jamaica; Papua New Guinea; the Rockies (USA); Syria & Jordan; Turkey.

The Lonely Planet TV series is produced by:
Pilot Productions
Duke of Sussex Studios
44 Uxbridge St
London W8 7TG UK

Lonely Planet videos are distributed by:
IVN Communications Inc
2246 Camino Ramon
California 94583, USA

107 Power Road, Chiswick
London W4 5PL UK

Music from the TV series is available on CD & cassette.
For ordering information contact your nearest Lonely Planet office.

PLANET TALK

Lonely Planet's FREE quarterly newsletter

We love hearing from you and think you'd like to hear from us.

When...*is the right time to see reindeer in Finland?*
Where...*can you hear the best palm-wine music in Ghana?*
How...*do you get from Asunción to Areguá by steam train?*
What...*is the best way to see India?*

For the answer to these and many other questions read PLANET TALK.

Every issue is packed with up-to-date travel news and advice including:

* a letter from Lonely Planet co-founders Tony and Maureen Wheeler
* go behind the scenes on the road with a Lonely Planet author
* feature article on an important and topical travel issue
* a selection of recent letters from travellers
* details on forthcoming Lonely Planet promotions
* complete list of Lonely Planet products

To join our mailing list contact any Lonely Planet office.

Also available: Lonely Planet T-shirts. 100% heavyweight cotton..

LONELY PLANET ONLINE

Get the latest travel information before you leave or while you're on the road

Whether you've just begun planning your next trip, or you're chasing down specific info on currency regulations or visa requirements, check out the Lonely Planet World Wide Web site for up-to-the-minute travel information.

As well as travel profiles of your favourite destinations (including interactive maps and full-colour photos), you'll find current reports from our army of researchers and other travellers, updates on health and visas, travel advisories, and the ecological and political issues you need to be aware of as you travel.

There's an online travellers' forum (the Thorn Tree) where you can share your experiences of life on the road, meet travel companions and ask other travellers for their recommendations and advice. We also have plenty of links to other Web sites useful to independent travellers.

With tens of thousands of visitors a month, the Lonely Planet Web site is one of the most popular on the Internet and has won a number of awards including GNN's Best of the Net travel award.

http://www.lonelyplanet.com

LONELY PLANET PRODUCTS

Lonely Planet is known worldwide for publishing practical, reliable and no-nonsense travel information in our guides and on our web site. The Lonely Planet list covers just about every accessible part of the world. Currently there are eight series: *travel guides*, *shoestring guides*, *walking guides*, *city guides*, *phrasebooks*, *audio packs*, *travel atlases* and *Journeys* – a unique collection of travellers' tales.

EUROPE

Austria • Baltic States & Kaliningrad • Baltic States phrasebook • Britain • Central Europe on a shoestring • Central Europe phrasebook • Czech & Slovak Republics • Denmark • Dublin city guide • Eastern Europe on a shoestring • Eastern Europe phrasebook • Finland • France • Greece • Greek phrasebook • Hungary • Iceland, Greenland & the Faroe Islands • Ireland • Italy • Mediterranean Europe on a shoestring • Mediterranean Europe phrasebook • Poland • Prague city guide • Russia, Ukraine & Belarus • Russian phrasebook • Scandinavian & Baltic Europe on a shoestring • Scandinavian Europe phrasebook • Slovenia • St Petersburg city guide • Switzerland • Trekking in Greece • Trekking in Spain • Ukranian phrasebook • Vienna city guide • Walking in Switzerland • Western Europe on a shoestring • Western Europe phrasebook

NORTH AMERICA

Alaska • Backpacking in Alaska • Baja California • California & Nevada • Canada • Hawaii • Honolulu city guide • Los Angeles city guide • Mexico • Pacific Northwest USA • Rocky Mountain States • San Francisco city guide • Southwest USA • USA phrasebook

CENTRAL AMERICA & THE CARIBBEAN

Central America on a shoestring • Costa Rica • Eastern Caribbean • Guatemala, Belize & Yucatán: La Ruta Maya • Jamaica

SOUTH AMERICA

Argentina, Uruguay & Paraguay • Bolivia • Brazil • Brazilian phrasebook • Buenos Aires city guide • Chile & Easter Island • Colombia • Ecuador & the Galápagos Islands • Latin American Spanish phrasebook • Peru • Quechua phrasebook • Rio de Janeiro city guide • South America on a shoestring • Trekking in the Patagonian Andes • Venezuela

ALSO AVAILABLE:

Travel with Children • Traveller's Tales

AFRICA

Arabic (Moroccan) phrasebook • Africa on a shoestring • Cape Town city guide • Central Africa • East Africa • Egypt & the Sudan • Ethiopian (Amharic) phrasebook • Kenya • Morocco • North Africa • South Africa, Lesotho & Swaziland • Swahili phrasebook • Trekking in East Africa • West Africa • Zimbabwe, Botswana & Namibia • Zimbabwe, Botswana & Namibia travel atlas

MAIL ORDER

Lonely Planet products are distributed worldwide. They are also available by mail order from Lonely Planet, so if you have difficulty finding a title please write to us. North American and South American residents should write to Embarcadero West, 155 Filbert St, Suite 251, Oakland CA 94607, USA; European and African residents should write to 10 Barley Mow Passage, Chiswick, London W4 4PH; and residents of other countries to PO Box 617, Hawthorn, Victoria 3122, Australia.

NORTH-EAST ASIA

Beijing city guide • Cantonese phrasebook • China • Hong Kong, Macau & Canton • Hong Kong city guide • Japan • Japanese phrasebook • Japanese audio pack • Korea • Korean phrasebook • Mandarin phrasebook • Mongolia • Mongolian phrasebook • North-East Asia on a shoestring • Seoul city guide • Taiwan • Tibet • Tibet phrasebook • Tokyo city guide

INDIAN SUBCONTINENT

Bengali phrasebook • Bangladesh • Delhi city guide • Hindi/Urdu phrasebook • India • India & Bangladesh travel atlas • Karakoram Highway • Kashmir, Ladakh & Zanskar • Nepal • Nepali phrasebook • Pakistan • Sri Lanka • Sri Lanka phrasebook • Trekking in the Indian Himalaya • Trekking in the Nepal Himalaya

SOUTH-EAST ASIA

Bali & Lombok • Bangkok city guide • Burmese phrasebook • Cambodia • Ho Chi Minh city guide • Indonesia • Indonesian phrasebook • Indonesian audio pack • Jakarta city guide • Java • Laos • Lao phrasebook • Malaysia, Singapore & Brunei • Myanmar (Burma) • Philippines • Pilipino phrasebook • Singapore city guide • South-East Asia on a shoestring • Thailand • Thailand travel atlas • Thai phrasebook • Thai audio pack • Thai Hill Tribes phrasebook • Vietnam • Vietnamese phrasebook • Vietnam travel atlas

AUSTRALIA & THE PACIFIC

Australia • Australian phrasebook • Bushwalking in Australia • Bushwalking in Papua New Guinea • Fiji • Fijian phrasebook • Islands of Australia's Great Barrier Reef • Melbourne city guide • Micronesia • New Caledonia • New South Wales & the ACT • New Zealand • Outback Australia • Papua New Guinea • Papua New Guinea phrasebook • Queensland • Rarotonga & the Cook Islands • Samoa • Solomon Islands • South Australia • Sydney city guide • Tahiti & French Polynesia • Tonga • Tramping in New Zealand • Vanuatu • Victoria • Western Australia

Travel Literature: Islands in the Clouds • Sean & David's Long Drive

MIDDLE EAST & CENTRAL ASIA

Arab Gulf States • Arabic (Egyptian) phrasebook • Central Asia • Iran • Israel • Jordan & Syria • Middle East • Turkey • Turkish phrasebook • Trekking in Turkey • Yemen

Travel Literature: The Gates of Damascus

ISLANDS OF THE INDIAN OCEAN

Madagascar & Comoros • Maldives & Islands of the East Indian Ocean • Mauritius, Réunion & Seychelles

THE LONELY PLANET STORY

Lonely Planet published its first book in 1973 in response to the numerous 'How did you do it?' questions Maureen and Tony Wheeler were asked after driving, bussing, hitching, sailing and railing their way from England to Australia.

Written at a kitchen table and hand collated, trimmed and stapled, *Across Asia on the Cheap* became an instant local bestseller, inspiring thoughts of another book.

Eighteen months in South-East Asia resulted in their second guide, *South-East Asia on a shoestring*, which they put together in a backstreet Chinese hotel in Singapore in 1975. The 'yellow bible', as it quickly became known to backpackers around the world, soon became *the* guide to the region. It has sold well over half a million copies and is now in its 8th edition, still retaining its familiar yellow cover.

Today there are over 180 titles, including travel guides, walking guides, language kits & phrasebooks, travel atlases and travel literature. The company is one of the largest travel publishers in the world. Although Lonely Planet initially specialised in guides to Asia, we now cover most regions of the world, including the Pacific, North America, South America, Africa, the Middle East and Europe.

The emphasis continues to be on travel for independent travellers. Tony and Maureen still travel for several months of each year and play an active part in the writing, updating and quality control of Lonely Planet's guides.

They have been joined by over 70 authors and 170 staff at our offices in Melbourne (Australia), Oakland (USA), London (UK) and Paris (France). Travellers themselves also make a valuable contribution to the guides through the feedback we receive in thousands of letters each year.

The people at Lonely Planet strongly believe that travellers can make a positive contribution to the countries they visit, both through their appreciation of the countries' culture, wildlife and natural features, and through the money they spend. In addition, the company makes a direct contribution to the countries and regions it covers. Since 1986 a percentage of the income from each book has been donated to ventures such as famine relief in Africa; aid projects in India; agricultural projects in Central America; Greenpeace's efforts to halt French nuclear testing in the Pacific; and Amnesty International.

'I hope we send the people out with the right attitude about travel. You realise when you travel that there are so many different perspectives about the world, so we hope these books will make people more interested in what they see. These are guidebooks, but you can't really guide people. All you can do is point them in the right direction.'
– Tony Wheeler

LONELY PLANET PUBLICATIONS

Australia
PO Box 617, Hawthorn 3122, Victoria
tel: (03) 9819 1877 fax: (03) 9819 6459
e-mail: talk2us@lonelyplanet.com.au

USA
Embarcadero West, 155 Filbert St, Suite 251,
Oakland, CA 94607
tel: (510) 893 8555 TOLL FREE: 800 275-8555
fax: (510) 893 8563
e-mail: info@lonelyplanet.com

UK
10 Barley Mow Passage, Chiswick,
London W4 4PH
tel: (0181) 742 3161 fax: (0181) 742 2772
e-mail: 100413.3551@compuserve.com

France:
71 bis rue du Cardinal Lemoine, 75005 Paris
tel: 1 44 32 06 20 fax: 1 46 34 72 55
e-mail: 100560.415@compuserve.com

World Wide Web: http://www.lonelyplanet.com